A PEOPLE AND A NATION

◆

Brief Edition

A People and
a Nation

A HISTORY OF THE UNITED STATES

Brief Edition ◆ *Fourth Edition*

Mary Beth Norton
Cornell University

David M. Katzman
University of Kansas

Paul D. Escott
Wake Forest University

Howard P. Chudacoff
Brown University

Thomas G. Paterson
University of Connecticut

William M. Tuttle, Jr.
University of Kansas

and

William J. Brophy
Stephen F. Austin State University

HOUGHTON MIFFLIN COMPANY

Boston   Toronto

Geneva, Illinois   Palo Alto   Princeton, New Jersey

Senior Sponsoring Editor: Sean W. Wakely
Senior Associate Editor: Jeffrey Greene
Senior Project Editor: Carol Newman
Senior Production/Design Coordinator: Carol Merrigan
Senior Manufacturing Coordinator: Priscilla Bailey
Marketing Manager: Pamela Shaffer

Cover designed by Minko Dimov.

Text photographs researched by Pembroke Herbert and
Sandi Rygiel/Picture Research Consultants.

Cover image: "The Quilting Party," c. 1854, Abby
Aldrich Rockefeller Folk Art Center, Williamsburg, VA.

Printed in the U.S.A.

Library of Congress Catalog Card Number: 95-76969

ISBN: 0-395-74158-0

123456789-VH-99 98 97 96 95

Brief Contents

Contents

Maps

Charts

Preface to the Brief Fourth Edition

This text is a condensation and updating of the highly successful Fourth Edition of *A People and a Nation*. We have preserved all the strengths of the full-length edition—its readability, scholarship, comprehensiveness, and, most important, its dynamic blend of social, political, foreign-relations, and economic history—in a form approximately half as long. This condensation of the whole story of American history is ideally suited for short courses or courses in which additional readings are assigned.

The brief edition is available in both one-volume and two-volume formats. The two-volume format divides as follows: Volume A contains Chapters 1–16, beginning with a discussion of three cultures—Native American, African, and European—that intersected during the exploration and colonization of the New World and ending with a discussion of the Reconstruction era; Volume B contains Chapters 16–34, beginning its coverage at Reconstruction and extending to the present. The chapter on Reconstruction appears in both volumes to provide greater flexibility in matching a volume to the historical span covered by a specific course.

This brief edition is not a simple revision of the previous brief version: we have ensured that it reflects changes in content and organization incorporated into the full-length **Creation of the Brief Edition** Fourth Edition (see the preface to the full-length edition, which follows). William J. Brophy, who prepared the condensation, collaborated closely with the six authors of the full-length edition to make all deletions with great care. Rather than simply cut entire sections, we took a line-by-line approach to the removal of material, paring down detail. Where two examples were given in the full-length edition, we deleted one; where many statistics were presented, we used a few. Although we abridged or deleted some excerpts from diaries and letters, we have retained many quotations and many individual accounts of everyday life.

One of the major changes in *A People and a Nation* is the addition of considerable new material at the beginning of the book. Mary Beth Norton, who had primary responsibility **Major Changes in this Edition** for Chapters 1–8, wrote the new first chapter with expanded treatment of American peoples before Columbus, voyages of exploration and discovery, colonization of the Atlantic islands, the origins of slavery, and the development of fishing in the New World. The recast second chapter more fully covers the Caribbean islands and the sugar industry, New France, and New Netherland. This chapter also includes a revised discussion of the introduction of slavery into the mainland English colonies. Her other chapters reflect recent scholarly works.

David M. Katzman, who had primary responsibility for Chapters 9, 10, 12, and 13, integrated new literature on western expansion and the impact of settlement and manufacturing on the environment, wrote a new and more focused assessment of the War of 1812, gave greater emphasis to population changes, social diversity, and education and the spread of literacy, and added a fuller explanation of the banking system.

Paul D. Escott, who had primary responsibility for Chapters 11, 14, and 15–16, expanded coverage of Supreme Court cases. He also explored in greater detail aspects of military history—strategy, tactics, technology, and the experience of soldiers.

Howard P. Chudacoff, who had primary responsibility for Chapters 17–21 and 24, like others introduced new material on the environment, especially water issues. He has redistributed the material of the previous edition's Chapter 19 (Everyday Life and Culture, 1877–1920) to two other chapters, Chapter 18 on the Machine Age and the dawn of consumerism and the current Chapter 19 on cities in the late nineteenth and early twentieth centuries. This change provides a greater chronological flow in these chapters. Also, the discussion of bosses and reformers in Chapter 19 has been substantially revised and reorganized to take into account new perspectives on urban politics.

Thomas G. Paterson, who served as the coordinating author for this book and who prepared the Appendix, had primary responsibility for Chapters 22–23, 26, 29, 31, and the new Chapter 34 on the Bush-Clinton years. With the end of the Cold War came the opportunity to rethink post-1945 foreign-relations history and to reorganize it into two chapters that address the two most prominent characteristics of the period—the Soviet-American confrontation of the Cold War and the rise of the Third World through decolonization, revolution, and war. The declassification of documents—such as those on the Cuban missile crisis—has permitted the recasting of many events. He also expanded discussion of cultural relations, military events, and U.S.-Puerto Rican affairs.

William M. Tuttle, Jr., who had primary responsibility for Chapters 25, 27, 28, 30, and 32–33, expanded treatment of the impact of government policies and economic growth on the environment, the domestic impact of war, the baby boom, child care issues, women's employment, the rise of the sunbelt, technological change (including home computers), the Watergate scandal, and immigration. He also reorganized post-1945 domestic history to coordinate it with the new foreign-relations chapters.

This edition also includes a new feature introduced in the full-length edition, *How Do Historians Know?* It is designed to help students understand how historians go about using evidence to arrive at conclusions. This innovative feature appears in every chapter. A brief highlighted paragraph, coupled with an illustration, explains how historians have drawn generalizations from particular kinds of sources—census data, political cartoons, letters, maps, autobiographies, artifacts, labor records, government documents. This feature also helps us to understand how scholars can claim knowledge about particular historical events or trends.

The Brief Edition is also updated to contain material on Clinton's healthcare and welfare proposals, the 1994 Congressional elections, North Korean nuclear weapons production, and the Republican Contract with America. In addition, we have also used the occasion of a new edition to update the end-of-chapter bibliographies.

Many instructors and students who have used this book in their courses have found its many learning and teaching aids very useful.

The *Study Guide*, prepared by George Warren and Cynthia Ricketson of Central Piedmont Community College, includes an introductory chapter on studying history that focuses on interpreting historical facts, test-taking hints, and critical analysis. The guide also includes learning objectives, a thematic guide, lists of terms, multiple-choice and essay questions for each chapter, as well as map exercises and sections on organizing information for some chapters. An answer key alerts students to the correct response and also explains why the other choices are wrong.

Study and Teaching Aids

A *Computerized Study Guide* is also available for students. It provides approximately 15 multiple-choice questions for each chapter and functions as a tutorial that gives students information on incorrect as well as correct answers. The computerized guide is available in IBM and IBM-compatible formats.

"Places in Time" Map Software, an animated map program, consists of four computer sessions, each focusing on a specific time period (1763, 1860, 1920, and 1980), in which the themes of population, territory, and economic development are ex-

plored. Available in Macintosh and IBM-PC compatible formats.

"Places in Time" Map Workbook, a printed version of the computer program, is available for students in workbook format and can be used independently of the computer program.

A new *Instructor's Resource Manual with Test Items*, prepared by Donald Frazier, Marvin Schultz, and Bruce Winders of Texas Christian University; Robert Pace of Longwood College; and George Warren of Central Piedmont Community College, contains ten chronological resource units in addition to teaching ideas for each chapter of the text. Each chronological resource unit includes sections on geography, technology, physical and material culture (artifacts), historical sites, documentary films, popular films, and music. The manual also includes for each text chapter an overview of material in the chapter, a brief list of learning objectives, a comprehensive chapter outline, ideas for classroom activities, discussion questions, and ideas for paper topics. There are also more than 1,000 new multiple-choice questions, identification terms, and essay questions.

A *Computerized Test Item File* is available to adopters for IBM and Macintosh computers. This computerized version of the printed *Test Items* file allows professors to create customized tests by editing and adding questions.

There is also a set of 50 *Map Transparencies* available on adoption. All of these maps appear in *A People and a Nation*, Brief Edition.

A variety of *videos*, documentaries and docudramas by major film producers, are available for use with *A People and a Nation*, including "The American Revolution: The Cause of Liberty," "Views of a Vanishing Frontier," "The Civil War: 1861: The Cause," "The Indomitable Teddy Roosevelt," "The Home Front," and "Awakenings" (from *Eyes on the Prize*).

Finally, we want to thank the many people who have contributed their thoughts and labors to this work, including the talented staff at Houghton Mifflin Company.

W. J. B.

Preface to the Full-Length Fourth Edition

When the authors of *A People and a Nation* began work on this fourth edition, we set several goals for ourselves. We wanted to preserve those features of the third edition that students and faculty have found attractive: our basic approach to American history as the story of all the people, our spirited narrative based upon letters, diaries, oral histories, and other sources that reveal the pulse of human experience, and our effort to challenge readers to think about the meaning of American history, not just to memorize it. We have appreciated hearing, too, that we have presented our interpretations openly and fairly and with a welcoming style that invites debate.

The Authors' Goals

The authors set out to write a thorough revision. We reexamined every paragraph, interpretation, map, illustration, chart, caption, bibliography, and each part of the appendix. We scrutinized the form of each chapter—opening vignette, introduction, chronology, conclusion, suggested readings. We rewrote throughout, condensing wherever possible. One-half of the opening vignettes are new. The concluding paragraphs of each chapter have been revised to become more explicit summaries. We reorganized chapters, and we added new ones at the beginning and end to account for advances in scholarship and for momentous changes in international relations. Finally, we have added a new critical thinking feature to the fourth edition. These many revisions are described in detail later.

Given the urgency of issues surrounding the natural environment and technology and the increasing availability of outstanding scholarship on these topics, the authors determined to expand coverage of these subjects. We immersed ourselves in the literature and sought expert advice from historians who have researched and explored these subjects. Throughout the book, then, readers will discover a greater integration of environmental and technological questions and their intersection with the experiences of the American people.

Eager to help students understand how historians go about using evidence to arrive at conclusions, the authors have introduced a new feature in each chapter: *How Do Historians Know?* A brief highlighted paragraph, coupled with an illustration, explains how historians have drawn generalizations from particular kinds of sources—census data, political cartoons, letters, maps, autobiographies, artifacts, labor records, government documents. This feature also helps us to understand how scholars can claim knowledge about particular historical events or trends.

Certain that one of the strengths of the book has been its incorporation of the very latest scholarship, the authors have drawn upon their own recent scholarly research and activities (see the biographical sketches of the authors) and the innovative work of other scholars. Changes in emphasis and interpretation mark every chapter. The Suggestions for Further Reading have been revised to present the new literature.

Determined to improve every aspect of the book, the authors and the Houghton Mifflin editors also developed a new design to make *A People and a Nation* more accessible. The graphs and charts have been redrawn, captions have been added to them and to the maps, the link between illustrative material and text has been defined more sharply, and a contemporary new look throughout reflects the freshness of this thoroughly revised edition.

In preparing this new edition, the authors maintained their tradition of enviable cooperation: They met in frank and friendly planning sessions, wrote critiques of each other's chapters, responded to many reports from instructors, and worked closely with Houghton Mifflin's talented staff to consider and reconsider every detail. We strove to give this multiauthored text a seamless quality.

As teachers and students we are always recreating our past, restructuring our memory, rediscovering the personalities and events that have

Our View of American History
———

shaped us, inspired us, and bedeviled us. This book is our rediscovery of America's past—its people and the nation they founded and have sustained. This history is sometimes comforting, sometimes disturbing. As with our own personal experiences, it is both triumphant and tragic, filled with both injury and healing. As memory, history is the way we identify ourselves. As this book reveals, there are many different Americans and many competing memories. We have sought to present all of them, in both triumph and tragedy.

A People and a Nation is a comprehensive book in its treatment of major subject areas—social, political, diplomatic, economic, military, environmental, intellectual, and more. Issues of gender, class, religion, race, work, sexual orientation, medicine, ecology, region, and ethnicity appear throughout, as does the friction that often arises from such a diverse people.

We emphasize the everyday life of the American people, from the ordinary to the exceptional— the factory worker, the slave, the immigrant, the sales clerk, the baseball player, the small-town merchant, the urban entrepreneur, the small farmer, the film celebrity, the scientist, the army general, the senator, the president. We pay particular attention to lifestyles, diet and dress, family life and structure, gender roles, workplace conditions, and childbearing and childrearing. We ask how Americans have entertained themselves through

sports, music, the graphic arts, reading, theater, film, radio, and television. We account for demographic change, geographic and social mobility, and peoples' adaptation to new environments.

Because the private sphere of everyday life intersects with public policies of government and the influential trends of a world economy, we explore the interactions of these different spheres. We also delve into Americans' expectations of their governments and the practices and impact of local, state, and federal institutions. We study not only politics, but also the culture of politics. We identify the mood and mentality of an era, searching for what Americans thought about themselves and others. We seek to understand why and how America goes to war and why diplomacy often fails. The sources of American expansion and empire abroad are plumbed throughout the book.

One of the major changes in *A People and a Nation* is the addition of considerable new material at the beginning of the book. Mary Beth Norton,

Major Changes in This Edition
———

who had primary responsibility for Chapters 1–8, wrote the new first chapter with expanded treatment of American peoples before Columbus, voyages of exploration and discovery, colonization of the Atlantic islands, the origins of slavery, and the development of fishing in the New World. The recast second chapter more fully covers the Caribbean islands and the sugar industry, New France, and New Netherland. This chapter also includes a revised discussion of the introduction of slavery into the mainland English colonies. Her other chapters reflect recent scholarly works.

David M. Katzman, who had primary responsibility for Chapters 9, 10, 12, and 13, integrated new literature on western expansion and the impact of settlement and manufacturing on the environment, wrote a new and more focused assessment of the War of 1812, gave greater emphasis to population changes, social diversity, and education and the spread of literacy, and added a fuller explanation of the banking system.

Paul D. Escott, who had primary responsibility for Chapters 11, 14, and 15–16, expanded coverage of Supreme Court cases. He also explored in greater detail aspects of military history—strategy, tactics, technology, and the experience of soldiers.

Howard P. Chudacoff, who had primary responsibility for Chapters 17–21 and 24, like others introduced new material on the environment, especially water issues. He has redistributed the material of the previous edition's Chapter 19 (Everyday Life and Culture, 1877–1920) to two other chapters, Chapter 18 on the Machine Age and the dawn of consumerism and the current Chapter 19 on cities in the late nineteenth and early twentieth centuries. This change provides a greater chronological flow in these chapters. Also, the discussion of bosses and reformers in Chapter 19 has been substantially revised and reorganized to take into account new perspectives on urban politics.

Thomas G. Paterson, who served as the coordinating author for this book and who prepared the Appendix, had primary responsibility for Chapters 22–23, 26, 29, 31, and the new Chapter 34 on the Bush-Clinton years. With the end of the Cold War came the opportunity to rethink post-1945 foreign-relations history and to reorganize it into two chapters that address the two most prominent characteristics of the period—the Soviet-American confrontation of the Cold War and the rise of the Third World through decolonization, revolution, and war. The declassification of documents—such as those on the Cuban missile crisis—has permitted the recasting of many events. He also expanded discussion of cultural relations, military events, and U.S.-Puerto Rican affairs.

William M. Tuttle, Jr., who had primary responsibility for Chapters 25, 27, 28, 30, and 32–33, expanded treatment of the impact of government policies and economic growth on the environment, the domestic impact of war, the baby boom, child care issues, women's employment, the rise of the sunbelt, technological change (including home computers), the Watergate scandal, and immigration. He also reorganized post-1945 domestic history to coordinate it with the new foreign-relations chapters.

Many instructors and students who have used this book in their courses have found its many learning and teaching aids very useful.

Study and Teaching Aids

The *Study Guide*, prepared by George Warren and Cynthia Ricketson of Central Piedmont Community College, includes an introductory chapter on studying history that focuses on interpreting historical facts, test-taking hints, and critical analysis. The guide also includes learning objectives, a thematic guide, lists of terms, multiple-choice and essay questions for each chapter, as well as map exercises and sections on organizing information for some chapters. An answer key alerts students to the correct response and also explains why the other choices are wrong.

A *Computerized Study Guide* is also available for students. It provides approximately 15 multiple-choice questions for each chapter and functions as a tutorial that gives students information on incorrect as well as correct answers. The computerized guide is available in IBM and IBM-compatible formats.

"Places in Time" Map Software, an animated map program, consists of four computer sessions, each focusing on a specific time period (1763, 1860, 1920, and 1980), in which the themes of population, territory, and economic development are explored.

"Places in Time" Map Workbook, a printed version of the computer program, is available for students in workbook format and can be used independently of the computer program.

A new *Instructor's Resource Manual*, prepared by Donald Frazier, Marvin Schultz, and Bruce Winders of Texas Christian University, and Robert Pace of Longwood College, contains ten chronological resource units in addition to teaching ideas for each chapter of the text. Each chronological resource unit includes sections on geography, technology, physical and material culture (artifacts), historical sites, documentary films, popular films, and music. The manual also includes for each text chapter an overview of material in the chapter, a brief list of learning objectives, a comprehensive chapter outline, ideas for classroom activities, discussion questions, and ideas for paper topics.

A *Test Items* file, also prepared by George Warren, provides approximately 1,700 new multiple-choice questions, more than 1,000 identification terms, and approximately 500 essay questions.

A *Computerized Test Item File* is available to adopters for IBM and Macintosh computers. This computerized version of the printed *Test Items* file allows professors to create customized tests by editing and adding questions.

There is also a set of 95 full-color *Map Transparencies* available on adoption. All of these maps appear in *A People and a Nation*.

A variety of *videos*, documentaries and docudramas by major film producers, are available for use with *A People and a Nation*, including "The American Revolution: The Cause of Liberty," "Views of a Vanishing Frontier," "The Civil War: 1861: The Cause," "The Indomitable Teddy Roosevelt," "The Home Front," and "Awakenings" (from *Eyes on the Prize*).

At each stage of this project, historians read drafts of our chapters. Their suggestions, corrections, and pleas helped guide us through our revisions. We could not include all of their recommendations, but the book is better for our having heeded most of their advice. We heartily thank:

Acknowledgments

Harriett Alonso, *Fitchburg State College*
Michael Bellesiles, *Emory University*
John D. Buenker, *University of Wisconsin, Parkside*
Ruth Schwartz Cowan, *State University of New York, Stony Brook*
Linda Ford, *Keene State College*
Duane Gage, *Tarrant County Junior College*
Roger Grant, *University of Akron*
Deborah E. Gray, *Worcester State College*
Barbara Green, *Wright State University*
David Hamilton, *University of Kentucky*
Theresa McGinley, *North Harris College*
Peter C. Mancall, *Kansas State University*
Martin Melosi, *University of Houston*
Eric Monkkonen, *University of California, Los Angeles*
Margaret Newell, *Ohio State University*
Stephen Norwood, *University of Oklahoma*
Magne Olson, *Chicago State University*
Barbara Posadas, *Northern Illinois University*
Louis Potts, *University of Missouri, Kansas City*
Henry Sage, *Northern Virginia Community College*
Richard Stott, *George Washington University*
Robert M. Weir, *University of South Carolina*
Marie Wiener, *University of Maine, Orono*

We are also pleased to thank others who helped us in various ways: Jan D. Emerson, Kathryn Nemeth Kretschmer, Brian Murphy, Gary Y. Okihiro, Noah Schwartz, Glenn Sheffield, and Samuel Watkins Tuttle. Finally, the fourth edition of this book received careful handling from several Houghton Mifflin people who have always set high standards and thrived on excellence: Jean Woy, Editor-in-Chief; Sean Wakely, Senior Sponsoring Editor; Ann Goodsell, Development Editor; Charleen Akullian, Project Editor; and Pat Mahtani, Art Editor. We thank them very much.

For the Authors, THOMAS G. PATERSON

A PEOPLE AND A NATION

◆

Brief Edition

1

The Meeting of Old World and New, 1492–1600

A T BIRTH, SHE WAS called Malinalli. The Spaniards christened her Doña Marina. History knows her as Malinche, a name formed by adding the Aztec suffix *che* to her original name. She has been both celebrated as the symbolic mother of the modern Mexican people and maligned as a traitor to that nation's ancient residents.

Born sometime between 1502 and 1505, Malinalli was the daughter of a village chief within the Aztec empire. Her father died while she was young, and her mother soon remarried. To protect the inheritance of the son born to that second marriage, the mother sold her daughter into slavery. Eventually, Malinalli came to live with Mayan-speaking people.

In 1519, she was presented as a gift to Hernán Cortés, the Spanish conquistador. Cortés, who first arrived in the Spanish West Indies in 1504, embarked for the mainland in search of wealthy cities rumored to exist there. Little did he know that the young woman whom the Spaniards baptized Doña Marina would be a key to his conquest of Mexico.

Doña Marina, who spoke both Nahuatl (the language of her birth and of the Aztecs) and Mayan (the language of her masters), and who soon learned Spanish, became Cortés's translator and mistress. She bore him a son, Martín—the first *mestizo*, or mixed-blood Mexican. Accompanying Cortés throughout his travels in Mexico, she did more than simply interpret words for him: she explained the meanings behind the language, opening the Aztec world to the Spaniards.

On one occasion, Doña Marina saved the Spaniards from an ambush. The European invaders had halted in a village en route to Tenochtitlán, the Aztec capital. Doña Marina learned that the villagers intended to attack the invaders as they departed. Forewarned, Cortés ordered all the local chiefs killed. The Aztecs and subsequent Mexican historians blame Malinché for betraying her people. But who were her people? The Aztecs, in whose empire she had been born and who had sold her as a slave? The Mayas, among whom she was raised? Or the Europeans, who relied on her translations?

Malinche's life history, and her dual image as betrayer of ancient Mexico and symbolic mother of the modern mixed-race nation, encapsulate many ambiguities of the initial encounter between

Europeans and Americans. Sold into slavery by her Aztec-connected family, she owed that people little loyalty, whereas the Spaniards gave her respect. Yet she did not become Spanish; Cortés never married her.

Until she died around 1540, Malinche was caught between two worlds, part of both and of neither. Many people from both sides of the Atlantic were to meet the same fate as they attempted to cope with the rapidly changing world of the fifteenth and sixteenth centuries.

As European explorers and colonizers sought to exploit the resources of the rest of the globe, peoples from different races and cultural traditions came into regular contact for the first time. All were profoundly changed by the resulting interaction. By the time Spanish troops invaded Mexico in 1519, the age of European expansion and colonization was already well under way. During the next 350 years, Europeans would spread their influence around the globe. The history of the tiny colonies in North America that became the first members of the United States must be seen in this broad context of European exploration and exploitation.

The continents that European sailors reached in the late fifteenth century had their own history, which the invaders largely ignored. The residents of the Americas were the world's most skillful plant breeders; they had developed vegetable crops more nutritious and productive than those grown in Europe, Asia, or Africa. They had invented systems of writing and mathematics and had created calendars fully as accurate as those used on the other side of the Atlantic. In the Americas, as in Europe, states rose and fell as leaders succeeded or failed at the goal of expanding their political and economic power. The Europeans' arrival in their world immeasurably altered the Americans' struggles with each other.

After 1400, European nations tried to improve their positions relative to neighboring countries, not only by waging wars on their own continent but also by acquiring valuable colonies and trading posts elsewhere. In response, nations in Asia, Africa, and the Americas attempted to use the alien intruders to their own advantage or, failing that, to adapt successfully to the Europeans' presence in their midst. All participants in the resulting interaction of divergent cultures were indelibly affected by the process.

The contest among Europeans for control of the Americas and Africa changed the course of history on four continents. Although in the end the Europeans emerged politically dominant, they by no means controlled all aspects of the interaction.

AMERICAN SOCIETIES

Human beings probably originated on the continent of Africa, where humanlike remains about three million years old have been found in what is now Ethiopia. Over many millennia, the growing human population slowly dispersed to the other continents. Some people crossed a now-submerged stretch of land that joined Asia and North America at the site of the Bering Strait.

The forerunners of the American population are known as *Paleo-Indians*. The earliest confirmed evidence of their presence in the Americas dates to approximately twenty-eight thousand years ago. The Paleo-Indians were nomadic hunters of game and gatherers of wild plants. They spread throughout North and South America, probably moving as extended families or bands. (Tribes were composed of allied bands.) By about 11,500 years ago, the Paleo-Indians were making fine stone projectile points, which they attached to wooden spears and used to kill and butcher the large mammals then living in the Americas. But as the Ice Age ended and the human population increased, all the large American mammals except the bison (buffalo) disappeared. Scholars cannot agree whether their demise was caused by overhunting or by a change in climate. In either case, deprived of their primary source of meat, the Paleo-Indians had to find new ways to survive.

Paleo-Indians

The most significant innovation was the development of agriculture. By approximately seven thousand years ago, the residents of what is now central Mexico began to cultivate food crops, especially maize (corn), squash, beans, and peppers. Centuries before, people living in the Andes Mountains of South America had started to grow potatoes. As knowledge of agricultural techniques improved and spread through the Americas, vegetables and maize proved more reliable sources of food than hunting

• *Important Events* •

ca. 1000 B.C.E.	Olmec civilization appears		**1497**	John Cabot reaches North American coast
ca. 300–600 C.E.	Height of influence of Teotihuacán		**1513**	Ponce de Léon explores Florida
ca. 600–900 C.E.	Classic Mayan civilization		**1518–1530**	Smallpox epidemic devastates Indian population of West Indies, Central and South America
1001	Norse establish settlement in "Vineland" (Newfoundland)		**1519**	Hernán Cortés invades Mexico
1050–1250	Height of influence of Cahokia; prevalence of Mississippian culture, midwestern and southeastern United States		**1521**	Tenochtitlán surrenders to Cortés; Aztec empire falls to Spaniards
14th century	Aztec rise to power		**1534–1535**	Jacques Cartier explores St. Lawrence River
1450s–1480s	Portuguese explore and colonize islands in the Mediterranean Atlantic and São Tomé in Gulf of Guinea		**1539–1542**	Hernando de Soto explores southeastern United States
			1540–1542	Francisco Vásquez de Coronado explores southwestern United States
1477	Publication of Marco Polo's *Travels*, describing China		**1565**	Spanish establish St. Augustine, first permanent European settlement within boundaries of present United States
1492	Christopher Columbus reaches Bahama Islands		**1587–1590**	Sir Walter Raleigh's Roanoke colony vanishes
1494	Treaty of Tordesillas divides land claims between Spain and Portugal in Africa, India, and South America		**1588**	Thomas Harriot publishes *A Briefe and True Report of the New Found Land of Virginia*

and gathering. Except for those living in the harshest climates, most Americans started to adopt a more sedentary style of life so they could tend fields regularly. Some established permanent settlements; others moved several times a year among fixed sites. They became adept at clearing forests through the use of controlled burning. All Native American cultures emphasized producing sufficient food to support themselves. Although they traded goods, no tribe ever became wholly dependent on another group for items vital to its survival.

Wherever agriculture dominated the economy, more complex civilizations flourished. Such societies were able to accumulate wealth, produce ornamental objects, and create elaborate rituals and ceremonies. In North America, the successful culti-

vation of nutritious crops seems to have led to the growth and development of all major civilizations: first the large city-states of Mesoamerica (modern Mexico and Guatemala), then the urban clusters known collectively as the Mississippian culture and located in the present-day United States. Each society reached its height of population and influence only after achieving success in agriculture, and each declined and collapsed after reaching the limits of its food supply. Even the powerful Aztec empire that the Spaniards encountered in 1519 is thought to have been approaching the point at which it could no longer sustain its population.

The Aztecs were the heirs of a series of Mesoamerican civilizations. The first great civilization in the region was that of the Olmecs, whose

Olmecs and Mayas

culture mysteriously appeared in the swampy lowlands near the Gulf of Mexico more than three thousand years ago and just as mysteriously disappeared about one thousand years later. The Olmecs created urban centers with ceremonial plazas flanked by temple pyramids, a construction style that would be adopted by all later Mesoamerican societies. Their chief deity was a jaguar god, an image that would reappear in the pantheons of later civilizations. The Olmec civilization, like its successors, was a highly stratified society ruled by an elite priestly caste that claimed the exclusive ability to communicate with the gods.

After the decline of the Olmec cities, the Mayan civilization developed in the Yucatán Peninsula. The Mayas also built large cities containing tall pyramids and constructed temples. They studied astronomy, created the first writing system in the Americas, and developed a richly symbolic religious life in which rituals of bloodletting played a major role. The kings of the great Mayan city-states vied with each other for power. By the fifth century C.E. (common era), or about fifteen hundred years ago, they had begun to engage in open warfare. But no king or city could win total victory. Eventually, the constant fighting combined with overpopulation and the resulting environmental stress to cause the collapse of the most powerful cities. By the time the Spaniards arrived, only a few remnants of the once-mighty Mayan civilization remained.

The largest Mesoamerican metropolis was a contemporary and a major trading partner of the Mayas. Teotihuacán, founded about 300 B.C.E. (before the common era)—

The City of Teotihuacán

some twenty-three hundred years ago—in the Valley of Mexico, was one of the largest cities in the world in the fifth century C.E., with an estimated population of up to two hundred thousand. The rulers of Teotihuacán gained their position through commerce rather than warfare, and their trading network extended hundreds of miles in all directions. Teotihuacán also served as a religious center; pilgrims must have come long distances to visit the impressive Pyramids of the Sun and Moon and the great temple of Quetzalcoatl—the feathered serpent, the primary god of central Mexico.

Teotihuacán's influence was felt so widely in Mesoamerica before its decline in the eighth century C.E. that some scholars have argued that this great Mexican city-state also influenced societies farther north, in what is now the United States. Although unproved, Teotihuacán and later Mesoamerican empires, like that of the Aztecs, may have affected the development of the Mississippian culture, which flourished around 1000 C.E. in what is now the midwestern and southeastern United States. Like those to the south, the civilization of Teotihuacán was based on the cultivation of maize, beans, and squash. Not until about 700 to 900 C.E. were these crops grown successfully in what is now the United States; soon after their introduction, large cities with plazas and earthen pyramids first appeared in the region. The largest of the cities was Cahokia, near modern St. Louis. At its peak (before 1250 C.E.), Cahokia had a population of about ten thousand—small by Mesoamerican standards but far larger than any other northern community. Like Teotihuacán, Cahokia seems to have been a center for religion and trade. Its main pyramid, today called the Monk's Mound, was the largest earthwork built in North America and stood about half as high as the Pyramid of the Sun. Other Mississippian sites were located in present-day Alabama and Georgia. Traces of this civilization remained when Spaniards first visited the area in the sixteenth century.

Aztec histories tell of the long migration of their people (who called themselves *Mexica)* into the Valley of Mexico during the twelfth century.

Aztecs

The uninhabited ruins of Teotihuacán, which by then had been deserted for at least two hundred years, awed and mystified the migrants. The Aztecs' primary god, Huitzilopochtli, was a god of war, represented by an eagle. Aztec chronicles record that Huitzilopochtli directed them to establish their capital at the spot on an island where they saw an eagle eating a serpent (thus symbolizing Huitzilopochtli's triumph over the traditional deity, Quetzalcoatl). That island city became Tenochtitlán, the center of a rigidly stratified society composed of hereditary classes of

How do historians know

warriors, merchants, priests, common folk, and slaves. The Aztecs conquered their neighbors and forced them to pay tribute in luxury items, raw materials, and human beings who could be sacrificed to Huitzilopochtli. The war god's taste for blood was not easily quenched. In the Aztec year Ten Rabbit (1502) at the coronation of Motecuhzoma II (Montezuma to the Spaniards), five thousand people were said to have been sacrificed by having their still-beating hearts torn from their bodies.

The Aztecs believed that they lived in the age of the Fifth Sun. Four times previously, they wrote, the earth and all people who lived on it had been destroyed. They predicted that their own world would end in earthquakes and hunger. In the Aztec year Thirteen Flint, volcanoes erupted, sickness and hunger spread, and an eclipse of the sun darkened the sky. Did some priest wonder whether the Fifth Sun was approaching its end? But nothing ominous happened, at least not immediately. Eventually, the Aztecs learned that their year Thirteen Flint was called 1492 by the Europeans.

NORTH AMERICA IN 1492

Over the centuries, the Americans who lived north of Mexico adapted their once-similar ways of life to quite different geographical settings, thus creating the diverse cultures that the Europeans encountered when they first arrived (see map). Hunter-gatherer bands lived in environments not well suited to agriculture. Within the area of the present-day United States, these tribes included the Paiutes and Shoshones, who inhabited the Great Basin (now Nevada and Utah). Because of the difficulty of finding food sufficient for more than a few people, such bands were small. Where large game was more plentiful and food supplies therefore more certain, as in present-day Canada and the Great Plains, bands of hunters were somewhat larger.

In more favorable environments, larger groups combined agriculture with gathering, hunting, and fishing. Tribes that lived near the seacoasts, like the Chinooks of present-day Washington and Oregon, consumed fish and shellfish in addition to growing crops and gathering seeds and berries. Tribes of the interior (for example, the Arikaras of the Missouri River valley) hunted large animals and cultivated maize, squash, and beans. The Algonkian tribes of what is now eastern Canada and the northeastern United States also combined hunting and agriculture. The Algonkians typically moved four or five times a year. Once crops were well established, villages broke into small mobile bands to engage in gathering, hunting, and fishing. Villages reassembled for harvest, then dispersed again for the fall hunting season. Finally, the people would spend the harsh winter months together in a protected location before returning to their fields in the spring. Every few

years, they would use controlled burning techniques to clear new fields and ensure continuing fertility.

Societies that relied primarily on hunting large animals like deer and buffalo assigned that task to men, allotting food-processing, clothing-production, and child-rearing chores to

Sexual Division of Labor in America

women. Before such nomadic bands acquired horses from the Spaniards, women—occasionally assisted by dogs—also carried the family's belongings whenever the band relocated. Such a sexual division of labor was universal among hunting tribes. By contrast, agricultural societies differed in how they assigned cultivating crops to the sexes. In what is now the southwestern United States, the Pueblo peoples defined agricultural labor as men's work. In the East, Algonkian, Iroquoian, and Muskogean peoples allocated agricultural chores to women, whereas men hunted and cleared the land. In all farming societies, women gathered wild foods, prepared food for consumption or storage, and cared for children.

The southwestern and eastern agricultural peoples had similar social organizations. They lived in villages, sometimes sizable ones with a thousand or more inhabitants. Pueblo villages had large, multistory buildings and were built on terraces along the sides of cliffs or other easily defended sites in what is now New Mexico and Arizona. Northern Iroquois villages (in modern New York State) were composed of large, rectangular, bark-covered structures, or longhouses; the word *Iroquois* means People of the Long House. In the present-day southeastern United States, Muskogeans and southern Algonkians lived in large houses made of thatch. Most eastern villages were surrounded by wood palisades and ditches to aid in fending off attackers. The defensive design of such villages and of the western pueblos suggests the significance of warfare in pre-Columbian America.

Native Cultures of North America   *The natives of the North American continent effectively used the resources of the regions in which they lived. As this map shows, coastal tribes relied on fishing, residents of fertile areas engaged in agriculture, and other tribes hunted (often combined with gathering) as a primary mode of subsistence.*

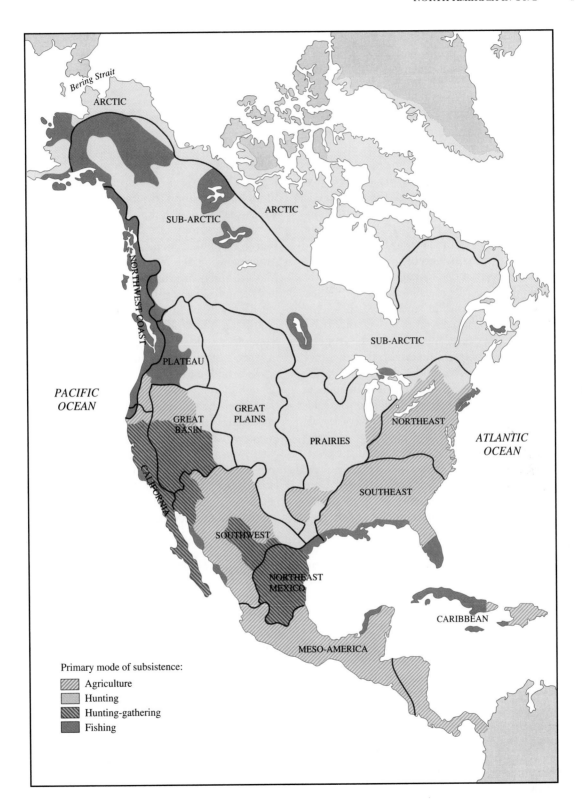

Bering Strait

ARCTIC

SUB-ARCTIC

ARCTIC

NORTHWEST COAST

SUB-ARCTIC

PACIFIC
OCEAN

PLATEAU

GREAT
BASIN

GREAT
PLAINS

PRAIRIES

NORTHEAST

ATLANTIC
OCEAN

CALIFORNIA

SOUTHWEST

SOUTHEAST

NORTHEAST
MEXICO

CARIBBEAN

MESO-AMERICA

Primary mode of subsistence:

- Agriculture
- Hunting
- Hunting-gathering
- Fishing

In all these agricultural societies, each dwelling housed an extended family defined matrilineally (through a female line of descent). Mothers, their married daughters, and their daughters' husbands and children lived together. Matrilineal descent did not imply matriarchy, or the wielding of power by women, but rather served as a means of reckoning kinship. Extended families were linked into clans, also defined by matrilineal ties. The nomadic bands of the Great Plains, on the other hand, were most often related patrilineally, through the male line.

The authority of American leaders rested ultimately on the consent of the other tribal members, but political structures in the various tribes differed

Native American Politics and Religion

considerably. Among Pueblo and Muskogean peoples, the village council was the highest political authority; there was no government at the tribal level. By contrast, the Iroquois had an elaborate political hierarchy that incorporated villages into tribes and tribes into a widespread confederation. All North American cultures divided political power between civil and war leaders who wielded authority only so long as they retained the confidence of the people. Consensus rather than autocratic rule characterized these political systems.

The political position of women varied from tribe to tribe. Women were more likely to assume leadership roles among agricultural peoples than among nomadic hunters. For example, women led certain Algonkian villages, but they were never chosen to lead hunting bands of the Great Plains. Iroquois women did not become chiefs, yet tribal matrons exercised political power. Probably the most powerful female chiefs were found in what is now the southeastern United States. In the mid-sixteenth century, a female ruler known as the Lady of Cofitachequi governed a large group of villages in what today is western South Carolina. Early English settlers in New England also noted in nearby villages the presence of female chiefs, most of whom were the wives, sisters, or widows of male leaders.

Americans' religious beliefs varied even more than did their political systems, but all the peoples were polytheistic, worshiping a multitude of gods. One common thread was their integration with nature. Thus each tribe's most important beliefs and rituals were closely tied to its economy. The major deities of agricultural peoples were associated with cultivation, and their chief festivals centered on planting and harvest. The most important gods of hunting tribes were associated with animals, and their major festivals were related to hunting. A tribe's economy and women's role in it helped to determine women's potential as religious leaders. Women held the most prominent positions in those agricultural societies (like the Iroquois') in which they were also the chief food producers.

A wide variety of cultures, comprising perhaps four to six million people, inhabited mainland North America when the Europeans arrived. In modern Mexico, hereditary rulers presided over vast agricultural empires. Along the Atlantic coast of the present-day United States, Americans likewise cultivated crops, but their political systems differed greatly from those of Mesoamerica. To the north and west, in what is now Canada and the Great Plains, lived nomadic and seminomadic societies primarily dependent on hunting large animals. Still farther west were the hunter-gatherer bands of the Great Basin and the agricultural villages of the Southwest. Finally, on the Pacific coast lived tribes that based their subsistence chiefly on fish. All told, these diverse groups spoke well over one thousand different languages. For obvious reasons, they did not consider themselves one people, nor did they, for the most part, think of uniting to repel the European invaders.

AFRICAN SOCIETIES

Fifteenth-century Africa also housed a variety of cultures adapted to different geographical settings (see map). In the north, along the Mediterranean Sea, lived the Berbers, a Muslim people. (Muslims are adherents of Islam, founded by the prophet

Africa and Its Peoples, ca. 1400 On the African continent resided many different peoples in a variety of ecological settings and political units. Even before Europeans began to explore its coastlines, Africa's northern regions were linked to the Mediterranean (and thus to Europe) via a network of trade routes.

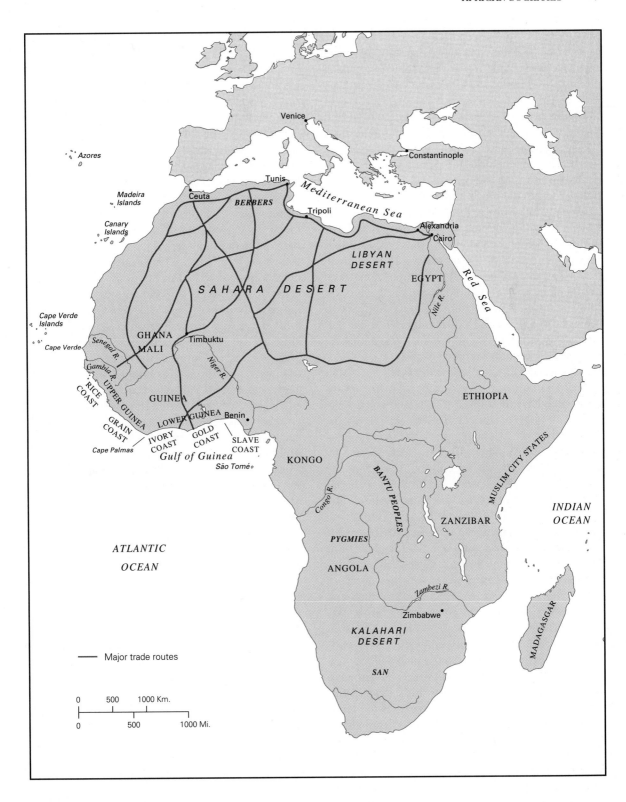

Azores

Madeira
Islands

Canary
Islands

Cape Verde
Islands

Cape Verde

Venice

Constantinople

Tunis

Ceuta

BERBERS

Mediterranean Sea

Tripoli

Alexandria
Cairo

LIBYAN
DESERT

EGYPT

Red Sea

SAHARA DESERT

Nile R.

GHANA
MALI

Timbuktu

Senegal R.

Gambia R.

UPPER GUINEA

RICE
COAST

GUINEA

Niger R.

ETHIOPIA

GRAIN
COAST

LOWER GUINEA

IVORY
COAST

GOLD
COAST

Benin

Cape Palmas

SLAVE
COAST

Gulf of Guinea

São Tomé

KONGO

BANTU PEOPLES

Congo R.

MUSLIM CITY STATES

ZANZIBAR

INDIAN
OCEAN

ATLANTIC

OCEAN

PYGMIES

ANGOLA

Zambezi R.

MADAGASGAR

Zimbabwe

KALAHARI
DESERT

SAN

—— Major trade routes

0   500   1000 Km.

0   500   1000 Mi.

Muhammad in the seventh century C.E.) On the east coast of Africa, Muslim city-states engaged in extensive trade with India, the Moluccas (part of modern Indonesia), and China. Through the East African city-states passed a considerable share of the trade between the eastern Mediterranean and the Far East; the rest followed the long land route across Central Asia known as the Silk Road.

In the African interior, south of the Mediterranean coast, lie the Sahara and Libyan deserts. Below the deserts, much of the continent is divided between tropical rain forests and grassy plains. People speaking a variety of languages and adopting quite different economies lived in a wide belt south of the deserts. Below the Gulf of Guinea, (see map, page 9) the grassy landscape came to be dominated by Bantu-speaking peoples, who left their homeland in modern Nigeria about two thousand years ago and slowly migrated south and east across the continent, gradually assimilating and conquering other ethnic groups.

West Africa (Guinea)

Most unwilling black migrants to North America came from West Africa. The Europeans called this land of tropical forests and small-scale agriculture Guinea. The northern region, or Upper Guinea, was heavily influenced by Islamic culture. As early as the eleventh century C.E., many of the region's inhabitants had become Muslims. The trans-Saharan trade between Upper Guinea and the Muslim Mediterranean was black Africa's major connection to Europe and the Middle East. For salt, dates, silk, and cotton cloth, Africans exchanged ivory, gold, and slaves with the northern merchants. (Slaves, who were mostly criminals and wartime captives, were in great demand as household servants in the homes of the Muslim Mediterranean elite.) This commerce was controlled by the great interior kingdoms of Ghana (ca. 900–1100 C.E.) and, later, Mali, which flourished in the fourteenth and fifteenth centuries. Black Africa and Islam intersected at the city that was the intellectual and commercial heart of the trade, the near-legendary Timbuktu. A cosmopolitan center, Timbuktu attracted merchants and scholars from all parts of North Africa and the Mediterranean.

On the Rice Coast of Upper Guinea (present-day Gambia, Senegal, and Guinea), people fished and cultivated rice in coastal swamplands. The Grain Coast, the next region to the south, was thinly populated and not readily accessible by sea, because it had only one good harbor. Its people concentrated on farming and raising livestock. Both the Rice and Grain Coasts supplied slaves destined for sale in the Americas, but even more enslaved migrants came from Lower Guinea.

The Ivory Coast and the Gold Coast in Lower Guinea were each named by the Europeans for the major trade goods they obtained there. Many of the first slaves destined for sale in the Americas came from the Gold Coast, comprising thirty little kingdoms known as the Akan States. By the eighteenth century, however, it was the area farther east, the modern nations of Togo and Benin, that supplied most slaves sold in the English colonies. The Adja kings of the region, which became known as the Slave Coast, encouraged the founding of slave-trading posts and served as middlemen in the trade, because access to valuable European trade goods enhanced their positions in their own societies and improved the kingdoms' standing relative to their neighbors. Initially, enslaved people sent to the Americas fell into the same categories as those previously traded to the Mediterranean: criminals, enemy captives, and individuals sold into slavery to repay debts. By the mid-eighteenth century, after the demand for enslaved labor in the American colonies had increased dramatically, raiding parties from the coast often attacked interior villages to acquire captives for the trade.

Sexual Division of Labor in West Africa

The societies of West Africa assigned different tasks to men and women. In general, the sexes shared agricultural duties. Men also hunted, managed livestock, and did most of the fishing. Women were responsible for child care, food preparation, and cloth manufacture. Everywhere in West Africa women were the primary local traders. They managed the extensive local and regional networks through which goods were exchanged among the various families, villages, and small kingdoms.

This decorative brass weight, created by the Asante peoples of Lower Guinea, was used for measuring gold dust. It depicts a family pounding fu-fu, a food made by mashing together plantains (a kind of banana), yams, and cassava. The paste was then shaped into balls to be eaten with soup. Thus a weight probably used in trading with Europeans showed a scene combining foods of African origin (plantains and yams) with an import from the Americas (cassava), bringing the three continents together in ways both symbolic and real. Courtesy of the Trustees of the British Museum. Photo by Michael Holford.

Despite their different economies and the rivalries among states, the peoples of Lower Guinea had similar social systems. In Lower Guinea, each sex handled its own affairs: just as male political and religious leaders governed the men, so females ruled the women. In the Dahomean kingdom, for example, every male official had his female counterpart; in the Akan States, chiefs inherited their status through the female line, and each male chief had a female assistant who supervised the other women. Religious beliefs stressed the complementary nature of male and female roles. Both women and men served as heads of the cults and secret societies that directed the spiritual life of the villages.

Thus the West Africans who were brought to the Americas were agricultural peoples, skilled at tending livestock, hunting, fishing, and manufacturing cloth from plant fibers and animal skins. Both men and women were accustomed to working communally, alongside other members of their own sex. They were also accustomed to a relatively egalitarian relationship between the sexes, especially within the context of religion. In the New World, they entered societies that used their labor but had little respect for their cultural traditions. Of the three peoples whose experience intersected in the Americas, the West Africans' lives were disrupted the most.

EUROPEAN SOCIETIES

In the fifteenth century, Europeans too were agricultural peoples. The daily lives of Europe's rural people had changed little for several hundred years. Split into numerous small, warring countries, that continent was divided linguistically, politically, and economically, yet in social terms Europeans' lives were more similar than different. European societies were hierarchical, with a few families wielding arbitrary power over the majority of people. Europe's kingdoms resembled those of Africa or Mesoamerica but differed from the more egalitarian, consensus-based societies then established in America north of Mexico.

Most Europeans, like most Africans and Native Americans, lived in small villages. European farmers, who were called peasants, owned or leased **Sexual Division of Labor in Europe** separate landholdings, but they worked the fields communally. Because fields had to lie fallow every second or third year to regain their fertility, a family could ensure a regular supply of food only if all villagers shared the work and the annual crop. Men did most of the field work; women helped out chiefly at planting and harvest. In some areas, men concentrated on herding livestock. Women's duties consisted primarily of child care and household tasks, including preserving food, milking cows, and caring for poultry. If a woman's husband was an artisan or a storekeeper in a city, she might assist him in business. Because Europeans kept domesticated animals (pigs, goats, sheep, and cattle) for meat, hunting had little economic importance in their cultures.

Unlike African and Native American societies, men dominated all areas of life in Europe. A few women from noble families—notably Queen Elizabeth I of England—achieved status or power, but the vast majority of European women were excluded from positions of political authority. In the Roman Catholic church, only men could become priests and bishops. At the familial level, husbands and fathers expected to control the lives of their wives, children, and servants (a patriarchal system of family governance). In short, European women held inferior stations in life.

When the fifteenth century began, the European nations were slowly beginning to recover from the devastating epidemic of plague known as the Black Death, which had first struck them in 1346. The bubonic plague, spread by rats and fleas as well as by human contact, arrived in Europe from China, traveling with long-distance traders along the Silk Road. The disease then recurred with particular severity in the 1360s and 1370s. An estimated one-third of Europe's population died from the plague during these years. That led to a precipitous economic decline and to severe social, political, and religious disruption because of the deaths of clergy and other leading figures.

As the plague ravaged the population, England and France were waging the Hundred Years' War (1337–1453), initiated because the English monarchy claimed the French throne. The war interrupted overland trade routes through France that connected northern Europe to the Italian city-states and thence to Central Asia. The merchants of the eastern Mediterranean sought new ways to reach their markets in Belgium and Holland, eventually forging a regular maritime link with the north to replace the overland route. Adding a triangular sail created by Arab mariners to the square-rigged mainsail developed by Europeans created more maneuverable ships that could sail out of the Mediterranean and into the North Sea. Also of key importance was the perfection of navigational instruments like the astrolabe and the quadrant, which allowed oceanic sailors to estimate their position on the high seas.

Political and Technological Changes

After the Hundred Years' War, ruthless European monarchs relied on nationalistic feelings fostered by the conflict to consolidate their once diffuse political power and to raise new revenues through increased taxation of an already hard-pressed peasantry. In England, Henry VII founded the Tudor dynasty in 1485 and began uniting a previously divided land. In France, the successors of Charles VII unified the kingdom. Most successful of all, at least in the short run, were Ferdinand of Aragon and Isabella of Castile. In 1469, they married and combined their kingdoms, thus creating the foundation of a strongly Catholic Spain. In 1492, they defeated the Muslims, who had lived in Spain and Portugal for centuries, and expelled all Jews and Muslims from their domain.

The fifteenth century also brought technological change to Europe. Movable type and the printing press, invented in Germany in the 1450s, made information more accessible than ever. Printing stimulated the Europeans' curiosity about fabled lands across the seas, lands they could now read about in books. The most important such work, Marco Polo's *Travels*, published in 1477, noted that China was bordered on the east by an ocean. Polo's book led many Europeans to believe that they could trade directly with China via ocean-going vessels instead of relying on the Silk Road or the Muslim merchants of East Africa.

Motives for Exploration

Thus the European explorations of the fifteenth and sixteenth centuries were made possible by technological advances and by the growing strength of newly powerful national rulers. The primary motivation for exploratory voyages was each country's craving for easy access to desirable African and Asian goods—spices like pepper, cloves, cinnamon, and nutmeg (needed to season the bland European diet), and goods like silk, dyes, perfumes, jewels, and gold. Another motive was to spread Christianity around the world. The linking of materialist and spiritual goals might seem contradictory today, but fifteenth-century Europeans saw no conflict.

EARLY EUROPEAN EXPLORATIONS AND THE COLUMBUS VOYAGES

Before European mariners could find new lands, they had to explore the oceans. Until 1291, when Genoese sailors defeated the Moroccans who had closed the Straits of Gibraltar to other nations' shipping, southern Europeans had sailed only in the Mediterranean. To reach Asia, seafarers needed not merely the maneuverable vessels and navigational aids increasingly used in the fourteenth century but also knowledge of the sea, its currents, and especially its winds. Wind would power their ships:

but how did the winds run? Where would Atlantic breezes carry their ships?

Europeans learned the answers to these questions in the region that has been called the Mediterranean Atlantic, the expanse of ocean that is south and west of Spain and is bounded by the island groups of the Azores (on the west) and the Canaries (on the south), with the Madeiras in their midst. Europeans reached all three sets of islands during the fourteenth century. The Canaries proved a popular destination for mariners from Iberia (the peninsula that includes Spain and Portugal). Sailing to the Canaries from Europe was easy, because strong winds known as the Northeast Trades blow south along the Iberian and African coastlines. The voyage took about a week. The

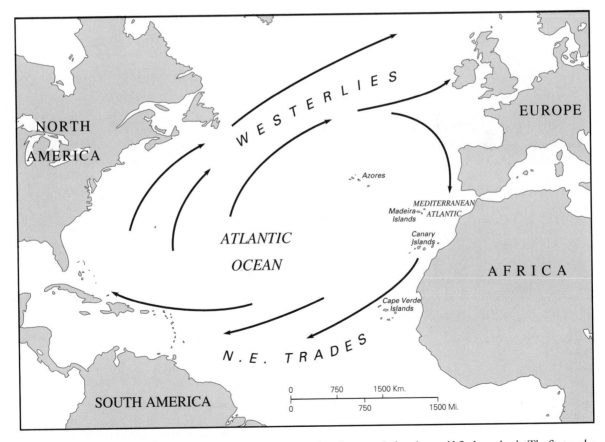

Atlantic Winds and Islands   *European mariners had to explore the oceans before they could find new lands. The first realm they investigated was the Atlantic winds and islands.*

problem was getting back. The very winds that had brought the Iberian sailor so quickly to the Canaries now blew directly at him.

What could be done? Some unknown seafarer figured out the answer: sail around the wind. If they could not sail against the trade winds, mariners had to sail as close as possible to the direction from which the wind was coming without being forced to tack. In the Mediterranean Atlantic, that meant pointing the vessel northwest into the open ocean, away from land, until—weeks later—it reached the winds that would carry it home, the so-called Westerlies (see map). Those winds blow north along the coast of North America before heading east toward Europe. This solution must at first have seemed to defy common sense, but it proved to be the key to successful exploration of both the Atlantic and Pacific oceans. Once sailors understood the winds and their allied currents, they no longer feared leaving Europe without being able to return.

Armed with knowledge of the winds and currents of the Mediterranean Atlantic, Iberian seamen regularly visited its islands during the fifteenth century. For Portugal's Prince Henry the Navigator, the islands were steppingstones to Africa. He knew that vast wealth awaited the first

The map produced in 1489 by Henricus Marcellus represented the world as it was known to Christopher Columbus, for it incorporated information obtained after Bartholomew Dias, a Portuguese sailor, rounded the Cape of Good Hope at the southern tip of Africa in 1488. Yet Marcellus did not try to estimate the extent of the ocean separating the west coast of Europe from the east coast of Asia.   Courtesy of the Trustees of The British Library.

European nation to tap the riches of Africa and Asia directly, and so each year he dispatched ships south along the African coast, attempting to find an oceanic route to Asia. But it was after Prince Henry died that Bartholomew Dias rounded the southern tip of Africa (1488) and Vasco da Gama finally reached India (1498). Before those voyages, Portuguese colonists in the Madeiras were using slaves (probably Jews and Muslims brought from Iberia) to grow large quantities of sugar for export to the mainland. Indeed, by the 1470s the Madeiras had developed into the world's first colonial plantation economy.

Although West African states successfully resisted European penetration of the interior, they allowed the Portuguese to establish trading posts along their coasts. Charging the traders rent and levying duties on the goods they imported, the African chiefs set the terms of exchange and benefited considerably from their new, easier access to European manufactures. The Portuguese gained too, for they no longer had to rely on the long trans-Saharan trade route. They earned immense profits by swiftly transporting African gold to Europe. Another valuable cargo was slaves. When they carried African Muslim prisoners of war back to the Iberian Peninsula, the Portuguese introduced black slavery to Europe.

Two groups of islands off the African coast, both previously uninhabited, proved critical to Portuguese success. The first, São Tomé, in the Gulf of Guinea was colonized

African Islands

in the 1480s. The soil of São Tomé proved ideal for raising sugar, and plantation agriculture there expanded rapidly. Many slaves were imported from the mainland to work in the cane fields, thus creating the first economy based primarily on the bondage of black Africans.

The second group, the Cape Verde Islands, served a different function for the Portuguese. Three hundred miles off the coast and too dry for sugar cultivation, the Cape Verdes became an important resupply station for ships in the Africa trade. Isolated from the diseases of the African continent—which devastated Europeans—the islands played host to a racially mixed population, the offspring of various African and European groups. The Cape Verdes and their inhabitants played an important role in the colonization of the Americas. There, the products and peoples of four continents mingled, and the islands became a primary staging area for the African slave trade.

By the 1490s, even before Christopher Columbus set sail to the west, Europeans had learned three important lessons of colonization from their experiences in the islands of the Mediterranean Atlantic and the African coast. First, they knew that they could transplant their crops and livestock successfully to exotic locations. Second, they had learned that the native peoples of unknown lands could be conquered or exploited to European advantage. Finally, they had successfully developed a model of plantation slavery and a system for supplying nearly unlimited quantities of workers held in perpetual bondage. The stage was set for a critical moment in world history, and the man of the hour was a sailor named Christopher Columbus.

Columbus was well schooled in the lessons of the Mediterranean Atlantic. Born in 1451 in the Italian city-state of Genoa, Columbus was by the

Christopher Columbus

1490s an experienced sailor and mapmaker. Like many mariners of the day, he was drawn to Portugal and its islands, especially the Madeiras, where he commanded a merchant vessel sailing in nearby waters. He sailed at least once to the Portuguese colony on the Gold Coast. There he acquired an obsession with gold and came to understand the economic potential of the slave trade.

Like all accomplished seafarers, Columbus knew the world was round. But he differed from other cartographers in his estimate of the earth's size: he thought that Japan lay only three thousand miles from the southern European coast. Thus, he argued, it would be easier to reach Asia by sailing west than by making the difficult voyage around the southern tip of Africa. Experts scoffed at this crackpot notion, accurately predicting that the two continents lay twelve thousand miles apart. When Columbus in 1484 asked the Portuguese authorities to back his plan to sail west to Asia, they refused.

Ferdinand and Isabella of Spain, ruling a newly united kingdom and jealous of the profits Portugal was earning in Africa, were more receptive to Columbus's ideas. Urged on by some Spanish nobles and a group of Italian merchants resident in Castile, the monarchs agreed to finance the risky voyage. And so, on August 3, 1492, in command of three ships—the *Pinta*, the *Niña*, and the *Santa Maria*—Columbus set sail from the southern Spanish port of Palos.

On October 12, he and his men landed on an island in the Bahamas, which its inhabitants called *Guanahaní*, but which he renamed San Salvador. (Because Columbus's sketchy description of his landfall can be variously interpreted, two different places—Watling Island and Samaná Cay—are today proposed as contenders for Columbus's landing site.) Later, he went on to explore the islands now known as Cuba and Hispaniola, which their residents, the Taíno people, called *Colba* and *Bohío*. Because he thought he had reached the Indies, Columbus referred to the inhabitants of the region as *Indians*.

Three themes dominate Columbus's log. First, he insistently asked the Taínos where he could find gold, pearls, and valuable spices. Each time, his informants replied (largely via signs) that such products could be obtained on other islands, on the mainland, or in cities in the interior. Eventually, he came to mistrust such answers.

Second, Columbus wrote repeatedly of the strange and beautiful plants and animals he was seeing. Yet Columbus's interest was not merely aesthetic. "I believe that there are many plants and trees here that could be worth a lot in Spain for use as dyes, spices, and medicines," he observed, adding that he was carrying home to Europe "a sample of everything I can," so experts could examine them.

Third, Columbus also described the islands' human residents, and he seized some to take back to Spain. The Taínos were, he said, handsome, gentle,

The Taíno People

and friendly, although they told him of fierce people who raided their villages and lived on other nearby islands. Those Caniba (today called Caribs), from whose name the word *cannibal* is derived, were reported to eat their captives. By contrast, Columbus

believed the Taínos to be likely converts to Catholicism. But he had more in mind than conversion. The islanders "ought to make good and skilled servants," Columbus declared.

Thus the first encounter between Europeans and America and its residents revealed a theme that would be of enormous significance for centuries to come: the Europeans' desire to extract profits from the continent by exploiting its natural resources, including plants, animals, and peoples.

Christopher Columbus made three more westward voyages, exploring most major Caribbean islands and sailing along the coasts of Central and South America. Until the day he died in 1506, Columbus believed that he had reached Asia. Even before his death, others knew better. Because the Florentine Amerigo Vespucci, who explored the South American coast in 1499, was the first to publish the idea that a new continent had been found, Martin Waldseemüller in 1507 labeled the land *America*. By then, Spain, Portugal, and Pope Alexander VI had signed the Treaty of Tordesillas (1494), confirming Portugal's dominance in Africa and Brazil in exchange for Spanish preeminence in the rest of the New World.

The first mariners to explore the region of North America that was to become the United States and Canada followed a different route. Some historians argue that European sailors probably found the rich Newfoundland fishing grounds in the 1480s, but that such men would have kept their findings a secret so that they alone could exploit the sea's bounty. Whether fishermen had crossed the entire width of the Atlantic or not, they had thoroughly explored its northern reaches. Just as the Portuguese traveled regularly in the Mediterranean Atlantic, fifteenth-century English seafarers and others voyaged among the European continent, England, Ireland, and Iceland.

Five hundred years before Columbus, in the year 1001, Leif Ericsson and other explorers from Greenland briefly established a settlement at a western site they named Vineland. (In the 1960s, archaeologists determined that this encampment was located at what is now L'anse aux Meadows, Newfoundland.) Attacks by local residents forced them to depart hurriedly, the tale of their exploits subsequently preserved in oral history sagas. As a result, the European generally credited with "discovering" North America is John Cabot. More precisely, Cabot brought to Europe the first formal knowledge of the northern coastline of the continent.

Like Columbus, Cabot was a master mariner from the Italian city-state of Genoa. He is known to have been in Spain when Columbus returned from his first trip to America. Calculating that England—which traded with Asia only through a long series of middlemen stretching from Belgium to Venice to the Muslim world—would be eager to sponsor exploratory voyages, Cabot sought and won the support of King Henry VII. He set sail from Bristol in late May 1497, reaching his destination on June 24. Scholars disagree

John Cabot's Northern Explorations

about where he landed (some say it was Cape Breton Island, others that it was Newfoundland), but all recognize the importance of his month-long exploration of the coast.

The voyages of Columbus, Cabot, and their successors finally brought the Eastern and Western Hemispheres together. The Portuguese explorer Pedro Alvares Cabral reached Brazil in 1500, John Cabot's son Sebastian followed his father to North America in 1507, France financed Giovanni da Verrazzano in 1524 and Jacques Cartier in 1534, and in 1609 and 1610 Henry Hudson explored the North American coast for the Dutch West India Company (see map). Although these men were primarily searching for the legendary, nonexistent Northwest Passage through the Americas, what they learned interested European nations in exploring the New World for its own sake.

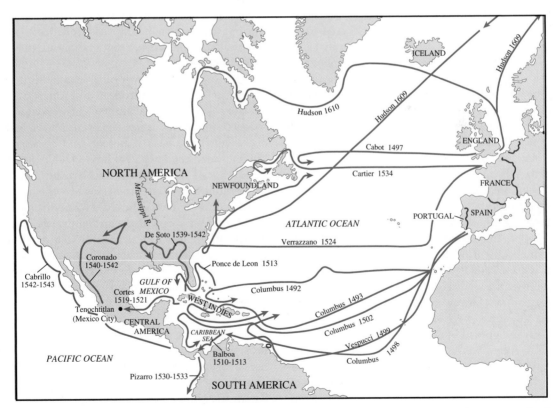

European Explorations in America   *In the century following Columbus's voyages, European adventurers explored the coasts and parts of the interior of North and South America.*

SPANISH COLONIZATION AND THE EXCHANGE OF DISEASES, PLANTS, AND ANIMALS

The Europeans' greatest effect on the Americas was unintended. Diseases carried from the Old World to the new by the alien invaders killed millions of Native Americans, who had no immunity to germs that had infested Europe, Asia, and Africa for centuries. Smallpox, which was spread by direct human contact, was the greatest killer. Other devastating diseases included measles and influenza. Their toll was staggering. When Columbus landed on Hispaniola in 1492, more than one million people probably lived there. Fifty years later, only five hundred were still alive.

The human destruction of a smallpox epidemic that began in Hispaniola in 1518 was felt far beyond the island's shore. Cortés and his army carried the disease to the mainland. When they failed to conquer the Aztec capital of Tenochtitlán in 1520, they left behind smallpox germs. The following year, the greatly weakened defenders surrendered, and the Spaniards built what is now Mexico City on the site of Tenochtitlán.

Far to the north, where smaller American populations encountered only a few European explorers, missionaries, traders, and fishermen, disease also ravaged the countryside. A great epidemic, most likely chicken pox, swept through the villages along the coast north of Cape Cod in 1616 to 1618. The mortality rate may have been as high as 90 percent. An English traveler several years later commented that the people had "died on heapes, as they lay in their houses," and that bones and skulls covered the remains of their villages. Because of this dramatic depopulation of the area, just a few years later English colonists were able to establish settlements virtually unopposed by Native Americans.

The Americans did take a revenge of sorts. They gave the Europeans syphilis. The first recorded case of the new disease in Europe occurred in Barcelona, Spain, in 1493, shortly after Columbus's return from the Caribbean. Although less likely than smallpox to cause immediate death, syphilis was extremely dangerous and debilitating. Carried by soldiers, sailors, and prostitutes, it spread quickly through Europe and Asia, reaching as far as China by 1505.

The exchange of diseases was only part of a broader mutual transfer of plants and animals that resulted directly from European voyages. Many

Exchange of Plants and Animals

large mammals, like cattle and horses, were native to the connected continents of Europe, Asia, and Africa, but the Americas contained no domesticated beasts larger than dogs and llamas. On the other hand, the vegetable crops of the New World—particularly corn, beans, squash, cassava, and potatoes—were more nutritious and produced higher yields than those of the old, like wheat and rye. In time, the Native Americans learned to raise and consume European livestock, and the Europeans and Africans became accustomed to planting and eating American crops. As a result, the diets of all three peoples were vastly enriched. One consequence was the doubling of the world's population in the next three hundred years.

The exchange of two other commodities significantly influenced European and American civilizations. In America, Europeans encountered tobacco, which was at first believed to have beneficial medicinal effects. Smoking and chewing the "Indian weed" became a fad in the Old World after it was sowed in Turkey in the sixteenth century. More immediately important was how the horse affected some Indian cultures. Horses brought to America by the Spaniards inevitably fell into the hands of Native Americans. Traded northward among the tribes, they eventually became essential to the life of the nomadic buffalo hunters of the Great Plains. Apaches, Comanches, and Blackfeet, among others, used horses for transportation and hunting, calculated their wealth in the number of horses they owned, and waged wars primarily from horseback. Women no longer had to carry the bands' belongings on their backs. Through the acquisition of horses, then, subsistence that had been based on hunting several different animals, combined with gathering and agriculture, became focused almost wholly on hunting buffalo.

The historian Alfred W. Crosby has coined the useful term *portmanteau biota* to describe the biological aspect of the European and African invasion of the Americas. That is, the invaders carried with them—in effect, in their luggage (or portmanteaus)—the plant and animal life with which they were familiar. Some creatures, such as livestock, they brought deliberately. Others, including rats, weeds, and diseases, arrived unexpectedly. And the same process occurred in reverse. When the Europeans packed to return home, they deliberately took back such crops as corn, potatoes, and tobacco, along with that unanticipated hitchhiker, syphilis.

All residents of the Americas would eventually feel the effects of the Europeans' portmanteau biota, but only in the areas explored and claimed by Spain did formal colonization begin immediately. On his second voyage in 1493, Columbus brought to Hispaniola seventeen ships loaded with twelve hundred men, seeds, plants, livestock, chickens, and dogs—along with germs and weeds. The settlement named Isabela (in the modern Dominican Republic) and its successors became the staging area for the Spanish invasion of America.

At first, Spanish explorers fanned out around the Caribbean basin. In 1513, Juan Ponce de León reached Florida, and Vasco Núñez de Balboa crossed the Isthmus of Panama **Conquistadores** to the Pacific Ocean. Eight years later, the Spaniards' dreams of wealth were realized when Cortés conquered the Aztec empire, seizing a fabulous treasure of gold and silver. Venturing north, conquistadores like Juan Rodriguez Cabrillo (who sailed along the California coast), Hernando de Soto (who journeyed to the Mississippi River), and Francisco Vásquez de Coronado (who explored the southwestern portion of what is now the United States) found few products the Spanish coveted. By contrast, Francisco Pizarro, who explored the western coast of South America, acquired the richest silver mines in the world by conquering and enslaving the Incas in 1535. By 1550, the Spanish monarchs controlled the richest, most extensive empire Europe had known since ancient Rome.

Spain established the model of colonization that other countries later attempted to imitate, a model with three major elements. First, the crown maintained tight control over the colonies, establishing a hierarchical government that allowed little autonomy to New World jurisdictions. Second, most colonists sent from Spain were male. They married Indian—and later black—women, thereby creating the racially mixed population that characterizes much of Latin America today. Third, the colonies' wealth was based on the exploitation of both the native population and slaves imported from Africa. The *encomienda* system, which granted tribute from Indian villages to individual conquistadores as a reward for their services to the crown, in effect legalized slavery. Laws adopted in 1542 reformed the system by forbidding Spaniards to enslave Indians. In response, the conquerors, familiar with slavery in Spain, began to import Africans to increase the labor force under their direct control.

Spanish wealth derived from American suffering. The Spaniards deliberately leveled American cities, building cathedrals and monasteries on sites once occupied by Aztec, Incan, and Mayan temples. Some conquistadores sought to erase all vestiges of the great Indian cultures by burning the written records they found. With traditional ways of life in disarray, devastated by disease, and compelled to labor for their conquerors, many demoralized residents of Mesoamerica accepted the Christian religion brought to New Spain by Franciscan and Dominican friars.

At first, the friars devoted their energies to persuading the Native Americans to move into new towns and to build Roman Catholic churches. In **Christianity in New Spain** such towns, they were exposed to European customs and to religious rituals newly elaborated in an attempt to assimilate Christianity and pagan beliefs. For example, the friars deliberately juxtaposed the cult of the Virgin Mary with that of the corn goddess. Their conversion efforts met with remarkable success.

The Spanish missionaries who ventured into the territory that is now the eastern United States were less able to win converts, for villages there resisted the invaders. After several failed attempts to colonize the Atlantic coast, the Spanish established St. Augustine, Florida, in 1565. Efforts to Christianize the local Indians succeeded only after the Franciscans, with the assistance of soldiers, forcibly moved them to mission towns; even then, many resisted the friars' message. Still, by the end of the sixteenth century, a chain of Spanish missions stretched across northern Florida.

EUROPEAN TRADERS, FISHERMEN, AND EARLY SETTLEMENTS

Unlike the Spanish, other European nations did not start at once to colonize the coasts their sailors had explored. They were more interested in exploiting natural wealth than in conquering territories or introducing alien crops. The first important natural resource of North America was fish. John Cabot had reported that fish were so plentiful they could be caught merely by lowering baskets over the side of a vessel. Europeans rushed to take advantage of the abundance of fish, a product in great demand in their homelands. By the 1570s, more than 350 ships were exploiting the bounty of the Newfoundland Banks each year.

Fishermen adopted different modes of working that were to have significant consequences for the history of the region. Mariners from Spain, Portugal, and southern France had abundant supplies of salt, produced in their home countries by evaporating sea water. Thus they used "wet" fishery techniques: the sailors filled cask after cask with salted, gutted fish until the ship could hold no more. English seafarers, lacking ready access to salt, were forced to use "dry" fishing. They set up camps on shore, where half the fishermen stayed to process and dry the fish the crew members caught. Because they needed more reliable sunshine to dry their catch than the foggy Newfoundland coast provided, they tended to fish in the more southerly waters off what is now Maine. As a result, when European nations moved to colonize what is now eastern Canada and the far northeastern United States, England had the best claim to the land, long although sporadically inhabited by its fishermen.

European fishermen soon learned that they could supplement their profits by exchanging cloth and metal goods such as pots and knives for the Native Americans' beaver pelts, which Europeans used to make fashionable hats. At first, the Europeans conducted their trading from ships sailing along the coast, but later they established permanent outposts on the mainland to centralize and control the traffic in furs.

Northern Traders

The Europeans' insatiable demand for furs, especially beaver, was matched by the Native Americans' desire for European goods that could make their lives easier and establish their superiority over neighboring tribes. Some tribes began to concentrate so completely on trapping for the European market that they abandoned their traditional economies. The Abenakis of Maine, for example, became partially dependent on food supplied by their neighbors to the south, the Massachusett tribe, because they devoted most of their energies to catching beaver to sell to French traders. The Massachusetts, in turn, intensified their production of foodstuffs, which they traded to the Abenakis in exchange for the European metal tools.

Although their nation was profiting handsomely from the fisheries and the fur trade, English merchants and political leaders watched enviously as Spain's American possessions enriched that country immeasurably. In the mid-sixteenth century, English sea dogs such as John Hawkins and Sir Francis Drake began to raid Spanish treasure fleets sailing home from the West Indies. Their actions caused friction between the two countries and helped to foment a war that culminated in the defeat of a huge invasion force—the Spanish Armada—off the English coast in 1588. As a part of their contest with Spain, English people started to think about planting colonies in the Western Hemisphere, thereby preventing their enemy from completely dominating the New World and simultaneously gaining better access to valuable American commodities.

The first English colonial planners hoped to reproduce Spanish successes by dispatching to America men who would similarly exploit the native

John White, an artist with Raleigh's 1585 expedition (and later the governor of the ill-fated 1587 colony), illustrated three fishing techniques used by Carolina Indians: to the left, the construction of weirs and traps; in the background, spearfishing in shallow water; and, in the foreground, fishing from dugout canoes. The fish are accurately drawn and can be identified by species today. Courtesy of the Trustees of the British Museum.

Raleigh's Roanoke Colony

peoples for their own and their nation's benefit. In the 1580s, a group that included Sir Humphrey Gilbert and Sir Walter Raleigh promoted a scheme to establish outposts that could trade with the Indians and provide bases for attacks on New Spain. Approving the idea, Queen Elizabeth I authorized Raleigh and Gilbert to colonize North America. Gilbert failed to plant a colony in Newfoundland, and Raleigh was only briefly more

successful. In 1587, he sent 117 colonists to the territory he named Virginia (for Elizabeth, the "Virgin Queen"). They established a settlement on Roanoke Island, in what is now North Carolina, but in 1590 a resupply ship could not find them. The colonists had vanished, leaving only the name of a nearby island carved on a tree.

Thus England's first attempt to plant a permanent settlement on the North American coast failed, as had earlier efforts by Portugal on Cape Breton Island (early 1520s) and France in northern Florida (mid-1560s). All three enterprises collapsed for the same two reasons: the inability to be self-sustaining with respect to food and the hostility of neighboring groups, both American and European. A Spanish attack wiped out the French colony in 1565, and neither the Portuguese nor the English were able to maintain friendly relations with local Indians for long.

The explanation for such failings becomes clear in Thomas Harriot's *A Briefe and True Report of the New Found Land of Virginia*, published in 1588 to publicize Raleigh's colony. Harriot was a noted English scientist who sailed on an exploratory voyage to Roanoke and who was charged with describing the animals, plants, and people of the region for an English readership. His account revealed that although the explorers had been almost wholly dependent on nearby villagers for food, they had needlessly antagonized their neighbors by killing some for what Harriot acknowledged were unjustifiable reasons.

Harriot's *Briefe and True Report* depicted for his English readers a bountiful land open to easy exploitation, full of opportunities for profit. The people already resident there would, he thought, "in a short time be brought to civilitie" through conversion to Christianity, admiration of European superiority, conquest, or, quite simply, death from disease. Harriot understood the key elements of the story, but his prediction was far off the mark. European dominance of North America was to be difficult to achieve.

The process of initial contact between Europeans and Americans that ended near the close of the sixteenth century had begun approximately 250 years earlier when Portuguese sailors first set out to explore the Mediterranean Atlantic and to settle on its islands. That region of the Atlantic, so close to European and African shores, nurtured mariners such as Christopher Columbus who ventured into previously unknown waters. When he first reached the Americas, Columbus thought he had found his intended destination, Asia. Later explorers knew better but, except for the Spanish, regarded the Americas primarily as a barrier that prevented them from reaching their long-sought goal of an oceanic route to the riches of China and the Moluccas. Ordinary European fishermen were the first to realize that the northern coasts had valuable products to offer: fish and furs, both much in demand in their homelands.

Of course, the wealth of the north could not compare to that of Mesoamerica. The Aztec empire, heir to the trading networks of Teotihuacán as well as to the intellectual sophistication of the Mayas, dazzled the conquistadores with the magnificence of its buildings and its seemingly unlimited wealth. Nonetheless, the Spaniards destroyed the temples and used their stone, as well as Indian laborers, to construct cathedrals honoring their God and his son Jesus rather than Huitzilopochtli. The conquerors used first Native Americans and, later, enslaved African workers to till the fields, mine the precious metals, and herd the livestock that earned immense profits for them and Spain.

The initial effect of Europeans on the Americas proved devastating. Flourishing civilizations were, if not entirely destroyed, markedly altered in just a few short decades. The Europeans' diseases and livestock, along with a wide range of other imported plants and animals, irrevocably changed the American environment, affecting the lives of the Western Hemisphere's inhabitants. By the end of the sixteenth century, many fewer people resided on the continent than had lived there before Columbus's arrival, even taking European immigration into account. And the people who did live there—Indian, African, and European—lived in a world that was literally new, a world engaged in the unprecedented process of combining foods, religions, economies, styles of life, and political systems that had developed separately for millennia. Conflict and dissension were to permeate that process.

SUGGESTIONS FOR FURTHER READING

General

Alfred W. Crosby, *Ecological Imperialism: The Biological Expansion of Europe, 800–1900* (1986), and *The Columbian Exchange: Biological and Cultural Consequences of 1492* (1972); William H. McNeill, *Plagues and Peoples* (1976); D. W. Meinig, *Atlantic America, 1492–1800* (1986); Zvi Dor Ner and William Scheller, *Columbus and the Age of Discovery* (1991); Kirkpatrick Sale, *The Conquest of Paradise: Christopher Columbus and the Columbus Legacy* (1990).

Mesoamerican Civilizations

Inga Clendinnen, *Aztecs* (1991); Michael Coe, *Mexico*, 3d ed. (1984); Brian Fagan, *Kingdoms of Gold, Kingdoms of Jade: The Americas Before Columbus* (1991); Charles Gallenkamp, *Maya: The Riddle and Rediscovery of a Lost Civilization*, 3d ed. (1985).

North American Indians

Brian Fagan, *The Great Journey: The Peopling of Ancient America* (1987); Alvin Josephy Jr., ed., *America in 1492* (1992); Robert Silverberg, *The Moundbuilders of Ancient America: The Archaeology of a Myth* (1968); Colin F. Taylor, ed., *The Native Americans: The Indigenous People of North America* (1992).

Africa

Philip Curtin et al., *African History* (1978); Richard Olaniyan, *African History and Culture* (1982); Roland Oliver and J. D. Fage, *A Short History of Africa* (1988).

Exploration and Discovery

Fredi Chiappelli et al., eds., *First Images of America: The Impact of the New World on the Old*, 2 vols. (1976); Felipe Fernández-Armesto, *Before Columbus: Exploration and Colonization from the Mediterranean to the Atlantic, 1229–1492* (1987); Samuel Eliot Morison, *The European Discovery of America: The Southern Voyages, a.d. 1492–1616* (1974), and *The European Discovery of America: The Northern Voyages, a.d. 1500–1600* (1971); J. H. Parry, *The Discovery of the Sea* (1974), and *The Age of Reconnaissance* (1963); William and Carla Phillips, *The Worlds of Christopher Columbus* (1992); David B. Quinn, *North America from Earliest Discovery to First Settlements* (1977).

Early European Settlements

Kenneth Andrews, *Trade, Plunder and Settlement: Maritime Enterprise and the Genesis of the British Empire, 1480–1630* (1984); Leslie Bethel, ed., *The Cambridge History of Latin America, vol. 2: Colonial Latin America* (1984); Charles Gibson, *Roanoke, the Abandoned Colony* (1984); David J. Weber, *The Spanish Frontier in North America* (1992).

Europeans Colonize North America, 1600–1640

R OBERT RYCE WAS WORRIED, for he had learned that a good friend was seriously considering emigrating to North America. In August 1629, he took up his pen to convince John Winthrop, a Suffolk justice of the peace, to think twice before embarking for the New World. "Plantations ar for yonge men, that can enduer all paynes and hunger," he advised Winthrop, who was then forty-one, with eight children born to three wives. "To adventure your wholle famylly vpon so many manifeste vncerteynties standeth not with your wysdome and longe experience."

Winthrop was not dissuaded. Like many of his pious contemporaries, he believed that England had become corrupt. In his opinion, the Church of England, which had split from Roman Catholicism during the sixteenth century, needed to be purified; hence, Winthrop and others like him were called Puritans. He thought the easiest way to avoid conflicts with the leaders of the English church and to worship as he pleased was to emigrate to America, a remote land beyond the immediate reach of English religious authorities.

Winthrop also believed that Protestants should become as active as Catholics in attempting to convert nonbelievers to Christianity. Puritan colonizers in America could work toward that goal. And why, Winthrop asked, should people continue to live in crowded England, when "whole countrys . . . lye waste without any improvement"? When someone pointed out to him that "other sonnes of Adam" already lived on the land he coveted, he responded confidently, "These salvadge peoples ramble over muche lande without title or propertye."

More than any other European people colonizing the Americas, the English tried to reproduce the society they had left. They did not, of course, want to copy it without any modifications; Winthrop and other Puritans sought to reform English religious practices, and other emigrants were trying to better their economic circumstances. Even so, the English colonists differed significantly from their Spanish, French, and Dutch counterparts. The American settlements of those nations were composed primarily of male emigrants who hoped to make a quick profit from the New World's lands and peoples and then return to their homelands.

The English were no less interested in profiting financially from North America. But especially to New England they emigrated as families, sometimes with friends and relatives from neighboring villages. Most English people came to America with the intention of staying. They recreated European society and family life to an extent not possible in the other, more thinly populated colonies, in which migrant men had to find their sexual partners within the Native American or African populations. Of the English colonies, those in the Chesapeake region and on the Caribbean islands most closely resembled colonies founded by other nations. Their economies, like those of New Spain, soon came to be based on large-scale production for the international market by a labor force composed of bonded servants and slaves.

Wherever they settled, the English, like other Europeans, failed to prosper until they had learned to adapt to the alien environment. The first permanent English colonies survived only because nearby Indians assisted the newcomers. The settlers had to learn to grow such unfamiliar American crops as maize and tobacco. They also had to develop extensive trading relationships with Native Americans and with colonies established by other European countries. In need of laborers for their fields, they eventually began to import African slaves. Thus the early history of the region that became the United States and the English Caribbean can best be understood as a series of complex interactions among a variety of European, African, and American peoples and environments rather than as the simple story of a triumph by only one group, the English colonists.

NEW FRANCE, NEW NETHERLAND, AND THE CARIBBEAN

In the early seventeenth century, the Netherlands and France also established permanent settlements in the region north of New Spain. Varying by location and economic goals, the French and Dutch colonies also for the most part developed quite differently from their English neighbors. The mass migration of English people to mainland North America had no counterpart in other nations' colonies; consequently, population and settlement patterns diverged significantly in the three countries' American possessions.

France's successful colonization in North America began in 1608 when Samuel de Champlain founded a trading post at a site he called Quebec.

New France

He had chosen well: Quebec was the most easily defended spot in the entire St. Lawrence River valley, a stronghold that controlled access to the heartland of the continent. In 1642, the French established a second post, Montreal, at the falls of the St. Lawrence (and thus at the end of navigation by ocean-going vessels).

Before the founding of Quebec and Montreal, French fishermen had served as the major conduits through which North American beaver pelts reached France, but the two new posts quickly took control of the lucrative fur trade. In an effort to attract settlers, the colony's leaders offered land grants along the river to prospective settlers, including wealthy seigneurs (nobles) who were expected to import tenants to work their farms. A small number of Frenchmen brought their wives and took up agriculture; even so, more than twenty-five years after Quebec's founding, it had just sixty-four resident families, along with traders and soldiers.

One other important group comprised part of the population of New France: missionaries of the Society of Jesus (Jesuits), a Roman Catholic order

Jesuit Missions in New France

dedicated to converting nonbelievers to Christianity. The first Jesuits arrived in the colony in 1625. In 1639, they were joined in New France by two orders of nuns, the most important of which were the Ursulines. The Jesuits, whom the Native Americans called Black Robes, initially tried to persuade the tribal peoples to live near French settlements and to adopt European lifestyles as well as the Europeans' religion. When that effort failed, the Jesuits learned Native American languages and traveled to remote regions in pursuit of their goal. By the early eighteenth century, they were living in present-day Illinois.

• *Important Events* •

1533	Henry VIII divorces Catherine of Aragon; English Reformation begins	**1624**	Dutch settle on Manhattan Island (New Amsterdam)
1558	Elizabeth I becomes queen		English colonize St. Christopher, first island in Lesser Antilles to be settled by Europeans
1603	James I becomes king		
1607	Jamestown founded; first permanent English settlement in North America	**1625**	Charles I becomes king
		1630	Massachusetts Bay colony founded
1608	Quebec founded by the French	**1634**	Maryland founded
1611	First Virginia tobacco crop	**1635**	Roger Williams expelled from Massachusetts Bay; founds Providence, Rhode Island
1614	Fort Orange (Albany) founded by the Dutch		
1619	First Africans arrive in Virginia	**1636**	Connecticut founded
	Virginia House of Burgesses established, first representative assembly in the English colonies	**1637**	Pequot War in New England
			Anne Hutchinson expelled from Massachusetts Bay colony; goes to Rhode Island
1620	Plymouth colony founded; first permanent English settlement in New England		
		ca. 1640	Sugar cultivation begins on Barbados
1622	Powhatan Confederacy attacks Virginia colony	**1642**	Montreal founded

In their pursuit of conversions, the Jesuits sought to undermine the authority of village shamans (the traditional religious leaders) and to gain the confidence of leaders who could influence others. The Black Robes used a variety of weapons to attain the desired end. Trained in rhetoric, they won admirers by their eloquence. Seemingly immune to smallpox, they explained epidemics among the Native Americans as God's punishment for sin. Drawing on European science, the Jesuits predicted solar and lunar eclipses. Perhaps most important, they amazed the villagers by communicating with each other over long distances and periods of time by using marks on paper. The Native Americans' desire to learn how to harness the extraordinary power of literacy was a critical factor in making them receptive to the Jesuits' message.

Although the process took many years, the Jesuits slowly gained thousands of converts. The converts replaced their own culture's traditional equal treatment of men and women with notions more congenial to the Europeans' insistence on male dominance and female subordination. Further, they altered their practice of allowing premarital sexual relationships and easy divorce, because Catholic doctrine prohibited both customs.

The Jesuit missionaries had no competition from other Europeans for the Native Americans' souls, but French traders confronted a challenge. In 1614, just five years after Henry Hudson sailed up the river that now bears his name, his Dutch sponsors established an outpost, Fort Orange, on the site of present-day Albany, New York. Like the French, they sought beaver pelts, and their presence so close to Quebec posed at least a potential threat to French domination of the region. Holland, at the time the world's dominant commercial power, was interested primarily in trade rather than colonization. Thus New Netherland, like New France, remained small. The colony's southern anchor was New Amsterdam, a town founded in 1624 on Manhattan Island.

The Founding of Permanent European Colonies in North America, 1565–1640

Colony	Founder(s)	Date	Basis of Economy
Florida	Pedro Menendez de Avilés	1565	farming
New Mexico	Juan de Oñate	1598	livestock
Virginia	Virginia Company	1607	tobacco
New France	France	1608	fur trading
New Netherland	Dutch West India Company	1614	fur trading
Plymouth	Pilgrims	1620	farming, fishing
Maine	Sir Ferdinando Gorges	1622	fishing
St. Kitts, Barbados, et al.	European migrants	1624	sugar
Massachusetts Bay	Massachusetts Bay Company	1630	farming, fishing, fur trading
Maryland	Cecilius Calvert	1634	tobacco
Rhode Island	Roger Williams	1635	farming
Connecticut	Thomas Hooker	1636	farming, fur trading
New Haven	Massachusetts migrants	1638	farming
New Hampshire	Massachusetts migrants	1638	farming, fishing

New Netherland

New Netherland, the Dutch West India Company's outpost in North America, was relatively unimportant, because the company's chief economic interests lay elsewhere. Autocratic directors-general ruled the colony for the company; with no elected assembly, settlers felt little loyalty to their nominal leaders. Migration was insignificant. Even a company policy of 1629 that offered a large land grant, or patroonship, to anyone who would bring fifty settlers to the province failed to attract takers. As late as the mid-1660s, New Netherland had only about five thousand inhabitants.

Despite their geographical proximity, New France and New Netherland did not come into serious conflict. Yet their respective American trading partners did. In the 1640s, the Iroquois, who traded chiefly with the Dutch and lived in modern upstate New York, went to war against their northern neighbors, the Hurons, who traded primarily with the French and lived in present-day Ontario. The Iroquois wanted to become the major supplier of pelts to the Europeans and to ensure the security of their hunting territories. They achieved both goals by practically exterminating the Hurons (whose population had already been decimated by a recent epidemic) by using guns they obtained from their Dutch allies. The Iroquois thus established themselves as a major force in the region, one that Europeans could ignore only at their peril.

It was in the Caribbean that France, Holland, and England clashed most openly in the first half of the seventeenth century. The Spanish had concentrated their colonization efforts on the larger islands, the Greater Antilles: Cuba, Hispaniola, Jamaica, and Puerto Rico. The smaller islands, ignored by the Spanish, were valuable targets for other European powers. The English, French, and Dutch saw such islands as bases from which they could attack each other and Spanish vessels loaded with gold and silver from the Americas. Moreover, they could also serve as sources of tropical products.

The English were the first of the northern European nations to establish a permanent foothold in the smaller islands of the West Indies, the Lesser Antilles. They founded a settlement on St. Christopher (St. Kitts) in 1624 and Barbados in 1627. In the 1630s, the French also moved on to St. Kitts, then to Guadeloupe and Martinique, and the Dutch settled on Curaçao (near the South American coast) in 1634 as well as on St. Eustatius. As a result of conflict among the European powers, most islands were attacked at least once during the century, and some changed hands. For example, the English drove the Spanish from Jamaica in 1655, and the French soon thereafter took over half of Hispaniola, creating the colony of St. Domingue (modern Haiti).

Why did the European powers devote so much energy to gaining control of the tiny bits of land Spain had neglected? After 1640, one product was the primary answer to that question: sugar.

Supplying Europe's Sweet Tooth

At the beginning of the seventeenth century, most American sugar came from Brazil. In 1630, the Dutch seized control of Brazil from Portugal, holding it until 1654. There the Dutch learned how to grow—and, more important—to process sugar cane. The Dutch then taught these skills to the English on Barbados, who by 1640 had found that their soil and climate were ideal for the cultivation of sugar cane. The Dutch were not being altruistic: they expected to sell African slaves to West Indian planters and to

In the 1660s, a French book illustrated the various phases of sugar processing for curious European readers. Teams of oxen (A) turned the mill, the rollers of which crushed the canes (C), producing the sap (D), which was collected in a vat (E), then boiled down into molasses (K). All phases of the process were managed primarily by African slaves, with minimal supervision by a few Europeans (foreground). Library Company of Philadelphia.

carry the barrels of sugar back to Europe. The results must have exceeded their wildest dreams. The Barbados sugar boom in the 1640s was both explosive and lucrative. Planters, slave traders, and Dutch shipping interests alike earned immense profits. Of course, as other Caribbean planters adopted sugar cane cultivation, the Barbadians' profits fell. Nevertheless, sugar remained the most valuable American commodity for more than one hundred years. In the eighteenth century, sugar grown in British Jamaica and French St. Domingue dominated the world market. Yet, in the long run, the economic importance of the Europeans' American colonies lay on the mainland rather than in the Caribbean.

ENGLAND COLONIZES MAINLAND NORTH AMERICA

The failure of Raleigh's attempt to colonize Virginia had halted English efforts to settle in North America for nearly two decades. When the English decided in 1606 to try once more, they again planned colonies that imitated the Spanish model. Success came only when they abandoned that model and sent large numbers of men and women to set up agricultural colonies on the mainland. Two major developments prompted approximately two hundred thousand ordinary English men and women to move to North America in the seventeenth century and led their government to encourage that migration.

The first development was a significant change in English religious practice, a transformation that eventually led large numbers of English dissenters to leave their homeland. In
English Reformation
1533, Henry VIII, wanting a male heir, sought to annul his marriage to his Spanish-born queen, Catherine of Aragon. When the pope refused to approve the annulment, Henry left the Roman Catholic church, founded the Church of England, and—with Parliament's concurrence—proclaimed himself its head. At first, the reformed Church of England differed little from Catholicism in its practices, but under Henry's daughter Elizabeth I, new currents of religious

belief, which had originated on the European continent early in the sixteenth century, dramatically affected the English church.

The leaders of the continental Protestant Reformation were Martin Luther, a German monk, and John Calvin, a French cleric and lawyer. Combating the Catholic doctrine that priests must serve as intermediaries between lay people and God, Luther and Calvin insisted that every individual could interpret the Bible. Both Luther and Calvin rejected Catholic rituals and denied the need for an elaborate church hierarchy. They also asserted that salvation came through faith alone, rather than—as Catholic teaching had it—through a combination of faith and good works. Calvin, though, went further than Luther in stressing God's absolute omnipotence and emphasizing the need for people to submit totally to God's will.

Elizabeth I tolerated religious diversity among her subjects so long as they generally acknowledged her authority as head of the Church of England.
Puritans
Accordingly, during her long reign (1558–1603), Calvin's ideas gained influence within the English church. By the late sixteenth century, many English Calvinists—those who, like John Winthrop, came to be called Puritans—believed that the English Reformation had not gone far enough. Henry had simplified the church hierarchy; they wanted to abolish it altogether. Henry had subordinated the church to the interests of the state; they wanted a church free from political interference. And the Church of England, like the Roman Catholic church, continued to include all English people in its membership. The Puritans preferred a more restricted definition; they wanted to confine church membership to persons believed to be "saved."

Elizabeth I's Stuart successors, her cousin James I (1603–1625) and his son Charles I (1625–1649), were less tolerant of Puritans than she. As Scots, they also had little respect for the traditions of representative government that had developed in England under the Tudors and their predecessors. The Stuarts insisted that a monarch's power came directly from God and that subjects had a duty to obey the monarch, whose authority was absolute. Both James I and Charles I believed that their authority included the power to enforce religious conformity among their subjects. Because Puritans were challenging many of the most important precepts of the English church, the monarchs authorized the removal of Puritan clergy from their pulpits. In the 1620s and 1630s, a number of English Puritans accordingly decided to move to America, where they hoped to put their religious beliefs into practice unmolested by the Stuarts or the church hierarchy.

The second major development that led English folk to move to North America was the onset of dramatic social and economic change caused

Social Change in England
_____

by the doubling of the English population in the 150-year period after 1530, largely as a result of the introduction of nutritious American crops in Europe. All those additional people needed food, clothing, and other goods. The competition for goods led to high inflation, coupled with a fall in real wages as the number of workers increased. In these new economic and demographic circumstances, some English people—especially those with sizable landholdings that could produce food and clothing fibers for the growing population—substantially improved their lot. Others, particularly landless laborers and those with very small amounts of land, fell into unremitting poverty.

Well-to-do English people reacted with alarm to what they saw as the disappearance of traditional ways of life. The streets and highways filled with steady streams of the landless and the homeless. Obsessed with the problem of maintaining order, officials came to believe that England was overcrowded. They concluded that colonies established in the New World could siphon off England's "surplus population," thus easing the social strains at home. For similar reasons, many English people decided that they could improve their circumstances by migrating to a land-rich continent. Such economic considerations affected English people's decisions to migrate to the colonies as much as, if not more than, a desire for escape from religious persecution.

The initial impetus for the establishment of what was to become England's first permanent colony in the Western Hemisphere came from a group of merchants and wealthy gentry. In 1606, envisioning the possibility of earning great profits from a New World settlement by finding precious metals and opening new trade routes, they set up a joint stock company, the Virginia Company, to plant colonies in America.

Joint stock companies had been developed in England during the sixteenth century as a mechanism for pooling the resources of many small

Joint Stock Companies
_____

investors. Until the founding of the Virginia Company, they had been used primarily to finance trading voyages; for that purpose they worked well. No one person risked too much money, and investors usually received quick returns. But joint stock companies turned out to be a poor way to finance colonies, because the early settlements required enormous amounts of capital and, with rare exceptions, failed to return much immediate profit. The colonies founded by joint stock companies consequently suffered from a chronic lack of capital.

The Virginia Company was no exception. Chartered by James I in 1606, the company tried but failed to start a colony in Maine and barely

Founding of Virginia
_____

succeeded in planting one in Virginia. In 1607, it dispatched 144 men and boys to North America. Ominously, the vessels were ravaged by disease, and only 104 passengers survived the voyage. In May of that year, they established the settlement called Jamestown on a swampy peninsula in a river they also named for their monarch.

Many of the first migrants were gentlemen unaccustomed to working with their hands and artisans with irrelevant skills like glassmaking. Having come to Virginia expecting to make easy fortunes, most could not adjust to the conditions they encountered. They resisted living "like savages," retaining English dress and casual work habits despite their desperate circumstances. Such attitudes, combined with the effects of chronic malnutrition and epidemic disease, took a terrible toll. Only when Captain John Smith, a founder of the colony, imposed military discipline on the colonists in 1608 was Jamestown saved from collapse. But after Smith's departure, the settlement experienced a severe "starving time" (the winter of 1609–1610), during which some colonists even resorted to cannibalism. Although a few wives and children of early settlers arrived in 1609 and living conditions began to improve, as late as 1624 only thirteen hundred of approximately eight thousand English migrants to Virginia remained alive.

That the colony survived at all was a tribute not to the English but to the Native Americans within whose territories they settled, a group of six Algonkian tribes known as the Powhatan Confederacy (see map). Powhatan, a powerful leader, was consolidating his authority over some twenty-five small tribes in the area when the Europeans arrived. Fortunately for the English, Powhatan at first viewed them as potential allies. He found the English colony a reliable source of such items as steel knives and guns, which gave him a technological advantage over his tribal neighbors. In return, Powhatan's tribes traded corn and other foodstuffs to the starving colonists. The initially cordial relationship soon deteriorated, however. The English colonists kidnapped Powhatan's daughter, Pocahontas, holding her hostage in retaliation for Powhatan's seizure of several settlers. In captivity, she agreed in 1614 to marry an Englishman, John Rolfe.

Powhatan Confederacy

Thereafter, the relationship between the Jamestown colony and the coastal tribes was an uneasy one. English and Algonkian peoples had much in common: deep religious beliefs, a lifestyle oriented to agriculture, clear political and social hierarchies, and sharply defined gender roles. Yet the English and the Powhatans usually focused on their cultural differences, not their similarities. English men thought that Indian men were lazy because they hunted (hunting was a sport in English eyes) and did not work in the fields. Indian men thought English men effeminate because they did "women's work" of cultivation. In the same vein, the English believed that Algonkian women were oppressed, because they did heavy field labor.

Other differences between the two cultures caused serious misunderstandings. Although both societies were hierarchical, the nature of the

Algonkian and English Cultural Differences

hierarchies differed considerably. Among the East Coast Algonkian tribes, people were not born to positions of leadership, nor were political power and social status necessarily inherited through the male line. The English gentry inherited their position from their fathers, and English leaders tended to rule autocratically. By contrast, the authority of Algonkian leaders rested on consensus of tribe members. Accustomed to the European concept of powerful kings, the English sought such figures within the tribes. Often (for example, when negotiating treaties) they willfully overestimated the ability of chiefs to make decisions independent of their people.

Furthermore, the Algonkians and the English had different notions of property ownership. In most eastern tribes, the entire group held land communally. It could not be bought or sold absolutely. The English, on the other hand, were accustomed to buying and selling land. In addition, the English refused to accept the validity of tribal claims to traditional hunting territories, insisting that only land intensively cultivated could be regarded as owned or occupied by a tribe.

Above all, the English settlers believed unwaveringly in the superiority of their civilization. They expected the Native Americans to adopt English customs and to convert to Christianity. The English thus showed little respect for traditional Indian ways of life, especially when the English believed their own interests were at stake. That attitude was clearly revealed in the Virginia colony's treatment of the Powhatan Confederacy in subsequent years.

What upset the balance between the English and the Indians was the spread of tobacco cultivation. In tobacco, the settlers and the Virginia

European Settlements and Indian Tribes in Eastern North America, 1650 The few European settlements established before 1650 were widely scattered, hugging the shores of the Atlantic Ocean and the banks of its major rivers. By contrast, America's native inhabitants controlled the vast interior expanse of the continent.

Lake Superior

OTTAWA

NEW FRANCE

Quebec

Montreal

St. Lawrence R.

Lake Huron

HURON
(WYANDOT)

Lake Michigan

POTAWATOMI

Lake Ontario

Lake Erie

ERIE

MIAMI

WINNEBAGO

MOHAWK
ONEIDA
ONONDAGA
CAYUGA
SENECA
IROQUOIS

MAHICAN

Connecticut R.

ABENAKI

MASSACHUSETTS
BAY

Salem

Fort Orange
(Albany)

Hudson R.

Hartford

Boston
POKA-
NOKET

Plymouth
PLYMOUTH

RHODE ISLAND
CONNECTICUT
NEW HAVEN
NEW NETHERLAND
New Amsterdam

MOHEGAN

SUSQUEHANNA

Susquehanna R.

Delaware R.

DELAWARE

Fort Christina (Wilmington)
NEW SWEDEN

NANTICOKE

MARYLAND

POWHATAN

St. Mary's

Chesapeake Bay

VIRGINIA
Jamestown

CHOWAN

Roanoke Island

SHAWNEE

CHEROKEE

TUTELO

TUSCARORA
PAMLICO

CATAWBA
PEDEE
WATEREE

WACCAMAW

SANTEE

CHICKASAW

CUSABO

ATLANTIC OCEAN

CREEK

YAMASEE

GUALE

CHOCTAW

St. Augustine

NEW SPAIN
(FLORIDA)

Extent of settlements

English

Dutch

Swedish

French

Spanish missions

| 0 | 100 | 200 miles |

| 0 | 100 | 200 | 300 kilometers |

Tobacco: The Basis of Virginia's Success

Company found the salable commodity for which they had been searching. John Rolfe planted the first crop in 1611. In 1620, Virginians exported 40,000 pounds of cured leaves, and by the end of that decade shipments had jumped dramatically to 1.5 million pounds. The great tobacco boom had begun, fueled by high prices and substantial profits for planters. Although the price of tobacco fluctuated wildly from year to year, it became the foundation of Virginia's prosperity, and the colony developed from a small outpost peopled exclusively by males into an agricultural settlement inhabited by both men and women.

Successful tobacco cultivation required abundant land, because the crop quickly drained soil of nutrients. Planters soon learned that a field could produce only about three satisfactory crops before it had to lie fallow for several years to regain its fertility. Thus the once small English settlements began to expand rapidly: eager planters applied to the Virginia Company for large land grants on both sides of the James River and its tributaries.

Opechancanough, Powhatan's brother and successor, watched the English colonists steadily encroaching on the confederacy's lands and attempting to convert its members to Christianity. Recognizing the danger his brother had overlooked, he launched coordinated attacks all along the river on March 22, 1622. By the end of the day, 347 colonists (about one-quarter of the total) lay dead, and only a timely warning from two Christian converts saved Jamestown from destruction. The colony survived both this war and one waged by Opechancanough in 1644. His defeat in the latter ended the Powhatan Confederacy's efforts to resist the spread of English settlements.

LIFE IN THE CHESAPEAKE: VIRGINIA AND MARYLAND

In 1624, James I revoked the charter and made Virginia a royal colony, ruled by the king through appointed officials. At the same time, though, he allowed the company's "headright" system and a representative assembly to continue. Under the headright system, every new arrival paying his or her own way was promised a land grant of fifty acres; those who financed the passage of others received headrights for each. To ordinary English farmers, the headright system offered a powerful incentive to migrate to Virginia. To wealthy gentry, it promised the possibility of establishing vast agricultural enterprises worked by large numbers of laborers. The assembly, called the House of Burgesses, had been created in 1619. It gave the landowning men of Virginia a representative government with considerable local autonomy. Thus the political structure of England's American possessions came to differ from that of New Spain, New France, and New Netherland, all of which were ruled autocratically.

By the 1630s, tobacco was firmly established in Virginia as the staple crop and chief source of revenue. It quickly became just as important in the second English colony planted on Chesapeake Bay: Maryland, chartered by Charles I in 1632 and given to the Calvert family as a personal possession (proprietorship). The Calverts intended the colony to serve as a haven for other Roman Catholics, who were being persecuted in England. Cecilius Calvert, second Lord Baltimore, became the first colonizer to offer freedom of religion to all Christian settlers.

Founding of Maryland

In everything but religion, the two Chesapeake colonies resembled each other. In both colonies, planters spread out along the region's deep, wide rivers, which served as the means of transporting imported and exported goods. With little need for commercial centers and with a dispersed population, few towns existed in the Chesapeake.

Because the tasks associated with tobacco culture were labor intensive, planters faced the problem of finding increasing numbers of workers. Nearby tribes could not supply the needed workers, because the region was not densely populated. Dutch traders carried a few Africans to the Chesapeake beginning in 1619, but such merchants could more easily and profitably sell slaves in the

How do historians know

West Indies. Moreover, most Virginians and Marylanders did not at first seek to acquire African workers. In the first half of the seventeenth century, only a few Africans, not all of them slaves, arrived in the Chesapeake. By 1650, only about three hundred blacks lived in Virginia.

Chesapeake tobacco planters thus looked primarily to England to supply their labor needs. When the headright system was adopted in Maryland in 1640, a prospective tobacco planter anywhere in the Chesapeake could simultaneously obtain both land and labor by importing workers from England. Through good management, a planter could use his profits to pay for the passage of more workers and thereby gain title to more land.

Because men did the agricultural work in European societies, planters and workers alike assumed that field laborers should be men. Such

Migrants to the Chesapeake male laborers, along with a few women, migrated to America as indentured servants—that is, in return for their passage, they contracted to work for planters for periods ranging from four to seven years. Indentured servants accounted for 75 to 85 percent of the approximately 130,000 English migrants to Virginia and Maryland during the seventeenth century. Roughly three-quarters of the servant migrants were males aged fifteen to twenty-four; only one in five or six was female. Most men had been farmers and laborers and were what their contemporaries called the common sort.

For such people, the Chesapeake appeared to offer good prospects. Once they had fulfilled the terms of their indentures, servants were promised "freedom dues" consisting of **Conditions of Servitude** clothes, tools, livestock, casks of corn and tobacco, and sometimes even land. Yet the migrants' lives were difficult. Servants typically worked six days a week, ten to fourteen hours a day. Their masters could discipline or sell them, and they faced severe penalties for running away. Even so, the laws did offer them some protection. For example, their masters were supposed to supply them with sufficient food, clothing, and shelter, and servants who were treated especially cruelly could turn to the courts for assistance.

Servants and planters alike had to contend with epidemic disease. Migrants first had to survive the process the colonists called seasoning—a bout with disease (probably malaria) that usually occurred during their first summer in the Chesapeake. They then had to endure recurrences of malaria, along with dysentery, typhoid fever, and other diseases. As a result, approximately 40 percent of male servants did not survive long enough to become freedmen.

For those who survived the term of their indentures, however, the opportunities for advancement were real. Until the last decades of the century, former servants were usually able to become independent planters (freeholders) and to live a modest but comfortable existence. Some even assumed such positions of political prominence as justice of the peace or militia officer. But after 1670,

tobbaco prices fell, good land became expensive, and Maryland dropped its requirement that servants receive land as part of their freedom dues. By 1700, the Chesapeake was no longer the land of opportunity it once had been.

Life in the seventeenth-century Chesapeake was hard for everyone. Farmers (and sometimes their wives) toiled in the fields alongside the servants. Most settlers lived in houses that were little more than shacks, had few material possessions, and consumed a diet based on pork and corn. Indeed, the lack of a nutritious diet magnified the health problems caused by epidemic disease. As a rule, planters devoted their income to improving their farms and buying more laborers rather than enhancing their standard of living.

The predominance of males, the incidence of servitude, and the high mortality rates combined to produce unusual patterns of family life. Female **Family Life in the Chesapeake** servants normally were not allowed to marry during their terms of indenture, because masters did not want pregnancies to deprive them of workers. Many male ex-servants could not marry at all, because there were so few women. On the other hand, nearly every adult free woman in the Chesapeake married, and widows usually remarried within a few months of a husband's death. Yet because their marriages were delayed by servitude or broken by death, Chesapeake women bore only one to three children, in contrast to English women, who normally had at least five.

As a result of the demographic patterns that led to a low rate of natural increase, migrants made up a majority of the Chesapeake population throughout the seventeenth century. That **Chesapeake Politics** fact had important implications for politics in Maryland and Virginia. Because migrants dominated the population, they also composed the vast majority of the membership of Virginia's House of Burgesses and Maryland's House of Delegates (established in 1635). So, too, in each colony they dominated the governor's council, which was simultaneously the colony's highest court, part of the legislature, and executive adviser to the governor.

English-born colonists naturally tended to look to England for solutions to their problems, and migrants frequently relied on English allies to advance their cause. The immigrant leaders of the Chesapeake colonies engaged in bitter and prolonged struggles for power and personal economic advantage; these struggles then crossed the Atlantic, and decisions made in America were laid open to reversal in London. The incessant quarreling and convoluted political tangles thwarted the Virginia and Maryland governments' ability to function effectively. Consequently, the existence of representative assemblies failed to create political stability. Indeed, instability may have been the political price for the Chesapeake's demographic patterns.

THE FOUNDING OF NEW ENGLAND

The economic motives that prompted English people to move to the Chesapeake colonies also drew men and women to New England. But two factors combined to make New England different from the Chesapeake. First, the northern climate and landscape were more conducive to diversified small farms than to large production units yielding staple crops. Second, Puritans organized the New England colonies, and their church became the region's most important institution. Neither the Church of England nor Roman Catholicism held that significance in the Chesapeake.

Religion was a constant presence in the lives of pious Puritans. As followers of John Calvin, they believed that an omnipotent God predestined souls to heaven or hell before birth **Puritan Beliefs** and that Christians could do nothing to change their ultimate fate. One of their primary duties as Christians, though, was to assess the state of their own souls. They thus devoted themselves to self-examination and Bible study. Yet even the most pious could never be absolutely certain that they were among the saved. Consequently, devout Puritans were filled with anxiety about their spiritual state.

Some Puritans (called Congregationalists) wanted to reform the Church of England rather than abandon it. Another group, known as Separatists, believed the Church of England to be so corrupt that it could not be salvaged. The only way to purify it, they believed, was to start anew, establishing their own religious bodies, with membership restricted to the saved, as nearly as they could be identified.

In 1620, some Separatists, many of whom had earlier migrated to Holland in quest of the right to practice their religion freely, received permission to settle in part of the territory **Founding of Plymouth** controlled by the Virginia Company. Later that year, more than one hundred people, only thirty of them Separatists, set sail from Plymouth, England, on the old and crowded *Mayflower.* Two months later, in November, they landed in America, but farther north than they had intended. Because winter was closing in, they decided to stay where they were. They established their colony on a fine harbor and named it Plymouth, after the city from which they had sailed.

Even before they landed, the Pilgrims had to surmount their first challenge—from the "strangers," or non-Puritans, who had sailed with them to America. Because they landed outside the jurisdiction of the Virginia Company, some strangers questioned the authority of the colony's leaders. In response, the Mayflower Compact, signed in November 1620 while everyone was still aboard the ship, established a "Civil Body Politic" and a rudimentary legal authority for the colony. The settlers elected a governor and at first made all decisions for the colony at town meetings. Later, after more towns had been founded and the population had increased, Plymouth, like Virginia and Maryland, created an assembly to which the landowning male settlers elected representatives.

A second challenge facing the Pilgrims in 1620 and 1621 was, quite simply, survival. Like the Jamestown settlers before them, they were poorly prepared to survive in the new environment. Their difficulties were compounded by the season of their arrival, for they barely had time to build shelters before winter descended on them. Only half the

Mayflower's passengers were still alive by spring. But again, like the Virginians, the Pilgrims benefited from the political circumstances of their Native American neighbors.

The Pokanokets (also called Wampanoags), who controlled the area in which the Pilgrims had settled, had suffered terrible losses in the epidemic of 1616–1618. To protect themselves from the powerful Narragansetts of the southern New England coast, the Pokanokets decided to ally themselves with the newcomers. In the spring of 1621, their leader, Massasoit, signed a treaty with the Pilgrims, and during the colony's first difficult years, the Pokanokets supplied the English with essential foodstuffs. The settlers were also assisted by Squanto. In the early 1610s, Squanto had been captured by fishermen and taken to England, where he learned to speak the language. He became the Pilgrims' interpreter and a major source of information about the unfamiliar environment.

Before the 1620s had ended, a group of Congregationalists launched the colonial enterprise that would come to dominate New England. The

Massachusetts Bay Company
——

event that stimulated their interest in the New World was the accession of Charles I to the throne in 1625. Charles was more hostile to Puritan beliefs than his father had been. After he appointed a prominent persecutor of Puritans to the most important position in the Church of England, some non-Separatists began to think about settling in America. A group of Congregationalist merchants sent a body of colonists to Cape Ann, north of Cape Cod, in 1628. The following year, the merchants obtained a royal charter, constituting themselves as the Massachusetts Bay Company.

The new company quickly attracted the attention of Puritans of the "middling sort" who were becoming increasingly convinced that they would no longer be able to practice their religion freely in England. They remained committed to the goal of reforming the Church of England but concluded that they should pursue that aim in America rather than at home. In a dramatic move, the Congregationalist merchants boldly decided to transfer the headquarters of the Massachusetts Bay Company to New England. The settlers would then be answerable to

no one in England and would be able to handle their affairs as they pleased.

The most important recruit to the new venture was John Winthrop. In October 1629, the members of the Massachusetts Bay Company elected

Governor John Winthrop
——

Winthrop as their governor. With the exception of a few scattered years, he served in that post until his death in 1649. It thus fell to Winthrop to organize the initial segment of the great Puritan migration to America. In 1630, more than one thousand English men and women came to Massachusetts, most of them to Boston, which soon became the largest town in British North America. By 1643, nearly twenty thousand compatriots had followed.

The society Winthrop foresaw in Puritan America was a true commonwealth, a community in which each person put the good of the whole ahead of private concerns. It was, furthermore, to be a society whose members all lived according to the precepts of Christian charity, loving and aiding friends and enemies alike. Of course, such an ideal was beyond human reach.

The Puritans expressed their communal ideal chiefly in the doctrine of the covenant. They believed God had made a covenant—that is, an

Ideal of the Covenant
——

agreement or contract—with them when they were chosen for the special mission to America. In turn, they covenanted with each other, promising to work together toward their goals. The founders of churches and towns in the new land often drafted formal documents setting forth the principles on which such institutions would be based. The same was true of the colonial governments of New England.

The leaders of Massachusetts Bay likewise transformed their original joint stock company charter into the basis for a covenanted community based on mutual consent. Under pressure from landowning male settlers, they gradually changed the General Court—officially the company's small governing body—into a colonial legislature. They also granted the status of freeman, or voting member of the company, to all property-owning adult male church members residing in Massachusetts. Less than two decades after the first large group of Puritans had arrived in Massachusetts Bay, the colony had a functioning system of self-government composed of a governor and a two-house legislature. The General Court also established a judicial system modeled on England's.

The colony's method of distributing land helped to further the communal ideal. Groups of families, often from the same region of England, applied

New England Towns

together to the General Court for grants of land on which to establish towns. The men who received the original town grant had the sole authority to determine how the land would be distributed. Understandably, they copied the villages from which they had come. First they laid out town lots for houses and a church. Then they gave each family parcels of land scattered around the town center: pasture here, a wood lot there, an arable field elsewhere. They also reserved the best and largest plots for the most distinguished among them (usually including the minister); people who had been low on the social scale in England were given much smaller and less desirable allotments. Even when migrants began to move beyond the territorial limits of the Massachusetts Bay colony into Connecticut (1636), New Haven (1638), and New Hampshire (1638), the same pattern of town land grants was maintained.

Thus New England settlements initially tended to be more compact than those of the Chesapeake. Town centers grew up quickly, developing in three distinctly different ways. Some, chiefly isolated agricultural settlements in the interior, tried to sustain Winthrop's vision of harmonious community life based on diversified family farms. A second group, the coastal towns like Boston and Salem, became bustling seaports. The third category, commercialized agricultural towns, grew up in the Connecticut River valley, where easy water transportation made it possible for farmers to sell surplus goods readily.

The migration to the Connecticut valley ended the Puritans' relative freedom from clashes with their Native American neighbors. The first English settlers in the valley moved there from Newtown (Cambridge, Massachusetts), under the direction of their minister, Thomas Hooker. Connecticut was

fertile, although remote from the other English towns, and the wide river promised ready access to the ocean. The site had just one problem: it fell within the territory controlled by the Pequots.

The Pequots' dominance was based on their role as primary middlemen in the trade between New England tribes and the Dutch in New Netherland. The arrival of

Pequot War

English settlers signaled the end of Pequot power over the regional trading networks, for their tributary bands could now trade directly with Europeans. Clashes between the Pequots and the English began even before the Connecticut valley settlements were established, but their founding tipped the balance toward war. After two English traders were killed (probably not by Pequots), the English raided a Pequot village. In retaliation, the Pequots attacked the new town of Wethersfield in April 1637, killing nine and capturing two colonists. The following month, an expedition from Massachusetts Bay attacked and burned the main Pequot town on the Mystic River. The English men and their Narragansett allies slaughtered at least four hundred Pequots, mostly women and children, and captured the few survivors.

Just five years later, the Narragansett leader Miantonomi realized that the Pequots had been correct in assessing the danger posed by the Puritan settlements. Miantonomi tried but failed to forge a pan-Indian alliance. He was killed in 1643 by other tribesmen acting at the English colonists' behest.

For the next thirty years, the New England Indians tried to accommodate themselves to the spread of white settlement. They traded with the whites and sometimes worked for them, but for the most part they resisted acculturation or incorporation in English society. The Native Americans clung to their traditional farming methods, which did not use plows, fertilizer, or fences; women rather than men continued to be the chief cultivators. The one European practice they did adopt was keeping livestock, for in the absence of game, domesticated animals provided excellent alternative sources of meat.

Although the official seal of the Massachusetts Bay colony showed an Indian crying, "Come over and help us," most colonists showed little interest in converting the New England Algonkians to

Christianity. Only a few Massachusetts clerics, most notably John Eliot, seriously undertook missionary activities. Eliot insisted that converts reside in towns, farm the land in English fashion, assume English names, wear European-style clothing and shoes, cut their hair, and stop observing a wide range of their own customs. Because Eliot was demanding a total cultural transformation from his adherents, he understandably met with little success. At the peak of Eliot's efforts, only eleven hundred Native Americans lived in the fourteen "Praying Towns" he established.

The Jesuits' successful missions in New France contrasted sharply with the Puritans' failure to win many converts. Three factors account for the difference. First, the small French outposts along the St. Lawrence did not substantially encroach on tribal lands and therefore did not alienate potential converts. Second, Catholicism had several advantages over Puritanism. It employed attractive rituals, instructed converts that through good works they could help to earn their salvation, and offered women in particular inspiring role models—the Virgin Mary and the communities of nuns who resided in Montreal and Quebec. Third, and perhaps most important, the Jesuits understood that Christian beliefs were to some extent compatible with Native American culture. Unlike the Puritans, the Jesuits were willing to accept converts who did not wholly adopt European styles of life.

Puritan and Jesuit Missions Compared

But what attracted Native Americans to these religious ideas? Surely one primary motive was a desire to use the Europeans' religion to cope with the dramatic changes the intruders had wrought. The combination of disease, alcohol, new trading patterns, and loss of territory disrupted customary ways of life to an unprecedented extent. Many Native Americans must have concluded that the Europeans' ideas could provide the key to survival in the new circumstances.

LIFE IN NEW ENGLAND

White settlers in New England adopted lifestyles that differed considerably from those of both their Indian neighbors and their European counterparts in the Chesapeake. Unlike the mobile Algonkians, who usually moved four or five times each year to take full advantage of their environment, English people lived year-round in the same location. And unlike residents of the Chesapeake, New Englanders constructed sturdy dwellings intended to last. They used the same fields again and again, believing it less arduous to use fertilizer than to clear new fields every few years. Furthermore, they had to fence their crop lands to prevent them from being overrun by the cattle, sheep, and hogs that were their chief sources of meat. When New Englanders began to spread out over the countryside, it was often to find additional pasturage for their livestock.

Puritans commonly moved to America in family groups, in contrast to the Chesapeake migrants, most of whom came individually. The age range of New Englanders was wide, and because many more women went there than to the tobacco colonies, the population could immediately begin to reproduce. Moreover, New England's climate was much healthier than the Chesapeake's. Indeed, New England proved to be even healthier than England. Although adult male migrants to the Chesapeake lost about ten years from their English life expectancy, their Massachusetts counterparts gained five or more years. Consequently, whereas Chesapeake population patterns gave rise to families that were few in number, small in size, and transitory, the demographic characteristics of New England made families there numerous, large, and long-lived. If seventeenth-century Chesapeake women could expect to rear one to three healthy children, New England women could anticipate raising five to seven.

Family Life in New England

The nature of the population had other major implications for family life. New England in effect created grandparents. And whereas early southern parents usually died before their children married, northern parents exercised a good deal of control over their adult children. Young men could not marry without acreage to cultivate, and given the communal land grant system they were dependent on their fathers to supply them with that land.

Daughters, too, needed the dowry of household goods that their parents would give them when they married. Yet parents needed their children's labor and often were reluctant to see them marry and start their own households. These needs at times led to considerable conflict between the generations. On the whole, children seem to have obeyed their parents' wishes, for they had few alternatives.

Another important difference lay in the influence of religion on New Englanders' lives. The governments of Massachusetts Bay, Plymouth, Connecticut, and the other early northern colonies were all controlled by Puritans. Congregationalism was the only officially recognized religion; except in Rhode Island, members of other sects had no freedom of worship. Some non-Puritans appear to have voted in town meetings, but in Massachusetts Bay and New Haven, church membership was a prerequisite for voting in colony elections. All households were taxed to build meetinghouses and pay ministers' salaries. Massachusetts's first legal codes (1641 and 1648) incorporated regulations drawn from Old Testament scriptures in the laws of the colony.

In addition, the Puritan colonies attempted to enforce a strict moral code of conduct. Maryland punished only sexually active couples who had bastard children. In New

Moral Codes
———

England, though, couples who had sex during their engagement—as revealed by the birth of a baby less than nine months after the wedding— were fined and humiliated, sometimes by a public whipping. More harshly treated in both regions were men—and a handful of women—who engaged in behaviors that today would be called homosexual. (The term did not then exist, nor were some people thought more likely to perform such acts than any others.) Several men who had consenting same-sex relationships were hanged, as were other men suspected of bestiality (sex with animals).

In the New England colonies, church and state were thus intertwined, for Puritans believed they were following Old Testament rules in assigning such penalties to those they believed to be moral miscreants. Puritans objected to secular interference in religious affairs but at the same time

expected the church to influence the conduct of politics and the affairs of society. They also believed that the state had an obligation to support and protect the one true church—theirs. As a result, although they came to America seeking freedom to worship as they wished, they saw no contradiction in their refusal to grant that freedom to others. Indeed, the two most significant divisions in early Massachusetts were caused by religious disputes and by Massachusetts Bay's unwillingness to tolerate dissent.

Roger Williams, a Separatist, migrated to Massachusetts Bay in 1631. Williams soon began to express the eccentric ideas that the king of England had no right to give away land

Roger Williams
———

already occupied by Native Americans, that church and state should be kept entirely separate, and that Puritans should not impose their religious beliefs on others. Banished from Massachusetts in 1635, Williams founded the town of Providence on Narragansett Bay. Because of Williams's beliefs, Providence, and other towns in what became the colony of Rhode Island, adopted a policy of tolerating all religions, including Judaism.

The other dissenter, and an even greater challenge to Massachusetts Bay orthodoxy, was Anne Marbury Hutchinson. She was a follower of John Cotton, a minister who stressed

Anne Hutchinson
———

the covenant of grace, or God's free gift of salvation to unworthy humans. By contrast, most Massachusetts clerics emphasized the need for Puritans to engage in good works, study, and reflection in preparation for receiving God's grace. In 1636, Hutchinson began holding women's meetings in her home to discuss Cotton's sermons. Soon men also started to attend. Hutchinson emphasized the covenant of grace more than did Cotton himself, and she even adopted the belief that the elect could communicate directly with God and be assured of salvation. Such ideas had an immense appeal for Puritans. Anne Hutchinson offered them certainty of salvation instead of a state of constant tension.

Hutchinson's ideas were a dangerous threat to Puritan orthodoxy, so in November 1637 she was brought before the General Court of Massachusetts.

For two days, she defended herself cleverly against her accusers, matching scriptural references and wits with John Winthrop. But Hutchinson then declared that God had spoken to her "by an immediate revelation," telling her that he would curse the Puritans' descendants for generations if they harmed her. That assertion assured her banishment to Rhode Island.

The authorities in Massachusetts Bay perceived Anne Hutchinson as doubly dangerous to the existing order: she threatened not only religious orthodoxy but also traditional gender roles. Puritans believed in the equality before God of all souls, but they considered actual women (as distinct from their spiritual selves) inferior to men. Christians had long followed Saint Paul's dictum that women should keep silent in church and be submissive to their husbands. Anne Hutchinson did neither. At her church trial, a minister told her bluntly: "You have stept out of your place, you have rather bine a Husband than a Wife and a preacher than a Hearer; and a Magistrate than a Subject."

The New England authorities' reaction to Anne Hutchinson reveals the depth of their adherence to European gender role concepts. To them, an orderly society required the submission of wives to husbands as well as the obedience of subjects to rulers. English people intended to change many aspects of their lives by colonizing North America but not the sexual division of labor or the assumption of male superiority.

By the middle of the seventeenth century, Europeans had unquestionably come to North America to stay, which signaled major changes for the peoples of both hemispheres. Europeans had indelibly altered not only their own lives but also those of the Native Americans. Europeans killed Indians with their weapons and diseases and had but limited success in converting them to European religions and styles of life. Contacts with the Native Americans taught Europeans to eat new foods, speak new languages, and recognize, however reluctantly, the persistence of other cultural patterns. The prosperity and even survival of many European colonies depended heavily on the cultivation of American crops (maize and tobacco) and an Asian one (sugar), thus attesting to the importance of post-Columbian ecological change.

European political rivalries, once confined to Europe, now spread around the globe. In America, France earned its primary profits from Indian trade and the cultivation of sugar cane. Sugar also enriched the Portuguese. The Netherlands concentrated on commerce—trading in furs and sugar as well as carrying African slaves to South America and the Caribbean.

Although they too at first sought to rely on trade, the English colonies quickly took another form altogether when so many English people of the middling sort decided to migrate to North America. To a greater extent than their European counterparts, the English transferred the society and politics of their homeland to a new environment. Yet both were English in origin, and in the years to come both regions would be drawn into the increasingly fierce rivalries besetting the European powers. Those rivalries would continue to affect Americans of all races until after France and England fought the greatest war yet known in the mid-eighteenth century and the Anglo-American colonies had won their independence.

SUGGESTIONS FOR FURTHER READING

General

Charles M. Andrews, *The Colonial Period of American History: The Settlements*, 3 vols. (1934–1937); David Hackett Fischer, *Albion's Seed: Four British Folkways in America* (1989). Gary B. Nash, *Red, White, and Black: The Peoples of Early America*, 2d ed. (1982).

New Netherland, New France, and the Caribbean

Karen Anderson, *Chain Her by One Foot: The Subjugation of Women in Seventeenth-Century New France* (1991); Charles R. Boxer, *The Dutch Seaborne Empire, 1600–1800* (1965); Richard S. Dunn, *Sugar and Slaves: The Rise of the Planter Class in the English West Indies, 1624–1713* (1972); William J. Eccles, *France in America*, rev. ed. (1990); Sidney Mintz, *Sweetness and Power: The Place of Sugar in Modern History* (1985).

England

Susan Dwyer Amussen, *An Ordered Society: Gender and Class in Early Modern England* (1988); Peter Laslett, *The World We Have Lost*, 3d ed. (1984); Michael Walzer, *The Revolution of the Saints* (1965); Keith Wrightson, *English Society, 1580–1680* (1982).

Early Contact Between Europeans and Indians

James Axtell, *The Invasion Within: The Contest of Cultures in Colonial North America* (1985); Philip Barbour, *Pocahontas and Her World* (1970); William Cronon, *Changes in the Land: Indians, Colonists, and the Ecology of New England* (1983); Francis Jennings, *The Invasion of America: Indians, Colonialism, and the Cant of Conquest* (1975); Karen O. Kupperman, *Settling with the Indians: The Meeting of English and Indian Cultures in America, 1580–1640* (1980); Neal Salisbury, *Manitou and Providence: Indians, Europeans, and the Making of New England, 1500–1643* (1982); Timothy Silver, *A New Face on the Countryside: Indians, Colonists, and Slaves in South Atlantic Forests, 1500–1800* (1990); Peter Wood, et al., eds., *Powhatan's Mantle: Indians in the Colonial Southeast* (1989).

Chesapeake Society and Politics

Lois Green Carr et al., *Robert Cole's World: Agriculture and Society in Early Maryland* (1991); Wesley Frank Craven, *The Southern Colonies in the Seventeenth Century, 1607–1689* (1949); David Galenson, *White Servitude in Colonial America: An Economic Analysis* (1981); Gloria L. Main, *Tobacco Colony: Life in Early Maryland, 1650–1720* (1983); Edmund S. Morgan, *American Slavery, American Freedom: The Ordeal of Colonial Virginia* (1975); Darrett Rutman and Anita Rutman, *A Place in Time: Middlesex County, Virginia, 1650–1750* (1984); Alden T. Vaughan, *American Genesis: Captain John Smith and the Founding of Virginia* (1975).

New England Communities, Politics, and Religion

Virginia DeJohn Anderson, *New England's Generation: The Great Migration and the Formation of Society and Culture in the Seventeenth Century* (1991); David D. Hall, *Worlds of Wonder, Days of Judgment: Popular Religious Belief in Early New England* (1989); Stephen Innes, *Labor in a New Land: Economy and Society in Seventeenth-Century Springfield* (1983); Sydney V. James, *Colonial Rhode Island* (1975); George Langdon, *Pilgrim Colony: A History of New Plymouth, 1620–1691* (1966); Kenneth A. Lockridge, *A New England Town: The First Hundred Years (Dedham, Massachusetts, 1636–1736)* (1970); John Frederick Martin, *Profits in the Wilderness: Entrepreneurship and the Founding of New England Towns in the Seventeenth Century* (1991); Edmund S. Morgan, *The Puritan Dilemma: The Story of John Winthrop* (1958).

New England Women and Family Life

John Demos, *A Little Commonwealth: Family Life in Plymouth Colony* (1970); Lyle Koehler, *A Search for Power: The "Weaker Sex" in Seventeenth-Century New England* (1980); Edmund S. Morgan, *The Puritan Family*, rev. ed. (1966); Roger Thompson, *Sex in Middlesex: Popular Mores in a Massachusetts County, 1649–1699* (1986).

American Society Takes Shape, 1640–1720

S TANDING ON A LADDER with the condemned man, the hangman tightened the noose around the neck of the notorious pirate Captain William Kidd—and pushed him off the ladder. Kidd died violently, as he had lived. It was May 23, 1701; the site was Wapping, near the London docks. Kidd's body was then left dangling from a gibbet as a warning to all who saw it.

William Kidd, born in Scotland, had made his home in New York, the port once known as New Amsterdam. Being none too choosy about how they earned their profits, Manhattan merchants eagerly provisioned pirates' ships and purchased their loot. In the 1690s, the economy of the town depended on this illegal trade. For years, Kidd and other pirates could even count on the complicity of New York's governors, who ignored their activities in exchange for shares of the bounty.

Then why was Captain Kidd condemned to die? His fatal enterprise began in London in early 1696, when he gained financial backing from several powerful and prominent English investors for a voyage to the Indian Ocean. After more than a year of buccaneering, Kidd returned to New York via the Caribbean, hoping to avoid prosecution for piracy by claiming he had taken only legal prizes and by repaying his investors in full (in addition to bribing the relevant officials). Unfortunately for Kidd, one of his financial backers, the Earl of Bellomont, had become the governor of New York. Bellomont had been waging a vigorous campaign against piracy and could not afford to protect Kidd. In addition, as governor he could claim one-third of any confiscated illegal cargo for his personal use. Kidd's fate was sealed when Bellomont ordered his arrest and shipped him back to England for trial.

The saga of William Kidd illustrates above all the involvement of the English mainland colonies in a growing network of trade and international contacts, not all of them legal. North America, like England itself, was becoming increasingly embedded in a worldwide matrix of exchange and warfare. The web woven by ocean-going vessels crisscrossed the globe, carrying West Indian sugar to Europe, Africans to America, cloth and spices from the East Indies to Africa, and New England fish and wood products to the Caribbean. Formerly tiny outposts, the

North American colonies expanded their territorial claims and embarked on a deliberate course of economic development. In response, the English government for the first time began to adopt policies to systematize colonial administration.

Three developments shaped life in the mainland colonies between 1640 and 1720: the introduction of a system of chattel slavery, especially in the south Atlantic coastal regions, changes in the colonies' relationship with England, and increasing conflicts with their North American neighbors, both European and Native American.

The explosive growth of the slave trade was of critical significance in the colonial economy. For slave trader and planter alike, slaves meant handsome profits. The arrival of large numbers of West African peoples dramatically reshaped colonial society and fueled the international trading system. Moreover, the burgeoning North American economy attracted new attention from officials in London who attempted to supervise the American settlements more effectively and thus ensure that England benefited from their economic growth.

Neither English colonists nor London administrators could ignore the other peoples living on the North American continent. As the English settlements expanded, they came into violent conflict not only with the powerful tribes of the interior but also with the Dutch, the Spanish, and especially the French. By 1720, war—between Europeans and Indians, among Europeans, and among Indians allied with different colonial powers—had become an all-too-frequent feature of American life.

THE ENGLISH CIVIL WAR, THE STUART RESTORATION, AND THE AMERICAN COLONIES

In 1640, Charles I, who had ruled England arbitrarily for eleven years, called Parliament into session because he needed money and wanted to propose new taxes. But Parliament instead enacted laws limiting his authority, and tensions heightened. In 1642, civil war broke out between royalists and the supporters of Parliament. Four years later, Parliament triumphed; Charles I was executed in 1649. Oliver Cromwell, the leader of the parliamentary army, then assumed control of the government, taking the title of Lord Protector in 1653. After Cromwell's death in 1658, Parliament decided to restore the monarchy if Charles I's son and heir would agree to certain restrictions on his authority. In 1660, Charles II ascended the throne, having promised to seek Parliament's consent for any new taxes and to support the Church of England. Thus ended the tumultuous chapter in English history known as the Interregnum (Latin for between reigns), or the Commonwealth period.

The English Civil War, the Interregnum, and the reign of Charles II (1660–1685) had far-reaching

The Founding of English Colonies in North America, 1664–1732

Colony	Founder(s)	Date	Basis of Economy
New York (formerly New Netherland)	James, Duke of York	1664	farming, fur trading
New Jersey	Sir George Carteret, John Lord Berkeley	1664	farming
North Carolina	Carolina Proprietors	1665	tobacco, forest products
South Carolina	Carolina Proprietors	1670	rice, indigo
Pennsylvania	William Penn	1681	farming
Georgia	James Oglethorpe	1732	rice, forest products

significance for the English colonies in the Americas. During the English Civil War and the Commonwealth period, Puritans dominated the English government. Therefore, the migration to New England largely ceased. During the subsequent reign of Charles II, six of the thirteen colonies that would eventually form the American nation were either founded or came under English rule: New York, New Jersey, Pennsylvania (including Delaware), and North and South Carolina. All were proprietorships granted in their entirety to one man or a group of men who held title to the soil and controlled the government. Charles II gave these vast American holdings as rewards to men who had supported him during his years of exile.

One of the first to benefit was Charles's younger brother James, the duke of York. In 1664, acting as though the Dutch colony of New Netherland did not exist, Charles II gave James the region between the Connecticut and Delaware Rivers, including the Hudson Valley and Long Island. James immediately organized an invasion fleet. In late August, the vessels anchored off Manhattan Island and demanded New Netherland's surrender. The colony's director-general, Peter Stuyvesant, complied without offering resistance.

Thus England acquired a tiny but heterogeneous possession. In 1664, an appreciable minority of English people (mostly Puritan New Englanders who had moved to Long Island)

New Netherland Becomes New York

already lived in the colony. New York, as it was now called, also included sizable numbers of Native Americans, Germans, French-speaking Walloons (from the southern part of modern Belgium), Scandinavians, and Africans, as well as a smattering of other European peoples. Because the Dutch had actively imported slaves to the colony, almost one-fifth of Manhattan's approximately fifteen hundred inhabitants were of African descent. Slaves constituted a higher proportion of New York's urban population than of the Chesapeake's at that time.

Recognizing the diversity of the population, the duke of York's representatives moved cautiously in their efforts to establish English authority. The Duke's Laws, a legal code proclaimed in 1665, at first applied only to the Puritan settlements on Long Island; they were later extended to the rest of the colony. Dutch forms of local government were maintained and Dutch land titles confirmed. A multiple establishment guaranteed religious toleration: each town was permitted to decide which church to support with its tax revenues. And the Dutch were allowed to maintain their customary legal practices, including the right of married women to draft wills. Much to the chagrin of English residents of the colony, the Duke's Laws made no provision for a representative assembly. James was suspicious of legislative bodies, and not until 1683 did he agree to the colonists' requests for an elected legislature.

The English takeover thus had little immediate effect on the colony. Its population grew slowly, barely reaching eighteen thousand by the time of the first English census in 1698. One chief reason the English conquest brought so little change to New York was that the duke of York quickly regranted the land between the Hudson and Delaware Rivers—East and West Jersey—to his friends Sir George Carteret and John Lord Berkeley. That left his own colony confined between Connecticut to the east and the Jerseys to the west and south, depriving it of much fertile land and hindering its economic growth. He also failed to promote migration. Meanwhile, the Jersey proprietors acted rapidly to attract settlers, promising generous land grants, limited freedom of religion, and—without authorization from the Crown—a representative assembly. New Jersey grew quickly; at the time of its first census as a united colony in 1726, it had 32,500 inhabitants, only eight thousand fewer than New York.

Founding of New Jersey

Within twenty years, Berkeley and Carteret sold their interests in the Jerseys to separate groups of investors. The purchasers of all of Carteret's share (West Jersey) and portions of Berkeley's (East Jersey) were members of the Society of Friends, seeking a refuge from persecution in England. The Society of Friends, also called the Quakers, denied the need for an intermediary between the individual and God. They believed anyone could receive the "inner light" and be saved, and all were equal in God's sight. They had no formally trained clergy;

• *I m p o r t a n t   E v e n t s* •

1642–46	English Civil War; end of first New England economic system based on furs and migrants	**1685**	James II becomes king
1649	Charles I executed	**1686–89**	Dominion of New England established, superseding all charters of colonies from Maine to New Jersey
1651	First Navigation Act passed to regulate colonial trade	**1688–89**	James II deposed in Glorious Revolution; William and Mary ascend throne
1660	Stuarts restored to throne; Charles II becomes king	**1689–97**	King William's War fought on northern New England frontier
1662	Halfway Covenant drafted in New England, creating category of partial membership in Congregational churches	**1692**	Witchcraft outbreak in Salem Village; nineteen executions result
1663	Carolina chartered	**1696**	Board of Trade and Plantations established to coordinate English colonial administration
1664	English conquer New Netherland; New York founded New Jersey established	**1701**	Iroquois adopt neutrality policy toward France and England
1670s	Jacques Marquette, Louis Jolliet, and Robert Cavelier de la Salle explore the Great Lakes and Mississippi Valley for France	**1702–13**	Queen Anne's War fought by French and English
1675–76	King Philip's (Metacomet's) War devastates New England	**1711–13**	Tuscarora War (North Carolina) leads to capture or migration of most Tuscaroras
1676	Bacon's Rebellion disrupts Virginia government; Jamestown destroyed	**1715**	Yamasee War nearly destroys South Carolina
1680–92	Pueblo revolt temporarily drives Spaniards from New Mexico	**1718**	New Orleans founded in French Louisiana
1681	Pennsylvania chartered	**1732**	Georgia chartered

any Quaker, male or female, could speak in meetings or become a "public Friend" and travel from meeting to meeting to discuss God's word. The Quaker message of radical egalitarianism was not welcome in the hierarchical society of either seventeenth-century England or Puritan New England.

The Quakers obtained their own colony in 1681, when Charles II granted the region between Maryland and New York to William Penn, one of the sect's most prominent members. Penn's father, Admiral William Penn, had originally served Oliver Cromwell; later, however, he joined forces with

Pennsylvania: A Quaker Haven

Charles II and loaned the monarch a substantial sum of money. The younger Penn became a Quaker in the mid-1660s, much to his father's dismay. But despite the younger Penn's radical political and religious beliefs, he and Charles II were close personal friends. Because of that friendship (and the desire of Charles's advisers to rid England of religious dissenters), Charles gave a huge tract of land to Penn, nominally as a repayment for the loan from his father.

William Penn held the colony as a personal proprietorship, and the vast property holdings earned profits for his descendants until the American Revolution. Even so, Penn saw the province not merely as a source of revenue but also as a haven for his persecuted coreligionists. Penn offered land to all comers on liberal terms, promised toleration of all religions (although only Christians were given the right to vote), guaranteed such English liberties as the right to bail and trial by jury, and pledged to establish a representative assembly. He also publicized throughout Europe the ready availability of land in Pennsylvania.

Penn's activities and the natural attraction of his lands for Quakers gave rise to a migration, the magnitude of which was equaled only by the Puritan exodus to New England in the 1630s. By mid-1683, more than three thousand people—among them Welsh, Irish, Dutch, and Germans—had already moved to Pennsylvania, and within five years the population reached twelve thousand. Philadelphia, carefully planned to be the major city in the province, drew merchants and artisans from throughout the English-speaking world. From mainland and West Indian colonies alike came Quakers seeking religious freedom. Pennsylvania's lands were both plentiful and fertile, and the colony soon began exporting flour and other foodstuffs to the West Indies. Practically overnight, Philadelphia acquired more than two thousand citizens and began to challenge Boston's commercial dominance.

A pacifist with egalitarian principles, Penn was determined to treat the Native Americans fairly. He purchased tracts of land from the Delawares (or Lenapes), the dominant tribe in the region, in order to sell them to settlers. Penn also established strict regulations for trade and forbade the sale of alcohol to the tribal people. His Indian policy illustrates the complexity of the interaction among Euroamericans and Amerindians. It prompted several tribes, most important the Tuscaroras from the Carolinas, to move to Pennsylvania. Likewise, Shawnees and Miamis chose to move east from the Ohio valley. By a supreme irony, however, the same toleration that attracted Native Americans to Penn's domains also brought non-Quaker Europeans who showed little respect for Indian claims to the soil. In effect, Penn's policy was so successful that it caused its own downfall. The Scotch-Irish, Palatine Germans, and Swiss who settled in Pennsylvania clashed repeatedly over land with tribes that had also recently migrated to the colony.

The other proprietary colony, granted by Charles II in 1663, encompassed a huge tract of land stretching from the southern boundary of Virginia to Spanish Florida. The area had great strategic importance; a successful English settlement there would prevent the Spanish from pushing farther north. The proprietors named their new province Carolina in honor of Charles, whose Latin name was Carolus. The "Fundamental Constitutions of Carolina," which they asked the political philosopher John Locke to draft for them, set forth an elaborate plan for a colony governed by a hierarchy of landholding aristocrats. But Carolina failed to follow the course the proprietors laid out. Instead, it quickly developed two distinct population centers, which in 1729 permanently split into two separate colonies.

Founding of Carolina

The Albemarle region that became North Carolina was settled by Virginia planters. They established a society much like their own, with an economy based on tobacco cultivation and the export of such forest products as pitch, tar, and timber. Because North Carolina lacked a satisfactory harbor, its planters continued to rely on Virginia's ports and merchants to conduct their trade, and the two colonies remained tightly linked. Although North Carolina planters held some slaves, they never became as dependent on slave labor as did the other population center in Carolina.

Charleston, South Carolina, was founded in 1670 by a group of settlers from the island of Barbados. The white Barbadians brought with them the slaves who had worked on their sugar plantations and the legal codes that had governed those laborers, thereby irrevocably shaping the future of South Carolina and the subsequent history of the United States.

THE FORCED MIGRATION OF AFRICANS

England had no tradition of slavery, so why did English settlers in North America and the Caribbean islands begin to enslave Africans around the middle of the seventeenth century? The answer lies in a combination of their need for labor and the customs of other Europeans.

Although the English had not practiced slavery, other Europeans had. Both the Spanish and Portuguese imported enslaved Africans as laborers to the islands of the Mediterranean Atlantic during the fifteenth century. They then extended that practice to their American possessions, New Spain and Brazil, especially after the Catholic church began actively discouraging enslavement of Native Americans. No free people were willing to toil for wages in the difficult and dangerous conditions of South American mines or Caribbean sugar plantations. To produce the profitable goods they had come to America to seek, the Europeans needed bound laborers—people who, by law or contract, could be forced to work at jobs that no person would do voluntarily.

Such a large proportion of the native inhabitants of North America and the Caribbean had died from imported diseases that they could not supply the labor needs of English set-

Slavery Established

tlers. English tobacco planters in the Chesapeake at first relied on indentured servants from their homeland. But by the mid-1660s, population pressures in England had eased. Accordingly, the supply of English servants began to dry up, and mainland planters had to find a new source of laborers.

They found their workers in the French, Dutch, and Spanish Caribbean islands, among the ranks of already enslaved Africans. Early in the history of the mainland English settlements, the few residents of African descent varied in status—some were free, some indentured, and some enslaved. Before the 1660s, none of the English colonies systematically categorized Africans as slaves. But the beginnings of large-scale importation of Africans to the mainland in the 1670s changed that situation decisively. As increasing numbers of enslaved Africans arrived each year, laws governing them were more comprehensively and tightly drawn. Most English colonies adopted codes to govern blacks' behavior. By the end of the century, African slavery was firmly established as the basis of the economy in the Chesapeake as well as in the Caribbean.

One remarkable aspect of the adoption of the slave system was the English enslavers' evident lack of moral qualms. No one at the time seems to have questioned—or even felt the need to justify with racist rationalizations—the decision to hold Africans and their descendants in perpetual bondage. That suggests the importance both of prior Spanish and Portuguese practice and of economic motives in leading to this momentous development.

Between 1492 and 1770, more Africans than Europeans were carried to the New World, the vast majority of them to Brazil or the Caribbean. At least ten million enslaved people were brought to the Americas—by 1775. Of these chattels, more than 260,000 were imported to the region that later became the United States. The magnitude of this trade raises three related questions. First, how did it affect West Africa and Europe? Second, how was the trade organized and conducted? Third, what was its effect on the people it carried and on the region to which they were taken?

The West African coast was a densely inhabited region. Despite the extent of forced migration to the Western Hemisphere, the area was not

West Africa and the Slave Trade

seriously depopulated by the trade in human beings. Even so, because American planters preferred to purchase male slaves, the trade did significantly affect the sex ratio of the remaining population. The relative lack of men increased the work demands on women and simultaneously encouraged polygyny (the practice of one man having several wives). In Guinea, the primary consequences of the trade were political and economic. Coastal rulers—such as those pictured on page 48—served as middlemen in the trade, using it as a vehicle to consolidate their power and extend their rule over larger territories. They controlled European traders' access to slaves and at the same time controlled inland peoples' access to desirable European trade goods. The centralizing tendencies of the trade thus helped in the formation of such powerful eighteenth-century kingdoms as Dahomey and Asante. At the same time, local manufactures declined in the face of European competition.

West African kings played a crucial role in the functioning of the slave trade. Europeans set up

At forts along the African coast, Europeans purchased slaves from local rulers. This contemporary illustration of such a transaction is taken from a book published in 1729.   Library of Congress.

permanent slave-trading posts in Lower Guinea under the protection of local rulers, who then supplied the resident Europeans with slaves to fill the ships that stopped regularly at the coastal forts. In Upper Guinea, the lack of good harbors promoted a somewhat different trading pattern: Europeans would sail along the coast, stopping when signaled from shore. Prisoners of war, criminals, debtors, and kidnap victims comprised the cargoes of the slave-trading vessels.

Europeans were the chief beneficiaries of this traffic in slaves, despite its importance to some African kings. The expanding network of trade between Europe and its colonies in the seventeenth and eighteenth centuries was fueled by the sale and transportation of slaves, the exchange of commodities produced by slave labor, and the need to feed and clothe so many bound laborers. The sugar planters of the Caribbean and Brazil, along with the tobacco and rice planters of North America, eagerly purchased slaves from Africa, dispatched shiploads of valuable staple crops to Europe, and bought large quantities of cheap food, much of it from elsewhere in the Americas. By the 1720s, more than 80 percent of English cotton textile exports were traded to Africa or slave-holding American colonies. The European economy, previously oriented to the Mediterranean and Asia, shifted its emphasis to the Atlantic Ocean. By the late seventeenth century, commerce in slaves and the products of slave labor constituted the basis of the European economic system. The irony of Columbus's voyages was thus complete: seeking the wealth of Asia, Columbus had found instead the lands that ultimately replaced Asia as the source of European prosperity.

Given the economic importance of the slave trade, it is hardly surprising that European nations fought bitterly to control it. The Portuguese, who initially dominated the trade, were supplanted by the Dutch in the 1630s. The Dutch in turn lost out to the English, who controlled the trade through the Royal African Company, a joint stock company chartered by Charles II in 1672. Holding a monopoly on all English trade with black Africa, the company transported more than 120,000 slaves to England's colonies in the Caribbean and on the North American mainland. Yet even before the company's monopoly expired in 1712, many individual English traders illegally entered the market for slaves. By the early eighteenth century, independent traders were carrying most of the Africans imported to the colonies and earning huge profits.

The experience of the Middle Passage (thus named because it was the middle section of the so-called triangular trade among England, Africa, and the Americas) was always trau-

The Middle Passage ──── matic and sometimes fatal for the Africans who made up a ship's cargo. An average of 10 to 20 percent of the slaves died en route. On voyages that were unusually long or plagued by epidemic diseases, the mortality rates were much higher. In addition, some slaves died either before the ships left Africa or shortly after their arrival in the New World. Their white captors died at the same, if not higher, rates, chiefly through exposure to diseases endemic to Africa. Once again, the exchange of diseases among the continents caused unanticipated death and destruction.

One of the most vivid accounts of the experience of the Middle Passage was written by Olaudah Equiano, who was eleven years old in 1756 when African raiders kidnapped him from his Ibo village in what is now Nigeria. Terrified by the light complexions, long hair, and strange language of the sailors on the slave ship, he was afraid that "I had gotten into a world of bad spirits and that they were going to kill me." Equiano thought about killing himself by jumping overboard but was too closely watched. At last, some other Ibos

told him that they were being taken to the whites' country to work. "I then was a little revived," Equiano remembered.

Equiano was not purchased in the West Indies, where planters preferred older, stronger slaves. Instead, he was carried to Virginia along with the other, less valuable Africans. There, on the plantation of his new owner, he was separated from the other Africans and put to work weeding and clearing rocks from the fields. But Equiano did not remain in Virginia for long. Bought by a sea captain, Olaudah Equiano became an experienced sailor. He learned to read and write English, purchased his freedom at the age of twenty-one, and later actively supported the English antislavery movement.

Equiano's voyage was typical, although his ability to eventually win his freedom was not. Most slave ships stopped in the Caribbean before

Slavery in the Chesapeake ──── heading north to Virginia. After about 1675, when the shortage of English indentured servants became acute, imports of Africans to the Chesapeake increased dramatically. As early as 1690, the Chesapeake colonies contained more black slaves than white indentured servants. Slaves usually cost about two-and-a-half times as much as servants, but they repaid the greater investment with a lifetime of service.

Yet not all planters could afford to purchase such expensive workers. Whites with enough money could acquire slaves and accumulate greater wealth, whereas the less affluent could not even buy indentured servants, whose price had been driven up by scarcity. As time passed, white Chesapeake society became more and more stratified—that is, the gap between rich and poor steadily widened.

In addition to demographic and economic change, the introduction of large numbers of Africans to the Chesapeake affected cultural values. Without realizing it, Chesapeake whites adopted African modes of thought about the use of time and the nature of work. Africans were more accustomed than European migrants to life in a hot climate, and whites soon learned the benefits of African patterns of time usage—working early and late, taking a long rest in the midday heat. And unlike the

How do historians know

that enslaved Africans were able to preserve at least some aspects of their cultural heritage in colonial North America? Although most enslaved people were illiterate and therefore did not leave written records of their cultural beliefs or practices, African-Americans did create objects that showed their connections to their homeland even more vividly than could words on a page. Many such objects have been found in the United States. The drum on the left was constructed on the Gold Coast of Africa in the nineteenth century, that on the right in Virginia sometime before the middle of the eighteenth century. The similarities of style and decoration suggest strong cultural affinities between the two drum builders, although they were separated by three thousand miles of ocean and at least one hundred years. Photo: Trustees of The British Museum; Smithsonian Institution, Washington, D.C.

colonists in New England, where the Puritan condemnation of leisure-time activities prevailed, Chesapeake whites learned, again from blacks, the importance of recreation.

African-Americans in South Carolina
In South Carolina, Africans were among the first colonists to come from Barbados. Indeed, one-quarter to one-third of South Carolina's early population was black. The Barbadian slave owners quickly learned that Africans had a variety of skills well suited to the semitropical environment of South Carolina.

African-style dugout canoes became the chief means of transportation in the colony, which was crisscrossed by rivers. Fishing nets copied from African models proved more efficient than those of English origin. Africans' skill at killing crocodiles equipped them to handle alligators as well. And, finally, Africans adapted their traditional techniques of cattle herding for use in the American context. Because meat and hides were the colony's chief exports in its earliest years, blacks contributed significantly to South Carolina's prosperity by drawing upon their African heritage.

The similarity of South Carolina's environment to West Africa's, coupled with the large number of blacks in the population, ensured that more aspects of West African culture survived in that colony than elsewhere on the mainland of North America. Only in South Carolina did black parents continue to give their children African names; only there did a dialect develop that combined English words with African terms. (Known as Gullah, it has survived to the present day in isolated areas.) African skills remained useful, and so techniques that in other regions were lost when the migrant generation died were instead passed down to their children. And in South Carolina, as in West Africa, black women were the primary traders, dominating the markets of Charleston as they did those of Guinea.

Significantly, the importation of large numbers of Africans near the end of the seventeenth century coincided with the successful introduction of rice as a staple crop in South Carolina. English people knew little about the techniques of growing and processing rice, and their first attempts to raise it were unsuccessful. But the former residents of Africa's Rice Coast had spent their lives working with the crop. Although the evidence is circumstantial, it seems likely that the Africans' expertise enabled their English masters to cultivate the crop profitably. After rice had become South Carolina's major export, 43 percent of the Africans imported to the colony came from rice-producing regions, and blacks' central position in the colony's economy was unchallenged.

South Carolina later developed a second staple crop, and it too made use of slaves' special skills. The crop was indigo, much prized in Europe as a blue dye for clothing. In the early 1740s, Eliza Lucas, a young white West Indian woman who was managing her father's South Carolina plantations, began to experiment with indigo cultivation. Drawing on the knowledge of white and black West Indians, she developed the planting and processing techniques later adopted throughout the colony. Indigo was grown on high ground, and rice was planted in low-lying swampy areas; rice and indigo also had different growing seasons. Thus the two crops complemented each other perfectly.

After 1700, white southerners thus were irrevocably committed to black slavery as their chief source of labor; white northerners were not.

Slavery in the North

Lacking large-scale agricultural enterprises, the rural North did not demand many bound laborers. In northern urban areas, though, white domestic servants were hard to find and slaves were often used. In some northern colonial cities (notably Newport, Rhode Island, and New York City), black slaves accounted for more than 10 percent of the population.

The introduction of large-scale slavery in the South, coupled with its near-absence in the rural North, accentuated regional differences that had already begun to develop in England's American colonies. To the distinction between diversified agriculture and staple-crop production was now added a difference in the status of most laborers. That difference was one of degree, but it was nonetheless crucial.

RELATIONS BETWEEN EUROPEANS AND INDIANS

Everywhere in North America, European colonizers depended heavily on the labor of native peoples, but their reliance took varying forms in different parts of the continent. In the Northeast, France, England, and the Netherlands competed for the pelts supplied by Indian trappers. In the Southeast, England, Spain, and later France each tried to control a thriving trade with the tribes in deerskins and Indian slaves. In the Southwest, meanwhile, Spain attempted to exploit the agricultural and artisan skills of the Pueblo peoples.

In 1598, drawn north by accounts that rich cities lay in the region, Juan de Oñate, a Mexican-born adventurer, led a group of about five hundred soldiers and settlers to New Mexico. When residents of Acoma pueblo resisted the Spaniards' demands for food and water, the invaders responded ferociously, killing more than eight hundred people and capturing the remainder. All captives older than the age of twelve were ordered enslaved for twenty years, and men older than twenty-five had one foot amputated. Not surprisingly, the other pueblos surrendered. But when it became apparent that New Mexico held little wealth and offered only a hard life, many Spaniards returned to Mexico. In 1609, Spanish authorities decided to maintain only a small military outpost and a few Christian missions in the area, with the capital at Santa Fe, founded in 1610 (see map).

Thereafter, Franciscan friars worked with mixed success to convert the residents of the pueblos. The Pueblo peoples were willing to add

Popé and the Pueblo Revolt

Christianity to their religious beliefs but not to give up their indigenous rituals. As the decades passed, the Franciscans adopted brutal tactics in an effort to wipe out all vestiges of the native religion. Friars and secular colonists who held *encomiendas* (grants of labor) also placed heavy demands on the Indians. Finally, in 1680 the Pueblos revolted under the leadership of Popé, a respected shaman, and successfully drove the Spaniards from New Mexico. Although Spanish authority was restored in 1692, Spain had learned its lesson. From that time on, Spanish governors stressed cooperation with the

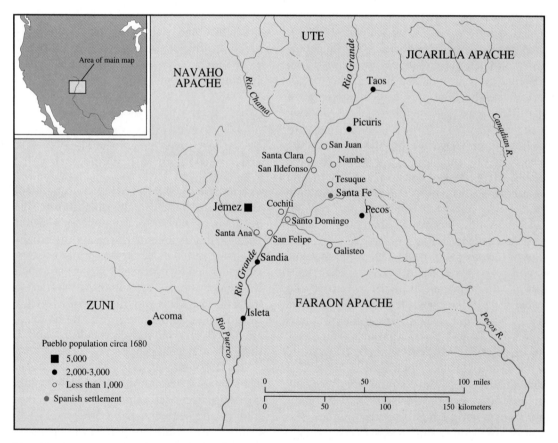

New Mexico, ca. 1680 *In 1680, the lone Spanish settlement at Santa Fe was surrounded and vastly outnumbered by the many pueblos nearby.* Source: Adapted from *Apache, Navaho, and Spaniard*, by Jack D. Forbes. Copyright © 1960 by the University of Oklahoma Press. Used by permission.

Pueblos, and no longer attempted to reduce them to bondage or to violate their cultural integrity. The Pueblo revolt was the most successful and longest-sustained Indian resistance movement in colonial North America.

When the Spanish expanded their territorial claims to the east and the north, they followed the same strategy they had used in New Mexico, establishing their presence through widely scattered military outposts and Franciscan missions. The army's role was to maintain order among the subject Indians and to guard the boundaries of the Spanish empire from incursions, especially by the French. By the late eighteenth century, Spain claimed a vast territory that stretched from California (initially colonized in 1769) through Texas (settled after 1700) to the Gulf coast.

Europeans along the eastern seaboard valued the Indians as hunters and traders rather than as agricultural workers, but they were no less dependent on Indian labor than were the Spanish. South Carolina provides a case in point. The Barbadians who colonized the region moved quickly to establish a vigorous trade in deerskins with nearby tribes. During the first decade of the eighteenth century, South Carolina exported to Europe an average of fifty-four thousand skins annually, a number that later climbed to a peak of 160,000. The trade gave rise to other exchanges that reveal the complexity of the economic relationships among Native Americans and Europeans. For example, white Carolinians carried the deerskins on horses they obtained from the Creeks, who had in turn acquired them from Spaniards in Florida through trade and capture.

Another important component of the Carolina trade was traffic in Indian slaves. The warring tribes of South Carolina (especially the Creeks)

Indian Slave Trade
_____

profited from selling their captive enemies to the whites, who either kept them as slaves or exported them to other mainland settlements or to the West Indies. There are no reliable statistics on the extent of the trade in Indian slaves, but in 1708 they made up 14 percent of the population of South Carolina.

A bitter conflict between white Carolinians and neighboring tribes added to the supply of Indian slaves. In 1711, the Tuscaroras, an Iroquoian people, attacked a Swiss-German settlement at New Bern, which had expropriated their lands without payment. The Tuscaroras had been avid slavers and had sold to the whites many captives from weaker Algonkian tribes. Those tribes seized the opportunity to settle old scores, joining with the English colonists to defeat their enemy in a bloody two-year war known as the Tuscarora War. In the end, more than a thousand Tuscaroras were sold into slavery, and the remnants of the tribe drifted north, where they joined the Five Nations Iroquois in New York.

The abuses of the slave trade led to the most destructive Indian war in Carolina. Colonial traders regularly engaged in corrupt, brutal, and fraudulent practices. They were notorious for cheating the Native Americans, physically abusing them, and selling friendly tribal peoples into slavery. In the spring of 1715, the Yamasees, aided by Creeks and a number of other tribes, retaliated by attacking English settlements. As the raids continued through the summer, refugees by the hundreds streamed into Charleston. Often guided by information from enslaved Indians held by the colonists, the Creek–Yamasee offensive at times came close to driving the intruders from the mainland altogether. But colonial reinforcements arrived from the north, and the Cherokees joined the English settlers against their ancient enemies the Creeks. The war pointed up both the difficulty of achieving unity among the tribes and the Indians' now critical dependence on European weapons. When the tribal allies ran out of ammunition and could not repair their broken guns, their cause was lost. The Yamasees moved south to seek Spanish protection, and the Creeks retreated to villages in the west.

That the Yamasees could escape by migrating south exposed the one remaining gap in the line of English coastal settlements, the area between the

Founding of Georgia
_____

southern border of South Carolina and Spanish Florida. The gap was plugged in 1732 with the chartering of Georgia, the last of the colonies that would become part of the United States. Intended as a haven for English debtors by its founder James Oglethorpe, Georgia was specifically designed as a garrison province. Because all its landholders were expected to serve as militiamen to defend English settlements, the charter prohibited women from inheriting or purchasing land in the colony. The charter also prohibited the use of alcoholic beverages and forbade the introduction of slavery. Such provisions reveal the founders' intention that Georgia be peopled by sturdy, sober yeoman farmers who could take up their weapons at a moment's notice against the Native Americans or Spaniards. None of the original conditions of the charter was enforced, however, and all were abandoned by 1752, when Georgia became a royal colony.

In the Northeast, relationships were complicated by the number of European nations and Indian tribes involved in the fur trade. The key players were

Iroquois Confederacy
———

the Iroquois, not one tribe but five—the Mohawks, Oneidas, Onondagas, Cayugas, and Senecas. (In 1722, the Tuscaroras became the sixth.) Under the terms of a defensive alliance forged early in the sixteenth century, decisions of war and peace for the entire Iroquois Confederacy were made by a council composed of tribal representatives. Each tribe retained some autonomy and could not be forced to comply with a council directive against its will. The Iroquois were unique among Native Americans, not only because of the strength and persistence of their alliance but also because of the role played by their tribal matrons. The older women of each village chose its chief and could either start wars (by calling for the capture of prisoners to replace dead relatives) or stop them (by refusing to supply warriors with necessary foodstuffs).

Before the arrival of the Europeans, the Iroquois had waged wars primarily to acquire captives to replenish their population. The arrival of Europeans created an economic motive for warfare: the desire to control the fur trade and gain unimpeded access to European goods. The war with the Hurons in the 1640s was but the first of a series of conflicts with other tribes known as the Beaver Wars, in which the Iroquois fought desperately to maintain a dominant position in the trade. In the mid-1670s, just when it appeared they would be successful, the French stepped in; an Iroquois triumph

would have destroyed France's plans to trade directly with the Indians of the Great Lakes and Mississippi valley regions. During the next twenty years, the French launched repeated attacks on Iroquois villages. The English offered little assistance other than weapons to their trading partners. Their people and resources depleted by constant warfare, the Iroquois in 1701 negotiated neutrality treaties with France, England, and their tribal neighbors. For the next half-century, they maintained their power through trade and skillful diplomacy.

The wars against the Iroquois Confederacy were crucial components of French Canada's plan to penetrate the heartland of North America. The

French Expansion
———

plan included the explorations of Father Jacques Marquette, Louis Jolliet, and Robert Cavelier de la Salle in the Great Lakes and Mississippi valley regions. Officials at home in France approved the expeditions, because they wanted to find a route to Mexico. By contrast, la Salle hoped to profit personally, monopolizing the fur trade by establishing trading posts along the Mississippi River.

Unlike the Spanish, the French adventurers did not attempt to subjugate the Native American peoples they encountered or even at first claim the territory formally for France. Still, when France decided to strengthen its presence near the Gulf of Mexico by founding New Orleans in the early eighteenth century—to counter both the westward thrust of the English colonies and the eastward moves of the Spanish—the Mississippi posts became the glue of empire (see map).

Most posts consisted of a small military garrison and a priest, surrounded by powerful nations such as the Choctaws, Chickasaws, Osages, and Illinois. The tribes permitted the French to remain among them, because the traders gave them ready access to precious European goods. The French, for their part, sought political as well as economic ends, attempting to prevent the English from encroaching too far into the interior. Their goals were limited; they did not engage in systematic efforts to convert the nearby tribal peoples to Christianity. Moreover, the French did not covet substantial amounts of Indian lands for agricultural purposes.

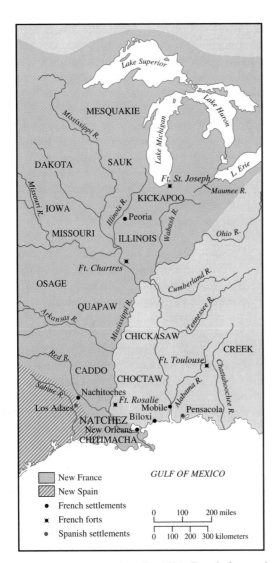

Louisiana, ca. 1720 By 1720, French forts and settlements dotted the Mississippi River and its tributaries in the interior of North America. Two isolated Spanish outposts were situated near the Gulf of Mexico. Source: Adapted from *France in America*, by William J. Eccles. Copyright © 1972 by William J. Eccles. Reprinted by permission of HarperCollins Publishers Inc.

Matters were different in the English colonies, where white colonists had an avid interest in acquiring more land. In Virginia, the conflict was especially acute because of the colonists' insatiable hunger for tobacco acreage.

By the early 1670s, some Virginians were eagerly eyeing the rich lands north of the York River that had been reserved for Native Americans under earlier treaties. Using as a pre-

Bacon's Rebellion
_____

text the July 1675 killing of a white servant by some members of the Doeg tribe, they attacked not only the Doegs but also the powerful Susquehannocks. In retaliation, Susquehannock bands began to raid frontier plantations in the winter of 1676. The land-hungry whites rallied behind the leadership of Nathaniel Bacon, a recently arrived planter, who wanted, in his words, "to ruine and extirpate all Indians in general." Governor William Berkeley, however, hoped to avoid setting off a major war.

Berkeley and Bacon soon clashed. After Bacon forced the House of Burgesses to authorize him to attack the tribes, Berkeley declared Bacon and his men to be in rebellion. As the summer of 1676 wore on, Bacon alternately pursued Indians and battled with the governor's supporters. In September, he marched on Jamestown and burned the capital to the ground. But when Bacon died of dysentery the following month, the rebellion collapsed. Even so, a new Indian treaty signed in 1677 opened much of the disputed territory to whites.

More than coincidentally, New England—also settled more than fifty years earlier—was wracked by conflict with Native Americans at precisely the same time. In both areas, the colonists' original accommodation with the tribes no longer satisfied both parties. In New England, though, it was the tribal peoples, rather than the colonists, who felt aggrieved.

In the half-century since the founding of New England, colonial settlement had spread far into the interior of Massachusetts and Connecticut. In

King Philip's War
_____

the process, the colonists had completely surrounded the ancestral lands of the Poka-nokets (Wampanoags) on Narragansett Bay. Their chief, Metacomet (known to the English as King Philip), was the son of Massasoit, who had signed the treaty with the Pilgrims in 1621. Troubled by the encroachments on Pokanoket lands and the effects of European culture and Christianity on his people, Metacomet led his warriors in attacks on nearby communities in June 1675.

Two more tribes, the Nipmucks and the Narragansetts, joined Metacomet's forces. In the fall, the three tribes jointly attacked settlements in the northern Connecticut River valley. In early 1676, they devastated well-established villages and even attacked Plymouth and Providence. Although the alliance totally destroyed twelve of the ninety Puritan towns and attacked forty others, the tide turned in the summer of 1676. The coalition ran short of food and ammunition. After Metacomet was killed in an ambush in August, the alliance crumbled. Many surviving Pokanokets, Nipmucks, and Narragansetts, including Metacomet's wife and son, were captured and sold into slavery in the West Indies. The power of New England's coastal tribes was broken. Thereafter, they lived in small clusters, subordinated to the colonists and often working as servants or sailors.

NEW ENGLAND AND THE WEB OF IMPERIAL TRADE

From the early years of colonization to the close of the seventeenth century, the New England settlements had changed in three major ways. The population had grown dramatically, the residents' relationship to the Puritan church had altered, and the economy had developed in unanticipated ways.

By 1700, New England's population had quadrupled to reach approximately one hundred thousand. Such an increase placed great pressure on the available land, and many

Population Pressures

members of the third and fourth generations of New Englanders had to migrate— north to New Hampshire or Maine, south to New York, west beyond the Connecticut River—to find sufficient farm land for themselves and their children. Others abandoned

agriculture and learned skills like blacksmithing and carpentry.

In addition, many second-generation Puritans seemed less willing to become church members than their parents had been. Some historians postulate that American-born Puritans were less fervent than their ancestors; other historians believe that such people were simply less willing to declare publicly that they had experienced the gift of God's grace, or "saving faith," a ritual required for full membership in the church. These New Englanders had been baptized as children, attended church services regularly, and wanted their own infants baptized, although the sacrament of baptism was supposed to be available only to the children of church members. At the same time, many clergy grew concerned about the increasing numbers of unchurched adults, who were not formally subject to religious supervision.

A synod of Massachusetts ministers, convened in 1662 to consider these problems, responded by establishing a category of "halfway" membership in

Halfway Covenant

the church. In a statement that has become known as the Halfway Covenant, the clergy declared that adults who had been baptized as children but were not full church members could acknowledge the authority of the church in a ceremony called owning the covenant, which obliged them to live according to moral precepts. If married, they could then have their children baptized. Halfway members, however, were not allowed to vote in church affairs or to take communion.

By 1660, another change in church membership was evident: the proportion of women in the typical congregation was increasing. Indeed, women comprised a majority of every congregation for which records still survive. In response, Cotton Mather, the most prominent member of a family of distinguished ministers, delivered sermons outlining women's proper role in church and society—the first formal examination of that theme in American history. Mather urged women to be submissive to their husbands, watchful of their children, and attentive to religious duty.

But why were New England's men so reluctant to acknowledge the church's authority over them? One historian hypothesizes that the connection between church membership and political obligation was critical, because in Massachusetts only male church members could vote in colony elections and hold office. Many seventeenth-century farmers sought to avoid the burden of holding public office. They did not want to have to arrest their acquaintances, round up stray cattle or hogs, or serve as militia officers. Thus Massachusetts men may have decided not to seek church membership, because unchurched men were unlikely to be elected to office.

Another hypothesis focuses on the male residents of such seaport towns as Boston and Salem. Men in these urban areas, some historians argue, became more worldly and less interested in religion as the economy of the New England colonies changed after the outbreak of the English Civil War.

New England's first commercial system had been based on two foundations: the fur trade and the constant flow of migrants. Together, these had allowed New Englanders to acquire the manufactured goods they needed: the fur trade gave them valuable pelts to sell in England, and the migrants were always willing to exchange clothing and other items for the earlier settlers' surplus seed, grains, and livestock. But New England's supply of furs was quickly exhausted, and the migrants stopped coming after the English Civil War began. Thus in the early 1640s that first economic system collapsed.

The Changing Economic System

The Puritans then began a search for new salable goods and markets. They found the goods in grain, wood products, and fish. By 1643, they had also found the markets. Among the markets were the English colonies in the Caribbean, which lacked precisely the goods that New England could produce in abundance: cheap food (corn and salted fish) to feed to slaves and wood for barrels to hold molasses (the form in which sugar was shipped).

Thus developed the series of transactions that has become known, inaccurately, as the triangular

Captain Thomas Smith, a Boston ship captain, painted this self-portrait in the late seventeenth century. The seafaring scene in the background disclosed his occupation, whereas the skull and religious verse portrayed under his right hand symbolized his piety. Probably few individuals succeeded as well as Smith did in this portrait in simultaneously reflecting the values of the two worlds. Worcester Art Museum, Worcester, Massachusetts.

trade. The northern colonists sold their goods in the West Indies and elsewhere to earn the money with which to purchase English imports. There soon grew up in New England's ports a cadre of merchants who acquired—usually through barter—cargoes of timber and foodstuffs, which they then dispatched to the West Indies for sale. In the Caribbean, the ships sailed from island to island, exchanging fish, barrel staves, and grains for molasses, fruit, spices, and slaves. Once they had a full load, the ships returned to Boston, Newport, or New Haven to dispose of their cargoes. New Englanders traded the items they did not use to other colonies or to England. Most important, they distilled West Indian molasses into rum. Rum was a key component of the only part of the trade that could be termed *triangular:* Rhode Islanders took rum to Africa and traded it for slaves, whom they

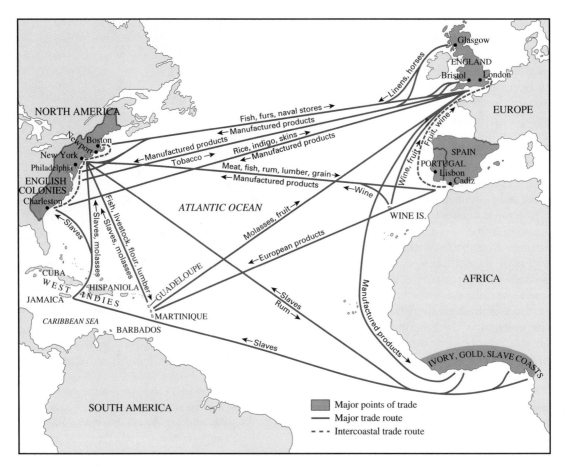

Atlantic Trade Routes   *By the late seventeenth century, the countries and colonies bordering the Atlantic Ocean were linked by an elaborate trade network. The most valuable commodities exchanged were enslaved people and the products of slave labor.*

carried to the West Indies to exchange for more molasses to produce still more rum. With that exception, the trading pattern was not a triangle but a shifting set of two-way voyages (see map).

The New Englanders who ventured into commerce were soon differentiated from their rural counterparts by their ties to a wider transatlantic world and their preoccupation with material endeavors. As time passed, increasing numbers of Puritans became involved in trade. Small investors who owned shares of voyages soon dominated the field numerically if not monetarily. The gulf be-

Puritans and Anglicans
—

tween commercial and farming interests widened after 1660, when Anglican merchants began to migrate to New England. Such men had little stake in the survival of Massachusetts Bay and Connecticut in their original form, and some were openly antagonistic to Puritan traditions. As non-Congregationalists they were denied the vote, but they were still taxed to support the church. Further, Anglicans were forbidden to practice their own religion freely. They resented their exclusion from the governing elite, believing that their wealth and social status entitled them to political power.

Congregationalist clergy returned their hostility in full measure and preached sermons called jeremiads lamenting New England's new commercial orientation. But the ministers spoke for the past, not the future, because by the 1670s New England and the other American colonies were deeply enmeshed in an intricate international trading network.

Colonial commerce also attracted the attention of English officials, who, seeking a new source of revenue after the disruptions of the English Civil War, realized that the colonies could make important contributions to England's economic well-being. Additional tax revenues could put the nation back on a sound financial footing, and English merchants wanted to ensure that they—not their Dutch rivals—reaped the benefits of trading with the English colonies. Parliament and the restored Stuart monarchs accordingly began to draft a system of laws designed to confine the profits of colonial trade primarily to England.

They based their commercial policy on a series of assumptions about the operations of the world's economic system. Collectively, these assumptions are usually called *mercantilism*, although neither the term itself nor a unified mercantilist theory was formulated until a century later. The economic world was seen as a collection of national states, each government actively competing for shares of a finite amount of wealth. Each nation's goal was to become as economically self-sufficient as possible while maintaining a favorable balance of trade with other countries (that is, exporting more than it imported). In such a scheme, colonies were to provide the home country with raw materials and to serve as markets for the home country's manufactured goods.

Parliament applied mercantilist thinking to the American colonies in a series of laws known as the Navigation Acts. The major acts—passed between 1651 and 1673—established **Navigation Acts** three main principles. First, only English or colonial merchants and ships could engage in trade in the colonies. Second, certain valuable American products could be sold only in England. At first, these "enumerated" goods were wool, sugar, tobacco, indigo, ginger, and dyes; later acts added rice, naval stores (masts, spars, pitch, tar, and turpentine), copper, and furs to the list. Third, all foreign goods destined for sale in the colonies had to be shipped via England and were subject to English import duties. Some years later, a new series of laws established a fourth principle: the colonies could not make or export items (such as wool clothing, hats, or iron) that competed with English products.

The intention of the Navigation Acts was clear: American trade was to center on England. England was to benefit from colonial imports and exports. England had first claim on the most valuable colonial exports, and all foreign imports to the colonies had to pass through England first, enriching its customs revenues in the process. Some colonies, such as those in the West Indies and the Chesapeake, were adversely affected by the laws, because they could not seek new markets for their staple crops. In others, the effect was less severe. The northern and middle colonies, for example, produced many nonenumerated goods such as fish, flour, and barrel staves that could be traded directly to foreign purchasers so long as they were carried in English or American ships.

The English authorities soon learned that it was easier to write mercantilist legislation than to enforce it. The many harbors of the American coast provided ready havens for smugglers, and colonial officials often looked the other way when illegally imported goods were offered for sale. Consequently, Parliament in 1696 enacted another navigation act designed to strengthen enforcement of the first four. This law established in America a number of vice admiralty courts, which operated without juries. Because American juries had already demonstrated a tendency to favor local smugglers over customs officers, Parliament decided to remove Navigation Act cases from the regular colonial courts.

England took another major step in colonial administration in 1696 by creating the Board of Trade and Plantations, which thereafter served as the chief organ of government concerned with the American colonies. (Previously, no single body had that responsibility.) It gathered information, reviewed Crown appointments in America, scrutinized legislation enacted by colonial assemblies, supervised trade policies, and advised successive ministries on colonial issues. Still, the Board of

Trade did not have any direct powers of enforcement. It also shared jurisdiction over American affairs with the customs service, the navy, and the secretary of state for the southern department, the member of the ministry responsible for the colonies. In short, although the Stuart monarchs' reforms considerably improved the quality of colonial administration, supervision of the American provinces remained decentralized and haphazard.

COLONIAL POLITICAL DEVELOPMENT AND IMPERIAL REORGANIZATION

English officials in the 1670s and 1680s were confronted not only by resistance to the Navigation Acts but also by a bewildering array of colonial governments. Massachusetts Bay and Plymouth functioned under their original charters, and neighboring Connecticut (including the formerly independent New Haven) and Rhode Island had been granted charters by Charles II in 1662 and 1663, respectively. Virginia was a royal colony, and New York also became one when its proprietor ascended the throne in 1685 as James II. All the other mainland settlements were proprietorships.

Still, in political structure the colonies shared certain characteristics. Most were ruled by a governor and a two-house legislature. In

Colonial Political Structures

New England, the governors were elected by property-holding men or by the legislature; in the Chesapeake and the middle colonies, they were appointed by the king or the proprietor. A council, either elected or appointed, advised the governor on matters of policy and sometimes served as the colony's highest court. The councils also served as the upper house of the colonial legislatures. At first, councillors and elected representatives met jointly to debate and adopt laws affecting the colony. But as time passed, the fundamental differences between the two legislative groups' purposes and constituencies led them to separate into two distinct houses. Thus

developed the two-house legislature still used in almost all states.

Meanwhile, local political institutions were taking shape. In New England, elected selectmen initially governed the towns, but by the end of the century the town meeting—held at least annually and attended by most free adult male residents, regardless of church membership—handled matters of local concern. In the Chesapeake, the same function was performed by the judges of the county court and by the parish vestry, a group of laymen charged with overseeing church affairs, whose power also encompassed secular concerns.

By late in the seventeenth century, therefore, the American colonists were accustomed to exercising a considerable degree of local political autonomy. The tradition of consent was especially firmly established in New England. Everywhere in the English colonies, free adult men who owned more than a stated minimum of property (which varied from province to province) expected to have an influential voice in how they were governed and especially in how they were taxed.

After James II became king, these expectations clashed with those of the monarch. The new king and his successors sought to bring order to the apparently chaotic state of colonial administration by tightening the reins of government and reducing the colonies' political autonomy. They began to chip away at the privileges granted in colonial charters and to reclaim proprietorships for the Crown. New Hampshire (1679), its parent colony Massachusetts (1691), New Jersey (1702), and the Carolinas (1729) all became royal colonies. The charters of Rhode Island, Connecticut, Maryland, and Pennsylvania were temporarily suspended but ultimately restored to their original status.

The most drastic reordering of colonial administration targeted Puritan New England. Reports from America convinced English officials that New

Dominion of New England

England was a hotbed of smuggling. Moreover, the Puritans refused to allow freedom of religion to non-Congregationalists and insisted on maintaining laws that ran counter to English practice. New England thus seemed an appropriate place to exert

English authority with greater vigor. The charters of all the colonies from New Jersey to Maine (then part of Massachusetts) were revoked, and a Dominion of New England was established in 1686. Sir Edmund Andros, the governor, was given immense power: all the assemblies were dissolved, and he needed only the consent of an appointed council to make laws and levy taxes.

New Englanders endured Andros's autocratic rule for more than two years. Then came the dramatic news that James II had been overthrown in a bloodless coup known as the Glorious Revolution and had been replaced on the throne by his daughter Mary and her husband, the Dutch prince William of Orange. James II had levied taxes without parliamentary approval. He had also announced his conversion to Roman Catholicism. When Parliament offered the throne to the Protestants William and Mary, the Glorious Revolution affirmed the supremacy of both Parliament and Protestantism.

Seizing the opportunity to rid themselves of the hated Dominion, New Englanders jailed Andros and his associates, proclaimed their loyalty to William and Mary, and wrote to England for instructions about the form of government they should adopt. In other American colonies too, the Glorious Revolution was a signal for revolt. In Maryland, the Protestant Association overturned the government of the Catholic proprietor, and in New York a militia officer of German origin, Jacob Leisler, assumed control of the government. Like the New Englanders, the Maryland and New York rebels allied themselves with the supporters of William and Mary. They saw themselves as carrying out the colonial phase of the English revolt against Stuart absolutism. But William and Mary, like James II, believed that England should exercise tighter control over its unruly American possessions.

Glorious Revolution in America

Consequently, the only American rebellion that received royal sanction was that in Maryland, primarily because of its anti-Catholic thrust. In New York, Leisler was hanged for treason, and Massachusetts (including the formerly independent

jurisdiction of Plymouth) became a royal colony with an appointed governor. The province was allowed to retain its town meeting system of local government and to elect its council, but the new charter issued in 1691 eliminated the traditional religious test for voting. An Anglican parish was set up in the heart of Boston.

Compounding New England's difficulties in a time of political upheaval and economic uncertainty was a war with the French and their Native American allies. King Louis XIV of France allied with the deposed James II, and England declared war on France in 1689. The conflict, which lasted until 1697, was known in Europe as the War of the League of Augsburg, but the colonists called it King William's War. The American war was fought chiefly on the northern frontiers of New England and New York.

In this period of extreme stress occurred an outbreak of witchcraft accusations in Salem Village (now Danvers), Massachusetts, a rural community adjoining the bustling port of Salem. Like their contemporaries elsewhere, seventeenth-century New Englanders believed in the existence of witches. If people could not find other explanations for their troubles, they tended to suspect they were bewitched. Before 1689, 103 New Englanders, most of them middle-aged women, had been accused of practicing witchcraft. Only a few of the accused were convicted, and fewer still were executed. Although most accusations were isolated incidents, a witchcraft panic occasionally resulted when one charge set off a chain reaction. But nothing in New England's history ever came close to matching the Salem Village cataclysm.

Witchcraft in Salem Village

The crisis began in early 1692 when a group of adolescent girls accused some older women of having bewitched them. Before the hysteria spent itself ten months later, nineteen people (including several men, most of them related to accused female witches) had been hanged, another pressed to death with heavy stones, and more than one hundred persons jailed. The events in Salem Village can best be understood when seen in the context of political and legal disorder, Indian war, and religious and economic crises. These factors undermined the sense of security that Puritan New Englanders had about their future.

Nowhere was that more true than in Salem Village, a farming town torn between old and new styles of life because of its position on the edge of a commercial center. And no residents of the village had more reason to feel insecure than the girls who made the initial accusations. Many had been orphaned in the recent Indian attacks on Maine; they were living in Salem Village as domestic servants. Their involvement with witchcraft began as an experiment with fortunetelling as a means of foreseeing their futures, in particular the identities of their eventual husbands. As the most powerless people in a town apparently powerless to direct its fate, they offered other New Englanders a compelling explanation for the seemingly endless chain of troubles afflicting them: their province was under direct attack from the devil and his legion of witches. Accordingly, it is not so much the number of witchcraft prosecutions that seems surprising but their abrupt cessation in the fall of 1692.

The crisis ended rapidly for two reasons. First, the accusers grew too bold. When they began to accuse some of the colony's most distinguished and respected residents of being in league with the devil, members of the ruling elite began to doubt their veracity. Second, the new royal charter was fully implemented in late 1692, ending the worst period of political uncertainty and eliminating a major source of psychological stress. King William's War continued and, although the Puritans were not entirely pleased with the charter, at least order had formally been restored.

During the course of the next three decades, Massachusetts and the rest of the English colonies in America accommodated themselves to the new imperial order. Most colonists resented alien officials who arrived in America determined to implement the policies of king and Parliament, but they adjusted to their demands and to the trade restrictions imposed by the Navigation Acts. They fought another imperial war—the War of the Spanish Succession, or Queen Anne's War—from 1702 to 1713, without enduring the psychological stress of the first. Colonists who allied with the royal government received patronage in the form of offices and land grants and composed "court parties" that supported English officials. Others, who were either less fortunate in their friends or more principled in defense of colonial autonomy (opinions differ), made up the opposition, or "country" interest. By the end of the first quarter of the eighteenth century, most men in both groups had been born in America and were members of elite families whose wealth derived from staple-crop production in the South and commerce in the North.

The eighty years from 1640 to 1720, then, established the basic economic and political patterns that were to structure all subsequent changes in colonial society. In 1640, there were just two isolated centers of English population, New England and the Chesapeake. In 1720, nearly the entire east coast of mainland North America was in English hands, and Indian power east of the Appalachian Mountains had been broken. What had been a migrant population was now mostly American born, economies originally based on the fur trade had become far more complex and more closely linked with England, and a wide variety of political structures had been reshaped into a more uniform pattern. Yet at the same time, the introduction of large-scale slavery to the Chesapeake and the Carolinas irrevocably differentiated their societies from those of the colonies to the north.

Meanwhile, from a small outpost in Santa Fe, New Mexico, the Spanish had expanded their influence throughout the region as far east as Texas and, just after midcentury, as far north as California. The French had moved from a few settlements along the St. Lawrence to dominate the length of the Mississippi River and the entire Great Lakes region. The extensive Spanish and French presence to the south and west of the English settlements meant that future conflicts among the European powers in North America were nearly inevitable.

By 1720, the essential elements of the imperial administrative structure that would govern the English colonies until 1775 were firmly in place. The regional economic systems originating in the late seventeenth and early eighteenth centuries also continued to dominate North American life for another century—until after independence had been won. And Anglo-Americans had developed the commitment to autonomous local government that would later lead them into conflict with Parliament and the king.

SUGGESTIONS FOR FURTHER READING

General

Carl Bridenbaugh, *Cities in the Wilderness: The First Century of Urban Life in America, 1625–1742* (1938); Wesley Frank Craven, *The Colonies in Transition, 1660–1713* (1968); W. J. Eccles, *France in America*, rev. ed. (1990), and *The Canadian Frontier, 1534–1760*, rev. ed. (1983); Jack P. Greene and J. R. Pole, eds., *Colonial British America* (1984); John J. McCusker and Russell R. Menard, *The Economy of British America, 1607–1789* (1985); Gary Walton and James Shepherd, *The Economic Rise of Early America* (1979).

New Netherland and the Restoration Colonies

Edwin Bronner, *William Penn's "Holy Experiment": The Founding of Pennsylvania, 1681–1701* (1962); Wesley Frank Craven, *New Jersey and the English Colonization of North America* (1964); Mary Maples Dunn, *William Penn: Politics and Conscience* (1967); Joyce Goodfriend, *Before the Melting Pot: Society and Culture in Colonial New York City, 1664–1730* (1992); Ronald Hutton, *Charles II: King of England, Scotland, and Ireland* (1990); Michael Kammen, *Colonial New York: A History* (1975); Oliver Rink, *Holland on the Hudson: An Economic and Social History of Dutch New York* (1986); Robert C. Ritchie, *The Duke's Province: A Study of Politics and Society in Colonial New York, 1660–1691* (1977); Robert M. Weir, *Colonial South Carolina: A History* (1983).

Africa and the Slave Trade

Philip D. Curtin, *The Atlantic Slave Trade: A Census* (1969); David Brion Davis, *The Problem of Slavery in Western Culture* (1966); Herbert Klein, *The Middle Passage* (1978); Robin Law, *The Slave Coast of West Africa, 1550–1750: The Impact of the Atlantic Slave Trade on an African Society* (1991); Daniel C. Littlefield, *Rice and Slaves: Ethnicity and the Slave Trade in Colonial South Carolina* (1981); James Rawley, *The Transatlantic Slave Trade: A History* (1981).

Africans in Anglo-America

T. H. Breen and Stephen Innes, *"Myne Owne Ground": Race and Freedom on Virginia's Eastern Shore, 1640–1676* (1980); Allan Kulikoff, *Tobacco and Slaves: The Development of Southern Cultures in the Chesapeake, 1680–1800* (1986); Edgar J. McManus, *Black Bondage in the North* (1973); Peter H. Wood, *Black Majority: Negroes in Colonial South Carolina from 1670 Through the Stono Rebellion* (1974).

European–Native American Relations

Russell Bourne, *The Red King's Rebellion: Racial Politics in New England 1675–1678* (1991); Verner W. Crane, *The Southern Frontier, 1660–1732* (1929); Ramón Gutiérrez, *When Jesus Came, the Corn Mothers Went Away: Marriage, Sexuality, and Power in New Mexico, 1500–1846* (1991); Francis Jennings, *The Ambiguous Iroquois Empire* (1984); Elizabeth A. H. John, *Storms Brewed in Other Men's Worlds: The Confrontation of Indians, Spanish, and French in the Southwest, 1540–1795* (1975); James Merrell, *The Indians' New World: Catawbas and Their Neighbors from European Contact Through the Era of Removal* (1989); Marc Simmons, *The Last Conquistador: Juan de Oñate and the Settling of the Far Southwest* (1991); Daniel H. Usner Jr., *Indians, Settlers, and Slaves in a Frontier Exchange Economy: The Lower Mississippi Valley Before 1783* (1992); Richard White, *The Middle Ground: Indians, Empires, and Republics in the Great Lakes Region, 1650–1815* (1991).

New England

Bernard Bailyn, *The New England Merchants in the Seventeenth Century* (1955); Christine Heyrman, *Commerce and Culture: The Maritime Communities of Colonial Massachusetts, 1690–1750* (1984); Carol Karlsen, *The Devil in the Shape of a Woman: Witchcraft in Early New England* (1987); Richard I. Melvoin, *New England Outpost: War and Society in Colonial Deerfield* (1990); Robert Pope, *The Half-Way Covenant* (1969); Laurel Thatcher Ulrich, *Good Wives: Image and Reality in the Lives of Women in Northern New England, 1650–1750* (1982).

Colonial Politics

Richard P. Johnson, *Adjustment to Empire: The New England Colonies, 1675–1715* (1981); David W. Jordan, *Foundations of Representative Government in Maryland, 1632–1715* (1987); David S. Lovejoy, *The Glorious Revolution in America* (1972); Stephen Saunders Webb, *1676: The End of American Independence* (1984).

Imperial Trade and Administration

Robert M. Bliss, *Revolution and Empire: English Politics and the American Colonies in the Seventeenth Century* (1991); Lawrence W. Harper, *The English Navigation Laws: A Seventeenth-Century Experiment in Social Engineering* (1939); Robert C. Ritchie, *Captain Kidd and the War Against the Pirates* (1986); I. K. Steele, *Politics of Colonial Policy: The Board of Trade in Colonial Administration* (1968).

Chapter

4

Growth and Diversity, 1720–1770

I N JUNE 1744, DR. Alexander Hamilton, a Scottish-born physician living in Annapolis, Maryland, paid his first visit to Philadelphia. There he encountered two quite different worlds. One consisted of men of his own status, the merchants and professionals he called "the better sort." The other comprised ordinary men from different ethnic backgrounds and religious beliefs. Hamilton thought of these men as rabble. To Hamilton, the "better sort" engaged in informed conversation, and the "rabble" spoke "ignorantly," regardless of subject.

And what of the women in Philadelphia? "The ladies," Hamilton explained, "for the most part, keep at home and seldom appear in the streets, never in publick assemblies except at the churches or meetings." Hamilton was referring to women of "the better sort." He could hardly have walked the streets of the city without seeing many female domestic servants, market women, and wives of ordinary laborers going about their daily chores.

Despite his obvious biases, Dr. Hamilton was an astute observer. The Philadelphians' chief employment, he wrote, "is traffick and mercantile busi-

ness," and the richest merchants of all were the Quakers. Members of that sect also controlled the colony's government, but, Hamilton noted, "The standing or falling of the Quakers in the House of Assembly depends upon their making sure the interest of the Palatines [Germans] in this province, who of late have turned so numerous that they can sway the votes which way they please." And Hamilton deplored the influence on the city of the Great Awakening, the religious revival then sweeping the colonies. "I never was in a place so populous where the gout [taste] for publick gay diversions prevailed so little," he remarked.

Hamilton's comments provide an excellent introduction to mid-eighteenth-century American life, for the patterns he observed in Philadelphia were not unique to that city. Although ethnic diversity was especially pronounced in urban areas, by midcentury non-English migrants were settling in many regions of the mainland colonies. Their arrival not only swelled the total population but also altered political balances and affected the religious climate by introducing new sects. The diverse group of men Hamilton encountered in that tavern could have been duplicated in other cities and even in some rural areas.

Hamilton correctly recognized that the Quakers maintained control of Pennsylvania politics because they had managed to win the support of recent German immigrants. The ruling elites in other provinces, however, often refused to allow immigrants adequate representation and government services. A series of violent clashes ensued after midcentury. By that time, native-born elites dominated each colony and contended with English-born governors and councillors for control of the governmental machinery.

Hamilton also accurately assessed the importance of commerce in Americans' lives. The web of imperial trade woven before 1720 became even more complex and all encompassing during the next fifty years. Americans of all descriptions were tied to an international commercial system that fluctuated wildly for reasons that had little to do with the colonies. As the colonies would learn when they attempted to break their trade ties with Great Britain, they were heavily dependent on England for both imported manufactured goods and markets for their exports.

Well-educated Americans like Dr. Hamilton were heavily influenced by the Enlightenment, the prevailing European intellectual movement of the day. The Enlightenment stressed reason and empirical knowledge, deliberately discarding superstition and instinct as guides to human behavior. Like other enlightened thinkers, Hamilton believed above all in rationality. To him, God was a distant presence who had ordered the world, setting forth natural laws that humans could discover through careful investigation and logical thought. From this perspective came Hamilton's distaste for the Great Awakening, because that revival drew primarily on the Calvinist concept of a God that people could never fully comprehend. Moreover, the hallmark of the Great Awakening was emotion, expressed in a conversion experience. To a believer in the primacy of reason, the passions of the newly converted were incomprehensible.

The Enlightenment also helped to create the elite world of which Hamilton was a part, a world quite different from that of ordinary folk. Wealthy, well-read Americans participated in a transatlantic intellectual community, whereas many colonists of "the lesser sort" could neither read nor write. Hamilton and his peers lived in comfortable houses and entertained at lavish parties; most colonists struggled just to make ends meet. The eighteenth century, then, brought an increasing gap between rich and poor. The colonies had always been composed of people of different ranks, but by the last half of the century, the social and economic distance between those ranks had widened noticeably.

After 1720, the population of the English colonies increased dramatically, and the area settled by whites and blacks expanded until it filled almost all the region between the Appalachian Mountains and the Atlantic Ocean, displacing the Native Americans who had previously lived there. At the same time, the colonies became more diverse; the two original regional economies (the Chesapeake and New England) became four (those two plus the middle colonies and the Lower South). Before 1720, the colonies were still inhabited mainly by English, African, and Indian peoples; just half a century later, a large proportion of the white population was of non-English origin. Many colonies were home to a variety of ethnic groups and religious sects. The urban population, although still tiny by today's standards, grew considerably after 1720, and the cities harbored the greatest extremes of wealth and poverty. Thus the colonies that revolted in unison against British rule after 1765 were different from the colonies that revolted separately against Stuart absolutism in 1689.

POPULATION GROWTH AND ETHNIC DIVERSITY

One of the most striking characteristics of the mainland colonies in the eighteenth century was their rapid population growth. Only about 250,000 European- and African-Americans resided in the colonies in 1700. Thirty years later, that number had more than doubled, and by 1775 it had become 2.5 million. Although migration accounted for a considerable share of the growth, most of it resulted from natural increase. Once the difficult early decades of settlement had passed, the

American population doubled approximately every twenty-five years. Such a rate of growth was then unparalleled in human history. It had a variety of causes, chief among them women's youthful age at marriage (early twenties for whites, late teens for blacks). Since married women became pregnant every two or three years, women normally bore five to ten children. Because the colonies were healthful places to live (especially north of Virginia), a large proportion of children reached maturity and began families of their own. As a result, about half the American population, white and black, was younger than sixteen in 1775. (By contrast, only about one-third of the American population was younger than sixteen in 1990.)

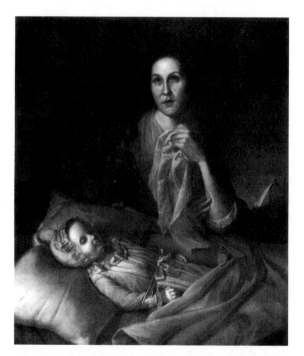

"Rachel Weeping," by Charles Willson Peale, conveys as few other colonial portraits can the affection of eighteenth-century parents for their children, and the grief they consequently felt when those children died (as was so often the case) at an early age. Peale movingly revealed his wife's sorrow at the death of their daughter; thus his painting helps to refute the interpretation—advanced by some historians—that high levels of infant mortality led colonists to avoid becoming too attached to their young children. Philadelphia Museum of Art, The Barra Foundation.

Africans (about 278,000 of them) constituted the largest racial or ethnic group that came to the mainland English colonies during the eighteenth century. In the slave-holding societies of South America and the Caribbean, a surplus of males over females and the appallingly high mortality rates meant that only a large, continuing flow of enslaved Africans could maintain the captive work force at constant levels. South Carolina, where rice cultivation was difficult and unhealthy, and where planters preferred to purchase men, bore some resemblance to such colonies. But in the Chesapeake, the number of black residents grew especially rapidly, because the new African workers were added to a population that began to sustain itself through natural increase after 1740.

Newcomers from Africa and Europe

The offspring of slaves were also slaves, whereas the children of servants were free. The consequences of this important difference between enslaved and indentured labor were not clear until after 1720. It then became evident that a planter who owned adult female slaves could watch the size of his labor force increase steadily—through the births of their children—without making additional major investments in workers. Not coincidentally, the first truly large Chesapeake plantations appeared in the 1740s.

In addition to the new group of Africans, about 585,000 Europeans moved to North America during the eighteenth century, most of them after 1730. Because some whites (for example, convicts sentenced to exile by English courts) and all blacks did not freely choose to come to the colonies, approximately one-third of the migrants moved to America against their will.

The largest group of white non-English immigrants to America—more than 100,000—came from Ireland. About 66,000 were Scotch-Irish, descended from Presbyterian Scots who had settled in the north of Ireland during the seventeenth century. Another 43,000 (both Protestants and Catholics) migrated from southern Ireland. Fleeing economic distress and religious discrimination, they were also lured by

Scotch-Irish, Germans, and Scots

• *Important Events* •

1720–40	Black population of Chesapeake begins to grow by natural increase, contributing to rise of large plantations	1760s	Baptist congregations take root in Virginia
1739	Stono Rebellion (South Carolina) leads to increased white fears of slave revolts	1760–75	Peak of eighteenth-century European and African migration to English colonies
	George Whitefield arrives in America; Great Awakening broadens	1765–66	Hudson River land riots pit tenants and squatters against large landlords
1739–48	King George's War disrupts American economy	1767–69	Regulator movement (South Carolina) tries to establish order in back-country
1741	New York City "conspiracy" reflects whites' continuing fears of slave revolts	1771	North Carolina Regulators defeated by eastern militia at Battle of Alamance

hopes of obtaining land. Irish immigrants often arrived in Philadelphia and other ports along the Delaware River. They moved west and south, settling chiefly in the western portions of Pennsylvania, Maryland, Virginia, and the Carolinas. Frequently unable to afford any acreage, they squatted on land belonging to Indian tribes, land speculators, or colonial governments.

Migrants from Germany numbered about eighty-five thousand. Most emigrated from the Rhineland between 1730 and 1755, also usually arriving in Philadelphia. Late in the century, German migrants and their descendants accounted for one-third of Pennsylvania's residents. But many other Germans moved west and then south along the eastern slope of the Appalachian Mountains, eventually finding homes in western Maryland and Virginia. Others sailed first to Charleston or Savannah and settled in the interior of South Carolina or Georgia. The Germans belonged to a wide variety of Protestant sects—primarily Lutheran, German Reformed, and Moravian—and therefore added to the already substantial religious diversity of the middle colonies.

The thirty-five thousand or more Scots who came directly to America from Scotland should not be confused with the Scotch-Irish. Many early Scottish immigrants were supporters of Stuart claimants to the throne of England (called Jacobites,

for the Latin version of James Stuart's name). After the death of William and Mary's successor Queen Anne in 1714, the British throne passed to the German house of Hanover, in the person of King George I. In 1715 and again in 1745, Jacobite rebels attempted unsuccessfully to capture the Crown for the Stuart pretender, and many were exiled to America as punishment. Most Jacobites settled in North Carolina. Ironically, they tended to become loyalists during the Revolutionary War because of their strong commitment to monarchy.

The most concentrated period of immigration to the colonies fell between 1760 and 1775. Tough times in Europe led many to decide to seek a better life in America. In those fifteen years alone arrived more than 220,000 persons—or 10 percent of the entire population of British North America. At least 90,000 migrants came from the British Isles: 34,000 Irish, 25,000 Scots, perhaps 11,000 Welsh, and about 20,000 English people. To them were added approximately 20,000 Germans, 100,000 Africans, and a smattering of people from other places, including a few from the West Indies. Late-arriving free immigrants had little choice but to remain in the cities or move to the peripheries of settlement; land elsewhere was fully occupied.

Because of the migration patterns of the various ethnic groups and the concentration of slave holding in the South, half the colonial population south of New England was of non-English origin by 1775. Whether the migrants assimilated readily into Anglo-American culture depended on patterns of settlement, the size of the group, and the strength of the migrants' ties to their common culture. For example, the Huguenots were French Protestants who settled in tiny enclaves in American cities but were unable to sustain either their language or their religious practices. Within two generations, they were almost wholly absorbed into Anglo-American culture. By contrast, the equally small group of colonial Jews maintained a distinct identity. They established synagogues and worked actively to preserve their culture (for example, by opposing intermarriage with Christians). Members of the larger groups of migrants (the Germans, Irish, and Scots) found it easier to sustain Old World ways. Countless localities were settled almost exclusively by one group or another.

Recognizing the benefits of keeping other racial and ethnic groups divided, the white elites on occasion deliberately fostered such antagonisms. When the targets of their policies were European migrants, the goal was the maintenance of political and economic power. When the targets were Indians and blacks, as they were in South Carolina, the stakes were considerably higher. In 1758, one official reported, "It has been allways the policy of this government to create an aversion in them [Indians] to Negroes." South Carolina whites, a minority of the population, wanted to prevent Indians and blacks from making common cause against them. To keep slaves from running away to join the Indians, whites hired Indians as slave catchers. To keep Indians from trusting blacks, whites used blacks as soldiers in Indian wars.

The elites would probably have preferred to ignore the colonies' growing racial and ethnic diversity, but they could not do so for long and still maintain their power. When such men decided to lead a revolution in the 1770s, they recognized that they needed the support of non-English Americans. Quite deliberately, they then began to speak of "the rights of man," rather than "English liberties," when they sought recruits for their cause.

ECONOMIC GROWTH AND DEVELOPMENT

The eighteenth-century American economy was characterized by sharp fluctuations rather than by a consistent long-term trend. Those fluctuations had two primary causes: the effect of European wars and variations in overseas demand for American products. The only source of stability in the shifting economic climate was the dramatic increase in the colonial population.

Each year, the rising population generated ever greater demands for goods and services, which led to the development of small-scale colonial manufacturing and a complex network of internal trade. As the area of settlement expanded, roads, bridges, mills, and stores were built to serve the new communities. A lively coastal trade developed; by the late 1760s, 54 percent of the vessels leaving Boston harbor were sailing to other mainland colonies rather than to foreign ports. Such ships not only collected goods for export and distributed imports but also sold items made in America. The colonies thus began to move away from their earlier pattern of near total dependence on Europe for manufactured goods. For the first time, the American population was generating sufficient demand to encourage manufacturing enterprises. The largest indigenous industry was iron making; by 1775, eighty-two American furnaces and 175 forges were producing more iron than was England. Almost all of that iron was for domestic consumption.

The major energizing, yet destabilizing, influence on the colonial economy was foreign trade. Colonial prosperity still depended heavily on overseas demand for American products like tobacco, rice, indigo, fish, and barrel staves; the sale of such items earned the colonists the credit they needed to purchase English and European imports. If demand for American exports slowed, the colonists' income dropped and so did their ability to buy imported goods.

Despite fluctuations, the economy grew slowly during the eighteenth century. That growth produced better standards of living for all property-

How do historians know

that wealthier Americans were starting to acquire more luxury goods in the eighteenth century? One way to learn what the colonists possessed is to examine documents, called probate inventories, which listed the belongings of recently deceased individuals before estates were distributed to heirs. Another way is to study material culture—that is, to find objects that were used in colonial homes and to determine their origins, chronology, and uses. The silver coffee pot pictured here, for example, was manufactured about 1755 in Charleston, South Carolina, by a silversmith named Alexander Petrie. It is important for two reasons. First, it provides evidence that by midcentury at least some well-to-do colonists had started to drink coffee, an exotic, expensive drink made from imported beans. Second, its elegant form revealed the refined taste of both its owner and its maker. Artisans like Petrie, with skills much in demand by wealthy colonial customers, could earn large sums of money by practicing their trades. By the time Petrie died in 1768, he had achieved the status of gentleman, one of the highest rungs on the ladder of colonial status. Photo: Museum of Early Southern Decorative Arts, Winston-Salem, N.C.

Rising Standard of Living

owning Americans. In the first two decades of the century, households began to acquire such amenities as chairs, knives and forks, and earthenware dishes. Diet also improved as trading networks brought access to more varied foodstuffs. After 1750, luxury items like silver plate could be found in the homes of the wealthy, and "the middling sort" started to purchase imported English ceramics and teapots. Even the poorest property owners had more and better household possessions.

Yet the benefits of economic growth were not evenly distributed: wealthy Americans improved their position relative to other colonists. The native-born elite families that dominated American political, economic, and social life by 1750 were those that had begun the century with sufficient capital to take advantage of the changes caused by population growth. They were urban merchants, large landowners, slave traders, and the owners of rum distilleries. The rise of this group of monied families helped to increase the stratification of the social and economic structure of mid-eighteenth-century America.

New immigrants did not have the opportunities for advancement that had greeted their predecessors. Even so, there seems to have been relatively little severe poverty among whites in rural areas, where 90 percent of the colonists lived. But in the cities, the story was different. Families of urban laborers lived on the edge of destitution. In Philadelphia, for instance, a

Urban Poverty

male laborer's average annual earnings fell short of the amount needed to supply his family with the bare necessities. Even in a good year, his wife or children had to do wage work; in a bad year, the family could be reduced to beggary. By the 1760s, applicants for assistance were overwhelming the public poor-relief systems, and some cities began to build workhouses or almshouses to shelter the growing number of poor people.

Within this overall picture, it is important to distinguish among the various regions: New England, the middle colonies, the Chesapeake, and the Lower South (the Carolinas and Georgia). Each region had its own economic rhythm derived from the nature of its export trade.

In New England, three elements combined to influence economic development: the nature of the

Regional Trading Patterns: New England *New England's major exports—dried fish, livestock, and wood products—were sold primarily in the West Indies.* Source: James F. Shepherd and Gary M. Walton, *Shipping, Maritime Trade, and the Economic Development of Colonial North America* (Cambridge: Cambridge University Press, 1972). Copyright 1972. Used by permission of Cambridge University Press.

landscape, New England's leadership in colonial shipping, and the imperial wars. New England's soil was rocky and thin, and farmers did not normally produce large agricultural surpluses to sell abroad. Farms were worked primarily by family members; the region had relatively few hired laborers. It also had the lowest average wealth per freeholder in the colonies. But New England had its share of wealthy men; they were the merchants and professionals who drew their income from trade in such items as fish and livestock, primarily with the West Indies (see figure).

Boston's central position in the New England economy and its role as a shipbuilding center ensured that it would be directly affected by any resumption of warfare. In 1739,

New England and King George's War

English vessels began clashing with Spanish ships in the Caribbean, setting off a conflict that became known in America as King George's War. Nominally, the war was fought to determine who would sit on the Austrian throne (in Europe it was called the War of the Austrian Succession), but one of its causes was European commercial rivalries over the lucrative West Indian trade. The war's first effect on Boston's economy was positive. Ships and sailors were in demand, and wealthy merchants profited from contracts to supply military expeditions.

But Boston suffered heavy losses of manpower. After France became Spain's ally, a Massachusetts force captured the French fortress of Louisbourg (in modern Nova Scotia), which guarded the sea lanes leading to New France. Afterward, though, the colony had to levy heavy taxes on its residents to pay for the expensive effort. For decades, Boston's economy felt the continuing effects of King George's War. The city was left with unprecedented numbers of widows and children on its relief rolls. The boom in shipbuilding ended when the war did, and taxes remained high. As a final blow to the colonies, Britain gave Louisbourg back to France in the Treaty of Aix-la-Chapelle (1748).

King George's War and its aftermath had a more positive effect on the middle colonies because of the greater fertility of the soil in New York and

Prosperity of the Middle Colonies

Pennsylvania, where commercial farming was the norm. With the outbreak of war, farmers in the middle colonies were able to profit from the wartime demand for grain and meat, especially in the West Indies. After the war, a series of poor grain harvests in Europe caused flour prices to rise even more rapidly. Philadelphia and New York, which could draw on large, fertile, grain- and livestock-producing areas, took the lead in the foodstuffs trade. Meanwhile, Boston, which had no such fertile hinterland, found its economy stagnating.

Increased European demand for grain had a significant effect on the Chesapeake as well. After 1745, some Chesapeake planters began to convert tobacco fields to wheat and corn (see figure). By diversifying their crops, they could avoid dependency on just one product for their income. Tobacco still ruled the region and remained the largest single export from the mainland colonies (see figure). Yet the conversion to grain cultivation brought about the first significant change in Chesapeake settlement patterns by encouraging the development of port towns (like Baltimore) to house the merchants who marketed the new products.

Like the Chesapeake, the Lower South depended on staple crops and an enslaved labor force, but its pattern of economic growth was distinctive

Chesapeake and the Lower South

(see figure). In contrast to tobacco prices, which rose slowly through the middle decades of the century, rice prices climbed steeply. The primary cause of the sharp rise was the heavy demand for rice in southern Europe. Because Parliament removed rice from the list of enumerated products in 1730, South Carolinians were able to do what colonial tobacco planters never could: trade directly with continental Europe. But dependence on European sales had its drawbacks, as rice growers learned at the outbreak of King George's War in 1739. Trade with the Continent was disrupted, rice prices plummeted, and South Carolina entered a depression. Still, prosperity returned by the 1760s; indeed, the Lower South experienced more rapid economic growth in that period than

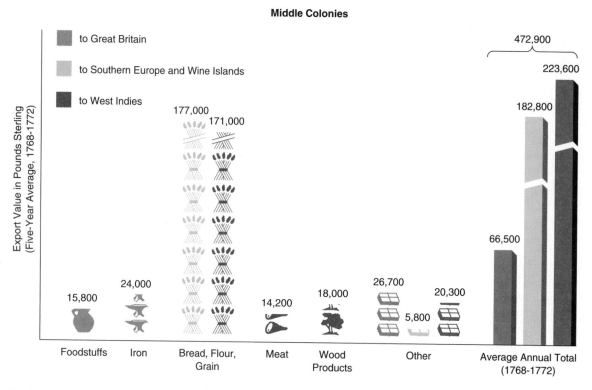

Regional Trading Patterns: Middle Colonies   *The middle colonies' major trading partners were the West Indies, the Wine Islands, and Southern Europe; bread, flour, and grains were the region's most valuable exports.*   Source: James F. Shepherd and Gary M. Walton, *Shipping, Maritime Trade, and the Economic Development of Colonial North America* (Cambridge: Cambridge University Press, 1972). Copyright 1972. Used by permission of Cambridge University Press.

the other regions of the colonies. Partly as a result, it had the highest average wealth per freeholder in Anglo-America by the time of the Revolution.

Although King George's War initially helped New England and hurt the Lower South, in the long run those effects were reversed. In the Chesapeake and the middle colonies, the war initiated a long period of prosperity. The variety of these economic experiences points up a crucial fact about the mainland colonies: they did not compose a unified whole. They were linked economically into regions, but they had few political or social ties beyond or even within those regions. Despite the growing coastal trade, the individual colonies' economic fortunes depended not on their neighbors in America but on the shifting markets of Europe and the West Indies.

THE DAILY LIVES OF EUROPEAN-AMERICANS

The basic unit of colonial society was the household. Headed by a white male (or his widow), the household was the chief mechanism of production and consumption. Its members—bound by ties of blood or servitude—worked together to produce goods for consumption or sale. The white male head of the household represented it to the outside world, serving in the militia or political posts, casting the household's sole vote in elections. He managed the finances and held legal authority over the rest of the family—his wife, his children, and his servants or slaves. (Eighteenth-century Americans used the word *family* for people who occupied one house, whether they were blood kin or not.) Such households were considerably larger than American families today; in 1790, the average home housed 5.7 whites. Most big families were nuclear—that is, they did not include extended kin like aunts, uncles, and grandparents.

The vast majority of colonial families lived in rural areas. As a result, nearly all adult white men were farmers, and nearly all adult white women were farm wives. In colonial America, household tasks were allocated by sex. The master, his sons, and his male servants or slaves performed one set of chores; the mistress, her daughters, and her

Sexual Division of Labor Among White Americans

female servants or slaves, an entirely different set. So rigid were these gender classifications that in households without a master or mistress, no one did those chores. Only in emergencies and for brief periods of time would women do men's work or men do women's.

The mistress of the rural household was responsible for what were termed *indoor affairs*. She and her female helpers prepared food, cleaned the house, did laundry, and often made clothing. In eighteenth-century America, these basic chores were complex and time consuming. Preparing food involved planting and cultivating a garden, harvesting and preserving vegetables, salting and smoking meat, drying apples and pressing cider, milking cows and making butter and cheese, not to mention

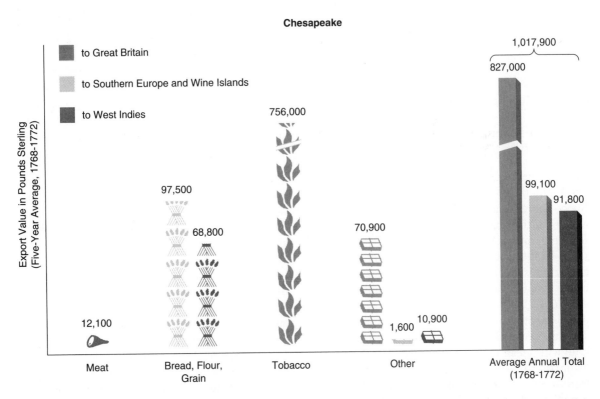

Chesapeake

■ to Great Britain

▨ to Southern Europe and Wine Islands

■ to West Indies

Export Value in Pounds Sterling (Five-Year Average, 1768-1772)

1,017,900
827,000

756,000

97,500
68,800

70,900

99,100
91,800

12,100

1,600 10,900

Meat | Bread, Flour, Grain | Tobacco | Other | Average Annual Total (1768-1772)

Regional Trading Patterns: The Chesapeake *Tobacco—legally exported only to Great Britain under the terms of the Navigation Acts—was the Chesapeake's dominant product, with grain making up an increasing proportion of the crops it sold to other destinations.* Source: James F. Shepherd and Gary M. Walton, *Shipping, Maritime Trade, and the Economic Development of Colonial North America* (Cambridge: Cambridge University Press, 1972). Copyright 1972. Used by permission of Cambridge University Press.

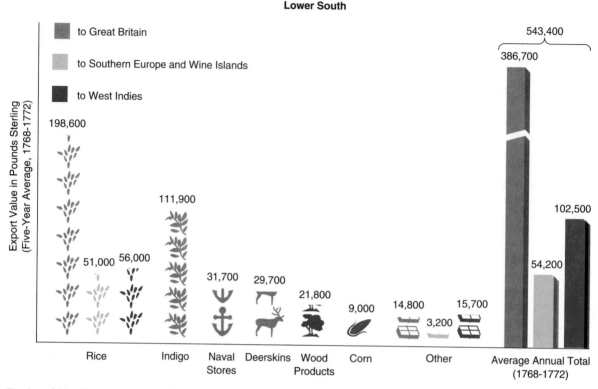

Regional Trading Patterns: The Lower South *Rice and indigo, sold primarily in England, dominated the exports of the Lower South.* Source: James F. Shepherd and Gary M. Walton, *Shipping, Maritime Trade, and the Economic Development of Colonial North America* (Cambridge: Cambridge University Press, 1972). Copyright 1972. Used by permission of Cambridge University Press.

cooking and baking. Making clothes (the chief job of daughters) meant processing raw wool and flax fibers, spinning thread, weaving cloth, dyeing and softening the cloth, and finally cutting out and sewing garments by hand.

The head of the household and his male helpers, responsible for outdoor affairs, also had heavy workloads. They had to plant and cultivate the fields, build fences, chop wood for the fireplace, harvest and market crops, care for livestock, and butcher cattle and hogs to provide the household with meat. Only on southern plantations and in northern cities could a few adult white males lead lives free from arduous physical labor.

The seasons and the hours of daylight governed farm households. Men and boys had the most leisure in winter, when no crops needed care.

Rhythms of Rural Life

Women and girls were most free in the summer, before embarking on autumn food preservation and winter spinning and weaving. Other activities, including education, had to be subordinated to seasonal work. Thus farm boys studied in the winter and their sisters did so in the summer. The seasons also affected travel plans. Because the roads were muddy in the spring and fall, most visiting took place in the summer and, in the North, winter, when sleighs could be used.

Because of the isolation and heavy workloads of farm households, rural folk took advantage of every opportunity for socializing. Men taking grain to a mill would stop at a crossroads tavern for a drink and conversation with friends. Women gathering to assist at childbirth would drink tea and exchange news. Barbecues and week-long house parties were popular among southern planter families. And work itself provided opportunities for visiting. Harvest frolics, corn-husking bees, and other communal endeavors drew neighbors from miles around, often for several days of work followed by feasting, dancing, and singing.

The few colonial cities were nothing but large towns by today's standards. In 1750, the largest, Boston and Philadelphia, had just seventeen thousand and thirteen thousand inhabitants, respectively. Still, city life differed considerably from rural life. City dwellers' lives were likely to be governed by clocks instead of the sun and by work schedules that did not depend so wholly on the seasons. Year-round, they could purchase foodstuffs and wood at city markets and cloth at dry goods stores. They could see friends whenever they wished. Wealthy urbanites had leisure time to visit taverns, read, take walks around town or rides in the countryside, play cards, or attend dances, plays, and concerts.

Rhythms of Urban Life

City people also had much more contact with the world beyond their homes than did their rural compatriots. By the 1750s, every major city had at least one weekly newspaper that printed the latest "advices from London," news from other English colonies, and local reports. Newspapers were available at taverns and inns, so people who could not afford to buy them could catch up on the news. Even illiterates could do so, because literate customers often read the papers aloud. However, contact with the outside world also had drawbacks. Sailors sometimes brought exotic and deadly diseases into port with them.

Cities attracted migrants from rural areas. Young men came to learn a skill through apprenticeship. Ordinary laborers came seeking work, and widows came looking for a means of supporting their families. Widows tended to congregate in port cities, where they could sell their services as nurses, teachers, laundresses, seamstresses, servants, or prostitutes; if they had some capital, they might open shops, inns, or boarding houses.

Only widows and the very few never-married women could legally run independent businesses. An unmarried colonial woman had the same legal rights as a man (with the exception of voting), but a wife was subordinate to her husband in law as well as custom. Under the common-law doctrine of coverture, a married woman became one person with her husband. She could not independently sue or be sued, make contracts, buy or sell property, or draft a will. Any property she owned before marriage became her husband's after the wedding; any wages she earned were legally his. Moreover, because divorces were practically impossible to obtain, men and women had little chance to escape from bad marriages.

Status of Women

The man's legal and customary authority extended to his children as well. Indeed, child rearing was the one task regularly undertaken by both sexes in colonial America. Women cared for infants and toddlers, but thereafter both parents disciplined the children. The father set the general standards by which they were raised and usually had the final word on such matters as education and vocational training. White parents usually insisted on unquestioning obedience from their offspring, and many freely used physical punishment to break a child's will. In the homes of elite families, servants performed most burdensome chores, which freed parents to spend more time with their offspring and reduced the need for strict disciplinary measures.

THE DAILY LIVES OF AFRICAN-AMERICANS

A white man's authority could include black families as well as his own kin. More than 95 percent of colonial blacks were held in perpetual bondage. In areas with high proportions of blacks in the population, most slaves resided on plantations with at least nine other bondspeople. Although many southern blacks lived on farms with only one or two other slaves, the majority had the experience of living and working in a largely black setting. In South

Carolina, a majority of the population was of African origin, in Georgia about half, and in the Chesapeake 40 percent.

The concentration of the slave population also had a profound effect on whites. Plantation housing styles, for example, were more African than English in origin, with clusters of small buildings—serving as kitchens, dairies, storage sheds, spinning rooms, and so forth—taking the place of one large structure encompassing all those functions. Just as blacks mimicked the whites' dances in their evening frolics, so too it became customary for whites to perform "Negro jigs" at the end of their cotillions. And words of African origin were incorporated in American English.

Large plantations allowed for the specialization of labor. Some African-American men and women became highly skilled at tasks whites believed appropriate to their sex. Each **Sexual Division** large plantation had its own **of Labor** male blacksmiths, carpenters, **Among African-** valets, shoemakers, and gar- **Americans** deners, and its female dairy- maids, seamstresses, cooks, and at least one midwife, who at- tended white and black women alike. These skilled slaves—10 to 20 percent of the black population— were essential to the smooth functioning of the plantation. But most slaves, male and female, worked in the fields.

The typical Chesapeake tobacco plantation was divided into small "quarters" located at some distance from one another. White overseers supervised work on the distant quarters, whereas the planter personally took charge of the home quarter, which included the planter's house. In the Carolina low country, where planters usually spent months in Charleston to avoid the malaria and yellow fever seasons, blacks often supervised their fellow slaves. Planters commonly assigned "outlandish" (African-born) slaves to do field labor in order to accustom them to plantation work routines and to enable them to learn some English. Artisans, on the other hand, were usually drawn from among the plantation's American-born blacks. Skills like carpentry and midwifery were typically passed down from father to son and

mother to daughter; such knowledge often constituted a slave family's most valuable possession.

Because all the English colonies legally permitted slavery, discontented blacks had few refuges from bondage. Some recently arrived Africans stole boats to try to return home or ran off in groups to the frontier, where they joined the Indians or attempted to establish traditional West African villages. Occasionally, slaves from South Carolina tried to reach Spanish Florida. But most slave runaways merely wanted to visit friends or relatives or to avoid their normal work routines for a few days or months. In a society in which blackness automatically connoted perpetual servitude, no black person anywhere could claim free status without being challenged. Violent resistance had even less to recommend it than running away. Whites may have been in the minority in some areas, but they controlled the guns and ammunition. Only in very unusual circumstances did colonial slaves attempt to rebel against their white oppressors.

African-Americans did try to improve the conditions of their bondage. Their chief vehicle for gaining some measure of control over their lives **African-** was the family. Planters' **American** records reveal how members of **Families** extended kin groups provided support, assistance, and comfort to each other. They protested excessive punishment of relatives, asked to live on the same quarter, and often requested special treatment for children or siblings. The extended kin ties that developed among African-American families that had lived on the same plantation for several generations served as insurance against the uncertainties of existence under slavery. If a sale broke up a nuclear family, other relatives could help with child rearing and similar tasks. Among colonial blacks, the extended family served a more important function than it did among whites.

Most black families managed to carve out a small measure of autonomy by a variety of means. Many plantations allowed or required slaves to plant their own gardens, hunt, or fish in order to supplement the standard diet of corn and salt pork. Some Chesapeake mistresses permitted their female slaves to raise chickens, which they then sold or exchanged for such items as extra clothing or blankets. In South Carolina, where most rice and indigo plantations operated on a task system, slaves were often able to accumulate personal property. Once they had completed their assigned tasks for the day, they were free to work for themselves. In Maryland and Virginia, where by the end of the century planters, and especially their widows, began to hire out slaves to others because of a surplus of bound laborers, blacks were sometimes allowed to keep a small part of the wages they earned. Such advances were slight, but against the bleak backdrop of slavery, they deserve to be highlighted.

Yet even the most autonomous enslaved African-Americans were always subject to white intrusions in their lives. In some households, masters and mistresses enforced their will chiefly through physical coercion. Other masters and mistresses were more lenient and respectful of slaves' property and their desire to live with their families. But even in households in which whites and blacks displayed genuine affection for one another, tensions were inescapable. Such tensions were caused by the dynamics of day-to-day relationships in which a small number of whites wielded arbitrary power over the lives of many African-Americans.

Master-Slave Relations

Thomas Jefferson was deeply concerned about this issue. In 1780, he observed, "The whole commerce between master and slave is a perpetual exercise of the most boisterous passions, the most unremitting despotism on the one part, and degrading submission on the other. Our children see this, and learn to imitate it." What troubled Jefferson most was the effect of the system on whites, not on the people they held in bondage. Before the Revolution, only a tiny number of Quakers criticized slavery out of sympathy for blacks. The other white colonists who questioned slavery took Jefferson's approach, stressing the institution's adverse effect on whites.

If the routines of daily life in the American colonies seemed fixed and unchanging, the wider context in which those routines unfolded did not. In both Europe and America, the eighteenth century was a time of great cultural and intellectual ferment. The movement known as the Enlightenment first influenced the educated elites; ordinary people seemed little touched by it. But enlightened thinking was to play a central role in the ideology of the American Revolution and thus eventually had a profound effect on the lives of all Americans.

COLONIAL CULTURE

Traditional colonial culture was oral, communal, and—at least through the first half of the eighteenth century—intensely local. The culture of the elite was increasingly print oriented, individualized, and self-consciously cosmopolitan. Although discussed separately here, the two cultures mingled in a variety of ways, for people of both descriptions lived side by side in small villages and cities.

Most residents of British America (almost all blacks, half the white women, and at least one-fifth of white men) could neither read nor write. That had important consequences for the transmission and development of American culture. In the absence of literacy, the primary means of communication was face-to-face conversation. Information tended to travel slowly and within relatively confined regions. Different locales developed divergent cultural traditions, and racial and ethnic variations heightened those differences. Public rituals served as the means through which the colonists forged their cultural identities.

Attendance at church was perhaps the most important such ritual. In Congregational (Puritan) churches, church leaders assigned seating to reflect standing in the community. In early New England, men and women sat on opposite sides of a central aisle, arranged in ranks according to age, wealth, and church membership. By the middle of the eighteenth century, wealthy men and their wives sat in privately owned pews; their children, servants, and the less fortunate still sat in sex-segregated fashion at the rear or sides of the church. In eighteenth-century Virginia, seating in Anglican parishes also conformed to the local status hierarchy. In

Religious Rituals

some parishes, the landed gentlemen customarily strode into church as a group just before the service, deliberately drawing attention to their exalted position. Quite a different message emanated from the egalitarian but sex-segregated seating system used in Quaker meetinghouses. Where one sat in colonial churches, in other words, symbolized one's place in society and the values of the surrounding community.

Communal culture also centered on the civic sphere. Particularly in New England, colonial governments proclaimed official days of thanksgiving and days of fasting and prayer.

Civic Rituals Everyone was expected to participate in the public rituals held in churches on such occasions. Monthly militia musters brought the community together, because all able-bodied men between the ages of sixteen and sixty were members of the militia.

In the Chesapeake, important cultural rituals occurred on court and election days. When the county court was in session, men would come from miles around to file suits, appear as witnesses, serve as jurors, or simply observe the goings-on. Attendance at court functioned as a method of civic education; from watching the proceedings, men learned what behavior their neighbors expected of them. Elections served the same purpose, for freeholders voted in public. An election official would call each man forward to declare his preference. The gentleman for whom the voter had cast his oral ballot would then thank him politely.

In such settings as church and courthouse, then, elite and ordinary folk alike participated in the oral culture that served as the cement holding their communities together. But the genteel residents of the colonies also took part in a newer kind of culture, one organized through the world of print.

Literacy was far less essential in eighteenth-century America than it is today. People, especially women, could live their entire lives without ever being called on to read a book or write a letter. Moreover, teaching slaves to read or write was forbidden as too subversive of the social order. Thus education

Attitudes Toward Education

beyond the bare rudiments of reading, writing, and "figuring" was usually regarded as a frill for either sex. Free men might have to know how to read a contract or keep rough accounts, and women might need or want to read the Bible. Beyond that, little learning appeared necessary. Thus public schools supported by taxes were few and far between. Children who learned to read usually did so in their own homes, taught by their parents or older siblings. A few months at a private "dame school" might complete their education by teaching them the basics of writing and simple arithmetic.

Accordingly, advanced education was primarily a sign of status. Only parents who wanted to distinguish their children from less-fortunate peers were willing to forgo their children's valuable labor to allow them to attend the few private schools. Girls ordinarily received little intellectual training beyond the rudiments, although they might learn music, dancing, or fancy needlework. Elite boys, on the other hand, studied with tutors or attended schools run by college graduates that prepared them to enter college at age fourteen or fifteen.

The colonial system of higher education for males was more fully developed than was basic instruction for either sex. The first American colleges were designed to train young men for the ministry. But during the eighteenth century, the curriculum and character of colleges changed considerably. Their students, the sons of the colonial elite, were now interested in careers in medicine, law, and business instead of the ministry. And the Enlightenment's stress on reason deeply affected the learned men who headed the colleges, although they were ministers..

In the seventeenth century, some European thinkers began to analyze nature in an effort to determine the laws that govern the universe. They used experimentation and abstract reasoning to discover the general principles behind such phenomena as the motions of the planets and stars, the behavior of falling objects, and the characteristics of light and sound. Above all, Enlightenment philosophers emphasized the acquisition of knowledge through reason.

The Enlightenment

The Enlightenment had an enormous influence on educated, well-to-do people in Europe and America. It supplied them with a common vocabulary and a unified view of the world. It joined them in a common endeavor, the effort to make sense of God's orderly creation. Thus American naturalists supplied European scientists with information about New World plants and animals so that they could be included in newly formulated universal classification systems. So too, Americans interested in astronomy took part in an international effort to learn about the workings of the solar system by studying a rare occurrence, the transit of Venus across the face of the sun in 1769.

Enlightenment rationalism affected politics as well as science. John Locke's *Two Treatises of Civil Government* (1691) challenged previous concepts of a divinely sanctioned political order. Governments, declared Locke, were created by men and so could be altered by them. If a ruler broke his contract with the people and did not protect their rights, they could legitimately use peaceful—or even violent—means to oust him from power. The aim of government was the good of the people, Enlightenment theorists proclaimed. A proper political order could prevent the rise of tyrants, and even the power of monarchs was subject to God's natural laws.

These intellectual currents had a dramatic effect on the curriculum of the colonial colleges. In the seventeenth century, Harvard courses had focused on ancient languages and theology. After the 1720s, however, colleges began to introduce courses in mathematics (including algebra, geometry, and calculus), the natural sciences, law, and medicine. The young men educated in such colleges—and their sisters at home, with whom they occasionally shared their books and ideas—developed a rational outlook on life that differentiated them from other colonists. This was the world of Dr. Alexander Hamilton and of those whom he called the "better sort."

Well-to-do graduates of American colleges, along with others educated in Great Britain, formed the core of genteel culture in the colonies.

Elite Culture

Men and women from these families wanted to set themselves apart from ordinary folk. Beginning in the 1720s, they constructed grandiose residences furnished with imported carpets, silver plate, and furniture. They entertained their friends at elaborate dinner parties and balls at which all present dressed in the height of European fashion. They cultivated polite manners and saw themselves as part of a transatlantic and intercolonial network.

How did this genteel, enlightened culture affect the lives of most colonists? Certainly no resident of the colonies could have avoided some contact with members of the elite. Ordinary folk were expected to doff their hats and behave deferentially when conversing with their "betters." Some were economically dependent on the gentry; for example, the elite's demand for consumer goods of all kinds led to the growth of artisan industries like fine furniture making. And, of course, elite men controlled the colonial governments, in which men of the "lesser" sort and women of all ranks played no role.

If the lives of genteel and ordinary folk in the eighteenth-century colonies seemed to follow different patterns, one man—Benjamin Franklin—appeared to combine their traits. Born in Boston in 1706, he was the perfect example of a self-made, self-educated man. Apprenticed at an early age to his older brother James, a Boston printer and newspaper publisher, Franklin ran away to Philadelphia in 1723. There he worked as a printer and eventually started his own publishing business, printing books, a newspaper, and *Poor Richard's Almanack*. The business was so successful that Franklin was able to retire from active control in 1748. He thereafter devoted himself to intellectual endeavors and public service. Franklin's *Experiments and Observations on Electricity* (1751) was the most important scientific work by a colonial American; it established the terminology and basic theory of electricity still in use today.

Benjamin Franklin, the Symbolic American

In 1749 and 1751, Franklin published pamphlets proposing the establishment of a new educational institution in Pennsylvania. The purpose of Franklin's English School was not to produce clerics or scholars but to prepare young men "for learning any business, calling or profession." The

College of Philadelphia (now the University of Pennsylvania), founded in 1755, was intended to graduate youths who would resemble Franklin—talented, practical men of affairs competent in a number of different fields.

Franklin and the students he envisioned thus fused the conflicting tendencies of colonial culture. Free of the Old World's restrictive traditions, the ideal American would achieve distinction through hard work and the application of commonsense principles. Like Franklin, he would rise from an ordinary family to the ranks of the genteel, thereby transcending the cultural boundaries that divided the colonists. The American would be a true child of the Enlightenment, knowledgeable of European culture yet not bound by its fetters, advancing through reason and talent alone.

The contrast with the original communal ideals of the early New England settlements could not have been sharper. John Winthrop's American had been a component of a greater whole that required his unquestioning submission. Franklin's American was an individual, free to make choices about his future. But the two visions did have one point in common: both described only white males. Not for many years would America formally recognize what had been true all along: that women and nonwhites had participated in the creation of the nation's cultural tradition.

POLITICS AND RELIGION: STABILITY AND CRISIS AT MIDCENTURY

In the first decades of the eighteenth century, colonial political life exhibited a new stability. Most residents of the mainland colonies had been born in America. Men from genteel families dominated the political structures in each province, for voters (property-holding white men) tended to defer to their well-educated "betters" on election days.

Throughout the colonies, political leaders sought to increase the powers of the elected assemblies relative to those of the governors and other appointed officials. Assemblies began to claim privileges associated with the British House of Commons, such as the rights to initiate all tax legislation and to control the militia. The assemblies also developed effective ways to influence British appointees, especially the threat to withhold their salaries. In some colonies (Virginia and South Carolina, for example), the elite members of the assemblies usually presented a united front to royal officials, but in others (like New York), they fought with each other. The latter province took the first steps on the road to modern American democracy. In their attempts to win hotly contested elections, New York's genteel leaders began to appeal to "the people," competing openly for the votes of ordinary freeholders. Yet in 1733, that same New York government imprisoned a newspaper editor, John Peter Zenger, who had too vigorously criticized its actions. Defending Zenger against the charge of seditious libel, his lawyer argued that the truth could not be defamatory, thus helping to establish American law's principle of a free press.

Eighteenth-century assemblies bore little resemblance to twentieth-century state legislatures. Much of their business would today be termed administrative; only on rare occasions did they formulate new policies or pass laws of real importance. Members of the assemblies also saw their roles differently than do modern legislators. In their minds, their primary function was to stop the governors or councils from enacting oppressive taxes, not to pass laws that would actively benefit their constituents.

By midcentury, politically aware colonists commonly drew analogies between their governments and Great Britain's balance of king, lords, and commons—a combination that was thought to produce a stable polity. Although the analogy was not exact, political leaders equated their governors with the monarch, their councils with the aristocracy, and their assemblies with the House of Commons. All three were thought essential to good government, but Americans saw the governors and appointed councils as aliens that posed a potential threat to colonial freedoms and customary ways of life. By contrast, colonists saw the assemblies as the people's

Rise of the Assemblies

protectors. And the assemblies in turn regarded themselves as representatives of the people.

Again, however, such beliefs should not be equated with modern practice. The assemblies, firmly controlled by dominant families, rarely responded to the concerns of their poorer constituents. Although settlement continually spread westward, assemblies failed to reapportion themselves to provide adequate representation for newer communities—a lack of action that led to serious grievances among frontier dwellers. Thus it is important to distinguish between the colonial ideal of protecting the people's liberties and the reality that those protected tended chiefly to be the wealthy and the assembly members themselves.

At midcentury, a series of crises confronted the political structures that had stabilized in a period of relative calm. None affected all the mainland provinces, but no colony escaped wholly untouched. The crises exposed the internal tensions building in the pluralistic American society, foreshadowing the greater disorder of the revolutionary era. Most important, they demonstrated that the political accommodations arrived at in the aftermath of the Glorious Revolution were no longer adequate to govern Britain's American empire.

One of the first and greatest crises occurred in South Carolina. Early one morning in September 1739, about twenty South Carolina slaves gathered near the Stono River south of Charleston. Seizing guns and ammunition from a store, they killed the storekeepers and some nearby planter families. Then, joined by other local slaves, they headed south toward Florida in hope of finding refuge in that Spanish colony. By midday, a troop of militia attacked the fugitives, who then numbered about a hundred, killing some and dispersing the rest. More than a week later, most remaining conspirators were captured. Those not killed on the spot were later executed.

Stono Rebellion

The Stono Rebellion shocked white South Carolinians and residents of other colonies as well. British America stiffened its laws governing the behavior of African-Americans. But the most immediate response came in New York City, which had suffered a slave revolt in 1712. There the news from the South, coupled with fears of Spain generated by the outbreak of King George's War, set off a reign of terror in the summer of 1741. Hysterical whites interpreted a biracial gang of thieves and arsonists as conspirators who wanted to foment a slave uprising under the guidance of a supposed priest in the pay of Spain. By summer's end, thirty-one blacks and four whites had been executed for participating in the "plot." The Stono Rebellion and the New York events exposed whites' deepest fears about the dangers of slave holding and revealed the assemblies' inability to prevent serious internal disorder. Events of the next two decades confirmed that pattern.

By midcentury, most fertile land east of the Appalachians had been purchased or occupied. As a result, conflicts over land titles and conditions of landholding grew in number and frequency as colonists competed for control of land good for farming. In 1746, for example, New Jersey farmers holding land under grants from the governor of New York (dating from the brief period when the duke of York owned both provinces) clashed violently with agents of the East Jersey proprietors. The proprietors claimed the land as theirs and demanded annual payments, called quitrents, for the use of the property. Similar violence occurred in the 1760s in the region that later became Vermont.

Land Riots

The most serious land riots of the period took place along the Hudson River in 1765 and 1766. Late in the seventeenth century, Governor Benjamin Fletcher of New York had granted several huge tracts in the lower Hudson valley to prominent colonial families. The proprietors in turn divided these estates into small farms, which they rented chiefly to poor Dutch and German migrants. After 1740, though, increasing migration from New England brought conflict to the great New York estates. The New Englanders squatted on vacant portions of the manors and resisted all attempts at eviction. In the mid-1760s, the Philipse family sued the New Englanders, some of whom had lived on Philipse land for twenty or thirty years. New York courts upheld the Philipse claim and ordered the squatters to make way for tenants with valid leases. Instead of complying, the farmers organized a rebellion against the proprietors. For nearly a year, the insurgent farmers controlled much of the Hudson valley, where they terrorized proprietors and loyal tenants. The rebellion was put down only after British troops dispatched from New York City captured its leaders.

Violent conflicts of a different sort erupted just a few years later in the Carolinas. The Regulator movements of the late 1760s (South Carolina) and early 1770s (North Carolina)

The Regulators

pitted backcountry farmers against the wealthy eastern planters who controlled the provincial governments. The frontier dwellers, most of whom were Scotch-Irish, protested their lack of an adequate voice in colonial political affairs. The South Carolinians for months policed the countryside in vigilante bands, contending that law enforcement in the region was too lax and biased against them. The North Carolinians, whose prime grievance was heavy taxation, fought and lost a battle with eastern militiamen at Alamance in 1771.

The most widespread crisis, however, was religious. From the late 1730s through the 1760s, waves of religious revivalism—today known

First Great Awakening

collectively as the Great Awakening—swept over various parts of the colonies, primarily New England (1735–1745) and Virginia (1750s and 1760s). Orthodox Calvinists were eager to combat Enlightenment rationalism, which denied innate human depravity. In addition, many recent immigrants and residents of the backcountry had no prior religious affiliation, thus presenting evangelists with a potential source of converts.

The first signs of what was to become the Great Awakening appeared in western Massachusetts, in the Northampton Congregational Church led by the Reverend Jonathan Edwards, a noted preacher and theologian. During 1734 and 1735, Edwards noticed a remarkable response among the youthful members of his flock to a message based squarely on Calvinist principles.

Individuals could attain salvation, Edwards argued, only through recognition of their own depraved natures and the need to surrender completely to God's will. Such surrender brought to members of his congregation an intensely emotional release from sin and came to be seen as a single identifiable moment of conversion.

The effects of such conversions remained isolated until 1739, when an English Methodist named George Whitefield arrived in America. For

George Whitefield

fifteen months, Whitefield preached to large audiences from Georgia to New England, and he became the chief generating force behind the Great Awakening. Thousands turned out to listen to him—and to experience conversion. At first, regular clerics welcomed Whitefield and the American-born itinerant evangelist preachers who sprang up to imitate him. Soon, however, many clergymen began to realize that "revived" religion, although it filled their churches, ran counter to their own approach to doctrine and matters of faith.

Opposition to the Awakening heightened rapidly, and large numbers of congregations splintered in its wake. "Old Lights"—traditional clerics and their followers—engaged in bitter disputes with the "New Light" evangelicals. American Protestantism, already characterized by numerous sects, became further divided as the major denominations split into Old Light and New Light factions and as new evangelical sects—Methodists and Baptists—gained adherents. Paradoxically, the angry fights and the rapid rise in the number of distinct denominations eventually led to an American willingness to tolerate religious diversity.

The most important effect of the Awakening was its influence on American modes of thought. The revivalists' message directly challenged the colonial tradition of deference.

Effect of the Awakening

Itinerant preachers, only a few of whom were ordained clergy, claimed they understood the will of God better than did the orthodox clerics. The Awakening's emphasis on emotion rather than learning undermined the validity of received wisdom, and New Lights

Phillis Wheatley, an African-born slave living in Massachusetts, was so moved by the death of George Whitefield in 1770 that she wrote "an elegiac poem" about the great evangelist, who had shown as much concern for black Americans as for their white compatriots. Although he did not condemn slavery as an institution, Whitefield urged slave holders to encourage the conversion of their slaves, and blacks, both slave and free, often attended his sermons. Historians credit Whitefield with bringing Christianity to the enslaved populations of South Carolina and Georgia. Library Company of Philadelphia.

questioned not only religious but also social and political orthodoxy. For example, New Lights began to defend the rights of groups and individuals to dissent from a community consensus, thereby challenging one of the most fundamental tenets of colonial political life.

Nowhere was this trend more evident than in Virginia, where the plantation gentry and their ostentatious lifestyle dominated society. By the 1760s, Baptists had gained a secure foothold in Virginia; their beliefs and behavior were openly at odds with the way most genteel families lived. They rejected as sinful the horse racing, gambling, and dancing that occupied much of the gentry's leisure time. They addressed each other as "brother" and "sister," regardless of social status, and they elected the leaders of their congregations. Moreover, almost all Virginia Baptist congregations included both black and white members. Church rules governed the behavior of both blacks and whites; interracial sexual relationships, divorce, and adultery were forbidden to all. In addition, Baptist churches directed masters not to break up slave marriages through sale. Biracial committees investigated complaints about church members' misbehavior. Churches excommunicated slaves for stealing from their masters, but they also excommunicated whites for physically abusing their slaves. One such slave owner, excommunicated in 1772, experienced a true conversion and became a preacher in a largely black church. Other white Baptists decided slave owning was "unrighteous" and freed their bondspeople; Robert Carter manumitted more than nine hundred slaves.

The Great Awakening thus injected an egalitarian strain in American life at midcentury and further disrupted traditional structures of existence. Although primarily a religious movement, the Awakening also had important social and political consequences, calling into question habitual modes of behavior in the secular as well as the religious realm. In short, the Great Awakening helped to break Americans' ties to their limited seventeenth-century origins. So too did the newcomers from Germany, Scotland, Ireland, and Africa, who brought their languages, customs, and religions to North America. Also important were the changes in the economy that enmeshed the colonies in an international network of trade, drawing them into European wars and creating the wealthy class of merchants and landowners who dominated colonial life.

A century and a half after English people had first settled in North America, the colonies were no longer exclusively English. Rather, they mixed diverse European, American, and African traditions in a novel cultural blend that owed much to the Old World but just as much, if not more, to the new. In the 1760s, Americans began to recognize that their interests were not necessarily identical to those of Great Britain or its monarch.

SUGGESTIONS FOR FURTHER READING

General

Jack P. Greene, *Pursuits of Happiness: The Social Development of the Early Modern British Colonies and the Formation of American Culture* (1988); David F. Hawke, *Everyday Life in Early America* (1988); Richard Hofstadter, *America at 1750: A Social Portrait* (1971); Stephen Innes, ed., *Work and Labor in Early America* (1988).

Rural Society

T. H. Breen, *Tobacco Culture* (1985); Carl Bridenbaugh, *Cities in Revolt: Urban Life in America, 1743–1776* (1955); Rhys Isaac, *The Transformation of Virginia, 1740–1790* (1982); Christopher Jedrey, *The World of John Cleaveland: Family and Community in Eighteenth-Century New England* (1979); Sung Bok Kim, *Landlord and Tenant in Colonial New York: Manorial Society, 1664–1775* (1978); Peter Mancall, *Valley of Opportunity: Economic Culture Along the Upper Susquehanna, 1700–1800* (1991); Gary B. Nash, *The Urban Crucible: Social Change, Political Consciousness, and the Origins of the American Revolution* (1979).

Economic Development

Alice Hanson Jones, *Wealth of a Nation to Be: The American Colonies on the Eve of the Revolution* (1980); John J. McCusker and Russell R. Menard, *The Economy of British America, 1607–1789* (1985); Edwin J. Perkins, *The Economy of Colonial America* (1980).

Politics

Bernard Bailyn, *The Origins of American Politics* (1968); Patricia U. Bonomi, *A Factious People: Politics and Society in Colonial New York* (1971); Richard Bushman, *King and People in Provincial Massachusetts* (1985); Jack P. Greene, *The Quest for Power: The Lower Houses of Assembly in the Southern Royal Colonies, 1689–1776* (1963).

Immigration

Bernard Bailyn, *Voyagers to the West* (1986); Bernard Bailyn and Philip Morgan, eds., *Strangers Within the Realm* (1991); A. Roger Ekirch, *Bound for America: The Transportation of British Convicts to the Colonies, 1718–1775* (1987); Ned Landsman, *Scotland and Its First American Colony* (1985); Sharon Salinger, *To Serve Well and Faithfully: Labor and Indentured Servants in Pennsylvania, 1682–1800* (1988).

African-Americans

Thomas J. Davis, *A Rumor of Revolt: The "Great Negro Plot" in Colonial New York* (1985); Gerald W. Mullin, *Flight and Rebellion: Slave Resistance in Eighteenth-Century Virginia* (1972); William Pierson, *Black Yankees: The Development of an Afro-American Subculture in Eighteenth-Century New England* (1988); Mechal Sobel, *The World They Made Together: Black and White Values in Eighteenth-Century Virginia* (1987).

Women and Family

Philip J. Greven, *The Protestant Temperament: Patterns of Child-rearing, Religious Experience, and the Self in Early America* (1977); Barry J. Levy, *Quakers and the American Family* (1988); Mary Beth Norton, *Liberty's Daughters: The Revolutionary Experience of American Women, 1750–1800* (1980); Daniel Blake Smith, *Inside the Great House: Planter Family Life in Eighteenth-Century Chesapeake Society* (1980).

Colonial Culture, Education, Science, and the Enlightenment

Richard Bushman, *The Refinement of America* (1992); Patricia Cline Cohen, *A Calculating People: The Spread of Numeracy in Early America* (1982); Lawrence A. Cremin, *American Education: The Colonial Experience, 1607–1783* (1970); Richard Beale Davis, *Intellectual Life in the Colonial South, 1585–1763*, 2 vols. (1978); Brooke Hindle, *The Pursuit of Science in Revolutionary America* (1956); Henry F. May, *The Enlightenment in America* (1976); Raymond P. Stearns, *Science in the British Colonies of America* (1970).

Religion and the Great Awakening

Patricia U. Bonomi, *Under the Cope of Heaven: Religion, Society, and Politics in Colonial America* (1986); J. M. Bumstead and John E. Van de Wetering, *What Must I Do to Be Saved? The Great Awakening in Colonial America* (1976); Jon Butler, *Awash in a Sea of Faith* (1990); Harry S. Stout, *The Divine Dramatist: George Whitefield and the Rise of Modern Evangelicalism* (1991); Patricia Tracy, *Jonathan Edwards, Pastor* (1980).

Severing the Bonds of Empire, 1754–1774

I N LATE OCTOBER 1769, the young Boston shopkeeper Betsy Cumming was visiting a sick friend when she heard "a voilint Skreeming Kill him Kill him." Cumming ran to the window and saw John Mein, a book seller and newspaper publisher, being chased by "a larg Croud of those who Call themselves Gentleman but in reality they ware no other then Murderers for there disigne was certainly on his life." That same night, Mein fled to a vessel anchored in the harbor. He later sailed to England and never returned to Boston.

Mein had aroused the wrath of the crowd by printing in his newspaper several lists of local merchants who had recently cleared imports through the Boston customs house. But why was the information Mein revealed so explosive? In the fall of 1769, many merchants had signed an agreement not to import goods from Great Britain; Mein's lists indicated that some of the most vocal supporters of nonimportation (including the patriot leader John Hancock) had been violating the agreement. That was why the gentlemen of Boston had to silence the outspoken publisher.

John Mein was not the first—and he would be far from the last—resident of the colonies who found his life wholly disrupted by the growing political antagonism between England and its American possessions. Long afterward, John Adams identified the years between 1760 and 1775 as the period during which the true American Revolution had occurred. The Revolution, Adams declared, was "in the Minds of the people," involving not the actual winning of independence but a shift of fundamental allegiance from England to America. Today, not all historians would agree with Adams's assertion that that shift constituted the Revolution. But none would deny the importance of the events of those crucial years.

The story of the 1760s and early 1770s describes an ever widening split between England and America. In the long history of British settlement in the Western Hemisphere, considerable tension had at times marred the relationship between individual provinces and the ruling country. Still, that tension had rarely been sustained for long, nor had it been widespread, except during the crisis that followed the Glorious Revolution in 1689. In the

1750s, however, a series of events began to draw the colonists' attention from domestic matters to their relations with Great Britain. It all started with the Seven Years' War.

Britain's overwhelming victory in that war forever altered the balance of power in North America. France was ousted from the continent, an event with major consequences for both the Indian tribes of the interior and the residents of the British colonies. Northern tribes could no longer play European powers off against one another and so lost a major diplomatic tool. Anglo-Americans, for their part, no longer had to fear a French threat on their borders. Some historians have argued that if the colonies had had to worry about the continuing presence of France on the North American mainland, the Revolution could never have occurred. The British colonies would never have dared to break with England, it is said, if an enemy nation and its Indian allies had controlled the interior of the continent.

The British victory in 1763, then, constituted a major turning point in American history because of its direct effect on white and Indian residents of North America. It also had a significant effect on Great Britain, one that soon affected the colonies as well. To win the war, Britain had gone heavily into debt. To reduce the debt, Parliament for the first time imposed revenue-raising taxes on the colonies in addition to the customs duties that had long regulated trade. That decision exposed differences in the political thinking of Americans and Britons.

During the 1760s and early 1770s, a broad coalition of white Americans, men and women alike, resisted new tax levies and attempts by British officials to tighten controls over the provincial governments. America's elected leaders became ever more suspicious of Britain's motives as the years passed. They laid aside intercolonial antagonisms to coordinate their response to the new measures, and they slowly began to reorient their political thinking. As late as the summer of 1774, though, most were still seeking a solution within the framework of the empire; few harbored thoughts of independence. When independence rather than loyal resistance became the issue, the coalition broke down. But that happened only after the battles of Lexington and Concord in April 1775. Before then, just a few Americans closely connected to colonial

administration or the Church of England opposed the trend of resistance.

RENEWED WARFARE AMONG EUROPEANS AND INDIANS

The English colonies along the Atlantic seaboard were surrounded by hostile, or potentially hostile, neighbors: Indians everywhere, the Spanish in Florida and along the coast of the Gulf of Mexico, the French along the great inland system of rivers and lakes that stretched from the St. Lawrence to the Mississippi. The Spanish outposts posed little threat to the English, for Spain's days as a major power had passed. The French were another matter. Their long chain of forts and settlements dominated the North American interior, facilitating trading partnerships and alliances with the tribes of the region. In none of the three wars fought between 1689 and 1748 was England able to shake France's hold on the American frontier. Under the Peace of Utrecht, which ended Queen Anne's War in 1713, the English won control of such peripheral northern areas as Newfoundland, Hudson's Bay, and Nova Scotia (Acadia). But Britain made no territorial gains in King George's War.

During both Queen Anne's War and King George's War, the Iroquois Confederacy adhered to its policy of neutrality. Rather than take sides, the

Iroquois Neutrality

Iroquois skillfully played the Europeans off against each other. When they went to war, it was against their traditional southern enemies, the Catawbas. Because France repeatedly urged them to attack the Catawbas, who were allied with England, the Iroquois achieved three desirable goals. They kept the French happy and simultaneously consolidated their control over the entire interior region north of Virginia. And the campaign against a common enemy enabled the confederacy to cement its alliance with its weaker tributaries, the Shawnees and Delawares, and to ensure the continued subordination of those tribes.

But even the careful Iroquois diplomats could not prevent the region inhabited by the Shawnees and Delawares (now western Pennsylvania and

• *Important Events* •

1754	Albany Congress meets to try to forge colonial unity Fighting breaks out with Washington's defeat at Fort Necessity	**1765**	Stamp Act requires stamps on all printed materials in colonies Sons of Liberty formed
1756	Britain declares war on France; Seven Years' War officially begins	**1766**	Stamp Act repealed Declaratory Act insists that Parliament can tax the colonies
1759	British forces take Quebec	**1767**	Townshend Acts lay duties on trade within the empire, send new officials and judges to America
1760	American phase of war ends with fall of Montreal to British troops George III becomes king	**1770**	Lord North becomes prime minister Townshend duties repealed, except for tea tax Boston Massacre kills five colonial rioters
1763	Treaty of Paris ends Seven Years' War Pontiac allies attack British forts in West Proclamation of 1763 attempts to close land west of Appalachians to English settlement	**1772**	Boston Committee of Correspondence formed
		1773	Tea Act aids East India Company Boston Tea Party protests the Tea Act
1764	Sugar Act lays new duties on molasses, tightens customs regulations Currency Act outlaws colonial paper money issues	**1774**	Coercive Acts punish Boston and the colony of Massachusetts Quebec Act reforms government of that province

eastern Ohio; see map) from providing the spark that set off a major war. That conflict spread from America to Europe and proved decisive in the contest for North America. Trouble began in 1752 when English fur traders ventured into the area known as the Ohio country. The French could not permit their English rivals to gain a foothold in the region, for a permanent English presence in the Ohio country could challenge France's control of the western fur trade and even threaten its prominence in the Mississippi valley. Accordingly, in 1753 the French pushed south from Lake Erie, building fortified outposts at strategic points along the rivers of the Ohio country.

In response to the French threat to their western frontiers, delegates from seven northern and middle colonies gathered in Albany, New York, in June 1754. With the backing of administrators in London, they sought to coordinate the defenses of the colonies and to

Albany Congress
———

persuade the Iroquois to abandon their traditional neutrality. In neither aim were they successful. The Iroquois saw no reason to change a policy that had served them well for half a century. And although the Albany Congress delegates adopted a Plan of Union (which would have established an elected intercolonial legislature with the power to tax), the plan was uniformly rejected by their provincial governments—primarily because those governments feared a loss of autonomy.

While the delegates to the Albany Congress deliberated, the war for which they sought to prepare was already beginning. Virginia claimed ownership of the Ohio country, and its governor had sent a small militia force west to counter the French moves. But the militiamen arrived too late. The French had already taken possession of the strategic point—now Pittsburgh—where the Allegheny and Monongahela Rivers meet to form the Ohio, and they were busily engaged in constructing Fort Duquesne. The foolhardy and inexperienced young

Lake Superior

CHIPPEWA

NEW FRANCE

Quebec

Montreal

St. Lawrence R.

Ft. Western
(Augusta)

MAINE
(Part of Mass.)

Falmouth
(Portland)

N.H.

Portsmouth

Lake Huron

Lake Michigan

CHIPPEWA

OTTAWA

Lake Ontario

Ft. Niagara

SENECA

Lake Erie

Ft. Detroit

POTAWATOMI

MIAMI

WYANDOT

MOHAWK

ONEIDA
TUSCARORA
ONONDAGA
CAYUGA

Ft. Stanwix

Albany

NEW
YORK

MASS.

Boston

Hartford

CONN.

Providence

R.I.

Allegheny R.

1720–1760

New York

PENNSYLVANIA

DELAWARE

Ft. Duquesne
(Pitt)

Philadelphia

N.J.

New Castle

Monongahela R.

Ft.
Necessity

Baltimore

M.D.

DEL.

OHIO COUNTRY

WEA

SHAWNEE

Ohio R.

Tuscarora Migration

Richmond

VIRGINIA

Williamsburg

ILLINOIS CONFEDERATION

Proclamation Line of 1763

Hillsboro

Salem

NORTH CAROLINA

New Bern

CHEROKEE

CATAWBA

Wilmington

ATLANTIC OCEAN

Camden

SOUTH CAROLINA

Mississippi R.

CHICKASAW

Ft. Augusta
(Augusta)

Charleston

GEORGIA

CREEK

Savannah

CHOCTAW

NEW SPAIN

St. Augustine

Total population of
English colonies: c. 1.5 million

Extent of settlement

| 0 | 100 | 200 miles |
| 0 | 100 | 200 | 300 kilometers |

colonel who commanded the Virginians attacked a French detachment and then allowed himself to be trapped in his crudely built Fort Necessity at Great Meadows, Pennsylvania. After a day-long battle (on July 3, 1754), twenty-two-year-old George Washington surrendered. He and his men were allowed to return to Virginia.

Washington had blundered grievously. He had started a war that eventually would encompass nearly the entire world. He had also ensured that the tribes of the Ohio valley would for the most part support France in the coming conflict. The Indians took Washington's mistakes as an indication of Britain's inability to win the war, and nothing that occurred in the next four years made them change their minds. In July 1755, a few miles south of Fort Duquesne, a combined force of French and Indians ambushed British and colonial troops led by General Edward Braddock. Braddock was killed and his men were demoralized by their complete defeat. After news of the debacle reached London, Britain declared war on France in 1756, thus formally beginning the conflict known as the Seven Years' War.

Seven Years' War

Although the early war years were disastrous for the British, the tide began to turn in 1757. In that year, William Pitt was named secretary of state. Under his leadership, the British mounted the effort that won them the war in North America. By agreeing to reimburse the colonies for their military expenditures and placing troop recruitment wholly in local hands, Pitt gained wholehearted American support for the war effort. Earlier in the war, British officers had usually tried to coerce the colonies into supplying men and materiel to the army.

In July 1758, British forces recaptured the fortress at Louisbourg. Then, in a surprise night attack in September 1759, General James Wolfe's soldiers defeated the French on the Plains of Abraham and took Quebec. Sensing a British victory, the Iroquois abandoned their policy of neutrality and allied with the British, hoping to gain some diplomatic leverage. A year later, the British captured Montreal, the last French stronghold on the continent, and the American phase of the war ended.

When the Treaty of Paris was signed in 1763, France ceded its major North American holdings to Britain. Spain, an ally of France toward the end of the war, gave Florida to the victorious English. Britain, fearing the presence of France on its western borders, also forced the French to cede the region west of the Mississippi (Louisiana) to Spain. The British thus gained control of the fur trade of the entire continent. And no longer would the English seacoast colonies have to worry about the threat to their existence posed by France's extensive North American territories.

Because most of the fighting had occurred in the Northeast, the war had especially pronounced effects on New Englanders. As many as one-third of all Massachusetts men between the ages of sixteen and twenty-nine served for a time in the provincial army. Wartime service left a lasting impression on these soldiers. For the first time, ordinary Americans came into extended contact with Britons—and they did not like what they saw. The provincials regarded the redcoats as haughty, profane Sabbath breakers who arbitrarily imposed overly harsh punishments on anyone who broke the rules.

American Soldiers

The New England soldiers also learned that British regulars did not share their adherence to principles of contract and consensus—the values that had governed their lives at home. Colonial regiments mutinied or rebelled en masse if they believed they were being treated unfairly, as happened, for example, when they were not allowed to leave at the end of their formal enlistments. One private in these circumstances grumbled in his journal in 1759, "Although we be Englishmen born, we are debarred Englishmen's liberty. . . . [The British soldiers] are but little better than slaves to their officers." Such men would later recall

European Settlements and Native American Tribes, 1750 By 1750, Europeans had expanded the limits of the English colonies to the eastern slopes of the Appalachian Mountains. Few independent tribal nations still existed in the East, but beyond the mountains they controlled the countryside. Only a few widely scattered English and French forts maintained the Europeans' presence there.

their personal experience of British tyranny when they were deciding whether to support the Revolution.

The overwhelming British triumph stimulated some Americans to think expansively about the colonies' future. People like Benjamin Franklin, who had long touted the colonies' wealth and potential, predicted a glorious new future for British North America. Such men were to lead the resistance to British measures in the years after 1763. They uniformly opposed any laws that would retard America's growth and persistently supported steps to increase Americans' control over their destiny.

1763: A TURNING POINT

The great victory over France had an irreversible effect on North America, and the interior tribes felt it first. With France excluded from the continent altogether and Spanish territory now confined to the area west of the Mississippi, the tribes could no longer use the diplomatic strategy that had served them well for so long. The consequences were immediate and devastating.

Even before the Treaty of Paris, southern Indians had to adjust to the new circumstances. After the British gained the upper hand in the American war in 1758, the Creeks and Cherokees lost their ability to force concessions by threatening to turn instead to the French or the Spanish. In desperation, and in retaliation for British atrocities, the Cherokees attacked the Carolina and Virginia frontiers in 1760. Although the tribes initially were victorious, a force of British regulars and colonial militia defeated them the following year. Late in 1761, the two sides concluded a treaty under which the Cherokees allowed the construction of English forts in tribal territories and opened a large tract of land to white settlement.

In the Ohio country, the Ottawas, Chippewas, and Potawatomis reacted angrily when Great Britain, no longer facing French competition, raised the price of trade goods and ended the practice of paying rent for forts. The British also allowed settlers to move into the Monongahela and Susquehanna valleys.

Pontiac, the war chief of an Ottawa village near Detroit, understood the implications of such British actions. Only unity among the western tribes, he realized, could prevent total dependence on and subordination to the victorious British. Using his considerable powers of persuasion, in the spring of 1763 he forged an unprecedented alliance among Hurons, Chippewas, Potawatomis, Delawares, Shawnees, and even some Mingoes (Pennsylvania Iroquois). Pontiac then laid siege to the fort at Detroit, while his war parties attacked other British outposts in the Great Lakes region. Detroit withstood the siege, but by the end of June all the other forts west of Niagara and north of Fort Pitt (old Fort Duquesne) had fallen to the tribal alliance. But they could not take the strongholds of Niagara, Fort Pitt, or Detroit. In early August, a combined force of Delawares, Shawnees, Hurons, and Mingoes was soundly defeated at Bushy Run, Pennsylvania. Conflict ceased when Pontiac broke off the siege of Detroit in late October. A treaty ending the war was finally negotiated three years later.

Pontiac's Uprising

Pontiac's uprising showed Great Britain that the huge territory it had just acquired from France would not be easy to govern. In October, in a futile attempt to assert control over the interior, the ministry issued the Proclamation of 1763, which declared the headwaters of rivers flowing into the Atlantic from the Appalachian Mountains to be the temporary western boundary for colonial settlement. The proclamation was intended to prevent clashes between Indians and colonists by forbidding whites to move onto Indian lands until the tribes had given up their land by treaty. But many whites had already established farms or purchased property west of the proclamation line, and the policy was doomed to failure from the outset.

Proclamation of 1763

Other decisions made in London in 1763 and thereafter had a wider effect in British North America. The victory in the Seven Years' War created both problems and opportunities for the British government. The most pressing problem was Britain's immense war debt. The men who had

Benjamin West, the first well-known American artist, engraved this picture of a prisoner exchange at the end of Pontiac's uprising, with Colonel Henry Bouquet supervising the return of whites captured during the war. In the foreground, a white child resists leaving the Indian parents he had grown to love. Many whites were fascinated by the phenomenon West depicted—the reluctance of captives to abandon their adoptive Indian families. Miriam and Ira D. Wallach Division of Art, Prints and Photographs, The New York Public Library.

to solve that problem were King George III and his new prime minister, George Grenville.

In 1760, George III, then twenty-two years old, assumed the English throne. The young king was a man of mediocre intellect and an erratic judge of character. During the crucial years between 1763 and 1770, when the rift with the colonies was widening, he replaced ministries with bewildering rapidity. Moreover, the king often substituted stubbornness for intelligence, and

George III
———

he regarded adherence to the status quo as the hallmark of patriotism.

The man he selected as prime minister in 1763, George Grenville, confronted a financial crisis: England's burden of indebtedness had nearly doubled since 1754, from £73 million to £137 million. Annual expenditures before the war had amounted to no more than £8 million; now the yearly interest on the debt alone came to £5 million. Obviously, Grenville's ministry had to find new sources of funds, and the English people were already heavily taxed. Because the colonists had been major beneficiaries of the wartime expenditures, Grenville concluded that the Americans should be asked to pay a greater share of the cost of running the empire.

It did not occur to Grenville to question Great Britain's right to levy taxes on the colonies. Like all his countrymen, he believed that the government's legitimacy derived ultimately from the consent of the people, but he defined *consent* far more loosely than did the colonists. Americans had come to believe that they could be represented only by men for whom they or their property-holding neighbors actually voted. To Grenville and his English contemporaries, Parliament—king, lords, and commons acting together—by definition represented all English subjects, wherever they resided (even overseas) and whether they could vote or not. According to this theory of government, called *virtual representation*, the colonists were seen as virtually, if not actually, represented in Parliament. Thus their consent to acts of Parliament could be presumed.

Theories of Representation

The Americans and the English began at the same theoretical starting point but arrived at different conclusions. In England, members of Parliament saw themselves as *collectively* representing the entire nation. Only members of the House of Commons were elected, and the particular constituency that chose a member had no special claim on his vote. By contrast, in the colonies members of the lower houses of the assemblies were viewed as *individually* representing the voters who had elected them.

The events of the 1760s threw into sharp relief Americans' attitudes toward political power. The colonists had become accustomed to a government that wielded only limited authority over them and affected their daily lives very little. In consequence, they believed that a good government was one that largely left them alone, a view in keeping with the theories of a group of British writers known as the Real Whigs. These writers stressed the dangers inherent in a powerful government, particularly one headed by a monarch. Some even favored republicanism, which proposed to eliminate monarchs altogether and rest political power more directly on the will of the people. They warned that political power was always to be feared, that rulers would try to corrupt and oppress the people, and that only the perpetual vigilance of the people and their elected representatives could preserve their fragile yet precious liberty, which was closely linked to their right to hold private property.

Britain's attempts to tighten the reins of government and raise revenues from the colonies in the 1760s and early 1770s convinced many Americans that the Real Whigs' reasoning applied to their circumstances, especially because of the link between liberty and property rights. Excessive and unjust taxation, they believed, could destroy their freedoms. They began to interpret British measures in light of the Real Whigs' warnings and to see oppressive designs behind the actions of Grenville and his successors. In the mid-1760s, however, colonial leaders did not immediately accuse Grenville of an intent to oppress them. They at first simply questioned the wisdom of the laws Grenville proposed.

The first such measures, the Sugar and Currency Acts, were passed by Parliament in 1764. The Sugar Act revised the existing system of customs regulations and laid new duties on certain foreign imports, including molasses, to the colonies. It also established a vice admiralty court at Halifax, Nova Scotia, and included provisions aimed at stopping the widespread smuggling of molasses, a chief commodity of American trade. Although the Sugar Act appeared to resemble the Navigation Acts, which the colonies had long accepted as legitimate, it broke with tradition, because it was explicitly designed to raise revenue, not to channel American trade through Britain. The Currency Act effectively outlawed colonial issues of paper money, because British merchants complained that Americans were paying their debts in inflated local currencies. Americans could accumulate little sterling, because they imported more than they exported; thus the act seemed to the colonists to deprive them of a useful medium of exchange.

Sugar and Currency Acts

Because the acts were imposed on an American economy that was in the middle of a postwar depression, it is not surprising that both individual colonists and colonial governments decided to protest the new policies. But, lacking any precedent for a united campaign against acts of Parliament, Americans in 1764 took only hesitant and uncoordinated steps. Eight colonial legislatures sent separate petitions to Parliament requesting repeal of the Sugar Act. They argued that the act placed severe restrictions on their commerce (and would therefore hurt Britain as well) and that they had not consented to its passage. The protests had no effect. The law remained in force, and Grenville proceeded with another revenue plan.

THE STAMP ACT CRISIS

The Stamp Act, Grenville's most important proposal, was modeled on a law that had been in effect in England for almost a century. It touched nearly every colonist by requiring tax stamps on most printed materials, but it placed the heaviest burden on merchants and other members of the colonial elite, who used printed matter more frequently than ordinary folk. Anyone who purchased a newspaper or pamphlet, made a will, transferred land, bought dice or playing cards, needed a liquor license, accepted a government appointment, or borrowed money would have to pay the tax. Never before had a revenue measure of such scope been proposed for the colonies. The act also required that tax stamps be paid in sterling, which was scarce, and that violators be tried in vice admiralty courts, which operated without juries. Finally, such a law would break decisively with the colonial tradition of self-imposed taxation.

The most important colonial pamphlet protesting the Sugar Act and the proposed Stamp Act was *The Rights of the British Colonies Asserted and Proved*, by James Otis Jr., a brilliant young Massachusetts attorney. Otis starkly exposed the ideological dilemma that was to confound the colonists for the next decade. How could they justify their opposition to certain acts of Parliament without questioning Parliament's authority over them? On the one hand, Otis asserted that

Otis's *Rights of the British Colonies*

Americans were "entitled to all the natural, essential, inherent, and inseparable rights" of Britons, including the right not to be taxed without their consent. On the other hand, Otis was forced to acknowledge that, under the British system, "the power of parliament is uncontrollable but by themselves, and we must obey."

Otis's first contention, drawing on colonial notions of representation, implied that Parliament could not constitutionally tax the colonies, because Americans were not represented in its ranks. Yet his second point both acknowledged political reality and accepted the prevailing theory of British government—that Parliament was the sole, supreme authority in the empire. The populace had to obey even unconstitutional laws enacted by Parliament until Parliament decided to repeal them. Otis tried to find such a middle ground by proposing colonial representation in Parliament, but his idea was never taken seriously on either side of the Atlantic. The British believed that the colonists were already virtually represented in Parliament, and the Americans quickly realized that a handful of colonial delegates to London would simply be outvoted.

Otis published his pamphlet before the Stamp Act was passed. When Americans first learned of its adoption in the spring of 1765, they were uncertain how to react. Few colonists publicly favored the law. But colonial petitions had already failed to prevent its adoption, and further lobbying appeared futile. Perhaps Otis was right that the only course open to Americans was to pay the stamp tax, reluctantly but loyally.

Not all colonists were resigned to paying the new tax. Among them was a twenty-nine-year-old lawyer serving his first term in the Virginia House of Burgesses. Patrick Henry later recalled that he was appalled by his fellow legislators' unwillingness to oppose the Stamp Act. Henry decided to act. "Alone, unadvised, and unassisted, on a blank leaf of an old law book," he wrote the Virginia Stamp Act Resolves.

Patrick Henry and the Virginia Stamp Act Resolves

Patrick Henry introduced his seven proposals near the end of the legislative session, when many members of the House of Burgesses had already departed for home. Henry's fiery speech led the Speaker of the House to accuse him of treason. (Henry denied the charge, contrary to the nineteenth-century myth that he exclaimed, "If this be treason, make the most of it!") The few burgesses remaining in Williamsburg adopted five of Henry's resolutions by a bare majority. Although they repealed the most radical of the five the next day, their action had far-reaching effects.

The four propositions adopted by the burgesses repeated Otis's arguments, asserting that the colonists had never forfeited the rights of British subjects, among which was consent to taxation. The other three resolutions went much further. The one that was repealed claimed for the burgesses "the only exclusive right" to tax Virginians, and the final two asserted that residents of the colony need not obey tax laws passed by other legislative bodies (namely Parliament), terming any opponent of that opinion "an Enemy to this his Majesty's Colony."

The burgesses' decision to accept only the first four of Henry's resolutions anticipated the position most Americans would adopt throughout the decade that followed. Although willing to contend for their rights, the colonists did not seek independence. They merely wanted some measure of self-government. Accordingly, they backed away from assertions that they owed Parliament no obedience and that only their own assemblies could tax them.

During the next ten years, America's political leaders searched for a formula that would enable them to control their internal affairs, especially taxation, but remain within the British Empire. The chief difficulty lay in British officials' inability to compromise on the issue of parliamentary power. The notion that Parliament could exercise absolute authority over all colonial possessions was basic to the British theory of government. In effect, the Americans wanted British leaders to revise their fundamental understanding of the workings of their government. That was simply too much to expect.

The ultimate effectiveness of Americans' opposition to the Stamp Act rested on more than ideological arguments over parliamentary power. What gave the resistance its primary force were the decisive and inventive actions of some colonists during the late summer and fall of 1765.

In August, the Loyal Nine, a Boston social club of printers, distillers, and other artisans, organized a demonstration against the Stamp Act. Hoping to

Loyal Nine
——

show that people of all ranks opposed the act, they approached the leaders of the city's rival laborers associations, based in the North End and South End. The Loyal Nine convinced them to lay aside their differences to participate in the demonstration. After all, the stamp taxes would have to be paid by all colonists, not just by affluent ones.

Early on August 14, the demonstrators hung an effigy of Andrew Oliver, the province's stamp distributor, from a tree on Boston Common. That night, a large crowd led by a group of about fifty well-dressed tradesmen tore down a small building they thought was intended as the stamp office and used wood from the structure to build a bonfire near Oliver's house. Members of the crowd broke most of Oliver's windows and threw stones at officials who tried to disperse them. In the middle of the melée, the North End and South End leaders drank a toast to their successful union. The Loyal Nine's demonstration achieved its objective when Oliver publicly promised not to fulfill the duties of his office. Twelve days later, another mob, reportedly led by the South End leader Ebenezer MacIntosh, attacked the homes of several customs officers. This time, the violence was almost universally condemned, for the mob completely destroyed Lieutenant Governor Thomas Hutchinson's townhouse.

The differences between the two Boston mobs of August 1765 exposed divisions that would continue to characterize subsequent colonial protests.

**Americans'
Divergent
Interests**
——

The skilled craftsmen who composed the Loyal Nine and members of the educated elite preferred orderly demonstrations confined to political issues. For the city's laborers, by contrast, economic grievances may have been paramount. Certainly, their "hellish Fury" as they wrecked Hutchinson's house suggests a resentment of his ostentatious display of wealth.

Colonists, like Britons, had a long tradition of crowd action in which disfranchised people took to the streets to redress deeply felt local grievances. But the Stamp Act controversy drew ordinary urban folk into the vortex of imperial politics for the first time. Matters that had previously been of concern only to the gentry or to members of colonial legislatures were now discussed on every street corner. Sally Franklin observed as much when she wrote to her father Benjamin, then serving as a colonial agent in London, that "nothing else is talked of, the Dutch [Germans] talk of the stompt act the Negroes of the tamp, in short every body has something to say."

The entry into the realm of imperial politics by lower-class whites, blacks, and women both threatened and afforded an opportunity to the elite white men who wanted to mount effective opposition to British measures. On the one hand, crowd action could have a stunning effect. Anti-Stamp Act demonstrations occurred in cities and towns stretching from Halifax, Nova Scotia, to the Caribbean island of Antigua. They were so successful that by November 1, when the law was scheduled to take effect, not one stamp distributor was willing to carry out the duties of his office. Thus the British could not enforce the act. But at the same time, wealthy men recognized that mobs composed of the formerly powerless could endanger their own dominance of society. What would happen, they wondered, if the crowd turned against them?

They therefore attempted to channel resistance into acceptable forms by creating an intercolonial association, the Sons of Liberty. The first such group was created in New York in early November, and branches spread rapidly through the coastal cities. Composed of merchants, lawyers, prosperous tradesmen, and others, the Sons of Liberty linked protest leaders from Charleston, South Carolina, to Portsmouth, New Hampshire, by early 1766.

Sons of Liberty

In Philadelphia, resistance leaders were dismayed when an angry mob threatened to attack Benjamin Franklin's house. The city's laborers believed Franklin to be partly responsible for the Stamp Act, because he had obtained the post of stamp distributor for a close friend. But Philadelphia's artisans—the backbone of the opposition movement there and elsewhere—were fiercely loyal to Franklin. They gathered to protect his home and family from the crowd. The house was saved, but the resulting split between the better-off tradesmen and the common laborers prevented the establishment of a successful workingmen's alliance like that of Boston.

During the fall and winter of 1765–1766, opposition to the Stamp Act proceeded on three separate fronts. Colonial legislatures petitioned Parliament to repeal the hated law and in October sent delegates to an intercolonial congress, the first since the Albany Congress of 1754. The Stamp Act Congress met in New York to draft a unified but conservative statement of protest. At the same time, the Sons of Liberty held mass meetings in an effort to win public support for the resistance movement. Finally, American merchants organized nonimportation associations to pressure British exporters. By the 1760s, one-quarter of all British exports were being sent to the colonies, and American merchants reasoned that London merchants whose sales suffered severely would lobby for repeal. Because times were bad, American merchants also saw nonimportation as a means of reducing bloated inventories.

In March 1766, Parliament repealed the Stamp Act. The nonimportation agreements had the anticipated effect, creating allies for the colonies among wealthy London merchants. But boycotts, formal protests, and crowd actions were less important in winning repeal than was the appointment of a new prime minister. Lord Rockingham, who replaced Grenville in summer 1765, had opposed the Stamp Act, not because he believed Parliament lacked power to tax the colonies but because he thought the law unwise and divisive. Rockingham, however, linked repeal to the passage of the Declaratory Act, which asserted Parliament's ability to tax and legislate for Britain's American possessions "in all cases whatsoever." As they celebrated the Stamp Act's repeal, few colonists saw the implications of the Declaratory Act.

Repeal of the Stamp Act

RESISTANCE TO THE TOWNSHEND ACTS

The colonists had accomplished their immediate aim, but the long-term prospects were unclear.

Another change in the ministry, in the summer of 1766, revealed how fragile their victory had been. The new prime minister, William Pitt, was ill much of the time, and the chancellor of the exchequer, Charles Townshend, became the dominant force in the ministry. Townshend, an ally of Grenville's, decided to renew the attempt to obtain additional funds from Britain's American possessions (see table).

The taxes proposed by Townshend in 1767 were to be levied on trade goods like paper, glass, and tea and thus seemed to be nothing more than extensions of the existing Navigation Acts. But the Townshend duties differed from previous customs taxes in two ways. First, they were levied on items imported to the colonies from Britain, not from foreign countries. Thus they were at odds with mercantilist theory. Second, they were designed to raise money to pay the salaries of certain royal officials in the colonies. That posed a direct challenge to the colonial assemblies, which derived considerable power from threatening to withhold officials' salaries. In addition, Townshend's scheme provided for the creation of an American Board of Customs Commissioners and of vice admiralty courts at Boston, Philadelphia, and Charleston. Last, Townshend proposed the appointment of a secretary of state for American affairs and the suspension of the New York legislature for refusal to comply with the Quartering Act of 1765, which required colonial governments to supply certain items to British troops stationed permanently in America.

The Townshend Acts drew a quick response. One series of essays in particular, *Letters from a Farmer in Pennsylvania*, by the prominent lawyer John Dickinson, expressed a broad consensus. Dickinson contended that Parliament could regulate colonial trade but could not exercise that power for the purpose of raising revenues. By drawing a distinction between the regulation of trade and unacceptable commercial taxation, Dickinson avoided the sticky issue of consent and how it affected the extent of colonial subordination to Parliament. But his argument suggested that the colonies would have to assess Parliament's motives in enacting any law pertaining to imperial trade before deciding whether to obey it. In the long run, that was an unworkable position.

The Massachusetts assembly responded to the Townshend Acts by drafting a circular letter to the other colonial legislatures, calling for unity and suggesting a joint petition of protest. Not the letter itself but the ministry's reaction to it united the colonies. When Lord Hillsborough, the first secretary of state for America, learned of the circular letter, he ordered Governor Francis Bernard of Massachusetts to insist that the assembly recall it. He also directed other governors

Massachusetts Assembly Dissolved

British Ministries and Their American Policies

Head of Ministry	Major Acts
George Grenville	Sugar Act (1764)
	Currency Act (1764)
	Stamp Act (1765)
Lord Rockingham	Stamp Act repealed (1766)
	Declaratory Act (1766)
William Pitt/Charles Townshend	Townshend Acts (1767)
Lord North	Townshend duties repealed (all but tea tax) (1770)
	Coercive Acts (1774)
	Quebec Act (1774)

to prevent their assemblies from discussing the letter. Hillsborough's order gave the colonial assemblies the incentive they needed to forget their differences and join forces to oppose the new threat to their prerogatives. In late 1768, the Massachusetts legislature met, debated, and resoundingly rejected recall by a vote of 92 to 17. Bernard immediately dissolved the assembly, and other governors followed suit when their legislatures debated the circular letter.

During the two-year campaign against the Townshend duties, the Sons of Liberty and other American leaders made a deliberate effort to involve ordinary folk in the formal resistance movement, not just in occasional crowd actions. The signers of a June 1769 Maryland nonimportation agreement, for instance, were identified as "Merchants, Tradesmen, Freeholders, Mechanics [artisans], and other Inhabitants"; all agreed not to import or consume items of British origin. Such tactics helped to increase the number of colonists who were publicly aligned with the protest movement.

Just as the pamphlets acquainted literate colonists with the issues raised by British action, public rituals taught illiterate Americans about the reasons for resistance. When Boston's Sons of Liberty invited hundreds of the city's residents to dine with them each August 14 to commemorate the first Stamp Act uprising, and the Charleston Sons of Liberty held their meetings in public, crowds gathered to watch and listen. Likewise, the public singing of songs supporting the American cause helped to spread the word. The participants in such events were openly expressing their commitment to the cause of resistance and encouraging others to join them.

Women, previously excluded from political activity, now played a part in resisting British policy. Young women, calling themselves Daughters of

Daughters of Liberty
——

Liberty, met to spin in public in an effort to spur other women to make homespun and end the colonies' dependence on English cloth. These symbolic displays of patriotism served an important purpose. When young ladies from well-to-do families sat publicly at spinning wheels all day, eating only American food and drinking local herbal tea, and later listening to patriotic sermons, they were serving as political instructors.

Women also took the lead in promoting nonconsumption of tea. In Boston, more than three hundred matrons publicly promised not to drink tea, "Sickness excepted." The women of Wilmington, North Carolina, burned their tea after walking through town in a solemn procession. Housewives throughout the colonies exchanged recipes for tea substitutes or drank coffee instead. The best known of the protests, the so-called Edenton Ladies Tea Party, actually had little to do with tea. It was a meeting of prominent North Carolina women who pledged formally to work for the public good and to support resistance to British measures.

But the colonists were by no means united in support of nonimportation. If the Stamp Act protests had occasionally revealed a division

Divided Opinion over Boycotts
——

between artisans and merchants on the one side and common laborers on the other, resistance to the Townshend Acts exposed new splits in the American ranks. The most significant divided the urban artisans and merchants, the former allies of 1765–1766, and it arose from a change in economic circumstances. The Stamp Act boycotts had helped to revive a depressed economy by creating a demand for local products and reducing merchants' inventories. But in 1768 and 1769, merchants were enjoying boom times and had no financial incentive to support a boycott. As a result, merchants signed the agreements only reluctantly. In contrast, artisans supported nonimportation enthusiastically, recognizing that the absence of British goods would create a ready market for their own manufactures. They also used coercion to enforce nonimportation.

Such tactics were effective: colonial imports from England dropped dramatically in 1769, especially in New York, New England, and Pennsylvania. But they also aroused heated opposition, creating a second major division among the colonists. Some Americans who supported resistance to British measures began to question the use of violence to force others to join the boycott. In addition, wealthier and more conservative colonists were frightened by the threat to private property inherent in the campaign. Moreover, political activism by ordinary colonists challenged the ruling elite's domination.

Americans were relieved when news arrived in April 1770 that the Townshend duties, with the exception of the tea tax, had been repealed. A new prime minister, Lord North, had persuaded Parliament that duties on trade within the empire were bad policy. Although some political leaders argued that nonimportation should continue until the tea tax was repealed, merchants quickly resumed importing. The rest of the Townshend Acts remained in force, but repeal of the taxes made the other laws appear less objectionable.

Repeal of the Townshend Duties

GROWING RIFTS

At first, the new ministry did nothing to antagonize the colonists. Yet on the very day Lord North proposed repeal of the Townshend duties, a clash between civilians and soldiers in Boston led to the deaths of five Americans. The origins of the event that patriots called the Boston Massacre lay in repeated clashes between customs officers and the people of Massachusetts. The decision to base in Boston the American Board of Customs Commissioners (created by a Townshend Act) was the source of the problem.

From the day of their arrival in November 1767, the customs commissioners were frequent targets of mob action. In June 1768, their seizure of the patriot leader John Hancock's sloop *Liberty* on suspicion of smuggling caused a riot in which prominent customs officers' property was destroyed. The riot in turn helped to convince the ministry in London to station two regiments in Boston. This act confirmed Bostonians' worst fears; the redcoats were a constant reminder of the oppressive potential of British power.

Accustomed to leading their lives with a minimum of interference from government, Bostonians now found themselves hemmed in at every turn. Guards on Boston Neck, the entrance to the city, checked all travelers and their goods. Redcoat patrols roamed the city day and night, questioning and sometimes harassing passers-by. But the greatest potential for violence lay in the uneasy relationship between the soldiers and Boston laborers. Many redcoats sought employment in their off-duty hours, competing for unskilled jobs with the city's ordinary workingmen. Members of the two groups brawled repeatedly.

Early on the evening of March 5, 1770, a crowd of laborers began throwing hard-packed snowballs at soldiers guarding the Customs House. Goaded beyond endurance, the sentries acted against express orders to the contrary and fired on the crowd, killing four and wounding eight, one of whom died a few days later. Resistance leaders idealized the dead rioters as martyrs for the cause of liberty, holding a solemn funeral and later commemorating March 5 annually with patriotic orations. Paul Revere's engraving of the massacre was part of the propaganda campaign.

Boston Massacre

The leading patriots wanted to make certain the soldiers did not become martyrs as well. Despite the political benefits the patriots derived from the massacre, it is unlikely that they approved of the crowd action that provoked it. Thus when the soldiers were tried for the killings in November, John Adams and Josiah Quincy Jr., both unwavering patriots, defended them. All but two of the accused men were acquitted, and those convicted were released after being branded on the thumb. Undoubtedly, the favorable outcome of the trials prevented London officials from taking further steps against the city.

For more than two years after the Boston Massacre and the repeal of the Townshend duties, a superficial calm descended on the colonies. The most outspoken colonial newspapers published essays accusing Great Britain of a deliberate plan to oppress the colonies. After repeal of the Stamp Act, the patriots had praised Parliament; following repeal of the Townshend duties, they warned of impending tyranny. What had seemed to be an isolated mistake, a single ill-chosen stamp tax, now appeared to be part of a plot against American liberties. Essayists pointed to the stationing of troops in

Engrav'd Printed & Sold by Paul Revere Boston

How do historians know

whether ordinary people were familiar with the ideas propounded by the leaders of the American Revolution? This is a difficult question to answer, because most evidence about the patriots' ideology comes from pamphlets and newspapers aimed at a well-educated public. Even people who could read at a basic level might not have been able to understand the sophisticated criticisms of British policies advanced in such writings. Because the engraver made his point visually rather than verbally, anyone, even illiterate folk, could interpret an image like Paul Revere's masterful portrayal of the Boston Massacre. The label Butcher's Hall on the customs house merely reinforces a patriot's view of the incident on March 5, 1770. The British soldiers are shown firing on an unresisting crowd (not the aggressive angry mob described at the soldiers' trial), and a gun with smoke drifting up from its barrel emerges from a window above the redcoats, suggesting the complicity of civilian officials in what the patriots interpreted as an outrageous act.   Photo: Library of Congress.

Boston, and the growing number of vice admiralty courts as evidence of plans to enslave the colonists.

Still, no one yet advocated complete independence from England. Although the patriots were becoming increasingly convinced that they should seek freedom from parliamentary authority, they continued to acknowledge their British identity and to pledge their allegiance to George III. They began, therefore, to try to envision a system that would enable them to be ruled by their own elected legislatures while remaining loyal to the king. But any such scheme was alien to Britons' conception of the nature of their government, which was that Parliament held sole undivided sovereignty over the empire. In the British mind, Parliament encompassed the king as well as lords and commons, and so separating the monarch from the legislature was impossible.

Then, in the fall of 1772, the North ministry began to implement the portion of the Townshend Acts that provided for governors and judges to be paid from customs revenues. In early November, voters at a Boston town meeting established a Committee of Correspondence to publicize the decision by exchanging letters with other Massachusetts towns. Samuel Adams, the man who had proposed the committee's formation, became its head. Adams was fifty-one in 1772, thirteen years older than his distant cousin John and a decade the senior of most other leaders of American resistance. An experienced political organizer, Adams continually stressed the necessity of prudent collective action. His Committee of Correspondence thus undertook the task of creating an informed consensus among all citizens of Massachusetts.

Committees of Correspondence ———

Such committees, which were eventually established throughout the colonies, represented the next logical step in the organization of American resistance. Until 1772, the protest movement was largely confined to the seacoast and primarily to major cities and towns. Adams realized that the time had come to attempt to involve the residents of the interior. Accordingly, the Boston town meeting directed the Committee of Correspondence "to state the Rights of the Colonists and of this Province in particular," to list "the Infringements and Violations thereof that have been, or from time to time may be made," and to send copies to the other towns in the province.

Samuel Adams, James Otis Jr., and Josiah Quincy Jr. prepared the statement of the colonists' rights. Declaring that Americans had absolute rights to life, liberty, and property, the committee asserted that the idea that "a British house of commons, should have a right, at pleasure, to give and grant the property of the colonists" was "irreconcileable" with

"the first principles of natural law and Justice . . . and of the British Constitution in particular." The list of grievances, drafted by another group of prominent patriots, complained of taxation without representation, the presence of unnecessary troops and customs officers on American soil, the use of imperial revenues to pay colonial officials, the expanded jurisdiction of vice admiralty courts, and even the nature of the instructions given to American governors by their superiors in London. No mention was made of obedience to Parliament. Patriots—at least in Boston—had placed American rights first, loyalty to Great Britain a distant second.

The response of the Massachusetts towns to the committee's pamphlet must have caused Samuel Adams to rejoice. Some towns disagreed with Boston's assessment of the state of affairs, but most aligned with the city. From Braintree came the assertion that "all civil officers are or ought to be Servants to the people and dependent upon them for their official Support, and every instance to the Contrary from the Governor downwards tends to crush and destroy civil liberty." The citizens of Petersham commented that resistance to tyranny was "the first and highest social Duty of this people." Such beliefs made the next crisis in Anglo-American affairs the final one.

THE BOSTON TEA PARTY

The only Townshend duty still in effect by 1773 was the tax on tea. Although a continuing tea boycott was less than fully effective, tea retained its explosive symbolic character. In May 1773, Parliament passed an act designed to save the East India Company from bankruptcy. The company, which held a legal monopoly on British trade with the East Indies, was of critical importance to the British economy (and to the financial well-being of many prominent British politicians). Under the Tea Act, certain duties paid on tea were to be returned to the company. Only designated agents were to sell tea, which would enable the East India Company to avoid colonial middlemen and undersell any competitors, even smugglers.

Tea Act ———

The net result would be cheaper tea for American consumers. But resistance leaders interpreted the new measure as a pernicious device to make them acknowledge Parliament's right to tax them, because the less expensive tea would still be taxed under the Townshend law. Others saw the Tea Act as the first step in the establishment of an East India Company monopoly of all colonial trade. Residents of the four cities designated to receive the first shipments of tea accordingly prepared to respond to what they perceived as a new threat to their freedom.

In New York City, the tea ships failed to arrive on schedule. In Philadelphia, the captain was persuaded to turn around and sail back to England. In Charleston, the tea was unloaded, stored under the direction of local tradesmen, and later destroyed. The only confrontation occurred in Boston, where both sides—the town meeting, joined by participants from nearby towns, and Governor Thomas Hutchinson—rejected compromise.

The first of three tea ships, the *Dartmouth*, entered Boston harbor on November 28. Under the customs laws, owners had to land a cargo and pay the appropriate duty within twenty days of a ship's arrival. Otherwise, customs officers would seize the cargo and sell it at auction. After a series of mass meetings, Bostonians voted to prevent the tea from being unloaded and to post guards on the wharf. Hutchinson, for his part, refused to permit the vessels to leave the harbor.

On December 16, one day before the cargo would have to be confiscated, more than five thousand people (nearly a third of the city's population) crowded into Old South Church. The meeting, chaired by Samuel Adams, made a final attempt to persuade Hutchinson to send the tea back to England. But Hutchinson remained adamant. At about 6 P.M., Adams reportedly announced "that he could think of nothing further to be done—that they had now done all they could for the Salvation of their Country." As if his statement were a planned signal, cries rang out from the back of the crowd: "Boston harbor a tea-pot tonight! The Mohawks are come!" Within a few minutes, about sixty men crudely disguised as Indians assembled at the wharf, boarded the three ships, and dumped the cargo into the harbor. By 9 P.M., their work was

Thomas Hutchinson was the governor of Massachusetts who helped to incite the Boston Tea Party by refusing to allow the tea ships to leave the harbor, a solution adopted in Pennsylvania by a governor less intent on seeking a confrontation with colonial resistance leaders. John Singleton Copley's portrait of the haughty Hutchinson reveals the governor's uncompromising character. Massachusetts Historical Society.

done: 342 chests of tea worth approximately £10,000 floated in splinters on the water.

When news of the Tea Party reached London, the North administration reacted by proposing the first of four laws that became known as the Coercive, or Intolerable, Acts.

Coercive and Quebec Acts
___

Passed in March 1774, it called for closing the port of Boston until the tea was paid for and prohibiting all but coastal trade in food and firewood. Colonial sympathizers in Parliament were easily outvoted by those who wished to punish the city that had been the center of opposition to British policies. Later in the spring,

Parliament passed three other punitive measures. The Massachusetts Government Act altered the province's charter, substituting an appointed council for the elected one, increasing the powers of the governor, and forbidding special town meetings. The Justice Act provided that a person accused of killing someone in the course of suppressing a riot or enforcing the laws could be tried outside the colony in which the incident had occurred. Finally, the new Quartering Act gave broad authority to military commanders seeking to house their troops in private dwellings. Thus the Coercive Acts punished not only Boston but Massachusetts as a whole and alerted other colonies to the possibility that their residents too could be subject to retaliation if they opposed British authority.

After passing the last of the Coercive Acts in early June, Parliament turned its attention to much-needed reforms in the government of Quebec. The Quebec Act, although unrelated to the Coercive Acts, thereby became linked with them in the minds of the patriots. Intended to ease the strains that had arisen since the British conquest of the formerly French colony, the Quebec Act granted greater religious freedom to Catholics, which alarmed the Protestant colonists, who equated Roman Catholicism with religious and political despotism. It also reinstated French civil law, and it established an appointed council as the governing body of the colony. Finally, in an attempt to provide the northern tribes some protection against white settlement, the act annexed to Quebec the area east of the Mississippi River and north of the Ohio River. That region, parts of which were claimed by individual seacoast colonies, was thus removed from their jurisdiction.

Members of Parliament who voted for the punitive legislation believed that colonists would obey the acts. But the patriots showed little inclination to bow to the wishes of Parliament. In their eyes, the Coercive Acts and the Quebec Act proved what they had feared since 1768: that Great Britain had embarked on a deliberate plan to oppress them. If the port of Boston could be closed, why not those of Philadelphia or New York? If the royal charter of Massachusetts could be changed, why not that of South Carolina? If certain people could be removed from their home colonies for trial, why not all

violators of all laws? If troops could be forcibly quartered in private houses, did not that pave the way for the occupation of all of America? If the Roman Catholic church could receive favored status in Quebec, why not everywhere? It seemed as though the full dimensions of the plot against American rights and liberties had at last been revealed.

The Boston Committee of Correspondence urged all the colonies to join in an immediate boycott of British goods. But the other provinces were not yet ready to take such a drastic step. They suggested that another intercolonial congress be convened to consider an appropriate response. Few people wanted to take hasty action; even the most ardent patriots remained loyal to Britain and hoped for reconciliation with its leaders. Despite their objections to British policy, they continued to see themselves as part of the empire. And so the colonies agreed to send delegates to Philadelphia in September.

During the preceding decade, momentous changes had occurred in the ways colonists thought about themselves and their allegiance. Once linked unquestioningly to Great Britain, they had begun to develop a sense of their own identity as Americans. They had started to realize that their concept of the political process differed from that held by people in England. They had also come to understand that their economic interests did not necessarily coincide with those of Great Britain. Colonial political leaders reached such conclusions only after a long train of events, some violent, had altered their understanding of the nature of their relationship with England.

In the late summer of 1774, the Americans were committed to resistance but not to independence. Even so, they had started to sever the bonds of empire. During the next decade, they would forge the bonds of a new American nationality to replace those rejected Anglo-American ties.

SUGGESTIONS FOR FURTHER READING

General

Ian R. Christie, *Crisis of Empire: Great Britain and the American Colonies, 1754–1783* (1966); Marc Egnal, *A Mighty Empire: The*

Origins of the American Revolution (1988); Merrill Jensen, *The Founding of a Nation: A History of the American Revolution, 1763–1776* (1968).

Colonial Warfare and the British Empire

Fred Anderson, *A People's Army: Massachusetts Soldiers and Society in the Seven Years' War* (1984); Robert C. Newbold, *The Albany Congress and Plan of Union of 1754* (1955); John Shy, *Toward Lexington: The Role of the British Army in the Coming of the American Revolution* (1965); James Titus, *The Old Dominion at War: Society, Politics, and Warfare in Late Colonial Virginia* (1991).

British Politics and Policy

John Brooke, *King George III* (1972); John L. Bullion, *A Great and Necessary Measure: George Grenville and the Genesis of the Stamp Act, 1763–1765* (1981); Bernard Donoughue, *British Politics and the American Revolution: The Path to War, 1773–1775* (1965); Michael Kammen, *A Rope of Sand: The Colonial Agents, British Politics, and the American Revolution* (1968).

Native Americans and the West

Richard Aquila, *The Iroquois Restoration: Iroquois Diplomacy on the Colonial Frontier, 1701–1754* (1983); David H. Corkran, *The Cherokee Frontier: Conflict and Survival, 1740–1762* (1962); Gregory Dowd, *A Spirited Resistance: The North American Indian Struggle for Unity, 1745–1815* (1992); Francis Jennings, *Empire of Fortune: Crowns, Colonies and Tribes in the Seven Years' War in America* (1988); Howard H. Peckham, *Pontiac and the Indian Uprising* (1947).

Political and Economic Thought

Bernard Bailyn, *The Ideological Origins of the American Revolution* (1967); J. E. Crowley, *This Sheba, Self: The Conceptualization of Economic Life in Eighteenth-Century America* (1974); Jay Fliegelman, *Prodigals and Pilgrims: The American Revolution Against Patriarchal Authority, 1750–1800* (1982); Clinton Rossiter, *Seedtime of the Republic: The Origin of the American Tradition of Political Liberty* (1953).

American Resistance

David Ammerman, *In the Common Cause: American Response to the Coercive Acts of 1774* (1974); Richard D. Brown, *Revolutionary Politics in Massachusetts: The Boston Committee of Correspondence and the Towns, 1772–1774* (1970); Benjamin W. Labaree, *The Boston Tea Party* (1964); Pauline R. Maier, *The Old Revolutionaries: Political Lives in the Age of Samuel Adams* (1980); Pauline R. Maier, *From Resistance to Revolution: Colonial Radicals and the Development of American Opposition to Britain, 1765–1776* (1972); Edmund S. Morgan and Helen M. Morgan, *The Stamp Act Crisis: Prologue to Revolution* (1953); Richard Ryerson, *The Revolution Has Now Begun: The Radical Committees of Philadelphia, 1765–1776* (1978); John W. Tyler, *Smugglers and Patriots: Boston Merchants and the Advent of the American Revolution* (1986); Richard Walsh, *Charleston's Sons of Liberty: A Study of the Artisans, 1763–1789* (1959); Hiller B. Zobel, *The Boston Massacre* (1970).

6

A Revolution, Indeed, 1775–1783

WHEN JOHN PROVEY AND Richard Weaver appeared before the loyalist claims commissioners in London at the end of the Revolution, the commissioners were not impressed with their descriptions of losses and loyal service to the king. Such men had "no right to ask or expect any thing from Government," the commissioners declared. So they denied Provey and Weaver any assistance from the funds allocated by Parliament to compensate loyalists for the damages they had incurred by opposing the Revolution. Why were Weaver and Provey treated thus? They were, quite simply, African-Americans.

Provey, a North Carolina slave, had served in a black corps of the British army during the war. Weaver, who claimed to be freeborn, had left Philadelphia with the British troops when they evacuated that city in 1778. Both had wives and children when they requested government assistance. Because they were denied the help they sought, they and their families, along with hundreds of other African-Americans, became dependent on charity disbursed by a group of civic-minded London merchants, the Committee to Aid the Black Poor.

Seeing no future in London, they both agreed to emigrate to West Africa, to the new colony of Sierra Leone. Provey died on shipboard, but Weaver went to Sierra Leone and was elected the first governor of the tiny colony, composed largely of exiled African-American loyalists. Conflicts with a nearby tribal chief and with slavers who established a post near the settlement almost destroyed it. But in 1792, the future of the colony was assured when an additional twelve hundred African-American refugees arrived from Nova Scotia, where they had fled immediately after the war.

The little-known tale of the black loyalists who returned to the homeland of their ancestors is but one dramatic example of the disruptive effects of the American Revolution. The Revolution uprooted thousands of families, disrupted the economy, reshaped society by forcing many colonists into permanent exile, led Americans to develop new conceptions of politics, and created a nation from thirteen separate colonies. Thus it marked a significant turning point in Americans' collective history.

The struggle for independence required revolutionary leaders to accomplish three tasks. The first was political and ideological: they had to transform a consensus among whites favoring loyal resistance into a coalition supporting independence. From African-Americans and Indians, the colonies' elected leaders hoped for cooperation at best, neutrality at worst, for they had reason to fear that Indians and blacks would unite with the English against them. The second task involved foreign relations. To win their independence, the patriot leaders knew they needed international recognition and aid, particularly from France. Thus they dispatched to Paris the most experienced American diplomat, Benjamin Franklin. Franklin skillfully negotiated the Franco-American alliance of 1778, which was to prove crucial to the winning of independence.

Only the third task directly involved the British. George Washington, commander in chief of the American army, quickly realized that his primary goal should not be to win battles but to avoid losing them decisively. So long as his army survived to fight another day, he saw, the outcome of any individual battle was more or less irrelevant. Accordingly, the story of the Revolutionary War reveals British action and American reaction, British attacks and American defenses. The American war effort was aided by the failure of British military planners to analyze accurately the problem confronting them. Until it was too late, they treated the war against the colonists as they did wars against other Europeans—that is, they concentrated on winning battles and did not consider the difficulties of achieving their main goal, retaining the colonies' allegiance. In the end, the Americans' triumph owed more to their endurance and to Britain's mistakes than to Americans' military prowess.

GOVERNMENT BY CONGRESS AND COMMITTEE

When the fifty-five delegates to the First Continental Congress convened in Philadelphia in September 1774, they knew that any measures they adopted were likely to enjoy support among many of their countrymen and countrywomen. That summer, open meetings held throughout the colonies had endorsed the idea of another nonimportation pact. The committees of correspondence that had

been established in many communities publicized these popular meetings so effectively that Americans everywhere knew about them. Extralegal provincial conventions chose most congressional delegates at local gatherings, because the royal governors had forbidden the regular assemblies to conduct formal elections. Thus the very act of designating delegates to attend the Congress involved Americans in open defiance of British authority.

The colonies sent their leading political figures—most of them lawyers, merchants, and planters—to the Philadelphia Congress. The Massachusetts delegation included both Samuel Adams and his younger cousin John, an ambitious lawyer. Among others, New York sent John Jay, a talented young attorney. From Pennsylvania came the conservative Joseph Galloway, speaker of the assembly, and his long-time rival John Dickinson. Virginia elected Richard Henry Lee and Patrick Henry, both noted for their patriotic zeal, as well as George Washington.

First Continental Congress

The delegates faced three tasks when they convened at Carpenters Hall on September 5, 1774. The first two were explicit: defining American grievances and developing a plan for resistance. The third—outlining a theory of their constitutional relationship with England—proved troublesome. The most radical delegates, like Lee of Virginia, argued that the colonists owed allegiance only to George III and that Parliament was nothing more than a local legislature for Great Britain with no authority over the colonies. The conservatives—Joseph Galloway and his allies—proposed a formal plan of union that would have required Parliament and a new American legislature to consent jointly to all laws pertaining to the colonies. After heated debate, the delegates rejected Galloway's proposal, but they were not prepared to accept the radicals' position, either.

Finally, they accepted a compromise position worked out by John Adams. The crucial clause that Adams drafted in the Congress's Declaration of Rights and Grievances read in part: "From the necessity of the case, and a regard to the mutual interest of both countries, we cheerfully consent to the

Declaration of Rights and Grievances

operation of such acts of the British parliament, as are bona fide, restrained to the regulation of our external commerce." Note the key phrases. "From the necessity of the case" declared that Americans had decided to obey Parliament only because they had decided that doing so was in the best interest of both countries. "Bona fide, restrained to the regulation of our external commerce" made it clear to Lord North that they would continue to resist taxes in disguise, like the Townshend duties. Most striking of all was that such language—which only a few years before would have been regarded as irredeemably radical—could be presented and accepted as a compromise in the fall of 1774.

With the constitutional issue resolved, the delegates readily agreed on the laws they wanted repealed (notably the Coercive Acts) and decided to implement an economic boycott while petitioning the king for relief. They adopted the Continental Association, which called for nonimportation of British goods (effective December 1, 1774), nonconsumption of British products (effective March 1, 1775), and nonexportation of American goods to Britain and the British West Indies (effective September 10, 1775, so that southern planters could market their 1774 tobacco crop).

To enforce the Continental Association, Congress recommended the election of committees of observation and inspection in every county, city, and town in America. By specifying that committee members be chosen by all persons qualified to vote for members of the lower house of the colonial legislatures, Congress guaranteed the committees a broad popular base. In some places, the committeemen were former local officeholders; in other towns, they were obscure men who had never before held office. The seven to eight thousand committeemen became the local leaders of American resistance.

Committees of Observation

Such committees were officially charged only with overseeing implementation of the boycott, but during the next six months they became de facto governments. They examined merchants' records and published the names of those who continued to import British goods. They also promoted home manufactures and encouraged Americans to adopt simple modes of dress and behavior to symbolize their commitment to liberty and virtuous behavior. Because expensive leisure-time activities were believed to reflect vice and corruption, Congress urged Americans to forgo dancing, gambling, horse racing, cock fighting, and other forms of "extravagance and dissipation." By enforcing these injunctions, the committees gradually extended their authority over many aspects of American life.

The committees also attempted to identify opponents of American resistance, developing elaborate spy networks, circulating copies of the Continental Association for signatures, and investigating reports of dissident remarks and activities. Suspected dissenters were first urged to convert to the colonial cause; if they failed to do so, the committees had them watched, restricted their movements, or tried to force them to leave the area. People engaging in casual political exchanges with friends one day could find themselves charged with "treasonable conversation" the next.

While the committees of observation were expanding their power during the winter and early spring of 1775, the established governments of the colonies were collapsing. Only in Connecticut, Rhode Island, Delaware, and Pennsylvania did colonial legislatures continue to meet without encountering patriot challenges to their authority. In every other colony, popularly elected provincial conventions took over the task of running the government, sometimes entirely replacing the legislatures and at other times holding concurrent sessions. In late 1774 and early 1775, these conventions approved the Continental Association, elected delegates to the Second Continental Congress (scheduled for May), organized militia units, and gathered arms and ammunition. Unable to stem the tide of resistance, the British-appointed governors and councils watched helplessly as their authority crumbled.

Provincial Conventions

Royal officials throughout the colonies found themselves politically impotent. Courts were prevented from holding sessions, taxes were paid to agents of the conventions rather than to provincial tax collectors, sheriffs' powers were questioned,

• *Important Events* •

1774	First Continental Congress meets in Philadelphia; adopts Declaration of Rights and Grievances		British evacuate Boston Declaration of Independence adopted New York City falls to British
	Continental Association implements economic boycott of Britain; Committees of Observation established to oversee boycott	**1777**	British take Philadelphia Burgoyne surrenders at Saratoga
1774–75	Provincial conventions replace collapsing colonial governments	**1778**	French alliance brings vital assistance to the United States British evacuate Philadelphia
1775	Battles of Lexington and Concord; first shots of war fired	**1779**	Sullivan expedition destroys Iroquois villages
	Second Continental Congress begins	**1780**	British take Charleston
	Lord Dunmore's Proclamation offers freedom to rebels' slaves if they join British forces	**1781**	Cornwallis surrenders at Yorktown
		1782	Peace negotiations begin
1776	Thomas Paine publishes *Common Sense,* advocating independence	**1783**	Treaty of Paris signed, granting independence to the United States

and militiamen refused to muster except by order of the local committees. In short, during the six months preceding the battles at Lexington and Concord, the colonists were winning independence at the local level, but without formal acknowledgment and for the most part without bloodshed. Not many Americans fully realized what was happening. The vast majority still proclaimed their loyalty to Great Britain and denied that they sought to leave the empire. Among the few who most clearly recognized the trend toward independence were those who opposed it.

CHOOSING SIDES: LOYALISTS, AFRICAN-AMERICANS, AND INDIANS

The first protests against British measures, in the mid-1760s, had won the support of most colonists. Only in the late 1760s and early 1770s did a significant number of Americans begin to question both the aims and the tactics of the resistance movement.

By 1774 and 1775, such people found themselves in a difficult position. Like their more radical counterparts, most objected to parliamentary policies and wanted some kind of constitutional reform. Nevertheless, if forced to a choice, these colonists sympathized with Great Britain rather than with an independent America. Their objections to violent protest, their desire to uphold the legally constituted colonial governments, and their fears of anarchy combined to make them especially sensitive to the dangers of resistance.

Some conservatives began in 1774 and 1775 to publish essays and pamphlets critical of the Congress and its allied committees. In New York City, a group of Anglican clergy jointly wrote pamphlets and essays arguing the importance of maintaining a cordial connection between England and America. In Pennsylvania, Joseph Galloway published *A Candid Examination of the Mutual Claims of Great Britain and the Colonies,* attacking the Continental Congress for rejecting his plan of union. In Massachusetts, the young attorney Daniel Leonard, writing under the pseudonym Massachusettensis, engaged in a prolonged newspaper debate with Novanglus

(John Adams). Leonard and the others realized that what had begun as a dispute over the extent of American subordination within the empire had now raised the question of whether the colonies would remain linked to Great Britain at all.

Some colonists heeded the conservative pamphleteers' warnings. About one-fifth of the white American population remained loyal to Great

Loyalists, Patriots, and Neutrals

Britain, actively opposing independence. With notable exceptions, most people of the following descriptions remained loyal to the Crown: British-appointed government officials, merchants whose trade depended on imperial connections, Anglican clergy everywhere and lay Anglicans in the North, former officers and enlisted men from the British army, non-English ethnic minorities (especially Scots), tenant farmers (particularly those whose landlords sided with the patriots), members of persecuted religious sects, and many backcountry southerners who had rebelled against eastern rule in the 1760s and early 1770s. All these people had one thing in common: the patriot leaders were their long-standing opponents. Local and provincial disputes thus helped to determine which side people chose in the imperial conflict.

The active patriots, who accounted for about two-fifths of the population, came chiefly from the groups that had dominated colonial society, either numerically or politically. Among them were yeoman farmers, members of dominant Protestant sects, Chesapeake gentry, merchants dealing mainly in American commodities, city artisans, elected officeholders, and people of English descent. Wives usually but not always adopted their husbands' political beliefs. Although all these patriots supported the Revolution, they pursued divergent goals within the broader coalition. Some sought limited political reform, others extensive political change, and still others social and economic reforms.

There remained in the middle perhaps two-fifths of the white population. Some who tried to avoid taking sides were sincere pacifists, such as Pennsylvania Quakers. Others opportunistically shifted their allegiance according to which side happened to be winning at the time. Still others

simply wanted to be left alone to lead their lives. Such persons made up an especially large proportion of the population in the southern backcountry, where Scotch-Irish settlers had little love for either the patriot gentry or the English authorities.

To American patriots, that sort of apathy or neutrality was a crime as heinous as loyalism. Those who were not for them were against them; in their minds, there could be no conscientious objectors. By the winter of 1775–1776, less than a year after the battles of Lexington and Concord, the Second Continental Congress was recommending to the states that all "disaffected" persons be disarmed and arrested. The state legislatures quickly passed laws prescribing severe penalties for suspected loyalists. Many began to require all voters (or, in some cases, all free adult males) to take oaths of allegiance; the punishment for refusal was usually banishment or extra taxes. After 1777, many states confiscated the property of banished loyalists and used the proceeds for the war effort. Perhaps as many as one hundred thousand white loyalists preferred to leave their homeland rather than live in a nation independent of British rule. They were not, however, the only Americans to concern the patriots.

Slaves faced a dilemma at the beginning of the Revolution: how could they best pursue their goal of escaping perpetual servitude? Should they fight

African-Americans' Dilemma

with or against their white masters? With no correct choice immediately apparent, African-Americans made different decisions. Some indeed joined the revolutionaries, but to most an alliance with the British appeared more promising. Thus news of slave conspiracies surfaced in different parts of the colonies in late 1774 and early 1775. All shared a common element: a plan to assist the British in return for freedom. One group of slaves futilely petitioned General Thomas Gage, the commander in chief of the British army in Boston, promising to fight for the redcoats if he would liberate them. The most serious incident occurred in 1775 in Charleston, where Thomas Jeremiah, a free black harbor pilot, was brutally executed after being convicted of attempting to foment a slave revolt.

A fear of such acts made white residents of the British West Indian colonies far more cautious in their opposition to parliamentary policies than their counterparts on the mainland. On most Caribbean islands, blacks outnumbered whites by six or seven to one. With the ever present threat of slave revolt or foreign attack hanging over their heads, the planters could not afford to risk opposing Britain, their chief protector.

Racial Composition and Patriotic Fervor

Racial composition affected politics in the continental colonies as well. In the North, where whites greatly outnumbered blacks, revolutionary fervor was at its height. Virginia and Maryland, where whites constituted a safe majority of the population, saw occasional alarm about potential slave revolts but no disabling fear. But in South Carolina, which was more than 60 percent black, and in Georgia, where the racial balance was nearly even, whites were noticeably less enthusiastic about resistance. Georgia sent no delegates to the First Continental Congress and reminded its representatives at the Second Continental Congress to consider its circumstances, "with our blacks and tories within us," when voting on the question of independence.

The whites' worst fears were realized in November 1775, when Lord Dunmore, the governor of Virginia, offered to free any slaves and indentured servants who would leave their patriot masters to join the British forces. Dunmore hoped to use African-Americans in his fight against the revolutionaries and to disrupt the economy by depriving white Americans of their labor force. But the African-Americans who rallied to the British standard in 1775 and 1776 were fewer than expected (at most two thousand), and many perished in a smallpox epidemic. Even so, Dunmore's proclamation led Congress in January 1776 to modify an earlier policy that had prohibited the enlistment of blacks in the Continental Army.

Although African-Americans did not pose a serious threat to the revolutionary cause in its early years, the patriots turned rumors of slave uprisings to their own advantage. In South Carolina, they won adherents by promoting white unity under the revolutionary banner. The Continental Association was needed, they argued, to protect whites from blacks at a time when the royal government was unable to muster adequate defense forces. Undoubtedly, many wavering Carolinians were drawn into the revolutionary camp by fear that an overt division among the colony's whites would encourage a slave revolt.

Similarly, the threat of Indian attacks helped persuade some reluctant westerners to support the struggle against Great Britain. In the years since the Proclamation of 1763, British officials had won the trust of the interior tribes by attempting to protect them from land-hungry whites. The British-appointed superintendents of Indian affairs, John Stuart in the South and Sir William Johnson in the North, lived among and understood the Indians. In 1768, Stuart and Johnson negotiated separate agreements modifying the proclamation line and attempting to draw realistic, defensible boundaries between tribal holdings and white settlements. The two treaties—signed at Hard Labor Creek, South Carolina, and at Fort Stanwix, New York—supposedly established permanent western borders for the colonies. But just a few years later, the British pushed the southern boundary even farther west to accommodate the demands of whites in western Georgia and Kentucky.

By the time of the Revolution, the tribes were impatient with white Americans' aggressive pressure on their lands. The relationship of the Indians and frontier whites was filled with bitterness, misunderstanding, and occasional bloody encounters. In combination with the tribes' confidence in Stuart and Johnson, such grievances predisposed most Indians to an alliance with the British. Even so, the latter hesitated to make full and immediate use of these potential allies. The superintendents were aware that neither tribal war aims nor the Indians' style of fighting was necessarily compatible with those of the British. Accordingly, they sought from the tribes nothing more than a promise of neutrality.

Indians' Grievances

Recognizing that their standing with the tribes was poor, the patriots also sought the Indians' neutrality. In 1775, the Second Continental Congress sent a general message to the tribes describing the war as "a family quarrel between us and Old England" and requesting that they "not join on either side," because "you Indians are not concerned in it." A branch of the Cherokee tribe, led by Chief Dragging Canoe, nevertheless decided that the whites' family quarrel would allow his people to settle some old scores. They attacked white settlements along the western borders of the Carolinas and Virginia in the summer of 1776. But a coordinated campaign by Carolina and Virginia militia destroyed many Cherokee towns, along with crops and large quantities of supplies. Dragging Canoe and his diehard followers fled west to the Tennessee River, where they established new outposts; the rest of the Cherokees agreed to a treaty that ceded more of their land to the whites.

The fate of the Cherokees foreshadowed the history of tribal involvement in the American Revolution. During the eighteenth century, the

Lack of Unity Among Native Americans
———

Iroquois had forcefully established their dominance over neighboring tribes. But the basis of their power started to disintegrate with the British victory over France in 1763, and their subsequent friendship with Sir William Johnson could not prevent the erosion of their position. Tribes long resentful of Iroquois power (or of the similar status of the Cherokees in the South) saw little reason to ally with those whose dominance they had just escaped, even to prevent white encroachment on their lands. Consequently, during the Revolution most tribes pursued a course that aligned them with neither side and kept them out of active involvement in the war.

Thus, although the patriots could never completely ignore the threats posed by loyalists, neutrals, slaves, and Indians, only rarely did fear of these groups seriously hamper the revolutionary movement. Occasionally, militia on the frontier refused to turn out for duty on the seaboard, because they feared Indians would attack in their absence. Sometimes, southern troops refused to serve in the North, because they (and their political leaders) were unwilling to leave the South unprotected against a slave insurrection. But the practical impossibility of a large-scale slave revolt, coupled with tribal feuds and the patriots' successful campaign to

disarm and neutralize loyalists, ensured that the revolutionaries would remain firmly in control as they fought for independence.

WAR BEGINS

On January 27, 1775, Lord Dartmouth, secretary of state for America, addressed a fateful letter to General Gage in Boston. Expressing his belief that American resistance was nothing more than the response of a "rude rabble without plan," Dartmouth ordered Gage to arrest "the principal actors and abettors in the provincial congress." If such a step were taken swiftly and silently, Dartmouth observed, no bloodshed need occur.

Because of poor sailing weather, Dartmouth's letter did not reach Gage until April 14. The main patriot leaders had by then left Boston, and Gage

Battles of Lexington and Concord
———

did not believe that arresting them would serve a useful purpose. The order nevertheless spurred him to action: he decided to send an expedition to confiscate provincial military supplies stockpiled at Concord. Bostonians dispatched two messengers, William Dawes and Paul Revere (later joined by Dr. Samuel Prescott), to rouse the countryside. Thus when the British vanguard of several hundred men approached Lexington at dawn on April 19, they found a ragtag group of seventy militiamen—about half the adult male population of the town—drawn up before them on the town common. The Americans' commander, Captain John Parker, ordered his men to withdraw, realizing they could not halt the redcoat advance. But as they began to disperse, a shot rang out; the British soldiers then fired several volleys. When they stopped, eight Americans lay dead and another ten had been wounded. The British moved on to Concord, five miles away.

The Americans allowed the British to enter Concord unopposed, but later in the morning they attacked the British infantry companies guarding the North Bridge. The brief exchange of gunfire there spilled the first British blood of the Revolution: three men were killed and nine were wounded. On their retreat to Boston, the British were attacked by thousands of militiamen, firing from behind trees, bushes, and houses along the road. By the end of the day, the redcoats had suffered 272 casualties, including 70 deaths. The patriots suffered just 93 casualties.

By the evening of April 20, perhaps as many as twenty thousand American militiamen had gathered around Boston, summoned by local committees that had spread the alarm across the New England countryside. Many did not stay long, because they were needed at home for spring planting, but those who remained dug in along siege lines encircling the city. For nearly a year, the two armies sat and stared at each other across those lines. The redcoats attacked their besiegers only once, on June 17, when they drove the Americans from trenches atop Breed's Hill in Charlestown. In that misnamed Battle of Bunker Hill, the British incurred their greatest losses of the entire war: more than eight hundred wounded and 228 killed. The Americans, though forced to abandon their position, lost less than half that number. During the

same eleven-month period, the patriots captured Fort Ticonderoga, a British fort on Lake Champlain, acquiring much-needed cannon. In the hope of bringing Canada into the war on the American side, they also mounted an uncoordinated northern campaign that ended in disaster at Quebec in early 1776. Most significant, the lull in the fighting at Boston gave both sides a chance to regroup, organize, and plan their strategies.

Lord North and his new American secretary, Lord George Germain, made three central assumptions about the war they faced. First, they concluded that patriot forces could not withstand the assaults of trained British regulars. Accordingly, they dispatched to America the largest force Great Britain had ever assembled anywhere: 370 transport ships carrying 32,000 troops and tons of supplies, accompanied by 73 naval vessels and 13,000 sailors. Such an extraordinary effort would, they thought, ensure a quick victory.

British Strategy
___

In 1775, Ralph Earle, an American artist and militiaman, painted the redcoat troops entering Concord. The fighting at North Bridge, which occurred just a few hours after this triumphal entry, signaled the start of open warfare between Britain and the colonies.   Concord Antiquarian Society.

Second, British officials and army officers treated this war as comparable to wars they had fought successfully in Europe. They adopted a conventional strategy of capturing major American cities and defeating the rebel army decisively without suffering serious casualties themselves. Third, they assumed that a clear-cut military victory would automatically bring about their goal of retaining the colonies' allegiance.

All these assumptions proved false. North and Germain, like Lord Dartmouth before them, vastly underestimated the Americans' commitment to armed resistance. Defeats on the battlefield did not lead the patriots to abandon their political aims and sue for peace. Although the British would control each of the most important American ports at one time or another during the war, less than 5 percent of the population lived in those cities. Furthermore, the coast offered so many excellent harbors that essential commerce was easily rerouted. In other words, the loss of cities did little to damage the American cause, whereas the desire for such ports repeatedly led redcoat generals astray.

Most of all, the British failed at first to understand that a military victory would not necessarily bring about a political victory. Securing the colonies permanently would require hundreds of thousands of Americans to return to their original allegiance. The British thus needed not only to overpower the patriots but also to convert them. After 1778, they adopted a strategy designed to achieve that goal through the expanded use of loyalist forces and the restoration of civilian authority in occupied areas. But the new policy came too late. The British never fully realized that they were not fighting a conventional European war but rather an entirely new kind of conflict: the first modern war of national liberation.

The British at least had a bureaucracy ready to supervise the war effort. The Americans had only the Second Continental Congress, originally

Second Continental Congress
———

intended merely as a brief gathering of colonial representatives to consider the British response to the Continental Association. Instead, the delegates who convened in Philadelphia on May 10, 1775, found that they had to assume the mantle of intercolonial government.

Yet as the summer passed, Congress slowly organized the colonies for war. It authorized the printing of money with which to purchase necessary goods, established a committee to supervise relations with foreign countries, and took steps to strengthen the militia. Most important, it created the Continental Army and appointed its generals.

Until Congress met, the Massachusetts provincial congress had taken responsibility for organizing the massive army of militia encamped at Boston. Because the cost of maintaining that army was too great, Massachusetts asked the Continental Congress to assume the task of directing the army. First, the Congress had to choose a commander in chief. Because the war had thus far been a wholly northern affair, many delegates recognized the importance of naming someone who was not a New Englander. There seemed only one obvious candidate: they unanimously selected their fellow delegate, the Virginian George Washington.

Washington was no fiery radical, nor was he a reflective political thinker. He had not played a prominent role in the prerevolutionary agitation,

George Washington: A Portrait of Leadership
———

but his devotion to the American cause was unquestioned. He was dignified, conservative, and respectable—a man of unimpeachable integrity. Although unmistakably an aristocrat, he was unswervingly committed to representative government, and he had other desirable traits as well. Moreover, he both looked and acted like a leader. Six feet tall in an era when most men were five inches shorter, his presence was stately and commanding. Other patriots praised his judgment, steadiness, and discretion, and even a loyalist acknowledged that Washington could "atone for many demerits by the extraordinary coolness and caution which distinguish his character."

Washington needed all the coolness and caution he could muster when he took command of the army outside Boston in July 1775. It took him months to impose hierarchy and discipline on the unruly troops and to bring order to the supply system. But by March 1776, when the arrival of cannon from Ticonderoga finally enabled him to put direct pressure on the redcoats in the city, the army was prepared to act. As it happened, an assault on Boston proved unnecessary. Sir William Howe, who had replaced Gage, had for some time been considering an evacuation; he wanted to transfer his troops to New York City. The patriots' bombardment of Boston early in the month decided the matter. On March 17, the British and more than a thousand of their loyalist allies abandoned Boston forever.

That spring of 1776, as the British fleet left Boston for the temporary haven of Halifax, Nova Scotia, the colonies were moving inexorably toward the unthinkable—a declaration of independence. Even months after fighting had begun, American leaders still denied seeking a break with the empire. But in January 1776, there appeared a pamphlet by a man who both thought the unthinkable and advocated it.

Thomas Paine's
Common Sense
———

Thomas Paine's *Common Sense* exploded on the American scene like a bombshell. Within three months of publication, it sold 120,000 copies. The author, a radical English printer who had lived in America only since 1774, called stridently and stirringly for independence. As an advocate of a republican form of government, Paine rejected the notion that a balance of monarchy, aristocracy, and democracy was necessary to preserve freedom. Instead of acknowledging the benefits of a connection with England, Paine insisted that Britain had exploited the colonies unmercifully. In place of the frequently heard assertion that an independent America would be weak and divided, he substituted an unlimited confidence in America's strength when freed from European control.

There is no way to know how many people were converted to the cause of independence by reading *Common Sense*. But by late spring 1776, independence had clearly become inevitable. On May 10, the Second Continental Congress formally recommended that individual colonies "adopt such governments as shall, in the opinion of the representatives of the people, best conduce to the happiness and safety of their constituents in particular, and America in general." From that source grew the first state constitutions.

Then, on June 7, came confirmation of the movement toward independence. Richard Henry Lee of Virginia, seconded by John Adams of Massachusetts, introduced the crucial resolution: "that these United Colonies are, and of right ought to be, free and independent States, that they are absolved of all allegiance to the British Crown, and that all political connection between them and the State of Great Britain is, and ought to be, totally dissolved." Congress debated the resolution and directed a committee composed of Thomas Jefferson, John Adams, Benjamin Franklin, Robert R. Livingston of New York, and Roger Sherman of Connecticut to draft a declaration of independence. The committee in turn assigned primary responsibility for writing the declaration to Jefferson, who was well known for his apt and eloquent style.

Thomas Jefferson was at the time thirty-four years old, a Virginia lawyer educated at the College of William and Mary. He had read widely in history and political theory and had been a member of the House of Burgesses. His broad knowledge was evident not only in the declaration but also in his draft of the Virginia state constitution. His beloved wife Martha's repeated difficulties in childbearing marked the early stage of his political career. While he wrote and debated in Philadelphia, she suffered a miscarriage at their home. Not until after her death in 1782, from complications following the birth of their sixth (but only third surviving) child, did Jefferson fully commit himself to public service.

Declaration of
Independence
———

The draft of the declaration was laid before Congress on June 28. The delegates officially voted for independence four days later, then debated the wording of the declaration for two more days, adopting it with some changes on July 4. Because Americans had long ago ceased to see themselves as legitimate subjects of Parliament, the Declaration of Independence concentrated on George III (see the Appendix). That focus also provided an identifiable villain. The document accused the king of attempting to destroy representative government in the colonies and of oppressing Americans through the unjustified use of excessive force.

The declaration's chief long-term importance, however, did not lie in its lengthy catalogue of grievances against George III but rather in its ringing statements of principle that have served ever since as the ideal to which Americans aspire. "We hold these truths to be self-evident: That all men are created equal; that they are endowed by their Creator with certain unalienable rights; that among these are life, liberty and the pursuit of happiness; that, to secure these rights, governments are instituted among men, deriving their just powers from the consent of the governed; that whenever any form of government becomes destructive of these ends, it is the right of the people to alter or to abolish it, and to institute new government." These phrases have echoed through American history like no others.

The delegates in Philadelphia who voted to accept the Declaration of Independence did not have the advantage of two hundred years of hindsight. When they adopted the declaration, they risked their necks: they were committing treason. Thus when they concluded the declaration with the assertion that they "mutually pledge[d] to each other our lives, our fortunes, and our sacred honor," they spoke no less than the truth. The real struggle still lay before them.

THE LONG STRUGGLE IN THE NORTH

In late June 1776, the first of the ships carrying Sir William Howe's troops from Halifax appeared off the coast of New York. On July 2, the day Congress voted for independence, the redcoats landed on Staten Island. But Howe waited until mid-August, after the arrival of more troops from England, to begin his attack on the city. The delay gave Washington sufficient time to march his army south to meet the threat. To defend New York, Washington had approximately seventeen thousand soldiers: ten thousand Continentals who had promised to serve until the end of the year and seven thousand militiamen who had enlisted for shorter terms. Neither he nor most of his men had ever fought a major battle against the British, and their lack of experience led to disastrous mistakes. The difficulty of defending New York City only compounded the errors.

Washington's problem was as simple as the geography of the region was complex (see map). To

Battle for New York City protect the city adequately, he would have to divide his forces among Long Island, Manhattan Island, and the mainland. But the British fleet under Admiral Lord Richard Howe, Sir William's brother, controlled the harbors and rivers that divided the American forces. The patriots thus constantly courted catastrophe, for swift action by the British navy could cut off the possibility of retreat and perhaps even communication. But despite these dangers, Washington could not afford to surrender New York to the Howes without a fight. Not only did the city occupy a strategic location but the region that surrounded it was known to contain many loyalist sympathizers. A show of force was essential if the revolutionaries were to retain any hope of persuading waverers to join them.

On August 27, Sir William Howe's forces attacked the American positions on Brooklyn Heights, pushing the untried rebel troops back to their defensive entrenchments. But Sir William failed to press his advantage, even neglecting to

The War in the North, 1775–1777 *The early phase of the Revolutionary War, as shown in this map, was dominated by British troop movements in the Boston area, the redcoats' evacuation to Nova Scotia in the spring of 1776, and the subsequent British invasion of New York and New Jersey.*

send his brother's ships into the East River to cut off a retreat. Consequently, the Americans were able to escape. Washington moved north on the island, retreating onto the mainland. But the nearly three thousand men left behind to defend the supposedly impregnable Fort Washington on the west shore of Manhattan had to surrender to Howe in early November.

Washington had defended New York but badly. He had repeatedly broken a basic rule of military tactics: never divide your force in the face of a superior enemy. In the end, though, the Howe brothers' failure to move quickly prevented a decisive defeat of the Americans. Although Washington's army had been seriously reduced by casualties, by the surrender of Fort Washington, and by the loss of most militiamen (who had returned home for the harvest), its core remained. Through November and December, Washington led his men in a retreat across New Jersey. Howe followed at a leisurely pace, setting up a string of outposts manned mostly by Hessian mercenaries. After Washington crossed the Delaware River into Pennsylvania, the British commander turned back and settled into comfortable winter quarters in New York City.

The British controlled most of New Jersey, and hundreds of Americans there accepted the pardons offered by the Howes. Occupying troops met little opposition, and the revolutionary cause appeared to be in disarray. "These are the times that try men's souls," wrote Thomas Paine in his pamphlet *The Crisis.*

In the aftermath of battle, as at its height, the British generals again let their advantage slip away. The redcoats stationed in New Jersey went on a rampage of rape and plunder. Because loyalists and patriots were indistinguishable to the British and Hessian troops, families on both sides suffered nearly equally. The troops seized the livestock, crops, and firewood they needed. They looted and burned houses and desecrated churches and public buildings. But nothing was better calculated to rally doubtful Americans to the cause than the wanton slaying of innocent civilians and the rape of women.

The soldiers' marauding alienated potentially loyal New Jerseyites and Pennsylvanians whose allegiance the British could ill afford to lose. It also

Battle of Trenton

spurred Washington's determination to strike back. The enlistments of most Continental troops were to expire on December 31, and Washington wanted to take advantage of short-term Pennsylvania militiamen who had recently joined him. Moving quickly, he attacked the Hessian encampment at Trenton early in the morning of December 26, while the redcoats were still reeling from their Christmas celebration. The patriots captured more than nine hundred Hessians and killed another thirty; only three Americans were wounded. A few days later, after persuading many men to stay beyond the term of their enlistments, Washington attacked again at Princeton. Having gained command of the field and buoyed American spirits with the two swift victories, Washington set up winter quarters at Morristown, New Jersey.

The campaign of 1776 established patterns that were to persist throughout much of the war, despite changes in British leadership and strategy. The British forces were usually more numerous and often better led than the Americans. But their ponderous style of maneuvering, lack of familiarity with the terrain, and inability to live off the land without antagonizing the populace partially offset those advantages. Furthermore, although Washington always seemed to lack regular troops—the Continental Army never numbered more than 18,500 men—he could usually count on the militia to join him at crucial times. American militiamen did not like to sign up for long terms of service or to fight far from home, but when their homes were threatened they rallied to the cause.

As the war dragged on, the Continental Army and the militia took on decidedly different characters. State governments, responsible for filling military quotas, found that most

The American Army

men willing to enlist for long periods in the regular army were young, single, and footloose. Farmers with families tended to prefer short-term militia duty. As the supply of whites willing to sign up with the Continentals diminished, recruiters in the northern states turned increasingly to African-Americans, both slave and free. Perhaps as many as five thousand blacks eventually served in the revolutionary army, and most won their freedom as a result. Also attached to the American forces were a number of women, who were the wives and widows of poor soldiers. Such camp followers worked as cooks, nurses, and launderers in return for rations and low wages. The American army was unwieldy and difficult to manage, yet the shapelessness provided an almost unlimited reservoir of manpower and womanpower.

The officers of the Continental Army developed an intense sense of pride and commitment to the revolutionary cause. The hardships they endured, the battles they fought, the difficulties they overcame all helped to forge an esprit de corps that was to outlast the war. The realities of warfare were often dirty, messy, and corrupt, but the officers drew strength from a developing image of themselves as professionals who sacrificed personal gain for the good of the entire nation.

In 1777, the chief British effort was planned by the flashy "Gentleman Johnny" Burgoyne, a playboy general and subordinate of William Howe, who had gained the ear of Lord George Germain. Burgoyne convinced Germain that he could lead an invading force of redcoats and Indians down the Hudson River from Canada, cutting off New England from the rest of the states. He proposed to rendezvous near Albany with a similar force that would move east from Niagara along the Mohawk River valley. The combined forces would then presumably link up with Sir William Howe's troops in New York City.

That Burgoyne's scheme would give "Gentleman Johnny" all the glory and relegate Howe to a supporting role did not escape Sir William's notice. While Burgoyne was plotting in London, Howe was laying his own plans to take Philadelphia. Just as Burgoyne left Howe out of his plans, Howe left Burgoyne out of his. Thus the two major British armies in America would operate independently in 1777, and the result would be a disaster.

Howe accomplished his objective: he captured Philadelphia. But he did so in an inexplicable way, delaying for months before beginning the campaign,

Howe Takes Philadelphia

then taking six weeks to transport his troops by sea to the head of Chesapeake Bay instead of marching them overland.

That maneuver cost him at least a month, debilitated his men, and depleted his supplies. Incredibly, at the end of the lengthy voyage, he was only forty miles closer to Philadelphia than when he started. By the time Howe was ready to move on Philadelphia, Washington had had time to prepare its defenses. Twice, at Brandywine Creek and again at Germantown, the two armies clashed near the patriot capital. Although the British won both engagements, the Americans handled themselves well. The redcoats took Philadelphia in late September but to little effect. The campaign season was nearly over, and far to the north, Burgoyne was going down to defeat.

Burgoyne and his men set out from Montreal in mid-June 1777, floating down Lake Champlain into New York in canoes and flatbottom boats.

Burgoyne's Campaign in New York

They easily took Fort Ticonderoga from its outnumbered and outgunned patriot defenders. Trouble began, however, as Burgoyne began his overland march. Because his clumsy artillery carriages and baggage wagons foundered in the heavy forests and ravines, Burgoyne's troops took twenty-four days to travel the twenty-three miles to Fort Edward, on the Hudson River. Short of supplies, the general dispatched eight hundred German mercenaries to forage the countryside. On August 16, American militia companies nearly wiped out the Germans near Bennington. Yet Burgoyne failed to recognize the seriousness of his predicament and continued to dawdle. By the time he finally crossed the Hudson in mid-September, bound for Albany, Burgoyne's fate was sealed. After several bloody clashes with the American force commanded by General Horatio Gates, Burgoyne was surrounded near Saratoga, New York. On October 17, 1777, he surrendered his entire force of more than six thousand men.

Two months before, the fourteen hundred redcoats and Indians marching along the Mohawk River from Niagara toward Albany had also been turned back. After they had laid siege to the isolated American outpost at Fort Stanwix in early August, they learned that a patriot relief column was en route. Leaving only a small detachment at Fort Stanwix, the British under Colonel Barry St. Leger ambushed and defeated the Americans at Oriskany on August 6. But they and their tribal allies abandoned the siege of Fort Stanwix in late August after the Americans tricked them into believing that another large patriot force was on the way.

The Battle of Oriskany revealed a split in the Iroquois Confederacy. In 1776, the Six Nations had formally pledged to remain neutral in the Anglo-American struggle. But two influential Mohawk leaders, Joseph Brant and Mary Brant, worked tirelessly to persuade the Iroquois to join the British.

Split of the Iroquois Confederacy

Mary Brant, a powerful tribal matron, was also the widow of the Indian superintendent Sir William Johnson. Her younger brother Joseph, a renowned warrior, was convinced that the Six Nations should ally with the British to prevent American encroachment on tribal lands. The Brants won over to the British the Senecas, Cayugas, and Mohawks, all of whom contributed warriors to St. Leger's expedition. But the Oneidas preferred the American side, bringing the Tuscaroras with them. The Onondagas split into three factions, one on each side and one supporting neutrality. At Oriskany, the three-hundred-year league of friendship was torn apart as confederation warriors fought on both sides.

The collapse of Iroquois unity and the confederacy's abandonment of neutrality had important consequences. In 1778, Iroquois warriors allied with the British raided the frontier villages of Wyoming, Pennsylvania, and Cherry Valley, New York. To retaliate, the Americans dispatched an expedition under General John Sullivan the following summer to burn Iroquois crops, orchards, and settlements. The destruction was so thorough that many bands had to leave their ancestral homeland to seek food and shelter with the British north of the Great Lakes. A large number of Iroquois people never returned to New York but settled permanently in British Canada.

The news of Burgoyne's surrender at Saratoga brought joy to patriots, discouragement to loyalists and Britons. The disaster prompted Lord North to authorize a peace commission to offer the Americans everything they had requested in 1774—in effect, a return to the imperial system of 1763. It was, of course, far too late for that: the patriots rejected the

Joseph Brant, the Iroquois leader who helped to persuade the Mohawks, Senecas, and Cayugas to support the British in the latter stages of the Revolution, as painted by Charles Willson Peale in 1797.   Independence National Historic Park Collection.

overture, and the peace commission sailed back to England empty handed in mid-1778.

Most important, the American victory at Saratoga drew France formally into the conflict. Ever since 1763, the French had sought to avenge their defeat in the Seven Years' War, and the American Revolution gave them that opportunity. Even before Benjamin Franklin arrived in Paris in late 1776, France was covertly supplying the revolutionaries with military necessities.

Franklin worked tirelessly to strengthen ties between the two nations. By presenting himself as a representative of American simplicity, he played on the French image of Americans as virtuous yeomen. Franklin's effort culminated in 1778 when the countries signed two treaties. In the Treaty of Amity and Commerce, France recognized American independence and established trade ties with the new nation; the second treaty instituted a formal alliance between

Franco-American Alliance of 1778

the two nations. In this Treaty of Alliance, France and the United States promised—assuming that France would go to war with Britain, which it soon did—that neither would negotiate peace with the enemy without consulting the other. France also abandoned all its claims to Canada and to North American territory east of the Mississippi River.

The French alliance had two major benefits for the patriot cause. First, France began to aid the Americans openly, sending troops and naval vessels in addition to arms, ammunition, clothing, and blankets. Second, the British could no longer concentrate their attention on the American mainland alone, for they had to fight the French in the West Indies and elsewhere. Spain's entry into the war in 1779 as an ally of France (but not of the United States) further magnified Britain's problems, for the Revolution then became a global war.

THE LONG STRUGGLE IN THE SOUTH

In the aftermath of the Saratoga disaster, Lord George Germain and the military officials in London reassessed their strategy. Maneuvering in the North had done them little good; perhaps shifting the field of battle southward would bring success. The new British commander in chief, Sir Henry Clinton, became convinced that a southern strategy would work. In late 1779, he sailed down the coast from New York with eighty-five hundred troops to attack Charleston, the most important city in the South (see map).

The Americans worked hard to bolster Charleston's defenses, but the city fell to the British on May 12, 1780. General Benjamin

Fall of Charleston

Lincoln surrendered the entire southern army—fifty-five hundred men—to the invaders. The redcoats then spread throughout South Carolina. As hundreds of South Carolinians proclaimed their loyalty to the Crown, Clinton organized loyalist regiments.

Yet the British triumph was less complete than it appeared. The success of the southern campaign

Campaign of 1777   *The crucial campaign of 1777 was fought on two fronts: along the upper Hudson and Mohawk River valleys, and in the vicinity of Philadelphia. The rebels won in the north, the British triumphed—at least nominally—in the south, but the capture of Philadelphia did the redcoats little good.*

depended on British control of the seas, for only by sea could the widely dispersed British armies remain in communication with one another. For the moment, the Royal Navy safely dominated the American coastline, but French naval power posed a threat to the entire southern enterprise. Moreover, the redcoats never managed to establish full control of the areas they seized. Patriot bands operated freely throughout the state, and loyalists could not be guaranteed protection against their enemies. Last but not least, the fall of Charleston did not dishearten the patriots; instead, it spurred them to greater exertions.

Nevertheless, the war in South Carolina went badly for the patriots throughout most of 1780. In August, a reorganized southern army under Horatio Gates was crushingly defeated at Camden by the forces of Lord Cornwallis, the new commander of British forces in the South. The redcoats were joined wherever they went by enslaved African-Americans seeking freedom on the basis of Lord Dunmore's proclamation. They had run away from their patriot masters in such numbers that they seriously disrupted planting and harvesting in 1780 and 1781. More than fifty-five thousand slaves were lost to their owners as a result of the war. Not all joined the British or won their freedom if they did, but their flight had exactly the effect Dunmore wanted.

After the defeat at Camden, Washington appointed General Nathanael Greene of Rhode Island to command the southern campaign. Greene adopted a conciliatory policy

Greene Rallies South Carolina
—

toward loyalists and neutrals, persuading the governor of South Carolina to offer complete pardons to those who had fought for the British if they would join the patriot militia. He also ordered his troops not to loot loyalist property and to treat captives fairly. Greene recognized that the patriots could win only by convincing the populace that they could bring stability to the region. He thus helped the shattered provincial congresses of Georgia and South Carolina to begin reestablishing civilian authority in the interior.

Greene also took a conciliatory approach to the southern tribes. With his desperate need for soldiers, he could not afford to have frontier militia companies occupied in defending their homes against Indian attacks. Because he had so few regulars (only sixteen hundred when he took command), Greene had to rely on western volunteers. Therefore, he negotiated with the tribes. By the end of the war, only the Creeks remained British allies.

Even before Greene took command of the southern army in December 1780, the tide had begun to turn. In October, at King's Mountain, near the border between the Carolinas, a force from the settlements west of the Appalachians defeated a large party of redcoats and loyalists. Then, in

January 1781, Greene's trusted aide Brigadier General Daniel Morgan brilliantly defeated the crack British regiment Tarleton's Legion at Cowpens, not far from King's Mountain. Greene himself confronted the main body of British troops under Lord Cornwallis at Guilford Court House, North Carolina, in March. Although Cornwallis controlled the field at the end of the day, most of his army had been destroyed. He had to retreat to the coast to receive supplies and fresh troops from New York.

Cornwallis had already ignored explicit orders not to leave South Carolina unless the state was safely in British hands. He headed north into Virginia, where he joined

Surrender at Yorktown
—

forces with a detachment of redcoats commanded by the American traitor Benedict Arnold. Instead of acting decisively with his new army of seventy-two hundred men, Cornwallis withdrew to the edge of the peninsula between the York and James Rivers, where he fortified Yorktown and in effect waited for the end. Seizing the opportunity, Washington quickly moved more than seven thousand troops south from New York City. When a French fleet under the Comte de Grasse arrived from the West Indies in time to defeat the Royal Navy vessels sent to rescue Cornwallis, the British general was trapped. On October 19, 1781, Cornwallis surrendered to the combined American and French forces.

When news of the surrender reached England, Lord North's ministry fell. Parliament voted to cease offensive operations in America and authorized peace negotiations. But guerrilla warfare between patriots and loyalists continued to ravage the Carolinas and Georgia for more than a year, and in the North vicious retaliatory raids by Indians and whites kept the frontier aflame. The persistence of conflict between frontier militia and Indians after the Battle of Yorktown, all too often overlooked in accounts of the Revolution, serves to underline the degree to which the Native Americans were the real losers in the war initiated by the colonists.

The fighting finally ended when Americans and Britons learned of the signing of a preliminary peace treaty at Paris in November 1782. The American

How do historians know

that Americans had only incomplete knowledge of the boundaries of their new nation? One way is to consult their written documents, another is to look at their early maps, like this one, "A New and Correct Map of the United States of North America," produced in 1784. New it certainly was, but correct it was not. A comparison with a standard map of the United States and Canada today shows many errors of scale, proportion, and placement of natural features. To point out just a few: the Ohio River is shown much too far south, the northern part of the Mississippi River is misplaced to the west, Lake Superior is too small and its islands too large, and the Nova Scotia peninsula is misshapen. What links all these features is that they were on the periphery of the new nation and thus on the margins of Americans' knowledge. But even so well known a waterway as Chesapeake Bay is inaccurately drawn, suggesting that residents of the United States still had much to learn about the geography of their country.   Photo: New Jersey Historical Society.

Treaty of Paris diplomats—Benjamin Franklin, John Jay, and John Adams—ignored their instructions from Congress to be guided by France and instead negotiated directly with Great Britain. Their instincts were sound: the French government was more an enemy to Britain than a friend to the United States. In fact, French ministers worked secretly behind the scenes to try to prevent the establishment of a strong and unified government in America. But the American delegates proved adept at playing the game of power politics and achieved their main goal: independence as a united nation. The new British ministry, headed by Lord Shelburne, was weary of war and made numerous concessions.

Under the Treaty of Paris, signed formally on September 3, 1783, the Americans were granted unconditional independence. The boundaries of the new nation were generous: to the north, approximately the present-day boundary with Canada; to the south, the thirty-first parallel (roughly the modern northern border of Florida); to the west, the Mississippi River. Florida, which the British had acquired in 1763, was returned to Spain. The Americans also gained unlimited fishing rights off Newfoundland. In ceding so much land to the United States, the British entirely ignored the territorial rights of their tribal allies. Once again, the tribes' interests were sacrificed to the demands of European power politics. Loyalists and British merchants were also poorly served by the British negotiators. The treaty's ambiguously worded clauses pertaining to the payment of prewar debts and the postwar treatment of loyalists caused trouble for years to come and proved impossible to enforce.

The long war finally over, the victorious Americans could look back on their achievement with satisfaction and awe. In 1775, with an inexperienced ragtag army, they had taken on the greatest military power in the world—and eight years later, they had won. They had accomplished their goal more through persistence and commitment than through brilliance on the battlefield. Actual victories had been few, but their army had always survived defeats and stand-offs to fight again. Ultimately, the Americans had simply worn their enemy down.

In the course of winning the war, the Americans had reshaped the landscapes in which they lived, both physically and mentally. They had abandoned the British identity that once had been important to them and had begun the process of creating loyalty to a new nation. They had also established a claim to most of the territory east of the Mississippi River and south of the Great Lakes, thereby greatly expanding the land potentially open to their settlements.

In achieving independence, Americans had surmounted formidable challenges. But they faced perhaps even greater ones: establishing stable republican governments at the state and national levels to replace the monarchy they had rejected and ensuring their governments' continued existence in a world of bitter rivalries among the major powers—England, France, and Spain. Those European rivalries had worked to the Americans' advantage during the war, but in the decades to come, they would pose significant threats to the survival of the new nation.

SUGGESTIONS FOR FURTHER READING

General

Colin Bonwick, *The American Revolution* (1991); Edward Countryman, *The American Revolution* (1985); Robert Middlekauff, *The Glorious Cause: The American Revolution, 1763–1783* (1982); Edmund S. Morgan, *The Challenge of the American Revolution* (1976).

Military

Jeremy Black, *War for America: The Fight for Independence, 1775–1783* (1991); Don Higginbotham, *The War of American Independence: Military Attitudes, Policies, and Practice, 1763–1789* (1971); Charles Royster, *A Revolutionary People at War: The Continental Army and American Character, 1775–1783* (1980); John Shy, *A People Numerous and Armed: Reflections on the Military Struggle for American Independence* (1976).

Local and Regional

Richard Buel, *Dear Liberty: Connecticut's Mobilization for the Revolutionary War* (1980); Edward Countryman, *A People in Revolution: The American Revolution and Political Society in New York, 1760–1790* (1981); Jeffrey Crow and Larry Tise, eds., *The Southern Experience in the American Revolution* (1978); Robert A.

Gross, *The Minutemen and Their World* (1976); Stephen Rosswurm, *Arms, Country, and Class: The Philadelphia Militia and the "Lower Sort" During the American Revolution* (1988).

Indians and African-Americans

Sylvia Frey, *Water from the Rock: Black Resistance in a Revolutionary Age* (1991); Barbara Graymont, *The Iroquois in the American Revolution* (1972); Isabel T. Kelsey, *Joseph Brant, 1743–1807: Man of Two Worlds* (1984); James H. O'Donnell III, *Southern Indians in the American Revolution* (1973); Benjamin Quarles, *The Negro in the American Revolution* (1961); Daniel K. Richter, *The Ordeal of the Longhouse* (1992).

Loyalists

Bernard Bailyn, *The Ordeal of Thomas Hutchinson* (1974); Robert McCluer Calhoon, *The Loyalists in Revolutionary America, 1760–1781* (1973); Mary Beth Norton, *The British-Americans: The Loyalist Exiles in England, 1774–1789* (1972); James W. St. G. Walker, *The Black Loyalists: The Search for a Promised Land in Nova Scotia and Sierra Leone, 1783–1870* (1976).

Women

Richard Buel and Joy Buel, *The Way of Duty: A Woman and Her Family in Revolutionary America* (1984); Linda K. Kerber, *Women of the Republic: Intellect and Ideology in Revolutionary America* (1980); Mary Beth Norton, *Liberty's Daughters: The Revolutionary Experience of American Women, 1750–1800* (1980).

Foreign Policy

Jonathan Dull, *A Diplomatic History of the American Revolution* (1985); Richard B. Morris, *The Peacemakers: The Great Powers and American Independence* (1965); Richard W. Van Alstyne, *Empire and Independence: The International History of the American Revolution* (1965).

Patriot Leaders

Verner W. Crane, *Benjamin Franklin and a Rising People* (1954); Marcus Cunliffe, *George Washington: Man and Monument* (1958); Noble Cunningham, *In Pursuit of Reason: The Life of Thomas Jefferson* (1987); Eric Foner, *Tom Paine and Revolutionary America* (1976).

Forging a National Republic, 1776–1789

O N JANUARY 25, 1787, an army of fifteen hundred farmers from the hills and valleys of western Massachusetts advanced on the federal armory at Springfield. Inside the arsenal, General William Shepard prepared his group of one thousand militiamen to resist the assault. First, though, he dispatched two aides to warn the farmers that they would soon "inevitably" draw the fire of men who had been their officers during the Revolutionary War. "That is all we want, by God!" replied one rebel. The farmers moved toward the armory, urged on by the commands of Daniel Shays, one of their leaders. Shepard fired two cannons over the heads of the farmers, and then—when that did not frighten them—ordered his men to shoot directly at the straggling ranks. Four men died, twenty were wounded, and the rebels withdrew from the field.

What caused this violent clash between former comrades in arms? The Massachusetts farmers were angered by high taxes and the scarcity of money. Since the preceding summer, they had organized committees and crowd actions—the tactics used so successfully in the 1760s and early 1770s—to halt state efforts to seize property for nonpayment of taxes. Many insurgents were respected war veterans. Daniel Shays, their nominal leader, had been a captain in the Continental Army. Clearly, the episode could not be dismissed as the work of an unruly rabble. What did the uprising mean for the future of the republic? Was it a sign of impending anarchy?

The protesters explained their position in an address to the governor and council of Massachusetts. They proclaimed their loyalty to the nation but objected to the state's fiscal policies, which, they said, prevented them from providing adequately for their families. One rebel sympathizer explained, "Whenever any encroachments are made either upon the liberties or properties of the people, if redress cannot be had without, it is virtue in them to disturb government." The Massachusetts government was "tyrannical," Shays asserted and, like that of Great Britain, deserved to be overthrown.

To the state's elected leaders, the most ominous aspect of the uprising was the rebels' attempt to forge direct links with the earlier struggle for independence. The state legislature issued an address to the people asserting that "in a republican government the majority must govern. If the minor part governs it becomes aristocracy; if every one opposed at his pleasure, it is no government, it is anarchy and confusion." Thus Massachusetts officials insisted that the crowd actions that had once been a justifiable response to British tyranny were no longer legitimate. In a republic, reform had to come about through the ballot box rather than by force.

The confrontation at the Springfield armory symbolized for many Americans the trials facing the new nation. That the rebels were dispersed easily, that their leaders (including Shays) had to flee to neighboring states for asylum, that two insurgents were hanged, and that a newly elected Massachusetts legislature adopted conciliatory measures—none of these outcomes altered American political leaders' interpretation of the events in western Massachusetts. In Shays' Rebellion they thought they discerned the first signs of disintegration of the republic they had worked so hard to establish.

Republicanism—the idea that governments should be based wholly on the consent of the people—originated with political theorists in ancient Greece and Rome. Republics, such writers declared, were desirable yet fragile forms of government. Unless their citizens were especially virtuous—that is, sober, moral, and industrious—and largely in agreement on key issues, republics were doomed to failure. When Americans left the British Empire, they committed to republicanism. Now they had to deal with the potentially unwelcome consequences of that decision. How could they best ensure political stability? How could they create a virtuous republic?

America's leaders worked hard to inculcate virtue in their countrymen and countrywomen. After 1776, American literature, theater, art, architecture, and education all pursued explicitly moral goals. The education of women was considered particularly important, for as the mothers of the Republic's children, they were primarily responsible for ensuring the nation's future. On such matters Americans could agree, but they disagreed on many other critical issues. Almost all white men

concurred that women, Indians, and African-Americans should be excluded from formal participation in politics, but they found it difficult to reach a consensus on how many of their own number should be included. And when should men's consent be sought: semiannually? annually? at intervals of two or more years? Further, how should governments be structured so as to reflect the people's consent most accurately?

Republican citizens had to answer many other questions as well. Should a republic conduct its dealings with Indian tribes and foreign countries any differently than other types of governments did? Were republics, in other words, obliged to negotiate fairly and honestly at all times? And how could white republicans reconcile the conflict between slavery and Jefferson's words in the Declaration of Independence: "all men are created equal." Some answered that question by freeing their slaves; others denied that blacks were *men* in the same sense as whites.

The most important task facing Americans in these years was the construction of a genuinely national government. Before 1765, the English mainland colonies had rarely cooperated on common endeavors. Many circumstances separated them: their diverse economies, varying religious traditions and ethnic compositions, competing land claims (especially in the West), and different political systems. But fighting the Revolutionary War brought them together and created a new nationalistic spirit. Wartime experiences broke down at least some boundaries that had previously divided Americans, replacing loyalties to state and region with loyalties to the nation.

Still, forging a national republic was neither easy nor simple. America's first such government, the Articles of Confederation, proved inadequate. But some of the nation's political leaders learned from their experiences and tried another approach when they drafted the Constitution in 1787. Some historians have argued that the Articles of Confederation and the Constitution reflect opposing political philosophies, the Constitution representing an aristocratic counterrevolution against the democratic Articles. The two documents are more accurately

• *Important Events* •

1776	Second Continental Congress directs states to draft constitutions	**1787**	Constitutional Convention drafts new form of government
1777	Articles of Confederation sent to states for ratification	**1788**	Hamilton, Jay, and Madison write *The Federalist* to urge ratification of the Constitution
1781	Articles of Confederation ratified		Constitution ratified
1784–87	Northwest Ordinances organize territory north of Ohio River and east of Mississippi River	**1794**	Defeat of Miami Confederacy at Fallen Timbers
1786	Annapolis Convention meets, discusses reforming government	**1795**	Treaty of Greenville opens Ohio to white settlement
1786–87	Shays' Rebellion in western Massachusetts raises questions about future of the Republic	**1800**	Mason Locke Weems publishes his *Life of Washington*

viewed as successive attempts to solve the same problems. Both applied theories of republicanism to practical problems of governance; neither was entirely successful in resolving those difficulties.

CREATING A VIRTUOUS REPUBLIC

When the colonies declared their independence from Great Britain, John Dickinson recalled many years later, "There was no question concerning forms of Government, no enquiry whether a Republic or a limited Monarchy was best. . . . We knew that the people of this country must unite themselves under some form of Government and that this could be no other than the republican form." But how should that goal be implemented?

Three different definitions of *republicanism* emerged in the new United States. The first, held chiefly by members of the educated elite, was based directly on ancient history and political theory. The histories of popular governments in Greece and Rome seemed to prove that

Varieties of Republicanism

republics could succeed only if they were small in size and homogeneous in population. Unless the citizens of a republic were willing to sacrifice their own private interests for the good of the whole, the government would inevitably collapse. In return for sacrifices, though, a republic offered its citizens equality of opportunity. Under such a government, society would be governed by a "natural aristocracy" of men whose rank would be based on merit rather than inherited wealth and status.

A second definition, advanced by other members of the elite but also by some skilled craftsmen, drew more on economic theory than political thought. Instead of perceiving the nation as an organic whole composed of people nobly sacrificing for the common good, this version of republicanism followed the English theorist Adam Smith in emphasizing individuals' pursuit of rational self-interest. When republican men sought to improve their economic and social circumstances, the entire nation would benefit. Republican virtue would be achieved through the pursuit of private interests rather than through their subordination to some communal ideal.

The third notion of republicanism was more egalitarian than the other two, both of which contained considerable potential for inequality. This view was less influential, because many of its proponents were illiterate or barely literate and thus wrote little to promote their beliefs. Americans who advanced this version of republicanism, the most prominent of whom was Thomas Paine, called for widening men's participation in the political process. They also wanted government to respond directly to the needs of ordinary folk and openly rejected any notion that the lesser sort should automatically defer to their betters. They were, in fact, democrats in more or less the modern sense.

It is important to recognize that the three strands of republicanism were part of a unified whole and shared many of the same assumptions. For example, all three contrasted a virtuous, industrious America to the corruption of England and Europe. In the first version, that virtue manifested itself in frugality and self-sacrifice; in the second, it would prevent self-interest from becoming vice; in the third, it was the justification for including even propertyless white men in the ranks of voters.

As the citizens of the United States set out to construct their republic, they believed they were embarking on an unprecedented enterprise. With great pride in their new nation, they expected to replace the vices of monarchial Europe with the sober virtues of republican America. They wanted to embody republican principles not only in their governments but also in their society and their culture. They looked to painting, literature, drama, and architecture to convey messages of nationalism and virtue to the public.

Virtue and the Arts

Americans faced a crucial contradiction at the outset of their efforts. To some republicans, the fine arts were manifestations of vice. What need did a frugal yeoman have for a painting or—worse yet—a novel? Why should anyone spend hard-earned wages to see a play in a lavishly decorated theater? The first American artists, playwrights, and authors thus confronted an impossible dilemma. They wanted to produce works embodying virtue, but many viewed those very works, regardless of their content, as corrupting.

Still, they tried. William Hill Brown's *The Power of Sympathy* (1789), the first novel written in the United States, was a lurid tale of seduction intended as a warning to young women, who made up a large proportion of America's fiction readers. In Royall Tyler's *The Contrast* (1787), the first successful American play, the virtuous conduct of Colonel Manly was contrasted (hence the title) with the reprehensible behavior of the fop Billy Dimple. The most popular book of the era, Mason Locke Weems's *Life of Washington*, published in 1800 shortly after George Washington's death, was intended by its author to "hold up his great Virtues . . . to the imitation of Our Youth."

Painting and architecture, too, were expected to embody high moral standards. Two of the most prominent artists of the period, Gilbert Stuart and Charles Willson Peale, painted innumerable portraits of upstanding republican citizens. John Trumbull's vast canvases depicted such milestones of American history as the Battle of Bunker Hill and Cornwallis's capitulation at Yorktown. Both portraits and historical scenes were intended to instill patriotic sentiments in their viewers. Architects likewise hoped to convey in their buildings a sense of the young Republic's ideals. When the Virginia government asked Thomas Jefferson, then ambassador to France, for advice on the design of the state capitol in Richmond, Jefferson unhesitatingly recommended copying a Roman building. "It is very simple," he explained, "but it is noble beyond expression." Jefferson set forth ideals that would guide American architecture for a generation to come: simplicity of line, harmonious proportions, a feeling of grandeur. Nowhere were these rational goals of republican art manifested more clearly than in Benjamin H. Latrobe's plans for the majestic domed United States Capitol in Washington, D.C., built in the early 1800s.

Despite the artists' efforts (or, some would have said, because of them), some Americans were beginning to detect signs of luxury and corruption by the mid-1780s. The end of the war and resumption of European trade brought a return to fashionable clothing for both men and women and abandonment of the simpler homespun garments patriots had once worn with pride. Elite families again attended balls

How do historians know

that American women were reading novels after the American Revolution? Modern best-seller lists and readers' surveys did not exist in late eighteenth-century America, so historians have to look to other sources to find the answer. Many types of evidence suggest the popularity of novels among a wide audience of females in the 1780s and 1790s. Women who kept diaries often took note of the titles of books they were reading; others mentioned novels in their letters to friends. Ministers preached sermons decrying young women's addiction to reading novels, and authors of advice books urged readers to turn their attention to more uplifting forms of literature. Perhaps most important is the evidence of the books themselves, like The Power of Sympathy, *the first novel written in the United States. After the Revolution, the new nation's printers published a myriad of British and American novels, finding in them a ready source of profit. Historians studying the phenomenon of novel-reading have linked it to women's increasing literacy and the availability of leisure time for reading, as well as to the useful messages about life's pitfalls and prospects the novels conveyed to their young readers.* Photo: American Antiquarian Society.

and concerts. Parties no longer seemed complete without gambling and card playing. Especially alarming to fervent republicans was the establishment in 1783 of the Society of the Cincinnati, a hereditary organization of Revolutionary War officers and their descendants. Many feared that the group would become the nucleus of a native-born aristocracy. All these developments directly challenged America's self-image as a virtuous republic.

Their deep-seated concern for the future of the infant Republic focused Americans' attention on their children, the "rising generation." Throughout

Educational Reform
___

the history of the colonies, education had been seen chiefly as a private means to personal advancement, of concern only to individual families. Now, though, education would serve a public purpose. If young people were to resist the temptations of vice, they would have to learn the lessons of virtue at home and at school. In fact, the survival of the nation depended on it. The early republican period was thus a time of major educational reform.

The 1780s and 1790s brought two significant changes in American educational practice. First, in contrast to the colonies, where nearly all education had been privately financed, some northern states began to be willing to use tax money to support public elementary schools. In 1789, Massachusetts became one of the first states to require towns to offer their citizens free public elementary education.

Second, schooling for girls was improved. Americans' recognition of the importance of the rising generation led to the realization that mothers would have to be properly educated if they were to instruct their children adequately. Therefore, Massachusetts insisted in its 1789 law that town elementary schools be open to girls as well as boys. Throughout the United States, private academies were founded to give teenage girls from well-to-do families an opportunity for advanced schooling. No one yet proposed opening colleges to women, but a few fortunate girls could study history, geography, rhetoric, and mathematics.

The chief theorist of women's education in the early Republic was Judith Sargent Murray of Gloucester, Massachusetts. In a series of essays

Judith Sargent Murray on Education
___

published in the 1780s and 1790s, Murray argued that women and men had equal intellectual capacities. Therefore, concluded Murray, boys and girls should be offered equivalent scholastic training. She further contended that girls should be taught to support themselves by their own efforts.

Murray's direct challenge to the traditional colonial belief that, as one man put it, girls "knew quite enough if they could make a shirt and a pudding" was part of a general rethinking of women's position

that occurred as a result of the Revolution. Male patriots who enlisted in the army or served in Congress were away from home for long periods of time. In their absence, their wives, who had previously handled only the indoor affairs of the household, shouldered the responsibility for outdoor affairs as well. This shift in responsibilities caused subtle but significant changes. John and Abigail Adams, for example, took great pride in Abigail's developing skills as a "farmeress." And like her female contemporaries, Abigail Adams stopped calling the farm "yours" in letters to her husband and began referring to it as "ours"— a revealing change of pronoun. Both men and women realized that female patriots had made a vital contribution to winning the war and that notions of proper gender roles had to be rethought. Americans began to develop new ideas about the role women should play in a republican society.

The best-known example of those new ideas is a letter Abigail Adams addressed to her husband in March 1776. "In the new Code of Laws which I

Abigail Adams: "Remember the Ladies"
___

suppose it will be necessary for you to make I desire you would Remember the Ladies," she wrote. "If perticuliar care and attention is not paid to the Laidies we are determined to foment a Rebelion, and will not hold ourselves bound by any Laws in which we have no voice, or Representation." With these words, Abigail Adams took a step that was soon to be duplicated by other disfranchised Americans. She deliberately applied the ideology developed to combat parliamentary supremacy to purposes white male leaders had never intended. For example, she called for reformation of the American law of marriage, which made wives subordinate to their husbands.

Abigail Adams did not ask that women be allowed to vote. But other women wanted to claim that right, as events in New Jersey proved. The men who drafted the state constitution in 1776 defined voters carelessly as "all free inhabitants" who met certain property qualifications. They thereby unintentionally gave the vote to property-holding white spinsters and widows, as well as to free blacks. Qualified women and African-Americans regularly voted in New Jersey's local and congressional elections until 1807, when they were disfranchised by the state legislature, which spuriously claimed that their votes could be manipulated too easily. Yet the fact that they had voted at all was evidence of their altered perception of their place in political life.

Such dramatic episodes were unusual. After the war, Americans still assumed that women's place was in the home and that their primary function

Women's Role in the Republic
___

was to be good wives and mothers. They perceived significant differences between male and female characters; that distinction eventually enabled Americans to resolve the conflict between the two most influential strands of republican thought. Because married women could not own property or participate directly in economic life, women in general came to be seen as the embodiment of self-sacrificing, disinterested republicanism. Through female-run charitable and other social welfare groups, they assumed responsibility for the welfare of the community as a whole. Yet because such public-spirited women worked chiefly with mothers and children in familial settings, women continued to be seen as private beings. Thus men were freed from the naggings of conscience as they pursued their economic self-interest (that other republican virtue), secure in the knowledge that their wives and daughters were fulfilling the family's obligation to the common good. The ideal republican man, therefore, was an individualist, seeking advancement for himself and his family; the ideal republican woman, by contrast, always put the well-being of others ahead of her own.

Together, white men and women established the context for the creation of a virtuous republic. But nearly 20 percent of the American population was black. How did approximately seven hundred thousand African-Americans fit into the developing national plan?

EMANCIPATION AND THE GROWTH OF RACISM

Revolutionary ideology exposed one of the primary contradictions in American society. Both blacks and whites saw the irony in slave-holding Americans'

claims that one of their aims in taking up arms was to prevent Britain from "enslaving" them. Many revolutionary leaders voiced that theme. In 1773, the Philadelphia doctor Benjamin Rush called slavery "a vice which degrades human nature" and warned that "liberty cannot thrive long in the neighborhood of slavery." Common folk also saw the contradiction. When Josiah Atkins, a Connecticut soldier marching south, saw Washington's plantation, he observed in his journal: "Alas! That persons who pretend to stand for the rights of mankind . . . can delight in oppression, & that even of the worst kind!"

African-Americans were quick to recognize the implications of revolutionary ideology. In 1779, a group of slaves from Portsmouth, New Hampshire, asked the state legislature "from what authority [our masters] assume to dispose of our lives, freedom and property" and pleaded "that the name of slave may not more be heard in a land gloriously contending for the sweets of freedom." The same year, several black residents of Fairfield, Connecticut, petitioned the legislature for their freedom, characterizing slavery as a "dreadful Evil" and "flagrant Injustice."

Both legislatures responded negatively. But the postwar years did witness the gradual abolition of slavery in the North. Vermont abolished slav-

Gradual Emancipation
___

ery in its 1777 constitution. Massachusetts courts decided in the 1780s that the clause in the state constitution declaring that "all men are born free and equal, and have certain natural, essential, and unalienable rights" prohibited slavery in the state. Pennsylvania passed an abolition law in 1780; four years later, Rhode Island and Connecticut provided for gradual emancipation, followed by New York (1799) and New Jersey (1804).

No southern state adopted similar general emancipation laws, but the legislatures of Virginia (1782), Delaware (1787), and Maryland (1790 and 1796) altered laws that had previously restricted slave owners' ability to free their slaves. South Carolina and Georgia never considered adopting such acts, and North Carolina insisted that all manumissions (emancipations of individual slaves) be approved by county courts.

Revolutionary ideology thus had limited influence on the well-entrenched economic interests of large slave holders. Only in the North, where slaves were relatively rare, could state legislatures vote to abolish slavery with relative ease. Even there, legislators' concern for property rights led them to favor gradual emancipation over immediate abolition. Most states provided only for the freeing of children born after passage of the law. And even those children were to remain slaves until reaching adulthood. Still, by 1840, in only one northern state—New Jersey—were African-Americans legally held in bondage.

Despite the slow progress of abolition, the number of free people of African descent in the United States grew dramatically in the first years

Growth of the Free Black Population

after the Revolution. Before the war, free blacks in America were few. Most blacks who had been freed before the war were mulattos, born of unions between white masters and enslaved black women and specifically granted freedom by their fathers. But wartime disruptions radically changed the size and composition of the freed population. Slaves who had escaped from plantations during the war, others who had served in the American army, and still others emancipated by their owners or by state laws were now free. Because most were not mulattos, dark skin was no longer an automatic sign of slave status. By 1790, nearly sixty thousand free people of color were living in the United States; ten years later, they numbered more than 108,000, nearly 11 percent of the total African-American population.

In the 1780s and thereafter, freed people often made their way to the port cities of the North. Boston and Philadelphia, where slavery was abolished sooner than in New York City, were particularly popular destinations. Women outnumbered men among the migrants by a margin of three to two. Like white females, black women found more opportunities for employment, particularly as domestic servants, in the cities than in the countryside. Some freedmen also worked in domestic service, but larger numbers were employed as unskilled laborers and seamen. A few of the women and a

sizable proportion of men (nearly one-third of those in Philadelphia in 1795) were skilled workers or retailers. As soon as possible, these freed people established independent two-parent nuclear families instead of continuing to live in white households. They also began to occupy distinct neighborhoods, probably as a result of both discrimination by whites and a desire for black solidarity.

Emancipation, however, did not bring equality. Even whites who recognized African-Americans' right to freedom were unwilling to accept them

Discrimination Against African-Americans

as equals. Laws discriminated against emancipated blacks as they had against slaves—South Carolina, for example, did not permit free blacks to testify against whites in court. Public schools often refused to educate their children. Freedmen found it difficult to purchase property and find good jobs. And whites rarely allowed them an equal voice in church affairs.

Gradually, free African-Americans developed separate institutions. In Charleston, mulattos formed the Brown Fellowship Society, which provided insurance coverage for its members, financed a school for free children, and helped to support black orphans. In 1794, blacks in Philadelphia and Baltimore founded societies that eventually became the African Methodist Episcopal (AME) denomination. AME churches later sponsored schools in a number of cities and, along with African Baptist, African Episcopal, and African Presbyterian churches, became cultural centers of the free black community.

Their endeavors were all the more necessary because the postrevolutionary years witnessed the development of a coherent racist theory in the

Development of Racist Theory

United States. Whites had long regarded their slaves as inferior, but the most influential writers on race had attributed that inferiority to environmental rather than hereditary factors. In the aftermath of the Revolution, white southerners needed to defend their enslavement of other human beings against the notion that all men are created equal. As a result, they began to argue that blacks were less than fully human and that the principles of republican equality applied only to whites.

This racism had several intertwined elements. First was the assertion that, as Thomas Jefferson suggested in 1781, blacks were "inferior to the whites in the endowments both of body and mind." Then came the belief that blacks were congenitally lazy, dishonest, and uncivilized (or uncivilizable). Third, and of crucial importance, was the notion that all blacks were sexually promiscuous and that black men lusted after white women. The specter of interracial sexual intercourse involving black men and white women haunted early American racist thought. The reverse situation, which occurred with far greater frequency (as white masters sexually exploited their female slaves), aroused little comment.

African-Americans did not allow these developing racist notions to go unchallenged. Benjamin Banneker, a free black surveyor, astronomer, and mathematical genius, directly disputed Thomas Jefferson's belief in blacks' intellectual inferiority. In 1791, Banneker sent Jefferson a copy of his latest almanac (which included his astronomical calculations) as an example of blacks' mental powers. Jefferson's response acknowledged Banneker's capability but implied that he regarded Banneker as an exception.

At its birth, then, the Republic was defined by whites as an exclusively white enterprise. Indeed, some historians have argued that the subjugation of blacks was a necessary precondition for equality among whites. They have pointed out that identifying a common racial antagonist helped to create white solidarity and to lessen the threat to gentry power posed by the enfranchisement of poorer whites. It was less dangerous to allow whites with little property to participate formally in politics than to open the possibility that they might join with freed blacks to question the rule of the better sort. That was perhaps one reason that, in the postrevolutionary years, the division of American society between slave and free was transformed into a division between blacks—some of whom were free—and whites. The white male wielders of power ensured their continued dominance in part

A Republic for Whites Only

by substituting race for enslavement as the primary determinant of African-Americans' status.

DESIGNING REPUBLICAN GOVERNMENTS

Drafting of State Constitutions

In May 1776, the Second Continental Congress directed the states to devise new republican governments to replace the provincial congresses and committees that had met since 1774. Thus Americans initially concentrated on drafting state constitutions and devoted little attention to their national government. They first faced the task of defining just what a constitution was. The British Constitution could not serve as a model, because it was an unwritten mixture of law and custom; Americans wanted tangible documents specifying the fundamental structures of government. Several years passed before the states concluded that their constitutions, unlike ordinary laws, could not be drafted by regular legislative bodies. Following the lead established by Vermont in 1777 and Massachusetts in 1780, they began to call conventions for the sole purpose of drafting constitutions. Thus the states sought direct authorization from the people—the theoretical sovereigns in a republic—before establishing new governments. After drawing up the new constitutions, delegates submitted them to the voters for ratification.

The framers of state constitutions were concerned primarily with outlining the distribution of and limitations on government power. Because of their experiences as colonists, Americans had learned to fear the power of the governor—usually, the appointed agent of the king or the proprietor—and to see the legislature as their defender. Accordingly, the first state constitutions typically provided for the governor to be elected annually, limited the number of terms any one governor could serve, and gave him little independent authority. At the same time, the constitutions expanded the powers of the legislature. Every state except Pennsylvania and Vermont retained a two-house structure and provided that members of the upper house would have longer terms and be required to meet higher standards of property holding. But they also redrew the lines of electoral districts to reflect population patterns more accurately, and they increased the numbers of members in both houses. Finally, most states lowered property qualifications for voting. Thus the revolutionary era witnessed the first deliberate attempt to broaden the base of American government.

But the authors of the state constitutions knew that governments designed to be responsive to the people would not necessarily provide sufficient protection if tyrants were elected to office. They consequently included explicit limitations on government authority in the documents they composed. Seven constitutions contained formal bills of rights, and the others had similar clauses. Most specifically guaranteed citizens freedom of the press and of religion, the right to a fair trial, the right of consent to taxation, and protection against general search warrants. An independent judiciary was charged with upholding such rights.

In sum, the constitution makers put far greater emphasis on preventing state governments from becoming tyrannical than on making them effective wielders of political authority. Their approach to the process of shaping governments was understandable, given the American experience with Great Britain. But establishing such weak political units, especially in wartime, practically ensured that the constitutions would soon need revision. When Americans realized that legislative supremacy was in itself no guarantee of good government, they began to develop a formal system of checks and balances. They would thus attempt to control government by balancing the powers of the legislative, executive, and judicial branches against one another.

The constitutional theories that Americans applied at the state level did not at first influence their conception of national government. Because American political leaders had little time to devote to legitimizing their de facto government while organizing the military struggle against Britain, the powers and structure of the Continental Congress evolved by default early in the war. Not until late 1777, after Burgoyne's defeat at Saratoga, did Congress send the Articles of Confederation to the states for ratification.

The chief organ of national government was a unicameral (one-house) legislature in which each state had one vote. Its powers included the conduct of foreign relations, the settlement of disputes between states, control over maritime affairs, the regulation of Indian trade, and the valuation of state and national coinage. The Articles did not give the national government the ability to tax effectively or to enforce a uniform commercial policy. The United States of America was described as "a firm league of friendship" in which each state "retains its sovereignty . . . and every Power . . . which is not by this confederation expressly delegated to the United States, in Congress assembled."

Articles of Confederation

The Articles required the unanimous consent of the state legislatures for ratification or amendment, and a clause concerning western lands turned out to be troublesome. The draft accepted by Congress allowed the states to retain all land claims derived from their original colonial charters. Because Maryland feared being overpowered by states with western land claims, it refused to accept the Articles until 1781. Only when Virginia promised to surrender its western holdings to the national government did Maryland accept the Articles. Other states followed suit, establishing the principle that western lands would be held by the nation as a whole.

The capacity of a single state to delay ratification for three years was a portent of the fate of American government under the Articles of Confederation. The authors of the Articles had not given adequate thought to the distribution of power within the national government or to the relationship between the Confederation and the states. The Congress they created was simultaneously a legislative body and a collective executive, but it had no independent income and no authority to compel the states to accept its rulings. What is surprising is not how poorly the Confederation functioned but how much the government was able to accomplish.

TRIALS OF THE CONFEDERATION

The most persistent problem faced by the American governments, state and national, was finance. Because of a reluctance to levy taxes, both Congress

Financial Problems

and the states tried to finance the war by printing currency. Although the money was backed by nothing but good faith, it circulated freely and without excessive depreciation during 1775 and most of 1776. But in late 1776, as the American army suffered major reverses in New York and New Jersey, prices began to rise and inflation set in (see figure). The value of the currency rested on Americans' faith in their government, a faith that was sorely tested in the years that

Depreciation of Continental Currency, 1777–1780

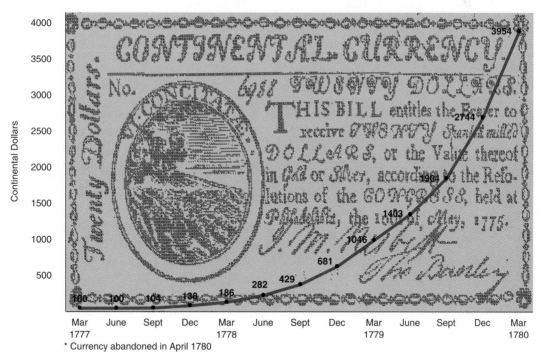

* Currency abandoned in April 1780

Depreciation of Continental Currency, 1777–1780 *The depreciation of Continental currency accelerated in 1778, as shown in this graph measuring its value against one hundred silver dollars. Thereafter, its value dropped almost daily.* Source: Data from John J. McCusker, "How Much Is That in Real Money? A Historical Price Index for Use as a Deflator of Money Values in the Economy of the United States," *Proceedings of the American Antiquarian Society*, Vol. 101, Pt. 2 (1991), Table C-1.

followed. Both Congress and the states attempted to control inflation, but in early 1780 it took forty paper dollars to purchase one silver dollar. Soon, Continental currency was worthless.

In 1781, faced with the total collapse of the monetary system, the delegates undertook ambitious reforms. After establishing a department of finance under the wealthy Philadelphia merchant Robert Morris, they asked the states to amend the Articles of Confederation to allow Congress to levy a duty of 5 percent on imported goods. Morris put national finances on a solid footing, but the customs duty was never adopted. First Rhode Island and then New York refused to agree to the tax. The states' resistance reflected genuine fear that a central government with permanent funds could become too powerful.

Congress also faced major diplomatic problems at the close of the war. Chief among them were issues involving the peace treaty. Article 4, which promised the repayment of prewar debts (most of them owed by Americans to British merchants), and Article 5, which recommended that states allow loyalists to recover their confiscated property, aroused considerable opposition. States passed laws denying British subjects the right to sue for recovery of debts or property in American courts, and because most of the purchasers of confiscated loyalist property were prominent patriots, the states had no desire to enforce Article 5.

Weakness in Foreign Affairs and Commerce

The refusal of state and local governments to comply with Articles 4 and 5 gave Britain an excuse to maintain military posts on the Great Lakes long after its troops were supposed to have withdrawn. Furthermore, Congress's inability to convince the states to implement the treaty pointed up its lack of power. Concerned nationalists argued publicly that enforcement of the treaty, however unpopular, was a crucial test for the Republic. "Will foreign nations be willing to undertake anything with us or for us," asked Alexander Hamilton, "when they find that the nature of our governments will allow no dependence to be placed on our engagements?"

Congress's weakness was especially evident in the realm of trade, because the Articles of Confederation specifically denied it the power to establish a national commercial policy. Immediately following the war, Britain, France, and Spain all restricted American trade with their colonies. When Britain closed the West Indies to American goods and flooded the United States with British products, Congress watched helplessly. Although Americans reopened trade with northern European countries and started a profitable trade with China in 1784, neither substituted for access to closer and larger markets.

Congress also had difficulty dealing with the threat posed by Spain's presence on the southern and western borders of the United States. Determined to prevent the new nation's expansion, Spain in 1784 closed the Mississippi River to American navigation. It thus deprived the growing settlements west of the Appalachians of their major access route to the rest of the nation and the world. If Spain's policy were not reversed, westerners might have to accept Spanish sovereignty as the necessary price for survival. Congress opened negotiations with Spain in 1785, but even John Jay, one of the nation's most experienced diplomats, could not win the necessary concessions on navigation. The talks collapsed the following year, after Congress divided sharply on the question of whether agreement should be sought on other issues. Southerners, voting as a bloc, insisted on navigation rights on the Mississippi; northerners were willing to abandon that claim in order to win commercial concessions. The impasse raised doubts about the possibility of a national consensus on foreign affairs.

Diplomatic problems of another sort confronted congressmen when they considered the status of the land on the nation's western borders.

Encroachment on Tribal Lands

Although tribal claims were not discussed by British and American diplomats at the end of the war, the United States assumed that the Treaty of Paris (1783) cleared its title to all land east of the Mississippi except the areas still held by Spain. But recognizing that some sort of land cession should be obtained from the most powerful tribes, Congress initiated negotiations with both northern and southern Indians. At Fort Stanwix, New York, in 1784, and at Hopewell, South Carolina, in late 1785 and early 1786, American diplomats signed separate treaties with chiefs purporting to represent the Iroquois and with emissaries from the Choctaw, Chickasaw, and Cherokee nations (see map). Later, both groups of Indians denied that the men who agreed to the treaties had been authorized to speak for them. But the United States still took the treaties as final confirmation of its sovereignty over the tribal territories and authorized settlers to move onto the land. Whites soon poured over the southern Appalachians, provoking the Creeks—who had not agreed to the Hopewell treaties—to defend their territory by declaring war. Only in 1790, when the Creek chief Alexander McGillivray traveled to New York to negotiate a treaty, did the Creeks finally come to terms with the United States.

In 1786, the Iroquois Confederacy formally repudiated the Fort Stanwix treaty and threatened new attacks on frontier settlements, but both whites and Indians knew the threat was an empty one. The flawed treaty was permitted to stand by default. At intervals until the end of the decade, the state of New York purchased large tracts of land from individual Iroquois tribes. By 1790, the once proud Iroquois Confederacy was confined to a few scattered reservations. In the West, tribes like the Shawnees, Chippewas, Ottawas, and Potawatomis formed their own confederacy and demanded direct negotiations with the United States. Their aim was to present a united front, so as to avoid the piecemeal surrender of land by individual tribes.

Congress ignored the western tribes' confederacy and organized the Northwest Territory, bounded by the Mississippi River, the Great Lakes, and the Ohio River. The **Northwest Ordinances** Northwest Ordinances, passed in 1784, 1785, and 1787, outlined the process through which the land could be sold to settlers and formal governments organized. To ensure orderly development, Congress in 1785 directed that the land be surveyed into townships six miles square, each divided into thirty-five sections of 640 acres (one square mile). Revenue from the sale of the sixteenth section of each township was to be reserved for the support of public schools—the first instance of federal aid to education in American

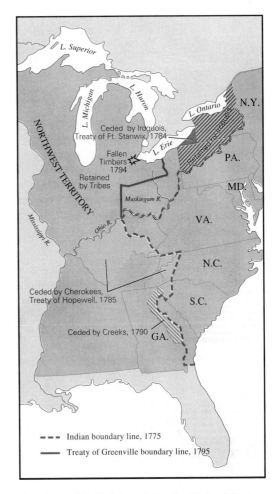

Cession of Tribal Lands to the United States, 1775–1790 *The land claims of the United States meant little so long as Indian nations still controlled vast territories within the new country's formal boundaries. A series of treaties in the 1780s and 1790s opened some lands to white settlement.* Source: From Lester J. Cappon et al., eds., *Atlas of Early American History: The Revolutionary Era, 1760–1790.* Copyright © 1976 by Princeton University Press. Reprinted by permission of Princeton University Press.

history. The minimum price per acre was set at $1, and the minimum sale was to be one section. Congress was not especially concerned about helping the small farmer: the minimum outlay of $640 was beyond the reach of ordinary Americans. The proceeds from the land sales were the first independent revenues available to the national government.

In 1784, Thomas Jefferson proposed a scheme for organizing the new nation's western lands that would have divided the region on a grid pattern, with fourteen new states (given such names as "Metropotamia" and "Pelisipia") composed of 10-mile-square "hundreds." After a year of debate, his plan was replaced by that adopted in the Land Ordinance of 1785, which is described in the text. Note that Jefferson's outline map contains some of the same errors evident in "A New and Correct Map" on page 120. William L. Clements Library.

The most important ordinance was the third, passed in 1787. The Northwest Ordinance contained a bill of rights guaranteeing settlers in the territory freedom of religion and the right to a jury trial, prohibiting cruel and unusual punishments, and forbidding the future importation of slaves. It also specified the process by which residents of the territory could eventually organize state governments and seek admission to the Union "on an equal footing with the original States." Early in the nation's history, therefore, Congress laid down a policy of admitting new states on the same basis as the old and assuring residents of the territories the same rights held by citizens of the original states.

In a sense, though, the ordinance was purely theoretical when it was passed. The Miamis, Shawnees, and Delawares refused to acknowledge American sovereignty and insisted on their right to the land. They opposed white settlement violently, attacking unwary pioneers who ventured too far north of the Ohio River. In 1788, the Ohio Company, to which Congress had sold a large tract of land at reduced rates, established the town of Marietta at the juncture of the Ohio and Muskingum Rivers. But the Indians prevented the company from extending settlement very far into the interior. After General Arthur St. Clair, the first governor of the Northwest Territory, failed to negotiate a meaningful treaty with the tribes in early 1789, it was apparent that the United States and the Miami-led western confederacy would clash.

Little Turtle, the able war chief of the Miami Confederacy, defeated first General Josiah Harmar (1790) and then St. Clair (1791) in major battles near the present border between Indiana and Ohio. More than six hundred of St. Clair's men were killed and scores more wounded; it was the whites' worst defeat in the entire history of the American frontier. In 1793, the Miami Confederacy declared that peace could be achieved only if the United States recognized the Ohio River as the boundary between white and Indian lands. But the national government refused to relinquish its claim to the Northwest Territory. A new army under the command of General Anthony Wayne defeated the tribesmen in August 1794 at the Battle of Fallen Timbers (near Toledo, Ohio). Peace negotiations began after the victory.

War in the Northwest

The Treaty of Greenville (1795) gave each side a portion of what it wanted. The United States gained the right to settle much of what was to become the state of Ohio, the tribes retaining only the northwest corner of the region. The Indians received the acknowledgment they had long sought: American recognition of their rights to the soil. At Greenville, the United States formally accepted the principle of Indian sovereignty, by virtue of residence, over all lands the tribes had not ceded. Never again would the U.S. government claim that it had acquired Indian territory solely through negotiation with a European or North American country.

The problems the United States encountered in ensuring safe settlement of the Northwest Territory pointed up, once again, the basic weakness of the Confederation government. Not until after the Articles of Confederation were replaced with a new constitution could the United States muster sufficient force to implement all the provisions of the Northwest Ordinance. Thus, although the ordinance is often viewed as one of the few lasting accomplishments of the Confederation Congress, it must be seen within a context of political impotence.

FROM CRISIS TO THE CONSTITUTION

The most obvious deficiencies of the Articles of Confederation involved overseas trade and foreign affairs. Congress could not impose its will on the states to establish a uniform commercial policy or to ensure the enforcement of treaties. The problems involving trade were particularly serious. Less than a year after the war ended, the American economy slid into a depression. The postwar restrictions that European powers imposed on American commerce harmed exporters of staple crops (especially tobacco and rice) and importers of manufactured goods. Although some restrictions were eased and recovery began by 1786, the war's effects proved impossible to erase entirely.

The war had wrought permanent change in the American economy. The near total cessation of foreign commerce in nonmilitary items during the war years stimulated domestic manufacturing. Consequently, despite the influx of European goods after 1783, the postwar period witnessed the stirrings of American industrial development—for example, the first American textile mill began production in Pawtucket, Rhode Island, in 1793. Moreover, foreign trade patterns shifted from Europe and toward the West Indies. Foodstuffs shipped to the French and Dutch Caribbean islands became America's largest single export.

Economic Change

Recognizing the Confederation Congress's inability to deal with commercial matters, Virginia invited the other states to a convention at Annapolis, Maryland, to discuss trade policy. Although eight states named representatives to the meeting in September 1786, only five delegations attended. Those present realized that they were too few in number to have any real influence on the political system. They issued a call for another convention, to be held in Philadelphia nine months later, "to devise such further provisions as shall . . . appear necessary to render the constitution of the federal government adequate to the exigencies of the Union." The other states did not respond immediately to the summons to another general meeting, but then Shays' Rebellion occurred.

The reaction to Shays' Rebellion hastened the movement toward comprehensive revision of the Articles of Confederation. After most states had already appointed delegates, the Confederation Congress belatedly endorsed the convention. In mid-May 1787, fifty-five men, representing all the states but Rhode Island, assembled in Philadelphia to begin their deliberations.

Constitutional Convention
———

The vast majority of delegates to the Constitutional Convention were men of property and substance. Among their number were merchants, planters, physicians, generals, governors, and especially lawyers. Most had been born in America, and many came from families that had arrived in the seventeenth century. In an era when only a tiny proportion of the population had any advanced education, more than half the delegates had attended college. A few had been educated in Britain, but most were graduates of American institutions. The youngest delegate was twenty-six, the oldest—Benjamin Franklin—eighty-one. Like George Washington, whom they elected chairman, most were in their vigorous middle years. A dozen men did the bulk of the convention's work. Of these, James Madison of Virginia was by far the most important; he truly deserves the title Father of the Constitution.

James Madison
———

Madison was unique among the delegates in his systematic preparation for the Philadelphia meeting. Through Jefferson in Paris, he bought more than two hundred books on history and government and carefully analyzed their accounts of past confederacies and republics. A month before the Constitutional Convention began, he summed up the results of his research in a lengthy paper entitled, "Vices of the Political System of the United States." After listing the flaws he perceived in the current structure of the government, Madison set forth the principle of checks and balances.

The government, he believed, had to be constructed in such a way that it could not become tyrannical or fall wholly under the influence of a particular interest group. He regarded the large size of a potential national republic as an advantage in that respect. Rejecting the common assertion that republics had to be small to survive, Madison argued that a large, diverse republic was in fact to be preferred. Because the nation would include many different interest groups, no one of them would be able to control the government. Political stability would result from compromises among the contending parties.

Virginia and New Jersey Plans
———

Madison's conception of national government was embodied in the so-called Virginia Plan, introduced on May 29 by his fellow Virginian Edmund Randolph. The plan provided for a two-house legislature, the lower house elected directly by the people and the upper house selected by the lower, with proportional representation in both houses, an executive elected by Congress, a national judiciary, and congressional veto over state laws. The Virginia Plan gave Congress the broad power to legislate "in all cases to which the separate states are incompetent." Had it been adopted intact, it would have created a government in which national authority reigned unchallenged and state power was greatly diminished. Proportional representation in both houses would also have given large states a dominant voice in the national government.

The convention included many delegates who recognized the need for change but believed the Virginians had gone too far in the direction of national consolidation. The disaffected delegates united under the leadership of William Paterson of New Jersey. On June 15, Paterson presented an alternative scheme, the New Jersey Plan, calling for modifications in the Articles of Confederation rather than a complete overhaul of the government. Paterson proposed retaining the unicameral Confederation Congress but giving it new powers of taxation and trade regulation. Although the delegates rejected Paterson's narrow interpretation of their task, he and his allies won a number of victories in the months that followed.

The delegates began their work by discussing the structure and functions of Congress. They readily agreed that the new national government should have a two-house (bicameral) legislature. But they then found that they differed widely in their answers to three key questions: Should representation in both houses of Congress be proportional to population? How was representation in either or both houses to be apportioned among the states? And, finally, how were the members of the two houses to be elected?

The last issue was the easiest to resolve. To quote John Dickinson, the delegates thought it "essential" that members of the lower branch of Congress be elected directly by the people and "expedient" that members of the upper house be chosen by the state legislatures. Because the legislatures had selected delegates to the Confederation Congress, they would expect a similar privilege in the new government.

Considerably more difficult was the matter of proportional representation in the Senate. The delegates accepted without much debate the principle of proportional representation in the lower house. But the smaller states, through their spokesman Luther Martin of Maryland, argued for equal representation in the Senate, whereas large states supported a proportional plan for the upper house. For weeks, the convention was deadlocked on the issue, neither side able to obtain a majority. A committee appointed to work out a compromise recommended equal representation in the Senate, coupled with a proviso that all appropriation bills originate in the lower house. But a breakdown was not averted until the convention accepted a suggestion that a state's two senators vote as individuals rather than as a unit.

Another critical question remained: how was representation in the lower house to be apportioned among the states? Delegates from states

Slavery and the Constitution

with large numbers of slaves wanted black and white inhabitants to be counted equally; delegates from states with few slaves wanted only free people to be counted. The issue was resolved by using a formula developed by the Confederation Congress in 1783 to allocate financial assessments among the states: three-fifths of the slaves would be included in the population totals. (The formula reflected the delegates' judgment that slaves were less efficient producers of wealth than free people, not that they were 60 percent human and 40 percent property.) The convention unanimously accepted the three-fifths compromise.

Although the words *slave* and *slavery* do not appear in the Constitution (the framers used euphemisms like *other persons*), direct and indirect protections for slavery were deeply embedded in the document. The three-fifths clause, for example, assured white southern voters not only congressional representation out of proportion to their numbers but also a disproportionate influence on the selection of the president, because the size of its congressional delegation determined the number of each state's electoral votes. Congress was prevented from outlawing the slave trade for at least twenty years. By guaranteeing that the national government would aid any states threatened with "domestic violence," the Constitution promised aid in putting down future slave revolts.

Once delegates agreed on the problems of slavery and representation, they readily achieved consensus on the other issues confronting them. They agreed to enumerate the powers of Congress but to allow it to pass laws "necessary and proper" to carry out those powers. Foreign policy was placed in the hands of the executive, who was also made commander in chief of the armed forces. Moreover, the Constitution plus national laws and treaties would constitute "the supreme law of the land; and the judges in every state shall be bound thereby." As another means of circumscribing state powers, the delegates drafted a long list of actions forbidden to the states—such as "impair[ing] the obligation of contracts." Finally, the delegates established the electoral college and a four-year term for the chief executive, who could seek reelection.

The key to the Constitution was the distribution of political authority—separation of powers among the executive, legislative, and judicial branches of the national government, and division of powers between the states and the nation. The system of checks and balances would make it difficult for the government to become tyrannical. At the same time, though, the elaborate system would sometimes prevent the government from acting quickly and decisively. Furthermore, the line between state and national powers was so ambiguously and vaguely drawn that the United States had to fight a civil war in the next century before the issue was fully resolved.

Separation of Powers
——

The convention held its last session on September 17, 1787. Of the forty-two delegates present, only three refused to sign the Constitution. (Two of the three declined in part because of the lack of a bill of rights.) Although the delegates had accepted the Constitution, whether the states would ratify it remained a question.

OPPOSITION AND RATIFICATION

The ratification clause of the Constitution provided for the new system to take effect once it was approved by special conventions in at least nine states. The qualified voters were to elect the delegates to each state convention. Thus the national Constitution, unlike the Articles of Confederation, would rest directly on popular authority.

As the states began to elect delegates to the special conventions, discussion of the proposed government grew more heated. Federalists—supporters of the Constitution—and Antifederalists, its opponents, published newspaper essays and pamphlets vigorously defending or attacking the convention's decisions. The extent of the debate was unprecedented, and it quickly became apparent that the disputes within the Constitutional Convention had been mild compared with the divisions of opinion within the populace as a whole. Indeed, many citizens believed that the proposed government, despite its built-in safeguards, held the potential for tyranny.

Federalists claimed that the nation did not need to fear centralized authority when good men were in charge and that the carefully structured government would preclude the possibility of tyranny. A republic could be large, they declared, if the government was designed to prevent any one group from controlling it absolutely. The separation of powers among legislative, executive, and judicial branches, and the division of powers between states and nation, would accomplish that goal. Thus the people did not need to be protected from the powers of the new government in a formal way.

Federalists
——

Antifederalists included those who emphasized the threat to the states embodied in the new national government and those who stressed the dangers to individuals posed by the lack of a bill of rights. They saw the states as the chief protectors of individual rights and their weakening as the onset of arbitrary power. Fearing a too-powerful central government, they rejected the Federalists' emphasis on the need for national leadership by a disinterested elite. Their arguments against the Constitution often consisted of lists of potential abuses of the national government's authority.

Antifederalists
——

The Antifederalists were the heirs of the Real Whig ideology of the late 1760s and early 1770s, which stressed the need for constant popular vigilance to avert oppression. Indeed, some Antifederalists were the very men who had originally promulgated those ideas—Samuel Adams and Richard Henry Lee were both leaders of the opposition to the Constitution. The Antifederalist ranks were also peopled by small farmers, who were preoccupied with guarding their property against excessive taxation, and ambitious, upwardly mobile men who would gain more from an economic and political system less tightly controlled than the one the Constitution promised to establish.

As the months passed and public debate continued, the Antifederalists focused more sharply on the Constitution's lack of a bill of rights. Even if the new system weakened the states, they believed, the people could still be protected from tyranny if their rights were specifically guaranteed. *Letters of a Federal Farmer*, perhaps the most widely read Antifederalist pamphlet, listed the rights that should be protected: freedom of the press and of religion, the right to trial by jury, and guarantees against unreasonable search warrants. From Paris, Jefferson added his voice to the chorus. Replying to Madison's letter conveying a copy of the Constitution, Jefferson declared, "I like much the general idea," but not "the omission of a bill of rights."

As the state conventions met to consider ratification, the lack of a bill of rights loomed larger and larger as a flaw in the proposed government. Four of the first five states to ratify did

Ratification of the Constitution

so unanimously, but serious disagreement then began to surface. Massachusetts, where Antifederalist forces had been bolstered by a backlash against the state government's heavy-handed treatment of the Shays rebels, ratified by a majority of only 19 votes out of 355 cast. In New Hampshire, the Federalists won by 57 to 47. When New Hampshire ratified, in June 1788, the requirement of nine states had been satisfied. But New York and Virginia had not yet voted, and everyone realized the new Constitution could not succeed unless those key states accepted it.

In Virginia, despite a valiant effort by the Antifederalist Patrick Henry, the pro-Constitution forces won 89 to 79. In New York, James Madison, John Jay, and Alexander Hamilton campaigned for ratification by publishing *The Federalist*, a political tract that explained the theory behind the Constitution and masterfully answered its critics. Their reasoned arguments, coupled with the Federalists' reluctant promise that a bill of rights would be added to the Constitution, helped win the battle. On July 26, 1788, New York ratified the Constitution by the slim margin of three votes. Although the last state (Rhode Island, which had not participated in the convention) did not formally

THE FEDERAL ALMANACK.

FEDERAL HALL.

LET Trumpets found, and fwift wing'd Fame,
Thefe glorious tidings far proclaim ;
On Virtue's bafe, by Wifdom plann'd ;
And rear'd by Union's facred hand ;
The FEDERAL DOME, is rais'd fublime :
Its PILLARS folid, ftrong as time ;
Rife ! Commerce ! rife ! unfurl the fail,
Rich Golden harvefts blefs the vale :
Arts ! Science ! Genius ! fpring to light ;
And Freedom burft on realms of Night

The Federal Almanack *for 1789 trumpeted the virtues of the new Constitution. Not all Americans were so certain that the national government, here symbolized as an edifice supported by thirteen pillars, was as "solid, strong as time" as the printer proclaimed.* American Antiquarian Society.

join the Union until 1790, the new government was a reality.

During the 1770s and 1780s, the nation took shape as a political union. It began to develop an economy independent of the British Empire and a foreign policy that attempted to chart its own course in the world, focusing primarily on the new nation's best interests. An integral part of the formation of the Union was the systematic formulation of American racist thought. Emphasizing race as a determinant of African-Americans' standing in the nation allowed white men to define republicanism to exclude all people but themselves and to ensure that they would dominate the country for the foreseeable future.

The experience of fighting a war and of struggling for survival as an independent nation in the 1780s had altered the political context of American life. At the outset of the war, most politically aware Americans believed that "that government which governs best governs least," but by the late 1780s many had changed their minds. These were the drafters and supporters of the Constitution, who had concluded from the Republic's vicissitudes under the Articles of Confederation that the United States needed a more powerful central government. They won their point when the Constitution was adopted, however narrowly.

SUGGESTIONS FOR FURTHER READING

General

Forrest McDonald, *Novus Ordo Seclorum: The Intellectual Origins of the Constitution* (1985), and *E Pluribus Unum: The Formation of the American Republic, 1776–1790* (1965); Edmund S. Morgan, *Inventing the People: The Rise of Popular Sovereignty in England and America* (1988); Robert R. Palmer, *The Age of the Democratic Revolution: A Political History of Europe and America, 1760–1800,* 2 vols. (1959, 1964); Gordon S. Wood, *The Radicalism of the American Revolution* (1992), and *The Creation of the American Republic, 1776–1787* (1969).

Continental Congress and Articles of Confederation

E. James Ferguson, *The Power of the Purse: A History of American Public Finance, 1776–1790* (1961); Merrill Jensen, *The Articles of Confederation,* 2d ed. (1959), and *The New Nation: A History of the United States During the Confederation, 1781–1789* (1950); Jack N. Rakove, *The Beginnings of National Politics: An Interpretive History of the Continental Congress* (1979).

State Politics

Willi Paul Adams, *The First American Constitutions: Republican Ideology and the Making of the State Constitutions in the Revolutionary Era* (1980); Robert Gross, ed., *In Debt to Shays* (1992); Jackson Turner Main, *The Sovereign States, 1775–1783* (1973); David P. Szatmary, *Shays' Rebellion: The Making of an Agrarian Insurrection* (1980); Ann Withington, *Toward a More Perfect Union: Virtue and the Formation of American Republics* (1992).

The Constitution

Charles A. Beard, *An Economic Interpretation of the Constitution of the United States* (1913); Frederick W. Marks III, *Independence on Trial: Foreign Affairs and the Making of the Constitution* (1973); Clinton Rossiter, *1787: The Grand Convention* (1973); Robert A. Rutland, *The Ordeal of the Constitution: The Antifederalists and the Ratification Struggle of 1787–1788* (1966).

Education and Culture

Joseph M. Ellis, *After the Revolution: Profiles of Early American Culture* (1979); Carl F. Kaestle, *Pillars of the Republic: Common Schools and American Society, 1780–1860* (1983); Kenneth Silverman, *A Cultural History of the American Revolution* (1976).

Women

Edith Gelles, *Portia: The World of Abigail Adams* (1992); Ronald Hoffman and Peter Albert, eds., *Women in the Age of the American Revolution* (1989); Linda K. Kerber, *Women of the Republic: Intellect and Ideology in Revolutionary America* (1980); Mary Beth Norton, *Liberty's Daughters: The Revolutionary Experience of American Women, 1750–1800* (1980).

Blacks and Slavery

David Brion Davis, *The Problem of Slavery in the Age of Revolution, 1770–1823* (1975); Carol V. R. George, *Segregated Sabbaths: Richard Allen and the Emergence of Independent Black Churches, 1760–1840* (1973); Gary Nash, *Forging Freedom: The Formation of Philadelphia's Black Community, 1720–1840* (1988); Donald L. Robinson, *Slavery in the Structure of American Politics, 1765–1820* (1971); Shane White, *Somewhat More Independent: The End of Slavery in New York City, 1770–1810* (1991).

Indians

Harvey L. Carter, *The Life and Times of Little Turtle* (1987); Francis Paul Prucha, *American Indian Policy in the Formative Years: The Indian Trade and Intercourse Acts, 1790–1834* (1962); Bernard Sheehan, *Seeds of Extinction: Jeffersonian Philanthropy and the American Indian* (1973); Anthony F. C. Wallace, *The Death and Rebirth of the Seneca* (1969).

Politics and Society in the Early Republic, 1789–1800

A BIGAIL ADAMS WAS FURIOUS. "I am at a loss to know how the people who were formerly so much alive to the usurpation of one Nation can crouch so tamely to a much more dangerous and dareing one," she wrote to her sister in January 1798. France, she asserted, "aims not only at our independance and libe[r]ty, but a total annihilation of the Christian Religion." Yet every state except one—Connecticut—had inexplicably elected French sympathizers to Congress.

Abigail Adams's anger stemmed from a deep division in American public opinion over the French Revolution, which had begun in 1789. Along with many others, she and her husband John—elected president in 1796—viewed the violent tactics of the French revolutionaries with deep alarm and saw the Republic's former ally as the major threat to freedom in the world, although other Americans continued to sympathize with the French. "There is no end to their audaciousness," she wrote her sister in the spring of 1798. "French emissaries are in every corner of the union sowing and spreading their Sedition."

Opinionated and fiercely loyal to her husband, Abigail Adams found her-self in the middle of an unprecedented phenomenon: the first truly heated partisan battle in the new Republic. She knew her husband had devoted his life to the nation's welfare. What then could explain the bitter invective directed at him by his opponents, the political faction now called Republicans? For her and her husband, there was only one answer: the criticism must have been instigated by France, the revolutionary government of which saw the Adams administration as its enemy.

The failure of Americans' quest for unity and unqualified independence during the 1790s was nowhere more evident than in the political battles that absorbed Abigail Adams's attention. The fight over the Constitution had been only the precursor of an even wider division over the major political, economic, and diplomatic questions confronting the young Republic. To make matters worse, Americans had not anticipated the political disagreements that characterized the decade. Believing that the Constitution would resolve the problems that had arisen during the Confederation period, they expected the new government to rule largely by consensus. They could not understand or fully accept the division of America's political leaders into two factions—not yet political parties—known as Federalists and Republicans, because factions were believed to be legitimate only in monarchies. In republics, it was thought, the rise of factions was a sign of decay and corruption.

Nor were prosperity and expansion easily attained. The American economy still depended on the export trade, as it had throughout the colonial era. When warfare between England and France resumed in 1793, Americans found commerce disrupted once again. Moreover, the strength of the Miami Confederacy blocked the westward expansion of white settlement north of the Ohio River until after the Treaty of Greenville in 1795. South of the Ohio, settlements were established west of the mountains as early as the 1770s, but the geographic barrier of the Appalachians tended to isolate them from the eastern seaboard. Not until the first years of the nineteenth century did those settlements become more fully integrated in American life through the vehicle of the Second Great Awakening, a religious revival that swept both East and West.

BUILDING A WORKABLE GOVERNMENT

Americans in many cities celebrated the ratification of the Constitution with a series of parades on July 4, 1788. Organizers carefully planned the processions to symbolize the unity of the new nation and to recall its history to the minds of the watching throngs. Like prerevolutionary protest meetings, the parades served as political lessons for literate and illiterate Americans alike. Men and women who could not read were thereby educated about the significance of the new Constitution in the life of the nation. They were also instructed about political leaders' hopes for industry and frugality on the part of a virtuous American public.

The nationalistic spirit expressed in the ratification processions carried over to the first session of Congress. Only a few Antifederalists ran for office in the congressional elections held late in 1788, and even fewer were elected. Thus

First Congress

the First Congress consisted chiefly of men who supported a strong national government. The Constitution had deliberately left many key issues undecided, so the nationalists' domination of Congress meant that their views on those points quickly prevailed.

Congress faced four immediate tasks when it convened in April 1789: raising revenue to support the new government, responding to the state ratification conventions' call for a bill of rights, setting up executive departments, and organizing the federal judiciary. The last task was especially important. The Constitution established a Supreme Court but left it to Congress to decide whether to have other federal courts as well.

James Madison, who had been elected to the House of Representatives, soon became as influential in Congress as he had been at the Constitutional Convention. A few months into the first session, he persuaded Congress to impose a 5 percent tariff on certain imports. Thus the First Congress quickly achieved what the Confederation Congress never had: an effective national tax law. The new government would have problems, but lack of revenue in its first years was not one of them.

Madison also took the lead on the issue of constitutional amendments. He placed nineteen proposed amendments before the House. Eventually,

Bill of Rights

the states ratified ten amendments, which officially became part of the Constitution on December 15, 1791. Not for many years did they become known collectively as the Bill of Rights.

The First Amendment specifically prohibited Congress from passing any law restricting the people's right to freedom of religion, speech, press, peaceable assembly, or petition. The next two arose directly from the former colonists' fear of standing armies as a threat to freedom. The Second Amendment guaranteed the people's right "to keep and bear arms" because of the need for a "well-regulated Militia." Thus the constitutional right to bear arms was based on the expectation that most able-bodied men would serve the nation as citizen soldiers; there would be little need for a standing army. The Third Amendment defined the circumstances in which troops could be quartered in private

• *Important Events* •

1789	George Washington inaugurated as first president
	Judiciary Act of 1789 organizes federal court system
	French Revolution begins
1790	Alexander Hamilton's *Report on Public Credit* proposes assumption of state debts
1791	First ten amendments (Bill of Rights) ratified
1793	France declares war on Britain, Spain, and Holland
	Washington's Neutrality Proclamation keeps the United States out of the war
	Democratic-Republican societies founded; first grassroots political organization
1794	Whiskey Rebellion in western Pennsylvania protests taxation
1795	Jay Treaty with England
1796	First contested presidential election: John Adams elected president, Thomas Jefferson vice president
1798	XYZ affair arouses American opinion against France
	Alien and Sedition Acts punish political dissenters
	Virginia and Kentucky Resolutions protest suppression of dissent
1798–99	Quasi-War with France
1800	Franco-American Convention ends the Quasi-War
	Jefferson elected president, Aaron Burr vice president
	Gabriel's Rebellion threatens Virginia whites
1801	Second Great Awakening sweeps through Kentucky

homes. The Fourth Amendment prohibited "unreasonable searches and seizures"; the Fifth and Sixth established the rights of accused persons; the Seventh specified the conditions for jury trials in civil (as opposed to criminal) cases; the Eighth forbade "cruel and unusual punishments." Finally, the Ninth and Tenth Amendments reserved to the people and the states other unspecified rights and powers. In short, the authors of the amendments made clear that, in listing some rights explicitly, they did not mean to preclude the exercise of others.

While debating the proposed amendments, Congress also considered the organization of the executive branch. It readily agreed to continue the three administrative departments established under the Articles of Confederation: War, Foreign Affairs (renamed State), and Treasury. Congress also instituted two lesser posts: the attorney general—the nation's official lawyer—and the postmaster general. Controversy arose over whether the president alone could dismiss officials whom he originally had appointed with the consent of the Senate. After some debate, the House and Senate agreed that he

had such authority. Thus was established the important principle that the heads of the executive departments are responsible to the president.

Aside from the constitutional amendments, the most far-reaching piece of legislation enacted by the First Congress was the Judiciary Act of 1789. That

Judiciary Act of 1789

act provided for the Supreme Court to have six members: a chief justice and five associate justices. It also defined the jurisdiction of the federal judiciary and established thirteen district courts and three circuit courts of appeal. The act's most important provision was its Section 25, which allowed appeals from state courts to the federal court system when certain types of constitutional issues were raised. This section was intended to implement Article VI of the Constitution, which stated that federal laws and treaties were to be considered "the supreme Law of the Land." For Article VI to be enforced uniformly, the national judiciary clearly had to be able to overturn state court decisions in cases involving the Constitution, federal laws, or treaties.

During the first decade of its existence, the Supreme Court handled few cases of any importance, and there was considerable turnover in its membership. But in a significant 1796 decision, *Ware* v. *Hylton*, the Court for the first time declared a state law unconstitutional. The same year, it also reviewed the constitutionality of an act of Congress, upholding its validity in the case of *Hylton* v. *U.S.* The most important case of the decade, *Chisholm* v. *Georgia* (1793), established that states could be sued in federal courts by citizens of other states. This decision, unpopular with the state governments, was overruled five years later by the Eleventh Amendment to the Constitution.

DOMESTIC POLICY UNDER WASHINGTON AND HAMILTON

George Washington did not seek the presidency. When in 1783 he returned to Mount Vernon, his plantation on the Potomac River, he was eager for the peaceful life of a Virginia planter. Yet Americans never regarded Washington as just another private citizen. He was unanimously elected the presiding officer of the Constitutional Convention. As such, he did not participate in debates, but he consistently voted for a strong national government. Once the proposed structure of the government was presented to the public, Americans agreed that only George Washington had sufficient stature to serve as the Republic's first president. The unanimous vote of the electoral college was just a formality.

Election of the First President

Washington acted cautiously during his first months in office, aware that whatever he did would set precedents. He held weekly receptions at which callers could pay their respects, and he toured different areas of the country. When the title by which he should be addressed aroused a good deal of controversy (Vice President John Adams favored "His Highness, the President of the United States of America, and Protector of their Liberties"), Washington said nothing; the accepted title soon became a plain "Mr. President." By using the heads of the executive departments collectively as his chief advisers, he created the cabinet. Washington also concluded that he should exercise his veto power over congressional legislation sparingly—indeed, only if he was convinced a bill was unconstitutional.

Washington's first major task as president was to choose the men who would head the executive departments. For the War Department, he selected an old comrade in arms, Henry Knox, who had been his reliable general of artillery during much of the Revolution. His choice for the State Department was his fellow Virginian Thomas Jefferson, who had just returned to the United States from his post as minister to France. And for the crucial position of secretary of the treasury, the president chose the brilliant, intensely ambitious Alexander Hamilton.

Two traits distinguished Hamilton from most of his contemporaries. First, he displayed an undivided, unquestioning loyalty to the nation as a whole. As a West Indian who had lived on the mainland only briefly before the war, Hamilton had no ties to a particular state. He showed little sympathy for, or understanding of, demands for local autonomy. Thus the aim of his fiscal policies was always the consolidation of power at the national level. Further, he never feared the exercise of centralized executive authority, as did older counterparts who had clashed repeatedly with colonial governors, nor was he afraid of maintaining close political and economic ties with Britain.

Alexander Hamilton

Second, he regarded other human beings with unvarnished cynicism. Perhaps because of his difficult early life and overriding ambition, Hamilton believed people to be motivated primarily, if not entirely, by self-interest—particularly economic self-interest. He placed absolutely no reliance on people's capacity for virtuous and self-sacrificing behavior. This outlook set him apart from those Americans who foresaw a rosy future in which public-spirited citizens would pursue the common good rather than their own private advantage.

In 1789, Congress ordered the new secretary of the treasury to assess the public debt and to submit recommendations for supporting the government's

National Debt

credit. Hamilton found that the country's remaining war debts fell into three categories: those owed by the national government to foreign governments and investors, mostly to France (about $11 million), those owed by the national government to merchants, former soldiers, holders of revolutionary bonds, and the like (about $27 million), and, finally, similar debts owed by state governments (roughly $25 million). With respect to the national debt, there was little disagreement: politically aware Americans recognized that if their new government was to succeed it would have to repay at full face value the financial obligations the nation had incurred while winning independence.

The state debts were quite another matter. Some states—notably Virginia, Maryland, North Carolina, and Georgia—had already paid off most of their war debts. They would oppose the national government's assumption of responsibility for other states' debts, because their citizens would be taxed to pay such obligations. Massachusetts, Connecticut, and South Carolina, on the other hand, still had sizable unpaid debts and would welcome a system of national assumption. The proposed assumption of state debts also had political implications. Consolidation of the debt in the hands of the national government would help to concentrate economic and political power at the national level. A contrary policy would reserve greater independence of action for the states.

Hamilton's First *Report on Public Credit*

Hamilton's first *Report on Public Credit*, sent to Congress in January 1790, reflected both his national loyalty and his cynicism. He proposed that Congress assume outstanding state debts, combine them with national obligations, and issue new securities covering both the principal and accumulated unpaid interest. Current holders of state or national debt certificates would have the option of taking a portion of their payment in western lands. Hamilton's aims were clear: he wanted to expand the financial reach of the U.S. government and reduce the economic power of the states. He also wanted to ensure that the holders of public securities—many of them wealthy merchants

and speculators—would have a significant financial stake in the survival of the national government.

Hamilton's plan stimulated lively debate in Congress. The opposition coalesced around his former ally James Madison. Well aware that speculators had purchased large quantities of debt certificates at a fraction of their face value, Madison proposed that the government also compensate the original holders of the debt. Madison's plan, although fairer than Hamilton's, would have been difficult, if not impossible, to administer. The House of Representatives rejected it.

At first, the House also rejected the assumption of state debts. The Senate, however, adopted Hamilton's plan largely intact, and a series of compromises followed. Hamilton agreed to changes in the assumption plan that would benefit Virginia in particular. The assumption bill also became linked in a complex way to the other highly controversial issue of that congressional session, the location of the permanent national capital. Both northerners and southerners wanted the capital in their region. The legend that Hamilton and Madison agreed over Jefferson's dinner table to exchange assumption of state debts for a southern site is not supported by the surviving evidence, but a political deal was undoubtedly struck. The Potomac River was designated as the site for the capital, and the first part of Hamilton's financial program became law in August 1790.

Four months later, Hamilton submitted to Congress a second report on public credit, recommending the chartering of a national bank.

First Bank of the United States

Hamilton modeled his bank on the Bank of England. The Bank of the United States was to be capitalized at $10 million, of which only $2 million would come from public funds. Private investors would supply the rest. The bank's charter was to run for twenty years, and one-fifth of its directors were to be named by the government. Its bank notes would circulate as the nation's currency; it would also act as the collecting and disbursing agent for the treasury and would lend money to the government. Most political leaders recognized that such an institution would benefit the country. But there was another issue: did the Constitution give Congress the power to establish such a bank?

James Madison, for one, answered that question with a resounding no. He pointed out that the delegates at the Constitutional Convention had specifically rejected a clause authorizing Congress to issue corporate charters. Consequently, he argued, that power could not be inferred from other parts of the Constitution.

Washington was sufficiently disturbed by Madison's contention that he decided to request other opinions before signing the bill. Edmund Randolph, the attorney general, and Thomas Jefferson, the secretary of state, agreed with Madison that the bank was unconstitutional. Jefferson referred to Article I, Section 8, of the Constitution, which gave Congress the power "to make all Laws which shall be necessary and proper for carrying into Execution the foregoing Powers." The key word, Jefferson argued, was *necessary:* Congress could do what was needed, but it could not do what was merely desirable without specific constitutional authorization. Thus Jefferson formulated the strict-constructionist interpretation of the Constitution.

Washington asked Hamilton to reply to these negative assessments of his proposal. Hamilton's *Defense of the Constitutionality of the Bank*, presented to the president in February 1791, was a brilliant exposition of what has become known as the broad-constructionist view of the Constitution. Hamilton argued forcefully that Congress could choose any means not specifically prohibited by the Constitution to achieve a constitutional end. In short, if the end was constitutional and the means was not unconstitutional, the means was constitutional. Washington was convinced and signed the bill.

In December 1791, Hamilton presented to Congress his *Report on Manufactures*, the third and last of his prescriptions for the American economy. In it, he outlined an ambitious plan for encouraging and protecting America's infant industries, like shoe-making and textile manufacturing. Hamilton argued that the nation could never be truly independent so long as it relied heavily on Europe for manufactured goods. He thus urged Congress to promote the immigration of technicians and laborers, to enact

John Trumbull, primarily noted for his larger-than-life portraits of patriot leaders, painted this miniature of George Washington, who posed for it during his presidency (ca. 1792–1794). Division of Political History, Smithsonian Institution, Washington, D.C.

protective tariffs, and to support industrial development. Most congressmen, convinced that America's future was agrarian, rejected Hamilton's report.

That same year, Congress did accept another feature of Hamilton's financial program, an excise tax on whiskey. Congressmen both recognized the

Whiskey Rebellion

————

need for additional government revenues and hoped to reduce the national consumption of distilled spirits. (Eighteenth-century Americans' annual per capita consumption of alcohol was about double today's rate.) The new tax most directly affected western farmers, who sold their grain crops in the form of distilled spirits to avoid the high cost of transporting wagonloads of bulky corn over the mountains.

News of the excise law set off protests in frontier areas of Pennsylvania. But matters did not come to a head until July 1794, when western Pennsylvania farmers resisted a federal marshal and a tax collector trying to enforce the law. About seven thousand rebels convened on August 1 to plot the destruction of Pittsburgh but decided not to face the heavy guns of the fort guarding the town. Unrest nevertheless continued for months on the frontiers of Pennsylvania, Maryland, and Virginia. Crowds of men drafted petitions protesting the excise, raised liberty poles (in deliberate imitation of the 1760s), and occasionally harassed tax collectors. But the Whiskey Rebellion remained largely leaderless and unorganized.

President Washington took decisive action to prevent a crisis reminiscent of Shays' Rebellion. On August 7, he called on the insurgents to disperse by September 1 and summoned nearly thirteen thousand militia from Pennsylvania and neighboring states. By the time the federal forces marched westward in October and November, the disturbances had long since ended.

The chief importance of the Whiskey Rebellion was the forceful message it conveyed to the American public. The national government, Washington had demonstrated, would not allow violent organized resistance to its laws. In the new Republic, change would be effected peacefully, by legal means. Those who were dissatisfied with the law should try to amend or repeal it, not take extralegal action.

By 1794, a group of Americans was already beginning to seek change systematically within the confines of electoral politics, although traditional political theory regarded organized opposition—especially in a republic—as illegitimate. Yet the opposition leaders Jefferson and Madison became convinced that Hamilton's policies of favoring wealthy commercial interests at the expense of agriculture aimed at imposing a corrupt, aristocratic government on the United States. They contended that they were the true heirs of the Revolution and that Hamilton was plotting to subvert republican principles. To dramatize their point, they and their followers in Congress began calling themselves Republicans.

Hamilton in turn accused Jefferson and Madison of the same crime: attempting to destroy the Republic. To legitimize their claims and link themselves with the Constitution, Hamilton and his supporters called themselves Federalists. In short, each group accused the other of being an illicit faction working to destroy the republican principles of the Revolution. (By traditional definition, a *faction* was a group opposed to the public good.)

At first, President Washington tried to remain aloof from the political dispute. Even so, the controversy helped persuade him to seek a second term of office in 1792 in hopes of promoting political unity. But in 1793 and thereafter, a series of developments in foreign affairs magnified the disagreements.

PARTISAN POLITICS AND FOREIGN POLICY

The first years under the Constitution were blessed by international peace. Eventually, however, the French Revolution, which began in 1789, brought about the resumption of hostilities between France, America's wartime ally, and Great Britain, America's most important trading partner.

Initially, Americans welcomed the news that France was turning toward republicanism. But by the early 1790s, the reports from France were disquieting. Outbreaks of violence continued; ministries succeeded each other with bewildering rapidity; executions were commonplace. The king was beheaded in early 1793. Although many Americans, including Jefferson and Madison, retained their sympathy for the French revolutionaries, others began to view France as a prime example of the perversion of republicanism. As might be expected, Alexander Hamilton fell into the latter group.

When France declared war on Britain, Spain, and Holland in 1793, the Americans faced a dilemma. The 1778 Treaty of Alliance with France bound them to that nation "forever," and a mutual commitment to republicanism created ideological bonds. Yet the United States was connected to Great Britain as well. Aside from their shared history and language, America and England were economic partners. Americans still purchased most of their manufactured goods from Great Britain.

Indeed, because the financial system of the United States depended heavily on import tariffs as a source of revenue, the nation's economic health in effect required uninterrupted trade with England.

The political and diplomatic climate was further complicated in April 1793, when Citizen Edmond Genêt, a representative of the French government, landed in Charleston.

Citizen Genêt

As Genêt made his way north to New York City, he recruited Americans for expeditions against British and Spanish possessions in the Western Hemisphere and distributed privateering commissions with a generous hand. Genêt's arrival raised a series of troubling questions for President Washington. Should he receive Genêt, thus officially recognizing the French revolutionary government? Should he acknowledge an obligation to aid France under the terms of the 1778 Treaty of Alliance? Or should he proclaim American neutrality in the conflict?

For once, Hamilton and Jefferson saw eye to eye. Both told Washington that the United States could not afford to ally firmly with either side. Washington agreed. He received Genêt but also issued the Neutrality Proclamation, informing the world that the United States would adopt "a conduct friendly and impartial toward the belligerent powers."

Genêt was removed from politics when his faction fell from power in Paris. But his disappearance from the diplomatic scene did not lessen the influence of the French Revolution in America. The domestic divisions Genêt helped to widen were perpetuated by clubs called Democratic-Republican societies, formed by Americans sympathetic to the French Revolution and worried about the policies of the Washington administration.

More than forty Democratic-Republican societies were organized between 1793 and 1800. Their members saw themselves as heirs of the Sons of Liberty, seeking the same goal as their predecessors: protection of the people's liberties against encroachments by corrupt and self-serving rulers. To that end, they publicly protested government policy and repeatedly proclaimed their belief in "the equal rights of man,"

Democratic-Republican Societies

particularly the rights to free speech, free press, and assembly. Like the Sons of Liberty, the Democratic-Republican societies were composed chiefly of artisans and craftsmen, although professionals, farmers, and merchants also joined.

The rapid growth of such groups, outspoken in their criticism of the Washington administration, deeply disturbed Hamilton and eventually Washington. Newspapers sympathetic to the Federalists charged that the societies were subversive agents of a foreign power. The climax of the counterattack came in the fall of 1794, when Washington accused the societies of having fomented the Whiskey Rebellion.

In retrospect, the reaction of Washington and Hamilton to the Democratic-Republican societies seems disproportionate to the threat they posed to the administration. But it must be recalled that factional disputes were believed to be dangerous to the survival of a republic. The Democratic-Republican societies were the first formally organized political dissenters in the United States. As such, they alarmed elected officials who had not yet accepted the idea that one component of a free government was an organized loyal opposition.

That same year, George Washington decided to send Chief Justice John Jay to England to try to reach agreement on four unresolved questions affecting Anglo-American affairs.

Jay Treaty

The first point at issue was recent British seizures of American merchant ships trading in the French West Indies. The United States wanted to establish the principle of freedom of the seas and to assert its right, as a neutral nation, to trade freely with both sides. Second, Great Britain had not yet carried out its promise in the 1783 Treaty of Paris to evacuate its posts in the American Northwest. Third and fourth, Americans hoped for a commercial treaty and sought compensation for the slaves who had left with the British army at the end of the war.

The negotiations in London proved difficult, because Jay had little to offer in exchange for the concessions he wanted. In the end, Britain did agree to evacuate the western forts and ease the restrictions on American trade to England and the West Indies. No compensation for slaves was agreed to, but Jay accepted a provision establishing an arbitration commission to deal with prewar debts owed to British creditors. A similar commission was to handle compensation for the seizures of American merchant ships. Under the circumstances, Jay did remarkably well: the treaty averted war with England. Nevertheless, most Americans, including the president, were dissatisfied with at least some parts of the treaty.

At first, potential opposition was blunted, because the Senate debated and ratified the treaty in secret. Not until after it was formally approved in June 1795 was the public informed of its provisions. The Democratic-Republican societies led protests against the treaty that were especially intense in the South. Once President Washington had reluctantly signed the treaty, though, there seemed to be little the Republicans could do to prevent it from taking effect. Just one opportunity remained: Congress had to appropriate funds to carry out the treaty provisions.

When the House took up the issue in March 1796, members opposing the treaty tried to prevent approval of the appropriations. To that end, they called on Washington to submit to the House all documents pertinent to the negotiations. In successfully resisting the House's request, Washington established the doctrine of executive privilege—the power of the president to withhold information from Congress if he believes circumstances warrant doing so. The treaty's opponents initially appeared to be in the majority. Frontier residents, however, were eager for evacuation of the British posts, and merchants wanted to reap the benefits of widened trade with the British Empire. Furthermore, Thomas Pinckney of South Carolina had negotiated a treaty with Spain giving the United States navigation privileges on the Mississippi, which would be an economic boost to the West and South. Its popularity (the Senate ratified Pinckney's Treaty unanimously) helped to overcome opposition to the Jay Treaty. For all these reasons, the House voted the necessary funds by the narrow margin of 51 to 48.

Analysis of the vote reveals both the regional nature of the division and the growing cohesion of the Republican and Federalist factions in Congress.

Republicans and Federalists Voting in favor of the appropriations were 44 Federalists and 7 Republicans; voting against were 45 Republicans and 3

Federalists. The final tally was also split by region. Southerners cast the vast majority of votes against the bill. The bill's supporters were from New England and the middle states, with the exception of two South Carolina Federalists.

The small number of defectors on both sides reveals a new force at work in American politics: partisanship. Voting statistics from the first four Congresses show the ever increasing tendency of members of the House of Representatives to vote as cohesive groups rather than as individuals. If *factional loyalty* is defined as voting together at least two-thirds of the time on national issues, the percentage of nonaligned congressmen dropped from 42 percent in 1790 to just 7 percent in 1796.

The terms used by Jefferson and Madison (*aristocrats* versus *the people*) or by Hamilton and Washington (*true patriots* versus *subversive rabble*) cannot accurately explain the growing division. Simple economic differences between agrarian and commercial interests do not provide the answer either, because more than 90 percent of Americans in the 1790s lived in rural areas.

Yet certain distinctions can be made. Republicans, who were especially prominent in the southern and middle states, tended to be self-assured, confident, and optimistic about both politics and the economy. Southern planters, firmly in control of their region, did not fear instability, at least among the white population. They foresaw a prosperous future based partly on continued westward expansion, which they expected to dominate. Republicans employed democratic rhetoric to win the allegiance of small farmers south of New England. Their ranks also included members of non-English ethnic groups, especially Irish, Scots, and Germans, and urban artisans. Republicans of all descriptions emphasized developing America's own resources and were less concerned about the nation's position in the world. Republicans also remained sympathetic to France in international affairs.

By contrast, Federalists, concentrated in New England, came mostly from English stock. They drew considerable support from commercial interests and were insecure, uncertain of the future. They stressed the need for order, authority, and regularity in the political world. Unlike Republicans, Federalists had no grassroots political organization and put little emphasis on involving ordinary people in government. Not all Federalists were wealthy merchants; many were farmers who, prevented from expanding agricultural production because of New England's poor soil, gravitated to the more conservative party. Federalists, like Republicans, assumed that southern interests would dominate the lands west of the mountains, so they had little incentive to work actively to develop that potentially rich territory. In Federalist eyes, the nation was perpetually threatened by potential enemies, both internal and external, and was best protected by a continuing alliance with Great Britain. Because the Federalist view held out little hope of a better future to the voters of any region, it is not surprising that the Republicans eventually prevailed.

The presence of the two organized groups—not yet parties in the modern sense but active contenders for office nonetheless—made the

Washington's Farewell Address
———

presidential election of 1796 the first that was seriously contested. Tired of the criticism to which he had been subjected, George Washington decided to retire from office. In September, Washington published his famous Farewell Address. In it, Washington outlined two principles that guided American foreign policy at least until the late 1940s: to maintain commercial but not political ties to other nations and to enter no permanent alliances. In doing so, he stressed the need for unilateralism (independent action in foreign affairs). He also lamented the factional division among the citizenry and attacked the legitimacy of the Republican opposition.

To succeed Washington, the Federalists in Congress put forward Vice President John Adams, with the diplomat Thomas Pinckney of South

Election of 1796
———

Carolina as his vice presidential running mate. Congressional Republicans caucused and chose Thomas Jefferson as their presidential candidate; the lawyer, Revolutionary War veteran, and active Republican politician Aaron Burr of New York agreed to run for vice president.

That the election was contested did not mean that the people decided its outcome. Voters could

cast their ballots only for electors, not for the candidates themselves. State legislatures, not the popular vote, chose more than 40 percent of the members of the electoral college. Moreover, the method of voting in the electoral college did not take into account the possibility of party slates. The authors of the Constitution had not foreseen the development of competing national political organizations, and the Constitution provided no way to express explicit support for one person for president and another for vice president. The electors simply voted for two people. The man with the highest total became president, the second highest vice president. Thus Adams, the Federalist with 71 votes, became the new president, and Jefferson, the Republican, with 68 votes, became the vice president.

JOHN ADAMS AND POLITICAL DISSENT

John Adams took over the presidency peculiarly blind to the partisan developments of the previous four years. As president, he never abandoned the outdated notion that the president should be above politics, an independent and dignified figure who did not seek petty factional advantage. Thus Adams kept Washington's cabinet intact, despite its key members' allegiance to his chief rival, Alexander Hamilton. Adams often adopted a passive posture, letting others (usually Hamilton) take the lead when he should have acted decisively. As a result, his administration gained a reputation for inconsistency. When Adams's term ended, the Federalists were severely divided, and the Republicans had won the presidency. But Adams's detachment from Hamilton's maneuverings did enable him to weather the greatest international crisis the Republic had yet faced: the so-called Quasi-War with France.

The Jay Treaty improved America's relationship with England, but it provoked retaliation by France. Angry that the United States had reached agreement with its enemy, the Directory (the coalition then in power in Paris) ordered French vessels to seize American ships carrying British goods. In response, Adams appointed three special commissioners to try to reach a settlement with France:

Elbridge Gerry, an old friend from Massachusetts; John Marshall, a Virginia Federalist; and Charles Cotesworth Pinckney of South Carolina. At the same time, Congress increased military spending.

For months, the American commissioners futilely sought negotiations with Talleyrand, the French foreign minister. Talleyrand's agents demanded a bribe of $250,000 before talks could begin. The Americans retorted, "No, no; not a sixpence," and reported the incident in dispatches that President Adams received in early March 1798. Adams informed Congress of the impasse and recommended increased appropriations for defense.

XYZ Affair
—

Convinced that Adams had deliberately sabotaged the negotiations, congressional Republicans insisted that he turn the dispatches over to Congress. Adams complied, aware that releasing the reports would work to his advantage. He withheld only the names of the French agents, referring to them as *X, Y,* and *Z.* The revelation that the Americans had been treated with utter contempt stimulated a wave of anti-French sentiment in the United States. Cries for war filled the air. Congress formally abrogated the Treaty of Alliance and authorized American ships to seize French vessels.

Thus began an undeclared war with France. The so-called Quasi-War was fought in the West Indies, between warships of the U.S. Navy and French privateers seeking to capture American merchant vessels. Although initial American losses of merchant shipping were heavy, by early 1799 the navy had established its superiority in Caribbean waters. Its ships captured eight French privateers and naval vessels, easing the threat to America's vital West Indian trade.

Alien and Sedition Acts
—

The Republicans, who opposed war and continued to sympathize with France, could do little to stem the tide of anti-French feelings. The Federalists saw this climate of opinion as an opportunity to deal a death blow to their Republican opponents. Now that the country seemed to see the truth of what they had been saying ever since the Whiskey Rebellion in 1794—that the Republicans were subversive foreign agents—the Federalists sought to codify that belief in law. In 1798, the Federalist-controlled Congress adopted a set of four laws known as the Alien and Sedition Acts, intended to suppress dissent and prevent further growth of the Republican party.

Three acts were aimed at immigrants, whom the Federalists accurately suspected of being Republican in their sympathies. The Naturalization Act lengthened the residency period required for citizenship and ordered all resident aliens to register with the federal government. The Alien Enemies Act provided for the detention of enemy aliens in time of war. The Alien Friends Act, to be in effect for two years, gave the president almost unlimited authority to deport any alien he deemed dangerous to the nation's security. (Adams never used that authority. The Alien Enemies Act was not implemented either, because Congress never formally declared war.)

The fourth law, the Sedition Act, sought to control both citizens and aliens. It outlawed conspiracies to prevent the enforcement of federal laws and set the maximum punishment for such offenses at five years in prison and a $5,000 fine. The act also tried to control speech. Writing, printing, or uttering "false, scandalous and malicious" statements against the government or the president "with intent to defame . . . or to bring them or either of them, into contempt or disrepute" became a crime punishable by as much as two years' imprisonment and a fine of $2,000.

In all, there were fifteen indictments and ten convictions under the Sedition Act. Most accused were outspoken Republican newspaper editors who failed to mute their criticism of the administration in response to the law. But the first victim—whose story may serve as an example of the rest—was a hot-tempered Republican congressman from Vermont, Matthew Lyon. The Irish-born Lyon was fined $1,000 and given a four-month prison sentence for declaring in print that John Adams had displayed "a continual grasp for power" and "an unbounded thirst for ridiculous pomp, foolish adulation, and selfish avarice." Lyon conducted his reelection campaign from jail, winning an overwhelming majority.

Faced with the prosecutions of their major supporters, Jefferson and Madison sought an effective means of combating the Alien and Sedition Acts.

Virginia and Kentucky Resolutions
———

They turned to constitutional theory and the state legislatures. Carefully concealing their own role—it would hardly have been desirable for the vice president to be indicted for sedition—Jefferson and Madison each drafted a set of resolutions. Introduced into the Kentucky and Virginia legislatures, respectively, in the fall of 1798, the resolutions differed somewhat, but their import was the same. Because the Constitution was created by a compact among the states, they contended, the people speaking through their states had a legitimate right to judge the constitutionality of actions taken by the federal government. Both sets of resolutions pronounced the Alien and Sedition Acts null and void and asked other states to join the protest.

Although no other state endorsed them, the Virginia and Kentucky Resolutions were nevertheless influential. First, they were superb political propaganda, rallying Republican opinion throughout the country. They placed the opposition party squarely in the revolutionary tradition of resistance to tyrannical authority. Second, the theory of union they proposed inspired southern states' rights advocates in the 1830s and thereafter. Jefferson and Madison had identified a key constitutional issue: how far could the states go in opposing the national government? How could a conflict between the two be resolved? These questions were not to be definitively answered until the Civil War.

Meanwhile, the Federalists split over the course of action the United States should take toward France. Hamilton and his supporters still called for a declaration legitimizing the undeclared naval war. But Adams received a number of private signals that the Directory regretted its treatment of the three American commissioners. Acting on these assurances, he dispatched an envoy to Paris. The United States asked two things of France: nearly $20 million in compensation for ships the French had seized since 1793 and abrogation of the treaty of 1778. The Convention of 1800, which ended the Quasi-War, provided for the latter but not the former. The results of the negotiations, however, were not known in America until after the election of 1800. By then, the split in Federalist ranks had already cost Adams his reelection.

In sharp contrast, the Republicans entered the 1800 presidential race firmly united behind Jefferson and Burr. Although they won the election,

Election of 1800
———

their lack of foresight almost cost them dearly. The problem was the system of voting in the electoral college. All Republican electors voted for both Jefferson and Burr, giving each 73 votes (Adams had 65). Because neither Republican had a plurality, the Constitution required that the contest be decided in the House of Representatives, with each state's representatives voting as a unit. Because the new House, dominated by Republicans, would not take office for some months, Federalist representatives decided the election by selecting Jefferson on the thirty-fifth ballot. In response to the tangle, the Twelfth Amendment to the Constitution (1804) changed the method of voting in the electoral college to allow for a party ticket.

———

WESTWARD EXPANSION, SOCIAL CHANGE, AND RELIGIOUS FERMENT

The United States experienced a dramatic increase in internal migration in the postrevolutionary years. As much as 5 to 10 percent of the population moved each year, approximately half relocating to another state. Young white men were the most mobile segment of the populace. The major population shifts were from east to west (see map): from New England to upstate New York and Ohio, from New Jersey to western Pennsylvania, from the Chesapeake to the new states of Kentucky and Tennessee, which entered the Union in 1792 and 1796, respectively. Few people moved north or south.

Western Expansion, 1785–1805 After the Revolutionary War, large numbers of white and black Americans ventured west of the Appalachian Mountains for the first time. Following certain distinct routes, they moved along rivers like the Mohawk (in New York) and the Ohio or through passes like the Cumberland Gap.

The first permanent white settlements beyond the Appalachian Mountains were established in western North Carolina in 1771. But not until after

White Settlement in the West

the defeat of the Shawnees in 1774 and the Cherokees in 1776 was the way cleared for a more general migration. By 1790, more than one hundred thousand residents lived in the future states of Kentucky and Tennessee. North of the Ohio River, white settlements grew more slowly because of the strength of the Miami Confederacy. Once the Treaty of Greenville was signed in 1795, however, the Ohio country grew rapidly.

The transplanted New Englanders in particular did their best to recreate the societies they had left behind, laying out farms and towns in neat checkerboard patterns and founding libraries and Congregational churches. Early arrivals' enthusiastic letters describing Ohio's rich soil and potential for growth recruited others to join them, setting off a phenomenon known in New England as Ohio Fever. The New Englanders, proud of their literate, orderly culture, viewed their neighbors with disdain. Ohioans, said one, were "intelligent, industrious, and thriving," whereas the Virginians who had settled across the river in Kentucky were "ignorant, lazy, and poor."

The westward migration of slave-holding whites, first to Kentucky and Tennessee and then later into the rich lands of western Georgia and eventually the Gulf Coast, had

African-Americans in the West

an adverse effect on African-Americans. The population movement tore apart the web of family connections built up over several generations of residence in the Chesapeake. Even those few large planters who moved their entire slave force west rarely owned all members of every family on their plantations. Most common, the white migrants were either younger sons of eastern slave holders, whose inheritance included only a portion of the family's slaves, or small farmers with just one or two slaves. In the early years of American settlement in the West, the population was widely dispersed; accordingly, African-Americans raised among large numbers of

kin in the Chesapeake had to adapt to lonely lives on isolated farms. The approximately one hundred thousand African-Americans forcibly moved west by 1810 had to begin to build new families there to replace those unwillingly left behind in the East.

The mobility of both blacks and whites created a volatile population mix in southern frontier areas (see map). Because most migrants were young single men just starting to lead independent lives, western society was at first unstable. Like the seventeenth-century Chesapeake, the late eighteenth-century American West was a society in which single women married quickly. The few women among the migrants lamented their lack of congenial female friends. Isolated, far from familiar surroundings, women and men strove to create new communities to replace those they had left behind.

Perhaps the most meaningful of the new communities was the affiliation supplied by evangelical religion. Among the migrants to Kentucky and

Second Great Awakening

Tennessee were clergy and committed lay members of the evangelical sects that arose in America after the First Great Awakening: Baptists, Presbyterians, and Methodists. At camp meetings, sometimes attended by thousands of people and usually lasting from three days to a week, clergymen exhorted their audiences to repent their sins and become genuine Christians. They declared that salvation was open to all, rejecting the doctrine of predestination that had characterized Calvinism. They stressed the emotional nature of the conversion experience far more than the need for careful study and preparation. Such preachers were in effect democratizing American religion, making it available to all rather than to a preselected and educated elite.

The most famous camp meeting took place at Cane Ridge, Kentucky, in 1801. At a time when the largest settlement in the state had no more than two thousand inhabitants, attendance at Cane Ridge was estimated at more than ten thousand. One witness, a Presbyterian cleric, recounted how people responded to the preaching with "loud ejaculations of prayer, . . . some struck with terror, . . . others, trembling, weeping and crying out, . . . others surrounding them with melodious songs, or fervent prayers

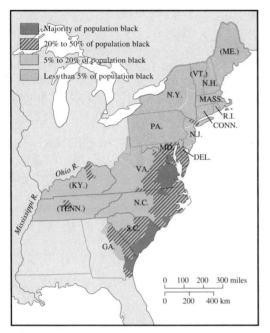

African-American Population, 1790: Proportion of Total Population The first census clearly indicated that the African-American population was heavily concentrated in just a few areas of the United States, most notably in coastal regions of South Carolina, Georgia, and Virginia. Although there were growing numbers of blacks in the backcountry—presumably taken there by migrating slave owners—most parts of the North and East, with the exception of the immediate vicinity of New York City, had few African-American residents. Source: From Lester J. Cappon et al., eds., *Atlas of Early American History: The Revolutionary Era, 1760–1790.* Copyright © 1976 by Princeton University Press. Reprinted by permission of Princeton University Press.

for their happy resurrection, in the love of Christ." Revivals swept different regions of the country until nearly midcentury, leaving an indelible legacy of evangelism to many American Protestant churches.

The established churches of the colonial era—supported, like the Congregationalists in Massachusetts or the Anglicans in Virginia, by tax revenues—came under vigorous attack from dissenters who used revolutionary ideology to great advantage. As a result, many states dissolved their ties

Attacks on Established Churches
——

to churches during or immediately after the war; others vastly reduced state support for established denominations. Without state support, they had to find other sources of revenue. Revivals, while representing a genuine outpouring of religious sentiment, had their more mundane side. They produced converts who in turn provided additional revenue.

An analysis of secular society can help to explain the conversion patterns of the Second Awakening. Unlike the First Great Awakening, when converts were evenly divided by sex, more women than men—particularly young women—answered the call of Christianity during the Second Awakening. The increase in female converts seems to have been directly related to fundamental changes in women's circumstances at the end of the eighteenth century. In some areas of the country, especially New England, women outnumbered men after 1790. Thus eastern women could no longer count on finding marital partners. The uncertainty of their social and familial position seems to have led them to seek spiritual certainty through religion. In the churches, they created hundreds of female associations to aid widows and orphans, collect money for foreign missions, and improve the quality of maternal care. Thus American women collectively assumed the role of keepers of the nation's conscience, taking the lead in charitable enterprises and freeing men from concern for such moral issues.

Women and the Second Awakening
——

The religious ferment among blacks and whites in frontier regions of the Upper South contributed to racial ferment as well. People of both races attended the camp meetings to hear both black and white preachers. When revivals spread eastward into more heavily slave-holding areas, white planters became fearful of the egalitarianism implied in the evangelical message of universal salvation and harmony. At the same time, revivals created a group of respected African-American leaders—preachers—and provided them a ready audience.

African-Americans and the Second Awakening
——

Events in the West Indies gave whites ample reason for apprehension. In 1793, mulattos and blacks in the French colony of Saint Domingue (Haiti) overthrew European rule under the leadership of a mulatto, Toussaint L'Ouverture. In an attempt to prevent the spread of such unrest to their own enslaved workers, southern state legislators passed laws forbidding white Haitian refugees from bringing their slaves with them. But North American blacks learned about the revolt anyway. And the preconditions for racial upheaval already existed in the South.

Like their white compatriots, African-Americans (both slave and free) had become familiar with notions of liberty and equality. They had also witnessed the benefits of fighting collectively for freedom rather than resisting individually or running away. The circumstances were ripe for an

explosion, and the Second Awakening was the match that lit the fuse.

In Virginia, a revolt was planned by Gabriel Prosser, a blacksmith who argued that blacks should fight to obtain the same rights as whites and who explicitly placed himself in the tradition of the French and Haitian revolutions. At revival meetings led by his brother Martin, a preacher, Prosser recruited other African-Americans like himself—urban artisans who moved easily in both black and white circles and who lived in semifreedom under minimal white supervision. The artisan leaders then enlisted rural blacks in the cause. The con-

Gabriel's Rebellion
———

In 1805, an unidentified artist painted Benjamin Hawkins, a trader and U.S. agent to the Indians of the Southeast, at the Creek agency near Macon, Georgia. Hawkins introduced European-style agriculture to the Creeks, who are depicted with vegetables from their fields. Throughout the eastern United States, Indian nations had to make similar adaptations of their traditional lifestyles in order to maintain their group identity.   Courtesy of Sumter Priddy and the Greenville County Art Museum, South Carolina.

How do historians know

that Americans were intensely patriotic in the early years of the Republic? One piece of evidence is supplied by the many items incorporating patriotic decorative motifs that were produced for use in the homes of middling and well-to-do American citizens. The artisans of the new nation quickly recognized that patriotism sold, and so they created a wide variety of objects to satisfy the demand—furniture, wallpaper, curtains, and pottery goods all drew on such themes. The owner of this four-foot-long parlor wall mirror, for example, would have seen Revolutionary War cannons and swords, a symbolic eagle, and George Washington himself, along with whatever household furnishings it reflected, each time she looked into it. Such reminders of national pride helped to confirm the new Republic's identity. Photo: Henry Francis du Pont Winterthur Museum.

spirators planned to attack Richmond on the night of August 30, 1800, setting fire to the city, seizing the state capitol, and capturing the governor. Their plan showed considerable political sophistication, but heavy rain made it impossible to carry out on schedule. Several whites then learned of the plan from their slaves and spread the alarm. Prosser avoided capture for some weeks, but most other leaders of the rebellion were quickly arrested and interrogated. The main conspirators, including

Prosser, were hanged, but in the months that followed, other insurrectionary scares continued to frighten Virginia slave owners.

The Iroquois too experienced a religious revival in the early nineteenth century. Led by their prophet Handsome Lake, the remaining American Iroquois, who were scattered on small reservations, embraced the traditional values of their culture and renounced such destructive white customs as drinking alcohol and gambling. At the same time, though, they began abandoning their ancient way of life. With Handsome Lake's approval, Quaker missionaries taught the Iroquois Anglo-American styles of agricultural subsistence; men were now to be cultivators rather than hunters and women housekeepers rather than cultivators. Because the tribes had lost their hunting territories to white farmers, Iroquois men accepted the changes readily. But many women, especially the powerful tribal matrons, resisted the shift in the gender division of labor. By surrendering control over food production, they realized, they would jeopardize their status in the tribe. But Handsome Lake branded as witches women who opposed the changes too vigorously, and eventually he triumphed.

Handsome Lake

As the new century began, the inhabitants of the United States were moving toward an accommodation to their new lives in the Republic. Native American peoples east of the Mississippi found that they had to give up some parts of their traditional culture to preserve others. Blacks and whites tried to create new lives in the West and to adjust to changed economic circumstances in the East. Building on successful negotiations with both Britain (the Jay Treaty) and France (the Convention of 1800), the United States developed its diplomatic independence, striving to avoid entanglement with the European powers. The 1790s spawned vigorous debates over foreign and domestic policy and saw the beginnings of a system of political parties. Religious revivals swept portions of the countryside, and again those revivals contributed to social unrest.

At the end of the decade, after years of struggle, the Jeffersonian interpretation of republicanism finally prevailed over Hamilton's approach. As a result, the country would be characterized in the years to come by a decentralized economy, minimal government (especially at the national level), and maximum freedom of action and mobility for individual white men. Jeffersonian Republicans, like white male Americans before them, failed to extend to white women, tribal people, and African-Americans the freedom and individuality they recognized as essential for themselves.

SUGGESTIONS FOR FURTHER READING

National Government and Administration

Kenneth Bowling, *The Creation of Washington, D.C.* (1991); Ralph Adams Brown, *The Presidency of John Adams* (1975); Morton Frisch, *Alexander Hamilton and the Political Order* (1991); Forrest McDonald, *The Presidency of George Washington* (1974); Merrill D. Peterson, *Thomas Jefferson and the New Nation* (1970).

Partisan Politics

Lance Banning, *The Jeffersonian Persuasion: Evolution of a Party Ideology* (1978); Richard Buel, *Securing the Revolution: Ideology in American Politics, 1789–1815* (1972); William Nisbet Chambers, *Political Parties in a New Nation: The American Experience, 1776–1809* (1963); Richard Hofstadter, *The Idea of a Party System: The Rise of Legitimate Opposition in the United States, 1780–1840* (1970); Adrienne Koch, *Jefferson and Madison: The Great Collaboration* (1950); Eugene P. Link, *Democratic-Republican Societies, 1790–1800* (1942).

Foreign Policy

Harry Ammon, *The Genêt Mission* (1973); Jerald A. Combs, *The Jay Treaty* (1970); Alexander DeConde, *The Quasi-War: Politics and Diplomacy of the Undeclared War with France, 1797–1801* (1966), and *Entangling Alliance: Politics and Diplomacy Under George Washington* (1958); Reginald Horsman, *The Diplomacy of the New Republic, 1776–1815* (1985); Lawrence Kaplan, *"Entangling Alliances with None": American Foreign Policy in the Age of Jefferson* (1987); William Stinchcombe, *The XYZ Affair* (1981).

Civil Liberties

Leonard W. Levy, *Emergence of a Free Press* (1985); Robert A. Rutland, *The Birth of the Bill of Rights, 1776–1791*, rev. ed. (1983); James Morton Smith, *Freedom's Fetters: The Alien and Sedition Laws and American Civil Liberties* (1956).

Women, African-Americans, and the Family

Nancy F. Cott, *The Bonds of Womanhood: "Woman's Sphere" in New England, 1780–1835* (1977); Douglas Egerton, *Gabriel's Rebellion: The Virginia Slave Conspiracies of 1800 and 1802* (1993); Laurel Thatcher Ulrich, *A Midwife's Tale* (1990).

Social Change and Westward Expansion

Andrew Cayton, *The Frontier Republic: Ideology and Politics in the Ohio Country, 1789–1812* (1986); Malcolm Rohrbough, *The Trans-Appalachian Frontier: Peoples, Societies, and Institutions, 1775–1850* (1979); Thomas Slaughter, *The Whiskey Rebellion* (1986); Charles G. Steffen, *The Mechanics of Baltimore: Workers and Politics in the Age of Revolution, 1763–1812* (1984); Sean Wilentz, *Chants Democratic: New York City and the Rise of the American Working Class, 1788–1850* (1984).

Religion

Catharine Albanese, *Sons of the Fathers: The Civil Religion of the American Revolution* (1976); Ruth Bloch, *Visionary Republic: Millennial Themes in American Thought* (1985); Paul Conkin, *Cane Ridge: America's Pentecost* (1990); Nathan O. Hatch, *The Democratization of American Christianity* (1990).

The Empire of Liberty,
1801–1824

ANDREW MERRY, THE BRITISH minister to the United States, stormed out of the executive mansion, certain that President Thomas Jefferson had insulted the British government and monarch. "I, in my official costume, found myself at the hour of reception he had himself appointed, introduced to a man as president of the United States, not merely in an undress, but *actually standing in slippers down at the heels*, and both pantaloons, coat, and under-clothes indicative of . . . indifference to appearances." Jefferson's predecessors, Washington and Adams, had appeared in public in wigs and breeches (knee-length trousers); Jefferson wore ordinary clothes. Jefferson had intended no insult, but he was making a statement. With the election of 1800, a revolution had swept the United States; aristocratic airs were a thing of the past.

The bitterness of the election of 1800 and the newness of the Republic had generated some anxiety about whether the transfer of power from the Federalists to the Republicans would be peaceful. Amid that uncertainty, Thomas Jefferson had strolled from his New Jersey Avenue boarding house in the new federal capital of Washington,

D.C., to take the oath as president at the Capitol. Though unaware that they were doing so, Republicans and Federalists were establishing the precedent of an orderly and peaceful change of government.

Jefferson was inaugurated at the beginning of a period in which Americans were struggling to assert and define their nationalism amid challenges, both foreign and domestic. Monarchial traditions inherited from Great Britain confronted the republican virtues of independence, self-reliance, and equality. In contrast to the formality of the Federalist presidencies of Washington and Adams, Jefferson, like other Republicans, preferred simplicity to pomp, equality to social distinctions. Republican virtue would be restored.

Chosen for its central location, the District of Columbia had been carved out of Maryland and Virginia. The capital was thus beholden neither to the colonial past nor to any single state. The small government, which essentially collected tariffs, delivered mail, negotiated with foreign governments, and defended the nation's borders, suited the Republic. In an age when it took some congressmen more than a

This portrait of President Thomas Jefferson was painted by Rembrandt Peale in 1805. Charles Willson Peale and his five sons helped establish the reputation of American art in the new nation. Rembrandt Peale was most famous for his presidential portraits; here he captures Jefferson in a noble pose without the usual symbols of office or power, befitting the Republican age. New York Historical Society.

week to travel from home to the capital, most Americans favored government closer to home. Although President Jefferson, after his inauguration in 1801, cut the federal budget and operations, he and his Republican successors, James Madison and James Monroe, invigorated the federal government during the next two decades.

The transfer of power to the Republicans from the Federalists intensified political conflict and voter interest. In the tradition of the Revolution, Republican presidents sought limited government, believing it would further republican virtue and encourage Americans to place obligations of citizenship and the public interest above private ambitions. The Federalists focused more on the market economy and economic individualism. Thus they prized a stronger national government with more centralized authority to promote economic development.

With both factions competing for popular support, the basis was laid for the evolution of democratic politics. But factionalism, personal animosities, and partisanship within each group prevented the development of cohesive political parties.

Events abroad and on the frontier encouraged and threatened the expansionism Americans had practiced from colonial times. Seizing one opportunity, the United States purchased the Louisiana Territory, pushing the frontier farther west. But then from the high seas came war. Caught between the warring British and French, the United States found its shipping rights as a neutral, independent nation ignored and violated. When the humiliation and threat to U.S. interests became too great, Americans took up arms in the War of 1812, both to defend their rights as a nation and to expand farther to the west and north.

The War of 1812 unleashed a wave of nationalism and self-confidence. War needs promoted the development of domestic manufacturing and internal transportation. With peace, the federal government championed business and construction of roads and canals. The new spirit encouraged economic growth and western expansion at home, trade abroad, and assertiveness throughout the Western Hemisphere. By the 1820s, the United States was no longer an experiment; a new nation had emerged.

Economic growth and territorial expansion, however, generated new problems. In 1819, a financial panic brought hardship and conflict that sowed the seeds for the Jacksonian movement in the 1820s and 1830s. More ominous, sectional differences and the presence of slavery created divisions that would widen in the wake of further westward expansion during the 1840s and 1850s.

JEFFERSON IN POWER

Jefferson delivered his inaugural address in the unfinished Capitol building. In an appeal for unity, he told the assembly, "We are all Republicans, we are all Federalists." Addressing those with little faith in the people's ability to govern themselves, he called America's republican government "the

Jefferson's Inaugural Address

world's best hope." The new president went on to outline his goals:

A wise and frugal government, which shall restrain men from injuring one another, which shall leave them otherwise free to regulate their own pursuits. . . . Equal and exact justice to all men, of whatever state or persuasion, religious or political. . . . The support of the state governments in all their rights, as the most competent administrators for our domestic concerns and the surest bulwarks against antirepublican tendencies.

At the same time, he assured Federalists that he shared their concerns:

The preservation of the general government in its whole constitutional vigor. . . . The honest payment of our debts and sacred preservation of the public faith. . . . Encouragement of agriculture and of commerce as its handmaid.

Still, the Federalists and Republicans distrusted each other. Republicans considered Federalists antidemocratic and antirepublican at heart and accused them of imitating the court society of England. Federalists accused Republicans of undermining social deference and favoring egalitarianism, which they believed had recently led to anarchy in France.

Almost immediately, Jefferson extended the Republicans' grasp over the federal government. Virtually all officials appointed under Washington and Adams were loyal Federalists. To restore government to those who shared his visions of an agrarian republic and individual liberty, Jefferson refused to recognize Adams's last-minute "midnight appointments" to local offices in the District of Columbia. He also dismissed Federalist customs collectors from New England ports and awarded vacant treasury and judicial offices to Republicans. By July 1803, Federalists still held only 130 of 316 presidentially controlled offices. Jefferson adroitly used patronage to build a party organization, compete with the Federalists, and restore political balance in government.

The Republican Congress proceeded to affirm its belief in limited government. Albert Gallatin, secretary of the treasury, and Representative John Randolph of Virginia put the federal government on a diet. Congress repealed all internal taxes, including the whiskey tax. Gallatin cut the army budget in half, to just under $2 million, and reduced the 1802 navy budget from $3.5 to $1 million. Gallatin planned to reduce the national debt—which Alexander Hamilton viewed as the engine of economic growth—from $83 million to $57 million, as part of a plan to retire it altogether by 1817.

More than frugality, however, distinguished Republicans from Federalists. Opposition to the Alien and Sedition Acts of 1798 had helped unite Republicans. Now Congress let the acts expire in 1801 and 1802. Congress also repealed the Naturalization Act of 1798, which had required fourteen years of residency for citizenship. The 1802 act that replaced it required only five years of residency, acceptance of the Constitution, and the forsaking of foreign allegiance and titles.

The Republicans turned next to the judiciary, the last stronghold of unchecked Federalist power. During the 1790s, not a single Republican had been appointed to the federal bench.

Attacks on the Judiciary

The Judiciary Act of 1801, passed in the final days of the Adams administration, had created fifteen new judgeships, which Adams filled by signing midnight appointments until his term was just hours from expiring. The act would also reduce by attrition the number of justices on the Supreme Court from six to five. Because that reduction would have denied Jefferson a Supreme Court appointment until two vacancies had occurred, the new Republican-dominated Congress repealed the 1801 act.

The Republicans also targeted opposition judges for removal. Federalist judges had refused to review the Sedition Act under which Federalists had prosecuted critics of the Adams administration. At Jefferson's prompting, the House impeached (indicted) federal District Judge John Pickering of New Hampshire, an emotionally disturbed alcoholic, and in 1804 the Senate removed him from office.

The day Pickering was convicted, the House impeached Supreme Court Justice Samuel Chase on several counts of judicial misconduct. Chase had repeatedly denounced Jefferson's administration from the bench. The Republicans, however, failed to muster the two-thirds majority of senators necessary to convict him. Their failure to remove Chase preserved the Court's independence: it established the

Important Events

1801	John Marshall becomes chief justice Jefferson inaugurated as first Republican president
1801–05	United States defeats Barbary pirates in Tripoli War
1803	*Marbury v. Madison* establishes judicial review U.S. purchases Louisiana Territory
1804	Jefferson reelected
1804–06	Lewis and Clark expedition reaches the Pacific Ocean
1805	Prophet emerges as Shawnee leader
1807	*Chesapeake* affair almost leads to war Embargo Act halts foreign trade
1808	Madison elected president
1808–13	Prophet and Tecumseh organize Native American tribal resistance
1812–15	War of 1812 is fought
1813	Death of Tecumseh ends effective pan-Indian resistance
1814	Treaty of Ghent ends the War of 1812
1814–15	Hartford Convention undermines Federalists
1815	Battle of New Orleans makes Andrew Jackson a hero
1816	Monroe elected president Second Bank of the United States chartered
1817	Rush-Bagot Treaty limits naval forces on Lakes Ontario and Champlain
1819	*McCulloch v. Maryland* establishes supremacy of federal over state law Adams-Onís Treaty gives Florida to United States and defines Louisiana territorial border
1819–23	Financial panic and depression: hard times for Americans
1820	Missouri Compromise creates a formula for admitting slave/free states Monroe reelected
1823	Monroe Doctrine closes Western Hemisphere to European intervention

precedent that criminal actions, not political disagreements, were the only proper grounds for impeachment. Although Jefferson did appoint three new Supreme Court justices, the Court remained a Federalist stronghold under Chief Justice John Marshall.

John Marshall

Marshall, a Virginia Federalist, was an astute lawyer with keen political sense. Under his domination, the Supreme Court retained a Federalist outlook even after Republican justices achieved a majority in 1811. Throughout his tenure (1801–1835), the Court consistently upheld federal supremacy over the states and protected the interests of commerce and capital. Of great importance, Marshall made the Court an equal branch of government in practice as well as theory. First, by his presence he made service on the Court a coveted honor. Second, he unified the

Court, influencing the justices to issue joint majority opinions rather than a host of individual concurring judgments. Marshall himself became the voice of the majority: from 1801 through 1810, he wrote 85 percent of the Court's opinions, including every important decision.

Marbury v. Madison

Marshall increased the Court's power, notably in the landmark case *Marbury* v. *Madison* (1803). William Marbury had been named a justice of the peace in the District of Columbia as one of Adams's midnight appointments. The new secretary of state, James Madison, declined to certify his appointment so that Jefferson could appoint a Republican. Marbury then sued, requesting a writ of mandamus (a court order forcing Madison to appoint him). The case presented a political dilemma. If the Supreme Court ruled in favor of Marbury and issued a writ of mandamus, the president might not comply. After all, why should the president, sworn to uphold the Constitution, allow the Court to decide for him what was constitutional? However, if the Court refused to issue the writ, it would be handing the Republicans a victory. Marshall avoided both pitfalls. Speaking for the Court, he ruled that Marbury had a right to his appointment but that the Court could not compel Madison to honor it, because the Constitution did not grant the Court power to issue a writ of mandamus. Marshall thus declared unconstitutional a section of the Judiciary Act of 1789, which authorized the Court to issue such writs. In *Marbury* v. *Madison*, the Supreme Court denied itself the power to issue writs of mandamus but established its great power to judge the constitutionality of laws passed by Congress.

In succeeding years, Marshall fashioned the theory of judicial review, the power of the Court to decide the constitutionality of legislation. Because the Constitution was the supreme law, he reasoned, any federal or state act contrary to the Constitution must be null and void. The Supreme Court, with the duty to uphold the law, thus had the responsibility to decide whether a legislative act contradicted the Constitution. If a conflict existed, the Court would declare the act unconstitutional. *Marbury* v. *Madison* ended criticism of the Court as a partisan instrument, and the power of judicial review permanently enhanced the independence of the judiciary.

While Marshall was enlarging the power of the Court, President Jefferson was keeping an eye on the Louisiana Territory to the west in hopes of enlarging the borders of the

Louisiana Purchase
———

nation. By 1800, hundreds of thousands of Americans in search of land had trekked into the rich Mississippi and Ohio Valleys. The settlers then floated their farm goods down the Mississippi and Ohio Rivers to New Orleans for export. Whoever controlled the port of New Orleans thus had a hand on the throat of the American economy. Spain owned Louisiana, but rumors of a transfer back to France persisted.

The rumors proved true in 1802. France had acquired the territory under secret pacts with Spain in 1800 and 1801, but the United States did not learn of the transfer until 1802, when the expansionist-minded Napoleon threatened to rebuild a French empire in the New World. The acquisition, Jefferson wrote to the American minister in Paris, Robert R. Livingston, "works most sorely" on the United States: "Every eye in the United States is now focused on the affairs of Louisiana." Then on the eve of ceding control to the French, Spain violated Pinckney's Treaty by denying Americans the privilege of storing their products at New Orleans before transshipment to foreign markets. Western farmers and eastern merchants alike thought a devious Napoleon had closed the port; they grumbled and talked war.

To relieve the pressure for war and to prevent westerners from joining Federalists in opposition to his administration, Jefferson simultaneously prepared for war and sent James Monroe to France to join Robert Livingston in negotiating to buy the port of New Orleans. Meanwhile, Congress authorized the call-up of eighty thousand militia should war become necessary. Arriving in Paris in April, Monroe was astonished to learn that France had already offered to sell all 827,000 square miles of Louisiana to the United States for a mere $15 million. Napoleon had lost interest in the New World. (France's dreams of reviving a Caribbean empire ended with its failure to suppress the slave revolt on Santo Domingo.) On April 30, Monroe and Livingston signed a treaty to purchase the vast territory, the borders of which were undefined and the land within which was uncharted (see map).

The Louisiana Purchase doubled the size of the nation and opened the way for westward expansion across the continent. It was also the most popular achievement of Jefferson's presidency. But its legality was questionable. The Constitution gave Jefferson no clear authority to acquire new territory and incorporate it in the nation. Although Jefferson considered requesting a constitutional amendment to allow the purchase, he finally justified it on the ground that he was exercising the president's implied powers to protect the nation. The people, he knew, would accept or reject the purchase on election day in 1804.

The president had a long-standing interest in Louisiana and the West. As secretary of state in 1793, he commissioned a French emigré botanist,

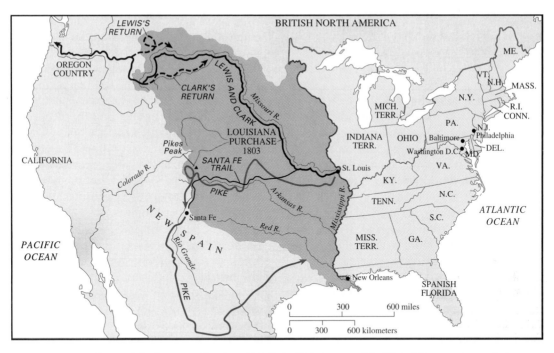

Louisiana Purchase *The Louisiana Purchase (1803) doubled the area of the United States and opened the trans-Mississippi West for American settlement.*

Lewis and Clark Expedition

André Michaux, "to find the shortest & most convenient route of communications between the U.S. & the Pacific Ocean." But allegations of Michaux's complicity in the Genêt affair aborted the mission. A decade later, Jefferson renewed Michaux's instructions when he sent an expedition headed by Meriwether Lewis and William Clark to the Pacific Ocean via the Missouri and Columbia Rivers. Because of American fears that the British intended to dominate the Far West, the 1804–1806 Lewis and Clark expedition assumed a political dimension. Because Jefferson had charged Lewis and Clark to collect specimens as they traveled, the expedition also had its scientific side. Lewis and Clark's fifty-strong "Corps of Discovery" was aided along the way by trappers and Native Americans, including a French-Canadian trader, Toussaint Charbonneau, and his young Shoshoni wife Sacagawea, who joined the expedition. Sacagawea helped negotiate safe passage in the Far West, and she interpreted the terrain and the languages of the West for the explorers.

The Lewis and Clark expedition reflected Jefferson's scientific curiosity and his interest in western commercial development. It also publicized the lands west of the Mississippi. Other explorers followed Lewis and Clark. In 1805 and 1806, Lieutenant Zebulon Pike set out in search of the source of the Mississippi and a navigable water route to the Far West. Pike and his men wandered into Spanish territory to the south, where the Spanish held them captive for several months in Santa Fe. After his release, Pike wrote an account of his experiences that set commercial minds spinning. During the next few decades, as Americans avidly read published accounts of western exploration, expansion seized their imagination. The vision of a road to the Southwest became a reality with the opening of the Santa Fe Trail in the 1820s.

REPUBLICANS VERSUS FEDERALISTS

Campaigning for reelection in 1804, Jefferson claimed credit for western expansion and the restoration of republican values. Jefferson considered

Election of 1804

Louisiana and the opening of the West among his greatest presidential accomplishments. Republicans bragged that they had ended the Federalist threat to liberty by repealing the Alien and Sedition and Judiciary Acts. They had also reduced the size and cost of government by cutting spending and had repealed Federalist excise and property taxes. Moreover, Jefferson had demonstrated that Republicans supported commerce and promoted free trade.

Jefferson's opponent was Charles Cotesworth Pinckney, a wealthy South Carolina lawyer and former Revolutionary War aide to George Washington. As Adams's vice presidential candidate in 1800, Pinckney had inherited the Federalist leadership. Jefferson swamped Pinckney in the electoral college by 162 votes to 14.

Jefferson's reelection was both a personal and an organizational triumph. The political dissenters of the 1790s had fashioned the Democratic-Republican societies into successful political organizations. More than anything else, opposition to the Federalists had given them cohesion. Indeed, in areas where the Federalists were strongest—in commercial New York and Pennsylvania in the 1790s and in New England in the 1800s—the Republicans had organized most effectively.

Until the Republican victory in 1800, most Federalists had disdained popular campaigning. They believed in government by the best people—those whose education, wealth, and experience qualified them to be leaders. For candidates to debate their merits in front of their inferiors—the voters—was demeaning. The Republicans' direct appeals struck the Federalists as a subversion of the natural political order.

After the resounding Federalist defeat in 1800, however, a younger generation of Federalists began to imitate the Republicans. Led by men like Josiah

Younger Federalists

Quincy, a young congressman from Massachusetts, they organized statewide and campaigned for popular support. Quincy cleverly presented the Federalists as the people's party, attacking Republicans as autocratic planters and slave holders. In attacking frugal government, the self-styled Younger Federalists played on fears of a weakened army and navy. Eastern merchants depended on a strong navy to protect ocean trade, whereas westerners looked for support from the army as they encroached on Native American tribes.

In states where both factions organized and ran candidates, people became more interested in politics generally, especially at the local level. In some states, about 90 percent of the eligible voters cast ballots between 1804 and 1816. As popular interest and participation in elections increased, the states expanded suffrage. But the popular base remained restricted: property qualifications for voting and holding office persisted, and in six states the legislatures still selected presidential electors in 1804.

Yet political competition and a vigorous press that saw its primary role as partisan advocacy prompted grassroots campaigning. Political barbecues symbolized the new style of campaigns. During the barbecues, candidates and party leaders delivered lengthy and uninhibited speeches. They often made wild accusations, which—given the slow speed of communications—might go unanswered until after the election.

Both factions adopted the political barbecue, but the Federalist party never fully mastered the art of wooing voters. Older Federalists still opposed blatant campaigning. And, although the Federalists were strong in a few states—Connecticut and Delaware, for example—they never offered the Republicans sustained competition. Divisions between Older and Younger Federalists often hindered the party, and the extremism of some Older Federalists tended to discredit the organization. A case in point was Timothy Pickering, a Massachusetts congressman who urged the secession of New England in 1803 and 1804. He won some support among the few Federalists in Congress, but most opposed his plan for secession. Ever the opportunist, Vice President Aaron Burr flirted with Pickering—

How do historians know

that popular interest in elections was increasing early in the nineteenth century? Election data are not available, but paintings like John Lewis Krimmel's Election Day in Philadelphia (1815) convey that popularity. Voting was limited to men at the time, and the crowd is composed mostly of white males, although at least one African-American and some women and children are present. The life of the street depicts a festive, holiday air that defines election day. Citizens on a float in the background carry their own flag; they have created a parade. A festive spirit seems to prevail as men cluster in groups talking, arguing, sharing jokes, and generally appearing to have a good time. There is a hint of excessive joy as well. The man sitting on a broken chair (left foreground), with his hat on the ground, seems to have fallen, perhaps from too much drink—a common affliction in the party atmosphere of election day. Among the spectators are the women (center foreground), who suggest a restraining force on the raucous scene. Dressed in white, the prominent woman and her child and caped friend offer a common female image of the time: the woman as emblem of republican virtue. The space between the women and male figures suggests that they stand apart not only as nonvoters but also as symbols of virtue and a seriousness absent in the male world. Over all, the painting depicts a popular event, mixing a party atmosphere with civic duty. From a sober exercise of democratic responsibility, voting had become a popular, festive occasion. Photo: Henry Francis du Pont Winterthur Museum.

Burr fantasized leading New York into secession, with other states following. When Burr lost his bid to become governor of New York in 1804, however, the dream evaporated.

Both Republicans and Federalists suffered from divisions and personal animosities. Aaron Burr and Alexander Hamilton, for instance, had

Hamilton-Burr Duel

long despised each other. Burr had an affinity for conspiracies, and Hamilton always seemed to block his path. Hamilton had thwarted Burr's attempt to steal the election of 1800 from Jefferson, and in the 1804 New York gubernatorial race Burr lost to a rival Republican faction backed by the Federalist Hamilton. Burr turned his resentment on Hamilton and challenged him to a duel. Hamilton accepted Burr's challenge, although he found dueling repugnant. Because New York had outlawed dueling, they met across the Hudson River at Weehawken, New Jersey. Hamilton deliberately fired astray and paid for that decision with his life. Burr was indicted for homicide in New York and New Jersey.

His political career in ruins, Burr plotted to create a new empire in the Southwest, using the Louisiana Territory as a base. With the collusion of General James Wilkinson, the U.S. army commander in the Mississippi Valley, Burr planned to raise a private army to grab land from the United States or from Spain (his exact plans remain uncertain). Wilkinson switched sides and informed President Jefferson of Burr's ambitions. Burr was tried and acquitted on the charge of treason. He then fled to Europe to avoid further prosecution.

The controversies surrounding Burr highlight some shortcomings of the emerging political system. Personal animosities were as strong a force as ideology, and temporary factions flourished. Moreover, although politicians courted voters, and participation in politics broadened, the electoral base remained narrow. As the election of 1804 revealed, the Federalists could offer only weak competition at the national level. And where Federalists were too weak to pose a threat, Republicans fought among themselves. Thus, although this period is commonly called the era of the first party system, parties as such were not fully developed.

PRESERVING AMERICAN NEUTRALITY IN A WORLD AT WAR

"Peace, commerce, and honest friendship with all nations, entangling alliance with none," President Jefferson had proclaimed in his first inaugural address. Jefferson's efforts to stand aloof from European conflict were successful until 1805. Indeed, for two years after the renewal of the Napoleonic wars in May 1803, American commerce

benefited from the conflict. As the world's largest neutral carrier, the United States became the chief supplier of food to Europe. American merchants also gained control of most of the West Indian trade, which was often transshipped through American ports to Europe.

Meanwhile, the U.S. victory in the Tripoli War on the north coast of Africa (the Barbary states) provided Jefferson his one clear success in protecting American trading rights. In 1801, the sultan of Tripoli had demanded payment to exempt American vessels and sailors in the Mediterranean from being taken hostage by his roving pirate ships. Jefferson refused and instead sent a naval squadron to protect American merchant ships. The United States signed a peace treaty with Tripoli in 1805 but continued to pay tribute to other Barbary states until 1815. That year, the navy, under Captain Stephen Decatur, forced Algiers and Tunis to renounce attacks against Americans.

American merchants grew more concerned about Anglo-French interference with trade. In October 1805, Britain tightened its control of the high seas by defeating the French and Spanish fleets at the Battle of Trafalgar. Two months later, Napoleon defeated the Russian and Austrian armies at Austerlitz. Stalemated, France and Britain launched a commercial war, blockading each other's trade. As a trading partner of both countries, the United States paid a high price.

Britain, which had the world's largest navy, was suffering a severe shortage of sailors. Few men enlisted, and those already in service frequently deserted, demoralized by poor food and living conditions and brutal discipline. The Royal Navy resorted to stopping American ships and forcibly removing British deserters, British-born naturalized American seamen, and other unlucky sailors suspected of being British. Perhaps six to eight thousand Americans were impressed (forcibly drafted) in this manner between 1803 and 1812.

Impressment of American Sailors

In February 1806, the Senate denounced British impressment as aggression and a violation of America's neutral rights. To protest the insult,

Congress passed the Non-Importation Act, prohibiting importation from Great Britain of a long list of cloth and metal articles. In November, Jefferson suspended the act temporarily while William Pinckney, a Baltimore lawyer, joined James Monroe in London in an attempt to negotiate a settlement. But the treaty Monroe and Pinckney carried home violated their instructions—it did not mention impressment—and Jefferson never submitted it to the Senate for ratification.

Less than a year later, the *Chesapeake* affair exposed American military weakness. In June 1807, the forty-gun frigate USS *Chesapeake* left Norfolk, Virginia. About ten miles out,

Chesapeake Affair

still inside American territorial waters, it met the fifty-gun British frigate *Leopard*. When the *Chesapeake* refused to be searched for deserters, the *Leopard* repeatedly emptied its guns broadside into the American ship. Three Americans were killed and eighteen wounded. The British impressed four deserters from the Royal Navy—three of them American citizens. Damaged and humiliated, the *Chesapeake* crept back to port.

Had the United States been better prepared militarily, the ensuing howl of public indignation might have brought about a declaration of war. But the United States was no match for the British navy. With Congress in recess, Jefferson was able to avoid hostilities. In July, the president closed American waters to British warships to prevent similar incidents, and soon thereafter he increased military and naval expenditures. In December, Jefferson again invoked the Non-Importation Act, followed eight days later by a new restriction, the Embargo Act.

Intended as a short-term measure, the Embargo Act forbade virtually all exports from the United States to any country. Imports

Embargo Act

came to a halt as well, because foreign ships delivering goods left American ports with empty holds. Smuggling blossomed overnight.

Few American policies were as well intentioned or as unpopular and unsuccessful as Jefferson's embargo. Mercantile New England, the heart of

Federalist opposition to Jefferson, felt the brunt of the resulting depression. Shipping collapsed as exports fell by 80 percent between 1807 and 1808. In the winter of 1808–1809, talk of secession spread through New England port cities. Some Americans, most notably merchants with ships abroad (thus not idled by the embargo) and U.S. manufacturers (the domestic market was now exclusively theirs), benefited from the embargo.

Great Britain, meanwhile, was only mildly affected by the embargo. And France used the policy as an excuse to set privateers against American ships that had managed to escape the embargo by avoiding American ports. The French argued that such ships must be British vessels in disguise, because the embargo barred American ships from the seas.

In the election of 1808, the Republicans found themselves facing not only the Federalists but also the embargo and factional dissent. Jefferson followed Washington's example in renouncing a third term and supported James Madison, his secretary of state, as the Republican standard-bearer. Madison won the endorsement of the congressional caucus. He and his running mate, Vice President George Clinton, defeated the Federalist ticket of Charles C. Pinckney and Rufus King.

The embargo eventually collapsed under the pressure of domestic opposition. In his last days in office, Jefferson had tried to lighten the burden by

Non-Intercourse Act

replacing the embargo with the Non-Intercourse Act of 1809. This act reopened trade with all nations except Britain and France, and it authorized the president to resume trade with either country if it ceased to violate neutral rights. But the new act solved only the problems created by the embargo; it did not prevent further British and French interference with American commerce.

When the Non-Intercourse Act expired in 1810, Congress substituted a variant, known as Macon's Bill Number 2, that exchanged the proverbial stick for a carrot. The bill reopened trade with both Great Britain and France but provided that when either nation stopped violating American commercial rights, the president could suspend American commerce with the other. Madison, eager to use the bill rather than go to war, was tricked at his own game. When Napoleon accepted the offer, Madison declared nonintercourse with Great Britain in 1811. Napoleon, however, did not keep his word. The French continued to seize American ships, and nonintercourse failed a second time. But because the Royal Navy dominated the seas, Britain, not France, became the main target of American hostility.

Angry American leaders tended to blame even tribal resistance in the West solely on British agitation, ignoring the Native Americans' legitimate protests against white en-

Shawnee Resistance
———

croachment and treaty violations. In the opening decade of the 1800s, the Shawnee brothers Prophet and Tecumseh had attempted to build a pan-Indian federation, taking advantage of Anglo-American friction. Prophet's early experiences mirrored the fate of many frontier tribes. Born in 1775, a few months after his father's death in battle, Prophet—called Lalawethika (Noisemaker) as a young man—was expelled to Ohio along with other Shawnees under the 1795 Treaty of Greenville, and he later moved to Indiana. Within the shrunken territory granted to the Shawnees under the treaty, game soon became scarce. Encroachment by whites and the periodic ravages of disease brought further misery to Native American villages and tribes.

In 1804, Lalawethika became a tribal medicine man. His medicine, however, could not stop the white man's virulent diseases from ravaging his village. Lalawethika then emerged from his own battle with illness in 1805 as a new man, called Prophet. Claiming to have died and been resurrected, Prophet traveled widely in the Northwest as a religious leader, attacking the decline of moral values among Native Americans, warning of damnation for those who drank whiskey, condemning intertribal battles, and stressing harmony and respect for elders. He urged the tribal peoples to return to the old ways and abandon white customs.

Prophet's message reassured the Shawnees, Potawatomis, and other peoples of the Old Northwest (Ohio, Indiana, Illinois, Michigan, and Wisconsin) who felt unsettled and threatened by whites. Prophet won converts by performing miracles—he darkened the sun by timing his invocations to coincide with a solar eclipse—and used opposition to federal Indian policy to draw others into his camp. His message spread to southern tribes as well, and the government and white settlers were alarmed.

By 1808, Prophet and his older brother Tecumseh talked less about spiritual renewal and more about resistance to American aggression. The

Prophet and Tecumseh
———

British encouraged the brothers' refusal to leave lands claimed by the government. In repudiating land cessions to the government under the Treaty of Fort Wayne (1809), Tecumseh told Indiana's governor William Henry Harrison at Vincennes in 1810 that "the only way to check and stop this evil is, for all the red men to unite in claiming a common and equal right in the land, as it was at first, and should be yet; for it never was divided, but belongs to all, for the use of each. . . . No part has a right to sell, even to each other, much less to strangers." Tecumseh, who had replaced his brother Prophet as the Shawnee leader, then warned Harrison that the tribes would resist white occupation of the 2.5 million acres on the Wabash that they had ceded in the Treaty of Fort Wayne.

THE WAR OF 1812

Conflict over Native American loyalties in the West and over impressment on the seas divided Britain and the United States. Frustrated, and having exhausted all efforts to alter British policy, the United States in 1811 and 1812 drifted into war with Great Britain. (Meanwhile, in June 1812, Britain opened the seas to American shipping. Hard times had hit the British Isles: the Anglo-French conflict had blocked much of British commerce with the European continent, and exports to the United States had fallen 80 percent. But two days later, before word had crossed the Atlantic, Congress declared war.)

The War of 1812 was the logical outcome of U.S. policy after the renewal of war in Europe in 1803. The grievances President Madison enumerated in his message to Congress on June 1, 1812, were old ones: impressment, interference with neutral commerce, and British alliances with the western tribes. Unmentioned was the resolve to defend American independence and honor—and the thirst of American expansionists for British Canada.

Yet Congress and the country were divided. Much of the sentiment for war came from the War Hawks, land-hungry southerners and westerners led by Henry Clay of Kentucky and John C. Calhoun of South Carolina. Most representatives from the coastal states (including all the Federalists) opposed war, because armed conflict with the great naval power threatened to interrupt American shipping. The vote for war—79 to 49 in the House, 19 to 13 in the Senate—reflected these sharp regional differences. The same split would be reflected in the way Americans fought the war.

Recruiting an Army

War was a foolish adventure for the United States in 1812. The navy had a corps of well-trained and experienced officers but next to the Royal Navy, the U.S. Navy was minuscule. Jefferson's warning that "our constitution is a peace establishment—it is not calculated for war" proved true. The army had neither an able staff nor an adequate force of enlisted men. The U.S. Military Academy at West Point, founded during Jefferson's administration in 1802, had produced only eighty-nine regular officers by 1812. The army thus turned to political leaders and state militia to organize volunteer companies, and not all states cooperated. Much of the war effort, including planning, was decentralized. The government offered enlistees a $16 sign-up bonus, $5 monthly pay, a full set of clothes, and a promise of three months' pay and 160 acres of western land upon discharge.

Invasion of Canada

Canada offered the United States the only readily available battlefront on which to confront Great Britain, as well as land to conquer. The mighty Royal Navy was useless on the Great Lakes separating the United States and Canada, because there was no river access from the Atlantic. Thousands of miles from British supply sources, Canada was vulnerable.

Begun with high hopes, the invasion of Canada ended in disaster. The American strategy concentrated on the West, hoping to split Canadian forces and isolate the Shawnees, Potawatomis, and other tribes that supported the British. Tecumseh had joined the British when the war began in return for the promise of an Indian nation in the Great Lakes region. General William Hull, governor of the Michigan Territory, marched his troops into Lower Canada, near Detroit. The British anticipated the invasion: they mobilized their Indian allies, moved troops into the area, and demanded Hull's surrender. When a pro-British, mostly Potawatomi, contingent captured Fort Dearborn near present-day Chicago, Hull capitulated. Farther to the west, other American forts surrendered. By the winter of 1812–1813, the British controlled about half of the Old Northwest.

The United States had no greater success on the Niagara front, where New York borders Canada. At the Battle of Queenstown, north of Niagara, the U.S. regular army met defeat, because the New York militia refused to leave the state. This scene was repeated near Lake Champlain, where American plans to attack Montreal were foiled when the militia declined to cross the border.

The navy provided the only bright ray in the first year of the war: the USS *Constitution*, the USS *Wasp*, and the USS *United States* all bested British warships on the Atlantic. In defeat, however, the British lost just 1 percent of their strength; in victory, the Americans lost 20 percent of their ships. The British admiralty simply shifted its fleet away from the American ships, and by 1813 the Royal Navy again commanded the seas.

The Royal Navy blockaded the Chesapeake and Delaware Bays in December 1812, and by 1814 the blockade covered nearly all U.S. ports along the Atlantic coast. American trade had declined nearly 90 percent since 1811, and the decline in revenues from customs duties threatened to bankrupt the federal government.

Great Lakes Campaign

The contest for control of the Great Lakes, the key to the war in the Northwest, was largely a shipbuilding race. Under Master Commandant Oliver Hazard Perry and shipbuilder Noah Brown, the United States outbuilt the British on Lake Erie and defeated them at the bloody Battle of Put-in-Bay on September 10, 1813. With this costly victory, the Americans gained control of Lake Erie.

General William Henry Harrison then began the march that proved to be America's most successful moment in the war. Harrison's force of forty-five hundred men, mostly Kentucky volunteers, crossed Lake Erie and pursued the British, Shawnee, and Chippewa forces into Canada, defeating them on October 5 at the Battle of the Thames. With this victory, the United States retained control of the Old Northwest. And when Tecumseh died in the Battle of the Thames, Native American unity also collapsed—as did the most significant resistance to the federal government's treaty-making tactics. Following the Battle of the Thames, the Americans razed York (now Toronto), the Canadian capital.

After defeating Napoleon in April 1814, the British stepped up the land campaign against the United States, concentrating their efforts in the Chesapeake Bay region. In retaliation for the burning of York—and to divert American troops from Lake Champlain, where the British planned a new offensive—royal troops occupied Washington, D.C., in August and set it ablaze. The attack on the capital, however, was only a diversion. The major battle occurred at Baltimore, where the Americans held firm. Francis Scott Key, witnessing the British fleet's bombardment of Fort McHenry in Baltimore harbor, was inspired to write the verses of "The Star-Spangled Banner" (which became the national anthem in 1931). Although the British inflicted heavy damage both materially and psychologically, they achieved little militarily. Equally unsuccessful was their offensive at Lake Champlain. The offensive was discontinued, and the war was essentially stalemated.

The last campaign of the war was waged in the South, along the Gulf of Mexico. Andrew Jackson, a Tennessee militia general, had raised his militia in December 1812 with the promise that they would serve one year. By late fall of 1813, his anti-Creek campaign was stalled by lack of supplies, and his men were talking about disbanding and going home. Jackson refused to discharge them; they could not, he claimed, leave their posts on enemy ground. In March 1814, Jackson executed John Woods, a militiaman, for disobedience and mutiny. This broke the opposition in the ranks, and his men

defeated the Creek nation at the Battle of Horseshoe Bend in March 1814. As a result, the Creeks had to cede two-thirds of their land and withdraw to southern and western Alabama. Jackson became a major general in the regular army and continued south toward the Gulf. To forestall a British invasion at Pensacola Bay, which guarded an overland route to New Orleans, Jackson seized Pensacola—in Spanish Florida—in November 1814. After securing Mobile, he marched on to New Orleans and prepared for a British attempt to capture the city.

The Battle of New Orleans was the final military engagement. Early in December, the British fleet landed fifteen hundred men east of the city, hoping to gain control of the Mississippi River. They faced American regular army troops, a larger contingent of Tennessee and Kentucky frontiersmen, and two companies of free African-American volunteers from New Orleans. For three weeks, the British and the Americans played cat-and-mouse, each trying to gain a major strategic position. Finally, on January 8, 1815, the two forces met head-on. In fortified positions, Jackson and his mostly untrained army held their ground against two suicidal frontal assaults from a reinforced British contingent of six thousand. At day's end, more than two thousand British soldiers lay dead or wounded. The Americans suffered only twenty-one casualties. Andrew Jackson emerged a national hero. Ironically, the Battle of New Orleans was fought two weeks after the end of the war; unknown to the participants, a treaty had been signed in Ghent, Belgium, on December 24, 1814.

Battle of New Orleans

The Ghent treaty made no mention of the issues that had led to war: the United States received no satisfaction on impressment, blockades, or other maritime rights for neutrals. Likewise, the treaty did not satisfy British demands for an independent Indian nation in the Northwest and territorial cessions from Maine to Minnesota. Essentially, the Treaty of Ghent restored the prewar status quo. It provided for an end to hostilities with the British and with Native American

Treaty of Ghent

tribes, release of prisoners, restoration of conquered territory, and arbitration of boundary disputes.

Why did the negotiators settle for so little? Events in Europe had made peace and the status quo acceptable at the end of 1814, as they had not been in 1812. Napoleon's fall from power allowed the United States to abandon its demands, because peace in Europe made impressment and interference with American commerce moot questions. Similarly, war-weary Britain—its treasury nearly depleted—stopped pressing for a military victory.

The War of 1812 reaffirmed the independence of the young American Republic. Although conflict with Great Britain continued, it never again led to war. The experience strength-

Results of the War of 1812

ened America's resolve to steer clear of European politics, for it had been the British-French conflict that had drawn the United States into war. For the rest of the century, the United States would shun involvement in European political issues and wars. The war also convinced the American government to maintain a standing army of ten thousand men—three times its size under Jefferson.

The war had disastrous results for most Native American tribes. Although they were not a party to the Treaty of Ghent, the ninth article pledged the United States to end hostilities and to restore "all the possessions, rights, and privileges" the tribes had enjoyed before the war. More than a dozen treaties were signed with midwestern tribal leaders in 1815, but they had little meaning. With the death of Tecumseh, the Indians had lost their most powerful political and military leader; with the withdrawal of the British, they had lost their strongest ally. The midwestern tribes had lost the resources with which they could have resisted American expansion.

Perhaps most important, the war stimulated economic growth. The embargo, the Non-Importation and Non-Intercourse Acts, and the war itself spurred the production of manufactured goods to replace banned imports. Unable to invest in embargoed cargoes or manufacturing abroad, New England capitalists began to invest in home

manufactures. The effects of these changes were to be far reaching.

And, finally, the war sealed the fate of the Federalist party. Its presidential nominee in 1812, DeWitt Clinton, lost to James Madison despite a hard campaign by the

Hartford Convention

Younger Federalists. The extremism of the Older Federalists was the party's undoing. During the war, Older Federalists had revived talk of secession, and Federalist delegates from New England met in Hartford, Connecticut, for three weeks in the winter of 1814–1815. With the war stalemated and trade in ruins, they plotted to revise the national compact or pull out of the Republic. Moderates prevented a resolution of secession, but convention members endorsed radical changes in the Constitution. They wanted to restrict the presidency to one term and to require a two-thirds congressional vote to admit new states. They also hoped to abolish the three-fifths compromise and to forbid naturalized citizens from holding office. These proposals were aimed at preserving New England Federalist political power by checking the growing strength of the West and South—the heart of Republican electoral strength—and that of Irish immigrants.

The timing of the Hartford Convention proved lethal. The victory at New Orleans and news of the peace treaty made the convention, with its talk of secession and proposed constitutional amendments, look ridiculous if not treasonous. Rather than harassing a beleaguered wartime administration, the Federalists found themselves in retreat before a rising tide of nationalism. Although Federalism survived in a handful of states until the 1820s, the Federalist party began to dissolve.

POSTWAR NATIONALISM AND DIPLOMACY

With peace came a new surge of American nationalism. Self-confidently, the nation asserted itself at home and abroad as Republicans aped Federalists in encouraging commerce and economic development.

In his message to Congress in December 1815, President Madison embraced Federalist doctrine by recommending expansion of the military and a program to stimulate economic growth. Wartime experiences, he said, had demonstrated the need for a national bank (the charter of the first Bank of the United States had expired) and for better transportation. To raise government revenues and perpetuate the wartime growth of manufacturing, Madison called for a protective tariff—a tax on imported goods designed to protect American manufactures. Although he strayed from Jeffersonian Republicanism, Madison did so within limits. Only a constitutional amendment, he argued, could give the federal government the authority to build roads and canals that were less than national in scope.

American System

The congressional leadership pushed Madison's nationalist program energetically in the belief that it would unify the country. Republican congressman John C. Calhoun of South Carolina and Speaker of the House Henry Clay of Kentucky, who named the program the American System, looked to the tariff on imported goods to stimulate industry. New mills would purchase raw materials; new mill workers would buy food from the agricultural South and West. New roads would make possible the flow of produce and goods, and tariff revenues would provide the money to build them. A national bank would facilitate all these transactions.

In 1816, Congress enacted much of the nationalistic program. The Second Bank of the United States was chartered. Like its predecessor, the bank had a twenty-year charter, was a blend of public and private ownership, and had one-fifth of its directors appointed by the government. To aid America's young industries, Congress also passed the nation's first substantial protective tariff. The act levied taxes on imported woolens and cottons (especially inexpensive ones) and on iron, leather, hats, paper, and sugar, in effect raising their cost. Some New England members of Congress viewed the tariff as interference in free trade, and southern members (except Calhoun and a few others) opposed it, because it raised the cost of imported goods to southern families. But the western and Middle Atlantic states backed it.

Congress did not share Madison's scruples about the constitutionality of using federal funds to build local roads. "Let us, then, bind the republic together," Calhoun declared, "with a perfect system of roads and canals." But Madison vetoed Calhoun's internal improvements bill, which provided for the construction of roads of mostly local benefit, declaring it unconstitutional. Internal improvements, Madison insisted, were the province of the states and of private enterprise. (He did, however, approve funds for the further extension of the National Road in Ohio, on the ground that it was a military necessity.)

James Monroe, Madison's successor as president, continued Madison's domestic program, supporting the national bank and tariffs and vetoing internal improvements on constitutional grounds. After he easily defeated Rufus King, the last Federalist candidate, Monroe declared that "discord does not belong to our system." The American people were, he said, "one great family with a common interest." A Boston newspaper dubbed the one-party period the "Era of Good Feelings." And throughout Monroe's first term, that label seemed appropriate.

McCulloch v. Maryland

Under the Federalist chief justice Marshall, the Supreme Court in this period became the bulwark of a nationalist point of view. In *McCulloch* v. *Maryland* (1819), the Court struck down a Maryland law taxing a branch of the federally chartered Second Bank of the United States. Maryland had imposed the tax in an effort to destroy the bank's Baltimore branch. The issue was thus one of state versus federal jurisdiction. Speaking for a unanimous Court, Marshall asserted the supremacy of the federal government over the states.

The Court went on to consider whether Congress could issue a bank charter; the Constitution did not spell out such power. But Marshall noted that Congress had the authority to pass "all laws which shall be necessary and proper for carrying into execution" the enumerated powers of the government. Echoing Alexander Hamilton's notion of implied powers, Marshall ruled that Congress could legally exercise "those great powers on which the welfare of the nation essentially depends." If the ends were legitimate and the means were not prohibited, Marshall ruled, a law was constitutional. The bank charter was declared legal.

McCulloch v. *Maryland* thus combined Federalist nationalism with Federalist economic views. By asserting federal supremacy, Marshall was protecting the commercial and industrial interests that favored a national bank; this was federalism in the tradition of Alexander Hamilton. The decision was only one in a series. In *Fletcher* v. *Peck* (1810), the Court voided a Georgia law that violated individuals' rights to make contracts. Similarly, in *Dartmouth College* v. *Woodward* (1819), the Court nullified a New Hampshire act altering the charter of Dartmouth College. Marshall ruled that the charter was a contract, and in protecting such contracts he thwarted state interference in commerce and business.

Monroe's secretary of state, John Quincy Adams, matched the self-confident Marshall Court in assertiveness and nationalist sentiments. From

John Quincy Adams as Secretary of State
———

1817 to 1825, he brilliantly managed the nation's foreign policy, stubbornly pushing for expansion, fishing rights for Americans in Atlantic waters, political distance from the Old World, and peace. An ardent expansionist, he nonetheless placed conditions on expansion, believing that it must come about through negotiations, not war, and that newly acquired territories must not permit slavery.

An Anglophobe, Adams nonetheless worked to strengthen the peace with Great Britain. In 1817, the two nations agreed in the Rush-Bagot Treaty to limit their Great Lakes naval forces to one ship each on Lakes Ontario and Champlain and to two vessels each on the other lakes. This first disarmament treaty of modern times led to the demilitarization of the U.S.-Canadian border. Adams then pushed for the Convention of 1818, which fixed the U.S.-Canadian border from Lake of the Woods in Minnesota west to the Rockies along the forty-ninth parallel. When agreement could not be reached on the territory west of the Rockies, Britain and the United States settled on joint occupation of Oregon for ten years (renewed indefinitely in 1827).

Adams's next move was to settle long-term disputes with Spain. During the War of 1812, the United States had seized Mobile and the remainder of West Florida. After the war, Adams took advantage of Spain's preoccupation with domestic and colonial troubles to negotiate for the purchase of East Florida. During the talks, which took place in 1818, General Andrew Jackson took it on himself to occupy much of present-day Florida on the pretext of suppressing Seminole raids against American settlements across the border. Adams was furious with Jackson but defended his brazen act.

The following year, Don Luís de Onís, the Spanish minister to the United States, agreed to cede Florida to the United States without payment.

Adams-Onís Treaty
———

The Adams-Onís, or Transcontinental, Treaty also defined the southwestern boundary of the Louisiana Purchase. In return, the United States government assumed $5 million worth of claims by American citizens against Spain and gave up its dubious claim to Texas. Expansion was thus achieved at little cost and without war, and American territorial claims now stretched from the Atlantic to the Pacific.

Conflict between the United States and European nations was temporarily resolved by the Rush-Bagot Treaty, the Convention of 1818, and the Adams-Onís Treaty, but events to the south still threatened U.S. interests. It was John Quincy Adams's desire to insulate the United States and the Western Hemisphere from European conflict that brought about his greatest achievement: the Monroe Doctrine.

The immediate issue was the recognition of new governments in Latin America. Between 1808 and 1822, the United Provinces of the Río de la Plata (present-day northern Argentina, Paraguay, and Uruguay), Chile, Peru, Colombia, and Mexico had all broken free from Spain. Although many Americans wanted to recognize the independence of these former colonies, Monroe and Adams moved cautiously. They sought to avoid conflict with Spain and its allies and to assure themselves of the stability of the revolutionary regimes. But in 1822, shortly after the Adams-Onís Treaty was signed and ratified, the United States became the first nation outside Latin America to recognize the new states.

Soon events in Europe again threatened the stability of the New World. Spain suffered a domestic revolt and, in an attempt to bolster the weak Spanish monarchy against the rebels, France occupied Spain. The United States feared that France would seek to restore the new Latin American states to Spanish rule. Great Britain, similarly distrustful of France, proposed a joint U.S.-British declaration against European intervention in the hemisphere and a joint disavowal of territorial ambitions in the region. Adams rejected the British overture; in accordance with Washington's admonition to avoid foreign entanglements, he insisted that the United States act independently.

The result was the Monroe Doctrine, a unilateral declaration against European interference in the New World. President Monroe presented the American position to Congress in December 1823. His message called for, first, *noncolonization* of the Western Hemisphere by European nations, a principle that addressed American anxiety not only about Latin America but also about Russian expansion on the West Coast. (Russia held Alaska and had built a chain of settlements and forts as far south as California.) Second, he demanded *nonintervention* by Europe in the affairs of independent New World nations. Finally, Monroe pledged *noninterference* by the United States in European affairs, including those of Europe's existing New World colonies.

Monroe Doctrine

Monroe's words, however, carried no force. Indeed, the policy could not have succeeded without the support of the British, who were already committed to keeping other European nations out of the hemisphere to protect their dominance in the Atlantic trade. Europeans ignored the doctrine; it was the Royal Navy they respected, not American policy.

THE PANIC OF 1819 AND RENEWED SECTIONALISM

Monroe's domestic record did not match the diplomatic successes of his administration. In 1819, financial panic subverted postwar confidence and revived sectional loyalties. Neither panic nor the resurgence of sectionalism hurt Monroe politically; without a rival political party to rally opposition, he won a second term in 1820 unopposed.

But hard economic times spread. The postwar expansion was built on loose money and widespread speculation. State banks extended credit and printed notes too freely, fueling speculative buying of western land. When economic expansion slowed, the manufacturing downturn that began in 1818 deepened and prices spiraled downward. To protect its assets, the Second Bank of the United States cut back on loans, thus accelerating the contraction of the economy. Distressed urban workers lobbied for easier credit and internal improvements and began to take a more active role in politics. Farmers clamored for lower tariffs on manufactured goods to reduce general price levels. Hurt by a sharp decline in the price of cotton, southern planters railed at the protective Tariff of 1816, which had raised prices on all imported goods while their incomes fell sharply. Manufacturers, on the other hand, demanded greater tariff protection—and eventually got it in the Tariff of 1824.

Hard Times

Western farmers suffered too. Those who had purchased public land on credit lacked sufficient income to repay their loans. To avoid mass bankruptcy, Congress delayed the deadlines for repayment, and western state legislatures passed "stay laws" restricting mortgage foreclosures. Many westerners blamed the panic on the Second Bank of the United States for tightening the money supply.

Far more divisive was the question of slavery. Ever since the drafting of the Constitution, political leaders had avoided the issue. The one exception was an act closing the foreign slave trade after January 1, 1808, which passed without much opposition. In 1819, however, slavery finally crept onto the political agenda when Missouri residents petitioned Congress for admission to the Union as a slave state. For the next two-and-a-half years, the issue dominated all congressional action.

Slavery Question

The debate transcended slavery in Missouri. At stake was the undoing of the compromises that had kept the issue quarantined since the Constitutional

Convention. Five new states had joined the Union since 1812: Louisiana (1812), Indiana (1816), Mississippi (1817), Illinois (1818), and Alabama (1819). Of these, Louisiana, Mississippi, and Alabama permitted slavery. Because Missouri was on the same latitude as free Illinois, Indiana, and Ohio (a state since 1803), its admission as a slave state would thrust slavery farther north. It would also tilt the uneasy political balance in the Senate toward the states committed to slavery. In 1819, the Union consisted of eleven slave and eleven free states. If Missouri entered as a slave state, the slave states would have a two-vote edge in the Senate.

What made the issue so highly charged was not the politics of admission to statehood but the debate about the morality of slavery. The settlers of Missouri were mostly Kentuckians and Tennesseeans who had grown up with slavery. But many northerners had concluded that slavery was evil.

When Representative James Tallmadge Jr. of New York introduced an amendment providing for gradual emancipation in Missouri, a passionate and sometimes violent debate ensued. The House, which had a northern majority, passed the Tallmadge amendment, but the Senate rejected it. The two sides were deadlocked.

A compromise emerged in 1820 under pressure from House Speaker Henry Clay: the admission of free Maine, carved out of Massachusetts, was linked with that of slave **Missouri Compromise** Missouri. In the rest of the Louisiana Territory north of 36°30' (Missouri's southern boundary), slavery was prohibited forever (see map). The compromise carried, but the agreement almost came apart in November when Missouri submitted a constitution that barred free blacks from settling in the

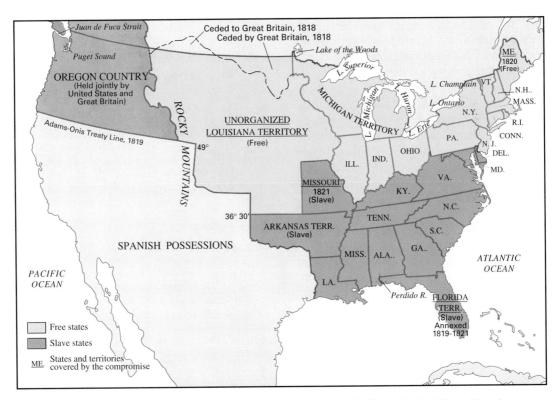

Missouri Compromise and the State of the Union, 1820 *Under House Speaker Henry Clay, the compromise established a formula that avoided debate over whether new states would allow or prohibit slavery. In the process, it divided the United States into northern and southern regions.*

state. Congressional arguments over Missouri's constitution were resolved when Clay produced a second compromise: Missouri guaranteed that none of its laws would discriminate against citizens of other states.

Although political leaders had succeeded in removing slavery from the congressional agenda, sectional issues would undermine Republican unity. The Republican party would come apart in 1824 as presidential candidates from different sections of the country scrambled for support.

Sectionalism and the question of slavery would ultimately threaten the Union itself. Still, the first decades of the nineteenth century were a time of self-definition and growth for the young Republic. Political parties broadened white male involvement in politics and quieted partisan divisions. Moreover, a tradition of peaceful transition of power through presidential elections was established. A second war with Britain—the War of 1812—had to be fought to reaffirm American independence and to thwart the Native American tribes' opposition to U.S. expansion; thereafter the nation was able to settle many disputes at the bargaining table.

The foreign-policy problems confronting the infant Republic from the turn of the century through the mid-1820s bear a striking resemblance to those that newly established underdeveloped nations have faced in the twentieth century. Empires often treat their former colonies as if they had not won their independence. Like underdeveloped nations, the young United States shunned alliances with the great powers, preferring neutrality and unilateralism.

After the war, all branches of government, responding to the popular mood, pursued a vigorous national policy. The Supreme Court promoted national unity by extending federal power over the states and encouraging commerce and economic growth. Moreover, disruption of trade during the war had promoted the manufacturing of goods in the United States, lessening dependence on imports from Europe. Developments in transportation further stimulated the economy.

The problem of sectionalism accompanied nationalism and geographic expansion. While manufacturers and merchants in the North and agricultural producers in the West became linked through transportation and trade, the South was developing its own economy and culture based on cotton, export markets, a plantation system, and slavery. Politicians kept the question of slavery off the national agenda as long as possible and worked out the Missouri Compromise as a stopgap measure. But territorial acquisitions and further westward expansion in the 1840s and 1850s collided with a rising tide of reform to make the question of slavery unavoidable.

At the same time, during the next two decades, the way Americans lived and worked changed at a quickening pace. Economic development, rising population, the spread of settlement, and the rise of cities were transforming people and their communities. In the face of religious revival, recognition of the imperfections in the new society, broad-based attempts to improve people and institutions, and conflict among groups, people turned to politics as an arena in which they could control, direct, or resist change.

SUGGESTIONS FOR FURTHER READING

General

George Dangerfield, *The Awakening of American Nationalism, 1815–1828* (1965), and *The Era of Good Feelings* (1952); Jean V. Matthews, *Toward a New Society: American Thought and Culture, 1800–1830* (1991); John Mayfield, *The New Nation, 1800–1845* (1981); Marshall Smelser, *The Democratic Republic, 1801–1815* (1968).

Party Politics

James Broussard, *The Southern Federalists, 1800–1816* (1978); Noble E. Cunningham Jr., *The Jeffersonian Republicans in Power: Party Operations, 1801–1809* (1963); Shaw Livermore, *Twilight of Federalism: The Disintegration of the Federalist Party, 1815–1830* (1962); Milton Lomask, *Aaron Burr,* 2 vols. (1979, 1983); Richard P. McCormick, *The Presidential Game: The Origins of American Presidential Politics* (1982); Drew McCoy, *The Elusive Republic* (1980); James Sterling Young, *The Washington Community, 1800–1828* (1966).

The Virginia Presidents

Noble E. Cunningham Jr., *In Pursuit of Reason: The Life of Thomas Jefferson* (1987); Ralph Ketcham, *Presidents Above Party: The First American Presidency, 1789–1829* (1984); Dumas Malone, *Jefferson and His Time,* 6 vols. (1948–1981); Drew R. McCoy, *The Last of* the *Fathers: James Madison and the Republican Legacy* (1989); Forrest McDonald, *The Presidency of Thomas Jefferson* (1976); Merrill D. Peterson, *The Jefferson Image in the American Mind* (1960); Robert Allen Rutland, *The Presidency of James Madison* (1990), and *James Madison: The Founding Father* (1987).

The Supreme Court and the Law

Leonard Baker, *John Marshall: A Life in Law* (1974); Robert Lowry Clinton, *Marbury v. Madison and Judicial Review* (1989); Morton J. Horowitz, *The Transformation of American Law, 1780–1860* (1977); R. Kent Newmyer, *The Supreme Court Under Marshall and Taney* (1968).

Expansionism and the War of 1812

R. David Edmunds, *Tecumseh and the Quest for Indian Leadership* (1984), and *The Shawnee Prophet* (1983); Clifford L. Egan, *Neither Peace nor War: Franco-American Relations, 1803–1812* (1983); Donald R. Hickey, *The War of 1812: A Forgotten Conflict* (1989); Bradford Perkins, *Prologue to War: England and the United States, 1805–1812* (1961); Julius W. Pratt, *Expansionists of 1812* (1925); James P. Ronda, *Lewis and Clark Among the Indians* (1984); J. C. A. Stagg, *Mr. Madison's War: Politics, Diplomacy, and Warfare in the Early Republic, 1783–1830* (1983).

The Monroe Doctrine

Samuel F. Bemis, *John Quincy Adams and the Foundations of American Foreign Policy* (1949); Ernest R. May, *The Making of the Monroe Doctrine* (1976); Dexter Perkins, *Hands Off: A History of the Monroe Doctrine* (1941).

Rails, Markets, and Mills: The North and West, 1800–1860

T HE HUTCHINSON FAMILY, ALSO known as the Tribe of Jesse, was the most popular musical group in nineteenth-century America. Abby, Asa, Jesse, John, and Judson Hutchinson performed throughout the United States and across the Atlantic, singing the patriotic, religious, and sentimental songs that had dominated popular music since the Revolution. But unlike most groups that just sang, the Tribe of Jesse presented well-rehearsed and elaborately produced performances. They used traditional airs that the audiences knew and found comforting, but they wrote political lyrics advocating, for example, abolitionism. Publishers considered "Get Off the Track" (first performed in 1844) too inflammatory to print. The Hutchinsons sang it on stage, and the abolitionist press carried its lyrics until a publisher finally printed songsheets.

> Ho! the Car Emancipation
> Rides majestic thro' our nation
> Bearing on its Train, the story.
> LIBERTY! a Nation's Glory.
>   Roll it along, thro' the Nation
>   Freedom's Car, Emancipation.

The song became one of the Hutchinsons' trademarks, electrifying anti-slavery audiences.

The Hutchinson Family was part of a new phenomenon: singers, songwriters, musicians, publishers, and managers who made a business of music and entertainment. Drawing their largest audiences in the growing cities, they entered the commercial world and made a living from writing and performing music. Each performance was planned and choreographed, and they had an entourage of managers, agents, publishers, and concert hall representatives. Hawkers sold sheet music, portraits, and song books at their concerts. A traditional rural pastime had become a big business.

The Hutchinsons were able to tour the nation in concert because of advances in transport and communications that linked the growing national economy between 1800 and 1860. The canal boat, steamboat, locomotive, and telegraph made possible a Hutchinson Family concert tour. But more enduring, these technological advances opened up the frontier and helped expand farm production for markets at home and abroad. Equally significant to improved transportation was the increased specialization in agriculture, manufacturing, and finance that fostered a nationwide, capitalist, market-oriented economy.

This dramatic transformation began early in the century and spread nearly everywhere. In 1800, most of the 5.3 million Americans earned their living working the land or serving those who did. Except in Kentucky and Tennessee, settlement had not stretched very far to the west. By 1860, 31.4 million Americans had spread across the continent. A continental nation had been forged. Meanwhile, an enormous commercial and industrial expansion was transforming the economy, although it still was primarily agricultural.

Promotion of economic growth became the hallmark of the federal government, which sought to encourage individual enterprise by promoting an environment in which farming and industry could flourish. New financial institutions amassed the capital for large-scale enterprises like factories and railroads. Mechanization took hold; factories and precision-made machinery competed successfully with home workshops and handmade goods, and reapers and sowers revolutionized farming.

Not everyone profited from economic expansion. The experience of a journeyman tailor displaced by retailers and less expensive labor was far different from that of the new merchant princes. The New England farm daughters who became wage workers found their world changing no less radically. Moreover, boom-and-bust cycles became part of the fabric of ordinary life. And canals, railroads, and urban and industrial growth brought with them destruction of the environment.

TRANSPORTATION AND REGIONALIZATION

The North, South, and West each followed a distinct economic path between 1800 and 1860. Everywhere, agriculture remained the foundation of the American economy. Nevertheless, the North was increasingly investing its resources in industry, commerce, and finance, the South in plantations and subsistence farms, and the West in commercialized family farms, agricultural processing, and implement manufacturing. This tendency toward regional specialization made the various sections of the country at once less similar and more dependent on each other.

The revolution in transportation and communications was probably the single overriding cause of these changes. The North's heavy investment in canals and railroads made it the center of American commerce. The South, with most of its capital invested in slave labor, built fewer canals, railroads, and factories and remained mostly rural and undeveloped.

Before the 1820s and 1830s, it was by no means certain that New England and the Middle Atlantic states would dominate American economic life. Indeed, the southward flowing Ohio and Mississippi Rivers oriented the frontier of 1800—Tennessee, Kentucky, and Ohio—to the South. Flatboats transported western grain and hogs south for consumption or transfer to ocean-going vessels at New Orleans. Steamboats, successfully introduced in 1807 when Robert Fulton's *Clermont* paddled up the Hudson River from New York City, began in 1815 to carry cargo upstream on the Mississippi and Ohio Rivers, further reinforcing ties between the South and the West.

Change in Trade Routes

But this pattern changed in the 1820s when new arteries opened up east-west travel. The National Road—a stone-based, gravel-topped highway originating in Cumberland, Maryland—reached Wheeling, Virginia (now West Virginia), in 1818 and Columbus, Ohio, in 1833. More important, the Erie Canal, completed in 1825, linked the Great Lakes with New York City and the Atlantic Ocean. Railroads and later the telegraph would solidify these east-west links. By contrast, at only one place—Bowling Green, Kentucky—did a northern railroad connect with a southern one. Although trade still moved south along the Ohio and Mississippi Rivers, the bulk of western trade flowed east by 1850. Thus, by the eve of the Civil War, the northern and Middle Atlantic states were closely linked to the former frontier of the Old Northwest.

Construction of the 363-mile-long Erie Canal was a visionary enterprise. When the state of New York authorized it in 1817, the longest existing

Canals

American canal was only twenty-eight miles long. Vigorously promoted by Governor DeWitt Clinton, the canal shortened the journey between Buffalo and New York City from twenty to six days and reduced freight charges from $100 to $5 a ton. By 1835, traffic was so heavy that the canal had to be widened from forty to seventy feet and deepened from four to seven feet.

Sensing the advantage the Erie Canal had given New York, other states and cities rushed to follow suit. By 1840, canals crisscrossed the Northeast and Midwest, and total canal mileage reached thirty-three hundred—an increase of more than two thousand miles in a single decade. Unfortunately for investors, none of these canals enjoyed the financial success achieved by the Erie. As a result, investment in canals began to slump in the 1830s. By 1850, more miles were being abandoned than built, and the canal era had ended.

Meanwhile, railroad construction boomed. The railroad era in the United States began in 1830 when Peter Cooper's locomotive Tom Thumb first steamed along thirteen miles of

Railroads

track constructed by the Baltimore and Ohio Railroad. In 1833, the nation's second railroad ran 136 miles from Charleston to Hamburg in South Carolina. By 1850, the United States had nearly nine thousand miles of railroad; by 1860, roughly thirty-one thousand (see figure). Canal fever stimulated this early railroad construction. Promoters of the Baltimore and Ohio believed that railroads would compete successfully with canals. Similarly, the line between Boston and Worcester in Massachusetts was intended as the first link in a line to Albany, at the eastern end of the Erie Canal. In Providence, Rhode Island, and other ports, the railroads extended to the ocean wharfs.

The earliest railroads connected two cities or a city and its surrounding area. But in the 1850s, technological improvements, competition, economic recovery, and a desire for national unity prompted development of regional and, eventually, national rail networks. By 1853, rail lines linked New York to Chicago. By 1860, rails stretched as far west as St. Joseph, Missouri—the edge of the

Railroad Mileage, 1830–1860

Miles (y-axis): 2,000 to 32,000
Year (x-axis): 1830, 1835, 1840, 1845, 1850, 1855, 1860

Data points: 23, 1,098, 2,818, 4,633, 9,021, 18,374, 30,626

Railroad Mileage, 1830–1860 *In the 1850s, railroads developed a natural rail network east of the Mississippi River.* Source: U.S. Bureau of the Census. *Historical Statistics of the United States, Colonial Times to 1970.* 2 Parts. (Washington, D.C., 1975), Part 2, p. 731.

frontier (see map). In 1853, seven short lines combined to form the New York Central system, and the Pennsylvania Railroad was unified from Philadelphia to Pittsburgh. Most lines, however, were still run by independents. Differences in gauge, scheduling, car design, and a commitment to serve their hometowns first and foremost prevented cooperation and mergers.

Railroads did not completely replace water transportation. At midcentury, steamships still carried bulk cargo less expensively than railroads, except during freezing weather.

Steamboats

The sealike Great Lakes could accommodate giant ships with propellers in place of paddle wheels; these leviathans carried heavy bulk cargoes like lumber, grain, and ore. On the high seas, steamships gradually replaced sailing vessels, which were dependent on prevailing winds and thus usually could not schedule regular crossings. The

• *Important Events* •

1807	Fulton's steamboat, *Clermont*, makes its debut
1812–15	The United States and Great Britain fight the War of 1812
1813	New England capitalists found the Boston Manufacturing Company and build the first large-scale American factory
1818	National Road reaches Wheeling, Virginia, opening the West
1819	*Dartmouth College* v. *Woodward* protects the sanctity of contracts
1819–23	Hard times bring unemployment and business bankruptcies
1820s	New England textile mills expand
1824	*Gibbons* v. *Ogden* affirms federal over state authority in interstate commerce
1825	Erie Canal completed
1830	Baltimore and Ohio Railroad begins operation
1831	McCormick invents the reaper
1834	Women workers strike at Lowell textile mills
1837	*Charles River Bridge* v. *Warren Bridge* encourages new enterprises
1839–43	Hard times strike again
1844	A government grant develops Baltimore-Washington telegraph line
1848	Regularly scheduled steamship passage begins between Liverpool and New York City
1849	California gold rush transforms the West Coast
1853	British study of American system of manufacturing
1857	Hard times mark end of third boom-or-bust cycle

biggest breakthrough occurred in 1848, when Samuel Cunard introduced regularly scheduled steamships between Liverpool and New York, reducing travel time across the Atlantic from twenty-five days eastbound and forty-nine days westbound to between ten and fourteen days each way. Sailing ships quickly lost first-class passengers and light cargo to steamships.

By far the fastest-spreading technological advance of the era was the magnetic telegraph. Invented by Samuel F. B. Morse, the telegraph made

Telegraph

it possible for long-distance messages to travel faster than any messenger could; instantaneous communication became possible even over long distances. By 1853, only nine years after construction of the first experimental line, twenty-three thousand miles of telegraph wire spread across the United States; by 1860, fifty

thousand miles were in use. In 1861, the telegraph bridged the continent, connecting the East and West Coasts, literally joining the nation together and ending the isolation that westerners felt. Rarely has an innovation had so great an influence so quickly: it revolutionized news gathering, provided advance information for railroads and steamships, and altered patterns of business and finance.

Time was key to the revolutionary changes in transportation and communications that took place from 1800 to 1860. In 1800, it took four days to travel by coach from New York City to Baltimore, and nearly four weeks to reach Detroit. By 1830, Baltimore was only a day-and-a-half away, and by 1857 Detroit was an overnight train ride from New York City. Not only did reduced travel time save money and facilitate commerce, it also brought frontier areas under the control of Chicago and eastern businesses. During the first two decades of

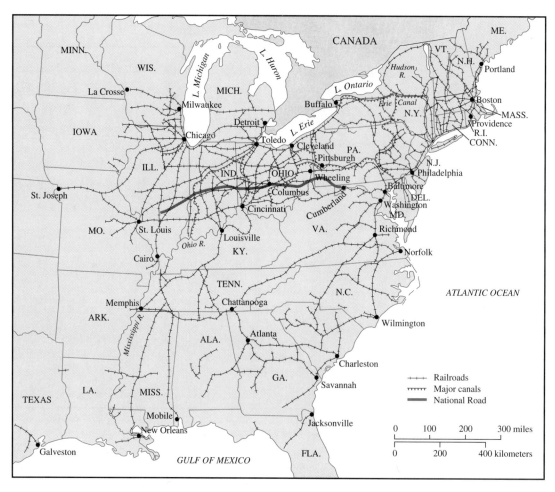

Major Railroads, Canals, and Roads in 1860 *Transportation networks linked port cities to the interior. These links were most dense in the North and the Old Northwest.*

the century, wagon transportation cost 30 to 70 cents per ton per mile. By 1860, railroads in New York State carried freight at an average charge of 2.2 cents per ton-mile. In sum, the transportation revolution transformed the economy.

THE MARKET ECONOMY

Before the transportation revolution, most farmers had geared production to family needs. They lived in interdependent communities and kept detailed accounts of labor and goods exchanged with neighbors.

Farm families produced much of what they needed, but they traded for or purchased items they could not produce. On most farms, men sold cordwood and women sold eggs and butter to generate the family's only cash. By the Civil War, however, the United States had an industrializing economy. An increasing number of men and women worked for wages, and most people outside the South—farmers and workers alike—purchased increasing amounts of store-bought goods produced in workshops and factories.

With the advent of a market economy, men and women grew crops and produced goods for sale at home or abroad. The money received in market

Definition of a Market Economy

transactions, whether the sale of goods or of a person's labor, purchased items produced by other people. Such a system encouraged specialization. Formerly self-sufficient farmers began to grow just one or two crops or to raise only livestock for market. Farm women gave up spinning and weaving and purchased fabric produced by wage-earning farm girls in Massachusetts textile mills.

Improvements in transportation and technology, the division of labor, and new methods of financing all fueled the expansion of the economy—that is, the multiplication of goods and services. This growth in turn prompted new improvements and greater opportunities for wage labor. The effect was cumulative; by the 1840s, the economy was growing at a faster rate than in the previous four decades. While per capita income doubled between 1800 and 1860, the price of manufactured goods and food fell.

The pace of economic growth, however, was uneven. Prosperity reigned during two long periods, from 1823 to 1835 and from 1843 to 1857. But

Boom-and-Bust Cycles

there were long stretches of economic contraction as well. Between Jefferson's 1807 embargo and the end of the War of 1812, the growth rate was negative—that is, fewer goods and services were produced. Contraction and deflation (decline in the general price level) occurred again during the hard times of 1819–1823, 1839–1843, and 1857. During these periods, banks collapsed, businesses went bankrupt, and wages and prices declined. For workers, the down side meant lower wages and higher unemployment rates.

Hard times were devastating for workers. In 1857, the Mercantile Agency—the forerunner of Dun & Bradstreet—recorded 5,123 bankruptcies, nearly double the number of the previous year. Contemporary reports estimated that twenty to thirty thousand people were unemployed in Philadelphia, and thirty to forty thousand in New York City. Female benevolent societies expanded their soup kitchens and distributed free firewood to the needy. In Chicago, charities reorganized to meet the needs of the poor; in New York, the city hired the unemployed to repair streets and develop Central Park. And in Fall River, Massachusetts, a citizens' committee disbursed public funds on a weekly basis to nine hundred families. The soup kitchen, the bread line, and public aid had become fixtures in urban America.

What caused the boom-and-bust cycles that brought about such suffering? Generally speaking, they were a direct result of the new market economy.

Cause of Boom-and-Bust Cycles

Prosperity stimulated greater demand for staples and finished goods, such as clothing and furniture. Increased demand in turn led not only to higher prices and still higher production but also, because of business confidence and expectation of higher prices, to speculation in land and to the flow of foreign currency into the country. Eventually, production surpassed demand, causing prices and wages to fall; in response, inflated land and stock values collapsed. The inflow of foreign money led first to easy credit and then to collapse when the unhappy investors withdrew their funds.

Some contemporary economists considered this process beneficial—a self-adjusting cycle that eliminated unprofitable economic ventures. In theory, people concentrated on the activities they did best, and the economy as a whole became more efficient. Advocates of the system also argued that it enhanced individual freedom, because theoretically each seller, whether of goods or labor, was free to determine the conditions of the sale. But in fact the system tied workers to a perpetual roller coaster; they became dependent on wages—and the availability of jobs—for their very existence.

The market economy also ushered in another type of boom-and-bust cycle: harvest and destruction. Canals and railroads stimulated demand for distant resources, then accelerated the destruction of forests, natural waterways, and any landscape features that represented obstacles. Railroads made possible large-scale lumbering of pinewood forests in northern Michigan, Wisconsin, and Minnesota. During the 1850s, forty million acres were cleared of lumber, leaving most of that land unfit even for agriculture. Similarly, the extension of railroads to

Kansas and Nebraska brought hunters who slaughtered the great herds of bison for sport. The result was a process that would eventually change the ecology of the United States.

GOVERNMENT PROMOTES ECONOMIC GROWTH

The eighteenth-century political ideas that had captured the imagination of the Revolutionary War generation and found expression in the ideal of republican virtue had economic counterparts in the writings of Adam Smith, a Scottish political economist. Smith's *The Wealth of Nations* first appeared in 1776, the year of the Declaration of Independence. Both works emphasized individual liberty, and both were reactions against forceful government: Jefferson denounced monarchy and distant government; Smith rejected mercantilism, or governmental regulation of the economy to benefit the state. Both declared that virtue resided in individual freedom and that the community would benefit most from individuals' pursuit of their own self-interest.

Jefferson believed that freedom thrived when individuals had scope for independence, creativity, and choice—individuals fettered by government, monopoly, or economic dependence could not be free. Limited government was not an end, according to Jefferson, but a means to greater freedom. Committed to the idea that a republican democracy would flourish best in a nation of independent farmers and artisans and in an atmosphere of widespread political participation, Jefferson recognized that government was a necessary instrument for promoting individual freedom. Beginning with the purchase of Louisiana in 1803, Republican policy, no less than that of the Federalists, endorsed using the federal government to promote economic growth.

After acquiring Louisiana, the federal government facilitated economic growth and geographic expansion by encouraging westward exploration and settlement and by promoting agriculture. The Lewis and Clark expedition was only the beginning of a continuing federal interest in geographic and geologic surveying and the first step in the opening of

western lands to exploitation and settlement. In subsequent decades, Henry Rowe Schoolcraft explored the Missouri and Arkansas region (1817–1818), Major Stephen Long the Great Plains (1819–1820), and John C. Frémont the areas along the Oregon Trail and then south to California (1843–1844). Frémont dispelled a long-standing myth that the center of the continent was a desert.

To encourage settlement and cultivation of western lands, the federal government evicted Indian tribes from their traditional lands and offered the land at reasonable prices. And because transportation was crucial to the development of the frontier, the government first financed roads and canals and later subsidized railroad construction by means of land grants. Even the State Department aided agriculture: its consular offices overseas collected horticultural information, seeds, and cuttings, and it published technical reports in an effort to improve American farming.

The federal government also played an active role in technological and industrial growth. Federal arsenals pioneered new manufacturing techniques and helped to develop the machine-tool industry. The U.S. Post Office provided a communications link that stimulated interregional trade and briefly played a crucial role in the development of the telegraph. The first telegraph line, from Washington to Baltimore, was constructed in 1844 under a government grant and briefly managed by the Post Office. And to create an atmosphere conducive to economic growth and individual creativity, the government protected inventions and domestic industries. Patent laws gave inventors a seventeen-year monopoly on their inventions, and tariffs protected American industry from foreign competition.

The federal judiciary validated government promotion of the economy and encouraged business enterprise. In *Gibbons* v. *Ogden* (1824), the

Legal Foundations of Commerce

Supreme Court overturned a New York State law that had given Robert Fulton and Robert Livingston a monopoly on the New York–New Jersey steamboat trade. Aaron Ogden, their successor, lost the monopoly when Chief Justice John Marshall ruled that the congressional prerogative of licensing new enterprises took precedence over New York's grant of monopoly rights to Fulton and Livingston. Marshall declared that Congress's power under the commerce clause of the Constitution extended to "every species of commercial intercourse," including transportation systems. In defining interstate commerce broadly, the Marshall Court expanded federal powers over the economy while restricting the ability of states to control economic activity within their borders.

Federal and state courts, in conjunction with state legislatures, also encouraged the proliferation of corporations—groups of investors entitled to hold property and transact business as if they were one person. Investors in corporations, called shareholders, were granted limited liability, or freedom from responsibility for the company's debts. In 1800, the United States had about three hundred incorporated companies; in 1817, there were about two thousand. By 1830, the New England states alone had issued nineteen hundred charters. At first, each company needed a special legislative act to incorporate, but after the 1830s applications became so numerous that states established routine procedures for companies to incorporate.

Another encouragement to corporate development and free enterprise was the Supreme Court's ruling in *Charles River Bridge* v. *Warren Bridge* (1837) that new enterprises could not be restrained by implied privileges under old charters. The case involved issues of great importance: should a new interest be allowed to compete against existing enterprises, and should the state protect existing privilege or encourage innovation and the growth of commerce through competition?

The Massachusetts legislature had chartered the Charles River Bridge Company in 1785 and six years later extended its charter for seventy years. In return for assuming the risk of building the bridge between Charlestown and Boston, the owners received the privilege of collecting tolls. In 1828, the legislature chartered another company to build the Warren Bridge across the Charles; the owner would have the right to collect tolls for six years, after which the bridge would be turned over to the state and be free of tolls. The Charles River Bridge Company sued in 1829, claiming that the new bridge breached the earlier charter. Speaking for the Court majority, Marshall's successor Roger Taney declared that the original charter did not confer the privilege of monopoly and that exclusivity could not therefore be implied. Focusing on the question of corporate privilege rather than the law of contracts, Taney ruled that charter grants should be interpreted narrowly and that ambiguities would be decided in favor of the public interest. Old charters should not restrict new enterprises.

State Promotion of the Economy

State governments far surpassed the federal government in promoting the economy. From 1815 through 1860, for example, 73 percent of the $135 million invested in canals was government money, most of it from the states. In the 1830s, the states started to invest in rail construction. Although the federal government played a larger role in constructing railroads than in building canals, state and local governments provided more than half the capital for southern rail lines. State governments also invested in corporate and bank stocks, providing those institutions with much-needed capital. In fact, states actually equaled or surpassed private enterprise in their investments.

Largely as a result of government efforts, the United States experienced uneven but sustained economic growth from the end of the War of 1812 until 1860. Political controversy raged over questions of state versus federal activity—especially with regard to internal improvements and banking—but all parties agreed on the general goal of economic expansion. Indeed, the major restraint on government action during these years was not philosophical but financial: the public purse was small.

THE RISE OF MANUFACTURING AND COMMERCE

In 1851, hundreds of American products made their international debut at the London Crystal Palace Exhibition, the first modern world's fair. The design and quality of American machines and wares astonished observers. Most impressive to the Europeans were three simple machines: Alfred C. Hobb's unpickable padlocks, Samuel Colt's revolvers, and Robbins and Lawrence's rifles with completely interchangeable parts. All were machine-tooled rather than handmade, products of what the British called the American system of manufacturing. The American system so impressed the British—whose nation was the leading industrial power of the time—that they sent a parliamentary committee to study it. Soon other nations were sending delegations across the Atlantic to bring back American machines.

The American system of manufacturing used precision machinery to produce interchangeable parts that needed no filing or fitting. Eli Whitney had promoted the idea of interchangeable parts in 1798 when he contracted with the federal government to make ten thousand rifles in twenty-eight months. By the 1820s, the U.S. Ordnance Department had contracted with private companies to introduce machine-made interchangeable parts for firearms. The American system quickly spread beyond the arsenals, giving birth to the machine-tool industry—the manufacture of machines for the purposes of mass production. One outcome was an explosion in the production of inexpensive consumer goods of uniformly high quality.

American System of Manufacturing
————

Interchangeable parts and the machine-tool industry were uniquely American contributions to the industrial revolution. Both paved the way for the swift industrialization that the nation experienced after the Civil War. The process of industrialization began, however, in a simple and traditional way, like that of other nations. In 1800, manufacturing was a relatively unimportant component of the American economy. Most took place in small workshops and homes, where master craftsmen supervised journeymen and taught apprentices, and women worked alone spinning thread and weaving cloth. Tailors, shoemakers, and blacksmiths made articles by hand, to order for specific customers.

The clothing trades illustrate well the nineteenth-century changes in manufacturing and distribution and the reliance on the market economy.

Clothing Trades
————

Tailors made wealthy men's clothing to order. The nineteenth-century machine-tool industry made textile and clothing production a function of mills and factories rather than kitchens and home workshops. First in England, then in the United States, cotton textile mills began processing cotton grown in the slave South. The first American textile mill, built in Pawtucket, Rhode Island, in 1790, used water-powered spinning machines constructed from British models by the English immigrant Samuel Slater. Soon other mills sprang up, stimulated by the embargo on British imports from 1807 through 1815.

By the 1820s and 1830s, clothing manufacturers had replaced much of the old system. Early mills used the "putting-out" system: typically, a journeyman tailor cut the fabric panels in the factory, and the sewing was put out at piece rates to unskilled or semiskilled labor, often women working in their homes. Although the work was familiar, women now worked for piece-rate wages, not to clothe their families.

In 1832, Boston manufacturers employed three hundred journeyman tailors at $2 per day and thirteen hundred women and one hundred boys at 50 cents a day. Apprentices, if used at all, were no longer learning a trade; they were a permanent source of cheap labor. Most women worked at home, sewing straight seams by hand. By the late 1850s, as many as seventeen different pairs of hands were involved in making a single pair of pants under the putting-out system.

Construction of the first American power loom and the chartering of the Boston Manufacturing Company in 1813 radically transformed textile manufacturing. The corporation was capitalized at $400,000—ten times the amount behind the Rhode Island mills—by Francis Cabot Lowell and other Boston merchants. Its goal was to eliminate the problems of timing, shipping, coordination, and quality control inherent in the putting-out system. The owners erected their factories in Waltham, Massachusetts, combining all the manufacturing processes at a single location. They also employed a resident manager to run the mill, thus separating ownership from

Waltham (Lowell) System
————

management. Workers were paid by the piece or by the hour, and the product—first cloth, then both cloth and finished clothing—was sold throughout the United States. The company's cloth was so inexpensive that many women began to purchase it rather than make their own.

When its managers could not find enough hands in rural Waltham to staff the mill, they recruited New England farm daughters, accepting responsibility for their living conditions. As inducements, they offered cash wages, company-run boarding houses, and such cultural events as evening lectures—none of which was available on the farm. This paternalistic approach, called the Waltham (or Lowell) system, was adopted in other mills erected alongside New England rivers.

Most of the first mass-produced clothes, crudely made and limited to a few loose-fitting sizes, were produced for men who lived in city boarding houses and rooming houses. Improvements in fit and changes in men's fashion, however, made ready-to-wear apparel more acceptable to white-collar and professional men. By the 1850s, the short sack coat, the forerunner of the modern suit jacket, had replaced the embroidered waistcoat. Now even upper-class men were willing to consider ready-made apparel. The New York City store of Henry Sands Brooks, which later became Brooks Brothers, opened in 1818 and offered tailoring services and ready-made apparel to the carriage trade.

Well-stocked retail clothing stores appeared in the 1820s. Their owners often bought goods wholesale, although many manufactured garments in their own factories. Lewis and Hanford of New York City boasted of cutting more than one hundred thousand garments in the winter of 1848–1849. The New York firm sold most of its clothing in the South and owned its own retail outlet in New Orleans. A New Orleans competitor, Paul Tulane, owned a New York factory that made goods for his Louisiana store. In the West, Cincinnati became the center of the new men's clothing industry. By midcentury, Cincinnati's ready-to-wear apparel industry employed fifteen hundred men and ten thousand women.

By 1860, a cotton mill resembled a modern factory. The work force consisted mainly of immigrant Irish women who lived at home, not in mill-

Textile Mills

subsidized housing. New England farm women continued to live in the few remaining boarding houses. Technological improvements in the looms and other machinery had made the work less skilled and more routine. The mills could thus pay lower wages, and increased immigration meant that mill owners always had a reservoir of unskilled labor from which to draw.

Textiles became the most important industry in the nation before the Civil War, employing 115,000 workers in 1860, more than half of whom were women and immigrants. The key to the success of the textile industry was that the machines, not the women, spun the yarn and wove the cloth. The workers watched the machines and intervened to maintain smooth operation. When a thread broke, the machine stopped automatically; the worker then found the break, pieced the ends together, and restarted the machine. The New England textile mills used increasingly specialized machines, relying heavily on advances in the machine-tool industry. Their application of the American system of manufacturing enabled American companies to compete successfully with British cotton mills.

Although cotton textile mills were the vanguard of industrialization, new manufacturing methods also transformed woolen textiles, farm implements, machine tools, iron, steel, glass, and finished consumer goods into major industries. "White coal"—water power—was widely used to run the machines. By 1860, manufacturing accounted for one-third of the nation's total production, an increase of 200 percent in twenty years.

Several factors stimulated industrial development. They included the demand for home manufactures created by the embargo and the War of 1812, population growth, government policy (protective tariffs, for example), the rise of commercial agriculture, and the transportation revolution. Moreover, the relative scarcity of skilled craftsmen encouraged mechanization. Commercial growth accompanied the rise in manufacturing and in many ways was essential to it.

Cotton, for instance, had once been traded by plantation agents, who handled all the crops produced and bought all the goods purchased by the

Specialization of Commerce

plantation owners, extending them credit when needed. As cotton became a great staple export following the invention of the cotton gin in 1793, exports rose from half a million pounds in that year to 83 million pounds in 1815. Gradually, some agents came to specialize in finance alone: these were cotton brokers, who for a commission brought together buyers and sellers. Similarly, wheat and hog brokers sprang up in the West—in Cincinnati, Louisville, and St. Louis. The distribution of finished goods also became more specialized as wholesalers bought large quantities of particular items from manufacturers, and jobbers broke down the wholesale lots for retail stores and country merchants.

Commercial specialization transformed some traders in big cities, especially New York, into virtual merchant princes. When the Erie Canal opened, New York City became a standard stop on every major trade route from Europe, the southern ports, and the West. New York traders were the middlemen for southern cotton and western grain trading; in fact, New York was the nation's major cotton-exporting city. Merchants in other cities played a similar role within their own regions.

Newly rich traders in turn invested their profits in processing enterprises and then manufacturing, further stimulating the growth of northern cities. Some cities specialized: Rochester became a milling center and Cincinnati—"Porkopolis"—became the first meat-packing center.

Banks and other financial institutions, which played a significant role in the expansion of commerce and manufacturing, also were a leading industry. Financial institutions

Banking and Credit Systems

(banks, insurance companies, and corporations) linked savers— those who deposited money in banks—with producers and speculators who wished to borrow money. The expiration of the first Bank of the United States in 1811, after Congress refused to renew its charter, acted as a stimulus to state-chartered banks, and during the next five years the number of such banks more than doubled. When state banks proved inadequate to spur national growth, Congress chartered the Second Bank of the United States in 1816.

Many farmers, local bankers, and politicians, however, denounced the bank as a monster, claiming that it served national, not local, interests. In 1836, critics succeeded in killing the bank.

The closing of the Second Bank in 1836 caused a nationwide credit shortage, which, in conjunction with the Panic of 1837, stimulated fundamental reforms in banking. Michigan and New York introduced charter laws promoting what was called *free banking*. Previously, every new bank had required a special legislative charter; thus each bank incorporation was in effect a political decision. Under the new laws, any proposed bank that met certain minimum conditions—capital invested, notes issued, and types of loans to be made—would automatically receive a state charter. Banks in Michigan and New York were thus freer to incorporate, but the states placed restrictions on their operation in order to reduce the risk of bank failure. Many other states soon followed suit.

Free banking proved to be a significant stimulus to the economy in the late 1840s and 1850s. New banks sprang up everywhere, providing merchants and manufacturers the credit they needed. The free-banking laws also served as a precedent for the general incorporation statutes that allowed manufacturing firms to receive state charters without special acts of the state legislature.

Changes in insurance companies also promoted industrialization by creating a new source of capital. In the course of business, insurance companies accumulated large amounts of money as reserves against future claims. Then as now, their greatest profits derived from investing those reserves. Beginning in the 1840s, insurance companies lent money for longer periods than did banks, and they bought shares in corporations.

In the 1850s, with credit and capital both easily obtainable, the pace of industrialization increased. In the North, industry began to rival agriculture and commerce in dollar volume. Meanwhile, commercial farming, financed by the credit boom, was integrating the early frontier and the northern economy. By 1860, six northern states—Massachusetts, New York, Pennsylvania, Connecticut, Rhode Island, and Ohio—were highly industrialized. Their clothing, textile, and shoe industries employed more than one hundred thousand workers each; lumber, seventy-five thousand; iron, sixty-five thousand; and woolens and leather, fifty thousand. Although agriculture still predominated even in these states, industrial employment would soon surpass it.

WORKERS AND THE WORKPLACE

Oh, sing me the song of the Factory Girl!
So merry and glad and free!
The bloom in her cheeks, of health how it speaks,
Oh! a happy creature is she!
She tends the loom, she watches the spindle,
And cheerfully toileth away,
Amid the din of wheels, how her bright eyes kindle,
And her bosom is ever gay.

This idyllic portrait of factory work appeared in the Chicopee, Massachusetts, *Telegraph* in 1850. It was a fitting anthem for the teenage single women who first left the villages and farms of New England to work in the mills. New England mill owners, convinced that the degradation of English factory workers arose from their living conditions and not from the work itself, designed model communities offering airy courtyards and river views, secure dormitories, prepared meals, and cultural activities.

The promise of steady work, good pay, and kinship ties at first lured eager rural young women into the mills. Many pairs of sisters and cousins worked in the same mill and lived in the same boarding house. They helped each other adjust, and their letters home drew other kin to the mills. Young women then had few opportunities for work outside their homes, and, at the same time, the commercial production of yarn and cloth had reduced their workload in New England farm households. Averaging 16.5 years of age when they entered the mills, the girls usually stayed only about five years—few intended to stay longer. Most left the mills to marry and were replaced by other women interested in earning a wage.

Between 1837 and 1842, most mills ran only part time because of a decline in demand for cloth; subsequently, managers applied still greater pressures on workers by means of the speed-up, the stretch-out, and the premium system. The speed-up increased the speed of the machines, the stretch-out increased the number of machines each worker had to operate, and premiums for the overseers whose departments produced the most cloth encouraged them to pressure workers for greater output. In mill towns like Lowell, concern for workers' living conditions gave way to a race for profits in which the owners lengthened hours, cut wages, and tightened discipline.

New England mill workers responded to their deteriorating working conditions by organizing and striking. In 1834, in reaction to a 25 percent wage cut, they unsuccessfully "turned out" (struck) against the Lowell mills. Two years later, when boarding house rates were raised, they turned out again. In the 1840s, however, mill women adopted a new method of resistance. They joined with other workers in a concerted effort to get the Massachusetts legislature to shorten the workday to ten hours.

Mill Women Protests

The short tenure of most workers weakened women's labor organizations. Few militant native-born mill workers stayed on to fight the managers and owners, and gradually fewer New England daughters entered the mills. The women who constituted the majority of mill workers by the end of the 1850s were mostly Irish immigrants, driven to the mills by the need to support their families and unable to afford to complain about their working conditions.

A growing gender division in the workplace, especially in the textile, clothing, and shoemaking industries, was one important outcome of industrialization. Although women and men tended to perform different tasks in traditional agricultural and artisan households, they worked as a family unit. As wage work spread, however, men's and women's work cultures became increasingly separate. The women and girls who left home to work in textile mills worked and lived in a mostly female world. In the clothing and shoemaking industries, male artisans, who had once worked at home assisted by unpaid family labor, began working outside the home, whereas women continued to work at home through the putting-out system.

Gender Divisions in Work

TIME TABLE OF THE LOWELL MILLS,

Arranged to make the working time throughout the year average 11 hours per day.

TO TAKE EFFECT SEPTEMBER 21st, 1853.

The Standard time being that of the meridian of Lowell, as shown by the Regulator Clock of AMOS SANBORN, Post Office Corner, Central Street.

From March 20th to September 19th, inclusive.

COMMENCE WORK, at 6.30 A. M. LEAVE OFF WORK, at 6.30 P. M., except on Saturday Evenings. BREAKFAST at 6 A. M. DINNER, at 12 M. Commence Work, after dinner, 12.45 P. M.

From September 20th to March 19th, inclusive.

COMMENCE WORK at 7.00 A. M. LEAVE OFF WORK, at 7.00 P. M., except on Saturday Evenings. BREAKFAST at 6.30 A. M. DINNER, at 12.30 P. M. Commence Work, after dinner, 1.15 P. M.

BELLS.

From March 20th to September 19th, inclusive.

Morning Bells.	Dinner Bells.	Evening Bells.
First bell,............4.30 A. M.	Ring out,.............12.00 M.	Ring out,............6.30 P. M.
Second, 5.30 A. M.; Third, 6.20.	Ring in,............12 35 P. M.	Except on Saturday Evenings.

From September 20th to March 19th, inclusive.

Morning Bells.	Dinner Bells.	Evening Bells.
First bell,............5.00 A. M.	Ring out,............12.30 P. M.	Ring out at............7.00 P. M.
Second, 6.00 A. M.; Third, 6.50.	Ring in,............1.05 P. M.	Except on Saturday Evenings.

SATURDAY EVENING BELLS.

During APRIL, MAY, JUNE, JULY, and AUGUST, Ring Out, at 6.00 P. M.
The remaining Saturday Evenings in the year, ring out as follows:

SEPTEMBER.	**NOVEMBER.**	**JANUARY.**
First Saturday, ring out 6.00 P. M.	Third Saturday ring out 4.00 P. M.	Third Saturday, ring out 4.25 P. M.
Second " " 5.45 "	Fourth " " 3.55 "	Fourth " " 4.35 "
Third " " 5.30 "		**FEBRUARY.**
Fourth " " 5.20 "	**DECEMBER.**	First Saturday, ring out 4.45 P. M.
OCTOBER.	First Saturday, ring out 3.50 P. M.	Second " " 4.55 "
First Saturday, ring out 5.05 P. M.	Second " " 3.55 "	Third " " 5.00 "
Second " " 4.55 "	Third " " 3.55 "	Fourth " " 5.10 "
Third " " 4.45 "	Fourth " " 4.00 "	**MARCH.**
Fourth " " 4.35 "	Fifth " " 4.00 "	First Saturday, ring out 5.25 P. M.
Fifth " " 4.25 "		Second " " 5.30 "
NOVEMBER.	**JANUARY.**	Third " " 5.35 "
First Saturday, ring out 4.15 P. M.	First Saturday, ring out 4.10 P. M.	Fourth " " 5.45 "
Second " " 4.05 "	Second " " 4.15 "	

YARD GATES will be opened at the first stroke of the bells for entering or leaving the Mills.

• *SPEED GATES commence hoisting three minutes before commencing work.*

Penhallow, Printer, Wyman's Exchange, 28 Merrimack St.

How do historians know

the nature of the working conditions experienced by New England mill workers? This 1853 timetable from the Lowell Mills is among the rich sources historians consult to reconstruct the workers' experiences in the mills. The textile factories were the first corporations to impose rigid work rules. The size of the labor force, the managerial structure, and the organization of the work made it necessary to print the work rules. The timetable illustrates the nature of the rules imposed. Exact times were established for beginning and ending work and for meals. Because few workers carried their own timepieces, a system of bells regulated the lives of the factory community. Thus from March 20 to September 19, when work began at 6:30 A.M., bells alerted the workers at 4:30 and 5:50 A.M. and again at 6:20, ten minutes before they had to be at the factory. For their main meal at midday, they had forty-five minutes away from work; the 12:35 bell warned that they had ten minutes to return. For young mill women from the New England countryside, and later for Irish women, such regimentation must have seemed a world apart from the rhythms of rural life.   Photo: Museum of American Textile History.

Tasks and wages too became rigidly differentiated: women sewed, whereas men shaped materials and finished products, receiving higher wages in shops employing only men.

The market system, wage labor, and the specialization of labor affected unpaid household labor as well. As home and workplace became separate and labor came to be defined in terms of wages (what could be sold in the marketplace) rather than production, the unpaid labor of women was devalued. Yet the family depended on women's work within the household. And as the family became more dependent on wage labor, more family members sought outside employment and had less time to do their share of household labor. Thus gender defined household labor and placed a low value on it.

The new textile mills, shoe factories, iron mills, insurance companies, wholesale stores, and railroads were the antithesis of the old tradition of workshop and household pro-

Changes in the Workplace
____

duction. Large factories created a workplace in which authority was hierarchically organized. Factory workers lost their sense of autonomy as impersonal market forces seemed to dominate their lives. Stiff competition among mills in the growing textile industry led to layoffs and the replacement of operatives with less expensive, less-skilled workers or children. The formal rules of the factory contrasted sharply with the more relaxed pace and atmosphere of artisan shops and farm households. Supervisors represented owners whom workers never saw. The division of labor and the use of machines narrowed the skills required of workers. And the bell, the steam whistle, or the clock governed the flow of work. Bells controlled when workers awoke, ate, began and ended work, and went to sleep. The central problem, of course, was the quickening pace of the work between the bells. Moreover, mill workers had to tolerate the roar of the looms, and all workers on power machines risked accidents that could kill or maim. Perhaps most demoralizing, opportunities for advancement in the new system were virtually nil.

Changes in the workplace in turn transformed the workers. Initially, mill women drew on kinship, village, and gender ties to build supportive networks in factories. In the 1840s and after, as recent Irish immigrant women came to predominate, more workers were strangers to each other before they entered the mills. Once employed, their only bases for friendship and mutual support were their work experiences. As a sense of distance from their employers took hold, so did deep-seated differences among workers. Nationality, religion, education, and future prospects separated Irish and Yankee mill workers. Many New England women resented the immigrants, and management set one group against the other through selective hiring and promotions. For most Irish women, mill work was permanent employment, not a stage in their lives, as it was for their Yankee sisters.

Organized labor's greatest achievement during this period was to gain relief from the threat of conspiracy laws. When journeyman shoemakers

Emergence of a Labor Movement
____

organized during the first decade of the century, their employers turned to the courts, charging criminal conspiracy. The cordwainers' (shoemakers') cases, which resulted in six trials between 1806 and 1815, left labor organizations in a tenuous position. Although the courts acknowledged journeymen's right to organize, they ruled unlawful any coercive action on the journeymen's part that would harm other businesses or the public. In other words, strikes were ruled illegal. Eventually, a Massachusetts case, *Commonwealth* v. *Hunt* (1842), effectively reversed this decision when Chief Justice Lemuel Shaw ruled that Boston journeyman boot makers could strike "in such manner as best to subserve their own interests." Conspiracy laws no longer thwarted unionization.

Yet permanent labor organizations were difficult to maintain. Most workers outside the crafts were unskilled or semiskilled at best. Moreover, religion, race, ethnicity, and gender divided workers. The first unions tended to be local in nature; the strongest resembled medieval guilds in that they sought to protect themselves against the competition of inferior workers by regulating apprenticeship and establishing minimum wages. They also excluded women and African-Americans.

Umbrella organizations composed of individual craft unions, like the National Trades Union (1834), arose in several cities in the 1820s and 1830s. But the movement fell apart in the hard times of 1839–1843. In the 1850s, the deterioration of working conditions strengthened the labor movement again, and affiliated craft unions began to organize into national unions. Workers won a reduction in hours, and the ten-hour day became standard. Although the Panic of 1857 wiped out the umbrella organizations, some new national unions in specific trades survived.

The effect of economic and technological change inevitably fell more heavily on individual workers than on their organizations. As a group, workers' share of the national wealth declined after the 1830s. Individual producers—craftsmen, factory workers, and farmers—had less economic power than they had had a generation or two earlier. And workers were increasingly losing control over their own work.

COMMERCIAL FARMING

Although urban areas were growing quickly, agriculture remained the backbone of the economy. America was still overwhelmingly rural. Indeed, it was rural population growth that transformed so many farm villages into bustling small cities. And in turn it was the new market orientation of farm families, and their ability to feed the growing town and village populations, that made possible these new concentrations of population.

In 1800, New England and Middle Atlantic farmers worked as their fathers and mothers had. Life centered around a household economy in which

Northeastern Agriculture

the needs of the family and the labor at its disposal determined what was produced and in what amounts. Then canals and railroads began transporting grain eastward from the fertile Old Northwest. At the same time, northeastern agriculture developed some serious problems. Northeastern farmers had already cultivated all the land they could; expansion was impossible. Moreover, small New England farms with their uneven terrain did not lend themselves to the new labor-saving farm implements introduced in the 1830s—mechanical sowers, reapers, threshers, and balers. Many northeastern farms also suffered from soil exhaustion.

In response to these problems and to competition from the West, many northern farmers either went west or gave up farming for jobs in the merchant houses and factories. Between 1820 and 1860, the percentage of the population of the North living on farms declined from 71 to 40 percent. The farmers who remained proved to be quite adaptable. By the 1850s, New England and Middle Atlantic farm families were adjusting successfully to competition from western agricultural products. Many abandoned the commercial production of wheat and corn and stopped tilling poor land. Instead, they improved their livestock, especially cattle, and specialized in vegetable and fruit production and dairy farming, financing these initiatives through land sales and borrowing. In fact, their greatest potential profit was from increasing land values, not from farming itself.

Farm families everywhere gradually adjusted to market conditions. In 1820, about one-third of all food produced was intended for market; by 1860, the fraction had increased to about two-thirds. Middlemen specializing in the grain and food trades replaced the country storekeepers who had handled transactions for local farmers, acting as both retailers and marketing and purchasing agents.

Women's earning power from wages or market sales was an important factor in the market economy. With increasing commercialization and

Women's Paid Labor

dependence on cash for both investment and purchases, women's earnings became essential to the survival of the family farm. The put-out work women did in New England had its parallel in the Middle Atlantic states and in women's dairy production, which was crucial to family income. Butter and cheese making for local and regional markets replaced spinning and weaving as farm women's major activity. The work was physically demanding and was added to the traditional home and farm chores. Yet women took pride in their work; it gave many a sense of independence.

Most farm families seemed to welcome the opportunities offered by the market economy. While continuing to take pride in self-sufficiency and to value rural serenity, they shifted toward specialization and market-oriented production. The rewards for such flexibility were great; produce sold at market financed land and equipment purchases and made credit arrangements possible. Many farm families flourished.

Others were less fortunate. The rising cost of land and of farming meant that by the 1850s it took ten to twenty years for a rural laborer to save enough money to farm for himself. Thus the number of tenant farmers increased, and the use of paid farm labor became commonplace.

Individually and collectively, Americans still valued agrarian life. State governments energetically promoted commercial agriculture in order to spur economic growth and sustain the values of an agrarian-based republic. Massachusetts in 1817 and New York in 1819 subsidized agricultural prizes and county fairs. New York required contestants to submit written descriptions of how they grew their prize crops; the state then published the best essays to encourage the use of new methods and promote specialization. Farm journals also helped familiarize farmers with developments in agriculture.

Even so, the Old Northwest gradually and inevitably replaced the northeastern states as the center of American family agriculture. Farms in the Old Northwest were much larger and better suited to the new mechanized farming implements than were their northeastern counterparts. The farmers of the region bought machines such as the McCormick reaper on credit and paid for them with the profits from their high yields. By 1847, Cyrus McCormick was selling one thousand reapers a year. By introducing interchangeable parts, he expanded production to five thousand a year. Similarly, John Deere's steel plow, invented in 1837, replaced the inadequate iron plow; steel blades kept the soil from sticking and were tough enough to break the roots of prairie grass. By 1856, Deere's sixty-five employees were making 13,500 plows a year.

Mechanization of Agriculture
—

Mechanized farming was the basis of expanded production. In the 1850s alone, wheat production surged 70 percent. By that time, the area that had been the western wilderness in 1800 had become one of the world's leading agricultural regions. Midwestern farm families fed an entire nation and still had enough food to export.

SETTLING AND CONQUERING THE WEST

Integral to the development of the market economy was the steady expansion of the United States. In 1800, the edge of settlement extended in an arc from western New York through the new states of Kentucky and Tennessee and south to Georgia. By 1820, it had shifted westward to Ohio, Indiana, and Illinois in the North and Louisiana, Alabama, and Mississippi in the South. By 1860, settlement reached the Southwest and the West Coast; the 1800 backcountry was long settled, and once-unexplored regions were dotted with farms and mines, towns and villages. Unsettled and sporadically settled land remained—mostly the plains and mountain territory between the Mississippi River and the Sierra Nevada—but elsewhere the land and its tribal inhabitants had given way to white settlement.

The lore of pioneers on the frontier was already becoming a part of the mythology of America. James Fenimore Cooper's *Leatherstocking Tales*, a series of novels that began to appear in 1823, introduced Hawkeye (Natty Bumppo), America's first popular fictional hero. At heart a romantic, Hawkeye preferred the freedom of the virgin forest to domesticated society. Legends, songs, and dime novels also glorified fur trappers, explorers and scouts, and pioneers. The reading public snapped up tales of pioneers crossing the arid plains and snow-covered Rockies to bring civilization to the wilderness, frontiersmen and settlers triumphing over the environment and the Indians, Mormons finding Zion in the Great American Desert, and gold seekers sailing on clipper ships to California.

Legends of Pioneers
—

Only recently have Americans come to recognize that these familiar stories had other sides. The frontier was more inclusive than legends suggest: not just white men, but white women and Indians and African-Americans of both genders were pioneers. Furthermore, explorers and pioneers did not find their way across North America by themselves, nor did the wagon trains fight their way across the Plains—Native Americans guided them along traditional paths and led them to food and water. And rather than civilizing the frontier lands, settlers at first brought a rather primitive economy and society, which did not compare favorably with the well-ordered Indian civilizations. And those who sought to farm the land, dig the gold, trap the furs, and cut the lumber destroyed the natural landscape and ecological balance in the name of progress and development.

The destruction of the environment illustrates the contrast between the idealized version of the frontier and the reality. If pioneers were attracted by the beauty and bounty of the American wilderness and lured by the opportunity to live a simple, rewarding life close to the soil, they were also destroying the land in the process. Settlers felled millions of trees to make way for farms, while lumbermen in Michigan denuded the land. Farther west, miners in search of gold leveled the hills.

No figure has come to symbolize the frontier more aptly than the footloose and rugged fur trapper who roamed the wilderness in search of pelts.

Fur Trade
———

The trapper, with his backpack, rifle, and kegs of whiskey, spearheaded America's manifest destiny, extending the U.S. presence to the Pacific Slope. Trappers sought the cooperation of the tribes in their territories, and nearly 40 percent wed Indian women. Many Native American wives of white trappers played important roles in bridging the trapper and tribal cultures. Moreover, an Indian woman shared her husband's special trading privileges as well as family ties and experiences of life on the frontier. Over time, *metís*, or mixed bloods (Indian–white offspring), and white women replaced Native American women as trappers' wives. This development not only changed trapper culture but was also a sign of the decline of the fur trade, signaling the arrival of settled agrarian society.

The complex history of trapping illustrates many characteristic elements in the conquest of the West. Early fur traders exploited friendly Indian

Alfred Jacob Miller's 1837 oil painting, "A Bourgeois & His Squaw," depicted mountain man Joseph Reddeford Walker and his Indian wife going to the rendezvous. A bourgeois supervised a group of trappers, and Walker was legendary as a bourgeois and scout, having led expeditions to the Great Salt Lake and Yosemite. Joslyn Art Museum, Omaha, Nebraska.

tribes, then mountain trappers monopolized the trade through the systematic organization and financial backing of trading companies, driven by demand in distant markets. Soon settlements and towns sprang up along the trappers' routes. Mining, lumbering, and ranching followed similar patterns as settlement intensified the exploration of the West's natural resources and land. Railroads would later accelerate the process.

Farther west, beyond the trails of the mountain men, it was gold that first stimulated a mass migration to the West Coast. Anglos settled newly

California Gold Rush

acquired California almost overnight. In January 1848, James Marshall, a carpenter, spotted a few goldlike particles in the millrace at Sutter's Mill (now Coloma, California). Word spread, and other Californians rushed to scrabble for instant fortunes.

By 1849, the news had spread eastward, and hundreds of thousands of fortune seekers flooded in. Success in the market economy required capital, hard labor, and time; by contrast, gold mining seemed to promise instant riches. Most "forty-niners" never found enough gold to pay their expenses. "The stories you hear frequently in the States," one gold seeker wrote home, "are the most extravagant lies imaginable—the mines are a humbug. . . . The almost universal feeling is to get home." But many stayed, either unable to afford the passage home or tempted by the growing labor shortage in California's cities and agricultural districts. San Francisco, the gateway from the West Coast to the interior, became an instant city, ballooning from one thousand people in 1848 to thirty-five thousand just two years later. The newcomers came for one reason: instant wealth. In search of gold and silver, they mined the lodes and washed away the surface soil with hydraulic mining, leaving the land unsuitable for anything after they abandoned it.

The forty-niners produced almost nothing, but they had to be fed. Thus began the great California agricultural boom. Wheat was the preferred staple; it required minimal investment, was easily planted, and offered a quick return at the end of a relatively short growing season. By the mid-1850s, California was exporting wheat.

Meanwhile, enterprising merchants rushed to supply, feed, and clothe the new settlers. One such merchant was Levi Strauss, a German Jewish immigrant, whose tough mining pants found an enduring and eventually worldwide market as blue jeans.

In the Midwest, family farms were the basic unit of production; in California, by contrast, gold and ore mining, grazing, and large-scale wheat farming were overwhelmingly

Women Settlers

male occupations. The experiences of women, who constituted about one-seventh of the travelers on the overland trails, differed from those of men moving west. Most men came alone, drawn by a sense of adventure and personal opportunity. Women most often accompanied their husbands, and they found their lives uprooted. It was a traumatic experience for many, as they left behind networks of friends and kin to journey, often with children, along an unknown path to a strange environment. Yet in the West they found their domestic skills in great demand. They received high fees for cooking, laundering, and sewing. Women ran boarding houses and hotels, because men shunned domestic work. But not all women were entrepreneurs. Some wives, at their spouses' behest, cooked for and served their husbands' friends; the women did the work while their husbands built reputations as hosts.

Gold altered the pattern of settlement along the entire Pacific coast. Before 1848, most overland traffic flowed north over the Oregon Trail; few pioneers turned south to California. By 1849, a pioneer observed that the Oregon Trail "bore no evidence of having been much traveled this year." Traffic was flowing south instead, and California was becoming the new population center of the Pacific Slope. One measure of this shift was the overland mail routes. In the 1840s, the Oregon Trail had been the main communications link between the Midwest and the Pacific. But the Post Office officials who organized mail routes in the 1850s terminated them in California, not Oregon; there was no route north of Sacramento.

By 1860, farmers and merchants in California, as in the Great Plains and prairies farther east, had become firmly linked to the market economy.

Western Farming

Although the experiences of these settlers were less dramatic than those of the trappers and forty-niners, theirs is the story of the overwhelming majority of westerners before 1860. They migrated from the Old Northwest and the Mississippi and Missouri Valleys. They cleared the land of trees or prairie grass, hoed in corn and wheat, fenced in animals, and constructed cabins of logs or sod. As settled areas expanded, farmers built roads to carry their stock and produce to market and bring back supplies they could not produce themselves. Growth brought specialization; as western farmers shifted from self-sufficiency to commercial farming, they too tended to concentrate on one crop.

What made farm settlements possible was the availability of land and credit. Some public lands were granted as a reward for military service: veterans of the War of 1812 received 160 acres; veterans of the Mexican War could purchase land at reduced prices. And until 1820, civilians could buy government land at $2 an acre (a relatively high price) on a liberal four-year payment plan. From 1800 to 1817, the government successively reduced the minimum purchase from 640 to eighty acres, bringing the land within the reach of more Americans. But when the availability of land prompted the flurry of land speculation that ended in the Panic of 1819, the government discontinued credit sales. Instead, it reduced the price further, to $1.25 an acre.

Land Grants and Sales

Some eager pioneers settled land before it had been surveyed and offered for sale. Such illegal settlers, or squatters, then had to buy the land at auction and faced the risk of being unable to purchase it. In 1841, to facilitate settlement and end property disputes, Congress passed the Preemption Act, which legalized settlement before surveying.

Because most settlers needed to borrow money, private credit systems arose: banks, private investors, country storekeepers, and speculators all extended credit to farmers. Railroads also sold land on credit—land they had received from the government

as construction subsidies. (The Illinois Central, for example, received 2.6 million acres in 1850.) Indeed, nearly all economic activity in the West involved credit, from land sales to the shipping of produce to railroad construction.

The agricultural West was dependent from the start on its links with towns and cities. The cities along the Ohio and Mississippi Rivers—Louisville, Cincinnati, and St. Louis—predated and promoted the earliest settlement of much of the West. A generation later, the lake cities of Cleveland, Detroit, and especially Chicago spearheaded settlement farther west. Steamboats connected these cities with eastern markets and ports, carrying grain east and returning with finished goods. As the center of a rail network, Chicago exercised sway over the settling and development of most of the middle United States. As in the Northeast, these western cities eventually developed into manufacturing centers as merchants shifted their investments from commerce to industry. Chicago became a center for the manufacture of farm implements, Louisville of textiles, and Cleveland of iron.

Frontier Cities

For the North and the West, the period from 1800 through 1860 was one of explosive growth. Population increased sixfold. Settlement now extended beyond the Mississippi and was spreading east from the Pacific Ocean by 1860. By then, Cincinnati, St. Louis, and Chicago each had populations exceeding one hundred thousand, and Buffalo, Louisville, San Francisco, Pittsburgh, Detroit, Milwaukee, and Cleveland had surpassed forty thousand. Thus commerce, urban growth, and industrialization overtook the farmers' frontier, wedding the West to the Northeast. By midcentury, agriculture was being challenged by a booming manufacturing sector. And agriculture was becoming market oriented and mechanized.

Economic development changed how people lived. Canals, railroads, steamboats, and telegraph lines linked economic activities hundreds and even thousands of miles apart. The market economy brought sustained growth and cycles of boom and bust. Hard times and unemployment became frequent occurrences. The growing economy also meant larger-scale destruction of the environment: while mills exploited New England waterways as a source of power, Michigan was denuded of its pine forests and the gold rush destroyed land in California.

Commercial and industrial growth also altered traditional patterns of production and consumption. Farmers began to purchase goods formerly produced by their wives and daughters, and farm families geared production to faraway markets. Farm women increasingly contributed income from market sales to the family farm. In New England, many young women left the family farm to become the first factory workers in the new textile industry. As the master–journeyman–apprentice system faded away, workplace relations became more impersonal and working conditions harsher. Industrial jobs began to attract large numbers of immigrants, and some workers organized labor unions.

The American people too were changing. Immigration and western expansion made the population more diverse. Urbanization, commerce, and industry were creating significant divisions among Americans, reaching deeply into the home as well as the workshop. The South was not totally insulated from these changes, but its dependence on slave rather than free labor set it apart. Above all else, slavery defined the South.

SUGGESTIONS FOR FURTHER READING

General

Stuart Bruchey, *The Roots of American Economic Growth, 1607–1861: An Essay in Social Causation* (1965); Jack Larkin, *The Reshaping of Everyday Life, 1790–1840* (1988); Douglass C. North, *Economic Growth of the United States, 1790–1860* (1966); Nathan Rosenberg, *Technology and American Economic Growth* (1972).

Transportation

Robert G. Albion, *The Rise of New York Port, 1815–1860* (1939); Louis C. Hunter, *Steamboats on the Western Rivers* (1949); Ronald E. Shaw, *Canals for a Nation: The Canal Era in the United States, 1790–1860* (1990); George R. Taylor, *The Transportation Revolution, 1815–1860* (1951); James A. Ward, *Railroads and the Character of America, 1820–1887* (1986).

Commerce and Manufacturing

Thomas C. Cochran, *Frontiers of Change: Early Industrialization in America* (1981); Louis Hartz, *Economic Policy and Democratic Thought: Pennsylvania, 1776–1860* (1954); David A. Hounshell, *From the American System to Mass Production, 1800–1932: The Development of Manufacturing Technology in the United States* (1984); Stanley I. Kutler, *Privilege and Creative Destruction: The Charles River Bridge Case* (1971); Theodore Steinberg, *Nature Incorporated: Industrialization and the Waters of New England* (1991); Barbara M. Tucker, *Samuel Slater and the Origins of the American Textile Industry, 1790–1860* (1984); Anthony F. C. Wallace, *Rockdale: The Growth of an American Village in the Early Industrial Revolution* (1978).

Agriculture

Jeremy Atack and Fred Bateman, *To Their Own Soil: Agriculture in the Antebellum North* (1987); Allen G. Bogue, *From Prairie to Corn Belt: Farming on the Illinois and Iowa Prairies in the Nineteenth Century* (1963); Clarence Danhof, *Change in Agriculture: The Northern United States, 1820–1870* (1969); John Mack Faragher, *Sugar Creek: Life on the Illinois Prairie* (1986); Paul W. Gates, *The Farmer's Age: Agriculture, 1815–1860* (1962); Joan M. Jensen, *Loosening the Bonds: Mid-Atlantic Farm Women, 1750–1850* (1986); Robert Leslie Jones, *History of Agriculture in Ohio to 1880* (1983).

The Frontier

William Cronon, *Nature's Metropolis: Chicago and the Great West* (1991); John Mack Faragher, *Women and Men on the Overland Trail* (1979); William H. Goetzmann, *Exploration and Empire: The Explorer and the Scientist in the Winning of the American West* (1966); Julie Roy Jeffrey, *Frontier Women: The Trans-Mississippi West, 1840–1880* (1979); Theodore J. Karamanski, *Fur Trade and Exploration: Opening the Far Northwest, 1821–1852* (1983); John D. Unruh Jr., *The Overland Emigrants and the Trans-Mississippi West, 1840–1860* (1979).

Workers

Mary H. Blewett, *Men, Women, and Work: Class, Gender, and Protest in the New England Shoe Industry, 1780–1910* (1988); Jeanne Boydston, *Home and Work: Housework, Wages, and the Ideology of Labor in the Early Republic* (1990); Alan Dawley, *Class and Community: The Industrial Revolution in Lynn* (1977); Thomas Dublin, *Women at Work: The Transformation of Work and Community in Lowell, Massachusetts, 1826–1860* (1979); Jonathan Prude, *The Coming of Industrial Order: Town and Factory Life in Rural Massachusetts, 1810–1860* (1983); Norman Ware, *The Industrial Worker, 1840–1860* (1924); Sean Wilentz, *Chants Democratic: New York City and the Rise of the American Working Class, 1788–1850* (1984).

11

Slavery and the Growth of the South, 1800–1860

SLAVERY AND RACISM PLAGUED Frederick Bailey from birth. He had no father, for his father was a white man—probably the master. He never knew his mother, for the master separated them before he was a year old. Raised by his grandmother, Bailey later recalled that as a young boy he often saw his aunt stripped to the waist and lashed until "the warm, red blood came dripping to the floor." On many mornings the "heart-rending shrieks" of a slave and the master's "horrid oaths" roused him from sleep. Yet somehow he formed "a deep conviction that slavery would not always be able to hold me within its foul embrace."

At about age fifteen, the young man was hired out to a violent man to be "broken"—to learn absolute obedience from a year of constant work and whippings. One day, as the slave breaker began again to beat him, Bailey seized his tormentor by the throat, and they struggled hand to hand for nearly two hours. When they parted, one knew his dominance was over, and the other felt "a glorious resurrection, from the tomb of slavery, to the heaven of freedom."

Two years later, he escaped from Baltimore, first to New York City and then to New Bedford, Massachusetts, where he took the name Frederick Douglass. In the North, he encountered prejudice. A few people treated him decently, but many despised his blackness. Although he knew how to caulk the seams of ships, white caulkers in New Bedford's shipyards refused to work with him.

Frederick Douglass made the most of the freedom that the North offered to study, to speak, and to agitate. He fled from bondage in 1838 and by 1841 had already begun his impressive career as an antislavery orator and editor. But he never escaped the prejudice that had grown so familiar to him in the South. Douglass's career illustrates both the differences that were developing between North and South and their similarities.

Racism was a national phenomenon, but attitudes on slavery were beginning to diverge in the 1820s and 1830s. Many northerners remained undisturbed by the idea of human bondage, but a growing number considered it shocking and backward. In the years after the Revolution, northerners—possessing few slaves and influenced by the revolutionary concept of natural rights—had adopted gradual emancipation laws. At the same time, they developed a dynamic market economy and embarked on an industrial revolution. The changes rendered forced labor obsolete.

While the North grew and changed between 1800 and 1860, economically the South merely grew. New lands were settled and new states peopled, but southern growth only reinforced existing economic patterns. Steadily, the South emerged as the world's most extensive and vigorous slave economy. Its people were slaves, slaveholders, and nonslaveholders rather than farmers, merchants, mechanics, mill workers, and manufacturers. Its well-being depended on agriculture alone, rather than on agriculture plus commerce and manufacturing. Its population was almost wholly rural rather than rural and urban.

MIGRATION, GROWTH, AND THE COTTON BOOM

Between 1800 and 1860, small farmers and slave-owning planters migrated westward and brought new territory under cultivation. As human labor, both voluntary and coerced, built a vastly larger slave-holding society, farms and plantations spread across the landscape.

The attraction of rich new lands drew thousands of southerners across the Appalachian Mountains. Both small farmers and ambitious slave owners poured across the mountains, pushing the Indians off their lands in the Gulf region. The floodtide of westward migration reached Alabama and Mississippi in the 1830s, then spilled into Texas in the 1850s.

The earliest settlers in the swelling stream of migration were often yeomen—small farmers, most of whom owned no slaves. Yeomen pioneered the southern wilderness, moving into undeveloped regions and building log cabins. After the War of 1812, they moved in successive waves down the southern Appalachians into new Gulf lands, first as herders of livestock and then as farmers. The herdsmen, who fattened their cattle and pigs on the abundant natural vegetation in the woods, moved on when farmers filled up an area and broke ground for crops. Yeoman farmers forced many herdsmen farther west and eventually across the Mississippi.

Migration became almost a way of life for some yeoman families. Lured by stories of good land beyond the horizon, many men uprooted their wives and children repeatedly. Women seldom shared the men's excitement about moving, but they labored in the household economy and patiently recreated the social ties—to relatives, neighbors, members of their church—that enriched experience.

Some yeomen acquired large tracts of level land and became wealthy planters. Others clung to the beautiful mountainous areas they loved or pressed farther into the wilds because, as one frontiersman told a European visitor, he disliked "seeing the nose of my neighbor sticking out between the trees." Those who moved tended to stick to the climate and soils they knew best. Yeomen could not afford the richest bottomlands, which were swampy and required expensive draining, but they acquired land almost everywhere else.

For slave-holding southerners, another powerful motive impelled westward movement: the chance to profit from a spectacular cotton boom.

Rise of the Cotton South

Southern planters were not sentimentalists, holding onto slavery while northerners grew rich from commerce and the industrial revolution. Like other Americans, slave-holding southerners were profit-oriented. But the cotton boom caused nonmechanized, slave-based agriculture to remain highly profitable in the South, sustaining the plantation economy.

This had not always seemed likely. At the time of the Revolution, slave-based agriculture was not very profitable in the Upper South, where most southerners then lived. Persistent debt hung heavily over Virginia's extravagant and aristocratic tobacco growers. Farther south, along the coast of the Carolinas and Georgia, slaves grew rice and some indigo. Cotton was a profitable crop only for the Sea Island planters of South Carolina and Georgia, who grew the luxurious long-staple variety. The short-staple cotton that grew readily in the interior was unmarketable, because its sticky seeds lay tangled in the fibers.

Then England's burgeoning textile industry demanded more and more cotton. Sea Island cotton became so profitable between 1785 and 1795 that thousands of farmers in the interior tried growing the short-staple variety. They grew most of this cotton in the hope that some innovation would make the crop salable to the English. Eli Whitney, an inventor from Connecticut, responded to the need in 1793 with a simple machine that removed the seeds from the fibers. By 1800, cotton was spreading rapidly west from the seaboard states.

The voracious appetite of English mills caused a meteoric rise in cotton production (see maps). Despite occasional periods of low prices, the demand for cotton surged ahead every decade. Southerners with capital bought more land and more slaves and planted ever more cotton. Cotton growers boosted production so successfully that by 1825 the South was the world's dominant supplier of cotton; by the 1850s, the South was the source of more than 70 percent of all cotton imported by Britain.

Thus the antebellum South—the Old South before the Civil War—became primarily a cotton South. Virginia and North Carolina continued to grow tobacco, and rice and sugar were important crops in certain coastal areas. But cotton was the largest and most widespread crop, and it fueled the South's hunger for new territory.

Small slave owners and wealthier planters (those who owned twenty bondsmen or more) sought out alluvial bottomland and other fertile soils, eager to grasp the opportunity for wealth the cotton boom offered. As demand for cotton increased, slave owners pushed feverishly to grow more. The desire to plant more cotton and buy more slaves often caused men with new wealth to postpone the enjoyment of luxuries. Many first-generation planters lived for decades in their original log cabins, improved only by clapboards or a frame addition. Yet the planters' wealth put ease and refinement within their grasp, and riches and high social status arrived quickly for some.

The rise of new aristocrats in the Gulf and the migration of thousands of aspiring slaveholders across the Appalachians meant another kind of migration—involuntary—for black southerners. Congress had closed the international slave trade in 1808, and, despite some smuggling, slave labor from abroad was essentially unavailable. Thus new slaves for the Lower South had to come from the older states of the Upper South.

As it happened, slave owners there often had more slaves than they needed. Their slave population had grown through natural increase, but tobacco prices had fallen and soil exhaustion had become a serious problem. Thus planters in Virginia and North Carolina were shifting toward wheat and corn, crops that were less labor intensive. Slave owners on worn-out tobacco lands were glad to sell excess slaves to the booming areas of fertile soil in the cotton South.

Between 1810 and 1820 alone, 137,000 slaves were forced to move from North Carolina and the Chesapeake states to Alabama, Mississippi, and other western regions. Interregional sales and transfers continued thereafter, as an estimated two million people were sold between 1820 and 1860 to satisfy the need for slave labor. Thousands of black families were disrupted every year to serve the needs of the cotton economy.

To white southerners, the period from 1800 to 1860 was a time of great change and progress, no less than in the North. The South was growing and expanding, driven by excitement over new lands and energies related to the cotton boom. But the South's growth was different: its distinguishing features were those of an agricultural and a slave society.

AN AGRARIAN SOCIETY

The South did exhibit some of the diversity of the bustling, urbanizing, commercial North. There were merchants, artisans, and craftsmen in the larger cities, as well as men of commerce who promoted railways and transportation improvements. Immigrants from Ireland and other parts of Europe arrived in Savannah and other southern ports in dramatically increasing numbers during the 1840s and 1850s. But these developments were only faint shadows of their northern counterparts and had

Cotton Production in the South   *The two maps illustrate the rapid westward expansion of cotton production and its importance to the antebellum South.*

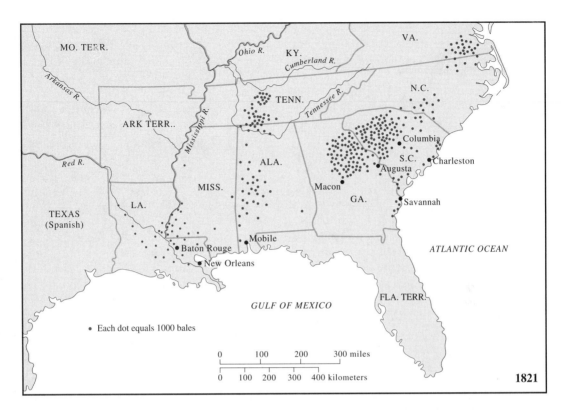

Each dot equals 1000 bales

1821

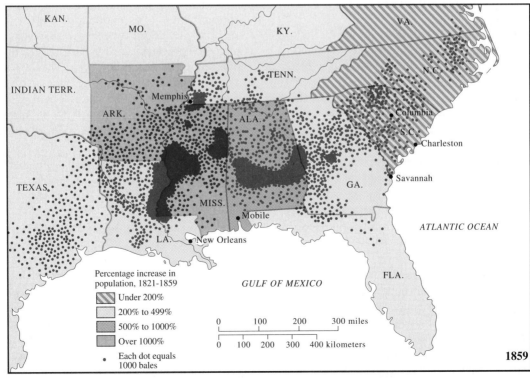

Percentage increase in
population, 1821–1859

Under 200%
200% to 499%
500% to 1000%
Over 1000%

Each dot equals
1000 bales

1859

relatively little effect. Agriculture and slavery and the prominence of rural slaves, slaveholders, and yeoman farmers in the population dominated Southern development.

Population distribution remained thin. Cotton growers spread out over as large an area as possible to maximize production and income. Farms were set

Population Distribution
───

far apart, rather than clustered around villages, and southern society remained predominantly rural. Because most immigrants to the United States sought urban locations, population growth fell behind the North's. Population density, low even in the older plantation states, was extremely low in the frontier areas being brought under cultivation. In 1860, there were only 2.3 people per square mile in vast and largely unsettled Texas, 15.6 in Louisiana, and 18.0 in Georgia. By contrast, population density in the nonslave-holding states east of the Mississippi River was almost three times higher. The Northeast had an average of 65.4 people per square mile. Massachusetts had 153.1 people per square mile, and New York City, where overcrowding reached epic proportions, compressed 86,400 people into each square mile.

Even in the 1850s, much of the South seemed a virtual wilderness. Frederick Law Olmsted, a northerner later renowned as a landscape architect, made several trips through the South in the 1850s as a journalist. Olmsted found that the few trains and stagecoaches available to travelers offered crude accommodations and kept their schedules poorly. Indeed, he had to do most of his traveling on horseback along primitive trails. Between Columbus, Georgia, and Montgomery, Alabama, Olmsted found "a hilly wilderness, with a few dreary villages, and many isolated cotton farms." Alabama, of course, had been frontier as recently as 1800, but Olmsted encountered the same conditions in parts of eastern Virginia.

Society in such rural areas was characterized by relatively weak institutions outside the family, for it takes a certain concentration of people to create and support organized activity. Where people were scarce, financing and operating schools, churches, libraries or even inns, restaurants, and other amenities was difficult. Southerners were strongly committed

to their churches, and some believed in the importance of universities, but all such institutions were far less fully developed than those in the North.

The South's cities were likewise smaller and less developed. Rather than engage in a broad commerce, they exported little beyond a staple crop, such as cotton or tobacco, and

Weak Urban Sector
───

imported only a few necessary supplies and luxuries. Factories were rare, because planters invested most of their capital in slaves. A few southerners did invest in iron or textiles on a small scale. But the largest southern industry was lumbering, and the largest factories made cigars using slave labor.

More decisively, the South was slower than the North to develop a unified market economy and a regional transportation network. Far less money was spent on canals, turnpikes, and railroads. The South had only 26 percent of the nation's railroad mileage in 1850 and, despite concerted efforts, only 35 percent in 1860. As a result, urban growth after 1820 was far less vigorous than in the North, and metropolitan centers were almost nonexistent. In 1860, only forty-nine thousand of 704,000 South Carolinians lived in towns with twenty-five hundred or more residents. Less than 3 percent of Mississippi's population lived in places of comparable size. The same year, the population of Charleston, South Carolina, was only forty-one thousand, that of Richmond, Virginia, thirty-eight thousand. New Orleans, by far the largest southern city, had only 169,000 residents, and it was being left behind, because it was not linked to the national railroad network.

Thus, although the South sold huge amounts of cotton on the international market, its economy at home was semideveloped relative to other sections of the country. Its white people were prospering but not as rapidly as most residents of the North. There, changes in commerce and industry brought unprecedented advances in productivity, raising the average person's standard of living. In the South, change was quantitative rather than qualitative. Southern planters continued to use the same farming techniques. They increased their acreage and hoped for continued high demand from foreign customers—but their region remained rural and its internal market undeveloped.

How do historians know

about the values and ways of life of the South's nonslave-holders? Letters, diaries, and family papers of these people, who generally were not rich or famous, have not been preserved as frequently as the records of the slave-holding elite. Therefore, historians have turned to a wide variety of sources—including travelers' accounts, folklore, and the U.S. census records—to learn more about them. This page from the manuscript "Population Schedules" of the U.S. census of 1850 supplies information on family structure and a variety of personal characteristics. The manuscript "Census of Agriculture" contains much additional information about the size of each family's farm and the crops grown there.   Photo: North Carolina Division of Archives & History.

Subsistence farmers merely worked harder and hoped to grow a bit more.

FREE SOUTHERNERS: FARMERS, PLANTERS, AND FREE BLACKS

A large majority of white southern families (three-quarters in 1860) owned no slaves. Some lived in towns and ran stores or businesses, but most were yeoman farmers who owned their own land and grew their own food. They were the typical whites, but the social distance between different groups of whites was great. Still greater was the distance between whites and blacks.

Although they were the majority of southern whites, subsistence farmers did not, as a rule, set the direction of the slave society. Normally, they occupied a relatively autonomous position within the slavery-based, staple-crop economy expanding around them. Independent and motivated by a hearty dose of frontier individualism, they provided for themselves in the traditional way of American farm families, prospering slowly from improvements on their acreage or the settlement of new and better land. The process meant steady progress for thousands of yeomen as the South expanded.

But the lives of most southern yeomen had not been transformed by improvements in transportation. Because few railroads penetrated the southern interior, yeomen generally had little contact with the market or the type of progress it could introduce. Families might raise a small surplus to sell for cash or trade for needed items, but they were remote from large market networks and therefore not particularly concerned about increasing their cash income. Yeomen constituted an important, although often silent, part of southern society. They valued their freedom from others' control, and if their rights were threatened, they could react strongly.

The yeomen enjoyed a folk culture based on family, church, and community. They spoke with a drawl, and their inflections were reminiscent of

Folk Culture of the Yeoman
_____

their Scottish and Irish backgrounds. Once a year, they flocked to religious revivals called protracted meetings or camp meetings, and in between they enjoyed house raisings, logrollings, quilting bees, and corn shuckings. Such occasions combined work with fun, offered food in abundance, and usually included liquor. They also provided a companionship that was especially welcome to isolated rural dwellers.

Social conventions imposed more uniformity on women of the yeoman class than on the men. A demanding round of work and family responsibilities shaped their lives in the home. At harvest time, yeoman women frequently helped in the fields, and throughout the year the drying, preserving, and preparing of food consumed much of their time. Household tasks continued during frequent pregnancies and the care of small children. Primary nursing and medical care also fell to the mother, who might have a book of remedies to aid her but often relied on family and folk wisdom. In some evangelical churches, women played respected roles

on certain committees, but overwhelmingly the busy life of the yeoman woman was tied to the home.

Among the men, many aspired to wealth, eager to join the race for slaves, land, and profits from cotton. Others were content with their independence, recreation, family life, and religion. But whether they strove to become rich or were satisfied with their status, they worked hard.

Ferdinand L. Steel, a North Carolinian who ultimately became a yeoman farmer in Mississippi, led a typical life. Each day, he worked from five in the morning until sunset. With the help of his family, Steel raised corn, wheat, pork, and vegetables for the family table. The family planted and picked enough cotton to yield five or six bales (about two thousand pounds). Cash from the sale of cotton enabled the family to buy sugar, coffee, salt, calico, gunpowder, and a few other store-bought goods.

Steel's life in Mississippi in the 1840s retained much of the flavor of the frontier. He made all the family's shoes; his wife and sister sewed dresses, shirts, and "pantiloons." The Steel women also rendered their own soap and spun and wove cotton into cloth; the men hunted game. A deeply religious man (he eventually became a traveling Methodist minister), Steel reflected that his life was "one of toil, but blessed be God that it is as well with me as it is."

Toil was also the lot of two other groups of free southerners: landless whites and free blacks. A sizable minority of white southern workers—from 25

Landless Whites
_____

to 40 percent, depending on the state—were unskilled laborers who owned no land and worked for others in the countryside and towns. Their property consisted of a few household items and some animals—usually pigs—that could feed on the open range. The landless included some immigrants, especially Irish, who did heavy and dangerous work such as building railroads and digging ditches.

In the countryside, white farm laborers struggled to become yeomen in the face of low wages or, if they rented, unpredictable market prices for their crops. Some fell into debt and were frequently sued. Others managed to climb into the ranks of yeomen. When James and Nancy Bennitt of North

Carolina succeeded in their ten-year struggle to buy land, they decided to avoid the unstable market in cotton; thereafter they raised extra corn and wheat as sources of cash.

For the nearly quarter-million free blacks in the South in 1860, conditions were generally worse than the yeoman's and often little better than the

Free Blacks
———

slave's. The free blacks of the Upper South were usually descendants of men and women emancipated by their owners in the 1780s and 1790s, a period of postrevolutionary idealism that coincided with a decline in tobacco prices. They usually did not own land and had to labor in someone else's fields, often beside slaves. By law, free blacks could not own a gun, buy liquor, violate curfew, assemble except in church, testify in court, or (throughout the South after 1835) vote. Despite the obstacles, a minority bought land, and others found jobs as artisans, draymen, boatmen, and fishermen. A few prospered and bought slave laborers, but most who owned slaves had purchased their own wives and children (whom they could not free, because laws required newly emancipated blacks to leave their state).

Farther south, in the cotton and Gulf regions, a large proportion of free blacks were mulattos, the privileged offspring of wealthy planters. Not all planters freed their mixed-race offspring, but those who did often recognized a moral obligation and gave their children good educations and financial backing. In a few cities like New Orleans and Mobile, extensive interracial sex had produced a mulatto population that was recognized as a distinct class. These people formed a society of their own and sought a status above slaves and other freedmen, if not equal to that of planters. But outside New Orleans, Mobile, and Charleston, such groups were rare, and most mulattos experienced more disadvantages than benefits from their light skin.

At the opposite end of the social spectrum from free blacks were slaveholders. As a group they lived well, on incomes that enabled them to

Planters
———

enjoy superior housing, food, clothing, and luxuries. But a few statistics tell the story: 50 percent of southern slave holders had fewer than five slaves, 72 percent had fewer than ten, 88 percent had fewer than twenty. Thus the average slaveholder was not a wealthy aristocrat but an aspiring farmer, usually a person of humble origins, with little formal education and many rough edges to his manner.

The wealth of the greatest planters gave ambitious men something to aspire to. Although most planters lived in spacious, comfortable farmhouses, some did own mansions. Most slave owners sat down at mealtimes to an abundance of tempting country foods—pork and ham, beef and game, fresh vegetables and fruits, breads and biscuits, cakes and jams—but the sophisticated elite consumed such delights as "gumbo, ducks and olives, *supreme de volaille*, chickens in jelly, oysters, lettuce salad, chocolate cream, jelly cake, claret cup, etc."

Slave-holding men dominated society and, especially among the wealthiest and oldest families, justified their dominance through a paternalistic

Southern Paternalism
———

ideology. Instead of stressing the profitable aspects of commercial agriculture, they focused on *noblesse oblige*, seeing themselves as custodians of the welfare of society as a whole and of the black families who depended on them in particular. The paternalistic planter viewed himself not as an oppressor but as the benevolent guardian of an inferior race. He developed affectionate feelings toward his slaves (so long as they knew their place) and was genuinely shocked at criticism of his behavior.

The letters of Paul Carrington Cameron, North Carolina's largest slaveholder, illustrate this mentality. After a period of sickness among his one thousand North Carolina slaves, Cameron wrote, "I fear the Negroes have suffered much from the want of proper attention and kindness under this late distemper . . . no love of lucre shall ever induce me to be cruel, or even to make or permit to be made any great exposure of their persons at inclement seasons." On another occasion, he described to his sister the sense of responsibility he felt: "I cannot better follow the example of our venerated Mother than in doing my duty to her faithful old slaves and their descendants."

It was comforting to the richest southern planters to see themselves in this way, and slaves—accommodating to the realities of power—encouraged their masters to think their benevolence was appreciated. Paternalism also served as a defense against abolitionist criticism. Still, paternalism affected the manner and not the substance of most planters' behavior. Its softness and warmth were a matter of style, covering harsher assumptions: blacks were inferior, and planters should make money.

Relations between men and women in the planter class were similarly paternalistic. An upper-class southern woman was typically raised and educated to be the subordinate companion of men. Her proper sphere was home management, not politics or other worldly affairs. In a social system based on the coercion of an entire race, women could not be allowed to challenge society's rules on sexual or racial relations. If she defied or questioned the status quo, she risked universal condemnation.

Elite Women's Role

Within the domestic circle, the husband reigned supreme, and many women were acutely conscious of that authority. "He is master of the house," wrote South Carolina's Mary Boykin Chesnut. "To hear is to obey. . . . All the comfort of my life depends upon his being in a good humor." In a darker mood, Chesnut once observed that "there is no slave . . . like a wife." For the fortunate women whose marriages joined two people of shared tastes and habits, like North Carolina diarist Catherine Devereux Edmondston, the husband's authority weighed lightly or not at all, but many women felt dissatisfaction.

The upper-class southern woman had to clear several barriers to happiness. The right choice of a husband was especially important. Once married, she ceded to her husband most of her legal rights, became part of his family, and was expected to get along with numerous in-laws during extended visits. On the plantation, she was expected to oversee the cooking and preserving of food, manage the house, supervise care of the children, and attend sick slaves. It is thus not surprising that an intelligent and perceptive young woman sometimes approached marriage with anxiety, for her future depended on the man she chose.

Childbearing brought grief and sickness, as well as joy, to southern women. In 1840, the birthrate for white southern women in their childbearing years was almost 30 percent higher than the national average. At the beginning of the nineteenth century, the average southern white woman could expect to bear eight children; by 1860, the figure had decreased only to six, and one or more miscarriages were likely among so many pregnancies. The high birthrate took a toll on women's health. Complications of childbirth were a major cause of death, occurring twice as often in the hot, moist South as in the Northeast. Moreover, a woman had to endure the loss of many of the infants she bore. In the South in 1860, almost five in ten children died before age five, and in South Carolina more than six in ten failed to reach age twenty.

Slavery was another source of problems that white women had to endure but were not supposed to notice. "Violations of the moral law . . . made mulattoes as common as blackberries," protested a woman in Georgia, but wives had to play "the ostrich game." "A magnate who runs a hideous black harem," wrote Chesnut, "under the same roof with his lovely white wife, and his beautiful accomplished daughters . . . poses as the model of all human virtues to these poor women whom God and the laws have given him. From the height of his awful majesty, he scolds and thunders at them, as if he never did wrong in his life."

In the early 1800s, some southern women, especially Quakers, had spoken out against slavery. Although most white women did not criticize "the peculiar institution," they often viewed it less as a system and more as a series of relationships among individuals. Perhaps sensing this, southern men tolerated no discussion by women of the slavery issue. In the 1840s and 1850s, as northern and international criticism of slavery increased, southern men published a barrage of articles stressing that women should restrict their concerns to the home.

But southern women were beginning to chafe at their customary exclusion from financial matters. A study of women in Petersburg, Virginia, a large tobacco-manufacturing town, revealed behavior amounting to an implicit criticism of the institution of marriage and the loss of autonomy it entailed. For several decades before 1860, the proportion of women who never married, or did not remarry after the death of a spouse, grew to exceed 33 percent. Likewise, the number of women who worked for wages, controlled their own property, and even ran businesses increased. In managing property, these women benefited from southern legal reforms—beginning with Mississippi's Married Women's Property Act of 1839—that had not been intended to increase female independence. Rather, the law gave married women some property rights in order to protect families from ruin caused by the husband's indebtedness.

For a large category of southern men and women, freedom was wholly denied and education in any form was not allowed. Male and female, slaves were expected to accept bondage and ignorance as their condition.

SLAVES AND THE CONDITIONS OF THEIR SERVITUDE

For African-Americans, slavery was a curse that brought no blessings other than the strengths they developed to survive it. Slaves knew a life of poverty, coercion, toil, heartbreak, and resentment. They had few hopes that were not denied, often they had to bear separation from their loved ones, and they were despised as an inferior race. That they endured and found loyalty and strength among themselves is a tribute to their courage, but it could not make up for a life without freedom or opportunity.

Southern slaves enjoyed few material comforts beyond the bare necessities. Although they generally had enough to eat, their diet was plain and monotonous. The basic ration

Slaves' Diet, Clothing, and Housing

was cornmeal, fat pork, molasses, and occasionally coffee. Many masters allowed slaves to tend gardens, which provided the variety and extra nutrition of greens and sweet potatoes, and some could fish and hunt. Despite the occasional supplements of green vegetables and fish, the diet was nutritionally deficient; many slaves suffered from beriberi and pellagra. Clothing too was plain, coarse, and inexpensive. The few clothes issued to slaves were made either of light cotton or a heavy, coarse material called *osnaburg*. Shoes were normally not issued until the weather became cool and were usually uncomfortable brass-toed brogans or stiff wraparounds made from leather tanned on the plantation.

Slaves typically lived in small one-room cabins, perhaps with a window opening but no glass. Logs chinked with mud formed the walls, dirt was the only floor, and a wattle-and-daub or stone chimney vented the fireplace, which provided both heat and light. Bedding consisted of heaps of straw, straw mattresses, or wooden bed frames lashed to the walls with rope. A few crude pieces of furniture and cooking utensils completed the furnishings. The gravest drawback of slave cabins, however, was not lack of comfort but their unhealthiness. Each small cabin housed one or two entire families. Crowding and lack of sanitation fostered the spread of infection and contagious diseases.

Hard work was the central fact of the slaves' existence. The long hours and large work gangs that characterized Gulf Coast cotton districts were

Slaves' Work Routines

more reminiscent of factories than of the small-scale, isolated work patterns of slaves in the eighteenth-century Chesapeake. Overseers rang the morning bell before dawn, making it possible for slaves to be in the fields at first light. Except in urban settings and on some rice plantations, where slaves were assigned daily tasks to complete at their own pace, working "from sun to sun" became universal in the South. Long hours and hard work were at the heart of the advantage that slave labor represented for slave owners. As one planter put it, slaves were the best labor, because "you could command them and *make* them do what was right." White workers, by contrast, couldn't be driven: "they wouldn't stand it."

Profit also took precedence over paternalistic "protection" of women: slave women did heavy field work, often as much as the men and even during pregnancy. Old people—of whom there were few—were kept busy caring for young children, doing light chores, or carding, ginning, and spinning cotton. Children had to gather kindling, carry water to the fields, or sweep the yard. But slaves had a variety of ways to keep from being worked to death. It was impossible to supervise every slave every minute, and slaves slacked off when they were not being watched.

Of course, slaves could not slow their pace too much, because the owner enjoyed a monopoly on force and violence. Whites throughout the South believed that Negroes "can't be governed except with the whip." Evidence suggests that whippings were less frequent on small farms than on large plantations, but the testimony of former slaves indicates that even most small farmers plied the lash. The beatings symbolized authority to the master and tyranny to the slaves, who made them a benchmark for evaluating a master. In the words of former slaves, a good owner was one who did not "whip too much," whereas a bad owner "whipped till he's bloodied you and blistered you."[1]

Physical and Mental Abuse of Slaves

As these reports suggest, terrible abuses could and did occur. The master wielded virtually absolute authority on his plantation, and courts did not recognize the word of a chattel. Pregnant women were whipped, and there were burnings, mutilations, tortures, and murders. Yet physical cruelty may have been less prevalent in the United States than in other slave-holding parts of the New World. In sugar-growing and mining regions of the Western Hemisphere in the 1800s, slaves were regarded as an expendable resource to be replaced after seven years. Treatment was so poor that death rates were high, and the heavily male slave

---

[1] Accounts by ex-slaves are quoted from *The American Slave: A Composite Autobiography*, edited by George P. Rawick (Westport, Conn.: Greenwood Press, First Reprint Edition 1972, Second Reprint Edition 1974), from materials gathered by the Federal Writers' Project and originally published in 1941. The spelling in these accounts has been standardized.

Coercion was the essence of slavery. To enforce their will, masters relied on whips and instruments like the pronged collar to inflict pain or restrict the slaves' movements. A slave woman in nineteenth-century New Orleans had to wear this collar as punishment for running away. The painting suggests that such sights were not unusual on the city's streets.   Painting: Historic New Orleans Collection; slave collar: Massachusetts Historical Society.

population rapidly shrank in size. In the United States, by contrast, the slave population experienced a steady natural increase as births exceeded deaths and each generation grew larger.

The greatest evil of American slavery was not its physical cruelty but the nature of slavery itself: coercion, lack of freedom, belonging to another person, virtually no hope for change. A woman named Delia Garlic cut to the core when she said, "It's bad to belong to folks that own you soul an' body. I could tell you 'bout it all day, but even then you couldn't guess the awfulness of it." American slaves hated their oppression and, contrary to some whites' perceptions, were not grateful to their oppressors. They had to be subservient and speak honeyed words to their masters, but they talked quite differently among themselves. The evidence of their resistant attitudes comes from their actions and their own life stories.

Former slaves reported some warm feelings between masters and slaves, but the prevailing picture was one of antagonism and resistance. Slaves mistrusted kindness from whites and saw the self-interest in it. One woman called her mistress "a mighty good somebody to belong to" but explained that the woman was kind "'cause she was raisin' us to work for her." Christmas presents of clothing from the master did not mean anything, observed another, "'cause he was going to [buy] that anyhow."

Slaves' Attitudes Toward Whites

Slaves were alert to the thousand daily signs of their degraded status. One man recalled the general rule that slaves ate cornbread and owners ate biscuits. If blacks did get biscuits, "the flour that we made the biscuits out of was the third-grade shorts." A woman reported that on her plantation "Old Master hunted a heap, but us never did get none of what he brought in." If the owner took his slaves' garden produce to town and sold it for them, the slaves suspected him of pocketing part of the profits.

Suspicion and resentment often grew into hatred. According to a former slave from Virginia, white people treated blacks "so mean that all the slaves prayed God to punish their cruel masters." When a yellow fever epidemic struck in 1852, many slaves saw it as God's retribution. As late as the 1930s, an elderly ex-slave named Minnie Fulkes cherished the conviction that God was going to punish white people for their cruelty to blacks. She described the whippings that her mother had had to endure and then exclaimed, "Lord, Lord, I hate white people and the flood waters goin' to drown some more."

SLAVE CULTURE AND EVERYDAY LIFE

The resource that enabled slaves to maintain such defiance was their culture: a body of beliefs and values born of their past and their present and of the companionship of their own community. It was not possible for slaves to change their world, but by drawing strength from their culture they could resist their condition and struggle on against it.

Slave culture changed significantly after the turn of the century. Between 1790 and 1808, when Congress banned further importation of slaves, there was a rush to import more Africans. After that, the proportion of native-born blacks rose steadily, reaching 96 percent in 1840 and almost 100 percent in 1860. Meanwhile, more and more slaves adopted Christianity as pure African culture faded and an African-American culture matured.

African influences remained strong, for African practices and beliefs reminded the slaves that they were and ought to be different from their oppressors and thus encouraged them to resist. The most visible features of African culture were the slaves' appearance and forms of recreation. Some slave men plaited their hair into rows and fancy designs; slave women often wore their hair "in string"—tied in small bunches secured by a string or piece of cloth. A few men and many women wrapped their heads in kerchiefs of the styles and colors of West Africa.

Influence of African Culture

Many slaves continued to see and believe in spirits. Whites too believed in ghosts, but the slaves' belief resembled the African concept of the living dead—the idea that deceased relatives visit the earth for many years until the process of dying is complete. Slaves also practiced conjuring, voodoo, and quasi-magical root medicine. By 1860, the most notable conjurers and root doctors were reputed to live in South Carolina, Georgia, Louisiana, and other isolated coastal areas of heavy slave importation.

For entertainment, slaves made musical instruments with carved motifs that resembled African stringed instruments. Their drumming and dancing clearly followed African patterns; whites marveled at them. One visitor to Georgia in the 1860s described a ritual dance of African origin: "A ring of singers is formed. . . . They then utter a kind of melodious chant, which gradually increases in strength, and in noise, until it fairly shakes the house, and it can be heard for a long distance."

These cultural survivals provided slaves with a sense of their separate past. Black achievement in music and dance was so exceptional that some whites became aware that the slave community was a different world and that they did not "know" their slaves. Conjuring and folklore also directly fed resistance; slaves could cast a spell or direct the power of a hand (a bag of articles belonging to the person to be conjured) against the master. Not all masters felt confident enough to dismiss such a threat.

Slaves fashioned Christianity into an instrument of support and resistance. Theirs was a religion of justice, quite unlike that of the propaganda their masters pushed at them.

Slaves' Religion   "You ought to have heard that preachin'," said one man. "'Obey your master and mistress, don't steal chickens and eggs and meat,' but nary a word about havin' a soul to save." The slaves believed that Jesus cared about their souls and their plight. They rejected the idea that in heaven whites would have "the colored folks . . . there to wait on 'em." Instead, the slaveholders would be "broilin' in hell for their sin" when God's justice came.

For slaves, Christianity was a religion of personal and group salvation. Beyond seeking personal guidance, the slaves prayed for deliverance. Some waited "until the overseer got behind a hill" and then laid down their hoes and called on God to free them. Others held fervent secret prayer meetings that lasted far into the night. Many slaves nurtured an unshakable belief that God would end their bondage. This faith—and the joy and emotional release that accompanied worship—sustained blacks.

Enslaved African-Americans also developed a sense of racial identity. They naturally drew together, helping each other in danger, need, and resistance. "We never told on each other," one woman declared. Although some slaves did betray others, former slaves were virtually unanimous in denouncing those who were disloyal to the group or sought personal advantage through allegiance to whites.

Of course, different jobs, talents, and circumstances created variations in status among slaves. But most slaves did not encounter a class system within the black community. Only one-quarter of all slaves lived on plantations of fifty or more blacks, so few knew a wide chasm between exalted house servants and lowly field hands.

The main source of support for individuals was the family. Slave families faced severe dangers. At any moment, the master could sell a husband or wife, give a slave child away as a wedding present, or die in debt, forcing a division of his property. Many families were broken up in such ways. Others were uprooted in the trans-Appalachian expansion of the South. When the Union Army registered thousands of black marriages in Mississippi and Louisiana in 1864 and 1865, fully 25 percent of the men older than forty reported that they had been forcibly separated from a previous wife.

Slaves' Family Life

But this did not mean that slave families could not exist. American slaves clung tenaciously to the personal relationships that gave meaning to life. Although American law did not protect slave families, masters permitted them; in fact, slave owners expected slaves to form families and have children. As a result, there was a normal ratio of men to women, young to old, even on the frontier.

Following African kinship taboos, African-Americans avoided marriage between cousins (commonplace among aristocratic slave owners). Adapting the West African custom of polygyny to American circumstances, they did not condemn unwed mothers but did expect a young woman to enter a monogamous relationship after one pregnancy, if not before. By naming their children after relatives of earlier generations, African-Americans emphasized their family histories. If they chose to bear the surname of a slave owner, it was often not that of their current master but of the owner under whom their family had begun in America.

Slaves abhorred interference in their family lives. Some of their strongest protests sought to prevent the breakup of a family. Rape was a horror for both men and women. Some husbands faced death rather than permit their wives to be sexually abused, and the women sometimes fought back. In other cases, slaves seethed with anger at the injustice but could do nothing except soothe each other with sympathy and understanding. Significantly, they condemned the guilty party, not the victim.

Slave men and women followed sex roles familiar to whites and similar to West African customs. After work in the fields was done, both men and women took part in activities.

Sex Roles in Slavery

Men's activities focused on traditional outdoor tasks and women did indoor work. Men hunted and fished for the family stewpot, fashioned rough furniture, and repaired implements; women cooked, mended, and cleaned house. It is clear too that slave families resembled white families in that African-American men held a respected place in their homes. They did not dominate their wives in a manner similar to white husbands, but it would be misleading to say that slave women enjoyed equality in sex roles and family life.

In addition to the heavy labor required on southern plantations, slaves performed work of fine craftsmanship in furniture making, needlework, and other areas. This dining room corner cupboard is walnut veneer on pine and cedar and was built around 1840. The quilt, emblazoned with chalice cups to celebrate the annual visit of an Anglican bishop, was made around 1860. Both are from Texas. Cupboard: Courtesy of the Witte Museum and the San Antonio Museum Association, San Antonio, Texas; quilt: The American Museum in Britain, photo courtesy of The Museum of the Confederacy.

The larger truth is that all enslaved people, men and women, were often deprived of the opportunity to provide for or protect their families. Under the pressures of bondage, men and women had to share parental and household responsibilities. At any time, each might have to stand in for the other and assume extra duties. Similarly, uncles, aunts, and grandparents sometimes raised the children of those who had been sold away.

Work routines frequently promoted close associations among slave women that heightened their sense of sisterhood. On plantations, young girls worked together as house servants. Nursing mothers got together to feed and care for their children, and adults worked together at tasks like soap making and stitching quilts. Old women gathered to spin thread or supervise a nursery. Female slaves thus spent significant portions of their lives as participants in a group of women, an experience that strengthened their ties to each other.

Resistance to Slavery

Slaves brought to their efforts at resistance the same common sense, determination, and practicality that characterized their family lives. American slavery produced some fearless and implacable revolutionaries. Gabriel Prosser's conspiracy was apparently known to more than a thousand slaves when it was uncovered in 1800, just before it was put into action. A similar conspiracy in Charleston in 1822, led by a free black named Denmark Vesey, involved many of the prominent whites' most trusted slaves. And the most famous rebel of all, Nat Turner, rose in violence in Southampton County, Virginia, in 1831.

The son of an African woman who passionately hated her enslavement, Turner was a precocious child who learned to read when he was very young. Encouraged by his first owner to study the Bible, he enjoyed certain privileges but also endured hard work and changes of masters. Eventually, young Turner became a preacher. He also developed a tendency toward mysticism and became increasingly withdrawn. After nurturing his plan for several years, Turner led a band of rebels from farm to farm in the predawn darkness of August 22, 1831. The group severed limbs and crushed skulls with axes or killed their victims with guns. Before they were stopped, Nat Turner and his followers had slaughtered sixty whites of both sexes and all ages. Turner and perhaps two hundred African-Americans, including many innocent victims of marauding whites, were killed in retaliation.

But most slave resistance was not violent, for the odds against revolution were especially poor in North America. Consequently, slaves directed their energies toward creating the means of survival and resistance within slavery. A desperate slave could run away for good, but it was more common for slaves to run off temporarily to hide in the woods. There, they were close to friends and allies who could help them escape capture in an area they knew well. Every day that a slave "lay out" in this way, the master lost a day's labor. Most owners chose not to mount an exhaustive search and instead sent word that the slave's grievances would be redressed. The runaway would then return to bargain with the master. Most owners let the matter pass, for, as the owner of a valuable cook put it, they were "glad to get her back."

Other modes of resistance had the same objective: to resist but survive under bondage. Appropriating food (stealing, in the master's eyes) was so common that even whites sang humorous songs about it. Blacks were also alert to the attitudes of individual whites and learned to ingratiate themselves and play one white person off against another. Field hands frequently tested a new overseer to intimidate him or win more favorable working conditions.

HARMONY AND TENSION IN A SLAVE SOCIETY

As the 1800s advanced, slavery impinged on laws and customs, individual values, and—increasingly—every aspect of southern politics. Legal restrictions on slaves, in effect since the seventeenth century, steadily increased. In all things, from their workaday movements to Sunday worship, slaves fell under the supervision of whites. State courts held that a slave "has no civil right" and could not even hold property "except at the will and pleasure of his master." In response to revolts, legislators tightened the legal straitjacket: after the Nat Turner insurrection of 1831, for example, they prohibited owners from teaching their slaves to read. As the sectional crisis developed, fears of slave revolt grew, and restrictions on slaves increased accordingly.

The law also required those who did not own slaves to help maintain the slave system. All white male citizens were legally obligated to ride in patrols to discourage slave movements at night. White ship captains and harbor masters were required to scrutinize the papers of African-Americans who might be attempting to escape bondage. Urban residents who did not supervise their domestic slaves as closely as planters did were subject to criticism for endangering the community. And the South's few manufacturers often felt pressure to substitute slave labor for the labor of free people.

Slavery had a deep effect on southern values precisely because it was the main determinant of wealth in the South. Ownership of slaves guaranteed the labor to produce cotton and other crops on a large scale. Slaves were therefore vital to the acquisition of a fortune. In fact, throughout southern society, slave holding indicated overall wealth with remarkable precision. Variations in wealth from county to county corresponded closely to variations in slave holding; important economic enterprises not based on slavery were too rare to have an effect on the pattern.

Slavery as the Basis of Wealth and Social Standing

Slave holding was the main determinant of a white man's social position. Wealth in slaves also translated into political power: a solid majority of political officeholders were slaveholders, and the most powerful were usually large-scale slaveholders. Lawyers and newspaper editors were sometimes influential, but they did not hold independent positions in the economy or society. Dependent on planters for business and support, they served planters' interests and reflected their outlook.

Slavery's influence spread throughout the social system until even the values and mores of nonslaveholders bore its imprint. For one thing, the availability of slave labor tended to devalue free labor. Consequently, nonslaveholders preferred to work for themselves, and those who had to sell their labor tended to resent or reject tasks that seemed degrading. Such thinking engendered an aristocratic value system ill suited to a newly established democracy.

The values of the aristocrat—lineage, privilege, pride, and refinement of person and manner—gained a considerable foothold among the masses. Some of those qualities were in short supply, however, in the recently settled portions of the cotton kingdom, where frontier values of courage and self-reliance modified the aristocratic ideal. Independence and defense of one's honor became highly valued traits for planter and frontier farmer alike. Thus, instead of gradually disappearing as it did in the North, dueling hung on in the South and gained acceptance throughout society.

Aristocratic Values and Frontier Individualism

Other aristocratic values of the planter class were less acceptable to the average citizen. Planters believed they were better than other people. In their pride, they expected not only to wield power but to receive special treatment. By the 1850s, some planters openly rejected the democratic creed, vilifying Thomas Jefferson for his statement that all men are equal.

The belief in their own superiority, which shaped the outlook of the southern elite for generations, was never acceptable to the individualistic members of the yeoman class. Independent and proud, yeomen resisted any infringement of their rights. They believed they were as good as anyone and knew that they lived in a nation in which democratic ideals were gaining strength. Thus occasional conflicts erupted between aristocratic pretensions and democratic zeal.

Yeomen farmers and other citizens resented their underrepresentation in state legislatures, the corruption in government, and the undemocratic control over local government. In the 1820s and 1830s, the reformers won most of their battles. Five southern states—Alabama, Mississippi, Tennessee, Arkansas, and Texas—adopted white manhood suffrage and other reforms, including popular election of governors,

Movements for Electoral Reform

legislative apportionment based on white popula-tion only, and locally chosen county government. Only South Carolina and Virginia effectively de-fended property qualifications for office, legislative malapportionment, appointment of county offi-cials, and selection of the governor by lawmakers. The formal structure of government thus became more democratic than many planters wished.

Slave owners knew that a more open govern-ment structure could permit troubling issues to arise. In Virginia, nonslave-holding westerners raised a basic challenge to the slave system in 1832, a year after the Nat Turner rebellion. Advocates of gradual abolition forced a two-week legislative de-bate on slavery, arguing that the institution was in-jurious to the state and inherently dangerous. When the House of Delegates finally voted, the motion favoring abolition lost by just 73 to 58. This was to be the last public debate on slavery in the antebellum South.

Given such tensions, it was perhaps remarkable that slaveholders and nonslaveholders did not ex-perience more overt conflict. Why were class con-frontations among whites so infrequent? Historians who have considered this question have given many answers. One of the most important factors was race. The South's racial ideology stressed whites' superiority to blacks and established race, not class, as the social dividing line. Besides, a rural society values family bonds and kinship ties, and some poor nonslave-holding whites were related to the rich new planters. The experience of frontier liv-ing, in which all were starting out together, must also have created a relatively informal, egalitarian atmosphere. Moreover, the South was an expand-ing mobile society in which yeoman and planter rarely depended on each other. Yeomen farmed mainly for themselves; planters farmed for them-selves and the market.

But suppression of dissent also played a signif-icant and increasing role. After 1830, white south-erners who criticized the slave system out of moral conviction or class resentment were intimidated, attacked, or legally prosecuted. Southern cities im-pounded abolitionist literature and sought to bar antislavery influences. Intellectuals developed elab-orate justifications for slavery as newspapers railed

at northern antislavery agitation. By the 1850s, the defense of slavery's interests dominated public dis-cussion, and all groups in society felt pressure to uphold the slave system.

Still, there were signs that the relative lack of conflict between slaveholders and nonslaveholders was coming to an end. As cotton lands filled up, nonslave holders saw their op-portunities narrowing; mean-while, wealthy planters enjoyed expanding profits. The risks of entering cotton production were becoming too great and the cost of slaves too high for many yeomen to rise in society. From 1830 to 1860, the percentage of white southern families holding slaves declined steadily from 36 to 25 per-cent. At the same time, the monetary gap between the classes was widening. Although nonslavehold-ers were becoming more prosperous, slave owners' wealth was increasing much faster. In 1860, slave owners' share of the South's agricultural wealth re-mained at 90 to 95 percent. The average slave holder was almost fourteen times as rich as the av-erage nonslave holder.

Hardening of Class Lines

Urban artisans and mechanics felt the pinch acutely. Their numbers were few, their place in so-ciety was hardly recognized, and in bad times they were often the first to lose work. Moreover, they faced stiff competition from urban slaves, whose masters wanted to hire them out to practice trades. White workers demanded that economic com-petition from slaves be forbidden, but they were ignored—slave owners would not tolerate interfer-ence with their property or the income they derived from it. But the angry protests of white workers re-sulted in harsh restrictions on *free* African-American workers and craftsmen.

Pre–Civil War politics reflected the tensions. Anticipating the prospect of a war to defend slav-ery, slave owners expressed growing fear about the loyalty of nonslaveholders. Schemes to widen slave ownership were discussed, including reopening the African slave trade. In North Carolina, a pro-longed and increasingly bitter controversy over the combination of high taxes on land and low taxes on slaves erupted, and a class-conscious nonslave holder named Hinton R. Helper denounced slavery in his book *The Impending Crisis*, published in New York in 1857. Discerning planters knew that such fiery controversies could easily erupt in every southern state.

But for the moment, slave owners stood secure. They occupied from 50 to 85 percent of the seats in state legislatures and a similarly high percentage of the South's congressional seats. They had also established their point of view in all major social institutions. Professors who criticized slavery had been dismissed from colleges and universities; schoolbooks that contained "unsound" ideas had been replaced. And almost all the Methodist and Baptist clergy had given up preaching against the institution. In fact, except for a few obscure persons of conscience, southern clergy had become slavery's most vocal defenders.

The South was a diverse society that embraced many contradictions, but the coercive influence of slavery was increasingly pressing it into a single mold. Powerful groups dependent on slavery worked tirelessly to promote unity and eradicate dissent. The potential for conflict linked to slavery persisted, but few southerners saw it. As the influence of the peculiar institution spread through the region, the evolving South took on the aspect of a conservative and traditional society wedded to slavery. The social order as southerners knew it seemed to be stable, with threats to the status quo under control.

In the nation generally, however, society was anything but stable. As market forces and the rise of industry produced a more diverse population, social and economic change became a central characteristic of the northern economy and society. The American people were changing, and the currents of change would eventually affect the South.

SUGGESTIONS FOR FURTHER READING

Southern Society

Clement Eaton, *The Growth of Southern Civilization, 1790–1860* (1961); William W. Freehling, *Prelude to Civil War* (1965); Eugene D. Genovese, *The Political Economy of Slavery* (1965);

Donald G. Mathews, *Religion in the Old South* (1977); Robert McColley, *Slavery and Jeffersonian Virginia* (1964); Charles S. Sydnor, *The Development of Southern Sectionalism, 1819–1848* (1948); Larry E. Tise, *Proslavery* (1987); Ralph A. Wooster, *The People in Power* (1969); Gavin Wright, *The Political Economy of the Cotton South* (1978); Bertram Wyatt-Brown, *Southern Honor* (1982).

Slave Holders and Nonslave Holders

Bennet H. Barrow, *Plantation Life in the Florida Parishes of Louisiana, as Reflected in the Diary of Bennet H. Barrow*, ed. Edwin Adams Davis (1943); Ira Berlin, *Slaves Without Masters* (1974); Joan E. Cashin, *A Family Venture* (1991); Bill Cecil-Fronsman, *The Common Whites* (1992); Everett Dick, *The Dixie Frontier* (1948); Drew Faust, *James Henry Hammond and the Old South* (1982); Eugene D. Genovese, "Yeoman Farmers in a Slaveholders' Democracy," *Agricultural History* 49 (April 1975): 331–342; John Inscoe, *Mountain Masters* (1989); Michael P. Johnson and James L. Roark, *Black Masters* (1984); James Oakes, *The Ruling Race* (1982); Frank L. Owsley, *Plain Folk of the Old South* (1949); J. Mills Thornton III, *Politics and Power in a Slave Society: Alabama, 1800–1860* (1978).

Southern Women

Carol Bleser, *In Joy and in Sorrow* (1990); Jane Turner Censer, *North Carolina Planters and Their Children, 1800–1860* (1984); Catherine Clinton, *The Plantation Mistress* (1982); Elizabeth Fox-Genovese, *Within the Plantation Household* (1988); Jean E. Friedman, *The Enclosed Garden* (1985); Harriet Jacobs, *Incidents in the Life of a Slave Girl*, ed. Jean Fagan Yellin (1987); Suzanne Lebsock, *Free Women of Petersburg* (1984); Mary D. Robertson, ed., *Lucy Breckinridge of Grove Hill* (1979); Deborah G. White, *Arn'n't I a Woman?* (1985).

Conditions of Slavery

Kenneth F. Kiple and Virginia H. Kiple, "Black Tongue and Black Men," *Journal of Southern History* 43 (August 1977): 411–428; Ronald L. Lewis, *Coal, Iron, and Slaves* (1979); Richard G. Lowe and Randolph B. Campbell, "The Slave Breeding Hypothesis," *Journal of Southern History* 42 (August 1976): 400–412; Todd L. Savitt, *Medicine and Slavery* (1978); Kenneth M. Stampp, *The Peculiar Institution* (1956); Robert S. Starobin, *Industrial Slavery in the Old South* (1970).

Slave Culture and Resistance

John W. Blassingame, *The Slave Community* (1979); Judith Wragg Chase, *Afro-American Art and Craft* (1971); Paul D. Escott, *Slavery Remembered: A Record of Twentieth-Century Slave Narratives* (1979); Eric Foner, ed., *Nat Turner* (1971); Eugene D. Genovese, *Roll, Jordan, Roll* (1974); Herbert G. Gutman, *The Black Family in Slavery and Freedom, 1750–1925* (1976); Vincent Harding, *There Is a River* (1981); Albert J. Raboteau, *Slave Religion* (1978); Robert S. Starobin, *Denmark Vesey* (1970).

Chapter

12

Among Strangers and Friends: People and Communities, 1800–1860

"I HOPE THAT THINGS will get better," Anna Maria Klinger wrote from New York to her family in Württemberg, Germany, in March 1849. "For it's always like that, no one really likes it at first, and especially if you are so lonely and forlorn in a foreign land like I am, no friends or relatives around." Twenty-eight-year-old Klinger had crossed the Atlantic alone among strangers. Her religious faith kept her going. "The dear Lord is my shield and refuge," she wrote home.

Klinger had left Germany during the political and economic crises of 1848. She was the first in her immediate family to emigrate. After arriving in New York, Klinger found work as a domestic servant at $4 a month. She also met and married Franz Schano, a deserter from the Prussian army. Over the next decade, she and Schano brought five of her siblings to New York: Babett, Gottlieb, Katharina, Daniel, and finally in 1858 the youngest, Rosina.

Work was not always easy to find—Franz, a stonecutter, was unemployed for a time—but teenagers like Babett and Katharina could always find work as servants. Babett, who now called herself Barbara, took a job as a servant and quickly repaid her sister for her fare to America. But within a year of Barbara's arrival, she became pregnant. Franz wrote home that they tried to get the young man to marry her, "but then he said he had never promised to marry her and he wouldn't ever marry her." He did provide a cash settlement of $80 to Barbara.

Anna Maria, assisted by Franz, guided the family, seeming to keep them together by sheer force of will. But the siblings' lives eventually diverged. In 1855, Anna Maria and Franz moved to Albany, New York, where Franz opened his own business and they bought a house for $1,000. But in 1860, Franz died of consumption. Thirteen months later, Anna Maria married Adam Plantz, a Prussian-born blacksmith; he too died of consumption, only five weeks after the wedding. Anna Maria now had a son and stepson to support. She feared losing her home, but she had been left enough money to prosper in the 1870s. As Anna Maria became more preoccupied with providing for her son and stepson, Gottlieb took over the role of head of the family.

When the Schanos moved to Albany, Barbara went west, leaving her son with Anna Maria and Franz. Within a year, she wrote that she was in Indiana, married and living in a log cabin on forty acres of land. She wanted her son, but it was too long a distance to travel. In the 1860s, a widow, she remarried and raised seven "Christian children" on her Indiana farm.

The Klingers represented both the old values of traditional culture and the new values of the market system. Anna Maria worked hard, saved money, and found success in Albany. Barbara lived a hard-scrabble life and was an unwed mother. She reestablished her life amid strangers, eventually finding peace in a rural German-American community. Katharina worked hard but spent most of her income on herself; her siblings complained of her selfishness. After losing contact with Rosina, the family heard she was living in New York and had "a whole brood of children" with her tinsmith husband. Even after years in the United States, the Klinger siblings were only partially Americanized. They always lived in German neighborhoods, and they socialized almost exclusively with family and other immigrants from Württemberg. Only rarely did they interact with anyone who was not German.

The Klinger family's experiences were similar to those of millions of other Americans. From the 1830s through the 1850s, millions of immigrants arrived on America's shores and hundreds of thousands of native-born Americans moved from farm to town and from town to city. The populations of the largest cities numbered in the hundreds of thousands and were highly diverse ethnically, religiously, and racially. Within large cities and in the countryside, whole districts became enclaves of ethnic groups. In hiring themselves out to build transportation and industry, immigrants reshaped American culture.

As economic opportunity increasingly attracted immigrants and energized the native born, the American people grew apart. People were on the move, and one year's frontier became the next year's settled town. Farm families felt a loss of cohesiveness, and some experimented with forming new utopian agrarian communities. The new

Mormon church combined spirituality with a strong sense of community, and its members eventually found an agrarian haven in Utah Territory.

The nature of community was changing in the United States. Civic and public institutions had to offer services, like education, that had once been provided by the family. In the nation's cities, opulent mansions rose within sight of notorious slums, and both wealth and poverty reached extremes previously unknown in agrarian America. The private sphere of the family also experienced change. With the growth of commerce and industry, the home began to lose its function as a workplace. Among the middle and upper classes, the home became woman's domain, although working-class women found no such refuge. At the same time, birth control was more widely practiced and families shrank in size.

Many Americans were uncomfortable with the new direction of American life. Antipathy toward immigrants was common among native-born Americans, who feared competition for jobs. Riots and violence became commonplace in cities. Free African-Americans fought unceasingly for equality, and tribal peoples tried unsuccessfully to resist forced removal to lands beyond the Mississippi River. In a society growing ever more diverse and complex, conflict became common.

Although the United States remained a predominantly agricultural country, the traditional economic and social arrangements were yielding to the influence of the market economy, urban growth, and immigration. The process would persist throughout the nineteenth century. Although it intensified in the final three decades of the century, the growth of an industrial, urban, and pluralist society began before the Civil War.

COUNTRY LIFE

Rural life changed significantly in the first half of the nineteenth century. Within a generation, many frontier settlements became sources rather than destinations of migrants. The villages of western New York State had lured the sons and daughters of New England in the first two decades of the century; in the 1820s and 1830s, young people moved from New York villages to the new frontier in the Old Northwest. Later, those Ohio and Michigan towns and farms would watch their young people move farther west. Their counterparts in the Upper South went to Illinois and Ohio, and those farther south settled the Gulf states.

Although most farm families lived in isolation, they did find community in the village. The farm village, with its churches, post office, general store, and tavern, was the center of rural life. But rural social life was not limited to trips to the village; families gathered on one another's farms to accomplish as a community what they could not manage individually. Barn raisings regularly brought people together. In preparation, the farmer and an itinerant carpenter built a platform and cut beams, posts, and joists. When the neighbors arrived, they constructed the walls and raised them into position. After the roof was erected, everyone celebrated with a communal meal and sometimes with singing, dancing, and games. Similar gatherings took place at harvest time and on special occasions.

Farm Communities

Women in particular sought to escape rural isolation. Men had frequent opportunities to meet at general stores, weekly markets, and taverns, and for hunting and fishing. Some women also attended market, but they more typically met at after-church dinners, prayer meetings, Bible study groups, sewing and corn-husking bees, and preparations for marriages and baptisms. These were occasions to exchange experiences, thoughts, and spiritual support and to swap letters, books, and news.

Traditional country bees had their town counterparts. Fredrika Bremer, a Swedish visitor to the United States, described a sewing bee in Cambridge, Massachusetts, in 1849, at which neighborhood women made clothes for "a family who had lost all their clothing by fire." Yet town bees were not the all-day family affairs typical of the countryside, and people who moved from farm to town often missed the country gatherings. Life was changing: town families seldom held bees, and they purchased most of their goods at the store.

Americans were increasingly conscious of such changes. Some turned to utopian experiments in an effort to find an antidote to the market economy and the untamed growth of large urban communities and have an opportunity to restore tradition and social cohesion. In the religious ferment of the Second Great Awakening, people reacted more favorably to new religious communities, whatever their philosophy. Virtually all the utopian experiments offered communal living, a cooperative rather than a competitive environment, and nontraditional work, family, and gender roles.

The Shakers, named for the way they danced at worship services, undertook one of the earliest utopian experiments. Founder Ann Lee imported this offshoot of the Quakers to America in 1774. While living in England, she had experienced a vision foretelling Jesus's second coming in America and urging her to go there. The Shakers believed that the end of the world was near and that sin entered the world through sexual intercourse. They considered existing churches too worldly and viewed the Shaker family as the instrument of salvation.

Shakers

In 1787, the Shakers "gathered in" at New Lebanon, New York, to live and work communally; other colonies soon followed. At its peak, between 1820 and 1860, the sect had about six thousand members and twenty settlements in eight states; it was the largest and most permanent of the utopian experiments. Although economically conservative, the Shakers were social radicals. They abolished individual families, practiced celibacy, and gave women new prospects for spiritual leadership. The Shaker ministry was headed by a woman, Lucy Wright, during its period of greatest growth. Celibacy, however, led inevitably to its demise.

By far the most successful communitarian group was the Church of Jesus Christ of Latter-day Saints, known as the Mormons. Joseph Smith, a young farmer in western New York, reported in 1827 that he had been visited by the angel Moroni, who gave him a set of gold plates engraved with divine revelation in an ancient language. Smith and his followers established headquarters in Ohio, but they were persecuted

Mormon Community of Saints

• *I m p o r t a n t   E v e n t s* •

1819	Congress passes "civilization act" to assimilate Native Americans	**1835–42**	Seminoles resist removal in Second Seminole War
1823	Catharine and Mary Beecher establish Hartford Female Seminary	**1837**	Boston employs paid policemen
1824	President Monroe proposes removal of Indians	**1837–48**	Horace Mann heads the Massachusetts Board of Education
1827	*Freedom's Journal*, first African-American newspaper, appears	**1841–47**	Brook Farm combines spirituality, work, and play in a utopian rural community
1830	Joseph Smith founds Mormon Church Congress passes Removal Act	**1842**	Knickerbocker baseball club formed
1830s–50s	Urban riots commonplace	**1845**	Start of the Irish potato famine
1831	Cherokees turn to courts to defend rights in *Cherokee Nation* v. *Georgia*	**1846–47**	Mormon trek to the Great Salt Lake
1831–38	Indian tribes resettled in West in Trail of Tears	**1847–57**	Peak period of immigration before the Civil War
		1848	Abortive revolutions in German states

there and in Illinois and Missouri because of their claims of continuous divine revelation and their practice of allowing men to have several wives at once. The Mormons trekked across the continent in 1846 and 1847 to found a New Zion in the Great Salt Lake Valley. There, under Brigham Young, head of the Twelve Apostles (their governing body), they established a cohesive community of Saints—a heaven on earth.

In Utah, the Mormons distributed agricultural land according to family size. An extensive irrigation system, constructed by men who contributed their labor in proportion to the quantity of land they received and the amount of water they expected to use, was the basis of their prosperity. As the colony developed, the church elders came to control water, trade, industry, and even the territorial government of Utah.

Not all utopian communities were founded by religious sects. In 1825, Robert Owen, a wealthy Scottish industrialist, attempted to found a socialist utopia in New Harmony, Indiana. According to his plan, its nine hundred members were to exchange their labor for goods at a communal store.

Handicrafts (hat and boot making) flourished at New Harmony, but its textile mill—the economic base of the community—failed after Owen gave it to the community to run. By 1827, the experiment had ended.

More successful were the New Englanders at the Brook Farm cooperative in West Roxbury, Massachusetts. Inspired by transcendentalism—the philosophy that the physical **Brook Farm** world is secondary to the spiritual realm—Brook Farm's members rejected materialism for a rural communal life combining spirituality, manual labor, intellectual growth, and play. Although short-lived (1841–1847), Brook Farm played a significant role in the flowering of a national literature. There Nathaniel Hawthorne, Ralph Waldo Emerson, and Margaret Fuller, the editor of the *Dial* (the leading transcendentalist journal), joined Henry David Thoreau, James Fenimore Cooper, Herman Melville, and others in creating what is known today as the American Renaissance. In its philosophical intensity and moral idealism, their work was both distinctively

American and an outgrowth of the European romantic movement. Their themes were universal, their settings and character American.

The essayist Ralph Waldo Emerson was the prime mover of the American Renaissance and a pillar of the transcendental movement. "We live in succession, in division, in parts, in particles," Emerson wrote. "We see the world piece by piece, as the sun, the moon, the animal, the tree; but the whole, of which these are the shining parts, is the soul." Intuitive experience of God is attainable, according to Emerson, because "the Highest dwells" within every individual in the form of the "Over-soul."

Utopian communities can be seen as attempts to recapture the cohesiveness of traditional agricultural and artisan life in reaction to the competitive pressures of the market economy and urbanization. Utopians resembled Puritan perfectionists; like the Separatists of seventeenth-century New England, they sought to begin anew in their own colonies.

CITY LIFE

The transportation revolution and the expansion of commerce and manufacturing caused the populations of American cities to grow geometrically between 1800 and 1860, especially in the North. The nation's population increased during this period from five million to thirty-one million. Meanwhile, settlement spread westward, and small rural settlements became towns. In 1800, the nation had only 33 towns with 2500 or more people and only 3 with more than 25,000. By 1860, 392 towns exceeded 2500 residents, 35 had more than 25,000, and 9 exceeded 100,000.

New York City became the nation's premier metropolis during these years, growing from 60,500 in 1800 to more than 800,000 in 1860.

New York City Across the East River, Brooklyn tripled in size between 1850 and 1860, becoming the nation's third-largest city with a population of more than 260,000. Many were just passing through; the majority would not stay ten years. Although contemporary depictions of New York appear almost pastoral, the city's energy and aromas of sweat, horse dung, and garbage would make twentieth-century cities seem sanitized in comparison. An immigrant port city, mostly Irish and German by the 1850s, New York City teemed with people.

New York City had literally burst its boundaries in the 1820s. Up to that time, New Yorkers could still regard the city as a village, because they could walk from one end of the city to the other in an hour. Until the 1820s, nearly all New Yorkers had lived within two miles of city hall. Mass transit, however, made it possible for the city to expand. Horse-drawn buses appeared in New York in 1827, and the Harlem Railroad, completed in 1832, ran the length of Manhattan. By the 1850s, all big cities had horse-drawn streetcars.

By modern standards, early nineteenth-century cities were disorderly, unsafe, and unhealthy. Expansion occurred so rapidly that few cities could handle the problems it brought. For example, migrants from rural areas were accustomed to relieving themselves outside and throwing refuse in any vacant area. In the city, such waste smelled, spread disease, and polluted water. New York City partially solved the problem in the 1840s by abandoning wells in favor of reservoir water piped into buildings and outdoor fountains. In some districts, scavengers and refuse collectors carted away garbage and human waste, but in much of the city it just rotted on the ground. Only one-quarter of New York City's streets had sewers by 1857.

New York and other cities lacked adequate taxing power to provide services for all. The best the city could do was to assess the adjoining property for the cost of sewers, street paving, and water mains. Thus the spread of new services and basic sanitation depended on residents' ability or willingness to pay. As a result, those most in need of services typically got them last. Another solution was to charter private companies to sell basic services. This worked well with gas service. Baltimore first chartered a private gas company in 1816; New York did so in 1842. By midcentury, every major city would be lit by a private gas supplier. The private sector, however, failed to supply the water the cities

The Lackawanna Valley *(1855), by George Inness. Hired by the Lackawanna Railroad to paint a railroad scene, Inness blended landscape and machine into an organic whole. American industrialism, Inness seemed to say, belonged to the landscape; it would neither overpower nor obliterate the land.*   Gift of Mrs. Huttleston Rogers, © National Gallery of Art, Washington, D.C.

needed. Private firms lacked the capital to build adequate systems, and they laid pipe only in commercial and well-to-do residential areas, ignoring the poor. As cities grew, water service did not keep pace. Eventually, city governments had to take over.

The civic service that had the greatest influence on American life was the provision of public or common schools. In 1800, there were no

Horace Mann and Public Schools

public schools outside New England; by 1860, every state offered some public education. Massachusetts, which had taken the lead in education since Puritan times, again led in expansion of schooling under Horace Mann, secretary of the state board of education from 1837 to 1848. Massachusetts established a minimum school term

of six months, formalized the training of teachers, and emphasized secular subjects and applied skills rather than religious training. In the process, school teaching became a woman's profession.

Horace Mann's preaching on behalf of free state-sponsored education changed schooling throughout the nation. "If we do not prepare children to become good citizens," Mann argued, "if we do not develop their capacities, . . . then our republic must go down to destruction." The abolition of ignorance, according to Mann, would end misery, crime, and suffering. "The only sphere . . . left open for our patriotism," he wrote, "is the improvement of our children—not the few, but the many; not a part of them but all." Mann and others were responding to the changes wrought by the market economy, urbanization, and immigration.

The typical city dweller was a newcomer, whether from abroad or from the country. The new public schools would take the children of this nation of strangers and inculcate them with shared values.

In laying the foundation for free public schools, Mann also broadened the scope of education. Schooling had previously focused on literacy, religious training, and discipline. Thus most parents were indifferent about whether their children continued their schooling. Under Mann's leadership, the school curriculum became more secular and more appropriate for future clerks, farmers, and workers. Students studied geography, American history, arithmetic, and science. Moral education was retained, but direct religious indoctrination was dropped.

The basic texts—*McGuffey's Eclectic Readers*—used Protestant Scriptures to teach children to accept their position in society. A good child, McGuffey taught, does not envy the rich: "It is God who makes some poor and others rich." Catholics, immigrants, blacks, and working-class people sought to have local control of their communities' schools, but the state legislatures established secular statewide standards under Protestant educators. Catholics in New York responded by building their own educational system during the next half-century.

New urban work and living patterns made for different uses of leisure than had been traditional in the countryside or in Europe. People worked long hours, found little space in the cities for recreation, and had limited opportunities for games and sports. Nonetheless, urban men engaged in traditional sports and recreations. Tavern games of skill and strength—arm wrestling, quoits (throwing a two-pound iron or stone ring at a pin), ninepins, and pitching coins—remained popular and often were accompanied by betting. Although city dwellers had less opportunity than their rural counterparts to ride and hunt, fishing remained popular. Space for recreation was scarce in cities, and the opportunities for games and sport were limited.

Leisure

Thanks to the expansion of public education, the vast majority of native-born white Americans were literate by the 1850s. Readers' appetites were fed by fiction and autobiographies as well as religious tracts. Newspapers and magazines printed fiction, and bookstores and stationers in large cities sold book-length novels and autobiographies. Susanna Rowson's 1794 novel *Charlotte Temple*, which offered a critique of women's dependence on men, and the powerful attack on slavery in the *Narrative of the Life of Frederick Douglass, an American Slave, Written by Himself* (1845), were widely read. Many popular novels written by women, often for women, were set in the home and upheld Christian values. Yet they can also be read as a challenge to prevailing values. Rowson's *Charlotte Temple*, for instance, never depicted the heroine performing domestic chores. And, although Susan Warners' *The Wide, Wide, Wide World* (1850), Nathaniel Hawthorne's *The House of the Seven Gables* (1851), and Fanny Fern's *Ruth Hall* (1855) did not challenge women's traditional domestic roles, they gave women a special moral bearing. In describing in positive terms community and republican virtue, they implicitly criticized the growing market economy.

Theater was a central institution in American life. A theater was often the second public building constructed in a town. (The first was usually a church.) Large cities boasted two or more theaters that catered to different social classes. Yet some theater cut across class lines. Shakespeare was performed so often and appreciated so widely that even illiterate theatergoers knew his blank verse well. In the 1840s, musical and dramatic presentations took on a more professional tone; the Hutchinson Family and their rivals and the newly popular minstrel shows offered carefully rehearsed routines.

Sports, like theater, increasingly involved city dwellers as spectators. Horse racing, boxing, pedestrianism (walking races), and, in the 1850s, baseball began to attract large urban male crowds. After New York State legalized horse racing in 1821, a track was built in Queens County across the East River from New York City. Two years later, an estimated crowd of more than fifty thousand came to the track to watch a single race. By 1849, boxing had gained enough popularity that round-by-round accounts of a match in Maryland were telegraphed throughout the East.

Sports

Sports and recreation mirrored the growing divisions in American urban society. They had become less spontaneous and relied increasingly on formal rules. Entertainment became not just recreation but a commodity to be purchased; one had to buy a ticket to go to the theater, the circus, P. T. Barnum's American Museum in New York City, the racetrack, or the ballpark. Sports and recreation also frequently depended on exclusive associations and clubs, which advanced the interests of particular groups. In 1829, for instance, a group of Ohio merchants organized the Cincinnati Angling Club, which had a formal constitution and bylaws and limited membership to twenty-five. A group of Wall Street office workers formed the Knickerbocker Club in 1842, and in 1845 they drew up rules for the game of baseball.

City Life

As cities grew, their populations seemed increasingly fragmented. Finding people similar to oneself required more of a conscious effort; groups of all sorts formed clubs and associations to get to know each other and to serve as a bulwark against the cultures of other groups—immigrants, migrants, blacks, and artisans. Middle- and upper-class New Yorkers, who felt alienated in the city of their birth, founded societies and clubs designed to be exclusive. Some joined the Masonic order, which provided everything the bustling city did not: an elaborate hierarchy, an orderly code of deference between ranks, harmony, and shared values. Members knew each other. Americans of all sorts—native and foreign born, black and white—also formed churches and church-associated clubs. Associations of these kinds brought together similar people, but they also formalized divisions between dissimilar groups.

Even a youth culture developed on the Bowery of the 1840s. Older New Yorkers feared the "Bowery boys and gals," whose ostentatious dress and behavior seemed threatening. The Bowery boys' swaggering gait frightened many in the middle class. Equally disturbing to old New Yorkers were the young working women who promenaded on the Bowery. Unlike more genteel ladies, who wore modest veils or bonnets, Bowery gals drew attention with bright outlandish clothes and ornate hats. Cities offered great diversity and anonymity. People interested in same-sex liaisons, although often publicly ostracized, could find each other in the city and live together in urban boarding houses.

Most working people spent much of their lives outdoors—they worked in the streets as laborers, shopped in open markets, and paraded on special occasions. Young people courted, neighbors argued, and ethnic groups defended their turf on the streets. Increasingly, urban streets served as a political arena as crowds formed to listen to speakers, to parade, and sometimes to form mobs.

Urban Riots

Rioting and incidents of violence became commonplace in the 1830s and 1840s as professionals and merchants, skilled craftsmen, and ordinary laborers vented their rage against political and economic rivals. "Gentlemen of property and standing," unnerved by antislavery proponents, sacked abolitionist and antislavery organizations, even killing newspaper editor Elijah Lovejoy in Alton, Illinois, in 1837. In the 1840s, "respectable" citizens drove the Mormons out of Illinois and Missouri. In Philadelphia, native-born workers attacked Irish weavers in 1828, and whites and blacks fought on the docks in 1834 and 1835. Philadelphia's disturbances climaxed in 1844 when mostly Protestant skilled workers attacked Irish Catholics. Smaller cities too became battlegrounds as nativist riots peaked in the 1850s. By 1840, more than 125 people had died in urban riots, and by 1860 fatalities exceeded one thousand.

As public disorder spread, Boston hired uniformed policemen in 1837 to supplement its part-time watchmen and constables, and New York in 1845 established an entirely uniformed force. Nonetheless, middle-class men and women did not venture out alone at night, and even during the day they avoided certain districts. Ironically, in the midst of so much dirt, noise, crime, and conflict, the opulent residences of the very rich rose like a deliberate affront to those struggling to survive.

EXTREMES OF WEALTH

Some observers, notably the young French nobleman Alexis de Tocqueville, characterized the United States before the Civil War as primarily a place of equality and opportunity. Tocqueville attributed

American equality—the relative fluidity of the social order in the United States—to Americans' mobility and restlessness. Geographic mobility offered people opportunities to start anew regardless of where they had come from or who they were. Wealth and family mattered little; a person could be known by deeds alone. Talent and hard work, many Americans believed, found their just reward in such an atmosphere.

Others disagreed with this egalitarian view of American life. Among those who traced the rise of a new aristocracy based on wealth and power and the growth of class and ethnic divisions was *New York Sun* publisher Moses Yale Beach. Author of twelve editions of *Wealth and Biography of the Wealthy Citizens of New York City*, Beach listed 750 New Yorkers with assets of $100,000 or more in 1845. John Jacob Astor led the list of nineteen millionaires with a fortune of $25 million. Ten years later, Beach reported more than one thousand New Yorkers worth $100,000, among them twenty-eight millionaires. Tocqueville himself, ever sensitive to the conflicting trends in American life, had described the growth of an American aristocracy based on industrial wealth. The rich and well educated "come forward to exploit industries," Tocqueville wrote, and become "more and more like the administrators of a huge empire. . . . What is this if not an aristocracy?"

Differences in Wealth

Wealth throughout the United States was becoming concentrated in the hands of a relatively small number of people. In New York City between 1828 and 1845, the wealthiest 4 percent of the city's population increased its holdings from an estimated 63 percent to 80 percent of all individual wealth. By 1860, the top 5 percent of American families owned more than half the nation's wealth.

Meanwhile, a cloud of uncertainty hung over working men and women. Many feared unemployment during hard times, and they resented the competition of immigrant and slave labor. They dreaded the insecurities and indignities of poverty, chronic illness, disability, old age, widowhood, and desertion. Women feared having to raise a family without a helpmate. And they had good reason: few women could earn sufficient money to support a family from full-time work in the few fields open to them.

Urban Poverty

Poverty and squalor dogged the urban working class. Cities were notorious for the dilapidated districts inhabited by newly arrived immigrants, indigent free blacks, the working poor, and thieves, beggars, and prostitutes. New York City's Five Points, a few blocks from City Hall, was the worst slum in pre–Civil War America. Dominated by the Old Brewery, which had been converted to housing for hundreds of adults and children in 1837, the neighborhood was predominantly Irish and black. Ill suited to human habitation, lacking such amenities as running water and sewers, Five Points exemplified the worst of urban life. Throughout the city, houses built for two families often held four; tenements built for six families held twelve. New York, like other large cities, harbored "street rats," children and young men who earned their living on the streets by bootblacking or petty thievery. They slept on boats, in haylofts, or in warehouses.

A world apart from Five Points and the people of the streets lived the upper-class elite society of Philip Hone, one-time mayor of New York. Hone's diary, meticulously kept from 1826 until his death in 1851, records the activities of an American aristocrat. On February 28, 1840, for instance, Hone attended a masked ball at the Fifth Avenue mansion of Henry Breevoort Jr. and Laura Carson Breevoort. The ball began at the fashionable hour of 10 P.M., and the five hundred ladies and gentlemen who filled the mansion wore costumes adorned with ermine and gold. At one time or another similar parties were held in Boston, Philadelphia, Baltimore, and Charleston.

The Urban Elite

Much of the new wealth was inherited. For every John Jacob Astor who made millions in the western fur trade, or George Law who left a farm to become a millionaire contractor and investor, ten others used the money they had inherited or married as a steppingstone to additional wealth. Many of the wealthiest New Yorkers bore the names of the colonial commercial elite—Beekman, Breevoort, Roosevelt, Van Rensselaer, and Whitney. The rich New Yorkers were not idle; they worked at increasing their fortunes and power.

Hardly an important canal, railroad, bank, or mill venture lacked the names and investments of the fashionable elite. Wealth begat wealth, and family ties were cemented through marriage.

Meanwhile, the hard-working middle class was becoming a distinct part of the urban scene. The growth and specialization of trade had rapidly increased their numbers. The men were businessmen or professionals, the women homemakers. Middle-class families enjoyed the fruits of advances in consumption: wool carpeting, fine wallpaper, rooms full of furniture, and indoor toilets. They filled the family pews in church on Sundays; their children pursued whatever educational opportunities were available. If they dreamed of entering Philip Hone's world, they were mindful to keep their distance from the working class and the poor.

The Middle Class

WOMEN AND THE FAMILY

Distinctions among women grew in the nineteenth century as a result of changes in work and gender roles. In the eighteenth century, women of different classes, race, and ethnicity had had much more in common. Women's and men's work also grew increasingly distinct. As manufacturing left the home, so did wage workers, except those doing putting-out work. On farms, women's and men's work still overlapped, but in the new stores and workshops their tasks diverged. Specialization in work tasks was an outcome of specialization in business and production; men acquired narrow new skills that they applied in set ways with purposefully designed tools and systems. Authority within the workplace became formal and impersonal.

Some women shared these experiences for brief periods. The New England farm daughters who were the first textile mill workers performed new specialized work tasks away from home. In the 1840s, the new urban department stores hired young women as clerks and cash runners. Many women worked for a time as teachers. Paid employment typically represented a brief stage in their

Working Women

lives before they left their paternal households and entered their marital households.

Working-class women—the poor, widows, and free blacks—worked to support themselves and their families. Leaving their parental homes as early as age twelve or thirteen, they earned wages most of their lives, with only short respites for bearing and rearing children. But unlike men and New England farm daughters, most of these women did not work in the new shops and factories. Instead, they worked as domestic servants in other women's homes and as laundresses, seamstresses, cooks, and boarding-house keepers. Few of these occupations enabled them to support themselves or a family at a respectable level. Widowhood in particular was synonymous with poverty.

Work was increasingly segregated and gender specific. Most women's work continued to center on the home. As the urban family lost its role in the production of goods, household upkeep and child-rearing claimed women's full-time attention. Devotion to education, religion, morality, domestic arts, and culture began to fill the void left by the decline in the economic functions of the family; these realms came to be known as woman's sphere. For a woman to achieve mastery in these areas was to live up to the middle-class ideal of the cult of domesticity.

Middle-class Americans idealized the family as a moral institution characterized by selflessness and cooperation. Women were idealized in turn as the embodiment of self-sacrificing republicanism. The role of the mother in this cult of domesticity was to strengthen the nation's future by rearing her children well and creating a spiritual and virtuous environment that contrasted sharply with the world outside the home. The world of work—the market economy—was seen as an arena of conflict increasingly identified with men and dominated by base self-interest. In a rapidly changing world, the family was assigned the role of representing stability and traditional values.

The domestic ideal in turn restricted the range of paying jobs available to middle-class women outside the home. Most paid work was viewed with disapproval, but one occupation came to be recognized as consistent with the genteel female role: teaching. In 1823, the Beecher sisters, Catharine and Mary, established the Hartford Female Seminary and offered philosophy, history, and science in addition to the traditional women's curriculum of domestic arts and religion. A decade later, Catharine Beecher successfully campaigned to establish training seminaries for female teachers by presenting such education as an extension of women's nurturing role. By the 1850s, school teaching was regarded as a woman's vocation, and most urban teachers were women, nearly all unmarried. Their pay, however, was about half that of male teachers.

Meanwhile, family size was shrinking. In 1800, American women bore an average of six to seven children; by 1860, the figure had dropped to five.

Decline in the Birthrate

A number of factors reduced family size. For one thing, small families were viewed as increasingly desirable in a market economy, in which the family was a unit of consumption rather than production. Children in smaller families would have greater opportunities: parents could give them more attention, better educations, and more financial help. Also, contemporary marriage manuals stressed that too many births had a harmful effect on a woman's health.

The evidence suggests that many couples made deliberate decisions to limit the size of their families. In areas where farmland was relatively expensive, for instance, families were smaller than in more affordable agricultural districts. Apparently, parents who foresaw difficulty setting up their children as independent farmers chose to have fewer children. In urban areas, children became more of an economic burden than an asset as the family lost its role as a producer of goods. As the length of the period before which children began contributing financially grew, so did their economic costs to parents.

How did men and women limit their families in the early nineteenth century? Average age at marriage rose, thus shortening the period of potential childbearing. Women also bore their last child at a younger age, suggesting that family planning was becoming more common.

Birth Control

Many couples used traditional forms of birth control, such as coitus interruptus (withdrawal of the male before completion of the sexual act) and breast feeding, which makes some women temporarily infertile. And cheap rubber condoms became popular after their introduction in the 1850s. Some couples used the rhythm method—attempting to confine intercourse to a woman's infertile periods. Awareness of the "safe period," however, was uncertain, even among physicians. For those desiring to terminate a pregnancy, surgical abortions became common after 1830. By 1860, however, twenty states had outlawed abortions.

Significantly, the birth-control methods that women controlled—douching, the rhythm method, abstinence, breast feeding, and abortion—were increasing in popularity. The new emphasis on domesticity encouraged women's autonomy in the home and by extension gave them greater control over their bodies. According to the cult of domesticity, the refinement and purity of women ruled the household, including the bedroom.

Sarah Ripley of Greenfield, Massachusetts, who grew up in the eighteenth century and reached adulthood in the nineteenth, traced the changes in her diaries. Daughter of a village shopkeeper, Ripley had a privileged childhood. After completing boarding school, she returned home to work as an assistant in her father's store. In 1812, she married Charles Stearns of Shelburn. "I have now . . . left the protection of my parents and given up the name I have always borne," she recorded in her diary. "May the grace of God enable me to fulfill with prudence and piety the great and important duties which now dissolve [fall] on me." Soon she confessed in her diary that she missed the bustle of the shop.

Sarah Ripley Stearns

Sarah Ripley Stearns's life was not a settled one; change was a constant. During the six years following her marriage, she bore three children, moved three times, became a widow, and found an anchor in religion. Sterns, like other middle-class women, found that social interaction within the church made it possible to extend the bounds of ideal domesticity. For example, she and her neighbors sponsored a school and a juvenile home. Such benevolent work both aided poor children and provided its female participants with experience in organizing and chairing meetings, raising funds, and cultivating an extended women's network.

Urban life and the market economy offered new roles for some women. Women who made a conscious decision to stay single rejected the cult of domesticity and intentionally **Single Women** departed from the centuries-old pattern whereby women moved from their fathers' households to those of their husbands. Louisa May Alcott (1832–1888), the author of *Little Women* (1868), sought independence and financial security for herself. Alcott worked as a seamstress, governess, teacher, and housemaid before her writing finally brought her success. "I think I shall come out right, and prove that . . . I *can* support myself," she wrote her father in 1856. "I like the independent feeling; and though not an easy life, it is a free one, and I enjoy it."

Louisa May Alcott had foresworn marriage to risk ridicule as a spinster. She and other like-minded women who chose to pursue their abilities shared a life defined by female relationships and activities. In large cities, they could establish independent relationships with other single women. Given the difficulty women had finding work that would allow them to be self-supporting, they undertook their independence at great risk. Nonetheless, the proportion of single women in the population increased significantly in the first three-quarters of the nineteenth century. Independent white women, in sum, were taking advantage of new opportunities offered by the market economy and urban expansion.

IMMIGRANT LIVES IN AMERICA

The five million strangers who came to the United States between 1820 and 1860 outnumbered the entire population of the country recorded in the first census in 1790. They came from every continent, although the vast majority were European. During the peak period of pre–Civil War immigration, from 1847 through 1857, 3.3 million immigrants entered the United States; 1.3 million were from Ireland and 1.1 million from the German states (see figure). By 1860, 15 percent of the white population was foreign born.

This massive migration had been set in motion decades earlier. The Napoleonic wars had initiated one of the greatest population shifts in history around the turn of the nineteenth century; it was ultimately to last more than a century. War, revolution, famine, religious persecution, and the lure of industrialization led many Europeans to leave home. Most Asian immigrants were from Southern China who left home to work in heavy construction. The United States beckoned, offering economic opportunity and religious freedom.

Meanwhile, both private enterprises and public entities in the United States actively recruited European emigrants. Midwestern and western states lured potential settlers in **Promotion of** the interest of promoting their **Immigration** economies. Two transplanted New Yorkers, Augustus and Joe Kirby Allen, for instance, set up in Houston in 1836 and advertised in newspapers for settlers. In the 1850s, the state of Wisconsin appointed a commissioner of emigration, who advertised the state's advantages in European newspapers. Wisconsin also opened an office in New York and hired European agents to compete with other states and with firms like the Illinois Central Railroad for immigrants' attention.

Large construction projects and mines needed strong young laborers. Textile mills and cities attracted young women workers. Europeans' awareness of the United States grew as employers, states, and shipping companies advertised opportunities across the Atlantic. The cost of the regularly scheduled sailing ships commuting across the ocean after 1848 was within easy reach of millions of Europeans.

So they came, enduring the hardships of travel and of settlement in a strange land. The average transatlantic crossing took six weeks; in bad weather it could take three months. Disease spread unchecked among people packed together like cattle in steerage. More than seventeen thousand immigrants, mostly Irish, died from "ship fever" in 1847. On arrival, immigrants became fair game for the con artists and swindlers who worked the docks. Aggressive agents representing boarding-house

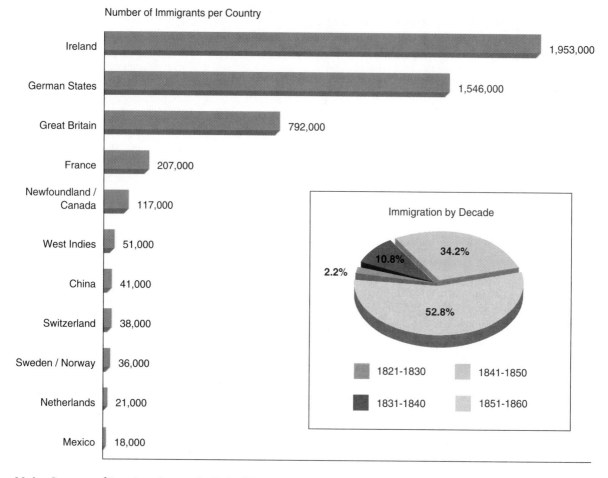

Major Sources of Immigration to the United States, 1821–1860

Number of Immigrants per Country

Country	Number
Ireland	1,953,000
German States	1,546,000
Great Britain	792,000
France	207,000
Newfoundland / Canada	117,000
West Indies	51,000
China	41,000
Switzerland	38,000
Sweden / Norway	36,000
Netherlands	21,000
Mexico	18,000

Immigration by Decade

34.2%
10.8%
2.2%
52.8%

1821-1830   1841-1850
1831-1840   1851-1860

Major Sources of Immigration to the United States, 1821–1860 *Most immigrants came from western Europe, and the five million immigrants who came to the United States between 1820 and 1860 outnumbered the entire population of the country at the first census in 1790. By 1860, 15 percent of the white population was of foreign birth.* Source: U.S. Bureau of the Census, *Historical Statistics of the United States, Colonial Times to 1970.* (2 Parts; Washington, D.C., 1975), Part I, pp. 206, 208.

owners and employers greeted them and tried to lure them from their chosen destinations. In response, New York State's commissioners of emigration established Castle Garden as an immigrant center in 1855. There, immigrants were somewhat sheltered from fraud. Authorized transportation companies maintained offices in the large rotunda and assisted new arrivals with their travel plans.

Most immigrants gravitated toward cities, because only a minority had farming experience or the means to purchase land and equipment. Many stayed in New York City. By 1855, 52 percent of its 623,000 inhabitants were immigrants. Boston, a major entry port for the Irish, took on a European tone; throughout the 1850s, the city was about 35 percent foreign born, of whom more than two-thirds were Irish. The South's largest cities also had sizable immigrant populations. In 1860, New Orleans was 44 percent foreign born, Savannah 33 percent, and the western city of St. Louis 61 percent. On the West Coast, San Francisco had a foreign-born majority.

Some immigrants did settle in rural areas. German, Dutch, and Scandinavian farmers, in particular, gravitated toward the Midwest. Greater percentages of Scandinavians and Netherlanders took up farming than did other nationalities; both groups came mostly as religious dissenters and migrated in family units. The Dutch who founded colonies in Michigan and Wisconsin, for instance, had seceded from the official Reformed Church of the Netherlands, fleeing persecution in their native land to establish new and more pious communities such as Holland and Zeeland in Michigan.

Not all immigrants found success in the United States; hundreds of thousands returned to their homelands disappointed. Before the potato blight hit Ireland, American re-

Immigrant Disenchantment
———

cruiters lured many Irish to swing picks and shovels on American canals and railroads and to work in construction. Among them was Michael Gaugin, who for thirteen years had been an assistant engineer in the construction of a Dublin canal. Gaugin was attracted to the United States by the promise that "he should soon become a wealthy man." The Dublin agent for a New York firm convinced him to quit his job, which included a house and an acre of ground, and emigrate. Gaugin had the misfortune to land in New York City during the financial panic of 1837, and within two months of arriving he became a pauper. Gaugin declared he was "now without means for the support of himself and his family, and has no employment, and has already suffered great deprivation since he arrived in this country; and is now soliciting means to enable him to return with his family home to Ireland."

Such experiences did not deter other Irish men and women from coming to the United States. Ireland was the most densely populated country in

Irish Immigrants
———

Europe and among the most impoverished. From 1815 on, small harvests prompted a steady stream of Irish to emigrate to America. Then in 1845 and 1846, potatoes—Ireland's staple food—rotted in the fields. From 1845 to 1849, death from starvation, malnutrition, and typhus spread. In all, one million died and about 1.5 million fled, two-

thirds to the United States. Ireland's major export was its people.

At the peak of Irish immigration, from 1847 to 1854, 1.2 million Irish men and women entered the United States. Every year between 1820 and 1854, with only two exceptions, the Irish constituted the largest single group of immigrants annually. By the end of the century, there would be more Irish in the United States than in Ireland.

The new Irish immigrants differed greatly from those who had left Ireland to settle in the American colonies. The Protestant Scotch-Irish who predominated in the eighteenth century had journeyed from one part of the British Empire to another. The nineteenth-century Irish immigrants to America, however, were mostly Roman Catholic, and they were also leaving a colony to settle in an independent republic. The political and religious differences made their cultural adaptation that much more difficult. In comparison with the Scotch-Irish, furthermore, the new immigrants from Ireland tended to be younger, increasingly female, and mostly from the rural provinces.

In the urban areas in which they clustered in poverty, Irish immigrants met growing anti-immigrant, anti-Catholic sentiment. "No Irish

Anti-Catholicism
———

Need Apply" signs were common. During the colonial period, white Protestants had feared "popery" as a system of tyranny and had discriminated against the few Catholics in America. After the Revolution, anti-Catholicism had receded, but it reappeared in the 1830s wherever the Irish did. Attacks on the papacy and the church circulated widely in the form of libelous texts like *The Awful Disclosures of Maria Monk* (1836), which alleged sexual orgies among priests and nuns. Nowhere was anti-Catholicism more overt and nasty than in Boston, but such sentiments were widespread.

The native born who embraced anti-Catholicism were motivated largely by anxiety. They feared that a militant Roman church would subvert American society, that unskilled Irish workers would displace American craftsmen, and that the slums inhabited in part by the Irish were undermining the nation's values. Every social problem from immorality and alcoholism to poverty and economic upheaval was blamed on immigrant Irish Catholics. Americans seemed to have adopted the negative British stereotypes of Irish people. Friction increased as Irish-American men fought back by entering politics.

In 1854, Germans replaced the Irish as the single largest group of new arrivals. The Klinger family was part of this migration. Potato blight had

German Immigrants

also prompted emigration from the German states to the United States in the 1840s; other hardships added to the steady stream. Many came from regions of Germany where small landholdings made it hard to eke out a living and to pass on adequate plots of land to their sons. Others were craftsmen displaced by the industrial revolution. The refugees were joined by middle-class Germans—a whole generation of liberals and freethinkers—who emigrated to the United States after the abortive revolution of 1848.

Unlike the Irish, who tended to congregate in towns and cities, Germans settled everywhere. Many came on cotton boats, disembarked at New Orleans, and traveled up the Mississippi. In the South, they became peddlers and merchants; in the North and West, they worked as farmers, urban laborers, and businessmen. They tended more than the Irish to migrate in families and groups; that tendency helped them maintain German culture and institutions in the New World.

Native-born Americans treated German immigrants with greater respect than they did the Irish, stereotyping Germans as industrious, hard working, self-reliant, and intelligent. Many believed that Germans would "harmonize" better with American culture. Nevertheless, Germans too encountered hostility. A significant number of German immigrants were Jewish, and they experienced anti-Semitism. More than half the German immigrants were Catholic, and their sabbath traditions differed from those of Protestants. On Sundays, urban German families customarily gathered at beer gardens to eat and drink beer, to dance, sing, and listen to band music and sometimes to play cards. Protestants were outraged by such violations of the Lord's day.

Not all immigrants came to the United States voluntarily. After the annexation of Texas, the Mexican War, and the Gadsden Purchase (the pur-

Hispanics

chase from Mexico of thirty thousand square miles in present-day New Mexico and Arizona), many Hispanics—people of Spanish or Mexican origin—found themselves residing in the United States because of boundary changes. The separation of Texas from Mexico after 1836, the discovery of gold in California, and the extension of railroad lines broke the linkage of the Southwest and Mexico and reoriented the Southwest to the United States.

Hispanic culture persisted in the region, but Anglos and European immigrants seized economic and political power. Hispanics retained their language, Roman Catholic religion, and community affiliations through newspapers, mutual aid societies, and the church, but they lost power and status to Anglos. In Nueces County, Texas, at the time of the Texas Revolution (1836), Mexicans held all the land; twenty years later, they had lost it all. Although many Hispanics had fought for Texas independence, arriving settlers tended to treat them as inferiors. Within two generations, Hispanics became strangers in their own land—second-class citizens on land where they had lived for generations.

For immigrants, becoming part of American society involved conflict, but once here they claimed their right to a fair economic and political share. Native Americans, however, like the Hispanics in the Southwest, were defending what they regarded as prior rights. Their land, their religions, and their ways of life came under constant attack, because they were viewed as obstacles to expansion and economic growth.

INDIAN RESISTANCE AND REMOVAL

Under the Constitution, the federal government had responsibility for dealing with Native Americans. For better or worse, there had to be a federal Indian policy. From the Indians' point of view, it was usually for the worse. U.S. territorial expansion took place at the tribal peoples' expense. The result was removal of the great Native American nations to lands west of the Mississippi. While the populations of other groups increased by leaps and bounds, the Indian population shrank. War, forced removal, disease—especially smallpox—and malnutrition reduced many tribes by half. More than half the Pawnee, Omaha, Ottoe, Missouri, and Kansas Indians died in the 1830s alone. Within tribes, the more traditional the family structure, the greater the toll; close contact spread disease.

As had the colonial powers in North America, the United States treated Native American tribes as sovereign nations until Congress ended the practice in 1871. In its relations with tribal leaders, the government followed international protocol. Indian delegations that visited Washington were received with the appropriate pomp and ceremony. Leaders exchanged presents as tokens of friendship, and commemorative flags and silver medals with presidents' likenesses became prized possessions among Indian chiefs. Agreements between a given tribe and the United States were signed, sealed, and ratified like any international pact.

In practice, however, Native American sovereignty was a fiction. Protocol appeared to signify mutual respect and independence, but treaty negotiations exposed the sham. Treaty making was essentially a process used by the American government to acquire Indian land. Instead of bargains struck between two equal nations, such treaties were often coerced agreements between the victor and the vanquished. Old treaties gave way to new ones in which Native Americans ceded their traditional holdings in return for different lands in the West.

The War of 1812 snuffed out whatever realistic hopes eastern Indian leaders might have had of resisting American expansion by means of warfare. Armed resistance persisted and blood was shed on both sides. Resistance, however, only delayed the inevitable. The Shawnee chiefs Prophet and Tecumseh led the most significant movement against the United States, but Prophet failed to sustain the movement after Tecumseh's death.

The experiences of Prophet and other Shawnees were typical of the wanderings of an uprooted people. When the Shawnees gave up seventeen million acres in Ohio in the 1795 Treaty of Greenville, they scattered to Indiana and eastern Missouri. After the War of 1812, Prophet's Indiana group withdrew to Canada. In 1822, other Shawnees sought Mexican protection and moved from Missouri to present-day eastern Texas. As the U.S. government began promoting removal to Kansas, Prophet returned from Canada to lead a group to the new Shawnee lands in eastern Kansas in 1825. When Missouri achieved statehood in 1821, the Shawnees there were also forced to move to Kansas, where they were joined in the 1830s by Shawnees removed from Ohio and others expelled from Texas. By 1854, Kansas was open to white settlement, and the Shawnees had to cede back seven-eighths of their land—1.4 million acres.

Indian Resistance

Removal had a profound effect on all Shawnees. The men had to give up their traditional role as providers; their methods of hunting and knowledge of woodland animals were useless on the prairies of Kansas. As grains became the tribe's dietary staple, Shawnee women played a greater role as providers, supplemented by government aid under treaty provisions. Remarkably, the Shawnees preserved their language and culture in the face of these drastic changes.

In the 1820s, Native Americans were pressured to cede their lands in Ohio, southern Indiana and Illinois, southwestern Michigan, most of Missouri, central Alabama, and southern Mississippi. They gave up nearly two hundred million acres for pennies an acre. But white settlers' appetites were insatiable and they wanted Native Americans to assimilate. The federal Indian agency system, which paid out the rations, supplies, and annuities they received in exchange for abandoning their land, served both purposes. With time, the tribes became dependent on the government payments—a dependency intended to make them docile in treaty negotiations. It also furthered assimilation by bringing them into the market system.

Indian Policy

Ever since the early days of European colonization, assimilation of Native Americans through education and Christianity had been an explicit goal. It took on renewed urgency as the United States expanded westward. In 1819, in response to missionary lobbying, Congress appropriated $10,000 annually for "civilization of the tribes adjoining the frontier settlements." This "civilization act" was intended to teach Indians to live like white settlers. Protestant missionaries administered the "civilizing fund" and established mission schools. In addition to English and the gospel, mission schools emphasized agriculture.

To settlers eyeing Native American land, assimilation through education seemed too slow a process. At any given time, there were never more than fifteen hundred students in all the schools; at that rate, it would take centuries to assimilate all the Indians. And Native Americans questioned the instruction. Some tribes found the missionary message repugnant. The Creek nation permitted the schools only after being assured that there would be no preaching. Zealous missionaries, however, violated the agreement, preaching to the Creeks and their black slaves. In response, a band of Creeks sacked the school.

It became apparent in the 1820s that neither economic dependency nor education nor Christianity could persuade Native Americans to cede much more land to meet the demands of expansionists. Attention focused on southern tribes—Cherokees, Creeks, Choctaws, Chickasaws, and Seminoles—because much of their land remained intact after the War of 1812 and because they aggressively resisted white encroachment.

In his last annual message to Congress in late 1824, President James Monroe suggested that all Indians be moved beyond the Mississippi River.

Indian Removal   Three days later, he sent a special message to Congress proposing removal. The southern tribes at which the program was aimed—the Cherokees, Creeks, Choctaws, and Chickasaws—unanimously rejected Monroe's offer.

Pressure from Georgia had prompted Monroe's policy. Most Cherokees and some Creeks lived in northwestern Georgia, and in the 1820s the state accused the federal government of not fulfilling its 1802 promise to remove the Indians in return for the state's renunciation of its claim to western lands. Georgia sought complete expulsion and was satisfied neither by Monroe's removal messages nor by further Creek cessions. Under federal pressure, the Creek nation ceded all but a small strip of its Georgia acreage in 1826. But Georgia's governor, George M. Troup, wanted all the Creek lands and sent surveyors to the one remaining strip. When President John Quincy Adams threatened to send the army to protect the Indians' claims, Troup countered with his own threats. Only the eventual removal of the Georgia Creeks to the West prevented a clash between the state and the federal government.

If "civilizing" Indians was the goal, no tribe met that test better than the Cherokees. Between 1819 and 1829, the tribe became economically self-sufficient and politically self-governing: during this

Cherokees   "Cherokee renaissance" the twelve to fifteen thousand adult Cherokees came to think of themselves as a nation and not a collection of villages. Between 1820 and 1823, the Cherokees created a formal government with a bicameral legislature, a court system, and a salaried bureaucracy. In 1827, they adopted a written constitution, modeled after that of the United States. Cherokee land laws, however, differed from U.S. law. The tribe owned all land, and complex provisions covered land sales (forbidden to outsiders). Nonetheless, the Cherokees assimilated American cultural patterns. By 1833, they held fifteen hundred black slaves whose legal status was the same as that of slaves held by southern whites. Moreover, missionaries had been so successful that the Cherokees could be considered a Christian community.

Although the tribe developed a political system similar to that of an American state, it failed to win respect or acceptance from southerners. Georgia pressed the Cherokees to sell the seventy-two hundred square miles of land they held in the state. Most Cherokees, however, preferred to stay where they were. Then Georgia annulled the Cherokee constitution, extended the state's sovereignty over the tribe, and ordered the tribal lands seized.

Backed by sympathetic whites but not by the new president, Andrew Jackson, the Cherokees turned to the federal courts to defend their treaty

Cherokee Nation v. Georgia

___

with the United States and prevent Georgia's seizure of their land. In *Cherokee Nation v. Georgia* (1831), Chief Justice John Marshall ruled that under the federal Constitution an Indian tribe was neither a foreign nation nor a state and therefore had no standing in federal courts. Nonetheless, said Marshall, the Indians had an unquestionable right to their lands; they could lose title only by voluntarily giving it up. A year later, in *Worcester v. Georgia,* Marshall defined the Cherokee position more clearly. The Indian nation was, he declared, a distinct political community in which "the laws of Georgia can have no force" and which Georgians could not enter without permission or treaty privilege.

But President Andrew Jackson ignored the Supreme Court's ruling, because it mandated action by Georgia, not the federal government. Keen to open up new lands for settlement, he was determined to remove the Cherokees at all costs. In the Removal Act of 1830, Congress provided Jackson with the funds he needed to negotiate new treaties and resettle the resistant tribes west of the Mississippi.

The infamous Trail of Tears had begun. The Choctaws were the first to go; they made the forced journey from Mississippi and Alabama to the West in the winter of 1831 and 1832 (see map). Other tribes soon joined the forced march. The Creeks in Alabama resisted removal until 1836, when the army pushed them westward. A year later, the Chickasaws followed. The Cherokees, having fought removal in the courts, found themselves divided. Some recognized the hopelessness of further resistance and accepted

Trail of Tears

___

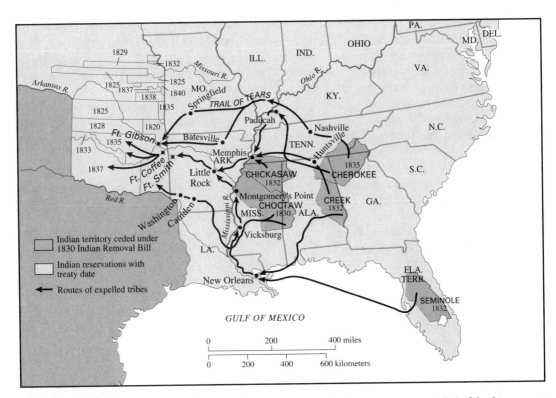

Removal of Native Americans from the South, 1820–1840 *During a twenty-year period, the federal government and southern states forced Native Americans to exchange their traditional homes for western land. Some tribal groups remained in the South, but most settled in the alien western environment.* Source: Acknowledgment is due to Martin Gilbert and George Weidenfeld and Nicholson Limited for permission to reproduce this map taken from *American History Atlas.*

removal as the only chance to preserve their civilization. The leaders of this minority agreed in 1835 to exchange their southern home for western land. But when the time for evacuation came in 1838, most Cherokees refused to move. President Martin Van Buren sent federal troops to round up the Native Americans. About twenty thousand Cherokees were evicted, held in detention camps, and marched to present-day Oklahoma under military escort. Nearly one-quarter died of disease and exhaustion on the Trail of Tears. When the forced march to the West ended, the Indians had traded about one hundred million acres east of the Mississippi for thirty-two million acres west of the river plus $68 million. Only a few scattered tribal remnants, among them the Seminoles in Florida and the Cherokees in the southern Appalachian Mountains, remained in the East and South.

The effect of the Trail of Tears on Native American life was drastic and disastrous. In the West, they encountered an alien environment: lacking generational ties with the new land, few felt at peace with it. The animals and plants they found there were unfamiliar. Native Americans no longer knew how to live off the land, and many became dependent on government payments for survival. Removal also brought new internal conflicts that would ultimately shatter Cherokee tribal unity. Finally, removal led to conflict between migrating tribes and western Indians and among migrants forced to share land and scarce resources.

In the Southeast, a small band of Seminoles successfully resisted removal and remained in Florida. Some Seminole tribal leaders agreed in the

Second Seminole War
———

1832 Treaty of Payne's Landing to relocate to the West within three years. A minority under Osceola refused to vacate their homes and fought the protreaty group. When U.S. troops were sent to suppress the intratribal war and impose removal in 1835, Osceola initiated a fierce guerrilla war against the federal troops. Although Osceola, who was captured under the white flag of truce, died in an army prison in 1838, the Seminoles continued the war. The army in turn attempted to exterminate the Seminoles. In 1842, the United States abandoned the removal effort. Most of Osceola's followers agreed to move

west to Indian Territory in 1858, but many Seminoles remained in the Florida Everglades, proud of having resisted conquest.

A complex set of attitudes drove whites to inflict removal on Native Americans. Most merely wanted the land and had little or no respect for the rights or culture of the tribes. Others were aware of the injustice but believed that Indians must inevitably give way to white settlement. Some, like John Quincy Adams, believed the only way to preserve Indian civilization was to remove the tribes and establish a buffer zone between them and white settlers. Others hoped to "civilize" Indians and assimilate them gradually into American culture. Whatever the source of white attitudes, their outcome was the devastation of Native American peoples and their cultures.

FREE PEOPLE OF COLOR

Free people of color also struggled for recognition and legal rights. Like Native Americans, they were involuntary participants in American society. Unlike Indians, however, they wished to partake fully in American life.

No black person was safe, wrote the abolitionist and former slave Frederick Douglass after the Philadelphia riot of 1849. "His life—his property—and all that he holds dear are in the hands of a mob." Between 1832 and 1849, five major antiblack riots had occurred in Philadelphia. Mobs stormed black dwellings and churches and set them on fire, killing the people inside. Such mobs could be made up of slave hunters seeking runaways but quite willing to kidnap a free black instead. Or they could represent civil authority: Cincinnati city officials, frightened by the growing black population, drove as many as two thousand blacks from the city in 1829 by enforcing a law requiring cash bonds for good behavior.

Under federal law, blacks' position was unclear. The Fifth Amendment specified that "no person shall . . . be deprived of life, liberty, or property, without due process of law." But eighteenth-century political theory defined a republic as consisting only of whites. Early federal legislation reflected the exclusionist thinking. Naturalization was limited to white aliens in 1790, and in 1792 the militia was limited to white male citizens. Moreover, Congress approved the admission to the Union of states that had constitutions that restricted the rights of African-Americans. After the admission of Missouri in 1821, every new state admitted until the Civil War banned blacks from voting. When the Oregon and New Mexico territories were organized, public land grants were reserved for whites.

In the North, African-Americans faced second-class legal status nearly everywhere. Many states barred free blacks or required bonds of $500 to $1,000 to guarantee their good behavior. Only in Massachusetts, New Hampshire, Vermont, and Maine could blacks vote on an equal basis with whites throughout the pre–Civil War period. In 1842, African-Americans gained the right to vote in Rhode Island, but they had lost it earlier in Pennsylvania and Connecticut. No state but Massachusetts permitted blacks to serve on juries; four midwestern states and California did not allow African-Americans to testify against whites. In Oregon, blacks could not own real estate, make contracts, or sue in court.

Exclusion and Segregation of African-Americans

Legal status was important, but practice and custom were crucial. Although Ohio repealed its law barring black testimony against whites in 1849, the exclusion persisted as custom in southern Ohio counties. Throughout the North, free people of color were either excluded from or segregated in public places. Hotels and restaurants were closed to them, as were most theaters and churches. Probably no practice inflicted greater injury than discrimination in hiring. Counting houses, retail stores, and factories refused to hire black men except as janitors and handymen. New England mills hired only whites.

Southern Free Blacks

Free people of color faced especially severe legal and social barriers in the southern slave states, where their presence was often viewed as an incentive to insurrection. Indeed, southern states responded to fear of mass rebellion by tightening restrictions on free blacks and forcing them out of small towns and interior counties. After the Nat Turner rebellion in 1831, the position of free blacks deteriorated even further. Within five years, nearly every southern state prohibited the freeing of slaves without legislative or court approval, and by the 1850s Texas, Mississippi, and Georgia had banned manumission altogether.

To restrict free blacks and encourage them to migrate north, southern states adopted elaborate "black codes." African-Americans, who provided most of the South's skilled labor, encountered licensing requirements and bans restricting work opportunities. Virginia and Georgia banned black river captains and pilots. Some states forbade blacks to assemble without a license; some prohibited them from learning to read and write. In the late 1830s, when the codes were enforced with vigor for the first time, free blacks began to move northward in growing numbers, although northern states discouraged the migration. Despite the obstacles, the free black population rose dramatically in the first part of the nineteenth century, from 108,000 in 1800 to almost half a million in 1860. Nearly half lived in the North, some in rural settlements, but far more in cities like Philadelphia, New York, and Cincinnati. Baltimore had the largest community, but sizable free black populations also existed in New Orleans, Charleston, and Mobile.

The ranks of free people of color were constantly increased by ex-slaves. Some, like Frederick Douglass and Harriet Tubman, were fugitives. Tubman, a slave in Maryland, escaped to Philadelphia in 1849 when it was rumored that she would be sold out of the state. Within the next two years, she returned twice to free her two children, her sister, her mother, and her brother and his family. Owners voluntarily freed other slaves. Some, like a Virginia planter named Sanders who settled his slaves as freedmen in Michigan, sought to cleanse their souls by freeing their slaves in their wills. Others freed elderly slaves after a lifetime of service rather than support them in old age.

Founding of Black Institutions

Free blacks founded strong, independent self-help societies as bulwarks against oppression. In every black community, African-Americans organized black churches, fraternal and benevolent associations, literary societies, and schools. More than half the black population in Philadelphia in the 1840s belonged to clubs and societies, and female benevolent societies and schools flourished. Their leaders believed that the mutual

CONSTITUTION

OF THE

AMERICAN SOCIETY

OF

FREE PERSONS OF COLOUR,

FOR IMPROVING THEIR CONDITION IN THE UNITED STATES;
FOR PURCHASING LANDS; AND FOR THE ESTABLISH-
MENT OF A SETTLEMENT IN UPPER CANADA.

ALSO

THE PROCEEDINGS OF THE CONVENTION,

WITH THEIR

ADDRESS

TO

THE FREE PERSONS OF COLOUR

IN THE

UNITED STATES.

PHILADELPHIA:
PRINTED BY J. W. ALLEN, NO 26, STRAWBERRY-ST.
1831.

How do historians know

about African-American political thought and activity in the early nineteenth century? One important source is the published minutes of the black conventions, first held in 1830.

Free people of color held at least eleven national conventions and about forty state conventions before the Civil War. The first national convention, a special meeting in Philadelphia in September 1830, presided over by Bishop Richard Allen, founder of the African Methodist Episcopal church, agreed to explore a settlement in Canada as a haven for free people of color and fugitive slaves. It also called for pursuing "all legal means for the speedy elevation of ourselves and brethren to the scale and standing of men."

Less than a year later, the "First Annual Meeting of the People of Colour" condemned the persecution of African-Americans, appealed for funds to support their work, called for the establishment of a college for poor blacks, and stressed the importance of education. The delegates were also self-consciously building a movement of annual conventions. This report, and the subsequent convention minutes and addresses, demonstrate the involvement of African-Americans in the reforms of the times and the stress they put on education and equality of opportunity. At later conventions in the 1850s, nationalism took hold among African-Americans.

The movement was democratic. Most communities elected their delegates to the national conventions at public meetings or at local and state conventions. Although the minutes reveal the wide range of opinion within black communities, they agreed on abolition of slavery, immediate emancipation, and equal rights for free people of color.

aid societies would encourage thrift, industry, and morality and thus equip their members to improve their lot. But no amount of effort could counteract white prejudice.

The network of voluntary organizations among urban free black men and women did provide a base for African-American protest. From 1830 to 1835, and irregularly thereafter, free blacks held national conventions with delegates drawn from city and state organizations. Under the leadership of the small black middle class, which included the Philadelphia sail manufacturer James Forten and the orator Reverend Henry Highland Garnet, the convention movement served as a forum to attack slavery and agitate for equal rights. Militant new black newspapers, such as *Freedom's Journal* (1827) and the *Weekly Advocate* (1837), joined the struggle.

The mood of free blacks began to shift in the late 1840s and 1850s. Many were frustrated by the failure of the abolitionist movement and angered

Black Nationalism
_____

by the passage of the Fugitive Slave Act of 1850. A rising tide of black nationalism stressed racial solidarity, self-help, and a growing interest in Africa. Before this time, efforts to send African-Americans "back to Africa" had originated with whites seeking to rid the United States of blacks. But blacks held emigrationist conventions of their own in the 1850s under the leadership of abolitionists Henry Bibb and Martin Delany. With the coming of the Civil War and emancipation, however, all but a few African-Americans lost interest in migrating to Africa.

The United States was a far more diverse and turbulent society in 1860 than it had been in 1800. The market economy, immigration, and the growth of cities had altered the ways people lived and worked. Economic growth not only created new jobs in towns and cities but also promoted clearer distinctions in wealth and status. Cities housed both ostentatious wealth and abject poverty, and disorder became commonplace.

In the midst of these changes, middle-class families sought to insulate their homes from the competition of the market economy. Many women found fulfillment in the domestic ideal, although others found it confining. Middle-class urban

women became associated with nurturing roles, first in homes and schools, then in churches and reform societies. Working-class women had more modest goals: escaping poverty and winning respect. Most Americans found some comfort in religion.

Famine and religious and political oppression in Europe propelled millions of people across the Atlantic. They were drawn to the United States by the promise of jobs and tolerance. Yet most found the going rough. In the process of adapting, immigrants changed the profile of the American people. Competition and diversity in turn bred intolerance. None suffered more painfully than Native Americans and free African-Americans, who were made to feel like aliens in their own land.

Conflict became increasingly commonplace in the public arena. The manifestations of division in America were many: utopian communities, conflicts over public space, backlash against immigrants, urban riots, black protest, and Indian resistance. Conflict also took the form of reform movements, which came to characterize American life from the 1820s through the 1850s. Through reform and political action, many Americans sought to harness and control the forces of change. Spurred on by religious revival and individualism, they turned to politics as a collective means of restoring harmony and order. In the process, divisions became even sharper.

SUGGESTIONS FOR FURTHER READING

Rural and Utopian Communities

Leonard J. Arrington and Davis Bitton, *The Mormon Experience: A History of the Latterday Saints* (1979); Priscilla J. Brewer, *Shaker Communities, Shaker Lives* (1986); John Mack Faragher, *Sugar Creek: Life on the Illinois Prairie* (1986); Steven Hahn and Jonathan Prude, eds., *The Countryside in the Age of Capitalist Transformation* (1985); Joan M. Jensen, *Loosening the Bonds: Mid-Atlantic Farm Women, 1750–1850* (1986); Anthony F. C. Wallace, *Rockdale: The Growth of an American Village in the Early Industrial Revolution* (1978); Kenneth H. Winn, *Exiles in a Land of Liberty: Mormons in America, 1830–1846* (1989).

Urban Communities and Inequality

Melvin A. Adelman, *A Sporting Time: New York City and the Rise of Modern Athletics, 1820–1870* (1986); Stuart M. Blumin, *The Emergence of the Middle Class: Social Experience in the American*

City, 1760–1900 (1989); Susan G. Davis, *Parades and Power: Street Theater in Nineteenth-Century Philadelphia* (1986); Timothy J. Gilfoyle, *City of Eros: New York City, Prostitution, and the Commercialization of Sex, 1790–1920* (1992); Elliott J. Gorn, *The Manly Art: Bare-Knuckle Prize Fighting in America* (1986); Carl Kaestle, *Pillars of the Republic: Common Schools and American Society, 1780–1860* (1982); Jack Larkin, *The Reshaping of Everyday Life, 1790–1840* (1988); Edward Pessen, *Riches, Class, and Power Before the Civil War* (1973); Christine Stansell, *City of Women: Sex and Class in New York, 1789–1860* (1986); Richard B. Stott, *Workers in the Metropolis: Class, Ethnicity, and Youth in Antebellum New York City* (1990); Stephen Thernstrom, *Poverty and Progress: Social Mobility in a Nineteenth-Century City* (1964); Alexis de Tocqueville, *Democracy in America*, 2 vols. (1835, 1840).

Women and the Family

Lee Virginia Chambers-Schiller, *Liberty, A Better Husband: Single Women in America: The Generations of 1780–1840* (1984); Nancy F. Cott, *The Bonds of Womanhood: "Woman's Sphere" in New England, 1780–1835* (1977); Hasia R. Diner, *Erin's Daughters in America: Irish Immigrant Women in the Nineteenth Century* (1983); Suzanne Lebsock, *The Free Women of Petersburg: Status and Culture in a Southern Town, 1784–1860* (1984); James C. Mohr, *Abortion in America: The Origins and Evolution of National Policy, 1800–1900* (1978); Mary P. Ryan, *Women in Public: Between Banners and Ballots, 1825–1880* (1990); Mary P. Ryan, *Cradle of the Middle Class: The Family in Oneida County, New York, 1790–1865* (1981); Robert V. Wells, *Revolutions in Americans' Lives* (1982); Barbara Welter, "The Cult of True Womanhood, 1820–1860," *American Quarterly* 18 (Summer 1966): 151–174.

Immigrants

Gunther Barth, *Bitter Strength: A History of Chinese in the United States, 1850–1870* (1964); Kathleen Neils Conzen, *Immigrant Milwaukee: 1836–1860* (1976); Arnoldo De León, *The Tejano Community, 1836–1900* (1982); Charlotte Erickson, *Invisible Immigrants* (1972); David A. Gerber, *The Making of an American Pluralism: Buffalo, New York, 1825–1860* (1989); Walter D. Kamphoefner, *The Westfalians: From Germany to Missouri* (1987); Walter D. Kamphoefner et al. (eds.), *News from the Land of Freedom: German Immigrants Write Home* (1991); Kerby A. Miller, *Emigrants and Exiles: Ireland and the Irish Exodus to North America* (1985); Stanley Nadel, *Little Germany: Ethnicity, Religion, and Class in New York City, 1845–1880* (1990); Harold Runblom and Hans Norman, *From Sweden to America* (1976); Philip Taylor, *The Distant Magnet: European Emigration to the United States of America* (1971); Mark Wyman, *Immigrants in the Valley: Irish, Germans, and Americans in the Upper Mississippi, 1830–1860* (1984).

Native Americans

Robert F. Berkhofer Jr., *The White Man's Indian* (1978); Grant Foreman, *Indian Removal: The Emigration of the Five Civilized Tribes of Indians*, rev. ed. (1953); John K. Mahon, *History of the Second Seminole War, 1835–1842* (1967); William G. McLoughlin, *Cherokee Renascence in the New Republic* (1986); Theda Perdue, *Slavery and the Evolution of Cherokee Society, 1540–1866* (1979); Francis P. Prucha, *American Indian Policy in the Formative Years* (1967); Ronald N. Satz, *American Indian Policy in the Jacksonian Era* (1975); Bernard Sheehan, *Seeds of Extinction: Jeffersonian Philanthropy and the American Indian* (1973); Anthony F. C. Wallace, *The Long, Bitter Trail: Andrew Jackson and the Indians* (1993); Richard White, *The Roots of Dependency: Subsistence, Environment, and Social Change Among the Choctaws, Pawnees, and Navajos* (1983).

Free People of Color

Ira Berlin, *Slaves Without Masters: The Free Negro in the Antebellum South* (1974); James Oliver Horton, *Free People of Color: Inside the African American Community* (1993); Luther Porter Jackson, *Free Negro Labor and Property Holding in Virginia, 1830–1860* (1942); David M. Katzman, *Before the Ghetto: Black Detroit in the Nineteenth Century* (1973); Leon Litwack, *North of Slavery: The Negro in the Free States, 1790–1860* (1961); Floyd J. Miller, *The Search for a Black Nationality: Black Colonization and Emigration, 1787–1863* (1975); Gary B. Nash, *Forging Freedom: The Formation of Philadelphia's Black Community, 1720–1840* (1988); Shirley J. Yee, *Black Women Abolitionists: A Study in Activism, 1828–1860* (1992).

13

Reform, Politics, and Expansion, 1824–1844

T HE TAPPAN BROTHERS, ARTHUR and Lewis, amassed a fortune in business but lived simple lives. They were not seen at the balls and elaborate dinners of the New York City elite. Instead, the brothers lived by their mother's Calvinist tenet that this world was preparation for the next. When the time came to submit their accounts to God, "luxurious living" and "vain show" would count against them.

Merchants and investors whose businesses included textile mills, an importing house, the *New York Journal of Commerce*, and the Mercantile Agency (the nation's first commercial credit-rating agency), the Tappans prospered with the expansion of the market economy. Although they did not indulge in luxuries, the Tappans nonetheless spent lavishly. Both contributed unselfishly to evangelical churches and missions, to temperance and antigambling societies, and to Bible printing and distribution. Disturbed by the wasteful habits of rural migrants and Irish Catholic immigrants, they considered education and self-improvement necessary preludes to assimilation.

The lives of the Tappan brothers and many like-minded reformers were changed by one compelling issue: antislavery. Drawn to abolitionism by their religious concerns and William Lloyd Garrison's calls for an immediate end to slavery, Arthur and Lewis Tappan became leaders of the religious antislavery movement. They deservedly earned their reputations as leading reformers in an age of reform.

The reform fervor of the 1820s to the 1850s was in part a response to the unsettling effect of the enormous transformation that the United States experienced after the War of 1812. Immigration, internal migration, urbanization, the spread of a market economy, growing inequality, loosening family and community ties, the westward advance of settlement, and territorial expansion all contributed to the remaking of the United States. Many Americans felt they were no longer masters of their own fate and that the changes in society were undermining traditional values.

Religious reformers like the Tappans sought to reimpose order on a society in which economic change and discord had reached a crescendo. Prompted by the evangelical ardor of the Second Great Awakening and convinced of their moral rectitude, they crusaded for individual self-improvement. Many renounced alcohol and gambling. Gradually, the personal impulse to reform led to the creation of benevolent and reform societies. Religious ardor drew men and women to reform, in time broadening democratic involvement. Reform soon eclipsed benevolent work and became an instrument for restoring discipline and order in a changing society. Women were prominent in the reform movement, and the role of women in public life became an issue.

Reform organizations eventually turned to government as an instrument of social and economic change. The line between social reform and politics was not always clear. Temperance, institutional reform, and, most notably, Antimasonry and abolition lured new voters into politics. Opponents of reform were no less concerned with social problems. What distinguished them from reformers was their skepticism about human perfectibility and their distrust of institutions and the exercise of power, both public and private. To them, coercion was the greater evil. They sought to reverse, not shape, change.

Two issues in particular served as bridges between reform and politics: the short-lived Antimasonry frenzy and the intense uncompromising crusade for immediate emancipation. Although Antimasons organized the first third-party movement, abolition eventually overrode all other concerns. No single issue evoked the depth of passion that slavery did. Politicians had recognized that slavery was a political powder keg, and they had adopted the Missouri Compromise of 1820 to avoid igniting it. Territorial expansion in the 1840s and 1850s, however, made slavery politically explosive.

The opponents of religious reform found a champion in Andrew Jackson and a home in the Democratic party in the late 1820s. Yet the Jacksonians too saw themselves as reformers; they responded to change by attempting to foster individualism and restore restraint in government. They opposed special privileges and the Second Bank of the United States. President Jackson believed that a strong federal government restricted individual freedom by favoring one group over another. In response, reformers rallied around the new

Whig party, which became the vehicle of humanitarian reform. Democrats and Whigs constituted the second party system, which was characterized by strong organizations, intensely loyal followings, energetic religious and ethnic competition, and popular bases among the electorate.

Both parties promoted westward expansion to further their goals during the economically prosperous 1840s. Democrats saw the agrarian West as an antidote to urbanization and industrialization; Whigs focused on the new commercial opportunities it offered. Expansion from coast to coast seemed to Americans to be the inevitable manifest destiny of the United States. Then race was added to the brew as the politics of territorial expansion and the antislavery movement boiled over in the 1850s and 1860s.

FROM REVIVAL TO REFORM

Religion was probably the prime motivating force behind organized benevolence and reform. A tremendous religious revival known as the Second Great Awakening galvanized Protestants, especially women, beginning in the late 1790s. The Awakening originated in small villages in the East, intensified after the War of 1812, then spread across western New York and continued to grow through the late 1840s. Under its sway, Christians in all parts of the country tried to right the wrongs of the world.

Revivals—the lifeblood of evangelical Christianity—won converts to a religion of the heart rather than the head. In 1821, New York lawyer Charles G. Finney, the father of modern revivalism, experienced a soul-shaking conversion that he interpreted as "a retainer from the Lord Jesus Christ to plead his cause." Using everyday language, Finney told his audiences that "God has made man a moral free agent." In other words, evil was avoidable—Christians were not doomed by original sin, and anyone could achieve salvation. The Second Great Awakening raised people's hopes for the Second Coming of the Christian messiah

Second Great Awakening

• *I m p o r t a n t   E v e n t s* •

1790s–1840s	Second Great Awakening spreads religious fervor
1820s	Reformers establish model penitentiaries
1825	House of Representatives elects John Quincy Adams president
1826	American Society for the Promotion of Temperance founded Morgan affair is catalyst for Antimasonry movement
1828	Protectionist Tariff of Abominations stirs nullification Andrew Jackson elected president
1830	Webster-Hayne debate explores nature of the Union
1830s–40s	Democratic-Whig competition gels in second party system
1831	*Liberator* begins publication First national Antimason convention
1832	Jackson vetoes recharter of the Second Bank of the United States Jackson reelected
1832–33	South Carolina nullifies the Tariff of 1832, prompting nullification crisis
1836	Republic of Texas established Specie Circular ends credit purchase of public lands Martin Van Buren elected president
1837	Financial panic ends boom of the 1830s
1838–39	United States and Canada mobilize militia over Maine–New Brunswick border dispute
1839–43	Hard times spread unemployment and deflation
1840	Whigs win presidency under William Henry Harrison
1841	Tyler assumes the presidency following death of Harrison Oregon fever attracts settlers to the Northwest and intensifies expansionism
1844	James K. Polk elected president
1845	Texas admitted to the Union
1848	Woman's Rights Convention, Seneca Falls, New York, calls for women's suffrage
1851	Maine adopts prohibition

and establishment of the Kingdom of God on earth. Revivalists resolved to speed the Second Coming by creating a heaven on earth, marshaling the forces of good and light—reform—to combat those of evil and darkness.

Regardless of theology, all shared a belief in individual self-improvement and self-reliance as forces for good. Thus the Second Great Awakening bred reform, and evangelical Protestants became missionaries for both religious and secular salvation. Wherever they preached, evangelists generated new religious groups and voluntary reform societies. Evangelical reformers organized an association to address each pressing issue—temperance, education, Sabbath observance, dueling, and later antislavery.

Collectively, the groups constituted a national web of benevolent and moral reform societies.

Women were the earliest converts to evangelism, and they tended to sustain the Second Great Awakening. Pious middle-class women in Rochester, New York, for instance, responded to Finney's prayer meetings by spreading the word to other women during the day while their husbands were away at work. Gradually, women brought their families and husbands into church and under the influence of reform. Women more than men tended to feel personally responsible for counteracting the increasingly secular orientation of the expanding market economy. Many

Role of Women

women felt guilty for neglecting their religious duties, and the emotionally charged conversion experience set them on the right path again.

Beyond conversion, the great influence of the Second Awakening was the spread of women's involvement in benevolent activities to ameliorate the growing social ills. In the larger cities, women responded both to their inner voices and to the growing inequality, turbulence, and wretched conditions around them. The poverty and vice that accompanied urbanization touched the hearts of women, especially those caught up in the fervor of revival. As early as the turn of the nineteenth century, most cities had women's benevolent societies to help needy women and orphans.

From Revival to Reform

Both female and male reformers sometimes acted in defiance of traditional political leaders. An exposé of prostitution in New York City illustrates the gulf between reform-minded men and women and the political establishment. In response to the report on how prostitution had taken hold in New York City, prominent businessmen and politicians united to defend the city's good name against "those base slanders." Reform-minded women, on the other hand, moved by the plight of "fallen women" and supported by the Tappan brothers, responded by organizing to fight prostitution. Whereas the male societies had made the prostitute the target, the new reform groups focused on the men who victimized young women. The newly organized Female Moral Reform Society, for example, publicized the names of men entering brothels in New York City.

The Female Moral Reform Society led the crusade against prostitution. New York based, the association expanded its activities and geographical scope during the 1830s as the American Female Moral Reform Society. By 1840, it had 555 affiliated female societies across the nation. They combated prostitution by focusing on men and by assisting poor women, whose economic desperation might lead them to turn to prostitution. They also entered the political sphere. In New York State in the 1840s, the movement fostered public morality by successfully crusading for criminal sanctions against men who seduced women into prostitution and against prostitutes.

As the pace of social change quickened in the 1830s and 1840s, so did religious fervor and efforts at reform. In western New York and Ohio, Finney's preaching acted as a catalyst to reform. Western New York experienced such continuous and heated waves of revivalism that it became known as "the burned-over district." The westward migration of New Englanders along the newly opened Erie Canal carried religious ferment as far west as Ohio. There, revivalist institutions—notably Ohio's Lane Seminary and Oberlin College—sent committed graduates out into the world to spread the gospel of reform. Their efforts stirred nonevangelical Protestants, Catholics, and Jews, as well as evangelical Christians. Reform-minded members of all these groups became involved in new grassroots political movements. In the late 1830s and 1840s, they rallied around the Whig party in hope of using government as an instrument of reform.

TEMPERANCE AND ASYLUMS

One of the most successful reform efforts was the campaign against the consumption of alcohol. Generally speaking, American men liked to drink. They gathered in public houses, saloons, and rural inns to gossip, discuss politics, play cards, escape work and home pressures, and drink. Respectable women did not drink in public, but many regularly tippled alcohol-based patent medicines promoted as cure-alls.

Why then did temperance become such a vital issue? And why were women especially active in the movement? Like all nineteenth-century reform, temperance had a strong religious foundation. To evangelicals, the sale of whiskey often involved a Sabbath violation, for workers commonly labored six days a week and spent Sunday at the public house drinking and socializing. Alcohol was seen as a destroyer of families. Temperance literature was laced with domestic images—abandoned wives, prodigal sons, drunken fathers. And in the new world of the factory, the habit of drinking could not be tolerated.

Demon rum thus became a prime target of reformers. As the movement gained momentum, their goal shifted from temperate use of alcohol to

Temperance Societies
——

voluntary abstinence and finally to prohibition. The American Society for the Promotion of Temperance, organized in 1826 to urge drinkers to sign a pledge of abstinence, shortly thereafter became a pressure group for state prohibition legislation. By the mid-1830s, more than one million people had taken the pledge, and the per capita consumption of alcohol underwent a sharp decline. From 1830 to the mid-1840s, the annual per capita consumption of alcohol fell from more than five gallons to less than two gallons. Furthermore, many northern states, beginning with Maine in 1851, prohibited the manufacture and sale of alcohol except for medicinal purposes.

Another aspect of the temperance movement was opposition to gambling. People who gathered at taverns to drink also gambled, and reformers believed that both vices undermined independence and self-reliance. Of special concern in the nineteenth century was the spread of lotteries.

English colonists had introduced lotteries at the turn of the eighteenth century. In the New World, lotteries were an effective way to sell costly

Lotteries
——

property in an age when few buyers could raise the purchase price. If hundreds of small investors participated in a lottery for the prize, a merchant could dispose of inventory or a homeowner could sell a valuable house. Local governments used lotteries to ease the tax burden by raising money for capital improvements. The Continental Congress had hoped to raise $1.5 million from a lottery to wage revolutionary war against England, but it failed to raise the revenue anticipated.

Lotteries became a target of reform, and between 1830 and 1860 every state in the Union banned them. Some people compared lotteries to such vices as slavery and alcohol. Others objected to the abuses inherent in the states' practice of delegating their lottery powers to private sponsors. An 1831 Pennsylvania investigation, for instance, revealed that a state-authorized lottery to raise $27,000 a year for internal improvements had generated enormous profits for the lottery company. On $5 million in annual sales, the state received its $27,000 and the sponsors $800,000.

The age of reform also brought about the construction of asylums and other institutions to house prisoners, the insane and ill, orphans, delinquent children, and the poor. Such institutions, reformers believed, would provide the victims of society's instability and turbulence with an environment of order, stability, and discipline, thus giving inmates opportunities to become self-reliant and responsible.

The penitentiary movement exemplified this outlook. In the 1820s, New York and Pennsylvania developed competing models for reforming

Penitentiaries
——

criminals. Both systems sought to remove criminals from evil societal and individual influences and to expose them to an ordered, disciplined regimen. It was widely believed that criminals came from unstable families in which lack of discipline and restraint led to vice and drink. Idleness was believed to be both a symptom and a cause of individual corruption and crime; thus the clock governed a prisoner's day, and idleness was banished.

Similar approaches were used in other kinds of asylums, from insane asylums and hospitals to orphanages and houses of refuge. Doctors attributed mental illness to the stress of urban life. Formerly, the prescribed treatment had been to remove disturbed individuals from their families and society and isolate them among strangers; they were often incarcerated with criminals. The new asylums removed them from society but attempted to impose discipline and order in a humane fashion. In response to the appeals of reform societies, states began in the 1830s to erect asylums for the insane in tranquil rural settings, away from the turbulent cities.

ANTIMASONRY

Far more intense than the asylum movement, although of shorter duration, was the crusade against Freemasonry, a secret middle- and upper-class fraternity that had come to the United States from England in the eighteenth century. Such sons of the Enlightenment as Benjamin Franklin and George Washington were attracted to Masonry, with its emphasis on individual belief in a deity (as opposed to organized religion) and on brotherhood (as opposed to one church). In the early nineteenth century, Freemasonry attracted many commercial and political leaders.

Opponents of Masonry charged that the order's secrecy was antidemocratic and antirepublican, as were its elite membership and its use of regalia and such offices as "knight" and "priest." As church leaders took up the moral crusade against Masonry, evangelicals labeled the order satanic. Antimasons argued that Masonry threatened the family, because it excluded women and encouraged men to neglect their families for alcohol and ribald entertainments at Masonic lodges.

The Antimasonry movement arose overnight in the burned-over district of western New York in 1826 and virtually disappeared in the 1830s. Foreshadowing abolitionism, it became more of a political than a reform movement. Antimasonry created the first third-party movement and drew new white voters into politics at a time when male suffrage was being extended. Antimasons sought to liberate society from the grip of what they considered a powerful and antirepublican secret fraternity. The political arena quickly absorbed Antimasonry, and its short life illustrates the close association of politics and reform between the 1820s and the 1840s.

The catalyst for Antimasonry as an organized movement was an incident known as the Morgan affair. In 1826, William Morgan, a disillusioned **Morgan Affair** Mason, published an exposé of Masonry, to which his printer David Miller added a scathing attack on the order. Just before the book appeared, a group of Masons abducted Morgan in Canandaigua, New York. It was widely believed that they killed Morgan, whose body was never found.

Events seem to confirm the Antimasonry crusade's characterization of Masonry as a secret conspiracy. Many officeholders in western New York, especially prosecutors, were Masons, and they appeared to obstruct the investigation of Morgan's abduction. The public pressed for justice, and the series of notorious trials that ensued from 1827 through 1831 led many to suspect a conspiracy. The cover-up became as much of an issue as distrust of Masonry itself, and the movement spread from the burned-over district to other states.

As a moral crusade, Antimasonry spilled over into the political arena almost immediately. The issue was political, because of the perceived obstruction of justice. Furthermore, Antimasonry attracted the lower and middle classes, pitting them against higher-status Masons and exploiting the general public's distrust and envy of local political leaders.

Unwittingly, the Masons stoked the fires of Antimasonry. Their silence seemed to condone the disappearance of Morgan. When newspaper editors who were Masons ignored the crusade against Masonry, the Antimasons founded their own newspapers. The conflict aroused a high level of public interest in politics. Wherever religious fervor flared and wherever families were entering the market economy for the first time, Antimasonry flourished.

As Antimasonry won a wider popular following, it introduced the convention system in place of caucuses for choosing political candidates. Invoking public morality and republican **Convention System** principles, the Antimasons held conventions in 1827 to oppose Masons running for public office. The next year, the conventions supported the National Republican candidate, John Quincy Adams, and opposed Andrew Jackson because he was a Mason. The Antimasons held the first national political convention in Baltimore in 1831 and a year later nominated William Wirt as their presidential candidate. Thus the Antimasons became a rallying point for those opposed to President Andrew Jackson.

By the mid-1830s, however, Antimasonry had lost momentum as a moral and political movement. A single-issue party, it declined along with Freemasonry. Yet the movement left its mark on the politics of the era. It inspired broad participation in the political process. The revivalist and reform impulses in movements like Antimasonry stimulated conflicts over values and ideology that were in turn reinforced by conflicts about class, religion, and status. The differences helped to polarize politics

How do historians know

about the activities of abolitionists, especially women and black abolitionists?

Abolitionists lived open lives. They used newspapers, pamphlets, speeches, and sermons to expose the evils of slavery, to mount a crusade for emancipation, and to build a network of like-minded people. Most of their speeches and even correspondence were printed in the pages of the abolitionist newspapers.

William Lloyd Garrison's Liberator, *which appeared from 1831 to 1866, recorded the weekly activities of immediatist abolitionists. The newspaper printed*

passionate attacks on slavery, reported meetings of anti-slavery societies, and published letters, especially from women and African-American abolitionists. Under the banners "No Union with Slaveholders" and "The United States Constitution is a 'covenant with death, and an agreement with hell,'" the Liberator *circulated to abolitionists advocating immediate emancipation. Throughout most of its history, a majority of its subscribers were probably African-Americans.*   Photo: David M. Katzman.

and to shape political parties as organizations to express those differences. Furthermore, the Antimasons contributed to party development more concretely by pioneering the convention system and stimulating grassroots involvement.

ABOLITIONISM AND THE WOMEN'S MOVEMENT

The issue of slavery eventually became so compelling that it consumed all other reforms. Passions would become so heated that they would threaten the nation itself. Those who advocated immediate emancipation saw slavery as, above all, a moral issue—evidence of the sinfulness of the American nation.

Before the 1830s, few whites advocated the immediate abolition of slavery. Some, most notably the Quakers, hoped that moral suasion would convince slaveholders to free their chattels. Others favored gradual abolition coupled with the resettling of former slaves in Africa. The American Colonization Society had been founded in 1816 with this in mind.

Only African-Americans demanded an immediate end to slavery. By 1830, there were at least fifty black abolitionist societies in urban African-American communities. The

Black Abolitionists

associations assisted fugitive slaves, lobbied for emancipation, exposed the evils of slavery, and reminded the nation that its mission as defined in the Declaration of Independence remained unfulfilled. A free black press helped to spread the word. Black abolitionists Frederick Douglass, Sojourner Truth, and Harriet Tubman then joined forces in the 1840s with white reformers in the American Anti-Slavery Society. Their militant and unrelenting campaign also won European support.

In the 1830s, a small minority of white reformers resolved to crusade for immediate emancipation. The most prominent and uncompromising immediatist, although far from the most representative, was William Lloyd Garrison. Recruited to the abolitionist cause in 1828 by Benjamin Lundy, a gradualist, Garrison broke with the moderate abolitionists in 1831. That year, contributions from the Tappan brothers and others helped him publish the first issue of the *Liberator*, which was to be his major weapon against slavery for thirty-five years. As he declared in the first issue, "I am in earnest—I will not equivocate—I will not excuse—I will not retreat a single inch—*and I will be heard.*" Garrison's staunch refusal to work with anyone who even indirectly tolerated delay of emancipation isolated him from most people who opposed or disliked slavery. Still, through sheer rhetorical power, Garrison helped to make antislavery a national issue.

William Lloyd Garrison

Most benevolent workers and reformers kept their distance from the immediatists. Many regarded the intensity of the immediatist approach as unchristian behavior. Although they shared the view that slavery was a sin, they believed that it had to be eradicated slowly, in a reasonable and patient manner. If they moved too fast, attacking sinners too harshly or interfering too aggressively in time-honored customs and beliefs, they would destroy the harmony and order they sought to bring about through benevolent and reform work.

Immediatists

Immediatists' greatest recruitment successes came about from defending their own constitutional and natural rights, not those of slaves. Wherever they went, immediatists found their civil rights at risk, especially their right of free speech. Antislavery speakers often faced hostile crowds, and their presses were under constant threat of attack.

At Utica, New York, merchants and professionals broke up the state Anti-Slavery Convention in 1835. Abolitionist conventions provoked hostility by welcoming both whites and blacks and by allowing women prominent roles. Fear and hatred moved proslavery proponents to take to the streets. In 1837, a mob in Alton, Illinois, killed the abolitionist editor Elijah P. Lovejoy. Public outrage at Lovejoy's slaying broadened the base of antislavery support in the North. Southern mobs seized and destroyed much of the propaganda mailed by the American Anti-Slavery Society (organized by the immediatists in 1833), and the state of South Carolina (with the approval of the U.S. postmaster general) intercepted and burned abolitionist literature that entered the state.

The opposition saw danger in abolitionism. Former Federalist Harrison Gray Otis portrayed abolitionists as subversives at a rally in Boston's Faneuil Hall in 1835. The abolitionists, he predicted, would soon turn to politics, causing unforeseeable calamity. "What will become of the union?" Otis asked. Others believed that the immediatists' opposition to black emigration undermined the best solution. Keeping blacks in America, they believed, would eventually lead to slave rebellions and racial amalgamation.

Another confrontation focused on Congress. Abolitionists, exercising their constitutional right to petition Congress, mounted a campaign to abolish slavery and the slave trade in the District of Columbia. Congress responded in 1836 by adopting the so-called gag rule, which automatically tabled abolitionist petitions, effectively preventing debate on them. In a dramatic defense of the right of petition, former president John Quincy Adams, a Massachusetts representative, took to the floor repeatedly to defy the gag rule and eventually succeeded in getting it repealed in 1844.

Gag Rule

Frustration with the federal government also fed northern support for antislavery. Generally speaking, politicians and government officials sought to avoid the question of slavery. The Missouri Compromise of 1820 had been an effort to make debate on the slave or free status of new states unnecessary. Censorship of the mails and the gag rule also represented attempts to keep the issue out of the political arena. Yet the more intensely national leaders, especially Democrats, worked to avoid the matter, the more they hardened the resolve of the antislavery forces.

The unlawful, violent, and obstructionist tactics used by opponents of abolition helped unify the movement by forcing the various factions to work together for mutual defense. Antislavery was not at the outset a unified movement. It was splintered and factionalized, and its adherents fought each other as doggedly and as often as they fought the defenders of slavery. They were divided over Garrison's emphasis on "moral suasion" versus the more practical political approach of James G. Birney, the Liberty party's candidate for president in 1844. They split over support of other reforms, especially the rights of women. And they disagreed about the place of free people of color in American society.

Women had less success when it came to their own position in society. At its inception, the American Anti-Slavery Society resembled most other benevolent societies in that

Women Abolitionists

women were in a subordinate role. Over time, the pattern changed. By the late 1840s, female abolitionists were breaking free of the domestic sphere—many were single women—and becoming genuine colleagues to men in the movement. Men like Garrison came to accept their women colleagues' contributions in providing moral direction. Lydia Maria Child, Maria Chapman, and Lucretia Mott all joined the American Anti-Slavery Society's executive committee; Child edited its official organ, the *National Anti-Slavery Standard*, from 1841 to 1843, and Chapman coedited it from 1844 until 1848. Many more women joined local female antislavery societies.

Negative reaction to the growing involvement of women in reform movements led some women to reexamine their position in society. In 1837, two antislavery lecturers, Angelina and Sarah Grimké, became particular objects of controversy. Natives of Charleston, South Carolina, they moved north in the 1820s to speak out more openly and forcefully against slavery, but they received a hostile reception for speaking before mixed groups of men and

Women played an activist role in reform, especially in abolitionism. A contemporary engraving shows women at an antislavery rally at Exeter Hall in 1840. Library of Congress.

women. The reaction turned the Grimkés' attention from slavery to the women's condition. The two attacked the concept of "subordination to man," insisting that men and women had the "same rights and same duties." Sarah Grimké's *Letters on the Condition of Women and the Equality of the Sexes* (1838) and her sister's *Letters to Catharine E. Beecher* (1838) were the opening volleys in the long war over the legal and social inequality of women.

Unlike other reform movements, which succeeded in building a broad base of individual and organizational support, the movement for women's rights was limited.

Women's Rights

The Woman's Rights Convention held at Seneca Falls, New York, in 1848—organized by Elizabeth Cady Stanton and Lucretia Mott—issued a much published indictment of the injustices suffered by women. Echoing the 1776 Declaration of Independence, the Seneca Falls Declaration of Sentiments asserted that "We hold these truths to be self-evident: that all men and women are created equal." The declaration documented the record of male tyranny over women and the inequalities and indignities that women suffered at the hands of government and the law. If women had the vote, the early advocates of women's rights argued, they could protect themselves and realize their potential as moral and spiritual leaders. Some men joined the ranks, notably Garrison and ex-slave Frederick Douglass, but most were actively opposed.

JACKSONIANISM AND THE BEGINNINGS OF MODERN PARTY POLITICS

The distinction between reform and politics began to erode in the 1820s as reform pushed its way into politics. No less than reformers, politicians also sought to control the direction of change in the expanding nation. After a brief flirtation with single-party politics following the War of 1812, the United States entered a period of intense and heated political competition. By the 1830s, politics had become the great nineteenth-century American pastime.

The election of 1824, in which John Quincy Adams and Andrew Jackson faced off for the first time, heralded a new, more open political system.

End of the Caucus System

From 1800 through 1820, the system whereby a congressional caucus chose Jefferson, Madison, and Monroe as the Republican nominees had worked well. Such a system limited voter involvement in choosing candidates, but this was not at first an anomaly, because in 1800 only five of the sixteen states selected presidential electors by popular vote. (In most cases, state legislatures selected the electors who voted for president.) By 1824, however, eighteen of the twenty-four states chose electors by popular vote.

The Republican caucus in 1824 chose William H. Crawford, secretary of the treasury. But other Republicans, emboldened by the opportunity to appeal directly to voters in most states, put themselves forward as sectional candidates. Secretary of State John Quincy Adams drew support from New England, and westerners backed Speaker of the House Henry Clay of Kentucky. Secretary of War John C. Calhoun looked to the South for support and hoped to win

Pennsylvania as well. And Andrew Jackson, a popular military hero whose political views were unknown, was nominated by resolution of the Tennessee legislature. Jackson had the most widespread support. By boycotting the deliberations of the caucus and by attacking it as being undemocratic, these men and their supporters ended the role of the congressional caucus in nominating presidential candidates.

Andrew Jackson led in both electoral and popular votes in the four-way presidential election of 1824, but no one received a majority in the electoral college (see map). Adams finished second, and Crawford and Clay trailed far behind. (Calhoun dropped out of the race before the election.) Under the Constitution, the selection of a president under such circumstances fell to the House of Representatives, on the basis of one vote to a state. Clay, who had received the fewest votes, was dropped; Craw-

President Andrew Jackson is portrayed here on a pendant and a cameo brooch, campaign paraphernalia from the 1820s that were mass produced and worn by partisan Jackson supporters. Museum of American Political Life, University of Hartford.

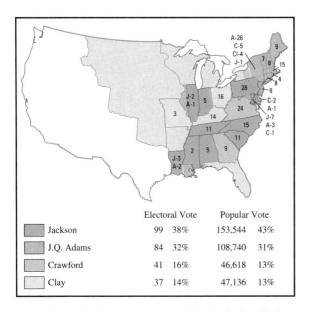

	Electoral Vote		Popular Vote	
Jackson	99	38%	153,544	43%
J.Q. Adams	84	32%	108,740	31%
Crawford	41	16%	46,618	13%
Clay	37	14%	47,136	13%

Presidential Election, 1824 Although Andrew Jackson led in both electoral and popular votes, he failed to achieve a majority of electoral college votes, and the House elected John Quincy Adams president.

ford, a stroke victim, never received serious consideration. The influential Clay, as Speaker of the House and leader of the Ohio Valley states, backed Adams, who received the votes of thirteen of twenty-four state delegations. Clay became secretary of state in the Adams administration—the traditional steppingstone to the presidency. With angry Jacksonians denouncing the arrangement as a "corrupt bargain" that had stolen the office from the clear front-runner, the Republican party divided. The Adams wing emerged as the National Republicans, and the Jacksonians became the Democratic-Republicans (shortened to Democrats).

The Jacksonians immediately began laying plans for 1828. After taking the oath as the sixth president, Adams proposed a strong nationalist policy incorporating Henry Clay's American System of protective tariffs, a national bank, and internal improvements. Adams believed the federal government should take an activist role not only in the economy but also in education, science, and the arts; he accordingly proposed a national university in Washington, D.C.

Brilliant as a diplomat and secretary of state, Adams was an inept president. He underestimated the lingering effects of the Panic of 1819 and the resulting bitter opposition to a national bank and protective tariffs. Meanwhile, supporters of Andrew Jackson sabotaged Adams's administration at every opportunity.

The 1828 campaign pitting Adams against Jackson was an intensely personal conflict. Whatever principles the two men stood for were obscured by mudslinging on both sides. A month after the election, Rachel Jackson died, and the president-elect attributed her death to the abuse heaped on him in the campaign. He never forgave her "murderers."

Jackson polled 56 percent of the popular vote and won in the electoral college by 178 to 83 votes. For him and his supporters, the will of the people had finally been served. Through a lavishly financed coalition of state parties, political leaders, and newspaper editors, a popular movement had elected a president. An era had ended, and the Democratic party became the first well-organized national political party in the United States. Tightly organized parties became the hallmark of nineteenth-century American politics.

Nicknamed "Old Hickory" after the toughest of the American hardwoods, Andrew Jackson was a rough-and-tumble ambitious man. He rose from humble beginnings to become a wealthy planter and slave holder. Jackson was the first American president from the West and the first born in a log cabin; he was a self-made man at ease among both frontiersmen and southern planters. Although given to violent displays of temper, he could charm away the suspicions of those opposed to him. He had an instinct for politics and shrewdly picked both issues and supporters.

Andrew Jackson
___

Jackson and his Democratic supporters offered a distinct alternative to the strong federal government advocated by John Quincy Adams. The Democrats represented a wide range of views but shared a fundamental commitment to the Jeffersonian concept of an agrarian society. They harkened back to the belief that a strong central government is the enemy of individual liberty, a tyranny to be feared. Like Jefferson, they favored

Democrats
___

limited central government. Jackson, symbol of the backwoodsman and the farmer, affirmed the familiar old values that predated the new party politics and the new market system.

Jacksonians feared the concentration of economic power as much as the concentration of political power. They saw government intervention in the economy as benefiting special interest groups and favoring the rich. Consequently, they sought to restore the independence of the individual—the artisan and the yeoman farmer—by ending federal support of banks and corporations and restricting the use of paper currency, which they distrusted.

Jackson and his supporters were also hostile to reform as a movement and an ideology. Reformers eager to turn their programs into legislation were calling for a more activist and interventionist government. But Democrats tended to oppose programs like educational reform and the establishment of public education. They believed, for instance, that public schools restricted individual liberty by interfering with parental responsibility and undermined freedom of religion by replacing church schools. Nor did Jackson share reformers' humanitarian concerns.

Jackson and the Jacksonians considered themselves reformers in a different way. By promoting restraint in government and emphasizing individualism, they sought to restore old republican virtues, such as industriousness, prudence, and economy. No less zealously than reformers, Jackson sought to encourage self-discipline and self-reliance and to restore a harmony and unity that he saw as having been disrupted by economic and social change.

Like Jefferson, Jackson strengthened the executive branch of government even as he weakened the federal role. Given his popularity and the strength of his personality, the concentration of power in the presidency was perhaps inevitable, but his deliberate policy of combining the roles of party leader and chief of state centralized even greater power in the White House. Invoking the principle that rotating officeholders would make government more responsive to the public will, Jackson used the spoils system to appoint loyal Democrats to office. He removed fewer than one-quarter of the federal officeholders he inherited, but his use of patronage nevertheless strengthened party organization and loyalty.

Jackson stressed his rejection of elitism and special favors, rotation of officeholders, and belief in popular government. Time and again, he declared that sovereignty resided with the people, not with the states or the courts. Summoning the electorate's support, he confidently claimed to represent the people's will. In this respect, Jackson was a reformer; he returned government to majority rule. Yet it is hard to distinguish between Jackson's belief in himself as the instrument of the people and simple egotism and demagogic arrogance. After all, his opponents too claimed to represent the people.

Animosity grew year by year among President Jackson's opponents. Daniel Webster feared the men around Jackson; Henry Clay most feared Jackson himself. Rotation in office, they contended, corrupted government. Opponents mocked Jackson as "King Andrew I," charging him with abusing his presidential powers by ignoring the Supreme Court's ruling on Cherokee rights, by his use of the spoils system, and by his dependence on the Kitchen Cabinet. Critics challenged his claim of restoring republican virtue and inheriting the mantle of Jefferson. They charged him with recklessly and impulsively destroying the economy.

Jackson injected new vigor into the philosophy of limited government. In 1830, he vetoed the Maysville Road bill—which would have funded construction of a sixty-mile turnpike from Maysville to Lexington, Kentucky—on the ground that a federally subsidized internal improvement confined to one state was unconstitutional; such projects were properly a state responsibility. The veto undermined Henry Clay's American System and personally embarrassed Clay, because the project was in his home district.

THE NULLIFICATION AND BANK CONTROVERSIES

Soon Jackson had to face the question of the proper division of sovereignty between state and central government more directly. The slave South, especially South Carolina, was fearful of federal power. To protect their interests, South Carolinian political leaders articulated the doctrine of nullification, according to which a state had the right to overrule, or nullify, federal legislation. The act that directly inspired this doctrine was the passage of the protectionist 1828 Tariff of Abominations. In his unsigned *Exposition and Protest*, John C. Calhoun argued that, in any disagreement between the federal government and a state, a special state convention—like the conventions called to ratify the Constitution—should decide the conflict by either nullifying or affirming the federal law. Only the power of nullification, Calhoun asserted, could protect the minority against the tyranny of the majority.

In public, Calhoun let others take the lead in advancing nullification. As Jackson's running mate in 1828, he avoided publicly endorsing nullification and thus embarrassing the ticket; he hoped to win Jackson's support as the Democratic presidential heir apparent. Thus Calhoun presided silently over the Senate and its packed galleries when Senators Daniel Webster of New Hampshire and Robert Y. Hayne of South Carolina debated nullification in early 1830. The debate explored North-South frictions and the question of the nature of the Union. Although ostensibly debating Hayne, Webster aimed his remarks at Calhoun in depicting the nation as a compact of people, not merely of states. Webster, at the climax of his career as a debater, invoked two powerful images. One was the outcome of nullification: "states dissevered, discordant, belligerent; on a land rent with civil feuds, or drenched . . . in fraternal blood!" The other was a patriotic vision of a great nation flourishing under the motto "Liberty *and* Union, now and forever, one and inseparable."

Webster-Hayne Debate

Although sympathetic to states' rights and distrustful of the federal government, Jackson rejected the idea of state sovereignty. It was his strong belief that sovereignty rested with the people. As a committed nationalist and patriot, he was deeply loyal to the Union. Thus he shared Webster's dread and distrust of nullification. Soon after the Webster-Hayne debate, the president made his position clear at a Jefferson Day dinner with the toast "Our Federal Union, it *must* and *shall be* preserved." Calhoun,

when his turn came, toasted: "The Federal Union—next to our liberty the most dear."

South Carolina invoked the theory of nullification against the Tariff of 1832, which reduced some duties but retained high taxes on imported iron, cottons, and woolens. Although a majority of southern representatives supported the new tariff, South Carolinians refused to go along. In their eyes, the constitutional right to control their own destiny had been sacrificed to the demands of northern industrialists. More than the tariff, they feared the consequences of accepting such an act; it could set a precedent for congressional legislation on slavery. In November 1832, a South Carolina state convention nullified the tariff, making it unlawful for officials to collect duties in the state.

Nullification Crisis

Old Hickory responded with toughness. In December, Jackson issued his own proclamation nullifying nullification. He moved troops to federal forts in South Carolina and prepared U.S. marshals to collect the required duties. At Jackson's request, Congress passed the Force Act, which gave Jackson renewed authority to call up troops but also offered a way to avoid using force by collecting duties before arriving ships reached South Carolina. At the same time, Jackson extended an olive branch by recommending tariff reductions. Calhoun, disturbed by South Carolina's drift toward separatism, resigned as vice president and was soon elected to represent South Carolina in the U.S. Senate. In that body, he worked with Henry Clay to draw up the compromise Tariff of 1833. Quickly passed by Congress and signed by the president, the new tariff lengthened the list of duty-free items and reduced duties over the course of nine years. Satisfied, South Carolina's convention repealed its nullification law. In a final salvo, it also nullified Jackson's Force Act. Jackson ignored the gesture.

The nullification controversy represented a genuine debate on the true nature and principles of the Republic. Each side believed it was upholding the Constitution. Neither side won a clear victory, although both claimed to have done so. It took another crisis, over a central bank, to define the powers of the federal government more clearly.

At stake was the rechartering of the Second Bank of the United States; its twenty-year charter expired in 1836. One of the bank's functions was to act as a clearing-house for state banks, keeping them honest by refusing to accept their notes if they had insufficient gold in reserve. Most state banks resented the central bank's police role—by presenting state bank notes for redemption all at once, the Second Bank could easily ruin a state bank. Moreover, with less money in reserve, state banks found themselves unable to compete on an equal footing with the Second Bank.

Second Bank of the United States

Many state governments also regarded the national bank, with its headquarters in Philadelphia, as unresponsive to local needs. Westerners and urban workers remembered with justifiable bitterness the bank's conservative credit policies during the Panic of 1819. Although the Second Bank served some functions of a central bank, it was a private profit-making institution, and its policies reflected the self-interest of its owners. Its president, Nicholas Biddle, controlled the bank completely. As an eastern patrician, Biddle symbolized all that westerners found wrong with the bank.

Although the bank's charter would not expire until 1836, Biddle convinced Congress to approve an early rechartering. This strategy, engineered by Clay, the National Republican presidential candidate, was designed to marshal public pressure either to force Jackson to sign the bill or to override his veto. The plan backfired when the president vetoed the rechartering bill and the Senate failed to override. Jackson's veto message was an emotional attack on the undemocratic nature of the bank. The bank thus became the prime issue in the presidential campaign of 1832, and Jackson used it to attack special privilege and economic power.

After his sweeping victory and second inauguration, Jackson moved in 1833 not only to dismantle the Second Bank of the United States but also to ensure that it would not be resurrected. He deposited federal funds in favored state-chartered ("pet") banks; without

Jackson's Second Term

federal money, the Second Bank shriveled. When its federal charter expired in 1836, it became just another Pennsylvania-chartered private bank. Five years later, it closed its doors.

In conjunction with this coup de grâce to the Bank of the United States, Congress passed the Deposit Act of 1836. Under this act, the secretary of the treasury designated one bank in each state and territory to provide the services formerly performed by the Bank of the United States. The act provided that the federal surplus in excess of $5 million be distributed to the states as interest-free loans beginning in 1837.

The surplus had derived from wholesale speculation in public lands: purchasers bought public land on credit, used the land as collateral to borrow more for additional acreage, and repeated the cycle. The banks providing the loans issued bank notes. Jackson, an opponent of paper money, feared that the speculative craze threatened the stability of state banks and worked against the interests of settlers, who could not compete with speculators in bidding for the best land.

In keeping with his hard-money instincts and his opposition to paper currency, President Jackson ordered Treasury Secretary Levi Woodbury to issue the Specie Circular. It provided that after August 1836 only specie—gold or silver—or Virginia land scrip would be accepted as payment for federal lands. By ending credit sales, it significantly reduced purchases of public lands and the budget surplus. As a result, the government suspended its loan payments to the states soon after they began.

Specie Circular

The policy was a disaster on many fronts. Although federal land sales were sharply reduced, speculation continued as available land for sale became scarce. The ensuing increased demand for specie squeezed banks, and many suspended specie payment (the redemption of bank notes for specie). Credit contracted further as banks issued fewer notes and gave less credit. In the waning days of Jackson's administration, Congress voted to repeal the circular, but the president pocket-vetoed the bill. Finally in mid-1838, a joint resolution of Congress overturned the circular. Restrictions on land sales ended, but the speculative fervor was over. The federal government did not revive loans to states.

From George Washington to John Quincy Adams, presidents had vetoed nine bills; Jackson vetoed twelve. Previous presidents believed that vetoes were justified only on constitutional grounds, but Jackson, as in the veto of the Second Bank of the United States, considered policy disagreement legitimate grounds as well. He made the veto an effective weapon for controlling Congress, because representatives and senators had to consider the possibility of a presidential veto in their deliberations on any bill. In effect, Jackson made the executive for the first time a rival branch of government, equal in power to Congress.

THE WHIG CHALLENGE AND THE SECOND PARTY SYSTEM

Historians used to call the 1830s and 1840s the Age of Jackson, and the personalities of leading political figures dominated their accounts of the era. Today, however, most historians view these years as an age of popularly based political parties and reformers. Only when the passionate concerns of reformers and abolitionists spilled over into politics did party differences become paramount and party loyalties solidify. Grassroots political groups, organized from the bottom up, set the tone of political life for the first time in American history.

Opponents of the Democrats found shelter under a common umbrella, the Whig party, in the 1830s. Resentful of Jackson's domination of Congress, the Whigs borrowed the name of the British party that had opposed the tyranny of Hanoverian monarchs in the eighteenth century. From 1834 through the 1840s, they and the Democrats competed on a nearly equal footing. They fought at every level—city, county, state, and national—and achieved a stability previously unknown in American politics. The organized political competition of this period—known as the second party system—resembled that of the first party system of Republicans and Federalists.

The two parties took different approaches to numerous fundamental issues during these years. Although both favored economic expansion, the Whigs sought it through an activist government and the Democrats through limited central government. The Whigs, for instance, supported corporate charters, a national bank, and paper currency; the Democrats were opposed. The Whigs also favored more humanitarian reforms than did the Democrats, including public schools, abolition of capital punishment, prison and asylum reform, and temperance.

Whigs were more optimistic than Democrats, generally speaking, and more enterprising. They had no objection to helping a specific group if doing so would promote the general welfare. The chartering of corporations, they argued, expanded economic opportunity for everyone, including laborers and farmers. The Democrats, meanwhile, distrustful of concentrated economic power and of moral and economic coercion, held fast to their Jeffersonian principle of limited government.

Interestingly, the basic economic issues of the era were not the key determinants of party affiliation. Instead, religion and ethnicity most influenced party membership. The Whigs' support for energetic government and humanitarian and moral reform won the favor of native-born and British-American evangelical Protestants in the North as well as the relatively small number of free black voters. Democrats, on the other hand, tended to be foreign-born Catholics and nonevangelical Protestants, both of whom preferred to keep religious and secular affairs separate.

The Whig party thus became the vehicle of revivalist Protestantism. The membership rolls of reform societies overlapped those of the party in many locales. Indeed, Whigs practiced a kind of political revivalism. Their rallies resembled camp meetings, their speeches employed evangelical rhetoric, their programs embodied the perfectionist beliefs of reformers.

Whigs and Reformers

In their appeal to evangelicals, the Whigs alienated members of other faiths. The evangelicals' ideal Christian state had no room for Catholics, Mormons, Unitarians, Universalists, or religious freethinkers. These groups opposed Sabbath laws and temperance legislation in particular and state interference in moral and religious questions in general. As a result, more than 95 percent of Irish Catholics, 90 percent of Reformed Dutch, and 80 percent of German Catholics voted Democratic.

Vice President Martin Van Buren, hand picked by Jackson, headed the Democratic ticket in the presidential election of 1836. The Whigs, who in 1836 had not yet coalesced into a national party, entered three sectional candidates: Daniel Webster of New England, Hugh White of the South, and William Henry Harrison of the West. By splintering the vote, they hoped to throw the election into the House, but Van Buren comfortably captured the electoral college, although he had only a 25,000-vote edge out of a total of 1.5 million votes cast.

Van Buren took office just weeks before the American credit system collapsed. In response to the effect of the Specie Circular, New York banks

Martin Van Buren and Hard Times
——

stopped redeeming paper currency with gold in mid-1837. Soon all banks suspended payments in hard coin. Thus began a cycle that led to curtailment of bank loans and reduced business confidence. The credit contraction only made things worse; after a brief recovery, hard times persisted from 1839 until 1843.

Ill-advisedly, Van Buren followed Jackson's hard-money policies. He curtailed federal spending, which caused prices to drop further, and opposed a national bank, which would have expanded credit. Even worse, Van Buren proposed a new regional treasury system for government deposits, replacing banks. The proposed treasury branches would accept and pay out only gold and silver coin; they would not accept paper currency or checks drawn on state banks. Van Buren's independent treasury bill passed in 1840. By creating a constant demand for hard coin, it deprived banks of gold and further accelerated the deflation of prices.

With the nation in the grip of hard times, the Whigs prepared confidently for the election of 1840. The Democrats renominated President Van

Election of 1840
——

Buren at a somber convention. The Whigs rallied behind the military hero General William Henry Harrison, conqueror of the Shawnees at Tippecanoe Creek in 1811. Harrison and his running mate, John Tyler of Virginia, ran a "log cabin and hard cider" campaign, a people's crusade against the aristocratic president in "the Palace." Although he presented himself as an ordinary farmer, Harrison was descended from a Virginia plantation family. In a huge turnout, 80 percent of eligible voters cast ballots—Harrison won the popular vote by a narrow margin but swept the electoral college 234 to 60.

Unfortunately for the Whigs, the sixty-eight-year-old Harrison died within a month of his inauguration. Tyler, his successor, was a former Democrat who had left the party to protest Jackson's nullification proclamation, and in office he turned out to be more of a Democrat than a Whig. He consistently opposed the Whig congressional program, vetoing bills that provided for protective tariffs, internal improvements, and a revived Bank of the United States. The only important measures that became law under his administration were repeal of the independent treasury system and passage of a higher tariff. Two days after Tyler's second veto of a bank bill, the entire cabinet except Secretary of State Daniel Webster resigned; Webster, busy negotiating a new treaty with Great Britain, left shortly thereafter. Tyler thus became a president without a party, and the Whigs lost the presidency without losing an election.

Hard times in the late 1830s and early 1840s deflected attention from a renewal of Anglo-American tensions that had multiple sources: the North's

Anglo-American Tensions
——

commercial rivalry with Britain, the default of state governments and corporations on British-held debts during the Panic of 1837, rebellion in Canada, boundary disputes, southern alarm over West Indian emancipation, and American expansionism.

A major dispute with Great Britain emerged over the imprecisely defined border between Maine and New Brunswick. In the winter of 1838–1839,

Using many techniques of twentieth-century politics, General William Henry Harrison in 1840 ran a "log cabin and hard cider" campaign—a popular crusade—against Jackson's heir, President Martin Van Buren. The campaign handkerchief shows Harrison welcoming two comrades to his log cabin, with a barrel of cider outside. The Log Cabin, *a newspaper edited by Horace Greeley, was the voice of the Harrison campaign, and it reached eighty thousand partisans.* Handkerchief: New York Historical Society; Newspaper: Smithsonian Institution, Division of Political History, Washington, D.C.

Canadian lumbermen moved into the disputed area. Shortly thereafter, the citizens of Maine attempted to expel them. The lumbermen captured the Maine land agent and posse, both sides mobilized their militia, and Congress authorized a call-up of fifty thousand men. Ultimately, no blood was spilled. General Winfield Scott, who was dispatched to Aroostook, Maine, arranged a truce. The two sides compromised on their conflicting claims in the Webster-Ashburton Treaty (1842).

The border dispute prefigured the conflicts that were to erupt in the mid- to late 1840s over the westward expansion of the United States. With Tyler's succession to power in 1841 and a Democratic victory in the presidential election of 1844, federal activism in the domestic sphere ended for the rest of the decade, and attention turned to the debate over territorial expansion.

MANIFEST DESTINY AND EXPANSIONISM

Ever since the colonists first turned their eyes westward, Americans had been hungry for new lands with fertile soil, valuable minerals, and the chance for a new beginning. Agrarian Democrats saw the West as an antidote to urbanization and industrialization; enterprising Whigs looked to the new commercial opportunities the West offered. Southerners envisioned the extension of slavery and more slave states. Equally important was a fierce national pride and a desire to acquire western lands to secure the nation from external enemies. Finally, Americans idealistically believed that westward expansion would extend American freedom and democracy "to less fortunate people." In the 1840s, manifest

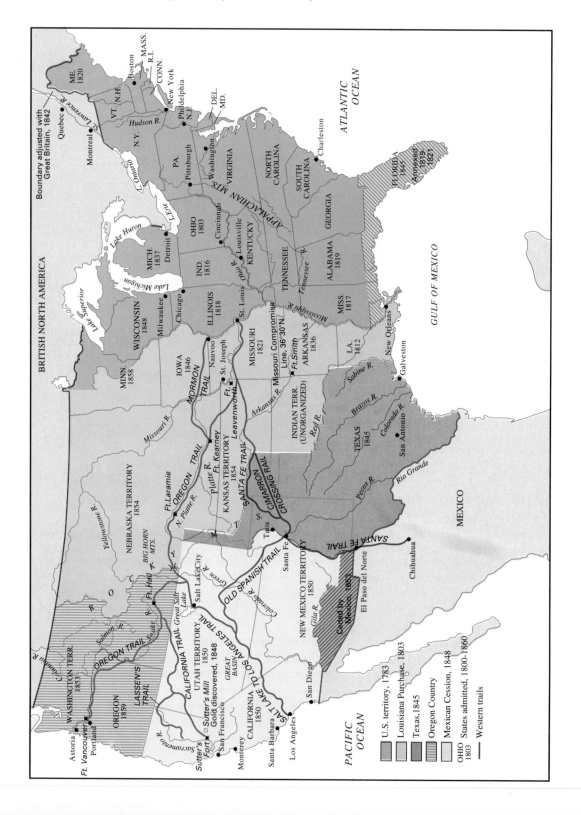

destiny—the belief that American expansion westward was inevitable, divinely ordained, and just—served the nation's expansionists (see map).

Manifest destiny was more than simply self-serving; it contained an undercurrent of racism. Native Americans were perceived as savages best confined to small areas in the West. Mexicans and Central and South Americans were also seen as inferior peoples, fit to be controlled or conquered. Thus the same racism that justified slavery in the South and discrimination in the North supported expansion in the West. Some also looked to expansion to solve the American race problem; free people of color, unwanted in the North and the South, could find refuge in distant territories.

Among the long-standing objectives of expansionists was the Republic of Texas, which in addition to present-day Texas included parts of present-day Oklahoma, Kansas, Colorado, Wyoming, and New Mexico.

Republic of Texas

This territory was originally part of Mexico. After winning its independence from Spain in 1821, the government of Mexico encouraged the development of these rich but remote northern provinces, offering large tracts of land virtually free to settlers called *empresarios*. The settlers in turn agreed to become Mexican citizens, adopt the Catholic religion, and bring two hundred or more families into the area.

By 1835, thirty-five thousand Americans, including many slave holders, lived in Texas. The new settlers ignored local laws and oppressed native Mexicans. When the Mexican government attempted to tighten control over the area, Anglos and Tejanos (Mexicans living in Texas) rebelled. At the Alamo mission in San Antonio in 1836, fewer than two hundred Texans made a heroic stand against three thousand Mexicans under General Antonio López de Santa Anna. When all the defenders of the mission died in the battle, "Remember the Alamo"

became the Texans' rallying cry. A few months later, Sam Houston's victory over Santa Anna in the Battle of San Jacinto gained Texas its independence.

Texas established an independent Lone Star republic but soon sought annexation to the United States. Sam Houston, the president of Texas, opened negotiations with Washington, but the issue quickly became politically explosive. Southerners favored annexing proslavery Texas; abolitionists, many northerners, and most Whigs opposed annexation. In recognition of the political dangers, President Jackson refused to recognize Texas and President Van Buren ignored annexation. Texans then began to talk about developing close ties with the British and extending their republic to the Pacific coast. President Tyler feared that a Texas alliance with the British might threaten American independence. He was also committed to expansion and hoped to build political support in the South by enlarging the area of slavery. But in a sectional vote, the Senate in April 1844 rejected a treaty of annexation.

To Texans, their War for Independence paralleled the American Revolution. Texans carried this banner of a lady of liberty, similar to images used during the American Revolution, in 1836. Archives Division, Texas State Library.

Westward Expansion, 1800–1860 *Through exploration, purchase, war, and treaty, the United States became a continental nation, stretching from the Atlantic to the Pacific oceans.*

Like southerners who sought expansion to the Southwest, northerners looked to the Northwest. "Oregon fever" struck thousands in 1841. Lured

Oregon Fever
———

by the glowing reports of missionaries, migrants organized hundreds of wagon trains and followed the Oregon Trail. The two-thousand-mile journey took six months or more, but within a few years five thousand settlers had arrived in the fertile Willamette Valley south of the Columbia River.

Britain and the United States had jointly occupied the disputed Oregon Territory since the Anglo-American Convention of 1818. Beginning with the administration of President John Quincy Adams, the United States had tried to fix the boundary at the forty-ninth parallel, but Britain refused. Time only sharpened the American appetite. In 1843, a Cincinnati convention of expansionists demanded the entire Oregon Country for the United States, up to its northernmost border of 54°40'. Soon "Fifty-four Forty or Fight" became the rallying cry of American expansionists.

Expansion into Oregon and the rejection of the annexation of Texas, both favored by antislavery forces, worried southern leaders. Anxious about

**Election
of 1844**
———

their diminishing ability to control the debate over slavery, they persuaded the 1844 Democratic convention to adopt a rule that the presidential nominee had to receive two-thirds of the convention votes. In effect, the southern states thus acquired a veto, and they used it to block Van Buren as the nominee; most southerners objected to Van Buren's antislavery stance and opposition to Texas annexation. Instead, the party chose House Speaker James K. Polk, a hard-money Jacksonian and avid expansionist from Tennessee. Henry Clay, the Whig nominee, believed the Democrats would provoke a war with Great Britain. He favored expansion through negotiation, not force.

With a well-organized campaign, Polk and the Democrats won the election by 170 electoral votes to 105. (They won the popular vote by just 38,000 out of 2.7 million votes cast.) Polk won New York's 36 electoral votes by just 6,000 votes; abolitionist

James G. Birney, the Liberty party candidate, had drawn almost 16,000 votes away from Clay, handing New York and the election to Polk. Abolitionist forces thus unwittingly brought about the choice of a slave holder as president.

Interpreting Polk's victory as a mandate for annexation, President Tyler proposed in his final days in office that Texas be admitted by joint resolution of Congress. Proslavery and antislavery congressmen debated the extension of slavery into the territory, and the resolution passed the House 120 to 98 and the Senate 27 to 25. Three days before leaving office, Tyler signed the measure. Mexico immediately broke relations with the United States; war was inevitable.

Religion, reform, and expansionism colored politics in the 1830s and 1840s. As the Second Great Awakening spread through villages and towns, the converts—especially women—changed American religion and organized to impose reform on a rapidly changing society. Claiming to personify republican values, reformers pursued perfectionism and republican virtue by doing battle with the evils of the growing cities, seeking to ban alcohol and gambling, and expanding education.

Once reform forced itself into politics, it generated a broader-based interest in politics that would remake the political system. The ensuing conflicts, and the highly organized parties that came into being during this era, stimulated even greater interest in campaigns and political issues. The Democrats, rallying around Andrew Jackson, and his opponents who found shelter under the Whig tent competed almost equally for the loyalty of voters. Both parties favored economic expansion, but their differences reflected fundamentally opposing world views. Whigs were more optimistic and favored greater centralized government initiative. Democrats, on the other hand, harbored a deep-seated belief in limited government.

Territorial expansion would provide the kindling for the firestorm that would overtake the United States in 1861. Manifest destiny, the admission of Texas, and debates over territorial expansion awaited a spark. Ultimately, one issue would rivet the attention of nearly all Americans and ignite the fire that would threaten to sever the Union: slavery.

SUGGESTIONS FOR FURTHER READING

Religion, Revivalism, and Reform

Michael Barkun, *Crucible of the Millennium: The Burned-Over District of New York in the 1840s* (1986); Clifford S. Griffen, *Their Brother's Keepers: Moral Stewardship in the United States, 1800–1865* (1960); Keith J. Hardman, *Charles Grandison Finney, 1792–1875: Revivalist and Reformer* (1987); Nathan O. Hatch, *The Democratization of American Christianity* (1989); Leon A. Jick, *The Americanization of the Synagogue, 1820–1870* (1976); Paul E. Johnson, *A Shopkeeper's Millennium: Society and Revivals in Rochester, New York, 1815–1837* (1978); Randolph A. Roth, *The Democratic Dilemma: Religion, Reform, and the Social Order in the Connecticut Valley of Vermont, 1791–1850* (1987); Timothy L. Smith, *Revivalism and Social Reform in Mid-Nineteenth Century America* (1957); Alice Felt Tyler, *Freedom's Ferment* (1944); Ronald G. Walters, *American Reformers, 1815–1860* (1978).

Temperance, Asylums, and Antimasonry

Paul Goodman, *Towards a Christian Republic: Antimasonry and the Great Transition in New England, 1826–1836* (1988); W. J. Rorabaugh, *The Alcoholic Republic: An American Tradition* (1979); David J. Rothman, *The Discovery of the Asylum: Social Order and Disorder in the New Republic* (1971); Ian R. Tyrrell, *Sobering Up: From Temperance to Prohibition in Antebellum America, 1800–1860* (1979); William Preston Vaughn, *The Antimasonic Party in the United States, 1826–1843* (1983).

Women and Reform

Catherine Clinton, *The Other Civil War: American Women in the Nineteenth Century* (1984); Ellen C. Du Bois, *Feminism and Suffrage: The Emergence of an Independent Woman's Movement in America, 1848–1869* (1978); Lori D. Ginzberg, *Women and the Work of Benevolence: Morality, Politics, and Class in the Nineteenth-Century United States* (1990); Elisabeth Griffith, *In Her Own Right: The Life of Elizabeth Cady Stanton* (1984); Nancy A. Hewitt, *Women's Activism and Social Change: Rochester, New York, 1822–1872* (1984); Mary P. Ryan, *Cradle of the Middle Class: The Family in Oneida County, New York, 1790–1865* (1981); Shirley J. Yee, *Black Women Abolitionists: A Study in Activism, 1828–1860* (1992).

Antislavery and Abolitionism

Frederick Douglass, *Life and Times of Frederick Douglass* (1881); George M. Fredrickson, *The Black Image in the White Mind: The Debate on Afro-American Character and Destiny, 1817–1914* (1971); Aileen S. Kraditor, *Means and Ends in American Abolitionism: Garrison and His Critics on Strategy and Tactics* (1967); Lewis Perry and Michael Fellman, eds., *Antislavery Reconsidered* (1979); Benjamin Quarles, *Black Abolitionists* (1969); Leonard L. Richards, *"Gentlemen of Property and Standing": Anti-Abolition Mobs in Jacksonian America* (1970); Ronald G. Walters, *The Antislavery Appeal: American Abolitionism After 1830* (1976); Bertram Wyatt-Brown, *Lewis Tappan and the Evangelical War Against Slavery* (1969).

Andrew Jackson and the Jacksonians

Lee Benson, *The Concept of Jacksonian Democracy: New York as a Test Case* (1964); Donald B. Cole, *Martin Van Buren and the American Political System* (1984); Michael F. Holt, *Political Parties and American Political Development from the Age of Jackson to the Age of Lincoln* (1992); Richard B. Latner, *The Presidency of Andrew Jackson* (1979); Edward Pessen, *Jacksonian America: Society, Personality, and Politics*, rev. ed. (1979); Robert V. Remini, *The Life of Andrew Jackson* (1988); Arthur M. Schlesinger Jr., *The Age of Jackson* (1945); Charles Sellers, *The Market Revolution: Jacksonian America, 1815–1846* (1991); Harry L. Watson, *Jacksonian Politics and Community Conflict: The Emergence of the Second American Party System in Cumberland County, North Carolina* (1981).

Democrats and Whigs

William J. Cooper, *The South and the Politics of Slavery, 1828–1856* (1978); Ronald P. Formisano, *The Transformation of Political Culture: Massachusetts Parties, 1790s–1840s* (1983); William W. Freehling, *Prelude to Civil War: The Nullification Controversy in South Carolina* (1966); Daniel Walker Howe, *The Political Culture of the American Whigs* (1979); Richard P. McCormick, *The Second American Party System: Party Formation in the Jacksonian Era* (1966); Merrill D. Peterson, *The Great Triumvirate: Webster, Clay, and Calhoun* (1987); Robert V. Remini, *Henry Clay: Statesman for the Union* (1991).

Manifest Destiny and Foreign Policy

John M. Belohlavek, *"Let the Eagle Soar!" The Foreign Policy of Andrew Jackson* (1985); Reginald Horsman, *Race and Manifest Destiny* (1981); Michael Hunt, *Ideology and U.S. Foreign Policy* (1987); David M. Pletcher, *The Diplomacy of Annexation: Texas, Oregon, and the Mexican War* (1973); William Earl Weeks, *John Quincy Adams and American Global Empire* (1992); Albert K. Weinberg, *Manifest Destiny* (1935).

Slavery and America's Future:
The Road to War, 1845–1861

CELIA WAS ONLY FOURTEEN when Robert Newsom bought her in 1850. Newsom, a sixty-year-old widower, lived on an eight-hundred-acre farm near Fulton, Missouri, with his two adult daughters. Almost immediately, he raped Celia and made it clear that he would continue to demand her sexual services. Newsom installed Celia in a small house only fifty yards behind his home. For the next five years, he visited her often, fathering two children. Newsom's two adult daughters and the neighbors knew what was happening but said nothing. He was a respected man, and these things happened.

In 1855, however, something else happened on the Newsom farm. Celia began a relationship with George, another Newsom slave. Moved by her own feelings and by George's insistence, Celia tried to end the relationship with her master. She appealed first to Newsom's daughters. They were troubled by Celia's story and by her threat to hurt Newsom, but they could do nothing to stop their father's behavior.

One evening in June 1855, Robert Newsom walked to Celia's door. When he brushed aside her objections to sex, she grabbed a club and struck Robert Newsom on the skull. As he sank to the floor, she struck him again. He never arose. Celia, panicked at having killed her master, proceeded to burn his body all through the night in her large fireplace. The physical evidence of Newsom's murder soon came to light. Her attorneys argued to no avail that laws against rape entitled her to defend herself. After a jury of twelve white men convicted her, Celia went to the gallows four days before Christmas.

By the time Celia was hanged, her drama was overshadowed by escalating violence in the territory of Kansas, where warfare had broken out between advocates and foes of slavery. Pro-slavery men, intent on spreading the peculiar institution and preserving a balance of free and slave states in the U.S. Senate, rode across the border from Missouri, stole elections, and physically attacked those who wanted Kansas to be free soil. Antislavery activists organized the New England Emigrant Aid Company to send opponents of slavery to Kansas. The passions aroused by slavery were intense, and in the 1850s they pulled Americans deeper and deeper into the maelstrom of conflict.

What brought these issues to center stage was territorial expansion. Between 1845 and 1853, the United States added Texas, the West Coast, and the Southwest to its domain and launched the settlement of the Great Plains. Each time the nation expanded, it confronted a thorny issue—should new territories and states be slave or free? The question spawned disagreements too extreme for compromise. A host of political leaders, including Henry Clay, Lewis Cass, Stephen A. Douglas, and Presidents Jackson and Van Buren, tried to postpone or resolve disagreements about slavery in the territories. Repeatedly, though, these disputes injected into national politics the bitterness surrounding slavery. Indeed, battles over slavery in the territories broke apart the second party system and then shaped a realigned system that emphasized sectional conflict. Sectional parties replaced nationwide organizations that had promoted compromise about slavery.

The ensuing political storms gave rise to a feeling in both North and South that America's future was at stake. The new Republican party charged that southerners were taking over the federal government and planning to make slavery legal throughout the Union. Republicans believed that America's future depended on the free labor of free men, whose rights were protected by a government devoted to liberty. Southern leaders defended slavery and charged the North with lawless behavior in violation of the Constitution. To these southerners, enslavement of blacks was the foundation of equality and republicanism among whites, and a government that failed to protect slavery was un-American and unworthy of their loyalty.

Not all citizens were obsessed with these conflicts. In fact, the results of the 1860 presidential election indicated that most voters wanted neither disunion nor civil war. Within six months, however, they had both. What had begun as a dark cloud over the territories became a storm engulfing the nation. Each section felt threatened by the other, and both believed that the future was at stake. The victorious Republican party and defensive southerners could not agree on desperate last-minute compromise measures, and, as a result, a vast civil war began.

CONFLICT BEGINS: THE MEXICAN WAR

Territorial expansion surged forward under the leadership of President James K. Polk. The annexation of Texas just before his inauguration did not weaken Polk's determination to acquire California and the Southwest, and he desired Oregon as well. The effective Polk achieved his goals, but he was unaware of the price in domestic harmony that expansion would exact. The expansion of the nation's boundaries had serious repercussions. It divided the Whig party, drove southern Whigs into a full embrace of slavery, and brought into the open an aggressive new southern theory about slavery's position in the territories. Expansion also sparked northern protests and proposals that generated further conflict between the sections.

Although his campaign supporters had threatened war with Great Britain to gain all the Oregon Territory, Polk as president found that diplomacy had its advantages. The annexation of Texas had outraged Mexican leaders, who severed relations with the United States. Aware that war with Mexico could break out at any time, Polk tried to avoid bloodshed in the Northwest, where America and Britain had jointly occupied disputed territory since 1818. Dropping the demand for a boundary at 54°40', he pressured the British to accept the forty-ninth parallel. In 1846, Great Britain agreed. In the Oregon Treaty, the United States gained all of present-day Oregon, Washington, and Idaho and parts of Wyoming and Montana.

Toward Mexico, Polk was much more aggressive. He ordered American troops to defend the border claimed by Texas but contested by Mexico and attempted to buy from the angry Mexicans a huge tract of land in the Southwest. When purchase failed, Polk resolved to ask Congress for a declaration of war. As he was drawing up a list of grievances, word arrived that Mexican forces had engaged American troops on disputed territory. American blood had been shed. Eagerly, Polk declared that "war exists by the act of Mexico itself" and summoned the nation to arms.

Congress recognized a state of war between Mexico and the United States in May 1846, but controversy soon arose. Public opinion about the war was sharply divided, with southwesterners enthusiastic and New Englanders strenuously opposed. In Congress, Whigs charged that Polk had "literally provoked" an unnecessary war and "usurped the power of Congress by making war upon Mexico." The aged John Quincy Adams denounced the war and a tall young Illinois Whig named Abraham Lincoln questioned its justification. Moreover, a small minority of antislavery Whigs agreed with abolitionists who charged that the war was no less than a plot to extend slavery.

These charges fed northern fear of the so-called Slave Power. Abolitionists had long warned of a Slave Power—a slave-holding oligarchy that controlled the South and intended to dominate the nation. The Slave Power's assault on northern liberties, abolitionists argued, had begun in 1836, when Congress passed the gag rule. Many white northerners, even those who saw nothing wrong with slavery, had praised John Quincy Adams's fight against the rule as a valiant defense of free speech and the right of petition. It was the battle over free speech that first made the idea of a Slave Power credible.

Idea of a Slave Power

Now the Mexican War fed fears of this sinister power. Antislavery northerners asked why the United States had abandoned claims to part of Oregon while undertaking a questionable war for slave territory. Northern opinion began to shift, but the influence of events on southern opinion and southern leaders was even more dramatic.

At first, many southern leaders criticized the war with Mexico. Southern Whigs attacked the Democratic president for causing the war, and few southern congressmen saw defense of slavery as the paramount issue. But no southern Whig could oppose it once slavery became the central issue. That happened in August 1846, when David Wilmot, a Pennsylvania Democrat, proposed an amendment, or proviso, to a military appropriations bill: that "neither slavery nor involuntary servitude shall ever exist" in any

Wilmot Proviso

territory gained from Mexico. His proviso did not pass both houses of Congress, but it immediately transformed the debate.

John C. Calhoun drew up resolutions about the territories that staked out a radical new southern position. According to the resolutions, the territories belonged to all the states, and the federal government could do nothing to limit the spread of slavery there. Southern slave holders had a constitutional *right*, Calhoun claimed, to take their slaves anywhere in the territories. This position, which quickly became orthodox for every southern politician, was a radical reversal of history. In 1787, the founders, in the Confederation Congress, had excluded slavery from the Northwest Territory. Article IV of the federal Constitution authorized Congress to make "all needful rules and regulations" for the territories, and the Missouri Compromise had barred slavery from most of the Louisiana Purchase. Now, however, southern leaders demanded protection for slavery.

In the North, the Wilmot Proviso became a rallying cry for abolitionists. Eventually, the legislatures of fourteen northern states endorsed it—and not because all its supporters were abolitionists. Like Wilmot, most white northerners were racists, not abolitionists. Wilmot's goal, for instance, was to defend "the rights of white freemen" and to obtain California "for free white labor." His fight was for "the sons of toil, of my own race and own color." Fear of the Slave Power, however, was building a potent antislavery movement that united abolitionists and antiblack voters. The latter's concern was to protect themselves, not southern blacks, from the Slave Power.

Meanwhile, events on the battlefield went well for American forces. The troops—as in previous wars, mainly volunteers furnished by the states—proved unruly and undisciplined, and their politically ambitious commanders often quarreled. Nevertheless, progress was steady. General Zachary Taylor's forces attacked and occupied Monterrey, securing northeastern Mexico (see map). Polk then ordered Colonel Stephen Kearny and a small detachment to invade the remote and thinly populated provinces of New Mexico and California. Taking Santa Fe without opposition, Kearny pushed into California, where he joined

• *Important Events* •

1846	War with Mexico begins Oregon Treaty negotiated Wilmot Proviso inflames sectional divisions
1847	Lewis Cass proposes idea of popular sovereignty
1848	Treaty of Guadalupe Hidalgo gives U.S. new territory in southwest Zachary Taylor elected president Free-Soil party formed
1849	California applies for admission to Union as free state
1850	Compromise of 1850 passed in separate bills
1852	Publication of *Uncle Tom's Cabin*, by Harriet Beecher Stowe Franklin Pierce elected president
1854	Kansas-Nebraska Act wins approval and ignites controversy Republican party formed Democrats lose ground in congressional elections
1856	Preston Brooks attacks Charles Sumner in Senate chamber

	"Bleeding Kansas" troubles nation James Buchanan elected president
1857	*Dred Scott* v. *Sanford* endorses southern views on race and territories Lecompton Constitution proposed; president supports it
1858	Kansas voters reject Lecompton Constitution Lincoln-Douglas debates attract attention Douglas proposes Freeport Doctrine
1859	John Brown raids Harpers Ferry
1860	Democratic party splits in two Lincoln elected president Crittenden Compromise fails South Carolina secedes from Union
1861	Six more Deep South states secede Confederacy established at Montgomery, Alabama Attack on Fort Sumter begins Civil War Four states in the Upper South join the Confederacy

forces with rebellious American settlers, led by Captain John C. Frémont, and a couple of U.S. naval units. A quick victory was followed by reverses, but American soldiers soon reestablished their dominance in distant California.

Because losses on the periphery had not broken Mexican resistance, General Winfield Scott carried the war to the enemy's heartland. From Veracruz on the Gulf of Mexico, he led **Treaty of Guadalupe Hidalgo** fourteen thousand men toward Mexico City. After a series of hard-fought battles, U.S. troops captured the Mexican capital and brought the war to an end. Representatives of both countries signed the Treaty of Guadalupe Hidalgo in February 1848. The United States gained California and New

Mexico (including present-day Nevada, Utah, and Arizona) and recognition of the Rio Grande as the southern boundary of Texas. In return, the American government agreed to settle the claims of its citizens against Mexico and to pay Mexico a mere $15 million.

The costs of the war included the deaths of thirteen thousand Americans (mostly from disease) and fifty thousand Mexicans, plus Mexican-American enmity that endured into the twentieth century. But the domestic cost was even higher. The slavery question divided southern Whigs from antislavery northern Whigs. President Polk tried to unify the Democrats by renouncing a second term and pursuing traditional Jacksonian economic policies, but even these steps did not prevent dissension in his party.

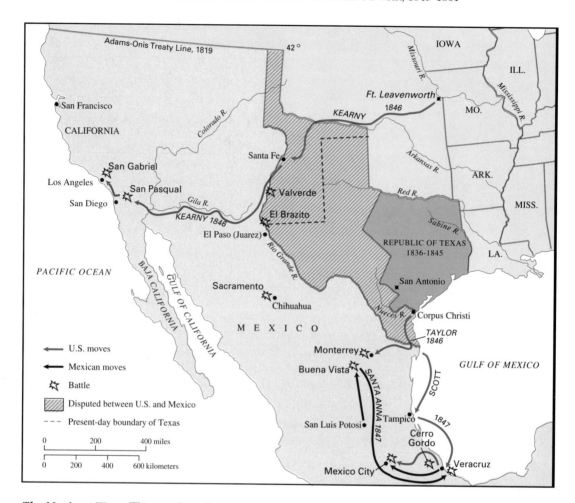

The Mexican War *This map shows the territory disputed between the United States and Mexico. After U.S. gains in northeastern Mexico and in New Mexico and California, General Winfield Scott captured Mexico City in the decisive campaign of the war.*

Slavery in the territories was the overriding issue in the presidential election of 1848. Both parties tried to push the question into the background,

Election of 1848 and Popular Sovereignty

but it dominated the conventions, the campaign, and the election. Seeking sectional balance, the Democrats nominated Senator Lewis Cass of Michigan for president and General William Butler of Kentucky for vice president. Cass devised the idea of "popular sovereignty" for the territories—letting residents in the territories decide the question of slavery for themselves. His party's platform de-

clared that Congress lacked the power to interfere with slavery and criticized those who pressed the question. The Whigs nominated General Zachary Taylor, a southern slave holder and the conqueror of Monterrey, with Congressman Millard Fillmore of New York as his running mate. Their convention similarly refused to assert that Congress had power over slavery in the territories. But the issue would not stay in the background.

Among northerners, concern over slavery led to the formation of a new party. New York Democrats committed to the Wilmot Proviso rebelled against Cass and nominated former president Van Buren. Antislavery Whigs and former supporters of the Liberty party then joined them to organize the Free-Soil party, with Van Buren as its candidate. This party, which adopted the slogan "Free soil, free speech, free labor, and free men," won almost three hundred thousand northern votes. Taylor polled 1.4 million votes to Cass's 1.2 million and won the White House, but the results were ominous. The North-South division in public opinion was deepening, and sectional issues were dividing both parties.

The conflicts of 1848 would dominate politics throughout the 1850s, as slavery in the territories colored every other national issue. The nation's uncertain attempts to deal with economic and social change gave way to more pressing questions about the nature of the Union itself. Soon, the second party system succumbed to the crisis over slavery and the future.

TERRITORIAL PROBLEMS ARE COMPROMISED BUT REEMERGE

The first sectional battle of the decade involved the territory of California. More than eighty thousand Americans flooded into California during the gold rush of 1849. With Congress unable to agree on a formula to govern the territories, President Taylor urged the settlers to apply directly for admission to the Union. The proposed state constitution submitted by California, however, prohibited slavery, and southerners objected. At a minimum, southerners wanted the Missouri Compromise line extended through California.

Henry Clay sensed that the Union was in peril. Twice before—in 1820 and 1833—Clay, the "Great Pacificator," had taken the lead in shaping sectional compromise; now he struggled one last time to preserve the nation. To hushed Senate galleries, Clay presented a series of compromise measures. In the weeks that followed, he and Senator Stephen A. Douglas of Illinois steered through Congress compromises balancing the issues of California and the nearby territories, the Texas boundary claim, fugitive slaves, and the slave trade in the District of Columbia. The problems to be solved were thorny

indeed, made more so by conflicting theories about settlers' rights in the territories. These theories proved most troublesome in the continuing debate over the territories.

Clay and Douglas hoped to avoid a specific formula and to preserve the ambiguity inherent in Lewis Cass's notion of popular sovereignty. Cass's idea possessed a vagueness that appealed to practical politicians. Like many others, Cass wanted Congress to stay out of the territorial wrangle. Ultimately, Congress would have to approve statehood for a territory, but "in the meantime," he said, it should allow the people living there "to regulate their own concerns in their own way." His few words, apparently clear enough, proved highly ambiguous.

When could settlers prohibit slavery? Southerners claimed that neither Congress nor a territorial legislature could bar slavery. Only when settlers assumed sovereignty under a state constitution could they take that step. Northerners insisted that Americans living in a territory could outlaw slavery at any time. To avoid dissension within their party, northern and southern Democrats had explained Cass's statement to their constituents in these two incompatible ways.

The cause of compromise gained a powerful supporter when Senator Daniel Webster committed his prestige and eloquence to Clay's bill. Yet even Webster's influence was not enough. After months of labor, when Clay and Douglas finally brought their legislative package to a vote, they met defeat. Then, with Clay sick and absent from Washington, Douglas reintroduced the compromise measures one at a time. Although there was no majority for compromise, Douglas shrewdly realized that different majorities might be created for each measure. The strategy worked, and the Compromise of 1850, as it was called, became the law.

Under its various measures, California became a free state, and the Texas boundary was set at its present limits. The United States paid Texas $10 million in consideration of the **Compromise of 1850** boundary agreement. The territories of New Mexico and Utah were organized with power to legislate on "all rightful subjects . . . consistent with the Constitution." A stronger fugitive slave law and an act to suppress the slave trade in the District of Columbia completed the compromise.

Jubilation greeted passage of the Compromise of 1850, but in reality, there was less cause for celebration than people hoped. Fundamentally, the Compromise of 1850 was not a settlement of sectional disputes; at best, it was an artful evasion. Rather than solve the problems, it merely postponed them. Furthermore, the compromise had two basic flaws. The first concerned the ambiguity of territorial legislation: what were "rightful subjects of legislation, consistent with the Constitution"? During debate, southerners said the words meant slavery would not be prohibited during the territorial stage; northerners declared that settlers could bar slavery whenever they wished. The compromise acknowledged the disagreement by providing for the appeal of a territorial legislature's action to the Supreme Court, but no such case ever arose.

The second flaw lay in the Fugitive Slave Act, which empowered slave owners to go to court in their own states to present evidence that a slave

Fugitive Slave Act

who owed them service had escaped. The resulting transcript and a description of the fugitive would then serve as legal proof of a person's slave status, even in free states and territories. Legal authorities would decide only whether the person brought before them was the person described, not whether he or she was indeed a slave. Fees encouraged U.S. marshals to assist in apprehending fugitives, and penalties discouraged citizens from harboring them. (Authorities were paid $10 if the alleged fugitive was turned over to the slave owner, $5 if not.) These provisions, in the eyes of some northerners, violated the basic American right to a trial by jury.

At this point, a book by a relatively unknown writer portrayed the humanity and suffering of slaves in a way that captured the sympathies of millions of northerners. Harri-

Uncle Tom's Cabin

et Beecher Stowe, whose New England family had produced many prominent ministers, wrote *Uncle Tom's Cabin* out of deep moral conviction. Her book, serialized in 1851 and published in 1852, conveyed the agony

slaves felt as husbands, wives, and parents. Stowe also portrayed slavery's evil effects on slave holders, indicting the institution more harshly than the southerners caught in its web. In nine months, the book sold more than three hundred thousand copies; by mid-1853, more than one million. Stowe brought home the evil of slavery to many who had never given it much thought.

The popularity of *Uncle Tom's Cabin* alarmed and appalled sensitive southern whites. In the territorial controversies and now in popular literature, they saw threats to their way of life. Behind the South's aggressive claims about territorial rights lay fear—fear that if nearby areas became free soil, they would be used as bases from which to spread abolitionism to the slave states. To defend slavery against political threats, southern leaders relied on Calhoun's territorial theories and on the familiar dogmas of states' rights and strict construction.

To protect slavery in the arena of ideas, southerners needed to counter indictments of the institution as a moral wrong. Accordingly, proslavery

Proslavery Theories

theorists elaborated numerous arguments based on partially scientific or pseudoscientific data. They discussed anthropological evidence suggesting separate origins of the races and physicians' views on the inferiority of the black body. Other proslavery spokesmen expounded the new "science" of phrenology, citing data on the external dimensions of human skulls and the volume of the cranial cavity that "proved" blacks were an inferior race. Yet in private and in their hearts, most southern leaders fell back on two rationales for slavery: the belief that blacks were inferior and biblical accounts of slave holding. Some, like Jefferson Davis, reverted to the eighteenth-century argument that southerners were doing the best they could with a situation they had inherited.

Antislavery denunciations troubled Davis, but he was far from despair in 1852. That year's elections gave him and other southerners hope that

Election of 1852

slavery would be secure under the administration of a new president. Franklin Pierce, a Democrat from New Hampshire, won an easy victory over the Whig presidential nominee, General Winfield Scott. Pierce had made no secret of his belief that the defense of each section's rights was essential to the nation's unity. And his strong endorsement of the Compromise of 1850 seemed to confirm national support for the compromise.

That interpretation of the election was, however, erroneous. Pierce's victory derived less from his strengths than from the Whig party's weakness. The Whigs were a congressional and state-based party that had never achieved much success in presidential politics. Sectional discord was splitting the party in two, and the deaths of President Taylor, Daniel Webster, and Henry Clay had deprived Whigs of the few dominant personalities they had. In 1852, the Whig party ran on little but its past reputation, and many predicted its demise.

In 1854, Pierce, who learned that a runaway slave named Anthony Burns was in custody in Boston, acted decisively to enforce the Fugitive Slave Act. He telegraphed local officials to "incur any expense to insure the execution of the law" and sent marines, cavalry, and artillery to Boston. When Burns's owner seemed willing to sell his property, the U.S. attorney blocked this solution and won a decision that Anthony Burns must return to slavery. U.S. troops marched Burns to the harbor through streets draped in black and hung with American flags at half mast. At a cost of $100,000, equivalent to roughly $2 million today, a single black man was returned to slavery through the power of federal law.

This demonstration of federal support for slavery radicalized opinion, even among many conservatives. Textile manufacturer Amos A. Lawrence observed that "we went to bed one night old fashioned, conservative, Compromise Union Whigs & waked up stark mad Abolitionists." Juries refused to convict some abolitionists who had stormed Boston's federal courthouse, and New England states passed personal liberty laws designed to impede or block federal enforcement. Where northerners saw evidence that the Slave Power was dominating American government, white southerners felt outrage over northern "faithlessness" to the Fugitive Slave Act.

Pierce seemed unable to avoid sectional conflict in other arenas as well. His proposal for a transcontinental railroad ran into congressional dispute over whether its location would be in the North or South. His attempts to acquire foreign territory stirred up more trouble. An annexation treaty with Hawaii failed, because southern senators would not vote for another free state, and Pierce's efforts to annex slave-holding Cuba angered antislavery northerners. Then another territorial bill threw Congress and the nation into a bitter conflict that was to have significant results.

TERRITORIAL PROBLEMS SHATTER THE PARTY SYSTEM

In 1854, Stephen A. Douglas, one of the architects of the Compromise of 1850, introduced a bill to establish the Kansas and Nebraska territories. As a senator from Illinois, Douglas hoped for a midwestern transcontinental railroad to boost Chicago's economy and encourage settlement of the Great Plains. A necessary precondition for such a railroad was the organization of the territory it would cross. Thus it was probably for the sake of railroad promotion that Douglas introduced a bill that inflamed sectional passions, finished off the Whig party, damaged the northern Democrats, gave birth to the Republican party, and thwarted his own ambitions for national office.

Kansas-Nebraska Bill

The Kansas-Nebraska bill exposed the first flaw of the Compromise of 1850—the conflicting interpretations of popular sovereignty. Douglas's bill left "all questions pertaining to slavery in the Territories . . . to the people residing therein," but northerners and southerners still disagreed violently about what territorial settlers could constitutionally do. Moreover, the Kansas-Nebraska bill opened another Pandora's box by repealing the Missouri Compromise of 1820. Douglas's bill, which became law in May 1854, threw land open to slavery where it had been prohibited (see map).

Northern reaction to the law was immediate and widespread. Abolitionists charged a sinister aggression by the Slave Power, and northern fears of

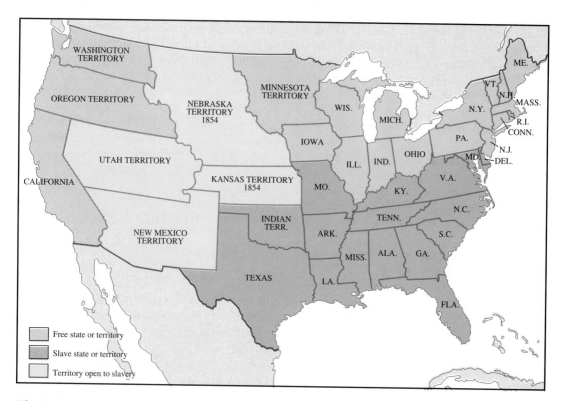

The Kansas-Nebraska Act, 1854 *Stephen Douglas's bill raised a storm of opposition in the North, because it repealed the Missouri Compromise's limitation on slavery. In Kansas and Nebraska, land where slavery had been prohibited now was open to it.*

slavery's influence deepened. Opposition to the Fugitive Slave Act grew dramatically; between 1855 and 1859, Connecticut, Rhode Island, Massachusetts, Michigan, Maine, Ohio, and Wisconsin enacted personal liberty laws. These laws interfered with the Fugitive Slave Act by providing counsel for alleged fugitives and requiring trial by jury. They enraged southern leaders, who saw them as a refusal to honor the Compromise of 1850.

More important was the devastating effect of the Kansas-Nebraska Act on political parties. The weakened Whig party broke apart into northern

The New Republican Party

and southern wings that could no longer cooperate as a national organization. One of the two foundations of the second party system was now gone. The Democrats survived, but their support in the North fell drastically in the

1854 elections. Moreover, anger over the territorial issue created a new political party. During the summer and fall of 1854, antislavery Whigs and Democrats, Free-Soilers, and other reformers throughout the Northwest met to form the new Republican party, dedicated to keeping slavery out of the territories. The Republicans' influence rapidly spread to the East, and they won a stunning victory in the 1854 elections by capturing a majority of northern House seats.

For the first time, too, a sectional party had gained significant power in the political system. Previously, every major party was a national organization with leaders that patched up sectional differences to achieve partisan goals. Now the Whigs were gone, and only the Democrats struggled to maintain a national following. The sectional Republican party, which absorbed the weaker Free-Soil party now grew rapidly in the North by raising a number of moral issues that repelled southern voters.

Nor were Republicans the only new party. An anti-immigrant organization, the American party, briefly seemed likely to replace the Whigs. This

Know-Nothings

party, popularly known as the Know-Nothings (because its members at first kept their purposes secret, answering "I know nothing" to all questions), exploited nativist fear of foreigners. By the mid-1850s, the American party was powerful and growing; so many candidates won congressional office in 1854 with anti-immigrant as well as antislavery support that Know-Nothings claimed to outnumber Republicans. But like the Whigs, the Know-Nothings could not keep their northern and southern wings together, and they melted away after 1856. That left the field to the Republicans (see table).

Republicans, Know-Nothings, and Democrats were all scrambling to attract former Whig voters. The demise of that party ensured a major

Realignment of Political System

realignment of the political system, with nearly half the old electorate up for grabs. To woo the homeless Whigs, the remaining parties addressed a variety of issues to appeal to various segments of the electorate. Immigration, temperance, homestead bills, the tariff, internal improvements—all played important roles in attracting voters during the 1850s.

The Republicans appealed strongly to those interested in the economic development of the West. Commercial agriculture was booming in the

Republican Appeals

Ohio–Mississippi–Great Lakes area, but residents of that region needed more canals, roads, and river and harbor improvements to reap the full benefit of their labors. Also, interest was widespread in a federal land grant program that would provide free western land to homesteaders. Whigs had favored and Democrats opposed all these things. Following long-standing party principles, Democratic presidents vetoed internal improvements bills and a homestead bill as late as 1859. Seizing their opportunity, the Republicans added internal improvements and land grant planks to their platform. They also backed higher tariffs as an enticement to industrialists and businessmen.

Partisan ideological appeals, which had a significant influence on the sectional crisis, were another major feature of the realigned political system. In the North, Republicans attracted many voters through effective use of ideology. When they preached "Free Soil, Free Labor, Free Men," they invoked an image that northerners had of themselves and their future. The phrases resonated with traditional ideals of equality, liberty, and opportunity under self-government—the heritage of republicanism.

Free Soil, Free Labor, Free Men" seemed an appropriate motto for a northern economy that was

New Political Parties

Party	Period of Influence	Area of Influence	Outcome
Liberty party	1839–1848	North	Merged with other antislavery groups to form Free-Soil party
Free-Soil party	1848–1854	North	Merged with Republican party
Know-Nothings (American party)	1853–1856	Nationwide	Disappeared, freeing some northern voters to join Republican party
Republican party	1854–present	North (later nationwide)	Became rival of Democratic party in third-party system

energetic, expanding, and prosperous. The key to progress appeared, to many people, to be free labor. Any hard-working and virtuous man, it was thought, could improve his condition and achieve economic independence by applying himself to opportunities that the country had to offer. Republicans pointed out that the South, which relied on slave labor and had little industry, was backward and retrograde compared with the North. Praising both laborers and opportunity, the Republicans captured much of the spirit of the age in the North.

The Republican party thus attracted support from a variety of sources. Opposition to the extension of slavery had initially brought the party into being, but party members carefully broadened their appeal by adopting the causes of other groups. They were wise to do so. As the New York newspaper editor Horace Greeley wrote in 1860, "an Anti-Slavery man *per se* cannot be elected." But, he added, "a Tariff, River-and-Harbor, Pacific Railroad, Free Homestead man, *may* succeed *although* he is Anti-Slavery." As these elements joined the Republican party, they also learned more about the dangers of slavery. Thus the process of party building deepened the sectional conflict.

A similar process was under way in the South. The disintegration of the Whig party had left many southerners at loose ends politically. Some gravitated to the American party but not for long. In the increasingly tense atmosphere of sectional crisis, these people were highly susceptible to strong states' rights positions, which provided a handy defense for slavery. Democratic leaders emphasized such appeals and managed to convert most of the formerly Whig slave holders, who responded to their class interests.

Southern Democrats

In the South, however, yeomen rather than slave holders were the heart of the party. Thus, Democratic politicians, although often slave owners, had lauded the common man and argued that their policies advanced his interests. Yeomen were told that the well-ordered South was the true defender of constitutional principles and that runaway change in the North was threatening to subvert the nation. According to the southern version of re-publicanism, white citizens in a slave society enjoyed liberty and social equality because the black race was enslaved. As Jefferson Davis put it in 1851, slavery elevated every white person's status and allowed the nonslaveholder to "*stand upon the broad level of equality with the rich man.*" Slave-holding Democrats warned that the overriding issue was "shall negroes govern white men, or white men govern negroes?"

The arguments had their effect. Racial fears and traditional political loyalties helped keep the political alliance between yeoman farmers and planters intact through the 1850s. No viable party emerged in the South to replace the Whigs. The result was a one-party system that emphasized sectional issues. In the South, as in the North, political realignment sharpened sectional divisions.

In both sections, political leaders argued that racial change threatened opportunity. The *Montgomery* (Alabama) *Mail* warned southern whites in 1860 that the Republicans intended "to free the negroes and force amalgamation between them and the children of the poor men of the South." Similarly, Republicans warned northern workers that if slavery entered the territories, it would poison the great reservoir of opportunity for decent people without means. Such charges aroused fears and anxieties in both sections. But events in Kansas did even more to deepen the conflict. Put into practice, the Kansas-Nebraska Act spawned hatred and violence. Abolitionists and religious groups sent armed Free-Soil settlers; southerners sent their reinforcements to establish slavery and prevent "northern hordes" from stealing Kansas. Clashes between the two groups caused bloodshed, and soon the whole nation was talking about "Bleeding Kansas."

Politics in the territory resembled war more than democracy. During elections for a territorial legislature in 1855, thousands of proslavery Missourians invaded the polls and ran up a large but fraudulent majority for slavery candidates. The resulting legislature legalized slavery, and in response Free-Soilers held an unauthorized convention at which they created their own government and constitution. A proslavery posse sent to arrest

Bleeding Kansas

the Free-Soil leaders sacked the town of Lawrence; in revenge, John Brown, an antislavery zealot who saw himself as God's instrument to destroy slavery, killed five proslavery settlers. Soon armed bands of guerrillas roamed the territory.

The passion generated by the conflict erupted in violence in the chamber of the U.S. Senate in May 1856, when Charles Sumner of Massachusetts denounced "the Crime against Kansas." In doing so, Sumner bitterly assailed the president, the South, and Senator Andrew P. Butler of South Carolina. Soon thereafter, Butler's cousin, Representative Preston Brooks, approached Sumner at the latter's Senate desk, raised his cane, and began to beat Sumner on the head. Shocked northerners recoiled from what they saw as another southern assault on free speech and the South's readiness to use violence to have its way. South Carolina voters reelected Brooks and sent him dozens of new canes. The country was becoming polarized.

The election of 1856 showed how extreme that polarization had become. When Democrats met to select a nominee, they shied away from prominent leaders whose views on the territories were well known. Instead, they chose James Buchanan of Pennsylvania, whose chief virtue was that for the past four years he had been ambassador to Britain, uninvolved in territorial controversies. His anonymity and superior party organization helped Buchanan win the election, but he owed his victory to southern support. The Republican candidate, John C. Frémont, won eleven of the sixteen free states; Republicans had become the dominant party in the North. The Know-Nothing candidate, Millard Fillmore, won more than 20 percent of the vote, but the election was to be his party's last hurrah. Only a sectional Republican party and a divided Democratic party remained.

SLAVERY AND THE NATION'S FUTURE

For years, the issue of slavery in the territories had convulsed Congress, and for years Congress had tried to settle the issue with vague formulas. In 1857, the Supreme Court stepped onto the scene and attempted to silence controversy with a definitive verdict.

A Missouri slave named Dred Scott had sued his owner for his freedom. Scott based his claim to freedom on the fact that his former owner, an army surgeon, had taken him for several years into Illinois, a free state, and into the Wisconsin Territory, from which slavery had been barred by the Missouri Compromise. Scott first won and then lost his case as it moved on appeal through the state courts, into the federal system, and finally after eleven years to the Supreme Court.

Dred Scott Case

Was a black person like Dred Scott a citizen of the United States and thus eligible to sue in federal court? Had residence in a free state or free territory made him free? Did Congress have the power to prohibit slavery in a territory or to delegate that power to a territorial legislature?

In March 1857, Chief Justice Roger B. Taney of Maryland answered each of these questions in *Dred Scott* v. *Sanford.* Taney declared that Scott was not a citizen of either the United States or Missouri, that residence in free territory did not make Scott free, and that Congress had no power to bar slavery from a territory, as it had done in the Missouri Compromise. The decision not only overturned a sectional compromise that had been honored for years but also invalidated the basic ideas of the Wilmot Proviso and probably popular sovereignty as well.

The Slave Power seemed to have gained vital constitutional ground. African-Americans were especially dismayed, for Taney's decision also declared that the nation's founders had never intended for black people to be citizens. Taney was mistaken; African-Americans had been citizens in several of the original states. Nevertheless, the Dred Scott decision seemed to shut the door permanently on their hopes for justice and equal rights.

A storm of angry reaction broke in the North. The decision alarmed a wide variety of northerners—abolitionists, would-be settlers in the West, and those who scorned black people but feared the influence of the South. Every charge against the aggressive Slave Power seemed now to be confirmed. "There is such a thing as the slave power," warned

of suffrage, for a reason of a very different character than the one supposed. The principle of freehold suffrage seems to have been brought
over from England with the first colonists, and to have been preserved
almost invariably in the colony ever afterwards. In the act of 1743,
ch. 1 (Swann's Revisal, 171), it will be seen that a freehold of fifty acres
was necessary to entitle the inhabitant of a county to vote, and by the
act of 2d Sept. of 1746, ch. 1, *ibid.*, 223, the *freeholders* only of the respective towns of Edenton, Bath, Newbern, and Wilmington were declared entitled to vote for members of the Colonial Legislature. The very
Congress which framed our Constitution was chosen by freeholders.
That Constitution extended the elective **franchise** to every freeman
who had arrived at the age of 21, and paid a public tax, and it is a
matter of universal notoriety that under it free persons without regard to color claimed and exercised the franchise until it was taken
from free men of color a few years since by our amended Constitution. But surely the possession of political power is not essential to
constitute a citizen. If it be, then women, minors, and persons who have
not paid public taxes are not citizens—and free white men who have
paid public taxes and arrived at full age, but have not a freehold of fifty

How do historians know

*that African-Americans played a role in government
at the nation's founding? In the Dred Scott decision,
Chief Justice Roger Taney declared that black people
were never considered part of the political community,
either in state or nation. Justice Benjamin Curtis,
who dissented from the decision, argued that Taney
was wrong. Curtis asserted that several original states*

*based voting on the ownership of property and that
blacks who qualified did indeed vote. This passage,
from a decision of the North Carolina Supreme Court
in 1838, confirms that black freeholders in North
Carolina voted until amendments were made to the
state's constitution in 1835.* Photo: Martine Sherrill,
courtesy Wake Forest University Law Library.

the *Cincinnati Daily Commercial.* And the *Cincinnati Freeman* asked, "What security have the Germans and the Irish that their children will not, within a hundred years, be reduced to slavery in this land of their adoption?" And the *Atlantic Monthly* asked, "Where will it end?"

To Abraham Lincoln, the territorial question affected every citizen. "The whole nation," he declared as early as 1854, "is interested that the best

Abraham Lincoln on the Slave Power

——

use shall be made of these Territories. We want them for homes of free white people. This they cannot be, to any considerable extent, if slavery shall be planted within them."

The territories must be reserved, he insisted, "as an outlet for *free white people everywhere, as well as a new home for immigrants coming to America.*"

After the Dred Scott decision, Lincoln charged that slavery's advocates were trying to "push it forward, till it shall become lawful in *all* the states . . . *North* as well as *South.*" He further asserted that the next step in the unfolding Slave Power conspiracy would be a Supreme Court decision "declaring that the Constitution does not permit a State to exclude slavery from its limits." This charge was not mere imagination, for cases soon reached the courts challenging state laws that freed slaves brought within their borders.

Lincoln's most eloquent statement against the Slave Power was his famous "House Divided" speech, in which he declared:

> I do not expect the Union to be dissolved—I do not expect the House to fall—but I do expect it to cease to be divided. It will become all one thing or all the other. Either the opponents of slavery will arrest the further spread of it, and place it where the public mind shall rest in the belief that it is in the course of ultimate extinction; or its advocates will push it forward, till it shall become alike lawful in all the States, old as well as new, North as well as South.

Lincoln warned repeatedly that the latter possibility was real, and events convinced countless northerners that slave holders were close to their goal of making slavery a national institution.

Politically, these forceful Republican arguments offset the difficulties that the Dred Scott decision posed. By endorsing Calhoun's theories, the Court had in effect declared that the central position of the Republican party—no extension of slavery—was unconstitutional. Republicans could only repudiate the decision, appealing to a "higher law," or hope to change the personnel of the Court. They did both and probably gained politically as fear of the Slave Power grew.

Meanwhile, Stephen Douglas, a northern Democrat, faced an awful dilemma. He had to find a way to ease the fear of northerners without alienating southern Democrats. Douglas chose to stand by his principle of popular sovereignty, which encountered a second test in 1857. In Kansas, after Free-Soil settlers boycotted an election, proslavery forces met at Lecompton and wrote a constitution that permitted slavery. New elections to the territo-rial legislature, however, returned an antislavery majority, and the legislature called for a popular vote on the new constitution. It was defeated by more than ten thousand votes. The evidence was overwhelming that Kansans did not want slavery, yet President Buchanan tried to force the Lecompton Constitution through Congress. Breaking with the administration, Douglas threw his weight against the Lecompton Constitution. He gauged opinion in Kansas correctly, for in 1858 voters there rejected the constitution a third time. But his action infuriated southern Democrats.

Douglas further alienated the southern wing of his party in his well-publicized debates with Abraham Lincoln, who challenged him for the Illinois Senate seat in 1858. Speaking at Freeport, Illinois, Douglas attempted to revive the notion of popular sovereignty with some tortured extensions of his old arguments. Asserting that the Supreme Court had ruled only on the powers of Congress, not on the powers of a *territorial* legislature, Douglas claimed that a territorial legislature could bar slavery either by passing a law against it or by doing nothing. Without the patrol laws and police regulations that support slavery, he reasoned, the institution could not exist. This argument, called the Freeport Doctrine, temporarily shored up Douglas's crumbling position in the North. But it gave southern Democrats further evidence that Douglas was unreliable, and many viciously turned against him. Some, like Representative William L. Yancey of Alabama, studied the trend in northern opinion and concluded that southern rights would be safe only in a separate nation.

Stephen Douglas Proposes the Freeport Doctrine

The immediate consequence for politics, however, was the likelihood of formal division in the Democratic party. Northern Democrats could not support the territorial protection for slavery that southern Democrats insisted was theirs as a constitutional right. Thus the issue of slavery in the territories continued to generate wider conflict, although it had little immediate, practical significance. In territories outside Kansas, the number of settlers was small, and everywhere the number of

African-Americans was negligible—less than 1 percent of the populations of Kansas and New Mexico. Nevertheless, the general public in both North and South moved from anxiety to anger and alarm. The situation had become explosive.

THE BREAKUP OF THE UNION

One year before the 1860 presidential election, John Brown, who had slain proslavery settlers in Kansas, led a small band of whites and blacks in an attack on Harpers Ferry, Virginia. Hoping to trigger a slave rebellion, Brown failed miserably and was quickly captured, tried, and executed. Yet his attempted insurrection struck fear in the South even before it came to light that Brown had had financial backing from several prominent abolitionists. When northern intellectuals such as Ralph Waldo Emerson and Henry David Thoreau praised Brown as a hero and a martyr, southerners' fears and anger multiplied many times over. The unity of the nation was now in peril.

Many observers feared that the election of 1860 would decide the fate of the Union. By that year, the Democratic party was the only remaining organization that was truly national in scope. Even religious denominations had split into northern and southern wings during the 1840s and 1850s. "One after another," wrote a Mississippi newspaper editor, "the links which have bound the North and South together, have been severed . . . [but] the Democratic party looms gradually up, its nationality intact, and waves the olive branch over the troubled waters of politics." At its 1860 convention, however, the Democratic party broke in two.

Stephen A. Douglas wanted the party's presidential nomination, but he could not afford to alienate northern voters by accepting the southern position on the territories. **Splintering of the Democratic Party** Southern Democrats like William L. Yancey, on the other hand, insisted on recognition of their rights—as Roger Taney had defined them—and they

moved to block Douglas's nomination. When Douglas obtained a majority for his version of the platform, delegates from eight slave states walked out of the convention hall in Charleston. After efforts at compromise failed, the Democrats presented two nominees: Douglas for the northern wing and Vice President John C. Breckinridge of Kentucky for the southern. The Republicans nominated Abraham Lincoln. A Constitutional Union party, formed to preserve the nation but strong only in the Upper South, nominated John Bell of Tennessee.

The results of the balloting were sectional in character, and although Lincoln won, Douglas, Breckinridge, and Bell together received most of the votes. Douglas had broad-based support but won few states; Breckinridge, whose strength was concentrated in the Deep South, carried nine southern states; Bell won pluralities in Virginia, Kentucky, and Tennessee. Lincoln prevailed in the North, but in the states that ultimately remained loyal to the Union he won only a plurality, not a majority (see table). Lincoln won in the electoral college.

Election of 1860

Given the heterogeneous nature of Republican voters, it is likely that many did not view the issue of slavery in the territories as paramount. But opposition to slavery's extension was the core issue of the Republican party, and Lincoln's alarm over slavery's growing political power was genuine. The slavery issue would not go away. While abolitionists and supporters of free soil in the North worked to keep the Republicans from compromising on their territorial stand, proslavery advocates and secessionists demanded that state conventions assemble to consider secession.

Lincoln made the crucial decision not to soften his party's position on the territories. His refusal to compromise probably derived both from conviction and from concern for the unity of the Republican party. Although many conservative Republicans—eastern businessmen and former Whigs who did not feel strongly about slavery—hoped for a compromise, the original and most committed Republicans—antislavery voters and "conscience Whigs"—were adamant for free soil.

Presidential Vote in 1860

	Lincoln	Other Candidates
Entire United States	1,866,452	2,815,617
North plus border and southern states that rejected secession prior to war[1]	1,866,452	2,421,752
North plus border states that fought for Union[2]	1,864,523	1,960,842

[1]Kentucky, Missouri, Maryland, Delaware, Virginia, North Carolina, Tennessee, Arkansas

[2]Kentucky, Missouri, Maryland, Delaware

Source: From David Potter, *Lincoln and His Party in the Secession Crisis.* Copyright 1942, 1967 by Yale University Press. Reprinted by permission.

Lincoln chose to preserve party unity by standing firm against slavery's extension.

Southern leaders in the Senate were willing, conditionally, to accept a compromise formula drawn up by Senator John J. Crittenden of Kentucky. Crittenden, hoping to don the mantle of Henry Clay and avert disunion, proposed that the two sections divide the territories between them at 36°30'. But the southerners would agree to this *only* if the Republicans did. When Lincoln ruled out concessions on the territorial issue, Crittenden's peacemaking effort, known as the Crittenden Compromise, collapsed. Virginians called for a special convention in Washington, to which several states sent representatives. But this gathering too failed to find a solution.

Misjudgment by political leaders also played a role in the coming of war. Lincoln and other prominent Republicans believed that southerners were bluffing when they threatened secession; Republicans expected a pro-Union majority in the South to assert itself. On their side, moderate southern leaders had become convinced, more accurately, that

northern leaders were not taking them seriously and that a posture of strength was necessary to win respect for their position. Such attitudes made confrontation more likely than compromise.

Meanwhile, the Union was being destroyed. On December 20, 1860, South Carolina passed an ordinance of secession amid jubilation and cheering. This step marked the

Secession of South Carolina

inauguration of a strategy favored by secessionists called separate state secession. Foes of the Union, recognizing the difficulty of persuading all southern states to challenge the federal government simultaneously, had concentrated their efforts on the most extreme proslavery state. They hoped South Carolina's secession would induce other states to follow, with each decision building momentum for disunion.

Southern extremists soon got their way in the Deep South. Overwhelming their opposition, they quickly called separate state conventions and passed secession ordinances in Mis-

Confederate States of America

sissippi, Florida, Alabama, Georgia, Louisiana, and Texas. By February 1861, these states had joined South Carolina to form a new government in Montgomery, Alabama: the Confederate States of America. The delegates at Montgomery chose Jefferson Davis as their president, and the Confederacy began to function independent of the United States.

Yet the apparent unanimity of action was deceiving. Confused and dissatisfied with the alternatives, many southerners who had voted for president in 1860 stayed home a few months later rather than vote for delegates who would decide upon secession. In some state conventions, the vote to secede had been close, the balance tipped by overrepresentation of plantation districts. Furthermore, the conventions were noticeably reluctant to seek ratification of their acts by the people. Four states in the Upper South—Virginia, North Carolina, Tennessee, and Arkansas—flatly rejected secession and did not join the Confederacy until after fighting had begun. In the border states, popular sentiment was too divided for decisive action; minorities in Kentucky and Missouri tried to secede, but these

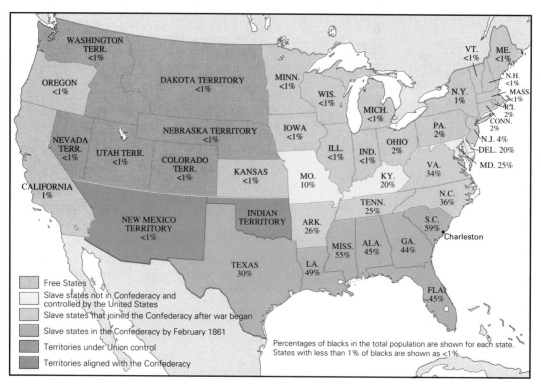

The Divided Nation—Slave and Free Areas, 1861   *After fighting began, the Upper South joined the Deep South in the Confederacy.*

slave states remained under Union control, along with Maryland and Delaware (see map).

Such misgivings were not surprising. Secession posed new and troubling issues for southerners, especially the possibility of war and death. Analysis of election returns from 1860 and 1861 indicates that slave holders and nonslave holders were beginning to part company politically. Heavily slave-holding counties strongly supported secession (see figure). But most counties with few slaves took an anti-secession position or were staunchly Unionist. In other words, nonslave holders were beginning to consider their class interests and to ask themselves how far they would go to support slavery and slave owners. Some still felt considerable love for the Union.

The dilemma facing President Lincoln on inauguration day in March 1861 was how to maintain the authority of the federal government without provoking war. He decided to proceed cautiously in the states that had left the Union. By holding onto federal fortifications in those states, he reasoned, he could assert federal sovereignty while waiting for a restoration of relations. But Jefferson Davis, who could not claim to lead a sovereign nation if its ports were under foreign control, was unwilling to be so patient. A collision was inevitable.

It arrived in the early morning hours of April 12, 1861, at Fort Sumter in Charleston harbor. A federal garrison there was running low on food, and

Attack of Fort Sumter

Lincoln notified the South Carolinians that he was sending a ship to resupply the fort. For the Montgomery government, the alternatives were to attack the fort or to acquiesce to Lincoln's authority. Accordingly, orders were sent to obtain a surrender or attack the fort. After two days of heavy bombardment, the federal garrison finally surrendered. No one died in battle, although an accident

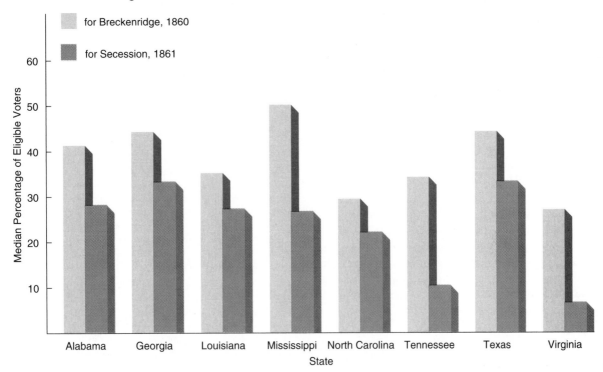

Voting Returns of Counties with Few Slaveholders, Eight Southern States,1860 and 1861

- for Breckenridge, 1860
- for Secession, 1861

Voting Returns of Counties with Few Slave Holders, Eight Southern States, 1860 and 1861 The chart depicts voting in counties in which the percentage of slave holders was smaller than in other counties in their state. How does voters' support for secession in 1861 compare with support for John Breckinridge, the southern Democratic candidate in 1860? Why was their support for secession so weak? At this time, counties with many slave holders were giving increased support to secession.

during later military ceremonies killed one Union soldier. Confederates permitted the U.S. soldiers to sail away on unarmed vessels while Charlestonians celebrated wildly. The Civil War—the bloodiest war in America's history—had begun.

Throughout the 1840s and 1850s, many able leaders had worked diligently to avert this outcome. Most people, North and South, had hoped to keep the nation together. As late as 1858, even Davis had declared, "This great country will continue united." He had explained sincerely that the United States "is my country and to the innermost fibers of my heart I love it all, and every part." Why, then, had war broken out? Why had all efforts to prevent it failed?

Slavery was an issue on which compromise was impossible. The conflict it generated was funda-

mental and beyond adjustment. The emotions bound up in attacking and defending it were too powerful, and the motives involved in maintaining or destroying it were too fundamental. It was deeply entwined with almost every major policy question of the present and the foreseeable future. Ultimately, each section regarded slavery as too important to put aside.

Even excluding extreme views, the North and the South had fundamentally different attitudes toward the institution. The logic of Republican ideology tended in the direction of abolishing slavery, although Republicans denied any such intention. Similarly, the logic of southern leaders' arguments led toward establishing slavery everywhere, although southern leaders denied that they sought any such thing. Lincoln put the problem succinctly.

Soon after the 1860 election, he assured his old friend Alexander Stephens of Georgia that the Republican party would not attack slavery in the states where it existed. But Lincoln continued, "You think slavery is *right* and ought to be expanded; while we think it is *wrong* and ought to be restricted. That I suppose is the rub."

The issue of slavery in the territories made conflict impossible to avoid. Territorial expansion generated disputes so frequently that the nation never enjoyed a breathing space. As the conflict recurred, its influence on policy and effect on the government deepened. Every southern victory increased fear of the Slave Power, and each new expression of Free-Soil sentiment made alarmed slave holders more insistent in their demands.

Concern over slavery had driven all other conflicts. But as the fighting began, this, the war's central issue, was shrouded in confusion. How would the Civil War affect slavery, its place in the law, and African-Americans' place in society?

SUGGESTIONS FOR FURTHER READING

Politics: General

Tyler Anbinder, *Nativism and Slavery* (1992); Paul Bergeron, *The Presidency of James K. Polk* (1987); Frederick J. Blue, *The Free Soilers: Third Party Politics, 1848–1854* (1973); Stanley W. Campbell, *The Slave Catchers* (1968); Don E. Fehrenbacher, *The Dred Scott Case* (1978); Holman Hamilton, *Prologue to Conflict: The Crisis and Compromise of 1850* (1964); Michael F. Holt, *The Political Crisis of the 1850s* (1978); Chaplain W. Morrison, *Democratic Politics and Sectionalism: The Wilmot Proviso Controversy* (1967); Russell B. Nye, *Fettered Freedom* (1949); David M. Potter, *The Impending Crisis, 1848–1861* (1976); Elbert B. Smith, *The Presidency of James Buchanan* (1975); Kenneth M. Stampp, *And the War Came* (1950); Gerald W. Wolff, *The Kansas-Nebraska Bill* (1977).

The South and Slavery

William L. Barney, *The Secessionist Impulse* (1974); Steven A. Channing, *A Crisis of Fear: Secession in South Carolina* (1970); William J. Cooper Jr., *The South and the Politics of Slavery, 1828–1856* (1978); Avery O. Craven, *The Growth of Southern Nationalism, 1848–1861* (1953); Daniel W. Crofts, *Reluctant Confederates: Upper South Unionists in the Secession Crisis* (1989); Drew G. Faust, *The Ideology of Slavery* (1981); Lacy K. Ford Jr., *Origins of Southern Radicalism* (1988); William W. Freehling, *The Road to Disunion* (1990); Eugene D. Genovese, *The Political Economy of Slavery* (1967); Michael P. Johnson, *Toward a Patriarchal Republic: The Secession of Georgia* (1977); David M. Potter, *The South and the Sectional Conflict* (1968); J. Mills Thornton III, *Politics and Power in a Slave Society* (1978); Ralph Wooster, *The Secession Conventions of the South* (1962).

The North and Antislavery

Eugene H. Berwanger, *The Frontier Against Slavery* (1967); Louis Filler, *The Crusade Against Slavery, 1830–1860* (1960); Eric Foner, *Free Soil, Free Labor, Free Men* (1970); William E. Gienapp, *The Origins of the Republican Party, 1852–1856* (1986); Henry V. Jaffa, *Crisis of the House Divided* (1959); Robert W. Johannsen, *Lincoln, the South, and Slavery* (1991); Aileen S. Kraditor, *Means and Ends in American Abolitionism* (1969); Lewis Perry and Michael Fellman, eds., *Antislavery Reconsidered* (1979); Richard Sewell, *Ballots for Freedom: Antislavery Politics in the United States, 1837–1860* (1976).

The Mexican War and Foreign Policy

Richard Griswold del Castillo, *The Treaty of Guadalupe Hidalgo* (1990); Neal Harlow, *California Conquered* (1982); Reginald Horsman, *Race and Manifest Destiny* (1981); Ernest M. Lander Jr., *Reluctant Imperialists: Calhoun, the South Carolinians, and the Mexican War* (1980); Robert E. May, *The Southern Dream of a Caribbean Empire, 1854–1861* (1973); Frederick Merk, *The Monroe Doctrine and American Expansion, 1843–1849* (1966); David M. Pletcher, *The Diplomacy of Annexation: Texas, Oregon, and the Mexican War* (1973); John H. Schroeder, *Mr. Polk's War: American Opposition and Dissent* (1973); Otis A. Singletary, *The Mexican War* (1960).

15

Transforming Fire:
The Civil War, 1861–1865

MONCURE CONWAY, A VIRGINIAN who had become an abolitionist and moved to New England, saw the Civil War as a momentous opportunity to promote social justice. But, he warned in a pamphlet, "Slavery, hoary tyrant of the ages," would try to drive justice "'back! back . . . into the chambers of Night!'" Urging northerners to defeat slavery, Conway lived for the day when "the rays of Freedom and Justice" would shine throughout America.

But Conway's lofty idealism was not what drove most federal soldiers to march grimly to their deaths. Although slaves believed they were witnessing God's "Holy War for the liberation of the poor African slave people," Union troops typically had a different perspective. When a Yankee soldier ransacked a slave family's cabin and stole their best quilts, the mother exclaimed, "Why you nasty, stinkin' rascal. You say you come down here to fight for the niggers, and now you're stealin' from 'em." The soldier replied, "You're a G-- D----- liar, I'm fightin' for $14 a month and the Union."

Southerners too had limited and pragmatic motives; many fought in self-defense or out of regional loyalty. A Union officer interrogating Confederate prisoners noticed the obvious poverty of one captive. Clearly, the man was no slave holder, so the officer asked him why he was fighting. "Because y'all are down here," was the Confederate's simple reply.

For these people and millions of others, the Civil War was a life-changing event. It obliterated the normal patterns and circumstances of life. Millions of men were swept into training camps and battle units. Armies numbering in the hundreds of thousands marched over the South, devastating once peaceful countrysides. Families struggled to survive without their men; businesses tried to cope with the loss of workers. Women in both North and South took on extra responsibilities in the home and moved into new jobs in the work force. No sphere of life was untouched.

Change was most drastic in the South, where the leaders of the secession movement had launched a revolution for the purpose of keeping things unchanged. Never were men more mistaken. The Civil War turned southern life upside-down and imperiled the very existence of slavery. And the leadership of Jefferson Davis, president of the Confederate States of America, resulted in policies more objectionable to the elite than any proposed by President Lincoln. Life in the Confederacy proved a shockingly unsouthern experience.

War altered the North as well but less deeply. Because most fighting took place on southern soil, northern farms and factories remained virtually unscathed. The drafting of workers and the changing needs for products slowed the pace of industrialization somewhat, but factories and businesses remained busy. Workers lost ground to inflation, but the economy hummed. A new probusiness atmosphere dominated Congress. To the alarm of many, the powers of the federal government and of the president increased during the war.

Ultimately, the Civil War forced on the nation new social and racial arrangements. Its greatest effect was to compel leaders and citizens to deal directly with the issue they had tried so hard to avoid: slavery. The issue had, in complex and indirect ways, given rise to the war. Now the scope and demands of the war forced reluctant Americans to confront it.

"FIGHTING MEANS KILLING"

Few Americans understood what they were getting into when the war began. The onset of hostilities sparked patriotic sentiments, optimistic speeches, and festive ceremonies in both regions. Northern communities, large and small, raised companies of volunteers eager to save the Union. In the cities, spectators cheered from flag-draped buildings as men marched off to war. In the South, confident recruits boasted of whipping the Yankees and returning home in time for dinner. Women sewed dashing uniforms for men who would soon be lucky to wear drab gray or butternut homespun.

Through the spring of 1861, both sides scrambled to organize and train their inexperienced undisciplined armies. On July 21, 1861, the first

Battle of Bull Run

battle took place outside Manassas Junction, Virginia, near a stream called Bull Run. General Irvin McDowell and thirty thousand federal troops attacked General P. G. T. Beauregard's twenty-two thousand southerners. As soldiers struggled amid the confusion of their first battle, federal forces began to gain ground. Then they ran into a line of Virginia troops under General Thomas Jackson. "There is Jackson standing like a stone wall," shouted one Confederate. "Stonewall" Jackson's line held, and the arrival of nine thousand Confederate reinforcements won the day for the South. Union troops fled back to Washington in disarray, and shocked northern congressmen and spectators, who had watched the battle from a point two miles away, suddenly feared their capital would be taken.

The unexpected rout at Bull Run gave northerners their first hint of the nature of the war to come. Victory would not be easy, although the United States enjoyed an enormous advantage in resources. Pro-Union feeling was growing in western Virginia, and loyalties were divided in the four border slave states—Missouri, Kentucky, Maryland, and Delaware. But the rest of the Upper South had joined the Confederacy. Moved by an outpouring of regional loyalty, a half-million southerners volunteered to fight.

The United States therefore undertook a massive build-up of troops in northern Virginia. Lincoln gave command of the army to General George McClellan, an officer who proved better at organization and training than at fighting. McClellan devoted the fall and winter of 1861 to readying a formidable force of a quarter-million men. The Union also initiated its plans to blockade southern ports and to eventually gain control of the Mississippi River (the "Anaconda" plan; see map, page 286). At first, the Union navy had too few ships to patrol the Confederacy's 3,550 miles of coastline. Gradually, however, the navy increased the blockade's effectiveness, although it never bottled up southern commerce completely.

Confederate strategy was essentially defensive. Not only was a defensive posture consistent with the South's claim that it merely wanted to be left alone, but it also took into account the North's advantage in resources (see figure, page 287). Jefferson Davis wisely rejected, however, a wholly defensive strategy. The South would pursue an "offensive defensive," taking advantage of opportunities to attack

• *Important Events* •

1861	Four more southern states secede from Union Battle of Bull Run takes place General McClellan organizes Union army Union blockade begins U.S. Congress passes first confiscation act
1862	Union captures Fort Henry and Fort Donelson U.S. Navy captures New Orleans Battle of Shiloh shows the war's destructiveness Confederacy enacts conscription Lee thwarts McClellan's offensive on Richmond U.S. Congress passes second confiscation act Confederacy mounts offensive Battle of Antietam ends Lee's drive into Maryland
1863	Emancipation Proclamation U.S. Congress passes National Banking Act Union enacts conscription African-American soldiers join Union army

Food riots occur in southern cities
Battle of Chancellorsville ends in Jackson's death
Union wins key victories at Gettysburg and Vicksburg
Draft riots take place in New York City

1864 Battle of Cold Harbor continues carnage in Virginia
Lincoln requests party plank abolishing slavery
General Sherman captures Atlanta
Lincoln wins reelection
Jefferson Davis proposes Confederate emancipation
Sherman marches through Georgia

1865 Congress approves Thirteenth Amendment
Hampton Roads conference
Lee abandons Petersburg and Richmond
Lee surrenders at Appomattox
Lincoln assassinated

---

and using its interior lines of transportation to concentrate troops at crucial points.

Strategic thinking on both sides slighted the importance of "the West," that vast expanse of territory between Virginia and the Mississippi River. Both sides were initially unprepared for large-scale and sustained operations in the West, but before the end of the war it would prove a crucial theater.

The last half of 1861 brought no major land battles, but the North made gains by sea. Late in the summer, Union naval forces began to come ashore in the South.

Union Naval Campaign Federal squadrons captured Cape Hatteras and then seized Hilton Head, one of the Sea Islands off Port Royal, South Carolina. A few months later, similar operations secured vital coastal points in North Carolina, as well as Fort Pulaski, which defended Savannah. The coastal victories, especially those off South Carolina's coast, caused frightened planters to abandon their lands and flee their homes. Their slaves greeted what they hoped to be freedom with rejoicing and broke the hated cotton gins. Ironically, the federal government, unwilling at first to wage a war against slavery, did not acknowledge the slaves' freedom.

These coastal incursions worried southerners, but the spring of 1862 brought even stronger evidence of the war's seriousness. In April, ships commanded by Admiral David Farragut smashed through log booms on the Mississippi River and fought their way upstream to capture New Orleans. Meanwhile, in northern Tennessee, land and river forces won significant victories for the Union. There, General Ulysses S. Grant captured Fort Henry and Fort Donelson, securing two prime routes to the Confederacy's heartland. A path into Tennessee, Alabama, and Mississippi now lay before the Union army.

Grant's Campaign in Tennessee

Grant moved on into southern Tennessee and the first of the war's shockingly bloody encounters,

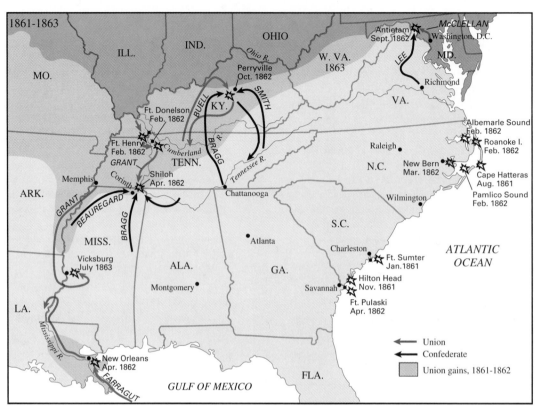

The Civil War, 1861–1863 *An overview of the Union's "Anaconda" plan and key battles in the West, 1861–1863.*

the Battle of Shiloh. On April 6, Confederate General Albert Sidney Johnston caught federal troops in an undesirable position on the Tennessee River. With their backs to the water, Grant's men were awaiting reinforcements. The Confederates inflicted heavy damage, but Johnston was killed. The next day, a reinforced Union army forced the Confederates to withdraw. There was no clear victor at Shiloh, but destruction reigned. Northern troops lost thirteen thousand (killed, wounded, or captured) of sixty-three thousand men; southerners sacrificed eleven thousand of forty thousand. Total casualties in this single battle exceeded those in all three of America's previous wars combined.

Meanwhile, on the Virginia front, Abraham Lincoln had a different problem. Conquest was im-

possible without battles, but he could not get General McClellan to move. Habitually overestimating the size of enemy forces, McClellan called repeatedly for reinforcements and ignored Lincoln's directions to advance. Finally, McClellan chose to move by a roundabout water route, sailing his troops to the York peninsula and advancing on Richmond from the east. By June, the sheer size of the federal armies outside the South's capital was highly threatening. But southern leaders foiled McClellan's legions. First, Stonewall Jackson moved north into the Shenandoah Valley behind Union forces and threatened Washington, drawing some federals from Richmond to protect their own capital. Then, in a series of engagements known as the Seven Days' battles, General Robert E. Lee

Comparative Resources, Union and Confederate States, 1861

■ Union States   ■ Confederate States

Total Population, 2.5 to 1

Naval Ship Tonage, 25 to 1

Farm Acerage, 3 to 1

Free Men 18-60 Yrs., 4.4 to 1

Factory Production Value, 10 to 1

Draft Animals, 1.8 to 1

44%   90%

Free Men in Military Service, 1864

Textile Goods Production, 14 to 1

Livestock, 1.5 to 1

Wealth Produced, 3 to 1

Iron Production, 15 to 1

Wheat Production, 4.2 to 1

Railroad Mileage, 2.4 to 1

Coal Production, 38 to 1

Corn Production, 2 to 1

Merchant Ship Tonnage, 9 to 1

Firearms Production, 32 to 1

Cotton Production, 1 to 24

Comparative Resources, Union and Confederate States, 1861 *The North had vastly superior resources. Although the North's advantages in workers and industrial capacity proved important, the South—like the colonies in the American Revolution—could not really be conquered until it chose to give up the fight.* Source: From *Times Atlas of World History.* Time Books, London, 1978. Used with permission.

struck at McClellan's army, and on August 3 McClellan withdrew to the Potomac. Richmond remained safe for almost two more years.

Buoyed by the results, Jefferson Davis conceived an ambitious plan to turn the tide of the war and compel the United States to recognize the Confederacy. He ordered a general offensive, sending Lee north into Maryland and Generals Kirby Smith and Braxton Bragg into Kentucky. The South would go on the offensive and carry the war north. Davis called on residents of Maryland and Kentucky to make a separate peace with his government and invited the Northwest, which sent much of its trade down the Mississippi to New Orleans, to leave the Union.

Davis Orders an Offensive
———

The plan was promising, but every part of the offensive failed. In the bloodiest day of the entire war, September 17, 1862, McClellan turned Lee back in the Battle of Antietam near Sharpsburg, Maryland. In Kentucky, Smith and Bragg were also forced to withdraw. The entire effort collapsed.

But 1862 did not end without painful lessons for the North as well. First, Confederate General James E. B. (Jeb) Stuart executed a daring cavalry raid into Pennsylvania in October. Then, on December 13, Union general Ambrose Burnside unwisely ordered his soldiers to attack Lee's army, which held fortified positions on high ground at Fredericksburg, Virginia. Lee's men controlled the engagement so thoroughly that Lee was moved to say, "It is well that war is so terrible. We should grow too fond of it."

WAR TRANSFORMS THE SOUTH

Disruptions in civilian life robbed southerners of their gaiety and nonchalance even more than did the fighting itself. The war altered southern society beyond all expectations. One of the first traditions to fall was the southern preference for local government.

The South had been characterized by limited government. States' rights had been its motto, but by modern standards even the state governments were weak and sketchy affairs. To withstand the massive power of the North, however, the South had to centralize. No one saw the necessity of centralization more clearly than Jefferson Davis. If the states insisted on fighting separately, said Davis, "We had better make terms as soon as we can."

From the outset, Davis pressed to bring all arms, supplies, and troops under his control. By early 1862, the scope and duration of the conflict required something more.

Centralization of Power in the South

When the states failed to attract enough troops, he secured the passage of the first national conscription (draft) law in American history. He adopted a firm leadership role toward the Confederate congress, which raised taxes and later passed a tax in-kind—a tax paid in farm products. Where opposition arose, the government suspended the writ of habeas corpus (which prevented individuals from being held without trial) and imposed martial law. In the face of political opposition that cherished states' rights, Davis proved unyielding.

Soon the Confederate administration in Richmond was exercising virtually complete control over the southern economy. Because it controlled the supply of labor through conscription, the administration could compel industry to work on government contracts and supply the military's needs. The Confederate congress also gave the central government almost complete control of the railroads; in 1864, shipping too came under extensive regulation. New statutes even limited corporate profits and dividends. A large bureaucracy sprang up to administer the operations. By the war's end, the southern bureaucracy was larger in proportion to population than its northern counterpart.

Clerks and subordinate officials crowded the towns and cities in which Confederate departments had their offices. The sudden population booms that resulted exceeded the existing housing supply and stimulated new construction. The pressure was especially great in Richmond, where the population increased 250 percent.

Effects of War on Southern Cities and Industry

Another prime cause of urban growth was industrialization. The Union blockade, which disrupted imports of manufactured products, caused the traditionally agricultural South to become interested in industry. Davis exulted that manufacturing was making the South "more and more independent of the rest of the world." Indeed, beginning almost from scratch, the Confederacy achieved tremendous feats of industrial development.

Southerners adopted new ways in response to the changes. Women, restricted to narrow roles in antebellum society, gained substantial new responsibilities. The wives and mothers of soldiers now headed households and performed men's work. Women in nonslave-owning families cultivated fields, whereas wealthier women suddenly had to manage field hands unaccustomed to female overseers. In the cities, white women—who had been virtually excluded from the labor force—found a limited number of respectable new paying jobs. Clerks had always been men, but the war changed that too. "Government girls" staffed the Confederate bureaucracy, and female school teachers became commonplace in the South for the first time. Such experiences undermined the image of the omnipotent male and gave thousands of women new confidence in their abilities.

Change in the Southern Woman's Role

The Confederate experience introduced and sustained many other new values. Legislative bodies yielded power to the executive branch of government, which could act more decisively in time of war. Aristocratic lineage gave way to achievement and bravery under fire, as many men of ordinary background distinguished themselves in industry and on the battlefield. Finally, sacrifice for the cause discouraged the pursuit of pleasure.

For the elite, such sacrifice was symbolic, but for millions of ordinary southerners it was terrifyingly real. Mass poverty descended for the first time on a large minority of the white population. Many yeoman families had lost their breadwinners to the army. As a South Carolina newspaper put it, "The duties of war have called away from home the sole supports of many, many families. . . . Help must be given, or the poor will suffer." The poor sought help from relatives, neighbors, friends—anyone they could. Sometimes they even pleaded their cases to the Confederate government.

Human Suffering in the South

Other factors aggravated the effect of the labor shortage. The South was in many places so sparsely populated that the conscription of one skilled craftsman could work a hardship on the people of an entire county. Often, they begged in unison for the exemption or discharge of the local miller, neighborhood tanner, or a blacksmith who was needed to repair farm implements.

Inflation raged out of control, fueled by the Confederate government's heavy borrowing and inadequate taxes, until prices had increased almost 7,000 percent. Inflation particularly imperiled urban dwellers and the many who could no longer provide for themselves. As early as 1861 and 1862, newspapers reported that "the poor of our . . . country will be unable to live at all" and warned that "want and starvation are staring thousands in the face."

Some concerned citizens tried to help. "Free markets," which disbursed goods as charity, sprang up in various cities; some families came to the aid of their neighbors. But other people would not cooperate: "It is folly for a poor mother to call on the rich people about here," raged one woman. "Their hearts are of steel." The need was so vast that it overwhelmed private charity. A rudimentary relief program organized by the Confederacy offered hope, but it was soon curtailed to supply the armies. Thus Southern yeomen sank into poverty and suffering.

As their fortunes declined, people of once modest means looked around and found abundant evidence that all classes were not sacrificing equally. They saw that the wealthy gave up only their luxuries, whereas many poor families went without necessities. And they noted that the government contributed to the inequities through policies that favored the upper class. Until the last year of the war, for example, prosperous southerners could avoid military service by hiring substitutes. More than fifty thousand upper-class southerners purchased such substitutes. Anger at such discrimination exploded in October 1862, when the Confederate congress exempted from military duty anyone who was supervising at least twenty slaves. Protests poured in from every corner of the Confederacy, and North Carolina's legislators formally condemned the law. Its defenders argued, however, that the exemption preserved order and aided food production, and the statute remained on the books.

Inequities of the Confederate Draft

Dissension spread as growing numbers of citizens concluded that the struggle was "a rich man's war and a poor man's fight." Alert politicians and newspaper editors warned that class resentment was building to a dangerous level. The bitterness of letters to Confederate officials during this period suggests the depth of the people's anger. "If I and my little children suffer [and] die while there Father is in service," threatened one woman, "I invoke God Almighty that our blood rest upon the South." Clearly, war was magnifying social tensions in the Confederacy.

THE NORTHERN ECONOMY COPES WITH WAR

With the onset of war, a tidal wave of change rolled over the North as well. Factories and citizens' associations geared up to support the war, and the federal government and its executive branch gained new powers. The energies of an industrializing capitalist society were harnessed to serve the cause of the Union. Idealism and greed flourished together, and the northern economy proved its awesome productivity.

At first, the war was a shock to business. With the sudden closing of southern markets, companies could no longer predict the demand for their goods, and many had to change their products and find new markets in order to remain open. Southern debts became uncollectible, jeopardizing not only northern merchants but also many western banks. In farming regions, families struggled with an aggravated shortage of labor. Initially, the war caused an economic slump.

Initial Slump in Northern Business

Overall, the war slowed industrialization in the North, but its economic effect was not all negative. Certain entrepreneurs, such as wool producers, benefited from shortages of competing products, and soaring demand for war-related goods swept some businesses to new heights of production. To feed the hungry war machine, the federal government pumped unprecedented sums into the economy. As a result, companies producing weapons, munitions, uniforms, boots, saddles, ships, and other war necessities prospered.

War production also promoted the development of heavy industry in the North. Coal output rose substantially. Iron makers improved the quality of their product while boosting the production of pig iron. Foundries developed new and less expensive ways to make steel. Although new railroad construction slowed, repairs helped the manufacture of rails to increase. Of considerable significance for the future was the railroad industry's adoption of a standard gauge (width) for track, which eliminated unloading and reloading of boxcars and created a unified transportation system.

Effects of War on Northern Industry and Agriculture

Another strength of the northern economy was the complementary relationship between agriculture and industry. Mechanization of agriculture had begun before the war. Wartime recruitment and conscription, however, gave western farmers an added incentive to purchase labor-saving machinery. The shift from human labor to machines created new markets for industry and expanded the food supply for the urban industrial work force. Finally, farm families whose breadwinners went to war did not suffer as their counterparts did in the South. "We have seen," one magazine observed, "a stout matron whose sons are in the army, cutting hay with her team . . . and she cut seven acres with ease in a day, riding leisurely upon her cutter."

Northern industrial and urban workers did not fare as well. Jobs were plentiful after the initial slump, but inflation ate up much of a worker's paycheck. Between 1860 and 1864, consumer prices rose at least 76 percent, whereas daily wages rose only 42 percent. Workers' families consequently suffered a substantial decline in their standard of living.

As their real wages shrank, industrial workers also lost job security. To increase production, some employers were replacing workers with labor-saving machines. Other employers urged the government to liberalize immigration regulations so they could import cheap labor. Workers responded by forming unions and sometimes by striking. Skilled craftsmen organized to combat the loss of their jobs and status to machines; women and unskilled workers, excluded by the craftsmen, formed their own unions. In recognition of the increasingly national scope of business activity, thirteen occupational groups—including tailors, coal miners, and railway engineers—formed national unions during the Civil War.

New Militancy Among Northern Workers

Employers reacted with hostility to the new spirit among workers. Manufacturers viewed labor activism as a threat to their property rights and freedom of action and accordingly formed statewide or craft-based associations to cooperate and pool information. The employers shared blacklists of union members and required new workers to sign "yellow dog" contracts (promises not to join a union). To put down strikes, they hired strikebreakers from the ranks of the poor and desperate—blacks, immigrants, and women—and sometimes received additional help from federal troops.

Troublesome as unions were, they did not prevent many employers from making a profit. The highest profits were made from profiteering on government contracts. Unscrupulous businessmen took advantage of the sudden immense demand for army supplies by selling clothing and blankets made of "shoddy"—wool fibers reclaimed from rags or worn cloth. Shoddy goods often came apart in the rain; most shoes purchased in the early months of the war were worthless too. Contractors sold inferior guns for double the usual price and passed off tainted meat as good. Corruption was so widespread that it led to a year-long investigation by the House of Representatives.

Legitimate enterprises also made healthy profits. The output of woolen mills increased so dramatically that dividends in the industry nearly tripled. Some cotton mills made record profits on what they sold, although they reduced their output. Railroads carried immense quantities of freight and passengers, increasing their business to the point that railroad stocks doubled or even tripled in value.

Wartime Benefits to Northern Business

Railroads were also a leading beneficiary of government largesse. Congress had failed in the 1850s to resolve the question of a northern versus a southern route for the first transcontinental railroad. With the South absent from Congress, the northern route quickly prevailed. In 1862 and 1864, Congress chartered two corporations, the Union Pacific Railroad and the Central Pacific Railroad, and assisted them financially in connecting Omaha, Nebraska, with Sacramento, California. Overall, the two corporations gained approximately twenty million acres of land and nearly $60 million in loans.

Other businessmen also benefited handsomely from the Morrill Land Grant Act (1862). To promote public education, Congress granted each state thirty thousand acres of federal land for each of its congressional districts. Hard-pressed to meet wartime expenses, some states sold their land cheaply to wealthy entrepreneurs. Nonetheless, the intent of Congress in passing the land grant act was fulfilled in that the law eventually fostered sixty-nine colleges and universities.

Higher tariffs also pleased many businessmen. Northern businesses did not uniformly favor high import duties; some manufacturers desired inexpensive imported raw materials more than they feared foreign competition. But northeastern congressmen traditionally supported higher tariffs, and after southern lawmakers left Washington, they had their way: the Tariff Act of 1864 raised tariffs generously. Some healthy industries earned artificially high profits by raising their prices to a level just below that of the foreign competition. By the end of the war, tariff increases averaged 47 percent, and rates were more than double those of 1857.

WARTIME SOCIETY IN THE NORTH

The outbreak of war stimulated patriotism in the North, just as it initially had in the South. Northern society, which had suffered the stresses associated with industrialization, immigration, and widespread social change, found a unifying cause in the preservation of the nation. In thousands of towns and communities, northern citizens had a long history of participation in local government. Secession threatened to destroy their system, and northerners rallied to its defense.

Such enthusiasm proved useful as northerners encountered a multitude of wartime changes. The powers of the federal government and the president grew steadily during the crisis. Abraham Lincoln, like Jefferson Davis, found that war required active presidential leadership. At the beginning of the conflict, Lincoln launched a major shipbuilding program without waiting for Congress to assemble. The lawmakers later approved his decision, and Lincoln continued to act in advance of Congress when he deemed it necessary. In one striking exercise of executive power, Lincoln suspended the writ of habeas corpus (which prevents the government from holding citizens without trial) for everyone living between Washington and Philadelphia. Lincoln also used his wartime authority to bolster his political fortunes. He and his generals proved adept at furloughing soldiers so they could vote in close

Wartime Powers of the U.S. Executive

elections; those whom Lincoln furloughed, of course, usually voted Republican.

Among the clearest examples of the wartime expansion of federal authority were the National Banking Acts of 1863, 1864, and 1865. Before the Civil War, the nation lacked a uniform currency, for the federal government had never exercised its authority in this area. Banks operating under state charters issued no fewer than seven thousand different kinds of notes. Now, acting on the recommendations of Secretary of the Treasury Salmon P. Chase, Congress established a national banking system empowered to issue national bank notes. At the close of the war in 1865, Congress imposed a prohibitive tax on state bank notes and forced most major state institutions to join the national system.

Social attitudes on the home front evolved in directions that would have shocked soldiers in the field. Amid the excitement of money making, a

Self-Indulgence Versus Sacrifice in the North
———

gaudy culture of vulgar display flourished in the largest cities. As William Cullen Bryant, the distinguished editor of the *New York Evening Post*, observed, "Extravagance, luxury, these are the signs of the times. . . . What business have Americans at any time with such vain show, with such useless magnificence? But especially how can they justify it . . . in this time of war?" The newly rich did not bother to justify it. *Harper's Monthly* reported that "the suddenly enriched . . . are spending money with a profusion never before witnessed in our country. . . . The men button their waistcoats with diamonds . . . and the women powder their hair with gold and silver dust."

Yet idealism coexisted with ostentation. Abolitionists, after initial uncertainty over whether to let the South go, campaigned to turn the war into a crusade against slavery. Free black communities and churches both black and white responded to the needs of slaves who flocked to the Union lines, sending clothing, ministers, and teachers in generous measure to aid the runaways.

Northern women, like their southern counterparts, took on new roles. Those who stayed home organized more than ten thousand soldiers' aid societies, rolled innumerable bandages, and raised $3 million to aid injured troops. Thousands served as nurses in front-line hospitals, where they pressed for better care of the wounded. Yet women were only a fraction of all nurses, and they had to fight for a chance to serve at all. The professionalization of medicine since the Revolution had created a medical system dominated by men, and many male physicians did not want their aid. Female nurses proved their worth, but only the wounded welcomed them. Even Clara Barton, the most famous female nurse, was ousted from her post in 1863.

Thus northern society embraced strangely contradictory tendencies. Materialism and greed flourished alongside idealism, religious conviction, and self-sacrifice. Whereas some men risked their lives on the battlefield out of a desire to preserve the Union or extend freedom, the sons of the wealthy often avoided military service by taking advantage of a law that allowed them to either hire a substitute or pay a $300 commutation fee. In all, 118,000 substitutes were provided and eighty-seven thousand commutations paid before Congress ended the commutation system in 1864.

THE STRANGE ADVENT OF EMANCIPATION

The highest levels of government had a similar lack of clarity about the purpose of the war. Both Davis and Lincoln studiously avoided references to slavery, the crux of the matter, throughout the first several months of the struggle. Davis, realizing that emphasis on the issue could increase class conflict in the South, told southerners they were fighting for constitutional liberty.

Lincoln avoided the issue, because he did not want to antagonize the border slave states. He also hoped that a pro-Union majority would assert itself in the South. It might thus be possible, he thought, to coax the South back into the Union and stop the fighting. Moreover, not all Republicans burned with moral outrage over slavery. A forthright stand by Lincoln on the subject of slavery could split the party, gratifying some groups and alienating others.

Circular No. 8.

WASHINGTON, D. C., *July* 14, 1862.

No candidate for service in the Women's Department for nursing in the Military Hospitals of the United States, will be received below the age of thirty-five years, nor above fifty.

Only women of strong health, not subjects of chronic disease, nor liable to sudden illnesses, need apply. The duties of the station make large and continued demands on strength.

Matronly persons of experience, good conduct, or superior education and serious disposition, will always have preference; habits of neatness, order, sobriety, and industry, are prerequisites.

All applicants must present certificates of qualification and good character from at least two persons of trust, testifying to morality, integrity, seriousness, and capacity for care of the sick.

Obedience to rules of the service, and conformity to special regulations, will be required and enforced.

Compensation, as regulated by act of Congress, forty cents a day and subsistence. Transportation furnished to and from the place of service.

Amount of luggage limited within small compass.

Dress plain, (colors brown, grey, or black,) and while connected with the service without ornaments of any sort.

No applicants accepted for less than three months' service; those for longer periods always have preference.

D. L. DIX.

Approved.
WILLIAM A. HAMMOND,
Surgeon General.

How *do historians know*

that women had to struggle to serve the nation as nurses? The records of the Surgeon General's Office in the National Archives in Washington, D.C., document the efforts of Dorothea Dix to organize female nurses for the Union cause. A veteran of two decades of reform efforts to provide state hospitals for the mentally ill, Dix went to Washington at age sixty and volunteered to help the cause. Commissioned as the nation's first superintendent of women nurses, she sought only serious care-givers who were not trying to be near their husbands and sweethearts. Her Circular Order, pictured here, reflects that intention as well as the need to convince male doctors and superiors that women would be helpful. Although Dix largely succeeded in her efforts, most Civil War nurses were men. Photo: National Archives.

Lincoln's Plan for Gradual Emancipation

Lincoln first broached the subject of slavery in a substantive way in March 1862, when he proposed that the states consider emancipation on their own. He asked Congress to pass a resolution promising aid to any state that decided to emancipate, and he appealed to border-state representatives to give serious thought to emancipation. What Lincoln proposed was gradual emancipation, with compensation for slave holders and colonization of the freed slaves outside the United States. To a delegation of freed blacks he explained, "it is better for us both . . . to be separated." Until well into 1864, Lincoln steadfastly promoted an unpromising and wholly impractical scheme to colonize blacks in some region like Central America. The plan was extremely conservative, and because the states would make the decision voluntarily, no responsibility for it would attach to Lincoln.

Others wanted to go much further. A group of congressional Republicans, known as the Radicals, had from the early days of the war concerned

Confiscation Acts
——

themselves with slavery. In August 1861, at the Radicals' instigation, Congress passed its first confiscation act. Designed to punish the Confederate rebels, the law confiscated all property used for "insurrectionary purposes"—that is, if the South used slaves in a hostile action, those slaves were declared seized and liberated. A second confiscation act (July 1862) was much more drastic: it confiscated the property of all those who supported the rebellion, even those who merely resided in the South and paid Confederate taxes. The act declared their slaves "forever free of their servitude, and not again [to be] held as slaves." Let the government use its full powers, free the slaves, and crush the revolution, urged the Radicals.

Lincoln would not go that far. He stood by his proposal of voluntary gradual emancipation by the states and made no effort to enforce the second confiscation act. His stance provoked a public protest from Horace Greeley, editor of the powerful *New York Tribune*. In an open letter to the president, Greeley pleaded with Lincoln to "execute the laws" and declared, "On the face of this wide earth, Mr. President, there is not one disinterested, determined, intelligent champion of the Union cause who does not feel that all attempts to put down the Rebellion and at the same time uphold its inciting cause are preposterous and futile."

Lincoln's letter in reply was an explicit statement of his complex and calculated approach to the question. "I would save the Union," announced Lincoln. "If I could save the Union without freeing *any* slave I would do it, and if I could save it by freeing *all* the slaves I would do it; and if I could save it by freeing some and leaving others alone I would also do that. What I do about slavery, and the colored race, I do because I believe it helps to save the Union."

When he wrote these words, Lincoln had already decided on a new step: issuing the

Emancipation Proclamations
——

Emancipation Proclamation. He waited until an opportune time arose. On September 22, 1862, shortly after the Battle of Antietam, Lincoln issued the first (and often forgotten) part of his two-part proclamation. Invoking his powers as commander in chief of the armed forces, he announced that on January 1, 1863, he would emancipate the slaves in states where people "shall then be in rebellion against the United States." The proclamation was less a declaration of the right of slaves to be free than a threat to southerners to end the war. Lincoln may not actually have expected southerners to give up their effort, but he was careful to offer them the option, thus putting the onus of emancipation on them.

When Lincoln designated the areas in rebellion on January 1, he excepted from his list every Confederate county or city that had fallen under Union control. Those areas, he declared, "are, for the present, left precisely as if this proclamation were not issued." Nor did Lincoln liberate slaves in the border slave states that remained in the Union. "The President has purposely made the proclamation inoperative in all places where . . . the slaves [are] accessible," charged the anti-administration *New York World*. "He has proclaimed emancipation only where he has notoriously no power to execute it." The exceptions, said the paper, "render the proclamation not merely futile, but ridiculous." Partisanship aside, even Secretary of State Seward, a moderate Republican, said sarcastically, "We show our sympathy with slavery by emancipating slaves where we cannot reach them and holding them in bondage where we can set them free."

As a moral document, the Emancipation Proclamation, which in fact freed no slaves, was inadequate. As a political document, it was nearly flawless. Because the proclamation defined the war as a war against slavery, radicals could applaud it, even if the president had not gone as far as Congress. Yet at the same time, it protected Lincoln's position with conservatives, leaving him room to retreat if he chose and forcing no immediate changes on the border slave states.

The need for men soon convinced the administration to recruit northern and southern blacks for the army. By spring 1863, African-American troops were proving their value. Lincoln came to see them as "the great *available* and yet *unavailed of* force for restoring the Union." African-American leaders hoped that military service would secure equal rights for their people. Once the black soldier had fought for the Union, wrote Frederick Douglass, "there is no power on earth which can deny that he has earned the right of citizenship in the United States."

In June 1864, Lincoln gave his support to a constitutional ban on slavery. On the eve of the Republican national convention, Lincoln called the party's chairman to the White House and instructed him to have the party "put into the platform as the keystone, the amendment of the Constitution abolishing and prohibiting slavery forever." The party promptly called for a new amendment, the thirteenth. Lincoln demonstrated his commitment by lobbying Congress for quick approval of the measure. The proposed amendment passed and was sent to the states for ratification or rejection. Lincoln's strong support for the Thirteenth Amendment—an unequivocal prohibition of slavery—constitutes his best claim to the title Great Emancipator.

Yet Lincoln soon clouded that clear stand, for in 1865 the newly reelected president considered allowing the defeated southern states to reenter the Union and delay or defeat the amendment. In February, he and Secretary of State Seward met with three Confederate commissioners at Hampton Roads, Virginia. With the end of the war in sight, Lincoln was apparently contemplating the creation of a new national party based on a postwar alliance with southern Whigs and moderate and conservative Republicans. The cement for the coalition would be concessions to planter interests.

Hampton Roads Conference

Pointing out that the Emancipation Proclamation was only a war measure, Lincoln predicted that the courts would decide whether it had granted all, some, or none of the slaves their freedom. Seward observed that the Thirteenth Amendment, which would be definitive, was not yet ratified; reentry to the Union would allow the southern states to defeat it. Lincoln did not contradict

Seward but spoke in favor of "prospective" ratification: approval with the effective date postponed for five years. He also promised to seek $400 million in compensation for slaveholders. The financial aid would provide an economic incentive for planters to rejoin the Union and capital to cushion the economic blow of emancipation. Such proposals were opposed in the North. In the South, they were not discussed because of Davis's total commitment to independence.

Before the war was over, the Confederacy too addressed the issue of emancipation. Jefferson Davis offered a strong proposal in favor of liberation. He was dedicated to independence, and he was willing to sacrifice slavery to achieve that goal. After considering the alternatives for some time, Davis concluded late in 1864 that independence with emancipation was preferable to defeat with emancipation. He proposed that the Confederate government purchase forty thousand slaves to work for the army as laborers, with a promise of freedom at the end of their service. Soon Davis upgraded his proposal, calling for the recruitment and arming of slaves as soldiers, who likewise would gain their freedom at the end of the war. The wives and children of the soldiers, he made plain, must also receive freedom from the states.

Davis's Plan for Emancipation

Confederate emancipation began too late to revive southern armies or win diplomatic advantages with antislavery Europeans. By contrast, Lincoln's Emancipation Proclamation stimulated a vital infusion of forces to the Union armies. Beginning in 1863, slaves shouldered arms for the North. Before the war was over, 134,000 slaves (and fifty-two thousand free African-Americans) had fought for freedom and the Union. Their participation was crucial to northern victory, and it discouraged recognition of the Confederacy by foreign governments.

THE SOLDIER'S WAR

The intricacies of policymaking were far from the minds of ordinary soldiers. Military service completely altered their lives. Army life meant tedium, physical hardship, and separation from loved ones even in the best of times. In battle, soldiers faced fear and the risk of death. For many, however, the war experience created a bond with their fellows and a connection to noble purpose that they cherished for years afterward.

Soldiers benefited from certain new products, such as canned condensed milk, but blankets, clothing, and arms were often of poor quality. Vermin were commonplace. Hospitals were badly managed at first. Rules of hygiene in large camps were badly written or unenforced; latrines were poorly made or carelessly used. Indeed, conditions were such that 224,000 Union troops died from disease or accidents, far more than the 140,000 who died as a result of battle.

On both sides, troops quickly learned that soldiering was far from glorious. In 1862, one North Carolina volunteer wrote: "We had no tents after the 6th of August, but slept on the ground, in the woods or open fields, without regard to the weather. . . . I learned to eat fat bacon raw, and to like it. . . .

Realities of a Soldier's Life
———

Without time to wash our clothes or our persons, and sleeping on the ground all huddled together, the whole army became lousy more or less with body lice." And the sight of the blasted bodies of friends and comrades left mental scars that even time often fails to heal.

Advances in technology made the Civil War particularly deadly. By far the most important were the rifle and the "minie ball." Bullets fired from a smoothbore musket tumbled and wobbled as they flew through the air and thus were not accurate at distances greater than eighty yards. Cutting spiraled grooves inside the barrel gave the projectile a spin and much greater accuracy, but rifles remained difficult to load and use until the Frenchman Claude Minie and the American James Burton developed a new kind of bullet. Civil War bullets were sizable lead slugs with a cavity at the bottom that expanded upon firing so that the bullet "took" the rifling and flew accurately. With these bullets, rifles were accurate at four hundred yards and useful up to one thousand yards.

This meant, of course, that soldiers assaulting a position defended by riflemen were in greater peril

than ever before. Thus the toll from Civil War battles was high. Never before in Europe or America had such massive forces pummeled each other with weapons of such destructive power. Yet the armies in the Civil War seemed virtually indestructible. Even in the bloodiest engagements, in which thousands of men died, the losing army was never destroyed.

Still, Civil War soldiers developed deep commitments to each other and to their task. The bonding may have been most dramatic among officers and men in the northern black regiments. Racism in the Union army was strong; one New Yorker objected to fighting beside African-Americans with the words, "We are a too superior race for that." Some white officers volunteered for black units only to gain faster promotion. But black troops had a mission to destroy slavery, and many of their white officers shared, or came to share, that commitment. One general reported that his "colored regiments" possessed "remarkable aptitude for military training," and another observer said, "They fight like fiends."

For their part, African-American troops appreciated the dedication and courage of white officers who treated them as men. Just before the 54th Massachusetts launched its famous and costly assault on Fort Wagner, a black soldier called out to abolitionist Colonel Robert Gould Shaw, "Colonel, I will stay by you till I die." "And he kept his word," noted a survivor of the attack. "He has never been seen since."

Such valor emerged despite persistent discrimination. The government, for instance, paid white privates $13 per month plus a clothing allowance of $3.50, whereas black privates earned only $10 per month less $3 deducted for clothing.

THE TIDE OF BATTLE BEGINS TO TURN

The fighting in the spring and summer of 1863 did not settle the war, but it began to place clear limits on the outcome. The campaigns began in a

These photographs capture the different personal styles of Generals Grant (left) and Lee (right). Their bloody battles in 1864 caused northern revulsion to the war but ultimately brought its end in sight. National Archives.

Battle of Chancellorsville
———

deceptively positive way for Confederates, as their Army of Northern Virginia performed brilliantly in the battle of Chancellorsville (May 2–3), where some 130,000 members of the Union Army of the Potomac bore down on fewer than sixty thousand Confederates. Acting as if they enjoyed being outnumbered, Lee and Stonewall Jackson boldly divided their forces, ordering thirty thousand men under Jackson on a day-long march westward and to the rear for a flank attack. Jackson's seasoned "foot cavalry" found unprepared Union troops laughing, smoking, and playing cards. The Confederate attack drove back in confusion the entire Union right wing, and Union forces left in defeat the next day. However, his own men had inadvertently killed Jackson. The victory was thus a costly one for the Confederacy.

In July 1863, two critical battles—at Vicksburg and Gettysburg—brought crushing defeats for the Confederacy and effectively circumscribed its hopes for independence. After finding an advantageous approach to Vicksburg, General Grant laid siege to that vital western fortification. If the city fell, U.S. forces would control the Mississippi, cutting the Confederacy in half and gaining an open

path to its interior. Meanwhile, Lee proposed a Confederate invasion of the North. Both movements drew toward conclusion in early July.

In the North, Lee's troops streamed through western Maryland and into Pennsylvania, threatening both Washington and Baltimore. The possibility of a major victory near the Union capital became more and more likely. But along the Mississippi, Confederate prospects darkened. Davis repeatedly wired General Joseph E. Johnston, urging him to concentrate his forces and attack Grant's army. Despite the prodding, Johnston did nothing to relieve the garrison. Grant's men, meanwhile, were supplying themselves from the agricultural riches of the Mississippi River valley and could continue their siege indefinitely. In such circumstances, the fall of Vicksburg was inevitable, and on July 4, 1863, its commander surrendered.

On the same day, a battle that had been raging for three days concluded at Gettysburg, Pennsylvania. On July 1, Confederate forces collided with part of the Union army. Heavy fighting on the second day left federal forces in possession of high ground along Cemetery Ridge. There, they enjoyed the protection of a stone wall and a clear view of their

Battle of Gettysburg
———

foe across almost a mile of open field. Undaunted, Lee believed his splendid troops could break the Union line, and on July 3 he ordered a direct assault. Full of foreboding, General James Longstreet warned Lee that "no 15,000 men ever arrayed for battle can take that position." But Lee stuck to his plan. Brave troops under General George E. Pickett methodically marched up the slope in a doomed assault known as Pickett's Charge. A hundred momentarily breached the enemy's line, but most fell in heavy slaughter. On July 4, Lee had to withdraw, having suffered almost four thousand dead and about twenty-four thousand missing and wounded.

Southern troops displayed unforgettable courage and dedication at Gettysburg, but the results there and at Vicksburg were disastrous. The Confederacy was split in two, its heartland exposed to invasion. Moreover, Lee's defeat spelled the end of major offensive actions by the South. Too weak to prevail in attack, the Confederacy would henceforth have to conserve its limited resources and rely on a prolonged defense. By refusing to be beaten, the South might yet win, but its prospects were more limited now than they had ever been before.

THE DISINTEGRATION OF CONFEDERATE UNITY

Both northern and southern governments waged the final two years of the war in the face of increasing opposition at home. Dissatisfactions that had surfaced earlier grew more intense and sometimes violent. The gigantic costs of a war that neither side seemed able to win fed the unrest. But protest also arose from fundamental stresses in the social structures of the North and the South.

One ominous development was the planters' increasing opposition to their own government, the actions of which often had a negative effect on them. Not only did the Richmond government impose new taxes and a tax in-kind, but Confederate military authorities also impressed slaves to build fortifications. And when Union forces advanced on plantation areas, Confederate commanders burned stores of cotton that lay in the enemy's path. Such interference with plantation routines and financial interests was not what planters had expected of their government, and they complained bitterly.

The Confederate constitution had in fact granted substantial powers to the central government, especially in time of war. But in many planters' minds, states' rights had become virtually synonymous with complete state sovereignty. In effect, years of opposition to the federal government within the Union had frozen southerners in a defensive posture. Now they erected the barrier of states' rights as a defense against change. Planters sought a guarantee that their plantations and their lives would remain untouched; they were deeply committed neither to building a southern nation nor to winning independence. If the Confederacy had been allowed to depart from the Union in peace and continue as a semideveloped cotton-growing region, they would have been content. When secession revolutionized their world, they could not or would not adjust to it.

Meanwhile, for ordinary southerners, the dire predictions of hunger and suffering were becoming a reality. Food riots occurred in the spring of 1863

Food Riots in Southern Cities

in Atlanta, Macon, Columbus, and Augusta, Georgia, and in Salisbury and High Point, North Carolina. On April 2, a crowd assembled in the Confederate capital of Richmond to demand relief. A passerby, noticing the excitement, asked a young girl, "Is there some celebration?" "There is," replied the girl. "We celebrate our right to live. We are starving. As soon as enough of us get together we are going to the bakeries and each of us will take a loaf of bread." Soon they did just that, sparking a riot that Davis had to quell at gunpoint.

Throughout the rural South, ordinary people resisted more quietly—by refusing to cooperate with conscription, tax collection, and impressments of food. "In all the States impressments are evaded by every means which ingenuity can suggest, and in some openly resisted," wrote a high-ranking commissary officer. Farmers who did provide food for the army refused to accept certificates of credit or government bonds in lieu of cash, as required by law. Conscription officers increasingly found no one to draft—men of draft age were hiding out in the forests.

Such civil discontent was certain to affect the Confederate armies. Spurred by concern for their loved ones and resentment of what they increasingly saw as a rich man's war, large numbers of men did indeed leave the armies, supported by their friends and neighbors. The problem of desertion became so acute that by November 1863 Secretary of War James Seddon admitted that one-third of the army could not be accounted for. The situation was to worsen.

Desertions from the Confederate Army

The defeats at Gettysburg and Vicksburg dealt a body blow to Confederate morale. In desperation, some leaders used racial scare tactics in hopes of getting greater sacrifices from southern whites. Instead, as the pace of the internal disintegration of the Confederacy quickened, Confederate leaders found that they were increasingly losing the support of the common people. Moreover, a few newspapers began to call openly for peace.

In North Carolina, a peace movement grew under the leadership of William W. Holden, a popular Democratic politician and editor. More than one hundred public meetings took place in the summer of 1863 in support of peace negotiations. In Georgia early in 1864, Governor Brown and Alexander H. Stephens, vice president of the Confederacy, led a similar effort. Ultimately, however, the movements came to naught. Nevertheless, their existence demonstrated deep disaffection.

Southern Peace Movements

By 1864, much of the opposition to the war had moved entirely outside the political sphere. Southerners were simply giving up the struggle and withdrawing their cooperation from the government. Deserters joined with ordinary citizens who were sick of the war to dominate whole towns and counties. Secret societies dedicated to reaffiliation with the Union sprang up. Active dissent spread throughout the South but was particularly common in upland and mountain regions. The government was losing the support of its citizens.

ANTIWAR SENTIMENT IN THE NORTH

In the North, opposition to the war was similar but less severe. Alarm over the growing centralization of government intensified, and war weariness was widespread. Resentment of the draft sparked protest, especially among poor citizens, and the Union army struggled with a desertion rate as high as the Confederates'. But the Union was so much richer than the South in human resources that none of these problems ever threatened the stability of the government. Fresh recruits were always available, and there were no shortages of food and other necessities.

Moreover, Lincoln possessed a talent that Davis lacked: he knew how to stay in touch with the ordinary citizen. Through letters to newspapers and to soldiers' families, he reached the common people and demonstrated that he had not forgotten them. Their grief was his also, for the war was his personal tragedy. His moving words helped to contain northern discontent, although they could not remove it.

Much of the wartime protest was political in origin. The Democratic party remained strong and fought to regain power by blaming Lincoln for the war's carnage, the expansion of federal powers, inflation and the high tariff, and the emancipation of blacks. Appealing to tradition, they called for an end to the war and reunion on the basis of "the Constitution as it is and the Union as it was." The Democrats denounced conscription and martial law and defended states' rights and the interests of agriculture. In the 1862 congressional elections, the Democrats made a strong comeback, and peace Democrats wielded influence in New York State and won majorities in the legislatures of Illinois and Indiana.

Peace Democrats

Led by outspoken men like Clement L. Vallandigham of Ohio, the peace Democrats made themselves highly visible. Vallandigham criticized Lincoln as a dictator who had suspended the writ of habeas corpus without congressional authority and had arrested thousands of innocent citizens. Like other Democrats, he condemned both conscription and emancipation. Vallandigham stayed carefully within legal bounds, but his attacks were so damaging to the war effort that military authorities arrested him for treason after Lincoln suspended habeas corpus. Lincoln wisely decided against punishment—and martyr's status—for Vallandigham and exiled him to the Confederacy.

Lincoln believed that antiwar Democrats were linked to secret organizations that harbored traitorous ideas. Likening such groups to a poisonous snake, Republicans branded them—and by extension the peace Democrats—as Copperheads. Although Democrats were connected with these organizations, most engaged in politics rather than treason.

More violent opposition to the government arose from ordinary citizens facing the draft, especially the urban poor and immigrants in strongly Democratic areas. The poor

New York City Draft Riot
———

resented the commutation fee that allowed many men to avoid military service, and many immigrants suspected (wrongly, on the whole) that they were called in disproportionate numbers. Such attitudes led to enrolling officers' receiving rough treatment in many parts of the North. They also contributed to the outbreak of riots in Ohio, Indiana, Pennsylvania, Illinois, Wisconsin, New Jersey, and New York. By far the most serious outbreak of violence occurred in New York City in July 1863, where three days of rioting left seventy-four people dead. The riots had racist and class overtones. Many working-class whites feared an influx of black labor from the South, and Irish immigrants resented being forced to serve in the place of others who could afford to avoid the draft.

Discouragement and war weariness reached a peak in the summer of 1864, when the Democratic party nominated the popular General George B. McClellan for president and inserted a qualified peace plank in its platform. Lincoln, running with Tennessee's Andrew Johnson on a "National Union" ticket, concluded that it was "exceedingly probable that this Administration will not be re-elected." The fortunes of war, however, soon changed the electoral situation.

NORTHERN PRESSURE AND SOUTHERN WILL

The success of the North's long-term diplomatic strategy was sealed in 1864. From the outset, the North's paramount diplomatic goal had been to

Northern Diplomatic Strategy
———

prevent recognition of the Confederacy by European nations and the military and financial aid it would bring. Confederate leaders, believing that England was dependent upon southern cotton, hoped to secure recognition through "king Cotton" diplomacy. Because British cotton mills had a 50 percent cotton surplus when the war began and because England developed new sources for cotton during the war, the South's strategy failed. The British government, refusing to be stampeded into recognition, kept its eye on the battlefield. France, although sympathetic to the South, was unwilling to act independent of the British.

More than once, the Union strategy nearly broke down. An acute crisis occurred in 1861 when the overzealous commander of an American frigate stopped the British steamer *Trent* and removed two Confederate ambassadors. The British reacted angrily, but Lincoln and Seward waited until public opinion cooled down enough for them to return the ambassadors. In a series of confrontations with Britain, the United States protested the sale of warships to the Confederacy. A few ships built in Britain, notably the *Alabama*, reached open water to serve the South. Over twenty-two months, the *Alabama* destroyed or captured more than sixty northern ships. But the British government soon began to bar delivery of warships such as the Laird rams, formidable vessels with pointed prows designed to break the Union blockade.

On the battlefield, the northern victory was far from won in 1864. The course of the war had demonstrated the advantages enjoyed by the defense and the extreme difficulty of destroying an opposing army. General William Tecumseh Sherman now realized that the North had to "keep the war South until they are not only ruined, exhausted, but humbled in pride and spirit." Yet military authorities throughout history have agreed that deep invasion is extremely risky: the farther an army penetrates enemy territory, the more vulnerable its own communications and support become. Moreover, observed the Prussian expert Karl von Clausewitz, if the invader encountered a "truly national" resistance, his troops would be "everywhere exposed to attacks by an insurgent population."

General Grant decided to test these conditions—and southern will—with a strategic innovation of his own: raids on a massive scale. Grant proposed to use whole armies, not just cavalry, to destroy Confederate railroads, thus ruining the enemy's transportation and damaging the South's economy. Abandoning their lines of support, federal armies would live off the land while they laid waste all resources useful to the Confederacy. After General George H. Thomas's troops won the Battle of Chattanooga in November 1863, the heartland of the South lay open. Moving to Virginia, Grant entrusted General Sherman with one hundred thousand men for a raid deep into the South, toward Atlanta.

Jefferson Davis countered by positioning the army of General Joseph E. Johnston in Sherman's path. Davis's entire political strategy for 1864 was based on demonstrating Confederate military strength and successfully defending Atlanta. With the federal elections of 1864 approaching, Davis hoped that a display of strength and resolve by the South would defeat Lincoln and elect a president who would sue for peace. When Johnston slowly but steadily fell back toward Atlanta, Davis grew anxious and pressed his commander for information and assurances that Atlanta would be held. From a purely military point of view, Johnston was conducting the defense skillfully, but Davis replaced him with the one-legged General John Hood, who knew his job was to fight. Hood attacked but was beaten, and Sherman's army occupied Atlanta on September 2, 1864. The victory buoyed northern spirits, assured Lincoln's reelection, and cleared the way for Sherman's march from Atlanta to the sea (see map).

As Sherman's men moved across Georgia, they cut a path fifty to sixty miles wide and more than two hundred miles long; the totality of the destruction was awesome. A Georgia woman described the "Burnt Country" this way: "The fields were trampled down and the road was lined with carcasses of horses, hogs, and cattle that the invaders, unable either to consume or to carry with them, had wantonly shot down to starve our people and prevent them from making their crops. The stench in some places was unbearable." Such devastation diminished the South's material resources and, more important, its faltering will to resist.

In Virginia, the preliminaries to victory proved protracted and ghastly. Throughout the spring and summer of 1864, Grant hurled his troops at Lee's army and suffered appalling losses: almost eighteen thousand casualties in the Battle of the Wilderness, more than eight thousand at Spotsylvania, and twelve thousand in the space of a few hours at Cold Harbor. Before the last battle, Union troops pinned scraps of paper bearing their names and addresses to their backs, certain they would be mowed down as they rushed Lee's trenches. In four weeks in May and June, Grant lost as many men as were enrolled in Lee's entire army. Although costly, Grant's strategy prepared the way for eventual victory: Lee's army shrank until offensive action was no longer possible, while the Union army kept replenishing its forces with new recruits.

The end finally came in the spring of 1865. Grant kept battering Lee, who tried but failed to break through the federal line. With the

Heavy Losses Force Lee's Surrender

numerical superiority of Grant's army now greater than two to one, Confederate defeat was inevitable. On April 2, Lee abandoned Richmond and Petersburg. On April 9, hemmed in by federal troops, short of rations, and with fewer than thirty thousand men left, Lee surrendered at Appomattox Courthouse (see map). Grant treated his rival with respect and paroled the defeated troops. Within weeks, Jefferson Davis was captured, and the remaining Confederate forces laid down their arms and surrendered. The war was over at last.

Lincoln did not live to see the last surrenders. On the evening of Good Friday, April 14, he went to Ford's Theatre in Washington, where an assassin named John Wilkes Booth shot him at pointblank range. The Union had lost its wartime leader, and millions publicly mourned the martyred chief.

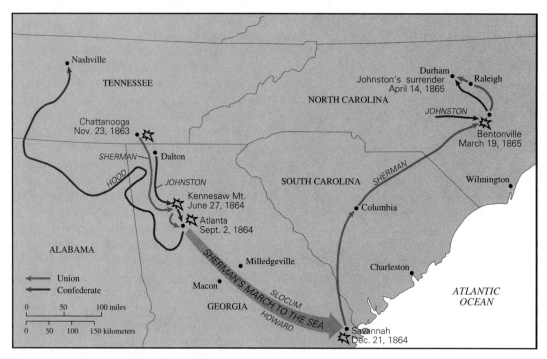

Sherman's March to the Sea *The West proved a decisive theater at the end of the war. From Chattanooga, Union forces drove into Georgia, capturing Atlanta. Then General Sherman embarked on his march of destruction through Georgia to the sea and then north through the Carolinas.*

Relief at the war's end now mingled uncomfortably with a renewed sense of loss and uncertainty about the future.

COSTS AND EFFECTS

The costs of the Civil War were enormous. The total number of military casualties on both sides exceeded one million—a frightful toll for a nation of thirty-one million people.

Casualties

Approximately 364,000 federal soldiers died, 140,000 from wounds suffered in battle. Another 275,175 Union soldiers were wounded but survived. On the Confederate side, an estimated 258,000 lost their lives, and almost as many suffered wounds. More men died in the Civil War than in all other American wars combined until Vietnam.

Although precise figures on enlistments are impossible to obtain, it appears that seven hundred thousand to eight hundred thousand men served in the Confederate armies. Far more, perhaps 2.3 million, served in the Union armies. All the men were taken from home, family, and personal goals and had their lives disrupted in ways that were not easily repaired.

Property damage and financial costs were also enormous, although difficult to tally. Federal loans and taxes during the conflict totaled almost $3 billion, and interest on the war debt was $2.8 billion. The Confederacy borrowed more than $2 billion but lost far more in the destruction of homes, crops, livestock, and other property. Scholars have noted that small farmers lost just as much, proportionally, as planters whose slaves were emancipated.

Financial Cost of the War

Estimates of the total cost of the war exceed $20 billion—five times the total expenditures of the federal government from its creation to 1861. The

The War in Virginia, 1864–1865 *At great cost, Grant hammered away at Lee's army until the weakened southern forces finally surrendered at Appomattox.*

northern government increased its spending by 700 percent in the first full year of the war; by the last year, its spending had soared to twenty times the prewar level. By 1865, the federal government accounted for more than 26 percent of the gross national product.

Many changes were more or less permanent. In the 1880s, interest on the war debt still accounted for approximately 40 percent of the federal budget and Union soldiers' pensions for as much as 20 percent. Thus, although many southerners had hoped to remove government from the economy, the war made such separation an impossibility. Federal expenditures shrank after the war, but they stabilized at twice the prewar level, or at 4 percent of the gross national product.

Economically, wartime measures had introduced new federal involvement in both the banking and transportation systems. The government had also exercised its power to support manufacturing and business interests by means of tariffs, loans, and subsidies. Industrialization and large economic enterprises clearly had arrived to stay. In political terms, national power increased permanently. Extreme forms of states' rights dogma clearly were dead, but serious questions remained to be answered. Would Americans continue to favor a state-centered federalism? How would white southerners respond to efforts to reconstruct the nation?

Closely related to these issues was a question of central importance: what would be the place of black men and women in American life? The Union victory provided a partial answer: slavery as it had existed before the war could not persist. But what would replace it? African-Americans eagerly awaited an answer, which would have to be found during Reconstruction.

SUGGESTIONS FOR FURTHER READING

The War and the South

Thomas B. Alexander and Richard E. Beringer, *The Anatomy of the Confederate Congress* (1972); Richard E. Beringer et al., *Why the South Lost the Civil War* (1986); William C. Davis, *Jefferson Davis* (1991), and *Diary of a Confederate Soldier* (1990); Robert F. Durden, *The Gray and the Black: The Confederate Debate on Emancipation* (1972); Paul D. Escott, *After Secession: Jefferson Davis and the Failure of Confederate Nationalism* (1978); Mary Elizabeth Massey, *Refugee Life in the Confederacy* (1964); Alan T. Nolan, *Lee Considered* (1991); Harry P. Owens and James J. Cooke, eds., *The Old South in the Crucible of War* (1983); Charles W. Ramsdell, *Behind the Lines in the Southern Confederacy*, ed. Wendell H. Stephenson (1944); James L. Roark, *Masters Without Slaves* (1977); Georgia Lee Tatum, *Disloyalty in the Confederacy* (1934); Emory M. Thomas, *The Confederate Nation* (1979); Bell Irvin Wiley, *The Life of Johnny Reb* (1943), and *The Plain People of the Confederacy* (1943); W. Buck Yearns, ed., *The Confederate Governors* (1985).

The War and the North

Ralph Andreano, ed., *The Economic Impact of the American Civil War* (1962); James W. Geary, *We Need Men* (1991); Frank L. Klement, *The Copperheads in the Middle West* (1960); James M. McPherson, *Battle Cry of Freedom* (1988); James H. Moorhead, *American Apocalypse* (1978); Phillip S. Paludan, *"A People's Contest": The Union and the Civil War, 1861–1865* (1989); Robert Hunt Rhodes, ed., *All for the Union: The Civil War Diary and*

Letters of Elisha Hunt Rhodes (1991); George Winston Smith and Charles Burnet Judah, *Life in the North During the Civil War* (1966); Paul Studenski, *Financial History of the United States* (1952); Bell Irvin Wiley, *The Life of Billy Yank* (1952).

Women

John R. Brumgardt, ed., *Civil War Nurse: The Diary and Letters of Hannah Ropes* (1980); Mary Elizabeth Massey, *Bonnet Brigades* (1966); George C. Rable, *Civil Wars: Women and the Crisis of Southern Nationalism* (1989); Mary D. Robertson, ed., *Lucy Breckinridge of Grove Hill: The Journal of a Virginia Girl, 1862–1864* (1979); C. Vann Woodward and Elisabeth Muhlenfeld, eds., *Mary Chesnut's Civil War* (1981).

African-Americans

Virginia M. Adams, ed., *On the Altar of Freedom: A Black Soldier's Civil War Letters from the Front* (1991); David W. Blight, *Frederick Douglass' Civil War* (1989); Joseph T. Glatthaar, *Forged in Battle* (1990); Leon Litwack, *Been in the Storm So Long* (1979); James M. McPherson, *The Negro's Civil War* (1965); Clarence L. Mohr, *On the Threshold of Freedom* (1986); Benjamin Quarles, *The Negro in the Civil War* (1953).

Military History

Nancy Scott Anderson and Dwight Anderson, *The Generals: Ulysses S. Grant and Robert E. Lee* (1987); Albert Castel, *Decision in the West* (1992); Benjamin Franklin Cooling, *Forts Henry and Donelson* (1988); Peter Cozzens, *This Terrible Sound* (1992); Shelby Foote, *The Civil War: A Narrative*, 3 vols. (1958–1974); Douglas Southall Freeman, *R. E. Lee*, 4 vols. (1934–1935); Joseph T. Glatthaar, *The March to the Sea and Beyond* (1985); Herman Hattaway and Archer Jones, *How the North Won* (1983);

Archer Jones, *Civil War Command and Strategy* (1992); Alvin M. Josephy Jr., *The Civil War in the American West* (1991); John F. Marszalek, *Sherman* (1992); Reid Mitchell, *Civil War Soldiers* (1988); Roy Morris Jr., *Sheridan* (1992); Emory M. Thomas, *Bold Dragoon: The Life of J. E. B. Stuart* (1987); Noah Andre Trudeau, *The Last Citadel* (1991); Warren Wilkinson, *Mother, May You Never See the Sights I Have Seen* (1990); Steven E. Woodworth, *Jefferson Davis and His Generals* (1990).

Diplomatic History

David P. Crook, *The North, the South, and the Powers, 1861–1865* (1974); Charles P. Cullop, *Confederate Propaganda in Europe* (1969); Norman A. Graebner, "Northern Diplomacy and European Neutrality," in David Donald, ed., *Why the North Won the Civil War* (1960); Gordon H. Warren, *Fountain of Discontent: The Trent Affair and Freedom of the Seas* (1981); Gordon H. Warren, "The King Cotton Theory," in Alexander DeConde, ed., *Encyclopedia of American Foreign Policy*, 3 vols. (1978).

Abraham Lincoln and the Union Government

Allan G. Bogue, *The Earnest Men: Republicans of the Civil War Senate* (1981); Richard N. Current, *The Lincoln Nobody Knows* (1958); Leonard P. Curry, *Blueprint for Modern America: Non-Military Legislation of the First Civil War Congress* (1968); Christopher Dell, *Lincoln and the War Democrats* (1975); Ludwell H. Johnson, "Lincoln's Solution to the Problem of Peace Terms, 1864–1865," *Journal of Southern History* 34 (November 1968): 441–447; Peyton McCrary, *Abraham Lincoln and Reconstruction: The Louisiana Experiment* (1978); James M. McPherson, *Abraham Lincoln and the Second American Revolution* (1990); Mark Neely, *The Fate of Liberty* (1991); Joel Silbey, *A Respectable Minority: The Democratic Party in the Civil War Era* (1977); Hans L. Trefousse, *The Radical Republicans* (1969).

16

Reconstruction: A Partial Revolution, 1865–1877

F OR BOTH MEN, WAR and Reconstruction brought stunning changes and swift reversals of fortune. In 1861, Robert Smalls was a slave in South Carolina, and Wade Hampton was a South Carolina legislator and one of the richest planters in the South. The events of the next fifteen years turned each man's world upside-down more than once.

When Smalls stole a Confederate ship from Charleston harbor and piloted it to the blockading federal fleet, he became a Union war hero. Thereafter, Smalls guided Union gunboats and toured the North recruiting black troops. By 1868, Smalls had begun a career in politics. He helped write his state's constitution, served in the legislature, and won election to Congress. There, he denounced white violence and worked for educational and economic opportunity for his people.

Hampton joined the Confederate army in 1861 and rose to the rank of lieutenant general. The South's defeat profoundly shocked him. For Hampton, the postwar years brought unexpected changes, including forced bankruptcy. By 1876, his fortunes were again on the rise: Democrats nominated him for gov-

ernor, promising that he would "redeem" South Carolina from Republican misrule. While Hampton spoke misleadingly of respect for blacks' rights, each member of the paramilitary Red Shirts who supported him pledged to "control the vote of at least one Negro, by intimidation, purchase," or other means. Hampton won the governor's chair and then a seat in the U.S. Senate.

As the careers of Smalls and Hampton suggest, Reconstruction changed much and yet changed little. Smalls rose from bondage to experience glory, emancipation, political power, and, ultimately, disappointment. Hampton fell from privilege to endure unaccustomed failure and powerlessness but eventually returned to a position of dominance. Similarly, American society experienced both extraordinary change and fundamental continuity. Unprecedented social, political, and constitutional changes took place, but the underlying realities of economic power, racial prejudice, and judicial conservatism limited Reconstruction's revolutionary potential.

Nowhere was the turmoil of Reconstruction more evident than in national politics. The president and

Congress fought bitterly about the shaping of a plan for Reconstruction. When Andrew Johnson succeeded Abraham Lincoln, his first actions convinced both southern aristocrats and northern Republicans that he intended to be tough on traitors. Formerly a Democrat from Tennessee, Johnson had always been a combative foe of the South's wealthy planters. Before the end of 1865, however, Johnson's policies changed direction. Jefferson Davis stayed in prison for two years, but no Confederate leaders were executed, and southern aristocrats soon came to view Johnson as their friend and protector. He pardoned rebel leaders liberally, allowed them to occupy high offices, and ordered tax officials to return plantations to their original owners, including abandoned coastal lands on which forty thousand freedmen had settled by order of General Sherman.

This turn of events alarmed northern voters. Republican congressmen began to discuss plans to keep rebels from regaining control of the South, and negotiations in Congress produced a new Reconstruction program, embodied in the Fourteenth Amendment. But southern intransigence blocked that program and forced the development of a more radical plan, the Reconstruction Act of 1867. When Congress put the act into effect, Johnson tried to subvert it, and by 1868 the president and Congress were bitterly antagonistic.

Before these struggles were over, Congress had impeached the president and enfranchised the freedmen. The nation also adopted the Fourteenth and Fifteenth Amendments. Yet nothing was done to open the doors of economic progress to black southerners. Moreover, the emergence of night-riding terrorist organizations such as the Ku Klux Klan reflected the extent to which many white southerners opposed Reconstruction. By 1877, hostile white Democrats in the South had regained control of every state government, undoing the political revolution. And judicially, the Supreme Court was adopting interpretations of the Thirteenth, Fourteenth, and Fifteenth Amendments that crippled their power for decades.

As the 1870s advanced, northern voters became increasingly weary and suspicious of the use of federal power to prop up failing Republican governments in the South. And other issues drew attention away from Reconstruction. Industrial growth accelerated, creating new opportunities and raising new problems. Interest in territorial expansion revived. Political corruption became a nationwide scandal and bribery a way of doing business. Eventually, these other forces triumphed. As politics moved on to new concerns, the courts turned away from civil rights, and even northern Republicans abandoned racial reforms in 1877.

Thus only limited change emerged from a period of tremendous upheaval. Congress asserted the principle of equality before the law for African-Americans and gave black men the right to vote. But more far-reaching measures to advance black freedom never had much support in Congress, and when suffrage alone proved insufficient to remake the South, the nation soon lost interest. Reconstruction proclaimed anew the American principle of human equality but failed to secure it in reality.

EQUALITY: THE UNRESOLVED ISSUE

For America's former slaves, Reconstruction had one paramount meaning: a chance to explore freedom. A southern white woman acknowledged in her diary that the black people "showed a natural and exultant joy at being free." Former slaves remembered singing far into the night after federal troops reached their plantations. The slaves on a Texas plantation jumped up and down and clapped their hands as one man shouted, "We is free—no more whippings and beatings." A few people gave in to the natural desire to do what had been impossible before. One grandmother who had long resented her treatment dropped her hoe and ran to confront the mistress. "I'm free!" she yelled. "Yes, I'm free! Ain't got to work for you no more!" Others "started on the move," either to search for family members or just to exercise their new-found freedom of movement.

Most freedmen reacted more cautiously and shrewdly, taking care to test the boundaries of their new condition. One sign of this shrewd caution was the way freedmen evaluated potential employers. If a white person had been relatively considerate to

• *Important Events* •

1865	President Johnson begins Reconstruction	**1870**	Congress passes first Enforcement Act
	Confederate leaders regain power	**1871**	Congress passes a second Enforcement Act and the Ku Klux Klan Act
	White southern governments pass restrictive black codes	**1872**	Amnesty Act frees almost all remaining Confederates from restrictions on holding office
	Congress refuses to seat southern representatives		Liberal Republicans organize
	Thirteenth Amendment ratified		Debtors urge government to keep greenbacks in circulation
1866	Congress passes Civil Rights Act and renewal of Freedmen's Bureau over Johnson's veto		Grant reelected
	Congress approves Fourteenth Amendment	**1873**	*Slaughter-House* cases limit power of Fourteenth Amendment
	Most southern states reject Fourteenth Amendment		Panic of 1873 damages economy
	In *Ex parte Milligan* the Supreme Court reasserts its influence	**1874**	Grant vetoes increase in paper money
1867	Congress passes Reconstruction Act and Tenure of Office Act		Democrats win majority in House of Representatives
	Constitutional conventions called in southern states	**1875**	Congress passes a weak Civil Rights Act
1868	House impeaches Johnson; Senate acquits him		Congress requires that after 1878 greenbacks be convertible to gold
	Most southern states gain readmission to Union	**1876**	*U.S. v. Cruikshank* and *U.S. v. Reese* further weaken Fourteenth Amendment
	Fourteenth Amendment ratified		Presidential election disputed
	Ulysses S. Grant elected president	**1877**	Congress elects Rutherford B. Hayes
1869	Congress approves Fifteenth Amendment (ratified in 1870)		Exodusters migrate to Kansas

blacks in bondage, they reasoned that he might prove a desirable employer in freedom. Others left their plantations all at once, for, as one put it, "that master am sure mean."

In addition to a fair employer, the freedmen wanted opportunity through education and, especially, through land of their own. Land represented their chance to farm for them-

African-Americans' Desire for Land
——

selves and to have an independent life. It represented compensation for generations of travail in bondage. A northern observer noted that freedmen in the Sea Islands of South Carolina and Georgia

made "plain, straight-forward" inquiries as they settled the land set aside for them by Sherman. They wanted to be sure the land "would be theirs after they had improved it."

But how much of a chance would whites, who were in power, give to blacks? Northerners' racial attitudes were evolving but remained generally unfavorable. Abolitionists and many Republicans helped African-Americans fight for equal rights, and they won some victories. In 1864, the federal courts accepted black testimony, and the next year the Thirteenth Amendment won ratification. And one state, Massachusetts, enacted a comprehensive public accommodations law. Nevertheless, signs of resistance to racial equality abounded. The Democratic party fought hard against equality, charging that Republicans favored race mixing and were undermining the status of the white worker. Voters in three states—Connecticut, Minnesota, and Wisconsin—rejected black suffrage in 1865.

Such evidence of northern prejudice was significant. The history of emancipation in the British Caribbean indicated that, if equality were to be won, the North would have to take a strong and determined stand. In 1833, Great Britain had abolished slavery in its possessions, providing slave owners with £20 million in compensation and requiring all former agricultural slaves to work the land for six more years as apprentices. Despite such generosity, British Caribbean planters had fought tenaciously to maintain control over their laborers and to keep them on the plantations. With equal determination, the former slaves had attempted to move onto small plots of land where they could raise food crops and be independent. The British, however—even abolitionists—judged the success of emancipation by the volume of sugar production for the world market. Their concern for the freedmen soon faded, and before long the authorities allowed planters to import indentured "coolie" labor from India.

In the United States, some of the same tendencies had appeared even before the war ended. When federal forces occupied the Sea Islands, local planters had fled, leaving their slaves behind. These black people wanted to move off the plantations and establish small self-sufficient farms. Northern soldiers, officials, and missionaries brought education and aid to the freedmen but also wanted them to grow cotton. "The Yankees preach nothing but cotton, cotton!" complained one Sea Island black. "We wants land," wrote another. This man complained that tax officials, who sold thousands of acres for nonpayment of taxes, "make the lots too big, and cut we out." Even after blacks pooled their earnings, they were able to buy only a small fraction of Sea Island lands sold in March 1863. Thus even from their northern supporters, the former slaves had received only partial support. How much opportunity would freedom bring? The answer depended on the evolution of policy in Washington.

JOHNSON'S RECONSTRUCTION PLAN

When Reconstruction began under President Andrew Johnson, many expected his policies to be harsh. Throughout his career in Tennessee, he had criticized the wealthy planters for holding down the small farmers, whose cause he championed. Northern Radicals and southern aristocrats thus had reason to believe that Johnson would deal sternly with the South. When one Radical suggested the exile or execution of ten or twelve leading rebels to set an example, Johnson replied, "How are you going to pick out so small a number? . . . *Treason* is a crime; and *crime* must be punished."

Through 1865, Johnson alone controlled Reconstruction policy, for Congress recessed shortly before he became president and did not reconvene until December. In the nearly eight months that intervened, Johnson devised and put into operation his own plan, forming new state governments in the South by using his power to grant pardons.

Wartime proposals for Reconstruction had produced much controversy but no consensus. In December 1863, Lincoln had proposed a "10 percent" plan for a government being organized in captured parts of Louisiana. Under the plan, a state government could be established as soon as 10 percent of those who had voted in 1860 took an oath of future loyalty to the Union. Only high-ranking Confederate officials would be denied a chance to take the oath, and Lincoln urged that at least a few well-qualified blacks be given the ballot. Radicals bristled, however, at such a mild plan, and Congress backed the much stiffer Wade-Davis bill, which required 50 percent of the voters to swear an "iron-clad" oath that they had never voluntarily supported the rebellion. Lincoln pocket-vetoed this measure. At the time of his death, he had given tentative approval to a plan, drafted by Secretary of War Stanton, to impose military authority and appoint provisional governors as steps

Lincoln's Reconstruction Plan

toward the creation of new state governments in the South.

Johnson began with Stanton's plan, but the president's advisers split evenly on the question of voting rights for freedmen in the South. Johnson claimed that he favored black suffrage, but *only* if the southern states adopted it voluntarily. A champion of states' rights and no friend of African-Americans, he regarded this decision as too important to be taken out of the hands of the states.

His racial conservatism had an enduring effect on Johnson's policies. Where whites were concerned, however, Johnson seemed to be pursuing radical changes in class relations. He proposed rules that would keep the wealthy planter class out of power. Every southern voter was required to swear an oath of loyalty as a condition of gaining amnesty or pardon, but Johnson barred several classes of southerners from taking the oath and gaining amnesty. Former federal officials who had violated their oaths to support the United States and had aided the Confederacy could not take the oath. Nor could graduates of West Point or Annapolis who had resigned their commissions to fight for the South. The same was true for high-ranking Confederate officers and political leaders. To this list, Johnson added another important group: all southerners who aided the rebellion and whose taxable property was worth more than $20,000. Such individuals had to apply personally to the president for pardon and restoration of their political rights; otherwise, they risked legal penalties that included confiscation of their land. Thus it appeared that the leadership class of the Old South would be removed from power and replaced by a new leadership of deserving yeomen.

Oaths of Amnesty and New State Governments

The provisional governors whom Johnson appointed began the Reconstruction process by calling constitutional conventions. The delegates chosen had to draft new constitutions that eliminated slavery and invalidated secession. After ratification of the constitutions, new governments could be elected, and the states would be restored to the Union with full congressional representation. No southerner could participate in the process if he had not taken the oath of amnesty or if he had been ineligible to vote on the day the state seceded. Thus unpardoned whites and former slaves were not eligible.

Johnson's plan, however, did not work as he hoped. Prominent Confederates won elections, and, surprisingly, Johnson started pardoning them. By the time the southern states drafted their constitutions and elected public officials, Confederate leaders had emerged in powerful positions. Johnson decided to endorse the new governments and declare Reconstruction completed. Thus in December 1865, many former Confederate congressmen traveled to Washington to claim seats in the U.S. Congress. Even Alexander Stephens, vice president of the Confederacy, returned to the capital as a senator-elect.

The election of such prominent rebels troubled many northerners, as did other results of Johnson's program. Some state conventions were slow to repudiate secession; others acknowledged only grudgingly that slavery was dead. Furthermore, to define the status of freedmen and control their labor, some legislatures merely revised large sections of the slave codes by substituting the word *freedmen* for *slave*. Laws written from scratch were also restrictive. According to the new black codes, former slaves who were supposed to be free were compelled to carry passes, observe a curfew, live in housing provided by a landowner, and give up hope of entering many desirable occupations. Stiff vagrancy laws and restrictive labor contracts bound supposedly free laborers to plantations. Finally, state-supported institutions in the South, such as schools and orphanages, excluded blacks entirely.

Black Codes

Thus it was not surprising that a majority of northern congressmen decided to take a closer look at the results of Johnson's plan. On reconvening, they voted not to admit the newly elected southern representatives, whose credentials were subject under the Constitution to congressional scrutiny. The House and Senate established a joint committee to examine Johnson's policies and advise on new ones. Reconstruction thus entered a second phase, one in which Congress would play the decisive role.

THE CONGRESSIONAL RECONSTRUCTION PLAN

Northern congressmen disagreed on what to do, but they did not doubt their right to play a role in Reconstruction. The Constitution mentioned neither secession nor reunion, but it gave Congress the duty to guarantee each state a republican government. The provision, the legislators thought, gave them the right to devise policies for Reconstruction.

They soon found that other constitutional questions had a direct bearing on the policies they adopted. What, for example, had rebellion done to the relationship between southern states and the Union? Lincoln had always insisted that states could not secede and that the Union remained intact. In contrast, congressmen who favored vigorous Reconstruction measures tended to the view that war *had* broken the Union. They maintained that the southern states had committed legal suicide and reverted to the status of territories or that the South was a conquered nation subject to the victor's will. Moderate members held that the states had forfeited their rights through rebellion and had thus come under congressional supervision.

These diverse theories mirrored the diversity of Congress. Northern legislators fell into four major groups: Democrats, conservative Republicans,

The Radicals

moderate Republicans, and those called Radical Republicans. No one group had decisive power. Although the Republican party had a majority, there was considerable distance between conservative Republicans, who favored a limited federal role in Reconstruction and were fairly happy with Johnson's actions, and the Radicals who wanted to transform the South. Although the Radicals were a minority within their party, they had the advantage of a clearly defined goal. They believed it was essential to democratize the South, establish public education, and ensure the rights of freedmen. They favored black suffrage, often supported land confiscation and redistribution, and were willing to exclude the South from the Union for several years if

necessary to achieve their goals. Between the conservative Republicans and the Radicals lay the moderates, who held the balance of power.

Through their actions, Johnson and the Democrats forced the diverse Republican factions to come together. The president and the northern Democrats, insisting that Reconstruction was over and that the southern delegates should be seated in Congress, refused to cooperate with conservative or moderate Republicans. Moreover, Johnson refused to support an apparent compromise on Reconstruction. Under its terms, Johnson would agree to two modifications of his program: an extension of the life of the Freedmen's Bureau, which Congress had established in 1865 to feed the hungry, negotiate labor contracts, and start schools, and passage of a civil rights bill to counteract the black codes. The bill would force southern courts to practice equality before the law by giving federal judges the power to move from state courts into federal courts cases in which blacks were treated unfairly. Its provisions applied to discrimination by private individuals as well as government officials. As the first major bill to enforce the Thirteenth Amendment's abolition of slavery, it was a significant piece of legislation.

Johnson destroyed the compromise, however, by vetoing both bills (they were later reenacted) and condemning Congress's action. In inflammatory language, he questioned the legitimacy of congressional involvement in policymaking. All hope of working with the president was now dead. Instead of a compromise program, the various Republican factions drew up a new Reconstruction plan. It took the form of a proposed amendment to the Constitution and represented a compromise between radical and conservative elements of the party. The Fourteenth Amendment was Congress's alternative to Johnson's program of Reconstruction.

Of the four points in the amendment, one had near-universal agreement: it declared the Confederate debt null and void and guaranteed

Fourteenth Amendment

the war debt of the United States. Prohibiting prominent Confederates from holding political office also had fairly general support. It meant that Confederate leaders were barred from state and federal office. Only Congress, by a two-thirds vote of each house, could remove the penalty.

The first section of the Fourteenth Amendment, which would have the greatest legal significance in later years, conferred citizenship on freedmen and prohibited states from abridging their constitutional "privileges and immunities." It also barred any state from taking a person's life, liberty, or property "without due process of law" and from denying "equal protection of the laws." These clauses were phrased broadly enough to become powerful guarantees of African-Americans' civil rights—indeed, of the rights of all citizens—in the twentieth century.

The second section of the amendment revealed the political motives that had produced the document. Northerners, in Congress and out, disagreed about whether black citizens should have the right to vote. A primary concern of Republicans was that emancipation, which made every former slave five-fifths of a person instead of three-fifths of a person for purposes of congressional representation, might increase the South's power in Congress. If it did, and if blacks were not allowed to vote, the former secessionists would gain seats in the House of Representatives.

Most northerners had never planned to reward the South for rebellion, and Republicans in Congress were determined not to hand over power to their political enemies. So they offered the South a choice. According to the second section of the Fourteenth Amendment, states did not have to grant black men the right to vote. But if they did not do so, their representation would be reduced proportionally. If they did enfranchise black men, their representation would be increased proportionally—but Republicans could seek the support of the new black voters.

The Fourteenth Amendment promoted the voting rights of black men but ignored female citizens, black and white. When legislators defined women as nonvoting citizens, prominent leaders such as Elizabeth Cady Stanton and Susan B. Anthony decided that it was time to end their alliance with abolitionists and fight more determinedly for themselves. Thus the amendment infused the independent women's rights movement with new determination.

In 1866, however, the major question in Reconstruction politics was how the public would respond to the amendment. Would the northern public support Congress's plan or the president's? Johnson did his best to block the Fourteenth Amendment and to convince northerners to reject it. Condemning Congress for its refusal to seat southern representatives, the president urged state legislatures in the South to vote against ratification. Every southern legislature except Tennessee's rejected the amendment by a wide margin.

Southern Rejection of the Fourteenth Amendment

To present his case to northerners, Johnson organized a National Union Convention and took to the stump. He boarded a special train for a "swing around the circle" that carried his message deep into the Midwest and then back to Washington. But increasingly, audiences rejected his views and hooted and jeered at him.

The election of 1866 was a resounding victory for Republicans in Congress. Radical and moderate Republicans whom Johnson had denounced won reelection by large margins, and the Republican majority increased. The North had spoken clearly: Johnson's policies were giving the advantage to rebels and traitors. Thus Republican congressional leaders won a mandate to pursue their Reconstruction plan.

Recognizing that nothing could be accomplished under the existing southern governments and with blacks excluded from the electorate, Congress passed the Reconstruction Act of 1867. The act called for a return to military authority in the South until new governments could be set up. It established five military districts, each headed by a Union general. Confederate leaders designated in the Fourteenth Amendment were barred from voting until new constitutions were ratified. The act guaranteed freedmen the right to vote in elections for state constitutional conventions and in subsequent elections under the new constitutions. In addition, it required each southern state to ratify the Fourteenth Amendment and its new constitution and submit it to Congress for approval.

Reconstruction Act of 1867

Plans for Reconstruction Compared

	Johnson's Plan	Radicals' Plan	Fourteenth Amendment	Reconstruction Act of 1867
Voting	Whites only; Confederate leaders must seek pardons	Give vote to black males	Southern whites may decide but can lose representation	Black men gain vote; whites barred from office by Fourteenth Amendment cannot vote while new governments being formed
Office-holding	Many prominent Confederates regain power	Only loyal white and black males eligible	Confederate leaders barred until Congress votes amnesty	Fourteenth Amendment in effect
Time out of Union	Brief	Years; until South is thoroughly democratized	Brief	Brief
Other changes in southern society	Little; gain of power by yeomen not realized	Expand public education; confiscate land and provide farms for freedmen	Probably slight	Depends on action of new state government

Thus African-Americans gained an opportunity to fight for a better life through the political process, but their only weapon was the ballot. The law required no redistribution of land and guaranteed no basic changes in southern social structure.

Congress's role as the architect of Reconstruction was not quite over. To restrict Johnson's influence and safeguard its plan, Congress passed a number of controversial laws. First, it set the date for its own reconvening—an unprecedented act, for the president traditionally summoned legislators to Washington. Then it limited Johnson's power over the army by requiring the president to issue military orders through the General of the Army, Ulysses S. Grant, who could not be sent from Washington without the Senate's consent. Finally, Congress passed the Tenure of Office Act, which gave the Senate power to interfere with changes in the president's cabinet. Designed to protect Secretary of War Stanton, who sympathized with the Radicals, the law violated the tradition that the president controlled the cabinet.

Johnson took several belligerent steps of his own. He issued orders to military commanders in the South limiting their powers and increasing the powers of the civil governments he had created in 1865. Then he removed officers who were conscientiously enforcing Congress's new law. Finally, he tried to remove Secretary of War Stanton. With that attempt, the confrontation reached its climax.

The House Judiciary Committee, which twice before had considered impeachment, again initiated the action. The 1868 indictment concentrated on his violation of the Tenure of Office Act, although modern scholars regard his efforts to impede enforcement of the Reconstruction Act of 1867 as a far more serious offense.

Impeachment of President Johnson

Johnson's trial in the Senate began promptly and lasted more than three months. The prosecution, led by such Radicals as Thaddeus Stevens and Benjamin Butler, attempted to prove that Johnson was guilty of "high crimes and misdemeanors." But they also argued that the trial was a means to judge Johnson's performance, not a judicial determination of guilt or innocence. The Senate ultimately rejected such reasoning, which could have made removal from office a political weapon against any chief executive who disagreed with Congress. Although a majority of senators voted to convict Johnson, the prosecution fell one vote short of the necessary two-thirds majority. Johnson remained in office, politically weakened and with only a few months left in his term. But his acquittal established the precedent that only serious misdeeds merited removal from office.

In 1869, in an effort to write democratic principles and colorblindness into the Constitution, the Radicals succeeded in presenting the Fifteenth Amendment for ratification.

Fifteenth Amendment

This measure forbade states to deny the right to vote "on account of race, color, or previous condition of servitude." Such wording did not guarantee the right to vote. It deliberately left states free to restrict suffrage on other grounds so that northern states could continue to deny suffrage to women and certain groups of men—Chinese immigrants, illiterates, and those too poor to pay taxes. Ironically, the votes of four uncooperative southern states—compelled by Congress to approve the amendment as an added condition to rejoining the Union—proved necessary to impose even this language on parts of the North. Although several states outside the South refused to ratify, the Fifteenth Amendment became law in 1870.

RECONSTRUCTION POLITICS IN THE SOUTH

From the start, Reconstruction encountered the resistance of white southerners. Their opposition to change appeared in the black codes and other

White Resistance

policies of the Johnson government as well as in private attitudes. Many whites stubbornly opposed emancipation, and the former planter class proved especially unbending. In 1866, a Georgia newspaper frankly observed that "most of the white citizens believe that the institution of slavery was right, and . . . they will believe that the condition, which comes nearest to slavery, that can now be established will be the best."

Fearing loss of control over their slaves, some planters attempted to postpone freedom by denying or misrepresenting events. Former slaves reported that their owners "didn't tell them it was freedom" or "wouldn't let [them] go." To hold on to their workers, some landowners claimed control over black children and used guardianship and apprentice laws to bind black families to the plantation. Whites also blocked blacks from acquiring land and used force to keep blacks submissive.

After President Johnson encouraged the South to resist congressional Reconstruction, white conservatives worked hard to capture the new state governments. Many whites also boycotted the polls in an attempt to defeat Congress's plans; because the new constitutions had to be approved by a majority of registered voters, registered whites could defeat them by sitting out the elections. This tactic was tried in North Carolina and succeeded in Alabama, forcing Congress to base ratification on a majority of those voting.

Few black men stayed away from the polls. They enthusiastically seized the opportunity to participate in politics, voting solidly Republican. Most agreed with one man who felt he should "stick to the end with the party that freed me."

Thanks to a large black turnout and the barring of prominent Confederates from politics, a new southern Republican party came to power in the constitutional conventions. Among the Republican delegates were a sizable contingent of blacks (265 out of the total of just over one thousand delegates throughout the South), some northerners who had moved to the South, and native southern whites who favored change. Together, these Republicans brought the South into line with progressive reforms that had been adopted in the rest of the nation. The new constitutions were more democratic. They eliminated property qualifications for voting and holding office, and they made elective state and local offices that had been appointive. They provided for public schools and institutions to care for the mentally ill, the blind, the deaf, the destitute, and the orphaned. They also put an end to imprisonment for debt and to barbarous punishments such as branding.

The conventions broadened women's rights in property holding and divorce. Usually, the main goal was not to make women equal with men but to provide relief to thousands of suffering debtors. In families left poverty stricken by the war and weighed down by debt, it was usually the husband who had contracted the debts. Thus giving women legal control over their property provided some protection to their families. However, some delegates aimed to elevate women. Blacks in particular called for laws to provide for women's suffrage, but they were ignored by their white colleagues.

Under the new constitutions, the southern states elected new governments. Again, the Republican party triumphed, putting new men in

Triumph of Republican Governments
———

positions of power. For the first time in history, the ranks of state legislators in 1868 included some black southerners. Congress's second plan for Reconstruction was well under way. It remained to be seen what the new governments would do and how much social change they would bring about.

One way to achieve radical change would have been to disfranchise substantial numbers of Confederate leaders. If the Republican regimes had used their new power to exclude many whites from politics as punishment for rebellion, they would have enjoyed a solid electoral majority based on black voters and their white allies. Land reform and the assurance of racial equality would have been possible. But none of the Republican governments did this or even gave it serious consideration.

Why did the new legislators reject this course of action? First, they appreciated the realities of power and the depth of racial enmity. In most states, whites were in the majority and former slave

owners controlled the best land and other sources of economic power. James Lynch, a leading black politician from Mississippi, candidly explained why African-Americans shunned what he called the folly of disfranchisement. Unlike northerners who "can leave when it becomes too uncomfortable," landless former slaves "must be in friendly relations with the great body of the whites in the state." Second, blacks believed in the principle of universal suffrage and the Christian goal of reconciliation. Far from being vindictive toward the race that had enslaved them, they treated leading rebels with generosity and appealed to white southerners to adopt a spirit of fairness and cooperation. For these, as well as other reasons, southern Republicans quickly restored the voting rights of former Confederates. Thus the South's Republican party committed to a strategy of winning white support. To put the matter another way, the Republican party condemned itself to defeat if white voters would not cooperate.

But for a time, both Republicans and their opponents, who called themselves Conservatives or Democrats, moved to the center and appealed for support from a broad range of groups. Some propertied whites accepted congressional Reconstruction as a reality and declared themselves willing to compete under the new rules. Whereas these Democrats angled for some black votes, Republicans sought to attract more white voters. And both parties found an area of agreement in economic policies.

The Reconstruction governments devoted themselves to stimulating industry. The policy reflected northern ideals, but it also sprang from

Industrialization
———

a growing southern eagerness to build up the manufacturing capacity of their region. Accordingly, Reconstruction legislatures designed many tempting inducements to investment. Loans, subsidies, and exemptions from taxation for periods as long as ten years helped to lure new industries to the region. The southern railroad system was rebuilt and expanded, and coal and iron mining made possible Birmingham's steel plants. Between 1860 and 1880, the number of manufacturing establishments in the South nearly doubled. The emphasis on big business, however, produced higher state debts and taxes, drew money away from schools and other programs, and multiplied possibilities for corruption.

Policies appealing to African-American voters never went beyond equality before the law. In fact, the whites who controlled the southern Republican party were reluctant to allow blacks a share of offices proportionate to their electoral strength. Aware of their weakness, black leaders did not push for revolutionary economic or social change. They refrained from advocating the confiscation and redistribution of land and, with the exception of some urban mulattos, did not press for civil rights. Instead, they led efforts to establish public schools but usually did not press for integrated facilities. These racially separate schools established a precedent. By the 1870s, segregation was becoming a common but not universal practice in theaters, trains, and other public accommodations in the South.

Other Republican Policies

Within a few years, as centrists in both parties met with failure, white hostility to congressional Reconstruction began to dominate. Some conservatives had always favored fierce opposition to Reconstruction through pressure and racist propaganda. Charging that the South had been turned over to ignorant blacks, conservatives deplored "black domination." The cry of "Negro rule" now became constant.

Such attacks were gross distortions. African-Americans participated in politics but did not dominate or control events. They were a majority in only two of ten state conventions (transplanted northerners were a majority in one). Of the state legislatures, only in the lower house in South Carolina did blacks ever constitute a majority; among officials, their numbers were generally far inferior to their proportion in the population. Sixteen blacks won seats in Congress before Reconstruction was over, but none was ever elected governor. Only eighteen served in a high state office such as lieutenant governor, treasurer, superintendent of education, or secretary of state. Freedmen were participating in government but did not dominate or control events.

Conservatives also stepped up their propaganda against the allies of black Republicans. *Carpetbagger*, a derisive name for whites from the North, suggested an evil and greedy northern politician, recently arrived with a carpetbag into which he planned to stuff ill-gotten gains before fleeing.

Carpetbaggers and Scalawags

A few northerners deserved the unsavory description. But of the thousands of northerners who settled in the postwar South, only a small proportion of them entered politics. Most wanted to democratize the South and to introduce northern ways, such as industry, free public education, and the spirit of enterprise.

Conservatives invented the term *scalawag* to discredit any native white southerner who cooperated with the Republicans. A substantial number of southerners did so, including some wealthy and prominent men. Most scalawags, however, were yeoman farmers, men from mountain areas and nonslave-holding districts who saw that they could benefit from the education and opportunities promoted by Republicans. Banding together with freedmen, they pursued common class interests and hoped to make headway against the power of long-dominant planters. Yet the black-white coalition was vulnerable to the issue of race, and most scalawags shied away from support for racial equality.

Taxation was a major problem for the Reconstruction governments. Financially, the Republicans were doomed to be unpopular despite their achievements. Republicans wanted to maintain prewar services, repair the war's destruction, stimulate industry, and support important new ventures such as public schools. But the Civil War had destroyed much of the South's tax base. Thus an increase in taxes was necessary even to maintain traditional services, and new ventures required still higher taxes.

Corruption was another serious charge levied against the Republicans. Unfortunately, it was true. Many carpetbaggers and black politicians engaged in fraudulent schemes, sold their votes, or padded expenses. Although white Democrats often shared in the guilt, and some Republicans tried to stop it, Democrats convinced many voters that scandal was the inevitable result of turning government over to unqualified blacks and greedy carpetbaggers.

All the problems hurt the Republicans, but in many southern states the deathblow came through violence. The Ku Klux Klan, a secret veterans' club that began in Tennessee, spread through the South and rapidly evolved into a terrorist organization. Violence against African-Americans had occurred throughout Reconstruction, but it became far more organized and purposeful after 1867. The Ku Klux Klan rode to frustrate Reconstruction and keep the freedmen in subjection. Nighttime harassment, whippings, beatings, and murder became common, and in some areas virtually open warfare developed.

Ku Klux Klan
————

Although the Klan persecuted blacks who stood up for their rights as laborers or individuals, its main purpose was political. Lawless nightriders made active Republicans the target of their attacks. The Klan killed prominent white Republicans and black leaders in several states. After freedmen who worked for a South Carolina scalawag started voting, terrorists visited the plantation and, in the words of one victim, "whipped every nigger man they could lay their hands on." Klansmen also attacked Union League Clubs—Republican organizations that mobilized the black vote—and school teachers who were aiding the freedmen.

Klan violence was not a spontaneous outburst of racism; specific social forces shaped and directed it. In North Carolina, for example, Alamance and Caswell Counties were the sites of the worst Klan violence. They were in the Piedmont, where slim Republican majorities rested on cooperation between black voters and white yeomen. In a successful effort to restore Democratic control, wealthy and powerful men organized a campaign of terror in the two counties. They served as Klan leaders at the county and local levels, recruited members, and planned atrocities. Their violence restored elite power and Democratic control.

Klan violence injured Republicans across the South. No fewer than one-tenth of the black leaders who had been delegates to the 1867–1868 constitutional conventions were attacked, seven fatally. In Eutaw, Alabama, a Klan raid left four dead and

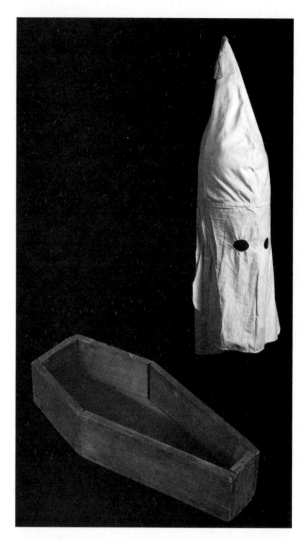

The Ku Klux Klan aimed to terrorize and intimidate its victims by violence and other methods. Mysterious regalia, such as the pointed hood (which was held up by a stick inside) contributed to a menacing atmosphere. The miniature coffin, typically left on a Republican's doorstep, conveyed a more direct threat. Collection of State Historical Museum, Mississippi Department of Archives and History. Photo by Gib Ford.

fifty-four wounded. In South Carolina, five hundred masked Klansmen lynched eight black prisoners at the Union County jail, and in nearby York County the Klan committed at least eleven murders and hundreds of whippings. According to historian Eric Foner, the Klan "made it virtually impossible for Republicans to campaign or vote in large parts of Georgia."

Thus a combination of difficult fiscal problems, Republican mistakes, racial hostility, and terror brought down the Republican regimes. In most southern states, so-called Radical Reconstruction lasted only a few years. The most enduring failure of Reconstruction, however, was not political; it was social and economic. Exploited as slaves, freedmen remained vulnerable to exploitation during Reconstruction. Without land of their own, they were dependent on white landowners who could and did use their economic power to compromise blacks' political freedom. Armed only with the ballot, African-Americans in the South had little chance to effect major changes.

Failure of Reconstruction

THE SOCIAL AND ECONOMIC MEANING OF FREEDOM

Black southerners entered life after slavery hopefully and determinedly but not naïvely. They had had too much experience with white people to assume that all would be easy. Expecting hostility, freedmen tried to gain as much as they could from their new circumstances. Often, the changes they valued the most were personal—alterations in location, employer, or living arrangements that could make an enormous difference to individuals or families.

One of the first decisions was whether to leave the old plantation or remain. This meant making a judgment about where opportunities for liberty and progress were likely to be greatest. Former slaves drew on their experiences in bondage. Not surprisingly, cruel slave holders usually saw their former property walk off en masse. Freedmen continued to seek fair employment throughout Reconstruction, and as many as one-third changed employers at the end of a crop year.

After choosing an employer, ex-slaves reached out for valuable things in life that had been denied them. One was education. Blacks of all ages hungered for the knowledge in books that had been permitted only to whites. With freedom, they started schools and filled classrooms both day and night.

Education for African-Americans

On log seats and dirt floors, freedmen studied their letters in old almanacs, discarded dictionaries, or whatever was available. Young children brought infants to school with them, and adults attended at night or after "the crops were laid by." The federal government and northern reformers of both races assisted the pursuit of education. In its brief life, the Freedmen's Bureau founded more than four thousand schools, and idealistic men and women from the North established and staffed others.

Blacks and their white allies also saw the need for colleges and universities. The American Missionary Association founded seven colleges, including Fisk University and Atlanta University, between 1866 and 1869. The Freedmen's Bureau helped to establish Howard University in Washington, D.C., and northern religious groups such as the Methodists, Baptists, and Congregationalists supported dozens of seminaries, colleges, and teachers' colleges. By the late 1870s, black churches had joined the effort, founding numerous colleges despite limited resources.

Even during Reconstruction, African-American leaders often were highly educated individuals, many of whom came from the prewar elite of free people of color. The group had benefited from its association with wealthy whites, who were often blood relatives; some planters had given their mulatto children outstanding educations. The two black senators from Mississippi, Blanche K. Bruce and Hiram Revels, for instance, had both had privileged educations. Bruce was the son of a planter who had provided tutoring at home; Revels was the son of free North Carolina mulattos who had sent him to Knox College in Illinois. These men and many self-educated former slaves brought to political office their experience as artisans, businessmen, lawyers, teachers, and preachers.

Meanwhile, millions of former slaves concentrated on improving life on their farms and in their neighborhoods. Surrounded by an unfriendly white

Freed from slavery, blacks of all ages filled the schools to seek the educations that had been denied them in bondage. Their education often cost one-tenth of each month's wages. William Gladstone Collection.

population, black men and women sought to insulate themselves from white interference and to strengthen the bonds of their community. Throughout the South, they devoted themselves to reuniting their families, moving away from the slave quarters, and founding black churches. Given the eventual failure of Reconstruction, the gains that African-Americans made in their daily lives often proved the most enduring.

The search for family members who had been sold during slavery was awe inspiring. With only shreds of information to guide them, thousands of freedmen embarked on odysseys in search of a husband, wife, child, or parent. By relying on the black community for help and information, many succeeded. Others walked through several states and never found loved ones.

Reunification of African-American Families

Husbands and wives who had belonged to different masters established homes together for the first time, and parents asserted the right to raise their children. One mother bristled when her old master claimed a right to whip her children, informing him that "he warn't goin' to brush none of her chilluns no more." Although the freedmen were too much at risk to act recklessly, they were tired of all the punishment and, as one man put it, they "sure didn't take no more foolishment off of white folks."

Many black people wanted to minimize all contact with whites. To avoid contact with overbearing whites who were used to supervising and controlling them, blacks abandoned the slave quarters and fanned out to distant corners of the land they worked. Some described moving "across the creek to [themselves]" or building a "saplin house . . . back in the woods." Others established small all-black settlements that still exist today along the back roads of the South.

The other side of movement away from whites was closer communion within the black community. Freed from the restrictions and regulations of

How do historians know

that African-Americans used strategies to progress in postwar southern society? Professor Peter Rachleff has studied the records of the Freedmen's Saving and Trust Company to illuminate the efforts of blacks in Richmond, Virginia. These records reveal that extended kinship networks were a major resource for aid and security. Parents opened accounts for their chil-dren, to prepare for their future, or to help parents in their old age. Individuals directed that relatives could have access to their savings in time of need. "Mutual support," notes Rachleff, "flowed back and forth between parents and children, tying them together for their entire lives."   Photo: National Archives.

Founding of Black Churches

———

slavery, blacks could build their institutions as they saw fit. The secret churches of slavery now came out into the open. Within a few years, independent branches of the Methodist and Baptist churches had attracted the great majority of black Christians in the South.

The desire to gain as much independence as possible also shaped the freedmen's economic arrangements. Because most former slaves lacked money to buy land, they preferred the next best thing: renting the land they worked. But few whites would consider renting land to blacks—social pressures against it were strong—and most blacks had no means to get cash before the harvest. Thus they had to try other approaches.

Northerners and officials of the Freedmen's Bureau favored contracts between owners and laborers. To northerners who believed in "Free soil, Free labor, Free men," contracts and wages seemed the key to progress. For a few years, the Freedmen's Bureau helped draw up and enforce such contracts, but they proved unpopular with both races. Owners often filled the contracts with detailed requirements that reminded blacks of their circumscribed lives under slavery. Disputes frequently arose over efficiency, lost time, and other matters. Besides, cash was not readily available in the early years of Reconstruction; times were hard, and the failure of Confederate banks had left the South with a shortage of credit facilities.

Black farmers and white landowners therefore turned to sharecropping, a system in which farmers kept part of their crop and gave the rest to the landowner while living on his property. The landlord or a merchant "furnished" food and supplies needed before the harvest, and he received payment from the crop. Landowners tried to set the laborers' share at a low level. Typical arrangements left half the crop to the landowner and half to the sharecropper.

Rise of the Sharecropping System

The sharecropping system originated as a desirable compromise. It eased landowners' problems with cash and credit; blacks accepted it, because it gave them more freedom from daily supervision. Instead of working under a white overseer, as in slavery, they farmed a plot of land on their own in family groups. But sharecropping later proved a disaster for all concerned. Because African-Americans were living in a discriminatory society, the system placed them at the mercy of unscrupulous owners and merchants who had many opportunities to cheat them. As for the South, sharecropping led to an overspecialization in cotton, just as the worldwide demand for the crop began to grow at a much slower rate than it had in the prewar years.

RECONSTRUCTION'S DECLINE AND FALL

Northerners had always been far more interested in suppressing rebellion than in aiding southern blacks, and by the early 1870s the North's partial commitment to bringing about change in the South was weakening. Criticism of the southern governments grew, new issues captured people's attention, and soon voters began to look favorably upon reconciliation with southern whites. In one state after another in the South, Democrats regained control, and they threatened to defeat Republicans in the North as well. Before long the situation had returned to "normal" in the eyes of southern whites.

The antagonism between Unionists and rebels was still strong in 1868. That year, Ulysses S. Grant, running as a Republican, defeated Horatio Seymour, a New York Democrat, for president. Grant was not a Radical, but he realized that Congress's program represented the wishes of most northerners. In office, Grant acted as an administrator of Reconstruction but not as its enthusiastic advocate. He vacillated in his dealings with the southern states, sometimes defending Republican regimes and sometimes currying favor with Democrats. On occasion, Grant called out federal troops to stop violence or enforce acts of Congress but only when he had to. Grant hoped to avoid confrontation with the South and to erase any image of dictatorship evoked by his military background.

Election of 1868

In 1870 and 1871, the violent campaigns of the Ku Klux Klan forced Congress to pass two Enforcement Acts and an anti-Klan law. The laws made acts by *individuals* against the civil and political rights of others a federal criminal offense for the first time. They also provided for election supervisors and permitted martial law and suspension of the writ of habeas corpus to combat killings, beatings, and threats by the Klan. But federal prosecutors used the laws rather selectively. In 1872 and 1873, Mississippi and the Carolinas saw many prosecutions, but the laws were virtually ignored in other states in which violence flourished. Southern juries often refused to convict Klansmen.

Some conservative but influential Republicans opposed the anti-Klan laws, basing their opposition on the charge that the laws infringed on states' rights. It was striking that some Republicans were echoing an old and standard line of the Democrats. The opposition foreshadowed a more general revolt within Republican ranks in 1872.

Disenchanted with Reconstruction, a group calling itself the Liberal Republicans bolted the party in 1872 and nominated Horace Greeley, the

**Liberal
Republicans
Revolt**
———

well-known editor of the *New York Tribune*, for president. The Liberal Republicans were a varied group, including civil service reformers, foes of corruption, and advocates of a lower tariff. They were united by two popular and widespread attitudes: distaste for federal intervention in the South and a desire to let market forces and the "best men" determine events there. The Democrats also gave their nomination to Greeley in 1872. The combination was not enough to defeat Grant, but it reinforced his desire to avoid confrontation with white southerners.

The Liberal Republican challenge reflected growing dissatisfaction with Grant's administration. Corruption within the administration had become widespread, and Grant foolishly defended some of the culprits. As the clamor against dishonesty in government grew, Grant's popularity and his party's prestige declined. In 1874, the Democrats recaptured the House of Representatives.

The Democratic gains further weakened congressional resolve on southern issues. Congress had already lifted the political disabilities of the

Amnesty Act
———

Fourteenth Amendment from many former Confederates. In 1872, it had adopted a sweeping Amnesty Act, which pardoned most remaining rebels and left only five hundred barred from political officeholding. The Civil Rights Act passed in 1875 purported to guarantee black people equal accommodations in public places, but the bill was watered down and contained no effective provisions for enforcement. Moreover, by 1876 the Democrats had regained control in all but three of the southern states.

Meanwhile, new concerns were capturing the public's attention. Industrialization had surged, hastening the pace of change in national life. Within only eight years, postwar industrial production had increased by an impressive 75 percent. For the first time, nonagricultural workers outnumbered farmers, and only Britain had a greater industrial output.

Then the Panic of 1873 ushered in more than five years of continuing economic contraction. The panic threw three million people out of work, and the clash between labor and capital became the major issue of the day. Businessmen, disturbed by the strikes and industrial violence that accompanied the panic, became increasingly concerned about the defense of property. Debtors and the unemployed sought easy-money policies to spur economic expansion.

The monetary issue aroused particularly strong controversy. Keeping Civil War paper money— called greenbacks—in circulation could expand the money supply and raise prices.

**Greenbacks
Versus Sound
Money**
———

In 1872, Democratic farmers and debtors had urged such a policy, but they were overruled by "sound money" men—businessmen, bankers, and creditors. Now hard times swelled the ranks of the "greenbackers," voters who favored greenbacks and easy money. Congress voted in 1874 to increase the number of greenbacks in circulation, but Grant vetoed the bill in deference to the opinions of financial leaders. The next year, sound-money interests prevailed in Congress, winning passage of a law requiring that greenbacks be convertible to gold after 1878. The law limited the inflationary effect of the greenbacks and aided creditors rather than debtors (such as the hard-pressed and angry farmers).

The Supreme Court also participated in the northern retreat from Reconstruction. During the Civil War, the Court had been cautious and reluctant to assert itself. Reaction to the Dred Scott decision had been so violent, and the Union's wartime emergency so great, that the Court had refrained from blocking or interfering with government actions.

But in 1866, a similar case, *Ex parte Milligan*, reached the Court through proper channels. Lambdin P. Milligan of Indiana had participated in a plot to free Confederate prisoners of war and overthrow state governments; for these acts, a military court had sentenced Milligan, a civilian, to death. Milligan challenged the authority of the military tribunal, claiming that he had a right to a civil trial. The Supreme Court declared that military trials were illegal when civil courts were open and functioning, and the sweeping language of the decision indicated that the Court intended to reassert itself as a major force in national affairs.

In the 1870s, interpretations by the Supreme Court narrowed the meaning and effectiveness of the Fourteenth Amendment. In 1873, the Court decided *Bradwell* v. *Illinois*, a case in which Myra Bradwell, a female attorney, had been denied the right to practice law in Illinois because of her gender. Pointing to the Fourteenth Amendment, Bradwell's attorneys contended that the state had unconstitutionally abridged her "privileges and immunities" as a citizen. The Supreme Court rejected her claim, alluding to women's traditional role in the home.

Supreme Court Decisions on Reconstruction

One day before, in the *Slaughter-House* cases, the Court had made its restrictive reading of the Fourteenth Amendment even more explicit. The *Slaughter-House* cases had arisen in 1869, when the Louisiana legislature granted one company a monopoly on the slaughtering of livestock in New Orleans. Rival butchers in the city promptly sued. Their attorney, former Supreme Court Justice John A. Campbell, argued that the Fourteenth Amendment had revolutionized the constitutional system by bringing individual rights under federal protection. Campbell thus articulated an original goal of the Republican party: to nationalize civil rights and guard them from state interference.

The Court not only rejected Campbell's argument but dealt a stunning blow to the scope and vitality of the Fourteenth Amendment and to the hopes of blacks. The justices interpreted the "privileges and immunities" of citizens so narrowly that it reduced them almost to trivialities. State citizenship and national citizenship were separate, the Court declared. National citizenship involved only such matters as the right to travel freely from state to state and to use the navigable waters of the nation, and only these narrow rights were protected by the Fourteenth Amendment. With this interpretation, the words "No state shall make or enforce any law which shall abridge the privileges or immunities of citizens of the United States" disappeared, from that day until now, as a meaningful and effective part of the Constitution.

The Supreme Court also concluded that the butchers who sued had not been deprived of their rights or property in violation of the due process clause of the amendment. The court's majority declared that the framers of the recent amendments had not intended to "destroy" the federal system, in which the states exercised "powers for domestic and local government, including the regulation of civil rights." Thus the justices dismissed Campbell's central contention and severely limited the amendment's potential for securing and protecting the rights of black citizens.

In 1876, the Court weakened the Reconstruction-era amendments even further by emasculating the enforcement clause of the Fourteenth Amendment and revealing deficiencies inherent in the Fifteenth Amendment. In *United States* v. *Cruikshank*, the Court dealt with Louisiana whites convicted under the 1870 Enforcement Act of attacking a meeting of blacks and conspiring to deprive them of their rights. The justices ruled that the Fourteenth Amendment did not empower the federal government to act against whites who were oppressing blacks. The duty of protecting citizens' equal rights "was originally assumed by the States; and it still remains there." As for the protection of "unalienable rights," the Court said that "Sovereignty, for this purpose, rests alone with the States." In *United States* v. *Reese*, the Court noted that the Fifteenth Amendment did not guarantee a citizen's right to vote but merely listed certain impermissible grounds for denying suffrage. Thus a path lay open for southern states to disfranchise blacks for supposedly nonracial reasons—lack of education, lack of property, or lack of descent from a grandfather qualified to vote before the Military Reconstruction Act. (So-called grandfather clauses became a means to give the vote to illiterate whites while excluding blacks, because the grandfathers of most black people had been slaves before Reconstruction and unable to vote.)

As the 1876 elections approached, it was obvious to most political observers that the North was no longer willing to pursue the goals of Reconstruction. The results of a disputed presidential election confirmed this fact. Samuel J. Tilden, the Democratic governor of New York, ran strongly

Election of 1876

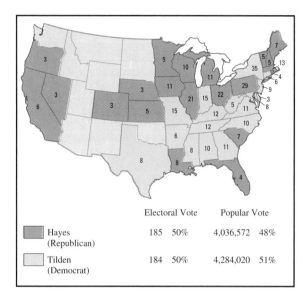

	Electoral Vote		Popular Vote	
Hayes (Republican)	185	50%	4,036,572	48%
Tilden (Democrat)	184	50%	4,284,020	51%

Presidential Election, 1876 *In 1876, a combination of solid southern support and Democratic gains in the North gave Samuel Tilden the majority of popular votes, but Rutherford B. Hayes won the disputed election in the electoral college.*

in the South and took a commanding lead in both the popular vote and the electoral college over Rutherford B. Hayes, the Republican nominee. Tilden won 184 electoral votes and needed only one more for a majority. Nineteen votes from Louisiana, South Carolina, and Florida were disputed; both Democrats and Republicans claimed to have won in those states despite fraud on the part of their opponents. One vote from Oregon was undecided because of a technicality.

To resolve this unprecedented situation, on which the Constitution gave no guidance, Congress established a fifteen-member electoral commission. In the interest of impartiality, membership on the commission was to be balanced between Democrats and Republicans. But one independent Republican, Supreme Court Justice David Davis, refused appointment in order to accept his election as a senator. A regular Republican took his place, and the Republican party prevailed 8 to 7 on every decision, along strict party lines. Hayes would become president if Congress accepted the commission's findings.

Congressional acceptance was not certain. Democrats, however, acquiesced in the election of Hayes. Scholars have found evidence of negotiations between Hayes supporters and southerners who wanted federal aid to railroads, internal improvements, federal patronage, and removal of troops from southern states. But studies of Congress conclude that the negotiations did not have a deciding effect on the outcome: neither party was well enough organized to implement and enforce a bargain between the sections. Northern and southern Democrats simply decided they could not win and did not contest the election. Hayes became president (see map), and southerners looked forward to the withdrawal of federal troops from the South. In 1877, Reconstruction was over.

Southern Democrats rejoiced, but African-Americans grieved over the betrayal of their hopes for equality. For many African-Americans, the only hope remaining after 1877 was **Exodusters Move West** "to go to a territory by ourselves." In South Carolina, Louisiana, Mississippi, and other southern states, thousands gathered up their possessions and migrated to Kansas. They were known as Exodusters, disappointed people still searching for their share in the American dream.

Thus the nation ended more than fifteen years of bloody Civil War and controversial Reconstruction without establishing full freedom for African-Americans. The contradictory record typified the results of Reconstruction in many other ways. A tumultuous period had brought tremendous change, and yet many things remained the same. Because extraordinary situations had, for a time, required revolutionary changes, the North had acted. The Union victory brought about an increase in federal power, stronger nationalism, unprecedented federal intervention in the southern states, and landmark amendments to the Constitution. Yet, because there was no commitment to make the changes endure, the revolution remained partial. The nation turned away from the needs of its African-American citizens and began to focus on issues related to industrialism and an increasingly interconnected national economy.

SUGGESTIONS FOR FURTHER READING

National Policy, Politics, and Constitutional Law

Richard H. Abbott, *The Republican Party and the South, 1855–1877* (1986); Herman Belz, *Emancipation and Equal Rights* (1978); Michael Les Benedict, *A Compromise of Principle: Congressional Republicans and Reconstruction, 1863–1869* (1974), and *The Impeachment and Trial of Andrew Johnson* (1973); Michael Kent Curtis, *No State Shall Abridge* (1987); Harold M. Hyman, *A More Perfect Union* (1973); Eric L. McKitrick, *Andrew Johnson and Reconstruction* (1966); James M. McPherson, *The Abolitionist Legacy* (1975); Brooks D. Simpson, *Let Us Have Peace* (1991); Kenneth M. Stampp, *The Era of Reconstruction* (1965); Hans L. Trefousse, *Andrew Johnson* (1989).

The Freed Slaves

Ira Berlin, ed., *Freedom: A Documentary History of Emancipation, 1861–1867* (1984); Orville Vernon Burton, *In My Father's House Are Many Mansions* (1985); Edmund L. Drago, *Black Politicians and Reconstruction in Georgia* (1982); Paul D. Escott, *Slavery Remembered* (1979); Gerald Jaynes, *Branches Without Roots: The Genesis of the Black Working Class in the American South, 1862–1882* (1986); Leon Litwack, *Been in the Storm So Long* (1979); Edward Magdol, *A Right to the Land* (1977); Robert Morris, *Reading, 'Riting, and Reconstruction* (1981); Howard Rabinowitz, ed., *Southern Black Leaders in Reconstruction* (1982); Emma Lou Thornbrough, ed., *Black Reconstructionists* (1972); Clarence Walker, *A Rock in a Weary Land* (1982).

Politics and Reconstruction in the South

Robert W. Coakley, *The Role of Federal Military Forces in Domestic Disorders, 1789–1878* (1988); Richard N. Current, *Those Terrible Carpetbaggers* (1988); W. E. B. Du Bois, *Black Reconstruction* (1935); Paul D. Escott, *Many Excellent People: Power and Privilege in North Carolina, 1850–1900* (1985); Michael W. Fitzgerald, *The Union League Movement in the Deep South* (1989); Eric Foner, *Reconstruction: America's Unfinished Revolution, 1863–1877* (1988); William C. Harris, *The Day of the Carpetbagger* (1979); Thomas Holt, *Black over White: Negro Political Leadership in South Carolina During Reconstruction* (1977); Michael Perman, *The Road to Redemption* (1984); George C. Rable, *But There Was No Peace* (1984); James Roark, *Masters Without Slaves* (1977); Mark W. Summers, *Railroads, Reconstruction, and the Gospel of Prosperity* (1984); Allen Trelease, *White Terror* (1967); Sarah Woolfolk Wiggins, *The Scalawag in Alabama Politics, 1865–1881* (1977).

Women, Family, and Social History

Virginia I. Burr, ed., *The Secret Eye* (1990); Ellen Carol Dubois, *Feminism and Suffrage* (1978); Herbert G. Gutman, *The Black Family in Slavery and Freedom, 1750–1925* (1976); Jacqueline Jones, *Labor of Love, Labor of Sorrow* (1985), and *Soldiers of Light and Love* (1980); Rebecca Scott, "The Battle over the Child," *Prologue* 10 (Summer 1978): 101–113.

The End of Reconstruction

Michael Les Benedict, "Southern Democrats in the Crisis of 1876–1877," *Journal of Southern History* 66 (November 1980): 489–524; William Gillette, *Retreat from Reconstruction, 1869–1879* (1980); Keith Ian Polakoff, *The Politics of Inertia* (1973); C. Vann Woodward, *Reunion and Reaction* (1951).

Reconstruction's Legacy for the South

Norman L. Crockett, *The Black Towns* (1979); Jay R. Mandle, *The Roots of Black Poverty* (1978); Nell Irvin Painter, *Exodusters* (1976); Howard Rabinowitz, *Race Relations in the Urban South, 1865–1890* (1978); Roger L. Ransom and Richard Sutch, *One Kind of Freedom* (1977); C. Vann Woodward, *Origins of the New South* (1951).

17

The Transformation of the West and South, 1877–1892

THEY CALLED THEMSELVES *DINÉ*, which meant The People. White Americans called them Navahos. They lived in what would become northern Arizona and New Mexico and devoted themselves to achieving *k'e*—a universal harmony of love, peace, and cooperation. K'e was symbolized by motherhood and by everything that was life giving. The People tried to achieve k'e by living in unity with the land and all other facets of nature.

White people did not share the Navaho reverence for the earth. When they moved into territory inhabited by Navahos and other tribal peoples, whites took more than they needed simply to survive. They cut open the earth to remove tons of minerals, cut down forests for lumber, dammed the rivers, and plowed the soil to grow crops to sell at distant markets. The Indians did not understand why white people urged them to adopt these practices and improve their lives by creating material wealth. When confronted with tribal resistance to their plans, whites responded with brutal violence.

Indian subsistence cultures withered in the face of coercive government policies and the triumph of market economies when white Americans transformed the western frontier in the late nineteenth century. Settlement of the West proceeded at a furious pace. Between 1870 and 1890, the population living between the Mississippi River and the Pacific Ocean swelled from seven million to nearly seventeen million. By 1890, farms, ranches, mines, towns, and cities could be found in almost every corner of the present-day continental United States, some of which consisted of territories not yet eligible for statehood. That year, the superintendent of the census acknowledged that a frontier line of settlement no longer existed.

In popular thought, the frontier represented the birthplace of American individualism. Conquering the wilderness and bringing forth food and raw materials, not to mention building cities within a single generation, filled white Americans with a sense of power and a faith that anyone eager and persistent enough could succeed. Their self-confidence, however, was easily transformed into an arrogant belief that white Americans were somehow special, and individualism often asserted itself at the expense of racial minorities and people without property—and at the expense of the environment. Americans rarely thought about conserving resources, because there was always more territory to exploit and bring into the market economy.

They spread their market economy across the North American continent—finding and extracting raw materials, harnessing water supplies for productive use, building railroads that carried raw materials to markets and manufactured products to farmers and miners, mechanizing agriculture to make the Great Plains the nation's breadbasket and meat supplier, and expanding both agriculture and industry in the South. In doing so, Americans exhibited their worst as well as their best characteristics.

THE TRANSFORMATION OF NATIVE AMERICAN CULTURES

Historians once defined the American frontier as "the edge of the unused," implying that the frontier faded when open land began to be used for farming or the building of cities. Now scholars emphasize that Native American tribes were using the land and shaping their environment long before other Americans migrated there. Nevertheless, almost all tribal economic systems failed in the late nineteenth century.

Western tribes' cultures varied, but all based their economies to differing degrees on four activities: raising crops; raising livestock; hunting,

This Sioux camp in South Dakota, photographed in 1891, typifies Sioux nomadic life; they carried out their subsistence economy in harmony with the natural environment. When they packed up and moved on, they left the landscape almost undisturbed. The photograph shows the temporary situation characteristic of their camps. Library of Congress.

• *I m p o r t a n t   E v e n t s* •

1862	Homestead Act grants free land to citizens who live on and cultivate the land for five years Morrill Land Grant Act gives states public lands to finance agricultural and industrial colleges
1869	First transcontinental railroad, the Union Pacific, completed
1874	Barbed-wire fence patented, enabling easier control of cattle herds
1876	Custer's Last Stand (Battle of Little Big Horn): Sioux annihilate white troops led by Colonel George A. Custer
1878	Timber and Stone Act allows citizens to buy timber land inexpensively but also enables large companies to acquire huge tracts of forest land
1880–81	Helen Hunt Jackson's *A Century of Dishonor* influences public conscience about poor government treatment of Indians
1882–83	Transcontinental routes of Santa Fe, Southern Pacific, and Northern Pacific railroads completed
1883	Supreme Court, in *Civil Rights Cases*, strikes down 1875 Civil Rights Act and reinforces claim that the federal government cannot regulate behavior of private individuals in matters of race relations National time zones standardized
1887	Dawes Severalty Act dissolves tribal lands and grants land allotments to individual families Hatch Act provides for agricultural experiment stations in every state
1889	Statehood granted to North Dakota, South Dakota, Washington, and Montana
1890	Census Bureau announces closing of the frontier Statehood granted to Wyoming and Idaho Yosemite National Park established
1896	*Plessy* v. *Ferguson* upholds doctrine of "separate-but-equal" among blacks and whites in public facilities Rural Free Delivery made available Statehood granted to Utah
1899	*Cummins* v. *County Board of Education* applies "separate-but-equal" doctrine to public schools

Subsistence Cultures

fishing, and gathering; and raiding. Corn was the most common crop; sheep and horses, acquired from Spanish colonizers, were the livestock. Buffalo were the primary prey of hunts. Tribes raided each other for food, hides, and slaves. The goal of all these activities was subsistence, the maintenance of life at its most basic level. To achieve subsistence, Indians tried to balance their economic systems. Thus when a buffalo hunt failed, a tribe could still subsist on crops; when its crops failed, the tribe could still hunt buffalo and steal food in a raid on another tribe. Indians also traded with each other and with whites.

For Indians on the Plains, everyday life focused on the buffalo. They cooked and preserved buffalo meat, fashioned hides into clothing, shoes, and blankets, used sinew for thread and bowstrings, and carved tools from bones and horns. The tribes also depended heavily on horses, which they used for transportation, hunting, and symbols of wealth. In the Southwest, Indians placed great value on sheep, goats, and horses. Old Man Hat, a Navaho, explained, "The herd is money. . . . You know that you have some good clothing; the sheep gave you that. And you've just eaten different kinds of food; the sheep gave that food to you. Everything comes from the sheep." To the Navahos, the herds were a means to achieve security.

The Indians' world of subsistence and ecological balance began to dissolve when whites, perceiving the buffalo and the Indians as hindrances to their

Slaughter of Buffalo

ambitions on the Plains, endeavored to eliminate both. As one U.S. army officer put it, "Kill every buffalo you can. Every buffalo dead is an Indian gone." Railroads sponsored hunts in which eastern sportsmen shot at the bulky targets from slow-moving trains. Some hunters collected $1 to $3 from tanneries for hides; others did not even stop to pick up their kill. By the 1880s, only a few hundred remained of the estimated thirteen million buffalo that had existed in 1850. The scarcity of buffalo disturbed the subsistence system by leaving Indians less food to supplement their diets if their crops failed or were stolen.

Government policy reinforced private efforts to remove Indians from the path of white ambitions. Since the Treaty of Greenville in 1795, American government officials had considered Indian tribes to be separate nations with which they could make treaties that ensured peace and defined the boundaries between tribal and white lands. But treaties seldom guaranteed the Indians' future land rights; whites assumed that eventually they could settle wherever they wished. Treaties made one week were violated the next. Some tribes acquiesced; others resisted with attacks on settlements, herds, and troops. Whites responded with slayings and massacres of entire villages. At Sand Creek, Colorado, in 1864 U.S. troops killed about 150 Cheyennes, mostly women and children.

By the 1870s, federal officials and humanitarians, seeking more peaceful means of dealing with western tribes, began promoting policies that would treat Indians more like blacks and immigrants; instead of being considered foreign nations, the tribes would be "civilized" and "uplifted" through education. White missionaries and teachers would attempt to inculcate in Indians the values of the white mobility ethic: ambition, thrift, and materialism. To achieve this transformation, however, Indians would have to abandon their traditional cultures.

From the 1860s to the 1880s, the federal government tried to force Indians onto reservations, where, it was thought, they could best be civilized. Reservations usually consisted of those areas of a

Reservation Policy

tribe's previous territory that were least desirable to whites. In assigning Indians to specific territories, the government promised protection from white encroachment and agreed to provide food, clothing, and other necessities.

Reservation policy had disturbing consequences. First, Indians had no say over their own affairs on reservations. Supreme Court decisions in 1884 and 1886 denied them the right to become U.S. citizens, leaving them unprotected by the Fourteenth and Fifteenth Amendments, which had extended to African-Americans the rights of citizenship. Second, it was impossible to protect reservations from the white farmers, miners, and herders who continually sought even remote Indian lands for their own purposes. Third, the government ignored tribal integrity, even combining on the same reservation tribes that had habitually waged war with each other. Rather than serving as civilizing communities, reservations came to resemble antebellum slave quarters.

Not all tribes succumbed to forces that undermined their way of life. Pawnees, for example, resisted extensive trading as well as the liquor that

Tribal Resistance

white traders deliberately used to addict Indians and tempt them into disadvantageous deals. And some tribes tried to preserve their traditional cultures even as they became dependent on whites. Navahos traded for food in order to restore their subsistence way of life, and Pawnees agreed to leave their Nebraska homelands for a reservation in the hope that they could hunt buffalo and grow corn as they once had.

Indians also actively defended their homelands against white intrusion in a series of bloody conflicts and revolts. The most famous battle occurred in June 1876, when twenty-five hundred Dakota Sioux led by chiefs Rain-in-the-Face, Sitting Bull, and Crazy Horse annihilated white troops led by the rash Colonel George A. Custer near the Little Big Horn River in southern Montana. Other Indian victories followed, but shortages of supplies and relentless pursuit by white troops eventually overwhelmed armed Indian resistance.

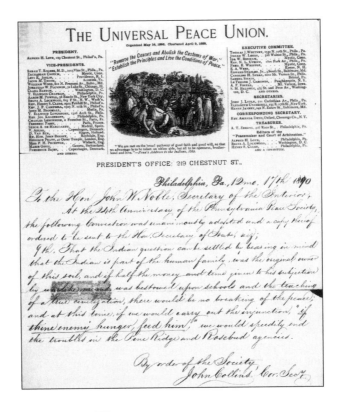

How do historians know

that the "Indian problem" of the late nineteenth century affected the public conscience? This letter was sent by the president of the Universal Peace Union, a humanitarian reform organization, to John W. Noble, secretary of the interior and the federal officer who ultimately oversaw U.S. policy toward the Native American tribes. The organization was forwarding its opinion that Indians were "part of the human family" and that the money and time being spent on subjugating them could be better spent on educating them. Although the organization was somewhat unusual, because its vice presidents included several women and foreigners, it was one of many that held meetings, passed resolutions, and printed publications that catalyzed public opinion to favor a more humane and peaceful approach to disputes between the government and Native Americans. Letters such as this reveal not only the method of petition the organization adopted but also the fervent language it used.   National Archives.

These conditions, the publication of Helen Hunt Jackson's *A Century of Dishonor* (1881), and unfavorable comparison with Canada's management of Indian affairs aroused the American conscience. Canada had granted tribal peoples the rights of British subjects, and the Royal Mounted Police defended them against whites. Canadian officials were more tolerant of tribal customs.

In the United States, the two most important Indian reform organizations were the Women's National Indian Association (WNIA) and the Indian Rights Association (IRA). The WNIA, a group composed mainly of white women who sought to put women's domestic skills and virtues at the service of people in need, urged gradual assimilation of Indians. The IRA supported citizenship and landholding by individual Indians.

Reform of Indian Policy

Reformers particularly deplored Indians' sexual division of labor. Women seemed to do all the work—tending crops, raising children, cooking, curing hides, making tools and clothes—and to be servile to men, who hunted but were otherwise idle. Groups such as the WNIA and IRA wanted Indian men to bear more responsibilities and to become more like the heads of white middle-class households.

Prodded by reformers, Congress in 1887 reversed its reservation policy and passed the Dawes Severalty Act. The act dissolved community-owned tribal lands, granted land allotments to individual families, and awarded citizenship (after a twenty-five-year waiting period) to all who accepted allotments. It also authorized the government to sell unallotted land and to set aside the proceeds for the education of Indians. These provisions applied to western tribes except the Pueblo peoples, who retained land rights granted to them by the Spanish.

**Dawes
Severalty Act**
———

U.S. Indian policy, as carried out by the Indian Bureau of the Interior Department, now took on three main features. First, land was distributed to individual families in the belief that they would acquire white people's wants and values by learning how to manage their property. Second, bureau officials believed that Indians would abandon their "barbaric" habits more quickly if their children were educated in boarding schools away from the reservations. Third, officials tried to suppress what they believed were dangerous religious ceremonies by funding white church groups to establish religious schools among the Indians and teach them to become good Christians.

In one crucial respect, the Dawes Act effectively accomplished what whites wanted and Indians feared: it reduced tribal control over land. Despite some protection against such practices, eager speculators induced Indians inexperienced in commercial dealings to sell their newly acquired property. Between 1887 and the 1930s, tribal landholdings dwindled from 138 million acres to fifty-two million. Land-grabbing whites were particularly cruel to the Ojibwas (Chippewas) of the northern Plains. In 1906, Senator Moses E. Clapp of Minnesota attached a rider to an Indian appropriations bill declaring that mixed-blood adults on the White Earth reservation were "competent" enough to sell their land without having to observe the twenty-five-year waiting period stipulated in the Dawes Act. When the bill became law, white speculators duped many Chippewas, declared mixed-bloods by white experts on the basis of fraudulent evidence, into signing away their land in return for counterfeit money and worthless merchandise.

The Dawes Act had other drawbacks as well. The boarding school program affected thousands of children, but most returned to their reservations rather than assimilate in white society. Efforts to suppress religious observances only drove them underground. Ultimately, however, the western tribes were overcome by political and ecological crises. By the end of the century, Indians had become what historian Richard White has called "a population without control over resources, sustained in its poverty by payments controlled by the larger society, and subject to increasing pressure to lose their group identity and disappear."

**Decline of
Western Tribes**
———

White military superiority was not the only factor contributing to defeat of the western tribes. Their economic systems had started to break down before the military defeats occurred. Although Indians tried to retain their culture by both adapting and yielding to the various pressures, the West was won at their expense, and they remain casualties of an aggressive age.

THE EXPLOITATION OF NATURAL RESOURCES

In sharp contrast to the Indians' use of the natural environment to meet subsistence needs, white migrants to the West and the Plains were driven by a get-rich-quick mentality. To their eyes, the continent's vast stretches of unsettled territory were untapped reservoirs of resources and profits. Extraction of the resources advanced settlement and created new markets; it also fueled the revolutions in transportation, agriculture, and industry that swept the United States in the late nineteenth century. At the same time, the exploitation of nature's wealth gave rise to a spirit of carelessness toward the environment, reinforced the sexual division of labor, and fed habits of racial oppression.

In the years just before the Civil War, eager prospectors began to comb remote forests and mountains for gold, silver, iron, coal, timber, oil,

Mining and Lumbering

and copper. The mining frontier advanced rapidly, drawing thousands of people to California, Nevada, Idaho, Montana, and Colorado. Prospectors tended to be restless optimists, willing to tramp mountains and deserts in search of precious metals.

The prospectors' ultimate goal was to find and sell a large quantity of minerals. But because excavating and transporting minerals were extremely expensive, prospectors who did find veins of metal seldom mined them. Instead, they sold their claims to mining syndicates that had ample capital to bring in engineers, heavy machinery, railroad lines, and work crews. Although gold and silver finds first drew attention to the West and its resources, mining companies usually moved into the Rocky Mountain states to exploit less romantic but equally lucrative metals.

Lumber production—another large-scale extractive industry—required vast amounts of forest land. As lumber companies moved into the Northwest, they grabbed millions of acres by exploiting the Timber and Stone Act (1878). This measure, passed by Congress to stimulate settlement in California, Nevada, Oregon, and Washington, allowed private citizens to buy (at the low price of $2.50 per acre) 160-acre plots "unfit for cultivation" and "valuable chiefly for timber." Taking advantage of the act, lumber companies hired seamen from waterfront boarding houses to register claims to timberland and turn them over to the companies. By 1900, claimants had bought more than 3.5 million acres, but most of that land belonged to corporations.

While lumbermen were acquiring timberlands in the Northwest, oilmen were beginning to sink wells in the Southwest. In 1900, most of the nation's petroleum still came from the Appalachians and Midwest, but rich oil reserves had been found in southern California and eastern Texas. Although oil and kerosene were still used mostly for lubrication and lighting, strikes in the Southwest later became a vital new source of fuel.

The natural resource frontier was largely a man's world. In 1880, white men outnumbered white women by more than two to one in Colorado, Nevada, and

Frontier Society

Arizona. Many western communities did have substantial populations of women, who had come for the same reason as men: to find a fortune. They usually accompanied a husband or father and seldom prospected themselves. Even so, many women recognized opportunities to earn money in the towns, where they provided cooking and laundering (and in some cases, sexual services) for the miners. Occasionally, a woman became the main breadwinner when her husband failed to strike it rich. Women also helped to bolster family and community life by campaigning against drinking, gambling, and prostitution.

Many mining and lumber communities had small numbers of Chinese, Mexican, Indian, and African-American residents. Most Chinese worked on the railroads, but some were employed in the camps to do cooking and cleaning. Blacks also held such jobs. Mexicans and Indians often had been the original settlers of land coveted by whites. Each group encountered prejudice. California, for instance, imposed a tax on foreign miners and denied blacks, Indians, and Chinese the right to testify or submit evidence in court. Just as land treaties with Indians were frequently broken, Mexicans' claims to land sought by white miners were often ignored or stolen.

Development of the nation's oil, mineral, and timber reserves raised serious questions about what resources belonged to the American people, as

Use of Public Lands

represented by the federal government, and what belonged to private interests. Two factors operated at cross-purposes. First, much of the undeveloped territory west of the Mississippi was in the public domain, and some people believed that the federal

Construction crews on western railroads contained workers from a variety of ethnic and racial backgrounds. This work gang, posing on a handcar on the Union Pacific tracks in 1869, includes Chinese and African-American laborers as well as a white foreman.   Lightfoot Collection.

government, as its owner, should receive some compensation for its exploitation. However, the government, lacking both the motivation and the means to dig mines, sink wells, and cut forests, sold the land to private interests that would take the initiative.

Developers of natural resources were seldom interested in landowning. They wanted trees, not forest land that would become useless once they had cut the trees. They wanted oil, not the scrubby plain that would be worthless if—as often happened—they dug wells but found no oil. To avoid purchase costs, oilmen and iron miners often leased property from private owners or the government and paid royalties on the minerals extracted. Some lumbermen simply cut trees on public lands without paying a cent (and used trickery to buy land cheaply under the Timber and Stone Act). Even when the government tried to prevent fraud, many communities resisted, fearing that such crackdowns would slow local economic growth.

Questions about natural resources caught Americans between the desire for progress and the fear of spoiling the land. By the late 1870s and early 1880s, people eager to protect the natural landscape began to coalesce in a conservation movement. Prominent among them was western naturalist John Muir, who helped establish Yosemite National Park in 1890. The next year, under pressure from Muir and others, Congress authorized President Benjamin Harrison to create forest reserves—public land protected from cutting by private interests. Such policies met with strong objections from those who wanted to exploit western resources. Public opinion split along sectional lines. Most supporters of regulation came from the eastern states; opposition was loudest in the West, where people were still eager to take advantage of nature's bounty.

Development of the mining and forest frontiers, and of the farms and cities that followed, brought western territories to the threshold of statehood. In

Admission of New States

1889, Republicans seeking to solidify their control of Congress pushed through an omnibus bill granting statehood to North Dakota, South Dakota, Washington, and Montana. Wyoming and Idaho were admitted the following year. Congress denied statehood to Utah until 1896, when the Mormon majority agreed to abandon polygamy.

The states' mining towns and lumber camps spiced American folk culture and fostered a go-getter optimism that distinguished the American spirit. The lawlessness and hedonism of places like Deadwood, in Dakota Territory, and Tombstone, in Arizona Territory, gave the West notoriety and romance. But violence and eccentricity were far from common. Most miners and lumbermen worked seventy hours a week and had little time, energy, or money for gambling, carousing, or gunfights. Women worked as long or longer as teachers, cooks, laundresses, storekeepers, and housewives; only a few were sharpshooters or dance hall queens. For most westerners, life was a matter of adapting and surviving.

WATER AND WESTERN AGRICULTURE

Glittering gold, tall trees, and gushing oil shaped the popular image of the West, but water gave it life. If the territories and states from the Rocky Mountains westward, plus Texas and Oklahoma, promised wealth from mining, cutting, and drilling, their agricultural potential promised more—if settlers could find a way to bring water to the arid land. Of most importance in the winning of the West is how engineering innovations, technology, and government and corporate effort developed the West's river basins and, in the process, made the land agriculturally productive.

For centuries, Native American tribes had irrigated the hot southwestern desert lands to sustain their subsistence farming. By the late sixteenth century, the Spanish had begun tapping the Rio Grande to irrigate their farms in southwest Texas and New Mexico. The first Americans of northern European ancestry to practice extensive irrigation were the Mormons. Arriving in Utah Territory in 1847, they quickly diverted streams and rivers into a network of canals, the water from which enabled them to farm the hard-baked soil.

Large-scale efforts at land reclamation through irrigation in Colorado and California raised controversies over rights to the precious streams that

Who Owns the Water?

flowed through the West. Americans had inherited the English common-law principle of riparian rights, which held that only people who owned land along the banks of a river could appropriate from the water's flow. The stream itself, according to riparianism, belonged to no one but God; those who lived on its banks could take water for normal needs, but they were not to diminish the river by damming or diverting water at the expense of others who lived along the banks.

Americans snubbed this Old World view. They rejected riparianism in favor of the doctrine of prior appropriation, which awarded a river's water to the first person who claimed it. Western farmers wanted to be allowed, as nonriparian property owners, to dam rivers and transport water as far as they wished. Moreover, they believed that anyone intending a beneficial or "reasonable" (economically productive) use of river water should have the right to appropriation. This doctrine, then, fostered a new attitude toward nature in the West, a belief that natural resources existed for human appropriation.

Without appropriated water, agriculture could not have flourished in the West. Most lands were too dry for the rainfall farming that characterized the eastern Plains. Allowing water-drawing rights only to farmers who lived along river banks would give them a monopoly and effectively prevent development of most of the land. The unspoken premise, however, was that all land existed for potential human development and that all natural resources should be used—even used up—to conquer the land and support maximum economic gain. Most white people assumed that the doctrine of appropriation made sense.

Under appropriation, those who dammed and diverted water could and often did reduce the flow of water available to potential users downstream. People disadvantaged by such action could protect their interests either by suing those who deprived them of water or by establishing a public authority to regulate water usage. Thus in 1879, Colorado created a number of water divisions, each with a commissioner to determine and regulate water rights. In 1890, Wyoming enlarged the concept of state control with a constitutional provision declaring that the state's rivers were public property subject to state supervision of their use.

California was the scene of the most dramatic water-related developments. Unlike other western states, California maintained a mixed legal system that upheld riparianism while allowing for some appropriation. Such a system put irrigators at a disadvantage and prompted them to seek a change in state law. In 1887, the state legislature passed such a law, permitting farmers to organize into irrigation districts that would sponsor construction and operation of irrigation projects. An irrigation district could use its public authority to purchase water rights, seize private property by power of eminent domain to build irrigation canals, and finance its projects through taxation or by issuing bonds. As a result of this legislation, California became the nation's leader in irrigated acreage, with more than one million irrigated acres by 1890. Each acre annually produced crops valued at $19, the most profitable agriculture in the country.

Although irrigation stimulated development, the federal government still owned most of the West in the 1890s. The states wanted the federal government to transfer to them all, or at least part, of its public domain lands. States could then make these lands profitable through reclamation—providing them with irrigated water—which would expand the states' tax bases. For the most part, Congress refused such transfers. Even if federal lands were transferred to state control for the purpose of water development, who would regulate waterways that flowed through more than one state or that could provide water to a nearby state? If, for example, California received control of the Truckee River, which flowed west out of Lake Tahoe, how would Nevadans be assured that California would give them any water? Only the federal government, it seemed, had the power to regulate water development.

In 1902, Congress passed the National, or Newlands, Reclamation Act. Named for Congressman Francis Newlands of Nevada, the act allowed

Newlands Reclamation Act

the federal government to sell western public lands to individuals in parcels not to exceed 160 acres and to use the proceeds from such sales solely to finance irrigation projects. The Newlands Act provided for control but not conservation of water, because about three-fourths of the water used in open-ditch irrigation, the most common form, was lost to evaporation. Thus the legislation fell squarely within the tradition of exploitation of nature for human profit. The law also represented a direct decision by the federal government to aid the economic development of the West, just as subsidies to railroads aided the settlement of the West.

THE AGE OF RAILROAD EXPANSION

The whole country knew what was happening at Promontory Summit in the mountains of Utah on May 10, 1869. On that day, the Central Pacific Railroad, built 689 miles eastward from Sacramento, California, joined with the Union Pacific Railroad, built 1,086 miles westward from Omaha, Nebraska, to form the nation's first transcontinental rail route.

The completion of the transcontinental railroad was part of a rapid expansion of the nation's rail system. Between 1865 and 1890, total track in

Effects of Railroad Construction

the United States grew from 35,000 to 200,000 miles (see map). By 1910, the nation had one-third of all the railroad track in the world. The construction of the rail network helped to boost the nation's steel industry to international leadership. Railroad expansion also spawned a number of related industries, including coal production, passenger and freight car manufacture, and depot construction.

Railroads also altered Americans' conceptions of time and space. First, by overcoming barriers of distance, railroads in effect transformed space into time. Instead of using miles to express the distance

The American West, 1860–1890   *The map shows the dispersed nature of economic activity in the trans-Mississippi West and the importance of railroads in linking those activities.*

PACIFIC OCEAN

GULF OF MEXICO

Mining centers
Gold
Silver
Copper
Indian reservations, 1890
Railroad routes
Cattle trails
Indian battles

between places, people began to refer to the amount of time it took to travel from one place to another. Second, railroad scheduling required nationwide standardization of time. Before railroads, each locale had its own time. Local church bells and clocks struck noon when the sun was directly overhead, and people set their clocks accordingly. But because the sun was not overhead at exactly the same moment everywhere, time varied from place to place. To impose some regularity, railroads created their own time zones. By 1880, there were still nearly fifty different standards, but in 1883 the railroads finally agreed—without consulting anyone in government—to establish four standard time zones for the whole country. Most communities adjusted their clocks accordingly, and railroad time became national time.

Third, railroad construction brought about technological and organizational reforms. By the late 1880s, almost all lines had adopted standard-gauge rails so that their tracks could connect with one another. Westinghouse air brakes, automatic car couplers, standardized handholds on freight cars, and other devices made rail transportation safer and more efficient. Organizational advances included systems for coordinating complex passenger and freight schedules and the adoption of uniform freight-classification systems.

Railroads accomplished these feats with the help of some of the largest government subsidies in American history. Executives argued that because

Government Subsidy of Railroads

railroads benefited the public, the government should aid them by giving them land from the public domain. Sympathetic governments at the national, state, and local levels responded by providing railroad companies with massive subsidies. The federal government gave the railroads more than 180 million acres; state grants totaled about fifty million acres. Counties, cities, and towns also assisted, usually by offering loans or by purchasing railroad bonds or stocks. Without such public help, few railroads could have prospered sufficiently to attract private investment. Nonetheless, railroad executives, while accepting government assistance, argued against government interference.

FARMING THE PLAINS

Settlement of the Great Plains and the West involved the greatest migration in American history. Most, although not all, migrants came from the eastern states or Europe. They were lured by

Migration to the Plains

offers of inexpensive land and credit from states and railroads eager to promote settlement. As a result of the migration, more acres were settled and put under cultivation between 1870 and 1890 than in the nation's previous 250 years. At the same time that the Plains and the West were being settled, the national population increased dramatically. As a result, the demand for farm products grew rapidly, and developments in transportation and storage made the prospects for commercial farming—growing crops for profit—more favorable than ever. Agricultural development of the West and the Plains turned the United States into the world's breadbasket.

Most migrants went west because opportunities there seemed to promise a better life but soon found that conditions on the Plains were much harder than

Hardships of Life on the Plains

the advertisements and railroad agents had suggested. Migrants often encountered scarcities of essentials they had once taken for granted. The open prairies contained little lumber for housing and fuel. Pioneer families were forced to build houses of sod and to burn manure for heat. Water was sometimes as scarce as timber.

Even more formidable than the terrain was the climate of the Plains. The expanse between the Missouri River and the Rocky Mountains divides climatologically along a line running from Minnesota southwest through Oklahoma, then south, bisecting Texas. East of the line, annual rainfall averages about twenty-eight inches, enough for most crops. To the west, life-giving rain was never certain.

Weather seldom followed predictable cycles. In summer, weeks of torrid heat and parching winds suddenly gave way to violent storms that washed away crops and property. Winter blizzards piled up mountainous snowdrifts that halted all outdoor movement. In March and April, melting snow swelled streams, and flood waters threatened millions of acres. In the fall, a week without rain could turn dry grasslands into tinder, and the slightest spark could ignite a raging prairie fire.

Even when the climate was favorable, nature could be cruel. Weather that was good for crops was also good for breeding insects. Worms and flying pests ravaged corn and wheat. In the 1870s and 1880s, swarms of grasshoppers virtually ate up entire farms. As one farmer lamented, the "hoppers left behind nothing but the mortgage."

Settlers of the Plains also had to contend with social isolation, a factor accentuated by the pattern of settlement. Under the Homestead Act of 1862 and other measures adopted to encourage western settlement, most plots of land were rectangular-shaped 160-acre tracts. The rectangular shape meant that at most four families could live near each other, but only if they congregated around the shared four-corner boundary intersection. In practice, farm families usually lived back from their boundary lines, and at least a half-mile separated farmhouses.

Social Isolation

Many observers wrote about the loneliness and monotony of life on the Plains. Men might find escape by working outdoors and taking occasional trips to sell crops or buy supplies. Women were more isolated, confined by domestic chores to the household, where, as one writer remarked, they were "not much better than slaves. It is a weary, monotonous round of cooking and washing and mending and as a result the insane asylum is 1/3d filled with wives of farmers."

Farm families survived by sheer resolve and by organizing churches and Grange clubs where they could socialize a few times a month. By the early 1900s, two developments had brought rural settlers into closer contact with modern consumer society. First, mail-order houses—Montgomery Ward and Sears, Roebuck—made new consumer products available to almost everyone by the 1870s and 1880s. Second, scores of rural communities petitioned

Mail-Order Companies and Rural Free Delivery

Congress for extension of the postal service during the 1890s, and in 1896 the government made Rural Free Delivery (RFD) widely available. Farmers would no longer lack news and information; they could receive letters, newspapers, and catalogues at home nearly every day. In 1913, the Post Office inaugurated parcel post, which enabled people to receive packages, such as orders from Ward's and Sears, less expensively.

The agricultural revolution that followed the Civil War would not have been possible without the expanded use of machinery. When the Civil War drew men away from farms in the upper Mississippi River valley, the women and men who remained began using reapers and other mechanical implements to satisfy demand and take advantage of high grain prices. After the war, continued demand and high prices encouraged farmers to depend more on machines, and inventors worked hard to develop new implements for farm use. Machines dramatically reduced the time and cost of farming various other crops as well.

Mechanization of Agriculture

Meanwhile, Congress and scientists worked to improve existing crops and develop new ones. The 1862 Morrill Land Grant Act granted each state federal lands (thirty thousand acres for each of a state's senators and representatives) to sell in order to finance agricultural and industrial colleges. (A second Morrill Act in 1890 aided more schools, including a number of public black colleges.) The Hatch Act of 1887 provided for agricultural experiment stations in every state, further encouraging the advancement of farming technology.

Legislative and Scientific Aid to Farmers

Meanwhile, scientific advances enabled farmers to use the soil more efficiently. Agricultural researchers developed the technique of dry farming, a system of plowing and harrowing that prevented precious moisture from evaporating. Botanists perfected several varieties of "hard" wheat that had seeds that could withstand northern winters, and millers invented an efficient process for grinding the tougher wheat kernels into flour. Californian Luther Burbank developed a wide range of new plants by cross-breeding. Chemist George Washington Carver of the Tuskegee Institute created hundreds of new products from peanuts, soybeans, sweet potatoes, and cotton wastes and taught methods of soil improvement. Other scientists developed new means of combating plant and animal diseases. Turbulent times lay ahead for farmers, but in the meantime development of the agricultural hinterland by virtue of settlement, science, and technology made America what one journalist called "the garden of the world."

THE RANCHING FRONTIER

While commercial farming was spreading, one of the West's most romantic industries, cattle ranching, was evolving. Early in the nineteenth century, huge herds of cattle, introduced by the Spanish and developed by Mexican ranchers, roamed southern Texas and bred with cattle brought by Anglo settlers. The resulting longhorn breed multiplied and became valuable by the 1860s, when population growth increased demand for beef and railroads facilitated the transportation of food. By 1870, drovers were herding thousands of Texas cattle north to railroad connections in Kansas, Missouri, and Wyoming. On these long drives, mounted cowboys (as many as 25 percent of whom were African-American) supervised the herds, which fed on open grassland along the way.

The long drive gave rise to romantic lore, but it was not very efficient. Trekking fifteen hundred miles made cattle sinewy and tough. Herds traveling through Indian lands and farmers' fields were sometimes shot at, and state laws later prohibited such trespass. The ranchers' only alternative was to eliminate long drives by raising herds nearer to railroad routes.

Cattle raisers needed vast stretches of land to graze their herds, and they wanted to incur as little expense as possible in using such land. Thus they often bought a few acres bordering streams and turned their herds loose on adjacent public domain that no one wanted

Open-Range Ranching

because it lacked water access. By this method, called open-range ranching, a cattle raiser could control thousands of acres by owning only a hundred or so.

Cowboy crews rounded up the cattle twice each year to brand new calves in the spring and to drive mature animals to market in the fall. Roundups delighted easterners with colorful images of western life: bellowing cattle, mounted rope-swinging cowboys, and smoky campfires. But roundups and open-range ranching proved short lived, because they lured too many ranchers to the business. Opportunities for profit at first enriched Civil War veterans in Texas and other states. But as demand for beef kept rising and ranchers and capital flowed into the Plains, cattle began to overrun the range.

Meanwhile, the farming frontier was advancing and generating new demands for land. Fearing loss of control, ranchers began to fence in pastures with barbed wire, a recent invention, although they had no legal title to the land. Fences eliminated the open range and often provoked disputes between competing ranchers, between cattle raisers and sheep raisers, and between ranchers and farmers who claimed use of the same land. In 1885, President Grover Cleveland ordered the removal of illegal fences on public lands and Indian reservations. Enforcement was slow, but the order signaled that free use of public domain was ending.

Open-range ranching made beef a staple of the American diet and created a few fortunes, but its extralegal features could not survive the rush of history. By 1890, big businesses were taking over the cattle industry and applying scientific methods of breeding and feeding. Most ranchers owned or leased the land they used, although some illegal fencing persisted.

THE SOUTH AFTER RECONSTRUCTION

While the Plains and West were being transformed, the South was developing its own forms of resource exploitation and market economies. Ravaged by the

Civil War, which had killed one-third of all draft animals and destroyed half of the region's farm equipment, southern agriculture recovered slowly. Rather than diversify, farmers concentrated on growing cotton even more single-mindedly than before the war. High prices for seed and implements, declining prices for crops, taxes, and, most of all, debt trapped many families in poverty.

To achieve sectional independence, some southern leaders tried to promote industrialization. Their efforts partially succeeded, but by the early 1900s many southern industries were mere subsidiaries of northern firms. Moreover, southern planters, shippers, and manufacturers depended heavily on northern banks to finance their operations. Equally important, low wages and stunted opportunities prevented inflows of people—laborers, farmers, businesspeople, and professionals—who would have brought inflows of capital. Thus although in some ways the South grew as rapidly as the North, it remained an isolated region, poorly integrated in the national economy.

During and after Reconstruction, a significant shift in the nature of agriculture swept the South. Between 1860 and 1880, the total number of farms in southern states more than doubled, but the size of the average farm decreased from 347 to 156 acres. Moreover, the number of landowners did not increase, because a growing proportion of southern farmers rented, rather than owned, their farms. Southern agriculture became dominated by landlords, and the system was characterized by sharecropping and tenant farming. More than one-third of the farmers counted in the 1880 census were sharecroppers and tenants, and the proportion increased to two-thirds by 1920.

Sharecropping and tenant farming entangled millions of southerners in a web of humiliation, at the center of which was the crop lien. Most farmers, too poor ever to have cash on hand, borrowed in order to buy necessities. They could offer as collateral only what they could grow. A farmer in need of supplies would deal with a nearby "furnishing merchant," who would exchange supplies for a certain

Crop-Lien System
_____

portion, or lien, of the farmer's forthcoming crop. After the crop was harvested and brought to market, the merchant collected his debt. All too often, the farmer's debt exceeded his crop's value. Thus the farmer paid off the merchant, received no cash for the crop, and still needed food and supplies. His only choice was to commit his next crop to the merchant and sink deeper into debt.

The merchants frequently took advantage of the customer's powerlessness by inflating prices and charging credit customers interest ranging from 33 to 200 percent on the advances they received. Suppose, for example, that a farmer needed a 20-cent bag of seed and had no cash. The furnishing merchant would extend credit for the purchase but would also boost the price to 28 cents. At year's end, that 28-cent loan would have accumulated interest, raising the farmer's debt to, say, 42 cents. The farmer, having pledged more than his crop's worth against scores of such debts, fell behind in payments and never recovered. His only choice was to commit his next crop to the merchant and sink deeper into debt. If he fell too far behind, he could be evicted.

The lien system caused hardship in former plantation areas where tenants and sharecroppers—black and white—grew cotton for the same markets that had existed before the Civil War. In the southern backcountry, which in the antebellum era had been characterized by small farms, relatively few slaves, and diversified agriculture, the crop-lien problem was compounded by other economic changes.

New spending habits of backcountry farmers illustrate the most important changes. In 1884, Jephta Dickson, of Jackson County in the northern Georgia hills, bought $53.37 worth of flour, meal, peas, meat, corn, and syrup from one merchant and $2.53 worth of potatoes, peas, and sugar from another. Such expenditures would have been rare in the upcountry before the Civil War, when most farmers grew almost all the food they needed. The war and Reconstruction, however, left yeoman farmers in debt, and that indebtedness forced men like Jephta Dickson to shift from semisubsistence agriculture to more commercialized farming. Simply put, they had to plant a cash crop and in the South that meant cotton. As backcountry yeomen devoted more acres to cotton, they raised less of what they needed on a day-to-day basis and found themselves more frequently at the mercy of merchants.

At the same time, backcountry farmers suffered from new laws that essentially closed the southern range (those lands owned by the federal government but used freely by southern herders). This change too resulted from the commercialization of agriculture. Before the 1870s, southern farmers, like open-range ranchers in the West, had let their livestock roam freely on other people's land in search of food and water. By custom, farmers who wished to protect their crops from foraging animals were supposed to build fences around those crops. But as commercial agriculture reached the backcountry, large landowners and merchants induced county and state legislative bodies to require the fencing-in of animals rather than crops. These laws hurt poor farmers who had little land, requiring them to use more of their precious land for pasture.

Closing the Southern Range

Poor whites in the rural South also feared that newly enfranchised blacks could undermine whatever political and social superiority (real and imagined) they enjoyed. Wealthy white landowners and merchants fanned the fears, using racism to divide poor whites and blacks and to distract poor whites from protesting their economic subjugation.

The majority of the nation's African-Americans still lived in the South, worked in agriculture, and found that freedom had not improved their opportunities relative to those of whites. In 1880, 90 percent of all southern blacks depended for a living on farming or personal and domestic service—the same occupations they had held as slaves.

Condition of African-Americans

Moreover, the New South proved as violent a place for African-Americans as the Old South had been. Between 1889 and 1909, for instance, more than seventeen hundred African-Americans were lynched in the South. Most lynchings occurred in sparsely populated rural districts in which whites felt threatened by an influx of blacks and where fast-changing communities left migrant blacks with no friends, black or white, to vouch for them. Most victims of lynchings were vagrants who had accidentally crossed the bounds of acceptable behavior, usually involving an alleged assault—rarely proved—on a white woman.

Threatened by violence, pushed into sharecropping, and burdened with crop liens, African-Americans also had to contend with new forms of social and political oppression. With slavery dead, white supremacists fashioned new ways to keep blacks in a position of inferiority. As part of this effort, southern leaders instituted measures to discourage blacks from voting and to segregate them legally from whites.

The end of Reconstruction did not stop blacks from voting. Despite increasing threats and intimidation, blacks still formed the backbone of the Republican party and some still won elective offices. White politicians, however, began to seek ways to discourage the "Negro vote." Beginning with Georgia in 1877, southern states levied taxes of $1 to $2 on all citizens wishing to vote. The poll taxes proved prohibitive to most black voters, who were so deeply in debt to merchants and landlords that they never had cash for any purpose. Other schemes disfranchised black voters who could not read. Voters might be required, for instance, to deposit ballots for different candidates in different ballot boxes. To do so correctly, however, voters had to be able to read the instructions. Although aimed at African-Americans, such measures also disqualified many poor whites.

Racial discrimination also grew worse in social affairs. Under slavery, a widespread informal system of separation had governed race relations. After the Civil War, the law formalized the system. In a series of cases during the 1870s, the Supreme Court opened the door to discrimination by ruling that the Fourteenth Amendment protected citizens' rights only against infringement by state governments. The federal government, according to the Court, had no authority over the actions of individuals or organizations. If blacks wanted protection under the law, the Court said, they must seek it from the states.

Spread of Jim Crow Laws

The climax to the rulings came in 1883, when in the *Civil Rights Cases* the Court struck down the 1875 Civil Rights Act, which had prohibited segregation in public facilities such as streetcars, hotels, theaters, and parks. Subsequent lower-court cases in the 1880s established the principle that blacks could be restricted to "separate-but-equal" facilities. The Supreme Court upheld the separate-but-equal doctrine in *Plessy* v. *Ferguson* (1896) and officially applied it to schools in *Cummins* v. *County Board of Education* (1899).

Thereafter, segregation laws—popularly known as Jim Crow laws—multiplied throughout the South, confronting African-Americans with daily reminders of their inferior status. State and local laws restricted them to the rear of streetcars, to separate drinking fountains and toilets, and to separate sections of hospitals, asylums, and cemeteries. Segregation reached such extremes that Atlanta required separate Bibles for the swearing-in of black witnesses in court.

In industry, new initiatives brought breezes of change, but there too a distinctively southern quality prevailed. Two of the South's leading industries in the late nineteenth century relied on traditional staple crops—cotton and tobacco. In the 1870s, textile mills began to appear in the Cotton Belt. Staffed inexpensively by poor whites eager to escape crop liens, and aided by low taxes, such mills multiplied. By 1900, the South had four hundred mills, and twenty years later the region was eclipsing New England in textile-manufacturing supremacy. Proximity to raw materials and inexpensive labor also aided the tobacco industry, and the invention in 1880 of a cigarette-making machine immensely enhanced the marketability of tobacco.

Industrialization of the South

Black and white workers (although in segregated sections of the factories) manufactured cigarettes in cities; textile mills were concentrated in small towns and developed their own exploitative labor system. Financed mostly by local investors, mills employed women and children from poor white families and paid 50 cents a day for twelve or more hours of work. Such wages were barely half the wage paid to northern workers. Many companies built villages around their mills and controlled the housing, stores, schools, and churches. Criticism of the company was forbidden, and attempts at union organization were squelched.

Northern and European capitalists financed other industries in the South. In the Gulf states, the lumber industry became significant, and iron and steel production made Birmingham, Alabama, a boom city. Yet in 1900, the South remained as rural as it had been in 1860. A New South eventually would emerge but not until after a world war and a massive black exodus had shaken up old attitudes.

The development of the West was accomplished with courage and creativity that amazed the rest of the world. The extraction of raw minerals, the use of irrigation and mechanization to bring forth agricultural abundance from the land, and the construction of railroads to tie the nation together transformed half the continent within half a century. The optimistic conquerors, however, employed power, violence, and greed that overwhelmed the culture of the land's original inhabitants, left many farmers feeling cheated and betrayed, and sacrificed environmental balance for market profits. In the South, recovery and growth kindled new optimism, but careless exploitation exhausted the soil and left poor farmers as downtrodden as ever. In an age of expansion, African-Americans saw their rights and opportunities narrowing. Industrialization failed to lessen the dominance of southern staple-crop agriculture, and by 1900 the South was more dependent economically on the North than it had been before the Civil War.

SUGGESTIONS FOR FURTHER READING

The Western Frontier

Ray A. Billington and Martin Ridge, *Westward Expansion*, 5th ed. (1982); Sara Deutsch, *No Separate Refuge: Culture, Class, and Gender on an Anglo-Hispanic Frontier in the American Southwest* (1987); Julie Roy Jeffrey, *Frontier Women* (1979); Patricia Limerick, *The Legacy of Conquest: The Unbroken Past of the American West* (1987); Rodman W. Paul, *The Far West and the Great Plains in Transition, 1859–1900* (1988); Henry Nash Smith, *Virgin Land: The American West as Symbol and Myth* (1950, 1958).

Water and the Environment

Roderick Nash, *American Environmentalism* (1990); Donald Worster, *Rivers of Empire: Water, Aridity, and the Growth of the American West* (1985).

Railroads

Alfred D. Chandler, ed., *Railroads: The Nation's First Big Business* (1965); George R. Taylor and Irene Neu, *The American Railroad Network* (1956); Alan Trachtenberg, *The Incorporation of America* (1982).

Native American Tribes

Frederick E. Hoxie, *A Final Promise: The Campaign to Assimilate the Indians, 1880–1920* (1984); Francis Paul Prucha, *The Great Father: The United States Government and the American Indians* (1984); Robert M. Utley, *The Indian Frontier of the American West, 1846–1890* (1984); Philip Weeks, *Farewell, My Nation: The American Indian and the United States* (1990); Richard White, *The Roots of Dependency* (1983).

Ranching and Settlement of the Plains

Allan G. Bogue, *From Prairie to Corn Belt* (1963); David Dary, *Cowboy Culture: A Saga of Five Centuries* (1981); Gilbert C. Fite, *The Farmer's Frontier* (1963); J. Stanford Rikoon, *Threshing in the Midwest* (1988).

The New South

Edward L. Ayers, *The Promise of the New South* (1992); Orville Vernon Burton and Robert C. McMath Jr., eds., *Toward a New South?: Post–Civil War Southern Communities* (1982); Paul Gaston, *The New South Creed* (1970); Steven Hahn, *The Roots of Southern Populism: Yeoman Farmers and the Transformation of the Georgia Upcountry, 1850–1890* (1983); C. Vann Woodward, *The Strange Career of Jim Crow* (1966), and *Origins of the New South*, rev. ed. (1951); Gavin Wright, *Old South, New South* (1986).

18

The Machine Age, 1877–1920

I T WAS 1882, AND Conrad Carl, a tailor who for nearly thirty years had done piecework in his New York City tenement apartment, was appearing before a Senate committee that was investigating the causes of recent labor unrest. Acknowledging that his testimony would probably cost him his job, Carl nevertheless testified candidly. When he first began tailoring, Carl explained, he and his wife and children had pieced together garments by hand. The pace of their work was relaxed, yet he was able to save a few dollars each year. Then, said Carl, "in 1854 or 1855, . . . the sewing machine was invented and introduced, and it stitched very nicely, nicer than the tailor could do; and the bosses said: 'We want you to use the sewing machine; you have to buy one.' "

Carl and other tailors used their meager savings to buy machines, hoping they could earn more by producing more. But then employers cut wages. The tailors "found that we could earn no more than we could without the machine; but the money for the machine was gone now, and we found that the machine was only for the profit of the bosses; that they got their work quicker, and it was done nicer."

Conrad Carl's testimony to the Senate committee was one worker's account of the industrialization that was relentlessly overtaking American society. The new order was both inspiring and ominous. The factory and the machine broke manufacturing down into routine tasks and organized work according to the dictates of the clock. Workers, who had long thought of themselves as valued producers, found they were struggling to avoid becoming slaves to machines. Meanwhile, in the quest for productivity and profits, corporations merged and amassed awesome power. Defenders of the new system devised new theories to justify it, whereas critics tried to combat what they thought were abuses of power.

Industrialization was and is a complex process; its chief feature is the production of goods by machine rather than by hand. In America, industrialization was characterized by the following phenomena:

- Concentration of production in large, intricately organized factories

- Growth of large enterprises and specialization in all forms of economic activity

- Involvement of an increasing proportion of the work force in manufacturing
- Increased accumulation of capital for investment in the expansion of production
- Accelerated technological innovation, emphasizing new inventions and applied science
- Expanded markets, no longer merely local and regional in scope
- Growth of a nationwide transportation network based on the railroad, and an accompanying communications network based on the telegraph and telephone
- Rapid increase in population
- Steady increase in the size and predominance of cities

In 1860, about one-fourth of the American labor force worked in manufacturing and transportation; by 1900, more than half did so. By the dawn of the twentieth century, the United States was not only the world's largest producer of raw materials and food but also the most productive industrial nation. Accelerated migration from farms and mass immigration from abroad swelled the industrial work force, but machines, more than people, boosted American productivity. Moreover, business innovations, in organization and marketing as well as in technology, drove the quest for profits.

These developments had momentous effects on standards of living and on the nature of everyday life. During the half-century between the end of Reconstruction and the end of the First World War, a new consumer society took shape. The nation's farms and factories were producing so much that Americans could afford to satisfy their material wants. What had once been accessible only to a few was becoming available to many. Yet the accomplishments of industrial expansion involved waste and greed.

TECHNOLOGY AND THE TRIUMPH OF INDUSTRIALISM

In 1876, Thomas A. Edison and his associates moved into a long wooden shed in Menlo Park, New Jersey, where Edison intended to turn out "a minor invention every ten days and a big thing every six months or so." Edison envisioned his laboratory as an invention factory, where creative people would pool their ideas and skills to fashion marketable products. Here was the brash American spirit adapting to a more systematic work ethic. If Americans wanted new products, they had to organize and work purposefully to bring about progress. Such efforts reflected a forward-looking energetic spirit that enlivened American industrialization at the end of the nineteenth century.

In the years between 1865 and 1920, the machine fired American optimism (see map on page 346). The machine, like the West, embodied opportunity. Technological adaptation of existing devices, such as the steam engine and sewing machine, plus new inventions in fields like electricity and industrial chemistry, enabled the United States to surpass all rivals in industrial and agricultural production. As innovative as the inventions was the marriage between technology and business organization. The harnessing of electricity, internal combustion, and industrial chemistry illustrates how this marriage worked.

Perhaps the biggest of Edison's "big thing" projects began in 1878 when he formed the Edison Electric Light Company and embarked on a search for a cheap, efficient means of indoor lighting. His major contribution was the perfection of an incandescent bulb that used a filament in a vacuum. At the same time, he worked out a system of power production and distribution—an improved dynamo and a parallel circuit of wires—to provide inexpensive, convenient power to a large number of customers.

Birth of the Electricity Industry

To make his ideas marketable, Edison acted as his own publicist. During the 1880 Christmas season, he illuminated Menlo Park with forty incandescent bulbs, and in 1882 he built a power plant that would light eighty-five buildings in New York's financial district around Wall Street. When the Pearl Street Station began service, a *New York Times* reporter marveled that working in his office at night "seemed almost like writing in daylight."

Because Edison's system used direct current at low voltage, it could send electric power only a mile

• *Important Events* •

1873–78	Overly rapid expansion causes economic decline
1877	Widespread railroad strikes protest wage cuts
1879	Henry George's *Progress and Poverty* argues against economic inequality Edison perfects incandescent light bulb
1880s	Chain-pull toilets spread across U.S. Doctors accept germ theory of disease Mass production of tin cans begins
1881	First federal trademark law begins spread of brand names
1882	Standard Oil Trust formed
1884–85	Economic decline results from numerous causes
1886	Haymarket riot in Chicago protests police brutality against labor demonstrators; seven people killed, eight anarchists tried and convicted American Federation of Labor (AFL) founded
1888	Edward Bellamy's *Looking Backward* depicts utopian world free of monopoly, politicians, and class divisions
1890	Sherman Anti-Trust Act outlaws "combinations in restraint of trade"
1892	Homestead (Pennsylvania) steel workers strike against Carnegie Steel Company
1893–97	Severe economic depression causes high unemployment and numerous business failures
1894	Workers at Pullman Palace Car Company in company town of Pullman, Illinois, strike against exploitative policies
1895	*U.S.* v. *E. C. Knight Co.* limits Congress's power to regulate manufacturing
1896	*Holden* v. *Hardy* upholds law regulating miners' working hours because of mining dangers
1898	Frederick W. Taylor promotes scientific management (rigid schedules and repetitive routines) as efficiency measure in industry
1901–03	U.S. Steel Corporation founded Ford Motor Company founded
1905	*Lochner* v. *New York* overturns law limiting bakery workers' work hours and limits scope of labor protection laws Industrial Workers of the World founded
1908	*Muller* v. *Oregon* upholds law limiting women to ten-hour workday First Ford Model T built
1913	First moving assembly line begins operation at Ford Motor Company

or two. George Westinghouse, a young inventor from Schenectady, New York, who had become famous for devising an air brake for railroad cars, solved the problem. Westinghouse purchased patent rights to generators that used alternating current and transformers that reduced high-voltage power to lower voltage levels, thus making transmission over long distances less expensive.

Once Edison and Westinghouse had made their technological breakthroughs, others introduced new business practices to market and refine their inventions. Samuel Insull, Edison's private secretary, deftly attracted investments and organized Edison power plants across the country, turning energy into big business. In the late 1880s and early 1890s, financiers Henry Villard and J. P. Morgan consolidated patents in electric lighting and merged small equipment-manufacturing companies into the General Electric Company. Equally important, General Electric and Westinghouse Electric established research laboratories that paid scientists to find new everyday uses for electricity.

A number of inventors, however, continued to work independently and tried to sell their handiwork

The idea of the assembly line, as perfected at the Ford plant in Highland Park, Michigan, outside Detroit, was to break down the production process so that individual workers efficiently repeated the same task. In this photograph, taken around 1914, assembly-line workers are installing pistons in engines of the Ford Model T. Henry Ford Museum and Greenfield Village.

to manufacturing companies. One such inventor was Granville T. Woods, an African-American engineer from Columbus, Ohio. Working in machine shops, Woods patented thirty-five devices vital to electronics and communications. Among his inventions, most of which he sold to companies such as General Electric, were an automatic circuit breaker, electric incubator, electromagnetic brake, and various

Industrial Production, 1919 By the early twentieth century, one or a few kinds of industrial production dominated each state. Although the value of goods produced was still highest in the Northeast, states like Minnesota and California had impressive dollar values of outputs. Source: © American Heritage Publishing Co., Inc., *American Heritage Pictorial Atlas of United States History;* data from U.S. Bureau of the Census, *Fourteenth Census of the United States, 1920.* Vol. IX: *Manufacturing* (Washington: U.S. Government Printing Office, 1921).

instruments to aid communications between railroad trains.

The era's most visionary manufacturer was Henry Ford. In the 1890s, Ford, then an electrical engineer in Detroit's Edison Company, experimented in his spare time with a gasoline-burning internal combustion engine to power a vehicle. Like Edison, Ford had a scheme as well as a product.

Mass Production of the Automobile

His plan was to reduce production costs by manufacturing millions of identical cars in exactly the same way. The key to mass production was flow. On Ford's assembly lines, production was broken down so that each worker was given responsibility for only one task, performed repeatedly, using the same specialized machine. By means of a continuous flow of these tasks, workers fashioned each component part and progressively assembled the car. In 1908, the first year the famous Model T was built, Ford sold ten thousand cars. By 1914, the year after the first moving assembly line was inaugurated, 248,000 Fords had been sold. The value of automobiles manufactured, only $6 million in 1900, reached $420 million by 1914. Moreover, rising automobile production created more jobs, higher earnings, and higher profits in such related industries as oil, paint, rubber, and glass.

By 1914, many mass-produced Ford cars cost $490, only about one-fourth of their cost a decade earlier. Yet even $490 was too much for many workers, who earned at best $2 a day. In 1914, however, Ford tried to spur productivity, prevent high labor turnover, head off unionization, and better enable his workers to buy the cars they produced by offering them the Five-Dollar-Day Plan—combined wages and profit sharing equal to $5 a day.

Although the timing of technological innovation varied from one industry to another, machines altered the nation's economy and everyday life in a pervasive way between 1865 and 1900 by creating new industries. The telephone and typewriter revolutionized communications. Sewing machines made mass-produced clothing available to almost everyone. Refrigeration changed American dietary habits by making it easier to preserve meat, fruit, vegetables, and dairy products. Streetcars, elevated railroads, and subways enabled people to live farther from their workplaces.

Higher production at lower costs made the products profitable. As technological innovations made large-scale production more economical, some owners used part of their profits to replace small factories with larger ones. Between 1850 and 1900, the average capital investment in a manufacturing company increased from $700,000 to $1.9 million. Only large factories could afford to buy new machines and operate them at full capacity. And large factories could best take advantage of discounts for shipping products in bulk and for buying raw materials in quantity. Economists call such advantages economies of scale.

But profitability was a matter of organization as well as mechanics. Running a successful factory depended as much on how production was arranged as

New Emphasis on Efficiency

on the machines in use. Where once shop-floor workers had made basic decisions about how a product was to be made, by the 1890s engineers and managers with specialized scientific knowledge had assumed this responsibility and planned every work task to increase output. Their efforts standardized tasks and quality in mass production, which then required less skill and independent judgment from workers.

The most influential advocate of efficient production was Frederick W. Taylor. In 1898, Taylor took his stopwatch to the Bethlehem Steel Company to illustrate how his principles of scientific management worked. His experiments, he explained, involved identifying the "elementary operations of motions" used by specific workers, selecting better tools, and devising "a series of motions which can be made quickest and best." Applying the technique to the shoveling of ore, Taylor designed fifteen kinds of shovels and prescribed the proper motions for using each one. He succeeded in reducing a crew of 600 men to 140, who received higher wages, although their new jobs were more stressful.

Time, as much as quality, became the measure of acceptable work as a result of Taylor's writings and experiments, and science rather than tradition determined the right ways of doing things. As integral features of the assembly line, where work was divided into specific time-determined tasks, employees had become another kind of interchangeable part.

MECHANIZATION AND THE CHANGING STATUS OF LABOR

By 1880, the course of a single generation had seen a dramatic shift in the status of labor. Almost five million Americans now worked in manufacturing, construction, and transportation, an increase of more than 300 percent. Most workers could no longer accurately be termed *producers*, as craftsmen and farmers had traditionally thought of themselves. The enlarged working class consisted mainly of *employees*—people who worked only when someone else hired them. Producers were paid by consumers according to the quality of what they produced; employees were paid wages based on time spent on the job.

As mass production subdivided manufacturing into small tasks, workers spent their time repeating one specialized operation. By reducing the manufacturing process to numerous simplified tasks constantly repeated, and by coordinating production to the running of machinery, assembly-line production also deprived employees of their independence. Workers could no longer decide when to begin and end the workday, when to rest, and what tools and techniques to use. And workers were now surrounded by others who labored at the same rate for the same pay, regardless of the quality of their work.

Men and women affected by the changes did not accept them passively. Workers struggled to retain independence and self-respect in the face of employers' ever increasing power. Some artisans, for instance, fought to preserve the pace and quality of their jobs and to retain such customs as appointing another worker to read aloud while they worked. Employers, on the other hand, sought to control workers' lives by supporting temperance and moral reform societies, dedicated to combating supposed drinking and debauchery on and off the job.

As machines and assembly-line production reduced the need for skilled workers, employers cut wage costs by hiring more women and children.

Employment of Women

Between 1880 and 1900, the numbers of employed women grew from 2.6 million to 8.6 million, and at the same time their occupational patterns underwent striking changes. The proportion of women in domestic service jobs (maids, cooks, laundresses)—traditionally the most common and lowest-paid form of female employment—dropped dramatically as jobs opened in other sectors. In manufacturing, these jobs were usually menial positions in textile mills and food-processing plants that paid women as little as $1.56 a week for seventy hours of labor.

More important, a major shift was occurring that set the pattern for female workers in the twentieth century. The numbers and percentages of women in clerical jobs—typists, bookkeepers, sales clerks—skyrocketed. By 1920, nearly half of all clerical workers were women; in 1880, only 4 percent had been women. Previously, when sales and office positions had demanded accounting, drafting, and letter-writing skills, men had dominated such jobs. Then new inventions such as the typewriter and adding machine simplified such tasks. Companies eagerly hired women who streamed into the labor market, having taken courses in typing and shorthand to prepare for the better pay and conditions that these jobs offered relative to factory and domestic work.

In sales, as in the office, women needed little training and could be paid low wages. The respectability, pleasant surroundings, and contact with affluent customers attracted women to sales jobs. In department stores, men handled all the money. Sex discrimination thus pervaded the clerical sector. The new jobs offered women some opportunities for advancement to supervisory positions, but women posed no threat to men's managerial jobs.

Although most working children toiled on their parents' farms, the number in nonagricultural occupations tripled between 1870 and 1900. In 1890,

Employment of Children

more than 18 percent of all children aged ten to fifteen were gainfully employed. Mechanization created a number of light tasks, such as running errands and helping machine operators, that children could handle at a fraction of adult wages. Conditions were especially bad for child laborers in the South, where burgeoning textile mills needed unskilled hands. Mill owners induced poor white farm families, which otherwise might not have had any jobs or income, to bind their children over to the factories at miserably low wages.

Several states, especially in the Northeast, had laws specifying the minimum age and maximum workday hours for child labor. But because state statutes did not apply to firms engaged in interstate commerce, most large companies could avoid state regulations. Furthermore, it was difficult to enforce age requirements, and to supplement the family income many parents lied about children's ages. By 1900, state laws and further automation had reduced the number of children working in manufacturing, but many more worked at street trades—shining shoes and peddling newspapers—and as helpers in stores.

Although working conditions were often dangerous and unhealthy, low wages were usually the immediate catalyst of worker unrest. Many employers believed in "the iron law of wages," which dictated that employees be paid according to conditions of supply and demand. In practice the iron law meant that employers did not have to raise wages—and could even cut them—so long as there were workers who would accept low pay. Employers justified the system by invoking individual freedom: a worker who did not like the wages being offered was free to quit and find a job elsewhere. Courts reinforced the principle, denying workers the right to organize and bargain collectively on the grounds that an employee's wages should be the result of an individual negotiation between employee and employer.

Even steady employment was insecure. Repetitive tasks using high-speed machinery dulled concentration, and the slightest mistake could cause serious injury. Industrial acci-

Industrial Accidents

dents rose steadily before 1920, killing or maiming hundreds of thousands of people each year. As late as 1913, after factory owners had installed safety devices, some twenty-five thousand people died each year in industrial mishaps, and close to one million were injured.

Because disability insurance and pensions were almost nonexistent, families stricken by such accidents suffered acutely. Prevailing free market views stifled protective legislation for workers, and employers denied responsibility for employees' well-being. As one railroad manager declared, "The regular compensation of employees covers all risk or liability to accident. If an employee is disabled by sickness or any other cause, the right to claim compensation is not recognized." The only recourse for a stricken family was to sue and prove in court that the dead or injured worker had not understood the risks involved and had not caused the accident.

Reformers and union leaders lobbied Congress successfully for laws to improve working conditions, but the Supreme Court limited the scope of

Courts Restrict Labor Reform

such legislation by narrowly defining what jobs were dangerous and which workers needed protection. Initially, in *Holden* v. *Hardy* (1896), the Court upheld a law regulating the working hours of miners, because their work was so dangerous that overly long hours would increase the threat of injury. In *Lochner* v. *New York* (1905), however, the Court struck down a law limiting bakery workers to a sixty-hour week and a ten-hour day. In response to the argument that states had the authority to protect workers' health and safety, the Court ruled that baking was not a dangerous enough occupation to justify restricting the right of workers to sell their labor freely.

In *Muller* v. *Oregon* (1908), the Court used a different rationale to uphold a law limiting women to ten hours of work a day. In this case, the Court asserted that women's health and reproductive functions required protection. According to the Court, a woman's health "becomes an object of public interest and care in order to preserve the strength and vigor of the race." As a result, women were barred from such occupations as printing and transportation, which required long hours or night work.

Throughout the nineteenth century, workers confronting mechanization reacted in different ways. Some people bent to the demands of the factory, machine, and time clock. Some tried to blend old ways of working into the new system. Some never adjusted and wandered from job to job. Others, however, turned to organized resistance.

The year 1877 was in many ways a watershed. In July, a series of strikes broke out among unionized railroad workers who were protesting wage

Strikes of 1877

cuts, layoffs, and increased workloads. Violence spread from Pennsylvania to the Midwest, Texas, and California. Venting pent-up anger, rioters attacked railroad property, derailing trains and burning railroad yards. State militia companies, organized and commanded by employers, broke up picket lines and fired into threatening crowds.

The worst violence occurred in Pittsburgh, where on July 21 militiamen from Philadelphia bayoneted and fired on a crowd of rock-throwing demonstrators, killing ten. Infuriated, the mob drove the soldiers into a railroad roundhouse and set a series of fires that destroyed 39 buildings, 104 engines, and 1,245 freight and passenger cars. The next day, the troops shot their way out of the roundhouse and killed twenty more citizens before fleeing the city. After more than a month of unprecedented carnage, President Rutherford B. Hayes sent federal troops to end the strikes—the first significant use of troops to quell labor unrest.

THE UNION MOVEMENT

The union movement had precedents but few successes. Craft unions composed of skilled workers in a particular trade dated from the early nineteenth century, but the narrowness of their membership left them without broad power. The National Labor Union, founded in 1866, claimed 640,000 members in 1868 but died during the hard times of the 1870s. The only broad-based labor organization to survive that depression was the Knights of Labor. Founded in 1860 by Philadelphia garment cutters, the Knights opened their doors to other workers in the 1870s. In 1879, Terence V. Powderly, a machinist and former mayor of Scranton, Pennsylvania, was elected grand master. Under his forceful guidance, the Knights recruited women, African-Americans, immigrants, and unskilled and semiskilled workers. Membership mushroomed from 10,000 in 1879 to 730,000 in 1886.

Strikes presented a dilemma for the Knights. Some leaders, including Powderly, believed that using strikes to pursue immediate goals would detract from the union's long-range

Knights of Labor

objective—a cooperative society—and that workers lost more strikes than they won. But other Knights leaders and the rank and file did engage in militant actions, including a demand for higher wages and union recognition from railroads in the Southwest in 1886. Railroad magnate Jay Gould refused to negotiate, and a strike that began on March 1 in several Texas communities spread to Kansas, Missouri, and Arkansas. As violence increased, Powderly began to denounce radicalism and violence. In reaction to Powderly's compromising position, the more militant craft unions broke away and Knight membership dwindled. The special interests of craft unions thus overcame the Knights' broad-based and often vague appeal, and dreams of labor unity faded.

As the hard times of the 1870s gave way to better conditions in the early 1880s, a number of labor groups, including the Knights, began to campaign for an eight-hour workday,

Haymarket Riot

partly to create more jobs so as to reduce unemployment. The effort by laborers to regain control of their work gathered momentum in Chicago, where radical anarchists—who believed that voluntary cooperation should replace all government—as well as various craft unions agitated for the cause.

Finally, on May 1, 1886, mass strikes and the largest spontaneous labor demonstration in the country's history took place. Some 100,000 workers turned out, and Chicago police mobilized to prevent disorder, especially among striking workers at the huge McCormick reaper factory. The day passed calmly, but two days later police stormed an area near the McCormick plant and broke up a battle between striking unionists and nonunion strikebreakers. Police shot and killed two unionists and wounded several others. The next evening, labor groups rallied at Haymarket Square, near downtown Chicago, to protest police brutality. As a company of police officers approached, a bomb exploded near their front ranks, killing seven and injuring sixty-seven. Mass arrests followed. Eventually eight men, all anarchists, were tried and convicted of the bombing, although the evidence of their guilt was questionable. Four were executed and one committed suicide in prison. The remaining three were pardoned in 1893 by Illinois governor John P. Altgeld, who believed they had been victims of the "malicious ferocity" of the courts.

The Haymarket bombing drew public attention to the growing discontent of labor and also revived middle-class fear of radicalism. Several cities strengthened their police forces and armories. Employer associations—coalitions of manufacturers in the same industry—worked to counter labor militancy by agreeing to resist strikes and by purchasing strike insurance.

The American Federation of Labor (AFL) emerged from the 1886 upheavals as the major workers' organization. A federation of national craft unions, the AFL initially had about 140,000 members, most of them skilled native-born workers. Led by Samuel Gompers, the pragmatic and opportunistic immigrant who headed the Cigar Makers' Union, the AFL avoided the idealistic rhetoric of worker solidarity to press for concrete goals—specifically higher wages, shorter hours, and the right to bargain collectively. The AFL also avoided party politics, adhering instead to Gompers's dictum to support labor's friends and oppose its enemies, regardless of party. By 1917, the organization included 111 national unions, 27,000 local unions, and 2.5 million members. In contrast to the Knights of Labor, the AFL accepted industrialism and worked to achieve better conditions within the wage-and-hours system. Member unions retained autonomy in their own areas of interest but tried to develop a general policy that would suit all members. Because these unions were organized by craft (skill) rather than by workplace, they had little interest in including unskilled workers.

American Federation of Labor

The AFL and the labor movement in general suffered a series of setbacks in the early 1890s, when once again labor violence stirred public fears. In July 1892, when the AFL-affiliated Amalgamated Association of Iron and Steelworkers refused to accept pay cuts and went on strike in Homestead, Pennsylvania, Henry C. Frick, the president of Carnegie Steel Company, closed the plant. Shortly thereafter, angry workers attacked and routed three hundred Pinkerton guards hired to protect the plant. State militia were summoned, and after five months the strikers gave in.

In 1894, workers at the Pullman Palace Car Company walked out in protest over exploitative policies at the company town near Chicago. The paternalistic George Pullman owned and controlled all land and buildings, the school, the bank, and the water and gas systems in his so-called model company town. As one laborer grumbled, "We are born in a Pullman

Pullman Strike

house, fed from the Pullman shop, taught in the Pullman school, catechized in the Pullman church, and when we die we shall be buried in the Pullman cemetery and go to the Pullman hell."

When the hard times that began in 1893 threatened his business, Pullman maintained profits and stock dividends by cutting wages 25 to 40 percent while holding firm on rents and prices in the model town. Enraged workers, most of whom had joined the American Railway Union, called a strike; Pullman retaliated by closing the plant. When the American Railway Union, led by the charismatic young organizer Eugene V. Debs, voted to aid the strikers by refusing to handle all Pullman cars, Pullman stood firm and rejected arbitration. The railroad owners' association then enlisted the aid of U.S. Attorney General Richard Olney, who obtained a court injunction to prevent the union from "obstructing the railways and holding up the mails." President Grover Cleveland sent troops to Chicago, ostensibly to protect the mails but in reality to crush the strike. Within a month, the strike was over and Debs was jailed for contempt in defying the injunction.

In the West, metal miners in Colorado participated in a series of bitter struggles and violent strikes. Their union, the Western Federation of Miners, helped form a new labor organization, the Industrial Workers of the World (IWW). Unlike the AFL, the IWW strove like the Knights of Labor to unify all American laborers, including the unskilled who were not in craft unions. But the Wobblies, as the IWW was known, went beyond the goals of the Knights and espoused the goal of socialism and the tactics of violence and sabotage. Using the rhetoric of class conflict—"The final aim is revolution," according to an IWW organizer—the Wobblies believed workers should seize and run the nation's industries. Although their anticapitalist goals and aggressive tactics attracted considerable publicity, IWW members probably never exceeded 150,000. The organization faded during the First World War when federal prosecution—and persecution—sent many of its leaders to jail.

Many unions, notably those of the AFL, were openly hostile to women. Of the 6.3 million employed women in 1910, fewer than 2 percent

Women and the Labor Movement

belonged to unions. Fear of competition was the crucial issue. Because women were paid less than men, men worried that their own wages would be lowered or that they would lose their jobs altogether if women invaded the workplace. Moreover, male workers accustomed to sex segregation in employment could not imagine women and men working side by side.

Yet female employees could organize and fight employers as strenuously as men could. Since the early years of industrialization, female workers had formed their own unions. Some, such as the Collar Laundry Union of Troy, New York, organized in the 1860s, had successfully struck for higher wages. The first women's labor federation to parallel the AFL was the Women's Trade Union League (WTUL), founded in 1903. The WTUL worked for protective legislation for female workers, sponsored educational activities, and campaigned for women's suffrage. In 1909, it supported the International Ladies Garment Workers Union's massive strike against New York City sweatshops. Initially, the union's highest offices were held by middle-class women who sympathized with female wage laborers, but control shifted in the 1910s to forceful working-class leaders—notably Agnes Nestor, a glove maker, Rose Schneiderman, a cap maker, and Mary Anderson, a shoe worker. The WTUL advocated such changes as opening apprenticeship programs to women so they could enter skilled trades and providing leadership training for female workers. It served as a vital link between the labor and women's movements into the 1920s.

Women did dominate, however, both the membership and leadership of one union—the Telephone Operators' Department of the International Brotherhood of Electrical Workers. First organized in Montana and San Francisco early in the twentieth century, the union spread throughout the Bell system, the nation's major telephone company and single largest employer of women. Although the union sponsored both social and educational programs, its main focus was workplace issues. Intent on developing pride in the craft of telephone operators, the union opposed scientific management

techniques and tightening of supervision. In 1919, several particularly militant unions paralyzed phone service in five New England states. The union collapsed after a failed strike, again in New England, in 1923, but not until women had proved that they could advance their cause.

Organized labor also excluded most immigrant and African-American workers. Some trade unions welcomed skilled immigrants, but only the Knights of Labor and the IWW had firm policies of accepting immigrants and blacks. Blacks were among the organizers of the coal miners' union, and they were partially unionized in such trades as construction, barbering, and dock work, which had large numbers of black workers. But they could belong only to segregated local unions in the South, and the majority of northern AFL unions also had exclusion policies. Long-held prejudices were reinforced when blacks and immigrants worked as strikebreakers.

Immigrants, African-Americans, and the Labor Movement

The drama that characterized the struggles of the labor movement in the half-century after the Civil War makes it easy to forget that only a fraction of American workers belonged to unions. In 1900, only about one million out of a total of 27.6 million workers were unionized. By 1920, total union membership had grown to five million—still only 13 percent of the work force. For many workers, issues of wages and hours were meaningless; getting and holding a job was the first priority. Job instability and the seasonal nature of work seriously hindered union organizing efforts. Few companies employed a full work force all year round; most employers hired workers during peak seasons and laid them off during slack periods. Thus employment rates often fluctuated wildly. And organizers took no interest in large segments of the industrial labor force and intentionally excluded others.

For most American workers, then, the machine age had mixed results. Industrial wages rose between 1877 and 1914, boosting purchasing power and creating a mass market for standardized goods. Yet in 1900, most employees worked sixty hours a week at wages that averaged 20 cents an hour for skilled work and 10 cents an hour for unskilled. Moreover, as wages rose, living costs increased even faster.

STANDARDS OF LIVING

Although some Americans were deeply suspicious of the advent of machines and the pursuit of profits, few could resist the changes that mechanization brought to everyday life. Mass production and mass marketing made available myriad goods that had not previously existed or had been the exclusive property of the wealthy. This new material well-being, brought about by the advent of such products as ready-made clothes, canned foods, and home appliances, had a dual effect: it drew Americans of differing status into communities of consumers—communities defined not by place or class but by possessions—and it accentuated differences between those who could afford such goods and services and those who could not.

If a society's affluence can be measured by how quickly it converts luxuries into commonplace articles, the United States was indeed becoming affluent in the years between 1880 and 1920. In 1880, for example, only wealthy women could afford silk stockings and only residents of Florida, Texas, and California could enjoy fresh oranges. By 1921, Americans ate 248 crates of oranges per 1,000 people and bought 217 million pairs of silk stockings. How did people afford to make these changes in their standard of living?

What people can afford obviously depends on their resources and incomes. Data for the period are incomplete, but there is no doubt that incomes rose. The rapidly expanding economy spawned massive fortunes. By 1920, for instance, the richest 5 percent of the population was receiving almost one-fourth of all earned income and 85 percent of all stock and bond dividends. Within the middle class, turn-of-the-century employees of the federal executive branch were averaging $1,072 a year and college professors $1,100. And the yearly income of clerical workers increased from $848 in 1890 to $1,156 in 1910. With such incomes, the middle class, which

Rising Personal Income

was increasing in number as a result of new job opportunities, could afford relatively comfortable housing. A six- or seven-room house cost about $3,000 to buy or build and $15 to $20 per month to rent.

Although wages for industrial workers increased as well, income figures were deceptive, because jobs were not always stable and workers had to expend a disproportionate amount of their income on necessities. On average, annual wages of factory workers rose from $486 in 1890 to $630 in 1910. In industries with large female work forces, hourly rates remained lower than in male-dominated industries. Regional variations were also wide. Nevertheless, most wages increased (see table). Income for farm laborers followed the same trend, although wages remained relatively low, because farm workers generally received free room and board.

Wage increases mean little, however, if living costs rise as fast as or faster than wages, and that is what happened. According to one economic index, the weekly cost of living for a typical wage earner's family of four rose more than 47 percent between 1889 and 1913. In few working-class occupations did income rise at the same rate as the cost of living.

Cost of Living

How then could working-class Americans afford the new goods and services that the machine age offered? Some working-class families raised their income and partook modestly in the consumer society by sending children and women into the labor market. In a household in which the father made $600 a year, the wages of other family members might lift total income to $800 or $900. Many families also rented rooms to boarders and lodgers, a practice that could yield as much as $200 a year. These means of increasing family income enabled people to spend more and save more.

Supplements to Family Income

Scientific and technological developments eased some of life's struggles, and their effect on living standards increased after 1900. Advances in medical care, better diets, and improved living conditions sharply reduced death rates and extended the life span. Between

Higher Life Expectancy

American Living Standards, 1880–1920

	1880	1890	1900	1910	1920
Income and earnings					
Annual income:					
Clerical worker		$848		$1,156	
Public school teacher		$256		$492	
Industrial worker		$486		$630	
Farm laborer		$233		$336	
Hourly wage:					
Soft-coal miner		$0.18[a]		$0.21	
Iron worker		$0.17[a]		$0.23	
Shoe worker		$0.14[a]		$0.19	
Paper worker		$0.12[a]		$0.17	
Labor statistics					
Number of people in labor force	17.4 million	28.5 million			41.7 million
Average workweek, manufacturing		60 hours		51 hours	47.4 hours
Food costs					
10 pounds potatoes		$0.16		$0.17	
1 dozen eggs		$0.21		$0.34	
1 pound bacon		$0.12½		$0.25	
Demographic data					
Life expectancy at birth:					
Women			48.3 years		54.6 years
Men			46.3 years		53.6 years
Death rate per 1,000 people			172		130
Birthrate per 1,000 people	39.8		32.3		27.7
Other					
Number of students in public high schools		203,000			2.3 million
Advertising expenditures	$20 million		$95 million		$500 million
Telephones per 100 people		0.3[b]	2.1[c]		12.6 [d]

[a]1892 [b]1891 [c]1901 [d]1921

1900 and 1920, life expectancy increased by fully six years and the death rate dropped by 24 percent (see table). During the same period, there were notable declines in death from typhoid, diphtheria, influenza (except for a harsh pandemic in 1918 and 1919), tuberculosis, and intestinal ailments—diseases that had been scourges of earlier generations. There were, however, significantly more deaths from cancer, diabetes, and heart disease, afflictions of an aging population and perhaps also of new environmental factors. Americans also found more ways to kill one another: although the suicide rate remained about the same, homicides and automobile deaths increased dramatically between 1900 and 1920.

Not only were amenities and luxuries more readily available in the early 1900s than they had been a half-century earlier, but the means to upward mobility seemed more accessible as well. Education was increasingly becoming the key to success. The spread of public education—particularly high schools—helped equip young people to achieve a standard of living higher than their parents'. Between 1890 and 1922, the number of students enrolled in public high schools grew dramatically. Yet the inequities that had pervaded earlier eras remained in place. Race, gender, religion, and ethnicity still determined access to opportunity.

THE QUEST FOR CONVENIENCE

One of the most representative agents of the revolution in American lifestyles at the end of the nineteenth century was the toilet. In the 1880s, Americans adopted the chain-pull washdown water closet, invented in England around 1870. Shortly after 1900, the flush toilet appeared; thanks to the mass production of enamel-coated fixtures, it soon became standard in American homes and buildings.

The indoor toilet brought about a shift in habits and attitudes. Before 1880, only luxury hotels and estates had private bathrooms. By the 1890s, however, acceptance of the germ theory of disease had raised fears about careless disposal of human waste as a source of infection and water contamination. Much more rapidly than Europeans did, Americans combined a desire for cleanliness with an urge for convenience, and water closets became common, especially in middle-class urban houses. Now bodily functions took on an unpleasant image, and the home bathroom became a place of utmost privacy. At the same time, the toilet and the private bathtub gave Americans new ways to use—and waste—water. The advances in plumbing were part of a broader democratization of convenience that accompanied mass production and consumerism.

The machine age also brought changes in the dietary habits of Americans. By 1880, for instance, inventors had fashioned stamping and soldering machines to mass produce cans from tin plate. The tin can, when combined with existing knowledge about the cooking-and-sealing process and the condensing and preserving of milk, made a variety of foods available to the public. Moreover, railroad refrigerator cars made it possible to ship perishables greater distances, and iceboxes made it possible for middle-class families to store perishables. In the meantime, growing urban populations encouraged fruit and vegetable farmers to produce more. As early as the 1890s, northern urban dwellers were enjoying southern and western strawberries, grapes, and tomatoes for up to six months a year.

Processed and Preserved Foods

Even the working class enjoyed a more diversified diet. As in the past, the poorest people still ate cheap foods, heavy in starches and carbohydrates. Now, however, many could buy previously unavailable fruits, vegetables, and dairy products. Workers had to spend a high percentage of their income on food—almost half the breadwinner's wages—but they never suffered the severe malnutrition that plagued other developing nations.

Just as tin cans and iceboxes made many foods widely available, the sewing machine was bringing about a revolution in clothing. In the 1850s, the sewing machine, invented in Europe but refined by Americans Elias Howe Jr. and Isaac M. Singer, came into use in the

Ready-Made Clothing

clothing and shoe industries. Manufacturers were soon mass producing quality apparel at relatively low cost and standardizing sizes to fit different body shapes. By 1900, only the poorest families could not afford "ready-to-wear" clothes.

With mass-produced clothing and the advent of dress patterns came a concern for style. Restrictive Victorian fashions still dominated women's clothing, but some of the most burdensome features were beginning to be abandoned. As women's participation in work and leisure activities became more active, dress styles began to place greater emphasis on comfort. By the end of the nineteenth century, long sleeves and skirt hemlines receded, and high-boned collars disappeared. By the First World War, when many women worked in hospitals and factories, shorter and more manageable styles had become fashionable.

Men's clothes too became more lightweight and stylish. Before 1900, among the middle and affluent working classes, a man would have owned no more than two suits, one for Sundays and special occasions and one for everyday wear. After 1900, manufacturers began to produce garments from fabrics of different weights and for different seasons, and dark-blue serge gave way to softer shades and more intricate weaves. Workingmen's clothes did not change markedly: laborers still needed the most durable, least expensive overalls, shirts, and shoes. But even for those of modest means, clothing was becoming something to be bought instead of made and remade at home.

Department stores and chain stores helped to create and serve the new consumerism. The great boom occurred between 1865 and 1900,

Department Stores

when companies like Macy's, Wanamaker's, and Jordan Marsh became fixtures of metropolitan America. Previously, working-class people had bought their goods in shabby stores, and wealthier types had patronized fancy shops. Now department stores, with their open displays of clothing, housewares, and furniture, as well as home deliveries and charge accounts, caused a merchandising revolution.

THE TRANSFORMATION OF MASS COMMUNICATIONS

With so many new things to do and buy, how did Americans decide what they wanted? Two new types of communication, modern advertising and popular journalism, were influencing consumer tastes and public opinion.

A society of scarcity does not need advertising. When demand exceeds supply, producers have no trouble selling what they market. But in a society of abundance such as industrial

Advertising

America, supply frequently outstrips demand, making necessary a means of increasing or even creating demand. The aim of advertising is to invent a need by convincing entire groups that everyone in that group should buy a specific product. Indeed, the growth in the late nineteenth century of large companies that mass produced consumer goods gave advertisers the task of creating "consumption communities"—bodies of consumers loyal to a particular brand name.

The prime vehicle for advertising was the newspaper. In the mid-nineteenth century, publishers began to pursue higher revenues from advertising by selling more ad space, especially to big urban department stores. Wanamaker's placed the first full-page ad in 1879, and at about the same time newspapers began to allow advertisers to print pictures of products. Such attention-getting techniques transformed advertising into information. More than ever before, people read newspapers to find out what was for sale as well as what was happening.

At the same time, large manufacturers were adding new marketing techniques to their technological and organizational innovations. Meat processor Gustavus Swift used branch slaughterhouses and refrigeration to enlarge the market for fresh meat. The American Tobacco Company made cigarettes a big business by saturating communities with billboards and free samples. Companies like International Harvester and Singer

How do historians know

what turn-of-the-century Americans thought about big business? Political cartoons and the symbols used by cartoonists often represent prevailing attitudes and can serve as a kind of shorthand for understanding how the same historical circumstance can arouse differing opinions. These two cartoons illustrate two quite different points of view. The one at top depicts the Standard Oil Trust as a greedy octopus with sprawling tentacles that are snaring Congress, state legislatures, and the taxpayer in their grasp and are reaching for the White House. The cartoonist obviously saw dangerous and wide-reaching power being exercised by such an economic giant. The second cartoon portrays a much more benevolent view. In this version, the cartoonist depicts John D. Rockefeller of Standard Oil and Andrew Carnegie of U.S. Steel at work, using their profits to nurture a garden of colleges and libraries, thereby showing the social good that could result from trusts. Octopus: Library of Congress; garden: Baker Library, Harvard Business School.

Sewing Machine set up systems for servicing their products and introduced financing schemes to permit customers to buy the machines more easily. Some producers began to sell directly to retailers, squeezing out wholesalers and eliminating the excess costs that wholesaling entailed.

THE CORPORATE CONSOLIDATION MOVEMENT

Neither the wonders of industrial production nor the new techniques of market promotion masked unsettling factors in the American economy. In each of the last three decades of the nineteenth century, the economy suffered from financial panics. The economic declines that began in 1873, 1884, and 1893 each lingered for several years. Business leaders disagreed on what caused them. Some blamed overproduction; others pointed to underconsumption; still others blamed lax credit and investment practices. Whatever the explanation, businesspeople began seeking ways to combat the uncertainty of the boom-and-bust business cycle. Many turned to centralized and cooperative forms of business organization, notably corporations, pools, trusts, and holding companies.

The corporation proved to be the best instrument for businesspeople to raise capital for industrial expansion. Under existing state laws, almost anyone could start a company and raise money by selling stock to investors. Stockholders could share in profits without high risk, because the laws limited their liability for company debts to the amount of their own investment. Nor did they need to concern themselves with the day-to-day operation of the firms; full responsibility for company administration was left in the hands of managers. Moreover, corporations won broad judicial protection in the 1880s and 1890s when the Supreme Court ruled that they, like individuals, are protected by the Fourteenth Amendment. In other words, states could not deny corporations equal protection under the law and could not deprive them of rights or property without due process of law. Such rulings

Role of Corporations

insulated corporations against vigorous government interference in their operations.

But as both economic disorder and the urge for profits mounted, corporation managers began to seek greater stability in new and larger forms of economic concentration. At first, such efforts were tentative and informal, consisting mainly of cooperative agreements among firms that manufactured the same product or offered the same service. Through these arrangements, called pools, competing companies tried to control the market by agreeing how much each should produce and what prices should be charged. Such "gentlemen's agreements" worked during good times when there was enough business for all; during slow periods, the desire for profits often tempted pool members to evade their commitments by secretly reducing prices or by selling more than the agreed quota. The Interstate Commerce Act of 1887 outlawed pools, but by then their usefulness was already fading.

Pools, Trusts, and Holding Companies

John D. Rockefeller disliked pools, calling them "ropes of sand." In 1879, one of his lawyers, Samuel Dodd, devised a more stable means of dominating the market. Because state laws prohibited one corporation from holding stock in another corporation, Dodd adapted an old device called a trust, which in law existed as an arrangement whereby responsible individuals would manage the financial affairs of a person unwilling or unable to handle them alone. Dodd reasoned that one company could achieve control of an industry by luring or forcing the stockholders of smaller companies in the industry to yield control of their stock "in trust" to the larger company's board of trustees. This device allowed Rockefeller to achieve horizontal integration of the highly profitable petroleum industry by combining his Standard Oil Company of Ohio with other refineries he bought up.

In 1888, New Jersey adopted new laws allowing corporations chartered there to own property in other states and to own stock in other corporations. This facilitated the creation of the holding company, which owned a partial or complete interest in other companies. Holding companies could in turn merge their constituent companies' assets as well as their management. Under this arrangement, Rockefeller's holding company, Standard Oil of New Jersey, merged forty constituent companies. Holding companies also encouraged vertical integration. This allowed companies to seek control over all aspects of their operations, including raw materials, production, and distribution.

Mergers became the answer to industry's search for order. Between 1889 and 1903, some three hundred combinations were formed. The most spectacular was the U.S. Steel Corporation, formed in 1901 and financed by J. P. Morgan. This new enterprise, made up of iron-ore properties, freight carriers, wire mills, plate and tubing companies, and other firms, was capitalized at more than $1.4 billion.

Role of Financiers

The merger movement created a new species of businessman, whose vocation was financial organizing rather than producing a particular good or service. Shrewd operators sought opportunities for combination, formed corporations, and then persuaded producers to sell their firms to the new company. The financiers usually raised money by selling stock and borrowing from banks. Uncommitted to any particular industry, their attention ranged widely. Investment bankers like J. P. Morgan and Jacob Schiff piloted the merger movement, inspiring awe with their financial power and organizational skills.

THE GOSPEL OF WEALTH AND ITS CRITICS

Business leaders turned to consolidation under new corporate forms not to promote competition but to minimize it. To justify the size and power of the resulting monopolistic companies to a public raised on the ideology of open competition, defenders of business eagerly embraced the doctrine of Social Darwinism. The doctrine loosely grafted Charles Darwin's theory of the evolutionary survival of the fittest onto laissez faire, the doctrine that govern-

Social Darwinism

ment should not interfere in economic private affairs. Social Darwinists reasoned that in an unconstrained economy, power would flow naturally to the most capable. The acquisition and possession of property were therefore sacred rights. Wealth was a mark of well-deserved power and responsibility, and monopolies resulted from the natural accumulation of economic power by those most capable of wielding it.

Social Darwinists reasoned too that wealth carries moral responsibilities: captains of industry should provide for the needs of those less fortunate or less capable. Steel baron Andrew Carnegie asserted what he called the Gospel of Wealth—that he and other powerful industrialists were trustees for society's wealth and that they had a duty to fulfill that trust in humane ways through philanthropic activities. Such philanthropy, however, implied a right for men like Rockefeller and Carnegie to define what they believed was good and necessary for society. It meant that the wealthy could and should endow churches, hospitals, and schools; it also meant that government should not tax or regulate the rich or their activities.

Paradoxically, business executives who extolled individual initiative and independence also pressed for government assistance. While denouncing measures to aid unions or regulate factory conditions, they lobbied for subsidies, loans, and tax relief to encourage business growth. By far the most extensive form of government assistance to American industry was tariffs, which raised the price of foreign products by placing an import tax on them. High duties on imported products allowed American producers to sell their goods at relatively high prices. Industrialists argued that tariff protection encouraged the development of new products and the founding of new enterprises. But tariffs also forced consumers to pay artificially high prices for many goods.

Government Assistance to Business

Critics who opposed trusts argued within the same framework of values as the corporate leaders they opposed. Defenders of trusts insisted that they were a natural and efficient outcome of economic development; critics charged that trusts were unnatural because

Dissenting Voices

they were created by greed and inefficient because they stifled opportunity. Such charges gave voice to an ardent fear of monopoly. Those who feared monopoly believed that large corporations could manipulate consumers by fixing prices, exploit workers by cutting wages, destroy opportunity by crushing small businesses, and threaten democracy by corrupting politicians.

Many believed there was a better way to achieve progress. By the mid-1880s, a number of young professors began to challenge Social Darwinism and laissez faire economics. Brown University sociologist Lester Ward attacked the application of evolutionary theory to social and economic relations. In *Dynamic Sociology* (1883), Ward argued that human control of nature, not natural law, accounted for the advance of civilization. To Ward, a system that guaranteed survival only to the fittest was wasteful and brutal; instead, he reasoned, cooperative activity fostered by planning and government intervention was the best route to progress. Economists Richard Ely, John R. Commons, and Edward Bemis agreed that natural forces should be harnessed for the public good. Instead of a laissez faire system, they sought one of positive assistance by the state.

While academics endorsed intervention in the natural economic order, others proposed more utopian schemes for combating monopolies.

Utopian Economic Schemes
_____

Reformer Henry George, the author of *Progress and Poverty* (1879), declared that economic inequality stemmed from the ability of a few to profit from rising land values. George argued that rising land values made owners rich simply because of increased demand for living and working space, especially in cities. To prevent profiteering, George proposed to replace all taxes with a single tax on the "unearned increment"—the rise in property values caused by increased market demand rather than by owners' improvements.

Unlike George, who accepted private ownership, novelist Edward Bellamy envisioned a state in which government would own and oversee the means of production and unite all citizens under moral laws. Bellamy outlined his dream in *Looking Backward, 2000–1887* (1888). The novel depicted Boston in the year 2000 as a peaceful community in which everyone belonged to an industrial army and people were paid not in money but in credits enabling them to obtain consumer goods and entertainment. By depicting a utopian world free of politicians and class divisions, Bellamy tried to convince readers that a "principle of fraternal cooperation" could replace vicious competition and wasteful monopoly.

Meanwhile, state governments began to take steps to prohibit monopolies and regulate big business. By 1900, fifteen states had constitutional provisions outlawing trusts, and

Antitrust Legislation
_____

twenty-seven had laws forbidding pools. Most were agricultural states in the South and West that were responding to antimonopolistic pressure from various farm organizations. But state attorneys general lacked the staff and judicial support for an effective attack on big business, and corporations always found ways to evade restrictions. Consequently, a need for national legislation became more pressing.

Congress moved hesitantly toward such legislation in the 1880s and in 1890 finally passed the Sherman Anti-Trust Act. The law made illegal "every contract, combination in the form of trust or otherwise, or conspiracy in the restraint of trade." People found guilty of violating the law faced fines and jail terms, and those wronged by illegal combinations could sue for triple damages. However, the law was left purposely vague so all factions could support at least part of it. It did not define clearly what a restraint of trade was. Moreover, it consigned interpretation of its provision to the courts, which at the time were strong allies of business.

Judges thus used the law's vagueness to blur distinctions between reasonable and unreasonable restraints of trade. When in 1895 the federal government prosecuted the so-called Sugar Trust for owning 98 percent of the nation's sugar-refining capacity, the Supreme Court ruled that control of manufacturing did not necessarily mean control of trade (*U.S. v. E. C. Knight Co.*). According to the Court, the Constitution empowered Congress to regulate interstate commerce but not manufacturing. Ironically, courts that did not consider monopolistic production a restraint on trade willingly applied antitrust provisions against labor unions engaged in strikes.

Mechanization and a burst of new inventions thrust the United States into the vanguard of industrial nations and immeasurably altered daily life between 1877 and 1920. Other effects were less positive. In industry, as in farming and mining, bigness and consolidation engulfed the individual, changing the nature of work from individual activity undertaken by producers to mass production undertaken by employees. Workers fought to regain control of their efforts, but they failed to develop well-organized unions that could meet their needs on a large scale. A maldistribution of power existed among American interest groups. Corporate enterprises controlled great resources of economic and political power. Other groups—farmers, laborers, and reformers—lacked power. Almost all members of these groups desired the material gains that technology and large-scale production were providing, but they increasingly feared that business was acquiring too much influence.

SUGGESTIONS FOR FURTHER READING

General

Daniel J. Boorstin, *The Americans: The Democratic Experience* (1973); Thomas J. Schlereth, *Victorian America: Transformations in Everyday Life* (1991).

Technology and Invention

David Hounshell, *From the American System to Mass Production* (1984); Thomas Parke Hughes, *American Genesis: A Century of Technological Enthusiasm* (1989); John P. Kasson, *Civilizing the Machine: Technology and Republican Values in America* (1976); Leo Marx, *The Machine in the Garden: Technology and the Pastoral Ideal* (1964); Andre Millard, *Edison and the Business of Innovation* (1990); David E. Nye, *Electrifying America* (1990).

Industrialism, Industrialists, and Corporate Growth

W. Eliot Brownlee, *Dynamics of Ascent: A History of the American Economy*, 2d ed. (1979); Stuart Bruchey, *Growth of the Modern Economy* (1973); Alfred D. Chandler, *The Visible Hand: The Managerial Revolution in American Business* (1977); Thomas C. Cochran, *Business in American Life* (1972); David F. Hawkes, *John D.: The Founding Father of the Rockefellers* (1980); Robert Higgs, *The Transformation of the American Economy, 1865–1914* (1971); Harold C. Livesay, *Andrew Carnegie and the Rise of Big Business* (1975); Glen Porter, *The Rise of Big Business* (1973); Martin J. Sklar, *The Corporate Reconstruction of American Capitalism* (1988).

Work and Labor Organization

Melvin Dubofsky, *We Shall Be All: A History of the Industrial Workers of the World* (1969); Leon Fink, *Workingmen's Democracy: The Knights of Labor and American Politics* (1982); Philip S. Foner, *The Great Labor Uprising of 1877* (1977); Herbert G. Gutman, *Work, Culture, and Society in Industrializing America* (1976); Tamara K. Hareven, *Family Time and Industrial Time: The Relationship Between the Family and Work in a New England Industrial Community* (1982); Alice Kessler-Harris, *Out to Work: A History of Wage Earning Women in the United States* (1982); Milton Meltzer, *Bread and Roses: The Struggle of American Labor, 1865–1915* (1967); Ruth Milkman, ed., *Women, Work, and Protest* (1985); David Montgomery, *The Fall of the House of Labor: The Workplace, the State, and American Labor Activism, 1865–1925* (1987); Stephen H. Norwood, *Labor's Flaming Youth: Telephone Operators and Worker Militancy* (1990); Elizabeth Ann Payne, *Reform, Labor, and Feminism: Margaret Dreier Robins and the Women's Trade Union League* (1988).

Living Standards and New Conveniences

Susan Porter Benson, *Counter Cultures: Saleswomen, Managers, and Customers in American Department Stores, 1890–1940* (1986); T. J. Jackson Lears and Richard W. Fox, eds., *The Culture of Consumption* (1983); Harvey A. Levenstein, *Revolution at the Table: The Transformation of the American Diet* (1988); Daniel Pope, *The Making of Modern Advertising* (1983); Susan Strasser, *Satisfaction Guaranteed: The Making of the American Mass Market* (1989); Gwendolyn Wright, *Building the Dream: A Social History of Housing in America* (1983).

Attitudes Toward Industrialism

Sidney Fine, *Laissez Faire and the General Welfare State* (1956); Louis Galambos and Barbara Barron Spence, *The Public Image of Big Business in America* (1975); Richard Hofstadter, *Social Darwinism in American Thought*, rev. ed. (1955).

Chapter

19

The Vitality and Turmoil of Urban Life, 1877–1920

FOR NEARLY THIRTY YEARS, Frank Ventrone had successfully pursued his dream. One night his world literally shattered. Ventrone had emigrated in the 1880s from southern Italy to Providence, Rhode Island. By saving money and buying property, Ventrone became a prominent businessman in the city's fast-growing Italian immigrant community. Ventrone's biggest success was a pasta business that furnished the community's staple food. The business was also the source of his trouble.

Food prices were rising in the summer of 1914, and Ventrone followed the trend by raising the price of his pasta. Angered by the pressure added to their already overburdened incomes, the people of Providence's Italian section vented their frustration on Ventrone. One August weekend, they marched through the neighborhood, broke windows in a block owned by Ventrone, broke into his shop, and dumped his stock of macaroni in the street. When police arrived, the rioters insisted that the matter was an internal one to be resolved by their community. Ventrone had violated the code of ethnic loyalty. The next Monday, Ventrone's agent

met with community members and agreed to lower his prices.

The urban America revealed by the Providence "macaroni riot," with its various dimensions—the transfer of immigrant cultures from Old World to new, the mobility of some people from rags to respectability, the continued poverty of others amid economic uncertainty, the eruption of violence—did not begin to truly emerge until the 1880s. By 1900, the United States was the most rapidly urbanizing nation in the Western world. By 1920, a symbolic milestone of urbanization had been passed: that year's census showed that, for the first time, a majority of Americans (51 percent) lived in cities (any settlement with more than twenty-five hundred people).

Cities served as marketplaces and forums, bringing together the people, resources, and ideas responsible for many of the changes American society was experiencing. By 1900, a network of small, medium, and large cities spanned every section of the country and attracted exuberant admirers and sneering detractors. Some people relished the opportunities and excitement cities offered. Others found the crudeness of American cities disquieting. Regardless of whether people liked or disliked the city, it had become central to American life. Modern American society has been shaped by the ways people built their cities and adjusted to the new urban environment.

TRANSPORTATION AND INDUSTRIAL GROWTH IN THE MODERN CITY

By 1900, the compact American city of the early nineteenth century, which mixed residences in among shops, factories, and warehouses, had burst open. From Boston to Los Angeles, development had sprawled several miles beyond the original central core. No longer did walking distance determine a city's size, and no longer did different social groups live close together: poor near rich, immigrant near native born, black near white. Instead, cities subdivided into distinct districts: working-class neighborhoods, African-American ghettos, business districts, a ring of suburbs.

Two forces, mass transportation and economic change, were responsible for these new neighborhood patterns. During the 1850s and 1860s,

Mechanization of Mass Transportation

steam-powered commuter railroads had appeared in a few cities, but not until the late 1870s did mechanized mass transit begin to appear. The first power-driven devices were cable cars, carriages that clamped onto a moving underground wire. Less expensive than horse cars, cable cars were also more efficient at hauling passengers up and down steep hills. By the 1880s, cable car lines operated in Chicago, San Francisco, and many other cities. A decade later electricity-powered streetcars began replacing early forms of mass transit. Between 1890 and 1902, total mileage of electrified track grew from thirteen hundred to twenty-two thousand miles.

In a few cities, trolley companies raised part of the track onto stilts, enabling vehicles to travel without interference above jammed downtown districts.

In Boston, New York, and Philadelphia, transit companies dug underground passages for their cars, also to avoid delays. Because elevated railroads and subways were extremely expensive to construct, they appeared only in the few cities in which transit companies could amass enough capital to lay track and buy equipment and where there were enough riders to ensure profits.

Mass transit lines launched millions of urban dwellers into outlying neighborhoods and created a commuting public. Those who could afford the fare—usually 5 cents a ride—

Beginnings of Urban Sprawl

could live outside the crowded central city but return there for work, shopping, and entertainment. Working-class families—their incomes rarely topped $1 a day—found the fare too high and could not benefit from streetcars. But for the growing middle class, a home in a quiet, tree-lined neighborhood became a real possibility. Real estate development boomed around the peripheries of scores of cities. Between 1890 and 1920, for example, developers in the Chicago area opened 800,000 new lots—enough to house at least three times the city's 1890 population.

Urban sprawl was essentially unplanned, but certain patterns did emerge. Investors who bought land in anticipation of settlement paid little attention to the need for parks, traffic control, and public services. Construction of mass transit was guided by the profit motive and thus benefited the urban public unevenly. Streetcar lines serviced mainly those districts that promised the most riders—whose fares, in other words, would increase dividends for stockholders.

Streetcars, elevateds, and subways altered commercial as well as residential patterns. When consumers moved outward, businesses followed. Branches of department stores and banks joined groceries, theaters, drugstores, taverns, and specialty shops to create neighborhood shopping centers. Meanwhile, the urban core became the work zone, where offices and stores loomed over streets clogged with traffic.

Cities also became the main arenas for industrial growth. As centers of resources, labor, transportation, and communications, cities provided

• *Important Events* •

1867	First law regulating tenements passes, in New York State	**1898**	Race riot erupts in Wilmington, North Carolina
1880s	"New" immigrants from eastern and southern Europe begin to arrive in large numbers	**1900–10**	Immigration reaches peak Vaudeville rises in popularity
1883	Joseph Pulitzer buys *New York World* and creates a major vehicle for yellow journalism	**1903**	Boston plays Pittsburgh in first baseball World Series
1885	Safety bicycle invented	**1905**	Intercollegiate Athletic Association, forerunner of National College Athletic Association (NCAA), is formed and restructures rules of football
1886	First settlement house opens in New York City		
1889	Thomas A. Edison invents the motion picture and viewing device	**1906**	Race riot erupts in Atlanta, Georgia
1890s	Electric trolleys replace horse-drawn mass transit	**1915**	D. W. Griffith directs *Birth of a Nation*, one of first major technically sophisticated movies
1895	William Randolph Hearst buys the *New York Journal*, another major popular yellow press newspaper	**1920**	Majority (51.4 percent) of Americans now live in cities

Urban-Industrial Development

everything factories needed. Once mass production became possible, capital accumulated by the cities' commercial enterprises fed industrial investment. Urban populations also furnished consumers for new products. Thus urban growth and industrialization wound together in a mutually beneficial spiral. The further industrialization advanced, the more opportunities it created for work and investment in cities. Increased opportunity in turn drew more people to cities; as workers and as consumers, they fueled further industrialization.

Urban and industrial growth transformed the national economy and freed the United States from dependence on European capital and manufactured goods. Imports and foreign investments still flowed into the United States. But by the early 1900s, cities and their factories, stores, and banks were converting America from a debtor agricultural nation into a major industrial, financial, and exporting power.

PEOPLING THE CITIES: MIGRANTS AND IMMIGRANTS

The population of a place can grow in three ways: by extension of its borders to annex land and people, by natural increase (an excess of births over deaths), and by net migration (an excess of in-migrants over out-migrants). Between the 1860s and early 1900s, many cities annexed nearby suburbs, thereby instantly increasing their populations. The most notable consolidation occurred in 1898 when New York City, which had previously consisted only of Manhattan and the Bronx, merged with Brooklyn, Staten Island, and part of Queens and grew overnight from 1.5 million to more than 3 million people. Annexation increased urban populations and added vacant land where new city

How Cities Grew

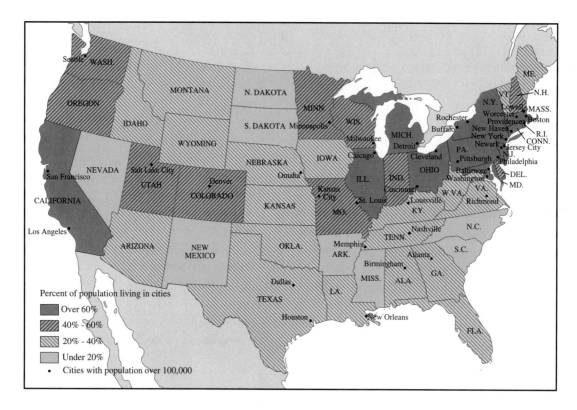

Percent of population living in cities

- Over 60%
- 40% - 60%
- 20% - 40%
- Under 20%
- • Cities with population over 100,000

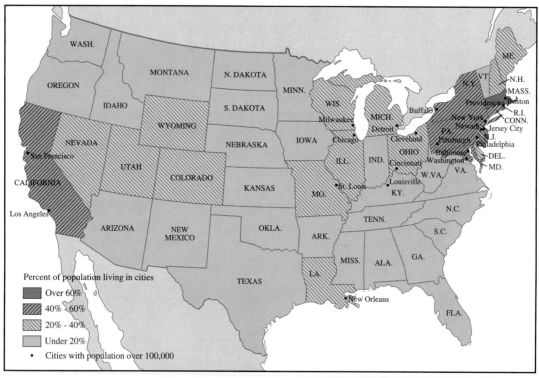

Percent of population living in cities

- Over 60%
- 40% - 60%
- 20% - 40%
- Under 20%
- • Cities with population over 100,000

dwellers could live, but its major effect was to enlarge the physical size of cities.

Natural increase did not account for much of any city's population growth. In the late nineteenth century, death rates declined in most regions of the country, but birthrates fell rapidly as well. In cities, the number of people who were born in a given year was roughly equal to the number who died that year.

Migration and immigration made by far the greatest contribution to urban population growth. In fact, migration to cities nearly matched the massive migration to the West that was occurring at the same time. Urban newcomers arrived from two major sources: the American countryside and Europe. Asia, Canada, and Latin America also supplied immigrants, although in smaller numbers.

In general, rural populations were declining as urban populations burgeoned. A variety of factors such as low crop prices and high debts dashed American farmers' hopes and drove them off the land toward the opportunities that cities seemed to offer. Many more newcomers, however, were immigrants who had fled foreign farms, villages, and cities for American shores. The dream of a large number was not to stay but to make enough money to return home and live in greater comfort and security. For every hundred foreigners who entered the country, about thirty left. Still, most of the twenty-six million immigrants who arrived between 1870 and 1920 remained, and the great majority settled in cities, where they helped reshape American culture (see figure).

Major Waves of Migration and Immigration
———

The United States had been the destination of immigrants from northern and western Europe since the 1840s, but after 1880 economic and demographic changes propelled a second massive wave of immigrants from other regions. Northern and western Europeans continued to arrive, but

The New Immigration
———

the new wave brought more people from eastern and southern Europe, plus smaller contingents from Canada, Mexico, and Japan. Two-thirds of the newcomers who arrived in the 1880s were from Germany, England, Ireland, and Scandinavia; between 1900 and 1909, two-thirds were from Italy, Austria-Hungary, and Russia. By 1910, arrivals from Mexico were beginning to outnumber arrivals from Ireland, and large numbers of Japanese had moved to the West Coast and Hawaii. Foreign-born blacks, chiefly from the West Indies, also increased in number, from forty thousand in 1910 to seventy-four thousand in 1920.

The immigrants varied widely in age, marital status, and other social characteristics, but certain traits stand out. Approximately two-thirds of the newcomers were men, especially after 1900, and about two-thirds were between the ages of fifteen and thirty-nine. Not all groups were equally educated, but almost three-fourths of the immigrants could read and write, at least in their native languages. About half identified themselves as unskilled laborers or domestic workers (maids, cooks, cleaners).

Many Americans feared the strange customs, Catholic and Jewish faiths, illiteracy, and poverty of "new" immigrants, considering them less desirable and assimilable than "old" immigrants, whose languages and beliefs seemed less alien. In reality, however, old and new immigrants resembled each other more closely than many Americans believed. The majority of both groups came from a world in which family was the focus of all decisions and undertakings. Whether and when to emigrate was decided in light of the family's needs, and family bonds and interests continued to prevail after immigrants reached the New World. New arrivals often received aid from relatives who had already immigrated. In many instances, workers helped kin obtain jobs, and family members pooled their resources to maintain, if not improve, their standard of living.

Perhaps most important, all immigrants brought with them memories and customs of their homelands. In their new surroundings—where the language was a struggle and housing and employment were often uncertain—immigrants anchored their lives to the rock they knew best: their culture.

Immigrant Cultures
———

Urbanization, 1880; Urbanization, 1920 Whereas in 1880 the vast majority of states still were heavily rural, by 1920 only a few had less than 20 percent of their population living in cities.

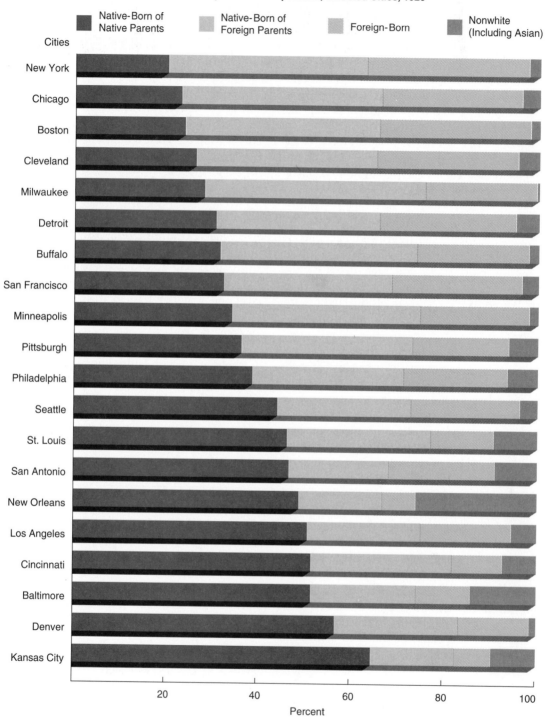

Composition of Population, Selected Cities, 1920

Arriving at Ellis Island in New York Harbor, probably to rejoin their husband and father who already had settled in the United States, this mother and her children put on their best clothes to match their determined look. Relatives and other villagers often advised immigrants to do everything possible to impress inspectors who examined them upon arrival. Brown Brothers.

Old World customs persisted in immigrant enclaves of Italians from the same province, Japanese from the same island district, or Russian Jews from the same shtetl (village). People practiced religion as they always had, held traditional feasts and pageants, married within their group, and pursued old feuds with people from rival villages and provinces.

Yet the very diversity of American cities forced immigrants to modify their attitudes and habits. Few newcomers could avoid contact with people

Composition of Population, Selected Cities, 1920

As a result of immigration and migration, in almost every major city by the early twentieth century native-born whites of native-born parents were distinct minorities. Moreover, foreign-born residents and native-born whites of foreign parents constituted absolute majorities in numerous places.

different from themselves, and few could prevent such contacts from altering their traditional ways of life. Although many foreigners identified themselves by their village or region of birth, native-born Americans categorized them by nationality. People from County Cork and County Limerick were lumped together as Irish; those from Schleswig and Württemberg were Germans; those from Calabria and Campobasso were Italians. Immigrant institutions, such as newspapers and churches, found they had to appeal to the entire nationality in order to survive.

Everywhere, Old World culture persisted alongside New World realities. Although immigrants struggled to maintain their native languages and to pass them down to younger generations, English was taught in the schools and needed on the job. Foreigners cooked ethnic meals using

American foods and fashioned American fabrics in European styles. Italians went to American doctors but still carried traditional amulets in their pockets to ward off evil spirits. Chinese expanded their traditional gambling games to include poker. Music especially revealed adaptations. Polka bands still entertained at Polish social gatherings, but their repertoires expanded to blend American and Polish folk music. Mexican ballads acquired new themes that described the adventures of border crossing and the hardship of labor in the United States. Eventually, most immigrants grew accustomed to trusting American institutions.

The influx of so many immigrants between 1870 and 1920 transformed the United States from a basically Protestant nation into one composed of Protestants, Catholics, and Jews. Newcomers from Italy, Hungary, Poland, and the present-day Czech Republic and Slovakia joined Irish and Germans to boost the proportion of Catholics in a number of cities, and German and Russian immigrants gave New York one of the largest Jewish populations in the world. Catholic Mexicans constituted more than half the population of El Paso.

Influence on Religion

In the 1880s, another group of migrants began to move into American cities. Thousands of rural African-Americans moved northward and westward, seeking better employment and fleeing crop liens, racial violence, and political oppression. Although black urban dwellers would grow more numerous after 1915, thirty-two cities had ten thousand or more black residents by 1900, and 79 percent of all blacks outside the South lived in cities. These migrants resembled foreign immigrants in their rural backgrounds and economic motivations, but they differed in several important ways. Because few factories would employ African-Americans, most found jobs in the service sector—cleaning, cooking, and driving. Also, because most domestic and personal service openings were traditionally female jobs, black women outnumbered black men in many cities.

African-American Migration to the Cities

Each of the three major migrant groups that peopled American cities—native-born whites, foreigners of various races, and native-born blacks—helped build modern American culture. The cities nurtured rich cultural variety: American folk music and literature, Italian and Mexican cuisine, Irish comedy, Yiddish theater, African-American jazz and dance, and much more. Like their predecessors, newcomers in the late nineteenth century changed their environment as much as they were changed by it.

LIVING CONDITIONS IN THE INNER CITY

Urban population growth created intense pressures on the public and private sectors. The masses of people who jammed inner-city districts were known more for the problems they bred than for their cultural contributions. American cities seemed to harbor all the afflictions that plague modern society: poverty, disease, crime, and other unpleasant conditions that develop when large numbers of people live close together. City dwellers adjusted as best they could. Although technology, science, private enterprise, and public authority failed to relieve all the problems, some remarkable successes were achieved. In the late nineteenth and early twentieth centuries, construction of buildings, homes, streets, sewers, and schools proceeded at a furious pace. American cities set world standards for fire protection and water purification. But many other hardships and ills still await solution.

One of the most persistent shortcomings of American cities—their failure to provide adequate housing for all who need it—has its roots in nineteenth-century urban development. Despite massive construction in the 1880s and early 1900s, population growth outpaced housing supplies. This situation weighed most heavily on working-class families. As cities grew, landlords took advantage of shortages in low-cost rental housing by splitting up existing buildings to house more people, constructing multiple-unit tenements, and hiking rents. Low-income families adapted to high costs and short supply by sharing space and expenses. Thus "one-

Housing Problems

family" apartments were often occupied by two or three families or a single family plus a number of boarders. Such conditions created unprecedented crowding. In 1890, for instance, New York City's immigrant-packed Lower East Side averaged 702 people per acre.

Inside many buildings, living conditions were harsh. The largest rooms were barely ten feet wide, and interior rooms either lacked windows or opened onto narrow shafts that bred vermin and rotten odors. Few buildings had indoor plumbing, and the only source of heat was dangerous, polluting, coal-burning stoves.

Housing problems aroused concerned citizens to mount reform campaigns in several places. New York State took the lead by legislating light, ventilation, and safety codes for **Housing** new tenement buildings in **Reform** 1867, 1879, and 1901. A few ——— reformers, such as journalist Jacob Riis and humanitarian Lawrence Veiller, advocated housing low-income families in "model tenements," with more spacious rooms and better facilities. Model tenements, however, required landlords to accept lower profits—a sacrifice few were willing to make. Neither reformers nor public officials would consider government financing of better housing, fearing that such a step would undermine private enterprise. Still, the housing codes and regulatory commissions that resulted from reform campaigns did strengthen the power of local government to oversee construction.

Efforts at housing reform had only limited success, but scientific and technological advances eventually enabled city dwellers and the nation in general to live and work in greater comfort and safety. By the 1880s, most doctors had accepted the germ theory of disease. In response, cities established more efficient systems of water purification and sewage disposal. Public health regulations helped to control such dread diseases as cholera, typhoid fever, and diphtheria. And modernized firefighting equipment and electric street lighting made the cities safer places in which to live. None of these improvements, however, lightened the burden of poverty.

Ever since colonial days, Americans have disagreed on how much responsibility the public should assume for poor relief. According to traditional

Urban Poverty beliefs, still widespread in the ——— late nineteenth and early twentieth centuries, anyone could escape poverty through hard work and clean living; poverty was inevitable only because some people were weaker than others. Such reasoning bred fear that aid to poor people would encourage paupers to rely on public relief rather than their own efforts. This attitude hardened as poverty increased, and city governments discontinued direct grants of food, fuel, and clothing to needy families. Instead, cities provided relief in return for work on public projects and sent special cases to such state-run institutions as almshouses, orphanages, and homes for the blind, deaf, and mentally ill.

Close observation of the poor, however, caused some welfare workers to conclude that people's environments, not their personal shortcomings, caused poverty. This new attitude, which had been gaining ground since the mid-nineteenth century, fueled drives for building codes, factory regulations, and public health measures. But most middle- and upper-class Americans continued to endorse the creed that in a society of abundance only the unfit were poor and that poverty relief should be tolerated but never encouraged.

Even more than crowding and pauperism, crime and disorder nurtured fears that urban growth, especially the immigrant slums, threatened the nation. The more cities **Crime and** grew, it seemed, the more they **Violence** shook with violence. Although ——— homicide rates declined in industrialized nations like England and Germany, those in America rose alarmingly: 25 homicides per million people in 1881, 107 per million in 1898. Pickpockets, swindlers, and burglars roamed every city.

Despite the fear of increases in robberies and violence, urban crime may simply have become more conspicuous and sensational, rather than more prevalent. To be sure, concentrations of wealth and the mingling of different peoples provided new opportunities for organized thievery, petty larceny, vice, and violent grudge settling. Although native-born whites were quick to blame Irish bank-robbery gangs, German pickpockets, and Italian Black Hand killers for urban disorder, there is little evidence that more immigrant than native-born Americans populated the rogues' gallery.

Whatever the extent of criminality, city life in this period supported the thesis that the United States has a tradition of violence. Cities served as arenas for many of the era's worst riots. In addition to the violence that often erupted during the confrontations between labor and management, there were race riots: Wilmington, North Carolina, 1898; Atlanta, Georgia, 1906; Springfield, Illinois, 1908. In cities of the Southwest and Pacific coast, Chinese and Mexican immigrants often felt the sting of intolerance.

Since the mid-nineteenth century, city dwellers had gradually overcome their resistance to professional law enforcement and increasingly depended

Role of the Police

on the police to protect life and property. By the early 1900s, however, law enforcement had become complicated and controversial, because various groups differed in their views of the law and how it should be enforced. Some people clamored for crackdowns on drinking, gambling, and prostitution at the same time that others privately supported loose law enforcement so they could indulge in the so-called customer crimes. And inequities existed in the enforcement of laws. Disadvantaged groups—notably ethnic and racial minorities—could not escape arrest as easily as those with economic or political influence.

The mounting problems of city life seemed to demand greater government action. Thus city governments passed more ordinances that regulated housing, provided poverty relief, and expanded police power to protect health and safety. Yet public responsibility always ended at the boundaries of private property. Eventually, some advances in housing construction, sanitation, and medical care did reach slum dwellers. But for most people, the only hope was that their children would do better or that opportunities would be better somewhere else.

FAMILY LIFE

Although the overwhelming majority of Americans continued to live within families, this most basic of social institutions suffered considerable strain dur-

ing the era of urbanization and industrialization. New institutions—schools, social clubs, political organizations, and others—increasingly competed with the family to provide nurturance, education, and security. Many observers warned that rising divorce rates, the entrance of large numbers of women into the work force, and loss of parental control over children spelled peril for home and family. Yet the family retained its fundamental role as a cushion in a hard, uncertain world.

Throughout modern Western history, most people have lived in two overlapping social units: household and family. A household is a group of

Family and Household Structures

people, related or unrelated, who share the same residence. A family is a group of people related by kinship, some of whom typically live together. The distinction helps describe how Americans lived in the late nineteenth and early twentieth centuries.

At the most elementary level, Americans continued to group themselves in traditional ways. As in the past, the vast majority of households (75 to 80 percent) consisted of nuclear families—usually a married couple, with or without children. About 15 to 20 percent of households consisted of extended families—usually a married couple, with or without children, plus one or more relatives such as parents, adult siblings, grandchildren, aunts, uncles, or in-laws. About 5 percent of households consisted of people who lived alone.

The average size of nuclear families changed over time. In 1880, the birthrate was forty live births per thousand people; by 1900, it had dropped

Declining Birthrates

to thirty-two, by 1920 to twenty-eight. Several factors explain the decline. First, the United States was becoming an urban nation, and birthrates in cities are generally lower than in rural areas. On farms, where children could work at home or in the fields at an early age, each child born represented a new set of hands for the family work force. In the wage-based urban economy, children could not contribute significantly to the family income for many years, and a new child simply represented another mouth to feed. Second, infant mortality fell as diet and medical care improved, and families did not have to bear many children just to ensure that some would survive. Third, growing awareness that smaller families meant an improved quality of life seems to have stimulated decisions to limit family size. Although fertility was consistently higher among blacks, immigrants, and rural people than among white native-born city dwellers, birthrates of all groups fell. As a result, families with six or eight children became less common; three or four became more usual. Thus the nuclear family tended to reach its maximum size and then shrink faster than in earlier eras.

Although the nuclear family predominated, the household tended to expand and contract over the lifetime of a given family. Family size fluctuated as children were born and later left home. The process of leaving home also changed households; huge numbers of young people—and some older people—lived as boarders and lodgers, especially in cities. Middle- and working-class families commonly took in boarders to occupy rooms vacated by grown children and to help pay the rent. Housing reformers charged that boarding caused overcrowding and loss of privacy. Yet for those who boarded, the practice was highly useful.

Boarding

For immigrants and young people, boarding was a transitional stage, providing them with a quasi-family environment until they set up their own households. Also, growing numbers of young people lived independently, away from any family. The efficiency apartment—one room with a disappearing or folding bed and collapsible furniture—originated in San Francisco around 1900 to house such people and quickly spread eastward.

Some households took in extended-family members who lived as quasi-boarders. Especially in communities in which economic hardship or rapid growth made housing expensive or scarce, newlyweds sometimes lived temporarily with one spouse's parents. Families also took in widowed parents or unmarried siblings who would otherwise have lived alone. Even when relatives did not live together, they often lived nearby and aided each other with child care, meals, shopping, advice, and consolation. They also obtained jobs for each other. Thus in an

Importance of Kinship

era in which welfare and service agencies were rare, the family continued to be the institution to which people in need could turn.

But obligations of kinship were not always welcome or even helpful. Immigrant families often put pressure on last-born children to stay at home to care for aging parents, a practice that stifled opportunities for education, marriage, and economic independence. Tensions also developed when one relative felt another was not helping out enough. Nevertheless, for better or worse, kinship provided people a means of coping with the many stresses caused by an urban industrial society. Social and economic change did not burst family ties.

By the early 1900s, family life and its functions were both changing and holding firm. New institutions were assuming tasks formerly performed by the family. Schools were making education more of a community responsibility. Employment agencies, personnel offices, labor unions, and legislatures were taking responsibility for employee recruitment and job security. In addition, migration and a soaring divorce rate seemed to be splitting families apart: 19,633 divorces were granted nationwide in 1880; by 1920, that number had grown to 167,105. Yet in the face of these pressures, the family adjusted by expanding and contracting to meet temporary needs, and kinship remained a dependable although not always appreciated institution.

THE NEW LEISURE AND MASS CULTURE

On December 2, 1889, as hundreds of workers paraded through Worcester, Massachusetts, in support of shorter working hours, a group of carpenters hoisted a banner proclaiming, "Eight Hours for Work, Eight Hours for Rest, Eight Hours for What We Will." The phrase, "for What We Will," was significant, for it laid claim to a special segment of daily life that belonged to the individual. Increasingly, among all social classes, leisure activities filled this time segment.

American inventors had long tried to create labor-saving devices, but not until the late 1800s did technological development become truly time

Increase in Leisure Time

saving. Mechanization and assembly-line production helped to cut the average workweek in manufacturing from sixty hours in 1890 to forty-seven in 1920. The reductions meant both shorter workdays and freer weekends. White-collar workers spent eight to ten hours a day on the job and often worked only half a day or not at all on weekends. To be sure, thousands still spent twelve- or fourteen-hour shifts in steel mills and sweatshops and had no time or energy for leisure. But more Americans began to partake of a variety of diversions, and for the first time a substantial segment of the economy began providing for—and profiting from—leisure. By the early 1900s, many Americans were enmeshed in the business of play.

The vanguard of this trend was sports. Baseball was the most popular organized sport. The game was formalized in 1845 when a group of wealthy New Yorkers organized the Knickerbocker Club and codified the rules of play. By the 1880s, professional baseball was a big business. In 1887, more than fifty-one thousand people paid to watch a championship series between St. Louis and Detroit. In 1903, the National League (founded in 1876) and competing American League (formed in 1901) began the World Series between their championship teams (Boston and Pittsburgh). About the time that baseball was becoming entrenched as the national pastime, football began to attract public attention.

Baseball and Football

American football began as a sport for people of high social rank. As an intercollegiate sport, football attracted players and spectators wealthy enough to have access to higher education. By the end of the century, however, the game was appealing to a broader audience. The 1893 Princeton-Yale game drew fifty thousand spectators. As the game became increasingly popular, winning at virtually any cost became important. Colleges hired nonstudents—called tramp athletes—to play on their teams. Serious injuries and even death became common. In 1905, for instance, 18 players died and 150 were seriously injured. Such violence prompted President Theodore Roosevelt, a strong advocate of athletics, to convene a White House conference to discuss ways to eliminate brutality and foul play. The conference founded the Intercollegiate Athletic Association (renamed the National College Athletic Association in 1910) to police college sports. In 1906, the association altered the rules of football to make it less violent.

Baseball and football appealed mostly to men. But croquet, which also swept the nation after the Civil War, attracted both sexes. Middle- and upper-class people held croquet parties and even outfitted wickets with candles for night games. In an era in which the paid work away from the home had separated men's from women's spheres, croquet increased opportunities for social contact between the sexes.

Croquet and Cycling

Bicycling, which achieved a popularity rivaling that of baseball, also brought men and women together. Moreover, the bicycle played an influential role in freeing women from the constraints of Victorian fashions. In order to ride bikes, even the dropped-frame female models, women had to wear divided skirts and simple undergarments. Gradually, freer styles of cycling costumes began to have an influence on everyday fashions. As the 1900 census declared, "Few articles . . . have created so great a revolution in social conditions as the bicycle."

Meanwhile, college women began to pursue forms of physical activity other than croquet, horseback riding, and bicycling. Believing that to succeed intellectually they needed to be active and healthy, college women participated in such sports as rowing, track, and swimming. Eventually, basketball became the most popular sport among college women. Invented in 1891 as a winter sport for men, Senda Berenson of Smith College gave basketball women's rules (which limited dribbling and running and encouraged passing) in the 1890s, and intercollegiate games became common.

Paralleling the rise of sports, American show business also became a mode of leisure created by and for common people. Circuses—traveling shows of acrobats and animals—had existed since the 1820s. But after the Civil War, railroads enabled circuses to reach more of the country, and the popularity of "the big show" increased enormously. Circuses offered two main attractions: so-called freaks of nature, both human

Circuses

and animal, and the temptation and conquest of death. At the heart of their appeal was the sheer astonishment aroused by the trapeze artists, lion tamers, acrobats, and clowns.

Three branches of American show business matured with the growth of cities. Popular drama, musical comedy, and vaudeville offered audiences a

Popular Drama and Musical Comedy
——

chance to escape the harsh realities of urban-industrial life into melodrama, adventure, and comedy. The plots were simple, the heroes and villains recognizable. For urbanized people increasingly distant from the frontier, popular plays brought to life the mythical Wild West and Old South. Virtue, honor, and justice always triumphed in melodramas, reinforcing the popular faith that even in an uncertain and disillusioning world, goodness would nevertheless prevail.

Musical comedies raised audiences' spirits with song, humor, and dance. American musical comedy grew out of the lavishly costumed operettas popular in Europe. By introducing American themes (often involving ethnic groups), folksy humor, and catchy tunes and dances, these shows launched the nation's most popular songs and entertainers. George M. Cohan, a spirited singer, dancer, and songwriter born into an Irish family of vaudeville entertainers, became the master of American musical comedy after the turn of the century. Drawing on urbanism, patriotism, and traditional values in songs like "Yankee Doodle Boy" and "You're a Grand Old Flag," Cohan helped bolster national morale during the First World War. Comic opera too became a fad, and the talented, beautiful, dignified Lillian Russell was its most admired performer. The first American comic operas imitated European musicals, but by the early 1900s composers like Victor Herbert were writing for American audiences. Shortly thereafter, Jerome Kern began to write more sophisticated musicals, and American musical comedy came into its own.

Vaudeville, which originated in France as light drama with musical interludes, became a uniquely American entertainment form. Originally staged by

Vaudeville
——

saloonkeepers to attract customers, vaudeville variety shows were developed by skilled promoters who gave it respectability and mass appeal. Because of its variety, vaudeville was probably the most popular entertainment in early twentieth-century America. Shows included magic and animal acts, juggling, comedy (especially ethnic humor), and song and dance. Around 1900, the number of vaudeville theaters and troupes skyrocketed. Its most famous promoter, Florenz Ziegfeld, brilliantly packaged popular entertainment in a stylish format—the Ziegfeld Follies—and gave the nation a new model of femininity, the Ziegfeld Girl, whose graceful dancing and alluring costumes were meant to suggest a haunting sensuality.

Show business provided new economic opportunities for women, African-Americans, and immigrants, but it also encouraged stereotyping and exploitation. Lillian Russell, vaudeville singer and comedienne Fanny Brice, and burlesque queen Eva Tanguay attracted intensely loyal fans, commanded handsome fees, and won respect for their genuine talents. In contrast to the demure Victorian woman, they conveyed pluck and creativity. But lesser female performers were often exploited by male promoters and theater owners, many of whom wanted only to titillate the public with the sight of scantily clad women.

Before the 1890s, the chief form of commercial entertainment open to African-American performers was the minstrel show. By century's end, however,

African-Americans and Immigrants in Vaudeville
——

minstrel shows had given way to more sophisticated musicals, and blacks had begun to break into vaudeville. As stage settings shifted from the plantation to the city, music shifted from folk tunes to ragtime. Pandering to the prejudices of white audiences, composers and performers of both races ridiculed blacks. Burt Williams, a talented and highly paid black comedian and dancer who achieved success mainly by playing the stereotypical roles of darky and dandy, was tormented by the humiliation he had to suffer.

Much of the uniqueness of American mass entertainment arose from its ethnic flavor. Indeed, immigrants occupied the core of American show business. Vaudeville in particular drew on and embellished ethnic humor, exaggerating dialects and other national traits. Skits and songs reinforced ethnic stereotypes and made fun of ethnic groups, but such distortions were more self-conscious and sympathetic than those directed at blacks.

Shortly after 1900, live entertainment began to yield to an even more accessible form of amusement: moving pictures. Perfected by Thomas Edison in

Movies
——

the late 1880s, movies began as slot machine peepshows in penny arcades and billiard parlors. Eventually, images were projected onto a screen so that large audiences could view them, and a new medium was born.

By 1910, motion pictures had become a distinct art form, thanks to creative directors like D. W. Griffith. Griffith's most famous work, *Birth of a Nation* (1915), an epic film about the Civil War and Reconstruction, fanned racial prejudice by depicting African-Americans as a threat to white moral values. The infant National Association for the Advancement of Colored People (NAACP) led an organized black protest against it. But the film's innovative techniques—close-ups, fade-outs, and battle scenes—gave viewers heightened drama and excitement. From the beginning, movies were popular among all classes.

The still camera, modernized by inventor George Eastman, enabled ordinary people to make their own photographic images; the phonograph, another Edison invention, brought musical performances into the home. The spread of movies, photography, and phonograph records meant that access to live performances no longer limited people's exposure to art and entertainment. By making it possible to mass produce sound and images, technology dissolved the uniqueness of experience. Entertainment became a consumer good more widely available than ever before.

News also became a consumer good. Canny publishers made people crave news just as they craved amusements and new products. Joseph

Yellow Journalism
——

Pulitzer, a Hungarian immigrant who bought the *New York World* in 1883, pioneered journalism as a branch of mass culture. Believing that newspapers should be "dedicated to the cause of the people rather than to that of the purse potentates," Pulitzer filled the *World* with stories of disasters, crimes, and

scandals. Sensational headlines, set in large bold type like that used for advertisements, screamed from every page. Pulitzer's journalists not only reported news but sought it out—and sometimes even created it. Pulitzer also popularized the comics, and the yellow ink used to print them gave rise to the term *yellow journalism* as a synonym for sensationalism. The success enjoyed by Pulitzer (in a single year, circulation rose from 20,000 to 100,000) caused others, most notably William Randolph Hearst, to adopt his techniques.

Pulitzer and his rivals boosted circulation even further by emphasizing sports and women's news. Newspapers had always reported on sporting events, but yellow journalism papers gave such stories far greater prominence by printing separate, expanded sports sections. While they were expanding sports news, mostly for male readers, newspapers were adding special sections devoted to household tips, fashion, decorum, and club news to capture the interest of female readers. Like crime and disaster stories, sports and women's sections helped to make news a mass commodity.

By the early twentieth century, mass circulation magazines were overshadowing the expensive elitist journals of earlier eras. Publications like *McClure's*,

Magazines for the Mass Market
——

the *Saturday Evening Post*, and *Ladies' Home Journal* offered human interest stories, muckraking exposés, titillating fiction, numerous photographs, and eye-catching ads to a growing mass market. Meanwhile, the total number of books published more than quadrupled between 1880 and 1917. This rising popular consumption of news and books reflected growing literacy (94 percent in 1920).

Other forms of communication were also expanding. By 1920, increasing numbers of people were using the telephone and mailing letters. Little wonder, then, that the term *community* took on new dimensions. More than ever before, people in different parts of the country knew about and discussed the same news event. America was becoming a mass society.

To some extent, new amusements and pastimes had a homogenizing influence, bringing together disparate ethnic and social groups to share a common experience. Yet different groups often used them to reinforce their own cultural habits. In some communities, for example, working-class immigrants used parks and amusement areas as sites for family and ethnic gatherings. Much to the dismay of reformers who hoped that recreation would help assimilate newcomers and teach them habits of restraint, immigrants used picnics and Fourth of July celebrations as occasions for boisterous drinking.

The most provocative issue was the use of leisure time on Sunday, the Lord's day. In the Puritan tradition, native-born Americans supported blue laws designed to prevent desecration of the Sabbath by prohibiting various commercial and recreational activities. Immigrants, accustomed to feasting and playing after church, fought the closing of saloons and other restrictions on the only day they had free for fun and relaxation. Thus in 1913, when the New York legislature proposed a law granting cities authority to end restrictions on Sunday baseball games and liquor sales, both sides argued vehemently. At about the same time, the Illinois and Ohio legislatures split over whether to legalize boxing, which small-town Protestants opposed and urban Catholics and Jews favored. Similar splits developed over public versus parochial schools and prohibition versus free availability of liquor. Thus as Americans learned to play, their leisure—like their work and politics—was shaped by and expressed pluralistic forces.

PROMISES OF MOBILITY

Baptist minister Russell Conwell delivered the same sermon more than six thousand times to countless listeners across the United States between the Civil War and the First World War. Titled "Acres of Diamonds," his popular lecture affirmed the faith that any American could achieve success. People did not have to look far for riches, Conwell preached; acres of diamonds lay at everyone's feet. Night after night he would insist to his audience that it was one's "Christian and Godly" duty to attain riches. But how possible was it for people to improve their lot?

Basically, a person could get ahead in three ways: occupational advancement (and the higher income that accompanied it), acquisition of property (and the wealth it represented), and migration to an area that offered better conditions and greater opportunity. All these options were open chiefly to white men. Although many women held paying jobs, owned property, and migrated, their economic standing was usually defined by the men in their lives—husbands, fathers, or other kin. Women could improve their economic status by marrying men with wealth or potential, but other avenues were mostly closed. Men and women who were African-American, American Indian, Mexican-American, or Asian-American had even fewer opportunities. Pinned to the bottom of society by prejudice, these groups were forced to accept their station.

Occupational mobility was a reality, however, for large numbers of people, thanks to urban and industrial expansion. Thousands of small businesses were needed to supply goods

Occupational Mobility and services to burgeoning urban populations. And corporations required new managerial personnel. Relatively few Americans traveled the rags-to-riches track, but considerable movement occurred along the path from rags to moderate success.

Rates of occupational mobility in American communities were slow but steady between 1870 and 1920. Some people slipped from a higher to a lower rung on the occupational ladder, but rates of upward movement were almost always twice that of downward rates. Although patterns were not consistent, immigrants generally experienced less upward and more downward mobility than the native-born did. Still, regardless of birthplace, the chances for a white man to rise occupationally during the course of his career or to have a higher-status job than his father had were relatively good.

In addition to or instead of advancing occupationally, a person could achieve social mobility by acquiring property. But property was not easy to acquire. Banks and savings and

Acquisition of Property loan institutions were far stricter in their lending practices than they would become after the 1930s, when the federal government began to insure real estate financing. Before then, however, mortgage loans carried relatively high interest rates and short repayment periods. Thus renting, even of single-family houses, was common, especially in big cities. A general rise in wage rates nevertheless enabled many families to amass savings, which they could use as down payments on property. Ownership rates varied by region—higher in western cities, lower in eastern cities—but 36 percent of urban American families owned their homes in 1900, the highest homeownership rate of any Western nation with the exceptions of Denmark, Norway, and Sweden.

Following the maxim that movement means improvement, millions of families each year packed up and moved elsewhere. The urge to move affected every region, every **Residential Mobility** city. From Boston to San Francisco, from Minneapolis to San Antonio, no more than half the families residing in a city at any one time could be found there ten years later.

In addition to movement between cities, extraordinary numbers of people moved within the same city. Today, one in every five families changes residence in a given year. A hundred years ago, the proportion was closer to one in four, or even one in three. Population turnover affected almost every neighborhood, every ethnic and occupational group.

Rapid residential flux undermined the stability of even the most homogeneous neighborhoods. Rarely did a single nationality make up a clear majority in any large area, even **Ethnic Neighborhoods and Ghettos** when that area was known as Little Italy, Jewtown, Polonia, or Greektown. Residential change dispersed immigrants from their original areas of settlement to many different neighborhoods. In New York, Boston, and other eastern ports, ethnically homogeneous districts did exist, and people tended to change residences within those districts rather than move away from them. Elsewhere, however, most white immigrant families lived in ethnically mixed neighborhoods rather than in ghettos.

In most cities, an area's institutions and enterprises, more than the people who actually lived there, identified a district as an ethnic neighborhood. A Bohemian Town, for example, received its nickname because it was the location of Swoboda's

Bakery, Cermak's Drug Store, Cecha's Jewelry, Knezacek's Meats, St. Wenceslaus Church, and the Bohemian Benevolent Association. Such institutions gave the district an ethnic identity even if the surrounding neighborhood was mixed and unstable.

If a *ghetto* is defined as a place of enforced residence from which escape is difficult at best, only nonwhites experienced true ghetto life in this era. Wherever Asians and Mexicans settled, they encountered discrimination in housing, employment, and other facets of public life. Although these groups often preferred to remain separate in Chinatowns and *barrios*, white Americans also made every effort to keep them confined. In the 1880s, the city of San Francisco, for example, tried to prohibit Chinese laundries from locating in most neighborhoods, and its school board tried to isolate Japanese and Chinese children in Chinatown schools. In the *barrios* of Los Angeles and San Antonio, Anglo teachers and administrators who dominated the schools insisted on teaching in English even when the children had no knowledge of the language.

The same prejudice and discrimination that trapped African-Americans at the bottom of the occupational ladder also limited housing opportunities. Whites organized protective associations that pledged not to sell homes to blacks and occasionally used violence to scare them away from white neighborhoods. Such efforts seldom worked. Whites who lived on the edge of black neighborhoods often fled, leaving homes and apartments to be sold and rented to black occupants. By 1920, in Chicago, Detroit, Cleveland, and other cities outside the South, two-thirds or more of the total African-American population lived in only 10 percent of the residential area. Within these districts, they nurtured cultural institutions that helped them adjust to urban life. But the ghettos also bred frustration, the result of stunted opportunity and racial bigotry. Color, more than any other factor, made the urban experiences of blacks different from those of whites.

All groups, however, including blacks, could and did move—if not from one part of the city to another, then from one city to another. Americans were always seeking greener pastures, and hope that things might be better elsewhere acted as a safety valve, relieving some of the tensions and frustrations that simmered inside the city. If they did not find those greener pastures through migration, occupational mobility, or property acquisition, city dwellers could seek to improve the quality of urban life and their lives by turning to politics.

THE POLITICS OF BOSSISM AND CIVIC REFORM

The sudden growth and mounting rivalry among social and economic interest groups that occurred in the late nineteenth century mired cities in a governmental swamp. Burgeoning populations, business expansion, and technological change created urgent needs for sewers, police and fire protection, schools, parks, and other services. Such needs strained municipal governments beyond their capacities. Furthermore, city governments approached these needs in a disorganized fashion.

Power thrives on confusion, and out of this governmental chaos arose political machines, organizations that had as their main goals the rewards—whether money, influence, or prestige—of getting and keep-ing political power. Machine politicians routinely used bribery and graft to further their ends. But machines needed popular support, and they could not have succeeded if they had not provided relief, security, and services to large numbers of people. By doing so, machine politicians accomplished things that other agencies had been unable or unwilling to attempt.

Political Machines

Machines were also beneficiaries of new urban conditions. As cities grew larger and economically more complex, some business leaders vied to use local government to advance their interests; others withdrew from local affairs to pursue their interests through interurban or interregional economic organizations. At the same time, hordes of newcomers, often unskilled and foreign born, crowded into cities. As they acquired citizenship and voting rights, the men in these groups became a substantial political force. These circumstances bred a new kind of leader: the political boss. Special interest groups needed brokers who could facilitate their goals, and urban newcomers had needs that required public

attention. Moreover, as Martin Lomasney, boss of Boston's South End, explained, "There's got to be in every ward somebody that any bloke can come to—no matter what he's done—and get help. Help, you understand, none of your law and justice, but help." Bosses and machines filled these needs.

The system rested on a popular base and was held together by loyalty and service. City machines were coalitions of smaller machines that derived power directly from inner-city neighborhoods inhabited by native and immigrant working classes. In return for votes, bosses provided jobs, built parks and bathhouses, distributed food and clothing to the needy, and helped when someone ran afoul of the law. Such personalized service cultivated mass attachment to the boss; never before had public leaders assumed such responsibility for people in need.

To finance their largess and support the system they had created, bosses exchanged favors for votes or money. Power over local government enabled machines to control the letting of public contracts, the granting of utility or streetcar franchises, and the distribution of city jobs. Recipients of city business and jobs were expected to repay the machine with a portion of their profits or salaries and to cast supporting votes on election day. Critics called the process graft; bosses called it gratitude. Machines constructed public buildings, sewer systems, and mass transit lines that otherwise might not have been built, but bribes and kickbacks made such projects costly to taxpayers. In addition, machines dispersed favors to both legal and illegal businesses. Payoffs from gambling, prostitution, and illegal liquor traffic became important sources of machine revenue.

Techniques of Bossism

While bosses were consolidating their power, others were attempting to destroy political machines. Many middle- and upper-class Americans feared that immigrant-based political machines menaced the Republic and that unsavory alliances between bosses and businesses undermined municipal finances. Anxious about the poverty, crowding, and disorder that seemed to accompany population expansion, and convinced that urban services were making taxes too high, civic reformers organized to install more responsible leaders at the helm of urban administrations.

Urban reform arose in part from the industrial system's emphasis on eliminating waste and inefficiency. Government could be made more efficient, business-minded reformers were convinced, if it were run like a business. The only way to prevent civic decay, they believed, was to elect officials who would hold down expenses and prevent corruption. Thus their main goals were to reduce city budgets, make public employees work more efficiently, and cut taxes.

To impose sound business principles on government, civic reformers supported structural changes such as the city-manager and commission forms of government and non-partisan citywide election of officials. These reforms were meant to abolish party politics, put decision making in the hands of experienced experts, and undermine bosses' power bases in the wards and neighborhoods. They rarely realized, however, that bosses succeeded because they used government to meet people's needs. Reformers only noticed the waste and corruption that machines bred.

Structural Reforms in Government

A few reform mayors did look beyond structural changes to a genuine concern for social problems. Hazen S. Pingree of Detroit, Samuel "Golden Rule" Jones of Toledo, and Tom Johnson of Cleveland worked to provide jobs for poor people, reduce charges by transit and utility companies, and promote greater government responsibility for the welfare of all citizens. They also supported public ownership of gas, electric, and telephone companies, a quasi-socialist reform that alienated their business allies. But most civic reformers could not match the bosses' political savvy and soon found themselves out of power.

URBAN PROFESSIONALS: ENGINEERS AND SOCIAL WORKERS

Meanwhile, a different type of reform was beginning to take hold outside politics. Convinced that laissez faire ideology was not applicable in a complex

Social Reform

urban-industrial world, social reformers—mostly young and middle class—embarked on campaigns for social betterment. Housing reformers pressed local governments for building codes to ensure safety in tenements. Protestant reformers influenced by the Social Gospel movement, which emphasized social responsibility as a means to salvation, built churches in slum neighborhoods, and urged businesses to be socially responsible. Educational reformers saw public schools as a means of preparing immigrant children for citizenship by teaching them American values as well as the English language.

Perhaps the most ambitious and inspiring feature of the urban reform movement was the settlement house. Run mostly by women, settlements were efforts by educated, middle-class young adults to bridge the gulf between social classes by going to live in slum neighborhoods. The first American settlement house, patterned after London's Toynbee Hall, opened in New York City in 1886, and others quickly appeared in Chicago, Boston, and elsewhere. Early settlement leaders such as Jane Addams and Florence Kelley wanted to improve the lives of slum dwellers by helping them to obtain education, appreciation of the arts, better jobs, and better housing. Settlement workers offered activities ranging from vocational classes to child care for working mothers and ethnic art exhibits.

As they broadened their scope to fight for school nurses, building safety codes, public playgrounds, and support for labor unions, settlement workers became reform leaders in cities and in the nation. Their efforts to involve national and local governments in the solution of social problems later made them the vanguard of the Progressive era when a reform spirit swept the nation. Moreover, the activities of settlement houses helped create new professional opportunities for women in social work, public health, and child welfare. These professions enabled women reformers to build a dominion of influence over aspects of social policy independent of male-dominated professions and to make valuable contributions to national as well as inner-city life.

A contrast developed between white female reformers, who worked mainly in northern cities, and black female reformers who operated both in the

SCHEDULE OF OCCASIONS

LIST OF MEETINGS, CLASSES, CLUBS AND OTHER APPOINTMENTS OF
THE WEEK AT CHICAGO COMMONS AND THE TABERNACLE
DURING THE PAST WINTER.

AT THE COMMONS,

140 NORTH UNION STREET.

DAILY
All Day—House open for neighbors and friends.
9:00-12:00 a. m.—Free Kindergarten (except Saturday and Sunday). Mrs. Bertha Hofer Hegner, head kindergartner; Miss Alice B. Coggswell, assistant.
2:00-5:00 p. m.—Kindergarten Training Classes.
7:00 p. m.—Family Vespers (except Saturday).

SUNDAY
3:30 p. m.—Pleasant Sunday Afternoon.

MONDAY
4:00 p. m.—Manual Training (Girls.) Mr. N. H. Weeks.
7:30 p. m.—Penny Provident Bank.
8:00 p. m.—Girls' Clubs. Misses Coggswell, Taylor and Purnell.
Cooking Class (Girls). Miss Manning.
Girls' Progressive Club (Young Women). Classes in Art, Miss Cushman; Embroidery, Mrs. Gavit; Greek Mythology, Mrs. Follett; English History and Constitution, Miss Allen.
Shakspere Class. Mr. Gavit.

TUESDAY
2:00 p. m.—Woman's Club.
4:00 p. m.—Cooking Class (Girls). Miss Cookinham.
Manual Training. Mr. Weeks.
7:30 p. m.—Boys' Club. Mr. Weeks, Misses Alexander and Holdridge.
French. Miss Sayer.
Rhetoric. Mr. Wyatt.
Stenography. Mr. Fisher.
Cooking Class (Girls). Miss Thayer.
8:00 p. m.—Choral Club. Miss Hofer and Mr. C. E. Weeks.
8:15 p. m.—"The Tuesday Meeting," for Economic Discussion.

WEDNESDAY
4:00 p. m.—Kindergarten Clubs (children). Miss Purnell and Abbott.
Dressmaking Class (Girls). Miss Temple.
Piano. Miss Gavit.
7:00 p. m.—Piano. Miss Bemiss.
7:30 p. m.—Penny Provident Bank.
Girls' Clubs. Misses Coggswell, Gavit, Bosworth, Bemiss, Etheridge.
Boys' Club. Mr. Grant.
Cooking Class (Young Women). Miss Temple.

THURSDAY
4:00 p. m.—Cooking Class (for Women). Miss Temple.
Elocution. Miss Ellis.
Manual Training (Girls). Mr. Weeks.
7:30 p. m.—Girls' Club. Miss Chandler.
Good Will ("Blue Ticket") Club. Mr. Weeks.
Elocution. Miss Ellis.
Grammar. Mr. Carr.
Cooking (for Girls). Miss Manning.
Mothers' Club (Fortnightly).
Seventeenth Ward Municipal Club (Monthly).

FRIDAY
4:00 p. m.—Manual Training (Boys'). Mr. Weeks.
7:30 p. m.—Penny Provident Bank.
Cooking Class (Girls). Miss Manning.
Boys' Clubs. Messrs. Burt, Carr, Crocker, Young, C. E. Weeks. N. H. Weeks.
Dressmaking. Mrs. Strawbridge.

SATURDAY
10:00 a. m.—Manual Training (Boys). Mr. Weeks.
2:00 p. m.—Manual Training (Boys). Mr. Weeks.
3:00 p. m.—Piano Lessons. Miss Bemiss.
6:30 p. m.—Residents' Meeting (for residents only).

Other Appointments, for Clubs, Study Classes, Social Gatherings, etc., are made from time to time and for special occasions.

How *do historians know*

the intent of settlement house activities? This document presents an actual listing of one week's activities at the Chicago Commons settlement house in 1896. There are at least three ways to examine these activities. First is the nature of the activities themselves: a blend of practical (savings bank, cooking, manual training) with intellectual (Shakespeare, French, elocution). Second is the age factor: note that the majority of entries are for children.

Third is the gender factor: although a few activities are for males, they are almost exclusively for boys, not adult men. Moreover, the female activities reinforce prevailing stereotypes of women's role as housekeeper—although the daily kindergarten might be used as a form of child care for working mothers of young children. A reader might also consider the significance of the time for which each activity is scheduled. Photo: Library of Congress.

South and, increasingly, in northern cities. Middle-class white women lobbied for government programs to aid needy people and focused on "helping others"—that is, the immigrant and native-born working classes. Black women, barred by their race from white political institutions, raised funds from private institutions and focused on helping members of their own race. These African-American women were especially active in raising money for schools, old-age homes, and hospitals, but they also worked for advancement of the race and protection of black women from sexual exploitation. Their ranks included women such as Jane Hunter, who founded a home for unmarried black working women in Cleveland in 1911 and influenced the founding of similar homes in other cities, and Modjeska Simkins, who founded a program to address health problems among blacks in South Carolina.

Urban reformers wanted to save cities, not abandon them. They believed they could improve urban life by restoring cooperation among all citizens. They often failed to realize, however, that cities were places of great diversity and that different people held very different views about what reform actually meant. To civic reformers, distributing city jobs on the basis of civil service exams rather than party loyalty meant progress; to working-class men it signified reduced employment opportunities. Moral reformers tried to prohibit the sale of alcoholic beverages to prevent working-class breadwinners from wasting their wages and ruining their health, but immigrants saw such crusades as interference in their wine- and beer-drinking customs. Thus early urban reform merged idealism with naïveté and insensitivity.

At the same time, efforts that took place outside the context of bossism and reform were making cities more livable. Technical and professional crea-

Engineering Reforms

tivity, not political or humanitarian action, were required to address sanitation, street lighting, bridge and street building, and other such needs. In addressing these issues, American urban dwellers, and the engineering profession in particular, developed new systems and standards of worldwide significance.

To solve their problems, cities increasingly depended on engineers, who had become, except for teachers, the largest profession in the country by 1900. Engineers applied their technical expertise to devise systems for incinerating refuse, dumping trash while ensuring safe water supplies, constructing efficient sewers, and providing for regular street cleaning and snow removal. Engineers also advised officials on budgetary matters and contracts. They had similar influence in matters of street lighting, parks, fire protection, and more.

Much of what American society is today originated in the urbanization of the late nineteenth century. Through a blending of old-fashioned native inventiveness and the traditions of European,

African, and Asian cultures, a new kind of society—a culturally pluralistic one—emerged. It was not so much a melting pot as it was a salad bowl. Literary critic Randolph Bourne dubbed the United States "a cosmopolitan federation of national colonies." Such reasoning produced hyphenated identifications: people considered themselves Irish-American, Italo-American, Polish-American, and the like. This society seldom functioned smoothly. Yet its jumble of social classes, ethnic and racial groups, political organizations, and other components left important legacies.

Pluralism and its attendant interest group loyalties enhanced the importance of politics. If America was not a melting pot, then different groups were competing for power, wealth, and status. Adherents of diverse cultural traditions battled over how much control government should exercise over people's lives. Such conflicts, fueled by hard times as well as the ever growing diversity of the American population, illustrate why local politics and state politics were so heated. Some people carried polarization to extremes and tried to suppress everything allegedly un-American.

Efforts to enforce homogeneity generally failed, however, because the country's cultural diversity prevented domination by a single ethnic majority. By 1920, immigrants and their offspring outnumbered the native born in many cities, and the national economy depended on new workers and consumers. These new Americans had transformed the United States into an urban nation. They had given American culture its rich and varied texture and had laid the foundations for the liberalism that would characterize American politics in the twentieth century.

SUGGESTIONS FOR FURTHER READING

Urban Growth

Howard P. Chudacoff and Judith E. Smith, *The Evolution of American Urban Society*, 4th ed. (1993); David Goldfield and Blaine Brownell, *Urban America*, 2d ed. (1990); Kenneth T. Jackson, *The Crabgrass Frontier: The Suburbanization of the United States* (1985); Raymond A. Mohl, *The New City: Urban America in the Industrial Age* (1985).

Immigration, Ethnicity, and Religion

Josef J. Barton, *Peasants and Strangers: Italians, Rumanians, and Slovaks in an American City* (1975); John Bodnar, *The Transplanted* (1985); John Bodnar, Roger Simon, and Michael P. Weber, *Lives of Their Own: Blacks, Italians, and Poles in Pittsburgh, 1900–1960* (1982); Jack Chen, *The Chinese of America* (1980); John B. Duff, *The Irish in the United States* (1971); Elizabeth Ewen, *Immigrant Women in the Land of Dollars* (1985); Mario T. Garcia, *Desert Immigrants: The Mexicans of El Paso, 1880–1920* (1981); Oscar Handlin, *The Uprooted*, 2d ed. (1973); John Higham, *Strangers in the Land: Patterns of American Nativism* (1955); Yusi Ichioka, *The Issei: The World of the First Japanese Immigrants, 1885–1924* (1988); Alan M. Kraut, *The Huddled Masses: The Immigrant in American Society, 1880–1921* (1982); Matt S. Maier and Felciano Rivera, *The Chicanos* (1972); Humbert S. Nelli, *The Italians of Chicago* (1970); Werner Sollors, *Beyond Ethnicity* (1986).

Urban Needs and Services

Charles W. Cheape, *Moving the Masses* (1980); Lawrence A. Cremin, *American Education: The Metropolitan Experience* (1988); Martin V. Melosi, *Garbage in the Cities* (1981); James F. Richardson, *The New York Police* (1970); Barbara Gutmann Rosencrantz, *Public Health and the State* (1972); Stanley K. Schultz, *Constructing Urban Culture: American Cities and City Planning* (1989); Mel Scott, *American City Planning Since 1890* (1969).

Family and Individual Life Cycles

Howard P. Chudacoff, *How Old Are You? Age in American Culture* (1989); Carl N. Degler, *At Odds: Women and the Family in America* (1980); John D'Emilio and Estelle B. Freedman, *Intimate Matters: A History of Sexuality in America* (1988); Carole Haber, *Beyond Sixty-five: Dilemmas of Old Age in America's Past* (1983); Joseph Kett, *Rites of Passage: Adolescence in America* (1979).

Mass Entertainment and Leisure

Allen Guttmann, *A Whole New Ball Game: An Interpretation of American Sports* (1988); John F. Kasson, *Amusing the Millions: Coney Island at the Turn of the Century* (1978); Kathy Peiss, *Cheap Amusements: Working Women and Leisure in Turn-of-the-Century New York* (1986); Benjamin G. Rader, *American Sports* (1983); Roy Rosenzweig, *Eight Hours for What We Will! Workers and Leisure in an Industrial City, 1870–1920* (1983); Robert Sklar, *Movie-Made America* (1976); Ronald A. Smith, *Sports and Freedom: The Rise of Big-Time College Athletics* (1988); Robert V. Snyder, *The Voice of the City: Vaudeville and Popular Culture in New York City, 1880–1920* (1990).

Journalism

Frank L. Mott, *American Journalism*, 3d ed. (1962), and *A History of American Magazines*, 5 vols. (1930–1968).

Mobility and Race Relations

James Borchert, *Alley Life in Washington* (1980); Jacqueline Jones, *Labor of Love, Labor of Sorrow: Black Women, Work, and the Family from Slavery to the Present* (1985); Kenneth L. Kusmer, *A Ghetto Takes Shape* (1976); Howard N. Rabinowitz, *Race Relations in the Urban South* (1978); Stephan Thernstrom, *The Other Bostonians: Poverty and Progress in the American Metropolis* (1973); Olivier Zunz, *The Changing Face of Inequality: Urbanization, Industrial Development, and Immigrants in Detroit, 1880–1920* (1982).

Boss Politics

Leo Hershkowitz, *Tweed's New York: Another Look* (1977); Terrence J. McDonald, *The Parameters of Urban Fiscal Policy: Socioeconomic Change and Political Culture in San Francisco, 1860–1906* (1986); Zane L. Miller, *Boss Cox's Cincinnati* (1968); Bruce M. Stave and Sondra Stave, eds., *Urban Bosses, Machines, and Progressive Reformers* (1984).

Urban Reform

John D. Buenker, *Urban Liberalism and Progressive Reform* (1973); Allen F. Davis, *American Heroine: The Life and Legend of Jane Addams* (1973), and *Spearheads for Reform* (1967); Lori Ginzberg, *Women and the Work of Benevolence* (1991); Roy M. Lubove, *The Progressives and the Slums* (1962); Clay McShane, *Technology and Reform* (1974); Robyn Muncy, *Creating a Female Dominion in American Reform* (1991); Martin J. Schiesl, *The Politics of Efficiency: Municipal Administration and Reform in America* (1977).

20

Gilded Age Politics, 1877–1900

RUTHERFORD B. HAYES, NINETEENTH president of the United States (1877–1881), was a dignified man who tried hard to move the nation beyond the tumult of the Civil War and Reconstruction as well as the scandals of the Grant presidency. In his speeches and writings, he emphasized social harmony, individual effort, and "character," meaning qualities of virtue and morality, as the goals of human development. He also protested exploitative treatment of Indians, discrimination toward blacks, and the corrupt spoils system.

But soon after he left office, Hayes found that two obstacles thwarted his faith in individual character and his worship of the "self-made man." One was "a system that fosters the giant evils of great riches and hopeless poverty." The other was "a government the exact opposite of the popular government for which Lincoln had lived and died—'a government of the people, by the people, and for the people'—and instead of it . . . a 'government of the rich, by the rich, and for the rich.' " Hayes's faith in property ownership as a route to virtue eroded when he learned that property was becoming concentrated in the hands of a few and that economic opportunity was fading.

Hayes, however, would not abandon his faith in individualism. He rejected a view that government regulation in the name of the public interest could alleviate problems of poverty and the unequal distribution of wealth. Ironically, Hayes died in 1893, just as a mass democratic movement called populism was preparing the nation for a new century in which government was to take much greater responsibility for solving the problems that so troubled him.

Between 1877 and 1900, transformation of the nation by the commercialization of agriculture, industrialization, and urbanization generated forces that upset time-honored customs and values. Corruption and greed tugged at the fabric of democracy, and the era's venality prompted novelists Mark Twain and Charles Dudley Warner to dub the 1870s and 1880s the Gilded Age. Officeholders used their positions to amass personal fortunes and dispense patronage appointments to their supporters. Congress, although split by powerful partisan and regional rivalries, did grapple with important issues, but many of its accomplishments proved to be either weak compromises or favors to special interests. Meanwhile, the judiciary, by defending vested property rights against state and federal regulation, supported big business. The presidency was occupied by a series of honest, respectable men who seldom took initiative; when they did, they often found themselves blocked by Congress and the courts.

Several major themes characterized politics. The influence of powerful special interests and the conflict between these private interests and the public interests emerged as the most prominent theme. Corruption flourished as the special interests vied for favors. Vote fraud, bribery, and unfair influence sparked calls for reform and defined several major legislative issues. Exclusion was another theme of politics, because the majority of Americans—including women, southern blacks, Indians, uneducated whites, and unnaturalized immigrants—could not vote. These phenomena—powerful special interests, corruption, and exclusion—contributed to a delicate equilibrium characterized by a stable party system and a regional balance of power.

Then in the 1890s, two developments shattered the equilibrium: the rural discontent that accompanied the transformation of the West and South erupted, and a deep economic depression bared flaws in the industrial system. Amid these crises, a presidential campaign stirred Americans as they had not been stirred for a generation. A new party arose, old parties split, sectional unities dissolved, and fundamental questions about the nation's future came to a head. The nation emerged from the turbulent 1890s with new political alignments, just as it had developed new economic configurations.

THE NATURE OF PARTY POLITICS

The historian Henry Adams, a grandson and a great-grandson of presidents, observed that in American political history, the period between 1870 and 1895 "was poor in purpose and barren in results." From the voters' perspective, however, politics appeared anything but barren. At no other time in the nation's history was public interest in elections more avid. Consistently, 80 to 90 percent of eligible voters (white and black men in the North, mostly white men in the South) cast ballots in local and national elections. Even among those who could not vote, politics was a form of recreation, more popular than baseball, vaudeville, or circuses. Actual voting was only the final stage in a process that included rallies, parades, picnics, and speeches, all of which were as much public amusement as civic responsibility.

Politics was a personal as well as a community activity. People formed strong loyalties to individual politicians, loyalties that often overlooked crassness and corruption. These allegiances to parties and candidates were distributed so evenly on the national level that no major faction or party gained control for any sustained period of time. Between 1877 and 1897, Republicans held the presidency for three terms, Democrats for two. Only briefly and rarely did the same party control the presidency and both houses of Congress simultaneously: the Republicans twice, the Democrats once, for two years at a stretch.

Party Allegiances

Republicans and Democrats competed avidly for office, but quarrels split both parties from within. Among Republicans, factional feuds and personal rivalries often took precedence over national concerns. On one side stood "the Stalwarts," led by New York's pompous Senator Roscoe Conkling, who worked the spoils system to win government jobs for his supporters. On the other side stood "the Half Breeds," led by James G. Blaine of Maine. Blaine pursued influence with the Republican party as blatantly as Conkling did, but he disguised his self-serving aims by courting support from independents. On the sidelines were the more idealistic Republicans, or Mugwumps (an Indian term meaning "mug on one side of the fence, wump on the other"). Mugwumps such as Senator Carl Schurz of Missouri disliked the political roguishness that tainted their party and believed that only righteous educated men like themselves should govern. Meanwhile, the Democrats tended to subdivide into white-supremacy southerners, immigrant-stock urban machine members, and business-oriented advocates

Party Factions

of low tariffs. Like Republicans, Democrats eagerly pursued the spoils of office.

NATIONAL ISSUES

In Congress, parties split over long-standing political and economic issues such as sectional controversies, patronage abuses, railroad regulation, tariffs, and currency. Long after Reconstruction ended, the bitter hostilities that the Civil War had engendered continued to haunt Americans. Republicans capitalized on war memories by "waving the bloody shirt" in response to Democratic challenges. In the South, Democrats also waved the bloody shirt, calling Republicans traitors to white supremacy. Such emotional appeals persisted well into the 1880s.

Sectional Conflict

Politicians were not the only Americans who attempted to profit by invoking the war. The Grand Army of the Republic, an organization of Union army veterans numbering more than 400,000, allied with the Republican party in the 1880s and 1890s and lobbied Congress into legislating generous pensions for former Union soldiers and their widows. Many pensions were deserved: Union soldiers had been poorly paid, and thousands of wives had been widowed. But for many veterans, the war's emotional wake provided an opportunity to profit at the public's expense.

Few politicians could afford to oppose Civil War pensions, but a number of reformers attempted to dismantle the spoils system. The practice of awarding government jobs to party workers, regardless of their qualifications, had taken root before the Civil War and

Civil Service Reform

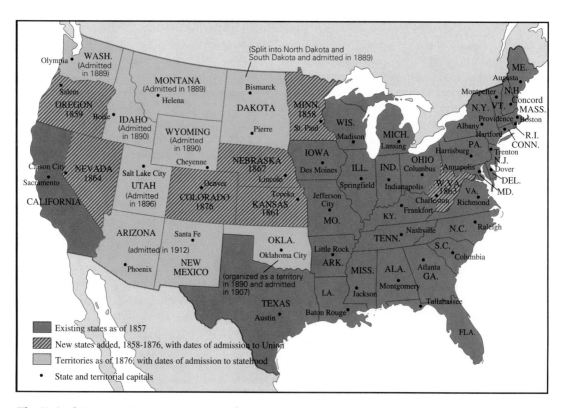

The United States, 1876–1912 *A wave of admissions between 1889 and 1912 brought remaining territories to statehood and marked the final creation of new states until Alaska and Hawaii were admitted in 1959.*

● I *m p o r t a n t* E *v e n t s* ●

1873	Congress ends coinage of silver dollars
1873–78	Economic hard times hit
1876	Rutherford B. Hayes elected president
	U.S. v. Reese affirms that Congress has no control over states wishing to disfranchise black voters
1877	*Munn* v. *Illinois* upholds state regulation of railroad rates
1878	Bland-Allison Act requires U.S. Treasury to buy $2 million to $4 million-worth of silver each month
	Susan B. Anthony-backed bill for women's suffrage amendment is defeated in Congress
1880	James Garfield elected president
1881	Garfield assassinated; Chester Arthur assumes the presidency
1883	Pendleton Civil Service Act creates Civil Service Commission to oversee competitive examinations for government positions
1884	Grover Cleveland elected president
1886	*Wabash* case declares that only Congress can limit interstate commerce rates
1887	Farm prices collapse
	Interstate Commerce Act creates commission to regulate rates and practices of interstate shippers
1888	Benjamin Harrison elected president
1890	McKinley Tariff raises tariff rates and introduces reciprocity
	Sherman Silver Purchase Act commits U.S. Treasury to buying 4.5 million ounces of silver each month
	"Billion-Dollar Congress" passes first federal budget surpassing $1 billion
	"Mississippi Plan" disfranchises African-Americans by imposing poll tax, property, and literacy requirements
1892	Populist convention in Omaha draws up reform platform
	Cleveland elected president
1893–97	Worst depression in country's history hits United States
1893	Sherman Silver Purchase Act repealed
1894	Wilson-Gorman Tariff attempts to reduce tariff rates; Senate Republicans restore cuts made by House
	Pullman strike; Eugene V. Debs arrested and turns to socialism
	Coxey's army marches on Washington, D.C.
1895	President Cleveland deals with bankers to save the gold reserve
1896	William McKinley elected president
1897	Dingley Tariff raises duties but expands reciprocity provisions
	Maximum Freight Rate decision rules that the Interstate Commerce Commission has no power to set rates
1898	Louisiana enacts first "grandfather clause," using literacy and property qualifications to prevent blacks from voting
1900	Gold Standard Act requires all paper money to be backed by gold
	McKinley reelected president

flourished after it. As the postal service, the diplomatic and consular corps, and other government activities expanded, so did the public payroll. Between 1865 and 1891, the number of federal government jobs tripled, from 53,000 to 166,000. Elected officials scrambled to control new appointments as a means of cementing support for themselves and their parties. In return for the comparatively short hours and high pay of government jobs, appointees pledged their votes and a portion of their earnings.

Shocked by such blatant corruption, a growing number of independents began advocating appointments and promotions based on merit rather than political connections. The movement for civil service reform grew during the 1870s, when scandals in the Grant administration exposed the defects of the spoils system. It became a fervent reform crusade in 1881 with the formation of the National Civil Service Reform League. The same year, a frustrated and demented job seeker assassinated President James Garfield. The murder hastened the drive for civil service reform.

The Pendleton Civil Service Act, passed by Congress in 1882 and signed by President Chester A. Arthur in 1883, outlawed political contributions by officeholders and created the Civil Service Commission to oversee competitive examinations for government positions. The act gave the commission jurisdiction, however, over only about 10 percent of federal jobs, although the president could expand the list.

Meanwhile, economic development was causing political problems at both the state and national levels. Railroad expansion was a particularly controversial area. As the nation's rail network spread, so did competition. In their quest for customers, railroad lines reduced rates to outmaneuver rivals, but rate wars soon cut into profits and wild vacillations of rates angered shippers and farmers.

Ironically, as rates generally fell, complaints about excessively high rates rose. On noncompetitive routes, railroads often boosted rates as high as possible to compensate for unprofitably low rates on competitive routes, making pricing disproportionate to distance. Charges on short-distance shipments served by only one line could be far higher than those on long-distance shipments served by competing lines. Railroads also played favorites: they gave reduced rates to large shippers and offered free passenger passes to preferred customers and politicians.

Such favoritism stirred farmers, shippers, and reform politicians to demand that government regulate railroad practices, especially rates. Attempts at regulation occurred first at the state level. By 1880, fourteen states had established commissions to limit freight and storage

Railroad Regulation
———

charges of state-chartered lines. Railroads bitterly fought these measures, arguing that rights of private property superseded public authority, but in 1877 the Supreme Court upheld the principle of rate regulation in *Munn* v. *Illinois.*

State agencies, however, could not regulate large interstate lines, a limitation affirmed by the Supreme Court in the *Wabash* case of 1886, in which the Court declared that only Congress could limit rates involving interstate commerce. Congress responded in 1887 by passing the Interstate Commerce Act. The act prohibited pools, rebates, and long haul–short haul rate discrimination, and it directed that "charges . . . shall be reasonable and fair." It also created the Interstate Commerce Commission (ICC) and empowered it to investigate railroad rate-making practices, issue cease-and-desist orders against illegal practices, and seek court aid to enforce compliance. But the law's lack of provisions for enforcement left the railroads ample room for evasion. Moreover, federal judges chipped away at ICC powers. In the *Maximum Freight Rate* case of 1897, the Supreme Court ruled that the ICC did not have the power to set rates, and in the *Alabama Midlands* case the same year the Court overturned prohibitions against long haul–short haul discrimination. Even so, the principle of government regulation, although weakened, remained in force.

Tariffs were another economic issue with political implications. Congress had initially created tariffs to protect American manufactured goods and some agricultural products from European competition. But tariffs quickly became a tool with which special interests could protect and enhance their profits. By the 1880s, separate tariffs applied to more than four thousand items. A few economists and farmers argued for free trade, but most politicians still insisted that tariffs were necessary to support industry and preserve jobs.

Tariff Policy
———

The Republican party, claiming responsibility for economic growth, put protective tariffs at the core of its political agenda. The Democrats complained that tariffs made prices artificially high by keeping out less expensive foreign goods, thereby benefiting manufacturers while hurting farmers whose crops were not protected and consumers who had to buy manufactured goods. Although Democrats acknowledged a need for some protection of manufactured goods and raw materials, they favored lower tariff rates to encourage foreign trade and to reduce the treasury surplus generated by high duties.

Manufacturing interests and their congressional allies successfully fought off objections and maintained control over tariff policy. The McKinley Tariff of 1890 boosted already high rates by another 4 percent. When House Democrats supported by President Grover Cleveland passed a bill to reduce tariff rates in 1894, Senate Republicans, aided by southern Democrats eager to protect their region's infant industries, added some six hundred amendments restoring most cuts (Wilson-Gorman Tariff). In 1897, a new tariff bill, the Dingley Act, raised rates further, although it expanded reciprocity provisions. Reciprocity, introduced in the McKinley Tariff of 1890 and designed to encourage foreign trade and discourage foreign retaliation against high American duties, authorized the president to remove items from the free list if their countries of origin placed unreasonable tariffs on American goods.

The currency controversy was even more tangled than the tariff issue. When prices fell after the Civil War, as a result of increased industrial and agricultural production, debtors

Monetary Policy and creditors had opposing reactions. Farmers, most of whom were debtors, suffered because they had to pay fixed mortgage and interest payments while prices for their crops were dropping. Correctly perceiving that an insufficient money supply made debts more expensive relative to other costs, farmers favored schemes like the coinage of silver to increase the amount of currency in circulation. With an expanded money supply, debts would be less burdensome, because interest rates would be lower. Thus farmers' costs would be lower relative to the prices they could receive for their crops. Creditors, on the other hand, believed that overproduction had caused prices to decline. They favored a more stable, limited money supply backed only by gold as a means of maintaining investors' confidence in the American economy.

But the issue involved more than economics. It grew from a series of conflicts—social, regional, and emotional. First, creditor-debtor conflict translated into haves versus have-nots. The debate also represented a sectional cleavage: western silver-mining areas and agricultural regions of the South and West against the more conservative industrial Northeast.

By the early 1870s, the currency controversy boiled down to gold versus silver. Until that time, the government had coined both gold and silver dollars. A silver dollar weighed sixteen times more than a gold dollar, meaning that gold was officially worth sixteen times as much as silver. Gold discoveries after 1848, however, had increased the supply and lowered gold's market price relative to that of silver. Because silver came to be worth more than one-sixteenth the value of gold, silver producers preferred to sell their metal on the open market rather than to the government. Silver dollars disappeared from circulation—because of their inflated value, owners hoarded them rather than spending them—and in 1873 Congress officially stopped coining silver dollars, an act that partisans of silver called "the Crime of '73." At about the same time, European nations also stopped buying silver. Thus the United States and many of its trading partners unofficially adopted the gold standard, meaning that their currency was backed chiefly by gold.

Within a few years, new mines in the American West began to flood the market with silver, and its price dropped accordingly. Once again gold was worth more than sixteen times the value of silver. It became profitable to spend silver dollars, and it would have been worthwhile to sell silver to the government in return for gold—but the government was no longer buying silver. Debtors, hurt by falling prices and the economic hard times of the mid-1870s, saw silver as a way to expand the currency supply. They joined with silver producers to denounce the Crime of '73 and press for the resumption of coinage at the old sixteen-to-one ratio.

Split into silver and gold factions, Congress tried to achieve a compromise. The Bland-Allison Act of 1878 required the treasury to buy $2 million- to $4 million-worth of silver each month, and the Sherman Silver Purchase Act of 1890 fixed the government's

Copyright 1893 by Henrietta Briggs-Wall

American Woman and Her Political Peers.

COPYRIGHT, 1893, BY HENRIETTA BRIGGS-WALL.

How do historians know

the different viewpoints on women's suffrage in the late nineteenth century? In addition to essays, editorials, and other publications, posters and cards often presented underlying themes, including those with mixed messages. This 1893 postcard supports women's suffrage in a cynical and partly racist manner by showing a dignified suffragist surrounded by individuals who, like her, were prohibited from voting (clockwise, from upper left): a mentally disabled man, a convict, a homeless immigrant, and a Native American. The artist has used stereotyped images in faces and clothing to convey the message that this prim white woman deserves a better status than being grouped with such undesirable and inferior characters. Photo: Sophia Smith Collection, Smith College.

monthly purchase of silver in weight (4.5 million ounces) rather than dollars. But neither act satisfied the different interest groups. The minting of silver dollars, which these laws allowed, failed to expand the money supply as substantially as debtors had hoped, and it also failed to erase the impression that the government favored the creditors' interests. Not until after a depression in the 1890s and an emotional presidential election did the money issue subside.

Amid debates over tariffs and money, supporters of women's suffrage pressed Congress and state legislatures more fervently than ever before. In

Women's Suffrage
—

1878, Susan B. Anthony, who had been rebuffed by the courts when she tried to vote in 1872, persuaded Senator A. A. Sargent of California, a proponent of women's suffrage, to introduce a constitutional amendment stating that "the right of citizens of the United States to vote shall not be denied or abridged by the United States or by any state on account of sex." A Senate committee killed the bill, but the National Women Suffrage Association (NWSA) had it reintroduced repeatedly over the next eighteen years. On the few occasions that the bill reached the Senate floor, it was voted down by senators who expressed fears that suffrage would interfere with women's family obligations and ruin female virtue.

While the NWSA fought for the vote on the national level, the American Women Suffrage Association worked for constitutional amendments at the state level. (The two groups merged in 1890 to form the National American Woman Suffrage Association.) Between 1870 and 1910, eleven states held referenda (all but three were west of the Mississippi River) to legalize women's suffrage. Although few of these attempts succeeded, women did win partial victories: by 1890, nineteen states allowed women to vote on school issues, and three granted suffrage on tax and bond issues.

Throughout the Gilded Age, legislators focused chiefly on protection of private property and the stability of the investment climate—deemed essential for economic progress. Debtors, farmers, laborers, women, racial minorities, and others who believed themselves disadvantaged expressed their political interests in increasingly organized and articulate ways, but Congress and the state legislatures catered to those who already had social and economic privileges.

THE PRESIDENCY IN ECLIPSE

American presidents in the years between 1877 and 1900 bore little resemblance to forceful predecessors like Andrew Jackson and Abraham Lincoln. Proper, honorable, and honest, Presidents Rutherford Hayes (1877–1881), James Garfield (1881), Chester Arthur (1881–1885), Grover Cleveland (1885–1889 and 1893–1897), Benjamin Harrison (1889–1893), and William McKinley (1897–1901) won respect but seldom elicited strong emotions. None of the era's presidents was an inspiring personality, nor could any dominate the factional chieftains of his party.

Rutherford B. Hayes emphasized national unity over sectional rivalry and opposed violence of all kinds. When Hayes ordered out troops to disperse railroad strikers in 1877, it was not to suppress their cause but because he believed the rioting and looting that accompanied the strikes threatened social harmony. He tried also to honor his pledge to overhaul the spoils system by appointing civil service reformer Carl Schurz to his cabinet and by battling New York's patronage king, Senator Roscoe Conkling. Hayes believed society was obligated to help those whom it had formerly oppressed, including American Chinese and Indians, and after retiring from the presidency he worked diligently to help former slaves.

Hayes, Garfield, and Arthur
—

When Hayes declined to run for reelection in 1880, the Republicans nominated another Ohio congressman and Civil War hero, James A. Garfield. After defeating Democrat Winfield Scott Hancock, also a Civil War hero, by just 40,000 votes out of more than 9 million cast, Garfield spent most of his brief presidency trying to secure an independent position among party potentates. He hoped to reduce the tariff and develop American economic interests in Latin America, but he had to spend most of his time dealing with hordes of office seekers. Garfield's chance to make lasting contributions ended with his assassination in 1881.

Garfield's vice president and successor was New York politician Chester A. Arthur, a spoilsman Hayes had fired in 1878. Although his elevation to the presidency made reformers shudder, he became a dignified and temperate executive. Arthur signed the Pendleton Civil Service Act, urged Congress to modify outdated tariff rates, and supported federal regulation of railroads. He wielded the veto aggressively, killing a number of bills that excessively benefited privileged interests. But congressional partisans frustrated his hopes for reducing the tariff and building up the navy. In 1884, he lost the Republican nomination to James G. Blaine.

To run against Blaine, the Democratic party named New York's Governor Grover Cleveland, a bachelor whose respectable reputation was tainted by his having fathered an illegitimate son—a fact he acknowledged openly during the campaign. On election day, Cleveland beat Blaine by only 23,000 popular votes; his tiny margin of 1,149 votes in New York gave him that state's 36 electoral votes, enough for a 219-to-182-vote victory in the electoral college. Cleveland may have won New York thanks to the last-minute efforts of a local Protestant minister, who publicly equated Democrats with "rum, Romanism, and rebellion" (drinking, Catholicism, and the Civil War). The Democrats eagerly publicized the slur among New York's large Irish-Catholic population, urging voters to protest by turning out for Cleveland.

Cleveland, the first Democratic president since James Buchanan (1857–1861), exerted more vigorous leadership than had his immediate predecessors. He used the veto against excessive

Cleveland and Harrison

pension bills—in fact, he vetoed two-thirds of all the bills Congress passed—and he expanded the merit-based civil service. His most forceful action was in the interest of tariff reform. Worried about the growing treasury surplus, Cleveland urged Congress to cut duties on raw materials and manufactured goods. When advisers warned him that his stand might weaken his chances for reelection, the president retorted, "What is the use of being elected or reelected, unless you stand for something?" But the Mills tariff bill of 1888, passed by the House in response to Cleveland's wishes, died in the Senate.

In 1888, the Democrats renominated Cleveland, and the Republicans ran Benjamin Harrison, an intelligent but stuffy former senator from Indiana and grandson of President William Henry Harrison (1841). The campaign was less savage than that of 1884 but far from clean. Bribery and multiple voting helped Harrison win Indiana by 2,300 votes and New York by 14,000. (Democrats also indulged in bribery and vote fraud, but this time Republicans proved more successful at it.)

Those crucial states assured Harrison's victory; although Cleveland outpolled Harrison by 90,000 popular votes, Harrison carried the electoral vote by 233 to 168.

Although Harrison was the first president since 1875 whose party had majorities in both houses of Congress, he had little control over legislators. He professed support for civil service and appointed the reformer Theodore Roosevelt a civil service commissioner. Harrison also signed the Dependents' Pension Act, which provided disability pensions for all Union veterans of the Civil War and granted aid for their widows and minor children. The bill doubled the number of pensioners from 490,000 to 966,000. As a consequence of the Pension Act and other grants and appropriations, the federal budget surpassed $1 billion in 1890 for the first time in the nation's history.

Democrats blamed the "Billion-Dollar Congress" on spendthrift Republicans. Voters reacted by unseating seventy-eight Republicans in the congressional elections of 1890. Seeking to capitalize on voter unrest, Democrats nominated Cleveland to run against Harrison again in 1892. This time, Cleveland attracted large contributions from business and beat Harrison by 380,000 popular votes and by 277 to 145 in the electoral college.

In office once more, Cleveland took bolder steps to address the problems of currency, tariffs, and labor unrest. But his actions reflected a narrow orientation toward the interests of business, and it bespoke political weakness. To protect the nation's dwindling gold reserve, which was shrinking during the Panic of 1893, Cleveland enlisted aid from bankers, who in 1895 bailed out the nation on terms highly favorable to themselves. During his campaign, Cleveland had promised sweeping tariff reform, but he made little effort to line up support for such reform in the Senate. And when 120,000 boycotting railroad workers paralyzed western commerce in the Pullman strike of 1894, Cleveland bowed to requests from railroad managers and Attorney General Richard Olney to send in troops. Throughout Cleveland's second term, events—particularly economic downturn and Populist ferment—seemed too much for the president.

STIRRINGS OF AGRARIAN UNREST AND POPULISM

While the federal government labored to sustain harmony and prosperity, inequities in the new agricultural and industrial order were stirring up a mass movement that was to shake American society. The agrarian revolt began in Grange organizations in the early 1870s. The revolt accelerated when farmers' alliances formed in Texas in the late 1870s and then spread across the Cotton Belt and Plains in the 1880s. The movement caught on chiefly in areas in which farm tenancy, crop liens, merchants, railroads, banks, weather, and insects threatened the ambitions and economic well-being of hopeful farmers. Once under way, the agrarian rebellion inspired visions of a truly cooperative and democratic society.

Agricultural expansion in the West and South exposed millions of people to the hardships of rural life. The uncertainties might have been more bearable if rewards had been more promising, but such was not the case. As growers put more land under cultivation, as mechanization boosted productivity, and as foreign competition increased, supplies exceeded national and worldwide demand for agricultural products. Consequently, prices for staple crops dropped steadily. Combined with social isolation, high expenses—for seed, fertilizer, manufactured goods, taxes, and mortgage interest—trapped many farm families in disadvantageous and sometimes desperate circumstances. In order to buy necessities and pay bills, farmers had to produce more, but the more they produced, the lower prices dropped.

Even before the full effect of these developments was felt, small farmers had begun to organize. With aid from Oliver H. Kelley of the U.S. Department of Agriculture, farmers founded a network of local organizations called Granges in almost every state during the 1860s and 1870s. By 1875, the Grange had nearly twenty thousand local branches and more than one million members. Strongest in the Midwest and South, Granges served a chiefly

Grange Movement

social function, sponsoring meetings and educational events to help relieve the loneliness of farm life.

As membership flourished, Granges moved into economic and political action. Encouraged by the national Grange, local branches formed cooperatives to buy equipment and supplies directly from manufacturers. Granges also organized sales cooperatives, whereby farmers would divide the profits from the sale of their pooled grain and dairy products. In politics, Grangers used their numbers to some advantage, electing sympathetic legislators and pressing for so-called Granger laws to regulate transportation and storage rates.

Despite their efforts, Granges declined in the late 1870s. A requirement that cooperatives run on a cash-only basis excluded large numbers of farmers who rarely had cash. Legislative efforts to regulate business and transportation withered when corporations won court support against such Granger laws. Politically, Granges disavowed third parties but could not withstand the power of business interests within the two major parties. Thus after a brief assertion of influence, the Grange reverted to an organization of farmers' social clubs.

Rural political activism then shifted to the Farmers' Alliances, two networks of organizations—one in the Plains and one in the South—that by 1890 constituted a genuine mass movement. The first Alliances sprang up in Texas, where hard-pressed small farmers rallied against crop liens, merchants, and railroads in particular and against "money power" in general. Using traveling lecturers to recruit members, Alliance leaders extended the movement to other southern states. By 1889, the Southern Alliance boasted more than three million members, including the powerful Colored Farmers' National Alliance, which claimed more than one million black members. A similar movement flourished in the Plains, where by the late 1880s two million members were organized in Kansas, Nebraska, and the Dakotas.

Farmers' Alliances

Alliances members not only pushed the Grange concept of cooperation but also proposed a scheme to relieve the most serious rural problems:

**Subtreasury
Plan**
———

lack of cash and lack of credit. The subtreasury plan called for the federal government to construct warehouses in every major agricultural county. At harvest time, farmers could store crops in these "subtreasuries" while awaiting higher prices, and the government would loan farmers treasury notes amounting to 80 percent of the market price the stored crops would bring. Farmers could use the treasury notes as legal tender to pay debts and make purchases. Once the stored crops were sold, farmers would pay back the loans plus small interest and storage fees.

Growing membership and rising confidence drew the Alliances more deeply into politics. By 1890, farmers had elected a number of officeholders sympathetic to their programs—especially in the South. In the Midwest, Alliance candidates often ran on independent third-party tickets and achieved some success in Kansas, Nebraska, and the Dakotas. During the summer of 1890, the Kansas Alliance held a "convention of the people" and nominated candidates who swept the state's fall elections. Formation of this People's party, members of which were called Populists (from *populus*, the Latin word for people), gave a name to Alliance political activism. Two years later, after overcoming regional differences, the People's party held a national convention in Omaha where members drafted a platform and nominated a presidential candidate.

**Rise of
Populism**
———

The new party's Omaha platform was one of the most comprehensive reform documents in American history. Most planks addressed the three central sources of rural unrest: transportation, land, and money. Frustrated with weak state and federal regulation, Populists demanded government ownership of railroad and telegraph lines. They urged the federal government to reclaim all land owned for speculative purposes by railroads and foreigners. The monetary plank called for a flexible currency system based on free and unlimited coinage of silver, which would increase the money supply and enable farmers to pay their debts more easily. Other planks advocated a graduated income tax, postal savings banks, direct election of U.S. senators, and shorter

hours for workers. As its presidential candidate, the party nominated James B. Weaver of Iowa, a former Union general.

Although Weaver lost badly in 1892, he garnered more than one million popular votes (8 percent of the total), majorities in four states and 22 electoral votes. Not since 1856 had a third party won so many votes in its first national effort. The party's central dilemma—whether to stand by its principles at all costs or compromise in order to gain power—still loomed ahead. But in the early 1890s, rural dwellers in the South and Plains had an emotional faith in the future. Although Populists were flawed democrats—their mistrust of blacks and foreigners gave them a reactionary streak—they sought change in order to fulfill their version of American ideals. Amid hardship and desperation, millions of people had begun to believe that a cooperative democracy in which government would ensure equal opportunity could overcome corporate power.

———

THE DEPRESSION OF THE 1890s

Shortly before Grover Cleveland became president for the second time in 1893, an apparently minor but ominous event occurred: the Philadelphia and Reading Railroad, once a thriving and profitable line, went bankrupt. Like other railroads, the Philadelphia and Reading had borrowed heavily to lay track and build stations and bridges. But overexpansion cut into profits, and ultimately the company was unable to pay its debts.

The same problem beset manufacturers. Output at McCormick farm machinery factories was nine times greater in 1893 than it had been in 1879, for example, but revenues only tripled. To compensate, the company bought more machines and squeezed more work out of fewer laborers. This strategy, however, only enlarged the debt and increased unemployment. The unemployed workers found themselves in the same plight as their employers: they could not pay their creditors. Banks suffered too when their customers defaulted. The failure of the

National Cordage Company in May 1893 accelerated a chain reaction of business and bank closings. During the first four months of 1893, 28 banks failed. By June, the number reached 128. The next year, an adviser warned President Cleveland, "We are on the eve of a very dark night." He was right; between 1893 and 1897, the nation suffered the worst economic depression it had ever experienced.

As the depression deepened, the currency problem reached a critical stage. The Sherman Silver Purchase Act of 1890 had committed the government to buy 4.5 million ounces of silver each month. Payment was to be in gold, at the ratio of one ounce of gold for every sixteen ounces of silver. But a western mining boom made silver more plentiful, causing its value relative to gold to fall. Thus every month, the government exchanged gold, the value of which remained fairly constant, for less valuable silver. Fearing a decrease in the value of the dollar, which was based on treasury holdings in silver and gold, merchants at home and abroad began to cash in paper money and securities for gold. As a result, the nation's gold reserve soon dwindled, falling below the psychologically significant level of $100 million in early 1893.

Currency Problems

President Cleveland, vowing to protect the gold reserve, called a special session of Congress to repeal the Sherman Silver Purchase Act. Repeal passed in late 1893, but the run on the treasury continued through 1894. By early 1895, gold reserves had fallen to $41 million. In desperation, Cleveland accepted an offer of 3.5 million ounces of gold in return for $62 million-worth of federal bonds from a banking syndicate led by financier J. P. Morgan. When the bankers resold the bonds to the public, they profited handsomely at the nation's expense. Cleveland claimed that he had saved the gold reserves, but discontented farmers, workers, silver miners, and even some members of Cleveland's own party saw only humiliation in the president's deal with big businessmen. Moreover, the deal between Cleveland and Morgan did not end the depression.

In the final years of the century, new gold strikes in Alaska, good harvests, and industrial growth brought relief. But the downturn of the 1890s had hastened the crumbling of the old economic system and the emergence of a new one. Since the 1850s, railroads had been the prime mover of American economic development, opening up new markets, boosting steel production, and invigorating banking. But the central features of the new business system—consolidation and a trend toward bigness—were beginning to solidify just when the depression hit.

Effect of New Economic Structures

The nation's economy had become interdependent rather than sectional; the fortunes of a large business in one part of the country now had repercussions elsewhere. By the 1890s, many companies had expanded too rapidly. When contraction occurred, their reckless assumption of debt dragged them down, and they pulled other industries down with them. In early 1893, for example, five hundred banks and sixteen thousand businesses filed for bankruptcy that year. European economies also slumped, and more than ever before the fortunes of one country affected those of other countries.

To complicate matters, American farmers had to contend not only with fluctuating transportation rates and falling crop prices at home but also with Canadian and Russian wheat growers, Argentine cattle ranchers, Indian and Egyptian cotton producers, and Australian wool producers. When farmers fell deeper into debt and lost purchasing power, their depressed condition in turn affected the economic health of railroads, farm implements manufacturers, banks, and other businesses. The downward spiral ended late in 1897, but the depression exposed problems that demanded reform and set an agenda for the years to come.

DEPRESSION-ERA PROTESTS

The depression exposed fundamental tensions in the industrial system. The gap between employees and employers had been widening steadily for half a century in response to technological and organizational changes. By the 1890s, workers' protests against exploitation were threatening to become a full-fledged economic and political upheaval. In

1894, the year the American economy plunged into depression, there were more than thirteen hundred strikes and countless riots. Labor violence reached an alarming pitch, and radical rhetoric escalated. Contrary to the fears of business leaders, only a few of the protesters were anarchists or communists from Europe come to sabotage American democracy. The disaffected included hundreds of thousands of men and women who believed that in a democracy their voices should be heard.

Socialism was part of this undercurrent, and small numbers of socialists did participate in some strikes and other confrontations. Furthermore, many workers who never became socialists had been convinced by their own experience to agree with Karl Marx (1818–1883), the German philosopher and father of communism, that whoever controls the means of production holds the power to determine how well people live. Marx predicted that workers throughout the world would become so discontented that they would revolt and seize factories, farms, banks, and transportation lines. The societies resulting from this revolution would establish a new socialist order of justice and equality.

Socialism

American socialism suffered from internal schisms and a lack of strong leadership. It splintered into a number of small groups, such as the Socialist Labor party, led by Daniel DeLeon, a fiery West Indian–born lawyer. DeLeon and other socialist leaders failed to attract the mass of unskilled workers. American socialists often focused on fine points of doctrine while ignoring the everyday needs of workers. Social mobility and the philosophy of individualism also undermined socialist aims. Workers hoped that they or their children would improve their lives through education or acquisition of property or by becoming their own boss. Thus most workers sought individual advancement rather than the betterment of all workers.

Events in 1894 triggered changes within the socialist movement. That year, the government's quashing of the Pullman strike and of the newly formed American Railway Union elevated an inspiring new socialist leader. Eugene V. Debs, the president of the railway union, had become a socialist while serving a six-month prison term for defying an injunction against the strike. Once released, Debs became the leading spokesman for American socialism, combining visionary Marxism with Jeffersonian and Populist antimonopolism. Although never good at organizing, Debs captivated huge audiences with his passionate eloquence and indignant attacks on the free enterprise system.

In 1894, however, Debs had to share public attention with a quiet businessman from Massillon, Ohio. Like Debs, Jacob S. Coxey had a vision.

Coxey's Army

Coxey was convinced that, to aid debtors, the government should issue paper money unbacked by gold—in other words, the government should deliberately stimulate inflation. As the depression deepened, Coxey also advocated a federal public works program—financed with $500 million of this "legal tender" paper money—to relieve unemployment and revive consumer spending. He planned to publicize his scheme by leading a march from Massillon to Washington, D.C., gathering a "petition in boots" of unemployed workers along the way.

Coxey's army, about two hundred strong, left Massillon in late March 1894. On April 30, Coxey's troops, including women and children, entered Washington. The next day (May Day, a date traditionally associated with socialist demonstrations), the citizen army of five hundred marched to the Capitol, armed with "war clubs of peace." When Coxey and a few others vaulted the wall surrounding the Capitol grounds, mounted police moved in and routed the crowd. Coxey tried to speak from the Capitol steps, but police dragged him away. As arrests and clubbings continued, Coxey's dream of a demonstration of 400,000 jobless workers dissolved. Like the strikes, the first people's march on Washington had yielded to police muscle.

Coxey's march expressed the frustration of people seeking relief from uncertainty. Unlike socialists, who wished to alter the economic system fundamentally, Coxey's troops merely wanted more jobs and better living standards. Yet the brutal reactions of officials reveal how threatening the dissenters, from Coxey to Debs, must have appeared to the defenders of the existing social order.

POPULISTS AND THE SILVER CRUSADE

The Populists did not elicit the kinds of suppression experienced by unions and Coxey's army, but they encountered problems just when their political goals seemed attainable. As late as 1894, Populist candidates made good showings in local and state elections in the West and South. Like earlier third parties, though, Populists were underfinanced and underorganized. They had strong and colorful candidates but not enough of them to wrest control from the major parties. Many voters were reluctant to abandon old loyalties to the Republicans or Democrats.

Moreover, the two major parties took steps to destroy Populist voting strength, especially in the South. The threat of biracial political dissent posed by the Farmers' Alliances in the 1890s prompted southern white Democrats to take urgent action. Southern legislatures had already enacted several measures to curtail black voting, including poll taxes and literacy tests. Not confident that these measures would thwart a Populist coalition of black and white voters, and fearful that northern Republicans might revive federal supervision of elections, southern white legislators took steps to prevent all blacks from voting.

Curtailment of African-American Voting

Disfranchisement was accomplished in clever and devious ways. The Supreme Court affirmed in 1876 that the Fifteenth Amendment prohibited states from denying the vote "on account of race, color, or previous condition of servitude." But, said the Court in *U.S.* v. *Reese*, Congress had no control over state elections other than the provisions of the Fifteenth Amendment. State legislatures thus found ways to exclude black voters without mentioning race, color, or servitude. For instance, an 1890 state constitutional convention established the "Mississippi Plan," which required all voters to pay a poll tax eight months before each election, to present the receipt at election time, and to prove that they could read and interpret the state constitution. Registration officials applied much stiffer standards to blacks than to whites. In 1898, Louisiana enacted the first "grandfather clause," which established literacy and property qualifications for voting but exempted sons and grandsons of those eligible to vote before 1867. Other southern states initiated similar measures. Poor whites, few of whom could meet poll tax, property, and literacy requirements, were often disfranchised. Blacks, however, bore the brunt of the attack on voting rights. By the early 1900s, African-Americans had effectively lost their political rights in every southern state except Tennessee.

White fears of a biracial Populist coalition were largely unjustified, for fundamental racism impeded the acceptance of blacks by white Populists. To be sure, some Populists sought a coalition of distressed black and white farmers. But even poor white farmers could not put aside their racism. Many came from families that had supported the Ku Klux Klan during Reconstruction. Some had once owned slaves, and they considered African-Americans a permanently inferior people. They seemed to take comfort in the belief that there would always be people worse off than they were. Thus few Populists addressed the needs of black farmers, and many used white supremacist rhetoric to avoid charges that they encouraged racial mingling.

In the national arena, the Populist crusade against "money power" settled on the issue of silver. Many people saw silver as a simple solution to the nation's complex ills. To them, free coinage of silver (not held to the gold standard) meant the end of special privileges for the rich and the return of government to the people. Populists made free coinage of silver their political battle cry. But as the election of 1896 approached, they had to settle on a strategy to translate their few previous electoral victories into larger success. Should they join forces with sympathetic factions of the major parties, thus risking a loss of identity, or should they remain an independent third party and settle for minor successes at best?

Free Silver

THE ELECTION OF 1896

The presidential election of 1896 brought the political turbulence to a climax. Each party was divided. Republicans, directed by political boss Marcus

McKinley and Bryan

Alonzo Hanna, a prosperous Ohio industrialist, had only minor problems. For more than a year, Hanna had been maneuvering to win the nomination for Ohio's governor, William McKinley. By the time the party convened in St. Louis, Hanna had corralled enough delegates to succeed. The Republicans' only distress occurred when the party

adopted a moderate platform supporting gold, rejecting a prosilver stance proposed by Senator Henry M. Teller of Colorado. Teller, who had been among the party's founders forty years earlier, walked out of the convention in tears, taking a small group of silver Republicans with him.

At the Democratic convention, prosilver delegates paraded through the Chicago Amphitheatre wearing silver badges and waving silver banners. A *New York World* reporter remarked that "All the silverites need is a Moses." They soon found one in William Jennings Bryan of Nebraska. Bryan, a former congressman whose support for free coinage of silver had annoyed President Cleveland, was only thirty-six years old, deeply religious, and

Critics of the free silver policy advocated by Populists and Democrats in the 1896 presidential election tried to convince voters that such a policy would result in poverty and low wages. The message of this broadside is that free silver would make Americans as downtrodden as peasants in the most underdeveloped countries. Smithsonian Institution, Division of Political History, Washington, D.C.

highly distressed by what the depression had done to midwestern farmers. As a member of the party's resolutions committee, Bryan helped write a platform calling for free coinage of silver.

When the committee presented the platform to the full convention, Bryan rose to speak on its behalf. In the heat and humidity of the Chicago summer, Bryan's now famous closing words ignited the delegates:

> Having behind us the producing masses of this nation and the world, supported by the commercial interests, the laboring interests, and the toilers everywhere, we will answer their [the wealthy classes'] demand for a gold standard by saying to them: You shall not press down upon the brow of labor this crown of thorns, you shall not crucify mankind upon a cross of gold.

The speech could not have been timed better; indeed, Bryan planned it that way. Friends who had been pushing Bryan for the presidential nomination now had no trouble enlisting support. Bryan won the nomination, a faction of gold Democrats split from the party, and the "great campaign" had begun in earnest.

Bryan's nomination presented the Populist party with a serious dilemma. Should Populists join Democrats in support of Bryan, or should they nominate their own candidate and preserve the party's independence? Tom Watson of Georgia, expressing southern sentiment against fusion with Democrats, warned that "the Democratic idea of fusion [is] that we play Jonah while they play whale." Others reasoned that supporting a different candidate would split the anti-McKinley vote and guarantee a Republican victory. In the end, the convention compromised, first naming Watson as its vice presidential nominee to preserve party identity and then nominating Bryan for president.

The election results revealed that the political stand-off had finally ended. McKinley, symbol of Republican pragmatism and a new economic order of corporate ascendancy, beat

Election Results

Bryan by more than six hundred thousand popular votes and won in the electoral college by 271 to 176. It was the most lopsided presidential election since 1872.

Bryan had worked hard to rally the nation. But lean campaign finances and obsession with silver undermined his effort. The silver issue in particular prevented Populists from building the urban-rural coalition that would have given them political breadth. Urban workers shied away from the silver issue out of fear that free coinage would inflate prices. Labor leaders like Samuel Gompers of the AFL, although partly sympathetic, would not join forces with Populists, because they viewed farmers as businessmen, not workers. And socialists such as Daniel DeLeon denounced Populists as "retrograde" because they, unlike socialists, still believed in free enterprise. Thus the Populist crusade collapsed in 1896.

As president, McKinley signed the Gold Standard Act (1900), which required that all paper money be backed by gold. He also supported the

The McKinley Presidency

Dingley Tariff of 1897, which raised duties even higher—although it did expand reciprocity provisions. Domestic tensions subsided during McKinley's presidency; an upward swing of the business cycle and a money supply enlarged by new gold discoveries in Alaska, Australia, and South Africa helped restore prosperity. A strong believer in the need to open new markets abroad in order to sustain prosperity at home, McKinley encouraged imperialistic ventures in Latin America and the Pacific. Good times and victory in the Spanish-American War enabled him to beat Bryan again in 1900.

The 1896 election destroyed the old equilibrium and realigned national politics. The Republican party had become the majority party by emphasizing freedom for big business and broadening its social base to include urban workers. The Democratic party had miscalculated on the silver issue and held onto its traditional support only in the South. After 1896, however, party loyalties were not as potent as they once had been. Suspicion of party politics increased, and voter participation rates declined. A new kind of politics was brewing, one in which technical experts and scientific organization would attempt to supplant the back-room deals and favoritism that had characterized the previous age.

The Populists had made a concerted effort to combat special privilege and corruption, but they foundered because too many people were benefiting from a generally expanding economy. Ironically, by 1920 many Populist reform goals would be achieved, including regulation of railroads, banks, and utilities; shorter working hours; a variant of the subtreasury system; a graduated income tax; direct election of senators; and the secret ballot. These reforms succeeded because a variety of groups in what had become a pluralistic society united behind them.

SUGGESTIONS FOR FURTHER READING

General

Sean Denis Cashman, *America in the Gilded Age* (1984); H. Wayne Morgan, ed., *The Gilded Age* (1970), and *From Hayes to McKinley* (1969); Nell Irvin Painter, *Standing at Armageddon: The United States, 1877–1919* (1987); Alan Trachtenberg, *The Incorporation of America: Culture and Society in the Gilded Age* (1982).

Parties and Political Issues

Paula Baker, *The Moral Framework of Public Life* (1991); Beverly Beeton, *Women Vote in the West: The Suffrage Movement, 1869–1896* (1986); Christine Bolt, *American Indian Policy and American Reform* (1987); Elisabeth Griffith, *In Her Own Right: The Life of Elizabeth Cady Stanton* (1984); Ari A. Hoogenboom, *Outlawing the Spoils: The Civil Service Movement* (1961); Robert D. Marcus, *Grand Old Party* (1971); Michael E. McGerr, *The Decline of Popular Politics* (1986); Walter T. K. Nugent, *Money and American Society* (1968); John G. Sproat, *The Best Men: Liberal Reformers in the Gilded Age* (1968).

Currents of Protest

William M. Dick, *Labor and Socialism in America* (1972); John P. Diggins, *The American Left in the Twentieth Century* (1973); Nick Salvatore, *Eugene V. Debs: Citizen and Socialist* (1982); Carlos A. Schwantes, *Coxey's Army* (1985); David Shannon, *The Socialist Party of America* (1955).

Populism and the Election of 1896

Paolo Coletta, *William Jennings Bryan: Political Evangelist* (1964); Paul W. Glad, *McKinley, Bryan, and the People* (1964), and *The Trumpet Soundeth: William Jennings Bryan and His Democracy* (1964); Lawrence Goodwyn, *Democratic Promise: The Populist Movement in America* (1976); Steven Hahn, *The Roots of Southern Populism* (1983); Richard Hofstadter, *The Age of Reform: From Bryan to FDR* (1955); J. Morgan Kousser, *The Shaping of Southern Politics* (1974); Walter T. K. Nugent, *The Tolerant Populists* (1963); Norman Pollack, *The Populist Response to Industrial America* (1962); Allan Weinstein, *Prelude to Populism: Origins of the Silver Issue* (1970).

Chapter

21

The Progressive Era, 1895–1920

A N ASSOCIATE DESCRIBED FLORENCE Kelley as a "guerrilla warrior" in the "wilderness of industrial wrongs." A woman of sharp wit and commanding presence who always dressed in black, Kelley accomplished as much as anyone in guiding the United States from the tangled swamp of unregulated industrial capitalism to the uncharted seas of the twentieth-century welfare state.

Raised in middle-class comfort in Philadelphia as the daughter of a Republican congressman, Kelley embarked on a tour of Europe in 1883 after graduating from Cornell. She had hoped to prepare for the study of law, but the University of Pennsylvania had denied her admission to its graduate school because of her gender. In Zurich, Kelley fell in with a group of socialists who opened her eyes to the plight of the underprivileged, especially working women and children. She married a Russian medical student and returned to the United States with her husband and infant son in 1886. When debts and other problems ended the marriage five years later, Kelley took her three children from New York to Chicago. There, she moved into Hull House, a residence in the slums where

middle-class reformers went to live in order to help and learn from working-class immigrants. At Hull House, she became immersed in a female-oriented world, where women sought to transfer their traditional helping skills to the betterment of society.

During the next decade, Kelley became one of the nation's most ardent advocates of better conditions for working-class women and children. She investigated and publicized abuses of the sweatshop system in Chicago's garment industry, lobbied for laws to prohibit child labor and regulate women's working hours, and served as Illinois's first chief factory inspector. Her work helped create new professions for women in social reform, and her strategy of investigating, publicizing, and crusading for action became a model for progressive reform initiatives. Perhaps most significant, she helped involve government in the solution of pressing social problems. These actions made Kelley a full participant in the era of progressive reform.

By 1900, the tumultuous events of the 1890s—a severe depression, bitter labor violence, political upheaval, and foreign entanglements—had passed, and reason for optimism had begun to emerge. The nation had just emerged victorious from a war (see Chapter 22), and a new political era of dynamic leaders such as Theodore Roosevelt and Woodrow Wilson was dawning. The resulting sense of renewal served both to heighten anxiety about continuing social and political problems and to raise hopes that such problems could somehow be fixed.

By the 1910s, many reformers were calling themselves progressives, and a new political party by that name had formed to embody their principles. Since that time, historians have used the term *progressivism* to refer to the era's reformist spirit, although they disagree about the movement's meaning and membership. The era between 1895 and 1920 can nonetheless be characterized by a series of movements, each aimed in one way or another at renovating or restoring American society, its values, and its institutions.

The urge for reform had many sources. Industrialization had brought awesome technology and unprecedented productivity. But it also brought labor strife, spoiling of natural resources, and abuse of corporate power. Rapidly growing cities facilitated the amassing and distribution of goods, services, and cultural amenities; they also bred poverty, disease, crime, and political corruption. Massive influxes of immigrants and the rise of a new class of managers and professionals shook the old social order. And the crippling depression of the 1890s forced many leading citizens to understand what working people had known for some time: the central promise of American life was not being kept. Equality of opportunity was a myth.

Progressives tried to address these problems by organizing their thinking and actions around three basic goals. First, they sought to end abuses of power. Trustbusting, consumers' rights, and good government became compelling political issues. Second, progressives aimed to supplant corrupt power with reformed versions of such traditional institutions as schools, charities, medical clinics, and the family. Third, they wanted to apply scientific principles and efficient management to economic, social, and political institutions. Their aim was cooperation, especially between business and government, that would end wasteful competition and labor conflict and minimize social and economic disorder.

THE CONTRADICTIONS OF PROGRESSIVISM

The Progressive era emerged in the aftermath of the election of 1896 to address the issues raised by urban reformers in the previous half-century. As the twentieth century dawned, party loyalty eroded and voter turnout declined. Parties and elections, it seemed, were losing their function of providing Americans with a way to influence government policies.

The political system was opening up to multiple and shifting interest groups, each of which championed its own brand of reform. These organizations **Issues of** included professional associations such as the American Bar **Reform** Association, women's organizations such as the National American Woman Suffrage Association, issue-oriented lobbies such as the National Consumers League, civic clubs such as the National Municipal League, and associations oriented toward minority groups, such as the National Negro Business League and the Society of American Indians. Because they were not usually tied to either of the established political parties, these organizations made politics much more fragmented and issue focused than in earlier eras.

Although some cherished values of the rural-based Populist movement lingered—notably moral regeneration, political democracy, and antimonopolism—the prevailing values of the Progressive era were urban. The progressive quest for social justice, educational and legal reform, and streamlining of government drew on the urban-reform goals of the previous half-century. Formation of the National Municipal League in 1895 and the National Civic Federation in 1900 signaled the beginning of the new reform era. The National Municipal League served as a forum for debate on civic reform issues such as civil service, nonpartisan elections, and municipal ownership of public utilities. The National Civic Federation fostered discussion of

• *Important Events* •

1895	Booker T. Washington gives Atlanta Compromise speech	**1912**	Theodore Roosevelt runs for president on the Progressive (Bull Moose) ticket
1900	William McKinley reelected		Woodrow Wilson elected president
1901	McKinley assassinated; Theodore Roosevelt assumes the presidency	**1913**	Sixteenth Amendment ratified; legalizes federal income tax
1904	*Northern Securities* case dissolves railroad trust		Seventeenth Amendment ratified; provides for direct election of U.S. senators
	Theodore Roosevelt elected president		Underwood Tariff institutes income tax
1905–06	Niagara Falls Convention promotes more militant pursuit of African-American rights		Federal Reserve Act establishes central banking system
	Lochner v. *New York* revoked, removes limits on bakers' work hours	**1914**	Federal Trade Commission created to investigate unfair trade practices
	Hepburn Act tightens control over railroads		Clayton Anti-Trust Act outlaws monopolistic business practices
	Pure Food and Drug Act requires ingredient labels on patent medicines		Margaret Sanger indicted for sending articles on contraception through the mail
1908	William H. Taft elected president	**1916**	Wilson reelected
1909	NAACP founded		Federal Farm Loan Act provides credit to farmers
	Payne-Aldrich Tariff passed	**1919**	Eighteenth Amendment ratified; prohibits manufacture, sale, and transportation of alcoholic beverages
1910	Mann-Elkins Act reinforces ICC powers		
	White Slave Traffic Act prohibits transportation of women for "immoral purposes"	**1920**	Nineteenth Amendment ratified; gives women the vote in federal elections
	Ballinger-Pinchot controversy angers conservationists		

social reforms, such as workers' compensation and arbitration of labor disputes.

Organizations and individuals who accepted the three progressive themes—opposition to abuse of power, reform of social institutions, quest for cooperation and scientific efficiency—existed in almost all levels of society. But the new middle class of professional men and women formed the vanguard of reform. Offended by inefficiency and immorality in business, government, and human relations, these people set out to apply the scientific techniques they had learned in their professions to the problems of the larger society.

Motivated by personal indignation at corruption and injustice, many middle-class progressive reformers sought an end to abuses of power. Their views were voiced by journalists whom Theodore Roosevelt dubbed muckrakers (after a character in the medieval allegory *Pilgrim's Progress* who rejected a crown for a muckrake). Muckrakers fed the public's taste for scandal and sensation by investigating and attacking social, economic, and political wrongs. Their fact-filled articles and books exposed such offenses as adulterated foods, fraudulent insurance, and prostitution. Lincoln Steffens's articles in *McClure's*, later published as *The Shame of the Cities* (1904), ranked among the highlights. Steffens hoped his exposés of bosses' misrule would inspire mass outrage and ultimately reform. Other well-known muckraking efforts included Upton Sinclair's

The Jungle (1906), a novel that attacked the meat-packing industry, and Ida M. Tarbell's scathing history of Standard Oil (1904).

Middle-class indignation also expressed itself as opposition to party politics. Male political reformers deplored the bargaining and self-serving that they

Political Reformers

believed infected boss-ridden parties. (Women could not vote and therefore were seldom involved in these discussions.) To improve the political process, the progressives advocated nominating candidates through direct primaries instead of party caucuses and holding nonpartisan elections to prevent the fraud and bribery bred by party loyalties.

To make legislators more responsible, they advocated three reforms: the initiative, which would permit voters to propose new laws on their own; the referendum, which would enable voters to accept or reject a law; and the recall, which would allow voters to remove offending officials and judges from office before their terms were up. Their goal was efficiency: they would reclaim government by replacing the boss system with rational, accountable management chosen by a responsible electorate.

Middle-class progressive reformers recoiled from party politics but not from government. In fact, they turned to government for aid in achieving most of their goals, for they were convinced that only government offered the leverage they needed. Science and scientific method—planning, control, and predictability—were central to their values. Just as corporations applied scientific management to achieve economic efficiency, progressives favored using expertise and planning to achieve social and political efficiency.

The progressive spirit also stirred some elite business leaders. Certain successful executives supported some government regulation and political

Upper-Class Reformers

reforms to protect their interests from more radical political elements. Others were humanitarians who worked unselfishly for social justice. Business-dominated organizations like the Municipal Voters League and U.S. Chamber of Commerce supported limited political and economic reform. They aimed to stabilize society by running schools, hospitals,

and local government like efficient businesses. Elite women often led reform organizations like the Young Women's Christian Association, which aided growing numbers of unmarried working women, and the Women's Christian Temperance Union, which participated in numerous causes in addition to abstinence from drinking.

But not all progressive reformers were middle- or upper-class. Vital elements of what would become modern American liberalism grew out of the

Working-Class Reformers

working-class urban experience in this era. By 1900, many urban workers were pressing for government intervention to ensure safety and promote welfare. They wanted safe factories, shorter working hours, workers' compensation, better housing, health safeguards, and other "bread-and-butter" reforms. Often these were the same people who supported political bosses, supposedly the enemies of reform. Workers understood that bosses needed to cultivate allegiance among their constituents and thus would cater to everyday needs. In fact, bossism was not necessarily at odds with humanitarianism.

After 1900, voters from inner-city districts populated by working-class families elected a number of progressive legislators who had trained in the trenches of machine politics. The chief goal of these legislators was to have government take responsibility for alleviating hardships that resulted from urban-industrial growth. They opposed such reforms as prohibition, Sunday closing laws, civil service, and nonpartisan elections, all of which conflicted with their constituents' interests.

Some deeply frustrated workers wanted more than progressive reform; they wanted a different society. They turned to the socialist movement, a

Socialists

blend of immigrant intellectuals, industrial workers, disaffected Populists, miners, lumbermen, and some women's rights activists. The majority of socialists united behind Eugene V. Debs. Although Debs failed to develop a consistent program beyond opposition to war and bourgeois materialism, he was a spellbinding speaker for the radical cause. His speaking tours activated increasing numbers of disenchanted workers and intellectuals. As the Socialist party's presidential candidate, Debs won 400,000 votes in 1904, and in 1912, at the pinnacle of his and his party's career, he polled more than 900,000.

With stinging rebukes of exploitation and unfair privilege, Debs and other socialists made compelling overtures to reform-minded people. Some, such as Florence Kelley, joined the socialist cause. But most progressives avoided radical attacks on free enterprise. Municipal ownership of public utilities was as far as they would go toward fundamental change in the system. Indeed, progressives had too much at stake in the capitalist system to overthrow it.

It would be a mistake to assume that a progressive spirit captured all of American society between 1895 and 1920. Large numbers of people who were heavily represented in Congress disliked government interference in economic affairs—except to strengthen the tariff—and they found no fault with existing power structures. "Old-guard" Republicans like Senator Nelson W. Aldrich of Rhode Island and House Speaker Joseph Cannon of Illinois championed this ideology. Outside Washington, D.C., this outlook was represented by tycoons like J. P. Morgan, John D. Rockefeller, and E. H. Harriman who insisted that the most genuine progress would result from maintaining the profit incentive.

Progressive reformers operated from the center of the ideological spectrum. Moderate, socially aware, sometimes contradictory, they believed on the one hand that the laissez faire system was obsolete and on the other that a radical shift away from capitalism was dangerous. Like Jeffersonians, they believed in the conscience and will of the people; like Hamiltonians, they opted for a strong central government to act in the interests of conscience.

GOVERNMENTAL AND LEGISLATIVE REFORM

By the turn of the century, professionals and intellectuals were rejecting the traditional American view that government should be small and unobtrusive, concluding instead that government should exert more power to ensure justice and well-being. Increasingly aware of the ineffectiveness of a simple, inflexible government in a complex industrial age, they reasoned that public authority was needed to counteract inefficiency, corruption, and exploitation. But before reformers could effectively use such power, they would have to capture government from politicians whose greed had soiled the democratic system.

Reformers first attacked corruption in cities. Between 1870 and 1900, opponents of the boss system tried to restructure government through reforms such as civil service hiring, nonpartisan elections, and tighter scrutiny of public expenditures. After 1900, growing momentum for reform brought into being the city-manager and city-commission forms of government (in which urban officials were chosen for professional expertise rather than political connections) and public ownership of utilities (to prevent gas, electricity, and streetcar companies from profiting at the public's expense).

Reformers found, however, that the city was too small an arena for the changes they sought. State and federal governments offered more opportunities for enacting sweeping reform through legislation. Because of their faith in a strong fair-minded executive, progressives looked to governors and other elected officials to extend and protect reforms achieved at the local level.

The reform movement produced a number of skillful, influential, and charismatic governors who used executive power to achieve change. Their ranks included Braxton Bragg

Progressive Governors

Comer of Alabama and Hoke Smith of Georgia, who introduced business regulation and other reforms in the South; Albert Cummins of Iowa and Hiram Johnson of California, who battled the railroads that dominated their states; and Woodrow Wilson of New Jersey, whose administrative reforms were imitated by other governors. Such men were not saints, however. Smith, bowing to prevailing racist sentiments, supported disfranchisement of African-Americans, and Johnson promoted discrimination against Japanese-Americans.

The most forceful of the progressive governors was Wisconsin's Robert M. La Follette. A self-made small-town lawyer, La Follette rose through the ranks of the state Republican party and won the governorship in 1900. As governor, he initiated a multipronged reform program distinguished by direct primaries, more equitable taxes, and regulation of railroad rates. He also appointed numerous commissions staffed by experts, whose investigations supplied La Follette with the facts and figures he used in fiery speeches to arouse public support for his policies. After three terms as governor, La Follette was elected to the U.S. Senate and carried his progressive ideals into national politics.

Few state leaders were as successful as La Follette. To be sure, the crusade against corrupt politics did bring about some permanent changes. By 1916, all but three states had direct primaries, and many had adopted the initiative, referendum, and recall. Political reformers achieved one of their major goals in 1912 when the states ratified the Seventeenth Amendment, which provided for direct election of U.S. senators (formerly elected by state legislatures). But political reforms did not always help. Party bosses, better organized and more experienced than reformers, were still able to control elections. And political reformers also found that the courts aided entrenched power in the stifling of change.

New state laws aimed at promoting social welfare had greater effect, especially in factories, than did political reforms. Broadly interpreting their constitutional powers to protect **Progressive** the health and safety of their **Legislation** citizens, many states enacted ——— factory inspection laws, and by 1916 nearly two-thirds of the states required compensation for victims of industrial accidents. Under pressure from the National Child Labor Committee, nearly every state set a minimum age for employment (varying from twelve to sixteen) and prohibited employers from working children more than eight or ten hours a day. Such laws were, however, hard to enforce.

Several groups also joined forces to limit working hours for women. After the Supreme Court upheld Oregon's ten-hour limit in 1908, many more states passed laws protecting female workers. Meanwhile, in 1914 efforts of the American Association for Old Age Security showed signs of success when Arizona established old-age pensions. The courts

struck down the law, but demand for pensions did not diminish, and in the 1920s many states enacted laws to provide for needy elderly people.

Defenders of free enterprise opposed most of the new regulatory measures out of self-interest and fear that such government programs would undermine the individual initiative and competition that they believed to be the basis of the free market system. The National Association of Manufacturers coordinated the campaign against regulation of business and working conditions. And legislators friendly to special interests connived to weaken new laws by withholding the funds for their enforcement.

Reformers themselves were not always certain about what was progressive, especially in human behavior. The main question was whether it was possible to create a desirable **Moral Reform** moral climate through legisla- ——— tion. Some reformers, notably adherents of the Social Gospel movement, believed that only church-based inspiration and humanitarian work, rather than legislation, could transform society. Others believed that state intervention was necessary to enforce purity, especially in drinking habits and sexual behavior.

The Anti-Saloon League, formed in 1893, intensified the long-standing campaign against drunkenness and its costs to society. This organization joined forces with the Women's Christian Temperance Union (founded in 1873) to publicize the role of alcoholism in liver disease and other health problems. But the league was especially successful in shifting attention from the individual's responsibility for temperance to the alleged link between the drinking that saloons encouraged and the accidents, poverty, and threat to industrial productivity that were consequences of drinking. Consequently, many states, counties, towns, and city wards moved to restrict the sale and consumption of liquor. In 1918, prohibitionists induced Congress to pass the Eighteenth Amendment (ratified in 1919 and implemented in 1920) outlawing the manufacture, sale, and transportation of intoxicating liquors.

Public outrage erupted in another area when muckraking journalists charged that interstate and international rings kidnaped young women and forced them into prostitution, a practice called white slavery. Middle-class moralists, already alarmed by a perceived link between immigration and prostitution, and fearful that prostitutes were producing genetically inferior children, prodded governments to investigate the problem and recommend corrective legislation. In 1910, Congress passed the White Slave Traffic Act, known as the Mann Act, prohibiting interstate and international transportation of women for immoral purposes. By 1915, nearly every state had outlawed brothels and solicitation of sex.

Like prohibition, the Mann Act reflected growing sentiment that government could improve human behavior by restricting it. Reformers believed that the source of evil was not original sin or human nature but the social environment. And if evil was created by human beings, it followed that it could be eradicated by human effort.

NEW IDEAS IN EDUCATION, LAW, AND THE SOCIAL SCIENCES

While legislation anchored the reform impulse, equally important changes occurred in schools, courts, and settlement houses. The prevailing preoccupation with efficiency and scientific management challenged educators, judges, and social scientists to come to grips with the problems of modern mass society. New ways of thinking and new forms of social organization were necessary. Darwin's theory of evolution had undermined traditional beliefs in a God-created world, immigration had replaced social uniformity with diversity, and technology had made old habits of production and consumption obsolete. Thoughtful people in a number of professions grappled with how to respond to the new era yet preserve what was best from the past.

Reformers had long envisioned education as a means of bettering society. In 1883, psychologist G. Stanley Hall noted that the experiences of modern urban schoolchildren differed greatly from those of their farm-bred parents and grandparents. In the early nineteenth

Progressive Education

century, school curricula had consisted chiefly of moralistic pieties. *McGuffey's Reader*, used throughout the nation, contained homilies such as "By virtue we secure happiness." Hall and the influential educational philosopher John Dewey asserted that modern education ought to prepare children for productive citizenship and fulfilling lives. The development of the child, not the subject matter, should be the focus of the curriculum. Moreover, schools should serve as community centers and instruments of social progress. Above all, said Dewey, education must relate directly to experience; children should be encouraged to discover knowledge for themselves. Learning relevant to students' lives should replace rote memorization and outdated subjects.

Personal growth became the driving principle behind college education as well. The purpose of American colleges and universities had traditionally been to train a select few for the professions of law, medicine, teaching, and religion. But in the late 1800s, institutions of higher education multiplied, spurred by land grants and more people who could afford tuition. Furthermore, curricula expanded as educators sought to make learning attractive and to keep up with technological and social changes. Harvard University, under President Charles W. Eliot, pioneered in substituting electives for required courses and experimenting with new teaching methods.

Growth of Colleges and Universities

As colleges and universities expanded, so did their female enrollments. Between 1890 and 1920, the number of women in institutions of higher learning swelled from 56,000 to 283,000, accounting for 47 percent of total enrollment. These numbers disproved earlier objections that women were unfit for higher learning because they were mentally and physically inferior to men, but discrimination lingered in admissions and curriculum policies. Women were encouraged (indeed, they usually sought) to take home economics and education courses rather than science and mathematics, and most medical schools refused to admit women.

The legal profession also embraced a new emphasis on experience and scientific principles. Harvard law professor Roscoe Pound, an influential

**Progressive
Legal Thought**
———

proponent of the new point of view, urged that social reality should influence legal thinking. Oliver Wendell Holmes Jr., an associate justice of the Supreme Court between 1902 and 1932, led the attack on the traditional view of law as universal and unchanging. Holmes's view, that law should reflect society's needs, challenged the practice of invoking legal precedents in an inflexible way that often obstructed social legislation. Louis D. Brandeis, a brilliant lawyer who later joined Holmes on the Supreme Court, carried legal reform one step further by insisting that judges' opinions be based on factual, scientifically gathered information about social realities.

The new legal thinking met with some resistance. Judges raised on laissez faire economic theory and strict construction of the Constitution continued to overturn the laws progressives thought necessary for effective reform. Thus despite Holmes's forceful dissent, the Supreme Court in 1905 revoked a New York law limiting bakers' working hours (*Lochner* v. *New York*). As in similar cases, the Court's majority argued that the Fourteenth Amendment protected an individual's right to make contracts without government interference and that this protection superseded reform sentiments. Judges also weakened federal regulations by invoking the Tenth Amendment, which prohibited the federal government from interfering in matters reserved to the states.

The judiciary was not entirely reactionary during the Progressive era. Courts upheld some regulatory measures, particularly those protecting general public safety. A string of decisions beginning with *Holden* v. *Hardy* (1898), in which the Supreme Court upheld Utah's mining regulations, supported the use of state police powers to protect health, safety, and morals. Judges also affirmed federal police powers and Congress's authority over interstate commerce in sustaining such federal legislation as the Pure Food and Drug Act, the Meat Inspection Law, and the Mann Act.

But the concept of general welfare posed thorny legal problems. Even if one agreed that laws should address society's needs, whose needs should prevail? The United States was a mixed nation, and religion and ethnicity deeply influenced law. In many localities, a native-born white Protestant majority imposed Bible reading in public schools (offending Catholics and Jews), required business establishments to close on Sundays, prohibited interracial marriage, and enforced racial segregation. Holmes asserted that laws should be made for "people of fundamentally differing views," but were such laws possible in a nation of so many ethnic, racial, and religious interest groups?

Meanwhile, social scientists joined with physicians and organizations like the National Consumers League (NCL) to bring about some of the most far-reaching progressive reforms.

National Consumers League and Public Health Reform
———

Founded by Josephine Shaw, a socially prominent Massachusetts widow, the NCL initially focused on improving the wages and working conditions of young women employed in department stores. After Florence Kelley became the NCL's general secretary, the organization expanded its activities to encompass women's suffrage, protection of child laborers, and elimination of potential health hazards. Local branches supported such consumer protection measures as the licensing of food vendors and inspection of dairies. They also urged city governments to fund neighborhood clinics that provided health education and medical care to the poor. The NCL's efforts spurred a broad-based consumer- and health-awareness movement that has persisted to the present day.

Thus a new breed of men and women pressed for institutional change as well as political reform between the end of the nineteenth century and the First World War. Largely middle class in background, trained by new professional standards, confident that new ways of thinking could bring about progress, these people helped to broaden government's role in meeting the needs of a mature industrial society. Their questioning of prevailing assumptions extended beyond their immediate goals and unsettled conventional attitudes toward race and gender.

CHALLENGES TO RACIAL AND SEXUAL DISCRIMINATION

W. E. B. Du Bois, the forceful black scholar and writer, ended an essay in *The Souls of Black Folk* (1903) with a call that heralded the twentieth-century civil rights movement: "By every civilized and peaceful method," Du Bois wrote, "we must strive for the right which the world accords to men."

By *men*, Du Bois meant all free human beings, not just one gender. But his assertion expresses well the circumstances of the two largest groups of underprivileged Americans in the early 1900s: women and people of color. Both lived in a society dominated by native-born white males. Both experienced disfranchisement, discrimination, and humiliation. And for these groups the progressive challenge to entrenched ideas and customs gave impetus to their struggle for rights, but it posed a dilemma as well. Should women and people of color strive to become just like white men, with white men's values and power as well as their rights? Or was there something unique about their racial and sexual identities that should be preserved at the risk of sacrificing some gains? African-American leaders differed sharply over how—and whether—to pursue assimilation. In the wake of emancipation, ex-slave Frederick Douglass had urged "ultimate assimilation through self-assertion, and on no other terms." Those who favored isolation from cruel white society supported migration to Africa or the establishment of all-black communities in Oklahoma Territory and Kansas. Others advocated militancy, believing, as one writer stated, "Our people must die to be saved and in dying must take as many along with them as it is possible to do with the aid of firearms and all other weapons."

Most blacks, however, could neither escape nor conquer white society. They had to find other routes to economic and social improvement. Self-help, a strategy articulated by educator Booker T. Washing-

Booker T. Washington
—

ton, was one of the most popular alternatives. Born to slave parents in 1856, Washington worked his way through school and in 1881 founded Tuskegee Institute in Alabama, a vocational school for blacks. There, he developed the philosophy that blacks' best hopes for assimilation lay in at least temporarily accommodating whites. Rather than fighting for political rights, he said, blacks should work hard, acquire property, and prove they were worthy of their rights. Washington

voiced his views in a widely acclaimed speech at the Atlanta Exposition in 1895, a speech that became known as the Atlanta Compromise. Whites, including progressives, welcomed Washington's policy of accommodation, because it urged patience and reminded black people to stay in their place.

But Booker T. Washington seemed to some blacks to favor second-class citizenship. In 1905, a group of "anti-Bookerites" convened near Niagara

W. E. B. Du Bois
—

Falls and pledged a more militant pursuit of such rights as unrestricted voting, equal economic opportunity, integration, and equality before the law. The spokesperson for the Niagara movement was W. E. B. Du Bois, an outspoken critic of the Atlanta Compromise. A New Englander with a Ph.D. from Harvard, Du Bois was both a progressive and a member of the black elite. He held an undergraduate degree from all-black Fisk University and had studied in Germany, where he learned about scientific investigation. Du Bois compiled rigorous fact-filled sociological studies of black ghetto dwellers and wrote poetically in support of civil rights. Du Bois treated Washington politely, but he could not accept white domination. Moreover, Du Bois could not accept disfranchisement, because he believed that the vote was essential to the protection of social and economic rights.

Du Bois demonstrated that accommodation was an unrealistic strategy, but his own solution may have been just as fanciful. A blunt elitist, Du Bois believed that an intellectual vanguard of cultivated, highly trained blacks, the "Talented Tenth," would save the race by setting an example to whites and uplifting other blacks. Such sentiment had more appeal for middle-class white liberals than for African-American sharecroppers. Thus in 1909, when Du Bois and his allies formed the National Association for the Advancement of Colored People (NAACP), which aimed to end racial discrimination by pursuing legal redress in the courts, the leadership consisted chiefly of white progressives.

Whatever their views, African-Americans faced continued oppression. Indeed, under the administration of Woodrow Wilson, discrimination within the federal government expanded—southern cabinet members supported racial separation in rest

During the Progressive era, African-Americans struggled to partake of the various advances in the reform of society. Part of the struggle involved their assertion of ability in science and economics. This photograph, taken at the surgical amphitheater of the Moorland-Spingarn Research Center at all-black Howard University, shows African-American medical personnel learning and performing medical skills.   Moorland-Spingarn Research Center, Howard University, Howard University Archives.

rooms, restaurants, and government office buildings, and they balked at hiring black workers.

Even as laws and social customs prevented blacks from becoming full-fledged citizens, they continued to seek to fulfill the American dream of success. Many, however, wondered whether their goals should include membership in a corrupt white society. Du Bois voiced these doubts poignantly, writing that "one ever feels his twoness—an American, a Negro, two souls, two thoughts, two unreconciled strivings, two warring ideals in one dark body." Somehow, blacks would have to reconcile that "twoness" by combining racial pride with national identity.

The dilemma of identity haunted Native Americans as well, but it had an added dimension of tribal loyalty. Since the 1880s, Native American reformers had belonged to white-led Indian organizations. In 1911, educated middle-class Indian men and women formed their own association, the Society of American Indians (SAI). SAI worked for better education, civil rights, and health care. It also sponsored American Indian Days to cultivate native pride and offset the Anglo images of tribal peoples promulgated in Wild West shows.

The SAI's emphasis on racial pride, however, was squeezed between pressures for assimilation from one side and tribal allegiance on the other. Its small membership did not genuinely represent the diverse and unconnected nations and tribes, and its attempt to establish a governing body representing all of them faltered. At the same time, the goal of achieving acceptance in white society proved elusive, and attempts to redress grievances through legal action bogged down for lack of funds. Ultimately, the SAI had to rely on rhetoric and moral exhortation, which had little effect on poor and powerless Indians. Torn by doubts and internal disputes, the association folded in the early 1920s.

During the same period, the progressive challenge to established social assumptions also stirred women to seek liberation from the confines of hearth and home. Their struggle raised questions of identity like those faced by blacks: what tactics should women use to achieve equality, and what should be their role in society? Could women achieve equality with men and at the same time change male-dominated society? Answers involved a subtle but important shift in women's politics. Before about 1910, those engaged in the quest for women's rights referred to themselves as "the woman movement." They used the label to characterize middle-class women striving to move beyond the home into social welfare activities, higher education, and paid labor. Like some African-American and Indian leaders, they argued that legal and voting rights were indispensable accompaniments to such moves. These women's rights advocates based their claims on the theory that women's special, even superior, traits as guardians of family and morality would humanize all of society.

"The Woman Movement"

The women's club movement represented a uniquely female dimension of Progressive era reform. Originating as literary and educational organizations, women's clubs consisted of middle-class women who began taking stands on public affairs in the late 1800s. Because they were excluded from holding office, these reformers were drawn less to efforts to revise government than to drives for social betterment. Rather than pressing for reforms such as trustbusting and direct primaries, women tended to work for goals such as factory inspection, regulation of children's and women's labor, housing reform, upgrading of education, and pure food and drug laws. Such efforts were not confined to white women. The National Association of Colored Women, founded in 1895, was the nation's first African-American social service organization; it concentrated on establishing nurseries, kindergartens, and retirement homes.

Women's Clubs

Around 1910, some of those concerned with women's place in society began using a new term, *feminism*, to refer to their efforts. Whereas members of the woman movement spoke of duties and moral purity, feminists, more explicitly conscious of their identity as women, spoke of rights and self-development. Feminism focused in particular on economic and sexual independence. Charlotte Perkins Gilman articulated feminist goals in *Women and Economics* (1898), declaring that domesticity and female innocence were obsolete and attacking the male monopoly on economic opportunity. Gilman argued that women must enter the modern age by taking paid jobs in industry and the professions.

Feminism

Feminists also supported what they called sex rights, or a single standard of social behavior for men and women in conjunction with recognition of women's sexual drives. A number of feminists joined the birth-control movement led by Margaret Sanger. As a visiting nurse in New York's East Side immigrant neighborhoods, Sanger distributed information about contraception, in hopes of preventing unwanted pregnancies and their tragic consequences among poor women. Sanger's crusade won the support of middle-class women who wanted both to limit their own families and to control the growth of immigrant masses. It also aroused the opposition of those who saw birth control as a threat to the family and to morality. In 1914, Sanger's opponents caused her to be indicted for defying an 1873 law that prohibited the sending of obscene literature (articles on contraception) through the mails, and she was forced to flee the country for a year. Sanger persevered and in 1921 formed the American Birth Control League, which enlisted physicians and social workers to convince judges to allow distribution of birth-control information. Most states still prohibited the sale of contraceptives, but Sanger had succeeded in introducing the issue into the realm of public discussion.

Feminist debates about work and class pervaded the suffrage movement, which achieved victory in 1920 when enough states ratified the Nineteenth Amendment to give women the vote in federal elections. Until the 1890s, the suffrage crusade was led by elite women who believed that the political system needed more participation by refined and educated people like themselves and that working-class

Women's Suffrage

BIRTH CONTROL REVIEW

Edited by Margaret Sanger

TWENTY CENTS A COPY   NOVEMBER, 1923   TWO DOLLARS A YEAR

Official Organ of
THE AMERICAN BIRTH CONTROL LEAGUE, INC., 104 FIFTH AVENUE, NEW YORK CITY

How do historians know

about Margaret Sanger and the birth-control movement of the Progressive era? The issue of unwanted pregnancy has long vexed American women, families, and all of society. In the early 1900s, the issue was fraught with moral and social controversy. Would common practice of birth control violate God's law and promote promiscuity? If women intentionally reduced the numbers of children born, would the American population eventually fail to replace itself or, as Theodore Roosevelt termed it, experience "race death"? Margaret Sanger, a young socialist and feminist mother of three living in New York City's Greenwich Village, did not believe so. She saw women dying from self-induced abortions, and she had been warned that she could die if she were to become pregnant again. Her response was to promote birth control (a term she first used in 1914) as a means of helping women, especially poor working-class women, to make choices about bearing children. After being forced to flee government prosecution for her ideas, Sanger returned to the United States and in 1916 organized the New York Birth Control League to lobby for the prerogative of physicians to advise women about contraception. In 1921, the movement nationalized when Sanger formed the American Birth Control League and began selling the "Birth Control Review," which contained articles on the medical, as well as the social, issues involved in contraception. Photo: The Schlesinger Library, Radcliffe College.

women would defer to better-educated women on political matters. But the younger generation of feminists ardently opposed this logic. To them, achievement rather than wealth and refinement was the best criterion for public influence. Thus women should exercise the vote not to increase the role of elites in public life but to promote and protect women's economic roles. This rationale implicitly (and sometimes explicitly) advocated that all women work for pay, especially outside the home.

Despite internal differences, suffragists achieved some successes. Nine states, all in the West, allowed women to vote in state and local elections by 1912, and women continued to press for national suffrage. Their tactics ranged from the moderate but persistent propaganda campaigns of the National American Woman Suffrage Association, led by Carrie Chapman Catt, to the open-air meetings and marches of the National Woman's party, led by feminist Alice Paul. All these activities heightened public awareness. More decisive, however, were women's efforts during the First World War as factory laborers, medical volunteers, and municipal workers. By convincing legislators that women could shoulder public responsibilities, women's wartime contributions gave final impetus to passage of the suffrage amendment.

The activities of women's clubs, suffragists, and feminists failed to create an interest group united or powerful enough to dent the political, economic, and social ascendancy of men. Like blacks, women knew that voting rights meant little until people's attitudes changed. The Progressive era helped women to clarify the issues that concerned them, but major reforms would have to await a later era.

THEODORE ROOSEVELT AND THE REVIVAL OF THE PRESIDENCY

The Progressive era's theme of reform—in politics, institutions, and social relations—drew attention to government, especially the federal government, as the foremost agent of change. At first, however, the federal government seemed incapable of assuming such responsibility. Dominated by two political parties that resembled private clubs more than bodies of statesmen, the federal government acted mainly on behalf of special interests when it acted at all. Then, in September 1901, the political climate suddenly changed. The assassination of President William McKinley vaulted Theodore Roosevelt, the vice president, into the White House.

Political manager Mark Hanna had warned fellow Republicans against nominating Roosevelt for the vice presidency in 1900. "Don't any of you realize," Hanna asked after the nominating convention, "that there's only one life between that madman and the presidency?" As governor of New York, Roosevelt had angered state Republican bosses by showing sympathy for regulatory legislation, so they had rid themselves of their pariah by pushing him into national politics.

As president, Roosevelt came to conclusions about the role of government similar to those reached by progressives. His sense of history convinced him that the small government Jefferson had envisioned would not suffice in the industrial era. Instead, economic development necessitated a Hamiltonian system of government powerful enough to guide national affairs. Like his progressive supporters, Roosevelt believed in the wisdom and talents of a select few whose superior backgrounds and education qualified them to coordinate public and private enterprise.

Theodore Roosevelt

Roosevelt became a hero, attracting the loyal support of those who believed his progressivism was heartfelt. In action, though, he deviated from the progressive path. His brash patriotism, admiration for big business, and dislike of anything he considered effeminate recalled the previous era of unbridled expansion, when raw power prevailed in social and economic affairs.

The federal regulation of economic affairs that has characterized twentieth-century American history began with Roosevelt's presidency. Roosevelt turned his attention first to big business. The combination movement had produced giant trusts that controlled almost every sector of the economy. Although Roosevelt won a reputation as a trustbuster, he actually considered consolidation the most efficient means to achieve material progress. Rather than tolerate uncontrolled competition, he believed in distinguishing between good and bad trusts and preventing bad ones from manipulating markets. Thus he instructed the Justice Department to use antitrust laws to prosecute the railroad, meat-packing, and oil trusts, which he believed had unscrupulously exploited the public.

Regulation of Trusts

Roosevelt's policy triumphed in 1904 when the Supreme Court, convinced by the government's arguments, ordered the breakup of the Northern

Securities Company, the huge railroad combination created by J. P. Morgan and his powerful business allies. In general, however, Roosevelt favored cooperation between business and government and the placing of pressure on business to regulate itself.

Roosevelt also pushed for regulatory legislation—especially after his resounding electoral victory in 1904, in which he won the votes of progressives and businesspeople alike. After a year of wrangling with business lobbyists in Congress, Roosevelt persuaded Congress to pass the Hepburn Act (1906), which imposed stricter control over railroads. The act gave the Interstate Commerce Commission (ICC) more authority to set railroad rates (although it did allow the courts to overturn rate decisions).

As he had done in securing passage of the Hepburn Act, Roosevelt showed a willingness to compromise on legislation to ensure the purity of food and drugs. Reformers had been

Pure Food and Drug Laws
———

urging government regulation of patent medicines and processed meat for decades. Public outrage at fraud and adulteration heightened in 1906 when Upton Sinclair published *The Jungle*, a fictionalized exposé of Chicago meat-packing plants. On reading the novel, Roosevelt ordered an investigation. Finding Sinclair's descriptions accurate, the president supported the Meat Inspection Act, which passed in 1906. Like the Hepburn Act, this law reinforced the principle of government regulation. But as part of the compromise to obtain its passage, the government had to pay for inspections, and meat packers could appeal adverse decisions in court.

The Pure Food and Drug Act (1906) addressed consumer abuses by the patent medicine industry. Makers of various tonics and pills were not only making wild claims about the effects of their products but also liberally using alcohol and narcotics as ingredients. Ads in popular publications claimed that such medicines had "cure-all" qualities. Although the Pure Food and Drug Act did not ban such products, it did require the use of labels listing the ingredients—a goal consistent with the progressives' confidence that if the people knew the truth, they would act on it and stop buying these medicines.

Roosevelt's approach to labor issues resembled his stance toward business. When the United Mine

Workers in Pennsylvania called a strike against coal mine owners in 1902 in pursuit of an eight-hour day and higher pay, the president employed the progressive tactics of investigation and arbitration. Owners stubbornly refused to recognize the union or arbitrate grievances. As winter approached and fuel shortages threatened, Roosevelt warned that he would use federal troops to reopen the mines and thus force management to accept arbitration of the dispute by a special commission. The commission decided in favor of higher wages and reduced hours and required management to deal with grievance committees elected by the miners, but it did not require recognition of the union. The decision, according to Roosevelt, provided a "square deal" for all. The settlement also embodied Roosevelt's belief that the president or his representatives should have a say in which labor demands were legitimate and which were not.

In matters of conservation and the environment, Roosevelt employed the same mix of flamboyant executive action and quiet compromise. He built a

Conservation and the Environment
———

reputation as a determined conservationist, using presidential authority to add almost 150 million acres to the national forests and to preserve vast areas of water and coal from private plunder. In 1902, he influenced passage of the National (Newlands) Reclamation Act, which set aside proceeds from western public land sales for the purpose of financing irrigation projects. True to the progressive spirit of efficiency, Roosevelt wanted a "well-conceived plan" for resource management—that is, for ordered growth rather than preservation of nature as it was. But compromises and factors beyond his control weakened his scheme. Timber and mining companies evaded supervision of their wasteful practices, and Congress never authorized enough funds to enforce regulations.

During his last year in office, Roosevelt drew away from the Republican party's traditional friendliness to big business. He lashed out at the irresponsibility of "malefactors of great wealth" and supported stronger regulation of business and heavier taxation of the rich. Having promised that he would not seek reelection, Roosevelt backed his friend William Howard Taft, secretary of war, for the nomination in 1908, hoping that Taft would continue to pursue Roosevelt's initiatives. Democrats nominated William Jennings Bryan for the third time, but "the Great Commoner" lost again.

Early in 1909, Roosevelt went to Africa to shoot game (he saw no contradiction between hunting and conservation), leaving Taft to face political problems that his pre-

Taft Administration

decessor had managed to postpone. Foremost among them was the tariff; rates had risen to excessive levels. Honoring Taft's pledge to cut rates, the House passed a bill sponsored by Representative Sereno E. Payne of New York that provided for numerous downward revisions. Protectionists in the Senate prepared to amend the House bill and revise rates upward. But Senate progressives, led by La Follette, organized a stinging attack on the tariff for benefiting vested interests. Taft was caught between reformers who claimed to be preserving Roosevelt's antitrust campaign and protectionists who still controlled the Republican party. In the end, Senator Aldrich and other protectionists restored many of the tariff cuts the Payne bill had made, and Taft signed what became known as the Payne-Aldrich Tariff. In the eyes of many progressives, Taft had failed the test of filling Roosevelt's shoes.

The progressive and conservative wings of the Republican party were rapidly drifting apart. Soon after the tariff controversy, a group of insurgents in the House mounted a challenge to Speaker "Uncle Joe" Cannon of Illinois, whose power over committee assignments and the scheduling of debates could make or break a piece of legislation. Taft first supported and then abandoned the insurgents, who nevertheless managed to liberalize procedures by enlarging the influential Rules Committee and removing selection of its members from Cannon's control. Taft also angered conservationists by allowing Secretary of the Interior Richard A. Ballinger to remove one million acres of forest and mineral land from the reserved list and to fire Gifford Pinchot when he protested a questionable sale of coal lands in Alaska.

In reality, Taft was as sympathetic to reform as Roosevelt was. He prosecuted more trusts than Roosevelt, expanded the national forest reserves, signed the Mann-Elkins Act of 1910 bolstering the regulatory powers of the ICC, and supported such labor reforms as the eight-hour day and mine safety legislation. The Sixteenth Amendment, which legalized a federal income tax, and the Seventeenth Amendment, which provided for the direct election of U.S. senators, were initiated during Taft's presidency (and ratified in 1913). Like Roosevelt, Taft was forced to compromise with big business, but unlike Roosevelt he lacked the ability to maneuver and publicize his positions.

In 1910, when Roosevelt returned from Africa, he found his party worn and tormented. Reformers angered by Taft's apparent insensitivity to their cause formed the National Progressive Republican League and rallied behind Robert La Follette for president in 1912. Another wing of the party remained loyal to Taft. Disappointed by Taft's performance, Roosevelt soon began to speak out and to rekindle public attention. When La Follette became ill early in 1912, Roosevelt, proclaiming himself fit as a "bull moose," threw his hat in the ring for the Republican presidential nomination.

Taft's supporters controlled the convention and nominated him for a second term, but Roosevelt forces formed a third party—the Progressive or Bull Moose party—and nominated the fifty-three-year-old former president. Meanwhile, it took Democrats forty-six ballots to select as their candidate New Jersey's progressive governor Woodrow Wilson. The Socialists, by now an organized and growing party, again nominated Eugene V. Debs.

WOODROW WILSON AND THE EXTENSION OF REFORM

Wilson won the election of 1912 with 42 percent of the popular vote—he was a minority president, although he did capture 435 of 531 electoral votes. Roosevelt received about 27 percent of the popular vote. Taft finished a poor third, polling 23 percent of the popular vote and only 8 electoral votes. Debs won 902,000 votes, or 6 percent of the total, but no electoral votes. Fully three-quarters of the electorate thus supported some alternative to the restrained approach to government that Taft represented.

Sharp debate over the fundamentals of progressive government had characterized the campaign. Roosevelt had offered voters a system called the New Nationalism. Roosevelt foresaw a new era of national unity in which governmental authority would coordinate and regulate economic activity. He would not destroy big business, which he saw as an efficient way to organize production. Instead, he would establish regulatory commissions, groups of experts who would protect citizens' interests and ensure wise use of concentrated economic power.

The New Nationalism and the New Freedom

Wilson offered a more idealistic scheme in the New Freedom. He believed that concentrated economic power threatened individual liberty and that monopolies had to be broken up so that the marketplace could again become genuinely open. But he did not want to restore laissez faire. Like Roosevelt, Wilson proposed to enhance governmental authority to protect and regulate. Wilson, however, stopped short of advocating the cooperation between business and government inherent in Roosevelt's New Nationalism.

Roosevelt and Wilson stood closer together than their rhetoric implied. Both men strongly supported equality of opportunity (although chiefly for white men), conservation of natural resources, fair wages, and social betterment for all classes. And neither would hesitate to expand the scope of government activity through strong personal leadership and bureaucratic reform. Thus, although he received a minority of the total vote in 1912, Wilson could interpret the election results as a popular mandate to subdue trusts and broaden the federal government's role in social reform.

As president, Wilson found it necessary to blend New Freedom commitment to competition with New Nationalism regulation, and in so doing he set the direction of federal economic policy for much of the twentieth century. The corporate merger movement had proceeded so far that restoration of free competition proved impossible. Thus Wilson could only acknowledge economic concentration and try to pre-

Wilson's Policy on Business Regulation

Looking sober and stubborn, Woodrow Wilson (1856–1924) used a preacher's moralism and an academic's reasoning to raise citizens' expectations for the fulfillment of his idealistic promises.   National Portrait Gallery, Smithsonian Institution. Transfer from the National Museum of American Art, Gift of the City of New York through the National Art Committee, 1923.

vent abuses by expanding government's regulatory powers. His administration moved toward that end with passage in 1914 of the Clayton Anti-Trust Act and a bill creating the Federal Trade Commission (FTC). The Clayton Act extended the Sherman Anti-Trust Act of 1890 by outlawing quasi-monopolistic practices such as price discrimination (efforts to destroy competition by lowering prices in some regions but not others) and interlocking directorates (management of two or more competing companies by the same executives). The FTC was to investigate corporations and issue cease-and-desist orders against unfair trade practices. As in ICC rulings, accused companies could appeal FTC orders in the courts. Nevertheless, the FTC represented a further step in consumer protection.

Wilson broadened federal regulation of finance with the Federal Reserve Act of 1913, which established the nation's first central banking system since Andrew Jackson had destroyed the Second Bank of the United States. Twelve new district banks were created to hold the reserves of member banks throughout the nation. (The act created many banks rather than one to allay the agrarian fear of a monolithic eastern banking power.) The district banks would loan money to member banks at a low interest rate called the discount rate. By adjusting this rate, district banks could increase or decrease the amount of money in circulation. In other words, depending on the nation's needs, the reserve bank could loosen or tighten credit. Monetary affairs would no longer depend on the supply of gold, and interest rates would be fairer, especially for small borrowers.

Perhaps the only act of Wilson's first administration that promoted free competition was the Underwood Tariff, passed in 1913. Rising prices had for years thwarted consumers' desires for the material benefits of the industrial age. Some prices were unnaturally high, because tariffs had discouraged the importation of less-expensive foreign materials and manufactured products. By drastically reducing or eliminating tariff rates, the Underwood Tariff encouraged imports. To replace revenues that were lost because of the reductions, the act levied a graduated income tax on U.S. residents—an option made possible when the Sixteenth Amendment was ratified earlier that year. The income tax was tame by today's standards. Incomes of less than $4,000 were exempt—almost all factory workers and farmers escaped taxation. Individuals and corporations earning $4,000 to $20,000 had to pay a 1 percent tax, and rates for higher incomes rose gradually to a maximum of 6 percent on earnings of more than $500,000.

Tariff and Tax Reform

The outbreak of the First World War in 1914 and the approaching presidential campaign prompted Wilson to support stronger reforms in 1916. Concerned that farmers needed a better system of long-term mortgage credit to sustain production, the president backed the Federal Farm Loan Act. This measure created twelve federally supported banks that would lend money at moderate interest to farmers who belonged to credit institutions. To stave off railroad strikes that might disrupt transportation at a time of national emergency, Wilson pushed passage of the Adamson Act, which mandated an eight-hour day and time-and-a-half overtime pay for railroad laborers. Finally, Wilson courted the support of social reformers by backing laws that outlawed child labor and provided workers' compensation for federal employees who suffered work-related injuries or illness.

In selecting a candidate to oppose Wilson in 1916, Republicans snubbed Theodore Roosevelt, who wanted the nomination, in favor of Charles Evans Hughes, a Supreme Court justice and former reform governor of New York. Acutely aware of the influence of the First World War on national affairs, Wilson ran on a platform of peace, progressivism, and preparedness, and his supporters used the campaign slogan "He Kept Us Out of War." Hughes and his fractured party could not muzzle Roosevelt, whose bellicose speeches suggested that Republicans would drag Americans into the world war. Wilson received 9.1 million votes to Hughes's 8.5 million, and the president barely won the electoral college—by 277 to 254.

Election of 1916

U.S. involvement in the First World War during Wilson's second term brought about a shift away from competition and toward interest group politics and government regulation. During his first term, Wilson had become convinced that regulatory commissions, which could easily fall under the influence of the very interests they were meant to regulate, should not govern social and economic behavior. The war effort, he came to believe, required government coordination of production, and cooperation between the public and private sectors.

By 1920, a quarter-century of reform had wrought momentous changes. Government, economy, and society as they had existed in the nineteenth century were gone forever. The progressives had established the principle of government intervention to ensure fairness, health, and safety for all citizens. Public concern over poverty and injustice had risen to new heights. But for every American who suffered some form of deprivation, three or four enjoyed unprecedented material comforts, and amid growing affluence reformers could not sustain their efforts indefinitely. Although progressive values lingered and even spread after the First World War, a mass consumer society had begun to refocus people's attention from reform to materialism.

The Progressive era was characterized by multiple and sometimes contradictory goals. By no means was there a single progressive movement. Reform programs on the national level ranged from Roosevelt's New Nationalism, with its faith in big government as a coordinator of big business, to Wilson's New Freedom, with its promise to dissolve economic concentrations and legislate open competition. At the state and local levels, reformers pursued causes as varied as neighborhood improvement, government reorganization, public ownership of utilities, betterment of working conditions, and moral revival.

The failure of many progressive initiatives testifies to the strength of opposition to reform, as well as to weaknesses within the reform movements. Courts asserted constitutional and liberty-of-contract maxims in striking down some key progressive legislation, notably the federal law prohibiting child labor. In states and cities, adoption of the initiative, referendum, and recall did not encourage greater participation in government as had been hoped; those mechanisms were either seldom used or became tools of special interests. On the federal level, regulatory agencies rarely had enough resources for thorough investigations; they had to obtain information from the companies they were meant to police. Progressives thus failed in many respects to redistribute power. In 1920, as in 1900, government remained under the influence of business and industry.

Yet the numerous reform movements that characterized the Progressive era did refashion the nation's future. Trustbusting, however faulty, forced industrialists to become more sensitive to public opinion, and insurgents in Congress partially diluted the power of dictatorial politicians. Progressive legislation equipped government with tools to protect consumers against price fixing and dangerous products. The income tax became a means for building government revenues and redistributing wealth. And perhaps most important, progressives challenged old ways of thinking: although the questions they raised about the quality of American life remained largely unresolved, they made the nation more acutely aware of its principles and its promise.

SUGGESTIONS FOR FURTHER READING

General

Richard Abrams, *The Burden of Progress* (1978); Arthur Ekirch, *Progressivism in America* (1974); Richard Hofstadter, *The Age of Reform: From Bryan to FDR* (1955); Morton Keller, *Regulating a New Economy* (1990); Gabriel Kolko, *The Triumph of Conservatism* (1963); David W. Noble, *The Progressive Mind*, rev. ed. (1981); Robert Wiebe, *The Search for Order* (1968).

Legislative Issues and Reform Groups

Allen F. Davis, *Spearheads for Reform: The Social Settlements and the Progressive Movement, 1890–1914* (1967); Ruth Rosen, *The Lost Sisterhood: Prostitution in America, 1900–1918* (1982); James H. Timberlake, *Prohibition and the Progressive Crusade* (1963); James Harvey Young, *Pure Food: Securing the Federal Food and Drug Act of 1906* (1989). (For works on socialism, see the listings under Currents of Protest at the end of Chapter 20.)

Education, Law, and the Social Sciences

Jerold S. Auerback, *Unequal Justice: Lawyers and Social Change in Modern America* (1976); Lawrence Cremin, *The Transformation of the School: Progressivism in American Education* (1961); Paula S. Fass, *Outside In: Minorities and the Transformation of American Education* (1989); Lynn D. Gordon, *Gender and Higher Education in the Progressive Era* (1990); Lawrence Veysey, *The Emergence of the American University* (1970).

Women

Ruth Borden, *Women and Temperance* (1980); Nancy F. Cott, *The Grounding of American Feminism* (1987); Carl N. Degler, *At Odds: Women and the Family in America* (1980); Linda Gordon, *Woman's Body, Woman's Right: A Social History of Birth Control in America* (1976); Alice Kessler-Harris, *Out to Work: A History of Wage-Earning Women in the United States* (1982); Robyn Muncy, *Creating a Female Dominion in American Reform* (1991); William L. O'Neill, *Everyone Was Brave: The Rise and Fall of Feminism in America* (1969); Rosalind Rosenberg, *Beyond Separate Spheres: Intellectual Roots of Modern Feminism* (1982).

African-Americans

George Frederickson, *The Black Image in the White Mind* (1971); Louis R. Harlan, *Booker T. Washington: The Making of a Black Leader, 1856–1901* (1972); Charles F. Kellogg, *NAACP* (1970); Elliot M. Rudwick, *W. E. B. Du Bois* (1969).

Roosevelt, Taft, and Wilson

Francis L. Broderick, *Progressivism at Risk: Electing a President in 1912* (1989); Paolo E. Coletta, *The Presidency of William Howard Taft* (1973); John Milton Cooper Jr., *The Warrior and the Priest: Woodrow Wilson and Theodore Roosevelt* (1983); Lewis Gould, *The Presidency of Theodore Roosevelt* (1991); August Heckscher, *Woodrow Wilson* (1991).

The Quest for Empire, 1865–1914

I N JANUARY 1893, MEMBERS of Hawaii's white American elite, who had been plotting against Queen Liliuokalani, made their treasonous move. The Americans constituted less than 10 percent of Hawaii's population but owned about three-fourths of the islands' wealth. They derived their wealth mostly from the cultivation of sugar cane and fruit.

Because diseases brought by foreigners had diminished the native population, causing a labor shortage, the American oligarchy imported Chinese and Japanese workers for the expanding sugar industry. By 1890, native Hawaiians accounted for only 40 percent of the islands' population. Hawaii became a multiracial society dominated by white Americans who subordinated its economy to that of the United States through sugar exports that entered the American marketplace duty free.

Many native Hawaiians joined King Kalakaua in the 1870s and 1880s in resisting the "grasping" foreigners, who were organizing secret clubs and military units to contest the royal government. In 1887, the American conspirators forced the king to accept a new constitution—the so-called Bayo-

net Constitution—which granted foreigners the right to vote and shifted decision-making authority from the monarchy to the legislature. The same year, Hawaii empowered the United States to develop Pearl Harbor.

The McKinley Tariff of 1890 created an economic crisis for Hawaii that further undermined the native government. The tariff eliminated Hawaiian sugar's favored status by admitting all foreign sugar to the United States duty free. The measure also provided a bounty of 2 cents a pound to domestic U.S. growers, making it possible for them to sell their sugar at a price lower than that charged for foreign sugar. With the new competition from other foreign producers and the advantage for U.S. producers, planters and their allies in Hawaii suffered declining profits. To relieve their economic woes, prominent Americans in Hawaii soon pressed for annexation of the Hawaiian Islands to the United States so that their sugar would be classified as domestic rather than foreign.

When Kalakaua's sister Princess Liliuokalani assumed the throne upon his death in 1891, "they were lying in wait," she remembered. In collusion with the chief U.S. diplomat in Hawaii, John L. Stevens, the conspirators struck in January 1893— but only after U.S. troops from the warship *Boston* had occupied key sites in Honolulu. The queen reluctantly surrendered to what she acknowledged as the "superior force" of the United States, but she refused to deal with the new regime headed by Sanford B. Dole, son of missionaries and a prominent attorney. On February 1, with Stevens's blessing, the American flag was raised over the Government Building in Honolulu.

Seizing foreign opportunities was common practice for those who governed the United States. In the early nineteenth century, Americans had purchased Louisiana; annexed Florida, Oregon, and Texas; pushed Indians out of the path of white migration westward; seized California and other western areas from Mexico; and acquired the Gadsden Purchase. Since the founding of the Republic, moreover, they had developed a lucrative foreign trade with most of the world.

From the Civil War to the First World War, the United States became one of the world's premier expansionist nations, ultimately building, managing, and protecting an overseas empire. The international system at the time was becoming multipolar, with several countries sharing power in an age of active imperialism throughout the world. Germany rose to challenge a declining Great Britain, the economic and military giant of the world; Japan in Asia and the United States in Latin America emerged as regional powers. The U.S. empire ultimately stretched from Latin America to Asia but not without opposition. Proud nationalists, commercial competitors, and other imperial nations tried to block the spread of U.S. influence, while anti-imperialists at home stimulated a momentous debate over the fundamental course of American foreign policy.

Most Americans applauded *expansionism*—the outward movement of goods, ships, dollars, people, and ideas—as a traditional feature of their nation's history. But many became uneasy whenever expansionism gave way to *imperialism*—the imposition of control over other peoples. Imperial control could be imposed either formally (by annexation, colonialism, or military occupation) or informally (by economic domination, political manipulation, or

the threat of intervention). As the informal methods indicate, imperialism did not necessarily mean the taking of territory.

Critics disparaged territorial imperialism as unbefitting the United States, and they opposed joining other great powers in the scramble for colonies in Asia and Africa. Would not an overseas territorial empire, with lands and peoples not contiguous to the United States, undermine institutions at home, invite perpetual war, and violate honored principles? Most Americans endorsed economic expansion as essential to the nation's prosperity and security, but anti-imperialists drew the line between expansionism and imperialism: profitable and fair trade relationships, yes; exploitation, no. And, some advised, American business activity abroad should not draw the United States into unwanted diplomatic crises and wars. But it did.

In the late nineteenth century, the federal government sometimes failed to fund adequately the vehicles of expansion, and most businessmen ignored foreign commerce in favor of the dynamic domestic marketplace. Still, the direction of American foreign policy after the Civil War became unmistakable: Americans intended to exert their influence beyond the continental United States, to reach for more land, more markets, and more international power. A pattern of accelerating activity abroad culminated in the tumultuous decade of the 1890s, when doubters' voices were drowned out by calls for war and foreign territory.

THE DOMESTIC ROOTS OF EXPANSIONISM AND EMPIRE

Foreign policy has always sprung from the domestic setting of a nation—its needs, wants, moods, prejudices, and ideals. The leaders who guided America's expansionist foreign relations were the same people who kindled the spirit of national growth at home, celebrated the machine age, forged the transcontinental railroad, shoved Native Americans aside, and built America's bustling cities and giant corporations.

Unlike domestic policy, foreign policy is seldom shaped by "the people." Most Americans simply do not follow international relations or express them-

• *Important Events* •

1861–69	Secretary of State Seward sets expansionist course		First Open Door note, calling for equal trade opportunity in China
1866	Transatlantic cable completed France withdraws from Mexico		Outbreak of Philippine Insurrection against the United States
1867	Alaska and Midway acquired	**1900**	Second Opened Door note requests respect for China's sovereignty
1871	*Alabama* claims settled with Great Britain		U.S. exports total $1.5 billion
1878	U.S. products monopolize awards at Paris World's Fair	**1901**	Theodore Roosevelt becomes president Hay-Pauncefote Treaty allows sole U.S. development of isthmian canal
1883	Advent of the New Navy	**1903**	Panama breaks from Colombia and grants canal rights to United States
1887	United States gains naval rights to Pearl Harbor		Platt Amendment subjugates Cuba
1889	First Pan-American Conference	**1904**	Roosevelt Corollary declares United States a "police power"
1890	Mahan's *The Influence of Sea Power upon History* is published McKinley Tariff hurts Hawaiian sugar exports	**1905**	Taft-Katsura Agreement gains Japanese pledge not to molest the Philippines Portsmouth Conference under Roosevelt's guidance ends Russo-Japanese War United States imposes financial supervision on the Dominican Republic
1893	Severe depression begins Turner's frontier thesis expounded Hawaiian revolution overthrows Queen Liliuokalani	**1906**	San Francisco segregates Asian school-children United States invades Cuba to put down rebellion
1894	Wilson-Gorham Tariff imposes tariff on Cuban sugar	**1907**	"Great White Fleet" makes world tour "Gentleman's agreement" with Japan restricts immigration
1895	Venezuelan crisis with Britain Cuban revolution against Spain begins Japan defeats China to become major Asian power	**1908**	Root-Takahira Agreement made with Japan for security of the Philippines
1896	William McKinley elected president on imperialist platform	**1912**	U.S. troops invade Cuba again U.S. troops occupy Nicaragua
1898	Sinking of the *Maine* heightens chances of war Spanish-American-Cuban-Filipino War Hawaii annexed	**1914**	U.S. troops invade Mexico First World War begins Panama Canal opens
1899	Treaty of Paris approved		

Foreign-Policy Elite

selves on foreign issues. Indeed, in the late nineteenth century, no more than 10 to 20 percent of the voting public was alert to world affairs. Thus the making of foreign policy was dominated by what scholars have labeled the for-

eign-policy elite—opinion leaders in politics, business, labor, agriculture, religion, journalism, education, and the military. This small group expressed the opinion that counted. Better read and better traveled than most Americans, more cosmopolitan in outlook, and politically active, they believed that

U.S. prosperity and security depended on the exertion of American influence abroad. Among the members of the foreign-policy elite were two future secretaries of state (John Hay and Elihu Root), a member of the Senate Foreign Relations Committee (Henry Cabot Lodge), and Theodore Roosevelt. Increasingly, especially in the 1890s, such men urged not only expansionism but both formal and informal imperialism.

American leaders understood the close relationship between domestic developments and foreign relations. They knew that railroads made it possible for midwestern farmers to transport their crops to seaboard cities and then on to foreign markets—"feeding the world." One result was that the farmers' livelihood became tied to world market conditions and the outcomes of foreign wars. Periodic depressions—especially the monster of the 1890s—fostered the belief among industrialists and others that the country's surplus production must be sold in foreign markets to restore and sustain economic well-being at home. By promoting economic health, the markets would also contribute to domestic social and political stability. The tariff question also linked domestic and world affairs. Tariff increases designed to protect American industry and agriculture from foreign competition adversely affected those who sold to America, prompting them to enact retaliatory tariffs on American products. American tariff revisions actually induced economic crises—in Hawaii and Cuba, for example—that helped ignite revolutions that ultimately served U.S. interests.

The Civil War had temporarily interrupted expansionism, but after that searing conflict leaders once again put the United States on an expansionist course. Their kindling of a spirit of nationalism helped heal sectional wounds as it resuscitated an expansionist mood. The 1876 centennial celebration emphasized national unity. Confederate and Union soldiers met to exchange captured flags. Pride welled up when, at the 1878 Paris World's Fair, American exhibitors won more awards than any other nation's representatives. Patriotic societies like

Nationalism and Exceptionalism

the Daughters of the American Revolution (founded in 1890) championed nationalism.

The inflated rhetoric of American exceptionalism and manifest destiny revived, giving intensified voice to racist explanations for expansion. The Reverend Josiah Strong's influential *Our Country* (1885) characterized Americans as a special God-favored Anglo-Saxon race destined to lead others. Social Darwinists saw Americans as a superior people who would surely overcome all competition and thrive. "The rule of the survival of the fittest applies to nations as well as to the animal kingdom," claimed the American diplomat John Barrett.

Missionaries, a majority of whom were women, contributed to expansionist ideology by spurring the transfer of American culture and power abroad. They taught the Bible, hoping to convert "natives" and "savages" to Christianity. The *Mother Goose Missionary Rhymes* captured the familiar blend of American evangelism, nationalism, and cultural arrogance:

Missionaries

> Ten little heathen standing in a line;
> One went to mission school, then there were but nine. . . .
> Three little heathen didn't know what to do;
> One learned our language, then there were two. . . .
> One little heathen standing all alone;
> He learned to love our flag, then there were none.

The arguments for expansion seemed all the more urgent when Americans anticipated the closing of the frontier at home. In 1893, the historian Frederick Jackson Turner of the University of Wisconsin postulated the thesis that an ever expanding continental frontier had shaped the American character. That "frontier has gone," Turner wrote, "and with its going has closed the first period of American history." He did not explicitly say that a new frontier had to be found overseas, but he did write that "American energy will continually demand a wider field for its exercise."

Turner's Frontier Thesis

With a mixture of self-interest and idealism, advocates of expansion and empire believed that imperialism benefited both Americans and those who

Remaking Societies

came under their control. When the United States intervened in other lands or lectured weaker states, Americans defended such behavior on the ground that they were extending the blessings of liberty and prosperity to less fortunate people. To the critics at home and abroad, however, American paternalism appeared hypocritical—a violation of cherished principles. Indeed, the persistent American belief that other peoples cannot solve their own problems and that only the American model of development is appropriate produced what the historian William Appleman Williams has called "the tragedy of American diplomacy."

FACTORY, FARM, AND FOREIGN AFFAIRS

American political leaders shared the views of the many businesspeople and farmers who believed that selling, buying, and investing in foreign marketplaces were important to the United States. Why? First, because of profits from foreign sales. Fear helped make the case for foreign trade as well, because the nation's farms and factories produced more than Americans could consume. Foreign commerce, it was thought, could serve as a safety valve to relieve the domestic pressures of overproduction, unemployment, and economic depression.

Growth of Foreign Trade

One of the major components of the tremendous economic growth of the United States after the Civil War was foreign trade. In 1865, U.S. exports totaled $234 million; by 1914, American exports had reached $2.5 billion. In the 1870s, the United States began to enjoy a long-term favorable balance (exporting more than it imported). Most of America's products went to Britain, other parts of Europe, and Canada, but increasing amounts flowed to new markets in Latin America and Asia. Agricultural goods accounted for about two-thirds of total exports in 1900. Manufactured goods led foreign sales for the first time in 1913, when the United States ranked third behind only Britain and Germany in such exports. Meanwhile, direct American investments abroad reached $3.5 billion by 1914, placing the United States among the top four investor countries.

Especially in Latin America, U.S. economic expansion grew impressively and aroused Washington's diplomatic interest in its neighbors to the

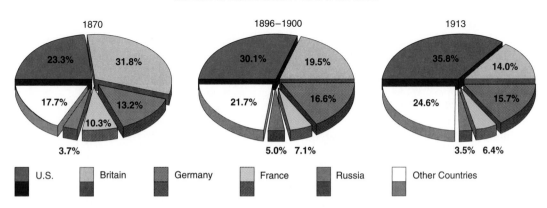

The Rise of U.S. Economic Power in the World *These data—percentage shares of world manufacturing production for the major nations of the world—demonstrate that the United States came to surpass Great Britain in this significant measurement of power.* Source: League of Nations data presented in Aaron L. Friedberg, *The Weary Titan: Britain and the Experience of Relative Decline, 1895–1905* (Princeton, N.J.: Princeton University Press, 1988), p. 26.

The Singer Manufacturing Company handed out this promotional postcard as a souvenir from the firm's display at the 1893 Columbian Exposition, a mammoth world's fair in Chicago where Americans showed off their technological and industrial genius. Singer sewing machines joined many other U.S. products in penetrating world markets, where three-quarters of all sewing machines sold were Singers. This machine was marketed in South Africa, where, the company advised, the "Zulus are a fine warlike people" who were moving toward "civilization" with Singer's help.   State Historical Society of Wisconsin.

Economic Links with Latin America

South. U.S. exports to Latin America, which exceeded $50 million in the 1870s, rose to more than $120 million in 1900 and reached $300 million in 1914. Investments by U.S. citizens in Latin America amounted to a towering $1.26 billion in 1914. In 1899, two large banana importers merged to form the United Fruit Company. In Central America, United Fruit owned much of the land (more than one million acres in 1913) and the railroad and steamship lines, and the company became an influential economic and political force in the region. As for Mexico, American capitalists came to own its railroads and mines. By 1910, Americans controlled 43 percent of Mexican property and produced more than half of Mexico's oil.

Economic expansion abroad became both a reason and a mechanism for exerting political influence. Indeed, by the early twentieth century, American economic interests were influencing policies on taxes and natural resources in Cuba and Mexico,

drawing Hawaii into the U.S. imperial net, and spreading American cultural values abroad. Religious missionaries and Singer executives, for example, joined hands in promoting the "civilizing medium" of the sewing machine. "The world is to be Christianized and civilized," declared Josiah Strong. "And what is the process of civilizing but the creating of more and higher wants?"

A WIDER FIELD ABROAD, 1860s–1880s

The American empire grew gradually, sometimes haltingly. One of its chief architects was William H. Seward. As secretary of state (1861–1869), he

Grand Expansionist: William H. Seward

envisioned a large, coordinated U.S. empire encompassing Canada, the Caribbean, Cuba, Central America, Mexico, Hawaii, Iceland, Greenland, and Pacific islands. This empire would be built not by war but by a natural process of gravitation toward the United States. Commerce would hurry the process, he thought, noting that in earlier centuries the merchants of Venice and Britain had become "masters of the world." To ensure the unity of this new empire, Seward appealed for a canal across Central America, a transcontinental American railroad to link up with Asian markets, and a telegraph system to speed communications.

Most of Seward's plans for acquiring territory were blocked by a combination of anti-imperialists and political foes. Anti-imperialists such as Senator Carl Schurz of Missouri and E. L. Godkin, editor of the magazine *The Nation*, argued that the country already had enough unsettled land and that the creation of a showcase of democracy and prosperity at home would best persuade other peoples to adopt American institutions and principles. Some anti-imperialists, sharing the racism of the times, opposed the annexation of territory populated by "inferior" dark-skinned people.

But Seward did enjoy some successes. In 1867, he paid Russia $7.2 million for the 591,000 square miles of Alaska—a real bargain for land twice the size of Texas. That same year, when an American naval officer seized the Midway Islands, Seward laid claim to them for the United States. He also shepherded the Burlingame Treaty (1868) through the Senate. This treaty with China provided for free immigration between the two countries and pledged Sino-American friendship.

The secretary's forceful handling of French interference in Mexico also furthered his reputation. Napoleon III had made Archduke Ferdinand Maximilian of Austria Mexico's monarch in 1861. Preoccupied with the Civil War, Seward could do little. But in 1866, as U.S. troops headed for the Mexican border, Seward cited the Monroe Doctrine and told the French to get out. Napoleon, troubled at home and now opposed by both Mexicans and Americans, abandoned his venture.

Seward realized his dream of a world knit together into a giant communications system. In 1866, an underwater transatlantic cable linked

International Communications European and American telegraph networks. In 1903, a submarine cable reached across the Pacific to the Philippines and, three years later, to Japan and China. Meanwhile, Americans strung telegraph lines to Latin America, reaching Chile in 1890. Information about markets, crises, and war flowed steadily and quickly.

Seward's successor, Hamilton Fish (1869–1877), inherited the knotty and emotional problem of the *Alabama* claims. The *Alabama* and other vessels built in Great Britain for the Confederacy during the Civil War had preyed on Union shipping. Senator Charles Sumner of Massachusetts demanded that Britain pay $2 billion in damages or cede Canada to the United States, but Fish favored negotiations. In 1871, Britain and America signed the Washington Treaty, whereby the British apologized and agreed to the creation of a tribunal, which later awarded the United States $15.5 million. Disputes over fishing rights along the North Atlantic coast and the hunting of seals in the Bering Sea near Alaska also dogged Anglo-American relations and would continue to do so for decades. Yet the two powers were coming to the conclusion that rapprochement rather than confrontation best served their interests.

Anglo-American Issues

The convening in 1889 of the first Pan-American Conference in Washington, D.C., bore witness to the growing ties between the United States and its hemispheric neighbors. Conferees from Latin America toured U.S. factories and then negotiated several commercial agreements. To encourage inter-American cooperation, they founded the Pan American Union. But Pan-Americanism did not prevent growing Latin American resentment toward U.S. influence in the hemisphere.

Pan-American Conference

As the United States acquired new territories and markets, expansionists bemoaned the condition of the U.S. Navy. Captain Alfred T. Mahan became a major popularizer for a "New Navy." Because foreign trade was vital to U.S. well-being, he argued, the nation required an

Mahan and the New Navy

efficient navy to protect its shipping; in turn, a navy required colonies for bases. Mahan became president of the Naval War College in Newport, Rhode Island, founded in 1884, and there gave lectures that were published as *The Influence of Sea Power upon History* (1890). This widely read book sat on every serious expansionist's shelf. Theodore Roosevelt and Henry Cabot Lodge eagerly consulted Mahan, sharing his belief in the links between trade, navy, and colonies.

Until its modernization, the navy was in a sorry state. Many of its wooden ships were rotting. But in 1883, Congress authorized construction of the first steel-hulled warships. American factories went to work to produce steam engines, high-velocity shells, powerful guns, and precision instruments. The navy gradually shifted from sail to steam and from wood to steel. Often named for states and cities to kindle patriotism and local support for naval expansion, New Navy ships like the *Maine*, the *Oregon*, and the *Boston* thrust the United States into naval prominence. When the United States faced crises in the 1890s, the New Navy warships were put to the test.

CRISES IN THE 1890s: HAWAII, VENEZUELA, AND CUBA

In the depression-plagued 1890s, crises in Hawaii, Venezuela, and Cuba gave expansionist Americans opportunities to act on their zealous arguments for what Senator Lodge called a "large policy." The Hawaiian Islands had long commanded American attention—commercial, missionary, naval, and diplomatic. Secretary of State James G. Blaine warned other nations away from the archipelago, declaring the islands "essentially a part of the American system." In 1893, wealthy Americans overthrew Queen Liliuokalani and immediately sought annexation to the United States.

Against the fervent protests of Queen Liliuokalani and of Japan (Japanese nationals far outnumbered Americans in Hawaii's population),

Annexation of Hawaii

President Benjamin Harrison hurriedly sent a treaty of annexation to the Senate. But incoming President Grover Cleveland,

who disapproved of forced annexation, withdrew it. After an investigation confirmed the conspiracy of the white economic elite and the diplomat John Stevens, the American flag came down.

When the Cleveland administration tried diplomacy to reverse this "abuse of power," the Dole government rejected U.S. attempts to restore the monarchy. Dole and his co-conspirators in Honolulu arrested the queen and confined her to her quarters for months. After gaining her freedom, she spoke out against annexation. But, in 1898, during the Spanish-American-Cuban-Filipino War, Hawaii gained renewed attention as a strategic and commercial way station to Asia and the Philippines. On July 7, President William McKinley successfully maneuvered annexation through Congress by means of a majority vote rather than by a treaty, which would have required a two-thirds count.

The Venezuelan crisis of 1895 also saw the United States in an expansive mood. For decades, Venezuela and Great Britain had squabbled over

Venezuelan Crisis

the border between Venezuela and British Guiana. The disputed territory contained rich gold deposits, and the mouth of the Orinoco River ranked as the commercial gateway to northern South America. Venezuela asked for American help. President Cleveland decided that the "mean and hoggish" British had to be warned away. In July 1895, Secretary of State Richard Olney sent the British a brash message that Cleveland compared to a twenty-inch gun—in the naval parlance of the time, a huge weapon. After lecturing the British that the Monroe Doctrine prohibited European intervention in the Western Hemisphere, Olney declared: "To-day the United States is practically sovereign on this continent, and its fiat is law upon the subjects to which it confines its interposition."

This bold statement of U.S. hegemony did not impress the British. American jingoists clamored for action. But neither London nor Washington wanted war. The British, seeking international friends to help counter intensifying competition from Germany, quietly retreated from the crisis. In 1896, an Anglo-American arbitration board divided the disputed territory between Britain and

How do historians know

that wealthy white Americans in Hawaii plotted in 1893 to overthrow the native government of Queen Liliuokalani? Both the queen (on the right) and the new president after her ouster, Sanford B. Dole (shown with Anna, his wife), wrote memoirs. Autobiographies must be read with skepticism, for their authors often embellish their performances and hide their blemishes. Memoirs are too frequently self-serving, presenting selective and faulty memories. Still, autobiographies can be valuable sources. Their accuracy can be tested and corroborated through comparison with other accounts and records, including private papers in archives. Memoirs also reveal the flavor of the times and the factors that influenced decisions. Sanford B. Dole (1844–1926) actually left several memoirs. After writing the unpublished "Reminiscences" for his family, he recalled events for the librarian of the Hawaiian Archives. Then, about 1914, he prepared articles

for a Honolulu newspaper that never published them. In 1936, ten years after Dole's death, the articles were published as Memoirs of the Hawaiian Revolution. Dole detailed the revolution against the queen, whom he called corrupt and politically inept, and claimed that he was a reluctant participant in the scheme. He also downplayed contacts with U.S. officials who welcomed the plot. Queen Liliuokalani (1838–1917) also left her recollections—in letters, diaries, interviews, and a memoir, Hawaii's Story by Hawaii's Queen (1898). She chastised Dole as a conspirator, defended Hawaiian nationalism, and emphasized the interventionist role of the U.S. diplomat John L. Stevens. The Dole and Liliuokalani autobiographies differ markedly, but together with contemporary official documents they have helped historians explain the great divide between foreigners and Hawaiians in the 1890s.   Photo: Hawaiian Historical Society.

Venezuela. The Venezuelans were barely consulted. Thus the United States displayed a trait common to imperialists: a disregard for the rights and sensibilities of smaller nations.

In 1895, another crisis rocked Latin America: the Cuban revolution against Spain. From 1868 to 1878, the Cubans had battled their ancestral country.

Economic and Cultural Ties with Cuba
——

Slavery was abolished but independence denied. While the Cuban economy suffered depression, Spanish rule continued to be repressive. Insurgents committed to *Cuba Libre* waited for another chance. José Martí, one of the heroes of Cuban history, collected arms and men in the United States. This was but one of the many ways the lives of Americans and Cubans were linked, a popular attraction to baseball being another. Their economies also became integrated. U.S. investments of $50 million, mostly in sugar plantations, dominated the Caribbean island. More than 90 percent of Cuba's sugar was exported to the United States, and most island imports came from the United States.

As in the case of Hawaii, a change in American tariff policy hastened the Cuban revolution and the island's further incorporation into "the American system." The Wilson-Gorman Tariff (1894) imposed a duty on Cuban sugar, which had been entering the United States duty free under the McKinley Tariff (1890). The Cuban economy, highly dependent on exports, plunged into deep crisis.

From American soil, Martí launched a revolution in 1895 that became gruesome in its human and material costs. Rebels burned sugar-cane fields and razed mills, conducting an economic war and using guerrilla tactics to avoid head-on clashes with Spanish soldiers. The Spanish retaliated under the command of the ruthless General Valeriano Weyler, who instituted a policy of "reconcentration": to separate the insurgents from their supporters among the Cuban people, an estimated three hundred thousand Cubans of all ages were herded into fortified towns and camps. Hunger, starvation, and disease led to deaths of tens of thousands. Weyler's forces also ransacked the

Martí and the Cuban Revolution
——

countryside. U.S. investments became jeopardized and Cuban-American trade dwindled. As reports of atrocity and destruction became headline news in the U.S. yellow press, Americans sympathized increasingly with the insurrectionists. In late 1897, a new government in Madrid modified reconcentration and promised some autonomy for Cuba.

President William McKinley had come to office an imperialist. The 1896 Republican platform on which McKinley ran demanded an enlarged American empire—Hawaii, the Virgin Islands, and a Nicaraguan canal. As for Cuba, if at all possible McKinley wanted to achieve independence without a U.S. war.

Events in early 1898 sabotaged the Spanish reforms and exhausted American patience. In January, antireform pro-Spanish loyalists and army personnel rioted in Havana. After the riots, Washington officials ordered the battleship *Maine* to Havana harbor to demonstrate U.S. concern and protect American citizens. On February 15, an explosion under the enlisted men's quarters ripped the *Maine*, killing 266 of 354 American officers and crew.

Sinking of the *Maine*
——

A week earlier, Spain's image in the United States had become further tarnished when William Randolph Hearst's inflammatory *New York Journal* published a stolen private letter from the Spanish minister in Washington, Enrique Dupuy de Lôme. The letter scorned McKinley and revealed Spain's determination to fight on in Cuba. An irritated McKinley soon asked for $50 million in defense funds, and Congress complied unanimously. The naval board created to investigate the sinking of the *Maine* then reported that a mine had caused the explosion. (A study by Admiral Hyman G. Rickover in 1976 challenged that conclusion, blaming the explosion on an internal accident.)

The impact of these events narrowed McKinley's diplomatic options. He decided to send Spain an ultimatum. In late March, the United States insisted that Spain accept an armistice, end reconcentration altogether, and designate McKinley as arbiter. Implicit was the demand that Spain grant Cuba its independence. No Spanish government could have given up Cuba and remained in office, but Madrid nonetheless made concessions. It abolished reconcentration and accepted an armistice on the condition that the insurgents agree first.

Wanting more, McKinley began to draft a war message to Congress. Then he received news that Spain had gone a step further and declared a unilateral armistice. McKinley hesitated, but he would no longer tolerate chronic disorder just ninety miles off the American coast. On April 11, the president asked Congress for authorization to use force against Spain.

On April 19, Congress declared Cuba free and independent and directed the president to use force to remove Spanish authority from the island. The legislators also passed the Teller Amendment, which disclaimed any American intention to annex Cuba. McKinley beat back a congressional amendment to recognize the rebel government. Believing that the Cubans were not ready for self-government, he argued that they needed a period of American tutoring.

THE SPANISH-AMERICAN-CUBAN-FILIPINO WAR

The motives of Americans who favored war were mixed and complex. McKinley's April 11 message expressed a humanitarian impulse to stop the bloodletting, a concern for commerce and property, and the need to end the nightmarish anxiety once and for all. Republican politicians advised McKinley that their party would lose the upcoming congressional elections unless the Cuban question was solved. Many businesspeople, who had been hesitant before the crisis of early 1898, joined many farmers in the belief that ejecting Spain from Cuba would open new markets for surplus production—to which the depression of the 1890s had given urgency.

Motives for War

Inveterate imperialists saw war as an opportunity to fulfill expansionist dreams. Naval enthusiasts could prove the worth of the New Navy. Conservatives, alarmed by populism and violent labor strikes, welcomed war as a national unifier. Sensationalism also figured in the march to war, with the yellow press in particular exaggerating stories of Spanish misdeeds. Some of those too young to remember the bloody Civil War looked on war as an adventure. Anglo-Saxon supremacists like the politician Albert Beveridge shouted, "God's hour has struck." Overarching all explanations for this war were expansionism and imperialism, the momentum of which had been moving the nation ever outward in the last half of the nineteenth century.

Secretary of State John Hay called it "a splendid little war," but it was hardly splendid. More than 5,400 Americans died but only 379 of them in combat. The rest fell to malaria and yellow fever spread by mosquitoes. Food was bad and medical care was unsophisticated. African-American troops, about 10,000 in number, served in segregated units and saw no relief from racism. Southern whites were especially resentful of the appearance of status that the military uniform gave to blacks.

U.S. Military Forces

To the surprise of most Americans, the first war news actually came from faraway Asia, from the Spanish colony of the Philippines. On May 1, 1898, Commodore George Dewey's New Navy ship the *Olympia*, leading an American squadron, steamed into Manila Bay and wrecked the outweighed and outgunned Spanish fleet. Dewey's sailors had to be handed volumes of the *Encyclopaedia Britannica* to acquaint them with this strange land, but officials in Washington knew better. Manila ranked with Pearl Harbor as a choice harbor, and the Philippines sat conveniently on the way to China and its potentially huge markets.

Dewey in the Philippines

Facing rebels and Americans in both Cuba and the Philippines, Spanish resistance collapsed rapidly. American ships had blockaded Cuban ports early to prevent Spain from reinforcing and resupplying its army on the island. American troops saw their first ground-war action on June 22, the day several thousand of them landed near Santiago de Cuba and laid siege to the city. On July 3, the Spanish Caribbean squadron, trapped in Santiago harbor, made a desperate attempt to escape but was destroyed by American warships. Two weeks later, the Spanish garrison at Santiago capitulated. Several days after that dramatic U.S. victory, American forces assaulted the Spanish Caribbean colony of Puerto Rico. Losing on all fronts, Madrid sued for peace. On August 12, Spain and the United States signed an armistice to end the Spanish-American-Cuban-Filipino War.

In Paris in December 1898, American and Spanish negotiators agreed on the peace terms: independence for Cuba; cession of the Philippines,

Treaty of Paris

Puerto Rico, and Guam (an island in the Pacific) to the United States; and American payment of $20 million to Spain for the territories. Filipino nationalists failed to persuade U.S. officials to grant their nation its freedom. The American empire now stretched deep into Asia, and the contemporaneous annexations of Wake Island (1898), Hawaii (1898), and Samoa (1899) gave American traders, missionaries, and naval promoters other steppingstones to China.

THE TASTE OF EMPIRE: IMPERIALISTS VERSUS ANTI-IMPERIALISTS

During the war, the *Washington Post* had detected "a new appetite, a yearning to show our strength. . . . The taste of empire is in the mouth of the people." But as the nation debated the Treaty of Paris, it became evident that many Americans found the taste bitter. Anti-imperialists like Mark Twain, William Jennings Bryan, Jane Addams, Andrew Carnegie, and Senator George Hoar of Massachusetts argued vigorously against annexation of the Philippines. They were disturbed that a war to free Cuba had led to empire.

Some critics of U.S. policy appealed to principle, citing the Declaration of Independence and the Constitution: the conquest of people against their will

Anti-Imperialist Arguments

violated the concept of self-determination. Other anti-imperialists argued that the United States could acquire markets

without having to subjugate foreign peoples. Still others claimed that to maintain empire, the president would repeatedly have to dispatch troops overseas. Because he could do so as commander in chief, he would not have to seek congressional approval, thus subverting the constitutional checks-and-balances system. And reform-minded critics emphasized domestic priorities over foreign ventures.

The anti-imperialists entered the debate with many handicaps and never launched an effective campaign. Although they organized the Anti-Imperialist League, they differed so profoundly on domestic issues that they found it difficult to speak with one voice on a foreign question. They also appeared inconsistent: Carnegie would accept colonies if they were not acquired by force; Hoar voted for annexation of Hawaii but not of the Philippines. Finally, possession of the Philippines was an established fact, hard to undo.

The imperialists answered their critics with appeals to patriotism, destiny, and commerce. They sketched a scenario of American greatness:

The Case for Empire

merchant ships plying the waters to boundless Asian markets, naval vessels cruising the Pacific to protect American interests, missionaries uplifting inferior peoples. Furthermore, insurgents were beginning to resist U.S. rule, and it was cowardly to pull out under fire. Germany and Japan, two powerful international competitors, were snooping around the Philippine Islands, apparently ready to seize them if the United States did not. National honor dictated that Americans keep what they had shed blood to take.

In February 1899, the Senate passed the Treaty of Paris by a vote of 57 to 27. Except for Hoar and Senator Eugene Hale of Maine, Republicans voted with their president; twenty-two Democrats voted no, but ten voted for the treaty. The latter group was probably influenced by Bryan, who had served as a colonel during the war; he urged a favorable vote in order to end the war and then push for Philippine independence. But an amendment promising independence as soon as the Filipinos formed a stable government was defeated only by the tie-breaking ballot of the vice president.

ASIAN ENCOUNTERS: OPEN DOOR IN CHINA, PHILIPPINE INSURRECTION, AND JAPAN

Meanwhile, the Germans, Japanese, Russians, French, and British were creating spheres of interest in China (see map). Within their spheres, the imperial powers built fortified bases and claimed exclusive economic privileges. American religious leaders, whose missions in China had doubled to one thousand in the 1890s, and business interests, which saw trade opportunities threatened, petitioned Washington to halt the dismemberment before they were closed out. What good were the Philippines as steppingstones to China if there was nothing left to step into?

Open Door Policy

Secretary Hay knew that the United States could not force the imperial powers out of China, but he was determined to protect American commerce. In September 1899, Hay sent the imperial nations a note asking them to respect the principle of equal trade opportunity—an Open Door—for all nations in their spheres. The recipients sent evasive replies, privately complaining that the United States was seeking for free the trade rights they had gained at considerable military and administrative cost. The next year, a Chinese secret society called the Boxers laid siege to the foreign legations in Beijing (Peking). The United States joined the imperial powers in sending troops to lift the siege and sent a second Open Door note in July that instructed other nations to preserve China's territorial integrity and to honor "equal and impartial trade."

Although Hay's foray into Asian politics settled little, the Open Door policy became established as a cornerstone of U.S. diplomacy. Actually, the Open Door had long been an American principle, for as a trading nation the United States opposed barriers to international commerce and demanded equal access to markets. After 1900, however, when the United States began to emerge as the premier world trader, the Open Door policy became an instrument first to pry open markets and then to dominate them, not just in China but throughout the world. But the Open Door was not just a policy. It was also an ideology with several tenets: first, that America's domestic well-being required exports; second, that foreign trade would suffer interruption unless the United States intervened abroad to implant American principles and keep foreign markets open; and third, that the closing of any area to American products, citizens, or ideas threatened the survival of the United States itself.

Philippine Insurrection

In the Philippines, meanwhile, the United States soon antagonized its new "wards," as McKinley labeled them. Emilio Aguinaldo, the Philippine nationalist leader who had been battling the Spanish for years, believed that U.S. officials had promised independence for his country. But after the victory, Aguinaldo was ordered out of Manila and isolated from decisions affecting his nation. American racial slurs and paternalistic attitudes infuriated nationalistic Filipinos, and they felt betrayed by the Treaty of Paris.

In January 1899, Aguinaldo proclaimed an independent Philippine Republic and took up arms. Before the Philippine Insurrection was suppressed in 1902, more than two hundred thousand Filipinos and five thousand Americans lay dead. After the defeat of the Filipinos came the Americanization of the islands (including the introduction of English) and the growth of the Philippine economy as a satellite of the U.S. economy. In 1916, the Jones Act promised independence to the Philippines, but it did not become a reality until thirty years later.

Japanese-American Rivalry

As the United States disciplined the Filipinos, Japan was becoming the dominant power in Asia. Gradually, the United States had to make concessions to Japan in efforts to protect the vulnerable Philippines and to salvage the Open Door policy. Japan smashed the Russians in the Russo-Japanese War (1904–1905). Roosevelt mediated the crisis at the Portsmouth Conference in New Hampshire in the hope that the peace settlement would preserve a balance of power in Asia. Although the president won the Nobel Peace Prize

for his efforts, peace did not come to Asia, and U.S. interests remained jeopardized. In 1905, in the Taft-Katsura Agreement, the United States conceded Japanese hegemony over Korea in return for Japan's pledge not to undermine the American position in the Philippines. Two years later, in the Root-Takahira Agreement, the United States recognized Japan's interests in Manchuria, whereas Japan again pledged the security of American possessions in the Pacific and promised to honor the Open Door in China. Roosevelt also built up U.S. naval power to deter the Japanese; in 1907, he sent the "Great White Fleet" on a world tour. Duly impressed, the Japanese began to build a bigger navy of their own.

President William Howard Taft thought he might counter Japanese advances in Asia through *dollar diplomacy*—the use of private funds to serve American diplomatic goals and at the same time to garner profits for American financiers. In this case, Taft induced American bankers to join an international consortium to build a Chinese railway. Taft's venture seemed only to embolden Japan.

Japanese-American relations also became tense over the treatment of Japanese citizens in the United States. In 1906, the San Francisco School Board, reflecting the anti-Asian bias of many West Coast Americans, ordered the segregation of all Chinese, Koreans, and Japanese in a special school. Tokyo protested the discrimination against its citizens. The following year, President Roosevelt quieted the crisis by striking a "gentleman's agreement" with Tokyo, restricting the influx of Japanese immigrants; San Francisco then rescinded its segregation order.

When World War I broke out in Europe, Japan seized Shandong and some Pacific islands from the

Imperialism in Asia: Turn of the Century   *China and the Pacific region had become imperialist hunting grounds by the turn of the century. The European powers and Japan controlled more areas than the United States did, but it participated in the race for influence by annexing the Philippines, Wake, Guam, and Hawaii, announcing the Open Door policy, and expanding trade in the area. As the "spheres" in China demonstrate, that besieged nation succumbed to imperial outsiders despite the Open Door policy.*

Germans. In 1915, Japan issued its Twenty-One Demands, virtually insisting on hegemony over all of China, then in the throes of a nationalistic revolution that had begun four years earlier. The Chinese door was being slammed shut. Americans—angry but lacking adequate countervailing power in Asia—could only protest.

THE FRUITS AND TASKS OF EMPIRE IN LATIN AMERICA

If the United States demonstrated feebleness in Asia, it revealed strength in Latin America (see map). Although the Teller Amendment outlawed annexation, it did not rule out U.S. control of postwar Cuba. American troops remained there until 1902. American officials also forced the Cubans to append to their constitution a frank avowal of U.S. hegemony known as the Platt Amendment. This statement prohibited Cuba from making a treaty with another nation that might impair its independence; in practice, this meant that all treaties had to have U.S. approval. Most important, another Platt Amendment provision granted the United States "the right to intervene" to preserve the island's independence and to maintain domestic order. Cuba was also required to lease to the United States a naval base (at Guantánamo Bay). Formalized in a 1903 treaty, the Platt Amendment governed Cuban-American relations until 1934.

Platt Amendment for Cuba

The Cubans, like the Filipinos, chafed under their U.S. masters. A revolution in 1906 prompted Roosevelt to order another invasion of Cuba. The marines stayed until 1909, returned briefly in 1912, and occupied Cuba again from 1917 to 1922. All the while, North Americans helped to develop a transportation system, expand the public school system, found a national army, and increase sugar production. Meanwhile, U.S. citizens and corporations soon acquired title to more than 60 percent of Cuba's rural lands and came to dominate the island's sugar, mining, tobacco, and utilities industries.

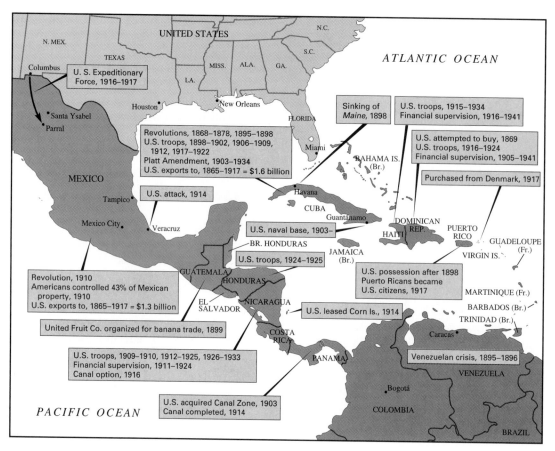

U.S. Hegemony in the Caribbean and Latin America *Through a great number of interventions and persistent economic expansion, the United States became the predominant power in Latin America in the early twentieth century. The United States often backed up the Roosevelt Corollary and its declaration of U.S. "police power" by dispatching troops to Caribbean nations, where they met nationalist opposition.*

Soon after the turn of the century, Panama, a province of Colombia, became the site of a much bolder U.S. expansionist venture—an isthmian canal.

Panama Canal

Before a waterway could be cut across Panama, three obstacles had to be overcome. First, the Clayton-Bulwer Treaty with Britain (1850) provided for joint control of a Central American canal. President Roosevelt persuaded the British, who were cultivating U.S. friendship as a counterweight to Germany, to step aside in the Hay-Pauncefote Treaty (1901). Second, when Colombia drove a hard bargain in talks about a canal in Panama, the Roosevelt administration encouraged Panamanian rebels to declare independence from

Colombia. He then sent American warships to the isthmus to ensure the success of the rebellion. In 1903, the United States signed a treaty with the new nation of Panama: the United States was awarded a canal zone and long-term rights to its control, and Panama was guaranteed its independence. Colombians would not soon forget this despoiling of their sovereignty, and nationalistic Panamanians could never forget that a foreign power sat astride their nation. Third, the cost of constructing a canal was enormous. Roosevelt, having overcome the British and Colombian hurdles, successfully pressed Congress for substantial funds.

The completion of the Panama Canal in 1914 marked a major technological achievement. People apparatus. The United States fortified the zone with conspicuous sixteen-inch guns, the nation's largest.

As for the rest of the Caribbean, Roosevelt's motto was "Speak softly and carry a big stick." Worried that Latin American nations' defaults on huge debts owed to European banks were provoking European intervention (England, Germany, and Italy sent warships to Venezuela in 1902), the president issued the Roosevelt Corollary to the Monroe Doctrine in 1904. He warned Latin Americans to stabilize their politics and finances. "Chronic wrongdoing," the corollary lectured, might require "intervention by some civilized nation," and "in flagrant cases of such wrongdoing or impotence" the United States would have to assume the role of "an international police power." Roosevelt and his successors were not bluffing. From 1900 to 1917, U.S. troops intervened in Cuba, Panama, Nicaragua, the Dominican Republic, Mexico, and Haiti. U.S. officials took over customs houses to control tariff revenues, renegotiated foreign debts, trained national guards, and ran elections. In Puerto Rico, moreover, U.S. governors imposed what some Puerto Ricans called the "Yankee model" and others tagged the "Yankee peril."

Roosevelt Corollary

Order became the byword of the U.S. managers of empire. The United States possessed few colonies, but it had developed an empire nonetheless—an informal one characterized by economic and political control rather than formal annexation. North Americans deemed order a necessary precondition for guaranteeing U.S. prosperity and security (especially the Panama Canal). The United States landed marines, developed national guards, manipulated politics and economies, and practiced dollar diplomacy. Americans were also eager to promote their values by remaking Latin American societies in the image of the United States.

In its relations with Europe, the United States reaffirmed the Monroe Doctrine and demonstrated the power to enforce it. Another guiding principle of U.S.-European relations was that the United States should stand outside continental embroilments. A third principle of American-European relations was that America's best interests lay in cooperation with Great Britain.

President Theodore Roosevelt visited the busy work site for the Panama Canal in 1906, just three years after he had engineered Panama's secession from Colombia and gained a treaty that gave the United States rights to a zone for the waterway that, upon its opening in 1914, linked the Pacific and Atlantic Oceans. Roosevelt vigorously defended himself against critics of his intervention in Panama. On one occasion, when he asked Secretary of War Elihu Root whether he had defended himself well, Root replied: "You have shown that you were accused of seduction and you have conclusively proved that you were guilty of rape." Collection of the Theodore Roosevelt Collection, Harvard College Library.

greeted the canal's opening the way people in the 1960s hailed the landing on the moon. American industry figured impressively in the accomplishment. Pittsburgh factories and shops made the various bolts and steel girders; the special bearings and gears used to operate the locks were manufactured by a Wheeling, West Virginia, company; and the General Electric Company produced the electrical

One outcome of the German-British rivalry was London's quest for American friendship. The makings of rapprochement had been developing since the late nineteenth century as Britain grew more wary of Germany and recognized the increasing power of the United States. Americans warmed to Britain when the British supported the United States in the war of 1898, stepped aside in the Hay-Pauncefote Treaty (1901) to permit construction of a U.S. canal, virtually endorsed the Roosevelt Corollary, and withdrew their warships from the Caribbean. The British overtures were to pay off in 1917 when the United States threw its weapons and soldiers into the First World War on the British side.

Anglo-American Rapprochement

In the years from the Civil War to World War I, expansionism and imperialism had elevated the United States to the status of a major world power. By 1914, Americans held extensive economic, strategic, and political interests in a world made smaller by modern technology. The belief that the nation needed foreign markets to absorb surplus production so that the domestic economy could thrive joined a missionary zeal to reform other societies. Notions of racial supremacy and emotional appeals to national greatness also fed the appetite for foreign adventure and commitments.

The outward reach of U.S. foreign policy from Secretary of State Seward to President Wilson sparked opposition from domestic critics, other imperial nations, and foreign nationalists, but the trend was never seriously diverted. In the future, Americans who sincerely believed that they had been helping foreign peoples to enjoy a better life would come to feel betrayed when their foreign clients questioned American tutelage or openly rebelled. Meanwhile, August 1914 presented a much different problem: the outbreak of war in Europe.

SUGGESTIONS FOR FURTHER READING

General

Robert L. Beisner, *From the Old Diplomacy to the New, 1865–1900,* 2d ed. (1986); Willard B. Gatewood Jr., *Black Americans and the*

White Man's Burden (1975); David Healy, *United States Expansionism* (1970); Patricia Hill, *The World Their Household* (1985) (on women missionaries); Michael H. Hunt, *Ideology and U.S. Foreign Policy* (1987); Paul Kennedy, *The Rise and Fall of the Great Powers* (1987); Walter LaFeber, *The American Search for Opportunity, 1865–1913* (1993), and *The New Empire* (1963); Ernest R. May, *American Imperialism* (1968); Thomas G. Paterson and Stephen G. Rabe, eds., *Imperial Surge* (1992); Emily Rosenberg, *Spreading the American Dream* (1982); William Appleman Williams, *The Tragedy of American Diplomacy*, new ed. (1988).

Theodore Roosevelt and Other Expansionists

Howard K. Beale, *Theodore Roosevelt and the Rise of America to World Power* (1956); John M. Cooper Jr., *The Warrior and the Priest: Woodrow Wilson and Theodore Roosevelt* (1983); Lewis L. Gould, *The Presidency of William McKinley* (1981); William H. Harbaugh, *The Life and Times of Theodore Roosevelt* (1975); Frederick Marks III, *Velvet on Iron* (1979) (on Roosevelt); Edmund Morris, *The Rise of Theodore Roosevelt* (1979); William C. Widenor, *Henry Cabot Lodge and the Search for an American Foreign Policy* (1980).

Economic Expansion

See the works by Beisner and LaFeber cited previously; William H. Becker, *The Dynamics of Business-Government Relations* (1982); Tom Terrill, *The Tariff, Politics, and American Foreign Policy, 1874–1901* (1973); Mira Wilkins, *The Emergence of the Multinational Enterprise* (1970); William Appleman Williams, *The Roots of the Modern American Empire* (1969).

The U.S. Navy

Benjamin F. Cooling, *Gray Steel and Blue Water Navy* (1979); Frederick C. Drake, *The Empire of the Seas* (1984); Kenneth J. Hagan, *This People's Navy* (1991); Robert Seager II, *Alfred Thayer Mahan* (1977); Ronald Spector, *Admiral of the New Empire* (1974) (on Dewey).

The Spanish-American-Cuban-Filipino War

Graham A. Cosmas, *An Army for Empire* (1971); Gerald F. Linderman, *The Mirror of War* (1974); Ernest R. May, *Imperial Democracy* (1961); John Offner, *An Unwanted War* (1992); David F. Trask, *The War with Spain in 1898* (1981).

Anti-Imperialism and the Peace Movement

Robert L. Beisner, *Twelve Against Empire* (1968); Charles Chatfield, *The American Peace Movement* (1992); Charles DeBenedetti, *Peace Reform in American History* (1980); Thomas J. Osborne, *"Empire Can Wait": American Opposition to Hawaiian Annexation, 1893–1898* (1981); David S. Patterson, *Toward a Warless World* (1976); E. Berkeley Tompkins, *Anti-Imperialism in the United States* (1970).

Cuba, Mexico, Panama, and Latin America

Arturo M. Carrión, *Puerto Rico* (1983); Richard H. Collin, *Theodore Roosevelt's Caribbean* (1990); David Healy, *Drive to Hege-*

mony: *The United States in the Caribbean, 1898-1917* (1989); Walter LaFeber, *Inevitable Revolutions*, 2d ed. rev. (1993) (on Central America), and *The Panama Canal*, rev. ed. (1990); Lester D. Langley, *The United States and the Caribbean, 1900–1970* (1980); David McCullough, *The Path Between the Seas* (1977) (on the Panama Canal); Louis A. Pérez Jr., *Cuba and the United States* (1990), and *Cuba Under the Platt Amendment, 1902–1934* (1986); Brenda G. Plummer, *Haiti and the Great Powers, 1902–1915* (1988); Josefina Vázquez and Lorenzo Meyer, *The United States and Mexico* (1985).

Hawaii, China, Japan, and the Pacific

Helena G. Allen, *The Betrayal of Queen Liliuokalani* (1982); Charles S. Campbell, *Special Business Interests and the Open Door Policy* (1951); Warren I. Cohen, *America's Response to China*, 3d ed. (1990); Michael Hunt, *The Making of a Special Relationship* (1983) (on China); Jane Hunter, *The Gospel of Gentility: American Women Missionaries in Turn-of-the-Century China* (1984); Akira Iriye, *Across the Pacific* (1967); Thomas J. McCormick, *China Market* (1967); Charles E. Neu, *The Troubled Encounter* (1975) (on Japan); Merze Tate, *The United States and the Hawaiian Kingdom* (1965); Marilyn Blatt Young, *The Rhetoric of Empire* (1968).

The Philippines: Insurrection and Colony

John M. Gates, *Schoolbooks and Krags: The United States Army in the Philippines, 1898–1902* (1973); Stanley Karnow, *In Our Image: America's Empire in the Philippines* (1989); Glenn A. May, *Battle for Batangas* (1991); Stuart C. Miller, *"Benevolent Assimilation"* (1982); Richard E. Welch, *Response to Imperialism: American Resistance to the Philippine War* (1972).

Great Britain and Canada

Kenneth Bourne, *Britain and the Balance of Power in North America, 1815–1908* (1967); Robert C. Brown, *Canada's National Policy, 1883–1900* (1964); Charles S. Campbell, *From Revolution to Rapprochement: The United States and Great Britain, 1783–1900* (1974); Adrian Cook, *The* Alabama *Claims* (1975); Bradford Perkins, *The Great Rapprochement* (1968).

Chapter

23

Americans at War,
1914–1920

T HE MEDICAL CASE FILES listed him as A.P. An eighteen-year-old Marine Corps private who had volunteered to fight in the First World War, A.P. was ordered to the western front in France. In early 1918, the Germans relentlessly bombarded his position at Château-Thierry, where screeching shells and deafening explosions punished the fresh American troops.

In June, A.P.'s company trudged closer to the forward battle lines, past the bodies of French soldiers dismembered by the big guns. His commanding officer detailed him to bury the mangled corpses. For several nights thereafter, A.P. could not sleep. During a bombardment on June 14, he began to tremble uncontrollably. A.P. was evacuated to a hospital, where noise easily startled him and horrifying dreams haunted him.

Doctors diagnosed such patients as suffering from a mental illness they called war neurosis or war psychosis. Almost everyone else called it shell shock. The symptoms became all too familiar: a fixed empty stare, violent tremors, paralyzed limbs, listlessness, jabbering, screaming, and terrifying dreams. Their nervous systems shattered by explosives,

some one hundred thousand victims went to special military hospitals staffed by psychiatrists. The very ill were sent home to the United States. According to follow-up studies, even cured shell-shock victims suffered lingering mental problems—flashbacks, nightmares, and a persistent disorientation that made it difficult for them to make decisions or organize their lives. Thousands of the most severely afflicted remained in veterans' hospitals.

For the generation that lived through the First World War, the glory of saving civilization from the Germans dissolved into the tragedy of human hurt. For many Americans who had heeded President Woodrow Wilson's call to "make the world safe for democracy," the war's results seemed more a national disaster than an ennobling experiment. Still, for many Progressive era professionals and reformers, the war presented an opportunity. The psychiatrists who treated the shell-shock victims, for example, hoped to use their wartime medical experience later, at home, to improve care for the mentally ill. For them, the cataclysm of foreign crisis and the opportunity for domestic social betterment went hand in hand.

The outbreak of the Great War in Europe in 1914 at first stunned Americans. For years, they had witnessed and participated in the international competition for colonies, markets, and weapons supremacy. But full-scale war seemed unthinkable in the modern age of progress. "Civilization is all gone, and barbarism come," moaned one social reformer.

For almost three years, President Wilson kept America out of the war. During this time, he sought to protect U.S. interests as a neutral trader and to improve the nation's military posture. He lectured the belligerents to rediscover their humanity and to respect international law. But American neutrality, lives, and property fell victim to British and German naval warfare. In early 1917, with his characteristic crusading zeal, the president asked Congress for a declaration of war. America entered the battle not just to win the war but to reform the postwar world.

Even after more than a decade of progressive reform, Americans remained a heterogeneous and fractious people at the start of the Great War. Headlines still trumpeted labor-capital confrontations like the Ludlow Massacre in Colorado, in which two women and eleven children were killed when state militia attempted to break a miners' strike. Racial antagonisms were evident in Wilson's decision to segregate federal buildings in Washington and in the continued lynchings of African-Americans (fifty-one in 1914). Ethnic groups eyed one another suspiciously. German-Americans were denounced as traitors, and war hawks harassed pacifists. Many women argued for equality among the sexes and for female suffrage, whereas many men wanted to sustain the tradition of the subordination of women. And the federal government, eager to stimulate patriotism, trampled on civil liberties to silence critics. The war experience thus accentuated the nation's social divisiveness.

America's participation in the war wrought massive changes and accelerated trends already in motion. Wars are emergencies, and during such times normal ways of doing things surrender to the extraordinary and exaggerated. The period witnessed greater powers for the presidency, unprecedented centralization and integration of the economy, increased standardization of products, and unusual cooperation between government and business. The war experience also helped splinter and thus undermine the progressive movement.

The United States emerged from the war a major power in a disrupted and economically hobbled world. Yet Americans who had marched to battle as if on a crusade grew disillusioned. They recoiled from the spectacle of the victors squabbling over the spoils, and they chided Wilson for failing to deliver the "peace without victory" he promised. As in the 1790s, the 1840s, and the 1890s, Americans engaged in a searching national debate about the fundamental direction of their foreign policy. The president appealed for American membership in the League of Nations, which he touted as a vehicle for reforming world politics. But the Senate killed his diplomatic offspring, fearful that the League might entangle Americans once again in Europe's problems, impede the growth of the U.S. empire, and compromise the country's traditional unilateralism. On many fronts, then, Americans during the era of the First World War were at war with themselves.

STRUGGLING WITH NEUTRALITY

The war that erupted in August 1914 grew from years of European competition over trade, colonies, allies, and armaments. Two powerful alliance systems had formed: the Triple Alliance of Germany, Austria-Hungary, and Italy, and the Triple Entente of Britain, France, and Russia. All had imperial ambitions, but Germany seemed particularly bold as it rivaled Britain for world leadership. Strategists said that Europe enjoyed a balance of power, but a series of crises in the Balkans of southeastern Europe started a chain of events that shattered the "balance" and propelled the European nations into battle.

Slavic nationalists in the Balkans sought to enlarge Serbia, an independent Slavic nation, by annexing regions like Bosnia, then a province of the Austro-Hungarian Empire. In

Outbreak of the First World War

In June 1914 at Sarajevo, the heir to the Austro-Hungarian throne was assassinated by a member of a Slavic terrorist group. Austria-Hungary, long worried about the prospect of a large Slavic state—an enlarged Serbia—on its southern border, consulted Germany, which urged toughness. Serbia called on its Slavic friend Russia for help; Russia in turn looked to its ally France. When Austria-Hungary declared war against Serbia, Russia began to mobilize its armies.

Certain that war was heading Berlin's way, Germany struck first, declaring war against Russia on August 1 and against France two days later. The British hesitated, but when Germany slashed into Belgium to get at France, Britain declared war against Germany on August 4. Eventually, Turkey joined Germany and Austria-Hungary (the Central Powers), and Japan and Italy teamed up with Britain, France, and Russia (the Allies). Japan took advantage of the European war to seize Germany's Chinese sphere of influence, Shandong. The world was aflame.

President Wilson at first sought to distance America from the conflagration by issuing a proclamation of neutrality. He also asked Americans to refrain from taking sides. But

**Ethnic Ties
to Europe**
——

Wilson's lofty appeal for American neutrality and unity at home collided with three realities. First, ethnic groups in the United States naturally took sides. Many German-Americans and anti-British Irish-Americans (Ireland was then trying to break free from British rule) cheered for the Central Powers. Americans of British and French ancestry and others with roots in Allied nations championed the Allied cause. Germany's attack on neutral Belgium at the start of the war confirmed in many people's minds that Germany had become the archetype of unbridled militarism and autocracy.

Second, U.S. economic links with the Allies also rendered neutrality difficult. England had long been one of the nation's best customers. Now the

**Trade and
Loans**
——

British flooded the United States with new orders for products, including arms. Sales to the Allies helped pull the American economy out of its recession. Between 1914 and 1916, American exports to England and France grew 365 percent, from $753 million to $2.75 billion. In the same period, however, exports to Germany dropped from $345 million to only $29 million. Loans from private American banks financed much of the U.S. trade with the Allies. The loans totaled $2.3 billion during the period of neutrality; Germany received only $27 million in the same period. The Wilson administration, which at first frowned on these transactions, came to see them as necessary to the economic health of the United States.

From Germany's perspective, the linkage between the American economy and the Allies meant that the United States had become the unneutral Allied arsenal and bank. Under international law, Britain—which controlled the seas—could buy both contraband (war-related goods) and noncontraband from neutrals. It was Germany's responsibility, not America's, to stop such trade in ways that international law prescribed—that is, by an effective blockade of the enemy's territory, by the seizure of contraband from neutral (American) ships, or by the confiscation of any goods from belligerent (British) ships.

The pro-Allied sympathies of Woodrow Wilson and his advisers were the third reason why neutrality did not work. Wilson believed that a German

**Pro-Allied
Sympathies**
——

victory would destroy free enterprise and government by law. If Germany won the war, he prophesied, "it would change the course of our civilization and make the United States a military nation." Wilson's chief advisers and diplomats—his assistant Edward House, Secretary of State Robert Lansing, and Ambassador to London Walter Hines Page—held similar anti-German views that often translated into pro-Allied policies.

The president and his aides also believed that Wilsonian principles stood a better chance of international acceptance if Britain, rather than the

Wilsonianism
——

Central Powers, sat astride the postwar world. Wilsonianism—the cluster of ideas Wilson espoused—consisted of traditional American principles and an evolving ideology of internationalism, the central tenet of which was that the United States had become such a special nation that it could best lead world affairs into a new peaceful era. Wilson's ideal world was to be open in every sense: no barriers to commerce

• *Important Events* •

1914	During Mexican Revolution U.S. troops invade Mexico
	First World War begins in Europe
1915	Germany declares war zone around British Isles
	Wilson denounces German U-boat sinking of *Lusitania*
	Secretary of State Bryan resigns in protest against Wilson's policies
1916	Gore-McLemore resolution barring Americans from travel on belligerent ships is defeated
	U.S. troops invade Mexico again
	After *Sussex* is torpedoed, Germany pledges not to attack merchant ships without warning
	National Defense Act provides for larger military
	Wilson reelected on platform of peace, progressivism, and preparedness
1917	Germany declares unrestricted submarine warfare
	Zimmermann telegram tries to stir up Mexican-U.S. troubles
	Russian Revolution ousts the czar, Bolshevik Revolution begins
	U.S. enters First World War
	Selective Service Act sets up compulsory military service (the draft)
	Espionage Act limits First Amendment rights
	War Industries Board created to manage the economy
	War Revenue Act raises taxes to avoid war profiteering
1918	Wilson announces Fourteen Points to guide future international relations
	Sedition Act further limits free speech
	Eugene Debs imprisoned for speaking against the war
	U.S. troops intervene in Russian civil war
	Deadly flu epidemic sweeps world and the United States
	Republicans hand Wilson setback by winning congressional elections
	Armistice ends the First World War
1919	Paris Peace Conference punishes Germany and plans new world order
	May Day bombings contribute to fears and stimulate Red Scare
	Chicago race riot one of many in the "Red Summer"
	Workers strike against the steel industry
	Wilson suffers stroke after speaking tour
	Senate rejects Treaty of Paris and U.S. membership in League of Nations
	Schenck v. *U.S.* upholds Espionage Act
1920	Palmer Raids of the Red Scare round up suspected radicals
	Nineteenth Amendment ratified, giving women the vote

and democratic politics and no secret diplomatic deals. Empires were to be dismantled in keeping with the principle of self-determination. Armaments were to be reduced. Wilson envisioned free-market nonexploitative capitalism and political constitutionalism for all nations, to ensure the good society and world peace. He also articulated the traditional belief in American exceptionalism. America had a mission, he believed, to restructure international relations and to reform other societies. American progressivism was to be projected onto the world. "We created this Nation," Wilson intoned, "not to serve ourselves, but to serve mankind." His critics charged that Wilson often violated his own tenets in his eagerness to force them on others. All agreed, though, that such ideals served the American national interest; in this way, idealism and realism were married.

To say that American neutrality was never a real possibility given ethnic loyalties, economic ties, and Wilsonian preferences is not to say that Wilson sought to enter the war. He emphatically wanted to keep the United States out. But go in the United States finally did. Why?

Americans got caught in the Allied–Central Power crossfire. The British, "ruling the waves and waiving the rules," declared a blockade of water entrances to Germany and

British Naval Policy
——

mined the North Sea. They also harassed neutral shipping by seizing cargoes and defined a broad list of contraband (including foodstuffs) that they prohibited neutrals from shipping to Germany; American vessels bearing goods for Germany seldom reached their destination. Furthermore, to counter German submarines (U-boats), the British flouted international law by arming their merchant ships and flying neutral (sometimes American) flags. Wilson frequently protested British violations of neutral rights, but London often deftly defused American criticism by paying for confiscated cargoes. Moreover, German provocations made British behavior appear less offensive by comparison.

Germany, unable to win the war on land and determined to lift the blockade and halt American-Allied commerce, looked for victory at sea by using submarines. In February 1915, Berlin announced that it was creating a war zone around the British Isles; it would sink all enemy ships in the area. Neutral vessels were warned to stay out so as not to be attacked by mistake, and passengers from neutral nations were advised to stay off Allied ships. Wilson stiffly informed Germany that the United States was holding it to "strict accountability" for any losses of American life and property.

Wilson was interpreting international law in the strictest sense possible. The law stated that an attacker had to warn a passenger or merchant ship

The Submarine and International Law
——

before attacking, so that passengers and crew could disembark safely into lifeboats. The rule predated the emergence of the submarine—a frail and sluggish vessel that based its effectiveness on the element of surprise. When Wilson refused to make adjustments, the Germans thought him unfair. Berlin frequently complained to Wilson that he was denying the Germans the one weapon they could use to break the British economic stranglehold, disrupt the Allies' substantial connection with U.S. producers and bankers, and win the war.

WILSON, THE SUBMARINE, AND THE DECISION FOR WAR

During the next few months, the U-boats sank ship after ship. In May 1915, the luxurious British passenger liner *Lusitania* left New York City carrying more than 1,200 passengers and

Sinking of the *Lusitania*
——

a cargo of food and contraband, including 4.2 million rounds of ammunition for Remington rifles. Before "Lucy's" departure, newspapers printed an unusual announcement from the German embassy: it warned travelers on British vessels that Allied ships in war-zone waters "are liable to destruction." Few passengers paid attention to the notice; few shifted to an American vessel for the transatlantic trip. On May 7, off the Irish coast, submarine U-20 unleashed torpedoes at the vessel. The *Lusitania* sank quickly, taking to their deaths 1,198 people, 128 of them Americans.

Even if the ship was carrying armaments, argued Wilson, the sinking was a brutal assault on innocent people. But he ruled out a military response. Secretary of State William Jennings Bryan advised that Americans be prohibited from travel on belligerent ships and that passenger vessels be prohibited from carrying war goods. The president rejected Bryan's counsel, insisting on the right of Americans to sail on belligerent ships and demanding that Germany cease its inhumane submarine warfare. When the president refused to ban American travelers from belligerent ships, Bryan resigned in protest. (The pro-Allied Robert Lansing took Bryan's place.) When criticized for pursuing a double standard in favor of the Allies, Wilson responded that the British were taking cargoes and violating property rights, but the Germans were taking lives and violating human rights. Wilson's attitude toward Germany had noticeably hardened.

Germany, seeking to avoid war with America, ordered its U-boat commanders to halt attacks on passenger liners. But in mid-August, another British vessel, the *Arabic*, was sunk and two Americans died. The Germans hastened to pledge that they would never again attack an unarmed passenger ship without warning. But the sinking of the *Arabic* fueled debate about American passengers on belligerent vessels. Why not require Americans to sail on American craft? asked critics.

In early 1916, Congress began to debate the Gore-McLemore resolution to prohibit Americans from traveling on armed merchant vessels or ships carrying contraband. The reso-

Gore-McLemore Resolution
———

lution, it was hoped, would prevent incidents like the sinking of the *Lusitania* from hurtling the United States into war. But Wilson would tolerate no interference in the presidential making of foreign policy (he had just sent Edward House to Europe to mediate an end to the war) and no restrictions on American travel. The resolution, he argued, would destroy the "whole fine fabric of international law." After heavy politicking, Congress rejected the resolution.

In March 1916, a U-boat attack on the *Sussex*, a French vessel crossing the English Channel, took the United States a step closer to war. Four Americans were injured on that ship. Stop the marauding submarines, Wilson lectured Berlin, or he would sever diplomatic relations. Again the Germans backed off, pledging not to attack merchant vessels without warning.

As the United States became more entangled in the Great War, many Americans urged Wilson to keep the nation out of the conflict. The various messages of antiwar advocates

Peace Movement
———

were that war drained a nation of its youth, resources, and impulse for reform; that it fostered a repressive spirit at home; that it violated Christian morality; and that wartime business barons reaped huge profits at the expense of the people. Although the peace movement was splintered—some of its followers endorsing peace but not pacifism—it carried political and intellectual weight that Wilson could not ignore and articulated several ideas that he shared. In fact, he campaigned on a peace platform in the 1916 presidential election. After his triumph, Wilson futilely labored once again to bring the belligerents to the conference table. In early 1917, he advised them to temper their acquisitive war aims, appealing for a "peace without victory."

In early February 1917, Germany launched unrestricted submarine warfare. All vessels—belligerent or neutral, warship or merchant—would be

Unrestricted Submarine Warfare
———

attacked if sighted in the declared war zone. This bold decision represented a calculated risk that submarines could impede U.S. munitions shipments to England and thus defeat the Allies before American troops could be ferried across the Atlantic. Wilson quickly broke diplomatic relations with Berlin.

The German challenge to American neutrality rights and economic interests was soon followed by an apparent German threat to U.S. security. In late February, British intelligence intercepted and passed to officials in Washington a telegram addressed to the German minister in Mexico from German Foreign Secretary Arthur Zimmermann. If the Mexican government joined a military alliance against the United States, the minister was instructed to tell Mexican leaders, Germany would help Mexico recover the territories it had lost to its northern neighbor in 1848.

American officials took the message seriously, because Mexican-American relations had recently deteriorated. The Mexican Revolution, a bloody civil

Mexican Revolution and Zimmermann Telegram
———

war with strong anti-Yankee overtones, threatened U.S. interests when the Mexican government began to take steps toward the nationalization of extensive American-owned properties. Wilson had twice ordered U.S. troops onto Mexican soil: in 1914, at Veracruz, to avenge a slight to the American uniform and flag and to destabilize a government he did not like, and again in 1916, in northern Mexico, where General John J. "Black Jack" Pershing spent months pursuing the elusive Pancho Villa after the Mexican rebel had raided an American border town.

Soon after learning of Zimmermann's ploy, Wilson asked Congress for "armed neutrality" to defend American lives and commerce. He requested authority to arm American merchant ships and to "employ any other instrumentalities or methods that may be necessary." In the midst of the debate, Wilson released Zimmermann's telegram to the press; Americans expressed outrage. Still, antiwar senators saw the armed-ship bill as a blank check for the president to move the country to war, and they filibustered it to death. Wilson proceeded to arm America's commercial vessels anyway. The action came too late to prevent the sinking of several American ships. War cries echoed across the nation.

On April 2, 1917, the president stepped before a hushed Congress. Passionately and eloquently, Wilson explained American grievances: Germany's violation of freedom of the seas, disruption of commerce, attempt to stir up trouble in Mexico, and breach of human rights by killing innocent Americans. Wilson's most famous words rang out: "The world must be made safe for democracy." Congress quickly declared war against Germany by a vote of 373 to 50 in the House and 82 to 6 in the Senate. The first woman ever to sit in Congress, Montana's Jeannette Rankin, cast a ringing vote of no that won her high ranking in the pantheon of American pacifism. "Peace is a woman's job," she declared.

Wilson's War Message

For principle, for morality, for honor, for commerce, for security, for reform—for all these reasons, Wilson took the United States into World War I. The submarine was certainly the culprit that drew a reluctant president and nation into the maelstrom. Yet critics did not attribute the American descent into war to the U-boat alone. They emphasized Wilson's rigid definition of international law, which did not take account of the submarine's tactics. They faulted his contention that Americans should be entitled to travel anywhere, even on a belligerent ship loaded with contraband, in time of war. They criticized his policies as unneutral. But they lost the debate.

In the broadest sense, America went to war to reform world politics, not to destroy Germany. By early 1917, Wilson seemed to believe that America would not be able to claim a seat at the postwar peace conference unless it had become a combatant. At the peace conference, Wilson intended to promote the principles he thought essential to a stable world order, to advance democracy and the Open Door, and to outlaw revolution and aggression. In the end, Woodrow Wilson decided for war to gain an American-fashioned peace.

TAKING UP ARMS AND WINNING THE WAR

Even before the U.S. declaration of war, the Wilson administration had been beefing up the military. "Preparedness" seemed prudent to many. The National Defense Act of 1916 provided for increases in the army and National Guard and for summer training camps modeled on the one in Plattsburg, New York, where a slice of America's social and economic elite had trained in 1915 as "citizen soldiers." The Navy Act, providing for a three-year naval expansion program, soon followed. To pay part of the huge cost of these undertakings, Congress passed the Revenue Act in 1916. The act raised the surtax on high incomes and corporate profits, imposed a federal tax on large estates, and significantly increased the taxes on munitions manufacturers.

To raise an army after the declaration of war, Congress in May 1917 passed the Selective Service Act, requiring the registration of all men aged twenty to thirty (later changed to eighteen to forty-five). National service, proponents believed, would not only prepare the nation for battle but instill respect for order, democracy, personal sacrifice, and nationalism. Critics, on the other hand, feared that "Prussianism," not democratization, would be the likely outcome.

The Draft

On June 5, 1917, more than 9.5 million men signed up for the "great national lottery." By war's end, local draft boards had registered 24 million men and more than 4.8 million had served in the armed forces, 2 million of them in France (see figure). In addition to the draftees, hundreds of thousands of citizens volunteered for military service. At the same

American Soldiers in the First World War

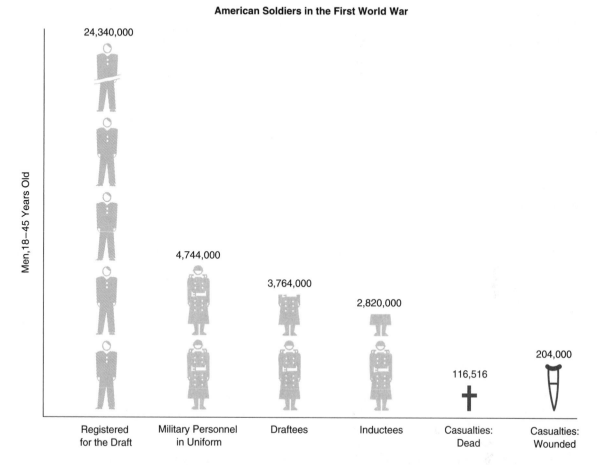

American Soldiers in the First World War   *As this figure shows, although many men were required to register for the draft under the Selective Service Act, only a small number (about 15 percent) were actually drafted and even fewer (about 12 percent) were inducted into the military. About half the deaths were caused by disease (especially by the flu).*

time, 3 million men evaded draft registration. Another 338,000 men who had registered and been summoned by their draft boards failed to show up for induction. Nearly 65,000 draftees initially applied for conscientious objector status (refusing to bear arms on religious or pacifistic grounds). Of these, approximately 4,000 were actually classified as conscientious objectors.

The typical American soldier in World War I was a draftee aged twenty-one to twenty-three, single, and poorly educated (most had not attended high school). Perhaps as many as 18 percent were foreign born, and 400,000 were African-American. Although women were excluded from military service, some women became navy clerks; others served as telephone operators in the Army Signal Corps or as nurses and physical therapists. On college campuses, 150,000 students joined the Student Army Training Corps or similar navy and marine units.

American leaders worried that the young soldiers, once away from home, would be tempted by vice—especially by the saloons and houses of prostitution that quickly surrounded training centers. To protect the supposed novices with "invisible armor," the government created the Commission on Training

Commission on Training Camp Activities

——

Camp Activities to coordinate the work of the YMCA and other groups that dispensed food, showed movies, held athletic contests, and distributed books. Men in uniform were not permitted to drink. Alarmed by the spread of venereal disease, commission officials declared "sin-free" zones around military bases and exhorted soldiers to abstain from sex.

Jim Crow was in the army too. Fearing "strutting representatives of black soldiery," as Senator James K. Vardaman of Mississippi growled, many politicians opposed the drafting of African-Americans. But the army needed men, white and black. The NAACP urged blacks to join the fight for "world liberty," in the hope that a war to make the world safe for democracy might also blur the color line at home. Instead, blacks encountered conscious discrimination. Military leaders segregated camp facilities and assigned black soldiers to menial labor. Racist slang became common in the camps. In August 1917 in Houston, Texas, angry African-American soldiers retaliated against whites who had been harassing them, killing sixteen. Nineteen black soldiers were ultimately executed; others were court-martialed and given long prison terms.

In Europe, General John J. Pershing, the head of the American Expeditionary Forces (AEF), insisted that his troops remain an independent army. He was not about to put his "doughboys" under the leadership of Allied commanders, who had become wedded to unimaginative and deadly trench warfare, producing a military stalemate and ghastly casualties on the western front. Zigzag trenches fronted by barbed wire and mines stretched across France. Beyond the muddy and stinking trenches lay "no man's land," denuded by artillery fire. When ordered out, soldiers would charge the German lines, also a maze of trenches. Machine guns mowed them down; chlorine gas, first used by Germany in 1915, poisoned them. Little was gained. At the Battle of the Somme in 1916, the British and French suffered 600,000 dead or wounded to earn only 125 square miles; the Germans lost 500,000 men.

The influx of American men and materiel decided the outcome of World War I. With both sides virtually exhausted, the Americans tipped the

AEF Battles in France

balance toward the Allies. American forces did not actually engage in much combat until after the lull in the fighting during the severe winter of 1917–1918. The Germans launched a major offensive in March 1918, after they had knocked Russia out of the war and shifted troops from the eastern front to France. By May, Kaiser Wilhelm's forces had stormed to within fifty miles of Paris. American troops helped blunt the German advance at Cantigny. In June, the U.S. Second Division defeated the Germans west of Château-Thierry in the Belleau Wood, but 5,183 of 8,000 marines died or were wounded after they made almost sacrificial frontal assaults against German machine guns. From this costly victory, the AEF learned to adopt more flexible attack methods. Still, casualties—including shell-shocked victims—mounted.

Allied victory in the Second Battle of the Marne in July 1918 seemed to turn the tide against the Germans. In September, the Allies began their massive Meuse-Argonne offensive. More than one million Americans joined British and French troops in weeks of fierce combat made all the more difficult by cold rainy weather. More than twenty-six thousand Americans died before the Allies claimed the Argonne Forest on October 10. For Germany, with its ground war a shambles, its submarine warfare a dismal failure, its troops and cities mutinous, and its allies Turkey and Austria dropping out, peace became imperative. The Germans accepted an armistice on November 11, 1918.

The belligerents counted awesome casualties: 8 million soldiers and 6.6 million civilians dead and 21.3 million people wounded. Fifty thousand

Casualties

American soldiers died in battle, and another 62,000 died from disease—many from the worldwide influenza epidemic of 1918. More than 200,000 Americans were wounded.

President Wilson welcomed the armistice, not only because it ended the bloodletting but also because the combatants agreed that his Fourteen

The Fourteen Points

Points, which he had enunciated in January, would guide the peace negotiations. The Fourteen Points summarized

Wilsonian internationalism. The first five called for diplomacy "in the public view," freedom of the seas, lower tariffs, reductions in armaments, and the decolonization of empires. The next eight points specified the evacuation of foreign troops from Russia, Belgium, and France and appealed for self-determination for nationalities in Europe. For Wilson, the fourteenth point was the most important— the mechanism for achieving all the others: "a general association of nations," or League of Nations. Having won the war, Wilson set out to win the peace and build a stable world order in accordance with American principles.

MANAGING THE HOME FRONT

"It is not an army that we must shape and train for war," declared President Wilson, "it is a nation." The United States was a belligerent for only nineteen months, but the war had a tremendous impact at home. The federal government quickly geared the economy to war needs and marshaled public opinion for sacrifices and adjustments. The state intervened in American life as never before. An unprecedented concentration of bureaucratic power developed in Washington as the federal government sought to manage the economy, the labor force, the military, public opinion, and more. In the period from 1916 to 1919, annual federal expenditures increased 2,500 percent, and war expenses ballooned to $33.5 billion. The total cost of the war was probably triple that figure, because future generations would have to pay veterans' benefits and interest on loans.

The federal government and private business became partners during the war. Dollar-a-year executives flocked to the nation's capital from major companies; they retained their **Business-** corporate salaries while serving **Government** in official administrative and **Cooperation** consulting capacities. Early in the war, the government relied on several industrial committees for advice on purchases and prices. But evidence of self-interested businesspeople cashing in on the national interest aroused public protest. The committees were disbanded in July 1917 in favor of the War Industries Board. But the government continued to work closely with business through trade associations. Business-government cooperation was also stimulated by the suspension of antitrust laws and by cost-plus contracts, which guaranteed companies a healthy profit and a means to pay higher wages to head off labor strikes. Competitive bidding was virtually abandoned and a floor was placed under prices to ensure profits.

Hundreds of new government agencies, staffed largely by businesspeople, placed controls on the economy in order to shift the nation's resources to the war effort. The Food Administration, led by Herbert Hoover, launched voluntary programs to increase production and conserve food; it also set prices and regulated distribution. The Railroad Administration took over the snarled railway industry. The Fuel Administration controlled coal supplies and rationed gasoline. When strikes threatened the telephone and telegraph companies, the federal government seized and ran them.

The largest of the superagencies was the War Industries Board (WIB), headed by the financier Bernard Baruch. Designed as a clearing-house to coordinate the national economy, the WIB made purchases, **War Industries** allocated supplies, and fixed **Board** prices at levels that business requested. Although the WIB seemed all powerful, in reality it had to conciliate competing interest groups and compromise with the businesspeople whose advice it so valued.

The performance of the mobilized economy was mixed, but it delivered enough men and materiel to France to ensure the defeat of the Central Powers. About a quarter of all American production was diverted to war needs. Farmers enjoyed boom years as they put more acreage into production and received higher prices. Encouraged to produce more at a faster pace, farmers mechanized as never before. Wartime demand also brought increased productivity and profits to some industries. Steel production in 1917, for example, was twice the prewar figure.

Mistakes were made nonetheless. Weapons deliveries fell short of demand; the bloated bureaucracy of the War Shipping Board failed to build enough ships. In the severe winter cold of 1917–1918, millions of Americans could not get coal, because the coal companies had held back on production to raise prices and railroads did not have enough coal cars. And, by adopting liberal credit policies and setting prices at high levels, the government encouraged inflation. The wholesale price index was 98 percent higher in 1918 than it had been in 1913.

Tax policies during the war were designed to pull some of the profits reaped from high prices into the treasury. Still, the government financed only one-third of the war through taxes. The other two-thirds came from loans, including Liberty Bonds sold to the American people. The War Revenue Act of 1917 provided for a more steeply graduated personal income tax, a corporate income tax, and an excess profits tax. Although the taxes did curb excessive corporate profiteering, they had several loopholes. Sometimes, companies inflated costs to conceal profits or paid high salaries and bonuses to their executives.

Labor and the War

For unions, the war seemed to offer opportunities for recognition and better pay. Samuel Gompers threw the AFL's loyalty to the Wilson administration, promising to deter strikes. He and other moderate labor leaders were rewarded with appointments to high-level wartime government agencies. The National War Labor Board, created to mediate labor disputes, forbade strikes and lockouts and required management to negotiate with existing unions. Union membership climbed from roughly 2.5 million in 1916 to more than 4 million in 1919. The AFL could not curb strikes by the radical Industrial Workers of the World (IWW) or rebellious AFL locals. In the nineteen war months, more than six thousand strikes expressed workers' discontent with their wages, working conditions, and inflation. Laborers benefited from the full-employment wartime economy, which increased their total earnings, but the high cost of living denied them an appreciable improvement in their economic standing.

Women in the Work Force

With 16 percent of the male work force in the military and declining immigration, business recruited women to fill vacancies. Although the total number of women in the work force increased slightly, the real story was that many changed jobs, sometimes moving into formerly male domains. Some white women left domestic service for factories and left textile mills for employment in firearms plants. At least 20 percent of all workers in the wartime electrical machinery, airplane, and food industries were women. As white women took advantage of new opportunities, black women took some of their places in domestic service and in textile factories. Overall, most working women remained concentrated in sex-segregated occupations ("women's jobs") as typists, nurses, teachers, and domestic servants.

Some men, unaccustomed to working beside women, complained that women were destabilizing the work environment with their higher productivity; women answered that they were used to seasonal employment and piecework and hence worked at a faster pace. Some men protested that women were undermining the wage system by working for lower pay; women pointed out that male-dominated companies discriminated against them and unions denied them membership. Finally, male employees resented the spirit of independence evident among women, whose labor was now greatly valued.

When the war was over, women lost many of the gains they had made. The attitude that women's proper sphere was the home had changed little. Married working women found their family relationships growing tense; their husbands and children resented the disruption of home life. Reformers complained, moreover, that working mothers were neglecting their children. Day nurseries were scarce and beyond the means of most working-class families, and few employers provided child-care facilities. Whether married or single—and the great majority of working women were unmarried—women lost their jobs to the returning veterans.

African-American Migration to the North

Because wartime jobs provided an escape from social, economic, and political oppression, southern blacks undertook a great migration to the industrial North to work in railroad yards, packing houses, steel mills, shipyards, and coal mines. Between 1910 and 1920, about a half-million African-Americans uprooted themselves to move to the North. Most migrants were males—young (in their early twenties), unmarried, and skilled or semiskilled.

New opportunities could not erase the fact that African-Americans continued to experience blatant discrimination in both the North and the South. When the United States entered World War I, there was not one black judge in the entire country. Segregation was social custom. The Ku Klux Klan was reviving, and racist films like D. W. Griffith's *Birth of a Nation* (1915) fed prejudice. Lynching statistics exposed the wide gap between wartime declarations of humanity and the American practice of inhumanity at home: between 1914 and 1920, 382 blacks were lynched, some of them in military uniform.

Northern whites who resented "the Negro invasion" vented their anger in riots. In East St. Louis, Illinois, whites opposed to black employment in a defense plant rampaged through the streets in July 1917; forty blacks and nine whites lost their lives. During the bloody "Red Summer" of 1919, race riots rocked two dozen cities and towns. The worst violence occurred in Chicago, where thirty-eight people died in a riot after a black youth swimming at a segregated white beach was hit by a thrown rock and drowned. In response to continued racism, W. E. B. Du Bois vowed a struggle: "We return. We return from fighting. We return fighting."

TRAMPLING ON CIVIL LIBERTIES

"Woe be to the man that seeks to stand in our way in this day of high resolution," warned President Wilson. An official and unofficial campaign soon began to silence dissenters who questioned Wilson's decision for war or protested the draft. The targets of abuse were the hundreds of thousands of Americans, including reformers like Jane Addams and Senator Robert La Follette, and aliens who refused to support the war.

Shortly after the declaration of war in 1917, the president appointed George Creel, a progressive journalist, to head the Committee on Public

Committee on Public Information

Information (CPI). Employing some of the nation's most talented writers and scholars, the CPI set out to shape and mobilize public opinion by means of anti-German tracts, speeches, films, and "self-censorship" of the press. The committee also urged people to spy on their neighbors and report any suspicious behavior. Exaggeration, fear mongering, distortion, half-truths—such were the stuff of the CPI's "mind mobilization."

The Wilson administration also guided through an obliging Congress the Espionage Act (1917) and the Sedition Act (1918). The first statute forbade

Espionage and Sedition Acts

"false statements" designed to impede the draft or promote military insubordination and banned from the mails materials considered treasonous. The Sedition Act made it unlawful to obstruct the sale of war bonds and to use "disloyal, profane, scurrilous, or abusive" language to describe the government, the Constitution, the flag, and the military uniform. These loosely worded laws gave the government wide latitude to crack down on those with whom it differed. More than two thousand people were prosecuted under the acts, and many others were intimidated into silence. Among them was the Socialist party leader Eugene Debs, who received a ten-year sentence for his criticism of the war.

State and local governments joined the campaign. School boards dismissed teachers who questioned the war. German-Americans suffered floggings and other public humiliations; some were tarred and feathered. The governor of Iowa prohibited the use of any language but English in schools, and Pittsburgh banned Beethoven's music. In Tulsa, a mob whipped IWW members and poured tar into their bleeding sores. A German-American miner in Illinois was wrapped in a flag and lynched. And at Columbia University, Professor J. M. Cattell, a distinguished psychologist, was fired for his antiwar views. His colleague Charles Beard, a historian with a prowar perspective, resigned in protest: "If we have to suppress everything we don't like to hear, this country is resting on a pretty wobbly basis."

President Wilson and U.S. officials tried to crush what they did not like to hear. They concentrated their efforts on the IWW and the Socialist party. The war emergency and the frank opposition of those two radical organizations gave progressives and conservatives alike an opportunity to throttle their political rivals. The IWW, which stood for revolution against capitalism and was often violent in its tactics, aroused bitter opposition. Government agents raided union meetings and arrested IWW leaders. The army was dispatched to western mining and lumber regions to put down IWW strikes. Alien members of the IWW were deported. By the end of the war, most of the union's leaders were in jail.

The Supreme Court, itself attuned to the pulse of the times, upheld the Espionage Act. Justice Oliver Wendell Holmes, in *Schenck* v. *U.S.* (1919), expressed the Court's unanimous opinion that in time of war the First Amendment could be restricted: "Free speech would not protect a man falsely shouting fire in a theater and causing panic." If, according to Holmes, words "are of such a nature as to create a clear and present danger that they will bring about the substantial evils that Congress has a right to prevent," free speech could be limited. In another case, *Abrams* v. *U.S.* (1919), the Court upheld the Sedition Act.

THE RED SCARE

In the last few months of the war, guardians of Americanism began to label dissenters not only pro-German but pro-Bolshevik. After the Bolshevik Revolution in the fall of 1917, American hatred for the Kaiser's Germany was readily transferred to Communist Russia. When the new Russian government under V. I. Lenin made peace with Germany in early 1918, Americans grew angry that the closing of the eastern front would permit the Germans to move troops west. Many lashed out at American radicals, casually applying the term *Red* to people of varying beliefs, including anarchists, Wobblies, Socialists, pacifists, Communists, union leaders, and reformers.

The Wilson administration's ardent anti-Bolshevism became clear in mid-1918 when the president ordered five thousand American troops to

Intervention in Russian Civil War

northern Russia and ten thousand more soldiers to Siberia, where they joined other Allied contingents, including a large one from Japan. Wilson did not consult Congress. He announced that the military expeditions were intended to guard Allied supplies and Russian railroads from German seizure and to rescue a group of Czechs who wished to return home to fight the Germans. Worried that the Japanese were building influence in Siberia and closing the Open Door, Wilson also hoped to deter Japan from further advances in Asia. Mostly, he wanted to smash the infant Bolshevik government. The United States joined an economic blockade of Russia, sent arms to anti-Bolshevik forces, refused to recognize the Bolshevik government, and later helped block Russian participation in the Paris Peace Conference. These interventions in civil war-torn Russia immediately embittered Washington-Moscow relations—a legacy that would persist deep into the twentieth century.

At home, too, the Wilson administration moved against radicals and others imprecisely defined as Bolsheviks or Communists. By the war's close, Americans had become edgy. The war had exacerbated racial tensions. It had disrupted the workplace and the family. Americans had suffered an increase in the cost of living, and postwar unemployment loomed. To add to Americans' worries, the Russian Communists in 1919 established the Comintern to promote world revolution. Already hardened by wartime violations of civil liberties, Americans found it easy to blame their postwar troubles on new scapegoats.

A rash of labor strikes in 1919 sparked the Red Scare. All told, more than thirty-three hundred strikes involving four million laborers jolted the nation that year, including the

Labor Strikes, 1919

Seattle general strike in January. On May 1, traditionally a day of celebration for workers around the world, bombs were sent through the mails to prominent Americans. Although most devices were intercepted and dismantled, police never captured the conspirators. Next came the Boston police strike in September.

Some sniffed a Bolshevik conspiracy. The conservative governor of Massachusetts, Calvin Coolidge, gained fame by proclaiming that nobody had the right to strike against the public safety. State guardsmen were brought in to replace the striking police.

Especially ominous was the September walkout of 350,000 steel workers, many of whom still put in twelve-hour days, seven days a week, and lived in squalid housing. To defeat the strike, management hired agents club strikers, employed strikebreakers, and depicted strike leaders as Bolsheviks.

One leader of the steel strike was William Z. Foster, an IWW member and militant labor organizer who later joined the Communist party. His presence in a labor movement seeking bread-and-butter goals permitted political and business leaders to dismiss the steel strike as a foreign threat orchestrated by American radicals. There was in fact no conspiracy. The American left was in fact badly splintered and incapable of mounting a serious threat to the established order.

But Wilson's attorney general, A. Mitchell Palmer, claimed that "the blaze of revolution" was "burning up the foundations of society." To stamp out the radical fire, Palmer created a new Bureau of Investigation and appointed J. Edgar Hoover to run it. Hoover compiled index cards bearing the names of allegedly radical individuals and organizations. During 1919, agents jailed IWW members; Palmer also saw to it that 249 alien radicals were deported to Soviet Russia. Again, state and local governments took their cue from Washington. The New York State legislature expelled five duly elected members. States passed peacetime sedition acts under which hundreds of people were arrested.

The Red Scare reached a climax in January 1920 when the attorney general staged his Palmer Raids. Using Hoover's file, government agents in

Palmer Raids

thirty-three cities broke into meeting halls and homes without search warrants. More than four thousand people were jailed and denied counsel. Of this number, nearly six hundred were deported.

Palmer's disregard for elementary civil liberties drew criticism. Civil libertarians and lawyers charged that his tactics violated the Constitution.

Many of the arrested "Communists" had committed no crimes. When Palmer called for a peacetime sedition act, he alarmed leaders of many political persuasions. His dire prediction that serious violence would mar May Day 1920 proved mistaken. Palmer's exaggerated scenarios of Bolshevik conspiracy simply exceeded the truth so much that he lost credibility.

The campaigns against free speech in the period from 1917 through 1920 left casualties. Antiwar critics, radicals, and others became afraid to speak their minds. Debate, so essential to democracy, was wounded. Reform suffered as reformers either joined in the antiradicalism or became victims of it. Radical groups were badly weakened: the IWW became virtually extinct and the Socialist party became paralyzed. Wilson's intolerance of those who disagreed with him seemed to bespeak a fundamental distrust of democracy. At the very least, it illustrated that some progressives were willing to use coercion to achieve their goal of a reformed society.

THE PEACE CONFERENCE, LEAGUE FIGHT, AND POSTWAR WORLD

As the Red Scare threatened American democracy, Woodrow Wilson was struggling to make his Fourteen Points a reality. When the president departed for the Paris Peace Conference in December 1918, he faced obstacles erected by his political enemies, by the Allies, and by himself. Some observers suggested that the ambitious and self-confident Wilson underestimated his task.

During the 1918 congressional elections, Wilson had urged a vote for the Democrats as a sign of support for his peace goals. But the American people did just the opposite, although probably less in response to foreign-policy issues than to domestic questions like inflation. The Republicans gained control of both houses, signaling trouble for Wilson in two ways. First, he would have to submit a peace treaty for approval to a potentially hostile Senate. Second, Wilson's stature had been diminished in the eyes of foreign leaders. Wilson aggravated his political problems by not naming a senator to his advisory American Peace Commission, refusing to take any prominent Republican with him to Paris, and failing to consult with the Senate Foreign Relations Committee before the conference.

Another obstacle in Wilson's way was the Allies' determination to impose a harsh vengeful peace on the Germans. Georges Clemenceau of France, David Lloyd George of Britain, and Vittorio Orlando of Italy—with Wilson, the Big Four—became formidable adversaries. They had signed secret treaties during the war to grab German-controlled territories, and they scoffed at the pious, headstrong, self-impressed president who wanted to deny them the spoils of war.

The victors demanded that Germany pay a huge reparations bill. Wilson instead called for a small indemnity, fearing that a resentful and eco-

**Paris Peace
Conference**

——

nomically hobbled Germany might turn to Bolshevism or disrupt the postwar community in some other way. Unable to moderate the Allied position, the president reluctantly gave way, agreeing to a clause blaming the war on the Germans and to the creation of a commission to determine the amount of reparations (later set at $33 billion).

As for the breaking up of empires and the principle of self-determination, Wilson could deliver on only some of his goals. Creating a League-administered "mandate" system, the conferees placed former German and Turkish colonies under the control of other imperial nations (see map). France and Britain, for example, obtained parts of the Middle East, and Japan gained authority over Germany's colonies in the Pacific. In other arrangements, Japan replaced Germany as the imperial overlord of China's Shandong peninsula, and France was permitted occupation rights in Germany's Rhineland. Elsewhere in Europe, Wilson's prescriptions fared better. Out of Austria-Hungary and Russia came the newly independent states of Austria, Hungary, Yugoslavia, Czechoslovakia, and Poland. Wilson and his colleagues also built a *cordon sanitaire* (buffer zone) of new westward-looking nations (Finland, Estonia, Latvia, and Lithuania) around Russia to quarantine the Bolshevik contagion.

Wilson worked hardest on the charter for the League of Nations. In the long run, he believed, such an organization would moderate the harshness

**League of
Nations**

——

of the Allied peace terms and temper imperial ambitions. The League reflected the power of large nations like the United States: it consisted of an influential council of five permanent members and elected delegates from smaller states, an assembly of all members, and a World Court. The "backbone" of the League covenant was the collective security provision contained in Article 10. In this provision, League members agreed to "respect and preserve as against external aggression the territorial integrity and existing political independence of all Members of the League."

Americans vigorously debated the treaty. Criticism mounted that Wilson had bastardized his own principles, conceded Shandong to Japan, and

**Critique of
the Treaty**

——

personally killed a provision affirming the racial equality of all peoples. The treaty did not mention freedom of the seas, and tariffs were not reduced. Negotiations had been conducted in private, and reparations promised to be punishing. And Article 10 raised serious questions: Would the United States be obligated to use armed force to ensure collective security?

Wilson pleaded for understanding and lectured his opponents that compromises were necessary given the stubborn resistance of the Allies, who had threatened to jettison the conference unless Wilson made concessions. Did they not recognize that the League would rectify wrongs? Could they not see that membership in the League would give the United States "leadership in the world"? Senator Lodge remained unimpressed. A Harvard-educated Ph.D. and a partisan Republican, Lodge packed the Foreign Relations Committee with critics and prolonged public hearings. He introduced reservations to the treaty: one stated that Congress had to approve any obligation under Article 10.

In September 1919, Wilson embarked on a speaking tour of the United States. Growing more exhausted every day, he dismissed his antagonists as

Legend:
- ----- Boundaries of German, Russian, and Austro-Hungarian Empires in 1914
- Areas lost by Austro-Hungarian Empire
- Areas lost by Russian Empire
- Areas lost by German Empire
- Areas lost by Bulgaria
- Demilitarized Zone
- ——— Boundaries of 1926

Europe Transformed by War and Peace *After President Wilson and the other conferees at Versailles negotiated the Treaty of Paris, empires were broken up. In Eastern Europe, in particular, new nations were established.*

"absolute, contemptible quitters." In Colorado, while delivering another passionate speech, the president collapsed. A few days later, back in Washington, he suffered a stroke that paralyzed his left side. He became peevish and stubborn, increasingly unable to conduct the heavy business of the presidency.

How do historians know

that President Woodrow Wilson's ill health contributed to the Senate's defeat of U.S. membership in the League of Nations? Although scholars differ on whether Woodrow Wilson's ill health and behavior stemmed primarily from physiological or psychological conditions, they agree that Wilson had been an ill man long before a massive stroke on October 2, 1919, incapacitated him during national debate on the League of Nations. His medical history included arteriosclerosis (hardening of the arteries) and several strokes (the first in 1896). He and his doctors conspired to keep the information from the American people, who might have hesitated to vote him into the presidency had they known how frail he was. During the League fight, Wilson's health deteriorated further. Nervous and trembling, he suffered headaches and insomnia. After a speech in Colorado, he collapsed. In tears, the president muttered, "I seem to have gone to pieces." After Wilson returned to Washington, D.C., a massive stroke soon left him paralyzed and haggard. He could not lead, because he could seldom concentrate on any subject for very long and he secluded himself from cabinet members. But this irascible, stubborn, very sick man would not resign. Nor would he compromise with senators who said they would vote for U.S. membership in the League of Nations if only the president would accept changes in the Treaty of Paris. Given the serious issues raised by the collective security provision of the treaty, some historians continue to wonder whether even a healthy Wilson could have changed the outcome of the Senate vote. Photo: Brown Brothers.

Advised to placate senatorial critics so the treaty would have a chance of passing, Wilson rejected "dishonorable compromise." From Senate Democrats, he demanded utter loyalty—a vote against all reservations.

Twice in November the Senate rejected the Treaty of Paris. In the first vote, Democrats joined a group of sixteen "Irreconcilables," mostly Republicans who opposed any treaty whatsoever, to defeat the treaty with reservations. In the second vote, Republicans and Irreconcilables turned down the treaty without reservations. Had Wilson permitted Democrats to compromise—to accept reservations—he could have achieved his fervent goal of U.S. membership in the League of Nations.

Senate Rejection of the Treaty

Who or what was responsible for the defeat of the treaty? Wilson's poor health incapacitated him, but at the core of the debate lay a basic issue in American foreign policy: whether the United States would endorse collective security or continue to travel its traditional path. Wilson lost because, in a world dominated by imperialist states unwilling to subordinate their selfish acquisitive ambitions to an international organization, Americans preferred their traditional nonalignment and freedom of choice over binding commitments to collective action.

Collective Security Versus Unilateralism

In the end, Woodrow Wilson failed to create a new world order through reform. He promised more than he could deliver. Still, the United States emerged from the First World War an even greater world power. By 1920, the United States had become the world's leading economic power, producing 40 percent of its coal, 70 percent of its petroleum, and half of its pig iron. Rising to first rank in world trade, the United States shifted from being a debtor to a creditor nation, becoming the world's leading banker.

The international system born in these years was unstable and fragmented. Espousing decolonization and taking to heart the Wilsonian principle of self-determination, nationalist leaders like Ho Chi Minh of Indochina and Mohandas K. Gandhi of India vowed to achieve independence for their peoples. Communism became a disruptive force in world politics, and the Russians bore a grudge against those invaders who had tried to thwart their revolution. The new states in central and eastern Europe proved weak, dependent on outsiders for security. Germans bitterly resented the harsh peace settlement, and the war debts and reparations problems would dog international order for years. As it entered the 1920s, the international system that Woodrow Wilson vowed to reform seemed extremely unstable on many fronts.

Unstable International System

America emerged from the war years an unsettled mix of the old and the new. The war exposed deep divisions among Americans: white versus black, nativist versus immigrant, capital versus labor, "dry" versus "wet," men versus women, radical versus progressive and conservative, pacifist versus interventionist, nationalist versus internationalist. It is little wonder that Americans—having experienced race riots, labor strikes, disputes over civil liberties, and the League fight—wanted to escape from what the education reformer John Dewey called the "cult of irrationality" to what President Warren G. Harding called "normalcy."

During the war, the federal government intervened in the economy and influenced people's everyday lives as never before. Centralization of control in Washington, D.C., and mobilization of the home front served as a model for the future. The partnership of government and business in managing the wartime economy contributed to the further development of a mass society through the standardization of products and the promotion of efficiency. Wilsonian wartime policies also nourished the continued growth of oligopoly through the suspension of antitrust laws. After a short postwar recession, business power revived to dominate the next decade. American labor, by contrast, entered what one historian has called its lean years.

The war experience also changed Americans' mood. The war was grimy and ugly. People recoiled from photographs of shell-shocked faces and of bodies dangling from barbed wire. American soldiers, tired of idealism and cynical about their ability to right wrongs, craved the latest baseball scores, their regular jobs, and renewed participation in America's famed consumer culture. Those progressives who had believed that entry into the war would deliver the millennium, later marveled at their naïveté. Many lost their enthusiasm for crusades, and many others turned away in disgust from the bickering of the victors.

Woodrow Wilson had remarked, soon after taking office in 1913 before the Great War, that "there's no chance of progress and reform in an administration in which war plays the principal part." From the perspective of 1920, looking back on distempers at home and abroad, Wilson would have to agree with other Americans that progress and reform had sustained blows.

SUGGESTIONS FOR FURTHER READING

General

John W. Chambers, *The Tyranny of Change*, 2d ed. (1992); Ellis W. Hawley, *The Great War and the Search for a Modern Order*, 2d ed. (1992); Henry F. May, *The End of American Innocence* (1964); Emily S. Rosenberg, *Spreading the American Dream* (1982); Ronald Steel, *Walter Lippmann and the American Century* (1980).

Woodrow Wilson, His Diplomacy, and the First World War

Lloyd E. Ambrosius, *Wilsonian Statecraft* (1991); Frederick S. Calhoun, *Power and Principle* (1986); Kendrick A. Clements, *The Presidency of Woodrow Wilson* (1992); John W. Coogan, *The End of Neutrality* (1981); John M. Cooper Jr., *The Warrior and the Priest* (1983); Patrick Devlin, *Too Proud to Fight* (1975); Robert H. Ferrell, *Woodrow Wilson and World War I* (1985); Ross Gregory, *The Origins of American Intervention in the First World War* (1971); Thomas J. Knock, *To End All Wars* (1992); N. Gordon Levin Jr., *Woodrow Wilson and World Politics* (1968); Arthur S. Link, *Woodrow Wilson: Revolution, War and Peace* (1979), and *Wilson*, 5 vols. (1947–1965); J. W. Schulte Nordholt, *Woodrow Wilson: A Life in World Peace* (1991); Edwin A. Weinstein, *Woodrow Wilson: A Medical and Psychological Biography* (1981).

The U.S. Military

John W. Chambers, *To Raise an Army* (1987); J. Garry Clifford, *The Citizen Soldiers* (1972); Edward M. Coffman, *The War to End All Wars* (1968); Donald Smythe, *Pershing* (1986); Russell F. Weigley, *The American Way of War* (1973).

The Home Front

Valerie Jean Conner, *The National War Labor Board* (1983); Alfred W. Crosby, *America's Forgotten Pandemic: The Influenza of 1918* (1989); Robert D. Cuff, *The War Industries Board* (1973); David M. Kennedy, *Over Here* (1980); Seward W. Livermore, *Politics Is Adjourned* (1966); Frederick C. Luebke, *Bonds of Loyalty: German-Americans and World War I* (1974); Ronald Schaffer, *America in the Great War: The Rise of the War Welfare State* (1991); Stephen L. Vaughn, *Holding Fast the Inner Lines* (1979) (on CPI); Neil A. Wynn, *From Progressivism to Prosperity: World War I and American Society* (1986).

Women, the War, and the Peace

Allen F. Davis, *American Heroine* (1974) (on Addams); Maurine W. Greenwald, *Women, War, and Work* (1980); Dorothy Schneider and Carl J. Schneider, *Into the Breach: American Women Overseas in World War I* (1991); Barbara J. Steinson, *American Women's Activism in World War I* (1982).

African-Americans at Home and Abroad

Arthur E. Barbeau and Florette Henri, *The Unknown Soldiers: Black American Troops in World War I* (1974); Marvin E. Fletcher, *The Black Soldier and Officer in the United States Army, 1891–1917* (1974); James B. Grossman, *Land of Hope: Chicago, Black Southerners, and the Great Migration* (1989); Robert V. Haynes, *A Night of Violence: The Houston Riot of 1917* (1976); Carole Marks, *Farewell—We're Good and Gone: The Great Black Migration* (1989); Elliot M. Rudwick, *Race Riot at East St. Louis, July 2, 1917* (1964); William M. Tuttle Jr., *Race Riot* (1970) (on Chicago).

Antiwar Critics, Antiradicalism, Civil Liberties, and the Red Scare

David Brody, *Labor in Crisis: The Steel Strike of 1919* (1965); Charles Chatfield, *The American Peace Movement* (1992); Charles DeBenedetti, *Origins of the Modern Peace Movement* (1978); Sondra Herman, *Eleven Against War* (1969); C. Roland Marchand, *The American Peace Movement and Social Reform, 1898–1918* (1973); Paul L. Murphy, *World War I and the Origin of Civil Liberties* (1979); Robert K. Murray, *Red Scare* (1955); H. C. Peterson and Gilbert C. Fite, *Opponents of War, 1917–1918* (1968); Richard Polenberg, *Fighting Faiths* (1987) (the *Abrams* case); William Preston, *Aliens and Dissenters* (1966); James Weinstein, *The Decline of Socialism in America, 1912–1923* (1967).

The United States and the Bolshevik Revolution

John Lewis Gaddis, *Russia, the Soviet Union, and the United States*, 2d ed. (1990); Christopher Lasch, *The American Liberals and the Russian Revolution* (1962); David McFadden, *Alternative Paths: Soviets and Americans, 1917–1920* (1993); Betty M. Unterberger, *The United States, Revolutionary Russia, and the Rise of Czechoslovakia* (1989).

Paris Peace Conference and League Fight

Lloyd Ambrosius, *Woodrow Wilson and the American Diplomatic Tradition* (1987); Herbert Hoover, *The Ordeal of Woodrow Wilson* (1958); Warren F. Kuehl, *Seeking World Order* (1969); Arno Mayer, *Politics and Diplomacy of Peacemaking* (1967); Ralph A. Stone, *The Irreconcilables* (1970); Arthur Walworth, *Wilson and the Peacemakers* (1986); William C. Widenor, *Henry Cabot Lodge and the Search for an American Foreign Policy* (1980).

The Aftermath of War

Malcolm Cowley, *Exile's Return* (1951); Paul Fussell, *The Great War and Modern Memory* (1975); Stuart I. Rochester, *American Liberal Disillusionment in the Wake of World War I* (1977); Stephen R. Ward, ed., *The War Generation: Veterans of the First World War* (1975).

24

The New Era of the 1920s

I T WAS A TRIAL that riveted national attention. The defendants were seven members of the Chicago White Sox and two alleged gamblers accused of conspiring to defraud the public by intentionally losing the 1919 World Series to the Cincinnati Reds. The Black Sox scandal had wracked baseball, the national pastime, for almost two years. Among the accused was outfielder Joe Jackson, who rivaled Ty Cobb and Babe Ruth as the game's greatest hitter. The jury's August 2, 1921, decision of not guilty caused an eruption in the courtroom. Even the judge joined the crowd in whistling and cheering. For a people recovering from a world war and eager to partake in new opportunities for amusement and consumer comfort, reaction to the verdict reflected the public's desire to put the darker realities behind it.

But was exoneration the answer? Judge Kennesaw Mountain Landis, a former federal judge who was baseball's newly appointed commissioner, did not think so. An accumulation of evidence, including three confessions that mysteriously disappeared before the trial, had prompted a grand jury to indict the players. The day after the trial, Landis declared, "Regardless of the verdict of juries, no player that throws a ball game; no player that undertakes or promises to throw a ball game; no player that sits in a conference with a bunch of crooked players and gamblers where the ways and means of throwing games are planned and discussed and does not promptly tell his club about it, will ever play professional baseball." With the same fearless rectitude and controlled temper he had used as judge in the trustbusting case against Standard Oil, Landis banned all eight from ever playing professional baseball again. Landis's act illustrates the clash of values that characterized the decade of the 1920s: the tension between the urge for release, fun, and consumerism and the tug of old-fashioned values, moral purity, and order.

During the 1920s, the flower of consumerism reached full bloom. Although poverty dogged small farmers, workers in declining industries, and nonwhites in inner cities, most of the population enjoyed a high standard of living. Spurred by advertising and new forms of credit, Americans eagerly bought radios, automobiles, real estate, and stocks. As in the Gilded Age, government policies supported the interests of business; Congress, three Republican presidents, and even the Supreme Court acted to maintain a favorable climate for profits. Yet state and local governments were undertaking important reforms.

Complexity characterized the 1920s. Its frivolous stunts and fads were accompanied by an outburst of creativity in the arts and by significant advances in science and technology. Changes in work habits, family responsibilities, and health care fostered new uses of time and new attitudes about proper behavior. While material bounty and increased leisure time enticed Americans into a variety of new amusements, winds of change stirred up waves of reaction. New liberal values repelled various groups such as the Ku Klux Klan, immigration restrictionists, and religious fundamentalists.

Other troubling clouds were gathering as well. The consumer culture that dominated everyday life caused Americans to ignore rising debts and other negative economic signs. Just before the decade closed, the whole system came crashing down.

BIG BUSINESS TRIUMPHANT

The decade of business ascendancy began with a frightening economic decline. For two years after the First World War, heavy consumer spending drove prices up. Then, in 1920, people abruptly stopped buying. Export trade and industrial output both dropped as wartime orders dried up. Farm income also plunged because of falling exports. Unemployment, about 2 percent in 1919, passed 12 percent in 1921. Profits declined in the railroad and mining industries, and layoffs spread through New England as textile companies abandoned outdated factories for the raw materials and inexpensive labor of the South.

Electric motors helped drive the recovery that began in 1922 and continued unevenly until 1929. By that year, electricity powered 70 percent of American industry. Assembly-line production also contributed to economic health, adding countless new consumer products to the market. As Americans acquired more spending money and leisure time, service industries boomed. More people could afford the goods and services of department stores, restaurants, beauty and barber shops, and movie theaters. The new consumerism was fueled by refined methods of credit, especially the installment or time-payment plan.

Beneath the prosperity, an economic revolution was rumbling. The consolidation movement that had bred trusts and holding companies in the late nineteenth century had reached a new stage. Although Progressive era trustbusting had to some extent harnessed big business, it had not eliminated oligopoly—control of an entire industry by a few large companies. By the 1920s, oligopolies dominated not only production but also marketing, distribution, and even finance. In such basic industries as automobile manufacturing, steel production, and electrical equipment, a few sprawling companies such as General Motors, U.S. Steel, and General Electric predominated.

The organizational movement that had begun around 1900 also matured in the 1920s. Myriad business and professional associations sprang up to protect members' interests. Retailers and manufacturers formed trade associations to pool information and coordinate planning. Farm bureaus promoted scientific agriculture, lobbied for government protection, and tried to stabilize markets. Lawyers, engineers, and social scientists cooperated with business to promote economic growth. Big business had dominated American economic life since the late nineteenth century; these consolidated, corporate forms of initiative that now pervaded so many segments of the economy were what distinguished the twentieth century from the nineteenth.

In the course of this expansion, many Americans shed their fears of big business, swayed in part by the testimonials of probusiness propagandists. "Among the nations of the earth today," one writer proclaimed in 1921, "America stands for one idea: *Business.*"

Government reflected this outlook. Congress reduced taxes on corporations and wealthy individuals in 1921, and the next year it raised tariff rates. Presidents Warren G. Harding, Calvin Coolidge, and Herbert Hoover appointed influential cabinet officers who pursued policies favorable to business. Regulatory agencies such as the Federal Trade Commission and Interstate Commerce Commission cooperated with corporations more than they regulated them. And the Supreme Court, by voiding restrictions on child labor (*Bailey* v. *Drexel Furniture*

Company, 1922) and overturning a minimum-wage law for women (*Adkins* v. *Children's Hospital*, 1923), struck down attempts at reform. Other Supreme Court decisions ruled that a striking union, like a trust, could be prosecuted for illegal restraint of trade but that trade associations could collect and disseminate antiunion information.

Organized labor, which had gained ground during the Progressive era, suffered setbacks during the 1920s. Public opinion, influenced by a fear of Bolshevism, turned against workers who disrupted everyday life with strikes. The federal government frequently stifled union attempts to exercise power. In 1922, for instance, the Harding administration obtained a severe and sweeping court injunction to quash a strike by 400,000 railroad shop workers. The same year, the Justice Department helped put down a nationwide strike by 650,000 miners.

Meanwhile, large corporations counteracted the appeal of unions by offering pensions, profit sharing, and company-sponsored social and sporting events, a policy known as welfare capitalism. State legislators lent their support to employers by prohibiting closed shops (workplaces where union membership was mandatory). In such a climate, union membership fell from 5.1 million in 1920 to 3.6 million in 1929.

A BUSINESS-MINDED PRESIDENCY

A symbol of the decade's good will toward business was President Warren G. Harding, a Republican elected in 1920 when the populace had no appetite for national or international crusades. He selected some capable assistants, notably Secretary of State Charles Evans Hughes, Secretary of Commerce Herbert Hoover, Secretary of the Treasury Andrew Mellon, and Secretary of Agriculture Henry C. Wallace. Harding also backed some reforms that represented an extension of progressivism into the 1920s. He helped streamline the federal budget with the Budget and Accounting Act of 1921, supported antilynching legislation, approved bills assisting farm cooperatives and liberalizing farm

credit, and, unlike his predecessor Wilson, was generally tolerant on civil liberties issues.

Harding's problem was that he appointed some predatory friends to positions from which they infested the government with corruption. Charles Forbes of the Veterans Bureau served time in federal prison after being convicted of fraud and bribery in connection with government contracts. Thomas W. Miller, custodian of alien property, was jailed for accepting bribes. Attorney General Harry Daugherty was implicated in a bribery scheme and in other fraudulent acts; he escaped prosecution only by refusing to testify against himself. In the most notorious case, a congressional inquiry in 1923 and 1924 revealed that Secretary of the Interior Albert Fall had accepted bribes to lease government property to private oil companies. For his role in the affair—called the Teapot Dome scandal after a Wyoming oil reserve that had been turned over to Mammoth Oil Company—Fall was fined $100,000 and spent a year in jail, the first cabinet officer ever to be so disgraced.

In mid-1923, few Americans knew how corrupt Harding's administration had become. The president, however, was disillusioned. Amid rumors of mismanagement and crime, he told journalist William Allen White, "My God, this is a hell of a job. I have no trouble with my enemies. . . . But my friends, my God-damned friends . . . they're the ones that keep me walking the floor nights." On a speaking tour that summer, Harding became ill, and he died in San Francisco on August 2. Vice President Calvin Coolidge succeeded Harding. A dour New Englander, the former governor of Massachusetts gained national attention and the 1920 vice presidential nomination because of his firm stand against striking Boston police in 1919.

Coolidge had great respect for private enterprise, and his presidency coincided with unusual business prosperity. Aided by Andrew Mellon, whom he retained as secretary of the treasury, Coolidge's administration balanced the budget, reduced government debt, lowered income-tax rates (especially for the rich), and began construction of a national highway system. The only disruptions

Coolidge Prosperity

• *Important Events* •

1919	Eighteenth Amendment ratified, establishing Prohibition
1920	Nineteenth Amendment ratified, legalizing the vote for women in federal elections
	Warren G. Harding elected president
	KDKA transmits first commercial radio broadcast
1920–21	Postwar deflation and depression occurs
1921	Federal Highway Act funds national highway system
	Johnson Act establishes immigration quotas
	Sacco and Vanzetti convicted
1922	Economic recovery raises standard of living
1923	Harding dies; Calvin Coolidge assumes the presidency
	Ku Klux Klan activity peaks
	Equal rights amendment introduced in Congress but not passed
1923–24	Government scandals exposed
1924	Johnson-Reid Act revises immigration quotas
	Coolidge elected president
1925	Scopes trial highlights battle between religious fundamentalists and religious liberals
1927	Sacco and Vanzetti executed
	Lindbergh pilots solo transatlantic flight
	Babe Ruth hits sixty home runs
	The Jazz Singer, the first movie with sound, is released
1928	Stock market soars
	Herbert Hoover elected president
1929	Stock market crashes; Great Depression begins

arose over farm policy. Responding to farmers' complaints of falling prices, Congress twice passed bills to establish government-backed price supports for staple crops (the McNary-Haugen bills of 1927 and 1928). Coolidge, however, vetoed the measure both times.

"Coolidge prosperity" was the decisive issue in the presidential election of 1924. Both major parties ran candidates who accepted business supremacy. Republicans nominated Coolidge with little dissent. At their national convention, Democrats first debated heatedly whether to condemn the Ku Klux Klan, voting 542 to 541 against condemnation. They then endured 103 ballots before settling on John W. Davis, a corporation lawyer from New York, as their presidential nominee. Remnants of the progressive movement, along with various farm, labor, and socialist groups, formed a new Progressive party and nominated Robert M. La Follette, the aging reformer from Wisconsin. Coolidge beat Davis by 15.7 million to 8.4 million popular votes, 382 to 136 electoral votes. La Follette finished a poor third, receiving a respectable but ineffective 4.8 million popular votes and only 13 electoral votes.

EXTENSIONS OF REFORM

Some political analysts, struck by the triumph of business influence, claimed that progressivism had died. They were partly right; the urgent thrust for political and economic reform that had moved the previous generation faded in the 1920s. Yet many of the Progressive era's achievements were sustained and extended in these years. Federal trustbusting declined, but regulatory commissions and other government agencies still monitored business activities and worked to reduce wasteful business practices. A corps of congressional reformers kept progressive causes alive by supporting labor legislation, aid to farmers, and a government-owned hydroelectric dam at Muscle Shoals, Alabama.

Most reform, however, occurred at state and local levels. Following initiatives begun before the

First World War, thirty-four states instituted or expanded workers' compensation laws in the 1920s. Many states established employee-funded old-age pensions and welfare programs for the indigent. In the cities, social scientists gathered data in a systematic effort to identify and solve urban problems. By 1926, every major city and many smaller ones had planning and zoning commissions that aimed to harness physical growth to the common good. Social workers continued to strive for better housing and poverty relief. During the 1920s, the nation's state houses, city halls, and universities trained a new generation of reformers who would later influence national affairs during the New Deal.

Indian affairs also stirred reformers, who were forced by the generally apathetic stance of the federal government to take adversarial positions toward federal officials. No

Indian Affairs

longer a threat to whites' ambitions, Native Americans were now treated like other minorities: as objects of discrimination and pressures to assimilate. Severalty, the policy of allotting land to individuals rather than to tribes, had failed. Indian farmers had to contend with poor soil, lack of irrigation, poor medical care, and cattle thieves. Deeply attached to their land, they showed little inclination to move to cities. Whites remained insensitive to indigenous cultures. Reformers were especially critical of Indian women, who refused to adopt middle-class homemaking methods and balked at sending their children to boarding schools.

Reform organizations such as the Indian Rights Association, the Indian Defense Association, and the General Federation of Women's Clubs worked to obtain racial justice and social services, including better education and return of tribal lands. Meanwhile, the federal government struggled to clarify Indians' citizenship status. The Dawes Act had conferred citizenship on all Indians who accepted land in severalty but not on those who remained on reservations. Congress finally clarified the issue in 1924 with a law granting full citizenship to all Indians who had not previously received it. And under President Herbert Hoover, expenditures for health, education, and welfare were increased. Much of the money, however, went to enlarge the bureaucracy rather than into Indian hands.

Even after the achievement of suffrage in 1920, politically active women tended to shun party politics in favor of voluntary organizations that helped

Women and Politics

develop the techniques of modern pressure-group politics. Whether the issue was birth control, peace, education, Indian affairs, or opposition to lynching, women active in these associations publicized their cause and lobbied legislators rather than trying to elect their own candidates. At times, they allied with men's organizations working for similar ends and achieved legislative victories especially valuable to women. The Cable Act of 1922, for example, reversed an old law under which an American woman who married a foreigner assumed her husband's citizenship; under the new law such a woman could retain U.S. citizenship.

As new voters, however, women faced a dilemma in electoral politics. Male party leaders were not likely to yield their power and would welcome only those women who accepted the party's platform and candidates. Should women form their own party? The National Woman's party, which before suffrage had been the champion of feminism, still stressed female solidarity in the quest for equal rights. Other groups, such as the League of Women Voters, did not attempt to create a female voting bloc. Instead, they preferred to lobby for issues of interest to women while integrating women into politics with men. To the dismay of women's political groups, however, newly enfranchised female voters participated in elections in the same small proportions as did men. Like men, they seemed preoccupied by the diversions of the new era's materialism.

MATERIALISM UNBOUND

Poor Richard's Almanac would have sold poorly in the 1920s. Rather than adhere to such traditional Franklin homilies as "Waste not, want not," Americans of the 1920s succumbed to the advice of an advertising executive: "Make the public want what you have to sell. Make 'em pant for it." And, although poverty and social injustice still blighted the country, the belief prevailed that, as journalist

Joseph Wood Krutch put it, "The future was bright and the present was good fun at least."

Between 1919 and 1929, the gross national product—the total value of all goods and services produced in the United States—swelled by 40 percent. Wages and salaries also grew (although not as drastically), while the cost of living remained relatively stable. People had more purchasing power, and they spent as Americans had never spent. By 1929, two-thirds of all Americans lived in dwellings that had electricity, compared with one-sixth in 1912. In 1929, one-fourth of all families owned electric vacuum cleaners and one-fifth had toasters. Many could afford these and other goods such as radios, washing machines, and movie tickets only because more than one family member worked or because the breadwinner took a second job. Nevertheless, new products and services were available to more than just the rich.

Expansion of the Consumer Society

Of all the era's material wonders, the automobile was the vanguard. During the 1920s, automobile registrations soared from eight million to twenty-three million. Mass production and competition brought down prices, making cars affordable even to some working-class families. A Ford Model T cost less than $300 and a Chevrolet sold for $700 by 1926—when workers in manufacturing earned about $1,300 a year and clerical workers about $2,300. At these prices, people could consider the car a necessity rather than a luxury.

Effects of the Automobile

The car altered American life as much as the railroad had seventy-five years earlier. Women achieved newfound independence as high numbers learned to drive. Changes in design provided new opportunities for youths to escape from watchful parents: by 1927, most autos were enclosed (most had had open tops in 1919), making for a privacy that bred fears of "houses of prostitution on wheels." And most important, the car was the ultimate symbol of social equality.

Americans' new passion for driving necessitated extensive construction of roads and abundant supplies of fuel. Important advances came in 1921 when Congress passed the Federal Highway Act, which provided federal aid for state roads, and in 1923 when the Bureau of Public Roads planned a national highway system. The advent of the automobile forced public officials to pay more serious attention to safety regulations and traffic control.

More than ever, advertising whetted demand for automobiles and other goods and services. By 1929, total advertising expenditures reached $3.4 billion, more than was spent on all types of formal education. Advertising became a new gospel for many business-minded Americans. In his best-selling *The Man Nobody Knows* (1925), advertising executive Bruce Barton called Jesus "the founder of modern business," because he "picked up twelve men from the bottom ranks of business and forged them into an organization that conquered the world."

Advertising

Although daily newspaper circulation declined in the 1920s, more than ten million families owned radios at the decade's end. A new advertising medium had been discovered. Station KDKA in Pittsburgh pioneered commercial radio broadcasting beginning in 1920; within two years there were 508 such stations. By 1929, the National Broadcasting Company, which had begun to assemble a network of radio stations three years earlier, was charging advertisers $10,000 to sponsor an hour-long show. Highway billboards and commercials projected during intermissions at movie houses also reminded viewers to buy.

CITIES, MIGRANTS, AND SUBURBS

Consumerism signified not merely an economically mature nation but an urbanized one. The 1920 federal census revealed that for the first time a majority of Americans, 51.4 percent, lived in urban areas (defined as places with twenty-five hundred people or more), a sign that the city had become the locus of national experience. The most explosive growth occurred in cities with warm climates—notably Miami

Continuing Urbanization

and San Diego—where the promise of comfort and profit attracted thousands of speculators.

The trend toward urbanization continued during the 1920s, when an estimated six million Americans left their farms for nearby or distant cities. African-Americans accounted for a sizable portion of the migrants. Pushed out of cotton farming by a plague of boll weevils and lured by industrial jobs, 1.5 million blacks moved cityward during the 1920s, accelerating a trend that had begun a decade earlier (see Chapter 23). The African-American populations of New York, Chicago, Detroit, and Houston doubled during these years. Forced by low wages and discrimination to seek the cheapest housing, newcomers squeezed into ghettos—low-rent districts from which escape was difficult at best. When overcrowding burst the boundaries of the ghetto and blacks spilled into nearby white neighborhoods, racial violence often was the result.

In response to discrimination, race riots, and threats, thousands of blacks in northern cities joined movements that glorified black independence. The

Marcus Garvey

most influential of the black nationalist groups was the Universal Negro Improvement Association (UNIA), headed by Marcus Garvey, a Jamaican immigrant who believed blacks should separate from corrupt white society. Proclaiming "I am the equal of any white man," Garvey cultivated racial pride with mass meetings and parades. He also promoted black capitalism. His newspaper, the *Negro World*, refused to publish ads for hair straighteners and skin-lightening cosmetics, and his Black Star shipping line was intended to help blacks emigrate to Africa.

The UNIA declined in the mid-1920s when the Black Star line went bankrupt (unscrupulous dealers had sold the line dilapidated ships) and when anti-radical fears prompted government prosecution (ten of the organization's leaders were arrested on charges of anarchism, and Garvey was deported for mail fraud). Black middle-class leaders like W. E. B. Du Bois opposed the UNIA. Nevertheless, in New York, Chicago, Detroit, and other cities, the organization attracted a huge following, and it served notice that blacks had their own aspirations, which they could and would translate into action.

The newest immigrants to American cities came from Mexico and Puerto Rico. As in the nineteenth century, Mexicans continued to move north

Mexican and Puerto Rican Immigrants

to work as agricultural laborers in the Southwest, but in the 1920s many were also drawn to growing cities like Denver, San Antonio, Los Angeles, and Tucson. Like other immigrant groups, Mexicans generally lacked resources and skills, and men greatly outnumbered women. Victims of Anglo prejudice, Mexicans crowded into low-rent inner-city districts plagued by poor city services. Yet in their communities, called *barrios*, immigrants could maintain the customs and values of the homeland and develop businesses and social organizations to help them adapt to American society.

The influx of Puerto Ricans to the mainland was caused by a shift in the island's economy from sugar to coffee production. The change created a surplus of workers, who were attracted by contracts from employers seeking inexpensive labor. Most Puerto Rican migrants moved to New York City where they created *barrios* in parts of Brooklyn and Manhattan. In both Puerto Rican and Mexican *barrios*, the educated elite—doctors, lawyers, business owners—tended to serve as community leaders.

As urban growth peaked, suburban growth accelerated. Although towns had clustered around the edges of urban centers since the nation's earliest

Growth of the Suburbs

years, prosperity and easier transportation—mainly the automobile—made the urban fringe more accessible in the 1920s. Between 1920 and 1930, the suburbs of Chicago, Cleveland, and Los Angeles grew five to ten times as fast as did the central cities. Most suburbanites were middle- and upper-class families motivated by a desire to escape big-city crime, dirt, and taxes. They resisted annexation to core cities and fought to preserve local control over their police, fire protection, and water and gas services. Both bulging cities and suburbs fostered the mass culture that gave the decade its character. Most consumers who jammed shops, movie houses, and sporting arenas, and embraced fads like crossword puzzles, miniature golf, and marathon dancing, were city and suburban dwellers. Cities and suburbs were the places where people defied law and morality by patronizing speakeasies (illegal saloons), wearing outlandish clothes, and listening to jazz. They were also the places where women, ethnic and racial minorities, and devout moralists strained hardest to adjust to the new era. Yet the sentimental ideal of small-town society survived, and Americans reminisced about the innocence and simplicity of a world gone by. This was the dilemma the modern nation faced: how does one anchor oneself in a world of rampant materialism and social change?

NEW RHYTHMS OF EVERYDAY LIFE

Amid all the change, Americans developed new ways of using time. People increasingly split their daily lives into distinct compartments: work, family, and leisure. Each type of time was altered in the 1920s. For many people, time on the job shrank. Among industrial workers, the five-and-a-half-day workweek (half a day on Saturday) was becoming common. Many white-collar employees worked a forty-hour week and enjoyed two days off. Annual vacations were becoming a standard job benefit for white-collar workers, whose numbers grew by 40 percent.

Family time is harder to measure, but certain trends are clear. Birthrates dropped noticeably between 1920 and 1930 and, as a result, family size decreased. Meanwhile, the divorce rate rose. In 1920, there was one divorce in every 7.5 marriages; by 1929, the national ratio was one in six, and in many cities it was two in seven. Because of longer life expectancy, lower birthrates, and more divorce, adults devoted a smaller portion of their lives to parental and other family tasks.

The availability of ready-to-wear clothes, canned foods, and mass-produced furniture meant that family members spent less time producing household necessities. Wives

Household Management

still spent long hours cleaning, cooking, and raising children, but machines—electric irons,

washing machines, and hot water heaters, for example—now lightened some of their tasks. And instead of being a producer of food and clothing as her predecessors had been, the wife now became the chief consumer, responsible for making sure the family spent its money wisely.

In addition, the availability of washing machines, hot water, and commercial soap put pressure on wives to keep everything clean. Advertisers tried to coax women to buy products by making them feel guilty for not giving enough attention to cleaning the home, caring for children, and tending to personal hygiene. Thus, while the industrial and service sectors became more specialized as a result of technological advances, housewives retained a wide variety of tasks and added new ones as well.

Better diets and shorter workdays made Americans generally healthier. Life expectancy at birth increased from fifty-four to sixty years between

Older Americans and Retirement

1920 and 1930. During those same years, the total population older than sixty-five grew 35 percent, whereas the rest of the population increased only 15 percent. The rising numbers and the worsening economic status of the elderly stirred interest in old-age pensions and other forms of assistance. Recognizing the needs of aging citizens, most European countries had established state-supported pension systems in the early 1900s. Many Americans believed, however, that individuals should prepare for old age by saving in their youth; pensions, they felt, smacked of socialism.

Yet something had to be done. Most inmates of state poorhouses were older people, and almost one-third of Americans aged sixty-five and older depended financially on someone else. Most employers, including the federal government, did not have pension plans for retired employees. Resistance to pension plans finally broke at the state level in the 1920s, when reformers persuaded voluntary associations, labor unions, and legislators to endorse the principle of old-age assistance through pensions, insurance, and retirement homes. By 1933, almost every state provided at least minimal assistance to needy elderly people, and a path had been opened for a national program of old-age insurance.

DEPARTMENT OF COMMERCE-BUREAU OF THE CENSUS

FOURTEENTH CENSUS OF THE UNITED STATES: 1920-POPULATION

STATE _Massachusetts_   ENUMERATOR _Harry Hoffman_

COUNTY _Suffolk_   ENUMERATED BY ME AN THE _7_ DAY OF _Jan._ 1920

TOWNSHIP OR OTHER DIVISION OF COUNTY _Tract 53 14,13_   NAME OF INCORPORATED PLACE _Boston_

Street	House Number	Name	Relation	Sex	Color or Race	Age	Single, Married, Widowed or Divorced	Citizenship	Year of Immigration	Person Place of Birth	Father Place of Birth	Mother Place of Birth	English Speaking	Occupation
	22	Carrigan, James	step-son	M	W	20	S			Mass.	New York	Ireland	yes	Chauffeur
		— Ellen	step-dghter	F	W	16	S			Mass.	New York	Ireland	yes	Laundry
	16	Bradley, George	Head	M	W	53	M			Mass.	Mass.	Mass.	yes	Railroad
		— Phila A.	wife	F	W	52	M		1880	New Brunswick	New Brunswick	New Brunswick	yes	none
		Hart, Dennis	Lodger	M	W	49	wd.			Mass.	Ireland	Ireland	yes	Painter
Stamford Street	12	Sidlinger, Albert	Head	M	W	65	M			Maine	Maine	Maine	yes	none
		— Catherine	wife	F	W	49	M		1886	Scotia	Ireland	Scotia	yes	none
		— Albert K	son	M	W	29	S			Mass.	Maine	Scotia		Insurance broker
	10	Milkowski, Harri	Head	M	W	34	M		1906	Russia	Russia	Russia	yes	Cook
		— Mary	wife	F	W	27	M		1908	Russia	Russia	Russia	yes	none
		— Helen	dghter	F	W	6½	S			Mass.	Russia	Russia		none
		— Jennie	dghter	F	W	5½	S			Mass.	Russia	Russia		none
		— Peter	son	M	W	1½	S			Mass.	Russia	Russia		none
		McQuard, Francis	Lodger	M	W	33	M			Mass.	Ireland	Ireland	yes	Reporter
		— Frieda	wife	F	W	22	M		1899	Switzerland	Italy	Germany	yes	none
		White, Irwin	Lodger	M	W	37	M		1897	England	England	England	yes	Hospital
		Blake, John	Lodger	M	W	38	M		1894	Ireland	Ireland	Ireland	yes	Laborer
		Miller, Harry	Lodger	M	W	44	S		1910	Norway	Norway	Norway	yes	Waiter
	8	Ling, Chinturg	Head	M	Ch	60	M		1890	China	China	China	no	Laundry
	6	Coss, Frank	Head	M	W	45	M		1889	Italy	Italy	Italy	yes	Master Fletcher
		— Effie	wife	F	W	43	M			New Hampshire	New Hampshire	Maine	yes	none

How do historians know

about individual and family life in the 1920s? The manuscript census schedules (the pages on which census takers actually recorded information) from the 1920 federal census contain extraordinarily rich information. By sampling, tabulating, and analyzing large numbers of census entries—after trying to decipher often illegible handwriting—historians raise and attempt to answer questions about everyday life and the environments in which ordinary people lived. The excerpt on this page reproduces the records from a few families living on Stamford Street in Boston and yields numerous insights into how their households were organized. For example, the Bradley household at 16 Stamford contained only a middle-aged husband, who was born in Massachusetts and worked as a railroad baggage master; his wife, born in New Brunswick (Nova Scotia) and of British descent, and a middle-aged boarder, who worked as a painter. Why was the boarder living there? Did the Bradleys have extra space because their children had grown up and moved away? The Milkowski household at 10 Stamford was larger and more complex. It contained ten people, including three young children and five lodgers. Mr. and Mrs. Milkowski were from Russia, but their lodgers came from a variety of places. What kinds of social and economic relationships might have existed in this household? A lone Chinese man lived at 8 Stamford. He worked in a laundry, and the census notes that he was married. But where was his wife? Census data often must be combined with other sources in order to answer these questions, but manuscript censuses have helped to illuminate the lives of people previously excluded from the historical record because they did not leave diaries or letters and were not famous enough to be the subject of newspaper stories.

Photo: National Archives Records and Census Bureau.

As people spent more time away from both work and family, new habits and values were inevitable. Especially among the middle class, but

Social Values

among the working class, too, clothes became a means of self-expression and freedom. Both men and women wore more casual and gaily colored styles than their parents would have considered. The line between acceptable and inappropriate behavior blurred as smoking, swearing, and frankness about sex became fashionable. Thousands who had never read psychoanalyst Sigmund Freud's theories were certain that he prescribed an uninhibited sex life as the key to mental health. Birth-control advocate Margaret Sanger, who a decade earlier had been accused of promoting race suicide, gained a large following in respectable circles. Newspapers, magazines, motion pictures, and popular songs made certain that Americans did not suffer from "sex starvation."

Other trends contributed to the breakdown of old values. Because child-labor laws and compulsory school-attendance laws kept children in school longer than ever before, peer groups played a more influential role in socializing children. In earlier eras, different age groups had shared the same activities: children had worked with older people in the fields, and young apprentices had worked with older journeymen and craftsmen. Now, graded school classes, sports, and other organized activities constantly brought together children of the same age, separating them from the company and influence of adults. Meanwhile, parents tended to rely less on family tradition and more on child-care manuals in raising children. Old-age homes, public health clinics, and workers' compensation reduced family responsibilities even further.

After the First World War, women continued to stream into the labor force. By 1930, 10.8 million women held paying jobs, an increase of more than 2 million since the war's end. The

Jobs for Women ───

sex segregation that had long characterized the workplace persisted; most female workers held jobs in which men were rare. Wherever they were employed, women's wages seldom exceeded half the wages paid to men.

For many women, employment outside the home represented an extension of their family roles. Although women worked for a variety of reasons, the economic needs of their families were paramount. The consumerism of the 1920s tempted working-class and middle-class families to satisfy their wants by sending women and children into the labor force. In earlier eras, most of these extra wage earners had been young and single. In the 1920s, the number of employed married women swelled from 1.9 million to 3.1 million. The vast majority of married women remained outside the work force (only 12 percent were employed in 1930), largely because of social pressure—it was a confession of failure if a wife had to take a paid job—and because the demands of housework and child care prevented them from joining. African-American women were the exception; the proportion of black women who worked for pay was double that of white women.

A group of women known as economic feminists in the 1920s addressed the issue of women in the labor force. They were concerned that women

Economic Feminism ───

who had formerly functioned as producers of food and clothes had lapsed into passive roles as child nurturers and homemakers; the result was economic dependency. The way to restore married women's sense of worth in a money-oriented society, they argued, was through gainful employment. Moreover, economic feminists believed all women should challenge the sexual division of labor and try to enter male-dominated jobs that had higher pay and required greater skill levels. Instead of seeking protective legislation for women workers, feminists wanted equal pay for equal work. In the 1920s, their goals were voiced by Alice Paul, leader of the National Woman's party, who in 1923 supported an equal rights amendment to the Constitution. But other women, including some from the working class, had doubts. Raised in cultures that assigned women the responsibility of fostering cooperation within their families and neighborhoods, they did not trust the competitive, individualistic environment of the job market.

Employed or not, women confronted choices among alternative images of femininity. Short skirts and bobbed hair, symbols of the independent-minded and sexually free flap-

Alternative Images of Femininity ───

per, became fashionable among office workers and store clerks as well as college students. As models of female behavior, chaste, modest heroines were eclipsed by movie vamps like Clara Bow, known as the "It Girl," and Gloria Swanson, known for her torrid love affairs on and off the screen. Many women—not just flappers—were asserting a new social equality with men.

These new trends represented a sharp break with the more restrained culture of the nineteenth century. But social change rarely proceeds smoothly. As the decade wore on, various groups prepared to defend against threats to older and more familiar values.

LINES OF DEFENSE

Early in 1920, the leader of a newly formed organization hired two public relations experts to recruit members. Using modern advertising techniques, the promoters canvassed communities in the South, Southwest, and Midwest, where they found thousands of men eager to pay a $10 membership fee and another $6 for a white uniform. By 1923, the organization, the Ku Klux Klan, claimed five million members.

The Klan was the most sinister reactionary movement of the 1920s. Reconstituted in 1915 by William J. Simmons, an Atlanta evangelist and insurance salesman, the new

Ku Klux Klan

Invisible Empire revived the hoods, intimidating tactics, and mystical terminology of its forerunner. But the new Klan had broader membership and objectives than the old. Its chapters fanned outward from the deep South and for a time wielded frightening power in every region of the country. One brief phrase summed up the Klan's goals: "Native, white, Protestant supremacy." Thus, unlike the original Klan, which directed its terrorist tactics at emancipated blacks, the new Klan targeted a variety of racial and religious groups.

Assuming the role of moral protector, the Klan meted out vigilante justice to suspected bootleggers, wife beaters, and adulterers; forced schools to adopt Bible reading and to stop teaching the theory of evolution; and campaigned against Catholic and Jewish political candidates. By the mid-1920s, however, the Invisible Empire was on the wane, outnumbered by immigrants and their offspring and rocked by scandal. (In 1925, Indiana Grand Dragon

David Stephenson kidnaped and raped a woman who later died, either from taking poison or from infection caused by bites on her body; Stephenson was convicted of second-degree murder on the ground that he was responsible for her suicide.)

The Ku Klux Klan had no monopoly on bigotry in the 1920s; intolerance pervaded American society. A number of groups had been urging an end to free immigration since the 1880s. Nativists charged that Catholic and Jewish immigrants clogged city slums, flouted community norms, and stubbornly held to alien religious and political beliefs.

Fear of radicalism, left over from the Red Scare of 1919, fueled antiforeign sentiment. The most notorious outburst of hysteria occurred in 1921,

Sacco and Vanzetti

when a court convicted Nicola Sacco and Bartolomeo Vanzetti, two immigrant anarchists, of murdering a guard and paymaster during a robbery in South Braintree, Massachusetts. Sacco and Vanzetti's main offenses seem to have been their political beliefs and Italian origins. Although the evidence failed to prove their involvement in the robbery, Judge Webster Thayer openly sided with the prosecution and privately called the defendants "anarchist bastards." The execution of the two in 1927 chilled those who had looked to the United States as the land that nurtured freedom of belief.

Meanwhile, Congress responded to the mounting pressure to restrict immigration by enacting legislation that set yearly immigration quotas for

Immigration Quotas

each nationality. The quotas favored northern and western Europeans, reflecting nativist prejudices against immigrants from southern and eastern Europe. By stipulating that annual immigration of a given nationality could not exceed 3 percent of the number of immigrants from that nation residing in the United States in 1910, the Quota (Johnson) Act of 1921 made it more difficult for immigrants from southern and eastern Europe, whose numbers were small in 1910 relative to those from northern Europe, to enter the country.

The Johnson Act, meant to be temporary, did not satisfy restrictionists, so Congress replaced it with the Immigration Act (Johnson-Reid Act) in 1924. This law limited annual immigration to 165,000 (less than one-fifth of prewar annual totals) and set quotas at 2 percent of each nationality residing in the United States in 1890. The act also established a "national origins" system. Instead of basing quotas on the 1890 census, national origins policy fixed an annual limit of 150,000 immigrants, with each country receiving a fraction of that number equal to the percentage of people in the U.S. population in 1920 who derived from that country

by birth or descent. This system fixed quotas of roughly 66,000 from Great Britain and 26,000 from Germany, but it allowed only 6,000 from Italy and 2,700 from Russia. It also excluded almost all Asians but set no quotas for peoples from the Western Hemisphere. Soon Canadians, Mexicans, and Puerto Ricans became the largest groups of newcomers (see figure).

While various groups lobbied for racial purity, the pursuit of moral purity stirred religious fundamentalists. In 1925, Christian fundamentalism

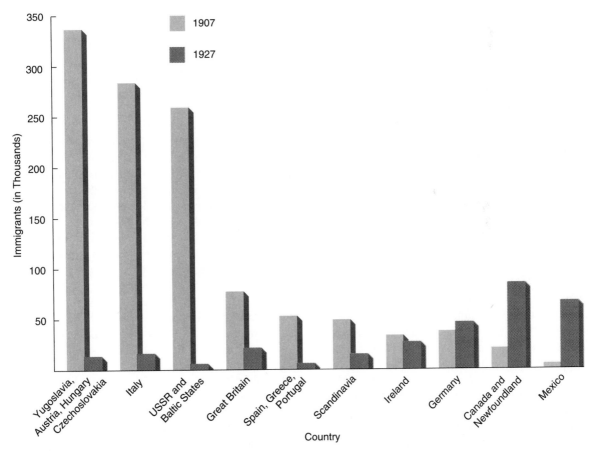

Sources of Immigration, 1907 and 1927 *Immigration peaked in the years 1907–1908, when newcomers from southern and eastern Europe poured into the United States. Then, after the immigration restriction laws were passed in the 1920s, the greatest number of immigrants came from the Western Hemisphere (Canada and Mexico), which was exempted from the quotas, whereas the number coming from eastern and southern Europe shrank.*

Scopes Trial clashed with new scientific theory in a celebrated case in Dayton, Tennessee. Early that year, the state legislature passed a law forbidding public school instructors to teach the theory that humans had evolved from lower forms of life rather than from Adam and Eve. Shortly thereafter, high school teacher John Thomas Scopes was arrested for violating the law. (He had volunteered to serve in a test case.) Scopes's trial that summer became a headline event, with William Jennings Bryan, the former secretary of state and three-time presidential candidate, arguing for the prosecution and a team of civil liberties lawyers headed by Clarence Darrow arguing for the defense. Hordes of reporters crowded into town, and radio stations broadcast the trial. Although Scopes was convicted—clearly he had broken the law—modernists claimed victory. The testimony, they believed, had shown fundamentalism to be illogical.

Americans' emotional responses to events in the 1920s represented an attempt to sustain time-tested ways in a fast-moving and materialistic world. Even as they worried about the decline of old values, however, most Americans tried to adjust to the new order in one way or another. They went to the movies, listened to the radio, attended sporting events, and generally sought release from societal pressures in a world of leisure.

THE AGE OF PLAY

Americans had an almost insatiable thirst for recreation in the 1920s and entrepreneurs responded quickly. New games and fancies particularly attracted middle-class families. Mahjong, a Chinese tile game, was all the rage in the early 1920s. By the mid-1920s, people were turning to crossword puzzles; a few years later, fun seekers adopted miniature golf as their new craze. Throughout the decade, dance crazes like the Charleston riveted public attention, aided by live and recorded band music on radio and the growing popularity of jazz.

In addition to participating actively in leisure activities, Americans were avid spectators, particularly of movies and sports. In 1922, movies attracted

Movies 40 million viewers a week; by 1930, that number had reached 100 million—at a time when the total population was just over 120 million and total weekly church attendance was less than 60 million. The introduction of sound in *The Jazz Singer* in 1927, and of color a few years later, made movies even more attractive and realistic. The most popular films were mass spectacles such as Cecil B. DeMille's *The Ten Commandments* (1923), lurid dramas such as *A Woman Who Sinned* (1924), and slapstick comedies. Ironically, the comedies, with their poignant satire of the human condition, carried the most thought-provoking messages.

Spectator sports also boomed. Each year, millions packed stadiums and parks to watch athletic events. Gate receipts from college football alone had surpassed $21 million by the late 1920s. In an age in which technology and mass production had robbed experiences and objects of their uniqueness, sports provided the unpredictability and drama that people craved. Baseball with its drawn-out suspense, infinite variety of plays, and potential for keeping statistics attracted a huge following. Newspapers and radio captured and magnified the drama of sports, feeding news to an eager public and glorifying events with unrestrained narrative.

Sports, movies, and the news gave Americans a galaxy of heroes. As society became more anonymous and the individual less significant, people clung to heroic personalities as

Sports Heroes a way to identify with the unique. Boxing, football, and baseball produced the most popular sports heroes. Heavyweight champion Jack Dempsey, a powerful brawler from Manassa, Colorado, attracted the first of many million-dollar gates in his fight with Georges Carpentier in 1921. Harold "Red" Grange, the running back for the University of Illinois football team, thrilled thousands and became the idol of sportswriters. Baseball's foremost hero was George Herman "Babe" Ruth, who began his career as a pitcher but found he could use his prodigious strength to better advantage hitting home runs. Ruth hit twenty-nine in 1919, fifty-four in 1920, fifty-nine in 1924, and sixty in 1927—each year a record. His exaggerated gestures on the field, defiant lifestyle, and boyish grin endeared him to millions and made him a national legend.

Although they identified with the physical exploits of sports stars, Americans fulfilled a yearning for romance and adventure through movie stars.

Movie Stars and Public Heroes

People discussed the films and personal lives of Douglas Fairbanks, Gloria Swanson, and Charlie Chaplin in parlors and pool halls across the country. The decade's most ballyhooed personality probably was Rudolph Valentino, whose smooth Latin seductiveness made women swoon and men imitate his pomaded hairdo and slick sideburns.

The news media also created heroes. Flagpole sitters, marathon dancers, and other record seekers regularly occupied the front pages. The most notable news hero was Charles A. Lindbergh, the pilot whose daring nonstop solo flight across the Atlantic in 1927 excited millions. A modest, independent midwesterner whom writers dubbed the Lone Eagle, Lindbergh accepted fame but did not try to profit from it. The stark contrast between his personality and the ballyhoo that surrounded him made Americans admire him even more fervently.

Americans' adulation of Lindbergh may have arisen in part from guilt at having abandoned the traditional virtues of restraint and moderation. In

Prohibition

their quest for fun and self-expression, Americans had become lawbreakers and supporters of crime. The Eighteenth Amendment (1919) and federal law (1920) that prohibited the manufacture, sale, and transportation of alcoholic beverages worked well at first. Per capita consumption of liquor dropped, as did arrests for drunkenness, and the price of illegal booze rose higher than average workers could afford. But after about 1925, the so-called noble experiment broke down in cities, where the desire for personal freedom overwhelmed weak enforcement.

Criminal organizations quickly capitalized on public demand. The most notorious of such mobs belonged to Al Capone, a burly tough who seized control of illegal liquor and vice in Chicago and maintained his grip through intimidation, bribery, and violence. It is important to recognize that Prohibition and its weak enforcement did not create organized crime. Gangs like Capone's had provided illegal goods and services long before the 1920s. As Capone put it, "Prohibition is a business. All I do is supply a public demand."

Al Capone

Thus during the 1920s, Americans were caught between two value systems. The Puritan tradition of hard work, sobriety, and restraint still prevailed, especially in rural areas in which new diversions were unavailable. Elsewhere, however, liberating opportunities to play beckoned. Never before in American history had so many types of commercial recreation existed.

The consumerism and ballyhoo of the 1920s inspired a diverse array of fads and stunts, and the popular media were all too eager to publicize every impulsive event, such as this 1927 ride by newlyweds on an "aquaplane" in New York Harbor. Underwood & Underwood.

CULTURAL CURRENTS

The tension between conflicting value systems pulled artists and intellectuals in new directions. In literature, art, and music, rejection of old beliefs prompted experimentation. Concern over materialism and conformity gave the era's artistic output a bitterly critical tinge. Yet artists seldom voiced a radical message; they wanted not so much to destroy modern society as to fend off the era's rampant vulgarity.

The disillusioned writers who found crass materialism at odds with art became known as the Lost Generation. A number of them, including novelist Ernest Hemingway and poets Ezra Pound and T. S. Eliot, moved to Europe. Others, such as novelists William Faulkner and Sinclair Lewis, remained in America but assailed the racism and irrationality they saw around them. Along with innovative forms of expression and realistic portrayals of emotion, these writers produced biting social commentary.

Literature of Alienation

Indictments of materialism and the impersonality of modern society dominated literature. F. Scott Fitzgerald's novels and Eugene O'Neill's plays exposed Americans' preoccupation with money. Edith Wharton explored the clash of old and new moralities in novels such as *The Age of Innocence* (1921). John Dos Passos's *Three Soldiers* (1921) and Ernest Hemingway's *Farewell to Arms* (1929) skillfully interwove antiwar sentiment with passionate critiques of the impersonality of modern relationships.

A spiritual discontent quite different from that of white writers inspired a new generation of young African-American artists. Middle-class, well-educated, and proud of their African heritage, these writers rejected the amalgamation of black and white cultures and exalted the militantly assertive "New Negro." Most of them lived in Harlem, in upper Manhattan; in this "Negro Mecca," black intellectuals and artists, aided by a few white patrons, celebrated modern black culture during what became known as the Harlem Renaissance.

Harlem Renaissance

Harlem in the 1920s also fostered a number of gifted writers, among them Langston Hughes, whose poems captured the mood and rhythm of blues and jazz; Countee Cullen, a poet of moving lyrical skill; and Claude McKay, whose militant verses urged rebellion against bigotry. Jean Toomer's poems and his novel *Cane* (1923) portrayed black life with passionate realism, and Alain Locke's essays defined the spirit of the artistic renaissance. The movement included visual artists, such as James A. Porter, whose paintings were shown in every important exhibition of black artists, and Augusta Savage, who sculpted busts of many famous black personalities.

Issues of identity troubled the Harlem Renaissance. Although intellectuals and artists cherished their African cultural heritage, they realized that blacks had to come to terms with themselves as Americans. Thus Locke urged that the New Negro "lay aside the status of beneficiary and ward for that of a collaborator and participant in American civilization."

The Jazz Age, as the decade of the 1920s is sometimes called, owed its name to music that developed from black urban experience. Evolving from African and black American folk music, early jazz communicated an exuberance, humor, and authority that African-Americans seldom expressed in their public, working, and political lives. With its emotional rhythms and emphasis on improvisation, jazz blurred the distinction between composer and performer and created intimacy between performer and audience. Jazz also endowed America with its most distinctive art form.

Jazz

In many ways, the 1920s were the most creative years the nation had yet experienced. Influenced by jazz and experimental writing, painters such as Georgia O'Keeffe and John Marin tried to forge a unique American style of painting. European composers and performers still dominated classical music, but Americans such as Henry Cowell, who pioneered electronic music, and Aaron Copland, who built orchestral and vocal works around native folk motifs, began careers that later won wide acclaim. George Gershwin blended jazz rhythms, classical forms, and folk melodies in his serious compositions, musical dramas, and numerous hit tunes. In architecture, the skyscraper boom drew worldwide attention, and Frank Lloyd Wright's "prairie-style" houses, churches, and schools celebrated the magnificence of the American landscape. At the beginning of the decade, essayist Harold Stearns had complained that "the most . . . pathetic fact in the social life of America today is emotional and aesthetic starvation." By 1929, that contention was hard to support.

THE ELECTION OF 1928 AND THE END OF THE NEW ERA

Intellectuals' uneasiness about the materialism of the 1920s had no place in the confident rhetoric of politics. Herbert Hoover epitomized that confidence in his speech accepting the Republican nomination for president in 1928. "We in America today," Hoover boasted, "are nearer to the final triumph over poverty than ever before in the history of any land. . . . We have not yet reached the goal, but, given a chance to go forward with the policies of the last eight years, we shall soon, with the help of God, be in sight of the day when poverty will be banished from this nation."

As Hoover's opponent, Democrats chose Governor Alfred E. Smith of New York, whose background contrasted sharply with Hoover's. Hoover had rural, native, Protestant, business roots and had never run for public office. Smith was an urbane, gregarious politician of immigrant stock with a career rooted in New York City's Tammany Hall. Smith was the first Roman Catholic to run for president on a major party ticket. His religion contributed to his considerable appeal among urban ethnic groups, which were voting in increasing numbers, but intense anti-Catholic sentiments lost him southern and rural votes.

Al Smith

Smith waged a spirited campaign, but Hoover, who stressed the nation's prosperity under Republican administrations, won the popular vote by

21 million to 15 million, the electoral vote by 444 to 87. Smith's candidacy nevertheless had beneficial effects on the Democratic party. He carried the nation's twelve largest cities, which formerly had given majorities to Republican candidates, and he lured millions of immigrant-stock voters to the polls for the first time. From 1928 on, the Democratic party would solidify this urban base, which in conjunction with its traditional strength in the South made the party a formidable force in national elections.

Democrats and Republicans both had reason to be encouraged in 1928. In his inaugural address, Hoover proclaimed a New Day, "bright with hope." His cabinet, composed mostly of businessmen committed to the existing order, included six millionaires. To the lower ranks of government, Hoover appointed young professionals who agreed with him that scientific methods could be applied to solve national problems.

Hoover's Administration

If the Hoover administration was optimistic, so were most Americans. Reverence for what Hoover called "the American system" ran high. The belief was widespread that individuals were responsible for their own situations and that unemployment or poverty suggested personal failing. Prevailing opinion also held that the ups and downs of the business cycle were natural and therefore not to be tampered with by the government.

This confidence was jolted in the fall of 1929 when stock prices suddenly plunged. Analysts explained the drop as a temporary condition caused by a "lunatic fringe." But on October 24, "Black Thursday," panic selling set in. The prices of many stocks hit record lows; some sellers could find no buyers. At noon, leading bankers met at the headquarters of J. P. Morgan and Company. To restore faith, they put up $20 million and ceremoniously began buying stocks like U.S. Steel. The mood changed and some stocks rallied.

Stock Market Crash

But as news of Black Thursday spread across the country, fearful investors decided to sell their stocks rather than risk further losses. On "Black

Tuesday," October 29, stock prices plummeted again. The market settled into a grim pattern of declines and weak rallies. Hoover, who had never approved of what he called "the fever of speculation," assured Americans that the economy was sound. He shared the popular assumptions that the stock market's ills could be quarantined and that the economy was strong enough to endure until the market righted itself.

But instead of reversing, the crash ultimately helped to unleash a devastating depression. The economic downturn did not arrive suddenly; it was more like a slow leak than a blowout. Had conditions been as sound as businesspeople maintained, the nation would have stood a better chance of weathering the Wall Street crash. In fact, however, some historians suggest that the stock market collapse merely moved an ongoing recession into depression.

The economic weakness that underlay the Great Depression had several interrelated causes. The first was declining demand. Some industries, like coal, railroads, and textiles, were in **Declining** distress long before 1929, but **Demand** the major growth industries— automobiles, construction, and mechanized agriculture—had been able to expand as long as consumers bought their goods and services. But the frenzied expansion could not continue unabated. When demand leveled off, unsold inventories stacked up in warehouses, and laborers were laid off. As wages and purchasing power lagged behind industrial production, workers became increasingly unable to buy consumer products in sufficient quantities to sustain the economy's momentum. Farmers too had to trim their purchases. Thus by 1929, significant underconsumption was causing serious repercussions.

Underconsumption also resulted from the maldistribution of income. Between 1920 and 1929, average per capita disposable income rose about 9 percent, but the income of the wealthiest 1 percent rose 75 percent, accounting for most of the increase. Much of this increase was put into luxuries, savings, and stock market investments instead of being spent on consumer goods.

Furthermore, American businesses were overloaded with debt. In 1929, the top two hundred nonfinancial corporations controlled 49 percent

Corporate Debt of corporate wealth. Many corporations built pyramidlike empires supported by shady, although legal, manipulation of assets and weakly supported liabilities. When one part of the edifice collapsed, the entire structure crumbled.

The depression also derived from largely unregulated pell-mell speculation on the stock market. Corporations and banks invested huge sums in stocks. Brokers sold stocks to **Speculation** buyers who borrowed in order **on the Stock** to purchase them, putting up **Market** little or no cash, and then used the stocks they had bought but not fully paid for as collateral for more loans. When stock prices collapsed, loan obligations could not be met and brokerage firms, banks, and investment companies failed.

International economic troubles also contributed to the crash and depression. As the world's leading creditor and trader, the United States was deeply bound up with the **International** world economy. Billions of dol- **Economic** lars in loans had flowed to Eu- **Troubles** rope during the First World War and during postwar reconstruction. By the late 1920s, however, American investors were beginning to keep their money at home in order to invest it in the more lucrative U.S. stock market. Europeans, unable to borrow more funds and unable to sell their goods easily in the American market because of high tariffs, began to buy less from the United States and to default on their debts. Pinched at home, they raised their own tariffs, further disabling international commerce, and withdrew their investments from America.

Finally, government policies and practices contributed to the crash and depression. The federal government failed to regulate wild speculation, contenting itself with occasionally **Failure of** scolding bankers and business- **Federal Policies** people. The Federal Reserve Board pursued easy credit policies before the crash, although easy money was financing the speculative mania.

Partly because of their optimism and partly because of the relatively undeveloped state of economic analysis and statistics gathering, neither the experts nor people on the street understood in 1929 what factors had brought on the depression. Conventional wisdom, based on the experience of previous depressions, held that little could be done to correct economic problems—that they simply had to run their course. So in 1929 people waited for the deflation to bottom out, never realizing that the era of expansion and frivolity had come to an end and that the nation's culture and politics, as well as its economy, would have to be rebuilt.

SUGGESTIONS FOR FURTHER READING

Overviews of the 1920s

William E. Akin, *Technocracy and the American Dream* (1977); Paul A. Carter, *Another Part of the Twenties* (1977); William E. Leuchtenburg, *The Perils of Prosperity* (1958); Donald R. McCoy, *Coming of Age* (1973).

Business and the Economy

William W. Barber, *Herbert Hoover, the Economists, and American Economic Policy, 1921–1933* (1986); Irving L. Bernstein, *The Lean Years: A History of the American Worker, 1920–1933* (1960); Peter Fearon, *War, Prosperity, and Depression* (1987); Morton Keller, *Regulating a New Economy* (1990).

Politics and Law

Christine Bolt, *American Indian Policy and American Reform* (1987); David Burner, *The Politics of Provincialism* (1968); Allan J. Lichtman, *Prejudice and the Old Politics: The Presidential Election of 1928* (1979); Donald R. McCoy, *Calvin Coolidge* (1967); Robert K. Murray, *The Harding Era* (1969); Joan Hoff Wilson, *Herbert Hoover: The Forgotten Progressive* (1975).

African-Americans and Hispanics

Rodolfo Acuna, *Occupied America: A History of Chicanos* (1980); Gilbert Osofsky, *Harlem: The Making of a Ghetto* (1965); Mark Reisler, *By the Sweat of Their Brows* (1976) (on Mexican-Americans); Virginia E. Sanchez, *From Colonia to Community: The History of Puerto Ricans in New York, 1917–1948* (1983); Judith Stein, *The World of Marcus Garvey* (1986).

Women and the Family

W. Andrew Achenbaum, *Shades of Gray: Old Age, American Values, and Federal Policies Since 1920* (1983); Howard P. Chudacoff, *How Old Are You? Age in American Culture* (1989); Nancy F. Cott, *The Grounding of Modern Feminism* (1987); Ruth Schwartz Cowan, *More Work for Mother* (1983); Linda Gordon, *Woman's Body, Woman's Right: A Social History of Birth Control in America* (1976); Lois Scharf, *To Work and to Wed* (1980); Winifred D. Wandersee, *Women's Work and Family Values, 1920–1940* (1981).

Lines of Defense

David M. Chalmers, *Hooded Americanism: The History of the Ku Klux Klan* (1965); Norman F. Furnis, *The Fundamentalist Controversy* (1954); Joseph R. Gusfeld, *Symbolic Crusade* (1963); John Higham, *Strangers in the Land: Patterns of American Nativism* (1955).

Mass Culture

Stanley Coben, *Rebellion Against Victorianism* (1991); Kenneth S. Davis, *The Hero, Charles A. Lindbergh* (1959); Susan J. Douglas, *Inventing American Broadcasting* (1987); Paula Fass, *The Damned and the Beautiful: American Youth in the 1920s* (1977); James J. Flink, *The Car Culture* (1975); Roland Marchand, *Advertising the American Dream* (1985); John Rae, *The Road and the Car in American Life* (1971); Robert Sklar, *Movie-Made America* (1976).

Literature and Thought

Robert Crunden, *From Self to Society: Transition in American Thought, 1919–1941* (1972); Nathan I. Huggins, *Harlem Renaissance* (1971); David L. Lewis, *When Harlem Was in Vogue* (1981); Roderick Nash, *The Nervous Generation: American Thought, 1917–1930* (1969); Cecilia Tichi, *Shifting Gears: Technology, Literature and Culture in Modernist America* (1987).

Boom and Bust: The Crash

William W. Barber, *Herbert Hoover, the Economists, and American Economic Policy, 1921–1933* (1986); Peter Fearon, *War, Prosperity, and Depression* (1987).

Chapter

25

The Great Depression and
the New Deal, 1929–1941

BUTCH BEUSCHER WAS FIFTY-SIX years old when he was laid off from the job he had held for twenty-nine years. The year was 1931, and businesses and farms across the country were collapsing. Butch's wife Tessie was a part-time seamstress, but because her customers were also unemployed or irregularly employed, her earnings declined to $3 or $4 a week. Four of the Beuschers' ten children still lived at home. As their income plummeted, the family lived off loans against an insurance policy, Tessie's earnings, and credit from the grocery store. Their unpaid bills mounted, as did the overdue notices for mortgage and property tax payments. Then, in the fall of 1933, Butch Beuscher announced that the family would have to face facts and "try to get relief" from the government. Tessie Beuscher recalled gasping at the suggestion that they ask for welfare, but there was no alternative.

Statistics suggest the magnitude of the Great Depression's human tragedy. Between 1929 and 1933, one hundred thousand businesses failed, corporate profits fell from $10 billion to $1 billion, and the gross national product was cut in half. Banks failed by the thousands. Americans who believed that saving was a virtue learned that their deposits had disappeared with the banks.

Americans lost jobs as well as savings. Thousands of men and women received severance slips every day. The number of unemployed increased from four million at the beginning of 1930 to thirteen million (about one-fourth of the work force) in early 1933. And millions more were underemployed. Unemployment strained relations within the family. African-Americans and other minorities sank deeper into destitution. Overall, the economic catastrophe aggravated old tensions: labor versus capital, white versus black, male versus female.

Elected amid prosperity and optimism, Herbert Hoover spent the years from late 1929 to his departure from office in early 1933 presiding over a gloomy and sometimes angry nation. Although he activated more of the federal government's resources than had any of his predecessors in an economic crisis, he opposed direct relief payments for the unemployed.

When Hoover refused to take measures strong enough to relieve people's hardships, voters turned him out of office in 1932. His successor in the White House was Franklin D. Roosevelt, the governor of New York.

From the first days of his presidency, Roosevelt displayed a buoyancy and willingness to experiment that helped to restore public confidence in the government and the economy. He acted not only to reform the banks and securities exchanges but also to provide central planning for industry and agriculture and direct government relief for the jobless. His sweeping emergency legislation was based on the concept of "pump priming," or deficit financing, to stimulate consumer buying power, business and industrial activity, and ultimately employment by pouring billions of federal dollars into the economy. Roosevelt's New Deal was opposed from both the left and the right. Ultimately, Roosevelt prevailed, vastly expanding the scope of the federal government and the popularity of the Democratic party, and in the process establishing America's welfare system.

During these years, several million workers seized the chance to organize for better wages and working conditions. The new Congress of Industrial Organizations (CIO) established unions in the automobile, steel, meat-packing, and other major industries. Blacks registered political and economic gains, too, although they benefited less from the New Deal than did whites. Two-and-a-half million additional women workers joined the labor force during the 1930s. But female workers were segregated in low-income jobs, and New Deal legislation excluded many women from Social Security coverage and minimum-wage protection.

The New Deal was not a revolution, but it transformed the United States. Farmers still plant according to federal crop allotments. The elderly and disabled still collect Social Security payments. The Federal Deposit Insurance Corporation still insures bank deposits. The Securities and Exchange Commission still monitors the stock exchanges. But the New Deal did not accomplish one of its goals—putting back to work all the people who wanted jobs. That would await the nation's entry into the Second World War in 1941.

HOOVER AND HARD TIMES: AMERICA'S WORSENING DEPRESSION, 1929–1933

As the Great Depression deepened in the early 1930s, its underlying causes—principally overproduction and underconsumption—grew in severity. So too did instability in the banking industry. What happened to America's banks illustrates the cascading nature of the depression. Banks tied in to the stock market or foreign investments were badly weakened. When nervous Americans made runs on banks to salvage their threatened savings, a powerful momentum—panic—set in. In 1929, 659 banks folded; in 1930, the number of failures more than doubled to 1,350. The Federal Reserve Board blundered after the crash, drastically raising the discount rate and thus tightening the money market when just the opposite was needed: loosening to spur borrowing and spending. In 1931, 2,293 banks shut their doors, and another 1,453 ceased to do business in 1932.

Causes of the Deepening Depression

During these years, people's diets deteriorated, malnutrition became common, and the undernourished frequently fell victim to disease. Some people quietly lined up at Red Cross and Salvation Army soup kitchens or in bread lines. Others ate only potatoes, crackers, or dandelions or scratched through garbage cans for bits of food. Millions of Americans were not only hungry and ill; they were cold. Unable to afford fuel, they huddled in unheated tenements and shacks. Families doubled up in crowded apartments, and those unable to pay the rent were evicted, furniture and all. From packing boxes and other debris, the homeless constructed makeshift communities that were bitterly called Hoovervilles.

Deterioration of Health

In the countryside, hobbled long before the depression struck, economic hardship deepened. Between 1929 and 1933, farm prices dropped 60

Plight of the Farmers

percent. At the same time, production decreased only 6 percent as individual farmers tried to make up for lower prices by producing more, thus creating an excess and depressing prices even further. They could not export the surplus, because foreign demand had shrunk. Drought, foreclosure, clouds of hungry grasshoppers, and bank failures further plagued American farmers. Some became transients in search of jobs or food. Dispossessed tenant farmers—husbands, wives, and children—wandered the roads of the South. Hundreds of thousands of other people jumped aboard freight trains or hitchhiked. The California Unemployment Commission reported in 1932 that an "army of homeless" had trooped into the state and was moving constantly from place to place, forced by one town after another to move on.

Economic woe also affected marriage patterns and family life. People postponed marriage, and married couples postponed having children. Divorces declined, but desertions rose as husbands unable to provide for their families simply took off. Families were beset in other ways as well. With less money available for outside recreation, families were forced to spend more time together, which further increased tension in those suffering unemployment and crowded living quarters.

Most Americans met the crisis not with protest or violence but with bewilderment and inability to fix the blame. They scorned businesspeople and bankers, of course, but often blamed themselves as well.

Farmers' Holiday Association

Some people were angry, though, and scattered protests raised the specter of popular revolt. Farmers in the Midwest prevented evictions and slowed foreclosures on farm properties by harassing sheriffs, judges, and lawyers. In Nebraska, Iowa, and Minnesota, farmers protesting low prices put up barricades of spiked logs and telegraph poles. They stopped trucks, smashed headlights, and dumped milk and vegetables in roadside ditches. Some of the demonstrations were organized by the Farmers' Holiday Association's leader, Milo Reno, who encouraged farmers to take a holiday—a farm strike that would keep their products off the market until they commanded a better price.

Isolated protests also sounded in cities and in mining regions. In Chicago, Los Angeles, and Philadelphia, the unemployed marched on city halls.

Bonus Expeditionary Force

When miners struck against wage reductions in Harlan County, Kentucky, mine owners responded with strikebreakers, bombs, the National Guard, the closing of relief kitchens, and evictions from company-owned housing.

The most spectacular confrontation shook Washington, D.C., in the summer of 1932. Congress was considering a bill to authorize immediate issuance of $2.4 billion in bonuses already allotted to World War I veterans but not due for payment until 1945. To lobby for the bill, fifteen thousand unemployed veterans and their families converged on the tense nation's capital, calling themselves the Bonus Expeditionary Force (BEF), or Bonus Army, and camping on vacant lots and in empty government buildings. President Hoover threw his weight against the bonus bill, but the House passed it. After the Senate rejected the measure, many bonus marchers left Washington. Several thousand, however, stayed on during the summer.

In July, General Douglas MacArthur, assisted by Major Dwight D. Eisenhower and Major George S. Patton, confronted the veterans and their families with cavalry, tanks, and bayonet-bearing soldiers. The BEF hurled back stones and bricks. What followed shocked the nation. Men and women were chased down by horsemen, children were tear-gassed, shacks were set afire. When presidential hopeful Franklin D. Roosevelt heard about the attack on the Bonus Army, he turned to his friend Felix Frankfurter and remarked: "Well, Felix, this will elect me."

With capitalism on its knees, American members of the Communist party in various parts of the nation organized "unemployment councils" to raise class consciousness and agitate

Communist Party

for jobs and food. In 1930, they led urban demonstrations, some of which ended in violent

• *Important Events* •

1931	Nine African-American men arrested in Scottsboro affair
	Hoover declares moratorium on First World War debts and reparations
1932	Reconstruction Finance Corporation established to make loans to businesses
	Bonus Expeditionary Force marches on Washington
	Franklin D. Roosevelt elected president
1933	13 million Americans unemployed
	National bank holiday suspends banking activities
	Agricultural Adjustment Act encourages decreased farm production
	Civilian Conservation Corps provides jobs to 300,000 people
	Tennessee Valley Authority established to aid economies of seven states
	Banking Act creates Federal Deposit Insurance Corporation (FDIC)
	National Industrial Recovery Act attempts to spur industrial growth
	Twenty-first Amendment repeals Eighteenth (Prohibition) Amendment
1934	Townsend devises Old Age Revolving Pensions plan
	Huey Long starts Share Our Wealth Society
	Indian Reorganization (Wheeler-Howard) Act restores lands to tribal ownership
	Democrats win victories in congressional elections
	Coughlin creates National Union for Social Justice
1935	Emergency Relief Appropriation Act authorizes establishment of public works programs

	Works Progress Administration creates jobs in public works projects
	Schechter v. *U.S.* invalidates NIRA
	National Labor Relations (Wagner) Act grants workers right to unionize
	Social Security Act establishes insurance for aged and unemployed
	Huey Long assassinated
	Committee for Industrial Organization (CIO) established
	Revenue (Wealth Tax) Act raises taxes on business and the wealthy
1936	*U.S.* v. *Butler* invalidates AAA
	Roosevelt defeats Landon
1937	United Auto Workers hold sit-down strikes
	Roosevelt's court-packing plan fails
	NLRB v. *Jones & Laughlin* upholds Wagner Act
	Memorial Day Massacre leaves ten steel strikers dead in Chicago
	Farm Security Administration established to aid farm workers
1937–39	Business recession
1938	AFL expels CIO unions
	Fair Labor Standards Act establishes minimum wage
	10.4 million Americans unemployed
1940	Roosevelt defeats Willkie
1941	African-Americans threaten to march on Washington to protest unequal access to defense jobs
	Fair Employment Practices Committee (FEPC) prohibits discrimination in war industries and government

clashes with local police, and in 1931 they led a hunger march on Washington, D.C. The Communists' tangles with authority publicized the human tragedy of the depression. Still, total party membership in 1932 remained small at twelve thousand.

The Socialist party, which took issue with both capitalists and Communists, fared better. More reformist than radical, the Socialists ran well in municipal elections after the stock market crash but scored few victories. Indeed, few Americans looked to left-wing doctrines, protest marches, or violence for relief from their misery. Americans were frightened and they were angry, but they were not revolutionaries. They turned instead to their local, state, and federal governments.

But when urgent daily appeals for government relief for the jobless reached the White House, Hoover at first became defensive if not hostile, rejecting direct relief in the belief that it would undermine character and individualism. To a growing number of Americans, Hoover seemed heartless and inflexible. True to his beliefs, the president urged people to help themselves and their neighbors. He applauded private voluntary relief through charitable agencies. Yet when the need was greatest, donations declined. State and urban officials found their treasuries drying up too. Meanwhile, those calling for federal action got no sympathy from Secretary of the Treasury Andrew Mellon, who advised Hoover to "let the slump liquidate itself. Liquidate labor, liquidate stocks, liquidate the farmers, liquidate real estate. . . . It will purge the rottenness out of the system."

As the depression intensified, Hoover's opposition to federal action gradually diminished. He rejected Mellon's insensitive counsel, hesitantly energizing the White House and federal agencies to take action—more action than the government had taken before. He won pledges from business and labor leaders to maintain wages and production and to avoid strikes. He urged state governors to increase their expenditures on public works. And he created the President's Organization on Unemployment Relief (POUR) to generate private contributions for relief of the destitute. Although POUR proved ineffective, Hoover's spurring of federal public works projects (including the Hoover and Grand Coulee Dams) did provide some jobs. Help also came from the Federal Farm Board, created under the Agricultural Marketing Act of 1929, which supported crop prices by lending money to cooperatives to buy products and keep them off the market. But the board soon found itself short of money, and unsold surplus commodities jammed

Hoover's Antidepression Remedies

warehouses. To retard the collapse of the international monetary system, Hoover announced a moratorium on the payment of World War I debts and reparations (1931).

The president also asked Congress to charter the Reconstruction Finance Corporation (RFC). Created in 1932 and eventually empowered with $2 billion, the RFC was designed to make loans to banks, insurance companies, and railroads and later to state and local governments. In theory, the RFC would lend money to large entities at the top of the economic system, and benefits would filter down to people at the bottom. It did not work; banks continued to collapse and small companies went into bankruptcy.

Reconstruction Finance Corporation

Despite warnings from prominent economists, Hoover also signed the Hawley-Smoot Tariff Act (1930). A congressional compromise serving special interests, the tariff raised duties by about one-third. Hoover argued that the tariff would help farmers and manufacturers by keeping foreign goods off the market. Actually, the tariff further weakened the economy by making it even more difficult for foreign nations to sell their products and thus to earn dollars to buy American products.

Hawley-Smoot Tariff Act

Like most of his contemporaries, Hoover believed that a balanced budget was sacred and deficit spending sinful. In 1931, he therefore appealed for a decrease in federal expenditures and an increase in taxes. The following year, he supported a sales tax on manufactured goods. The sales tax was defeated, but the Revenue Act of 1932 raised corporate, excise, and personal income taxes. Hoover seemed tangled in a contradiction: he urged people to spend to spur recovery, but his tax policies deprived them of spending money.

Although Hoover expanded public works projects and approved loans to some institutions, he vetoed a variety of relief bills presented to him by the Democratic Congress. In rejecting a public power project for the Tennessee River, he argued that its inexpensive elec-

Hoover's Traditionalism

tricity would compete with power from private companies. Hoover's traditionalism was also well demonstrated by his handling of Prohibition. Although the law was not and could not be enforced, Hoover resisted mounting public pressure for repeal. Opponents of Prohibition argued not only that it encouraged crime but also that its repeal would stimulate economic recovery by reviving the nation's breweries and distilleries. But the president refused to tamper with the Constitution; he declared that the liquor industry, having no socially redemptive value, was best left depressed. (After Hoover left office in 1933, Prohibition was repealed through the ratification of the Twenty-first Amendment.)

Still, President Hoover stretched government activism as far as he thought he could without violating his cherished principles. Because Hoover mobilized the resources of the federal government as never before, some historians have depicted him as a bridge to the New Deal of the 1930s. If nothing else, he prepared the way for massive federal activity by giving private enterprise the opportunity to solve the depression—and to fail in the attempt.

FRANKLIN D. ROOSEVELT AND THE ELECTION OF 1932

Herbert Hoover and the Republican party faced dreary prospects in 1932. The president kept blaming international events for the economic crisis, when Americans were less concerned with abstract explanations than with tomorrow's meal. He grumbled and grew impatient with his critics. But what soured public opinion most was that Hoover did not offer leadership when the times required innovative generalship. So unpopular had he become by 1932 that Republicans who did not want to be associated with a loser ran independent campaigns.

Franklin D. Roosevelt enjoyed quite a different reputation. Although born into the upper class of old money and privilege, the smiling, ingratiating governor of New York appealed to people of all classes, races, and regions, and he shared the American penchant

Franklin D. Roosevelt

for optimism. After serving as assistant secretary of the navy under Woodrow Wilson and running as the Democratic party's vice presidential candidate in 1920, Roosevelt was left totally paralyzed in both legs.

What should Roosevelt do next? Should he retire from public life, a rich invalid? His answer and his wife Eleanor's was no. Throughout the 1920s, the Roosevelts contended with his handicap. Rejecting self-pity, Roosevelt worked to rebuild his body. Friends commented that polio had made him a "twice-born man" and that his fight against the disease had given him new moral and physical strength.

For her part, Eleanor Roosevelt—who had grown up shy and sheltered in a distant branch of the Roosevelt family—launched her own career in public life. She worked hard to become an effective public speaker and participated in the activities of the League of Women Voters, the Women's Trade Union League, and the Democratic party. In a short time, she became the leading figure in a network of feminist activists. She became deeply committed to equal opportunity for women and for African-Americans and wanted to alleviate the suffering of the poor. On these issues, she served as her husband's conscience.

Eleanor Roosevelt

Elected governor of New York in 1928 and reelected in 1930, Roosevelt's terms coincided with Hoover's presidency. But whereas Hoover appeared hardhearted and unwilling to help the jobless, Roosevelt seemed quite the opposite. He endorsed unemployment insurance and direct relief payments for the jobless, as well as the creation of jobs in publicly funded reforestation, land reclamation, and hydroelectric power projects. He also advocated old-age pensions and protective legislation for labor unions. With this record, Roosevelt became an obvious prospect for the 1932 Democratic presidential nomination.

Roosevelt as Governor of New York

To prepare a national political platform, Roosevelt surrounded himself with a "Brain Trust" of lawyers and university professors. These experts

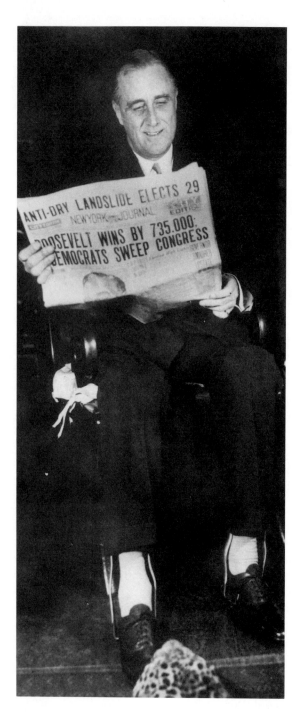

In November 1930, Franklin D. Roosevelt (1882–1945) read the good news. Reelected governor of New York by 735,000 votes, he immediately became a leading contender for the Democratic presidential nomination. Note Roosevelt's leg braces, rarely shown in photographs because of an unwritten agreement by photographers to shoot him from the waist up. UPI/Bettmann Archives.

Roosevelt's "Brain Trust" reasoned that bigness was unavoidable in the modern American economy. It thus followed that the cure for the nation's ills was not to go on a rampage of trustbusting but to place large corporations, monopolies, and oligopolies under effective government regulation. "We are no longer afraid of bigness," declared Columbia University professor Rexford G. Tugwell, speaking in the tradition of Theodore Roosevelt's New Nationalism.

Roosevelt and his Brain Trust agreed that it was essential to restore purchasing power to farmers, blue-collar workers, and the middle classes and that the way to do so was to cut production. If demand for a product remained constant and the supply were cut, they reasoned, the price would rise. Producers would make higher profits, and workers would earn more. This method of combating a depression has been called "the economics of scarcity," which the Brain Trust saw as the preferred alternative to deficit spending, or pump priming, in which the government borrowed money to prime the economic pump and thereby revive purchasing power. Indeed, Roosevelt and Hoover both campaigned as fiscal conservatives committed to a balanced budget. But unlike Hoover, Roosevelt also advocated immediate and direct relief to the unemployed. And Roosevelt demanded that the federal government engage in centralized economic planning and experimentation to bring about recovery.

Upon accepting the Democratic nomination, Roosevelt called for a "new deal for the American people." The two party platforms differed little, but **1932 Election Results** the Democrats were willing to abandon Prohibition and to launch federal relief. More people went to the polls in

1932 than in any election since the First World War. In a crisis-ridden moment, Americans followed their traditional pattern and exchanged one government for another. The presidential election of 1932 had never been much of a contest: Roosevelt's 22.8 million popular votes far outdistanced Hoover's 15.8 million. Democrats also won overwhelming control of the Senate and the House.

On March 2, 1933, President-elect Roosevelt and his family and friends boarded a train for Washington, D.C., and the inauguration ceremony. Roosevelt was carrying with him rough drafts of two presidential proclamations, one summoning a special session of Congress, the other declaring a national bank holiday, suspending banking transactions throughout the nation.

LAUNCHING THE NEW DEAL AND RESTORING CONFIDENCE

"First of all," declared the newly inaugurated president, "let me assert my firm belief that the only thing we have to fear is fear itself—nameless, unreasoning, unjustified terror." In his inaugural address, Roosevelt scored his first triumph as president, instilling hope and courage in the rank and file. He invoked "the analogue of war," asserting that, if need be, "I shall ask the Congress for the one remaining instrument to meet the crisis—broad Executive power to wage a war against the emergency, as great as the power that would be given to me if we were in fact invaded by a foreign foe."

The next day, Roosevelt declared a four-day national bank holiday and summoned Congress to an emergency session. Congress convened on

Launching the First New Deal

March 9 to launch what observers would call the First Hundred Days. This was also the beginning of the vast legislative output of 1933–1934 that historians would call the First New Deal. Roosevelt's first measure, the Emergency Banking Relief Bill, was introduced on March 9, passed sight unseen by unanimous House vote, approved 73 to

7 in the Senate, and signed by the president that evening. The act provided for the reopening, under Treasury Department license, of banks that were solvent and for the reorganization and management of those that were not. It also prohibited the hoarding and export of gold. It was, however, a fundamentally conservative law that upheld the status quo and left the same bankers in charge.

On March 12, a Sunday evening, the president broadcast the first of his "fireside chats," and sixty million people heard his comforting voice on their

First Fireside Chat

radios. His message: banks were once again safe places for depositors' savings. On Monday morning, the banks opened their doors, but instead of queuing up to withdraw their savings, people were waiting outside to deposit their money. The bank runs were over; Roosevelt had reestablished people's confidence in their political leadership, their banks, even their economic system.

In mid-March, Roosevelt sent to Congress the Agricultural Adjustment bill to restore farmers' purchasing power. If overproduction was the cause

Agricultural Adjustment Act

of farmers' problems—falling prices and mounting surpluses—the government had to encourage farmers to grow less food. Under the domestic allotment plan, the government would pay farmers to reduce their acreage or plow under crops already in the fields. Farmers would receive payments based on parity, a system of regulated prices for corn, cotton, wheat, rice, hogs, and dairy products that would provide them the same purchasing power they had had during the prosperous period of 1909 to 1914. In effect, the government was making up the difference between the actual market value of farm products and the income farmers needed to make a profit. The subsidies would be funded by taxes levied on the processors of agricultural commodities. Despite vehement opposition, the Agricultural Adjustment Act (AAA) was passed on May 12. A month later, the Farm Credit Act was passed, providing short- and medium-term loans that enabled many farmers to refinance their mortgages and hang onto their homes and land.

Meanwhile, other relief measures became law. On March 21, the president requested three kinds of massive relief: a job corps called the Civilian Conservation Corps (CCC),

Civilian Conservation Corps
——

direct cash grants to the states for relief payments to needy citizens, and public works projects. Ten days later, Congress approved the CCC, which ultimately put 2.5 million young men aged eighteen to twenty-five to work planting trees, clearing camping areas and beaches, and building bridges, dams, reservoirs, fish ponds, and fire towers. Then, on May 12, Congress passed the Federal Emergency Relief Act, which authorized $500 million in aid to state and local governments.

Roosevelt's proposed plan for public works became Title II of the National Industrial Recovery Act (NIRA). Passed on June 16, NIRA established the Public Works Administration (PWA) and appropriated $3.3 billion for hiring the unemployed to build roads, sewage and water systems, public buildings, ships, naval aircraft, and a host of other projects. The purpose of the PWA was to prime the economic pump to spur recovery.

If the AAA was the agricultural cornerstone of the New Deal, the National Industrial Recovery Act was the industrial cornerstone. The NIRA was

Economic Planning Under the NIRA
——

a testimony to the New Deal belief in national planning, as opposed to an individualistic, intensely competitive, laissez faire economy. It was essential, the planners argued, for businesses to end cutthroat competition and raise prices by limiting production. Like the War Industries Board (WIB) during the First World War, the NIRA exempted businesses from antitrust laws by establishing the National Recovery Administration (NRA). Under its auspices, competing businesses met with representatives of workers and consumers to draft codes of fair competition, which limited production and established prices. Finally, Section 7(a) of the NIRA guaranteed workers the right to unionize and to bargain collectively.

The New Deal also strengthened public confidence in the stock exchanges and banks. Roosevelt signed the Federal Securities Act, which compelled brokers to tell the truth about new securities issues, and the Banking Act of 1933, which set up the Federal Deposit Insurance Corporation for insuring bank deposits. During the First Hundred Days, Roosevelt also took the United States off the gold standard, no longer guaranteeing the gold value of the dollar abroad. Freed from the gold standard, the Federal Reserve System could expand the supply of currency in circulation, thus enabling monetary policy to become another weapon for economic recovery.

One of the boldest programs enacted by Congress addressed the badly depressed Tennessee River valley, which runs through Tennessee, North

TVA
——

Carolina, Kentucky, Virginia, Mississippi, Georgia, and Alabama. For years, progressives had advocated government operation of the Muscle Shoals electric power and nitrogen facilities on the Tennessee River. Roosevelt's Tennessee Valley Authority (TVA) was a much broader program. Its dams would not only control floods but also generate hydroelectric power. The TVA would produce and sell nitrogen fertilizers to private citizens and nitrate explosives to the government, dig a 650-mile navigation channel from Knoxville, Tennessee, to Paducah, Kentucky (see map), and construct public power facilities as a yardstick for determining fair rates for privately produced electric power. The goal of the TVA was nothing less than enhancement of the economic well-being of the entire Tennessee River valley.

The TVA achieved its goals, but it also became—largely in unforeseen ways—the most notorious polluter in the region. To power its coal-

TVA's Environmental Legacy
——

burning generators, the TVA engaged in massive strip mining that caused landslides and festering soil erosion. The generators also released sulfur oxides, which combined with water vapor to produce acid rain, a poison that not only killed aquatic life and destroyed forests in New England and Canada but also attacked human lungs and promoted heart disease. Above all, the TVA degraded

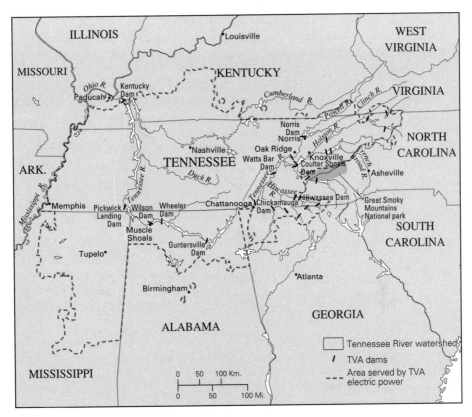

The Tennessee Valley Authority *For flood control and to generate electricity, the Tennessee Valley Authority constructed dams along the Tennessee River and its tributaries from Paducah, Kentucky, to Knoxville, Tennessee.*

the water by dumping untreated sewage, toxic chemicals, and metal pollutants from strip mining into streams and rivers. The TVA would prove to be a monumental disaster in America's environmental history.

Congress finally adjourned on June 16. During the First Hundred Days, Roosevelt had delivered fifteen messages to Congress, and fifteen significant laws had been enacted (see table). Within a few months of Roosevelt's succession to office, the United States had rebounded from hysteria and near collapse.

End of the First Hundred Days

Throughout the remainder of 1933 and the spring and summer of 1934, more New Deal bills became law, benefiting farmers, the unemployed, in-

Interest Group Democracy

vestors, homeowners, workers, and the environment. In 1934, additional hundreds of millions of federal dollars were appropriated for unemployment relief and public works. Legislation that year also established the Securities and Exchange Commission, the National Labor Relations Board, and the Federal Housing Administration. Here was interest group democracy at work, with New Deal legislation seeming to promise something for every group: industrial workers, urban dwellers, landowning farmers, and the jobless, not to mention industrialists, bankers, stockbrokers, educators, and social workers. In the midst of this coalition of special interests was President Roosevelt, the artful broker, who pointed to the economy as proof that his approach was working. Following the passage of

New Deal Achievements

	Labor	Agriculture	Business and Industrial Recovery	Relief	Reform
1933	Section 7(a) of NIRA	Agricultural Adjustment Act Farm Credit Act	Emergency Banking Act Beer and Wine Revenue Act Banking Act of 1933 (guaranteed deposits) National Industrial Recovery Act	Civilian Conservation Corps Federal Emergency Relief Act Home Owners Refinancing Act Public Works Administration Civil Works Administration	TVA Federal Securities Act
1934	National Labor Relations Board				Securities Exchange Act
1935	National Labor Relations (Wagner) Act	Resettlement Administration Rural Electrification Administration		Works Progress Administration and National Youth Administration	Banking Act of 1935 Social Security Act Public Utilities Holding Company Act Revenue Act (wealth tax)
1937		Farm Security Administration			
1938	Fair Labor Standards Act	Agricultural Adjustment Act of 1938			

Source: Adapted from Charles Sellers, Henry May, and Neil R. McMillen, *A Synopsis of American History*, 6th ed. Copyright © 1985 by Houghton Mifflin Company. Reprinted by permission.

New Deal legislation, unemployment fell steadily from thirteen million in 1933 to nine million in 1936. Net farm income rose from just over $3 billion in 1933 to $5.85 billion in 1935. Manufacturing salaries and wages also increased, from $6.25 billion in 1933 to almost $13 billion in 1937.

There was no question about the popularity of either the New Deal or the president during those early years of Roosevelt's presidency. In the 1934 congressional elections, the Democrats gained ten seats in the House and ten in the Senate. The New Deal, according to Arthur Krock of the *New York*

Times, had won "the most overwhelming victory in the history of American politics."

OPPOSITION TO THE FIRST NEW DEAL

There was more than one way to read employment and income statistics and election returns. For example, although unemployment had dropped from a high of 25 percent in 1933 to 16.9 percent in 1936, it had been only 3.2 percent in 1929. And although manufacturing wages and salaries had reached almost $13 billion in 1937, that figure was less than the total for 1929. Regardless of the New Deal's successes, in other words, it had a long way to go before reaching predepression standards.

Conservative Critics of the New Deal

With the arrival of partial economic recovery, many businesspeople and conservatives became vocal critics of the New Deal. Some charged that there was too much taxation and government regulation. Others criticized the deficit financing of relief and public works. In 1934, the leaders of several major corporations joined with Al Smith and disaffected conservative Democrats to establish the American Liberty League. Members of the Liberty League believed that the New Deal was subverting individual initiative and self-reliance by providing welfare payments.

Although businesspeople considered the government their enemy, others thought the government favored business too much. Critics argued that NRA codes favored industry's needs over those of workers and consumers. Farmers, labor unions, and individual entrepreneurs complained that the NRA set prices too high and favored large producers over small businesses. The federal courts also began to scrutinize the constitutionality of the legislation in cases brought by critics.

The AAA also came under attack for its encouragement of cutbacks in production. Farmers had plowed under 10.4 million acres of cotton and slaughtered 6 million pigs in 1933—a time when people were ill clothed and ill fed. Although for landowning farmers the program was successful, the average person found such waste shocking. Tenant farmers and sharecroppers were also supposed to receive government payments for taking crops out of cultivation, but very few received what they were entitled to, especially if they were African-American. Furthermore, the AAA's hopes that landlords would keep their tenants on the land even while cutting production were not fulfilled. In the South, the number of sharecropper farms dropped by 30 percent between 1930 and 1940. The result was a homeless population, dispossessed Americans heading to cities and towns in all parts of the country.

Joining the migration to the West Coast were "Okies" and "Arkies," many of whom were evicted from their tenant farms during the depression.

The Dust Bowl

They also took to the road to escape the drought that plagued the southern Plains states of Kansas, Colorado, New Mexico, Oklahoma, Arkansas, and Texas, known in the mid-1930s as the Dust Bowl. The Dust Bowl was the result of an environmental tragedy. For fifteen years, farmers on the southern Plains had bought tens of thousands of tractors and ploughed under millions of acres. In 1930, for instance, there were 66,000 tractors in just one state—Kansas. When the rain stopped in the 1930s, millions of acres of plowed land became vulnerable to the strong winds that caused the dust storms. From 1935 through 1938, 241 dust storms hit the southern Plains. One storm in 1934 carried 300 million tons of dust from the Plains and dropped it on East Coast cities and into the Atlantic Ocean. The tragedy of the Dust Bowl has been ranked as one of the three worst ecological mistakes in history.

Demagogic Attacks on the New Deal

Some farmers blamed the government for their woes, others blamed themselves. As dissatisfaction mounted, so too did the appeal of various demagogues, who presented an analysis of American society that people understood: the wealthy and powerful were ruling people's lives. Among the best-known demagogues were Father Charles Coughlin and Dr. Francis E. Townsend. Coughlin was a Roman Catholic priest whose weekly radio

sermons offered a curious combination of anticommunism and anticapitalism. In addition to criticizing the New Deal, Coughlin became increasingly anti-Semitic, telling his listeners that the cause of their woes was an international conspiracy of Jewish bankers. Townsend devised the Old Age Revolving Pensions plan, under which the government would pay monthly pensions of $200 to all citizens older than sixty on condition that they spent the money in the same month they received it. He claimed his plan, which was in reality fiscally impossible, would both aid the aged and cure the depression by pumping enormous purchasing power into the economy.

Then there was Huey Long, perhaps the most successful demagogue in American history. Long was elected governor of Louisiana in 1928 with the slogan "Every Man a King, But No One Wears a Crown." As a U.S. senator, Long at first supported the New Deal, but he found the NRA too conservative and began to believe that Roosevelt had fallen captive to big business. Long countered in 1934 with the Share Our Wealth Society, which advocated the seizure by taxation of all incomes greater than $1 million and all inheritances of more than $5 million. With the resulting funds, the government would furnish each family a homestead allowance of $5,000 and an annual income of $2,000. By mid-1935, Long's movement claimed seven million members, and few doubted that Long aspired to the presidency. An assassin's bullet extinguished his ambition in September 1935.

Some politicians, like Governor Floyd Olson of Minnesota, declared themselves socialists in the 1930s. In Wisconsin, the left-wing Progressive party reelected Robert La Follette Jr.

Left-Wing Critics of the New Deal
___

to the Senate in 1934, sent seven of the state's ten representatives to Washington, and placed La Follette's brother Philip in the governorship. And the old muckraker and socialist Upton Sinclair won the Democratic gubernatorial nomination in California in 1934 with the slogan "End Poverty in California."

Perhaps the most controversial alternative to the New Deal was the Communist party of the United States of America. Its membership remained small until 1935, when the party leadership changed its strategy. Proclaiming "Communism is Twentieth Century Americanism," the Communists disclaimed any intention of overthrowing the U.S. government; at its high point for the decade, in 1938, the party had fifty-five thousand members.

In addition to challenges from the right and the left, the New Deal was subject to challenge by the Supreme Court. Many New Deal laws had been hastily drafted, and the major-

Supreme Court Decisions Against the New Deal
___

ity of the justices feared that the legislation had vested too much power in the presidency. In 1935, the Court unanimously struck down the NIRA (*Schechter* v. *U.S.*) on the grounds that it granted the White House excessive legislative power and that the commerce clause of the Constitution did not give the federal government authority to regulate intrastate businesses. Roosevelt's industrial recovery program was dead. In early 1936, his farm program met a similar fate when the Court invalidated the AAA (*U.S.* v. *Butler*), deciding that agriculture was a local problem and thus, under the Tenth Amendment, subject to state, not federal, action.

As Roosevelt looked ahead to the presidential election of 1936, he foresaw the danger of losing his capacity to lead and to govern. His coalition of all interests was breaking up, radicals and demagogues were offering Americans alternative programs, and the Supreme Court was dismantling the New Deal. In early 1935, Roosevelt took the initiative once more. So impressive was the spate of new legislation that historians have called it the Second New Deal.

THE SECOND NEW DEAL AND THE ELECTION OF 1936

The Second New Deal differed in important ways from the First New Deal. When the chief legislative goal had been economic recovery, Roosevelt had cooperated with business.

Works Progress Administration
___

Beginning in 1935, however, he denounced business leaders for placing their selfish interests above the national welfare. The first triumph of the Second New Deal was an innocuous sounding but momentous law called the Emergency Relief Appropriation Act, which authorized the president to establish massive public works programs for the jobless. The first such program was the Works Progress Administration (WPA), later renamed the Work Projects Administration. The WPA ultimately employed more than 8.5 million people and built more than 650,000 miles of highways and roads, 125,000 public buildings, and 8,000 parks, as well as numerous bridges, airports, and other structures.

But the WPA did more than lay bricks. Its Federal Theater Project brought plays, vaudeville, and circuses to cities and towns across the country, and its Federal Writers' Project hired talent like John Steinbeck and Richard Wright to write local guidebooks and regional and folk histories.

The Emergency Relief Appropriation Act also funded the Resettlement Administration, which resettled destitute families and organized rural homestead communities and suburban greenbelt towns for low-income workers. The Rural Electrification Administration (REA) brought electricity to isolated rural areas. And the National Youth Administration (NYA) sponsored work-relief programs for young adults and part-time jobs for students.

Roosevelt also wanted new legislation aimed at controlling the activities of big business. The Supreme Court had condemned the government-business cooperation that had been the foundation of the First Hundred Days. In addition, business-people had become increasingly critical of Roosevelt and the New Deal. If big business would not cooperate with government, Roosevelt decided, government should "cut the giants down to size" through antitrust suits and heavy corporate taxes. In 1935, he asked Congress to enact several major bills, including a labor bill sponsored by Senator Robert Wagner of New York, a Social Security bill, and a "soak-the-rich" tax bill.

When the summer of 1935 that constituted the Second Hundred Days was over, the president had everything he had requested. The National Labor

Roosevelt's Second Hundred Days

Relations (Wagner) Act granted workers the right to unionize and bargain collectively with management. The act also empowered the National Labor Relations Board to guarantee democratic union elections and to penalize unfair labor practices by employers, such as firing workers for union membership.

The Social Security Act established old-age insurance for workers who paid Social Security taxes out of their wages. Social Security was a conservative measure: the government did not pay for old-age benefits; workers and their bosses did. The tax was also regressive in that the more workers earned, the less they were taxed proportionally, and it was deflationary, because it took out of people's pockets money that it did not repay for years. Finally, the law excluded from coverage farm workers, domestic servants, and many hospital and restaurant workers, occupations that included many women and people of color. Nevertheless, the Social Security Act was a milestone. With its passage, the federal government acknowledged its responsibility not only for the aged but also for the temporarily jobless, dependent children, and disabled people.

Social Security Act

As summer neared its end, Congress also passed the Revenue (Wealth Tax) Act of 1935, as Roosevelt had requested. The act, which some critics saw as the president's attempt to "steal Huey Long's thunder," did not result in a redistribution of income, although it did raise the income taxes of the wealthy. It also imposed a new tax on excess business profits and increased taxes on inheritances, large gifts, and profits from the sale of property.

The Second Hundred Days made it unmistakably clear that the president was once again in charge and preparing to run for reelection. The campaign was less heated than might have been expected. The Republican nominee, Governor Alf Landon of Kansas, criticized Roosevelt but did not advocate wholesale repeal of the New Deal. Roosevelt won by a landslide, carrying all but

Election of 1936

two states and polling 27.8 million votes to Landon's 16.7 million.

By 1936, Roosevelt and the Democrats had forged what observers have called the New Deal coalition. The coalition consisted of the urban masses, especially immigrants from southern and eastern Europe and their sons and daughters, organized labor, the eleven states of the Confederacy (the "Solid South"), and northern blacks. (Before the 1930s, most African-Americans had voted Republican.) With the New Deal coalition, the Democratic party had become the dominant half of the two-party system and would occupy the White House for most of the next thirty years.

New Deal Coalition

ROOSEVELT'S SECOND TERM: COURT PACKING AND OTHER FAILURES

Roosevelt faced a darkening horizon during his second term. The economy faltered again between 1937 and 1939, bringing renewed unemployment and suffering. And Europe drew closer to war, threatening to drag the United States into the conflict (see Chapter 26). To gain support for his foreign and military policies, Roosevelt began to court conservative opponents of his domestic reforms. The eventual result was the demise of the New Deal.

In several instances, Roosevelt brought about his own defeat. The Supreme Court had invalidated much of the work of the First Hundred Days; now Roosevelt feared it would do the same with the fruits of the Second Hundred Days. Four justices steadfastly opposed the New Deal; three generally approved of it; two were swing votes. What the federal judiciary needed, the president claimed, was a more enlightened and progressive world view. His Judiciary Reorganization Bill requested the authority to add a federal judge whenever an incumbent failed to retire within six

Roosevelt's Court-Packing Plan

months of reaching age seventy; he also wanted the power to name as many as fifty additional federal judges, including six to the Supreme Court. Roosevelt frankly envisioned using the bill to create a Supreme Court sympathetic to the New Deal. Liberals joined Republicans and conservative Democrats in resisting the bill, and Roosevelt had to concede defeat. The bill he signed into law provided pensions to retiring judges but denied him the power to increase the number of judges.

This episode had a final ironic twist. During the public debate over court packing, the two swing-vote justices on the Supreme Court began to vote in favor of liberal, pro–New Deal rulings. In short order, the Court upheld both the Wagner Act (*NLRB v. Jones & Laughlin Steel Corp.*, ruling that Congress's power to regulate interstate commerce also involved the power to regulate the production of goods for interstate commerce) and the Social Security Act. Moreover, the new pensions encouraged judges older than seventy to retire, and the president was able to appoint seven new associate justices in the next four years, including such notables as Hugo Black, Felix Frankfurter, and William O. Douglas.

Another New Deal setback was the renewed economic recession of 1937–1939. Roosevelt had never abandoned his commitment to a balanced budget. In 1937, confident that the depression had largely been cured, he began to order drastic cutbacks in government spending. At the same time, the Federal Reserve Board, concerned about a 3.6 percent inflation rate, tightened credit. The two actions sent the economy into a tailspin: unemployment climbed from 7.7 million in 1937 to 10.4 million in 1938. Soon Roosevelt was forced to resume deficit financing.

Recession of 1937–1939

In the spring of 1938, with conflict over events in Europe commanding more and more of the nation's attention, the New Deal came to an end. Roosevelt sacrificed further domestic reforms in return for conservative support for his programs of military rearmament and preparedness. The last significant New Deal laws enacted were the National Housing Act (1937), which established the U.S. Housing

Authority and built housing projects for low-income families; a new Agricultural Adjustment Act (1938); and the Fair Labor Standards Act (1938), which forbade labor by children younger than sixteen and established a minimum wage and forty-hour workweek for many, but by no means all, workers.

INDUSTRIAL WORKERS AND THE RISE OF THE CIO

Working people gained from the New Deal the right to organize labor unions and bargain collectively with their bosses. Enactment of Section 7(a) of the NIRA (1933) and the Wagner Act (1935) inspired vigorous recruitment of union members. Union membership in 1929 stood at 3.6 million; in mid-1938, it surpassed 7 million. The gains, however, did not always come easily. Management resisted vigorously in the 1930s, relying on the police or hiring armed thugs to intimidate workers and break up strikes.

Labor confronted yet another obstacle in the American Federation of Labor (AFL) craft unions' traditional hostility toward industrial unions. Craft

Rivalry Between Craft and Industrial Unions

unions typically consisted of skilled workers in a particular trade, such as carpentry or plumbing. Industrial unions represented all the workers, skilled and unskilled, in a given industry. The organizational gains of the 1930s were far more impressive in industrial unions than in craft unions, as hundreds of thousands of workers organized in such industries as autos, garments, rubber, and steel.

Attempts to reconcile the craft and industrial union movements failed, and in 1935 John L. Lewis of the United Mine Workers resigned as vice president of the AFL. He and other industrial unionists then formed the Committee for Industrial Organization (CIO). The AFL expelled the CIO unions in 1938, and the CIO reorganized as the Congress of Industrial Organizations. By that time, CIO membership had reached 3.7 million, more than the AFL's 3.4 million.

The CIO evolved during the 1930s into a pragmatic bread-and-butter labor organization that organized millions of workers, including women and African-Americans, who had

Sit-Down Strikes

never before had an opportunity to join a union. One union, the United Auto Workers (UAW), scored a major victory in late 1936. The UAW demanded recognition from General Motors, Chrysler, and Ford. When GM refused, workers at the Fisher Body plant in Flint, Michigan, launched a sit-down strike and refused to leave the building. To discourage the strikers, GM turned off the heat. When that tactic failed, GM called in the police, who were met by a barrage of iron bolts, coffee mugs, and bottles. The police then resorted to tear gas, and the strikers turned the plant's water hoses on them.

The strike lasted for weeks. GM obtained a court order to evacuate the plant, but the strikers stood firm, risking imprisonment and fines. With the support of their families, neighbors, and a women's "emergency brigade" that organized to deliver food and supplies to the strikers, the UAW prevailed. GM agreed to recognize the union. Chrysler signed a similar agreement, but Ford held out for four more years. As a tactic, the sit-down strike spread dramatically; it was used by workers in the textile, glass, and rubber industries and by dime-store clerks, janitors, dressmakers, and bakers.

In 1937, the Steel Workers Organizing Committee (SWOC) signed a contract with the nation's largest steel maker, U.S. Steel, that guaranteed an

Memorial Day Massacre

eight-hour day and a forty-hour week. Other steel companies refused to go along. Confrontations between the so-called little steel companies and the SWOC soon led to violence. On Memorial Day, strikers and their families joined with sympathizers in a picket line in front of the Republic Steel plant in Chicago. Violence erupted, and ten strikers were killed and forty suffered gunshot wounds. The police explained that the marchers had attacked them with clubs and bricks and that they had responded with reasonable force to defend themselves and disperse the mob.

How do historians know

who was responsible for the 1937 Memorial Day Massacre in Chicago? There is both photographic and medical evidence of the police's culpability. Covering the story at the Republic Steel plant were a cameraman from Paramount News and photographers from Life magazine and World Wide Photos (see photograph). Paramount News suppressed its film footage, claiming that releasing it "might very well incite local riots," but an enterprising reporter alerted a congressional committee to its existence, and a private viewing was arranged. Spectators at this showing, the reporter noted, "were shocked and amazed by scenes showing scores of uniformed policemen firing their revolvers pointblank into a dense crowd of men, women, and children, and then pursuing the survivors unmercifully as they made frantic efforts to escape." Medical evidence also substantiated the picketers' version: none of the ten people killed by police had been shot from the front. Clearly, the picketers were trying to flee the police when they were shot or clubbed to the ground.   Photo: World Wide Photos.

The strikers argued that the police, without provocation, had brutally attacked citizens who were peacefully asserting their constitutional rights.

Although senseless, the Memorial Day Massacre was not surprising. During the 1930s, industries had hired private police agents and accumulated large stores of arms and ammunition for use in deterring workers from organizing and joining unions. Meanwhile, the CIO continued to enroll new members. By the end of the decade, the CIO had succeeded in organizing most of the nation's mass production industries.

MIXED PROGRESS FOR PEOPLE OF COLOR

The depression plunged the vast majority of African-Americans deeper into fear, political disfranchisement, segregation, and privation. In 1930, about three-fourths of all blacks lived in the South. Almost all were prohibited from voting or serving on juries. They were routinely denied access to hospitals, universities, public parks, and swimming pools. And they were hired only for the least desirable, most menial jobs. Blacks living in rural areas in the South were sharecroppers, tenants, or wage hands. Their life expectancy was ten years less than that of whites. And the specter of the lynch mob was a continuing reality. Racism also plagued African-Americans living in the North. Southern blacks who migrated to northern cities found that employers discriminated against them. Black unemployment rates ran high; in Pittsburgh, 48 percent of black workers were jobless in 1933, compared with 31 percent of white laborers.

African-Americans in the Depression

As African-Americans were aware, Herbert Hoover shared prevailing white racial attitudes. Hoover sought a lily-white GOP and attempted to push blacks out of the Republican party in order to attract white southern Democrats. In 1930, the president demonstrated his racial insensitivity by nominating Judge John J. Parker of North Carolina to the Supreme Court. Ten years earlier, Parker had endorsed the disfranchisement of blacks. Pressure from the NAACP and the AFL helped to defeat Parker's nomination in the Senate.

Shortly thereafter, a celebrated civil rights case revealed the ugliness of race relations in the depression era. In March 1931, nine African-Americans who were riding a freight train near Scottsboro, Alabama, were arrested and charged with roughing up some white hoboes and throwing them off the train. Two white women removed from the same train claimed the nine men had raped them. Medical

Scottsboro Trials

evidence later showed that the women were lying. But within two weeks, eight of the so-called Scottsboro boys were convicted of rape by all-white juries and sentenced to death.

After several trials, the first defendant, Haywood Patterson, was condemned to die. A Supreme Court ruling intervened, however, on the ground that African-Americans were systematically excluded from juries in Alabama. Patterson was found guilty again in 1936 and was given a seventy-five-year jail sentence. Four of the other youths were sentenced to life imprisonment. Not until 1950 were all five out of jail—four by parole and Patterson by escaping from his work gang.

African-Americans coped with their white-circumscribed environment and fought racism in a variety of ways. The NAACP, although internally divided, lobbied quietly against a long list of injustices, and A. Philip Randolph's Brotherhood of Sleeping Car Porters fought for the rights of black workers. In Harlem, the militant Harlem Tenants League fought rent increases and evictions, and African-American consumers began to boycott white merchants who refused to hire blacks as clerks. Their slogan was, "Don't Buy Where You Can't Work." But America's white leaders made few concessions.

With the election of Franklin D. Roosevelt, blacks' attitudes toward government changed, as did their political affiliation. For African-Americans, Franklin D. Roosevelt would become the most appealing president since Abraham Lincoln. Part of the reason was the courageous way he bore his physical disability. Blacks suffered from their own handicap—racism—and knew what courage was. Moreover, Roosevelt was a decided improvement over Hoover. Blacks were heartened by photographs of African-American visitors at the White House and by news stories about Roosevelt's black advisers. Most important, New Deal relief programs aided black people in their struggle for economic survival.

The "Black Cabinet," or black brain trust, was unique in U.S. history. Never before had there been so many African-American advisers at the White House. There were black lawyers, journalists, and doctorates and black experts on housing,

Black Cabinet

Mary McLeod Bethune, pictured here with her friend and supporter Eleanor Roosevelt, became the first African-American woman to head a federal agency as director of the Division of Negro Affairs of the National Youth Administration.   UPI/Bettmann Newsphotos.

labor, and social welfare. William H. Hastie and Robert C. Weaver, holders of advanced degrees from Harvard, served in the Department of the Interior. Mary McLeod Bethune, educator and president of the National Council of Negro Women, was director of the Division of Negro Affairs of the National Youth Administration. There were also among the New Dealers some whites who had committed themselves to first-class citizenship for African-Americans. Foremost among these people was Eleanor Roosevelt.

The president himself, however, remained uncommitted to African-American civil rights. Fearful of alienating southern whites, he never endorsed two

The New Deal's Racism

————

key goals of the civil rights struggle: a federal law against lynching and abolition of the poll tax. Furthermore, some New Deal programs functioned in ways that were definitely damaging to African-Americans. The AAA, rather than benefiting black

tenant farmers and sharecroppers, had the effect of forcing many of them off the land. The Federal Housing Administration (FHA) refused to guarantee mortgages on houses purchased by blacks in white neighborhoods, and the CCC was racially segregated. Finally, Social Security coverage and the minimum-wage provisions of the Fair Labor Standards Act of 1938 excluded waiters, cooks, hospital orderlies, janitors, farm workers, and domestics, many of whom were African-Americans.

Confronted with the mixed message of the New Deal, African-Americans reacted in different ways. The large majorities they gave Roosevelt at

March on Washington Movement

————

election time demonstrated their appreciation of the benefits they received from New Deal programs. Their concern about continuing racism was reflected through self-help and direct-action movements. Nowhere was the trend toward direct action more evident than in the March on Washington Movement in 1941. That year, billions of federal dollars flowed into American industry as the nation prepared for the possibility of another world war. Thousands of new jobs were created, but discrimination deprived blacks of their fair share. One executive notified black job applicants that "the Negro will be considered only as janitors and other similar capacities." Randolph, leader of the porters' union, proposed that blacks march on the nation's capital to demand equal access to jobs in defense industries. Fearing that the march might provoke riots and that Communists might infiltrate the movement, Roosevelt announced that he would issue an executive order prohibiting discrimination in war industries and in the government if the march was canceled. The result was Executive Order No. 8802, which established the Fair Employment Practices Committee (FEPC).

Another group, American Indians, sank further into malnutrition and disease during the early 1930s. In Oklahoma, where the Choctaws, Cherokees, and Seminoles lived with more than twenty other tribes on infertile soil, three-fourths of all Native American children were undernourished. Tuberculosis swept through the reservations. At the heart of the problem was a 1929 ruling by the U.S. comptroller general that landless tribes were ineligible for federal aid. Not until 1931 did the Bureau of Indian Affairs take steps to relieve the suffering.

The New Deal approach to Native Americans differed greatly from that of earlier administrations; as a result, Indians benefited more directly than

A New Deal for Native Americans

blacks from the New Deal. As commissioner of Indian Affairs, Roosevelt appointed John Collier, the founder of the American Indian Defense Association. Collier had crusaded for tribal landownership and an end to the allotment policy established by the Dawes Severalty Act of 1887. Since that date, total Native American landholding had dropped from 138 million acres to 48 million acres, 20 million of which were arid or semiarid.

The Indian Reorganization (Wheeler-Howard) Act of 1934 aimed to reverse this process by restoring lands to tribal ownership and forbidding future division of Indian lands into individual parcels.

Other provisions of the act enabled tribes to obtain loans for economic development and to establish self-government. Under Collier, the Bureau of Indian Affairs also encouraged the perpetuation of Indian religions and cultures.

Mexican-Americans also suffered extreme hardship during the depression, but no government programs benefited them. During these

Depression Hardships for Mexican-Americans

years, many Mexicans and Mexican-Americans packed up their belongings and moved south of the border, sometimes willingly and sometimes deported by immigration officials or forced out by California officials eager to purge them from the relief rolls. According to the federal census, the Mexican-born population in the United States dropped from 617,000 in 1930 to 377,000 in 1940. Many employers had changed their minds about the desirability of hiring Mexican-American farm workers. Before the 1930s, farmers had boasted that Mexican-Americans were an inexpensive, docile labor supply and that they would not join unions. But in the 1930s, Mexican-Americans overturned the stereotype by engaging in prolonged and sometimes bloody strikes.

The New Deal offered Mexican-Americans little help. The AAA was created to assist property-owning farmers, not migratory farm workers. The Wagner Act did not cover farm workers' unions, nor did the Social Security Act or the Fair Labor Standards Act cover farm laborers. One New Deal agency, the Farm Security Administration (FSA), was established in 1937 to help farm workers, in part by setting up migratory labor camps. But the FSA came too late to help Mexican-Americans, most of whom had by then been replaced in the fields by dispossessed white farmers.

WOMEN, WORK, AND THE DEPRESSION

In *It's Up to the Women* (1933), Eleanor Roosevelt wrote that during depressions wives and mothers often bore a heavier burden than husbands and

Mothers and Households Face the Depression

fathers. Many women followed the maxim "Use it up, wear it out, make it do, or do without." In Eleanor Roosevelt's words, making do meant "endless little economies." Women bought day-old bread and cheap cuts of meat; they relined old coats with blankets and saved string, rags, and broken crockery for future use. Many families were able to maintain their standard of living only because of astute spending and because women substituted their own labor for goods and services they once purchased.

While they were cutting corners to make ends meet, women were also seeking paid work outside the home. In 1930, approximately 10.5 million women were paid workers; ten years later, the female labor force exceeded 13 million. Despite the social realities, most Americans continued to believe that women should not take jobs outside the home, that they should strive instead to be good wives and mothers, and that women who worked were doing so for "pin money" to buy frivolous things. When a 1936 Gallup poll asked whether wives should work if their husbands had jobs, 82 percent of the respondents (including 75 percent of the women) answered no.

These attitudes resulted in severe job discrimination. Most insurance companies, banks, railroads, and public utilities had policies against hiring married women. And from 1932 to 1937, federal law prohibited more than one family member from working for the civil service. Because wives usually earned less than their husbands, they were the ones who quit their government jobs.

Job Discrimination Against Married Women

In part, such thinking missed the point for two reasons. First, women were heavily concentrated in "women's jobs," including clerical positions, teachers, telephone operators, and nurses. Men rarely sought these jobs and probably would not have been hired had they applied. Second, most women workers (71 percent in 1930) were single and thus self-supporting. But this was changing. By 1940, married women constituted 35 percent of the female work force, up from 29 percent in 1930 and 15 percent in 1900. They worked to keep their families from slipping into poverty, but their assistance with family expenses did not improve their status. The prevailing pattern was that although women were making greater contributions to the family, their husbands, including those without jobs, still expected to rule the roost and to remain exempt from child care and housework.

The New Deal did take women's needs into account but only when forcefully reminded to do so by the activist women who advised the administration. These women, mainly government and Democratic party officials, formed a network united by their commitment to social reform and to the participation of women in politics and government. The network's most prominent member was Eleanor Roosevelt, who was her husband's valued adviser. Secretary of Labor Frances Perkins was the nation's first woman cabinet officer. Other historic New Deal appointments included the first woman federal appeals judge and the first women ambassadors.

Women in the New Deal

Even with increased participation by women, however, New Deal provisions for women were mixed. The maximum-hour and minimum-wage provisions mandated by the NRA won women's support. Women workers in the lowest-paying jobs, many of whom labored under sweatshop conditions, had the most to gain from these standards. Some NRA codes mandated pay differentials based on gender, however, making women's minimum wages lower than men's. Federal relief agencies, such as the Civil Works Administration and the Federal Emergency Relief Administration, hired only one woman for every eight to ten men placed in relief jobs. A popular New Deal program, the Civilian Conservation Corps, was limited to young men. And women in agriculture and domestic service were not protected by the 1935 Social Security Act or the 1938 Fair Labor Standards Act.

THE ELECTION OF 1940 AND THE LEGACY OF THE NEW DEAL

As the presidential election of 1940 approached, many Americans speculated about whether Roosevelt would run for a third term. (No president had ever served more than two terms.) Roosevelt seemed undecided until May 1940, when Adolf Hitler's military advances in Europe apparently convinced him to stay on. After being nominated on the first ballot, Roosevelt selected Henry A. Wallace, the secretary of agriculture, as his running mate.

The Republican candidate was Wendell Willkie, an Indiana lawyer and utilities executive who was once a Democrat but had become a prominent business opponent of the New Deal. Willkie campaigned against the New Deal, contending that its meddling in business had failed to return the nation to prosperity. He also criticized the government's lack of military preparedness. But Roosevelt preempted the defense issue by beefing up military and naval contracts. When Willkie reversed his approach and accused Roosevelt of warmongering, the president promised, "Your boys are not going to be sent into any foreign wars."

Willkie never did come up with an effective campaign issue, and on election day Roosevelt received twenty-seven million popular votes to Willkie's twenty-two million. As in 1936, the New Deal coalition triumphed in the cities, primarily among blue-collar workers, ethnic Americans, and African-Americans. He also won every state in the South. Although the New Deal was over at home, Roosevelt was still riding a wave of public approval.

Any analysis of the New Deal must begin with Franklin Delano Roosevelt. Assessments of his career varied widely during his presidency. Most historians consider him a truly

The New Deal Assessed

great president, citing his courage and buoyant self-confidence, his willingness to experiment, and his capacity to inspire the nation during the most somber days of the depression. Those who criticize him charge that he lacked vision and failed to formulate a bold and coherent strategy of economic recovery and political and economic reform.

Even scholars who criticize Roosevelt's performance agree that he transformed the presidency. "Only Washington, who made the office, and Jackson, who remade it, did more than Roosevelt to raise it to its present condition of strength, dignity, and independence," according to political scientist Clinton Rossiter. Some scholars, however, have charged that it was Roosevelt who initiated "the imperial presidency." Whether for good or ill, Roosevelt strengthened not only the presidency but the whole federal government. "For the first time for many Americans," the historian William Leuchtenburg has written, "the federal government became an institution that was directly experienced. More than state and local governments, it came to be *the* government."

The New Deal laid the foundation of the welfare system on which subsequent presidential administrations would build. For the first time, the federal government acknowl-

Origins of America's Welfare System

edged a responsibility to offer relief to the jobless and the needy, and for the first time it resorted to deficit spending to stimulate the economy. Millions of Americans benefited from government programs that are still operating today.

Limited change in the nation's power structure also occurred under the New Deal. Beginning in the 1930s, business interests had to share their political clout with others. Labor gained influence in Washington, and farmers got more of what they wanted from Congress and the White House. If people wanted their voices to be heard, they had to organize into labor unions, trade associations, or other special interest lobbies. Not everybody's voice was heard, however. Because of the persistence of racism, there was no real increase in the power of African-Americans and other minorities.

The New Deal failed in its fundamental purpose: to put people back to work. As late as 1939, more than ten million men and women were still jobless. That year, unemployment was 19 percent. In the end, it was not the New Deal but massive government spending during World War II that put people back to work. In 1941, as a result of mobilization for war, unemployment would drop to 10 percent, and in 1944, at the height of the war, only 1 percent of the labor force would be jobless.

The New Deal's most lasting accomplishments were its programs to ameliorate the suffering of unemployment. The United States has suffered several economic recessions since 1945, but even Republican presidents have primed the pump during the periods of slump. Before the New Deal, the United States had experienced a major depression every fifteen or twenty years. The Great Depression was the last of its kind. Since the New Deal, thanks to unemployment compensation, Social Security, and other measures, the United States has not reexperienced this national nightmare.

SUGGESTIONS FOR FURTHER READING

Hoover and the Worsening Depression

Michael A. Bernstein, *The Great Depression: Delayed Recovery and Economic Change in America, 1929–1939* (1988); David Burner, *Herbert Hoover* (1979); Martin L. Fausold, *The Presidency of Herbert C. Hoover* (1985); John A. Garraty, *The Great Depression* (1986); James S. Olson, *Herbert Hoover and the Reconstruction Finance Corporation, 1931–1933* (1977); Albert B. Romasco, *The Poverty of Abundance: Hoover, the Nation, the Depression* (1965); Jordan A. Schwarz, *Interregnum of Despair* (1970).

The New Deal

Anthony J. Badger, *The Deal: The Depression Years, 1933–1940* (1989); Roger Biles, *A New Deal for the American People* (1991); Steve Fraser and Gary Gerstle, eds., *The Rise and Fall of the New Deal Order, 1930–1980* (1989); William E. Leuchtenburg, *Franklin D. Roosevelt and the New Deal* (1963); Robert S. McElvaine, *The Great Depression* (1984); Albert U. Romasco, *The Politics of Recovery: Roosevelt's New Deal* (1983).

Franklin and Eleanor Roosevelt

James MacGregor Burns, *Roosevelt: The Lion and the Fox* (1956); Blanche Wiesen Cook, *Eleanor Roosevelt: Volume One, 1884–1933* (1992); Kenneth S. Davis, *FDR: Into the Storm, 1937–1940* (1993), and *FDR: The New Deal Years, 1933–1937* (1986); Frank Freidel, *Franklin D. Roosevelt: A Rendezvous with Destiny* (1990); Doris Kearns Goodwin, *No Ordinary Time: Franklin and Eleanor Roosevelt: The Home Front in World War II* (1994); Joseph P. Lash, *Eleanor and Franklin* (1971); (1983); Arthur M. Schlesinger Jr., *The Age of Roosevelt,* 3 vols. (1957–1960).

Voices from the Depression

James Agee, *Let Us Now Praise Famous Men* (1941); Federal Writers' Project, *These Are Our Lives* (1939); Robert S. McElvaine, ed., *Down and Out in the Great Depression: Letters from the Forgotten Man* (1983); Studs Terkel, *Hard Times: An Oral History of the Great Depression* (1970).

Alternatives to the New Deal

Alan Brinkley, *Voices of Protest: Huey Long, Father Coughlin, and the Great Depression* (1982); William Ivy Hair, *The Kingfish and*

His Realm: The Life and Times of Huey P. Long (1992); Robin D. G. Kelley, *Hammer and Hoe: Alabama Communists During the Great Depression* (1991); Mark Naison, *Communists in Harlem During the Depression* (1983); Leo Ribuffo, *The Old Christian Right: The Protestant Far Right from the Great Depression to the Cold War* (1983); T. Harry Williams, *Huey Long* (1969).

Labor

Irving Bernstein, *A Caring Society: The New Deal, the Worker, and the Great Depression* (1985), and *Turbulent Years: A History of the American Worker, 1933–1941* (1969); Lizabeth Cohen, *Making a New Deal: Industrial Workers in Chicago, 1919–1939* (1991); Melvin Dubofsky and Warren Van Tine, *John L. Lewis: A Biography* (1977); Sidney Fine, *Sit-Down: The General Motors Strike of 1936–1937* (1969).

Agriculture and the Environment

David E. Conrad, *The Forgotten Farmers: The Story of Sharecroppers in the New Deal* (1965); Theodore M. Saloutos, *The American Farmer and the New Deal* (1982); John L. Shover, *Cornbelt Rebellion: The Farmers' Holiday Association* (1965).

People of Color

Dan T. Carter, *Scottsboro,* rev. ed. (1979); Laurence C. Kelly, *The Assault on Assimilation: John Collier and the Origins of Indian Policy Reform* (1983); John B. Kirby, *Black Americans in the Roosevelt Era* (1980); Donald J. Lisio, *Hoover, Blacks, and Lily-Whites* (1985); Mark Reisler, *By the Sweat of Their Brow: Mexican Immigrant Labor in the United States, 1900–1940* (1976); Harvard Sitkoff, *A New Deal for Blacks* (1978); Nancy J. Weiss, *Farewell to the Party of Lincoln: Black Politics in the Age of FDR* (1983); Raymond Wolters, *Negroes and the Great Depression* (1970).

Women

Glen H. Elder Jr., *Children of the Great Depression* (1974); Lois Scharf, *To Work and to Wed: Female Employment, Feminism, and the Great Depression* (1980); Winifred Wandersee, *Women's Work and Family Values, 1920-1940* (1981); Susan Ware, *Holding Their Own: American Women in the 1930s* (1982), and *Beyond Suffrage: Women in the New Deal* (1981).

Cultural and Intellectual History

Daniel Aaron, *Writers on the Left: Episodes in American Literary Communism* (1961); Andrew Bergman, *We're in the Money: Depression America and Its Films* (1971); David P. Peeler, *Hope Among Us Yet: Social Criticism and Social Solace in Depression America* (1987); Richard H. Pells, *Radical Visions and American Dreams: Culture and Social Thought in the Depression Years* (1973); Warren I. Susman, "The Culture of the Thirties," in Warren I. Susman, ed., *Culture as History* (1984), pp. 150–183.

Foreign Relations in a Broken World, 1920–1941

PRISONER 9653 STRODE OUT of Atlanta's federal penitentiary on December 24, 1921. After a train ride to Washington, D.C., he met the man who had just pardoned him. "I have heard so damned much about you, Mr. Debs," said the congenial President Warren G. Harding as Debs entered the White House, "that I am now very glad to meet you personally." The release of Eugene V. Debs, the most prominent of the jailed antiwar critics, marked one of Harding's ways of saying that the troubled recent past should be shelved in favor of what he called normalcy.

In November 1921, the president took further steps to put the war behind the American people. To initiate "a new and lasting era of peace," he buried the Unknown Soldier in Arlington Cemetery. He then signed peace treaties with the defeated Central Powers, which had still been technically at war with the United States because of the Senate's rejection of the Treaty of Paris. Harding promoted these peace treaties "so that we may put aside the last remnant" of the war. The same month he opened an international conference in Washington. His goal: a reduction in naval armaments to ensure a stable world order.

Harding's desire to shove the war into the past, and his emphasis on avoiding entanglements with Europe, did not mean that Americans cut themselves off from international affairs after the First World War. To be sure, many Americans had become disillusioned with their war experience. But the United States remained quite active in the world in the 1920s.

The most apt description of interwar U.S. foreign policy is independent internationalism. The United States was active on a global scale but retained its independence of action, its traditional unilateralism. At the same time, many Americans called themselves *isolationists*, by which they meant that they wanted to isolate themselves from Europe's political squabbles, from military alliances and interventions, and from commitments like the League of Nations that might restrict their freedom of choice. Americans, then, were isolationists in their desire to avoid war but independent internationalists in their behavior.

In the aftermath of the First World War, Americans had grown disenchanted with military methods of achieving order and protecting American prosperity and security. American diplomats thus increasingly sought to exercise the power of the United States through conferences, moral lectures and calls for peace, nonrecognition of disapproved regimes, arms control, and economic and financial ties in accord with the principle of the Open Door. They pulled the marines out of Caribbean and Central American nations and fashioned a Good Neighbor policy for Latin America.

The United States failed, however, to create a stable world order. Severe economic problems undercut it, and many other nations schemed to disrupt it. The debts and reparations bills left over from World War I bedeviled the 1920s, and the Great Depression of the 1930s shattered world trade and finance. The depression also spawned revolutions in Latin America and political extremism, militarism, and war in Europe and Asia. As Nazi Germany marched toward world war, the United States tried to protect itself from the conflict by adopting a policy of neutrality. At the same time, the United States sought to defend its interests in Asia against Japanese aggression by invoking the venerable Open Door policy.

In the late 1930s, and especially after the outbreak of European war in September 1939, many Americans came to agree with President Franklin D. Roosevelt that Germany and Japan had become menaces to the national interest. Roosevelt first pushed for American military preparedness and then for the abandonment of neutrality in favor of aiding Britain and France. To deter Japanese expansion in the Pacific, the United States ultimately cut off supplies of vital American products such as oil. But economic warfare had the effect not of containing Japan but rather of intensifying antagonisms. Japan's surprise attack on Pearl Harbor in December 1941 finally brought the United States into the Second World War.

SEARCHING FOR PEACE AND ORDER IN THE 1920s

Europe lay in shambles at the end of the First World War. Between 1914 and 1921, Europe suffered sixty million casualties from world war, civil war, massacre, epidemic, and famine. Crops, live-stock, factories, trains, forests, bridges—little was spared. Americans responded with humanitarian aid. The American Relief Administration delivered food to needy Europeans, including Russians wracked by famine in 1921 and 1922.

American peace groups also worked to create international stability. During the 1920s and 1930s, peace societies advocated a variety of strategies to ensure world order: cooperation with the League of Nations, membership in the World Court, arbitration of international disputes, disarmament and arms reduction, curbs on exploitative business ventures, the outlawing of war, and strict neutrality in times of belligerency. Organizations like the Fellowship of Reconciliation and the Women's International League for Peace and Freedom reminded Americans of the carnage of the First World War and the futility of war as a solution to international problems.

American Peace Movement

The Washington Conference (November 1921–February 1922) seemed to mark a substantial step toward arms control. The United States and eight other nations (Britain, Japan, France, Italy, China, Portugal, Belgium, and the Netherlands) discussed limits on naval armaments. Britain, the United States, and Japan—the three major powers—were facing a costly naval arms race, and they welcomed the opportunity to deflect it.

Washington Conference

The conference produced three treaties. The Five-Power Treaty set a ten-year moratorium on the construction of capital ships (battleships and aircraft carriers) and established a total tonnage ratio of 5 for Britain, 5 for the United States, 3 for Japan, 1.75 for France, and 1.75 for Italy. The first three nations actually agreed to dismantle some existing vessels to satisfy the ratio. They also pledged not to build new fortifications in their Pacific possessions (such as the Philippines in the case of the United States). In the Nine-Power Treaty, the conferees reaffirmed the Open Door in China, recognizing Chinese sovereignty. In the Four-Power Treaty, the United States, Britain, Japan, and France agreed to respect each other's Pacific possessions. The three treaties represented a rare

• *Important Events* •

1921	Washington Conference opens to limit naval arms race
1922	Mussolini comes to power in Italy Fordney-McCumber Tariff Act raises duties
1924	Dawes Plan eases German reparations payments
1926	American troops occupy Nicaragua
1928	Kellogg-Briand Pact outlaws war
1929	Great Depression hits United States Young Plan reduces German reparations
1930	Hawley-Smoot Tariff raises duties
1931	Japan seizes Manchuria
1932	Stimson Doctrine protests Japanese control of Manchuria
1933	Hitler establishes Nazi government in Germany United States recognizes Soviet Union Good Neighbor policy announced for Latin America
1934	Batista comes to power in Cuba Reciprocal Trade Agreements Act attempts to spur foreign commerce by lowering tariffs U.S. troops withdraw from Haiti Export-Import Bank founded to expand foreign trade
1935	Italy invades and annexes Ethiopia Neutrality Act prohibits arms shipments
1936	Spanish Civil War breaks out between Loyalists and Franco's fascists Neutrality Act forbids loans to belligerents

1937	Neutrality Act creates cash-and-carry trade with warring nations Sino-Japanese War breaks out Roosevelt delivers quarantine speech against aggressors
1938	Mexico nationalizes American-owned oil companies Munich Conference grants part of Czechoslovakia to Germany
1939	Nazi-Soviet Pact Second World War begins United States repeals arms embargo to help Allies
1940	Committee to Defend America by Aiding the Allies formed Germany, Italy, and Japan join in Tripartite Pact Great Britain and the United States swap destroyers for bases Isolationists form America First Committee Selective Training and Service Act starts first peacetime draft
1941	Lend-Lease Act gives aid to Allies Germany attacks Soviet Union United States freezes Japanese assets Atlantic Charter produced at Roosevelt-Churchill meeting Roosevelt exploits *Greer* incident to convoy British ships Japanese flotilla attacks Pearl Harbor, Hawaii United States enters Second World War

example of mutual disarmament. But they did not limit submarines, destroyers, or cruisers, nor did they provide enforcement powers for the Open Door declaration. Subsequent conferences in the 1930s, moreover, produced meager results. Rearmament soon supplanted disarmament.

Peace advocates also placed their hopes on the Kellogg-Briand Pact of 1928, a treaty eventually signed by sixty-two nations. The signatories agreed

Kellogg-Briand Pact

to "condemn recourse to war for the solution of international controversies, and renounce it as an instrument of national policy." The backers billed the accord as a first step in a long journey toward international cooperation and the outlawing of war. Although weak, the Kellogg-Briand Pact reflected popular sentiment that war was barbaric and wasteful.

The League of Nations, envisioned as a peacemaker, exhibited conspicuous feebleness, not because the United States refused to join but because its members usually chose not to use it to settle disputes. Starting in the mid-1920s, American officials participated discreetly in League meetings on public health, prostitution, drug trafficking, and other questions. And American jurists served on the World Court in Geneva, although the United States also refused to join that international body.

THE WORLD ECONOMY AND THE GREAT DEPRESSION

While Europe struggled to recover from the ravages of the First World War, the international economy wobbled and then, in the early 1930s, collapsed. The Great Depression set off a political chain reaction that carried the world to war. Cordell Hull, secretary of state under Roosevelt from 1933 to 1944, often said that economic conditions defined the character of international relations. "We cannot have a peaceful world," he warned, "until we rebuild the international economic structure." Events proved Hull right.

U.S. leaders believed that American economic expansion and America's prominent position in the international economy would stabilize world politics. By the late 1920s, the **U.S. Economic Expansion** United States produced about half the world's industrial goods, ranked first among exporters ($5.2 billion-worth of shipments in 1929), and served as the financial capital of the world. During 1914–1930, private investments abroad grew fivefold to more than $17 billion. The federal government facilitated much of the American economic activity abroad. The overseas offices of the Department of Commerce, for example, gathered valuable market information, and the 1919 Edge Act permitted U.S. banks to open foreign branch banks.

As Europeans watched American economic expansion with wariness, they also branded the United States stingy for its handling of war debts

War Debts and reparations. Twenty-eight nations became entangled in the web of inter-Allied debts, which totaled $26.5 billion, about half of it owed to the United States. Europeans urged Americans to erase the debts as a magnanimous contribution to the war effort. During the war, they charged, Europe had bled while America profited. But U.S. leaders insisted on repayment.

The debts question was linked to Germany's $33 billion reparations bill. Hobbled by inflation and economic disorder, Germany began to default on its payments. To keep Germany afloat and to forestall the **German Reparations** radicalism that might thrive on economic troubles, American bankers loaned millions of dollars to the floundering nation. A triangular relationship developed: American investors' money flowed to Germany, Germany paid reparations to the Allies, the Allies then paid some of their debts to the United States. The American-crafted Dawes Plan of 1924 greased the financial tracks by reducing Germany's annual payments, extending the repayment period, and providing still more loans. The United States also gradually scaled down Allied obligations, cutting the debt by half during the 1920s.

But the triangular arrangement depended on continued German borrowing in the United States, and in 1928 and 1929 American lending abroad declined sharply in the face of more lucrative opportunities in the stock market at home. The U.S.-negotiated Young Plan of 1929, which reduced Germany's reparations, salvaged little as the international economy sputtered and collapsed. By 1931, when Hoover declared a moratorium on payments, the Allies had paid back only $2.6 billion, approximately 20 percent of their debt. Staggered

The United States in the World Economy In the 1920s and 1930s, the United States tried various ways to improve its economic position and stabilize the world economy, but global depression and war scuttled U.S. goals, as did its high tariff policy before the mid-1930s. The Reciprocal Trade Agreements program was designed to ease the tariff wars. Source: U.S. Department of Commerce, *Historical Statistics of the United States: Colonial Times to 1970* (Washington, D.C., 1975).

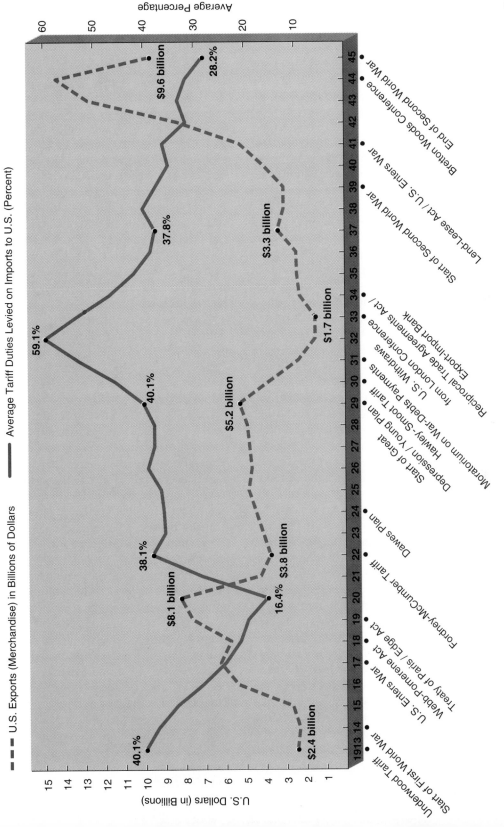

Average Percentage

- - - U.S. Exports (Merchandise) in Billions of Dollars

—— Average Tariff Duties Levied on Imports to U.S. (Percent)

U.S. Dollars (in Billions)

Underwood Tariff / Start of First World War

U.S. Enters War

Webb-Pomerene Act / Treaty of Paris / Edge Act

Fordney-McCumber Tariff

Dawes Plan

Start of Great Depression / Young Plan / Hawley - Smoot Tariff

U.S. Withdraws from London Conference

Moratorium on War-Debts Payments

Reciprocal Trade Agreements Act / Export-Import Bank

Start of Second World War

Lend-Lease Act / U.S. Enters War

Bretton Woods Conference / End of Second World War

40.1%

$2.4 billion

$8.1 billion

38.1%

16.4% $3.8 billion

40.1%

$5.2 billion

59.1%

$1.7 billion

37.8%

$3.3 billion

$9.6 billion

28.2%

by the Great Depression, they defaulted on the rest. World trade, heavily dependent on an easy and safe exchange of currencies, also faltered: from 1929 to 1933, it declined in value by some 40 percent. American merchandise exports slumped from $5.2 billion to $1.7 billion.

By the early 1930s, U.S. economic power had failed to sustain a healthy world economy. As the depression accelerated, so did economic nationalism.

Economic Nationalism

By 1932, some twenty-five nations had retaliated against rising American tariffs (created in the Fordney-McCumber Act of 1922 and the Hawley-Smoot Tariff Act of 1930) by imposing higher rates on U.S. imports. Critics argued that instead of raising their tariff rates, Americans might have lowered them so that Europeans could sell their goods in the United States and thus earn dollars to pay off their debts. Americans might have worked for a comprehensive multinational settlement. Selfish, vengeful Europeans might have trimmed Germany's huge indemnity. The Germans might have borrowed less from abroad and taxed themselves more. The Soviets might have agreed to pay rather than repudiate Russia's $4 billion debt. Many nations, in short, shared responsibility for the economic cataclysm.

Calling the protective tariff the "king of evils," Secretary of State Hull successfully pressed Congress to pass the Reciprocal Trade Agreements Act in 1934 (see figure). This important legislation, which would guide American economic foreign policy long into the future, empowered the president to reduce American tariffs by as much as 50 percent through special agreements with foreign countries. In 1934, Hull also created the Export-Import Bank, a government agency that provided loans to foreigners for the purchase of American goods. The central feature of the act was the *most-favored-nation principle*, whereby the United States was entitled to the lowest tariff rate set by any nation with which it had an agreement. But in the short term, Hull's ambitious programs—examples of America's independent internationalism—brought only mixed results.

Reciprocal Trade Agreements Act

U.S. SPHERE OF INFLUENCE IN LATIN AMERICA

Before World War I, the United States had thrown an imperial net over much of Latin America. Its tools for doing so were the Platt Amendment, the Roosevelt Corollary, control of the Panama Canal, military intervention, and economic domination. By the 1920s, U.S.-built schools, roads, telephones, and irrigation systems dotted Caribbean and Central American nations. U.S. advisers supervised government budgets; U.S. soldiers were occupying Cuba, the Dominican Republic, Haiti, Panama, and Nicaragua; and U.S. authorities maintained Puerto Rico as a colony.

Imperial behavior, however, drew increasing criticism at home and abroad. A distinguished Argentine writer, Manuel Ugarte, asserted that the United States had become a new Rome. Congressional critics protested the denial of self-determination to Latin Americans and the sending of troops abroad without a congressional declaration of war. Businesspeople feared that Latin American nationalists would attack Yankee property. And in 1932, Secretary of State Henry L. Stimson worried about a double standard. How could he effectively protest Japanese incursions in China, if the United States intervened in a similar way in Latin America?

Anti-Imperialism

Renouncing unpopular military intervention, the United States tried other methods to maintain its influence in Latin America: Pan-Americanism, support for strong local leaders, training of national guards, economic penetration, Export-Import Bank loans, and political subversion. Franklin D. Roosevelt gave the new approach a name in 1933: the Good Neighbor policy. It meant that the United States would be less blatant in its domination—less willing to defend exploitative business practices, less eager to launch military expeditions, and less reluctant to consult with Latin Americans.

Good Neighbor Policy

The training of national guards went hand in hand with support of dictators. Some Latin American dictators rose to power through the ranks of U.S.-trained national guards.

National Guard in the Dominican Republic

For example, before the United States withdrew its troops from the Dominican Republic in 1924, U.S. personnel created a guard. One of its first officers was Rafael Leonidas Trujillo, who became head of the national army in 1928 and, through fraud and intimidation, became president two years later. Trujillo ruled the Dominican Republic with an iron fist until his assassination in 1961. "He may be an S.O.B.," Franklin Roosevelt supposedly remarked, "but he is our S.O.B."

Nicaraguans endured a similar experience. U.S. troops occupied Nicaragua from 1912 to 1925 and returned in late 1926 during a civil war. Washington

Somoza and Sandino in Nicaragua

claimed that it was only trying to stabilize Nicaragua's politics, but critics at home and abroad saw a case of U.S. imperialism.

Nationalistic Nicaraguan opposition, led by César Augusto Sandino, who denounced the Monroe Doctrine as meaning "America for the Yankees," helped persuade Washington to end the occupation. In 1933, the U.S. Marines departed, but they left behind a powerful national guard headed by General Anastasio Somoza, who "always played the game fairly with us," according to the top-ranked American military officer there. With American backing, the Somoza family ruled Nicaragua from 1936 to 1979 through corruption, political suppression, and torture.

The marine occupation of the Afro-Caribbean nation of Haiti from 1915 to 1934 also left a negative legacy. U.S. officials censored the Haitian press,

These children in Nicaragua seem amused by the comic strips U.S. Marines are explaining to them in 1927, during the U.S. military occupation of that Central American nation. The marines actually spent most of their time chasing the troops of César Augusto Sandino, who fought the North American intruders until his death in 1934. National Archives.

Occupation of Haiti
_____

manipulated elections, wrote the constitution, jailed or killed thousands of protesters, managed government finances, and created a national guard. The National City Bank of New York became the owner of the Haitian Banque Nationale, and the United States became Haiti's largest trading partner.

African-American leaders decried this blatant manipulation of foreigners. The NAACP's James Weldon Johnson reported that Haitians forced to build roads without pay (the *corvée* system) "were in the same category with the convicts in the negro chain gangs" of the American South. Washington did not withdraw its soldiers until 1929, when Haitians protested violently against U.S. rule and an official U.S. investigative commission told President Hoover that the occupation had failed to bring benefits to the Haitian people.

The Cubans too grew restless under North American domination. By 1929, American investments in the Caribbean nation totaled $1.5 billion, and the U.S. military uniform

Cuban Revolution of 1933
_____

remained conspicuous at the Guantánamo Naval Base. In 1933, Cubans rebelled against the dictator and U.S. ally Gerardo Machado. In open defiance of U.S. warships cruising offshore, Professor Ramón Grau San Martín became president and declared the Platt Amendment null and void. His government also seized some North American–owned mills, refused to repay North American bank loans, and talked of land reform. Unsettled by this bold display of nationalism, U.S. officials refused to recognize the Grau government and successfully plotted with army sergeant Fulgencio Batista to overthrow it in 1934. During the Batista era, which lasted until 1959, Cuba attracted U.S. tourists and investments while it aligned with U.S. foreign-policy goals. In return, Havana received military aid, loans, the abrogation of the Platt Amendment, and a favorable sugar tariff. Cuba became a dependency of the United States.

Elsewhere in the Caribbean, Puerto Ricans chafed under U.S. tutelage. Throughout the 1920s and 1930s, incompetent American governors who could not speak Spanish disparaged Puerto Ricans as people of color unfit to govern them-

Puerto Rico
_____

selves. The Jones Act of 1917 granted Puerto Ricans U.S. citizenship, but the United States rejected calls for the colony's independence or statehood. Under U.S. paternalism, schools and roads were improved, but 80 percent of the island's rural folk were landless in the sugar economy. The per capita income of Puerto Rico in 1930 was $122 (one-fifth of the U.S. figure).

Students, professors, and graduates of the University of Puerto Rico formed the nucleus of islanders critical of U.S. tutelage. Some founded the Nationalist party under the leadership of the Harvard-trained lawyer Pedro Albizo Campos, who eventually advocated the violent overthrow of U.S. rule. Other Puerto Ricans followed the socialist Luis Muñoz Marín, whose Popular Democratic party ultimately settled for the compromise of "commonwealth" status (officially conferred in 1952). To this day, Puerto Ricans remain divided into statehood, commonwealth, and independence factions.

Mexico, torn by revolution and civil war, was a unique case in inter-American relations. In 1917, Mexicans adopted a new constitution specifying

U.S. Clash with Mexican Nationalism
_____

that all "land and waters" and all subsoil raw materials (like oil) belonged to Mexico. This nationalistic document represented a threat to U.S. landholdings and petroleum interests there. If Mexico succeeded, Washington officials worried, other Latin Americans might attempt to follow the Mexican model of defying U.S. hegemonic power.

Washington and Mexico City wrangled for years over the rights of U.S. economic interests. Then, in 1938, Mexico boldly expropriated the property of all foreign-owned petroleum companies. The United States encouraged a business boycott of the nation. But President Roosevelt decided to compromise, because he feared the Mexicans would sell their oil to Germany and Japan. In 1942, the United States conceded that Mexico owned its raw materials and could treat them as it saw fit, and Mexico compensated U.S. companies for their lost property.

The Good Neighbor policy paid off. In the Declaration of Panama (1939), for instance, Latin American governments drew a security line around the hemisphere and warned aggressors away. And in exchange for more U.S. trade and foreign aid, Latin Americans also reduced their sales of raw materials to Germany, Japan, and Italy and increased shipments to the United States. On the eve of the Second World War, then, the U.S. sphere of influence was virtually intact, and most Latin American regimes backed U.S. diplomatic objectives.

NAZI GERMANY AND APPEASEMENT IN EUROPE

Adolf Hitler came to power in depression-wracked Germany in 1933. Like Benito Mussolini, who had gained control of Italy in 1922, Hitler was a fascist. Fascism (called nazism, or National Socialism, in Germany) was a collection of ideas and prejudices that celebrated supremacy of the state over the individual, of dictatorship over democracy, of authoritarianism over freedom of speech, of a regulated state-oriented economy over a free-market economy, and of militarism and war over peace. The Nazis vowed not only to revive German economic and military strength but also to cripple communism and "purify" the German "race" by expelling or destroying those people Hitler disparaged as inferior: Jews, homosexuals, and gypsies.

Resentful of the punitive terms of the 1919 Treaty of Paris, Hitler pulled Germany out of the League of Nations, ended reparations payments, and began to rearm. While secretly laying plans for the conquest of neighboring states, he watched admiringly as Mussolini's troops invaded the African nation of Ethiopia in 1935. The next year, Hitler ordered his goose-stepping troopers into the Rhineland, an area that the Treaty of Paris had declared demilitarized. Germany's timid neighbor France did not attempt to reverse this aggressive act.

Hitler's Aggression

Soon the aggressors joined hands. In 1936, Italy and Germany formed an alliance called the Rome-Berlin Axis. Shortly thereafter, Germany and Japan united against the Soviet Union in the Anti-Comintern Pact. Britain and France responded to these events with a policy of appeasement, hoping to curb Hitler's expansionist appetite by permitting him a few nibbles. The policy of appeasing Hitler proved disastrous, for Hitler continually raised his demands.

In those hair-trigger times, a civil war in Spain soon turned into an international struggle. From 1936 to 1939, the Loyalists defended Spain's elected republican government against Francisco Franco's fascist movement. Hitler and Mussolini sent military aid to Franco; the Soviet Union backed the Loyalist Republicans. France and Britain held to the fiction of a nonintervention pledge that even Italy and Germany had signed. About three thousand American volunteers known as the Lincoln Battalion joined the fight on the side of the republicans. When Franco won in 1939, his victory tightened the grip of fascism on the European continent.

Spanish Civil War

Early in 1938, Hitler sent soldiers into Austria to annex the nation. Then, in September, he seized the Sudeten region of Czechoslovakia. Appeasement reached its apex that month when France and Britain, without consulting the helpless Czechs, agreed at the Munich Conference to allow Hitler this one last territorial bite. In March 1939, Hitler swallowed the rest of Czechoslovakia.

Poland was next on the German leader's list. Scuttling appeasement, London and Paris announced that they would stand by their ally Poland. Undaunted, Berlin signed the Nazi-Soviet Pact with Moscow in August and launched attacks against Poland on September 1. Britain and France declared war on Germany two days later. The Second World War had begun.

The Second World War Begins

As the world hurtled toward war, the Soviet Union posed a special problem for American foreign relations. Following Wilsonian precedent, the Republican administrations of the 1920s had not recognized the Soviet government, arguing that the Bolsheviks had failed to pay $600 million for confiscated American-owned property and had repudiated preexisting Russian debts. American businesses nonetheless began to enter the Soviet marketplace, and by 1930 the Soviet Union had become the largest buyer of American farm and industrial equipment.

In the early 1930s, when trade began to slump, some U.S. businesspeople began to lobby for diplomatic recognition of the Soviet Union to stimulate trade and help the United States pull out of the depression. Practicing personal one-on-one diplomacy, Roosevelt negotiated in 1933 with Soviet Commissar for Foreign Affairs Maxim Litvinov. They hammered out agreements, some of them vaguely phrased: U.S. recognition of the Soviet Union, future discussion of the debts question, a Soviet promise to forgo subversive activities in the United States, and religious freedom and legal rights for Americans in the Soviet Union. Within just a few years, however, Soviet-American relations once again became embittered. The Nazi-Soviet Pact and the Soviet Union's grabbing of half of Poland especially upset Americans.

U.S. Recognition of the Soviet Union

ISOLATIONISM AND ROOSEVELT'S LEADERSHIP

As authoritarianism, racial hatred, and military expansion descended on Europe and Asia in the 1930s, Americans affirmed their isolationist beliefs. A 1937 Gallup poll found that nearly two-thirds of the respondents thought U.S. participation in the First World War had been a mistake. Conservative isolationists feared higher taxes and increased executive power if the nation went to war again. Liberal isolationists worried that domestic problems might go unresolved as the nation spent more on the military. Many isolationists predicted that in attempting to spread democracy abroad, Americans would lose it at home. The vast majority of isolationists opposed fascism and condemned aggression, but they did not think the United States should have to do what Europeans refused to do: block Hitler.

Isolationism was a nationwide phenomenon that cut across socioeconomic, ethnic, party, and sectional lines and attracted a majority of the American people. Some liberal isolationists, critical of business practices at home, charged that

Isolationists

corporate "merchants of death" were assisting the aggressors. From 1934 to 1936, a congressional committee chaired by Senator Gerald P. Nye of North Dakota held hearings on the role of business interests and financiers in the U.S. decision to enter the First World War. The hearings did not prove that American business had dragged a reluctant nation into that war, but they did uncover evidence that corporations had bribed foreign politicians to bolster arms sales in the 1920s and 1930s, had signed contracts with Nazi Germany and fascist Italy, and had lobbied against arms control.

President Roosevelt shared isolationist views in the early 1930s. Like his older cousin Theodore, Franklin as a young man had believed that the United States should ensure American security and prosperity by exerting leadership in the world community and flexing its military muscle. FDR was an expansionist and interventionist, but during the interwar period, like most Americans, he talked less about preparedness and more about disarmament and the horrors of war.

Roosevelt acted on his and the nation's preference for avoiding European squabbles when he signed a series of neutrality acts. Congress sought to protect the nation by outlawing the kinds of contacts that had compromised U.S. neutrality two decades earlier. The Neutrality Act of 1935 prohibited arms shipments to either side in a war once the president had declared the existence of belligerency. The Neutrality Act of 1936 forbade loans to belligerents. After a joint resolution in 1937 declared the United States neutral in the Spanish Civil War, Roosevelt embargoed arms shipments to both sides. The Neutrality Act of 1937 introduced the cash-and-carry principle: warring nations wishing to trade with the United States would have to pay cash for their nonmilitary purchases and carry the goods away in their own ships. The act also forbade Americans from traveling on the ships of belligerent nations.

Neutrality Acts

In a stirring speech in August 1936 at Chautauqua, New York, Roosevelt expressed prevailing isolationist opinion: "I have seen war. . . . I have seen blood running from the wounded. I have seen men coughing out their gassed lungs. . . . I have seen the agony of mothers and wives. I hate war."

The United States, he promised, would remain distant from European conflict. During the Czech crisis of 1938, Roosevelt actually endorsed appeasement. The United States, he wrote to Hitler, had "no political involvements in Europe."

All the while, Roosevelt was becoming increasingly troubled by the arrogant behavior of Germany, Italy, and Japan, the aggressors he tagged the "three bandit nations." He condemned the Nazi persecution of the Jews and the Japanese slaughter of Chinese civilians. He privately chastised the British and French for failing to collar Hitler, and he worried that the United States was militarily ill-prepared to confront the aggressors.

Roosevelt's Changing Views

Roosevelt did not neglect the U.S. military. New Deal public works programs included millions for the construction of new ships. In 1935, the president requested the largest peacetime defense budget in American history; three years later, in the wake of Munich, he asked Congress for funds to build up the air force. The president also began to cast about for ways to encourage the British and French to show more backbone. One result was his agreement in January 1939 to sell bombers to France.

Early in 1939, the president lashed out at the international lawbreakers. Soon afterward, he failed to persuade Congress to repeal the arms embargo and permit the sale of munitions to belligerents on a cash-and-carry basis. When Europe descended into the abyss of war in September 1939, Roosevelt both declared neutrality and pressed again for repeal of the arms embargo. After much debate, Congress in November lifted the embargo on contraband and approved cash-and-carry exports of arms. Short of going to war, Roosevelt was ready to aid the Allies.

Repeal of the Arms Embargo

JAPAN, CHINA, AND A NEW ORDER IN ASIA

If U.S. power and influence were massive in Latin America and limited in Europe, they were minuscule in Asia. Still, the United States had Asian interests that needed protection: the Philippines and Pacific islands, religious missions, trade and investments, and the Open Door in China. Americans came to believe that Japan was bent on subjugating China and unhinging the Open Door doctrine of equal trade and investment opportunity.

In the late 1920s, civil war broke out in China when Jiang Jieshi (Chiang Kai-shek) ousted Mao Zedong and his Communist followers from the ruling Guomindang party. Americans applauded this display of anti-Bolshevism and Jiang's conversion to Christianity in 1930. Warming to Jiang, U.S. officials abandoned one imperial vestige by signing a treaty in 1928 restoring control of tariffs to the Chinese. American gunboats and marines, however, remained in China.

Rise of Jiang Jieshi in China

The Japanese grew increasingly suspicious of U.S.-Chinese ties. Japan also resented the Immigration Act of 1924, which excluded Japanese entry into the United States. On the other hand, Japan's increasing intrusions in China collided with America's Open Door policy. Japanese-American relations were thus seldom cordial.

Relations deteriorated further after the Japanese military seized Manchuria in 1931 (see map). Only nominally a Chinese region, Manchuria was important to the Japanese both as a buffer against the Soviets and as a vital source of coal, iron, timber, and food. Although the seizure of Manchuria violated the Nine-Power Treaty and the Kellogg-Briand Pact, the United States did not have the power to compel Japanese withdrawal. The American response therefore went no further than a moral lecture known as the Stimson Doctrine (1932), which declared that the United States would not recognize any impairment of China's sovereignty or of the Open Door policy.

Japanese Seizure of Manchuria

Hardly cowed by protests from Western capitals, Japan continued to harry China. In mid-1937, full-scale Sino-Japanese war erupted. To help China, Roosevelt refused to declare the existence of war, thus avoiding activation of the Neutrality Acts and allowing the Chinese to buy weapons in the United States. And in a stirring speech denouncing the aggressors in

October 1937, he called for a "quarantine" to curb the "epidemic of world lawlessness." Yet Roosevelt had formulated no program to halt the Japanese.

Japan's declaration of a "New Order" in Asia, in the words of one American official, "banged, barred, and bolted" the Open Door. Alarmed, the Roosevelt administration found small ways to assist China and thwart Japan in 1938 and 1939. Military equipment flowed to the Chinese, as did a $25 million loan. Secretary of State Hull declared a moral embargo on the shipment of airplanes to Japan. Meanwhile, the U.S. Navy continued to grow, aided by a billion-dollar congressional appropriation in 1938. In mid-1939, the United States abrogated the 1911 Japanese-American

trade treaty, yet America continued to ship oil, cotton, and machinery to Japan. The administration hesitated to initiate economic sanctions, because such economic pressure might spark a Japanese-American war at a time when Germany posed a more serious threat.

COLLISION COURSE, 1939–1941

Polls showed that Americans strongly favored the Allies and that most supported aid to Britain and France—but the great majority emphatically

Japanese Expansion Before Pearl Harbor   *The Japanese quest for predominance began at the turn of the century and intensified in the 1930s, with China suffering the most at the hands of Tokyo's military. Vulnerable U.S. possessions in Asia and the Pacific proved no obstacle to Japan's ambitions for a Greater East Asian Co-Prosperity Sphere.*

wanted the United States to remain at peace. Troubled by this conflicting advice—oppose Hitler, aid the Allies, but stay out of the war—the president gradually moved the nation from neutrality to undeclared war and then to full-scale war itself.

Because the stakes were so high, Americans vigorously debated the direction of their foreign policy from 1939 to 1941. Unprecedented numbers of Americans paid attention to foreign affairs. The internationalist Committee to Defend America by Aiding the Allies and the isolationist America First Committee (both organized in 1940), as well as such groups as the

National Debate

League of Women Voters and the American Legion, provided outlets for citizen participation in the national debate.

In September 1939, Poland succumbed to German storm troopers, while the Red Army seized Poland's eastern district (see map). In November, Soviet troops invaded Finland. The following spring, Germany invaded Denmark, Norway, the Netherlands, and Belgium. In May, several German divisions attacked France. By early June, they had pushed French and British forces back to the English Channel. At Dunkirk, more than three hundred thousand Allied soldiers, abandoning their equipment on the

Fall of France

The German Advance, 1939–1942 *Hitler's drive to dominate Europe carried German troops deep into France and the Soviet Union. Great Britain took a beating but held on with the help of U.S. economic and military aid before the United States itself joined the Second World War.*

beaches, frantically escaped to Britain on a flotilla of small boats. Would Britain be next?

Meanwhile, isolationist sentiment in the United States waned, and Roosevelt charged that some of his critics were pro-Nazi subversives. Of greater significance, Roosevelt began to aid the beleaguered Allies to prevent the fall of Britain. In May 1940, he ordered the sale of old surplus military equipment to Britain and France. In July, he cultivated bipartisan support by naming Republicans Henry L. Stimson and Frank Knox, ardent backers of aid to the Allies, secretaries of war and the navy, respectively. In September, by executive agreement, the president traded fifty old American destroyers for leases to

eight British bases, including those in Newfoundland, Bermuda, and Jamaica. Two weeks later, Roosevelt signed into law the hotly debated and narrowly passed Selective Training and Service Act, the first peacetime military draft in U.S. history.

Roosevelt claimed that the United States could stay out of the war by enabling the British to win. The United States must, he said, become the "great arsenal of democracy." In Janu-

Lend-Lease Act
————

ary 1941, the administration sent to Congress the Lend-Lease bill. Because Britain was broke, the president explained, the United States should lend rather than sell weapons, much as a

President Franklin D. Roosevelt (left) and British Prime Minister Winston Churchill (1874–1965) confer aboard a ship near Newfoundland during their summit meeting of August 1941 when they signed the Atlantic Charter. Upon his return to England, Churchill told his advisers that Roosevelt had promised to "wage war" against Germany and do "everything" to "force an incident." Franklin D. Roosevelt Library, Hyde Park, New York.

neighbor lends a garden hose to fight a fire. In March 1941, with pro-British sentiment running high, the House passed the Lend-Lease Act 317 to 71; the Senate followed suit, 60 to 31. The initial appropriation was $7 billion, but by the end of the war the amount had reached $50 billion, more than $31 billion of it for England.

To ensure the safe delivery of Lend-Lease goods, Roosevelt ordered the navy to patrol halfway across the Atlantic and sent American troops to Greenland. And after the German invasion of the Soviet Union in June 1941, Roosevelt sent Lend-Lease aid to the Soviets. He calculated that if the Soviets could hold off two hundred German divisions in the east, Britain would gain some breathing time.

In August 1941, Churchill and Roosevelt met for four days on a British battleship off the coast of Newfoundland. The two leaders issued the Atlantic

"Atlantic Charter" Conference
———

Charter, a set of war aims reminiscent of Wilsonianism: collective security, disarmament, self-determination, economic cooperation, and freedom of the seas. On January 1, 1942, twenty-six nations signed the Declaration of the United Nations, pledging allegiance to the charter.

In September 1941, there occurred an incident Roosevelt could exploit: a German submarine fired on (but did not hit) the U.S. destroyer *Greer*. In a special national radio broadcast, the president protested German "piracy" and announced a policy he had already privately promised Churchill: American naval vessels would now convoy British merchant ships all the way to Iceland and would shoot German submarines, the "rattlesnakes of the Atlantic," on sight. Roosevelt did not mention that the *Greer* had been tailing a German U-boat for hours, signaling the submarine's location to British airplanes hunting the ship with depth charges. The next month, when the destroyer *Reuben James* went down with the loss of more than one hundred American lives, Congress scrapped the cash-and-carry policy and further revised the Neutrality Acts to permit transport of munitions to England on armed American merchant ships.

WHY WAR CAME: PEARL HARBOR AND THE INTERWAR ERA

In retrospect, it seems ironic that the Second World War came to the United States by way of Asia. Roosevelt had wanted to avoid war with Japan

Cutoff of Trade with Japan
———

in order to concentrate American resources on the defeat of Germany. In September 1940, after Germany, Italy, and Japan had signed the Tripartite Pact, Roosevelt slapped an embargo on shipments of aviation fuel and scrap metal to Japan. Because the president believed the petroleum-thirsty Japanese would consider a cutoff of oil a life-or-death matter, he did not embargo that vital commodity. But after Japanese troops occupied French Indochina in July 1941, Washington froze Japanese assets in the United States, virtually ending trade (including oil) with Japan.

Tokyo recommended a summit meeting between President Roosevelt and Prime Minister Prince Konoye, but the United States rejected the idea. American officials insisted that the Japanese first agree to respect China's sovereignty and territorial integrity and to honor the Open Door policy—in short, to get out of China. Roosevelt told his advisers to string out ongoing Japanese-American talks to gain time—time to fortify the Philippines and check the fascists in Europe. According to polls in the fall of 1941, the American people seemed willing to risk war with Japan to thwart further aggression, but Roosevelt was not ready for an Asian war; Europe claimed first priority. Still, he would not back down in Asia, and he supported Secretary Hull's hard-line policy against Japan's pursuit of the Greater East Asian Co-Prosperity Sphere—the name Tokyo gave to the vast Asian region it intended to dominate.

By breaking the Japanese code and deciphering intercepted messages through Operation MAGIC, American officials learned that Tokyo's patience with diplomacy was fast dissipating. In late November, the Japanese rejected U.S. demands that

How do historians know

that American leaders knew in December 1941, before the attack on Pearl Harbor, that Japan intended to go to war with the United States? In September 1940, U.S. cryptanalysts, or code breakers, of the Signal Intelligence Service cracked the most secret diplomatic cipher of the Japanese government, a machine they called PURPLE. The code breakers found patterns in the incoherent letters of telegraphed messages, produced texts, and even duplicated the complicated PURPLE machine (shown here). Thereafter, under Operation MAGIC, they decoded thousands of intercepted messages sent by Japanese officials around the world. Important intercepts were delivered to a handful of top U.S. leaders, including the president. The dispatches made increasingly clear through 1941 that Tokyo expected all-out war with the United States. An intercept on December 3,

just a few days before the surprise attack on Pearl Harbor, revealed that Tokyo had ordered the Japanese embassy in Washington to destroy all codes and machines, a sure sign that war was imminent. After the onslaught against Pearl Harbor, and after it became public knowledge that the United States had broken the Japanese diplomatic code, the cry sounded that President Roosevelt must have known what was coming and yet failed to prepare for the Japanese attack. The many intercepted messages of fall and winter 1941, however, never revealed Japan's military plans. Not one intercepted message mentioned an attack on Pearl Harbor; indeed, Japanese diplomats in Washington were never told that Pearl Harbor would be hit. And few Americans expected the Japanese to attack Hawaii or the United States itself. Photo: National Archives.

they withdraw from Indochina. An intercepted message that U.S. experts decoded on December 3 instructed the Japanese embassy in Washington to burn codes and destroy cipher machines—a sure sign that war was coming. Secretary Stimson ex-

plained later that the United States let Japan fire the first shot so as "to have the full support of the American people" and "so that there should remain no doubt in anyone's mind as to who were the aggressors."

The Japanese plotted a daring raid on Pearl Harbor in Hawaii. An armada of 60 Japanese ships, with a core of 6 carriers bearing 360 airplanes, crossed 3,000 miles of the Pacific Ocean. To avoid detection, every ship maintained radio silence. In the early morning of December 7, Japanese planes swept down on the unsuspecting U.S. naval base and nearby airfields, killing 2,403 people, sinking or damaging 8 battleships, and smashing more than 160 aircraft on the ground. Three aircraft carriers were out of port and thus escaped the disaster.

Surprise Attack on Pearl Harbor

How could the stunning attack on Pearl Harbor have happened? After all, U.S. cryptanalysts had broken the Japanese diplomatic code. Although the intercepted Japanese messages told code breakers and policymakers that war lay ahead because Japanese-American relations had so deteriorated, the intercepts never revealed naval or military plans and never specifically mentioned Pearl Harbor. Roosevelt did not, as some critics charged, conspire to leave the fleet vulnerable to attack so that the United States could enter the Second World War through the "back door" of Asia. The base was not ready—not on red alert—because a message sent from Washington warning of the imminence of war had been too casually transmitted by a slow method and had arrived too late. Base commanders were too relaxed, believing Hawaii too far from Japan to be a target for all-out attack. Like Roosevelt's advisers, they expected an assault at British Malaya, Thailand, or the Philippines. The Pearl Harbor calamity stemmed from mistakes and insufficient information, not from conspiracy.

Explaining Pearl Harbor

On December 8, referring to the previous day as "a date which will live in infamy," Roosevelt asked Congress for a declaration of war against Japan. A unanimous vote in the Senate and a 388 to 1 vote in the House thrust America into war. (Only Representative Jeannette Rankin of Montana voted no, matching her vote against entry into World War I.) Three days later, Germany and Italy, honoring the Tripartite Pact they had signed with Japan in 1940, declared war against the United States. "Hitler's fate was sealed," Britain's Winston Churchill wrote. "Mussolini's fate was sealed. As for the Japanese, they would be ground to powder. . . . I went to bed and slept the sleep of the saved and thankful."

Americans, remembering the bitter experience of the First World War, had tried to stay out. Diplomacy and economic sanctions had not stopped the aggressors, who kept pushing on, threatening U.S. interests. A fundamental clash of systems explains why diplomacy failed and war came. Germany and Japan preferred a world divided into closed spheres of influence. The United States sought conditions that would ensure its continued international stature and domestic well-being: a liberal capitalist world order in which all nations enjoyed the freedom to trade with and invest in all other nations. U.S. principles manifested a respect for human rights; fascists in Europe and militarists in Asia defiantly trampled on the rights of individuals and groups. The United States prided itself on its democratic system; Germany and Japan embraced authoritarian regimes backed by the military.

Clash of Systems

The Second World War offered yet another opportunity for Americans to set things right in the world. As publisher Henry Luce put it in *American Century* (1941), the United States must "exert upon the world the full impact of our influence, for such purposes as we see fit and by such means as we see fit." As they had so many times before, Americans flocked to the colors. Isolationists now joined the president in spirited calls for victory. "We are going to win the war, and we are going to win the peace that follows," Roosevelt predicted.

SUGGESTIONS FOR FURTHER READING

Interwar Issues and the Road to War

Warren I. Cohen, *Empire Without Tears* (1987); Frank Costigliola, *Awkward Dominion* (1984) (on Europe); Justus D. Doenecke and John E. Wilz, *From Isolation to War, 1931–1941*, 2d ed. (1991); Melvyn P. Leffler, *The Elusive Quest* (1979); Elting E. Morison, *Turmoil and Tradition* (1964) (on Stimson); Emily S. Rosenberg,

Spreading the American Dream (1982); James C. Schneider, *Should America Go to War?* (1989); Michael S. Sherry, *The Rise of American Airpower* (1987); Raymond Sontag, *A Broken World, 1919–1939* (1971).

The Peace Movement and Kellogg-Briand Pact

Charles Chatfield, *For Peace and Justice: Pacifism in America, 1914–1941* (1971); Charles DeBenedetti, *The Peace Reform in American History* (1980), and *Origins of the Modern American Peace Movement, 1915–1929* (1978); Lawrence Wittner, *Rebels Against War* (1984).

The United States in the World Economy

Derek H. Aldcroft, *From Versailles to Wall Street, 1919–1929* (1977); Michael J. Hogan, *Informal Entente* (1977) (on Anglo-American relations); Charles Kindleberger, *The World in Depression* (1973); Mira Wilkins, *The Maturing of Multinational Enterprise* (1974); Joan Hoff Wilson, *American Business and Foreign Policy, 1920–1933* (1971).

Latin America

Bruce J. Calder, *The Impact of Intervention* (1984) (on Dominican Republic); Arturo Morales Carrión, *Puerto Rico* (1983); Irwin F. Gellman, *Good Neighbor Diplomacy* (1979); Walter LaFeber, *Inevitable Revolutions*, 2d ed. rev. (1993) (on Central America); Lester D. Langley, *The United States and the Caribbean, 1900–1970* (1980); Neil Macaulay, *The Sandino Affair* (1967); Richard Millett, *Guardians of the Dynasty* (1977) (on Nicaragua); Louis A. Pérez, *Cuba and the United States* (1990), and *Cuba Under the Platt Amendment* (1986); Brenda G. Plummer, *Haiti and the United States* (1992); Stephen G. Rabe, *The Road to OPEC* (1982) (on Venezuela and oil); Bryce Wood, *The Making of the Good Neighbor Policy* (1961).

Isolationism and Isolationists

Wayne S. Cole, *Roosevelt and the Isolationists, 1932–1945* (1983); Manfred Jonas, *Isolationism in America, 1935–1941* (1966); Richard Lowitt, *George W. Norris*, 3 vols. (1963–1978); John Wiltz, *In Search of Peace: The Senate Munitions Inquiry, 1934–1936* (1963).

Europe, the Coming of World War II, and Roosevelt

Edward Bennett, *Recognition of Russia* (1970); J. Garry Clifford and Samuel R. Spencer Jr., *The First Peacetime Draft* (1986); James V. Compton, *The Swastika and the Eagle* (1967); Robert Dallek, *Franklin D. Roosevelt and American Foreign Policy, 1932–1945* (1979); Robert A. Divine, *The Reluctant Belligerent*, 2d ed. (1979), and *Roosevelt and World War II* (1969); Manfred Jonas, *The United States and Germany* (1984); Warren F. Kimball, *The Most Unsordid Act* (1969) (on Lend-Lease); Douglas Little, *Malevolent Neutrality* (1985) (on Spanish Civil War); Arnold A. Offner, *American Appeasement* (1969); David Reynolds, *The Creation of the Anglo-American Alliance, 1937–1941* (1982); David F. Schmitz, *The United States and Fascist Italy, 1922–1944* (1988); Donald C. Watt, *How War Came* (1989).

China, Japan, and the Coming of War in Asia

Dorothy Borg and Shumpei Okomoto, eds., *Pearl Harbor as History* (1973); R. J. C. Butow, *Tojo and the Coming of War* (1961); Warren I. Cohen, *America's Response to China*, 3d ed. (1990); Hilary Conroy and Harry Wray, eds., *Pearl Harbor Reexamined* (1990); Waldo H. Heinrichs Jr., *Threshold of War* (1988); Akira Iriye, *The Origins of the Second World War in Asia and the Pacific* (1987); Paul W. Schroeder, *The Axis Alliance and Japanese-American Relations, 1941* (1958); Jonathan Utley, *Going to War with Japan* (1985).

Pearl Harbor

David Kahn, *The Codebreakers* (1967); Martin V. Melosi, *The Shadow of Pearl Harbor* (1977); Gordon W. Prange, *Pearl Harbor* (1986), and *At Dawn We Slept* (1981); John Toland, *Infamy* (1982); Roberta Wohlstetter, *Pearl Harbor* (1962).

The Second World War at Home and Abroad, 1941–1945

HENRIETTA BINGHAM WAS NINE when the Japanese attacked Pearl Harbor. In December 1941, she remembered later, "all the war meant to me . . . was excitement. By 1945 that excitement had turned our family to tragedy & sorrow & especially for a 13 year old." In 1942, her sixteen-year-old brother Gerald falsified his age to enlist and became a top turret gunner on a bomber. The next year, he was killed on a mission in the Pacific. Her brother Gene enlisted in the Air Corps the day after his graduation from high school in 1943. He too became a gunner on a bomber, and the next year he was killed in a mid-air collision. In 1945, when Gerald's class graduated from high school, an empty chair sat on the stage. Henrietta's parents had aged greatly; her "young pretty mother had turned almost white," and her father "appeared an old man." And Henrietta herself, watching the graduation ceremony, "remembered how excited I was at age 9 when the war began in 1941 & how I felt just a few short years later. I had lost my childhood."

Other children saw their fathers go to war. Ruth Wagner was born on a farm near Arapahoe, Nebraska, just a week after Pearl Harbor. The next spring, her father was inducted into the army. Ruth's mother went to work, as a teacher in a Nebraska country school, for the first time in her married life. Meanwhile, Ruth was cared for by her grandmother. Ruth Wagner was elated when the war ended and her father returned home from an island in the Pacific. But he was distant and "never talked about his job there, except that it was hot, primitive, and insect-infested." To put the army behind him, he threw himself into his work as the manager of a grocery store. Her mother stopped working and had two more babies. "I think the war did a lot for her too," Ruth wrote. "She was the sole provider and decision maker . . . but she had to take a far back seat to my Dad when he came home."

World War II was a turning point in Americans' lives and in the history of the United States. Most deeply affected were those who fought the war. For forty-five months, Americans fought abroad to subdue the Nazi and Japanese aggressors. After military engagements against fascists in North Africa and Italy, American troops joined the dramatic crossing of the English Channel on D-Day in June 1944. The massive invasion forced the Germans to retreat through France to Germany. They finally capitulated in May 1945. In the Pacific, Americans drove the Japanese from one island after another before turning to the just-tested atomic bombs that demolished Hiroshima and Nagasaki in August and helped spur a Japanese surrender.

Throughout the war, the Allies—Britain, the Soviet Union, and the United States—were held together by their common goal of defeating Germany. But they squabbled over many issues: when to open a second front, how to structure a new international organization, how Eastern Europe, liberated from the Germans, would be reconstructed, how Germany would be governed after defeat. At the end of the war, Allied leaders seemed more intent on retaining and expanding their own nations' spheres of influence than on building a community of mutual interest. The prospects for postwar international cooperation seemed bleak, and the advent of the atomic age frightened everyone.

The war transformed America's soldiers and sailors. Horizons expanded for the 16.4 million men and women who served in the armed forces, seeing new parts of the world and acquiring new skills. But at war's end, they were older than their years, both physically and emotionally, and many felt they had sacrificed the best years of their lives.

Americans at home united behind the war effort, collecting scrap iron, rubber, and old newspapers and planting "victory gardens." The federal government mobilized all traditional sectors of the economy—industry, finance, agriculture, and labor—as well as a couple of new ones: higher education and science. This was a scientific and technological war supported by the development of new weapons like the atomic bomb.

For millions of Americans, the war was a time to relocate in other parts of the country. Not only did sixteen million men and women serve in the armed forces, but African-Americans, Mexican-Americans, whites, and women of all races migrated to war-production centers in the North and the West. Employers' negative attitudes toward women workers eased during the war, and millions of women took jobs in defense industries. For all these reasons, World War II was a watershed in American history.

WINNING THE SECOND WORLD WAR IN EUROPE

"We are now in the midst of a war, not for conquest, not for vengeance, but for a world in which this Nation, and all that this Nation represents, will be safe for our children." President Franklin D. Roosevelt was speaking just two days after the surprise attack on Pearl Harbor. Americans agreed with Roosevelt that they were defending their homes and families against aggressive, even satanic, Japanese and Nazis.

America's men and women responded eagerly to Roosevelt's call to arms. In 1941, although Selective Service had been functioning for a full year, only 1.8 million people were serving on active duty. In 1945, the number of women and men serving in the army, navy, and marines peaked at 12.1 million. Fighting a world war on two fronts required such a massive force.

Despite nearly unanimous support for the war effort, various government leaders worried that public morale would lag during a lengthy war. The army therefore hired prominent Hollywood director Frank Capra to produce a series of propaganda films called *Why We Fight*. In these widely distributed films, and in the popular mind, the Allies were heroic partners in a common effort against evil.

In actuality, wartime relations among the United States, Great Britain, and the Soviet Union ran hot and cold. Although winning the war was the top priority, Allied leaders knew that military decisions also had political consequences. If one ally became desperate, for instance, it might destroy the alliance by pursuing a separate peace. Moreover, the positions of troops at the end of the war might determine the politics of the regions they occupied. Thus an undercurrent of mutual suspicion ran just beneath the surface of Allied cooperation.

Important Events

1941	Japan attacks Pearl Harbor; United States enters Second World War
1942	National War Labor Board created to deal with labor-management conflict
	War Production Board begins to oversee conversion to military production
	West Coast Japanese-Americans interned in prison camps
	War Manpower Commission created to manage labor supply
	Office of Price Administration created to control inflation
	Bataan Death March intensifies anti-Japanese sentiment
	U.S. defeats Japanese forces at battles of Coral Sea and Midway
	Office of War Information created
	Manhattan Project set up to produce atomic bomb
	Allies invade North Africa
	Republicans gain in Congress
	Synthetic rubber program begins
1943	Russian Red Army defeats German troops at Stalingrad
	Soft-coal and anthracite miners strike
	Office of War Mobilization established
	Congress passes War Labor Disputes (Smith-Connally) Act
	Race riots break out in Detroit, Harlem, and forty-five other cities
	Allies invade Italy
	Roosevelt, Churchill, and Stalin meet at Teheran Conference
1944	War Refugee Board established
	Supreme Court upholds Japanese-American internment
	Allied troops land at Normandy; D-Day
	Dumbarton Oaks Conference approves charter for United Nations
	Roosevelt reelected
	United States retakes the Philippines
1945	Roosevelt, Stalin, and Churchill meet at Yalta Conference
	Battles of Iwo Jima and Okinawa result in heavy U.S. and Japanese losses
	Roosevelt dies; Harry S Truman assumes the presidency
	United Nations founded
	Germany surrenders
	Potsdam Conference calls for Japan's "unconditional surrender"
	First atomic bomb exploded in test at Alamogordo, New Mexico
	Atomic bombs devastate Hiroshima and Nagasaki
	Japan surrenders

Roosevelt, British Prime Minister Winston Churchill, and Soviet Premier Josef Stalin differed vigorously over the opening of a second, or western, front. After Germany invaded Russia in 1941, the Russians bore the brunt of the war until mid-1944, suffering heavy casualties. To ease the pressure on his nation, Stalin pressed for a British-American landing on the northern coast of Europe to draw German troops away from the eastern front, but Churchill would not agree. The Russians therefore did most of the fighting and dying on land, while

Second-Front Controversy

the British and Americans concentrated on getting Lend-Lease supplies across the Atlantic and harassing the Germans from the air with attacks on factories and civilians alike.

Roosevelt was both sensitive to the Soviet's burden and fearful that Russia might be knocked out of the war, leaving Hitler free to invade England. In 1942, he told the Russians that they could expect the Allies to cross the English Channel and invade France later that year. But Churchill, fearing heavy losses in a premature invasion, balked. His preference was a series of small jabs at the enemy's Mediterranean forces.

Nov. 1942 boundaries
Hitler's Greater Germany
Other Axis Nations
Axis-occupied areas
Allied nations
Neutral nations
Limit of Axis advance, November 1942
Allied advance
Limit of Allied advance, May 1945
Major battles

ATLANTIC OCEAN

NORTH SEA

BALTIC SEA

BLACK SEA

MEDITERRANEAN SEA

NORWAY
SWEDEN
FINLAND
DENMARK
GREAT BRITAIN
IRELAND
U. S. S. R.
GERMANY
FRANCE
VICHY FRANCE
SWITZ.
SPAIN
PORTUGAL
ITALY
CZECHOSLOVAKIA
HUNGARY
YUGOSLAVIA
RUMANIA
BULGARIA
ALBANIA
GREECE
TURKEY
SYRIA (France)
LEBANON
PALESTINE (Great Britain)
TRANSJORDAN (Great Britain)
SAUDI ARABIA
IRAQ
EGYPT
LIBYA
TUNISIA (Vichy France)
ALGERIA (Vichy France)
MOROCCO (Vichy France)

Stalingrad Aug. 1942-Feb. 1943
Kursk July 1943
Berlin Apr.-May 1945
Warsaw Aug. 1944-Jan. 1945
Normandy June 1944
Battle of the Bulge Dec. 1944-Jan. 1945
Liberated Aug. 1944
Apr. 1945
Anzio Jan. 1945
Sept. 1943
July 1943
Kasserine Pass Feb. 1943
El Alamein Oct.-Nov. 1942
Allied landings Nov. 1942

Volga R.
Don R.
Dnieper R.
Rhine R.
Elbe R.
Po River
Danube R.

Moscow
Leningrad
Helsinki
Oslo
Stockholm
Copenhagen
Hamburg
Cologne
Berlin
Munich
Vienna
Prague
Budapest
Belgrade
Sofia
Bucharest
Athens
Rome
Naples
Tunis
Tripoli
Algiers
Oran
Casablanca
Gibraltar (Great Britain)
Madrid
Lisbon
London
Dublin
Paris
Vichy
Marseilles
Riga
Minsk
Kiev
Odessa
Kharkov
Rostov
Yalta
Ankara
Cyprus (Great Britain)
Cairo
Alexandria
Sicily
Malta (Great Britain)
Sardinia
Corsica
Crete

0   300   600 miles
0   300   600 kilometers

Churchill won the debate. Instead of attacking France, the British and Americans invaded North Africa in November 1942 (see map). "We are striking back," Roosevelt declared. The news from Russia also buoyed Roosevelt. In the battle for Stalingrad (September 1942–January 1943)—probably the turning point of the European war—the Red Army defeated the Germans, forcing Hitler's divisions to retreat. But shortly thereafter, the president once again angered the Russians by declaring another delay in launching the second front. Marshal Stalin was not mollified by the Allied invasion of Italy in the summer of 1943. Italy surrendered in September to American and British officers; Russian officials were not invited to participate. Stalin grumbled that the arrangement smacked of a separate peace.

With the alliance badly strained, Roosevelt sought reconciliation through personal diplomacy. The three Allied leaders met in Teheran, Iran, in December 1943. Stalin dismissed Churchill's repetitious justifications for further delaying the second front. Roosevelt had had enough too; he also rejected Churchill's proposal for another peripheral attack, this time through the Balkans to Vienna. The three finally agreed to launch Operation Overlord—the cross-Channel invasion of France—in early 1944.

D-Day

The second front opened in the dark morning hours of June 6, 1944—D-Day. In the largest amphibious landing in history, two hundred thousand Allied troops under the command of General Eisenhower scrambled ashore at Normandy, France. After digging in at now famous places like Utah and Omaha Beaches, reinforced Allied forces broke through disorderly German lines and gradually pushed inland, reaching Paris in August. The same month another force invaded southern France and threw the stunned Germans back.

The Allies on the Offensive in Europe, 1942–1945
The United States pursued a "Europe first" policy: first defeat Germany, then focus on Japan. American military efforts began in North Africa in late 1942 and ended in Germany in 1945 on V-E Day (May 8).

Allied troops soon spread across the countryside, liberating France and Belgium and entering Germany itself in September. In December, German armored divisions counterattacked in Begium's Ardennes Forest, hoping to push on to Antwerp to halt the flow of Allied supplies through that Belgian port. After weeks of heavy fighting in what has come to be called the Battle of the Bulge—because of a noticeable bulge in the Allied line—the Allies pushed the enemy back once again. Meanwhile, battle-hardened Russian troops marched through Poland and cut a path to Berlin. American forces crossed the Rhine in March 1945 and captured the heavily industrial Ruhr Valley. Several units peeled off to enter Austria and Czechoslovakia, where they met up with Russian soldiers. As the Americans marched east, a new president took office in Washington: Franklin D. Roosevelt died on April 12, and Harry S Truman became commander in chief. Eighteen days later, in bomb-ravaged Berlin, Adolf Hitler killed himself. On May 8, Germany surrendered.

WINNING THE SECOND WORLD WAR IN THE PACIFIC

Allied strategists had devised a "Europe first" formula: knock out Germany and then concentrate on an isolated Japan. Nevertheless, the Pacific theater claimed headlines throughout the war, for the U.S. people regarded Japan as America's chief enemy. By mid-1942, Japan had seized the Philippines, Guam, Wake, Hong Kong, Singapore, Malaya, and the Netherlands East Indies. In the Philippines in 1942, Japanese soldiers forced American and Filipino prisoners weakened by insufficient rations to walk sixty-five miles, clubbing, shooting, or starving to death about ten thousand of them. The so-called Bataan Death March intensified American hatred of the Japanese.

In April 1942, Americans began to hit back, initially by bombing Tokyo. In May, in the momentous Battle of the Coral Sea, carrier-based U.S. planes halted a Japanese advance toward Australia (see map). The next month, American forces defeated the Japanese

Battle of Midway

at Midway, sinking four of the enemy's valuable aircraft carriers. The Battle of Midway was a turning point in the Pacific war, breaking the Japanese momentum and relieving the threat to Hawaii. Thereafter, Japan was never able to match American manpower, sea power, air power, or economic power.

American strategy was to "island-hop" toward Japan, skipping the most strongly fortified points whenever possible and taking the weaker ones. In an effort to strand the Japanese armies on their island outposts and to cut off raw materials from the home islands, Americans also set out to sink the Japanese merchant marine. The first American offensive—at Guadalcanal in the Solomon Islands in mid-1942—gave troops their first taste of jungle

warfare: thick vegetation, mosquitoes, scorpions, tropical heat, and rotting gear. In 1943 and 1944, American troops attacked the Gilberts, Marshalls, and Marianas. And in October 1944, General Douglas MacArthur landed at Leyte to reclaim the Philippines for the United States. Early the next year, both sides took heavy losses at Iwo Jima and Okinawa. Acting out of desperation, Japanese pilots began kamikaze (suicide) attacks by flying their planes directly into American ships.

Still, Japanese leaders refused to admit defeat. Hoping to avoid a humiliating unconditional surrender (and to preserve the emperor's sovereignty), they hung on even while American bombers leveled their cities. In one staggering attack on Tokyo on

The Pacific War *U.S. strategy was to "island-hop" from Hawaii in 1942 to Iwo Jima and Okinawa in 1945. Naval battles were also decisive, notably the Battles of the Coral Sea and Midway in 1942. The war ended with Japan's surrender on V-J Day (August 15).* Source: From Paterson et al., *American Foreign Policy: A History*, vol. 2, 3rd ed. rev., copyright 1991, page 494. Reprinted by permission of D.C. Heath.

How do historians know

whether photographs tell the truth? On February 23, 1945, U.S. Marines planted the American flag atop Mount Suribachi on the island of Iwo Jima. This was trumpeted as the first American flag to fly over conquered Japanese territory. The Associated Press's Joe Rosenthal's famous photo (left) not only won a Pulitzer Prize but also inspired the building of the Marine Corps monument in Arlington, Virginia. The truth is that three hours earlier, before Mount Suribachi had been secured, another group of marines had climbed to the summit and raised a smaller flag atop a fifteen-foot section of drainage pipe. Fearing that this historical flag might be stolen by other marines, the commander had ordered a replacement flag. The right-hand photograph shows the first flag coming down and the famous replacement going up. Photos: National Archives.

May 23, 1945, American planes dropped napalm-filled bombs that engulfed the city in a firestorm, killing eighty-three thousand people.

Impatient for victory, American leaders began to plan a fall invasion of the Japanese islands, an expedition that was sure to incur high casualties. But a secret program, known as the Manhattan Project, led to the successful development of an atomic bomb by American scientists. On August 6, the Japanese city of Hiroshima was destroyed by an atomic blast that killed approximately 130,000 people. Three days later, another atomic bomb leveled Nagasaki, killing at least 60,000 people. A few days later, the Japanese, who had been sending out peace feelers since June, surrendered. The victors promised that the Japanese emperor could remain as the nation's titular head. Formal surrender ceremonies were held September 2 aboard the battleship *Missouri*. The Second World War was over.

The Atomic Bomb

Most Americans agreed with President Truman that the atomic bombing of two Japanese cities had been necessary to end the war as quickly as possible and to save American lives. Use of the bomb to achieve victory had, in fact, been the primary goal of the Manhattan Project. At the highest government levels and among atomic scientists, alternatives had been discussed: detonate the bomb on an unpopulated Pacific island, with international observers as witnesses; blockade and bomb Japan conventionally; follow up Tokyo's peace feelers; encourage a Russian declaration of war on Japan. But Truman's aides had rejected these options, because they would take too long and would not convince the tenacious Japanese that they had been beaten.

Why the Atomic Bomb Was Used

Diplomatic considerations also influenced the decision to use the bomb. U.S. leaders wanted the real and psychological power the bomb would bestow on the United States. It might serve as a deterrent against aggression; it might intimidate Russia into making concessions in Eastern Europe; it might end the war in the Pacific before the Soviet Union could claim a role in the postwar management of Asia. "If it explodes, as I think it will," Truman remarked, "I'll certainly have a hammer on those boys [the Soviets]."

ECONOMIC EFFECTS OF THE WAR AT HOME

World War II was won at great cost, not only abroad but also on the American home front. While the guns boomed in Europe and Asia, the war was changing American lives and institutions. One month after Pearl Harbor, President Roosevelt established the War Production Board (WPB) and assigned to it the task of converting the economy from civilian to military production. Factories had to be expanded and new ones built. The wartime emergency also spurred the establishment of totally new industries, most notably synthetic rubber. The Japanese, in their conquest of the South Pacific, had captured 90 percent of the world's supply of crude rubber.

New industries, however, brought with them new and hazardous pollutants. The production of synthetic rubber, whether from petroleum or grain alcohol, spewed forth dangerous gases like sulfur dioxide and carbon monoxide. War industries fouled the water with both solid and petrochemical wastes. The dumping of radioactive waste began at Hanford, Washington, where plutonium was produced for the atomic bomb. Sulfur vapors from the Kaiser steel plant in Fontana, California, burned the leaves off trees and killed the grapefruit crop. And air pollution—smog—was first detected in Los Angeles in 1943. Although these were ominous signs, few people worried during the war.

To gain the cooperation of business, the WPB and other government agencies met business more than halfway. The government guaranteed profits in the form of cost-plus-fixed-fee contracts, generous tax write-offs, and exemptions from antitrust prosecution. It also allowed prime contractors to distribute subcontracts as they saw fit.

Government Incentives to Business

From mid-1940 through September 1944, the government awarded contracts totaling $175 billion, no less than two-thirds of which went to the top one hundred corporations. General Motors alone received 8 percent of the total; big awards also went to other automobile companies and to aircraft, steel, electrical, and chemical companies. Although the expression "military-industrial complex" had not yet been coined—President Dwight Eisenhower would do so in 1961—the web of military-business interdependence had begun to be woven.

In science and higher education, too, the big got bigger. Massachusetts Institute of Technology received $117 million to develop radar and do other research. California Institute of Technology was in second place, with contracts totaling $83 million, followed by Harvard, Columbia, the University of California, Johns Hopkins, and the University of Chicago. The most spectacular result of government contracts with universities was the atomic bomb. The Manhattan Project, run by the army, financed research at the University of Chicago, which in 1942 was the site of the world's first sustained nuclear chain reaction. The University of California at Berkeley ran the testing of the atomic bomb. Some wartime contracts accelerated medical progress.

Labor also grew bigger during the war. Membership in unions ballooned from 8.5 million in 1940 to 14.75 million in 1945. Less than a week after Pearl Harbor, a White House labor-management conference agreed to a no-strike–no-lockout pledge to guarantee uninterrupted war production. To minimize labor-management conflict, President Roosevelt created the National War Labor Board (NWLB), sometimes referred to as the Supreme Court for labor disputes. Unions were permitted to enroll as many new members as possible, but workers were not required to join a union. Thus the NWLB forged a temporary compromise between the unions' demand for a closed shop, in which only union members could be hired, and management's interest in open shops.

But when the NWLB attempted in 1943 to limit wage increases to cost-of-living pay increases, workers responded with wildcat strikes and other work stoppages that tripled the amount of lost production time over that of the previous year. The worst labor disruptions of 1943 occurred in the coal fields, where 450,000 soft-coal miners and 80,000 anthracite miners struck. To discourage further work stoppages, Congress passed the War Labor Disputes (Smith-Connally) Act in June 1943. The act conferred on the president the authority to seize and operate any strike-bound plant deemed necessary to the national security, and it established a mandatory thirty-day cooling-off period before any new strike could be called. The Smith-Connally Act also gave the NWLB the legal authority to settle labor disputes for the duration of the war.

Wartime Labor Strikes

Agriculture made an impressive contribution to the war effort, through hard work and the introduction of labor-saving machinery to replace men and women who had gone to the front or migrated to war-production centers. Before the war, farming had been in the midst of a transition from

Wartime Changes in Agriculture

the family-owned and -operated farm to the large-scale mechanized agribusiness dominated by banks, insurance companies, and farm co-ops. The Second World War accelerated the trend, for wealthy financial institutions were better able than family farmers to pay for expensive new machinery. Like business and labor, agriculture was becoming more consolidated as it contributed to the war effort.

At the apex of the burgeoning national economy stood the federal government, the size and importance of which was mushrooming: from 1940 to 1945, the federal bureaucracy expanded from 1.1 million workers to 3.4 million. The WPB and the NWLB were only two of a host of new agencies that sprang up: others included the Office of Price Administration, the War Manpower Commission, the Office of War Information, and the Office of Scientific Research and Development. The bill for the war effort, like the acquisition of war materials, was expensive. The national debt skyrocketed from $49 billion in 1941 to $259 billion in 1945.

Growth in the Federal Government

THE MILITARY LIFE

To American servicepeople in Asia and in Europe, World War II was a grimy job. Like cartoonist Bill Mauldin's popular GI characters Willy and Joe, who were more interested in tasty food and dry socks than in abstractions, millions of GIs were simply eager to get it over with. The largest of the services was the army, in which a total of 11.3 million Americans served; 4.2 million were on active duty in the navy, and 670,000 in the Marine Corps. American troops served overseas for an average of sixteen months. Some never returned: total deaths exceeded 405,000.

Large numbers of women also served in America's armed forces during the war. The WACs (Women's Army Corps) enlisted 140,000 women, and 100,000 served in the navy's WAVES (Women Accepted for Volunteer Emergency Service) and 39,000 in

Women in the Armed Forces

the Marine Corps and Coast Guard. Another 75,000 women served in the U.S. Army and Navy's Nursing Corps. Women also served as pilots in the WASP (Women Air Service Pilots), teaching basic flying, towing aerial targets for gunnery practice, ferrying planes across the country, and serving as test pilots. WASP flying duty was often hazardous, and 38 women died.

Military service demanded enormous personal adjustments. Soldiers and sailors who had never been more than a few miles from home became homesick; GIs joked, somewhat bitterly, about having found a home in the army. But loneliness was inconsequential compared with the intense fear that soldiers acknowledged they felt in battle.

Among the millions of people who left home were men and women who had experienced homosexual attraction in peacetime. Serving in sex-segregated units, many acted on their feelings. The military court-martialed homosexuals, but gay relationships usually went unnoticed by the heterosexual world. "For many gay Americans," the historian John D'Emilio has written, "World War II created something of a nationwide coming out situation."

When many men and women returned home after two or three years abroad, they did so not knowing what to expect from civilian life. Earlier in the war, troops had been given orientation lectures and booklets introducing them to the historical backgrounds and social customs of the foreign nations where they would serve. Now they were coming home, "to a surprising degree," as one observer wrote, "foreigners in their own land." And although the American Psychiatric Association did not identify the illness known as posttraumatic stress disorder until 1980, it is clear in retrospect that many of America's World War II veterans suffered from it after the war. The symptoms included nightmares and flashbacks to the battlefield, depression and anger, and widespread alcoholism.

Many GIs also returned with the feeling that life at home had passed them by. They were much older in experience and exposure to brutality; many came back to the United States convinced that they had sacrificed their youth. And they found that home had changed as well. "Our friends are gone," one GI lamented. "The family and the town naturally had to go on even if we weren't there, and somehow it seems things have sort of closed in and filled that space we used to occupy."

THE INTERNMENT OF JAPANESE-AMERICANS

After America entered the war, U.S. leaders had to consider whether enemy agents were operating within the nation's borders and threatening the war effort. It was clear that not all Americans were enthusiastic supporters of the nation's involvement. After Pearl Harbor, several thousand "enemy aliens" were arrested and taken into custody, some of them Nazi agents. Other people had conscientious objections to the war. During the Second World War, conscientious objectors (COs) had to have a religious (as opposed to moral or ethical) reason for refusing military service. About twenty-five thousand qualified COs accepted noncombat service, most as medical corpsmen. An additional twelve thousand were sent to civilian public service camps, where they worked at forestry or conservation or as orderlies in public health hospitals. Approximately fifty-five hundred, three-fourths of whom were Jehovah's Witnesses, refused to participate in any way; they were imprisoned.

"An Enemy Race"

The one enormous exception to the nation's generally creditable wartime civil liberties record was the internment in "relocation centers" of, ultimately, 120,000 Japanese-Americans. Of these people, 77,000 were Nisei, or native-born citizens of the United States. Their imprisonment was based not on suspicion or evidence of treason; their crime was solely their ethnic origin—the fact that they were of Japanese descent. Charges of criminal behavior were never brought against any Japanese-Americans; none was ever indicted or tried for espionage, treason, or sedition.

"It was really cruel and harsh," recalled Joseph Y. Kurihara, a citizen and a veteran of World War I. "To pack and evacuate in forty-eight hours was an impossibility. Seeing mothers completely bewildered with children crying from want and peddlers taking advantage and offering prices next to robbery made me feel like murdering those responsible."

The internees were sent to flood-damaged lands at Relocation, Arkansas, to the intermountain terrain of Wyoming and the desert of western Arizona, and to other arid and desolate spots in the West. Although the names were evocative—Topaz, Utah; Rivers, Arizona; Heart Mountain, Wyoming; Tule Lake and Manzanar, California—the camps were bleak and demoralizing. Behind barbed wire stood tarpapered wooden barracks where entire families lived in a single room furnished only with cots, blankets, and a bare light bulb. Toilets and dining and bathing facilities were communal; privacy was almost nonexistent. Japanese-Americans were forced to sell property valued at $500 million, and they lost their positions in the truck-garden, floral, and fishing industries. Indeed, their economic competitors were among the most vocal proponents of their relocation.

Life in the Internment Camps

The Supreme Court upheld the government's policy of internment. In wartime, the Court said in the *Hirabayashi* ruling (1943), "Residents having ethnic affiliations with an invading enemy may be a greater source of danger than those of different ancestry." In the *Korematsu* case (1944), the Court approved the removal of the Nisei from the West Coast. One dissenter, Justice Frank Murphy, denounced the decision as the "legalization of racism."

In 1983, forty-one years after he had been sent to a government camp, Fred Korematsu had the satisfaction of hearing a federal judge rule that he—and by implication all detainees—had been the victim of "unsubstantiated facts, distortions and misrepresentations of at least one military commander whose views were affected by racism." A year earlier, the government's special Commission on Wartime Relocation and Internment of Civilians had recommended compensating the victims of this policy. Finally, in 1988, Congress voted to award $20,000 and a public apology to each of the surviving sixty thousand Japanese-American internees.

JOBS AND RACISM ON THE HOME FRONT

At peak enrollment, the army had more than 700,000 African-American troops. An additional 187,000 black men and women enlisted in the navy, the Coast Guard, and the once all-white Marine Corps. In response to the March on Washington Movement of 1941, the Selective Service System and the War Department agreed to draft black Americans in proportion to their presence in the population: about 10 percent.

Although they served in segregated units, African-Americans made real advances toward racial equality during these years. For the first time, the War Department sanctioned the training of blacks as pilots. After instruction at Tuskegee Institute in Alabama, pilots saw heroic service in such all-black units as the Ninety-ninth Pursuit Squadron, winner of eighty Distinguished Flying Crosses. In 1940, Colonel Benjamin O. Davis was the first African-American to be promoted to brigadier general. Wherever black people were offered opportunities to distinguish themselves, they proved that they could do the job.

African-American Troops

These accomplishments, however, were undercut by serious failures in race relations. Race riots instigated by whites broke out on military bases, and white civilians assaulted black soldiers and sailors throughout the South. When the War Department issued an order in mid-1944 forbidding racial segregation in military recreation and transportation, the *Montgomery Advertiser* replied, "Army orders, even armies, even bayonets, cannot force impossible and unnatural social relations upon us."

Experiences such as these caused black soldiers and sailors to wonder what, in fact, they were fighting for. They rankled at the remark of the governor of Tennessee, when blacks urged him to appoint African-Americans to local draft boards: "This is a white man's country. . . . The Negro had nothing to do with the settling of America." They noted that the Red Cross separated blood according to the race of the donor, as if there were some difference. Some even argued that World War II was a white man's war and that American racism was little different from German racism.

But there were persuasive reasons for African-Americans to participate in the war effort. Perhaps, as the NAACP believed, this was an opportunity "to persuade, embarrass, compel and shame our government and our nation . . . into a more enlightened attitude toward a tenth of its people." Proclaiming that in the Second World War they were waging a "Double V" campaign (for victory at home and abroad), blacks were more militant than before and readier than ever to protest. Membership in civil rights organizations soared.

The war also created opportunities in industry. To secure defense jobs, 1.2 million black Americans migrated from the South to the industrial cities of the

African-American War Workers

North and West in the 1940s. Almost three-fourths settled in the urban-industrial states of California, Illinois, Michigan, New York, Ohio, and Pennsylvania. More than half a million became active members of CIO unions. African-American voters in northern cities were beginning to constitute a vital swing vote, not only in local and state elections but also in presidential contests.

But the benefits of urban life came with a high price tag. The migrants had to make enormous emotional and cultural adjustments, and white hostility

Race Riots of 1943

and ignorance made their task difficult. Southern whites who had migrated north brought with them the racial prejudices of the Deep South. Equally hostile were the attitudes of northern whites, more than half of whom believed in 1942 that blacks should be segregated in separate schools and neighborhoods. Such attitudes caused many people to fear that the summer of 1943 would be like 1919, another Red Summer. Indeed, in 1943 almost 250 racial conflicts exploded in 47 cities. Outright racial warfare bloodied the streets of Detroit in June. At the end of 30 hours of rioting, 25 blacks and 9 whites lay dead.

The federal government did practically nothing to prevent further racial violence. From President Roosevelt on down, most federal officials put the war first, domestic reform second. But this time government neglect could not discourage African-Americans and their century-old civil rights movement. By war's end, they were ready—politically, economically, and emotionally—to wage a struggle for voting rights and for equal access to public accommodations and institutions.

Racial violence was not directed exclusively against blacks. To some whites, people of Mexican origin were as undesirable as those whose roots were African. In 1942, American farms and war industries needed workers, and the United States and Mexico had agreed to the *bracero* program, whereby Mexicans were admitted to the United States on short-term work contracts. Although the newcomers suffered racial discrimination and segregation, they seized the economic opportunities that had thus become available. In Los Angeles, seventeen thousand people of Mexican descent found shipyard jobs where before the war none had been available to them.

In 1943, Los Angeles witnessed the "zoot-suit riot," in which whites, most of them sailors and soldiers, wantonly attacked Mexican-Americans. Mexican-American street gangs (*pachucos*) had adopted ducktail haircuts and zoot suits: long coats ("drapes") with wide padded shoulders, pegged pants, wide-brimmed hats, and long watch chains. White racist anger at the presumed arrogance of the zoot-suiters boiled over in June, and for four days mobs invaded Mexican-American neighborhoods. Not only did white police officers look the other way during these assaults, but the city of Los Angeles passed an ordinance that made it a crime to wear a zoot suit within city limits. Although the war briefly provided economic opportunities for Mexican-Americans, these years were not the transformational experience that they were for African-Americans.

WOMEN WORKING: PARTICIPATION AND DISCRIMINATION ON THE HOME FRONT

The wartime need for industrial workers temporarily ended the depression-era hostility toward working women. The result was that more than six million women entered the labor force during the war years, increasing the number of working women by 57 percent. Moreover, the typical newcomer was not a young single woman; she was married and older than thirty-five.

Statistics, no matter how impressive, tell only part of the story. Attitudinal change was also important. Until early in the war, employers had insisted that women were not suited for industrial jobs. As labor shortages began to threaten the war effort, employers did an about-face. "Almost overnight," said Mary Anderson, head of the Women's Bureau of the Department of Labor, "women were reclassified by industrialists from a marginal to a basic labor supply for munitions making." Women became lathe operators, riveters, lumberjacks ("lumberjills"), welders, crane operators, keel benders, toolmakers, shell loaders, cowgirls, blast-furnace cleaners, locomotive greasers, and police officers.

Women in War Production

New employment opportunities also increased women's geographic and occupational mobility. Especially noteworthy were the gains made by African-American women; more than 400,000 quit work as domestic servants to enjoy the better working conditions, higher pay, and union benefits of industrial employment. To take advantage of the new employment opportunities, both black and white women willingly uprooted themselves. More than 7 million moved from their original counties of residence to war-production areas. Many sought jobs in the rapidly expanding aircraft industry, in which the female work force increased from 4,000 in December 1941 to 310,000 two years later.

As public opinion shifted to support women's war work, posters and billboards appeared urging women to "Do the Job HE Left Behind." Newspapers and magazines, radio and movies proclaimed Rosie the Riveter a war hero. But few people asserted that women's war work should bring about a permanent shift in sex roles: this was merely a response to a national emergency. Once the victory was won, women should go back to nurturing their husbands and children, leaving their jobs to returning GIs. Wartime surveys showed, however, that many of the women wanted to remain in their jobs—80 percent of New York's women workers felt that way, as did 75 percent in Detroit.

Although women's wages rose when they acquired better jobs, they still received lower pay than men. In 1945, women in manufacturing earned only 65 percent of what men were paid. And working women, particularly working mothers, suffered in other ways as well. Even as mothers were being encouraged to work in the national defense, opposition to their doing so remained. One form this campaign took was a series of exaggerated articles in mass circulation magazines about the suffering of "eight-hour orphans" or "latchkey children," left alone or deposited in all-night movie theaters while their mothers worked eight-hour shifts in war plants. Child-care centers were in short supply in some war-boom areas; communal or neighborhood kitchens were almost nonexistent.

Discrimination Against Women and Children

By and large, however, the home-front children of working women were not neglected or abused during the war. Congress addressed the child-care problem through the Lanham Act of 1940. The law provided federal aid, including funds for child-care centers, to communities that had to absorb large war-related populations. Another government program, Extended School Services, offered care for children before and after school. Many families made their own arrangements, which often involved leaving children in the care of their grandmothers.

While millions of women were entering the work force, hundreds of thousands of women were also getting married. The number of marriages rose from 73 per 1,000 unmarried women in 1939 to 93 in 1942. Some couples scrambled to get married so they could live together before the man was sent overseas; others doubtless married and had children to qualify for military deferments. Many of these hasty marriages did not survive long military separations, and divorces soared too—from 25,000 in 1939, to 359,000 in 1943, and 485,000 in 1945. As might be expected, the birthrate also climbed: total births

Increase in Marriage, Divorce, and Birth Rates

rose from about 2.4 million in 1939 to 3.1 million in 1943. Many births were "goodbye babies," conceived as a guarantee that the family would be perpetuated if the father died in battle overseas.

Ironically, women's efforts to hold their families together during the war posed problems for returning men. Women war workers had brought home the wages; they had taken over the budgeting of expenses and the writing of checks. In countless ways, they had proved they could hold the reins in their husbands' absence. Many husbands returned home to find that the lives of their wives and children seemed complete without them.

What of the women who wanted to remain in the labor market? Many were forced, by employers or by their husbands, to quit. Others chose to leave their jobs for a year or two but then returned to work. And throughout the rest of the 1940s and 1950s, millions more who had never worked took jobs.

THE DECLINE OF LIBERALISM AND THE ELECTION OF 1944

Even before Pearl Harbor, political liberals had suffered major defeats. Some Democrats hoped to revive the reform movement during the war, but Republicans and conservative Democrats were on guard against such a move. Conservatives did more than block additional reform; they dismantled significant New Deal programs like the Civilian Conservation Corps and the Work Projects Administration.

Aided by a small turnout in November 1942, the Republicans scored impressive gains, winning forty-four new seats in the House and nine in the

Republican Gains in 1942

Senate and defeating Democratic governors in New York, California, and Michigan. Part of the Democrats' problem was that the war years, unlike the 1930s, were a time of full employment. Once people had acquired jobs and gained some economic security, they began to be more critical of New Deal policies. The New Deal coalition had always been a loose and fragile alliance: southern white farmers had little in common with northern blacks

or white factory workers. In northern cities, blacks and whites who had voted for Roosevelt in 1940 were competing for jobs and housing and would soon collide in race riots.

But although Democratic liberalism was enfeebled, it was far from dead. At its head still stood Franklin D. Roosevelt, and it had a program to present to the American people. The liberal agenda began with a pledge to secure full employment. Roosevelt emphasized the concept in his Economic Bill of Rights, delivered as part of his 1944 State of the Union address. Every American had a right, the president declared, to a decent job; to sufficient food, shelter, and clothing; and to financial security in unemployment, illness, and old age. If to accomplish those goals the government had to operate at a deficit, Roosevelt was willing to do so. But first he had to be reelected. For his running mate, Roosevelt selected Senator Harry S Truman of Missouri. But there was little evidence that Truman possessed the capacities for national and world leadership that he would need as president. Nor did Roosevelt take Truman into his confidence, failing even to inform his running mate about the atomic bomb project.

In 1944, the Republicans were optimistic about their prospects for regaining the presidency. New York's Governor Thomas E. Dewey, who won the nomination on the first ballot, was moderate in his criticism of Roosevelt's foreign policy and did not advocate repeal of the essentials of the New Deal—Social Security, unemployment relief, collective bargaining, and price supports for farmers. But Dewey had one great liability—his public image. He was stiff in manner and bland in personality.

Despite rumors of ill health, Roosevelt won a fourth term. It was the urban vote that returned Roosevelt to the White House. Wartime population shifts had enhanced the cities' new political clout: southern whites who had been lifelong Democrats and southern blacks who had never before voted had migrated to the urban industrial centers. Added to the urban vote was a less obvious factor. Many voters seemed to be exhibiting what has been called depression psychosis. Fearful that hard times would return once war contracts were terminated, they remembered New Deal relief programs and voted for Roosevelt. Finally, the Republicans had "underestimated the difficulty of changing a President at the very height of a victorious war." With victory within grasp, many Americans wanted Roosevelt's experienced hand to guide the nation, and the world, to a lasting international peace. But Roosevelt's death in April 1945 rendered that choice moot. The new president who would deal with the postwar world was Roosevelt's running mate, Harry Truman.

WARTIME DIPLOMACY

The aftermath of World War I weighed heavily on the minds of American diplomats throughout the war. Americans vowed to make a peace that would ensure a postwar world free from economic depression, totalitarianism, and war. Thus American goals included the Open Door and lower tariffs, self-determination for liberated peoples, avoidance of the debts-reparations tangle that had plagued Europe after World War I, expansion of the U.S. sphere of influence, and management of world affairs by what Roosevelt once called the Four Policemen: Russia, China, Great Britain, and the United States.

Although the Allies concentrated on defeating the aggressors, their suspicions of one another undermined cooperation. Eastern European questions proved the most difficult. The

Allied Disagreement over Eastern Europe

Soviet Union sought to fix its boundaries where they had stood before Hitler attacked in 1941. This meant that the part of Poland that the Soviets had invaded and captured in 1939 would become Soviet territory. The British and Americans hesitated, preferring to deal with Eastern Europe at the end of the war. Yet in an October 1944 agreement, Churchill and Stalin struck a bargain: the Soviet Union would gain Rumania and Bulgaria as a sphere of influence, Britain would have the upper hand in Greece, and the two countries would share authority in Yugoslavia and Hungary.

Poland was a special case. In 1943, Moscow had broken off diplomatic relations with the conservative Polish government-in-exile in London. The Poles had angered Moscow by asking the International Red Cross to investigate German charges that the Soviets had massacred thousands of Polish army officers in the Katyn Forest in 1940. Then an uprising in Warsaw in July 1944 complicated matters still further. Encouraged by approaching Soviet troops to expect assistance, the Warsaw underground rose against the occupying Germans. To the dismay of the world community, Soviet armies stood by as German troops slaughtered 166,000 people and devastated the city. The Soviets then set up a pro-Communist government in Lublin. Thus, near the end of the war, Poland had two competing governments, one in London, recognized by America and Britain, and another in Lublin.

Early in the war, the Allies had begun talking about a new international peace-keeping organization. At Teheran in 1943, Roosevelt called for an

Creation of the United Nations Organization

institution controlled by the Four Policemen. The next year, at a Washington, D.C., mansion called Dumbarton Oaks, American, British, Russian, and Chinese representatives conferred on the details. The conferees approved a preliminary charter for a United Nations Organization, providing for a supreme Security Council dominated by the great powers and a weak General Assembly. The Security Council would have five permanent members, each with veto power. Britain had insisted that France be one of the permanent members. Meanwhile, the Soviet Union, hoping to counter pro-American and pro-British blocs in the General Assembly, asked for separate membership in the General Assembly for each of the sixteen Soviet republics. This issue was not resolved at Dumbarton Oaks, but the meeting proved a success nevertheless.

Diplomatic action on behalf of the European Jews, however, proved to be a tragic failure. Even before the war, Nazi officials had targeted Jews

Jewish Refugees from the Holocaust

throughout Europe for extermination. By war's end, about 6 million Jews had been forced into concentration camps and had been systematically killed. The Nazis also exterminated as many as 250,000 gypsies and about 60,000 gay men. During the depression, the United States and other nations had refused to relax their immigration

When the British liberated the Bergen-Belsen concentration camp near Hanover, Germany, in April 1945, they found this mass grave, which held the remains of thousands of Holocaust victims who had been starved, gassed, and machine-gunned by their Nazi jailers. This photograph and many others provide irrefutable proof of the Holocaust's savagery. Imperial War Museum.

restrictions to save Jews fleeing persecution. The American Federation of Labor argued that new immigrants would compete with American workers for scarce jobs, and public opinion polls supported their position. This fear of economic competition was fed by anti-Semitism. Bureaucrats applied the rules so strictly—requiring legal documents that fleeing Jews could not possibly provide—that otherwise-qualified refugees were kept out of the country. From 1933 to 1945, less than 40 percent of the German-Austrian immigration quota was filled.

Even the tragic voyage of the *St. Louis* did not change government policy. The vessel left Hamburg in mid-1939 carrying 930 desperate Jewish refugees who lacked proper immigration documents. Denied entry to Havana, the *St. Louis* headed for Miami, where Coast Guard cutters prevented it from docking. The ship was forced to return to Europe. Some of those refugees took shelter in countries that were later overrun by Hitler's legions.

When evidence mounted that Hitler intended to exterminate the Jews, British and American representatives met in Bermuda (1943) but came up with no plans. Secretary Hull submitted a report to the president that emphasized "the unknown cost of moving an undetermined number of persons from an undisclosed place to an unknown destination." Appalled, Secretary of the Treasury Henry Morgenthau Jr. charged that the State Department's foot-dragging made the United States an accessory to murder. Early in 1944, stirred by

American Inaction in the Face of the Holocaust

Morgenthau's well-documented plea, Roosevelt created the War Refugee Board, which set up refugee camps in Europe and played a crucial role in saving two hundred thousand Jews from death. But, lamented one American official, "By that time it was too damned late to do too much."

American officials had waited too long to act, and they also missed a chance to destroy the gas chambers and ovens at the extermination camp at Auschwitz in occupied Poland. They possessed aerial photographs and diagrams of the camp, but they argued that bombing it would detract from the war effort or prompt the Germans to step up the anti-Jewish terror. In 1944, American planes bombed factories in the industrial sector of Auschwitz but left untouched the gas chambers and crematoria that were only five miles away.

THE YALTA CONFERENCE AND A FLAWED PEACE

With the war in Europe nearing an end, Roosevelt called for another summit meeting. The three Allied leaders met at Yalta, in the Russian Crimea, in early February 1945. Controversy has surrounded the conference ever since. Roosevelt was obviously ill, and critics of the Yalta agreements later charged that Roosevelt was too weak to resist Stalin's cunning and that he struck a poor bargain. The evidence suggests, however, that Roosevelt was mentally alert and managed to sustain his strength during negotiations.

Each of the Allies arrived at Yalta with definite goals. Britain sought to make France a partner in the postwar occupation of Germany, to curb Soviet influence in Poland, and to ensure protection for the vulnerable British Empire. The Soviet Union wanted reparations from Germany to assist in the massive task of rebuilding at home, possessions in Asia, continued influence in Poland, and a permanently weakened Germany. The United States lobbied for the United Nations Organization, in which it believed it could exercise influence, for a Soviet declaration of war against Japan, for recognition of

Allied Goals at Yalta

China as a major power, and for compromise between rival factions in Poland.

Military positions at the time of the conference helped to shape the final agreements. Soviet troops had occupied much of Eastern Europe, including Poland, and Stalin insisted on a government friendly to Moscow—the Lublin regime. Churchill boiled over in protest; he wanted the London government-in-exile to return to Poland. With Roosevelt's help, a compromise was reached: a boundary favorable to the Soviet Union in the east, postponement of the western boundary issue, and the creation of a "more broadly based" coalition government that would include members of the London regime. Free elections would be held sometime in the future. The agreement was vague but, given Soviet occupation of Poland, Roosevelt considered it "the best I can do."

As for Germany, the Big Three agreed that it would be divided into four zones, the fourth to be administered by France. Berlin, within the Soviet zone, would also be divided among the four victors. On the question of reparations, Stalin wanted a precise figure, but Churchill and Roosevelt insisted on determining Germany's ability to pay. With Britain abstaining, the Americans and Russians agreed that an Allied committee would consider the sum of $20 billion as a basis for discussion in the future.

Other issues led to trade-offs. Stalin promised to declare war on Japan two or three months after Hitler's defeat. The Soviet premier also agreed to sign a treaty of friendship and alliance with Jiang Jieshi (Chiang Kai-shek), America's ally in China, rather than with the Communist Mao Zedong. In return, the United States agreed to the Soviet Union's taking of the southern part of Sakhalin Island and Lushun (Port Arthur). Regarding the new world organization, Roosevelt and Churchill granted the Soviets three votes in the General Assembly. (Fifty nations officially launched the United Nations Organization three months later.) Finally, the conferees issued the Declaration of Liberated Europe, a pledge to establish order and to rebuild economies by democratic methods.

Yalta marked the high point of the Grand Alliance; each of the Allies came away with something it wanted. But as the great powers jockeyed for

Potsdam Conference

influence at the close of the war, neither the spirit nor the letter of Yalta held firm. The crumbling of the alliance became evident almost immediately, at the Potsdam Conference, which began in mid-July. Roosevelt had died in April. Truman, who replaced him, was a novice at international diplomacy and less patient with the Soviets. Truman also was emboldened by learning during the conference that the atomic test in New Mexico had been successful.

Despite major differences, the Big Three did agree on general policies toward Germany: complete disarmament, dismantling of industry used for military production, and dissolution of Nazi institutions and laws. In a compromise over reparations, they decided that each occupying nation should extract reparations from its own zone, but they could not agree on a total figure. To resolve other issues, such as peace treaties with Italy, Finland, and Hungary, the Big Three created the Council of Foreign Ministers.

Hitler once said, "We may be destroyed, but if we are, we shall drag a world with us—a world in flames." Indeed, *rubble* was the word most often invoked to describe the European landscape at the end of the war. Hamburg, Stuttgart, and Dresden had been laid waste; three-quarters of Berlin was in ruins. In England, Coventry and parts of London were bombed out. Everywhere, ghostlike people wandered about, searching desperately for food and mourning those who would never come home. Russia had lost more than 20 million people, Poland 5.8 million, Germany 4.5 million. In all, some 35 million Europeans died as a result of the war. In Asia, untold millions of Chinese and 2 million Japanese died.

Only one major combatant escaped such grisly statistics: the United States. Its cities were not burned and its fields were not trampled. Amer-

Postwar Strength of the United States

ican deaths from the war—405,399—were few compared with the losses of other nations. In fact, the United States emerged from the Second World War more powerful than it had ever been. It alone had the atomic bomb. The U.S. Air Force and Navy were the largest anywhere.

What is more, only the United States had the capital and economic resources to spur international recovery. America, gloated Truman, was "a giant."

Life for many Americans was fundamentally different in 1945 from what it had been before Pearl Harbor. The Academy Award for 1946 went to *The Best Years of Our Lives*, a painful film about the postwar readjustments of three veterans and their families and friends. Many men returned home suffering deep emotional distress. One girl remembered that her father had flashbacks and nightmares. He even "seemed afraid to touch us," she said.

The Second World War also stimulated the trend toward bigness, not only in business and labor but also in government, agriculture, higher education, and science. And it was during these years that the seeds of the military-industrial complex were sown. Moreover, with the advent of the Cold War, millions of younger men would be inducted into the armed forces during the next thirty years. War and the expectation of war would become part of American life.

At the same time, World War II was a powerful engine of social change in the United States. The gains made during the war by African-Americans and women were overdue. And by blending New Deal ideology and wartime urgency, the government assumed the responsibility of ensuring prosperity and stepping in when capitalism faltered. Finally, Americans emerged from the war fully confident that theirs was the greatest country in the world. Clearly, the Second World War was a turning point in the nation's history.

SUGGESTIONS FOR FURTHER READING

Fighting the War

Robert H. Abzug, *Inside the Vicious Heart: Americans and the Liberation of Nazi Concentration Camps* (1985); Stephen A. Ambrose, *Eisenhower: Soldier, General of the Army, President-Elect* (1983); A. Russell Buchanan, *The United States in World War II*, 2 vols. (1964); John W. Dower, *War Without Mercy: Race and Power in the Pacific War* (1986); Richard B. Frank, *Guadalcanal* (1991); Paul Fussell, *Wartime* (1989); B. H. Liddell Hart, *History of the Second World War* (1970); Max Hastings, *OVERLORD: D-Day and the Battle of Normandy* (1984); D. Clayton James, *A Time for Giants: Politics of the American High Command in World War II*

(1987); John Keegan, *The Second World War* (1989); Eric Larabee, *Commander in Chief* (1987); Richard M. Leighton and Robert W. Coakley, *Global Logistics and Strategy, 1940–1945*, 2 vols. (1955–1968); Karal Ann Marling and John Wetenhall, *Iwo Jima* (1991); Samuel Eliot Morison, *The Two-Ocean War* (1963); Forrest C. Pogue, *George C. Marshall*, 4 vols. (1963–1987); Bill D. Ross, *Iwo Jima* (1985); Ronald Schaffer, *Wings of Judgment: American Bombing in World War II* (1985); Ronald H. Spector, *Eagle Against the Sun: The American War with Japan* (1984).

Grand Alliance Diplomacy

Russell Buhite, *Decisions at Yalta* (1986); James MacGregor Burns, *Roosevelt: The Soldier of Freedom* (1970); Winston S. Churchill, *The Second World War*, 6 vols. (1948–1953); Diane Clemens, *Yalta* (1970); Robert Dallek, *Franklin D. Roosevelt and American Foreign Policy, 1932–1945* (1979); Robert A. Divine, *Roosevelt and World War II* (1969); George C. Herring, *Aid to Russia, 1941–1946* (1973); Gary R. Hess, *The United States at War, 1941–1945* (1986); Akira Iriye, *Power and Culture: The Japanese-American War, 1941–1945* (1981); Keith Sainsbury, *The Turning Point* (1985); Gaddis Smith, *Diplomacy During the Second World War, 1941–1945*, 2d ed. (1985); Michael Stoff, *Oil, War, and American Security* (1980); Mark Stoler, *The Politics of the Second Front* (1977); Christopher Thorne, *Allies of a Kind* (1977); David S. Wyman, *The Abandonment of the Jews* (1984).

The Home Front

Allan Berube, *Coming Out Under Fire: The History of Gay Men and Women in World War II* (1990); John Morton Blum, *V Was for Victory: Politics and American Culture During World War II* (1976); John D'Emilio, *Sexual Politics, Sexual Communities: The Making of a Homosexual Minority in the United States, 1940–1970* (1983); Mark Jonathan Harris et al., *The Homefront* (1984); Richard R. Lingeman, *Don't You Know There's a War On?* (1970); Gerald D. Nash, *The American West Transformed* (1985); Geoffrey Perrett, *Days of Sadness, Years of Triumph: The American People, 1939–1945* (1973); Richard Polenberg, *War and Society* (1972); Studs Terkel, ed., *"The Good War": An Oral History of World War Two* (1984); William M. Tuttle Jr., *"Daddy's Gone to War": The Second World War in the Lives of America's Children* (1993).

Mobilizing for War

John Chambers, *To Raise an Army* (1980); George Q. Flynn, *The Draft, 1940–1973* (1993); Daniel J. Kevles, *The Physicists* (1977); Clayton R. Koppes and Gregory D. Black, *Hollywood Goes to War* (1987); Harold G. Vatter, *The U.S. Economy in World War II* (1985); Allen M. Winkler, *The Politics of Propaganda: The Office of War Information, 1942–1945* (1978).

Farmers and Workers, Soldiers and Sailors

Melvyn Dubofsky and Warren H. Van Tine, *John L. Lewis* (1977); Lee Kennett, *G.I.: The American Soldier in World War II* (1987); Nelson Lichtenstein, *Labor's War at Home: The CIO in World War II* (1983); Bill Mauldin, *Up Front*, rev. ed. (1968); Davis R. B. Ross, *Preparing for Ulysses: Politics and Veterans During World War II* (1969); Samuel A. Stouffer et al., *The American Soldier*, 2 vols. (1949).

Japanese-American Internment

Roger Daniels, *Prisoners Without Trial* (1993); Peter Irons, *Justice at War* (1983); Thomas James, *Exile Within: The Schooling of Japanese-Americans, 1942–1945* (1987); John Tateishi, ed., *And Justice for All: An Oral History of the Japanese-American Detention Camps* (1984); Michi Weglyn, *Years of Infamy* (1976).

African-Americans and Wartime Violence

A. Russell Buchanan, *Black Americans in World War II* (1977); Dominic J. Capeci Jr., *Race Relations in Wartime Detroit* (1984); Richard M. Dalfiume, *Desegregation of the U.S. Armed Forces* (1969); Mauricio Mazon, *The Zoot-Suit Riots* (1984); Patrick S. Washburn, *A Question of Sedition: The Federal Government's Investigation of the Black Press During World War II* (1986); Neil A. Wynn, *The Afro-American and the Second World War*, rev. ed. (1993).

Women at War

Karen T. Anderson, *Wartime Women* (1981); D'Ann Campbell, *Women at War with America* (1984); Sherna Berger Gluck, *Rosie the Riveter Revisited* (1987); Claudia Goldin, *Understanding the Gender Gap: An Economic History of American Women* (1990); Susan M. Hartmann, *The Home Front and Beyond* (1982); Ruth Milkman, *Gender at Work: The Dynamics of Job Discrimination by Sex During World War II* (1987); Leila J. Rupp, *Mobilizing Women for War: German and American Propaganda, 1939–1945* (1978); Peter A. Soderbergh, *Women Marines: The World War II Era* (1992).

The Atomic Bomb and Japan's Surrender

Gar Alperovitz, *Atomic Diplomacy*, rev. ed. (1985); Herbert Feis, *The Atomic Bomb and the End of World War II* (1966); Gregg Herken, *The Winning Weapon* (1980); John Hersey, *Hiroshima*, rev. ed., (1985); Richard Rhodes, *The Making of the Atomic Bomb* (1987); Martin J. Sherwin, *A World Destroyed* (1975); Leon V. Sigal, *Fighting to a Finish* (1988).

28

Cold War Politics, McCarthyism, and Civil Rights, 1945–1961

R AIN FELL ON CAPITOL Hill on the afternoon of April 12, 1945. The House of Representatives had adjourned for the day, and Speaker Sam Rayburn had invited the House parliamentarian to join him for a drink in his office. "Be there around five," the Speaker had said. "Harry Truman is coming over."

Rayburn's telephone rang as he sipped his first drink. The caller was the White House press secretary; would the vice president telephone the White House as soon as possible? Truman arrived shortly. At Rayburn's suggestion, he picked up the phone and called the White House. Truman's face drained of color. He rushed to the White House, where an usher announced that Eleanor Roosevelt was waiting for him. When he entered the second-floor sitting room, Eleanor Roosevelt walked toward him, touched his shoulder, and said, "Harry, the President is dead."

When Truman became president, his initial response to the challenge was a deep feeling of inadequacy. As vice president, moreover, Truman had been left in the dark by Roosevelt about cru-

cial foreign and military initiatives; nevertheless, he would have to deal with the onset of the Cold War. In domestic matters, too, the new president would need a crash course in the intricacies of governing the United States.

The nation's reconversion from war to peace was not smooth, and Truman managed to anger liberals, conservatives, farmers, consumers, and union members during his first year as president. In 1946, voters reacted to inflation and a wave of strikes by electing a Republican majority to Congress. Truman's actions also heightened fears that a Communist conspiracy was operating within the federal government. He issued an executive order in 1947 establishing the Employee Loyalty Program for the executive branch of the government. Henceforth, all agency directors had to ensure that each employee under their jurisdiction was a loyal American. In doubtful cases, the agency's chief had to appoint a loyalty board to hear evidence. Personal beliefs and past associations became criteria for employment, and those federal employees accused of disloyalty were presumed to be guilty.

In 1948, Truman was thought to be extremely vulnerable, but he confounded political experts by winning the presidency in his own right.

Truman's victory also demonstrated the volatility of postwar politics. The key domestic issues of the period—civil rights for African-Americans and the anti-Communist witch hunt led by Senator Joseph R. McCarthy and called McCarthyism—were both highly charged issues. Later, the outbreak of the Korean War in 1950 intensified discontent. The war, inflation, and corruption in the White House caused Truman's popularity to plummet. After twenty years of Democratic presidents, Americans in 1952 elected the Republican nominee and war hero, General Dwight D. Eisenhower.

During the 1950s, an age of consensus, Americans generally shared a belief in anticommunism and the primacy of economic progress over social agendas. President Eisenhower—hardly the passive, ill-informed chief executive the Democrats tried to depict—actively articulated both beliefs and worked hard to put them into action. But he moved cautiously and hesitantly, particularly in dealing with civil rights and McCarthyism.

To promote economic growth, Eisenhower pursued staunchly Republican goals: a balanced budget, reduced government spending, lower taxes, low inflation, private enterprise, a return of power to the states, and modest federal efforts to stimulate economic development. But Eisenhower administration officials did not attempt to roll back the New Deal. In fact, however reluctantly, they expanded the welfare state.

It was the infant civil rights movement that most vigorously challenged the national consensus. Not only were most African-Americans at the bottom of the economic ladder, they also were being denied their constitutional rights. How would blacks be incorporated into the consensus? The president, Congress, southern whites, and black civil rights activists all gave different answers as they debated *Brown* v. *Board of Education of Topeka*, the Supreme Court's momentous decision on school desegregation.

Still, however fragile, the age of consensus remained basically intact. President Eisenhower was succeeded in 1961 by a much younger man and a Democrat, Senator John F. Kennedy of Massachusetts. Eisenhower's vice president, Richard M. Nixon, had lost the election to Kennedy. Meanwhile, throughout the country, race relations and urban conditions continued to deteriorate. In the 1960s, the nation would have to deal with problems it had postponed in the 1950s.

A ROUGH TRANSITION AT HOME

After the initial joyous reaction to the Second World War's end, Americans faced a number of important questions. What would be the effect of reconversion—the cancellation of war contracts, termination of wage and price controls, and expiration of wartime labor agreements? Would depression recur as the artificial stimulus of the war was withdrawn, throwing people out of work and sending prices downward? Or would Americans spend the money they had saved during the war years and go on a buying spree, driving prices up?

Even before the war's end, cutbacks in production had caused layoffs. At Ford Motor Company's massive Willow Run plant outside Detroit, where

Postwar Job Layoffs

9,000 Liberator bombers had been produced, most workers were let go in the spring of 1945. Ten days after the victory over Japan, 1.8 million people nationwide received pink slips and 640,000 filed for unemployment compensation. The employment picture was, of course, made more complex by the return of millions of discharged GIs in 1945 and 1946. At the peak of postwar unemployment in March 1946, 2.7 million people searched for work.

Despite high unemployment immediately after the war, the United States was not teetering on the brink of depression. In fact, after a brief period of readjustment, the economy would soon blast off into a quarter-century of unprecedented boom. People had plenty of savings to spend in 1945 and 1946, and suddenly there were new houses and cars for them to buy. Easy credit and the availability of new products from such war-inspired industries as synthetic rubber and electronics promoted the buying spree. As a result, despite the winding down of war production that began in 1944, the gross national product

(GNP) continued to rise in 1945. The nation's postwar economic problem was not depression; it was inflation. Throughout 1945 and 1946, prices skyrocketed; inflation exceeded 18 percent in 1946.

Although prices were spiraling upward, many people were earning less in real income (actual purchasing power) than they had earned during the war.

Upsurge in Labor Strikes

Industrial workers had complained during the war that the National War Labor Board limited them to cost-of-living pay increases. In the immediate postwar period, they complained that the end of war production had eliminated much of their overtime work. A primary reason for workers' discontent was that as their wages and salaries declined slightly in 1946, net profits had reached all-time highs. Indignant that they were not sharing in the prosperity, more than 4.5 million men and women went on strike in 1946. Workers forced nationwide shutdowns in the coal, automobile, steel, and electricity industries and halted railroad and maritime transportation.

John L. Lewis's United Mine Workers was among the most powerful unions to walk off the job. Coal was the nation's primary source of energy in 1946. When soft-coal production stopped on April 1, steel and automobile output plummeted, railroad service was canceled, thousands of people were laid off, and twenty-two states reinstituted wartime "dim-outs" to conserve coal. The miners' demands were legitimate—higher wages, a federal safety code, and a royalty of 10 cents per ton to finance health services and welfare and pension funds. A two-week truce in May failed to produce a solution; with time running out and the country still desperate for coal, Truman ordered federal seizure of the mines. Lewis and the government reached an accord a week later, and the miners returned to work. But within six months, the agreement collapsed, and once again the government took over operation of the mines.

By 1946, there was no doubt about the growing unpopularity of labor unions and their leadership. Many Americans blamed the unions for strikes,

Truman's Attack on the Unions

which not only restricted the output of consumer goods and inflated prices but also threatened the national security. In May, when a nationwide railroad strike was threatened, Truman hopped aboard the anti-union bandwagon. A mediation board had managed to satisfy eighteen of the disgruntled unions, but two held out for a better settlement. In exasperation, Truman made a dramatic appearance before a joint session of Congress. If the government seized a strike-bound industry, he said, and the workers in that industry refused to honor a presidential order to return to work, "I [would] request the Congress immediately to authorize the President to draft into the Armed Forces of the United States all workers who are on strike against their government." He also requested authority to strip strikers of seniority benefits, to take legal action against union leaders, and to fine and even imprison them for contempt. Truman's speech alienated not just the railroad workers but union members in general. Many vowed to defeat him in the upcoming 1948 presidential election.

Truman fared little better in his direction of the Office of Price Administration (OPA). Now that the war was over, powerful interests wanted OPA

Consumer Discontent

controls lifted. Consumers grew impatient with shortages and black-market prices, and manufacturers and farmers wanted to jack up prices legally. Yet when most controls expired in mid-1946 and inflation rose further, consumers grumbled.

Republicans made the most of public discontent. "Got enough meat?" asked Republican Congressman John M. Vorys of Ohio. "Got enough houses? Got enough OPA? . . . Got enough inflation? . . . Got enough debt? . . . Got enough strikes?" In 1946, the Republicans won a majority in both houses of Congress and captured twenty-five of the thirty-two nonsouthern governorships. The White House in 1948 seemed within their grasp.

THE EIGHTIETH CONGRESS AND THE ELECTION OF 1948

The politicians who dominated the Eightieth Congress, whether Republicans or southern Democrats, were committed conservatives. They supported Truman's foreign policy but perceived the Republican

• *Important Events* •

1945	Roosevelt dies; Harry S Truman assumes presidency Japan surrenders	**1953**	Korean War ends Rosenbergs executed J. Robert Oppenheimer's security clearance is revoked Congress adopts termination policy for Native Americans Recession hits United States
1946	Coal miners strike Inflation reaches 18.2 percent Republicans win both houses of Congress	**1954**	*Brown* decision rules "separate but equal" is illegal Senate condemns Senator McCarthy
1947	Truman institutes Employee Loyalty Program Taft-Hartley Act limits power of unions *To Secure These Rights* issued by the President's Committee on Civil Rights	**1955**	Montgomery bus boycott begins
1948	Truman appoints President's Committee on Equality of Treatment and Opportunity in the Armed Services Truman elected president	**1956**	Highway Act launches interstate highway project Eisenhower reelected
1949	Russia explodes an atomic bomb Communists win revolution in China	**1957**	Little Rock has desegregation crisis Congress passes Civil Rights Act Recession recurs
1950	Klaus Fuchs arrested as an atomic spy Alger Hiss convicted of perjury Hydrogen bomb project announced McCarthy alleges Communists in government Korean War begins Julius and Ethel Rosenberg charged with conspiracy to commit treason Internal Security (McCarran) Act passed	**1958**	National Defense Education Act passed Sherman Adams resigns over scandal St. Lawrence Seaway opens for traffic
1951	*Dennis et al.* v. *U.S.* upholds Smith Act	**1960**	Sit-in in Greensboro, North Carolina SNCC formed John F. Kennedy elected president Recession hits again
1952	Eisenhower elected president Republicans win both houses of Congress	**1961**	Eisenhower warns against "military-industrial complex"

landslide as a mandate to reverse the New Deal—that is, to curb the power of government and of labor. Truman had had little success with the previous Congress; he would have even less success with this one. Ironically, however, the Eightieth Congress would ultimately help him win the presidency in 1948. For if Truman had alienated labor, farmers, and liberals, the Eightieth Congress made them livid.

Particularly unpopular was the Taft-Hartley Act, which Congress approved over Truman's veto in 1947. A revision of the Wagner Act of 1935, the law prohibited the "closed shop," a workplace where membership in a particular union was a pre-

Taft-Hartley Act

requisite for being hired. It also permitted the states to enact "right-to-work" laws banning union-shop agreements, which required all workers to join if a majority voted in favor of a union shop. In addition, the law forbade union contributions to political candidates in federal elections, required union leaders to sign non-Communist affidavits, and mandated an eighty-day cooling-off period before carrying out strikes that imperiled the national security. Taft-Hartley became labor's litmus test for political candidates. Thus Truman's veto of the measure vindicated him in the eyes of labor.

Throughout 1947 and into 1948, the conservative Eightieth Congress offended a raft of interest groups, which in turn swung back to Truman. The president asked Congress for continued price supports for farmers; the Eightieth Congress responded with weakened price supports. The president requested nationwide health insurance; the Eightieth Congress refused. The pattern was the same with federal funding of public housing and aid to public education; with unemployment compensation, old-age and survivors' benefits, and the minimum wage; with funds for land reclamation, irrigation, and public power; and with antilynching, anti-poll tax, and fair employment legislation. Truman proposed; Congress rejected or ignored his requests.

Republicans seemed oblivious to public opinion. Not since 1928 had they been so confident of capturing the presidency, and most political experts

Campaign of 1948
———

Third Parties
———

agreed. "Only a political miracle or extraordinary stupidity on the part of the Republicans," according to *Time*, "can save the Democratic party." At their national convention, Republicans strengthened their position by nominating the governors of two of the nation's most populous states: Thomas E. Dewey of New York for president and Earl Warren of California for vice president.

Truman, who received the Democratic nomination, found himself fighting more than just Republicans. Leftist elements of the party, especially those critical of Truman's policy toward the Soviet Union, started a new Progressive party and

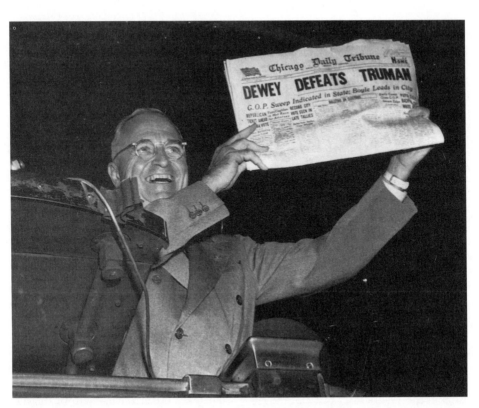

So few pollsters predicted that President Harry S Truman (1884–1972) would win in 1948 that the Chicago Daily Tribune *announced his defeat before all the returns were in. Here, a victorious Truman pokes fun at the newspaper for its premature headline.* UPI/Bettmann Archives.

nominated former vice president Henry Wallace. Segregationists, angered over the Democratic party's adoption of a civil rights plank, formed the States Rights Democratic party (Dixiecrats) and nominated Governor Strom Thurmond of South Carolina. If Wallace's candidacy did not destroy Truman's chances, experts said, the Dixiecrats certainly would.

Truman's Upset Victory

But Truman had a few ideas of his own. He called the Eightieth Congress into special session and challenged it to enact all the planks in the Republican platform. If Republicans really wanted to transform their convictions into law, said Truman, this was the time to do it. After Congress had debated for two weeks and accomplished nothing of significance, Truman took to the road. Traveling more than thirty thousand miles by train, he delivered scores of whistle-stop speeches denouncing the "do-nothing" Eightieth Congress. Still, no amount of furious campaigning by Truman seemed likely to change the predicted outcome.

As the votes were counted, it was clear by early morning that Truman had confounded the experts. The final tally was 24 million popular votes and 303 electoral votes for Truman, 22 million popular votes and 189 electoral votes for Dewey. How and why did the upset occur? First, the United States was prosperous, at peace, and essentially united on foreign policy. Second, Roosevelt's legacy—the New Deal coalition—had endured.

Truman began his new term brimming with confidence. It was time, he believed, for government to fulfill its responsibility to provide economic security for the poor and the elderly. As he worked on his 1949 State of the Union message, he penciled in an expression of his intentions: "I expect to give every segment of our population a fair deal." Little did Truman know that he had chosen the label that historians would hereafter associate with his presidency: Fair Deal.

PRESIDENTIAL AND JUDICIAL ACTIVISM IN CIVIL RIGHTS

Truman and other politicians knew they would have to compete for the growing African-American vote in urban-industrial states like California, Illinois, Michigan, Ohio, Pennsylvania, and New York. Many Republicans cultivated the black vote. Dewey, who as governor of New York had pushed successfully for a fair employment practices commission, was particularly popular with African-Americans. In Harlem, which had gone Democratic by a four-to-one margin in 1938, Dewey won by large margins in 1942 and 1946.

Clearly, then, Truman had compelling political reasons for supporting African-American civil rights. But he also felt a moral obligation to blacks. For one thing, he genuinely believed it was only fair that every American, regardless of race, should enjoy the full rights of citizenship. More than that, Truman was horrified by a report that police in Aiken, South Carolina, had gouged out the eyes of a black sergeant just three hours after he had been discharged from the army. Several weeks later, in December 1946, Truman signed an executive order establishing the President's Committee on Civil Rights.

President's Committee on Civil Rights

The committee's report, *To Secure These Rights*, would become the agenda for the civil rights movement for the next twenty years. Among its recommendations were the enactment of federal antilynching, antisegregation, and anti-poll tax laws. *To Secure These Rights* also called for laws guaranteeing voting rights and equal employment opportunity and for the establishment of both a permanent commission on civil rights and a civil rights division within the Department of Justice. Although Congress failed to act and some evidence suggests that Truman's real goal was the African-American vote in 1948, his action was significant. For the first time since Reconstruction, a president had acknowledged the federal government's responsibility to protect blacks and strive for racial equality.

Truman took this responsibility seriously, and in 1948 he issued two executive orders declaring an end to racial discrimination in the federal government. One proclaimed a policy of "fair employment throughout the federal establishment" and created the Employment Board of the Civil Service Commission to hear charges of discrimination. The other ordered the racial desegregation of the armed forces and appointed the Committee on Equality of Treatment and Opportunity in the Armed Services to oversee this change.

African-Americans also benefited from a series of Supreme Court decisions. The trend toward judicial support of civil rights had begun in the late 1930s, when the NAACP established its Legal Defense Fund. At the time, the NAACP was trying to destroy the separate-but-equal doctrine by insisting on its literal interpretation. In higher education, the NAACP calculated, the cost of true equality in racially separate schools would be prohibitive. "You can't build a cyclotron for one student," as the president of the University of Oklahoma acknowledged. As a result of NAACP lawsuits in the 1930s and 1940s, African-American students

Supreme Court Decisions on Civil Rights

won admission to professional and graduate schools at a number of state universities. In *Smith* v. *Allwright* (1944), the Supreme Court also outlawed the whites-only primaries held by the Democratic party in some southern states, branding them a violation of the Fifteenth Amendment's guarantee of the right to vote. Two years later, the Court struck down segregation in interstate bus transportation *(Morgan* v. *Virginia)*. And in *Shelley* v. *Kraemer* (1948), the Court held that a racially restrictive covenant (a private agreement among white homeowners not to sell to blacks) violated the equal protection clause of the Fourteenth Amendment.

A change in social attitudes accompanied these gains in black political and legal power. Books like Gunnar Myrdal's social science study *An American Dilemma* (1944) and Richard Wright's novels *Native Son* (1940) and *Black Boy* (1945) had in-

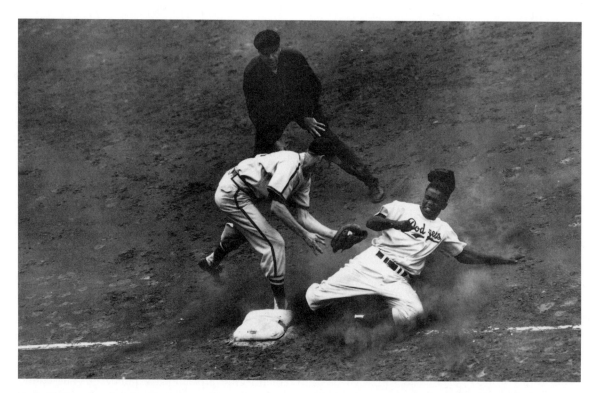

Jackie Robinson cracked the color line in major league baseball when he joined the Brooklyn Dodgers for the 1947 season. Sliding safely into third base, Robinson flashes the aggressive style that won him rookie-of-the-year honors. He was later elected to the Baseball Hall of Fame.   Hy Peskin, LIFE Magazine © Time Warner Inc.

creased white awareness of the social injustice that plagued African-Americans. A new black middle class had emerged, composed of college-educated activists, war veterans, and union workers. Blacks and whites also worked together in CIO unions and service organizations such as the National Council of Churches. In 1947, a black baseball player, Jackie Robinson, broke the major league color barrier.

Cold War pressures also benefited blacks. As the Soviet Union was quick to point out, the United States could hardly pose as the leader of the free world or condemn the denial of human rights behind the iron curtain if it condoned racism at home. Nor could the United States convince new African and Asian nations of its dedication to human rights if African-Americans were subjected to segregation, disfranchisement, and racial violence. To win the support of nonaligned nations, the United States would have to live up to its ideals.

McCARTHYISM

It is a common misconception that anti-Communist hysteria began in 1950 with the furious speeches of Senator Joseph R. McCarthy of Wisconsin. Actually, anticommunism had been a prominent strand in the American political fabric since World War I and the Red Scare of 1919 and 1920. But the Cold War heightened anti-Communist fears, and McCarthy manipulated the fears to his advantage. He became the most successful and frightening redbaiter the country had ever seen.

To a great extent, President Truman initiated the postwar anti-Communist crusade. He was bothered by the revelation in 1945 that classified government documents had been found during a raid on the offices of *Amerasia*, a little-known magazine where the editors sympathized with the Chinese Communists. Who had supplied the documents to the magazine, and why? Similar concern was mounting in Canada, where in 1946 a royal commission issued a report claiming that Soviet spies were operating there. Among them, the report said, was a scientist who had transmitted atomic secrets to a Soviet agent.

Spurred by these revelations, Truman in 1947 ordered investigations into the loyalty of the more than three million employees of the U.S. government. In 1950, the government began discharging people deemed "security risks," among them alcoholics, homosexuals, and debtors thought to be susceptible to blackmail; others became victims of guilt by association. None was allowed to confront his or her accusers.

Truman's Loyalty Probe

The wellspring of this fear of communism was the Cold War: fear of internal subversion was intertwined with fear of external attack. Truman was not alone in peddling fear; conservatives and liberal Democrats joined him. Republicans used the same methods to attack the Democratic candidates for president in 1948 and 1952; liberal Democrats used them to discredit the far-left, pro-Wallace wing of their party. The anti-Communist hysteria of the late 1940s, created by professional politicians, was embraced and promoted by labor union officials, religious leaders, Hollywood moguls, and other influential figures.

People began to point accusing fingers at each other. Hollywood film personalities who had been ardent left-wingers such as Will Geer and Zero Mostel were blacklisted. School teachers and college professors were fired for expressing dissenting viewpoints, and in some communities "pro-Communist" magazines and books were removed from school libraries. In labor union elections and even in local parent-teacher associations, redbaiting became a convenient tactic for discrediting the opposition.

Victims of Anti-Communist Hysteria

Despite the rampant false accusations, there was cause for alarm—especially in 1949. In that year, the Soviets detonated their first atomic bomb, and the Chinese Communists, finally victorious in their civil war, proclaimed the People's Republic of China. Furthermore, a former State Department official, Alger Hiss, was on trial for perjury, charged with swearing to a grand jury that he had never passed

Hiss Trial

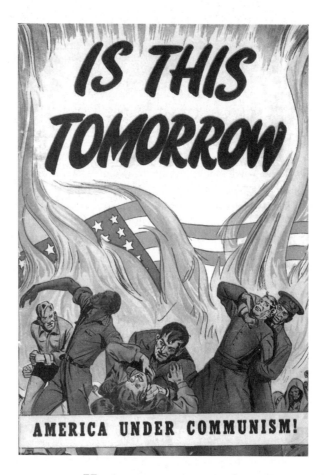

How do historians know

that public anxiety about communism was heightened by the media? This comic book, published in 1947 by the Catechetical Guild Educational Society, enjoyed several reprintings; four million copies were distributed free to church groups. Claiming that Communists had already "wormed their way into . . . government offices, trade unions, and other positions of trust," it warned Americans that, unless they were vigilant, they might be "living in Communist slavery." Films such as Invasion U.S.A. (1952) also featured Communist-takeover scenarios, as did newspaper and magazine articles and television specials, like Red Nightmare (1962). Photo: The Michael Barson Collection, Glen Ridge, N.J.

classified documents to his accuser, former American Communist spy Whittaker Chambers, and that he in fact had not seen Chambers since 1936. When Truman and Secretary of State Dean Acheson came to Hiss's defense, some people began to suspect that the Democrats had something to hide. In 1950, Hiss was convicted of perjury. That same year, a British court sentenced Klaus Fuchs, a nuclear scientist and Nazi refugee, to fourteen years in prison for turning over to Soviet agents secrets from the atomic bomb project at Los Alamos, New Mexico.

It was in this atmosphere that Senator Joseph McCarthy mounted a rostrum in Wheeling, West Virginia, in February 1950 and gave a name to the hysteria: McCarthyism. The

McCarthy's Attack on the State Department

State Department, he asserted, was "thoroughly infested with Communists," and the most dangerous person in the State Department was Dean Acheson. The senator claimed to have a list of 205 Communists working in the department; McCarthy later lowered the figure to "fifty-seven card-carrying members," then raised it to eighty-one. But the number did not matter. What McCarthy needed was a winning campaign issue, and he had found it. Republicans, distraught over losing what had appeared to be a sure victory in 1948, were eager to support his attack.

Widespread support for anti-Communist measures was also apparent in the adoption, over Truman's veto, of the Internal Security (McCarran) Act of 1950. The act made it unlawful to "contribute to the establishment . . . of a totalitarian dictatorship"; it also required members of "Communist front" organizations to register with the government and prohibited them from holding defense jobs or traveling abroad. In a telling decision in 1951 (*Dennis et al.* v. *U.S.*), the Supreme Court upheld the Smith Act, under which eleven Communist party leaders had been convicted and imprisoned.

McCarthy and McCarthyism gained momentum throughout 1950. Nothing seemed to slow the senator down, not even attacks by other Republicans. Seven Republican senators broke with their colleagues in 1950 and publicly condemned McCarthy for his "selfish political exploitation of fear, bigotry, ignorance, and intolerance"; a Senate committee reported that his charges against the State Department were "a fraud and a hoax." But McCarthy had much to sustain him, including Julius and Ethel Rosenberg's 1950 arrest for conspiracy to commit espionage; during the war, they allegedly had recruited and supervised a spy who worked at the Los Alamos atomic laboratory. Perhaps even more helpful to McCarthy than the

Rosenberg case was the outbreak of the Korean War in June 1950.

THE ELECTION OF 1952 AND THE TRUMAN RECORD

As the 1952 presidential election approached, the Democrats foundered. Americans were frustrated over a stalemated war, in a state of unrest over communism, and concerned by

Truman's Unpopularity

the revelation of influence peddling by some of Truman's cronies. Known as "five percenters," they had offered government contracts in return for 5 percent kickbacks. In exchange for expediting the import of perfume ingredients, Truman's military aide and friend, Major General Harry Vaughn, had accepted a freezer. Another presidential appointee acknowledged under oath, "I have only one thing to sell and that is influence." In 1951, Truman's public approval rating slumped to an all-time low of 23 percent and hovered at that level for a year. Once again, the Democratic party appeared doomed along with its leader.

What sealed the fate of the Democratic party was the Republican candidacy of General Dwight D. Eisenhower. A bona fide war hero with a winning smile, "Ike" seemed to embody the virtues Americans most admired: humble origins, integrity, decency, lack of pretense, and native ability. His running mate, Senator Richard M. Nixon of California, was less likable. Accused during the campaign of having received money from a secret slush fund raised by wealthy Californians, Nixon went on television to deny the charge. The only gift his family had received, he said, was a puppy named Checkers. His daughters loved the little dog, and "we're gonna keep it."

Eisenhower's unlucky Democratic opponent was Adlai Stevenson, the thoughtful, cerebral, and witty governor of Illinois. Eisenhower's supporters derided him as an "egghead,"

Eisenhower's Victory

and from the outset it was never much of a contest. Eisenhower promised to end the Korean War. He remained cautiously silent on the subject of McCarthyism, but his running mate did not. Nixon scrambled for political points by referring to Stevenson as "Adlai the appeaser . . . who got a Ph.D. from Dean Acheson's College of Cowardly Communist Containment." The result was a landslide: Eisenhower won almost 34 million popular votes and 442 electoral votes, to the Democrats' 27 million popular and 89 electoral votes. Eisenhower even captured four states in the once solid Democratic South. Moreover, his coattails were long enough to carry other Republicans to victory; the party gained control of both houses of Congress.

Truman's Presidential Legacy

Although Truman was highly unpopular when he left office in 1953, historians now rate him among the nation's ten best presidents. Having come to office suddenly and with little experience, in eight years he strengthened the powers of the presidency. During the Truman administration, agencies that had been established for temporary duty during the Second World War were made permanent. The Atomic Energy Act of 1946 established the Atomic Energy Commission. Legislation in 1947 created a unified Department of Defense, the National Security Council, and a permanent intelligence service, the Central Intelligence Agency (CIA). Truman's main shortcomings stemmed from his overreaction to the alleged threat of Communist subversion in government. His loyalty program ruined innocent people's lives and careers, and his rhetoric helped pave the way for McCarthyism. He also sent American troops to fight in Korea without a declaration of war from Congress.

At the same time, Truman was a New Dealer who fought for social welfare programs and legislation to benefit farmers, workers, homeowners, retired persons, and people in need of health care. His Fair Deal—most of which was enacted during subsequent presidential administrations—represented a commitment to first-class citizenship for African-Americans. When Truman left office in 1953, he had set the United States on a course from which it would not veer, and he had cast a long shadow across the country's twentieth-century history.

CONSENSUS AND THE POLITICS OF THE EISENHOWER PRESIDENCY

Smiling Ike, with his folksy style, garbled syntax, and frequent escapes to the golf course, provoked Democrats to charge that he failed to lead. But it was not that simple. Dwight D. Eisenhower was no stranger to hard work. His low-key, hidden-hand style was a way of playing down his role as politician and highlighting his role as chief of state. He was also timid about tangling directly with the Republican party's vocal right wing. Eisenhower relied heavily on staff work, delegated authority to departments, and shied away from close involvement in the legislative process. This approach sometimes meant that he was not well informed on details, and it gave the impression that he was out of touch with his own government. In fact, he was not, and he remained a very popular president.

The Consensus Mood

During Eisenhower's presidency, most Americans clung to the status quo. Demand for reform at such a time seemed to most Americans not only unnecessary but downright unpatriotic. The country was engaged in a moral struggle with communism, people believed, and during such a crusade they should support, not criticize, the government. The historian Henry Steele Commager saw conformity everywhere—"the uncritical and unquestioning acceptance of America as it is." A weak minority on the left advocated checks on the political power of corporations, and a noisy minority on the right accused the government of a wishy-washy campaign against communism. But both liberal Democrats and moderate Republicans avoided extremism, satisfied to be occupying what historian Arthur M. Schlesinger Jr. called "the vital center."

Consensus Historiography

During the 1950s, scholars who subscribed to the prevailing consensus proclaimed "the end of ideology" in America. Since the early twentieth century, historians had told the American story as one of conflict—rich against poor, North against South, farmer against industrialist and banker. They focused on rebellions, strikes, moral crusades, and wars. The historians of the 1950s, on the other hand, wrote about stability, continuity, and cultural unity. Although the consensus historians of the 1950s did not deny the existence of conflict in the American past, they ascribed it less to flaws in society than to disturbed personalities. Among the groups historians identified as maladjusted were abolitionists, feminists, Populists, and progressive reformers. The consensus perspective thus shifted the focus away from society's faults—slavery, sexism, political corruption—and placed it on those who demanded reform.

In this age of consensus, President Eisenhower approached his duties with a philosophy he called "dynamic conservatism," by which he meant being

"Dynamic Conservatism"
———

"conservative when it comes to money and liberal when it comes to human beings." Eisenhower's was unabashedly "an Administration representing business and industry," as Interior Secretary Douglas McKay acknowledged. The president and his appointees gave priority to reducing the federal budget, but they did not always succeed. They recognized that dismantling New Deal and Fair Deal programs was politically impossible. And most government expenditures consisted of fixed built-in costs such as veterans' pensions, Social Security benefits, and interest payments on the national debt. The administration did try to remove the federal government from agriculture, but the effort failed. Despite several changes in federal farm price-support policy, the government found itself spending more money and stockpiling increased amounts of surplus farm commodities.

Eisenhower made more headway in other spheres. In 1954, Congress passed legislation to construct a canal, the St. Lawrence Seaway, between Montreal and Lake Erie. This inland waterway was intended to spur the economic development of the Midwest by linking the Great Lakes to the Atlantic Ocean. The president also made a Cold War–inspired case for the joint Canadian-American project: it would strengthen the security of both nations. The same year, Eisenhower signed into law amendments to the Social Security Act that raised benefits and added 7.5 million workers,

mostly self-employed farmers, to the program's coverage. The Housing Act of 1954, the first of many such measures during the decade, provided federal funds to construct houses for low-income families displaced by urban renewal's destruction of their neighborhoods. Congress also obliged the president with tax reform that increased deductions and raised business depreciation allowances and with the Atomic Energy Act of 1954, which granted private companies the right to own reactors and nuclear materials for the production of electricity.

The Eisenhower administration presided over a dramatic change in the lives of Native Americans. In 1953, Congress adopted a policy of *termination:*

Termination Policy for Native Americans
———

the liquidation of Indian reservations and an end to federal services. Another act of the same year made Indians subject to state laws. Native Americans were not asked their opinions of these departures from policies established a century before. Administration officials applauded the changes, because they would reduce federal costs and serve states' rights. Critics—including most Indians—denounced termination as one more attempt to grab Indian lands and further exploit Native Americans.

Between 1954 and 1960, the federal government withdrew its benefits from sixty-one tribes. About one in eight Indians abandoned their reservations, many to join the ranks of the urban poor in low-paying jobs. By the time termination was halted in the 1960s, so much human tragedy had struck Native Americans that observers compared the situation to the devastation their forebears had endured in the late nineteenth century.

McCarthyism caused another form of devastation. During Eisenhower's first term, McCarthy's conduct was one of the most vexing problems facing the administration. The

Eisenhower on McCarthy
———

Republican senator's no-holds-barred search for subversives in government turned up none, but it was an affront to political fair play, decency, and civil liberties. Eisenhower avoided confronting McCarthy, saying privately that he would not "get into the gutter with that guy"; the president also feared that a showdown would splinter the Republican party. Instead, he denounced unnamed "demagogues thirsty for personal power" and hoped the media and Congress would bring McCarthy down.

While Eisenhower pursued this indirect strategy to undermine the senator, his administration practiced its own brand of anticommunism. A new executive order in 1953 expanded the criteria under which federal workers could be dismissed as "security risks." In its first three years in office, the Eisenhower administration dismissed fifteen hundred people, more than Truman had fired in twice the time. One of Eisenhower's most controversial decisions was his denial of clemency to Julius and Ethel Rosenberg. The two, having received the death penalty for espionage, were executed in 1953. Later that year, at the urging of the chairman of the Atomic Energy Commission, the president suspended the security clearance of J. Robert Oppenheimer, the celebrated physicist who had directed the Manhattan atomic bomb project at Los Alamos during the Second World War. Oppenheimer's "crimes" were not that he was either disloyal to his nation or a risk to its security but rather that he had lied about the details of a 1943 conversation with a friend on Soviet interest in atomic secrets and that he had later opposed the government's crash program to develop the hydrogen bomb. In 1954, the Communist Control Act, which received a unanimous vote in the Senate and only two dissenting votes in the House, demonstrated that both liberals and conservatives shared in the consensus on anticommunism. For all practical purposes, the measure made membership in the Communist party illegal.

As for Senator McCarthy, he finally undercut himself by taking on the U.S. Army in front of millions of television viewers. At issue was the senator's wild accusation that the army was shielding and promoting Communists; he cited the case of one army dentist. The so-called Army-McCarthy hearings, held by a Senate subcommittee in 1954, became a showcase for the senator's abusive treatment of witnesses. McCarthy, apparently drunk, alternately ranted and slurred his words. Finally, after he maligned a young lawyer who was not even involved in the hearings, Joseph

Army-McCarthy Hearings
——

Welch, counsel for the army, protested, "Have you no sense of decency, sir?" The gallery erupted in applause, and McCarthy's career as a witch-hunter plummeted. The Senate finally condemned McCarthy, in a 67-to-22 vote in December 1954, not for defiling the Bill of Rights but for sullying the dignity of the Senate. He remained a senator, but exhaustion and alcohol took their toll. McCarthy died in 1957 at the age of forty-eight.

President Eisenhower's reluctance to discredit McCarthy publicly had given the senator, other right-wing members of Congress, and some private and public institutions enough rein to divide the nation and destroy the careers of many innocent people. McCarthyism demoralized and frightened federal workers, some of whom were driven from public service. The anti-Communist campaigns of the 1950s also discouraged people from freely expressing themselves and hence from debating critical issues. Fear and a contempt for the Bill of Rights, in short, helped sustain consensus.

McCarthyism disgusted many voters, and the 1954 congressional elections revealed that, although they still liked Ike, they remained loyal to the Democratic party. Voters gave the Democrats control of both houses of Congress. Lyndon B. Johnson of Texas became the Senate's new majority leader. An energetic, pragmatic politician, Johnson tried to work with the Republican White House to pass legislation. A notable accomplishment was the Highway Act of 1956, which launched the largest public works program in American history. The law authorized the spending of $31 billion over the next thirteen years to build a forty-one-thousand-mile interstate highway system, intended to facilitate commerce and enable the military to move around the nation more easily. The interstate highways invigorated the tourist industry and spurred the growth of suburbs farther and farther from the central cities.

Interstate Highway System
——

Eisenhower suffered a heart attack in 1955 but regained his strength and declared his intention to run again. The Democrats nominated Adlai E. Stevenson once more. Eisenhower won a landslide victory in 1956: 36 million votes and 457 electoral votes to Steven-

Election of 1956
——

son's 26 million and 73. Still, the Democrats continued to dominate Congress.

Eisenhower faced rising federal expenditures in his second term, in part because of the tremendous expense of America's global activities. In the first three years of his presidency, he had managed to trim the budget, largely by controlling defense spending. But the president learned that he had to tolerate deficit spending to achieve his goals. In fact, Eisenhower balanced only three of his eight budgets. The administration's resort to deficit spending was also fueled by the need to cushion the effect of three recessions—from 1953 to 1954, 1957 to 1958, and 1960 to 1961. A sluggish economy and unemployment also reduced the tax dollars collected by the federal government.

Setbacks of 1958

A series of setbacks in 1958 made that year the low point for the administration. In addition to a lingering recession, scandal unsettled the White House when the president's chief aide, Sherman Adams, resigned under suspicion of influence peddling. Then came large Republican losses in the 1958 congressional elections. The Democrats—boosted by the Adams affair, the economic slump, discontent among farmers, and their own exaggerated claims that the administration had let the United States fall behind in the arms race—took the Senate 64 to 34 and the House 282 to 154. For the last two years of his presidency, then, Eisenhower had to confront what he called congressional "spenders," who proposed "every sort of foolish proposal" in the name of "national security and the 'poor' fellow."

AN AWAKENED CIVIL RIGHTS MOVEMENT

Brown v. Board of Education of Topeka

In May 1954, the NAACP won a historic victory that stunned the white South and energized African-Americans to challenge segregation on several fronts. *Brown v. Board of Education of Topeka* incorporated cases from several states, all involving segregated schools. Written by Earl Warren, whom Eisen-

hower had named chief justice in 1953, the Court's unanimous decision concluded that "in the field of public education the doctrine of 'separate but equal' has no place. Separate educational facilities are inherently unequal." Such facilities, Warren wrote, produced in black children "a feeling of inferiority . . . that may affect their hearts and minds in a way unlikely ever to be undone." Because of segregation, the Court said, blacks were being "deprived of the equal protection of the laws guaranteed by the Fourteenth Amendment." But the ruling did not demand immediate compliance. A year later, the Court finally ordered school desegregation but only "with all deliberate speed." This vague timetable encouraged the southern states to resist.

Some border states quietly implemented the order, and many southern moderates advocated a gradual rollback of segregation. But the forces of resistance soon came to dominate, urging southern communities to defy the Court. Business and professional people created White Citizens' Councils for the express purpose of resisting the order. Known familiarly as uptown Ku Klux Klans, the councils brought their economic power to bear against black civil rights activists. The Klan experienced another resurgence, and defiant whites formed new resistance groups, such as the so-called National Association for the Advancement of White People. One of the most effective resistance tactics was enactment of state laws that paid the private-school tuition of white children who had left public schools to avoid integration. In some cases, desegregated public schools were ordered closed.

Eisenhower on Civil Rights

Eisenhower, who personally disapproved of segregation, objected to "punitive or compulsory federal law." He also feared that the ugly public confrontations likely to follow rapid desegregation would jeopardize Republican inroads in the South. Thus Eisenhower did not state forthrightly that the federal government would enforce the Court's decision as the nation's law—in short, instead of leading, he spoke ambiguously and thereby tacitly encouraged massive resistance.

Events in Little Rock, Arkansas, forced the president to stop sidestepping the issue. In September 1957, Governor Orval E. Faubus intervened to

Crisis in Little Rock, Arkansas

halt a local plan for the gradual desegregation of Little Rock's Central High School. Faubus mobilized the Arkansas National Guard to block the entry of black students. Eisenhower made no effort to impede Faubus's actions. Late that month, bowing to a federal judge's order, Faubus withdrew the guardsmen. As hundreds of jeering whites threatened to storm the school, eight black children entered Central High. The next day, fearing violence, Eisenhower federalized the Arkansas National Guard and dispatched paratroopers to Little Rock to ensure the children's safety. Troops patrolled the school for the rest of the year; in response, Little Rock officials closed all public high schools in 1958 and 1959 rather than desegregate them.

Elsewhere, African-Americans did not wait for Supreme Court or White House decisions to claim equal rights. In 1955, Rosa Parks, a department

Montgomery Bus Boycott

store seamstress and active member of the NAACP, was arrested for refusing to give up her seat to a white man on a public bus in Montgomery, Alabama. Local black leaders decided to boycott the city's bus system, and they elected Martin Luther King Jr., a local minister, as their leader. King launched the boycott with a moving speech in which he declared: "If we are wrong, the Constitution is wrong. If we are wrong, God Almighty is wrong. If we are wrong, Jesus of Nazareth was merely a utopian dreamer. . . . If we are wrong, justice is a lie."

Martin Luther King Jr. was an Atlanta-born, twenty-six-year-old Baptist minister who had recently earned a doctoral degree at Boston University.

Martin Luther King Jr.

Disciplined and analytical, he was committed to nonviolent peaceful protest in the spirit of India's leader Mahatma Gandhi. Although he was jailed and a bomb blew out the front of his house, King persisted. "Absence of fear," according to civil rights leader Bayard Rustin, was what King gave to black Americans. In 1957, King became president of the Southern Christian Leadership Conference, organized to coordinate civil rights activities.

Bolstered by a 1956 Supreme Court decision that declared Alabama's Jim Crow laws unconstitutional, Montgomery blacks triumphed. They and others across the nation were further heartened when Congress passed the Civil Rights Act of 1957, which created the U.S. Commission on Civil Rights to investigate systematic discrimination, such as voting discrimination. But this measure, like a voting rights act passed three years later, proved ineffective. Critics charged that the Eisenhower administration was more interested in quelling the civil rights question than in addressing it.

African-Americans responded by adopting more aggressive tactics. In February 1960, four black students from North Carolina Agricultural and

The Sit-Ins

Technical College in Greensboro ordered coffee at a department store lunch counter. Told that "we do not serve Negroes," the students refused to budge. Thus began the sit-in movement, which quickly spread northward. Inspired by the sit-ins, southern black college and high school students met on Easter weekend in 1960 and organized the Student Nonviolent Coordinating Committee (SNCC). In the face of angry white mobs, SNCC members challenged the status quo.

King personally joined the sit-in movement, and in October 1960 he was arrested in a sit-in to desegregate an Atlanta snack bar. Sent to a cold, cockroach-infested state penitentiary where he faced four months at hard labor, he became ill. As an apathetic Eisenhower White House looked on, King was rescued when Senator John F. Kennedy, running for the presidency, persuaded the sentencing judge to release King on bond.

THE ELECTION OF 1960 AND THE EISENHOWER RECORD

The election of 1960 was one of the closest and most hard fought in the twentieth century (see map). The forty-three-year-old Democratic candidate, Senator Kennedy,

John F. Kennedy

injected new vigor and glamour into presidential politics. Kennedy had been born to wealth, had graduated from Harvard, and had served as a member of Congress before joining the Senate in 1953. His running mate in 1960 was Senator Lyndon B. Johnson of Texas, added to the ticket to keep white southerners loyal to the Democratic party as the civil rights issue heated up. The Republican candidate was Richard M. Nixon, the forty-seven-year-old vice president from California. He and his running mate, Ambassador Henry Cabot Lodge of Massachusetts, expected a rugged campaign.

Kennedy, exploiting the media to great advantage, ran a risky but ultimately brilliant race. Aware that his major liability with voters was his Roman

How and Why Kennedy Beat Nixon

Catholicism, he addressed the issue head-on: he went to the Bible Belt to tell a group of Houston ministers that he respected the separation of church and state and would take his or-

ders from the American people, not the pope. Seeing opportunity in the African-American vote and calculating that Johnson could keep the white South loyal to the Democrats, Kennedy courted black voters. A major asset to Kennedy was the unsavory image that Nixon presented in the nation's first televised debate between presidential candidates; he came across as heavy jowled and surly. Perhaps worse, Eisenhower gave him only a tepid endorsement.

Foreign policy became a major issue. Nixon claimed that he alone knew how to deal with Communists, and he charged that Kennedy lacked experience in foreign affairs and could not stand up to Khrushchev. Kennedy shot back, "I was not the vice president of the United States who presided over the communization of Cuba." The Democratic nominee hit hard on Cuba, but his most effective theme was that Eisenhower and Nixon had let American prestige and power erode. Kennedy offered voters victory instead of stalemate in the Cold War, and he vowed to win over Third World countries as allies of the United States. Kennedy subscribed to the two fundamental tenets of the 1950s consensus—economic growth and anticommunism—and asserted that he could expand the benefits of economic progress and win foreign disputes through more vigorous leadership.

In an election characterized by the highest voter participation (63 percent) in half a century, Kennedy defeated Nixon by the razor-slim margin of 118,000 votes. Kennedy's electoral college margin, 303 to 219, was much closer than the numbers suggest. Slight shifts in the popular vote in Illinois and Texas—two states in which electoral fraud helped produce narrow Democratic majorities—would have made Nixon president. Although Kennedy's Catholicism lost him votes, especially in the Midwest, he won about 80 percent of Catholic voters. Religious bigotry did not decide the election, and Kennedy became the first Roman Catholic president.

Assessments of the Eisenhower administration once emphasized its conservatism, passive style, limited achievements, and reluctance to confront difficult issues. In recent years,

Eisenhower Presidency Assessed

however, interpretations have been changing as scholars have begun examining the now declassified documents of the

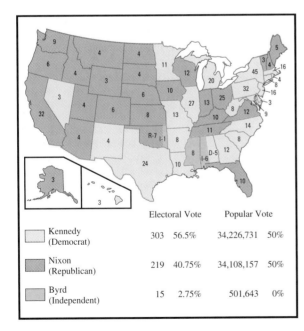

	Electoral Vote		Popular Vote	
Kennedy (Democrat)	303	56.5%	34,226,731	50%
Nixon (Republican)	219	40.75%	34,108,157	50%
Byrd (Independent)	15	2.75%	501,643	0%

Presidential Election, 1960 *In 1960, John F. Kennedy won the closest presidential election in twentieth-century American history. In fact, Richard M. Nixon won the popular votes of 26 states to Kennedy's 24. In the electoral college, 15 southerners voted for neither Kennedy nor Nixon but cast protest votes for Harry F. Byrd, a conservative senator from Virginia.*

consensus era. Many now stress Eisenhower's command of policymaking, sensibly moderate approach to most problems, political savvy, and great popularity. Many historians now argue that Eisenhower was not an aging bystander in the 1950s but a competent, pragmatic, compassionate leader.

The record of Eisenhower's presidency is nonetheless mixed. At home, he failed to deal with racism, poverty, and urban decay—problems that would wrack the country in the next decade. He dragged his feet on civil rights. He exacerbated McCarthyism by refusing to come down hard on the reckless senator, and his own loyalty program was excessive. On the other hand, in comparison with his successors in the 1960s, Eisenhower was measured and cautious. He kept military budgets under control and managed crises adroitly so that the United States avoided major military ventures abroad. At home, he curbed inflation and kept the nation prosperous. He strengthened the infrastructure by building an interstate highway system, and he expanded Social Security coverage. Eisenhower brought dignity to the presidency, and the American people respected him.

Just before leaving office in early 1961, Eisenhower went on national radio and television to deliver his farewell address to the nation. Because of

The "Military-Industrial Complex"

the Cold War, he observed, the United States had been "compelled to create a permanent industry of vast proportions," as well as a standing army of 3.5 million. "This conjunction of an immense military establishment and a large arms industry is new in the American experience," Eisenhower noted. "The total influence—economic, political, even spiritual—is felt in every city, every statehouse, every office of the federal government." Then Eisenhower issued a direct warning, urging Americans to "guard against . . . the military-industrial complex." They did not.

Although both ranked as excellent presidents, Truman and Eisenhower presided over an era during which serious social problems—racism, poverty, and urban decay—were allowed to fester. It was a time of consensus and conformity, which went hand in hand with trust in and respect for established authority. In government, business, labor,

the military, religion, and education, Americans were content to let those at the top decide on their behalf. They chose to pursue economic goals more than moral ones, seeming to believe that the latter were divisive and, in any case, seldom attainable.

Like their leaders, Americans were suspicious of mass movements, viewing even those with democratic goals like the civil rights movement as threats

An Age of Consensus

to stability. Rather than working for idealistic causes, people preferred to focus on earning a living, raising a family, and contributing their tax dollars to strengthen America. On the surface, the age of consensus remained intact throughout the 1950s, reinforced not only by economic development but also by the baby boom, the growth of suburbs, and an emphasis on patriotism, fads, and family togetherness. During the 1960s, the nation would finally have to deal with the daunting social, economic, and political problems postponed since the end of World War II. Meanwhile, consensus prevailed.

SUGGESTIONS FOR FURTHER READING

The Truman-Eisenhower Era

John Patrick Diggins, *The Proud Decades* (1988); Marty Jezer, *The Dark Ages* (1982); William L. O'Neill, *American High: The Years of Confidence, 1945–1960* (1986).

The Truman Administration

Robert J. Donovan, *Tumultuous Years: The Presidency of Harry S Truman, 1949–1953* (1982), and *Conflict and Crisis: The Presidency of Harry S Truman, 1945–1948* (1977); Alonzo L. Hamby, *Beyond the New Deal: Harry S Truman and American Liberalism* (1973); Maeva Marcus, *Truman and the Steel Seizure Case* (1977); Allen J. Matusow, *Farm Policies and Politics in the Truman Years* (1967); Donald R. McCoy, *The Presidency of Harry S Truman* (1984); David McCullough, *Truman* (1992).

Truman and Civil Rights

Richard M. Dalfiume, *Desegregation of the U.S. Armed Forces* (1969); Richard Kluger, *Simple Justice: The History of Brown v. Board of Education and Black America's Struggle for Equality* (1975); Donald R. McCoy and Richard T. Ruetten, *Quest and Response: Minority Rights and the Truman Administration* (1973); Mark V. Tushnet, *The NAACP's Legal Strategy Against Segregated*

Education (1987); Jules Tygiel, *Baseball's Great Experiment: Jackie Robinson and His Legacy* (1983).

McCarthyism

David Caute, *The Great Fear* (1978); Richard M. Fried, *Nightmare in Red* (1990); Robert Griffith, *The Politics of Fear: Joseph R. McCarthy and the Senate*, rev. ed. (1987); Maurice Isserman, *If I Had a Hammer . . . : The Death of the Old Left and the Birth of the New Left* (1987); Stanley I. Kutler, *The American Inquisition* (1982); David M. Oshinsky, *A Conspiracy So Immense: The World of Joe McCarthy* (1983); Thomas C. Reeves, *The Life and Times of Joe McCarthy* (1982); Ellen W. Schrecker, *No Ivory Tower: McCarthyism in the Universities* (1986); Athan Theoharis, *Seeds of Repression: Harry S Truman and the Origins of McCarthyism* (1971).

An Age of Consensus

Paul A. Carter, *Another Part of the Fifties* (1983); David Halberstam, *The Fifties* (1993) ; Douglas T. Miller and Marion Novak, *The Fifties* (1977); Richard H. Pells, *The Liberal Mind in a Conservative Age* (1985); Stephen J. Whitfield, *The Culture of the Cold War* (1987).

Eisenhower and the Politics of the 1950s

Charles C. Alexander, *Holding the Line* (1975); Stephen E. Ambrose, *Eisenhower: The President* (1984); Robert F. Burk, *Dwight D. Eisenhower* (1986); Donald L. Fixico, *Termination and Relocation: Federal Indian Policy, 1945–1970* (1986); Fred I. Greenstein, *The Hidden-Hand Presidency* (1982); Chester J. Pach Jr. and Elmo Richardson, *The Presidency of Dwight D. Eisenhower* (1991); Herbert Parmet, *Eisenhower and the American Crusades* (1972); Gary W. Reichard, *The Reaffirmation of Republicanism* (1975); Mark H. Rose, *Interstate: Express Highway Politics, 1941–1956* (1979).

The Civil Rights Movement and Martin Luther King Jr.

Taylor Branch, *Parting the Waters: America in the King Years, 1954–1963* (1988); Robert F. Burk, *The Eisenhower Administration and Black Civil Rights* (1984); William H. Chafe, *Civilities and Civil Rights: Greensboro, North Carolina, and the Black Struggle for Freedom* (1980); David J. Garrow, *Bearing the Cross: Martin Luther King Jr. and the Southern Christian Leadership Conference* (1986); Stephen B. Oates, *Let the Trumpet Sound: The Life of Martin Luther King Jr.* (1982); Stephen J. Whitfield, *A Death in the Delta: The Story of Emmett Till* (1991).

The Cold War Era,
1945–1991

PRESIDENT HARRY S TRUMAN'S speech writers considered his March 12, 1947, speech to a joint session of Congress as important as any since Pearl Harbor. Yet they were worried. Truman had a selling job to do if he wanted the fiscally conservative Eightieth Congress to approve his request for $400 million in aid to Greece and Turkey. In his effort to persuade the Republican Congress, Truman used alarmist language. Communism, he claimed, imperiled the world. "If Greece should fall under the control of an armed minority," he gravely concluded in an early version of the "domino theory," "the effect upon its neighbor, Turkey, would be immediate and serious. Confusion and disorder might well spread throughout the entire Middle East." Civil war, in which Communists played a prominent role, rocked Greece, and Turkey bordered the hostile Soviet Union. Events in these faraway places, Truman argued, threatened the United States.

Especially momentous in the dramatic speech were the words that would guide U.S. policymakers for almost a half century: "I believe that it must be the policy of the United States to support free peoples who are resisting attempted subjugation by armed minorities or by outside pressures." Two young members sitting in the House of Representatives, John F. Kennedy and Richard M. Nixon, heard the "Truman Doctrine" speech that day, and when they assumed the presidency years later, the doctrine still guided their policies.

The Truman Doctrine helped launch the containment doctrine: the United States had to draw the line against communism everywhere. American presidents from Truman to George Bush believed that a ruthless Soviet Union was masterminding a worldwide Communist conspiracy against peace, free-market capitalism, and political democracy. Soviet leaders from Josef Stalin to Mikhail Gorbachev protested that a militarized, economically aggressive United States sought nothing less than domination of the globe. The contest between the United States and the Soviet Union soon acquired the name Cold War.

The primary feature of world affairs for more than four decades, the Cold War was fundamentally a bipolar contest between the United States and the Soviet Union over spheres of influence. The two nations never fought one another directly on the battlefield. Instead, they waged the Cold War through competing alliances (the capitalist "West" versus the Communist "East"), regional wars between client states, rival ideologies, foreign aid and economic sanctions, and the stockpiling of nuclear weapons. The contest took the lives of more than twenty million people, emptied the treasuries of the combatants, spawned fears of doomsday, and destabilized politics in one nation after another, dragging localized conflicts into its path. Sometimes, the two superpowers negotiated at summit conferences and signed agreements to temper the arms race; at other times, they went to the brink of war and armed allies to fight vicious wars in the Third World (see Chapter 31). Decisions made in Moscow and Washington dominated world politics.

Ultimately, the two great powers, weakened by the huge costs of their competition and challenged by other nations and blocs, faced an international system in which power had become diffused. In an effort to stem their relative decline, the two adversaries began in the late 1980s to take steps to end the Cold War. Its end finally came in 1991 with the disintegration of the Soviet Union, the collapse of other Communist regimes in Eastern Europe, and the reunification of Germany. Gloating Americans claimed victory in the Cold War, but slumping U.S. competitiveness in world markets, the faltering U.S. infrastructure, and the failure of many U.S. foreign interventions suggested that the Cold War had no winners.

THE SOURCES OF THE COLD WAR

After the Second World War, the international system was so unsettled that conflict became virtually inevitable. Economic chaos rocked Europe and Asia. Factories had been reduced to rubble, agricultural production plummeted, and displaced persons wandered around in search of food and family. How would the devastated economic world be pieced back together? America and the Soviet Union offered very different answers and models.

Unsettled International System

The collapse of Germany and Japan had also created power vacuums that drew the two major powers into collision as they both sought influence in countries where the Axis had once held sway. And the political turmoil that some nations experienced after the war also spurred Soviet-American competition.

The international system was also unstable, because empires were disintegrating. Financial constraints and nationalist rebellions forced the European imperial states to set their colonies free. As new nations were born in the Middle East and Asia, America and Russia vied to win these Third World states as friends that might provide military bases, resources, and markets. The shrinkage of the globe also ensured conflict. With the advent of the airplane, the world had become more compact. Faster travel brought nations closer and made them more vulnerable to surprise attack from the air. The Americans and the Soviets collided as they strove to establish defensive positions, sometimes far from home.

Driven by different ideologies and different economic and strategic needs in this volatile international climate, the United States and the Soviet Union shelved diplomacy to build what Secretary of State Dean Acheson (1949–1953) called "situations of strength." Both nations marched into the Cold War with convictions of righteousness that gave the contest an almost religious character. Each saw the other as the world's bully. Americans feared "Communist aggression"; Soviets feared "capitalist encirclement."

American leaders also determined never to repeat the experience of the 1930s. They vowed to accept no more Munichs, no more appeasement, and no more depressions that might spawn political extremism and war. To Americans after the Second World War, it seemed that Soviet Russia had simply replaced Nazi Germany, that communism was simply the flip side of the totalitarian coin. The popular term *Red fascism* captured this sentiment.

American officials also knew that the nation's economic well-being depended on an activist foreign policy. In the postwar years, the United States was the largest supplier of goods to world markets, but that trade was jeopardized by the postwar economic paralysis

U.S. Economic Needs

• *Important Events* •

1945	Yalta Conference accords chart postwar order	**1949**	North Atlantic Treaty Organization founded
	Soviet-American clash over Poland		Soviet Union explodes an atomic bomb
	Roosevelt dies; Truman assumes presidency		Communist victory occurs in China
	Japan surrenders and U.S. occupation begins	**1950**	U.S. hydrogen bomb project announced
1946	Soviets and Americans compete for influence in Iran		Secret NSC-68 document calls for huge military build-up
	Kennan's "long telegram" depicts Soviet Union as uncompromising foe		Korean War begins; China enters in fall
	Churchill gives "iron curtain" speech	**1951**	Armistice talks begin in Korea
	Baruch Plan for control of atomic weapons fails	**1952**	U.S. hydrogen bomb exploded
1947	Truman Doctrine establishes containment doctrine against communism	**1953**	Dwight D. Eisenhower becomes president
			Stalin dies
	Communists take over in Hungary		Korean War ends
	Kennan's "Mr. X" article articulates containment doctrine	**1954**	Sino-American crisis occurs over Jinmen and Mazu
	Marshall Plan announced to reconstruct Europe	**1956**	Soviets crush Hungarian revolt
	National Security Act creates Defense Department and Central Intelligence Agency	**1957**	Soviets launch *Sputnik* into outer space
		1958	National Aeronautics and Space Administration (NASA) established
	Rio Pact organizes alliance in Latin America		Berlin crisis erupts
1948	Communist coup takes place in Czechoslovakia	**1959**	Castro ousts Batista in Cuba
	Truman recognizes new nation of Israel	**1960**	Cuba and the United States feud; Castro looks to Soviet Union for help
	United States organizes airlift to break Berlin blockade		U-2 incident occurs

of Europe and by discriminatory trade practices that violated the Open Door doctrine. "Any serious failure to maintain this flow," declared an assistant secretary of state, "would put millions of American businessmen, farmers, and workers out of business." Indeed, exports constituted about 10 percent of the gross national product. And the United States needed to import essential minerals such as zinc, tin, and manganese. Thus economic expansionism, so much a part of pre–Cold War history, remained a central feature of postwar foreign relations.

New strategic theory also propelled the United States toward an expansionist, globalist diplomacy. To be ready for a military challenge in the postwar

American Strategic Thinking

"air age," American strategists believed that the nation's defenses had to extend far beyond its borders. Thus the United States sought overseas bases to guard the approaches to the Western Hemisphere. The bases would also permit the United States to launch offensive attacks with might and speed.

President Truman, who shared all these assumptions, also had a personality that tended to increase international tensions. Whereas Franklin D. Roosevelt had been ingratiating, patient, and evasive, Truman was brash, impatient, and direct. He seldom displayed

Truman's "Get-Tough" Style

• *Important Events* •

1961	John F. Kennedy becomes president
	CIA-sponsored Bay of Pigs invasion fails in Cuba
	Berlin Wall goes up
1962	Cuban missile crisis brings world to brink of nuclear war
1963	Limited Test Ban Treaty prohibits atmospheric testing of nuclear weapons
	Lyndon B. Johnson becomes president
1965	U.S. escalates Vietnam War
1967	Glassboro summit
1968	Nuclear nonproliferation treaty signed
	Soviets invade Czechoslovakia
1969	Richard M. Nixon becomes president and, with Kissinger, launches détente policy
1972	Nixon visits China and ends years of Sino-American isolation
	SALT-I Treaty limits ABMs and strategic nuclear weapons
1977	Jimmy Carter becomes president and presses human rights policy
1979	SALT-II treaty acknowledges Soviet-American nuclear parity
	Soviets invade Afghanistan
1980	Carter Doctrine declares U.S. will defend Persian Gulf area
	Grain embargo and boycott of Olympic Games imposed against Soviets
1981	Ronald Reagan becomes president
	Soviet crackdown in Poland prompts U.S. trade restrictions on Soviet Union
1982	START negotiations begin on reducing strategic nuclear forces
1983	Strategic Defense Initiative ("Star Wars") announced by Reagan
	Nuclear freeze movement grows around the world
	Soviets shoot down Korean airliner
	U.S. Pershing missiles deployed in Western Europe
1985	Reagan Doctrine promises aid to anti-Soviet "freedom fighters"
	Gorbachev initiates *glasnost* and *perestroika* reforms in the Soviet Union
1987	Gorbachev, Reagan sign INF treaty at Washington summit meeting
1989	George Bush becomes president
	Berlin Wall opens and East German Communist regime collapses
1990	Communist regimes in Eastern Europe fall
	Germany reunified
1991	Soviet Union dissolves into independent states
	Cold War ends

Note: For events in the Third World, see Chapter 31.

the appreciation of subtleties so essential to successful diplomacy. For example, in his first meeting with the Soviet commissar of foreign affairs, V. M. Molotov, Truman sharply berated the Soviet Union for violating the Yalta agreement on Poland, although the agreement was given to interpretation. The president was pleased with what he called his "tough method": "I gave it to him straight 'one-two to the jaw.'" This simplistic display of toughness would become a trademark of American Cold War diplomacy.

As for the Soviets, they were not easy to get along with, either. Dean Acheson found them rude and abusive. But more than the Soviets' style bothered Americans. Soviet territorial acquisitions included a portion of eastern Poland; the Baltic states of Lithuania, Latvia, and Estonia; and parts of Finland and Rumania. In Eastern Europe, Soviet officials began to suppress non-Communists and install Communist clients.

The Soviets remembered that since the Bolshevik Revolution the hostile West had attempted to defeat and then ostracize them. Driven by memories of the past, fear of a revived Germany, a monumental task of reconstruction, and Marxist-Leninist doctrine, the Soviets suspected capitalist nations of

Europe may have been liberated from Nazi Germany's grasp in 1945, but the survivors faced a bleak future. The Second World War left factories mangled and fields cropless. Millions of people grew weak and sick from hunger, crying out for relief supplies from one of the few belligerents to escape the war's devastation at home—the United States. Cold War tensions soon sprang from the massive task of postwar reconstruction. Daniel Robert Fitzpatrick, *St. Louis Post-Dispatch.* Victoria Schuck Collection, John F. Kennedy Library.

Yet the public statements of President Truman and other U.S. officials often sounded alarmist, exaggerating the Soviet threat. Why? First, Truman liked things in black and white. Nuances, ambiguities, and counterevidence were often glossed over to satisfy Truman's penchant for the simple answer. Second, military officers overplayed the Soviet threat to persuade Congress to pass larger defense budgets. Third, some Americans fixed their attention, as they had since 1917, on the utopian Communist goal of world revolution rather than on actual Soviet behavior. Fourth, American leaders feared that the ravaging postwar economic and social unrest abroad would leave U.S. strategic and economic interests vulnerable to political disorders that the Soviets might exploit. In other words, Americans feared direct Soviet attack less than Soviet seizure of opportunities to challenge American interests. Most telling, the United States, flushed with its own strength, took advantage of the postwar power vacuum to expand its overseas interests and shape a peace on American terms.

Question of the Soviet Threat

CONFRONTATION AND CONTAINMENT IN EUROPE

One of the first Soviet-American clashes came in Poland in 1945, when the Soviets refused to admit conservative Poles from London to the Communist government in Lublin, as Americans believed they had agreed to do at Yalta. The Soviets also snuffed out civil liberties in the former Nazi satellite of Rumania. They initially allowed free elections in Hungary and Czechoslovakia, but as the Cold War accelerated and U.S. influence in Europe expanded, the Soviets encouraged Communist coups: first Hungary (1947) and then Czechoslovakia (1948) succumbed to Soviet subversion. Yugoslavia was a unique case: its independent Communist government, led by Josip Broz Tito, successfully broke with Stalin in 1948.

Soviet Domination of Eastern Europe

plotting once again to extinguish the Communist flame. The Americans, they protested, were surrounding them with hostile bases and practicing atomic and dollar diplomacy.

Throughout the Cold War era, Americans debated Soviet intentions and capabilities. Some believed that the well-armed aggressive Soviet Union was always opportunistic and could never be trusted. Others charged that American officials exaggerated the Soviet/Communist threat. The Soviet Union actually emerged from the war with a weak military establishment, a hobbled economy, and obsolete technology. It was a regional power in Eastern Europe, not a global menace. Aware of all this, American leaders did not expect the Soviets to attack Western Europe or to provoke a war that the Soviet Union was incapable of sustaining.

To justify their actions, the Soviets pointed out that the United States was reviving their traditional enemy, Germany. The Soviets also protested that the United States was pursuing a double standard—intervening in the affairs of Eastern Europe but demanding that the Soviet Union stay out of Latin America and Asia. American officials called for free elections in the Soviet sphere, Moscow noted, but not in the U.S. sphere in Latin America, where several military dictatorships ruled.

The atomic bomb also divided the two major powers. The Soviets believed that the United States was practicing "atomic diplomacy"—maintaining a nuclear monopoly and bragging about it to scare the Soviets into diplomatic concessions. At a stormy foreign ministers' conference in London in fall 1945, Molotov teased Byrnes by asking if he had an atomic bomb in his side pocket. Byrnes replied that southerners "carry our artillery in our hip pocket. If you don't cut out all this stalling . . . , I am going to pull an atomic bomb out of my hip pocket and let you have it."

Atomic Diplomacy

In this atmosphere of suspicion and distrust, the United States and the Soviet Union could not agree on international control of atomic energy. The U.S. proposal, called the Baruch Plan, provided for U.S. abandonment of its monopoly once the world's fissionable materials were brought under the authority of an international agency. Moscow retorted that this plan would require it to shut down its atomic bomb development project while the United States continued its own. The Soviets argued that the first step toward control must be the destruction of the U.S. atomic arsenal. Unable to agree in 1946, the two sides became locked into an expensive and frightening nuclear arms race.

Soviets and Americans clashed on every front that year. When the United States turned down a Soviet request for a reconstruction loan but gave a loan to Britain, Moscow denounced Washington for using its dollars to manipulate foreign governments. The two Cold War powers also backed different groups in Iran, where the United States helped bring the pro-West shah to the throne. Unable to agree on the unification of Germany, they built up their zones independently. The new World

Bank and International Monetary Fund, created at the 1944 Bretton Woods Conference to stabilize trade and finance, also became tangled in the Cold War struggle. The Soviets refused to join, because the United States so dominated both institutions.

After Josef Stalin gave a speech in February 1946 that depicted the world as threatened by capitalist acquisitiveness, the American chargé d'affaires in Moscow, George F. Kennan, asserted that Soviet fanaticism made even a temporary understanding impossible. His pessimistic "long telegram" to Washington fed U.S. toughness toward the Soviets. The following month, Winston Churchill delivered a stirring speech in Fulton, Missouri, in which he warned that Eastern European countries were being cut off from the West by an "iron curtain" erected by the Soviets.

The Cold War escalated further in early 1947, when the British requested American help in Greece to defend their conservative client government against a leftist insurgency. The president responded by asking Congress for aid to Greece and Turkey and enunciating the Truman Doctrine. Critics pointed out that there was no evidence the Soviet Union was involved in the civil war in Greece. Nor was the Soviet Union threatening Turkey. After much debate, however, the Senate approved Truman's request. Using American dollars and military advisers, the Greek government defeated the insurgents in 1949, and Turkey became a staunch U.S. ally on the Soviets' border.

Greek Civil War and Truman Doctrine

Four months after Truman's speech, George F. Kennan, who had become director of the State Department's policy-planning staff, published an influential statement of the containment doctrine. Writing as "Mr. X" in the magazine *Foreign Affairs*, Kennan advocated a "policy of firm containment, designed to confront the Russians with unalterable counterforce at every point where they show signs of encroaching upon the interests of a peaceful and stable world." Such counterforce, Kennan argued, would check Soviet expansion and eventually foster a "mellowing" of Soviet behavior. With the Truman Doctrine, Kennan's "X"

George F. Kennan's "X" Article

article became a key manifesto of Cold War policy. The highly regarded journalist Walter Lippmann took issue with the containment doctrine, because it failed to distinguish between areas vital and peripheral to U.S. security.

Invoking the containment doctrine, the United States began in 1947 and 1948 to build an international economic and defensive network to protect American prosperity and security and to advance U.S. hegemony. In Western Europe, the region of primary American concern, U.S. diplomats pursued several objectives: economic reconstruction; ouster of Communists from governments, as occurred in 1947 in France and Italy; blockage of "third force" or neutralist tendencies; creation of a military alliance; and unification of the western zones of Germany.

The first instrument designed to achieve these goals was the Marshall Plan. Announced by Secretary of State George C. Marshall (1947–1949) in June 1947, the Marshall Plan **Marshall Plan** called for a massive European recovery program to be financed by the United States. Although Marshall did not exclude the Soviet Union or Eastern Europe, few American leaders believed that the Soviets and their allies would want to join a U.S.-dominated project. Indeed, they did not join (see map). Launched in 1948, the Marshall Plan sent $12.4 billion to Western Europe before the program ended in 1951. To stimulate business at home, the legislation provided that the foreign aid dollars must be spent in the United States on U.S. products. The Marshall Plan proved a mixed success. The program caused inflation, failed to solve a balance-of-payments problem, and took only tentative steps toward economic integration. But it sparked impressive Western European industrial production and investment and started the region toward self-sustaining economic growth.

To streamline the administration of U.S. defense, Truman worked with Congress on the National Security Act (July 1947). The act created the Department of Defense **National Security Act** (replacing the Department of War), the National Security Council (NSC) to advise the president, and the Central Intelligence Agency (CIA) to conduct spying and information gathering. By the early 1950s, the CIA had expanded its functions to include covert (secret) operations aimed at overthrowing unfriendly foreign leaders and to stir up economic trouble in "the camp of the enemy."

American officials also reached out to cultivate new foreign friends and build new bases. The United States granted the Philippines independence in 1946 but retained military and economic hegemony. The following year, U.S. diplomats created the Rio Pact—a military alliance with Latin American countries. Under this and other agreements, the Truman administration sent several military missions to Latin America and to Greece, Turkey, Iran, China, and Saudi Arabia to improve the armed forces of those nations. In May 1948, Truman quickly recognized the newly proclaimed state of Israel, which had been carved out of British-held Palestine after years of Arab-Jewish dispute. Despite State Department objection that recognition would alienate oil-rich Arab nations, Truman made the decision for three reasons: he believed that after the Holocaust Jews deserved a homeland, he desired Jewish American votes in the upcoming election, and he sought another international ally.

One of the most electric moments in the Cold War came in June 1948 after the Americans, French, and British had agreed to fuse their German zones, including their **Berlin Blockade and Airlift** three sectors of Berlin. They sought to integrate West Germany (the Federal Republic of Germany) into the Western European economy, complete with a reformed German currency. Fearing a resurgent Germany tied to the American Cold War camp, the Soviets cut off

Divided Europe *After the Second World War, Europe broke into two competing camps. When the United States launched the Marshall Plan in 1948, the Soviet Union countered with its own economic plan the following year. When the United States created NATO in 1949, the Soviet Union answered with the Warsaw Pact in 1955. On the whole, the two camps held firm until the late 1980s.*

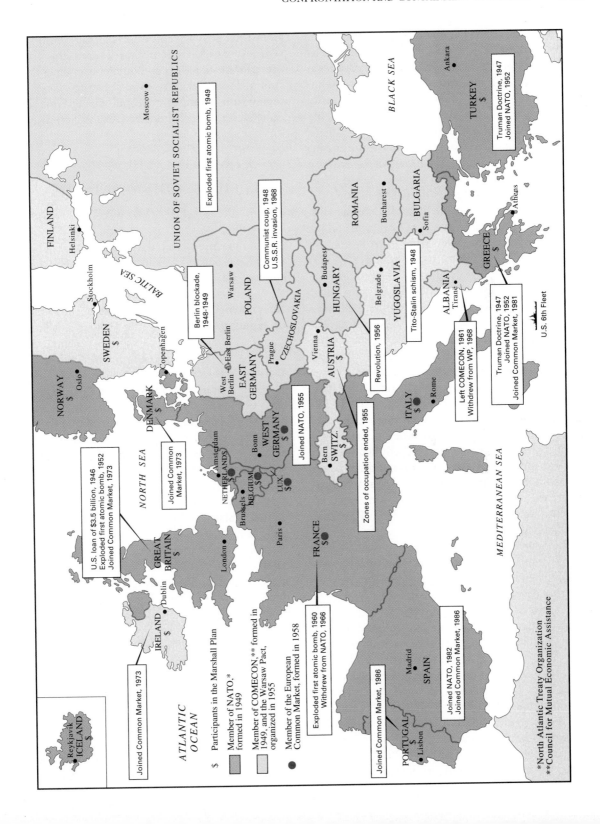

BLACK SEA

TURKEY
$

Ankara

Truman Doctrine, 1947
Joined NATO, 1952

Moscow

UNION OF SOVIET SOCIALIST REPUBLICS

Exploded first atomic bomb, 1949

ROMANIA

Bucharest

BULGARIA

Sofia

Communist coup, 1948
U.S.S.R. invasion, 1968

GREECE
$

Athens

FINLAND

Helsinki

Warsaw

POLAND

Budapest

HUNGARY

Belgrade

YUGOSLAVIA

Tito-Stalin schism, 1948

ALBANIA

Tiranë

Truman Doctrine, 1947
Joined NATO, 1952
Joined Common Market, 1981

Berlin blockade,
1948-1949

Stockholm

BALTIC SEA

SWEDEN
$

Copenhagen

East Berlin

West
Berlin

EAST
GERMANY

Prague

CZECHOSLOVAKIA

Vienna

AUSTRIA
$

Revolution, 1956

Left COMECON, 1961
Joined NATO, 1952
Withdrew from WP, 1968

U.S. 6th Fleet

NORWAY
$

Oslo

DENMARK
$

WEST
GERMANY
$

Bonn

SWITZ.
$

Bern

Joined NATO, 1955

Zones of occupation ended, 1955

ITALY
$

Rome

NORTH SEA

Amsterdam

NETHERLANDS

BELGIUM
$

LUX.
$

Brussels

U.S. loan of $3.5 billion, 1946
Exploded first atomic bomb, 1952
Joined Common Market, 1973

Joined Common
Market, 1973

London

GREAT
BRITAIN
$

Paris

FRANCE
$

MEDITERRANEAN SEA

Joined Common Market, 1973

Dublin

IRELAND
$

Reykjavik

ICELAND
$

ATLANTIC
OCEAN

Exploded first atomic bomb, 1960
Withdrew from NATO, 1966

Member of NATO,*
formed in 1949

Member of COMECON,** formed in
1949, and the Warsaw Pact,
organized in 1955

Member of the European
Common Market, formed in 1958

Participants in the Marshall Plan

$

Joined Common Market, 1986

Madrid

SPAIN

Joined NATO, 1982
Joined Common Market, 1986

PORTUGAL
$

Lisbon

*North Atlantic Treaty Organization
**Council for Mutual Economic Assistance

Western access to the jointly occupied city of Berlin, located well inside the Soviet zone. In response to this bold move, President Truman ordered a massive airlift of food, fuel, and other supplies to Berlin. Their spoiling effort blunted, the Soviets finally lifted the blockade in May 1949 and founded the German Democratic Republic, or East Germany.

The Berlin crisis also accelerated the movement toward a security pact. Convinced that a military shield should join the economic shield pro-

Creation of NATO

vided by the Marshall Plan, the United States, Canada, and many western European nations founded the North Atlantic Treaty Organization (NATO) in April 1949. The treaty aroused considerable domestic debate, for not since 1778 had the United States entered a formal European military alliance. Critics protested that NATO would provoke an accelerated arms race or war with the Soviet Union, cost too much, and empower the president to send troops into combat without a congressional declaration of war. Administration officials responded that, should the Soviets ever probe westward, NATO would function as a "tripwire," bringing the full force of the United States to bear on the Soviet Union. Truman officials also hoped that NATO would give Western Europeans the confidence to resist communism and neutralism. The Senate ratified the treaty, and the United States soon began to spend billions of dollars under the Mutual Defense Assistance Act.

In September 1949, the Soviets exploded an atomic bomb, breaking the American nuclear monopoly. Truman responded early the next year by ordering development of the hydrogen bomb.

Worried about Mao's victory in China and the Soviet acquisition of the atomic bomb, Truman asked his advisers to give him a comprehensive

NSC-68

study of world affairs. The National Security Council delivered to the president in April 1950 a significant top-secret document tagged NSC-68. Predicting continued tension with the Communists and describing "a shrinking world of polarized power," the report appealed for an enlarged military budget to counter an alleged Soviet ambition for global domination. Officials worried about how to sell this strong prescription to voters and budget-conscious members of Congress. "We were sweating over it, and then—with regard to NSC-68—thank God Korea came along," recalled one of Dean Acheson's aides.

CONFRONTATIONS IN ASIA: JAPAN, CHINA, AND THE KOREAN WAR

Asia too became ensnared in the Cold War. The victors in the Second World War dismantled Japan's empire. The United States and the Soviet Union

Reconstruction of Japan

divided Korea into competing spheres of influence. Pacific islands (the Marshalls, Marianas, and Carolines) came under American control and Formosa (Taiwan) was returned to the Chinese. As for Japan itself, the United States monopolized its reconstruction. General Douglas MacArthur, the director of the U.S. occupation, wrote a democratic constitution for Japan, revitalized its economy, and destroyed the nation's weapons. In 1951, despite Soviet protests, the United States and Japan signed a separate peace. The treaty restored Japan's sovereignty, ended the occupation, and granted the United States a military base on Okinawa and the right to station troops in Japan. Further expanding its global military network, Washington also initialed a defense pact with Tokyo.

Meanwhile, America's Chinese ally was faltering. The United States had long backed the Nationalists of Jiang Jieshi (Chiang Kai-shek) against

Chinese Civil War

Mao Zedong's and Zhou Enlai's Communists. But after the Second World War, Generalissimo Jiang became an unreliable partner who rejected U.S. advice. His government was corrupt, inefficient, and out of touch with the rebellious peasants, whom the Communists enlisted with promises of land redistribution. Jiang also subverted U.S. efforts to negotiate a cease-fire and a coalition government. Still, seeing Jiang as the only alternative to Mao, Truman backed him to the end.

On the question of whether Mao was a puppet of the Soviet Union, American officials were divided. Some considered him independent, but most believed him to be part of an international Communist movement that would give the Soviets a springboard into Asia. Acheson went so far as to claim that China's "Communist leaders have foresworn their Chinese heritage and have publicly announced their subservience to a foreign power." Thus, when the Chinese Communists made secret overtures to the United States to begin diplomatic talks in 1945 and again in 1949, American officials rebuffed them. Mao soon decided that he was "leaning to one side" in the Cold War—the Soviet side. But China always maintained a fierce independence that rankled the Soviets.

In the fall of 1949, Jiang fled to the island of Formosa and Mao proclaimed the People's Republic of China (PRC). For several reasons, the United

Nonrecognition of the People's Republic of China

States decided not to recognize the new government. American officials became alarmed by a Sino-Soviet treaty of friendship signed in early 1950, and Mao's followers had harassed Americans and seized American-owned property in China. Mao antagonized the United States by blaming it for prolonging the bloody civil war. Truman also chose nonrecognition because a vocal group of Republican critics, the so-called China lobby, was winning headlines by charging that the United States had "lost" China. The nonrecognition policy lasted well beyond the Truman era; not until 1979 did official Sino-American relations resume.

In the early morning hours of June 25, 1950, thousands of troops under the banner of the Democratic People's Republic of Korea (North

Outbreak of Korean War

Korea) moved across the thirty-eighth parallel into the Republic of Korea (South Korea). Since 1945, when the great powers divided Korea, the two halves had skirmished along the supposedly temporary border. Both regimes sought

reunification of their nation, but each on its own terms. Now it appeared that the North Koreans, heavily armed by the Soviets, would realize their goal by force.

For Truman, it was the 1930s all over again. "Communism was acting in Korea just as Hitler, Mussolini, and the Japanese had acted," he said. The president first ordered General MacArthur to send arms and troops to South Korea. Worried that Mao might attempt to take Formosa, Truman also directed the Seventh Fleet to patrol the waters between the Chinese mainland and Jiang's sanctuary on Formosa, thus inserting the United States once again into Chinese politics. After the U.N. Security Council voted to assist South Korea, MacArthur became commander of U.N. forces in Korea (90 percent of them American).

Although Truman acted decisively for war because he believed that the Soviets had masterminded the North Korean attack, unanswered

Who Started the War?

questions dog the thesis that Moscow started the Korean War. When the Security Council voted to defend South Korea, the Soviet representative was not present to veto the resolution, because the Soviets were then boycotting the United Nations to protest its refusal to seat the People's Republic of China as a member. And why did the Soviets give so little aid to the North Koreans once the war broke out? Why, when the Soviets were scoring important propaganda points by advocating peaceful coexistence, would they destroy their gains by igniting a war? Some scholars, emphasizing the Korean rather than international origins of the conflict, believe that the North Koreans began the war for their own nationalistic reasons.

The war went badly at first. Within weeks after the initial North Korean attack, the South Koreans and Americans found themselves pushed into

Inchon Landing

the tiny Pusan perimeter at the base of South Korea, where they dug in. Then, on September 15, 1950, MacArthur launched a highly successful amphibious landing at Inchon, several hundred miles behind North

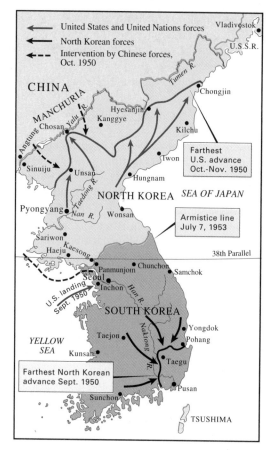

The Korean War, 1950–1953 *Beginning as a civil war between North and South Korea, the war became international when the United States, under the auspices of the United Nations, and the Peoples Republic of China intervened.* Source: Adapted from Paterson et al., *American Foreign Policy: A History*, vol. 2, 3rd ed. rev., © 1991, page 474. Reprinted by permission of D.C. Heath and Company.

Korean lines (see map). The American goal soon shifted from the containment of North Korea to the reunification of Korea by force.

Within several weeks, U.S. troops had driven deeply into North Korea, and in early November American aircraft began strikes against bridges on the Yalu River, the border between North Korea and China. Mao warned that China could not permit the bombing of its transportation links with Korea

Chinese Entry into the Korean War

or the annihilation of North Korea itself. Both MacArthur and officials in Washington shrugged off the warnings.

In late October, American troops had tangled with some Chinese soldiers, who pulled back quickly after the encounter. This may have been one of many Chinese signals to the United States that American advances to the Sino-Korean border should halt. Undeterred, the U.S. Eighth Army marched north in a new offensive. On November 26, tens of thousands of Chinese troops counterattacked, surprising American forces and driving them south. Embarrassed, MacArthur demanded that Washington order a massive air attack on China. Truman, reflecting on the costs and consequences of a wider war, rejected MacArthur's advice.

By early 1951, the military lines had stabilized around the thirty-eighth parallel. Both Washington and Moscow welcomed negotiations, but MacArthur had other ideas. The general recklessly called for an attack on China and for Jiang's return to the mainland. MacArthur also hinted that the president was practicing appeasement. On April 10, Truman fired MacArthur for insubordination.

Truman Fires MacArthur

MacArthur returned home to a hero's welcome and Truman's popularity sagged. The chairman of the Joint Chiefs of Staff, General Omar Bradley, spoke against MacArthur's provocative ideas. Bradley pointed out that escalation could bring the Soviet Union into battle. And it was unwise to exhaust America's resources in an Asian war that promised no victory when there were allies in Europe to be protected.

Armistice talks began in July 1951, but the fighting and dying went on for two more years. Dwight D. Eisenhower, elected president in 1952, went to Korea before his inauguration to fulfill a campaign pledge, but his visit brought no settlement. As president, Eisenhower let it be known that he was considering using atomic weapons in Korea. The most contentious point in the negotiations was the fate of prisoners of war (POWs): thousands of

The POW Question

North Korean and Chinese captives did not want to return home.

An armistice was finally signed in July 1953. The combatants agreed to hand over the POW question to a special panel of neutral nations (which later gave prisoners their choice of staying or leaving). The North Korean–South Korean line was set near the thirty-eighth parallel, the prewar boundary. Thus ended a frustrating war—a limited war that Americans, accustomed to victory, had not won. American casualties reached 34,000 dead in battle and another 103,000 wounded. Total killed and wounded for all combatants was 1.9 million.

The Korean War carried major political consequences. The failure to achieve victory and the public's impatience with a limited war undoubtedly helped to elect Eisenhower. The powers of the presidency grew. The president had never asked Congress for a declaration of war, believing that as commander in chief he had the authority to send troops wherever he wished.

The Korean War set off a great national debate. Conservative critics of globalism suggested that America should reduce its overseas commitments and draw its defense line in the Western Hemisphere. But Eisenhower's future secretary of state, John Foster Dulles, countered that "a defense that accepts encirclement quickly decomposes." The advocates of global defense won the debate, and the implementation of containment worldwide became entrenched as U.S. policy. Increased aid flowed to allies around the world, and defense budgets remained high. In sum, Truman's legacy was a highly militarized U.S. foreign policy active on a global scale.

Debate over Globalist Policy

EISENHOWER AND THE NUCLEAR ARMS RACE

As president, Dwight D. Eisenhower essentially perpetuated Truman's Cold War policies, applying the containment doctrine worldwide. He brought considerable experience in foreign affairs to his presidency. As a general during World War II, he had negotiated with world leaders. After the war, as Army Chief of Staff and NATO Supreme Commander, he learned the essentials of nuclear weapons development and secret intelligence operations. Like most Americans, Eisenhower accepted the Cold War consensus about the threat of communism and the need for global vigilance.

Eisenhower relied heavily on his trusted secretary of state, the strong-willed John Foster Dulles. Like the president, Dulles conceded much to the anti-Communist McCarthyites of the early 1950s. Dulles appointed one of McCarthy's henchmen, Scott McLeod, as chief security officer of the State Department. Making few distinctions between New Dealers and Communists, McLeod and Dulles forced many innocent talented officers out of the Foreign Service. Among them were Asian specialists whose expertise was thus denied to the American decision makers who later sent the United States to war in Vietnam.

State Department Purge

Dulles considered containment too defensive. He called instead for liberation, although he never explained precisely how the countries of Eastern Europe could be freed from Soviet control. "Massive retaliation" was the administration's phrase for the nuclear obliteration of the Soviet state or its assumed client, the People's Republic of China, if they took aggressive actions. Eisenhower said it "simply means the ability to blow hell out of them in a hurry if they start anything." The ability of the United States to make such a threat was thought to provide deterrence, or the prevention of hostile Soviet behavior.

In their "New Look" for the American military, Eisenhower and Dulles emphasized air power and nuclear weaponry. The president's preference for heavy weapons stemmed in part from his desire to trim the federal budget ("more bang for the buck," in the words of the time). With its huge military arsenal, the United States in the 1950s practiced brinkmanship, not backing down in a crisis, even if it meant taking the nation to the brink of war. Eisenhower also popularized the domino theory, according to which small weak nations would fall to communism like a row of dominoes if they were not propped up by the United States. Eisenhower increasingly ordered CIA covert operations against governments in the Third World, where new states were emerging from colonialism to nationhood. Americans feared that revolutionary nationalism and unrest in underdeveloped countries would threaten U.S. economic interests and also be exploited by Communists linked to a Soviet-led international conspiracy.

After Stalin's death in 1953, hopes ran high for a relaxation of Soviet-American relations. Instead, the nuclear arms race accelerated as the two superpowers developed new military technology and nuclear delivery systems. In November 1952, the United States detonated the first hydrogen bomb. Then, in early 1954, the largest bomb the United States has ever tested destroyed the Pacific island of Bikini. This H-bomb packed the power of 15 million tons of TNT (750 times as powerful as the atomic bomb that leveled Hiroshima).

Hydrogen Bomb

The Soviets tested their first H-bomb in 1953. Four years later, they fired the world's first intercontinental ballistic missile (ICBM) and then propelled the world's first man-made satellite, *Sputnik*, into outer space. Americans now felt more vulnerable to air attack and inferior to the Russians in rocket technology. The United States soon tested its own ICBMs. It also enlarged its fleet of long-range bombers (B-52s) and deployed intermediate-range missiles in Europe, targeted against the Soviet Union. By the end of 1960, the United States had added Polaris missile-bearing submarines to its navy. To foster future technological advancement, the National Aeronautics and Space Administration (NASA) was created in 1958.

Development of Missiles

The CIA's U-2 spy planes collected information demonstrating that the Soviets had deployed very few ICBMs. Yet critics charged that Eisenhower had allowed the United States to fall behind in the missile race. The "missile gap" was actually a false notion inspired in part by political partisanship. As the 1950s closed, the United States enjoyed overwhelming strategic dominance over the Soviet Union.

President Eisenhower had long been uneasy about the arms race. He feared nuclear war, and the cost of the new weapons made it difficult to balance the budget. He also doubted the need for more and bigger nuclear weapons. How many times, he once asked, "could [you] kill the same man?" Spurred by such thoughts and by neutralist and Soviet appeals, the president cautiously initiated arms-control proposals. But Eisenhower's distrust of the Soviets prevented arms control from becoming a top priority. In response to worldwide criticism of radioactive fallout, however, the two powers unilaterally suspended atmospheric testing from 1958 until 1961, when the Soviets resumed it. The United States began testing again at the same time but underground.

In 1956, Soviet Premier Nikita Khrushchev called for "peaceful coexistence" between capitalists and Communists, denounced Stalin, and suggested that Moscow would tolerate different brands of communism. Soon, however, events in Eastern Europe revived the customary acrimony of the Cold War. Revolts against Soviet power erupted in Poland and Hungary. After a new Hungarian government announced its withdrawal from the Warsaw Pact that the Soviets had formed in 1955, Soviet troops and tanks battled students and workers in the streets of Budapest and crushed the rebellion. The Eisenhower administration, on record as favoring the liberation of Eastern Europe, found itself unable to aid the rebels without igniting a world war. The United States could only welcome Hungarian immigrants in greater numbers than American quota laws allowed.

Hungarian Uprising

Hardly had the turmoil subsided in Eastern Europe when the divided city of Berlin once again became a Cold War flash point. The Soviets railed against the placement in West Germany of U.S. bombers capable of carrying nuclear warheads, and they complained that West Berlin had become an escape route for disaffected East Germans. In 1958, Khrushchev announced that the Soviet Union would recognize East German control of all of

Berlin unless the United States and its allies began talks on German reunification and rearmament. The United States refused to give up its hold on West Berlin or to break West German ties with NATO. The two sides talked of war; finally Khrushchev backed away from his ultimatum, promising to raise the issue at future conferences.

Berlin and Germany were on the agenda of a summit meeting planned for Paris in 1960. Shortly before the conference, an American U-2 spy plane crashed twelve hundred miles inside the Soviet Union. Moscow claimed credit for shooting down the aircraft and displayed the captured CIA pilot, Francis Gary Powers, and the pictures he had been snapping of Soviet military installations. Moscow demanded an apology, Washington refused, and the Soviets walked out of the Paris summit.

U-2 Incident

While sparring over Europe, both sides kept a wary eye on the People's Republic of China. Despite growing evidence of a Sino-Soviet split, most American officials still treated communism as a unified world movement. Washington continued to prop up Jiang on Formosa, which the Chinese claimed as part of the People's Republic, and to fret about China's encouragement of anti-imperialist rebellions in the Third World.

Dispute over two tiny islands off the Chinese coast brought the United States and the People's Republic to the brink of war. Jiang's forces used Jinmen (Quemoy) and Mazu (Matsu) as bases for commando raids against the mainland. China bombarded the islands in 1954. Eisenhower decided to defend the outposts and let it be known that he was considering the use of nuclear weapons. Why massive retaliation over such an insignificant issue? "Let's keep the Reds guessing," advised John Foster Dulles. But what if they guessed wrong? critics replied. Congress passed the Formosa Resolution (1955), authorizing the president to deploy U.S. forces to defend Formosa and adjoining islands, and two years later the United States installed on Formosa missiles capable of carrying nuclear warheads. War loomed again in 1958 over Jinmen and

Jinmen and Mazu

Mazu. The crisis passed, but one consequence was China's decision to develop nuclear weapons.

In eight years of adopting a globalist perspective and applying the containment doctrine worldwide, Eisenhower held the line—against the Soviet Union, Communist China, neutralism, communism, nationalism, and revolution everywhere. The Cold War tensions that Eisenhower had inherited and sustained, as well as an accelerated nuclear arms race, passed to his successor, John F. Kennedy.

KENNEDY, JOHNSON, AND THE CRISES OF THE 1960s

John F. Kennedy's diplomacy owed much to the past. He often invoked the tragedy of appeasement in the 1930s and the triumph of containment in the late 1940s. He vowed to rout communism in the 1960s. That there would be no halfway measures was apparent in Kennedy's inaugural address: "Let every nation know that we shall pay any price, bear any burden, meet any hardship, support any friend, oppose any foe to assure the survival and the success of liberty."

Kennedy as Cold War Activist

Khrushchev matched Kennedy's rhetoric with an endorsement of "wars of national liberation" in the Third World. Khrushchev also bragged about Soviet ICBMs, raising American anxiety over Soviet capabilities. Intelligence data soon demonstrated that there was no missile gap—except the one in America's favor. Kennedy nonetheless sought to fulfill his campaign commitment to a military build-up based on the principle of flexible response. Junking Eisenhower's concept of massive retaliation, Kennedy sought ways to meet any kind of warfare, from guerrilla combat to nuclear showdown. Thus the United States could contain both the Soviet Union and Third World revolutionary movements. In 1961, the military budget shot up 15 percent and ICBM arsenals swelled further. Although Kennedy could claim credit for the Limited Test Ban Treaty with the Soviet Union (1963), which banned nuclear testing in the atmosphere, in outer space, and under water, his real legacy was an accelerated arms race.

Once again, in 1961, the Soviets demanded negotiations to end Western occupation of West Berlin. Calling the city "the great testing place of Western courage and will,"

Berlin Wall
━━━━━

Kennedy rejected negotiations and asked Congress for an additional $3.2 billion for defense and the authority to call up reservists. Events took an ugly turn in August 1961, when the Soviets, upon the urging of the East German regime, erected a concrete-and-barbed-wire barricade designed to halt the exodus of East Germans to West Berlin. The Berlin Wall inspired protests throughout the non-Communist world. The crisis passed, but the wall remained.

U.S. hostilities with Cuba provoked Kennedy's most serious confrontation with the Soviet Union. Cold War and Third World issues dramatically intersected in Cuba. In early

**The Cuban
Revolution**
━━━━━

1959, Fidel Castro's rebels had ousted Fulgencio Batista, a long-time U.S. ally. From the start, Castro sought to break the economic power of U.S. business, which had invested some $1 billion on the island, to end U.S. domination of Cuban trade, and to expunge the gambling and prostitution that U.S. tourists supported. His increasing authoritarianism and anti-Yankee declarations alarmed Washington. In early 1960, after Cuba signed a trade treaty with the Soviet Union, Eisenhower ordered the CIA to organize an invasion force of Cuban exiles to overthrow the Castro government. The president also drastically cut U.S. purchases of Cuban sugar. Castro responded by seizing all North American–owned companies that had not yet been nationalized. Threatened by U.S. decisions designed to bring him and his revolution down, Castro appealed to the Soviet Union, which offered loans and expanded trade.

Just before leaving office, Eisenhower broke diplomatic relations with Cuba and advised Kennedy to advance plans for the invasion. Kennedy, who preferred victory over compromise, never attempted to negotiate Cuban-American troubles

Bay of Pigs
━━━━━

with Castro. He instead listened to the CIA, which sketched an appealing scenario: Cuban exiles would land at the Bay of Pigs and secure a beachhead, and the Cuban people would rise up against Castro and welcome a new U.S.-backed government. When the Bay of Pigs attack began in April 1961, however, the Cuban people did not rise up in sympathy with the invaders. Within two days, the poorly planned and poorly executed invasion collapsed.

Kennedy did not suffer defeat easily. He vowed to bring Castro down. As part of a plan called Operation Mongoose, government agents disrupted the island's trade, supported raids on Cuba from Miami, and plotted with organized crime bosses to assassinate Castro. The United States also tightened its economic blockade, engineered Cuba's eviction from the Organization of American States, and undertook military maneuvers that Castro read as preparations for another invasion.

Had there been no Bay of Pigs invasion, no Operation Mongoose, no assassination plots, and no program of diplomatic and economic isolation, there probably would have

**Cuban Missile
Crisis**
━━━━━

been no Cuban missile crisis. For Castro, the relentless U.S. hostility represented a real threat to Cuba's independence. For the Soviets, American actions challenged the only pro-Communist regime in Latin America. Premier Khrushchev also saw an opportunity to improve the Soviet position in the nuclear arms race. So Castro and Khrushchev devised a daring plan to deter any new U.S. intervention, especially an invasion: they agreed to install in Cuba nuclear-armed missiles capable of hitting the United States. The world soon faced a frightening episode of brinkmanship.

Although the Kennedy administration was aware of a military build-up on the island, it was not until October 1962 that a U-2 plane photographed sites for medium-range mis-

**Executive Com-
mittee Debate**
━━━━━

siles. Whether the Soviets had acted to protect Cuba, to improve their own nuclear capability, to trigger negotiations over Berlin, or to force the United States to pull its missiles out of Turkey remains debatable. In any

How do historians know

that at the outset of the Cuban missile crisis President John F. Kennedy insisted that the Soviet missiles had to be forced from Cuba, even at the risk of nuclear war? Long before the 1962 crisis, Kennedy had ordered the Secret Service to install a taping system throughout the White House. Listening devices were placed in meeting rooms and on telephones. Neither Secretary of State Dean Rusk (with the window behind him to Kennedy's right) nor Secretary of Defense Robert McNamara (with the flag behind him to Kennedy's left) knew that their remarks were being taped. Only a few members of the presidential staff knew about the secret system. Whether Kennedy wanted the tapes because he sought an accurate record for the memoirs he intended one day

to write or because he hoped to protect himself against public misrepresentations of what he said to others in private, he left historians a rich source. During the missile crisis of October 1962, he regularly convened and taped meetings of the advisory Executive Committee, shown gathered here. The John F. Kennedy presidential library in Boston has declassified and transcribed several tapes of that time and others, although many more remain to be opened to researchers. Because of such tapes (some of Kennedy's predecessors and successors also made recordings), historians can study the minute-by-minute, hour-by-hour handling of a crisis that brought the Soviet Union and the United States to the nuclear brink.

Photo: John F. Kennedy Presidential Library.

case, the president immediately organized the "Executive Committee" to find a way to force the removal of the missiles from Cuba. Some members advised a surprise air strike. The Joint Chiefs of

Staff recommended a full-scale military invasion, an option that risked a prolonged war with Cuba, a Soviet attack against West Berlin, or even nuclear holocaust. The Soviet expert Charles Bohlen unsuccessfully urged quiet direct negotiations with Soviet officials. Secretary of Defense Robert S. McNamara proposed the formula that the president found most acceptable: a naval quarantine of Cuba that left the administration free to attack or negotiate, depending on the Soviet response.

Kennedy addressed the nation on television on October 22 to demand that the Soviets retreat. U.S. warships began criss-crossing the Caribbean, while B-52s loaded with nuclear bombs took to the skies and U.S. military forces around the globe went on alert. Khrushchev replied that he would withdraw the missiles if Washington pledged never to attack Cuba. He then added that American Jupiter missiles, aimed at the Soviet Union, must be removed from Turkey. Kennedy accepted the first condition but rejected the second. On October 28, Khrushchev finally accepted the U.S. pledge to respect Cuban sovereignty. Soviet technicians began to dismantle the missiles for shipment back to the Soviet Union. Kennedy informally and privately promised to withdraw the Jupiters from Turkey and did so. This was, many said, Kennedy's finest hour.

But critics then and now have raised questions. Was the crisis really necessary? Why did the president attempt to solve the crisis with brinkmanship instead of private negotiations? Was Kennedy motivated by the forthcoming congressional elections? What if Castro, whom Khrushchev considered "an impetuous hothead," had decided to provoke war on his own? Finally, critics have argued that the strategic balance of power was not seriously altered by the placement of Soviet missiles in Cuba. Did Kennedy risk doomsday unnecessarily?

National Security Affairs Adviser McGeorge Bundy recalled that the crisis was in danger of "spinning out of control." Each day, the chances for error grew greater. The missiles were armed with warheads, and the Soviet commander in Cuba had the authority to fire them.

The Cuban missile crisis did produce some relaxation in Soviet-American relations. The adversaries signed a treaty banning nuclear tests in the atmosphere, and Washington and Moscow installed a teletype "hot line" staffed around the clock by translators and technicians. They also refrained from further confrontation in Berlin. In June 1963, Kennedy spoke at American University in conciliatory terms about Soviet-American relations, urging cautious steps toward disarmament. Some analysts predicted a thaw in the Cold War, but the assassination of President Kennedy left unresolved the question of whether he was shedding his cold warriorism.

President Lyndon B. Johnson shared the Cold War traditions of his predecessors. He saw the world in simple terms—them against us—and privately disparaged both his enemies and his allies. Johnson dismissed Vietnam as a "raggedy-ass fourth-rate country." Johnson often exaggerated and sometimes lied, creating what became known as a credibility gap. He also held firmly to fixed ideas about American superiority, the menace of communism, and the necessity of global intervention in the Cold War.

Johnson and the Cold War

Although Johnson improved Soviet-American relations somewhat by meeting with Soviet Premier Alexei Kosygin at Glassboro State College in New Jersey in 1967 and by pushing for a nonproliferation treaty to curb the spread of nuclear weapons (signed in 1968), the Cold War hardly relented. The Soviets—having vowed to catch up with the United States after the Cuban missile crisis—reached numerical parity with the United States by the end of the decade. The Soviets' invasion of Czechoslovakia in 1968 caused Johnson to shelve further arms-control talks. Meanwhile, Johnson had become preoccupied by the war in Southeast Asia. With the Soviet Union and the United States backing opposing forces in the Vietnam War, opportunities for relaxing the Cold War seemed to diminish.

NIXON, KISSINGER, AND DÉTENTE

Richard M. Nixon, Johnson's successor, had been an ardent cold warrior as a congressman, senator, and vice president, and few observers expected him to produce a thaw in the Cold War when he became president in 1969. Nixon's chief foreign-policy aide was the ambitious Henry A. Kissinger, a German-born political scientist teaching at Harvard. Kissinger served as Nixon's national security adviser until 1973, when he became secretary of state.

Together, Nixon and Kissinger pursued a grand strategy designed to promote a global balance of power, which they called equilibrium. The

The Pursuit of Détente
———

first part of the strategy was détente: measured cooperation with the Soviets through negotiations within a general environment of rivalry. Détente's primary purpose, like that of the containment doctrine it resembled, was to check Soviet expansion and limit the Soviet arms build-up. The second part of the strategy was curbing revolution and radicalism in the underdeveloped world so as to quash threats to U.S. interests.

Critics faulted the Nixon-Kissinger posture for its arrogant assumption that the United States had the ability and the right to manipulate a disorderly

SALT Talks
———

world. But Nixon and Kissinger pursued détente with extraordinary energy and fanfare. They expanded trade relations with the Soviet Union; a 1972 deal sent $1 billion-worth of American grain to the Soviets at bargain prices. To slow the costly arms race, they initiated the Strategic Arms Limitations Talks (SALT). In 1972, Soviet and American negotiators produced a SALT treaty that limited antiballistic missile (ABM) systems. (By making offensive missiles less vulnerable to attack, these defensive systems had accelerated the arms race, because both sides built more missiles to overcome the ABM protection.) A second agreement imposed a five-year freeze on the number of offensive nuclear missiles each side could possess. At the time of the agreement, the Soviets held an advantage in total missiles, but the United States had more warheads per missile because of its MIRVs (multiple independently targeted reentry vehicles). In short, the United States

had a two-to-one advantage in deliverable warheads. Because SALT did not restrict MIRVs, the nuclear arms build-up continued.

Nixon and Kissinger also cultivated détente with the People's Republic of China, ending almost three decades of Sino-American hostility. In 1972,

Opening to China
———

the president made a historic trip to China. The Chinese welcomed him, because they sought to improve trade and hoped that friendlier Sino-American relations would make their enemy, the Soviet Union, more cautious. Nixon reasoned the same way. Official diplomatic recognition and the exchange of ambassadors came in 1979.

Global economic issues bedeviled the Nixon-Kissinger grand design for world order. Kissinger explained that "international political stability

International Economic Instability
———

requires international economic stability." But in the 1970s, there was little economic stability. A severe global recession, high oil prices, and increased tariff rates affected national economies. And the debt-ridden developing nations of the Third World—sometimes called the "South"—insisted that the wealthier, industrial "North" share economic resources.

The United States could not escape these problems. It began to suffer a trade deficit—importing more goods than it exported (see figure). America's economic standing had declined since the Olympian days of the 1940s and 1950s as other nations, notably Japan and West Germany, recovered from wartime devastation and as underdeveloped countries gained more control over their raw materials. Americans nonetheless remained the richest people in the world. The United States produced about one-third of the world's goods and services. The U.S. economy also depended on imports of raw materials such as tin, manganese, and zinc. Such ties, as well as American investments abroad totaling more than $133 billion in the mid-1970s, explain in part why the United States welcomed détente as a means to calm international relations and protect the U.S. stake in the world economy.

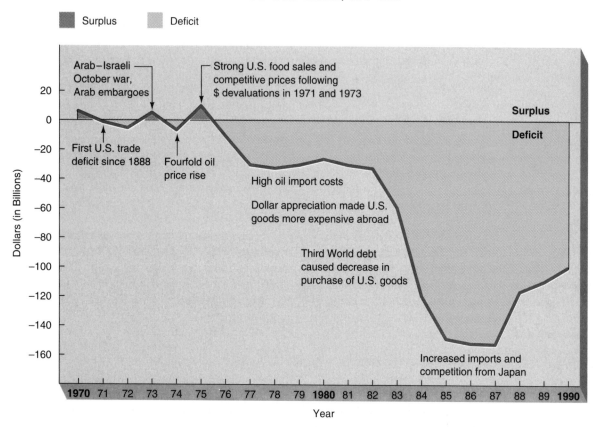

U.S. Trade Balance, 1970–1990   *Importing more than it exports, the United States has suffered trade deficits for years. Foreign political and economic crises and growing competition from Japanese products in the U.S. marketplace weakened the U.S. position in the world economy. Trade deficits must be financed by borrowing. One result has been a mounting U.S. external debt ($650 billion by 1989).*   Source: U.S. Department of State.

CARTER AND A REINVIGORATED COLD WAR

President Jimmy Carter promised fresh initiatives and diplomatic activism when he took office in 1977. He asked Americans to put their "inordinate fear of Communism" behind them. The old Cold War consensus had appeared fractured two years earlier when the Vietnam War finally ended, and Americans seemed uncertain about their nation's place in the world. Some wanted Carter to spare no expense to expand the military to face down U.S.

adversaries. Others wanted an end to bluster, reductions in the military, and less interventionism.

With reformist zeal, Carter set out to address long-range issues so as not to become trapped by a reactive foreign policy controlled by day-to-day

Carter's Foreign-Policy Goals

crises. The new president pledged to devote as much attention to North-South as to East-West issues, to reduce the American military presence overseas, to cut back arms sales, and to slow the nuclear arms race. He also promised preventive diplomacy: advancing the peace process in the Middle East, mediating conflict in the Third

World, and creating worldwide economic stability through agreements on the law of the sea, energy, and clean air and water. A deeply religious man, Carter said he intended to infuse international relations with moral force. "The soul of our foreign policy," he declared, would be the championing of individual human rights abroad—the freedom to vote, worship, travel, speak out, and get a fair trial.

Almost from the start, Carter spoke and acted inconsistently, and his advisers squabbled among themselves. One source of the problem was Zbigniew Brzezinski, Carter's Polish-born national security adviser. The stern-faced Brzezinski was an old-fashioned cold warrior who viewed foreign crises in globalist terms—that is, he blamed them on the Soviet Union. Carter gradually listened more to Brzezinski than to Secretary of State Cyrus Vance, an experienced, widely respected public servant who advocated quiet diplomacy to find avenues toward Soviet-American cooperation.

Under Carter, détente deteriorated and the Cold War deepened. The president first angered the Soviets by demanding that they respect their citizens' human rights and tolerate dissent. American officials then denounced the Soviets for sponsoring Cuban troops in Angola, where a leftist government was struggling against U.S.-backed rebels. Soviet leaders worried too that the United States was playing its "China card"—building up China in order to threaten the Soviet Union.

Despite this rocky start, a new treaty, SALT-II, codified Soviet-American nuclear parity in 1979. The agreement placed a ceiling of 2,250 delivery vehicles on each side. The So-

SALT-II

viet Union had to dismantle more than 250 existing delivery vehicles, whereas the United States was permitted to expand from its existing 2,060 to the new ceiling. The treaty did not affect nuclear warheads, which stood at 9,200 for the United States and 5,000 for the Soviet Union. Critics on the right charged that verification of compliance was difficult; critics on the left protested that the treaty did not go far enough to quell the arms race. Carter tried to win votes from skeptical conservatives by announcing an expensive military expansion program and deployment of Pershing II missiles and cruise missiles in the NATO nations of Western Europe.

As Senate ratification of SALT-II stalled and Moscow fumed over the Pershings, events in Afghanistan led to Soviet-American confrontation. In late 1979, the Red Army bludgeoned its way into Afghanistan to shore up a faltering Communist government under siege by Muslim rebels. An embittered Carter shelved SALT-II (the two powers nonetheless unilaterally honored its terms later), suspended shipments of grain and high-technology equipment to the Soviet Union, and initiated an international boycott of the 1980 Summer Olympics in Moscow. The president also announced the Carter Doctrine: the United States would intervene, unilaterally and militarily if necessary, against Soviet aggression in the petroleum-rich Persian Gulf. But all of Carter's efforts proved fruitless: the Soviets refused to withdraw their forces from Afghanistan.

Carter lost the 1980 presidential election to Ronald Reagan, not because the Cold War had become more frigid but because the Iranian hostage crisis had paralyzed the administration and because Carter seemed to have contradicted many of his own goals. As Chapter 31 shows, Carter enjoyed some diplomatic successes in the Middle East, Africa, and Latin America. But his legacy also included a revived Cold War.

REAGAN, DEVIL THEORY, AND MILITARY EXPANSION

Ronald Reagan assumed the presidency in 1981 with no experience in foreign relations and no firm grasp of international issues, history, or geography. Reagan and the conservatives around him believed in a devil theory: that a malevolent Soviet Union—Reagan branded it the "evil empire"—was the source of the world's troubles. Charging that the Soviets were prepared "to commit any crime" to achieve a Communist world, the president attributed Third World disorders to Soviet intrigue. He rejected arguments that the civil wars in Central America derived from deep-seated economic instability, poverty, and class oppression.

Reagan asserted that a substantial military build-up would thwart the Soviet threat and intimidate Moscow into negotiating on terms favorable to the United States. He sponsored multitrillion-dollar defense spending and an antimissile defense system in space he called the Strategic Defense Initiative (SDI), which critics soon dubbed Star Wars. As the veteran diplomat George Ball observed when U.S. forces overthrew a leftist pro-Cuban government on the tiny Caribbean island of Grenada in 1983, once again "we shiver in the icy winds of the Cold War."

Reagan Emphasis on Military Expansion

To gain public support for a more interventionist, militarized foreign policy, Reagan used his exceptional communicating skills to stimulate emotional patriotism. Most Americans shared Reagan's feeling that the nation had been ignobly retreating from global leadership. He made Americans feel good about themselves and their place in the world. Reagan also argued that the United States could win the Cold War by pressing other nations to embrace capitalism.

The Reagan Doctrine also drove U.S. foreign policy. The term derived from the president's declaration in 1985 that the United States would openly support anti-Communist movements wherever they were battling the Soviets or Soviet-backed governments. Under this doctrine, the CIA funneled aid to insurgents in Afghanistan, Nicaragua, Angola, and Ethiopia. In open defiance of the sovereignty of these nations, Reagan vowed the overthrow of governments deemed hostile to the interests of the United States.

Reagan Doctrine

In this atmosphere, Soviet-American relations became "white hot, thoroughly white hot," in the words of a Soviet leader. Actually, Reagan's first decision affecting the Soviets was friendly: fulfilling a campaign pledge to help American farmers, he lifted Carter's grain embargo and sold the Soviet Union grain worth $3 billion. But the decision was followed by hostility when the Soviets cracked down on the Solidarity labor movement in Poland. In response, Washington placed restrictions on Soviet-American trade and hurled angry words at Moscow. In 1983, Reagan restricted commercial flights to the Soviet Union after a Soviet fighter pilot mistakenly shot down a South Korean commercial jet that had strayed some three hundred miles off-course into Soviet air space.

Reagan's expansion of the military, his careless utterances about winning a limited nuclear war, and his quest for nuclear supremacy stimulated worldwide debate. In 1981, hundreds of thousands of marchers in London, Rome, Bonn, and other European cities demanded Soviet-American negotiations to prevent a nuclear holocaust. The next year, a million people marched through New York City to support a nuclear arms freeze, and in 1983 the U.S. Roman Catholic bishops condemned nuclear weapons as immoral.

Debate over Nuclear Weapons

Responding to public opinion and pressure from NATO allies, and believing that reinvigorated military power had created a strong U.S. bargaining position, Reagan officials in 1981 began talks with the Soviets on limiting intermediate-range nuclear forces (INF) based in Europe. The Soviets had SS-20 missiles targeted at Western Europe, and the United States had cruise missiles and Pershing-IIs aimed at the Soviet Union. A year later, Reagan substituted the Strategic Arms Reduction Talks (START) for the inactive SALT talks. At a 1985 Geneva summit meeting, Reagan and the new Soviet leader Mikhail S. Gorbachev agreed in principle that strategic weapons should be substantially reduced. But summit meetings in subsequent years failed to produce a treaty. The sticking point was SDI. Gorbachev insisted that the United States shelve SDI, but Reagan persisted in pushing it, despite widespread scientific opinion that it would cost billions of dollars and never work.

Near the end of Reagan's presidency, Soviet-American relations markedly improved. The turnaround stemmed more from changes abroad than from Reagan's decisions. Under Gorbachev, a younger generation of Soviet leaders came to power in 1985. They were

Mikhail S. Gorbachev

"CONGRATULATIONS.... YOU WON THE COLD WAR!"

The cartoonist Jim Borgman captured the complexity of what many interpreted as a simple matter: U.S. victory in the Cold War. Borgman reminded his readers that the Cold War had cost the United States a great deal—neglect of its domestic problems, including economic malaise, deteriorating infrastructure, unemployment, and millions of people defined by the U.S. government as poor and homeless. Given the domestic crisis, some analysts argue, it is difficult to claim that either side won the Cold War. Jim Borgman for the *Cincinnati Enquirer.* Reprinted with special permission of King Features Syndicate.

determined to restructure and modernize the highly bureaucratized, decaying economy (*perestroika*) and to liberalize the suffocatingly authoritarian political system (*glasnost*). These new Soviet officials understood that a reduction in military spending made possible by reduced international tensions would free up resources for their reform efforts. In 1987, Gorbachev and Reagan signed a treaty banning all land-based intermediate-range missiles in Europe (totaling twenty-eight hundred). Gorbachev's 1989 decision to remove the remaining Soviet troops from Afghanistan also eased tensions. To reduce the chances that nuclear war could start by accident, Soviet and American officials established in their capitals Nuclear Risk

Reduction Centers with direct hookups operated around the clock.

Reagan had at first judged Gorbachev to be another untrustworthy Kremlin ideologue, but the president warmed to "Gorby" and toned down his strident anti-Soviet rhetoric in the late 1980s. Other American conservatives remained suspicious that Gorbachev might be hoodwinking Americans. Reagan's vice president and successor, George Bush, warned that "the Cold War isn't over." Dramatic events in the Soviet Union, Germany, and Eastern Europe, however, soon persuaded most Americans that the Cold War was winding down, including a skeptical President George Bush, who seemed a bystander to the events sweeping Europe.

THE END OF THE COLD WAR

Mikhail Gorbachev had set loose cascading changes in his own country, but he had also encouraged the people of East Germany and Eastern Europe to go their own ways. No longer would Moscow prop up unpopular Communist regimes. In 1989, East Germans startled the world by repudiating their Communist government, and in November joyful Germans scaled the Berlin Wall to dance atop it and then tear it down, opening East to West. The next year, the two Germanys reunited and veteran Communist oligarchs fell—in Poland, Hungary, Czechoslovakia, and Rumania. Bulgaria and Albania soon held elections.

Collapse of Communism in Eastern Europe

Meanwhile, the Union of Soviet Socialist Republics was unraveling. In 1990, the Baltic states of Lithuania, Latvia, and Estonia declared independence. The following year, after Gorbachev himself denounced communism, the Soviet Union disintegrated into independent successor states—Russia, Ukraine, and many others. With no government to lead, and muscled aside by reformers who thought he was moving too slowly toward democracy and free-market economics, Gorbachev lost power.

The break-up of the Soviet empire, the dismantling of the Warsaw Pact, the repudiation of communism by its own leaders, the shattering of the myth of monolithic communism, the reunification of Germany, and the significant reduction in the risk of nuclear war signaled the end of the Cold War.

Why the Cold War Ended

The Cold War ended because of the relative decline of the United States and the Soviet Union in the international system from the 1950s through the 1980s—the contest had undermined the power of its two major protagonists. They moved gradually toward a cautious cooperation; its urgent goals were the restoration of both powers' economic well-being and the preservation of their diminishing global positions.

Four influential trends explain the gradual decline and the resulting attractions of détente. First was the burgeoning economic cost of the Cold War—trillions of dollars spent on weapons and interventions rather than on improving domestic infrastructures. Foreign ventures starved domestic programs and strained budgets. Second, challenges to the two major powers from within their own spheres of influence also help explain why the United States and the Soviet Union welcomed détente. Cuba's revolution and France's withdrawal from NATO in the 1960s are but two pieces of evidence that the United States was losing power. The Hungarian and Czech revolutions and the Sino-Soviet rift undercut the Soviet Union's hegemony within its network of allies. Détente seemed to offer a means to restore superpower management of unruly states.

Third, the Cold War ended because of the emergence of the Third World, which introduced new players into the international game, further diffused power, and eroded bipolarism (see Chapter 31). Soviet-American détente represented a means to deal with the volatile Third World, a fulcrum by which to apply leverage to those nations. Finally, the worldwide antinuclear movement of the 1980s pressed leaders, especially in Western Europe, to seek détente—to persuade Washington and Moscow to stop the arms race.

By the early 1990s, the world had experienced the functional equivalent of a third world war: the two major Cold War combatants had not fought to the death, but the international system had been fundamentally transformed. An empire collapsed, boundaries were redrawn, and the Communist ideology was discredited. All three worlds were breaking up. The First World, or capitalist world, was subdividing into trading blocs and rivals—North America (evidenced by the 1988 U.S.-Canada Free Trade Agreement), Japan, and Europe's Economic Community, or Union. The Second World of communism was disintegrating. The Third World too was fragmenting, into newly industrializing countries, oil-rich nations, and yet a Fourth World—the poorest of nations. The Cold War had no winners. Both sides—and all the peoples of the world—paid an enormous price for waging the Cold War. At best, the United States had merely outlasted the Soviet Union.

The legacy of the Cold War cast a long shadow. For the United States, long-neglected domestic needs begged for attention and resources. A large arms industry had secured a firm hold on the American economy, and a massive military establishment had tenaciously built a base of power within the American system. The power of the presidency had expanded greatly at the expense of the checks-and-balances system; presidents launched covert operations, dispatched troops, and ordered invasions while barely consulting Congress. The Cold War also bequeathed a record of government secrecy, political extremism, cover-ups, lies, and scandals that made many Americans feel either cynical about their government and the political process or helpless to influence their leaders.

Throughout the world, the two great powers had intervened in civil wars, transforming local class, racial, religious, and economic conflicts into Cold War contests. Given these conflicts, millions would probably have died whether there had been a Cold War or not, but millions more surely died because of it. After some forty years, although the world had been spared nuclear war, the list of nuclear nations grew. The Cold War had ended, but its consequences ensured continued international disorder.

SUGGESTIONS FOR FURTHER READING

For U.S. relations with the Third World since 1945, see Chapters 31 and 34. For George Bush's foreign policy, see Chapter 34.

The Cold War: General and Origins

Stephen Ambrose, *Rise to Globalism*, 5th ed. (1988); John Lewis Gaddis, *Russia, the Soviet Union, and the United States*, 2d ed. (1990), *The Long Peace* (1987), and *Strategies of Containment* (1982); Francis Harbutt, *The Iron Curtain* (1986); Robert C. Hilderbrand, *Dumbarton Oaks* (1990) (on United Nations); Walter Isaacson and Evan Thomas, *The Wise Men* (1986); Robert C. Johansen, *The National Interest and the Human Interest* (1980); Paul Kennedy, *The Rise and Fall of the Great Powers* (1988); Walter LaFeber, *America, Russia, and the Cold War, 1945–1990*, 6th ed. (1991); Melvyn Leffler, *A Preponderance of Power* (1992); Thomas McCormick, *America's Half-Century* (1989); Thomas

G. Paterson, *On Every Front* (1992), and *Meeting the Communist Threat* (1988); Michael Schaller, *The American Occupation of Japan* (1985); William Taubman, *Stalin's American Policy* (1982).

Early Containment in Europe: Truman Doctrine, Marshall Plan, and NATO

Walter Hixson, *George F. Kennan* (1990); Michael Hogan, *The Marshall Plan* (1987); Lawrence S. Kaplan, *The United States and NATO* (1984); Alan Milward, *The Reconstruction of Western Europe* (1984); Wilson D. Miscamble, *George F. Kennan and the Making of American Foreign Policy, 1947–1950* (1992); Mark A. Stoler, *George C. Marshall* (1989); Imanuel Wexler, *The Marshall Plan Revisited* (1983); Lawrence S. Wittner, *American Intervention in Greece, 1943–1949* (1982).

Nuclear Arms Race

Howard Ball, *Justice Downwind: America's Nuclear Testing Program in the 1950s* (1986); Paul Boyer, *By the Bomb's Early Light* (1986); McGeorge Bundy, *Danger and Survival* (1988); Lawrence Freedman, *The Evolution of Nuclear Strategy* (1981); Gregg Herken, *Counsels of War* (1985), and *The Winning Weapon* (1981); Richard G. Hewlett and Jack M. Hall, *Atoms for Peace and War, 1953–1961* (1989); Fred Kaplan, *The Wizards of Armageddon* (1983); John Newhouse, *War and Peace in the Nuclear Age* (1989); Martin Sherwin, *A World Destroyed* (1975); Strobe Talbott, *The Master of the Game: Paul Nitze and the Nuclear Peace* (1988), *Deadly Gambit* (1984) (on Reagan), and *Endgame* (1979) (SALT-II); Marc Trachtenberg, *History and Strategy* (1991); Spencer Weart, *Nuclear Fear* (1988).

America and the People's Republic of China

Gordon Chang, *Friends and Enemies* (1990); Warren I. Cohen, *America's Response to China*, 3d ed. (1990); Robert P. Newman, *Owen Lattimore and the "Loss" of China* (1992); William W. Stueck Jr., *The Road to Confrontation* (1981); Nancy B. Tucker, *Patterns in the Dust* (1983); Shu Guang Zhang, *Deterrence and Strategic Culture: Chinese-American Confrontations, 1949–1958* (1993).

The Korean War

Clay Blair, *The Forgotten War* (1988); Bruce Cumings, *The Origins of the Korean War*, 2 vols. (1980, 1991); Rosemary Foot, *A Substitute for Victory* (1990), and *The Wrong War* (1985); John Halliday and Bruce Cumings, *Korea: The Unknown War* (1989); Burton I. Kaufman, *The Korean War* (1986); Peter Lowe, *The Origins of the Korean War* (1986); Callum A. MacDonald, *Korea* (1987).

Eisenhower-Dulles Foreign Policy

Stephen E. Ambrose, *Eisenhower*, 2 vols. (1982, 1984); Robert A. Divine, *Eisenhower and the Cold War* (1981); Fred Greenstein, *The Hidden-Hand Presidency* (1982); Townsend Hoopes, *The Devil and John Foster Dulles* (1973); Richard Immerman, ed., *John Foster Dulles* (1990).

Foreign Relations under Kennedy and Johnson

Michael Beschloss, *The Crisis Years: Kennedy and Khrushchev, 1960–1963* (1991); Philip Geyelin, *Lyndon B. Johnson and the World* (1966); James N. Giglio, *The Presidency of John F. Kennedy* (1991); David Halberstam, *The Best and the Brightest* (1972); Doris Kearns, *Lyndon Johnson and the American Dream* (1976); Herbert S. Parmet, *JFK* (1983); Thomas G. Paterson, ed., *Kennedy's Quest for Victory* (1989); Arthur M. Schlesinger Jr., *Robert Kennedy and His Times* (1978); Thomas J. Schoenbaum, *Waging Peace and War* (1988).

Cuba and the Missile Crisis

Graham Allison, *Essence of Decision* (1971); James G. Blight and David A. Welch, *On the Brink* (1989); Dino Brugioni, *Eyeball to Eyeball* (1991); Trumbull Higgins, *The Perfect Failure* (1987) (on the Bay of Pigs); Morris Morley, *Imperial State and Revolution* (1987); James Nathan, ed., *The Cuban Missile Crisis Revisited* (1992); Thomas G. Paterson, *Contesting Castro* (1994); Louis A. Pérez Jr., *Cuba and the United States* (1990); Tad Szulc, *Fidel* (1986).

Nixon, Kissinger, and Détente

Stephen Ambrose, *Nixon* (1987); Raymond L. Garthoff, *Détente and Confrontation* (1985); John R. Greene, *The Limits of Power* (1992); Seymour Hersh, *The Price of Power* (1983); Walter Isaacson, *Kissinger* (1992); Herbert S. Parmet, *Richard Nixon and His America* (1990); Robert D. Schulzinger, *Henry Kissinger* (1989).

The United States in the World Economy and Environment

Richard J. Barnet, *The Lean Years* (1980); Richard J. Barnet and Ronald Müller, *Global Reach:* (1974); David P. Calleo, *The Impe-* *rious Economy* (1982); Alfred E. Eckes, *The U.S. and Global Struggle for Minerals* (1979); Stephen D. Krasner, *Defending the National Interest* (1978); John McCormick, *Reclaiming Paradise: The Global Environmental Movement* (1989); Robert K. Olson, *U.S. Foreign Policy and the New International Economic Order* (1981); Herman Van Der Wee, *The Search for Prosperity: The World Economy, 1945–1980* (1986).

Carter Foreign Policy and Human Rights

Erwin C. Hargrove, *Jimmy Carter as President* (1988); Ole R. Holsti and James N. Rosenau, *American Leadership in World Affairs: Vietnam and the Breakdown of Consensus* (1984); Burton I. Kaufman, *The Presidency of James Earl Carter* (1993); David S. McLellan, *Cyrus Vance* (1985); A. Glenn Mower Jr., *Human Rights and American Foreign Policy* (1987); Kenneth A. Oye et al., *Eagle Entangled* (1979); Gaddis Smith, *Morality, Reason, and Power* (1986).

Reagan, Bush, and the End of the Cold War

Michael R. Beschloss and Strobe Talbott, *At the Highest Levels* (1993); Lou Cannon, *President Reagan* (1991); Robert Dallek, *Ronald Reagan* (1984); John Lewis Gaddis, *The United States and the End of the Cold War* (1992); Michael Hogan, ed., *The End of the Cold War* (1992); Haynes Johnson, *Sleepwalking Through History* (1991); Robert G. Kaiser, *Why Gorbachev Happened* (1991); David E. Kyvig, ed., *Reagan and the World* (1990); Michael McGwire, *Perestroika and Soviet National Security* (1991); Don Oberdorfer, *The Turn* (1991); Kenneth A. Oye et al., eds., *Eagle Resurgent?* (1987); David Remnick, *Lenin's Tomb* (1993); Michael Schaller, *The Reagan Years* (1992). For other works on the Bush foreign policy, see Chapter 34.

30

American Society During the Postwar Boom, 1945–1970

ONE OF THE FIRST things Staff Sergeant Samuel Goldenberg did when he returned from World War II was to make love to his wife Eve. One of her first questions was whether he had been unfaithful. Sam told her that only one man in his entire unit "didn't fool around." When Sam came home to Eve and the daughter who had been born during his absence, he had one overriding goal: to build a happy life for his family.

Two more daughters and a son were born to Sam and Eve Goldenberg over the next few years, contributing to the postwar baby boom. Sam worked hard as an electrician, commuting daily from the Bronx to Manhattan. He was determined to succeed, so his children could grow up in grassy suburban yards and attend good public schools. For business reasons, he changed his name to Gordon. In 1952, the family bought a car and moved to a new suburb on the south shore of Long Island. Sam was the first member of his family to own either a house or a car. For the Gordons, the American Dream was coming true. As part of the American dream of the 1950s, Eve was a homemaker. She devoted herself to her family and did

volunteer work for a theater group and the Jewish Center Sisterhood.

Ensconced in their suburban home, Sam and Eve Gordon were unprepared for the cultural turmoil of the 1960s. In 1964, their seventeen-year-old daughter Lorraine told them she was pregnant and was leaving home to marry her boyfriend and live in a squalid walk-up on the Lower East Side of New York City. Lorraine's choice of poverty seemed to mock their own aspirations for middle-class comfort and respectability. All four Gordon children joined the "hippie" counterculture and participated in sit-ins opposing the Vietnam War. And their son told them he was gay. The Gordon children were consumers like their parents, but their favorite products were drugs and rock 'n' roll.

Material comfort was the hallmark of the postwar middle classes. In terms of both income level and lifestyle, more Americans were better off than ever before—and most expected their good fortune to continue. The most obvious expression of postwar optimism was the baby boom. From 1946 through 1964, births hit record highs.

During this period, seventy-six million babies were born in the United States, compared with only forty-four million during the period of depression and war from 1929 through 1945.

Beginning with its size, this generation of newborns was different. During their childhoods, "family togetherness" took on almost religious significance. And as this vast age group grew older, it had successive influences on housing, elementary and secondary education, fads and popular music, higher education, and the adult job market.

Although the baby boom began to taper off in 1964, the economic boom lasted until 1970. The cornerstones of the twenty-five-year economic boom that began in 1946 were the automobile, construction, and defense industries. Although the nation's economic progress was disrupted four times by recessions (1950, 1953–1954, 1957–1958, 1960–1961), most Americans enjoyed an increasingly comfortable standard of living. And whatever the nation's shortcomings, Americans heralded it as the world's foremost land of opportunity. They boasted of their political self-determination and social mobility. And public education guaranteed a better life to all who were willing to study and work hard.

Most Americans did not notice the exceptions to the American Dream. An emphasis on femininity, piety, and family togetherness concealed the lack of equal opportunities for women. The affluent ignored evidence of poverty. Yet it became clear by the early 1960s that the American poor were much more numerous than people in the complacent 1950s had imagined: one in every four Americans was poor in the early 1960s.

During the late 1960s, the twenty-five-year economic boom slowed, and by 1970 it was over. But between 1945 and 1970, booms in business and babies had transformed the economic, social, and cultural life of the American people.

THE POSTWAR BOOMS: BUSINESS AND BABIES

When the postwar era began, many Americans wondered whether it would resemble the most recent postwar epoch, the Roaring Twenties. Most Americans, however, expected a replay of the 1930s—not the 1920s. After all, it was the war that had created jobs and prosperity; surely the end of war would bring a slump.

Neither prediction was correct: in 1945, the United States entered one of its longest, steadiest periods of growth and prosperity, the keys to which were increasing production and increasing demand. Between 1945 and 1970, the American economy grew at an average annual rate of 3.5 percent. Despite occasional recessions, the gross national product seldom faltered, rising from just under $210 billion in 1946 to almost $1 trillion in 1970.

When the economy produced more, Americans generally brought home bigger paychecks and had more money to spend. Between 1946 and 1950, per capita real income (based on actual purchasing power) rose 6 percent—but that was only the beginning. In the 1950s, it jumped another 15 percent; in the 1960s, the increase was even greater—32 percent. The result was a noticeable increase in the standard of living. To the vast majority of Americans, such prosperity was a vindication of the American system of free enterprise.

Increased Purchasing Power

The baby boom was both a cause and an effect of prosperity. It was natural for the birthrate to soar immediately following a war; what was unusual was that it continued to do so throughout the 1950s (see figure). During the 1950s, the annual total exceeded four million, reversing the downward trend in birthrates that had prevailed for 150 years. Births began to decline after 1961 but continued to exceed four million per year through 1964. The baby boom generation was the largest by far in the nation's history.

Baby Boom

The baby boom meant business for builders, manufacturers, and school systems. "Take the 3,548,000 babies born in 1950," wrote Sylvia F. Porter in her syndicated newspaper column. "Bundle them into a batch, bounce them all over the bountiful land that is America. What do you get?"

• *Important Events* •

1946	Baby boom begins Spock's *Baby and Child Care* changes child-rearing practices More than one million GIs enroll in colleges		Ginsberg's poem *Howl* published, symbolizing the Beat generation Elvis Presley releases first single
1947	Gross national product ($231.3 billion) begins postwar rise	**1957**	Baby boom peaks (4.3 million births) Soviet Union launches *Sputnik* Kerouac criticizes white middle-class conformity in *On the Road*
1948	Kinsey's *Sexual Behavior in the Human Male* sparks controversy	**1958**	National Defense Education Act emphasizes math, science, and language education Galbraith's *The Affluent Society* published
1952	Ellison's *Invisible Man* shows African-Americans' exclusion from the American Dream	**1960**	Gross national product reaches $503.7 billion
1953	Kinsey causes a public uproar with *Sexual Behavior in the Human Female*	**1962**	Harrington's *The Other America* creates awareness of America's poor Carson's *Silent Spring* warns of dangers of DDT
1955	Salk polio vaccine approved for use AFL and CIO merge *Rebel Without a Cause* idealizes youth subculture	**1970**	Gross national product reaches $977.1 billion Suburbs surpass central cities in population
1956	Highway Act launches national network of highways		

Porter's answer: "Boom. The biggest, boomiest boom ever known in history. Just imagine how much these extra people, these new markets, will absorb—in food, clothing, in gadgets, in housing, in services. Our factories must expand just to keep pace."

Of the three cornerstones of the postwar economic boom (construction, automobiles, and defense), two were directly related to the upsurge in births. Demand for housing

Housing and Auto Sales

and schools for all these children generated a building boom, furthered by construction of office buildings, shopping centers, factories, airports, and stadiums. Much of the construction took place in suburbs. The postwar suburbanization of America would in turn have been impossible without automobile manufacturing, for in the sprawling new communities a car was a necessity.

The third cornerstone of the postwar economic boom was military spending. When the Defense Department was established in 1947, the

Military Spending

nation was spending just over $10 billion a year on defense. By 1953, it was more than $50 billion; in 1970, it exceeded $80 billion. Defense contracts also went to industries and universities to develop weapons. The government also supported space research; funds spent on space research alone zoomed from $76 million in 1957 to almost $6 billion in 1966.

Defense spending helped stimulate rapid advances in the electronics industry. The ENIAC computer, completed at the University of Pennsylvania in 1946, weighed 30 tons, required 18,000 vacuum tubes, and worked 1,000 times as quickly as its wartime predecessor, the Mark I. The introduction of the transistor in the 1950s accelerated the computer revolution; the silicon microchip in the 1960s inaugurated even more stunning advances in electronics.

The microchip facilitated the shift from heavy manufacturing to "high-tech" industries in fiber optics, lasers, video equipment, robotics, and

Birthrate, 1940–1970

Birthrate, 1940–1970 *The birthrate began to rise in 1942 and 1943, but it skyrocketed during the postwar years beginning in 1946. Reaching its peak in 1957, the birthrate thereafter subsided throughout the 1960s.*   Source: Adapted from U.S. Bureau of the Census, *Historical Statistics of the United States, Colonial Times to 1970,* Bicentennial Edition (Washington, D.C.: U.S. Government Printing Office, p. 49).

The Computer Revolution
———

genetic engineering. Sales of office and business equipment reflected the growth in technology-based production. In 1965, almost $3 billion-worth of computing equipment was sold; by 1970, the figure had almost doubled to $5.7 billion. And this was just the beginning.

The evolution of electronics meant a large-scale trade-off for the American people. As industries automated, computerized processes replaced slower mechanical ones, generating a rapid rise in productivity. But in doing so, they brought about technological unemployment. Electronic technology also

promoted concentration of ownership in industry. Sophisticated technology was expensive. Typically, only large corporations could afford it; small corporations were shut out of the market. Indeed, large corporations with capital and experience in high-technology fields expanded into related industries.

Another kind of corporate expansion also marked the early 1950s as the third great wave of mergers swept across American business. Unlike

Conglomerate Mergers
———

the first two such movements in the 1890s and 1920s, which had tended toward vertical and horizontal integration, respectively, this era was distinguished by conglomerate mergers. A conglomerate merges companies in unrelated industries as a hedge against instability in a particular market. The new wave of mergers resulted in unprecedented concentration of industry: the two hundred largest manufacturing corporations held the same proportion of total manufacturing assets in 1968 as had the thousand largest in 1941.

The labor movement also experienced a postwar merger. In 1955, the American Federation of Labor and the Congress of Industrial Organizations finally put aside their differences and formed the AFL-CIO. Union membership remained fairly constant, increasing from just around 18 million at the time of the merger to only 20.7 million in 1970. The main reason for the slow growth of union membership was a shift in employment patterns. Most new jobs were being created not in the heavy industries that hired blue-collar workers but in the union-resistant white-collar service trades.

The postwar economic boom was good for unionized blue-collar workers, many of whom won real increases in wages, sufficient to enjoy a middle-class lifestyle that previously had been the exclusive province of white-collar workers, businesspeople, and professionals. Union workers could qualify for mortgages for suburban homes, especially if their spouses also worked. Many enjoyed job security, paid vacations, and retirement plans. And they were more protected against inflation: in 1948, General Motors and the United Auto Workers agreed on automatic cost-of-living adjustments (COLAs) in workers' wages, a practice that spread to other industries.

Union Workers' Benefits

The trend toward economic consolidation also changed agriculture. New machines, such as mechanical cotton-, tobacco-, and grape-pickers and crop-dusting planes revolutionized farming methods, and the increased use of fertilizers and pesticides raised the total value of farm output from $29 billion in 1946 to (in constant dollars) $54 billion in 1970. Meanwhile, labor productivity tripled. The resulting improvement in profitability drew large investors into agriculture. By the 1960s, it took money—sometimes big money—to become a farmer. In many regions, only banks, insurance companies, and large businesses could afford the necessary land, machinery, and fertilizer.

The movement toward consolidation threatened the survival of the family farm. From 1946 to 1970, the nation's farm population declined from about twenty-four million to just under ten million—from 18 percent of the population to just 5 percent. When the harvesting of cotton in the South was mechanized in the 1940s and 1950s, for example, more than four million people were displaced. One result was that many of the displaced farmers traded southern rural poverty for northern urban poverty.

Decline of the Family Farm

Economic growth also exacted environmental costs, to which most Americans were oblivious. All aspects of the environment—air, water, soil, wildlife—suffered degradation. Steel mills, coal-powered generators, and internal-combustion car engines polluted the air and imperiled people's health. In 1948, for example, twenty people in the steel town of Donora, Pennsylvania, died of respiratory failure caused by air pollution. The smoke and sulfur gases pouring from the zinc smelter in Donora became so thick that people could not see or breathe.

Environmental Costs of Economic Growth

America's water supplies also suffered. Human and industrial waste befouled many rivers and lakes, making them unfit for consumption or recreation. Municipalities were at fault as well as industries. Vast quantities of water were diverted from lakes and rivers to meet the needs of America's burgeoning Sun Belt cities, including the swimming pools that dotted Arizona and southern California. Arid lands bloomed for the first time, but once fertile areas—such as Owens Valley on the eastern slope of the Sierras, which was pumped dry to supply water to Los Angeles—became dust bowls. The extraction of natural resources—strip-mining of coal, for example—also scarred the landscape, and toxic waste from chemical plants seeped deep into the soil. America was becoming a dumping ground as never before.

Among the country's worst polluters were defense contractors and farmers. Nuclear-processing plants that produced plutonium for atomic bombs

DDT
___

also produced radioactive waste with a half-life of two thousand years. Refuse from nuclear weapons facilities at Hanford, Washington, and at Colorado's Rocky Flats arsenal polluted soil and water resources for years. Agriculture began using massive amounts of pesticides and other chemicals. A chemical called DDT, for example, which had been used on Pacific islands during the war to kill mosquitoes and lice, was released for public use in 1945. During the next fifteen years, farmers eliminated chronic pests with DDT. In 1962, however, *Silent Spring* by Rachel Carson, a wildlife biologist, alerted Americans to the dangers of massive and indiscriminate use of farm chemicals; Carson specifically indicted DDT for the deaths of mammals, birds, and fish. DDT accumulates in the fatty tissues of eagles, trout, and other animals, causing cancer and leukemia. Because of her book, many Americans finally realized that there were costs to human conquest of the environment. The federal government banned the domestic sale of DDT in 1972.

Much of America's continued economic growth, however, was based on encouraging habits that would make the country a throwaway society. The auto industry, for example, intentionally made cars less durable ("planned obsolescence") and through advertising urged consumers to buy a new car every year or two. And increasing numbers of disposable products such as plastic cups and paper diapers were marketed as conveniences.

THE GROWTH OF SUBURBS

A combination of motives drew people to the suburbs. One was racism, as white families fled urban neighborhoods in which African-American families had just settled. Others wanted to leave behind the noise and smells of the city and live closer to nature and further from their neighbors. They also wanted homes with yards so that, as one suburbanite put it, "every kid [would have] an opportunity to grow up with grass stains on his pants." They wanted family rooms, extra closets, and utility rooms. Many were also looking for a community of like-minded people and a place where they could have a measure of political influence. Big-city government was dense

and impenetrable; in the suburbs, citizens could become involved in government and have an impact, particularly on the education their children received. Indeed, the focus of suburbanites' lives was their children. And for this generation of adults— one that had suffered economic deprivation during the depression and separation from loved ones during the war years—the home became a refuge and "family togetherness" a psychological need.

Government funding helped new families to settle in the suburbs. Low-interest GI mortgages and Federal Housing Administration (FHA) mortgage insurance made the differ-

Housing Boom
___

ence for people who otherwise would have been unable to afford a home. It was this easy credit, combined with postwar prosperity, that produced a construction boom. From 1945 to 1946, housing starts climbed from 326,000 to more than 1 million; they approached 2 million in 1950 and remained close to 1.5 million as late as 1970. Never before had new starts exceeded 1 million. Not until the early 1980s would they again dip below that level.

At the same time, highway construction opened up previously remote rural lands for transformation into suburbs. In 1947, Congress authorized con-

Highway Construction
___

struction of a 37,000-mile chain of highways. In 1956, President Eisenhower signed the Highway Act, which launched a 41,000-mile nationwide network. Federal expenditures on highways swelled from $79 million in 1946 to $2.9 billion in 1960 and $4.6 billion in 1970. State and local spending on highways also mushroomed. Highways not only hastened suburbanization, they also promoted more uniformity in lifestyles and homogenized the landscape. The high-speed trucking that highways made possible also accelerated the integration of the South into the national economy.

Highway construction in combination with the growth of suburbia produced a new phenomenon, the *megalopolis*, a term coined by urban experts in the early 1960s to refer to the almost uninterrupted metropolitan complex stretching along the northeastern seaboard from Boston six hundred miles south through New York, Philadelphia, and Baltimore all the way to Washington, D.C. "Boswash" encompassed parts of eleven states and a population of forty-nine million people, all linked by interstate highways. Other megalopolises that took shape following the Second World War were "Milipitts," a band of heavy industry and dense population stretching from Milwaukee to Pittsburgh, and "San-San," the area between San Francisco and San Diego.

Socially, the suburbs' emphasis on family togetherness tended to isolate families. Sociologist David Riesman, writing in 1957, criticized "the

Critics of Suburban Life

decentralization of leisure in the suburbs . . . as the home itself, rather than the neighborhood, becomes the chief gathering place for the family—either in the 'family room' with its games, its TV, its informality, or outdoors around the barbecue." The floor plan of the ranch-style home, the centerpiece of which was the TV set enthroned on a swivel, was suited to the stay-at-home lifestyle.

Other observers denounced the suburbs for breeding conformity and status seeking. Some writers criticized suburbanites for trying to keep up with the Joneses by buying new cars and appliances. William H. Whyte's *The Organization Man* (1956), a study of Park Forest, Illinois, pronounced the suburbanites mindless conservatives and extreme conformists. Their value system featured a belief in the group as "the source of creativity" and "in 'belongingness' as the ultimate need of the individual." And C. Wright Mills, a sociologist, castigated white-collar suburbanites who "sell not only their time and energy but their personalities as well. They sell . . . their smiles and their kindly gestures."

Nonetheless, most residents of suburbia preferred family togetherness to any other lifestyle of which they were aware. Of the college students interviewed by Riesman in the 1950s, the vast majority looked forward to settling in the suburbs.

IDEALS OF MOTHERHOOD AND THE FAMILY

Change, much of it the result of the publication in 1946 of Dr. Benjamin Spock's *Baby and Child Care*, also occurred within the American family. Unlike

Dr. Spock on Child Rearing

earlier manuals, *Baby and Child Care* urged mothers always to think of their children first. (Spock assigned fathers little formal role in child rearing.) He based his advice on new findings about the importance of responding to a baby's needs. Spock's predecessors had advised mothers to consider their own needs as well as their children's. But the millions of women who embraced Dr. Spock's teachings tried to be mother, teacher, psychologist, and playmate to their children. If they "failed" in any of the roles, guilt was the inevitable outcome.

Meanwhile, the social critic Philip Wylie denounced such selfless behavior as "Momism." In the guise of sacrificing for her children, Wylie wrote in *Generation of Vipers,* Mom was pursuing "love of herself." She smothered her children with affection to make them emotionally dependent on her and reluctant to leave home. But women were caught in a double bind, for if they pursued a life outside the home they were accused of being "imitation men" or neurotic feminists. Echoing the psychoanalyst Sigmund Freud, critics of working mothers contended that a woman could be happy and fulfilled only through domesticity.

The conflicting roles women were expected to fulfill created a dilemma. On the one hand, the home was premised on a full-time housewife who,

Women's Conflicting Roles

with little regard for her own needs, provided her children and husband with a haven from the outside world. On the other hand, women continued to enter the labor force for a variety of reasons. Many women worked because they were their families' sole source of income; they had to work. Others took jobs to supplement their husbands' income. Thus despite the cult of motherhood, the wartime trend toward work outside the home accelerated. Indeed, the female labor force rose from seventeen million in 1946 to thirty-two million in 1970. And most new entrants to the job market were married and had children.

Immediately after the Second World War, many former GIs had enrolled in college and set up housekeeping with their wives and babies in abandoned

The GI Bill

military barracks on college campuses. The legislation that made this possible was the Servicemen's Readjustment Act of 1944, popularly known as the GI Bill of Rights, which provided living allowances and tuition payments to college-bound veterans. More than one million veterans enrolled in 1946—accounting for one out of every two students. Despite pessimistic predictions, the veterans succeeded as students. (The downside of this success story was that colleges made places for male veterans by turning away qualified women.)

As the baby boom became a grade-school boom, American families became preoccupied with education. Convinced that their children's success in school was a prerequisite for

Education of the Baby Boom Generation

economic and social success in adult life, parents joined the parent-teacher association so they would have a voice in the educational process. Then in 1957, education became a matter of national security. In that year, the Soviet Union launched *Sputnik*, the first earth-orbiting satellite. The Russian triumph threw into question American military and technological superiority, based ultimately on the nation's school system. Congress responded in 1958 with the National Defense Education Act (NDEA), which funded public school enrichment programs in mathematics, foreign languages, and the sciences, as well as fellowships and loans to college students. Public education was characterized as "the engine of democracy," crucial to both upward social mobility and military superiority. One of the clearest indications of this belief was the surge in college enrollments, which jumped from 2.3 million in 1950 to 7.4 million in 1970.

But even as college enrollments swelled, women lost ground. In an era in which wives tended to subordinate their career goals to those of their husbands, the percentage of women earning college degrees declined. The proportion of women among college graduates dropped from 40 percent in 1940 to 25 percent in 1950. At the postgraduate level, only 11 percent of doctorates earned in the United States went to women, compared with 16 percent in 1920. The 1960s reversed the trend; by 1970 the figure had again reached the 1920 level.

As education became intertwined with national security, religion became a matter of patriotism. As President Eisenhower put it, "Recognition of the

Religion in Postwar America

Supreme Being is the first, the most basic expression of Americanism." In America's Cold War with an atheistic enemy, religious leaders emphasized traditional values like family togetherness. "The family that prays together stays together" was a familiar refrain in the 1950s and 1960s. The Bible topped the best-seller lists, and membership in religious congregations nearly doubled in the twenty-five years after the Second World War.

Although Americans were eager to improve their minds and souls, they were not ready until the 1960s to acknowledge their sexuality. When Dr. Alfred Kinsey, director of the Institute for Sex Research at Indiana University, published his pioneering study *Sexual Behavior in the Human Male* (1948), the American public was shocked. On the basis of interviews with twelve thousand men, Kinsey estimated that 95 percent of all American men had engaged in masturbation, premarital or extramarital intercourse, or homosexual behavior. Five years later, Kinsey caused an uproar with *Sexual Behavior in the Human Female*, which revealed that 62 percent of women masturbated and 50 percent had had intercourse before marriage. Some angry Americans condemned the report as a slanderous attack on motherhood and the family.

Movies and magazines reinforced the prevailing notion that sex was wrong and dangerous outside of marriage. Family, church, state, and media alike warned Americans that

Sexual Taboos

premarital, extramarital, and homosexual behavior would bring "familial chaos and weaken the country's moral fiber," and it blamed women for the impending disaster. Despite any evidence of significant increases in women's sexual activity from the 1920s to the 1960s, female lust was perceived to pose the greatest sexual threat to the future of the family. From Momism to promiscuity, American women were the victims of male-inspired stereotypes.

THE AFFLUENT SOCIETY

As U.S. productivity grew by leaps and bounds in the postwar years, so did Americans' appetite for goods and services. During the depression and the Second World War, many Americans had dreamed of buying a home or a car. In the affluent postwar years, they could finally satisfy those deferred desires. Some families bought two cars and equipped their new homes with dishwashers, television sets, and stereophonic sound systems. When they lacked cash to buy what they wanted, they borrowed money. Consumer credit to support the nation's shopping spree grew from about $8 billion in 1946 to $127 billion in 1970. Easy credit was the economic basis of the consumer culture.

As Americans consumed goods and services, they were using up the world's resources. Consumption of crude petroleum soared 118 percent from 1946 to 1970. Electricity use jumped too, from 270 billion kilowatt-hours to 1.6 trillion. By the mid-1960s, the United States, with only 5 percent of the world's population, produced and consumed more than one-third of the world's goods and services.

By contrast, advances in public health were a particularly happy effect of postwar prosperity. The average life span increased from sixty-seven years in 1946 to seventy-one in 1970, largely because of a dramatic decline in the infant mortality rate. (Racial differences, however, continued to be significant. In 1970, whites lived more than six years longer than blacks.) Regular prenatal and pediatric care led to a major reduction in the infant mortality rate. At the same time, the postwar discovery of wonder drugs such as streptomycin (1945) and aureomycin (1948) reduced deaths from influenza and postsurgical infection. The Salk polio vaccine, approved for public use in 1955, reduced reported cases of polio 97 percent by 1962.

Improvements in Public Health

Millions of Americans began their search for affluence by migrating to the Sun Belt—roughly, the southern third of the United States, running from southern California across the Southwest and South all the way to the Atlantic coast (see map). This mass migration had started during the war, when GIs and their families were ordered to new duty stations and war workers moved to the shipyards and aircraft factories of San Diego and other cities of the West and South. The economic bases of the Sun Belt's spectacular growth were agribusiness, the aerospace industry, the oil industry, real estate development, recreation, and defense spending. Industry was also drawn to the southern rim by right-to-work laws, which outlawed closed shops, and by low taxes and low heating bills.

Growth of the Sun Belt

The millions of people who left the chilly industrial cities of the North and East in the 1940s and 1950s strengthened the political clout of the Sun Belt. In 1969, Kevin Phillips, a conservative Republican political analyst, predicted an emerging Republican majority based on the conservatism of the South and West. Richard Nixon's triumph in the presidential election of 1968 seemed to support Phillips's thesis. So does the tendency of political parties to nominate Sun Belt candidates for national office. (All six of the nation's most recently elected presidents have hailed from the West or South—two from Texas, two from California, one from Georgia, and one from Arkansas.)

THE OTHER AMERICA

In an age of abundance, most Americans dismissed poverty, if they noticed it at all, as the fault of the poor people themselves. But in 1962, about 42.5 million Americans (nearly one of every four) were poor. These were people who earned less than $4,000 per year for a family of four or $2,000 per year for a single person living alone. Age, race, sex, education, and marital status were all factors in their poverty. One-fourth of the poor were older than sixty-five. One-fifth were people of color, including almost half the nation's African-American

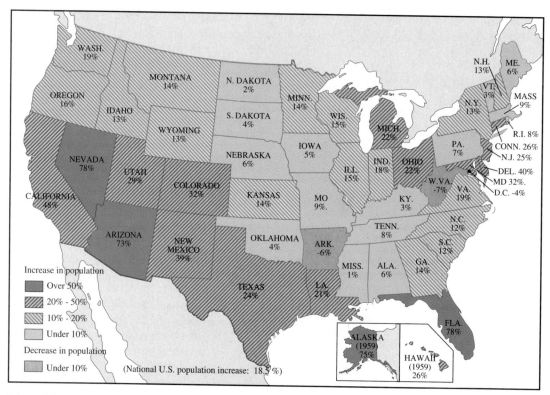

Rise of the Sun Belt, 1950–1960   *The years after the Second World War saw a continuation of the migration of Americans to the Sun Belt states of the Southwest and the West Coast.*

population and more than half of all Native Americans. Two-thirds lived in households headed by a person with an eighth grade education or less and one-fourth in households headed by a single woman. More than one-third were younger than eighteen. None of these people had much reason for hope.

While millions of Americans (most of them white) were settling in the suburbs, the poor were congregating in the inner cities. Almost 4.5 million

Poor People in the Inner Cities

African-Americans migrated to the cities from the South between the war years and the end of the 1960s. The black population, which had been 49 percent urban in 1940, was 81 percent urban by 1970. Joining African-Americans in the exodus to the cities were poor whites from the southern Appalachians, many of whom moved to Cincinnati, Baltimore, St. Louis, Columbus, Detroit, and Chicago. Mean-

while, Latin Americans were arriving in growing numbers from Mexico, the Dominican Republic, Colombia, Ecuador, and Cuba. And New York City's Puerto Rican population exploded from 70,000 to more than 600,000 in just twenty years.

Second only to African-Americans in numbers of urban newcomers were Mexican-Americans. Millions came as farm workers during and after the

Mexican-Americans

war, and increasing numbers remained to make their lives in the United States. Despite the initiation in 1953 of Operation Wetback, a federal program to find and deport illegal aliens, Mexicans continued to enter the country in large numbers, many of them illegally. Most settled in cities. According to the 1960 census, more than five hundred thousand Mexican-Americans had migrated to the *barrios* of the Los Angeles–Long Beach area since 1940. Estimates of uncounted illegal aliens suggest that the

The Moreira family gathered for an Easter celebration in Los Angeles in 1960. By the end of the 1950s, many Mexican-American families had established businesses, bought homes, and entered the middle class. The photograph shows three generations of the Moreira family. Security Pacific National Bank Collection, Los Angeles Public Library.

actual total was far higher. The same was true of the *barrios* in southwestern and northern cities.

Native Americans, whose average annual income was barely half the amount designated as poverty level, were the country's poorest people. Many

Native Americans

Native Americans moved to the cities in the 1950s and 1960s, particularly after Congress in 1953 adopted a policy called termination, which abolished the status of certain tribes as wards of the United States. Accustomed to semicommunal rural life on the reservation, many had difficulty adjusting to the urban environment. Like other groups that migrated to the cities in hope of finding a place to prosper, they found only a dumping ground for the poor.

Not all of the poor, however, lived in cities. In 1960, 30 percent lived in small towns and 15 percent on farms. Tenant farmers and sharecroppers, both black and white, continued to suffer severe economic hardship. Migratory farm workers lived in abject poverty. Elderly people tended to be poor regardless of where they lived.

A disproportionate share of the poor were women. Occupational segregation was still pervasive, and the better-paying positions were reserved

Women in Poverty

for men. In 1945, many women who wanted to remain in the factories and shipyards were pushed out to make way for returning veterans. Those who tried later to return to high-paying industrial work were discouraged, and many were forced into low-paying jobs in restaurants and laundries. Median annual earnings for full-time women workers stood at 60 percent of men's earnings in 1960. Ten years later, women's earnings had dropped to 59 percent of men's. Moreover, many women's jobs were not covered by either the minimum wage or Social Security. Finally, if divorce, desertion, or death did break up a family, the woman was usually left with responsibility for the children. Many divorced fathers did not keep up their regular child-support payments. Single mothers and their children, dependent on welfare or low wages, more often than not slipped into poverty.

One of the least-acknowledged effects of economic hardship was physical and emotional illness. A study in New Haven, Connecticut, in the late 1950s found that the rate of treated psychiatric illness was three times as high among the lowest-paid fifth of the population as it was among the upper-middle and upper classes. Psychiatrists at Cornell University's Medical School described the "low social economic status individual" as rigid, suspicious, with "a fatalistic outlook on life. . . . They are prone to depression, have feelings of futility, lack of belongingness . . . and a lack of trust in others." During the recession of 1960, a social worker from Rochester, New York, reported a direct correlation between loss of jobs and sharp rises in "marital discord and desertions of families by the father, increased welfare dependency, increased crime, especially robberies, burglaries and muggings, and alcoholism."

Poverty and Emotional Distress

With the publication of Michael Harrington's *The Other America* in 1962, people became aware of the contradiction in their midst. America's poor, wrote Harrington, were "the strangest poor in the history of mankind." As Harrington put it, they "exist within the most powerful and rich society the world has ever known." Whether living in urban obscurity or rural isolation, the poor had "dropped out of sight and out of mind," particularly the minds of comfortable suburbanites.

MIDDLE-CLASS AMERICA AT PLAY

Having satisfied their basic needs for food, clothing, and shelter, many Americans began turning their attention to conveniences and luxury items. "More appliances make mom's work easier," read a typical 1950s advertisement. As families strove to acquire the latest conveniences, shopping became a form of recreation.

Of the new luxuries, television was the most revolutionary in its effects. "And so the monumental change began in our lives and those of millions of other Americans," recalled a man whose parents bought their first TV set in 1950. "More than a year passed before we again visited a movie theater. Money which previously would have been spent for books was saved for the TV payments. Social evenings with friends became fewer and fewer still because we discovered we did not share the same TV program interests."

TV Enters the American Home

Entertainment was TV's number one product, and situation comedies and action series were among the most popular shows. Topping these categories in the 1950s were "I Love Lucy," starring Lucille Ball, and "Dragnet," a detective series. "Father Knows Best" and "Leave It to Beaver" celebrated family life. As average TV-viewing time reached five hours a day in 1956 and continued to increase, critics worried that TV's distorted presentation of the world would significantly define people's sense of reality.

Advertising bankrolled the television industry, as it had radio. The first TV commercial, made by the Bulova Watch Company in 1941, was a one-minute effort that cost $9. By the end of the decade, the bargain rates had vanished; annual expenditures for TV advertising totaled $171 million in 1950. By 1970, the figure had soared to $3.6 billion.

The more television brought the world into their living rooms, the less attentively Americans read newspapers and news magazines and listened to the radio. Nevertheless, book readership went up, in part because of the mass marketing of inexpensive paperbound books. Pocket Books hit the market in 1939; soon westerns, detective stories, and science fiction appeared at newsstands, supermarkets, and drugstores. The comic book, which had become popular in 1939 with the introduction of *Superman*, became another drugstore standard. Reprints of hardcover books and condensed books also sold well.

An obvious casualty of the stay-at-home suburban culture was the motion picture. From 1946 to 1948, Americans had attended movies at the rate of

How do historians know

that the suburbs stimulated the postwar American economy? For one thing, they can point to census data that document the spiraling sales of houses and automobiles. There is also anecdotal evidence. In 1953, Leo Ferguson and his family moved into Los Angeles's fastest-growing suburb, Lakewood. During the first week in their new home, they were visited by more than seventy-five representatives selling everything from Venetian blinds to hot water heaters, and from Fuller Brush products to weather stripping.   Photo: J.R. Eyerman, LIFE Magazine @ Time Warner Inc.

**Rise of
the Youth
Subculture**

nearly ninety million a week. By 1950, that figure had dropped to sixty million a week; by 1960, to forty million. The postwar years saw the steady closing of movie theaters—with the notable exception of the drive-in, which appealed to car-oriented suburban families and teenagers. In fact, teenagers were the one exception to the downturn in movie going. By the late 1950s, the first wave of the postwar baby boom had reached adolescence, and they were flocking to the theaters. No less than 72 percent of movie goers during the 1950s were younger than thirty. Hollywood catered to the new audience with films portraying young people as sensitive and insightful, adults as boorish and hostile. *Rebel Without a Cause* (1955), starring James Dean, was one such movie. The cult of youth had been born.

Soon the music industry began catering to teens with inexpensive 45-rpm records. Bored with the era's syrupy music, young Americans were electrified by the driving energy and hard beat of Bill Haley and the Comets, Chuck Berry, the Everly Brothers, Jerry Lee Lewis, Little Richard, and Buddy Holly. The release of Elvis Presley's first single, "Heartbreak Hotel," in 1956, and his appearance on Ed Sullivan's Sunday night TV show, touched off a frenzy of adoration and hero worship; so much the better that parents were scandalized by his suggestive gyrations.

African-American Roots of Rock 'n' Roll
___

Although the roots of rock 'n' roll lay in African-American rhythm-and-blues, few white musicians acknowledged the debt. Presley's "Hound Dog," for example, had originally been performed by the black singer Big Mama Thornton, but she received little credit for her contribution.

Meanwhile, serious black jazz artists like Charlie Parker and Dizzy Gillespie were experimenting with bebop. In the 1950s, jazz became increasingly fused with classical themes, compositions, and instrumentation. Intellectuals began to appreciate jazz, once considered vulgar, as a uniquely American art form.

America's cultural influence grew worldwide in the 1950s and 1960s. In dance, Martha Graham was lauded in international circles, and in painting Jackson Pollock became the pivotal figure of the abstract expressionist movement, which in the 1950s established New York City as the center of the art world. Rather than work with the traditional painter's easel, Pollock spread his canvas on the floor, where he was free to walk around it, "work from the four sides and literally be in the painting." In the 1960s, artists of the Pop Art movement rejected abstract expressionism and satirized the consumer society, using commercial techniques to depict everyday objects. Andy Warhol painted Campbell's soup cans;

other artists did blowups of ice-cream sundaes, hamburgers, and comic strip panels.

Consumerism was also evident in Americans' postwar play and in the era's fads. The Slinky, selling for $1, began loping down people's stairs in 1947; Silly Putty was introduced in 1950. The 1950s and 1960s also had 3-D movies and Hula-Hoops. Although most crazes were short lived, they created multimillion-dollar industries and effectively promoted dozens of movies and TV shows. Another postwar fad was the family vacation. With more money and leisure time and a much improved highway system, middle-class families took vacations that formerly had been restricted to the rich. The destination of many family vacations was Disneyland, which opened in Anaheim, California, in 1955.

The consumer society was unreceptive to social criticism. The film-going public preferred noncontroversial doses of Doris Day and Rock Hudson and Dean Martin and Jerry Lewis. Readers of fiction escaped into the criminal underworld, the wild West, or science fiction. Even serious artists tended to ignore the country's social problems.

There were exceptions. Ralph Ellison's *Invisible Man* (1952) gave white Americans a glimpse of the psychic costs to black Americans of exclusion from the American Dream. Two

Beat Generation
___

films—*Gentleman's Agreement* (1947) and *Home of the Brave* (1949)—examined anti-Semitism and white racism. And one group of writers noisily repudiated the materialistic and self-congratulatory world of the middle class and the suburbs. The Beat (for beatific) writers rejected both social niceties and literary conventions, and they flaunted their freewheeling sexuality and consumption of drugs. The Beats produced some memorable prose and poetry, including Allen Ginsberg's angry incantational poem *Howl* (1956) and Jack Kerouac's novel *On the Road* (1957). Although the Beats were largely ignored during the 1950s, millions of young Americans discovered their writings and imitated their lifestyle in the 1960s.

One of the period's most influential books was the best-selling *The Affluent Society* (1958), by John Kenneth Galbraith. Galbraith's thesis dovetailed with the prevalent belief that economic growth would bring prosperity to everyone. Some would have more than others, of course, but in time everybody would have enough. "Production has eliminated the more acute tensions associated with [economic] inequality," Galbraith wrote. He dismissed poverty as by no means "a universal or massive affliction" but "more nearly an afterthought."

Only a few years later, however, comfortable middle-class Americans learned that millions of poor people lived in their midst, and that most of them had been deprived of the civil rights the rest of the nation took for granted. Politically and culturally, the 1960s were to prove vastly different from the years that immediately preceded them. Ironically, it would be the children of suburbia—the generation of the baby boom—who would form the vanguard of the assault on racism, poverty, and the whole value system of the postwar American middle class.

SUGGESTIONS FOR FURTHER READING

The Baby Boom

Landon Y. Jones, *Great Expectations: America and the Baby Boom Generation* (1980); Donald Katz, *Home Fires: An Intimate Portrait of One Middle-Class Family in Postwar America* (1992); Elaine Tyler May, *Homeward Bound: American Families in the Cold War Era* (1988); John Modell, *Into One's Own: From Youth to Adulthood in the United States, 1920–1975* (1989).

Suburbia

Robert Fishman, *Bourgeois Utopias* (1987); Herbert J. Gans, *The Levittowners* (1967); Mark I. Gelfand, *A Nation of Cities* (1975); Dolores Hayden, *Redesigning the American Dream* (1984); Kenneth T. Jackson, *Crabgrass Frontier: The Suburbanization of the United States* (1985); Zane L. Miller, *Suburb* (1982).

The Spread of Education

Keith W. Olson, *The GI Bill, the Veterans, and the Colleges* (1974); Diane Ravitch, *The Troubled Crusade: American Education, 1945–1980* (1983); Joel Spring, *The Sorting Machine: National Educational Policy Since 1945* (1976).

Women, Work, and Family Togetherness

Wini Breines, *Young, White, and Miserable: Growing Up Female in the Fifties* (1992); Ruth Schwartz Cowan, *More Work for Mother* (1983); Myra Dinnerstein, *Women Between Two Worlds* (1992);

Barbara Ehrenreich, *The Hearts of Men: American Dreams and the Flight from Commitment* (1983); Betty Friedan, *The Feminine Mystique* (1963); Cynthia Harrison, *On Account of Sex: The Politics of Women's Issues, 1945–1968* (1988); Eugenia Kaledin, *Mothers and More: American Women in the 1950s* (1984); Glenna Matthews, *"Just a Housewife"* (1987); Leila J. Rupp and Verta Taylor, *Survival in the Doldrums: The American Women's Rights Movement, 1945 to the 1960s* (1987); Susan Strasser, *Never Done: A History of American Housework* (1982).

The Affluent Society

Loren Baritz, *The Good Life: The Meaning of Success for the American Middle Class* (1982); John Kenneth Galbraith, *The Affluent Society* (1958); David F. Noble, *Forces of Production: A Social History of Industrial Automation* (1988); David M. Potter, *People of Plenty* (1954); Kirkpatrick Sale, *Power Shift: The Rise of the Southern Rim and Its Challenge to the Eastern Establishment* (1975); Bruce J. Schulman, *From Cotton Belt to Sunbelt: Federal Policy, Economic Development, and the Transformation of the South, 1938–1980* (1991).

Farmers and Workers

Gilbert C. Fite, *American Farmers* (1981); James R. Green, *The World of the Worker* (1980); John L. Shover, *First Majority–Last Minority: The Transforming of Rural Life in America* (1976).

The Other America

Harry M. Caudill, *Night Comes to the Cumberland* (1963); Richard B. Craig, *The Bracero Program* (1971); J. Wayne Flint, *Dixie's Forgotten People: The South's Poor Whites* (1979); Michael Harrington, *The Other America*, rev. ed. (1981); Dorothy K. Newman et al., *Politics and Prosperity: Black Americans and White Institutions, 1940–1975* (1978); James T. Patterson, *America's Struggle Against Poverty, 1900–1985* (1986).

Postwar Culture

Peter Biskind, *Seeing Is Believing: How Hollywood Taught Us to Stop Worrying and Love the Fifties* (1983); Paul Boyer, *By the Bomb's Early Light: American Thought and Culture at the Dawn of the Atomic Age* (1985); James Gilbert, *A Cycle of Outrage: America's Reaction to the Juvenile Delinquent* (1986); Charlie Gillett, *The Sound of the City: The Rise of Rock and Roll*, rev. ed. (1983); William S. Graebner, *The Age of Doubt: American Thought and Culture in the 1940s* (1991); Serge Guilbaut, *How New York Stole the Idea of Modern Art* (1982); David Halberstam, *The Fifties* (1993); Nora Sayre, *Running Time: Films of the Cold War* (1982); Jane and Michael Stern, *Elvis World* (1987); John Tytell, *Naked Angels: The Lives and Literature of the Beat Generation* (1976).

Television

Michael Arlen, *The Camera Age* (1981); Erik Barnouw, *Tube of Plenty*, rev. ed. (1982); Todd Gitlin, *Inside Prime Time* (1983); Ella Taylor, *Prime-Time Families: Television Culture in Postwar America* (1989).

Chapter
31

Contesting Nationalism and Revolution: The Third World and the Vietnam War, 1945–1989

T HE JOINT CHIEFS OF Staff memorandum lay on the table. Its recommendation: add another 100,000 to the 80,000 American troops already in Vietnam, because the war was not going well. "Is there anyone here of the opinion we should not do what the memorandum says?" President Lyndon B. Johnson asked his advisers in a tense meeting on July 21, 1965. Only Under Secretary of State George Ball spoke up: "Take our losses, let their government fall apart, negotiate, discuss, knowing full well there will be a probable takeover by the Communists." Johnson recoiled from thoughts of losing. He simply could not accept that a small primitive country like Vietnam could deny the United States victory.

The next day, Johnson met with the military brass. The generals told him that they needed more men, more bombings, and more money to save America's South Vietnamese ally from defeat at the hands of North Vietnamese and Vietcong forces. The president asked tough questions: "But if we put in 100,000 men, won't they put in

an equal number, and then where will we be?" When an admiral claimed that if the United States did not back the faltering South Vietnamese regime, allies around the world would lose faith in America's word, Johnson knew better: "We have few allies really helping us now." And have the bombing raids hurt the enemy? Not really, the generals answered, but they would if the U.S. military added more sites to the target list. Johnson wondered, "Isn't this going off the diving board?"

President Johnson nonetheless decided in July to give the Joint Chiefs of Staff what they wanted. A turning point in the Vietnam War, the decision meant that the United States was for the first time assuming primary responsibility for fighting the war. Fearing a national debate, Johnson underplayed the decision's importance when he announced it. By the end of 1965, nearly 200,000 American combat troops were at war in Vietnam. Yet Congress had not passed a declaration of war, and most of the American people remained ignorant of the venture. Ball later called Johnson's July decision "the greatest single error that America had made in its national history."

Vietnam bedeviled the United States from 1945, the year Vietnamese nationalists declared independence from France, to well beyond 1975, the year the last Americans withdrew from Vietnam. President Truman backed the futile efforts of France, America's ally in the emerging Cold War, to save its Indochinese empire. After the French pulled out in defeat and Vietnam was divided, Eisenhower sent U.S. military advisers and foreign aid to shore up the anti-Communist South Vietnamese government. Kennedy, fearing that Communist China was expanding into Vietnam, greatly enlarged the U.S. presence to block Vietcong advances against the U.S.-backed regime. Johnson Americanized the war, and Nixon struggled to pull American soldiers out of the war without losing it. His successors had to deal with defeat and the anguished aftermath of America's longest war.

Vietnam was part of the *Third World*, a general term for those nations that during the Cold War belonged neither to the capitalist "West" (the United States and its allies) nor to the Communist "East" (the Soviet Union and its allies). Third World nations on the whole were nonwhite, nonindustrialized, and located in the southern half of the globe—in Asia, Africa, the Middle East, and Latin America. After the Second World War, when the United States and the Soviet Union coveted allies, the Third World became entangled in the Cold War. Although the highly diverse Third World peoples had their own histories, cultures, and aspirations, they often found that they could not escape the pervasive effects of the great-power rivalry.

Americans often interpreted Third World anti-imperialism, political instability, and restrictions on foreign-owned property as Soviet or Communist inspired, rather than as expressions of profound nationalism or consequences of indigenous developments. The Soviets did support guerrilla wars and revolution, but they seldom if ever initiated them. Had there been no Cold War, the Third World would still have challenged U.S. strategic and economic interests. Interventionism, U.S. leaders came to believe, was necessary to impress Moscow with American might and resolve

and to counter nationalist strivings for independence and radical social change that threatened U.S. interests worldwide.

To thwart nationalist, radical, and Communist challenges, the United States directed its massive resources toward the Third World. In the 1950s, technical assistance under the Point Four Program and development loans and grants flowed to developing nations. By 1961, more than 90 percent of American foreign aid went to the Third World. Washington also forged alliances with undemocratic but friendly regimes, meddled in civil wars, and unleashed CIA covert operations against unfriendly governments. Bitter resentments built up in the Third World, where millions died in conflicts aggravated by U.S. intervention.

The emergence of the Third World in the 1950s began to undermine the bipolar Cold War international system the United States and the Soviet Union had constructed at the end of the Second World War. By the 1980s, power had become diffused: great-power management of world affairs had diminished, and international relations had become less predictable as more and more nations demanded a voice and a vote. Secretary of State Henry Kissinger observed in the 1970s that the international order was coming "apart politically, economically, and morally." The world, he feared, was "tilting against us."

THE RISE OF THE THIRD WORLD

The process of decolonization began during the First World War but accelerated after the end of World War II, when the economically wracked imperial countries proved incapable of resisting their colonies' demands for freedom. A cavalcade of new nations earned independence. The United States granted independence to the Philippines in 1946. Britain freed India and Pakistan and present-day Bangladesh in 1947, Burma and Ceylon (Sri Lanka) in 1948. The Dutch reluctantly let go of Indonesia in 1949. From 1943 to 1989, a total of

Decolonization

• *Important Events* •

1861–87	French consolidate colonial rule in Indochina	**1956**	Suez crisis pits Nasser's Egypt against Israel, France, and Britain
1940	Japan occupies Indochina and weakens French influence	**1957**	Eisenhower Doctrine declares containment of communism in Middle East
1941	Vietminh organized as anti-French, anti-Japanese movement in Vietnam	**1958**	U.S. troops land in Lebanon
1945	Ho Chi Minh declares independence for Democratic Republic of Vietnam	**1959**	Castro launches Cuban Revolution
		1960	National Liberation Front (Vietcong) organized in South Vietnam
1946	Anticolonial war against France begins in Vietnam	**1961**	CIA-directed Bay of Pigs invasion fails to overthrow Castro
1947	Truman Doctrine declares policy of containment		Peace Corps founded
			Alliance for Progress announced to spur Latin American economies
1948	State of Israel founded amid Arab-Jewish hostilities		Kennedy increases aid and military "advisers" to Vietnam
1949	Communists win in China	**1962**	Cuban missile crisis leads to nuclear brinkmanship
1950	Korean War begins		
	Point Four Program of technical assistance to developing nations begins	**1963**	Strategic Hamlet Program established in South Vietnam
	United States recognizes Bao Dai and sends military aid to French for war in Vietnam		Diem assassinated
		1964	Tonkin Gulf Resolution authorizes Johnson to handle the war his way
1954	Siege of Dienbienphu in Vietnam persuades France to negotiate	**1965**	United States invades Dominican Republic
	CIA intervenes in Guatemala		Johnson Americanizes Vietnam War by sending large numbers of troops
	Geneva Accords partition Vietnam		Operation Rolling Thunder bombs North Vietnam
	SEATO created		
1955	United States backs government Ngo Dinh Diem		
	Bandung Conference organizes Nonaligned Movement		

ninety-six countries cast off their colonial bonds (see map). At the same time, the long-independent Third World nations of Latin America unsettled the world order by repeatedly challenging the hegemony of the United States.

By the early 1950s, when Cold War lines were drawn fairly tightly in Europe, Soviet-American rivalry shifted increasingly to the Third World. Much was at stake. Third World nations pos-

sessed strategic raw materials. They also attracted foreign investment and provided markets for American manufactured products and technology. The great powers looked to the new states for votes in the United Nations for military and intelligence bases.

Many Third World states—notably India, Ghana, Egypt, and Indonesia—did not wish to take sides in the Cold War. To the dismay of both Wash-

• *Important Events* •

1965–66	Teach-ins at universities oppose U.S. intervention in Vietnam
1967	Peace rallies staged across the nation Six-Day War in the Middle East
1968	Tet offensive in Vietnam sets back U.S. objectives My Lai massacre leaves many women and children dead Vietnam talks open in Paris
1969	543,400 U.S. troops in Vietnam Nixon begins withdrawal of troops from Vietnam
1970	Invasion of Cambodia sets off U.S. demonstrations
1971	*Pentagon Papers* indicate that administrations had lied about Vietnam
1972	In Christmas bombing, U.S. Air Force pounds North Vietnam
1973	Vietnam cease-fire agreement reached Allende ousted in Chile after U.S. subversive efforts Outbreak of Arab-Israeli war and imposition of Arab oil embargo War Powers Resolution restricts presidential warmaking authority
1974	New International Economic Order proposed by Third World
1975	Egyptian-Israeli accord authorizes U.N. peacekeeping force in Sinai Vietnam War ends Civil war breaks out in Angola after Portugal grants independence
1977	Carter announces human rights policy
1978	Panama Canal treaties approved by Congress Carter negotiates Egyptian-Israeli peace accord at Camp David
1979	Egyptian-Israeli Peace Treaty signed Shah of Iran overthrown; American hostages seized
1980	Carter Doctrine announced for Persian Gulf region
1981	American hostages in Iran released after 444 days United States steps up role in El Salvador's civil war CIA begins to train contras for attacks against Nicaragua
1982	U.S. troops ordered to Lebanon
1983	Terrorists kill U.S. Marines in Lebanon Reagan orders invasion of Grenada
1984	Reagan administration aids contras, despite congressional ban
1985	Reagan Doctrine declares U.S. aid to "freedom fighters"
1986	U.S. bombers attack Libya Iran-contra scandal breaks
1987	Third World debt reaches $1.2 trillion
1988	Palestinian uprising occurs in West Bank (*intifada*) George Bush elected president
1989	Cold War winds down

Note: See also "Important Events" in Chapter 29 for related events in the history of the Cold War.

The Nonaligned Movement

ington and Moscow, they declared themselves nonaligned, or neutral. Nonalignment became an organized movement in 1955 when twenty-nine Asian and African nations met in 1955 at the Bandung Conference in Indonesia. Secretary of State John Foster Dulles declared his opposition to neutralism—which he considered a first step on the road to communism. Both he and President Eisenhower argued that every nation should take a side in the life-and-death Cold War struggle.

If this negative view of neutralism inhibited U.S. efforts to strengthen relations with the Third World, so did America's domestic race relations. In

KOREA 1948
MALAYSIA 1957
VANUATU 1980
NAURU 1968
PAPUA NEW GUINEA 1975
BRUNEI 1984
SOLOMON ISLANDS 1978
PHILIPPINES 1946
INDONESIA 1949
BHUTAN 1949
BANGLADESH 1972
MYANMAR (BURMA) 1948
LAOS 1949
VIETNAM 1949
CAMBODIA 1949
SRI LANKA 1948
MALDIVES 1965
SINGAPORE 1965
SEYCHELLES 1976
PAKISTAN 1947
INDIA 1947
SYRIA 1944
LEBANON 1943
JORDAN 1946
KUWAIT 1961
BAHRAIN 1971
QATAR 1971
OMAN 1971
YEMEN 1967
DJIBOUTI 1977
SOMALIA 1960
UGANDA 1962
KENYA 1963
RWANDA 1962
BURUNDI 1962
COMOROS 1975
MADAGASCAR 1960
MAURITIUS 1968
MALAWI 1964
MALTA 1964
CYPRUS 1960
ISRAEL 1948
LIBYA 1951
UNITED ARAB EMIRATES 1971
SUDAN 1956
CHAD 1960
CENTRAL AFRICAN REP. 1960
ZAIRE 1960
TANZANIA 1961
ZAMBIA 1964
MOZAMBIQUE 1975
SWAZILAND 1968
LESOTHO 1966
ALGERIA 1962
NIGER 1960
CONGO 1960
ANGOLA 1975
NAMIBIA 1960
TUNISIA 1956
MALI 1960
NIGERIA 1960
BURKINA FASO 1960
BOTSWANA 1966
ZIMBABWE 1980
MOROCCO 1956
WESTERN SAHARA
MAURITANIA 1960
SENEGAL 1960
TOGO 1960
BENIN 1960
CAMEROON 1960
SAO TOME AND PRINCIPE 1975
EQUATORIAL GUINEA 1968
GABON 1960
GHANA 1957
CAPE VERDE 1975
GAMBIA 1965
GUINEA-BISSAU 1974
GUINEA 1958
SIERRA LEONE 1961
COTE D'IVOIRE 1960
ICELAND 1944
BAHAMAS 1973
ANTIGUA AND BARBUDA 1981
DOMINICA 1978
ST. LUCIA 1979
ST. VINCENT AND THE GRENADINES 1979
BARBADOS 1966
GRENADA 1974
GUYANA 1966
SURINAM 1975
FRENCH GUIANA (Fr.)
TRINIDAD AND TOBAGO 1962
JAMAICA 1962
BELIZE 1981

Newly independent nations

Possessions of colonial nations

(Dates shown are dates of independence)

KIRIBATI 1979
TUVALU 1978
WESTERN SAMOA 1962
FIJI 1970
TONGA 1970

(From Southern Pacific)

American Racism as Handicap

1955, the Indian ambassador to the United States was refused service in the whites-only section of a restaurant at Houston International Airport. The insult stung deeply and was not soon forgotten.

Because such embarrassments were not uncommon in the 1950s, Dulles complained that segregation was becoming a "major international hazard," spoiling U.S. efforts to gain the friendship of Third World countries. Americans stood publicly condemned as a people who did not honor their own ideal of equality. Thus when the U.S. attorney general appealed to the Supreme Court to strike down segregation in public schools, he underlined the international implications. He noted that racial discrimination "furnished grist for the Communist propaganda mills."

U.S. hostility toward revolution also obstructed the American quest for influence in the Third World. Despite its own history, the United

American Intolerance of Revolution

States has openly opposed most twentieth-century revolutions. Although Americans celebrated the Spirit of '76, they grew intolerant of revolutionary disorder, because Third World revolutions were often directed against America's Cold War allies. Such upheavals also threatened American investments, markets, and military bases. During revolutionary crises, therefore, the United States usually supported its European allies or the conservative propertied classes in the Third World.

Another obstacle in America's relations with the rising Third World was the country's great wealth. Foreigners both envied and resented Americans who had so much and wasted so much while poorer peoples went without. American movies offered enticing

The Rise of the Third World: Newly Independent Nations Since 1943 *The influx of new nations into the international system challenged the United States and Soviet Union. Often voting as a bloc, they pitted one superpower against the other and, suffering economic and political disorder, became targets of great-power intrigue, but they resisted efforts to control them and their assets.*

glimpses of middle-class materialism. And Americans stationed overseas often flaunted their higher standard of living. The popular novel *The Ugly American* (1958) spotlighted the "golden ghettos" where American diplomats lived in compounds separated by high walls from their poorer surroundings. Finally, the people of many countries resented the ample profits that American corporations extracted from them. For all these reasons, the United States often found itself the target of revolutionary nationalism rather than the model for Third World development.

The Soviet Union enjoyed only a slight edge, if any, in the great-power competition to win friends in the Third World. It was true that Communist

Obstacles to Soviet Influence

ideology encouraged anticolonialism and that the Soviet Union was free of association with the long years of Western European imperialism. But although Moscow kept up a heavy drumbeat of anti-imperialist propaganda, it could not easily explain away its subjugation of Eastern European countries. The Soviet invasion of Hungary in 1956 earned the Soviets international condemnation. Khrushchev toured India and Burma in the mid-1950s, but those nations refused to become Soviet clients. They were not about to replace one imperial master with another. Like Americans, the Soviets suspected that neutralist nations were playing the two superpowers off against one another in order to garner more aid and arms.

The Central Intelligence Agency became a major instrument of U.S. policy in the Third World. Although espionage and the gathering of information had been defined

CIA Covert Activities

as the CIA's primary functions at its birth in 1947, covert actions soon joined them. The CIA bribed foreign politicians, subsidized foreign newspapers, hired mercenaries, conducted sabotage, sponsored labor unions, dispensed "disinformation" (false information), plotted the assassination of foreign leaders, and staged coups. The CIA helped overthrow the governments of Iran (1953) and Guatemala (1954) but failed in attempts to topple regimes in Indonesia (1958) and Cuba (1961).

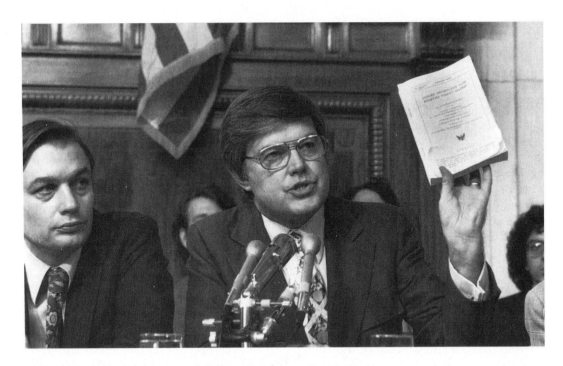

How do historians know

that the Central Intelligence Agency tried to assassinate foreign leaders? During the 1970s, Senator Frank Church (1924–1984), Democrat of Idaho, chaired a special investigating committee that looked into the activities of the CIA and other intelligence agencies. Although there had long been speculation that Washington headquarters ordered CIA agents to kill certain foreign leaders, incontrovertible evidence did not come to public light until Church's probe forced the CIA to declassify secret documents. Here, on November 20, 1975, Church holds a copy of his committee's report on assassination plots. Among other findings, the committee detailed several bungled attempts on the life of Fidel Castro, the revolutionary leader of Cuba. In this case, the CIA actually hired Mafia crime bosses to help with the unsuccessful schemes. In other cases, the Church committee found that the CIA tried to kill Patrice Lumumba of the Congo and either promoted or associated with plots against Rafael Trujillo of the Dominican Republic and Ngo Dinh Diem of South Vietnam. Most of the assassination plots, the committee concluded, failed. The committee could not confirm whether Presidents Eisenhower, Kennedy, and others personally ordered assassinations, although the report hinted that they gave orders that could only have been interpreted by underlings as licenses to kill. Because of such revelations, the CIA was later prohibited from conducting assassinations. But until another committee like Church's opens classified documents, the secrecy that enshrouds CIA operations makes it difficult for historians to know whether the ban has been observed. Photo: UPI/Bettmann Archives.

The CIA and other components of the American intelligence community followed the principle of "plausible deniability": covert operations should be conducted in such a way, and the decisions that launched them concealed so well, that the president could deny any knowledge of them. Thus President Eisenhower publicly denied the U.S. role in Guatemala, even though he had ordered the operation.

THE EISENHOWER INTERVENTIONS

Anti-Yankee feelings grew in Latin America, long a U.S. sphere of influence, where poverty, class warfare, overpopulation, illiteracy, economic sluggishness, and foreign exploitation fed discontent. In 1951, the leftist Jacobo Arbenz Guzmán was elected president of Guatemala, a poor country in which the largest landowner was the American-owned United Fruit Company. To fulfill his promise of land reform, Arbenz expropriated United Fruit's uncultivated land and offered compensation. United Fruit dismissed the offer and began an aggressive public relations campaign to rally Washington officials against what the company called a Communist threat to Guatemala.

Although lacking evidence of Communist control of Arbenz's government, U.S. officials cut off aid to Guatemala, and the CIA began a secret plot

CIA in Guatemala

to subvert its government. When Arbenz learned that the CIA was working against him, he turned to Moscow for military aid, thus reinforcing American suspicions. The CIA airlifted arms into Guatemala, dropping them at United Fruit facilities, and in mid-1954 CIA-supported Guatemalans struck from Honduras. American planes bombed the capital city, and the invaders drove Arbenz from power. The new pro-American regime returned United Fruit's land. Latin Americans wondered what had happened to the Good Neighbor policy.

In the volatile Middle East, the Eisenhower administration confronted challenges to U.S. influence from Arab nationalists (see map). American

U.S. Interests in the Middle East

interests were conspicuous: survival of the Jewish state of Israel and extensive oil holdings. Oil-rich Iran was a special friend; its shah had granted U.S. oil companies a 40 percent interest in a new petroleum consortium in return for CIA help in the successful overthrow of his rival, Mohammed Mossadegh, who had attempted to nationalize foreign oil interests.

Egypt's Gamal Abdul Nasser became a towering figure in a pan-Arabic movement to reduce Western interests in the Middle East. Nasser vowed to expel the British from the Suez Canal Zone and the Israelis from Palestine. The United States wished neither to anger the Arabs, for fear of losing valuable oil supplies, nor to alienate its ally Israel, which was supported at home by politically active American Jews. But when Nasser declared neutrality in the Cold War, Dulles lost patience. In 1956, the United States abruptly reneged on its offer to Egypt to help finance the Aswan Dam, a project to provide inexpensive electricity and water for thirsty farmlands. Nasser responded by nationalizing the British-owned Suez Canal, intending to use its profits to build the dam.

Fearing interruption of the Middle East oil trade, from which Western Europe received 75 percent of its oil, the British and French conspired

Suez Crisis

with Israel to bring down Nasser. On October 29, 1956, the Israelis invaded the Suez, joined two days later by Britain and France. Eisenhower fumed that U.S. allies had not consulted him. The president also speculated that the invasion would cause Nasser to seek help from the Soviets, inviting them into the Middle East. Eisenhower sternly demanded that London, Paris, and Tel Aviv pull their troops out, and they did. From the U.S. perspective, the results were negative: Egypt took possession of the canal and the Soviets built the Aswan Dam.

In an effort to improve the deteriorating Western position in the Middle East and to protect American interests there, the president proclaimed

Eisenhower Doctrine

the Eisenhower Doctrine in 1957. The United States would intervene in the Middle East, he declared, if any government threatened by a Communist takeover asked for help. The next year, fourteen thousand American troops scrambled ashore in Lebanon to quell an internal political dispute that Washington feared might be exploited by pro-Nasser groups or Communists. Some critics protested that the United States was wrongfully acting as the world's policeman. Others observed

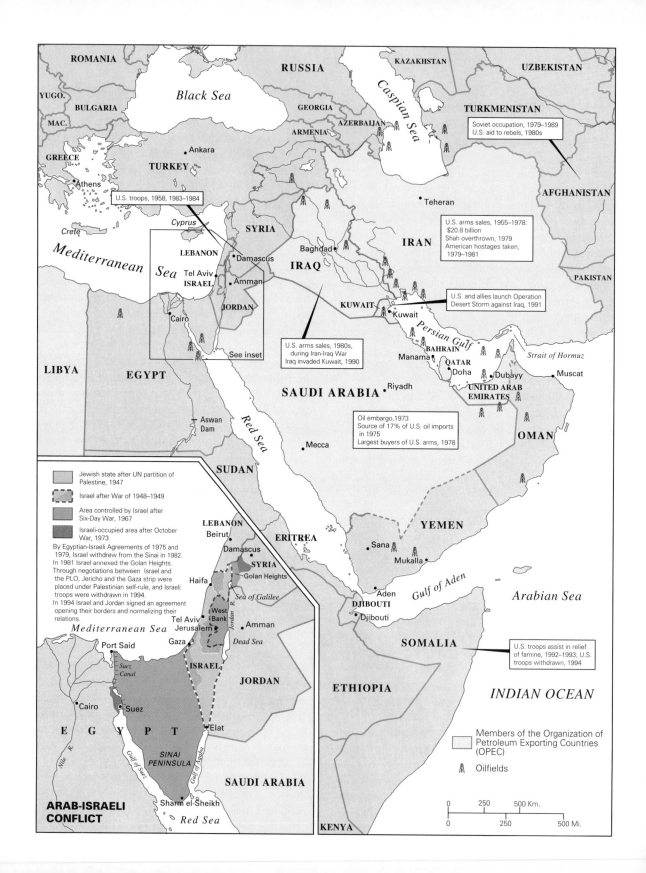

ROMANIA

RUSSIA

KAZAKHSTAN

UZBEKISTAN

YUGO.

Black Sea

BULGARIA

GEORGIA

TURKMENISTAN

MAC.

ARMENIA

AZERBAIJAN

Caspian Sea

GREECE

Ankara

Soviet occupation, 1979–1989
U.S. aid to rebels, 1980s

Athens

TURKEY

AFGHANISTAN

Crete

Cyprus

U.S. troops, 1958, 1983–1984

Mediterranean

SYRIA

Baghdad

Teheran

U.S. arms sales, 1955–1978:
$20.8 billion
Shah overthrown, 1979
American hostages taken,
1979–1981

LEBANON

Damascus

IRAQ

IRAN

PAKISTAN

Sea

Tel Aviv

Amman

ISRAEL

JORDAN

U.S. and allies launch Operation
Desert Storm against Iraq, 1991

Cairo

KUWAIT

Kuwait

Persian Gulf

See inset

U.S. arms sales, 1980s,
during Iran-Iraq War
Iraq invaded Kuwait, 1990

BAHRAIN

Strait of Hormuz

LIBYA

EGYPT

Manama

QATAR

Dubayy

Muscat

Doha

UNITED ARAB
EMIRATES

Aswan
Dam

Red Sea

SAUDI ARABIA

Riyadh

OMAN

Oil embargo, 1973
Source of 17% of U.S. oil imports
in 1975
Largest buyers of U.S. arms, 1978

Mecca

SUDAN

LEBANON

Beirut

ERITREA

YEMEN

Arabian Sea

Damascus

Sana

SYRIA

Golan Heights

Mukalla

Haifa

Sea of Galilee

Aden

Gulf of Aden

INDIAN OCEAN

By Egyptian-Israeli Agreements of 1975 and
1979, Israel withdrew from the Sinai in 1982.
In 1981 Israel annexed the Golan Heights.
Through negotiations between Israel and
the PLO, Jericho and the Gaza strip were
placed under Palestinian self-rule, and Israeli
troops were withdrawn in 1994.
In 1994 Israel and Jordan signed an agreement
opening their borders and normalizing their
relations.

Jordan R.

DJIBOUTI

Djibouti

SOMALIA

Mediterranean Sea

West
Bank

Tel Aviv

Jerusalem

Amman

Gaza

Dead Sea

U.S. troops assist in relief
of famine, 1992–1993; U.S.
troops withdrawn, 1994

Port Said

*Suez
Canal*

ISRAEL

JORDAN

ETHIOPIA

INDIAN OCEAN

Cairo

Suez

Nile R.

SINAI
PENINSULA

Gulf of Aqaba

Gulf of Suez

Elat

Members of the Organization of
Petroleum Exporting Countries
(OPEC)

Oilfields

SAUDI ARABIA

Jewish state after UN partition of
Palestine, 1947

Israel after War of 1948–1949

Area controlled by Israel after
Six-Day War, 1967

Israeli-occupied area after October
War, 1973

**ARAB-ISRAELI
CONFLICT**

Sharm el-Sheikh

Red Sea

KENYA

0   250   500 Km.

0   250   500 Mi.

that such a drastic resort to military intervention demonstrated that Eisenhower had failed miserably at thwarting challenges to American power and winning Cold War allies in the Third World.

KENNEDY'S QUEST FOR VICTORY

During the 1960 presidential campaign, John F. Kennedy hammered the Eisenhower administration for failing to align the Third World with the U.S. side in the Cold War. Kennedy vowed to win the race for influence in the Third World. After Khrushchev endorsed "wars of national liberation" such as that in Vietnam, Kennedy called for "peaceful revolution" based on the concept of nation building. Drawing on the ideas of the economist Walt W. Rostow, who joined the Kennedy administration, the president decided to win favor in Third World countries by helping them through the infant stages of nationhood with aid programs aimed at improving agriculture, transportation, and communications. Kennedy thus initiated the multibillion-dollar Alliance for Progress (1961) to spur economic development in Latin America.

Created for the same purpose, the Peace Corps sent American teachers, agricultural specialists, and health workers into developing nations. But the

Peace Corps

Peace Corps's humanitarian purpose sometimes competed with the administration's political agenda. Conflicts arose between corps members in the field, who identified with Third World peoples' desire for neutrality in the Cold War, and headquarters in Washington, where the goal was aligning those peoples with U.S. foreign policy.

The Middle East   Extremely volatile and often at war, the nations of the Middle East maintained precarious relations with the United States. To protect its interests, the United States extended large amounts of economic and military aid and sold huge quantities of weapons to the area. At times, Washington ordered U.S. troops to the region. The Arab-Israeli dispute particularly upended order.

Kennedy also relied on *counterinsurgency*—an organized effort to defeat revolutionaries who challenged Third World governments friendly with the United States. American military and technical advisers and CIA operatives trained native troops and police forces to quell unrest. And the United States deployed soldiers—especially the Special Forces units, or Green Berets—to provide a protective shield against insurgents while American civilian personnel worked on economic projects.

Nation building and counterinsurgency did not work. Americans assumed that the U.S. model of capitalism and government could be transferred successfully to foreign cultures. But as much as they craved U.S. economic assistance, many foreign peoples resented meddling by outsiders in their affairs. And because aid was usually funneled through a self-interested elite, it often failed to reach the very poor. To people who preferred the relatively quick solutions of a managed economy, moreover, the American emphasis on private enterprise seemed inappropriate.

DESCENT INTO THE LONGEST WAR: VIETNAM

In Southeast Asia, the belief that the United States could influence the internal affairs of Third World countries led to outright disaster. How Vietnam became the site of America's longest war (1950 to 1975), and how the world's most powerful nation failed to subdue a peasant people who suffered enormous losses, is one of the most remarkable and tragic stories of modern history.

For decades after the French takeover of Indochina (Vietnam, Cambodia, and Laos) in the late nineteenth century, France exploited Vietnam for

French Imperialism in Vietnam

its rice, rubber, tin, and tungsten. Although the French beat back recurrent peasant rebellions, Vietnamese nationalists dedicated to independence grew in strength. Their leader, Ho Chi Minh, was born in 1890, lived in France before the First World War, and at the close of the war joined the French Communist party to use it as a vehicle for Vietnamese independence.

Not until the Second World War, when the Japanese moved into Indochina, did French authority collapse. Seizing their chance, the Vietminh, an anti-imperialist coalition organized by Ho and other patriots, teamed up with agents of the American Office of Strategic Services (OSS) to harass the Japanese and their French collaborators. OSS officers who worked with Ho in Vietnam were impressed by his determination to win independence and by his frequent references to the United States as a revolutionary model. When Ho declared Vietnam's independence in September 1945, his words sounded familiar: "We hold these truths to be self-evident. That all men are created equal."

Yet the Truman administration never answered Ho's appeals for support; instead, it endorsed the restoration of French rule. The United States did not recognize Vietnamese independence for several reasons. First, Americans wanted France's cooperation in the Cold War. Second, Southeast Asia was an economic asset; its rice could feed America's soon-to-be ally Japan, and it was the world's largest producer of natural rubber and a rich source of other commodities. Third, the area seemed strategically vital to the defense of Japan and the Philippines. Finally, Ho Chi Minh was a Communist, who, Washington assumed, would assist Soviet expansionism. Thus Vietnam became another test for the containment of communism.

U.S. Rejection of Vietnamese Independence
———

In the 1940s, Vietnam was a French problem that few Americans followed with keen interest. But after Jiang Jieshi (Chiang Kai-shek) went down to defeat in China in 1949, the Truman administration made two crucial decisions, both in early 1950. First, it recognized the French puppet government of Bao Dai, a playboy and former emperor. In Vietnamese eyes, the United States thus became in essence a colonial power, an ally of the hated French. Second, the administration agreed to send weapons, and ultimately military advisers, to the French. By 1954, the United States was bearing three-fourths of the cost of the war.

U.S. Support for the French
———

Despite American aid, the French lost steadily to the Vietminh. Finally, in early 1954, Ho's forces surrounded the French fortress at Dienbienphu in northwest Vietnam. What would the United States do? President Eisenhower moved deliberately. Although the United States had been advising and bankrolling the French, it had not committed its own forces to the war. If American air power did not save the French, would ground troops be required next?

Dienbienphu Crisis
———

Worrying aloud about a Communist victory, Eisenhower compared the weak nations of the world to a row of dominoes, all of which would topple if just one fell (a concept later known as the domino theory). He decided to press the British to help form a coalition to address the Indochinese crisis, but they refused. At home, influential members of Congress warned him to avoid any American military commitment, especially in the absence of allied cooperation. The issue became moot on May 7, when the weary French defenders at Dienbienphu surrendered.

To compound the administration's problems, the French wanted out of the war. In April, they had entered into peace talks at Geneva with the United States, the Soviet Union, Britain, the People's Republic of China, Laos, Cambodia, and the two competing Vietnamese regimes of Bao Dai and Ho Chi Minh. The 1954 Geneva Accords, signed by France and Ho's Democratic Republic of Vietnam, temporarily divided Vietnam at the seventeenth parallel, with Ho's government confined to the North and Bao Dai's to the South. The parallel was meant to serve as a military truce line, not a national boundary; the country was scheduled to be unified after national elections in 1956. In the meantime, neither North nor South was to join a military alliance or permit foreign military bases on its soil.

Geneva Accords
———

Certain that the Geneva agreements would ultimately mean Communist victory, the United States and Bao Dai refused to accept the accords and set about to sabotage them. Soon after the conference, a CIA team entered Vietnam and undertook secret operations against the North, including commando raids across the seventeenth parallel. In the fall of 1954, the United States also joined Britain, France, Australia, New Zealand, the Philippines, Thailand, and Pakistan in the anti-Communist Southeast Asia Treaty Organization (SEATO), one purpose of which was to protect the southern part of Vietnam.

In the South, the United States helped Ngo Dinh Diem push Bao Dai aside. A Catholic in a Buddhist nation, Diem lacked popular support. But he was a nationalist and an anti-Communist, and with American aid he won a fraudulent election. When Ho called for national elections in keeping with the Geneva agreements, Diem and Eisenhower refused, fearing the charismatic Vietminh leader would win. From 1955 to 1961, the Diem government received more than $1 billion in U.S. aid, most of it military. Diem's Saigon regime became dependent on the United States for its very existence, and the culture of southern Vietnam became increasingly Americanized.

Meanwhile, Diem became increasingly dictatorial. He abolished village elections, appointed to public office people beholden to him, threw dissenters in jail, and shut down newspapers that criticized his regime. Non-Communists and Communists alike struck back. Encouraged by Ho's regime in the northern capital of Hanoi, southern insurgents embarked on a program of terror, assassinating hundreds of Diem's village officials. Then, in 1960, southern Communists organized the National Liberation Front, known as the Vietcong. The Vietcong in turn attracted other anti-Diem groups in the South. The war against imperialism had become a two-part civil war: Ho's North versus Diem's South, and Vietcong guerrillas versus the Diem government.

Having suffered the humiliations of the Bay of Pigs and the Berlin Wall, President Kennedy decided to stand firm in Vietnam. He feared further criticism if the United States

Kennedy's Escalation
——

backed down in Asia (where he was already seeking to negotiate an end to the civil war in Laos). He also sought a Cold War victory. By late 1963, Project Beef-up had sent more than 16,000 American "advisers." That year, 489 Americans were killed in Vietnam.

The United States in 1963 also unveiled the Strategic Hamlet Program. Intended to separate peasants from the Vietcong by relocating them to barbed-wire compounds, the project further alienated villagers from the Diem regime. At the same time, Buddhist priests began protests, charging Diem with religious persecution. In the streets of Saigon, protesting monks poured gasoline over their robes and set themselves afire.

American officials concluded that if Diem could not be reformed, he should be removed. Through the CIA, the United States quietly

Removal of Diem
——

encouraged disaffected South Vietnamese generals to stage a coup. With the ill-concealed backing of Ambassador Henry Cabot Lodge, the generals struck in November 1963. Diem was captured and slain—only a few weeks before Kennedy died by an assassin's bullet.

JOHNSON AND THE WAR WITHOUT VICTORY

With new governments in Saigon and Washington, some analysts thought it an appropriate time for reassessment. United Nations, Vietcong, and French leaders called for a coalition government in South Vietnam. But the new American president, Lyndon Johnson, would have none of it. America's purpose was victory, he declared.

Johnson, an old New Dealer, talked about building Tennessee Valley Authorities around the world. "I want to leave the footprints of America there [in Vietnam]. I want them to say, 'This is what Americans left—schools and hospitals and dams.'" The footprints America eventually left were those of soldiers, bombs, and chemical defoliants.

On August 2, 1964, the USS *Maddox*, in the Gulf of Tonkin to assist South Vietnamese commando raids against North Vietnam, came under

Tonkin Gulf Incident
——

attack from northern patrol boats (see map). The small craft suffered heavy damage while the unharmed *Maddox*

CHINA

MYANMAR
(BURMA)

Red R.

Black R.

• Dienbienphu

Hanoi •

Haiphong •

Harbor mined, 1972

Gulf of Tonkin

Communist-Pathet Lao victory, 1975

PLAIN OF JARS

⊙ *Maddox*
    incident, 1964

HAINAN

NORTH VIETNAM
• Vinh

Mu Gia Pass

**U.S. Seventh Fleet
operations during the war**

L   A   O   S

Vientiane •

Mekong R.

Ca R.

Udon Thani ■   ■ Nakhon Phanom ■

Demilitarized Zone

17°
Demarcation Line, July 1954

Khe Sanh •   ■ Quang Tri
Sépone •   A Chau   Hue
Lang Vei •

*SOUTH
CHINA
SEA*

Ta Khli ■

■ Khon Kaen

T   H   A   I   L   A   N   D

Kham Duc   Da Nang
                My Lai

Chu Lai

Ubon Ratchathani ■

Mekong R.

• Quang Ngai

Dak To •

■ Rachasima

Kontum
Pleiku
An Khe •
Duc Co •   • Qui Nhon

• Don Muang

• Bangkok

C   A   M   B   O   D   I   A
(KAMPUCHEA)

CENTRAL
HIGHLANDS

• Tuy Hoa

Ban Me Thout •

■ Sattahip

U.S. invasion, 1970

Nha Trang

Dalat •

• Bu Dop   **SOUTH VIETNAM**   ■ Can Ranh Bay

Vietnamese invasion, 1978

Communist-Khmer Rouge victory, 1975

Phnom Penh •

Cholon   ■ Bien Hoa
Tan Son Nhut   ■
Saigon   ■ Long Binh

Gulf of Siam

Chau Duc
My Tho
Vinh Long   Ben Tre

⊙   Vung Tau

**Vietcong and
North Vietnamese victory
and U.S. withdrawal, 1975**

Mayaguez incident, 1975

Can Tho   *Mekong Delta*
Ca Mau

CA MAU PENINSULA

0   100   200 miles

0   100   200   300 kilometers

→ Ho Chi Minh Trail

➡ Boat-People Refugees after 1975

✷ Major battles of the Tet Offensive,
   January 1968

■ Major U.S. bases during the war

sailed away. Two days later, the *Maddox*, now joined by another destroyer, moved toward the North Vietnamese shore once again, as if to bait the Communists. In bad weather, sonar technicians reported what they thought were enemy torpedoes; the two destroyers began firing ferociously. Yet when the captain of the *Maddox* asked his crew what had happened, not one had seen or heard hostile gunfire.

President Johnson seized the chance to go on national television; he announced retaliatory air strikes against North Vietnam. Congress promptly passed the Tonkin Gulf Resolution, 416 to 0 in the House and 88 to 2 in the Senate. The resolution authorized the president to "take all necessary measures to repel any armed attack against the forces of the United States and to prevent further aggression." By passing the Tonkin Gulf Resolution—which Johnson later argued amounted to a declaration of war—Congress essentially surrendered its powers in the foreign-policy process by giving the president wide latitude to conduct the war as he saw fit.

After winning the presidency in his own right in November 1964, Johnson directed the military to map plans for stepped-up bombing of both Laos and North Vietnam. (Unbeknown to Congress and the American public, U.S. aircraft were already bombing the supply routes from North Vietnam to the Vietcong that were known as the Ho Chi Minh Trail.) When the Vietcong, who controlled nearly half of South Vietnam, attacked the American airfield at Pleiku in February 1965, killing nine Americans, Johnson ordered carrier-based jets to ravage the North. Soon Operation Rolling Thunder—a sustained bombing program above the seventeenth parallel—was under way. Before the longest war was over, more bombs would fall on Vietnam than American aircraft had dropped in the Second World War.

In his momentous decision of July 1965, the president also sent more American troops to the South. America's troop commitment increased

Southeast Asia and the Vietnam War *To prevent Communists from coming to power in Vietnam, Cambodia, and Laos in the 1960s, the United States intervened massively in Southeast Asia. The interventions failed, and the remaining U.S. troops made a hasty exit from Vietnam in 1975, when the victorious Vietcong and North Vietnamese took Saigon and renamed it Ho Chi Minh City.*

Americanization of the War

from 184,300 at the end of 1965 to 543,400 in 1969. In 1967, the secret CIA-run Phoenix Program began to kill Vietcong leaders; probably 60,000 were assassinated. Undeterred, Ho increased the flow of arms and men to the rebels in the South. In this seemingly endless war of attrition, each American escalation begot a new Vietnamese escalation.

The Americanization of the war troubled growing numbers of Americans, especially as television coverage brought the war into their homes every night. The pictures and stories were not pretty. Innocent civilians were caught in the line of fire; refugees straggled into "pacification" camps; villages considered friendly to the enemy were burned to the ground. To expose and destroy Vietcong hiding places, pilots sprayed chemical defoliants like Agent Orange over the landscape to denude it. The Vietcong and North Vietnamese contributed to the carnage, but American guns, bombs, and chemicals took by far the greatest toll, and the Vietnamese people knew it.

Stories of atrocities made their way home. Most gruesome was the My Lai massacre of March 1968 (not made public until twenty months later because of a military cover-up).

My Lai Massacre

An American unit, frustrated by its inability to pin down an elusive enemy and eager to avenge the loss of some buddies, shot to death more than two hundred unarmed Vietnamese civilians, most of them women and children.

Many incidents of deliberate shooting of civilians, torturing and killing of prisoners, taking of Vietnamese ears as trophies, and burning of villages have been recorded, but most

American Soldiers in Vietnam

American soldiers were not committing atrocities. They were trying instead to save their own young lives (their average age was only nineteen) and to serve the U.S. mission by killing enemy troops. Many of these Americans made up the rear-echelon forces that supported the "grunts" or "boonie rats" in the field. But wherever they were, the environment was inhospitable, for no place in Vietnam was secure. Well-hidden booby traps blasted away body parts. And the enemy was everywhere yet nowhere, often burrowed into elaborate underground tunnels or melded into the population, where any Vietnamese might be a Vietcong terrorist.

As the war ground on to no discernible conclusion and became increasingly unpopular at home, morale in the U.S. armed forces sagged and discipline sometimes lapsed. The generals grew alarmed by reports of disobedience—and by peace symbols scratched on helmets. Desertions and absent-without-official-leave (AWOL) cases increased, especially near the end of the war in the 1970s, when no GI wanted to be the last man killed. Racial tensions between whites and blacks intensified. Drug abuse became serious. "Fragging"—killing of officers by enlisted men, usually using hand grenades—took at least 1,000 lives between 1969 and 1972.

At home, thousands of young men were expressing their opposition to the war by fleeing the draft. By the end of 1972, more than 30,000 draft resisters were living in Canada; thousands more had gone into exile in Sweden or Mexico or were living under false identities in the United States. In the course of the war, more than a half-million men committed draft violations, including a quarter-million who never registered and thousands who burned their draft cards.

As American military engagements in Vietnam escalated, so did protest at home. Teach-ins at universities began in 1965, and in April of that year, 25,000 people marched on the White House. In October, the National Committee to End the War in Vietnam mobilized more than 80,000 in nationwide demonstrations. In early 1966, Senator J. William Fulbright held public hearings on whether the national interest was being served by pursuing the war in Asia. What exactly was the threat? he asked. In October 1967, 100,000 people marched on Washington to protest the war. Disenchantment also rose in the administration. Secretary of Defense Robert McNamara worked quietly to scale back the American military presence in Vietnam and resigned when he failed to persuade President Johnson. "Ho Chi Minh is a tough old S.O.B.," McNamara told his

Antiwar Protest

aides. "And he won't quit no matter how much bombing we do."

Johnson dug in, dismissing his critics as "those little shits on the campuses." Cheered by opinion polls that showed Americans favored escalation over withdrawal, the president vowed to continue the battle. Although on occasion he halted the bombing to encourage Ho Chi Minh to negotiate, such pauses were often accompanied by increases in American troop strength. And the United States sometimes resumed or accelerated the bombing just when a diplomatic breakthrough seemed imminent—as in 1966, when a resumption of bombing cut short a Polish diplomat's efforts. The North demanded a complete suspension of bombing raids before sitting down at the conference table. And Ho could not accept American terms: nonrecognition of the Vietcong as a legitimate political organization, withdrawal of northern soldiers from the South, and an end to North Vietnamese military aid to the Vietcong—in short, abandonment of his life-long dream of an independent unified Vietnam.

In January 1968, a shocking event forced Johnson to reappraise his position. During Tet, the Vietnamese holiday of the lunar new year, Vietcong and North Vietnamese forces struck all across South Vietnam, hitting and capturing provincial capitals. Vietcong raiders even penetrated the American embassy compound in Saigon. U.S. and South Vietnamese units eventually regained much of the ground they had lost, inflicting heavy casualties on the enemy. But the Tet offensive jolted Americans. If all of America's air power and dollars and half a million troops couldn't defeat the Vietcong once and for all, could anything do so?

Tet Offensive

The Tet offensive and its influence on public opinion hit the White House like a thunderclap. The new secretary of defense, Clark Clifford, told Johnson the war could not be won, even if the 206,000 more soldiers now requested by the army were sent to Vietnam. The ultimate Cold Warrior, Dean Acheson—one of the "wise men" Johnson had brought in to advise him—bluntly told the surprised president that the military brass did not know what they were talking about.

President Lyndon B. Johnson, after the Tet offensive and his decision to end his political career by not running again for the presidency, reveals the strain of the office.   (Lyndon B. Johnson Library.)

The wise men had become aware that the nation was suffering a financial crisis prompted by rampant deficit spending, largely the result of heavy U.S. expenditures abroad to sustain the war and other global commitments. Nervous foreigners were exchanging their U.S. dollars for gold at an alarming rate. On March 14 alone, foreigners—especially Europeans—redeemed $372 million for gold. A post–Tet effort to take the initiative in Vietnam would surely cost billions more and thus further derange the budget, panic foreign owners of dollars, and wreck the economy.

Dollar/Gold Crisis

Strained by exhausting sessions with advisers, troubled by the economic implications of escalation, sensing that more soldiers and firepower would not bring victory, and faced with serious opposition within his own party, Johnson changed course. On March 31, he announced on television that he had stopped the bombing of most of North Vietnam and asked Hanoi to begin negotiations. Then he stunned the nation by dropping out of the presidential race. U.S. leaders, aware that they could not win the war, would at least try not to lose it.

DEFEAT AND EXIT: NIXON AND THE LEGACY OF VIETNAM

In July 1969, the new president, Richard M. Nixon, announced that the United States would help those nations that helped themselves. The Nixon Doctrine, as the policy was called, reflected official Washington's realization that it could no longer afford to sustain its many overseas commitments and that the United States would have to rely more on regional allies to maintain an anti-Communist world order. In Southeast Asia, the United States implemented this doctrine as "Vietnamization"—building up South Vietnamese forces to replace American troops. Nixon began a gradual withdrawal of U.S. troops from Vietnam, decreasing their number to 156,800 by the end of 1971. But he also increased the bombing of the North, hoping to pound Hanoi into concessions—"jugular diplomacy," in the words of Nixon's national security adviser, Henry Kissinger.

Nixon Doctrine

In April 1970, Nixon announced that South Vietnamese and American forces were invading Cambodia in search of arms depots and enemy forces that used the neutral nation as a sanctuary. This escalation of the war provoked angry demonstrations on college campuses. At Kent State University in Ohio, National Guardsmen ordered to suppress protest killed four people. Across the nation, students went "on strike" to protest the killing in Indochina and America. In June, the Senate joined the protest against Nixon's broadening of the war by terminating the Tonkin Gulf Resolution of 1964.

Cambodia and Antiwar Protest

Nixon's troubles at home mounted in June 1971 when the *New York Times* began to publish the *Pentagon Papers*, a top-secret official study of U.S. decisions in the Vietnam War. Secretary McNamara had ordered preparation of the study in 1967 to preserve a documentary record. Daniel Ellsberg, a former Defense Department official, working at the RAND Corporation (a think tank for analyzing defense policy), had leaked the report to the *Times*. The *Pentagon Papers* revealed that U.S. leaders had frequently lied to the American people.

Nixon and Kissinger continued to expand the war, ordering "protective reaction strikes" against the North, bombing of Cambodia, and mining of Haiphong harbor in North Vietnam. In December 1972, they launched a massive air strike on the North called the Christmas bombing. The air terror punished the Vietnamese. The campaign cost the United States twenty-six planes, including fifteen B-52 bombers.

In Paris, meanwhile, the peace talks begun in 1968 seemed to be going nowhere. But Kissinger was also meeting privately with Le Duc Tho, the chief delegate from North Vietnam. On January 27, 1973, Kissinger and Le Duc Tho signed a cease-fire agreement. The United States promised to withdraw all its troops within sixty days. Vietnamese troops would stay in place, and a coalition government that included the Vietcong would eventually be formed in the South. Critics of the war, pleased that peace had been made, nonetheless noted that if the same terms had been accepted in

Cease-Fire Agreement

1969, more than 20,000 American lives would have been spared. To prevent a future Vietnam, Congress passed the War Powers Resolution in late 1973: the president could commit American troops abroad for no more than sixty days without obtaining congressional approval.

The United States pulled its troops out of Vietnam, leaving behind some advisers, and reduced but did not end its aid program. Both North and South soon violated the cease-fire, and full-scale war erupted once more. As many had predicted, the feeble South Vietnamese government—for so long an American puppet—could not hold out. On April 29, 1975, the South Vietnamese government collapsed. Shortly thereafter, Saigon was renamed Ho Chi Minh City for the persevering patriot who had died in 1969.

The overall costs of the war were immense. More than 58,000 Americans and about 1.5 million Vietnamese had died. The war cost the United States more than $170 billion, and billions more would be paid out in veterans' benefits. At home, the war brought inflation, political schism, attacks on civil liberties, and retreat from reform. The war also had extremely negative consequences internationally: delay in improved relations with the Soviet Union and the People's Republic of China, friction with allies, and the alienation of Third World nations.

Costs of the Vietnam War

In 1975, Communists assumed control and instituted repressive governments in South Vietnam, Cambodia, and Laos, but the domino effect once predicted by pro-war U.S. officials never occurred. Acute hunger afflicted the people of those devastated lands. Soon, refugees were crowding aboard unsafe vessels in an attempt to escape their battered homelands. Many of these "boat people" eventually emigrated to the United States, where they were received with mixed feelings by Americans reluctant to be reminded of their defeat in Asia.

This sad conclusion prompted an American ambassador to pose a central question about the U.S. defeat: how was it that "so many with so much could achieve so little for so long against so few"? General Maxwell Taylor, summarizing the reasons Americans could not win the Vietnam War, said, "We didn't know our ally. Secondly, we knew even less about the enemy. And, the last, most inexcusable of our mistakes, was not knowing our own people."

Americans seemed both angry and confused about the nation's war experience. For the first time in their history, the historian William Appleman Williams observed, Americans were suffering from a serious case of "empire shock"—that is, shock over having had their overseas sphere of influence violently pushed back. Hawkish leaders claimed that America's failure in Vietnam undermined the nation's credibility and tempted enemies to exploit opportunities at the expense of U.S. interests. They pointed to a "Vietnam syndrome"—a suspicion of foreign entanglements—that they feared would inhibit the United States from exercising its power. Next time, they said, the military should be permitted to do its job, free from the constraints of whimsical public opinion, stab-in-the-back journalists, and meddlesome politicians. America lost in Vietnam, they asserted, because Americans lost their guts and will at home.

The Lessons of Vietnam

Dovish leaders drew different lessons. Some blamed the war on an imperial presidency that had permitted strong-willed men like Johnson to act without limits and on pusillanimous Congresses that had conceded too much power to the executive branch, as with the Tonkin Gulf Resolution. Others took a more hard-headed, even fatalistic, view: as long as the United States remained a major power with compelling ideological, strategic, economic, and political needs that could be satisfied only through activism abroad, the nation would continue to be expansionist and interventionist. The United States was destined to intervene abroad, they argued, to sustain its role as the world's policeman, teacher, social worker, banker, and merchant. Still others blamed the containment doctrine for failing to make distinctions between areas vital and peripheral to the national security and for relying too heavily on military means. Containment could not work, they believed, if there were no political stability and no effective popular government in the country where it was being applied.

Public discussion of the lessons of the Vietnam War was also stimulated by veterans' calls for help in dealing with post-traumatic stress disorder,

Post-Traumatic Stress Disorder

which afflicted thousands of the 2.8 million Vietnam veterans after returning home. They suffered nightmares and extreme nervousness. Doctors reported that the disorder stemmed primarily from the soldiers having seen so many children, women, and elderly people killed. Some GIs inadvertently killed these people, unable to distinguish the innocent from the enemy; some killed them vengefully and later felt guilt. By the early 1990s, about 60,000 veterans of the Vietnam War had committed suicide—more deaths than Americans had suffered during the war itself.

CONTENDING WITH THE THIRD WORLD IN THE 1970s

President Nixon called Vietnam a "short-term problem," and Henry Kissinger declared the war a mere historical "footnote"; both considered Soviet-American relations the central question of international affairs. They nonetheless valued the Third World for its resources and markets, and they repeatedly exerted U.S. power against it to preserve the administration's grand strategy to achieve a stable world order through détente.

Events in the Middle East revealed how fragile the Nixon-Kissinger grand strategy was. When Nixon took office in 1969, the Middle East was, in the president's words, a "powder keg." Israel, using American weapons, had scored victories against Egypt and Syria in the Six-Day War (1967), seizing the West Bank and the ancient city of Jerusalem from Jordan, the Golan Heights from Syria, and the Sinai Peninsula from Egypt (see map, page 602). To further complicate matters, Palestinians, many of them expelled from their homes in 1948 when the nation of Israel was created, had organized the Palestine Liberation Organization (PLO) and pledged to destroy Israel.

In October 1973, Egypt and Syria attacked Israel. Despite détente, Moscow, backing Egypt, and Washington, backing Israel, put their armed forces—

The 1973 War in the Middle East

including nuclear forces—on alert. In an attempt to pressure Americans into a pro-Arab stance, the Organization of Petroleum Exporting Countries (OPEC) imposed an embargo on shipments of oil to the United States.

Faced with an energy crisis at home that was due to dramatically higher oil prices, the Nixon administration had to find a way to end Mideast hostilities. Kissinger arranged a cease-fire and undertook "shuttle diplomacy," flying repeatedly between Middle Eastern capitals in search of a settlement. In March 1974, OPEC lifted the oil embargo. The next year, Kissinger persuaded Egypt and Israel to accept a United Nations peace-keeping force in the Sinai. But other problems, including Israel's insistence on building Jewish settlements in occupied lands and Arab threats to destroy the Jewish state, remained.

In Latin America, Nixon continued President Johnson's interventionist policies. (Johnson had dispatched twenty thousand American troops to the Dominican Republic in 1965 to prevent a leftist government from coming to power there.) In 1970, Nixon perceived a Communist threat in Chile, when the Chileans elected a Marxist president, Salvador Allende. The CIA began secret operations to disrupt the Chilean economy and apparently encouraged military officers to stage a coup. In 1973, a military junta ousted and killed Allende and installed an authoritarian regime in his place. Nixon and Kissinger privately pronounced their policy of "destabilization" successful, while publicly denying any role in the affair.

In Africa, the maneuvers of Nixon and Kissinger proved less successful. During the 1960s and early 1970s, while Washington publicly supported Portugal, the CIA hedged its bets by channeling funds to groups fighting to liberate Angola from Portuguese colonial rule. After Angola won its independence in 1975, civil war erupted. The United States and South Africa covertly backed one faction and the Soviets helped another. When Congress learned about the secret U.S. aid, it voted to cut off all funds. Although Kissinger claimed that the Soviets would gain a foothold in Africa, many members of

Angola

Congress argued that Americans could not decide the outcome of an African civil war, that the United States should not be aligned with the white racist regime of South Africa, and that the administration should have tried diplomacy. After a leftist government came to power in Angola, Washington took a keener interest in the rest of Africa, building economic ties, sending arms to friendly black nations, and distancing the United States from the white minority governments of Rhodesia (now Zimbabwe) and South Africa.

The United States was interventionist in part because the American economy depended on imports of strategic raw materials. Furthermore, American investments abroad totaled more than $133 billion by the mid-1970s. American leaders thus read threats to markets, investments, and raw materials as deadly stabs at the high U.S. standard of living.

U.S. Economic Interests Abroad

By the 1970s, multinational corporations had become a symbol of America's conspicuous economic position overseas. U.S.-based multinationals like Exxon and General Motors actually enjoyed budgets and incomes larger than those of most countries. These giant firms brought home profits and exported American culture, but they also provoked criticism. American workers protested that global oligopolies stole their jobs when the companies moved factories abroad in search of less expensive labor. Third World critics protested that multinationals robbed them of their natural resources, corrupted politics, provided "covers" for CIA agents, and evaded taxes by clever manipulations of their books.

Multinational Corporations

Multinational executives and U.S. government officials defended these enterprises, pointing out that they invested in risky ventures that promised economic progress, including the transfer of technology. Multinationals, they insisted, helped rationalize a chaotic world economy. Many nations nonetheless passed laws requiring a certain percentage of native ownership; India, for example, legislated that its nationals own a majority of voting shares in industrial firms. Other countries simply nationalized multinational properties.

In addition to imposing restraints on multinationals, the South—as the Third World has sometimes been called—demanded low-interest loans, lower prices for the technology and manufactured goods they bought abroad, and higher prices for the raw materials they sold. In 1974, the United Nations called for a "New International Economic Order" in order to encompass many of these points, but the industrial North made few concessions.

CARTER AND DIPLOMATIC INTERVENTION

When President Jimmy Carter took office in 1977, he promised no more Vietnams. Instead, he vowed new departures, including an emphasis on human rights and advancement of the North-South dialogue. Carter promised to be an interventionist too but through diplomacy instead of armed forces. The United States, he pledged, would respect Third World nations as never before. Like his predecessors, however, he frowned on radicalism and nationalism, because they threatened America's prominent global position.

Carter worked to improve relations with the Third World, where the opinion prevailed that the United States was a selfish imperial power. His appointment of Andrew Young, a black civil rights activist and member of Congress, as ambassador to the United Nations earned goodwill among developing nations. Third World leaders were shocked, however, when Carter forced Young to resign in

On March 26, 1979, Egypt's President Anwar el-Sadat (1918–1981) on the left, Israel's Prime Minister Menachem Begin (1913–1992) on the right, and U.S. President Jimmy Carter (1924–) signed a peace treaty known as the Camp David Accords. Studiously negotiated by Carter, the Egyptian-Israeli peace has held to this day—despite conflict in much of the rest of the Middle East. Jimmy Carter Presidential Library.

1979 after the ambassador had met privately with representatives of the PLO. (The United States refused to recognize the PLO as a legitimate entity.)

In the Middle East, Carter markedly advanced the peace process. Through tenacious personal diplomacy at a Camp David meeting in 1978 with Egyptian and Israeli leaders, the president gained Israel's promise to withdraw from the Sinai. The agreement was finalized the following year. Other Arab states denounced the agreement for not requiring Israel to relinquish additional occupied territories and for not guaranteeing a Palestinian homeland. But the treaty at least ended warfare along one frontier in that troubled area of the world.

Camp David Agreements
———

In 1979 in Nicaragua, leftist insurgents overthrew Anastasio Somoza, a member of the dictatorial family that had ruled the Central American nation since the mid-1930s. The revolutionaries called themselves Sandinistas in honor of the Nicaraguan who had fought U.S. Marines then. Carter welcomed Somoza's departure and recognized the new government, but he recoiled from the Sandinistas' radicalism. In early 1981, he halted aid to Nicaragua to express U.S. disapproval of the Sandinistas' curbing of civil liberties, ties with Castro's Cuba, and assistance to radical rebels in El Salvador.

Latin America
———

Elsewhere in Latin America, Carter concluded two treaties with Panama. Signed in 1977 and narrowly endorsed by the Senate in 1978, the treaties provided for the return of the Canal Zone to Panama in the year 2000 and guaranteed the United States the right to defend the canal after that time.

Carter met his toughest test in Iran, where in early 1979 the U.S.-supported shah was overthrown by revolutionaries led by the Ayatollah Ruhollah Khomeini, a bitterly anti-American Moslem cleric. Much of Khomeini's resentment stemmed from the CIA's training of the shah's ruthless secret police and the huge infusion of U.S. arms into their country. In November, after the exiled shah was admitted to the United States for medical treatment, mobs stormed the American embassy in

Iranian Hostage Crisis
———

Teheran. They took hostages, demanding the return of the shah to stand trial, along with his vast wealth. The Iranians eventually released a few of the American prisoners, but fifty-two others languished more than a year under Iranian guard.

President Carter would not return the shah to Iran or apologize for past U.S. aid to his regime. Unable to gain the hostages' freedom through diplomatic intermediaries, Carter took steps to isolate Iran economically, freezing Iranian assets in the United States and urging allies to sever trade links with the renegade state. In April 1980, Carter broke diplomatic relations with Iran and ordered a daring rescue mission. But the rescue effort miscarried after equipment failure in the sandy Iranian desert. The hostages were not freed until January 1981, after the United States unfroze Iranian assets and promised not to intervene again in Iran's internal affairs.

Carter's diplomatic record failed to meet his aspirations. More American military personnel were stationed overseas in 1980 than in 1976, and the defense budget climbed. Carter's human rights policy also proved inconsistent. He followed a double standard by applying the human rights test to some nations (the Soviet Union, Argentina, and Chile) but not to American allies (South Korea, the shah's Iran, and the Philippines).

Carter's Mixed Record
———

Carter's performance did not satisfy Americans who wanted a post-Vietnam reinstatement of the economic hegemony and military edge the United States once enjoyed. As one Tennessee woman mused, "Growing up we learned in history that America was the best in everything. We had the respect of the whole world. But where can you go today and be respected for being American?" During the 1980 presidential election, the nostalgia for old-fashioned American militancy and supremacy found a ringing voice in Ronald Reagan.

REAGAN CONFRONTS THE THIRD WORLD

Reagan blamed most Third World troubles on the Soviet Union and thought revolutionary movements took their orders from Communists. Invoking the Reagan Doctrine, the United States intervened both covertly and openly in civil wars in several Third World countries. The Reagan administration also preferred military solutions to negotiations with Third World states. In 1983, for example, the president ordered U.S. troops to invade the tiny Caribbean nation of Grenada to oust a leftist government that had developed ties with Castro's Cuba, and in 1986 U.S. warplanes bombed Libya to punish it for supporting terrorism.

Under the banner of private enterprise, Reagan pressed Third World nations to open their economies to competition and reduce the role of the state in managing economic affairs. The Law of the Sea Treaty, patiently composed in the 1970s through extended negotiations and compromise, became a test case. Developing nations argued that rich sea-bed resources of petroleum and minerals should be shared under international supervision among all nations as a "common heritage of mankind." The First World industrial states preferred private exploitation with minimal international management. The treaty represented a compromise, but the Reagan administration rejected the treaty. Angry Third World nations denounced the U.S. decision as selfish economic imperialism, whereas many American allies who supported the compromise predicted a chaotic future of competing claims of ownership, territorial disputes, and threats to freedom of navigation.

Law of the Sea Treaty

In Central America (Guatemala, Honduras, El Salvador, Nicaragua, and Costa Rica), Reagan officials believed that the Soviets (and their Cuban allies) were fomenting disorder (see map). They saw El Salvador as a textbook case of Communist aggression. In that small, very poor country, revolutionaries challenged the government, which was dominated by the military and a small landed elite. The regime used (or could not control) right-wing "death squads" that killed thousands of dissidents and other citizens, as well as some American missionaries who worked with landless peasants. Persuaded that a U.S.-funded counterinsurgency war could be

El Salvador

won in a short time, Reagan eschewed negotiations and instead increased military assistance to the Salvadoran regime. The controversial U.S. intervention in the Salvadoran civil war sparked a debate much like that which had erupted over Vietnam years before. Those who urged negotiations thought Reagan wrong to interpret the conflict as a Cold War contest. Oppression and poverty, not Communist plots, caused people to pick up guns to fight the regime, they argued. Resurrecting the discredited domino theory, Reagan retorted that the "Communists" would soon be at the Mexican-American border if they were not stopped in El Salvador. Reagan also made a strategic argument: Central America hugs the Caribbean Sea, "our lifeline to the outside world." After consistently intense debate, Congress repeatedly gave Reagan the funds he wanted for El Salvador. The civil war only continued, more bloody than before.

Reagan also intervened in Nicaragua, where the Sandinista leader Daniel Ortega defiantly explained that his people "have broken with their past history of servility to imperialist politics." When the Sandinistas bought Soviet weapons and invited Cubans to work in Nicaragua's hospitals and schools and to help reorganize their army, Reagan charged that Nicaragua was becoming a Soviet client and that it was sending arms to the rebels in El Salvador. Reagan therefore decided to topple the Nicaraguan regime. In 1981, the CIA began to train, arm, and direct more than ten thousand counterrevolutionaries, called *contras*. From CIA-managed bases in Honduras and Costa Rica, the contras crossed into Nicaragua to kill officials and destroy oil refineries, transportation facilities, medical clinics, and day-care centers.

Undeclared War Against Nicaragua

It became known in 1984 that the CIA had mined the harbors of Nicaragua, blowing up merchant ships. The World Court ruled that Nicaragua had the right to sue the United States for damages. At the same time, Congress voted to stop U.S. military aid to the contras. ("Humanitarian aid" was soon sent in its place.) The Reagan administration secretly lined up other countries, including Saudi Arabia, Panama, and Korea, to funnel money and weapons to the contras, and in 1985 Reagan imposed

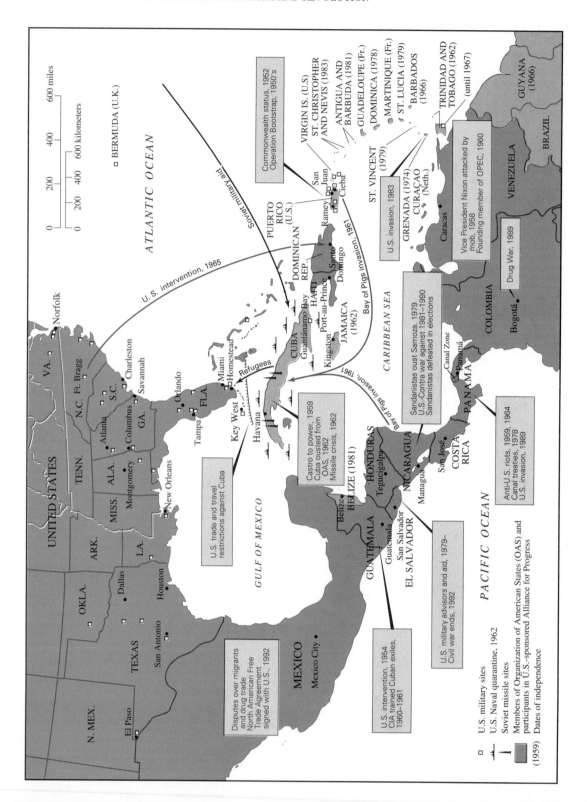

600 miles

□ BERMUDA (U.K.)

600 kilometers

600 kilometers

0   200   400   600

ATLANTIC OCEAN

Soviet military aid

Commonwealth status, 1952
Operation Bootstrap, 1950's

VIRGIN IS. (U.S)
ST. CHRISTOPHER
AND NEVIS (1983)
ANTIGUA AND
BARBUDA (1981)
GUADELOUPE (Fr.)
DOMINICA (1978)
MARTINIQUE (Fr.)
ST. LUCIA (1979)
BARBADOS
(1966)
TRINIDAD AND
TOBAGO (1962)

GUYANA
(1966)

San
Juan

Ramey   Ceiba

PUERTO
RICO
(U.S.)

ST. VINCENT
(1979)

CURAÇAO
(Neth.)

GRENADA (1974)
U.S. invasion, 1983

Vice President Nixon attacked by
mob, 1958
Founding member of OPEC, 1960

VENEZUELA

BRAZIL

Bay of Pigs invasion, 1961

U. S. intervention, 1965

DOMINICAN
REP.

HAITI
Port-au-Prince

Santo
Domingo

Caracas

Drug War, 1989

Norfolk

VA.

N.C. Ft. Bragg

CUBA

Guantánamo Bay

JAMAICA
(1962)

Kingston

CARIBBEAN SEA

COLOMBIA

Bogotá

Charleston

S.C.

Savannah

Atlanta
GA.

Orlando

Sandinistas oust Samoza, 1979
U.S.-Contra war against 1981–1990
Sandinistas defeated in elections

Canal Zone

Panamá

TENN.

Columbus

Tampa

FLA.

Miami

Homestead

PANAMA

ALA.

Montgomery

Key West

Havana

Refugees

Bay of Pigs invasion, 1961

NICARAGUA

Managua

San José

COSTA
RICA

Anti-U.S. riots, 1959, 1964
Canal treaties, 1978
U.S. invasion, 1989

UNITED STATES

MISS.

ARK.

LA.

New Orleans

U.S. trade and travel
restrictions against Cuba

Castro to power, 1959
Cuba ousted from
OAS, 1962
Missile crisis, 1962

BELIZE (1981)

HONDURAS

Tegucigalpa

OKLA.

Dallas

Houston

GULF OF MEXICO

Belize

GUATEMALA

San Salvador

Guatemala

EL SALVADOR

U.S. military advisors and aid, 1979–
Civil war ends, 1992

PACIFIC OCEAN

TEXAS

San Antonio

MEXICO

Mexico City

U.S. intervention, 1954
CIA trained Cuban exiles,
1960–1961

N. MEX.

El Paso

Disputes over migrants
and drug trade
North American Free
Trade Agreement
signed with U.S., 1992

□   U.S. military sites

⌐   U.S. Naval quarantine, 1962

┬   Soviet missile sites

▨   Members of Organization of American States (OAS) and
participants in U.S.-sponsored Alliance for Progress

(1959)   Dates of independence

an economic embargo against Nicaragua. The next year, Congress once again voted military aid for the contras. During the undeclared U.S. war against Nicaragua, critics around the world chastised U.S. leaders for rejecting opportunities for negotiations.

Scandal, popularly called Irangate or Contragate, tainted the North American crusade against the Sandinistas. It became known in 1986 that the president's national security af-

Iran-Contra Scandal

fairs adviser, John M. Poindexter, and an aide, Oliver North, in collusion with CIA Director William J. Casey, had covertly sold weapons to Iran and then diverted the profits to the contras so that they could purchase arms. The diversion had occurred during the period in which Congress had prohibited military assistance to the contras.

From any angle, the Iran-contra scandal made President Reagan look bad. If Reagan did not know that the National Security Council was running guns to both Iran and the contras, he looked incompetent. If he did know about arms deliveries to Iran, he was guilty of breaking his own pledge not to aid a government that supported terrorists and of violating the law—Congress's ban on military aid to the contras. The scandal irreparably tarnished Reagan's reputation. In late 1992, outgoing President George Bush pardoned several former government officials who had been convicted of lying to Congress. Critics smelled a cover-up, for Bush himself, as vice president, had participated in high-level meetings on Iran-contra deals.

In the 1980s, as before, the deeply divided Middle East continued to defy American solutions. An Iraqi-Iranian war threatened Persian Gulf shipping. Lebanon was disintegrating. And American leaders became upset that Arab states like Jordan and Saudi Arabia, recipients of substantial U.S. foreign aid, refused to help stabilize the region. The

The United States in the Caribbean and Central America   The United States often has intervened in the Caribbean and Central America. Geographic proximity, economic stakes, political disputes, security links, trade in illicit drugs, and especially Cuba's defiance of the United States and alliance with the Soviet Union have kept North American eyes fixed on events to the south.

Middle East was also a major source of the world's terrorism against U.S. citizens and property.

Even Israel gave the United States trouble. In retaliation for PLO shelling of Israel from Lebanon, the Israelis repeatedly bombed suspected PLO camps inside Lebanon, killing

Crisis in Lebanon

hundreds of civilians. And in 1981, without warning, Israel annexed the Syrian territory of the Golan Heights. The following year, Israeli troops invaded civil-war-torn Lebanon, reaching the capital Beirut and inflicting massive damage. The beleaguered PLO and various Lebanese factions called on Syria to contain the Israelis. Thousands of civilians died in the multifaceted conflict, and a million people became refugees. Reagan sent U.S. Marines to Lebanon to serve as part of a peace-keeping force. Their mission ill defined, the American troops soon became embroiled in a war between Lebanese factions. In October 1983, terrorist bombs demolished a marine barracks, killing 240 Americans. Four months later, Reagan recognized failure and pulled the remaining marines out.

Still, the United States had commitments (the defense of Israel), political friends (Saudi Arabia), and enemies (Iran and Libya). Mideast oil supplies fueled Western economies—this was such a critical concern that in 1988 American warships escorted both American and foreign commercial ships through the Persian Gulf.

Washington, which openly sided with Israel, continued to propose peace plans designed to persuade the Israelis to give back occupied territories and the Arabs to give up attempts to push the Jews out of the Middle East (the "land-for-peace" formula). As the peace process stalled in 1987, Palestinians living in the West Bank began an uprising called *intifada* against Israeli forces that had occupied the area since 1967. The Israelis used brute force to quell rock-throwing youths and sent bulldozers to knock down the houses of families whose sons or daughters were known to be active in the intifada. The unrest became more embittered. The PLO, meanwhile, declared the West Bank and Gaza Strip an independent Palestinian state. Israel refused to negotiate, but the United States decided to reverse its policy and talk with PLO leaders after PLO chief Yasser Arafat renounced terrorism and accepted Israel's right to live in peace and security. Still, the divide between Arabs and Jews remained wide and peace elusive.

In Africa, the Reagan administration struggled to define a policy toward South Africa, where a blatantly racist white minority imposed a rigidly

South Africa
———

segregationist system called *apartheid* on the predominantly (85 percent) black population. Blacks were kept poor, disfranchised, and geographically segregated in townships that resembled prisons. At first, the Reagan administration pursued a patient policy it called constructive engagement—asking the South African government to reform its repressive system. But many Americans demanded economic sanctions: cutting off imports from South Africa and pressing some 350 American companies to cease operations there. Some American cities and states passed divestment laws, withdrawing dollars (such as pension funds used to buy stock) from U.S. companies active in South Africa. Public protest and congressional legislation forced the Reagan administration in 1986 to impose economic restrictions against South Africa.

The staggering debt of Third World nations ($1.2 trillion by 1989) presented the United States with other problems. Having borrowed heavily in the 1970s, Third World nations were unable to repay the loans when world prices for sugar, coffee, and other commodities slumped. Indebtedness and falling prices, moreover, caused them to cut back on imports of U.S. goods. Hundreds of thousands of jobs in the United States were lost as a result, and economic instability spawned political unrest throughout the Third World.

From Truman to Reagan, the United States was at odds with the Third World. Foreign aid, trade and investment, CIA covert actions, military interventions—nothing seemed capable of closing the gap between the United States and the Third World. In fact, such activities widened the chasm. The clash was fundamentally a struggle for power, and it stemmed primarily from two sources: the Cold War and U.S. economic stakes.

Despite its own revolutionary past, the United States usually stood with its European Cold War allies to resist decolonization, slow the process toward independence, and preach evolution rather than revolution. Then the United States denounced the pref-

erence of many Third World nations for nonalignment in the Cold War. The U.S. globalist perspective also prompted Americans to interpret many Third World troubles as Cold War conflicts, inspired if not directed by Soviet-backed Communists. The intensity of the Cold War obscured for Americans the indigenous roots of most Third World troubles. Indeed, American attitudes and interests were such that the United States could not abide Third World nations' drive for economic independence—for gaining control of their own raw materials and economies.

The Third World, in short, challenged U.S. strategic power by forming a third force in the Cold War, and it challenged U.S. economic power by demanding a new economic order of shared interests. Overall, the rise of the Third World introduced new actors into the international system, challenging its bipolarity. The developing nations contested great-power superintendency of world affairs even as they often feuded among themselves. Even when the Cold War ended, Third World nations continued to challenge U.S. strategic and economic interests. Third World countries remained as resolute as ever about keeping their goals and problems high on the international agenda.

SUGGESTIONS FOR FURTHER READING

For Soviet-American relations, Sino-American relations, and the Cold War, see Chapter 29. Many works cited in Chapter 29 include discussion of issues related to the Third World.

The United States and the Third World: General

H. W. Brands, *The Specter of Neutralism* (1989); Gabriel Kolko, *Confronting the Third World* (1988); Gerald T. Rice, *The Bold Experiment: JFK's Peace Corps* (1985); Alvin Z. Rubenstein and Donald E. Smith, eds., *Anti-Americanism in the Third World* (1985). For global economic issues, see works cited in Chapter 29.

The CIA and Counterinsurgency

Douglas S. Blaufarb, *The Counterinsurgency Era* (1977); Rhodi Jeffreys-Jones, *The CIA and American Democracy* (1989); Loch K. Johnson, *America's Secret Power* (1989); Mark Lowenthal, *U.S. Intelligence* (1984); Thomas Powers, *The Man Who Kept the Secrets* (1979); John Prados, *Presidents' Secret Wars* (1986); John Ranelagh, *The Agency* (1986).

The Vietnam War and Southeast Asia: General

Loren Baritz, *Backfire* (1985); Eric M. Bergerud, *The Dynamics of Defeat* (1991); Frances FitzGerald, *Fire in the Lake* (1972); Leslie H. Gelb and Richard K. Betts, *The Irony of Vietnam* (1979); George C. Herring, *America's Longest War*, 2d ed. (1986); Gary R. Hess, *Vietnam and the United States* (1990); Arnold R. Isaacs, *Without Honor: Defeat in Vietnam and Cambodia* (1983); Stanley Karnow, *Vietnam*, rev. ed. (1991); Gabriel Kolko, *Anatomy of a War* (1986); Guenter Lewy, *America in Vietnam* (1978); William Shawcross, *Sideshow* (1979) (on Cambodia); Anthony Short, *The Origins of the Vietnam War* (1989); Marilyn B. Young, *The Vietnam Wars* (1991). For works on the antiwar movement, see Chapter 32.

Truman, Eisenhower, and Vietnam

David L. Anderson, *Trapped by Success* (1991); James R. Arnold, *The First Domino* (1991); Melanie Billings-Yun, *Decision Against War: Eisenhower and Dien Bien Phu, 1954* (1988); Lloyd C. Gardner, *Approaching Vietnam* (1988); Gary Hess, *The United States' Emergence as a Southeast Asian Power* (1987); Lawrence S. Kaplan et al., eds., *Dien Bien Phu and the Crisis of Franco-American Relations* (1990); Andrew Rotter, *The Path to Vietnam* (1987).

Kennedy, Johnson, and Escalation in Vietnam

Larry Berman, *Lyndon Johnson's War* (1989), and *Planning a Tragedy* (1982); William C. Berman, *William Fulbright and the Vietnam War* (1988); Larry Cable, *Unholy Grail* (1991); Charles DeBenedetti and Charles Chatfield, *An American Ordeal: The Antiwar Movement of the Vietnam Era* (1990); David L. DiLeo, *George Ball, Vietnam, and the Rethinking of Containment* (1991); George McT. Kahin, *Intervention* (1986); Thomas G. Paterson, ed., *Kennedy's Quest for Victory* (1989); Deborah Shapley, *Promise and Power: The Life and Times of Robert McNamara* (1993); Melvin Small, *Johnson, Nixon, and the Doves* (1988); Brian VanDerMark, *Into the Quagmire* (1991).

The Vietnam War: Military Aspects

Jeffrey J. Clarke, *United States Army in Vietnam* (1988); Mark Clodfelter, *The Limits of Power: The American Bombing of North Vietnam* (1989); Phillip B. Davidson, *Vietnam at War* (1988); Ronald H. Spector, *After Tet: The Bloodiest Year in Vietnam* (1992), and *United States Army in Vietnam* (1983).

The Vietnam Legacy

John Hellman, *American Myth and the Legacy of Vietnam* (1986); Herbert Hendin and Ann P. Haas, *Wounds of War: The Psychological Aftermath of Combat in Vietnam* (1984); Ole R. Holsti and James Rosenau, *American Leadership in World Affairs: Vietnam and the Breakdown of Consensus* (1984); David Levy, *The Debate over Vietnam* (1991); Myra MacPherson, *Long Time Passing* (1984); Norman Podhoretz, *Why We Were in Vietnam* (1982); Earl C. Ravenal, *Never Again* (1978); Harry G. Summers Jr., *On Strategy* (1982).

Latin America: General

Cole Blasier, *Hovering Giant* (1974); Thomas Carothers, *In the Name of Democracy* (1991) (on Reagan years); Richard Immerman, *The CIA in Guatemala* (1982); Lester Langley, *America and the Americas* (1989); Abraham F. Lowenthal, ed., *Exporting Democracy* (1991), and *Partners in Conflict* (1987); Stephen G. Rabe, *Eisenhower and Latin America* (1988); William F. Sater, *Chile and the United States* (1990); Lars Schoultz, *National Security and United States Policy Toward Latin America* (1987). Books on Cuba and the missile crisis are cited in Chapter 29.

Central America and Panama

Cynthia J. Arnson, *Crossroads: Congress, the Reagan Administration, and Central America* (1989); Morris J. Blachman et al., eds., *Confronting Revolution* (1986); Raymond Bonner, *Weakness and Deceit: U.S. Policy and El Salvador* (1984); Kenneth M. Coleman and George C. Herring, eds., *Understanding the Central American Crisis* (1991); Theodore Draper, *A Very Thin Line: The Iran-Contra Affairs* (1991); Roy Gutman, *Banana Diplomacy, 1981–1987* (1988) (on Nicaragua); J. Michael Hogan, *The Panama Canal in American Politics* (1986); Stephen Kinzer, *Blood of Brothers* (1991) (on Nicaragua); Michael Klare and Peter Kornbluh, eds., *Low Intensity Warfare* (1988); Walter LaFeber, *Inevitable Revolutions*, 2d ed. rev. (1993), and *The Panama Canal*, updated ed. (1989); Robert A. Pastor, *Condemned to Repetition: The United States and Nicaragua* (1987); Thomas W. Walker, ed., *Revolution and Counterrevolution in Nicaragua* (1991); Bob Woodward, *Veil: The Secret Wars of the CIA* (1987).

Middle East

James A. Bill, *The Eagle and the Lion* (1988) (on Iran); Mark Gasiorowski, *U.S. Foreign Policy and the Shah* (1991); Stephen Green, *Living by the Sword: America and Israel in the Middle East, 1968–87* (1988) (on Israel); Peter L. Hahn, *The United States, Great Britain, and Egypt, 1945–1956* (1991); Donald Neff, *Warriors at Suez* (1981); William B. Quandt, *Peace Process* (1993); Cheryl A. Rubenberg, *Israel and the American National Interest* (1986); David Schoenbaum, *The United States and the State of Israel* (1993); William Shawcross, *The Shah's Last Ride* (1988); Gary Sick, *October Surprise: America's Hostages in Iran and the Election of Ronald Reagan* (1991) (on Iran); Steven L. Spiegel, *The Other Arab-Israeli Conflict* (1985); William Stivers, *America's Confrontation with Revolutionary Change in the Middle East* (1986); Robert W. Stookey, *America and the Arab States* (1975); Daniel Yergin, *The Prize* (1991) (on oil).

Asia and Africa

Pauline H. Baker, *The United States and South Africa: The Reagan Years* (1989); Thomas Borstelmann, *Apartheid's Reluctant Uncle* (1993) (on South Africa); H. W. Brands, *India and the United States* (1989); Christopher Coker, *The United States and South Africa, 1968–1985* (1986); Stanley Karnow, *In Our Image* (1989) (on Philippines); Robert J. McMahon, *The Cold War on the Periphery* (1994); Dennis Merrill, *Bread and the Ballot* (1990) (on India); Thomas J. Noer, *Cold War and Black Liberation* (1985).

32

Reform and Conflict: A Turbulent Era, 1961–1974

T HE FIRST DREADFUL FLASH from Dallas clattered over newsroom Teletype machines across the country at 1:34 P.M. Eastern Standard Time. People still remember precisely where they were and what they were doing on November 22, 1963, when they heard that President John F. Kennedy had been assassinated. Time stopped for Americans, and they experienced what psychologists call flash bulb memory, the freeze-framing of an exceptionally emotional event down to the most incidental detail.

For four days, Americans wept, prayed, and gazed at their television sets, numbed by the unbelievable. Throughout the afternoon and night before the funeral, 250,000 people trod silently past the president's coffin in the Capitol Rotunda. The next day, one million people lined the streets of Washington, and millions more watched on television as the president's body was borne by horse-drawn caisson to Arlington Cemetery.

"In retrospect," the journalist Godfrey Hodgson has written, "people looked back to Friday, November 22, 1963, as the end of a time of hope, the beginning of a time of troubles." The

irony in America's outpouring of grief was that the Kennedy administration had failed to achieve many of its goals. In the final months of his presidency, Kennedy had been criticized for being ineffectual in domestic affairs and reckless in foreign affairs. Nevertheless, John Kennedy's assassination was a national tragedy. Grieving Americans remembered how he had inspired them to hope for peace, prosperity, and social justice.

Hope had run especially high among the nation's poor. Kennedy's presidency coincided with and was energized by the modern African-American civil rights movement. His call for a New Frontier had inspired liberal Democrats, idealists, and brave young activists to work to eliminate poverty, segregation, and voting rights abuses. Americans also supported Kennedy's desire to court the Third World and prevail in the Cold War.

Lyndon Johnson, Kennedy's successor in the White House, presided over what he called the Great Society, and Congress responded to Johnson's urgings with a flood of legislation. The 1960s witnessed more economic, political, and social reform than any period since the New Deal. But even during these years of liberal triumph, anger and social tension intermittently flared into violence. Beginning with Kennedy's assassination in 1963, ten years of bloodshed—race riots, the murders of other political and civil rights leaders, and the war in Vietnam—shattered the optimism of the Kennedy and Johnson eras.

Many urban blacks were angry that poverty and segregation persisted despite the civil rights movement and the passage of landmark civil rights laws. Their discontent exploded during the 1960s' "long hot summers." The social turbulence, in conjunction with the growing movement opposing the Vietnam War, brought down the presidency of Lyndon Johnson and gave rise to the Black Power movement, the radical politics of the New Left, a revived women's movement, and the "hippie" counterculture.

Lyndon Johnson's departure from office did not produce calm. Richard Nixon, elected president in 1968, polarized the nation still further. The presidencies of Nixon's two immediate predecessors had ended tragically: Dallas and Vietnam were the sites of their undoings. A third location, the Watergate apartment complex in Washington, D.C., would prove Richard Nixon's downfall. In 1974, he resigned from office, the only American president to do so. Battered by more than a decade of turmoil, many Americans ceased to believe in any version of the American Dream.

THE CIVIL RIGHTS MOVEMENT AND KENNEDY'S NEW FRONTIER

President John F. Kennedy was, as Norman Mailer wrote, "our leading man." Young, handsome, and vigorous, the new chief executive was the first president born in the twentieth century. Perceived by the public as an intellectual, he had a genuinely inquiring mind, and as a patron of the arts he brought wit and sophistication to the White House.

In a departure from the Eisenhower administration's staid conservative image, the new president surrounded himself with young men of intellectual

"The Best and the Brightest" verve who proclaimed that they had fresh ideas for invigorating the nation; the writer David Halberstam called them "the best and the brightest." (Kennedy appointed only one woman to a significant position.) Secretary of Defense Robert McNamara, age forty-four, had been an assistant professor at Harvard at twenty-four and later the whiz-kid president of the Ford Motor Company. Kennedy's special assistant for national security affairs, McGeorge Bundy, age forty-one, had become a Harvard dean at thirty-four with only a bachelor's degree. Kennedy was only forty-three, and his brother Robert, the attorney general, was thirty-five.

Kennedy's ambitious program, the New Frontier, promised more than Kennedy could deliver: an end to racial discrimination, federal aid to education, medical care for the elderly, and government action to halt the recession the country was suffering. Only eight months into his first year, it was evident that Kennedy lacked the ability to move Congress, which was dominated by a conservative coalition of Republicans and southern Democrats. In that year, Kennedy saw the defeat of bills providing for federal aid to education and a boost in the minimum wage.

Still struggling to appease conservative members of Congress, the new president pursued civil rights with a notable lack of vigor. Kennedy did establish the President's Committee on Equal Employment Opportunity to eliminate racial discrimination in government hiring. But he waited until late 1962 before honoring a 1960 campaign pledge to issue an executive order forbidding segregation in federally subsidized housing. Meanwhile, he appointed five die-hard segregationists to the federal bench in the Deep South. The struggle for racial equality was the most important domestic issue of the time, and Kennedy's performance disheartened civil rights advocates.

Despite the White House's lack of commitment, African-American civil rights activists continued their struggle through the tactic of nonviolent civil disobedience. Volunteers organized by the Southern Christian Leadership Conference (SCLC), headed by the

The Civil Rights Movement

Reverend Martin Luther King Jr., deliberately violated segregation laws by sitting in at whites-only lunch counters, libraries, and bus stations in the South. The Congress of Racial Equality (CORE) initiated the first Freedom Ride: in May 1961, an integrated group of thirteen people boarded a bus in Washington, D.C., and traveled into the South, where they braved attacks by white mobs for daring to desegregate interstate transportation. Meanwhile, black students in the South were organizing the Student Non-Violent Coordinating Committee (SNCC). It was these young people who walked the dusty back roads of Mississippi and Georgia, encouraging African-Americans to resist segregation and register to vote.

As the civil rights movement gained momentum, President Kennedy gradually made a commitment to first-class citizenship for blacks. In 1962, he ordered U.S. marshals to protect James Meredith,

the first African-American student to attend the University of Mississippi. And in June 1963, Kennedy finally requested legislation to outlaw segregation in public accommodations. When more than 250,000 people, black and white, gathered at the Lincoln Memorial for the March on Washington that August, they did so with the knowledge that President Kennedy was at last on their side.

Meanwhile, television news programs brought the civil rights struggles into Americans' homes. The story was sometimes grisly. In 1963, Medgar Evers, director of the NAACP in Mississippi, was gunned down in his own driveway. The same year, police in Birmingham, Alabama, under the command of Sheriff "Bull" Connor attacked nonviolent civil rights demonstrators, including many children, with snarling dogs, fire hoses, and cattle prods. Then two horrifying events helped to convince reluctant politicians that action on civil rights

A historic moment for the civil rights movement was the March on Washington of August 28, 1963. One-quarter million black people and white people stood together for racial equality. Waving to friends, the Reverend Martin Luther King Jr. is about to begin delivering his "I Have a Dream" speech. Francis Miller, *Life* magazine © 1963 Time, Inc.

• *Important Events* •

1960	Sit-ins begin at Greensboro, North Carolina Birth control pill approved for use John F. Kennedy elected president
1961	Freedom Rides protest segregation in transportation First President's Commission on the Status of Women established
1962	SDS makes Port Huron Statement James Meredith enters University of Mississippi *Baker* v. *Carr* establishes "one person, one vote" principle
1963	Friedan's *The Feminine Mystique* published Civil rights advocates march on Washington Birmingham, Alabama, Baptist church bombed Kennedy assassinated; Lyndon B. Johnson assumes the presidency
1964	Economic Opportunity Act allocates funds to fight poverty Civil Rights Act outlaws discrimination in jobs and public accommodations Riots break out in the first of the "long hot summers" Free Speech Movement begins at Berkeley Johnson elected president
1965	Malcom X assassinated Voting Rights Act allows federal supervision of voting registration Medicare program established Elementary and Secondary Education Act provides federal aid to education Watts race riot leaves thirty-four dead
1966	National Organization for Women (NOW) founded *Miranda* v. *Arizona* requires police to inform suspects of their rights
1967	Race riots erupt in Newark, Detroit, and other cities
1968	Tet offensive causes fear of losing Vietnam War Martin Luther King Jr. assassinated

	African-Americans riot in 168 cities and towns Civil Rights Act bans discrimination in housing Antiwar protests escalate Robert F. Kennedy assassinated Violence erupts at Democratic convention Richard M. Nixon elected president
1969	Stonewall riot sparked by police harassment of homosexuals 400,000 gather at Woodstock festival Moratorium Day calls for end to Vietnam War
1970	United States invades Cambodia Students killed at Kent State and Jackson State universities
1971	*Pentagon Papers* published Twenty-sixth Amendment extends vote to eighteen-year-olds *Swann* v. *Charlotte-Mecklenberg* upholds North Carolina desegregation plan
1972	Nixon visits China Equal Rights Amendment (ERA) approved by Congress "Plumbers" break into Watergate Nixon reelected
1973	Watergate burglars tried Senator Sam Ervin chairs Watergate hearings White House aides Ehrlichman and Haldeman resign *Roe* v. *Wade* legalizes abortion War Powers Resolution passed Agnew resigns; Nixon appoints Ford vice president Saturday Night Massacre provokes public outcry
1974	Supreme Court orders Nixon to release White House tapes House Judiciary Committee votes to impeach Nixon Nixon resigns; Ford becomes president Ford pardons Nixon

was long overdue. In September, white terrorists exploded a bomb during Sunday morning services at Birmingham's Sixteenth Street Baptist Church. Sunday school was in session, and four black girls were killed. A little more than two months later, John Kennedy was assassinated in Dallas. If ever the civil rights movement had the moral support of most of the American people, it was at this time of national tragedy and repugnance over violence.

Historians have wondered what John Kennedy would have accomplished had he lived. Although his legislative achievements were meager, he inspired genuine idealism in Americans. When Kennedy exhorted Americans in his inaugural address to "Ask not what your country can do for you; ask what you can do for your country," tens of thousands volunteered to spend two years of their lives in the Peace Corps. Kennedy also promoted a sense of national purpose through his vigorous support of the space program.

Kennedy in Retrospect

In recent years, writers have drawn attention to Kennedy's recklessness in world events, such as authorizing CIA attempts to assassinate Cuba's Premier Fidel Castro. They have also criticized his timidity in civil rights and have pointed to his extramarital sex life as evidence of a serious character flaw. It is clear, however, that Kennedy had begun to grow as president during his last few months in office. He made a moving appeal for racial equality and called for reductions in Cold War tensions. And in a peculiar way, he accomplished more in death than in life. In the post-assassination atmosphere of grief and remorse, Lyndon Johnson pushed through Congress practically the entire New Frontier agenda.

THE GREAT SOCIETY AND THE TRIUMPH OF LIBERALISM

In the aftermath of the assassination, the new president resolved to unite the country behind the unfulfilled legislative program of the martyred president.

More than that, he wanted to realize Roosevelt's and Truman's unmet goals. He called his new program the Great Society.

Johnson made civil rights his top legislative priority. "No memorial oration or eulogy," he told a joint session of Congress five days after the assassination, "could more eloquently honor President Kennedy's memory than the earliest passage of the civil rights bill." Within months, Johnson had signed into law the Civil Rights Act of 1964, which outlawed discrimination on the basis of race, color, religion, sex, or national origin, not only in public accommodations but also in employment. An Equal Employment Opportunity Commission was established the same year to investigate and judge complaints of job discrimination. The act also authorized the government to withhold funds from public agencies that discriminated on the basis of race, and it empowered the attorney general to guarantee voting rights and end school segregation.

Civil Rights Act of 1964

Johnson enunciated another priority in his first State of the Union address: "The administration today, here and now, declares unconditional war on poverty." Eight months later, he signed into law the Economic Opportunity Act of 1964, which allocated almost $1 billion to fight poverty. The act became the opening salvo in Johnson's War on Poverty.

In the year after Kennedy's death, Johnson sought to govern by a liberal consensus, appealing to the shared values and aspirations of the majority of the nation for continued economic growth and social justice. Judging by his lopsided victory over his conservative Republican opponent in 1964, Senator Barry Goldwater of Arizona, he succeeded. Johnson garnered 61 percent of the popular vote and the electoral votes of all but six states.

Election of 1964

Riding on Johnson's coattails, the Democrats won large majorities in both the House (295 to 140) and the Senate (68 to 32). Johnson recognized that the opportunity to push through further reform had arrived. "Hurry, boys, hurry," he told his staff just after the election. "Get that legislation up to the Hill and out. Eighteen months from now ol' Landslide Lyndon will be Lame-Duck Lyndon." Congress responded in 1965 and 1966 with the most sweeping reform legislation since 1935.

Three bills enacted in 1965 were legislative milestones: the Medicare program insured the elderly against medical and hospital bills, the Ele-
Voting Rights Act of 1965
mentary and Secondary Education Act provided for general federal aid to education for the first time, and the Voting Rights Act of 1965 empowered the attorney general to supervise voter registration in areas where fewer than half the minority residents of voting age were registered. In 1960, only 29 percent of the South's African-American population was registered to vote; when Johnson left office in 1969, the proportion was approaching two-thirds. Even in Mississippi, one of the most resistant states, black registration figures grew from 7 percent in 1964 to 60 percent in 1968.

The flurry of legislation during Johnson's presidency was staggering: establishment of the Department of Housing and Urban Development and the National Endowments for the Arts and Humanities, water- and air-quality improvement acts, liberalization of immigration laws, and appropriations for the most ambitious federal housing program since 1949, including rent supplements to low-income families. In 1968, Johnson signed his third civil rights act, banning racial and religious discrimination in the sale and rental of housing. Another provision of this legislation, known as the Indian Bill of Rights, extended those constitutional protections to Native Americans living under tribal self-government on reservations.

By far the most ambitious of Johnson's initiatives was the War on Poverty. Because the gross national product (GNP) had increased in the mid-
War on Poverty
1960s, Johnson and his advisers reasoned that the government could expect a "fiscal dividend" of several billion dollars in additional tax revenues. They decided to spend the extra money to wipe out poverty through education and job-training programs. Beginning with the $1 billion appropriation in 1964, the War on Poverty

evolved in 1965 and 1966 to include the Job Corps, a program to provide marketable skills, work experience, remedial education, and counseling for young people; Project Head Start, to prepare low-income preschoolers for grade school; and Upward Bound, for high school students from low-income families who aspired to a college education. Other antipoverty programs were Legal Services for the Poor; Volunteers in Service to America (VISTA); and the Model Cities program, which channeled federal funds to upgrade employment, housing, education, and health in targeted neighborhoods.

In tandem with a rising GNP, the War on Poverty substantially alleviated hunger and suffering in the United States. Its legislation directly addressed the debilitating housing, health, and nutritional deficiencies from which the poor suffered. Between 1965 and 1970, the GNP leapt from $685 billion to $977 billion, and federal spending for Social Security, health, welfare, and education more than doubled. Not only did some of this prosperity trickle down to the poor but also—and more important—millions of new jobs were created. The result was a startling reduction in the number of poor people, from 25 percent of the population in 1962 to 11 percent in 1973.

Successes in Reducing Poverty

There were, however, two notable exceptions to the general success of the War on Poverty. Little was done to reduce rural poverty. This failure contributed to a continuance of the South-to-North migration and the subsequent worsening of northern urban problems. The other large group that remained poor despite antipoverty initiatives consisted of women and children living in female-headed families, and they constituted 40 percent of the poor in the United States. The economic boom that lasted from 1963 to 1969 lifted twelve million people in male-headed families out of poverty. Left stranded in poverty were eleven million in families headed by women (the same number as in 1963).

The period of liberal ascendancy represented by the War on Poverty was short lived; its legislative achievements were limited to the years between 1964 and 1966. Disillusioned with America's deepening involvement in Vietnam, many of

Johnson's allies began to reject both him and his liberal consensus.

But one branch of government maintained the liberal tradition—the Supreme Court. Under the intellectual and moral leadership of Chief Justice Earl Warren, the Court in the 1960s was disposed by political conviction and a belief in judicial activism to play a central role in the resurgence of liberalism. After the 1954 and 1955 school desegregation cases, the liberal Warren Court did not disturb the political waters for the remainder of the 1950s. Beginning in 1962, however, the Court began handing down a series of important liberal decisions. *Baker* v. *Carr* (1962) and subsequent rulings established that the principle of "one person, one vote" must prevail at both the state and national levels. This decision required the reapportionment of state legislatures so that each representative would serve the same number of constituents. The Court also outlawed required prayers and Bible reading in public schools, explaining that such practices imposed an "indirect coercive pressure upon religious minorities."

The Warren Court

The Court also attacked the legal underpinning of McCarthyism, ruling in 1965 that a person need not register with the government as a member of a subversive organization, because doing so would violate constitutional safeguards against self-incrimination. In *Griswold* v. *Connecticut* (1965), the Court ruled that a state law prohibiting the use of contraceptives by married couples violated "a marital right of privacy" and was unconstitutional. The Court upheld the Civil Rights Act of 1964 and the Voting Rights Act of 1965. In other rulings that particularly upset conservatives, the Court decreed that books, magazines, and films could not be banned as obscene unless they were found to be "utterly without redeeming social value."

Civil Rights Rulings

Perhaps most controversial of all was the Court's transformation of the criminal justice system. Beginning with *Gideon* v. *Wainwright* (1963), the Court ruled that a poor person charged with a felony had the right to a state-appointed lawyer. In *Escobedo* v. *Illinois* (1964), it decreed that the accused had a right to counsel during interrogation and a right to remain silent. *Miranda* v. *Arizona* (1966) established that police had to inform criminal suspects that they had these rights and that any statements they made could be used against them.

Despite conservatives' demands for Warren's removal, constitutional historians consider him one of the two most influential chief justices in the nation's history. (The other was John Marshall.) Whether one approves of the decisions of the Warren Court (which ended with Warren's retirement in 1969) or not, its effect on the American people is undeniable.

CIVIL RIGHTS, RACE RIOTS, AND BLACK POWER

Even while the civil rights movement was winning legal and constitutional victories, some activists began to grumble that the federal government was not to be trusted. During the Mississippi Summer Project of 1964, hundreds of college-age volunteers from the North had joined SNCC and CORE field workers to establish "freedom schools," which taught African-American children their own history. Many volunteers believed that the Federal Bureau of Investigation was hostile to the civil rights movement. FBI Director J. Edgar Hoover was a racist, they charged, and they were disturbed by rumors (later confirmed) that Hoover had wiretapped and bugged King's hotel rooms and planted allegations in the newspapers about his sexual improprieties.

Indeed, some FBI informants were not only members of the Ku Klux Klan but worse: terrorists who instigated violence against civil rights volunteers. One informant had organized several atrocities, including the bombing of Birmingham's Sixteenth Street Baptist Church in 1963. Small wonder that during the summer of 1964 racist violence surged in the South, particularly in Mississippi. White vigilantes bombed and burned two dozen black churches there, and three civil rights workers were murdered by a group that included sheriff's deputies in Philadelphia, Mississippi.

Violent Attacks on Civil Rights Workers

The year 1964 also witnessed the first of the long hot summers of race riots in northern cities. In Harlem and Rochester in New York, and in several cities in New Jersey, brutal actions by white police officers, including vicious unprovoked beatings in police stations, sparked riots in black neighborhoods. African-Americans deeply resented the unnecessary force that police sometimes used.

Explosion of Black Anger

Whites wondered why African-Americans were venting their frustration violently when real progress was being made in the civil rights struggle. But the civil rights movement had been largely southern in focus, geared to abolishing Jim Crow and black disfranchisement. In the North, although African-Americans could vote, many were still living in deep poverty. The median income of blacks was little more than half that of whites, and their unemployment rate was twice that of whites (see figure). For black males aged eighteen to twenty-five, it was five times as high. Many African-American families, particularly those headed by women, lived in perpetual poverty. The primary assistance program, Aid to

Poverty in America for Whites, African Americans, and All Races, 1959–1974

Legend: All Races · Whites · African Americans · No Statistics Available

(y-axis: Percentage of Population Living Below Poverty Level — 5 to 60; x-axis: Year — 1959 to 1974)

Poverty in America for Whites, Blacks, and All Races, 1959–1974   Because of rising levels of economic prosperity, combined with the Great Society, the percentage of Americans living in poverty in 1974 was half that of 1959. African-Americans were still far more likely to be poor than white Americans. In 1959, more than half of all blacks (55.1 percent) were poor; in 1974, the figure remained high (30.3 percent). (The government did not record data on African-American poverty for the years 1960–1965.)

Families with Dependent Children (AFDC), failed to meet the needs of the poor. AFDC payments were inadequate to cover a family's rent, utilities, and household expenses, let alone its food. In 1970, it was estimated that more than 60 percent of African-American children were being raised in poverty.

Northern blacks, surveying the economic and civil rights gains of the 1960s, wondered when they too would benefit from the Great Society. Concentrated in the inner cities, they looked around the ghettos in which they lived and knew their circumstances were deteriorating. Their neighborhoods were more segregated than ever; in increasing numbers during the 1960s, whites had responded to the continuing black migration from the South by fleeing to the suburbs. And as inner-city neighborhoods became all black, so did the neighborhood schools.

If 1964 was fiery and violent, 1965 was even more so. In August, police brutality sparked rioting in the Los Angeles ghetto of Watts; thirty-four people were killed. Other cities exploded in riots between 1966 and 1968. Unlike race riots in 1919 and 1943, white mobs did not initiate the violence; instead, blacks exploded in anger over their joblessness and lack of opportunity, as well as police brutality. They looted white-owned stores, set fires, and threw rocks at police and firefighters.

The Watts Race Riot

In 1968, the National Advisory Commission on Civil Disorders, chaired by Governor Otto Kerner of Illinois, released its report blaming white racism for the riots: "The nation is rapidly moving toward two increasingly separate Americas . . . a white society principally located in suburbs . . . and a Negro society largely concentrated within large central cities."

Clearly, many blacks, especially in the North, were beginning to question whether the nonviolent civil rights movement was serving their needs. In 1963, King had appealed to whites' humanitarian instincts in his "I Have a Dream" speech. Now another voice was beginning to be heard, one that urged blacks to seize their freedom "by any means necessary." It was the voice of Malcolm X, a one-time pimp and street hustler who had converted while in prison to the Nation of Islam faith, commonly known as the Black Muslims.

The Black Muslims, a small sect that espoused black pride and separatism from white society, condemned "the white devil" as the chief source of evil in the world. They dissociated themselves from white society, exhorted blacks to lead sober lives and practice thrift, and sanctioned violence in self-defense. By the early 1960s, Malcolm X had become the Black Muslims' chief spokesperson, and his advice was straightforward: "If someone puts a hand on you, send him to the cemetery."

Malcolm X

Malcolm X was murdered in early 1965; his assassins were Black Muslims who believed he had betrayed their cause. In fact, he had modified some of his positions just before his death. He had met whites who were not devils, he said, and he had expressed cautious support for the nonviolent civil rights movement. Still, for both blacks and whites, Malcolm X symbolized black defiance and self-respect.

A year after Malcolm X's death, Stokely Carmichael, the intense and articulate chairman of SNCC, called on African-Americans to assert Black Power. To be truly free from white oppression, Carmichael believed, blacks had to control their own institutions. They had to elect black candidates and organize their own schools. Several influential organizations that had previously been committed to racial integration and nonviolence embraced Black Power. SNCC in 1966 and CORE in 1967 purged their white members and repudiated integration, arguing that black people needed power, not white friendship.

Black Power

The wellspring of the new militance was black nationalism, the concept that black peoples everywhere in the world share a unique history and cultural heritage that sets them apart from whites. College students pressed for black studies programs, and activists adopted the terms *black* and *Afro-American* in preference to *Negro*. To white America, one of the most fearsome of the new groups was the Black Panther party. Blending black nationalism and revolutionary communism, the Panthers dedicated themselves to destroying both capitalism and "the military arm of our oppressors," the police in the ghettos. They adopted Mao Zedong's revolutionary slogan: "Power flows from

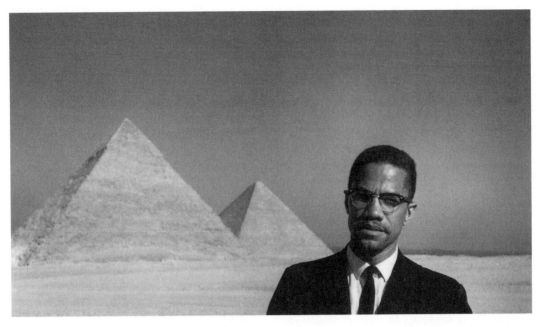

Malcolm X, as chief spokesperson for the Black Muslims, espoused African-American pride and separatism from white society. After a pilgrimage to Mecca in 1964, Malcolm X softened his hostility toward whites. Here he is pictured in Egypt, on his way to Mecca.   John Launois/Black Star.

the barrel of a gun." At the same time, a vocal minority of whites from the baby boom generation set out to "change the system."

THE NEW LEFT AND THE COUNTERCULTURE

In the fall of 1964, Mario Savio returned to Berkeley, California. He had spent the previous few months teaching in SNCC's Mississippi Summer Project. Savio and others returned to Berkeley convinced that the same power structure that dominated blacks' lives also controlled the bureaucratic machinery of the university. "Last summer I went to Mississippi to join the struggle there for civil rights," Savio wrote. "This fall I am engaged in another phase of the same struggle, this time in Berkeley. . . . The same rights are at stake in both places."

The University of California was in many respects a model university in 1964, with a worldwide reputation for excellence. Its chancellor, the econo-

Free Speech Movement

mist Clark Kerr, had likened the "multiversity," with its many separate colleges and research institutes, to a big business. The largest single campus in the country, with tens of thousands of students, Berkeley had become hopelessly impersonal by the 1960s. Rather than learning from the famous professors, undergraduates were herded into lecture classes taught by graduate students. Some students complained that they felt like cogs in a machine.

The struggle at Berkeley began when the university administration banned recruitment by civil rights and antiwar organizations in Sproul Plaza, the students' traditional gathering place. Militant students, calling themselves the Free Speech Movement, defied Kerr's ban; the administration suspended them or had them arrested. On October 1, several thousand students surrounded a police car in which a militant was being held, immobilizing it for thirty-two hours. In December, the Free Speech Movement seized and occupied the main administration building. Governor Pat Brown dispatched state police to Berkeley, and more than eight hundred people were arrested. Angry students shut down classes for several days in protest.

The willingness of those in positions of authority to mobilize the police against unruly but not violent students was profoundly shocking and radicalizing to many young people. Having grown up comfortable and even indulged, they found themselves treated like criminals for questioning what they considered a criminal war in Vietnam and racial injustice in their country. By the end of the decade, the activism born at Berkeley would spread to hundreds of other campuses.

Two years earlier, another group of students had met in Port Huron, Michigan, to found Students for a Democratic Society (SDS). Like their

Students for a Democratic Society (SDS)

leaders Tom Hayden and Al Haber, most SDS members were white middle-class college students. In their platform, the Port Huron Statement, they condemned racism, poverty in the midst of plenty, and the Cold War. SDS sought nothing less than the revitalization of democracy by taking power from the corporations, the military, and the politicians and returning it to the people.

Inspired by the Free Speech Movement and SDS, a minority of students allied themselves with the New Left. Although united in their hatred of racism and the Vietnam War, the New Left was divided along philosophical and political lines. Some radicals were Marxists, others black nationalists, anarchists, or pacifists. Some believed in pursuing social change through negotiation; others were revolutionaries who regarded compromise as impossible.

By calling into question the basic foundations of American society, the New Left indirectly gave rise to a phenomenon that observers called the counterculture. Exhorted by

Countercultural Revolution

Timothy Leary—a former Harvard instructor and advocate of expanded consciousness through use of LSD and other mind-altering drugs—to "turn on, tune in, drop out," millions of students experimented with marijuana and hallucinogenic drugs. They were persuaded by their political outrage, drug experiences, and experiments with communal living that they

lived in a new era unconnected to the past. The past in general and adults in particular had nothing to offer but moral bankruptcy and materialism.

It was music more than anything else that expressed the countercultural assault on the status quo. Bob Dylan promised revolutionary answers

Rock 'n' Roll

"blowin' in the wind," and young people cheered Jimi Hendrix, who sang of life in a drug-induced "purple haze," and Janis Joplin, who brought African-American blues to white Americans. Like sex and drugs, the music of the 1960s represented a quest to redefine reality and create a more just and joyful society. Rock festivals became cultural watersheds; in 1969 at the Woodstock Music and Art Festival in upstate New York, more than four hundred thousand people ignored or reveled in days of rain and mud, without shelter and without violence. A number of them began to dream of a peaceful "Woodstock nation" based on love, drugs, and rock music.

Some young people tried to construct alternative ways of life. In the Haight-Ashbury section of San Francisco, "flower children" created an urban subculture as distinctive as that of any Chinatown or Little Italy. "Hashbury" inspired numerous other communal living experiments. The counterculture attracted only a small proportion of the nation's youth, but to disconcerted middle-class parents hippies seemed to be everywhere. Parents were appalled by long hair, beards, and patched jeans. They complained that "acid rock" was loud, discordant, even savage. They feared their children would suffer lifelong damage from drugs.

The "generation gap" was yawning wide, but most disturbing to parents were the casual sexual mores that young people were adopting, partly as a

Sexuality

result of the widespread availability of birth-control pills, which in 1960 received governmental approval for use. For many young people, living together no longer equaled living in sin, and as attitudes toward premarital sex changed, so did notions about homosexuality and sex roles.

The militancy of the 1960s also helped inspire the gay rights movement. Homosexuals had long feared that disclosing their sexual orientation

Gay Rights Movement

——

would mean losing not only their jobs but even their friends and families. That attitude began to change in June 1969. In New York City's Greenwich Village, a riot erupted when police raided the Stonewall Inn, a gay bar on Christopher Street, and were greeted with a volley of beer bottles by patrons tired of police harassment. Rioting continued into the night. As the historian John D'Emilio has written, Stonewall "marked a critical divide in the politics and consciousness of homosexuals and lesbians. A small, thinly spread reform effort suddenly grew into a large, grass-roots movement for liberation."

As the slogan "Make Love, Not War" suggests, the New Left and the counterculture discovered a common cause as the war in Vietnam escalated. Students held teach-ins—open forums for discussion of the war by students, professors, and guest speakers—and antiwar marches and demonstrations became a widespread protest tactic. Some young men fled the draft by moving abroad—mostly to Canada and Scandinavia—and others protested, violently and nonviolently, at local draft board offices.

By this time, however, growing numbers of Americans, young and old, had quit believing their elected leaders. President Johnson claimed the United States was fighting for honorable reasons, but people wondered what goal could justify the murder of Vietnamese women and children. Johnson's credibility had evaporated.

1968: A YEAR OF PROTEST, VIOLENCE, AND LOSS

As stormy and violent as the years from 1963 through 1967 had been, many Americans were still trying to downplay the nation's distress in the hope that it would go away. But in 1968, a series of shocks hit them even harder. The first jolt came in January, when the USS *Pueblo*, a navy intelligence ship, was captured by the North Koreans. A week later came the Tet offensive in Vietnam. For the first time, many Americans believed that they might lose the war. Meanwhile, American casualties increased. By July 4, 1968, total American fatalities had surpassed thirty thousand.

Controversy over the war deepened. Within the Democratic party, two candidates rose to challenge Johnson for the 1968 presidential nomination. One, Senator Eugene McCarthy of Minnesota, entered the New Hampshire primary on March 12 solely to contest Johnson's war policies, and he won twenty of twenty-four convention delegates. Soon another Democrat, Senator Robert F. Kennedy of New York, the dead president's brother, entered the fray. On March 31, President Johnson went on national television to announce a scaling-down of the bombing in North Vietnam. Then he hurled a political thunderbolt—he would not be a candidate for reelection.

Less than a week later, a white man named James Earl Ray shot and killed Martin Luther King Jr. in Memphis. Ray's crime aroused instant rage in

Assassination of Martin Luther King Jr.

——

the nation's ghettos. Blacks rioted in 168 cities and towns, looting and burning white businesses and properties. Thirty-four blacks and five whites died in the violence. The terror provoked a white backlash. Tough talk was the response from Chicago's Mayor Richard Daley, who ordered police to shoot to kill arsonists.

Gallup polls in April and May reported Robert Kennedy to be the front-running Democratic presidential candidate. In June, he won the California primary. After addressing his

Assassination of Robert Kennedy

——

joyous supporters in a Los Angeles hotel, Kennedy took a short cut through the kitchen to a press conference. A young man stepped forward with a .22-caliber revolver and fired. The assassin was an Arab nationalist named Sirhan Sirhan who despised Kennedy for his unwavering support of Israel.

Violence erupted again in August at the Democratic national convention in Chicago. The Democrats were divided over the war, and thousands of antiwar protesters and members of the zany and anarchic Youth International Party ("Yippies") had traveled to Chicago. The Chicago police

Violence at the Democratic Convention

——

force was still in the psychological grip of Mayor Daley's shoot-to-kill directive. Twelve thousand police were assigned to twelve-hour shifts, and another twelve thousand army troops and National Guardsmen were on call with rifles, bazookas, and flame throwers. They attacked in front of the Hilton Hotel, wading into the ranks of demonstrators, reporters, and TV camera operators. Throughout the nation, viewers watched as club-swinging police beat protesters to the ground. When onlookers rushed to shield the injured, they too were clubbed.

The Democratic convention nominated Vice President Hubert Humphrey for president and Senator Edmund Muskie of Maine for vice president. Like Johnson and Kennedy before him, Humphrey was a political descendant of the New Deal, committed to the social welfare system, and an unstinting supporter of the war. Richard M. Nixon was at the top of the Republican ticket; his running mate was the tough-talking Governor Spiro Agnew of Maryland. Another tough-talking governor, George C. Wallace of Alabama, ran as the nominee of the American Independent party. Wallace was a segregationist, a proponent of reducing North Vietnam to rubble with nuclear weapons, and an advocate of "law and order."

When the votes were tabulated, Nixon emerged the winner by the slimmest of margins. Wallace collected nearly ten million votes, or almost 14 percent of the total, the best performance by a third party since 1924. His strong showing made Nixon a minority president, elected with 43 percent of the popular vote (see map). Moreover, the Democrats maintained control of the House and the Senate.

Election of 1968

Still, the election had been a triumph for conservatism, in that the combined vote for Nixon and Wallace was 57 percent. The war had hurt the Democrats' appeal, but even more politically damaging was the party's identification with the cause of racial justice. In 1968, Humphrey received 97 percent of the black vote but only 35 percent of the white vote. Among the defectors from the New Deal coalition were northern blue-collar ethnic voters. "In city after city," one observer noted,

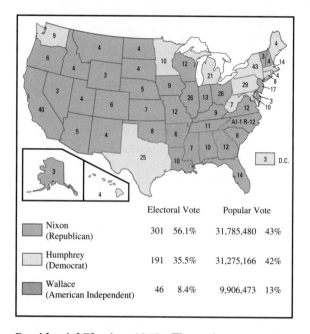

	Electoral Vote		Popular Vote	
Nixon (Republican)	301	56.1%	31,785,480	43%
Humphrey (Democrat)	191	35.5%	31,275,166	42%
Wallace (American Independent)	46	8.4%	9,906,473	13%

Presidential Election, 1968   *The popular vote was almost a dead heat between Richard M. Nixon and Hubert Humphrey, but Nixon won thirty-one states to Humphrey's fourteen and triumphed easily in electoral votes. Note the success of George Wallace's American Independent candidacy, which won five states in the Deep South.*

"racial conflicts had destroyed the old alliance. The New Deal had unraveled block by block."

THE REBIRTH OF FEMINISM

Another liberation movement gained momentum during the turbulence of the 1960s, at first quietly and then on the picket line. The women's rights movement had languished after the adoption of the Nineteenth Amendment in 1920. But in the 1960s, feminism was reborn. Many women were dissatisfied with their lives, and in 1963 they found a voice with the publication of Betty Friedan's *The Feminine Mystique*. According to Friedan, women across the country were deeply troubled by "the problem that has no name." Most women had grown up believing that "all they had to do was

The Feminine Mystique

devote their lives from earliest girlhood to finding a husband and bearing children." The problem was that this "mystique of feminine fulfillment" left many wives and mothers feeling empty and incomplete. Friedan quoted a young mother: "I've tried everything women are supposed to do—hobbies, gardening, pickling, canning, and being very social with my neighbors. . . . I love the kids and Bob and my home. . . . But I'm desperate. I begin to feel that I have no personality. . . . Who am I?"

The one woman President Kennedy had appointed to a policymaking post in his administration was an effective advocate of equal rights. As assistant secretary of labor and director of the Women's Bureau, Esther Peterson urged Kennedy to establish the first President's Commission on the Status of Women in the nation's history. Its report, *American Women* (1963), argued that every obstacle to women's full participation in society must be removed. By 1967, all fifty states had established commissions to promote women's equality. Still, little federal action had resulted from the release of *American Women*, and the government was failing to enforce the gender-equality provisions of the Civil Rights Act of 1964. The need for action inspired the founding in 1966 of the National Organization for Women (NOW). In the reform tradition, NOW battled for "equal rights in partnership with men" by lobbying for legislation and testing laws in the courts.

Not long after NOW's formation, a new generation of radical feminists emerged. Most radical feminists were white and well educated; many were

Radical Feminism

the daughters of working mothers. Most had been raised in the era of sexual liberation, taking for granted liberation from unwanted pregnancy. The intellectual ferment of their movement produced a new feminist literature. Radical feminists focused not only on legal barriers but also on cultural assumptions and traditions. In the process they introduced the term *sexism* to signify a phenomenon far more pervasive than lack of legal equality, and they challenged everything from women's economic and political inequality to sexual double standards and sex-role stereotypes.

Unlike NOW, the radical feminists practiced direct action, such as picketing the 1968 Miss America contest in Atlantic City. One woman auctioned off an effigy of Miss America: "Gentlemen, I offer you the 1969 model. . . . She walks. She talks. She smiles on cue. *And* she does the housework." Into the "freedom trash can" the pickets dumped false eyelashes, curlers, girdles, and *Playboy* to protest the prevailing view of women as domestic servants and sex objects.

Many radical feminists had joined the struggles for black civil rights and against the Vietnam War. In these movements, they found that instead of making policy, they were expected to make coffee, take minutes, and even provide sexual favors. Many of these feminists organized consciousness-raising groups to discuss such wide-ranging and sensitive matters as homosexuality, abortion, and power relationships in romance and marriage. The issue of homosexuality caused a split in the women's movement; in 1969 and 1970, NOW forced lesbians to resign from membership and offices in the organization. This rift was healed in 1971, largely because homosexuals had begun to fight back.

For working women in the 1960s, the most pressing problems were sex discrimination in employment, meager professional opportunities, unequal pay for equal work, lack

Occupational Segregation

of adequate day care for children, and prohibitions against abortion. The main cause of the disparity in pay was "occupational segregation," which became even more pronounced in the 1960s as baby boomers and mothers of baby boomers flooded entry-level jobs in female-dominated fields like secretarial and clerical work. Because many women with college educations routinely earned less than men with eighth grade educations, it was natural that the two primary feminist goals of the 1960s were equal job opportunity and equal pay for equal work.

Despite opposition, women made impressive gains. They entered professional schools in record numbers: from 1969 to 1973, the number of women law students almost quadrupled, and the number of women medical students more than doubled. Under Title IX of the Educational

Amendments of 1972, female college athletes gained the right to the same financial support as male athletes. The same year, Congress approved the Equal Rights Amendment (ERA) and sent it to the states for ratification. (The ERA states, "Equality of rights under the law shall not be denied or abridged by the United States or by any State on account of sex.")

The Supreme Court also ruled on several issues essential to women. In 1973, the Court struck down state laws that made abortion a crime (*Roe* v. *Wade*).

Roe v. Wade

The Court also addressed sex discrimination. In a 1971 ruling (*Reed* v. *Reed*), it held that legislation differentiating between the sexes "must be reasonable, not arbitrary," and in 1973 (*Frontiero* v. *Richardson*) the justices went a step further in declaring that job-related classifications based on sex, like those based on race, were "inherently suspect." These victories gave the women's movement new confidence in the 1970s.

NIXON AND THE PERSISTENCE OF CHAOS

Richard Nixon's presidency was born in chaos. Bloody confrontations occurred at Berkeley, San Francisco State, Wisconsin, and scores of other colleges and universities in 1969. At Cornell, a hundred black students armed with rifles and shotguns occupied the student union for thirty-six hours. In October, three hundred Weathermen—an SDS splinter group—raced through Chicago's downtown district, smashing windows and attacking police officers in an attempt to incite armed class struggle. A month later, half a million people assembled peacefully at the Washington Monument on Moratorium Day to call for an end to the Vietnam War.

If 1969 was bloody and turbulent, 1970 would prove to be even more so. President Nixon appeared on television on April 30 to announce that the United States had launched an "incursion" into Cambodia. Antiwar protest escalated. On May 4, National Guardsmen in

Kent State and Jackson State

Ohio fired into a crowd of fleeing students at Kent State University, killing four young people. Ten days later, police and state highway patrolmen armed with automatic weapons blasted a women's dormitory at Jackson State, an all-black university in Mississippi, killing two students and wounding nine others. The police claimed they had been shot at, but no evidence of sniping could be found; the police fired no tear gas or warning shots.

Many Americans, although disturbed by the increasing ferocity of campus confrontations, felt more personally endangered by street crime. Sales of pistols, burglar alarms, and bulletproof vests soared, as did demand for private guards and special police. Conservatives accused liberals and the Supreme Court of causing the crime wave by coddling criminals.

Fear of Crime

This new wave of riots, protests, and violent crime convinced Nixon that the nation was plunging into anarchy. Worried like Lyndon Johnson before him that the antiwar movement was Communist-inspired, he ordered the FBI, the CIA, the National Security Agency, and the Defense Intelligence Agency in mid-1970 to formulate a coordinated attack on "internal threats." Meanwhile, the administration also worked to put the Democratic party on the defensive. In a memorandum, Jeb Stuart Magruder, a White House assistant, set the theme for the upcoming congressional elections: "The Democrats should be portrayed as being on the fringes: radical liberals who . . . excuse disorder, tolerate crime, . . . and undercut the President's foreign policy." But Republican attempts to discredit the Democrats failed. The Democrats gained seats in both the House and the Senate.

Politics of Divisiveness

Nixon's fortunes declined further in 1971. In June, the *New York Times* began to publish the *Pentagon Papers*, a top-secret Defense Department study of the Vietnam War. Nixon also had to contend with inflation, a problem not entirely of his making; it was Lyndon Johnson's policy of "guns and butter"—massive deficit financing to support both the Vietnam War

Stagflation

and the Great Society—that had fueled inflation. By early 1971, the United States was suffering from a 5.3 percent inflation rate and a 6 percent unemployment rate. The word *stagflation* would shortly be coined to describe this coexistence of economic recession (stagnation) and inflation.

Nixon shocked both critics and allies by declaring in early 1971 that "I am now a Keynesian." (According to the British economist John Maynard Keynes, governments could stimulate economic growth in the private sector by means of "pump priming," or deficit financing.) Nixon's budget for fiscal 1971 would have a built-in deficit of $23 billion, just slightly less than the all-time high of $25 billion. Then in August, in an effort to correct the nation's balance-of-payments deficit, Nixon announced that he would devalue the dollar and allow it to "float" in international money markets. Finally, to curb inflation, the president froze prices, wages, and rents for ninety days and set limits on subsequent increases. Nixon's commitment to these controversial wage-and-price controls buckled the next year under pressure from businesses and unions.

Wage and price controls were just one facet of what surprised observers called Nixon's "great turnabout" from outspoken conservative to pragmatic liberal. Another was his announcement in 1971 that he would travel to the People's Republic of China, a Communist enemy Nixon had denounced for years. It was clear that the president was preparing for the 1972 presidential election.

NIXON'S SOUTHERN STRATEGY AND THE ELECTION OF 1972

Political observers believed that Nixon would have a hard time running for reelection on his first-term record. Having urged Americans to "lower our voices," he had ordered Vice President Agnew to denounce the press and student protesters. Having espoused unity, he had practiced the politics of polarization. Having campaigned as a fiscal conservative, he had authorized near-record budget deficits.

And having promised peace, he had widened the war in Southeast Asia.

Moreover, Congress's accomplishments were more despite Nixon than because of him. The Democrats had dominated both houses during his first term, and they continued to pursue a liberal agenda. The states ratified the Twenty-sixth Amendment, which extended the vote to eighteen-year-olds; Congress increased Social Security payments and food stamp funding and established the Occupational Safety and Health Administration to reduce hazards in the workplace.

Liberal Legislative Victories

The environmental movement also bore fruit during Nixon's first term. Books, especially Rachel Carson's *The Silent Spring* (1962) and Paul Ehrlich's *The Population Bomb* (1968), had begun to awaken Americans to ecological issues. The public was further sensitized by a 1969 oil spill that fouled the beaches and killed wildlife in Santa Barbara, California. Congress responded to the growing concern about the environment by establishing the Environmental Protection Agency (1970) and by passing the Clean Air Act (1970), Clean Water Act (1972), and Pesticide Control Act (1972). Each measure was signed into law by an unsympathetic president who recognized their political appeal.

Environmental Issues

In his campaign for reelection, Nixon used a "southern strategy" of political conservatism. A product of the Sun Belt, he was acutely aware of the growing political power of that conservative region. He thus appealed to "the silent majority," the suburbanites, white ethnic groups, and blue-collar workers of "middle America." As in the 1970 congressional elections, Nixon equated the Republican party with law and order and the Democrats with permissiveness, crime, drugs, pornography, the hippie lifestyle, student radicalism, black militancy, feminism, homosexuality, and dissolution of the family. Moreover, Attorney General John Mitchell had courted southern white voters by trying to delay school desegregation

Nixon's Southern Strategy

in Mississippi and to prevent extension of the 1965 Voting Rights Act.

The southern strategy had also guided Nixon's nomination of Supreme Court justices. After appointing Warren Burger, a conservative federal judge, to succeed Earl Warren as chief justice, Nixon had selected two southerners to serve as associate justices. The Senate rejected both men. By 1972, however, the president had managed to appoint three more conservatives to the Supreme Court. Ironically, the new appointees did not always vote as Nixon would have wished. The Court, for instance, in *Swann* v. *Charlotte-Mecklenburg* (1971) ordered massive cross-town busing to achieve racial integration. Nixon responded by seeking a congressional moratorium on busing and by denouncing busing as a reckless and extreme remedy for segregation.

Election of 1972

To a great extent, the inept campaign waged by Nixon's Democratic opponent, Senator George McGovern of South Dakota, handed victory to the Republicans. When McGovern endorsed a $30 billion cut in the defense budget, people began to fear that he was a neo-isolationist who would reduce the United States to a second-rate power. McGovern's proposals split the Democrats between his supporters—antiwar activists, blacks, feminists, young militants—and old-guard urban bosses, labor leaders, and white southerners.

Nixon's Landslide Victory

Nixon's victory in November was overwhelming: he polled 47 million votes, more than 60 percent of the votes cast. McGovern received only 29 million and won just one state, Massachusetts, and the District of Columbia. Nixon's southern strategy had been supremely successful: he carried the entire Deep South, which had once been solidly Democratic. He also gained the suburbs and won a majority of the urban vote, including such long-time Democrats as blue-collar workers, Catholics, and white ethnics. Only blacks, Jews, and low-income voters stuck by the Democratic candidate. The Democrats, however, retained control of both houses of Congress.

Watergate Break-in

Little noticed during the campaign was a break-in at the Watergate apartment-office complex in Washington, D.C., on June 17, 1972. A watchman telephoned the police to report an illegal late-night entry into the building through an underground garage. At 2:30 A.M., police arrested five men who were attaching listening devices to telephones in the sixth floor offices of the Democratic National Committee. The men had cameras and had been rifling through files.

One of those arrested was James W. McCord, a former CIA employee who had become security coordinator of the Committee to Re-Elect the President (CREEP). The other four were anti-Castro Cubans from Miami who had worked with the CIA before. Unknown to the police, two other men had been in the Watergate building at the time of the break-in. One was E. Howard Hunt, a one-time CIA agent who had become CREEP's security chief. The other was G. Gordon Liddy, a former FBI agent serving on the White House staff. What were these men trying to find in the Democrats' offices? What did they hope to overhear on the telephones? And most important, who had ordered the break-in?

WATERGATE AND NIXON'S RESIGNATION

The Watergate fiasco had actually begun in 1971, when the White House established not only CREEP but the Special Investigations Unit, known familiarly as the Plumbers, to stop the leaking of secret government documents to the press. After publication of the *Pentagon Papers*, the Plumbers burglarized the office of Daniel Ellsberg's psychiatrist in an attempt to discredit Ellsberg, who had leaked the top-secret report to the press. It was the Plumbers who broke into the Democratic National Committee's headquarters to photograph documents and install wiretaps; money raised by CREEP was used to pay the Plumbers' expenses both before and after the break-ins.

How do historians know

that President Richard M. Nixon was actually guilty of obstructing justice in the Watergate affair? What was the evidence—the "smoking gun"? The smoking gun was the tape recording of a June 23, 1972, White House conversation in which Nixon ordered his top aide to stop the Federal Bureau of Investigation's inquiry into the Watergate break-in. The Central Intelligence Agency, Nixon thundered, should call the FBI, claim that the break-in was a secret spy operation, and say, "'Don't go further into this case, period!'" That tape proved that Nixon had instigated a cover-up and obstructed justice almost from the outset of the scandal. Photo: "The Smoking Gun" by Oliphant, 1984. Reprinted courtesy of Susan Corn Conway Gallery.

The arrest of the Watergate burglars generated furious activity in the White House. Incriminating documents were shredded, E. Howard Hunt's name was expunged from the White House telephone directory, and President Nixon ordered his chief of staff, H. R. Haldeman, to discourage the FBI's investigation into the burglary on the pretext that it might compromise national security. Nixon also authorized CREEP "hush-money" payments in excess of $460,000 to keep Hunt and others from implicating the White House in the crime.

White House Cover-up

Because of successful White House efforts to cover up the scandal, the break-in was almost unnoticed by the electorate. Had it not been for the diligent efforts of reporters, government special prosecutors, federal judges, and members of Congress, President Nixon might have succeeded in disguising his involvement in Watergate. Slowly, however, the tangle of lies and distortions began to unravel. In early 1973, U.S. District Judge John Sirica tried the burglars, one of whom implicated his superiors in CREEP and at the White House. From May until November, the Senate Select Committee on Campaign Practices, chaired by Senator Sam Ervin of North Carolina, heard testimony from White House aides. John Dean, the White House counsel, acknowledged not only that there had been a cover-up but that the president had directed it. Another aide shocked the committee and the nation by disclosing that Nixon had had a taping system installed in his White House office and that conversations about Watergate had been recorded.

Watergate Hearings and Investigations

Nixon feigned innocence. In April, he tried to distance himself from the cover-up by announcing the resignations of his two chief White House aides, John Ehrlichman and H. R. Haldeman. The administration then appointed Archibald Cox, a Harvard law professor, to fill the new position of special Watergate prosecutor. But when Cox sought in October to obtain the White House tapes by means of a court order, Nixon decided to have him fired.

Saturday Night Massacre

Both Attorney General Elliott Richardson and his deputy resigned rather than carry out the dismissal order. It thus fell to the third-ranking person in the Department of Justice to fire Cox. The public outcry provoked by the so-called Saturday Night Massacre compelled the president to agree to the appointment of a new special prosecutor, Leon Jaworski. When Nixon still refused to surrender the tapes, Jaworski took him to court.

In the same month as the Saturday Night Massacre, the Nixon administration was stung by another scandal. Vice President Spiro Agnew resigned after pleading no contest to charges of income-tax evasion and acceptance of bribes. Under the provisions of the Twenty-fifth Amendment, Nixon nominated and Congress confirmed Gerald R. Ford, the House minority leader from Michigan, to replace Agnew.

Agnew's Resignation

Throughout 1973 and 1974, enterprising reporters uncovered more details of the break-in, the hush money, and the various people from Nixon on down who had taken part in the cover-up. White House aides and CREEP subordinates began to go on trial, with Nixon cited as their "unindicted co-conspirator." *Washington Post* reporters Carl Bernstein and Bob Woodward found an informant, known as Deep Throat, who provided damning information about Nixon and his aides. As Nixon's protestations of innocence became less credible, his hold on the tapes became more tenuous. In late April 1974, the president finally released an edited transcript of the tapes.

The edited tapes, however, were replete with gaps. They swayed neither the public nor the House Judiciary Committee, which had begun to draft articles of impeachment against the president. Nixon was still trying to hang on to the original tapes when the Supreme Court, in *U.S. v. Nixon*, unanimously ordered him in July to surrender the recordings to Judge Sirica. At about the same time, the Judiciary Committee began to conduct nationally televised hearings. After several days of testimony, the committee voted for impeachment on three of five counts: obstruction of justice through the payment of hush money to witnesses, lying, and withholding of evidence; defiance of a congressional subpoena of the tapes; and use of the CIA, the FBI, and the Internal Revenue Service to deprive Americans of their constitutional rights of privacy and free speech.

On August 5, the president finally handed over the complete tapes, which he knew would condemn him. Four days later, he resigned the presidency. The first substantive act of his successor, Gerald R. Ford, was to pardon Nixon. Some people concluded that Ford and Nixon had struck a deal.

The Watergate scandal prompted the reform of abuses of presidential power, some of which had predated the Nixon administration. The executive's usurpation of legislative pre-

Post-Watergate Restrictions on Executive Power

rogatives, which the historian Arthur M. Schlesinger Jr. called "the imperial presidency," dated from Franklin D. Roosevelt's administration. To remedy many of these abuses, Congress in 1973 passed the War Powers Resolution, which mandated that "in every possible instance" the president must consult with Congress before sending American troops into foreign wars. Under this law, the president could commit American troops abroad for no more than sixty days, after which he had to obtain congressional approval. The next year, Congress approved the Congressional Budget and Impoundment Control Act, which prohibited the president from impounding federal money.

In actions directly related to Watergate, Congress addressed campaign fund-raising abuses and the misuse of government agencies. The Federal Election Campaign Act of 1972 had restricted campaign spending to no more than 10 cents per constituent, and it required candidates to report individual contributions of more than $100. In 1974, Congress enacted additional legislation that set ceilings on campaign contributions and expenditures for congressional and presidential elections. Finally, to aid citizens who were victims of dirty tricks campaigns, Congress strengthened the Freedom of Information Act, originally enacted in 1966.

When John F. Kennedy delivered his inaugural address in 1961, he had challenged Americans to "pay any price, bear any burden, meet any hard-

ship" to defend freedom and inspire the world. Twelve years later, Richard M. Nixon echoed that rhetoric: "Let us pledge to make these four years the best four years in America's history, so that on its 200th birthday America will be as young and vital as when it began, and as bright a beacon of hope for all the world." But too much had happened in the intervening years for most Americans to see the nation as a bright beacon of hope. The urban riots, campus disorders, Vietnam, the assassinations of charismatic leaders, and Nixon's own unraveling tragedy—Watergate—had changed the nation and its people. Before the bicentennial celebration of 1976, America seemed bruised and battered—not young and vital.

SUGGESTIONS FOR FURTHER READING

The 1960s

David Chalmers, *And the Crooked Places Made Straight: The Struggle for Social Change in the 1960s* (1991); Godfrey Hodgson, *America in Our Time* (1976); Allen J. Matusow, *The Unraveling of America: A History of Liberalism in the 1960s* (1984); Charles R. Morris, *A Time of Passion: America, 1960–1980* (1984); Tom Shachtman, *Decade of Shocks: Dallas to Watergate, 1963–1974* (1983); Theodore H. White, *America in Search of Itself: The Making of the President, 1954–1980* (1982).

The Kennedy Administration

Irving Bernstein, *Promises Kept: John F. Kennedy's New Frontier* (1991); Thomas Brown, *JFK: History of an Image* (1988); David Burner, *John F. Kennedy and a New Generation* (1988); David Halberstam, *The Best and the Brightest* (1972); Bruce Miroff, *Pragmatic Illusions* (1976); Herbert S. Parmet, *J.F.K.: The Presidency of John F. Kennedy* (1983); Thomas C. Reeves, *A Question of Character* (1991); Arthur M. Schlesinger Jr., *Robert Kennedy and His Times* (1978), and *A Thousand Days: John F. Kennedy in the White House* (1965); Theodore C. Sorensen, *Kennedy* (1965); Gary Wills, *The Kennedy Imprisonment* (1982).

The Johnson Administration

Paul K. Conkin, *Big Daddy from the Pedernales: Lyndon Baines Johnson* (1986); Doris Kearns, *Lyndon Johnson and the American Dream* (1976); Sar A. Levitan and Robert Taggart, *The Promise of Greatness* (1976); Charles Murray, *Losing Ground: American Social Policy, 1950–1980* (1983); James T. Patterson, *America's Struggle Against Poverty, 1900–1985* (1986); John E. Schwarz, *America's Hidden Success: A Reassessment of Twenty Years of Public Policy* (1983).

Civil Rights and Black Power

Taylor Branch, *Parting the Waters: America in the King Years, 1954–1963* (1988); Clayborne Carson, *In Struggle: SNCC and the Black Awakening of the 1960s* (1981); William H. Chafe, *Civilities and Civil Rights: Greensboro, North Carolina, and the Black Struggle for Freedom* (1980); David J. Garrow, *Bearing the Cross: Martin Luther King Jr. and the Southern Christian Leadership Conference* (1986); Hugh Davis Graham, *Civil Rights and the Presidency* (1992); Malcolm X and Alex Haley, *The Autobiography of Malcolm X* (1965); August Meier and Elliott Rudwick, *CORE* (1973); Mark Stern, *Calculating Visions: Kennedy, Johnson, and Civil Rights* (1992).

The New Left and the Antiwar Movement

Wini Breines, *Community and Organization in the New Left, 1962–1968*, rev. ed. (1989); Charles DeBenedetti, *An American Ordeal: The Antiwar Movement of the Vietnam Era* (1990); Todd Gitlin, *The Sixties* (1987); Maurice Isserman, *If I Had a Hammer . . . : The Death of the Old Left and the Birth of the New Left* (1987); James Miller, *"Democracy Is in the Streets": From Port Huron to the Siege of Chicago* (1987); Thomas Powers, *Vietnam, the War at Home* (1984).

The Counterculture

Stanley Booth, *Dance with the Devil: The Rolling Stones and Their Times* (1984); Morris Dickstein, *Gates of Eden: American Culture in the Sixties* (1977); Philip Norman, *Shout! The Beatles in Their Generation* (1981); Charles Perry, *The Haight-Ashbury* (1984); Jay Stevens, *Storming Heaven: LSD and the American Dream* (1987); Jon Weiner, *Come Together: John Lennon in His Time* (1984); Tom Wolfe, *The Electric Kool-Aid Acid Test* (1968).

The Rebirth of Feminism

William H. Chafe, *The Paradox of Change: American Women in the Twentieth Century* (1991); Alice Echols, *Daring to Be Bad: Radical Feminism in America, 1965–1975* (1989); Sara Evans, *Personal Politics* (1978); Marian Faux, *Roe v. Wade* (1988); Jo Freeman, *The Politics of Women's Liberation* (1975); Cynthia Harrison, *On Account of Sex: The Politics of Women's Issues, 1945–1968* (1988); Judith Hole and Ellen Levine, *Rebirth of Feminism* (1971); Rosalind Rosenberg, *Divided Lives: American Women in the Twentieth Century* (1992); Gayle Graham Yates, *What Women Want: The Ideas of the Movement* (1975).

Year of Shocks: 1968

David Caute, *The Year of the Barricades* (1988); Lewis Chester et al., *An American Melodrama: The Presidential Campaign of 1968* (1969); David Farber, *Chicago '68* (1988).

The Nixon Administration

Stephen E. Ambrose, *Nixon*, 3 vols. (1987–1991); Roger Morris, *Richard Milhous Nixon* (1990); Herbert S. Parmet, *Richard Nixon and His America* (1990); James A. Reichley, *Conservatives in an Era of Change: The Nixon and Ford Administrations* (1981); Tom Wicker, *One of Us* (1991); Garry Wills, *Nixon Agonistes* (1970).

Watergate

Jim Hougan, *Secret Agenda: Watergate, Deep Throat and the CIA* (1984); Stanley I. Kutler, *The Wars of Watergate* (1990); J. Anthony Lukas, *Nightmare: The Underside of the Nixon Years* (1976); Kim McQuaid, *The Anxious Years: America in the Vietnam-Watergate Era* (1989); Theodore H. White, *Breach of Faith* (1975); Bob Woodward and Carl Bernstein, *The Final Days* (1976) and *All the President's Men* (1974).

33

A Turn to the Right,
1974–1989

On JANUARY 20, 1981, just 28 minutes after Ronald Reagan was sworn in as president of the United States, 52 Americans who had been held hostage in Iran for 444 days boarded a plane that flew them from Teheran to freedom. The hostage crisis had contributed to the nation's sense of impotence and frustration. Now the ordeal was over. On hearing the news, Bruce German's mother ran onto Main Street in Edwardsville, Pennsylvania, ringing a cowbell and shouting, "My Bruce is free! My Bruce is free!" Church bells rang, sirens wailed, people tied yellow ribbons everywhere, and the nation rejoiced.

Never had a presidential administration enjoyed a more auspicious beginning. But the challenges facing the new administration were immense. Reagan's 1980 victory took place during a period of economic decline; Americans, reeling under the one-two punch of stagflation, were filled with uncertainty. First, there was the economic stagnation known as a *recession*, which economists define as at least two consecutive quarters of no growth in the gross national product (GNP). Unemployment was on the upswing, particularly in heavy industry. Americans saw once proud automobile and steel plants close. As a result of such "deindustrialization," many jobs were jeopardized, whereas others disappeared forever. Second, there was *inflation*. As soaring prices eroded the purchasing power of workers' paychecks, people raided their savings, sacrificing future security to current needs.

America's economic dominance in the world had begun to decline in the 1970s. The 1973 Arab oil embargo led to the realization that the United States was not a fortress that could stand alone; it was dependent for its survival on imported oil. The postwar boom was over, but Presidents Gerald Ford and Jimmy Carter seemed unable to cope with the floundering economy.

By 1980, economic uncertainty was higher than at any time since the 1930s. The 1970s was the first decade since the Great Depression in which Americans' purchasing power declined. Women and people of color were particularly hard hit, for they were usually the last hired and the first to be laid off. Even when they had jobs, they were paid less than white men, and experts pointed to the growing "feminization" and "blackening" of poverty.

Changing economic conditions and the belief of people that they could no longer shape their personal destinies helped to create a wave of conservatism that Ronald Reagan rode into office. He promised a return to old-fashioned morality and a balanced budget, and he blamed government for fettering American economic creativity.

Ronald Reagan was successful during his first term. Although unemployment had risen between 1981 and 1983, the economy then rebounded, and by 1984 Reagan's policies had helped lower inflation and interest rates as well as unemployment. As the 1984 election approached, many Americans applauded Reagan's successes, including his foreign policy; they were proud that their nation was confronting the Soviets not only with strong words but with military interventions and a large military build-up. Patriotism was back in style, and so were traditional values. A proponent of prayer in the public schools and an opponent of abortion, Reagan argued for a return to the morality that had dominated American culture before the 1960s.

Reagan also provoked severe criticism as president. Opponents lambasted his economic policies ("Reaganomics") as favoring the rich and penalizing the poor. Reagan seemed to escape personal blame. He was a master at distancing himself not only from scandals in the White House but even from problems in foreign and domestic policy. Representative Patricia Schroeder, a Colorado Democrat, gave this phenomenon a memorable label: Reagan, she said, was "perfecting a Teflon-coated presidency. . . . He sees to it that nothing sticks to him."

Reagan's victory in 1984 was never in doubt, but his forty-nine-state sweep convinced some observers that he had transformed American politics by forging a New Right coalition that could dominate national politics for years.

Because of Reagan's economic policies, wealth in the United States was being redistributed upward. While the rich got richer in the 1980s, poverty deepened for many people. The United States was polarizing racially and economically, and societal divisions were being exacerbated by new problems: AIDS (acquired immune deficiency syndrome) and the cocaine-derived drug known as crack.

Reagan's influence collapsed during his final two years in office. But when the voters went to the polls in November 1988, the nation was at peace, and both unemployment and inflation were at low levels. George Bush, President Reagan's vice president, was the beneficiary of the Reagan legacy, and as the Republican candidate he rode it to victory.

THE ENERGY CRISIS AND END OF THE ECONOMIC BOOM

It was already evident in the early 1970s that the United States was suffering serious economic decline. Any lingering doubts about this assessment disappeared during the Arab oil embargo of 1973. Even before the embargo, the United States had suffered occasional shortages of natural gas, heating oil, and gasoline. But the American people, who had grown up on inexpensive and abundant energy, made no effort to conserve. By late 1973, the country had to import one-third of its oil supplies.

Price increases ordered by the Organization of Petroleum Exporting Countries (OPEC) struck the United States another blow. Oil prices rose 350 percent in 1973. As Americans grappled with the social and political costs of the price hikes, multinational oil companies prospered: their profits jumped 70 percent in 1973 and another 40 percent in 1974. Meanwhile, the boost in the price of imported oil reverberated through the entire economy. Inflation jumped from 3 percent in 1972 to a frightening 11 percent in 1974.

OPEC Price Increases Fuel Inflation

At the same time, recession hit the auto industry. In Detroit, General Motors laid off thirty-eight thousand workers indefinitely—6 percent of its domestic work force—and put another forty-eight thousand on leave for as long as ten days at a time. Sales of gas-guzzling American autos had plummeted as consumers rushed to purchase energy-efficient foreign subcompacts. Like Ford and Chrysler, GM was stuck with mostly

Recession in the Auto Industry

• *Important Events* •

1974	OPEC oil prices increase		Congress approves Reagan's budget cuts

1974   OPEC oil prices increase
       Gerald Ford becomes president
       Nelson Rockefeller appointed as vice president
       Ford pardons Nixon
       Ford creates WIN program to fight inflation
       Equal Credit Opportunity Act equalizes loan and credit card terms for men and women

1975   Nuclear accident occurs at Brown's Ferry
       Antibusing agitation erupts in Louisville and Boston
       Economic recession hits nation

1976   Hyde Amendment cuts off Medicaid funds for abortions
       Jimmy Carter elected president

1978   *Bakke* v. *University of California* outlaws quotas but upholds affirmative action
       California voters approve Proposition 13

1979   Three Mile Island nuclear accident raises fears of meltdown
       Moral Majority established
       Federal Reserve Board tightens money supply
       American hostages seized in Iran

1980   Economic recession recurs
       Race riots break out in Miami and Chattanooga
       Ronald Reagan elected president

1981   American hostages released after 444 days
       Prime interest rate reaches 21.5 percent
       AIDS first observed in the United States

       Congress approves Reagan's budget cuts
       Reagan breaks air traffic controllers strike
       Economic recession; unemployment hits 8 percent

1982   Prime interest rate at 14 percent
       Unemployment reaches 10 percent

1983   Prime interest rate at 10.5 percent
       More than half of adult women work outside the home
       ERA dies for lack of ratification

1984   Unemployment drops to 7.1 percent
       Reagan reelected
       Inflation falls to 4 percent

1985   Gramm-Rudman bill calls for balanced budget by 1991

1986   Tax Reform Act lowers personal income taxes
       Immigration Reform and Control Act provides amnesty to undocumented workers
       Iran-contra scandal breaks
       Republicans lose control of Senate in congressional elections

1987   Stock market prices drop 508 points in one day

1988   *Understanding AIDS* mailed to 107 million households
       Reagan travels to the Soviet Union
       George Bush elected president

1989   Bush inaugurated as president
       Federal deficit rises to $206 billion

---

large-car assembly plants. Moreover, the ailing American auto companies were not buying steel, glass, rubber, or tool-and-die products. Soon the recession in the auto industry had spread to other manufacturers, which quit hiring new workers and began laying off experienced employees.

Unlike earlier postwar recessions, this one did not fade away in a year or two. Part of the reason was inflation. In the earlier recessions, Republican as well as Democratic administrations had held to a policy of neo-Keynesianism. To minimize the swings

in the business cycle, they had manipulated federal policies—both fiscal policies (taxes and government spending) and monetary policies (interest rates and the money supply). They hoped by so doing to keep employment up and inflation down. Beginning in the 1970s, however, joblessness and prices both began to rise sharply. Policies designed to correct one problem only seemed to worsen the other.

Even in the best of times, the economy would have been hard-pressed to produce jobs for the millions of baby boomers who joined the labor market

The Shifting Occupational Structure

in the 1970s. As it was, economic activity created twenty-seven million additional jobs during the decade, a remarkable increase of 32 percent. But deindustrialization was causing a shift in the occupational structure. As heavy industries collapsed, laid-off workers took jobs in fast-food restaurants, all-night gas stations, and convenience stores—but at half their former wages. Workers who once had held high-paying blue-collar jobs saw their middle-class standard of living slipping away.

Another economic problem was a slowing of growth in productivity—the average output of goods per hour of labor. Between 1947 and 1965,

Decreased Productivity

American industrial productivity had increased an average of 3.3 percent a year, raising manufacturers' profits and lowering the cost of products to consumers. From 1966 to 1970, annual productivity growth averaged only 1.5 percent; it fell further between 1971 and 1975 and reached a mere 0.2 percent between 1976 and 1980. Economists blamed lack of business investment in state-of-the-art technology, the shift from an industrial to a service economy, and an alleged erosion of the work ethic. Whatever the causes, American goods cost more than those of foreign competitors.

The lag in productivity was not matched by a decrease in workers' expectations. Wage increases regularly exceeded production increases, and some economists blamed the raises for inflation. Indeed, wages that went up seldom came down again. Managers of the nation's basic industries—steel, autos, rubber—complained that the automatic cost-of-living adjustments in their labor contracts left them little margin to restrain price hikes.

Another spur to inflation was easy credit. Fearing scarcity, many people went on a buying spree; between 1975 and 1979, household and business borrowing more than tripled

Easy Credit and Inflation

(from $94 billion to $328 billion). More people had credit cards. The credit explosion helped bid up the price of everything, from houses to gold. Farmers bought new farmland and expensive machinery and irrigation equipment. The nation's farm debt, $55 billion in 1971, had reached $166 billion by 1980. Overburdened with debts, many farmers faced bankruptcy in the 1980s.

Every expert had a scapegoat to blame for the nation's economic doldrums. Labor leaders cited foreign competition and called for protective tariffs. Some businesspeople and economists blamed the cost of obeying federal health and safety laws and pollution controls. They urged officials to abolish the Environmental Protection Agency and the Occupational Safety and Health Administration. They also pressed for deregulation of the oil, airline, and trucking industries on the theory that competition would drive prices down. Above all, critics attacked the federal government's massive spending programs; the mounting national debt, they said, was the sad result.

By the time Gerald Ford became president in 1974, OPEC price increases had pushed the inflation rate to 11 percent. Appalled, Ford created

Government Response to the Economic Crisis

Whip Inflation Now (WIN), a voluntary program that encouraged businesses, consumers, and workers to save energy and organize grassroots anti-inflation efforts. In the 1974 congressional elections, voters responded to WIN, Watergate, and Ford's pardon of Nixon by giving the Democrats forty-three additional seats in the House and four in the Senate.

Ford's response to inflation was to curb federal spending and encourage the Federal Reserve Board to raise its interest rates to banks, thus tightening credit. As in the past, these actions prompted a recession—only this time, it was the worst in forty years. Unemployment jumped to 8.5 percent in 1975 and, because the economy had stagnated, the federal deficit for the fiscal year 1976–1977 hit a record $60 billion.

Ford devised no lasting solutions to the energy crisis, but the crisis seemed to pass when OPEC ended the embargo—and the incentive to prevent future shortages dissolved as

Nuclear Power

well. The energy crisis did, however, intensify public debate over nuclear power. For the sake of energy independence, advocates asserted, the United States had to rely more on nuclear energy. Environmental activists countered that the risk of nuclear accident was too great and that there was no safe way to store nuclear waste. Accidents in the nuclear power plants at Brown's Ferry in Alabama (1975) and Three Mile Island in Pennsylvania (1979) gave credence to the activists' cause. By 1979, however, ninety-six reactors were under construction throughout the nation, and thirty more were on order.

Meanwhile, the combined effects of the energy crisis, stagflation, and the flight of industry and the middle class to the suburbs and the Sun Belt were producing fiscal disaster in the nation's cities. Not since 1933, when Detroit defaulted on its debts, had a major American city gone bankrupt. But New York City was near financial collapse by late 1975. President Ford vowed "to veto any bill that has as its purpose a federal bail-out of New York City," but he relented after the Senate and House Banking Committees approved loan guarantees, and the city was saved. New York was not alone in its financial problems; other Frost Belt cities were in trouble, saddled with growing welfare rolls, deindustrialization, and a declining tax base. In 1978, Cleveland became the first major city to default since the Great Depression.

Throughout Ford's term, Congress enjoyed new power. Watergate and criticism of the imperial presidency accounted for Congress's new self-confidence. For the first time in the nation's history, furthermore, neither the president nor vice president had been popularly elected. One of Ford's first acts as president had been to select Nelson Rockefeller, former governor of New York, as his vice president. But Republican prospects for retaining the presidency in the 1976 election seemed gloomy.

THE FAILED PROMISE OF THE CARTER PRESIDENCY

While Ford struggled with a Democratic Congress, the Democratic party geared up for the presidential election of 1976. Against the background of

Election of 1976

Watergate secrecy and corruption, one candidate in particular promised honesty and openness. "I will never lie to you," pledged Jimmy Carter, an obscure former one-term governor of Georgia. When this born-again Christian promised voters efficiency and decency in government, they believed him. Carter secured the Democratic nomination and chose Senator Walter Mondale, a liberal from Minnesota, as his running mate.

Neither Carter nor President Ford, the Republican nominee, inspired much interest, and on election day only 54 percent of the electorate bestirred itself to vote. Nevertheless, an analysis of the turnout was instructive. One political commentator concluded that the vote was "fractured to a marked degree along the fault line separating the haves and have-nots." Although Carter won nearly 90 percent of the African- and Mexican-American vote, he squeaked to victory by a slim 1.7 million votes out of 80 million cast. Ford's appeal was strongest among middle- and upper-middle-class white voters.

Carter's most noteworthy domestic accomplishments were in energy, transportation, and conservation policy. To encourage domestic production of oil, he phased in decontrol of

Carter's Accomplishments

oil prices. To moderate the social effects of the energy crisis, he called for a windfall-profits tax on excessive profits resulting from decontrol and for grants to the poor and elderly for the purchase of heating fuel. Carter also deregulated the airline, trucking, and railroad industries and persuaded Congress to ease federal control of banks. His administration established a $1.6 billion "superfund" to clean up abandoned chemical waste sites and created two free-standing departments—those of energy and education. Finally, in what Carter called "the most important decision on conservation matters that the Congress will face in this century," he placed more than one hundred million acres of Alaskan land under the federal government's protection as national parks, national forests, and wildlife refuges.

Despite these accomplishments, Carter both failed to inspire Americans and alienated party members. Elected as an outsider, he remained one

Carter's Flagging Popularity

throughout his presidency. Moreover, his support of deregulation and his opposition to wage and price controls and gasoline rationing ran counter to liberal Democratic principles. Seeing inflation as a greater threat to the nation's economy than either recession or unemployment, Carter announced that his top priority would be to cut federal spending, although doing so would add to the jobless rolls. But inflation continued to rise.

Carter's problems were not entirely of his own making. The shah of Iran's government fell to revolutionary forces in 1979; the new government then cut off oil supplies to the United States. The same year, OPEC raised its prices again, and the cost of crude oil nearly doubled. As Americans waited in long lines at gasoline pumps, public approval of the president reached a new low.

Carter also inherited political problems. In the wake of Vietnam and Watergate, power had temporarily shifted from the White House to Capitol Hill. Meanwhile, Congress was

Decline of Presidential Authority

filling up with political newcomers, men and women unaccustomed to reflex obedience to established leadership. Despite the large Democratic majorities in Congress after the Watergate scandal, party discipline seemed to be a thing of the past. To further complicate matters, Capitol Hill was crawling with lobbyists from special interest groups: trade associations, corporations, labor unions, and single-issue groups like the National Rifle Association. In 1980, there were 2,765 political action committees (PACs), more than four times as many as in 1974.

By 1980, the economy was in a shambles. Inflation had jumped in 1979 to exceed 13 percent, and traders around the world had lost confidence in the dollar, causing unprece-

Economic Discomfort in 1980

dented increases in the price of gold. To steady the dollar and curb inflation, the Federal Reserve Board took drastic measures. First, the board cut the money supply—partly by selling treasury securities to take money out of circulation—thus forcing borrowers to bid up interest rates sufficiently to

dampen the economy and reduce inflation. Second, it raised the rate at which the Federal Reserve loaned money to banks. As a result, mortgage interest rates leaped beyond 15 percent, and the prime lending rate (the rate charged to businesses) hit an all-time high of 20 percent. Inflation fell but only to 12 percent. Worse still, by 1980 the nation

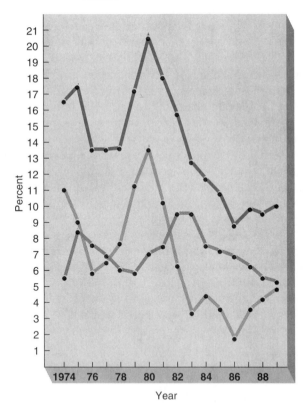

"Discomfort Index" (Unemployment Plus Inflation), 1974–1989

— "Discomfort Index"
— Unemployment Rate
— Inflation

Discomfort Index (Unemployment Plus Inflation), 1974–1989 Americans' economic discomfort (unemployment plus inflation) directly determined their political behavior. When the "discomfort index" was high in 1976 and 1980, Americans voted for a change in presidents. When the economic discomfort declined in 1984 and 1988, Ronald Reagan and George Bush were the political beneficiaries. Source: Adapted from *Economic Report of the President, 1992* (Washington, D.C.: U.S. Government Printing Office, 1992), pp. 340, 365.

was in a full-fledged recession. The 1980 unemployment rate of 7.5 percent, combined with the 12 percent inflation rate, had produced a staggeringly high "discomfort index" of just under 20 percent (see figure). In 1976, Carter had gibed at the incumbent president, Gerald Ford, by saying, "Anything you don't like about Washington, I suggest you blame on him." In 1980, Carter was the incumbent, and many Americans blamed him for the problems that beset the country.

RONALD REAGAN AND THE ELECTION OF 1980

The 1980 federal census revealed significant growth in the elderly population—24 percent—and a two-year rise in the median age. By 1980, as many

A Shifting Population

Americans were older than thirty as younger, and the number of retired people had increased by more than 50 percent since 1972. The census also documented the continuing shift of large numbers of people from the politically liberal Frost Belt states of the Northeast and Midwest to the more conservative Sun Belt states of the South and West (see map). The census findings meant that seventeen seats in the House of Representatives would shift from the Frost Belt to the Sun Belt by the 1982 elections.

A consequence of the shift of population to the Sun Belt was the resurgence of conservatism in the 1970s and 1980s. With doubt about government's capacity to serve the people, conservatives set out to repeal the social welfare system. California voters approved a 1978

Resurgence of Conservatism

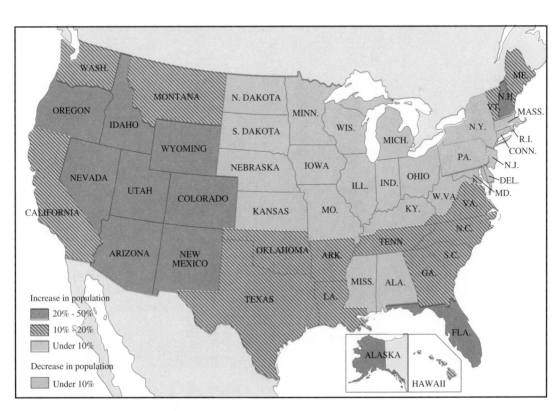

The Continued Shift to the Sun Belt in the 1970s *Throughout the 1970s, Americans continued to leave economically declining areas of the North and the East in pursuit of opportunity in the Sun Belt.*

tax-cutting referendum called Proposition 13, which reduced property taxes and put stringent limits on state spending for social programs. Proposition 13 set off shock waves: nearly a score of other states imposed similar ceilings on taxes and expenditures. On the national level, conservatives lobbied for a constitutional amendment to prohibit federal budget deficits.

A new political alignment was taking place. Economic conservatives were being joined by evangelical Christians, who believed they had a moral obligation to enter politics on the side of "a pro-life, pro-traditional family, pro-moral position." It was through the political system that evangelicals intended to oppose gay rights, abortion, sex in movies, and the Equal Rights Amendment (ERA). In 1979, the Reverend Jerry Falwell, a radio-TV minister from Lynchburg, Virginia, helped to found the Moral Majority, which quickly registered between two and three million new voters, started a newspaper, and bought daily time on 140 radio stations. Together with conservative think tanks like the Hoover Institution and conservative magazines like the *National Review*, these church groups formed a flourishing network of potential supporters for conservative candidates.

In the Republican primaries, Ronald Reagan, a former actor and two-term governor of California, triumphed easily over Representative John Anderson and former CIA director George Bush. His appeal to the voters in the presidential campaign was much broader than experts had predicted. Reagan

Election of 1980

A former movie actor and host of television shows, Ronald Reagan made effective use of TV in arguing for "family values," an aggressive anti-Soviet foreign and military policy, and tax cuts. To numerous Americans, Reagan was "the great communicator." Ronald Reagan Presidential Library, TV courtesy of Zenith Electronics Corporation.

appealed to both the traditional economic conservatives and the new breed of social issue conservatives. Economic conservatives liked his commitment to economy in government, a balanced budget, and "supply-side" economics, or tax reductions to businesses to encourage capital investment. Reagan's stand against the ERA and legalized abortion recommended him to the "profamily" movement.

On election day, voters gave Reagan and his running mate George Bush 51 percent of the vote to 41 percent for Carter, the Democratic candidate. John Anderson, who ran as an independent, received almost 7 percent of the vote. Reagan's sweep was nationwide; Carter carried only six states and the District of Columbia. The vote was not only an affirmation of Reagan's conservatism but also a signal of the nation's deep dissatisfaction with Jimmy Carter's management of both the economy and foreign policy. As startling as Reagan's sweep was the capture of eleven Senate seats by Republican candidates, giving the party a majority in that house. Republicans also gained thirty-three seats in the House and four state governorships.

REAGANOMICS

Upon taking office, President Reagan wasted little time announcing what he called "a new beginning." He immediately launched a double-barreled attack on problems in the economy. First, he asked Congress to cut billions from domestic programs, including urban aid, Medicare and Medicaid, food stamps, welfare subsidies for the working poor, and school meals. Congress endorsed most of Reagan's demands. He soon initiated a second round of budget cuts, resulting among other things in the trimming of a million food stamp recipients from government rolls.

Tax cuts were the second facet of Reagan's economic plan. A fervent believer in supply-side economics, he called for reductions in the income taxes of the affluent and of cor-

Tax Cuts

porations in order to stimulate savings and investments. New capital would be invested, the argument went, and would produce new plants, new jobs, and new products. As prosperity returned, the profits at the top would "trickle down" to the middle classes and even to the poor. Congress responded with a five-year, $750 billion tax cut, the largest ever in American history, featuring a 25 percent reduction in personal income taxes over three years. Other provisions increased business investment tax credits and depreciation allowances and lowered the maximum tax on income from 70 to 50 percent. The wealthy gained the most from these tax cuts.

A third item occupied Reagan's agenda: a vigorous assault on federal environmental, health, and safety regulations that, Reagan believed, excessively reduced business profits and discouraged economic growth.

Weakened Environmental Enforcement

The president appointed opponents of these regulations to enforce them. Some critics likened such appointments to hiring foxes to guard the chicken coops. Reagan officials explained that slackened enforcement was necessary to reduce business costs and make American goods competitive in world markets, but environmentalists countered that such policies invited disaster, such as toxic waste poisoning or nuclear reactor accidents.

Reagan scored two notable economic successes during his first two years in office: the inflation rate plummeted, as did the cost of borrowing money.

Falling Inflation

The prime rate for bank loans, which had stood at a record high of 21.5 percent in early 1981, dropped to 10.5 percent by early 1983. Inflation fell from 12 percent in 1980 to less than 7 percent in 1982. Oil led the way in price declines; after eight years, OPEC had at last increased its oil production, thus lowering prices. In 1981, the United States was awash with oil, as world production exceeded demand by two million barrels a day.

But there was also a sobering explanation for the decline in inflation. By mid-1981, the nation was mired in a recession that not only persisted but deepened. During the last three months of the year, the GNP fell 5 percent, and sales of cars and houses dropped sharply. With declining economic activity, unemployment soared to 8 percent, the highest level in almost six years.

A year later, in late 1982, unemployment had reached 10 percent, the highest rate since 1940. Most of the jobless were adult men, particularly African-Americans who suf-

Rising Unemployment

fered an unemployment rate of 20 percent. Many unemployed were blue-collar workers in such ailing "smokestack industries" as autos, steel, and rubber. Reagan and his advisers had promised that his supply-side economics would produce demand-side results and that, by spending their tax cuts, consumers would lift the economy out of the recession. But as late as April 1983, unemployment still stood at 10 percent. Agriculture too was faltering and near collapse. Farmers suffered from floods and droughts and from burdensome debts they had incurred at high interest rates. Many lost their property through mortgage foreclosures and farm auctions. Others filed for bankruptcy.

As the recession deepened in 1982, poverty rose to its highest level since 1965. The Bureau of the Census reported that the number of Americans

Resurgence of Poverty

living in poverty had increased from twenty-six million in 1979 to thirty-four million in 1982. Poverty had increased most among African-Americans (36 percent of whom were poor) and Hispanic-Americans (30 percent). Predictably, the largest single category of poor families consisted of households headed by women (36 percent). With one exception, poverty continued its rise in 1983, returning to the level that had prevailed before the enactment of President Johnson's Great Society. That exception was the elderly; politicians had begun paying attention to the needs of this vocal and rapidly growing group.

President Reagan had announced that his administration would halt the expansion of social and health programs but would retain a "safety net" for the "truly needy." But he reneged on this promise, and Congress, unwilling to buck the popular president, sustained most of his decisions. Facing a budget deficit in excess of $200 billion in mid-1982, Reagan had three choices, and in each case he made a conservative decision. First, he could cut back on his rearmament plans to spend $1.7 trillion over five years. This he refused to do; in fact, the budget he signed raised defense spending another 13 percent.

Second, he could suspend or reduce the second installment of his tax cut. This choice too he found unacceptable. Third, he could—and did—cut welfare and social programs, pushing through Congress further cuts in Medicare and Medicaid, food stamps, federal pensions, and government-guaranteed home mortgages. Nevertheless, in the absence of other budget cuts, the deficit continued to grow.

REAGAN TRIUMPHANT: THE ELECTION OF 1984

President Reagan prepared for his 1984 reelection campaign with the knowledge that, although most white men supported him, the majority of women and people of color opposed him. Joining them in the anti-Reagan camp were most of the nation's labor unions.

Even without Reagan in the White House, hard times would have hit the unions in the 1980s. Faced with recession and unemployment, union

Hard Times for Labor Unions

negotiators had to settle for less than they were accustomed to receiving. American workers who ratified contracts during the first three months of Reagan's term settled for pay increases averaging only 2.2 percent, the biggest drop in wage settlements since the government began collecting such data in 1954. Unions had suffered large membership losses when unemployment hit the smokestack industries, and their efforts to unionize the high-growth electronics and service sectors of the economy were failing.

Reagan made the unions' hard times worse. He presided over the government's busting of the Professional Air Traffic Controllers Organization (PATCO) during the union's 1981 strike. His appointees to the National Labor Relations Board consistently voted against labor and for management. Although Reagan appeared to be an enemy of labor, an estimated 44 percent of union families had voted for Reagan in 1980; many still responded positively to his genial personality, espousal of old-fashioned values, and anticommunism. And by 1984, the economy was showing signs of recovery.

In 1984, the GNP rose 7 percent, the sharpest increase since 1951, and midyear unemployment fell to a four-year low of 7 percent. The economy was heating up but without sparking inflation. Indeed, inflation (4 percent in 1984) fell to its lowest level since 1967. A second factor in Reagan's favor was people's perception of him as a strong leader in foreign as well as national affairs. Reagan was the enthusiastic choice not only of political conservatives but also of social and religious conservatives across the country. He won the approval of millions of other Americans who agreed with his television ads that "America is back" after two decades of turmoil and self-doubt.

Reagan's Reelection Assets

Aiding Reagan was the Democrats' failure to field a convincing alternative. The Democratic nominee—former Vice President Walter Mondale—did not inspire Americans. Even the policies that Mondale espoused seemed timeworn and out of step with the nation's conservatism. Adding to Mondale's woes was the disarray of the Democratic party; it had fragmented into separate caucuses of union members, blacks, women, Jews, homosexuals, Hispanics, and other groups. Each caucus had its own agenda. The one bright spot for the Democrats was Mondale's historic selection of Representative Geraldine Ferraro of New York as his vice presidential running mate. Ferraro showed herself to be an intelligent indefatigable campaigner.

Mondale attempted to debate the federal deficit and the nuclear arms race, but Reagan preferred to invoke the theme of leadership and rely on slogans. Mondale chastised Reagan for the deficit, which had reached $175 billion in fiscal year 1984 (see figure). But when Mondale announced that he would raise taxes to cut the deficit, he lost

America's Rising National Debt, 1974–1989 *America's national debt, which rose sporadically throughout the 1970s, soared to record heights during the 1980s. Under President Reagan, large defense expenditures and tax cuts caused the national debt to grow by $1.5 trillion. The years in this illustration are budget years, which begin in preceding calendar years (the 1989 budget year, for example, began October 1, 1988).* Source: Adapted from U.S. Bureau of the Census, *Statistical Abstract of the United States* (Washington, D.C.: U.S. Government Printing Office, 1992), p. 315.

votes. Mondale also attacked Reagan's foreign policy as militaristic, but Americans were attracted to Reagan's pledge to restore American global power.

Voters in 1984 had a clear choice, and in every state but Minnesota—Mondale's home state—they chose the Republican ticket. The election returns were the most convincing evidence yet that the nation had shifted to the right. The only groups still loyal to the Democratic ticket were African-Americans, Hispanics, Jews, the poor, and the unemployed. Reagan scored solid victories with all other voting groups, including young people, whites in both the North and the South, high school and college graduates, Protestants and Catholics, and families with incomes exceeding $12,500.

Reagan's Victory

In his second inaugural address, Reagan announced that his "new American Emancipation" would eradicate the excesses of fifty years of Democratic liberalism and thus "tear down economic barriers to liberate the spirit of enterprise." Whether Reagan had forged a lasting conservative coalition—one that would eventually repeal the New Deal—remained to be seen. What was not debatable was that he had succeeded in his principal aims during his first term and had restored the presidency to its central role in politics and the government.

Columnist David Broder noted, however, that "Reagan's issue-free, feel-good 1984 campaign created no policy mandate," and for much of 1985 the president was on the defensive. Reagan had assailed President Carter's $73 billion deficit during the 1980 campaign, but the deficit exceeded $222 billion in fiscal 1985. Although Republicans blamed the deficit on the Democrats, almost half the national debt derived from fiscal years 1982 through 1986, when Reagan occupied the White House and the Republicans controlled the Senate. Because of tax reductions and upwardly spiraling defense budgets, the national debt grew by $954 billion during this five-year period. In response, Reagan and Congress reluctantly agreed to the 1985 Gramm-Rudman bill, which called for a balanced federal budget by

Mounting Fiscal Deficit

fiscal 1991 through a gradual reduction of the annual deficit. The deficit did drop—for one year, 1987—but then rose again to $206 billion in 1989.

Reagan was more successful in confronting other challenges. Following Warren Burger's decision to retire from the Supreme Court, he nominated William Rehnquist to serve as chief justice and Antonin Scalia to fill Rehnquist's seat; the Senate confirmed both choices. Another victory was the Tax Reform Act of 1986, which lowered personal income taxes, closed some flagrant loopholes, and eliminated six million poor people from the tax rolls.

Meanwhile, economically and racially, American society became increasingly polarized. People of color and new immigrants found themselves battling not only rising poverty levels but also white hostility. Large numbers of women and children also slipped into poverty in the 1980s, a decade of growing economic inequality and social problems. Hard drugs brought devastation to entire neighborhoods, and AIDS killed tens of thousands of Americans.

PEOPLE OF COLOR AND NEW IMMIGRANTS

Many people of color saw their economic fortunes decline during the 1970s and 1980s. Joblessness plagued blacks, Native Americans, and Hispanics, as well as new immigrants. As a result of the sluggish economy, poverty was still a national problem in 1989, and African-Americans made up a disproportionate share of the poor. The overall poverty rate was 13 percent by 1980, but the rate among blacks was 33 percent and among Hispanics 26 percent, compared with 10 percent for whites. These figures had barely changed by the end of Reagan's presidency in 1989.

The weight of poverty fell most heavily on African-American children, almost half of whom lived below the poverty line in the 1980s. A 1981 Children's Defense Fund survey reported that black children in the United States were four times more likely than whites to be born into poverty, twice as likely to drop out of school before twelfth grade, five times as likely as white teenagers to be murdered, and three times as likely to be unemployed. Many of these children lived in families headed by single women who were forced to rely on welfare or earned meager incomes as domestic servants, laundresses, and kitchen helpers.

Some whites and even other blacks grumbled that poor blacks were responsible for their own poverty. But the job market was far different in the 1970s and 1980s from that of twenty-five, fifty, or seventy-five years before. Deindustrialization had eliminated many blue-collar jobs; job demand in the 1970s and 1980s was greatest for skilled workers such as computer operators, bank tellers, secretaries, and bookkeepers. Most jobless people could not qualify.

Declining Job Opportunities for African-Americans

Even as the plight of the African-American poor worsened, the black middle class expanded. The number of black college students increased from 282,000 in 1966 to more than one million in 1980; by 1980, about one-third of all black high school graduates were going on to college, the same proportion as among white youths. And by 1990, the number of black college students had increased further, to 1.3 million. At least at the upper levels of black society, the dream of equality was being realized.

African-American Middle Class

As middle-class African-Americans made gains, however, resentful whites complained that they were being victimized by "reverse discrimination." To meet federal affirmative action requirements, some schools and companies had established quotas for minorities and women; in some cases, the requirements were lower than those for whites. When Allan Bakke, a white man, was denied admission to medical school, he sued on the ground that less-qualified black applicants had been admitted. In a 5-to-4 ruling in 1978, the Supreme Court outlawed quotas but upheld the principle of affirmative action, explaining that race or ethnicity could be counted

White Backlash

as "a 'plus' in a particular applicant's file" (*Bakke* v. *University of California*). In 1989, however, the Court ruled that past discrimination did not "justify a rigid racial quota" and that white workers could sue to reopen affirmative action cases settled in federal courts years earlier (*Richmond* v. *Croson*, *Martin* v. *Wilks*).

White anger over affirmative action and busing combined with the effects of stagflation to produce an upsurge in racism. In Boston, where busing provoked numerous riots, a group of white students attacked a black passer-by outside city hall. "Get the nigger; kill him," one shouted, and they ran at him with the sharp end of a flagstaff flying an American flag. Tension rose not only in Boston but in cities across the nation.

African-Americans were tense, and they showed it more openly than in the past. Charles Silberman wrote in *Criminal Violence, Criminal Justice* (1978) that "black Americans have discovered that fear runs the other way, that whites are intimidated by their very presence. . . . The taboo against expression of anti-white anger is breaking down, and 350 years of festering hatred has come spilling out." That hatred erupted several times in 1980, most notably in Miami and Chattanooga, after all-white juries acquitted whites in the killings of blacks. Miami's three days of rioting left eighteen dead and four hundred injured.

Black Anger

African-American civil rights leaders denounced not only the judicial system but also the executive branch headed by President Ronald Reagan. Appointments were one issue: whereas 12 percent of President Jimmy Carter's high-level appointees had been black and 12 percent women, Reagan's were 4 percent black and 8 percent women. (Reagan did appoint four women to his cabinet, and he made history by appointing Sandra Day O'Connor as the first woman associate justice of the Supreme Court.) Moreover, Reagan's civil rights chief in the Justice Department fought against renewing the Voting Rights Act of 1965, opposed busing and affirmative action, and was criticized for lax enforcement of fair housing laws and laws banning sexual and racial discrimination in federally funded education programs.

Every bit as angry as African-Americans were Native Americans. Their new militancy burst into the headlines in late 1969, when a small group of

Native American Militancy
———

Indians seized Alcatraz Island in San Francisco Bay. Arguing that an 1868 Sioux treaty entitled them to possession of unused federal lands, the group occupied the island until mid-1971. Two years later, members of the militant American Indian Movement (AIM), demanding the rights guaranteed Indians in treaties with the United States, seized eleven hostages and a trading post on the Pine Ridge Reservation at Wounded Knee, South Dakota, where troops of the Seventh Cavalry had massacred the Sioux in 1890. Their seventy-one-day confrontation with federal marshals ended with a government agreement to examine the treaty rights of the Oglala Sioux.

Like other people of color, Native Americans were trapped in poverty. Four in ten Native Americans were unemployed, and nine out of ten lived in substandard housing. Often, being an Indian also meant being unhealthy: Native Americans suffered the highest incidence of alcoholism, tuberculosis, and suicide of any ethnic group in the United States.

Since 1924, Indians have had dual legal status as U.S. citizens and as members of tribal nations subject to special treaty agreements with the

Indian Suits for Lost Lands
———

United States. Their dual status has proved a curse, in large part because the government found it easier to breach its treaty commitments. In 1946, Congress established the Indian Claims Commission to compensate Indians for lands stolen from them. Under the legislation, lawyers for the Native American Rights Fund and other groups scored notable victories. In 1980, for example, the Supreme Court ordered the government to pay $106 million plus interest to the Sioux Indian Nation for the Black Hills of South Dakota, stolen when gold was found there in the 1870s. Nevertheless, corporations and government agencies continued to covet Indian lands and disregard Indian religious beliefs: a coal company strip-mined a portion of the Hopi Sacred Circle, which according to tribal religion is the source of all life.

As Indians fought to regain old rights, Hispanic-Americans struggled to make a place for themselves. An influx of immigrants unequaled since the turn of

Hispanic-Americans
———

the century, coupled with a high birthrate, made Hispanic peoples America's fastest-growing minority by the 1970s. Of the more than twenty million Hispanics living in the United States in the 1970s, eight million were Mexican-Americans concentrated in Arizona, California, Colorado, New Mexico, and Texas. Several million Puerto Ricans and Cubans clustered principally on the East Coast.

These officially acknowledged Hispanics were joined by millions of undocumented workers, or illegal aliens. Beginning in the mid-1960s, large numbers of poverty-stricken Mexicans began to cross the poorly guarded two-thousand-mile border. The movement north continued in the 1970s and 1980s. By 1990, one out of three Los Angelenos and Miamians was Hispanic, as was 20 percent of the population of San Diego, 48 percent of San Antonio, and 70 percent of El Paso.

Poverty awaited the new immigrants, as it had previous groups of newcomers. Like many earlier groups, Hispanics faced a language barrier. Most inner-city schools did not provide bilingual education for Spanish-speaking students. Finally, the larger the Hispanic population has become, the more widespread has been the discrimination.

Most of these new Americans preferred their family-centered culture to Anglo culture and for that reason resisted assimilation. "We want to be

Hispanic Cultural Pride
———

here," explained Daniel Villanueva, a TV executive, "but without losing our language and our culture. They are a richness, a treasure that we don't care to lose."

Like other minorities, Hispanics wanted political power—"brown power." Cesar Chavez's United Farm Workers was the first Hispanic interest group to gain national attention. The militant Brown Berets also attracted notice for their efforts to provide meals to preschoolers and courses in Chicano studies and consciousness raising to older students. And throughout the 1970s, the Mexican-American political party La Raza Unida was a potent force in the Southwest and East Los Angeles. Still, for the group that was becoming the nation's largest minority, Hispanics exercised a disproportionately small share of political power.

During the 1980s, Hispanic and Native Americans joined African-Americans in denouncing the Reagan administration. The League of United Latin American Citizens censured Reagan for his "very, very dismal record" in dealing with their problems, and the National Tribal Chairmen's Association charged that under Reagan "the delivery of services by federal agencies to Indians was in a shambles."

During the 1970s and 1980s, people of color immigrated to the United States in record numbers from Indochina, Mexico, Central and South America, and the Caribbean. **New Influx of Immigrants** Refugees of the Vietnam War arrived, other immigrants came from the Philippines, Korea, Taiwan, India, the Dominican Republic, and Jamaica, and boat people poured in from the islands of Cuba and Haiti. Between 1970 and 1980, the United States absorbed more than 4 million immigrants and refugees and perhaps twice that number of illegal aliens. High as these figures were, they doubled again during the next decade. With 9 million new arrivals, the 1980s surpassed the historic high mark set by the 8.7 million immigrants who had reached American shores between 1901 and 1910. The new immigrants consisted largely of families. Among the varied peoples who were seeking opportunity in a new land, Asian-Americans were by far the most successful.

The arrival of so many newcomers put pressure on Congress to curtail the flow and perhaps offer amnesty to aliens already living illegally in the United States. In 1978, Congress authorized a comprehensive reexamination of America's immigration policy. The immigration commission completed its study in 1981, but legislative solutions were delayed until 1986, when Congress passed the Immigration Reform and Control (Simpson-Rodino) Act. The act provided amnesty to undocumented workers who had arrived before 1982. The act's purpose was to discourage illegal immigration by imposing sanctions on employers who hired undocumented workers, but it failed to stem the flow of people fleeing Mexico's economic woes. In 1988, the number of new immigrants from Mexico approached the record numbers reached just before the reform law went into effect.

WOMEN AND CHILDREN LAST

Feminists scored some impressive legislative victories in the 1970s. In 1974, Congress passed the Equal Credit Opportunity Act, which enabled women to get bank loans and obtain credit cards on the same terms as men. Even more significant were women's gains from affirmative action in hiring. As mandated by the Civil Rights Act of 1964 and the establishment of the Equal Employment Opportunity Commission, women and people of color applying for jobs had to receive the same consideration as white males. In the field of criminal law, many states revised their statutes on rape, prohibiting defense lawyers from discrediting rape victims by revealing their previous sexual experience.

Still, women continued to encounter opposition in their quest for equality. Particularly formidable was the antifeminist or "profamily" movement, which contended that men should lead and women should follow, especially within the family. The backlash against feminism became an increasingly powerful political force in the United States. In defense of the family—especially the patriarchal, or father-led, family—antifeminists campaigned against the Equal Rights Amendment, the gay rights movement, and abortion on demand.

Antifeminists blamed the women's movement for the country's spiraling divorce rate; they charged that feminists would jettison their husbands and even their children in their quests for job fulfillment and sexual equality. Although the number of divorces almost tripled from 1960 to 1976, the decision to divorce was often made by the husbands. According to Barbara Ehrenreich, a feminist scholar, men started walking out on their families in large numbers in the 1950s, well before the rebirth of feminism. Tired of fulfilling the role of husband, father, and financial provider, many men came to see their wives as the agent of their entrapment; divorce was their escape.

Antifeminists successfully stalled ratification of the Equal Rights Amendment, which after quickly passing thirty-five state legislatures fell three states short of success in the late 1970s. Phyllis Schlafly's "Stop ERA" campaign falsely claimed that the ERA would abolish alimony and legalize homosexual marriages. The debate was occasionally vicious. Refusing to acknowledge gender-based discrimination, Schlafly derided ERA advocates as "a bunch of bitter women seeking a constitutional cure for their personal problems."

Equal Rights Amendment

Many antifeminists also participated in the anti-abortion or "prolife" movement, which sprang up almost overnight in the wake of the Supreme Court's 1973 decision in *Roe* v. *Wade*. Along with Catholics, Mormons, and other religious opponents of abortion, the prolife movement supported the successful legislative effort of Representative Henry Hyde of Illinois in 1976 to cut off most Medicaid funds for abortions.

Feminists fought back. They assailed Reagan for failing to reverse "the feminization of poverty" and for approving cuts in food stamps and school meals. The Reagan administration's opposition to federally subsidized child care and the goal of "comparable worth" also drew feminists' ire. Because of persistent occupational segregation, 80 percent of all working women in 1985 were concentrated in such low-paying "female" occupations as clerking, selling, teaching, and waitressing. Recognizing this, feminists supplemented their earlier rallying cry of "equal pay for equal work" with a call for "equal pay for jobs of comparable worth." Why, women asked, should a grade school teacher earn less than an electrician, if the two jobs require comparable training and skills and involve comparable responsibilities? By the end of the 1980s, female workers still took home only 70 cents to every male worker's dollar.

Women Opponents of Reagan's Conservatism

Activists in the women's struggle had to acknowledge certain harsh realities. One was the tight job market created by the economic recessions of

Increased Burdens on Women

the 1970s and 1980s. Other problems included a rising divorce rate that left increasing numbers of women and their children with lower standards of living and a high teenage pregnancy rate. The tandem of divorce and teenage pregnancy meant that a progressively smaller proportion of America's children lived with two parents. Another disturbing trend was "the Superwoman Squeeze." According to a report by the Worldwatch Institute, most working wives and mothers, even those with full-time jobs, "retained an unwilling monopoly on unpaid labor at home."

A POLARIZED PEOPLE: AMERICAN SOCIETY IN THE 1980s

The United States became an increasingly polarized society in the 1980s. The rich got even richer, while the poor sank deeper into despair. Indeed, by 1989 the top 1 percent (834,000 households with $5.7 trillion in net worth) was worth more than the bottom 90 percent (84 million households with $4.8 trillion in net worth).

By the end of the 1980s, as many Americans lived in poverty as in 1964, when thirty-six million were poor and President Johnson declared war on poverty. The poverty of the 1980s, explained the authors of a 1988 report of the Social Science Research Council, "is found less among the elderly and people living in nonurban areas and more among children living with one parent—in households headed principally by young women." As inequality grew, the gap widened between affluent whites and poor blacks, Indians, and Hispanics, between the suburbs and the inner cities, between the country's social and defense needs, and culturally between liberal lifestyles and religious conservatism. And as inequality increased, so too did social pathology. Violent crime, particularly homicides and gang warfare, grew alarmingly, as did school dropout rates, crime rates, and child abuse.

Increasing Inequality

Poverty stemmed from a variety of causes. Certainly it was the result of economic recessions. Race was another significant factor. African- and Hispanic-Americans were much more likely than whites to be poor. Similarly, women were more likely than men to be poor. By 1990, one woman in six lived in poverty, compared with one man in eight.

Poverty also resulted from the changing structure of the labor market. As deindustrialization took hold, the job market shifted from high-paying unionized blue-collar jobs to low-paying service jobs. Minimum-wage employment burgeoned in fast-food restaurants, but such jobs meant a substantial drop in workers' standard of living. Thus by the end of the 1980s, 40 percent of the nation's poor

Changing Job Market

were working, but few had full-time year-round jobs. At the same time, social workers reported that more and more of the nation's homeless were families. Estimates of the number of homeless varied from 350,000 to more than one million in 1988.

About a third of the homeless were former psychiatric patients who found themselves living on the streets after psychiatric hospitals emptied their wards in a burst of enthusiasm for "deinstitutionalization." By 1985, 80 percent of the total number of beds in state mental hospitals had been eliminated on the premise that small neighborhood programs would be more responsive than large state hospitals to people's needs. Few provisions were made for medical treatment, however, and these troubled people increasingly found that they had nowhere to go except the street.

For this family, which includes a one-week-old baby, homelessness came suddenly. Home had been a squalid motor inn in North Bergen, New Jersey, but the board of health condemned the motel and the police put the family out on the street. In 1988, as many as a million people were homeless.   Eugene Richards/Magnum.

Drugs were the scourge of the urban underclass. Mired in hopelessness, poverty-stricken men and women tried to find forgetfulness in hard drugs, especially cocaine and

Tragic Effects of Drugs
___

its derivative, crack. Crack first struck New York City's poorest neighborhoods in 1985. Users included children eleven and twelve years old and young single mothers. Crack's legacy included destroyed families, abused children, and drug dealers who were too young for a driver's license but who had access to submachine guns and other state-of-the-art firearms. Gang shootouts were deadly: the toll in Los Angeles in 1987 was 387 deaths, and more than half the victims were innocent bystanders.

Another lethal by-product of the 1980s drug epidemic was the spread of AIDS. First observed in the United States in 1981, AIDS is a disease

AIDS
___

transmittable through the exchange of infected body fluids, often during sexual contact or sharing of intravenous needles by drug users. Caused by a virus that attacks cells in the immune system, AIDS makes its victims susceptible to deadly infections and cancers. In the United States, AIDS initially was linked to the sexual practices of male homosexuals, but the disease spread to heterosexuals. Between 1981 and 1988, of the fifty-seven thousand AIDS cases reported, nearly thirty-two thousand resulted in death. But because it takes seven years or more for symptoms to appear, the worst has not yet revealed itself. A 1988 study reported that half of the gay men in San Francisco would develop AIDS and another 25 percent would develop the AIDS-related complex within about nine years of infection.

AIDS—along with such other sexually transmitted diseases as genital herpes and chlamydia—affected Americans' sexual behavior. Caution replaced the mores of "the sexual revolution." "Safe sex" campaigns urged the use of condoms.

For several years, Americans pretended the disease was limited to promiscuous homosexuals and drug addicts. But as writers, artists, athletes, actors, and relatives and friends died, people began to confront the horrifying epidemic. Nonetheless, AIDS divided communities. Conservative Protestant sects joined the Roman Catholic Church in warning that condom advertising implicitly sanctioned contraception and encouraged promiscuity. Sex education should not be offered in the schools, they contended, citing their deep belief that any sexual activity other than heterosexual matrimonial monogamy was wrong. Gay men expected little assistance from the conservative executive branch, but they were partly wrong. In 1988, the federal government mailed a booklet entitled *Understanding AIDS* to 107 million households. Nevertheless, AIDS continued to be one of several unsolved social problems dividing the nation as the presidential election drew near in 1988.

___

REAGAN'S DECLINE AND THE ELECTION OF 1988

During his second term, Ronald Reagan lost his mastery; the "great communicator" had taken on the appearance of a tired bumbling old man. "Who's in Charge Here?" asked a *Time* magazine headline. His political troubles began at the time of the 1986 elections. Two events took place on election day. First, the Republicans lost control of the Senate. Second, from Lebanon came a bizarre story that the president's national security adviser had traveled to Iran with a Bible, a cake, and a planeload of weapons seeking the release of Americans held hostage in the Middle East. "No comment," Reagan told reporters. As details of the Iran-contra scandal began to surface, half the people in the country came to believe that Reagan was lying about his lack of involvement in the affair.

Reagan's problems continued in 1987 and 1988. Congress overrode his veto of a massive highway construction bill, and twice his nominees for

Reagan's Political Woes
___

the Supreme Court failed to win confirmation by the Senate. His first nominee, federal Judge Robert Bork, failed to convince the Senate that he was not a right-wing ideologue; his second nominee, another federal judge, withdrew his name from consideration after revelations that he had smoked marijuana while a professor at Harvard Law School.

Scandals continued to tarnish the White House as well. Then, on October 19, 1987, the stock market went into a nose dive and fell 508 points.

As the 1988 elections approached, however, there was some good political and economic news for Republicans. First, Reagan had moderated his anti-Soviet rhetoric and in 1988, to the applause of most Americans, had traveled to the Soviet Union—the first American president to visit Moscow since Richard Nixon in 1972. Second— and of greater importance to voters—after the economic recession of 1981 and 1982, the United States had embarked on a six-year business recovery. The discomfort index, which had risen alarmingly in the 1970s and early 1980s, dropped to more comfortable levels in the later 1980s. And although unemployment dropped to a decade-low 5.4 percent in April 1988, it did so without refueling inflation.

Continuing Economic Recovery

The Reagan administration pointed to the economy as proof of the success of supply-side economics. Critics retorted that Reagan's policy of pursuing massive tax cuts while greatly increasing the defense budget was just another form of Keynesianism—deficit financing to stimulate the economy. But the average American, caring little about this kind of debate, was content to enjoy the economic recovery. It was true that the poor had little to rejoice over and that Americans viewed the economic future with uncertainty. But it was also true that in the 1980s most Americans had jobs and lived very comfortably.

George Bush

Had Reagan been allowed by the Constitution to run for a third term, he probably would have ridden the economic boom to victory. But this election was for his successor, and the competition in both parties was intense. The candidates on the Republican side included Vice President George Bush, Senate minority leader Bob Dole, and Pat Robertson, a television evangelist. Bush emerged with the nomination after bitter Republican infighting in state primaries.

On the Democratic side, there was also a scramble for the presidential nomination. Beginning with a half-dozen campaigners, the race narrowed to a two-person contest between Michael Dukakis, under whose governorship Massachusetts had seemed a model of economic recovery and welfare reform, and Jesse Jackson, a former colleague of the Reverend Martin Luther King Jr., who had moved to Chicago to organize economic and educational programs for the poor. An eloquent preacher, Jackson campaigned on his dream of forming a "Rainbow Coalition" of the "rejected"— African-Americans, women, and Hispanics. Jackson was the first African-American to win mass support in seeking the presidential nomination of a major political party.

Presidential Campaign of 1988

Both Bush and Dukakis avoided serious debate of the issues: child care, drugs, environmental collapse, corruption in government, poverty, rising medical and educational costs, and the fiscal and trade deficits. Despite the gravity of these problems, the candidates relied on clichés and negative campaigning. Television dominated the presidential election as never before. Bush aimed his appeals at the "Reagan Democrats" by pushing such emotional "hot buttons" as patriotism and the death penalty. A Republican advertisement for television appealed to racism and fear by accusing Dukakis of being soft on crime for furloughing Willie Horton, a black convict.

But with America at peace and inflation and unemployment both low, Bush's victory was seldom in doubt. His margin over Dukakis was substantial: 53 percent of the popular vote to 46 percent. The election confirmed that the Solid South, once a Democratic stronghold, had become solidly Republican. Bush won every state in the region. And across the nation, race was a key factor, as it had been in every presidential election since 1964: for twenty-five years, the Republican vote had been almost exclusively white and almost all blacks had voted Democratic.

Legacies of the 1980s

George Bush was inaugurated as the forty-first president of the United States on January 20, 1989. The American people prepared to greet not only a new presidency but also a new decade. "Ronald Reagan leaves no Vietnam War, no Watergate, no hostage crisis," reported the

Southern States in Presidential Elections, 1960–1988

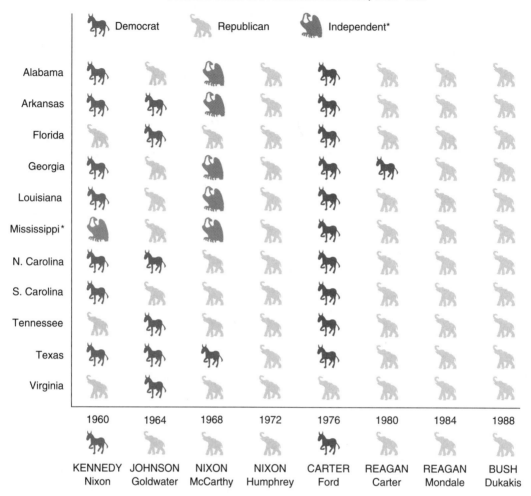

*Mississippi voters elected Harry Byrd in 1960. In 1968, George Wallace carried Alabama, Arkansas, Georgia, Louisiana, and Mississippi.

How do historians know

that the South was a key factor in presidential elections? This figure illustrates that the once solid Democratic South had become Republican by 1972, when Richard M. Nixon won every state in the region. In the aftermath of the Watergate scandal, a southern Democrat, Jimmy Carter of Georgia, did win all of the South but one state. But the Republicans' ascendancy returned in 1980, when Ronald Reagan won every southern state but Georgia. And in 1984 and 1988, the Republican ticket handily won all of the South. Note that in each of these presidential elections, whoever won the South won the general election as well.   Data: New York Times, October 18, 1992. Copyright © 1992 by the New York Times Company. Reprinted by permission.

New York Times. "But he leaves huge question marks—and much to do." First, inequality had escalated in the 1980s, as the poor got poorer and the rich got richer. The poorest Americans of all were children, and economics and racism had conspired to widen the gap between the races. Second, the effects of mismanagement and deception were beginning to show in certain industries, forcing the federal government to consider massive bailouts and threatening greater fiscal deficits. In 1989, Congress debated putting up $157 billion to rescue insolvent savings-and-loan associations. Third, the country was losing control of its economic destiny. Between 1983 and 1989, foreigners invested $700 billion more in America than Americans invested abroad. It was clear that the American people and their leaders would have to make difficult economic, political, diplomatic, and social choices in the 1990s.

SUGGESTIONS FOR FURTHER READING

Deficits, Deindustrialization, and Other Economic Woes

Donald L. Bartlett and James B. Steele, *America: What Went Wrong?* (1992); Barry Bluestone and Bennett Harrison, *The Deindustrialization of America* (1982); Richard Feldman and Michael Betzold, *End of the Line: Autoworkers and the American Dream* (1988); Gregory Pappas, *The Magic City: Unemployment in a Working-Class Community* (1989).

The Ford and Carter Administrations

Betty Glad, *Jimmy Carter* (1980); John Robert Greene, *The Limits of Power: The Nixon and Ford Administrations* (1992); Erwin C. Hargrove, *Jimmy Carter as President* (1989); Charles O. Jones, *The Trusteeship Presidency: Jimmy Carter and the United States Congress* (1988); Burton I. Kaufman, *The Presidency of James Earl Carter Jr.* (1993).

Women and Children's Struggles

Marian Wright Edelman, *Families in Peril* (1987); Barbara Ehrenreich, *The Hearts of Men: American Dreams and the Flight from Commitment* (1983); David T. Ellwood, *Poor Support: Poverty in the American Family* (1988); Susan Faludi, *Backlash: The Undeclared War Against American Women* (1991); Sylvia Ann Hewlett, *When the Bough Breaks: The Cost of Neglecting Our Children* (1991); Arlie Russell Hochschild, *The Second Shift: Working Parents and the Revolution at Home* (1989); Kristin Luker, *Abortion and the Politics of Motherhood* (1984); Ruth Sidel, *Women and Children Last* (1986);

Winifred D. Wandersee, *On the Move: American Women in the 1970s* (1988); Lenore J. Weitzman, *The Divorce Revolution* (1985).

People of Color and New Immigrants

James D. Cockcroft, *Outlaws in the Promised Land: Mexican Immigrant Workers and America's Future* (1986); John Crewdson, *The Tarnished Door: The New Immigrants and the Transformation of America* (1983); Roger Daniels, *Coming to America* (1990); Reynolds Farley and Walter R. Allen, *The Color Line and the Quality of Life in America* (1987); Gil Loescher and John A. Scanlan, *Calculated Kindness: Refugees and America's Half-Open Door* (1986); Peter Matthiessen, *In the Spirit of Crazy Horse* (1983); David M. Reimers, *Still the Golden Door: The Third World Comes to America* (1985); William Julius Wilson, *The Truly Disadvantaged: The Inner City, the Underclass, and Public Policy* (1987).

The New Conservatism and the Election of 1980

Sidney Blumenthal, *The Rise of the Counter-Establishment* (1986); Alan Crawford, *Thunder on the Right* (1980); Thomas Byrne Edsall, *The New Politics of Inequality* (1984); Jack W. Germond and Jules Witcover, *Blue Smoke and Mirrors: How Reagan Won and Why Carter Lost the Election of 1980* (1981); Gillian Peele, *Revival and Reaction* (1984); Peter Steinfels, *The NeoConservatives* (1979).

Ronald Reagan and His Presidency

Lou Cannon, *President Reagan* (1991); Hodding Carter, *The Reagan Years* (1988); Paul D. Erickson, *Reagan Speaks: The Making of an American Myth* (1985); Jane Mayer and Doyle McManus, *Landslide: The Unmaking of the President, 1984–1988* (1988); Michael Rogin, *Ronald Reagan, the Movie* (1987); Michael Schaller, *Reckoning with Reagan* (1992); John Kenneth White, *The New Politics of Old Values* (1988).

Reaganomics

Benjamin Friedman, *Day of Reckoning: The Consequences of American Economic Policy Under Reagan and After* (1988); William A. Niskanen, *Reaganomics* (1988); Kevin Phillips, *The Politics of Rich and Poor* (1990); Frances Fox Piven and Richard Cloward, *The New Class War* (1982).

A Polarized Society in the 1980s

Chandler Davidson, *Race and Class in Texas Politics* (1990); Michael Harrington, *The New American Poverty* (1984); Randy Shilts, *And the Band Played On: Politics, People, and the AIDS Epidemic* (1987); Studs Terkel, *The Great Divide* (1988).

The Presidential Elections of 1984 and 1988

Sidney Blumenthal, *Pledging Allegiance: The Last Campaign of the Cold War* (1990); Richard Ben Cramer, *What It Takes* (1992); Thomas Byrne Edsall and Mary D. Edsall, *Chain Reaction: The Impact of Race, Rights, and Taxes on American Politics* (1991); Thomas Ferguson and Joel Rogers, *Right Turn: The Decline of the Democrats and the Future of American Politics* (1986).

34

A New Century Beckons: America and the World in the 1990s

"I FEEL LIKE THEY rob me without a gun," remarked Jo Harris, a seventy-nine-year-old Montana widow in early 1993. She had just paid $89.95 for a month's supply of the pills she needed to alleviate her severe arthritis pain. "When I paid the drugstore clerk, I told him, 'You know Bill Clinton's watching you, don't you?'" Indeed, the new president was watching. Shortly after taking office, he lambasted drug firms for "shocking" overcharges on prescriptions. Hillary Rodham Clinton echoed her husband's views. Makers of childhood vaccines, she protested, had shamefully raised prices 1,000 percent over the last decade.

Having promised health-care reform during the campaign, President Clinton set two goals for his new administration. He pledged to extend care to the millions of Americans who lacked medical insurance. Most were middle-class working people, for the poor received Medicaid and the rich could afford coverage. He also vowed to control the soaring costs of medical care, which had reached more than $900 billion a year. One in every seven dollars Americans spent went to medical care, and

health care accounted for one-seventh of the federal government's budget.

The health-care system in the United States was in crisis. Insurance companies cut benefits to control their costs. Employers shifted a greater share of health-care expenses to their workers, many of whom could not afford the burden and had to drop insurance policies. Doctors, fearing malpractice suits, often ordered expensive and unnecessary tests.

President Clinton named his talented wife Hillary, an attorney who had skillfully led the fight for education reform in Arkansas, to head a task force to reform the health-care system. After the work of the task force was completed, unanswered questions remained. Would Americans accept higher taxes to help pay for the program? Would health-care providers—doctors, hospitals, and insurance companies—and drug companies accept restrictions on their freedom? Could a president whose popularity was waning move the plan through Congress?

More than health care troubled the Clinton administration. In 1993 and

1994, Republicans attempted to discredit the president. Republicans demanded a broad investigation of a scandal involving a failed savings and loan bank and the Whitewater Development Company. (Whitewater was a real estate development company in which Clinton and his wife had been partners with the owner of a failed savings and loan while Clinton was governor of Arkansas.) Leading Republicans also attacked Clinton's plan to reform the nation's welfare system when he unveiled it in mid-1994. The spring and summer of 1994 saw the president and his aides dealing with a continuing civil war in Bosnia, the possibility that North Korea was developing a nuclear device, and a military junta that for months refused to step down in impoverished Haiti. Foreign affairs issues kept pushing onto the national agenda.

The president whom Democrat Bill Clinton had defeated in the 1992 election, Republican George Bush, had offered no solutions to the health-care crisis. Bush opted for inaction on this and so many other issues that observers called his administration a status quo presidency. He certainly had his chances to lead. With the collapse of the Soviet empire and the end of the Cold War, there arose a need to redefine the international role of the United States. Many Americans also envisioned a "peace dividend"—a shift of federal resources from weaponry and interventionism to domestic needs. But Bush did not redefine the nation's priorities, insisting that trouble still stalked the world.

Nor did the president's interpretation of U.S. interests in the Third World change with the end of the Cold War. President Bush ordered military interventions in Panama and the Middle East, and he dispatched a military expedition to Africa to ensure the distribution of food to starving Somalis. Meanwhile, environmental ruin, political instability, massive debt, large-scale population growth and migration, and illicit drug trafficking in the Third World threatened the prosperity and health of the United States. Bush seldom took the initiative to help resolve these problems. He seemed more comfortable as commander in chief than as long-range planner, and the domestic political benefits of military victory abroad seemed rewarding. For example, after triumph in the Persian Gulf War in 1991, Bush's popularity rating soared to 89 percent despite rising unemployment, factory closings, massive federal debt, heightening racial tensions, drug abuse, decaying cities, collapse of real estate markets, and the costly bailout of failed savings-and-loan institutions.

Bush's reelection seemed guaranteed, but it was not. His administration continued to drive up the federal debt through deficit spending, and its tax policies favored the wealthy. The economy continued to slump, and layoffs climbed. Bush pandered to the right wing of his party on issues like abortion and school prayer. He appointed highly conservative justices to the Supreme Court, one of whom, Clarence Thomas, became the source of controversy when a former employee charged him with sexual harassment, highlighting women's rights issues that President Bush had ignored.

In the topsy-turvy political year of 1992, many voters embraced an anti-incumbent mood and endorsed the third-party candidacy of H. Ross Perot. In the end, the electorate defeated George Bush and elected Clinton. The voters also changed Congress, electing more women, African-Americans, and Hispanics. People with fresh ideas, high optimism, and a mandate for change moved into Washington, D.C.

BUSH'S FOREIGN POLICY IN THE POST–COLD WAR ORDER

George Bush preferred foreign policy to domestic affairs and considered himself an expert on international relations. Still, he hardly anticipated the transformation of the Cold War world he had come to know so well as a member of Congress, ambassador to the United Nations and to China, CIA director, and vice president. When the Cold War ended, Bush spoke vaguely of a "new world order," but he seemed hesitant to explain its dimensions or shape its agenda. He and Secretary of State James A. Baker III conducted a largely reactive foreign policy, short on new ideas, wedded to the "truths" of the past.

This posture became particularly evident in the Bush administration's use of military force in Latin America, the Middle East, and Africa. Although the end of the Cold War eliminated a superpower threat to U.S. security, Bush cut back only minimally on the large defense

Declinists

The United States among the Economic Superpowers, 1980–1991

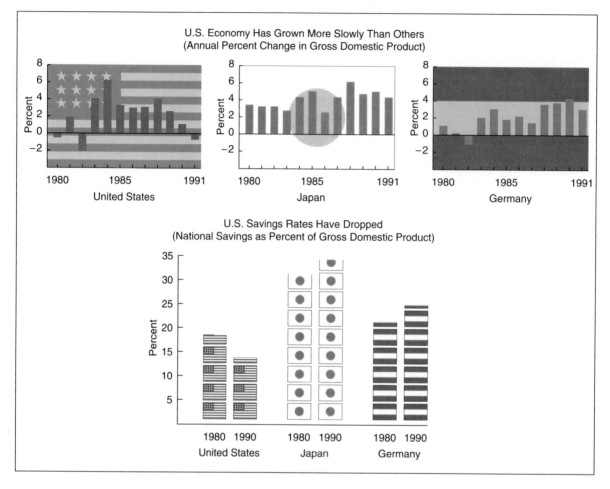

How do historians know

that the United States has suffered relative decline? Scholars who argue that the United States has declined use comparative statistics like those shown. Handicapped by a falling savings rate, which meant that fewer dollars were available for long-term investment,

and unable to maintain a growth rate to match its economic rivals—Germany and Japan—the United States, some scholars have concluded, appeared to be slipping in the 1980s.   Data: U.S. government and U.N. publications.

budget and discouraged hopes for a "peace dividend." Critics known as "declinists" spotlighted a fundamental legacy of the Cold War: the United States still spent heavily on its military and neglected its domestic development. According to the historian Paul Kennedy's *The Rise and Fall of the Great Powers*

(1987), the United States suffered from "imperial overstretch." Kennedy argued that U.S. power, like that of Spain and Great Britain in earlier centuries, would continue to erode unless it restored its productive vitality and marketplace competitiveness to compete with Japan and Germany (see figure),

• *Important Events* •

1989   George Bush inaugurated president
        Helsinki agreement outlines phase-out of
            ozone-destroying chemicals
        Berlin Wall is opened
        U.S. troops invade Panama

1990   Sandinistas defeated in Nicaraguan elections
        Clean Air Act requires reduction in emission
            of pollutants
        Communist regimes in Eastern Europe col-
            lapse
        Iraq invades Kuwait
        Bush orders U.S. armed forces to Persian
            Gulf region
        Bush-Congress budget agreement raises taxes
        Americans with Disabilities Act prohibits dis-
            crimination
        Reunification of Germany signals Cold War's
            end

1991   Persian Gulf War
        Antarctica agreement bans oil exploration and
            mining
        Military ousts elected government in Haiti;
            more Haitians flee to the United States
        START I treaty reduces nuclear warheads in
            Soviet Union and United States
        Soviet Union disintegrates; Yeltsin ousts
            Gorbachev
        Confirmation hearings of Clarence Thomas
            to Supreme Court spotlight issue of sexual
            harassment

1992   World population reaches 5.4 billion
        Federal deficit hits $4 trillion
        Perot third-party candidate
        Los Angeles riots erupt
        Twenty-seventh Amendment prohibits mid-
            term congressional pay raises

        United States opposes many resolutions at
            Rio "Earth Summit"
        Clinton elected president
        U.S. troops sent to Somalia to ensure delivery
            of relief supplies
        North American Free Trade Agreement signed
            by Canada, Mexico, and the United States
        START II agreement calls for cuts in war-
            heads and ICBMs

1993   Clinton and Gore inaugurated
        Hillary Rodham Clinton heads task force on
            health-care reform
        Clinton lifts restrictions on abortions
        President's proposal to lift ban on homosexuals
            in the military stirs controversy
        Congress modifies and passes Clinton's eco-
            nomic proposals
        Clinton appoints Ruth Bader Ginsburg to the
            Supreme Court
        Motor-voter and family-leave bills are signed
        Brady Bill passed
        Clinton health-care plan released

1994 $30.2 billion crime bill enacted
        Clinton appoints Stephen G. Breyer to the
            Supreme Court
        Nelson Mandela becomes president of South
            Africa
        PLO-Israeli agreement over the Gaza Strip
            and Jerico implemented
        Aristide returned to power in Haiti
        Republicans win control of the House and
            Senate
        Clinton proposes reform of the welfare system

reduced its huge federal debt, put more resources into long-term investment, and improved its educational system. One way to stem economic decline was to curb America's global interventionism.

Bush dismissed the declinists as "gloomsayers." He seemed to agree with those commentators who envisioned the United States as the supreme power

**International
Environmental
Issues**

in a unipolar world. But the list of world problems and domestic ills that Reagan had bequeathed to Bush was daunting. Reagan had paid little attention to global environmental issues, for example. Warming of the earth's climate from the "greenhouse effect"—the build-up of carbon dioxide and other gases in the atmosphere—threatened a rise in ocean levels, flooding farmlands and dislocating millions of people. In addition, scientists found a growing hole in the earth's protective ozone layer over the South Pole. This expanding hole allows deadly ultraviolet rays to reach the earth's surface. Methane, chlorofluorocarbons, and other harmful gases cause the depletion of the ozone layer, and Americans release about one-third of all chlorofluorocarbons in the world.

In the early 1990s, the human costs of environmental damage mounted, and governments found themselves hard-pressed to feed and care for their people. As the world's population was growing at a rate of more than 80 million a year, reaching 5.4 billion in 1992, soil erosion was reducing food production. Acid rain, overcutting of forests, and overgrazing of fields destroyed livelihoods and drove people into overcrowded cities. Food riots and migrations of refugees from environmentally damaged areas became common.

Meanwhile, the Bush administration withheld monies from the U.N. Fund for Population Activities and International Planned Parenthood, because, U.S. officials claimed, those agencies supported abortion. Washington also continued to oppose the Law of the Sea Treaty (see Chapter 31), because Bush believed that the provisions governing the marine environment would hamper American private business. He addressed the global warming problem by warning against policies that would interfere with the free marketplace. Some advances were achieved: in 1989, eighty-six nations, including the United States, agreed to phase out use of ozone-destroying chemicals by 2000, and Bush signed a tougher Clean Air Act in 1990. The next year, the United States and twenty-five other nations agreed to protect the fragile environment of Antarctica by banning oil exploration and mining there for fifty years.

As the world split into competing economic spheres—Europe's Economic Community, Japan's Asian trading community, and the U.S.-dominated Western Hemispheric community—the Bush administration negotiated the North American Free Trade Agreement (NAFTA) with Canada and Mexico. Signed in late 1992, the pact envisioned tariff-

free trade among the three nations. Critics claimed that the agreement would cost many U.S. workers their jobs, because corporations would move south to exploit less expensive Mexican labor and minimal environmental controls. Bush called it "the first giant step" toward a free-trade zone encompassing the entire Western Hemisphere. NAFTA faced acrimonious debate.

Trade issues lay at the heart of tense U.S.-Japanese relations. Most nettlesome was the huge trade deficit in Japan's favor (about $50 billion in 1989). Japanese products flooded American stores and won customers who appreciated their price and quality. The best-selling car in the United States in 1989 was the Honda Accord (many of which were assembled by American workers in the United States). American manufacturers complained that Japan's tariffs, cartels, and government subsidies made it difficult for American goods to penetrate Japanese markets. The Japanese countered that obsolete equipment, poor education, and inadequate spending on research and development undercut U.S. competitiveness.

Tense Japanese-American Relations

In 1990, the world's ten largest banks were all in Japan, as were seven of the world's largest public companies (ranked by market value). It stung Americans when Japanese leaders claimed that the United States was no longer number one in the world economy and that U.S. workers were illiterate and lazy. Many Americans feared that the dollar-rich Japanese were buying up too many U.S. businesses. Japanese and other foreign investors used their accumulating dollars to buy U.S. Treasury bonds, companies, stock, and real estate.

As the U.S. economy slipped, protectionists championed "Buy American" campaigns. Auto workers in Michigan and others practiced "Japan bashing," blaming U.S. woes on the Japanese. Was a damaging economic war in the offing? Some thought not, because the two economies were so interdependent that economic warfare would be mutually destructive. Furthermore, many American products did manage to penetrate the Japanese market. McDonald's fast food, Schick razor blades, and Coca-Cola became preeminent in their markets, suggesting a Japanese embrace of American culture. And Japan and the United States remained security partners. Still, as economic competitors, neither nation seemed willing to give much ground.

Elsewhere in Asia, Sino-American relations took a turn for the worse in June 1989, when Chinese armed forces stormed into Beijing's Tiananmen Square. They slaughtered hundreds—perhaps thousands—of unarmed students and other citizens who had for weeks been holding peaceful prodemocracy rallies. Bush officials initially expressed revulsion, but their response gradually became muted. They believed that America's global security needs required friendly Sino-American ties. Critics charged that the United States was short-sightedly allying with China's elderly governing clique and alienating the nation's progressive future leaders. Bush cheered such leaders in Bucharest, Prague, and Warsaw but snubbed them in Beijing.

Tiananmen Square Massacre

In European affairs, the Bush administration seemed unprepared when Eastern Europeans disengaged from the Soviet empire and jettisoned communism. And the American reaction to the 1991 disintegration of the Soviet Union was passive rather than proactive. U.S. aid to the Soviet Union's successor states, which descended into ethnic warfare, political upheaval, and economic recession, was slowly granted and comparatively small in amount.

The Strategic Arms Reduction Talks (START) on limiting strategic nuclear forces gradually produced substantive results. In mid-1991, Russia and the United States signed the START I pact to reduce each's nuclear warheads to six thousand and each country's strategic delivery systems to sixteen hundred. In late 1992, Bush signed a START II agreement with Russia's President Boris Yeltsin, who had ousted Gorbachev. This accord provided for the reduction of warheads to about three thousand each by the year 2003 and the elimination of land-based intercontinental ballistic missiles (ICBMs) with more than one warhead, leaving each with about five hundred ICBMs. Arms-control advocates welcomed START

START

II, but the proliferation of nuclear weapons promised a dangerous future. Iran, Iraq, North Korea, Pakistan, and Israel, for example, seemed close to acquiring them.

One of many events that signaled an end to the Cold War was the reunification of Germany on October 2, 1990. U.S. officials grew wary that Germany would dominate the continent—that it could not be anchored in or controlled by NATO or the European Community and that its economic prowess would further diminish U.S. competitiveness in world markets.

German Reunification

INTERVENTIONS AND RECURRENT ISSUES IN THE THIRD WORLD

The Cold War may have ended, but America's stormy relations with Third World countries did not relent. In Latin America, the Bush administration tried to cool the zeal with which Reagan had intervened, for the interventions had largely failed. The costly U.S.-financed contra war had not forced the Sandinista National Liberation Front from power in Nicaragua. In 1989, the Central American presidents devised a workable plan for free elections in Nicaragua and disbanding the contras. In the elections that followed in 1990, the Sandinista Front lost to the U.S.-backed National Opposition Union. Elsewhere in Central America, Bush's efforts to dampen crises came to fruition in 1992 when Salvadoran leftists agreed to lay down their arms in favor of pressing their agenda through the political process.

Poverty-wracked Haiti held its first free elections in decades in 1990. But the next year, the army overthrew the newly elected government of Jean-Bertrand Aristide. Although the United States imposed economic sanctions, the military regime refused to restore Aristide to the presidency. Thousands of Haitians fled in boats for the United States, but the

Haiti

U.S. government classified them as economic rather than political refugees, rejecting their pleas for asylum and sending many back. Critics charged Washington with discriminating against the Haitians because they are black.

Debt joined political instability to burden Latin America. By 1990, Latin American nations owed more than $400 billion. Brazil, Mexico, and

Debt Burdens

Argentina owed the most, much of it to U.S. banks. The debt crisis hurt the United States when debtors trimmed their imports as they struggled to meet debt-service payments. As a result, U.S. exports slumped by billions of dollars and North American jobs were lost. Required by the International Monetary Fund to restructure their economies in order to qualify for assistance, Latin American governments drastically cut budgets. As they reduced health services and educational outlays, political unrest increased. Migrants fleeing grinding poverty pressed against U.S. immigration gates, sometimes entering illegally by sneaking across the Mexican-American border.

The profitable trade in illicit drugs also troubled inter-American relations. By 1990, the U.S. drug market was probably worth $100 billion. In an

The "Drug War"

effort to combat the influx of drugs, Washington used the U.S. military to quash drug producers and traffickers in Colombia, Bolivia, and Peru, sources of cocaine and crack. Bush officials thus concentrated on interrupting supply more than on halting demand inside the United States.

The drug issue became conspicuous as Panamanian-U.S. relations deteriorated. Soon after General Manuel Antonio Noriega took power in Panama in 1983, he cut deals with Colombia's cocaine barons and laundered drug money in Panamanian banks. By the late 1980s, his dictatorial rule and drug running had angered North Americans eager to blame the swaggering Panamanian for U.S. drug problems. The American people were unaware—although Bush knew—that Noriega had long been on the CIA payroll and that he had helped the United States aid and train the contras. Grateful for his cooperation, Washington had long turned a blind eye to Noriega's links with drug traf-

fickers. When exposés of Noriega's sordid record provoked protests in Panama, the United States encouraged a coup that failed.

Then in late December 1989, an American force of 22,500 troops invaded Panama. The venture, named Operation Just Cause, became a

Invasion of Panama

blood-soaked success. At least 500 Panamanians and 23 American soldiers perished. Noriega was captured and taken to Miami, where he was later convicted of drug trafficking. Devastated Panama, meanwhile, like war-torn Nicaragua, became all the more dependent on the United States.

President Bush also took the United States to war in the Middle East. In August 1990, Iraq's dictator Saddam Hussein—resentful that Kuwait would not reduce the huge debt

Gulf War

Iraq owed to it and eager to acquire Kuwait's vast petroleum industry—ordered his troops to invade his peaceful neighbor. Oil-rich Saudi Arabia, long a U.S. ally, felt threatened. President Bush dispatched more than five hundred thousand U.S. forces to the region to defend Saudi Arabia and to press Saddam to pull out of Kuwait. If Iraq gained control of Kuwaiti and Saudi oil fields, the world would become vulnerable to Saddam's economic and military power, Bush argued. Declaring this the first post–Cold War "test of our mettle," Bush rallied to war a deeply divided Congress (the Senate vote was 52 to 47). The United Nations also voted for war and helped organize a coalition of forces. Many Americans believed that economic sanctions on Iraq should be given more time to persuade Saddam to retreat. "This will not be another Vietnam," the president assured Americans.

When Operation Desert Storm began on January 16, 1991, the greatest air armada in history began pummeling Iraq and Iraqi forces in Kuwait. U.S. missiles joined round-the-clock bombing raids on Baghdad, Iraq's capital. In late February, coalition forces launched a ground war that routed the Iraqis from Kuwait in just 100 hours. The war's toll: tens of thousands Iraqis dead, only 148 American service personnel killed. "By God," Bush exclaimed, "we've kicked the Vietnam syndrome once and for all."

On Thanksgiving Day 1991, George and Barbara Bush visited American soldiers after the success of Operation Desert Storm. The president had skillfully organized a multinational force to expel Iraqi forces from the oil-rich Persian Gulf state. Bush's popularity soared at first. By fall 1991, however, polls showed that Americans wanted him to shift his attention from world to domestic affairs. Diana Walker/Gamma Liaison.

The celebratory mood was short lived. Environmental disaster followed when the retreating Iraqis set fire to Kuwait's oil wells, polluting the air and releasing millions of barrels of the black riches into Persian Gulf waters. American bombs had so damaged Iraq's infrastructure that spreading disease and hunger took countless lives. Saddam Hussein remained in power and brutally suppressed revolts by Iraqi Shiites and Kurds; only after many people had been slaughtered did the United States declare certain areas of Iraq off-limits to Saddam's military. The U.S. military's heavy censorship of the news also concerned many Americans, as did their learning after the war that the United States, virtually up to the moment of the Iraqi onslaught

The Aftermath of War

against Kuwait, had actually been pursuing closer relations with the brutal Saddam as a counterweight to Iran. The Bush administration itself had sent foreign aid that enabled Saddam to buy arms.

In the Persian Gulf War, the United States had demonstrated that it possessed the most impressive high-technology military force in the world, but the war had cost the United States $1 billion a day as U.S. education, health, and economic competitiveness languished. "If we can make the best smart bomb, why can't we make the best VCR?" asked one senator. A larger question reverberated: Was war the means the United States was going to use to create a new post–Cold War world order? The prospects of both perpetual interventionism and economic decline took the spirit out of the U.S. victory.

The Persian Gulf War had some effect on the conflict between Arabs and Jews. Secretary Baker now demanded that Israel back off from its stern control of the Palestinians: "Forswear annexation. Stop settlement activity. . . . Reach out to the Palestinians as neighbors who deserve political rights," he implored. Baker's patient efforts led to a breakthrough in October 1991, when the Israelis sat down to negotiate with their Arab neighbors. Israel, however, came to the bargaining table vowing to give up no occupied territory.

Arab-Israeli Peace Talks

Operation Restore Hope was a Bush military expedition of a very different kind. The people of the African nation of Somalia had long suffered from the effects of soil erosion and famine. After Somalia jilted its Cold War ally the Soviet Union in the late 1970s, the Indian Ocean nation became a recipient of U.S. aid, including large amounts of weapons. When Somalia's repressive dictator was driven from power in early 1991, rival clans led by warlords vied for power and public authority broke down. Gun-toting bandits regularly stole the relief supplies sent by international agencies. "He [Bush] would not want to leave office with 50,000 people starving that he could have saved," a senior official remarked. After gaining United Nations approval, the president ordered more than twenty thousand American troops to Somalia in December 1992 to

Humanitarian Role in Somalia

ensure the delivery of relief aid. A U.N. peace-keeping force replaced U.S. troops in mid-1993.

Many Americans cheered this humanitarian work as an appropriate post–Cold War mission for the United States. But because Bush had neither looked very far into the future nor given direction to the "new world order," America's role in the tumultuous world remained unclear when he left office in early 1993.

THE BUSH PRESIDENCY AT HOME

Concluding his multivolume history of the United States in 1989, the political scientist James Mac-Gregor Burns took a final look at the American experiment and was discouraged by what he saw. The American people seemed mired in "political immobility." Indeed, Burns wrote, what the United States needed above all was "creative and transforming leadership" to mobilize the country and "carry through great projects." Burns, a Democrat, did not think Bush was up to the task.

Although Bush called for a "kinder, gentler nation" on inauguration day, expectations of a compassionate vigorous presidency soon dimmed. Shortly

Economic Crisis

after Bush took office, the economy began a nose dive. The gross national product increased on average only 0.7 percent a year, the slowest growth since the Great Depression of the 1930s. By 1992, several million Americans had joined the unemployment rolls and factory employment skidded. Even for Americans with jobs, personal income was stagnant. In 1991, median household income fell by 3.5 percent, the most severe decline since the 1973 recession. In 1992, the number of poor people in America reached the highest level since 1964. Bush seemed uncaring when he defended tax breaks for the rich but opposed extending relief payments to the long-term unemployed.

Because of the ever-mounting federal deficit spending ($220 billion in 1990, $269 billion in 1991, and $290 billion in 1992) and federal debt ($4 trillion in 1992), the president thought he could do little to stimulate the economy and create jobs. The total

cost of the federal bailout of the failed savings-and-loan industry alone had reached $130 billion in 1992. Reduced federal aid to city and state governments and the ailing economy, among other factors, pushed these governments to the brink of bankruptcy.

Businesses also became deeply burdened with debt. Companies of all kinds laid off workers as the recession deepened. In efforts to cut costs and increase productivity, many businesses replaced workers with computers and other machines. Some businesses moved their plants to countries where wages were lower, environmental controls weaker, and benefits packages nonexistent. The Bush administration did not invest in programs to retrain the many workers let go by the defense industry, which had seen contracts for weapons shrink at the end of the Cold War. Indeed, the president had a long-standing aversion to government action to solve economic and social problems. As the economy slumped more deeply and Bush refrained from attacking the crisis, his popularity declined.

The Persian Gulf War of early 1991 temporarily shored up Bush's floundering presidency. Just as the president's domestic inactivity was drawing the most severe criticism, he earned high praise for assembling the multinational force that drove Iraqi troops from Kuwait. Shortly after this victory, Bush's advisers told him that the stagnant economy was about to boom and that Americans distrusted government solutions to economic problems and wanted him to pursue further foreign-policy triumphs. "The idea," recalled a senior official, "was that he'd ride the wave from the war" to reelection. Bush's complacency and inactivity on unemployment, health care, and the environment, however, proved a serious miscalculation.

"Read my lips: no new taxes," Bush had proclaimed at the 1988 Republican convention. But during the 1990 budget negotiations with Congress,

Breaking the No-New-Taxes Pledge

the White House agreed to a trade-off to reduce the federal deficit: Democratic leaders accepted budget cuts and the president endorsed a tax hike. Bush's press secretary was shocked when he heard about the deal: "That means we've broken the pledge." Soon television newscasts began running the videotape of Bush's "Read my lips" statement, raising anew doubts about his consistency.

In his 1988 campaign, Bush had promised to be both "the environmental president" and "the education president." He became neither. Bush won plaudits for signing the 1990 reauthorization of the Clean Air Act, which required businesses to control emissions of sulfur dioxide and nitrogen oxides, but he gutted enforcement of the act by creating the Council on Competitiveness. Headed by Vice President Dan Quayle, the council undercut environmental regulations on the grounds that they slowed economic growth and cost jobs. In addition, the Justice Department overruled the Environmental Protection Agency when it sought to prosecute large corporate polluters.

Weakening of Environmental Regulations

As for education, President Bush had announced that by the year 2000 American students would rank second to none in science and mathematics. But other than argue for government vouchers that parents could use to pay tuition at public or private schools of their choice, Bush did little to improve education. The high school dropout rate increased, urban schools became battlegrounds of gangs and drug dealers, and an increasing number of illiterates entered the work force. Some observers charged that right-wing ideologues in the Bush administration were waging cultural war against universities, the National Endowment for the Humanities, and the National Endowment for the Arts, because these institutions tolerated dissenting and experimental views.

Bush provoked further controversy when he nominated Clarence Thomas to the Supreme Court in 1991 to replace the retiring Thurgood Marshall. Few people believed that Thomas, a young and inexperienced federal judge, was the best candidate. An African-American of extremely conservative views, he opposed affirmative action in hiring, believed in permitting prayer in the schools, and opposed abortion. Bush's nomination of a black conservative was a clever political move, "calculated," in the words of Eleanor Holmes Norton, the congressional delegate from Washington, D.C., to "mute the expected reaction to yet another conservative nominee."

Clarence Thomas and Sexual Harassment

Thomas nonetheless seemed likely to win confirmation. Then in October, Anita Hill, a black law professor at the University of Oklahoma, electrified the nation. She charged that Thomas had sexually harassed her when she worked for him in the early 1980s. The Senate confirmed Thomas, but Hill's testimony and many senators' disregard of it angered women, especially those who had suffered similar experiences of sexual harassment in the workplace. Many vowed to oppose the Republican party in 1992.

The social ills that had plagued the United States in the 1980s persisted into the new decade: AIDS, homelessness, drug and alcohol addiction, racism and inequality, poverty among children, the day-to-day struggle of single-parent families, child abuse, teen suicide, the income gap between rich and poor, inadequate health insurance coverage. In the 1990s, however, economic and social problems that had once afflicted only the poor now touched the lives of increasing numbers of middle-class people whose standard of living declined.

Social Problems

As unemployment and poverty rose, so did racial tensions. In April 1992, when a California jury acquitted four police officers charged with beating Rodney King, an African-American motorist, violence erupted in Los Angeles. In the bloodiest urban riot since the 1960s, forty-four people died and two thousand were injured. Entire blocks of houses and stores went up in flames, leaving $1 billion in charred ruins. According to a California legislative committee, the 1965 Watts riot had sprung from "poverty, segregation, lack of education and employment opportunities, [and] widespread perceptions of police abuse. . . . Little has changed in 1992 Los Angeles." Bush advocated emergency aid, but he passed up an opportunity to address the country's urban and racial problems.

Los Angeles Riots

In contrast, Bush did push for the progressive change represented by the Americans with Disabilities Act of 1990. The act banned job discrimination against blind, deaf, mentally retarded, and physically impaired people, as well as those who had cancer or tested positive for

Americans with Disabilities Act

human immunodeficiency virus (HIV), which causes AIDS. Applicable to companies with twenty-five or more employees, the act covered 87 percent of all jobs. The statute also required "reasonable accommodations," such as wheelchair ramps, for people with disabilities. Bush signed the bill, marking one of his presidency's few upbeat moments on domestic issues.

But the Republican president and the Democrat-controlled Congress seldom worked together. Instead of compromise and negotiated solutions, they produced stalemate. Beginning in 1989 with his rejection of a minimum-wage increase, Bush vetoed thirty-seven bills during his presidency, only one of which was overridden by the necessary two-thirds vote of both houses of Congress. Rarely in American history had legislative results been so meager.

Americans did not blame the gridlock solely on the president: they also grew impatient with a Congress that seemed mired in scandal and privilege.

Scandals in Congress

———

The most blatant example was the mismanagement of the House bank; representatives wrote thousands of bad checks that the bank covered at no fee. During the savings-and-loan scandal, information became public that still other senators had done favors for a money manipulator who had deceitfully misused the funds of unsuspecting small investors, costing them their savings. Many members of Congress received payments from corporate and other interest group lobbyists who offered free jet flights and high honoraria for speeches. The public grew angrier when members of Congress voted themselves a pay raise. In 1992, the necessary number of states ratified the new Twenty-seventh Amendment to the Constitution to prohibit mid-term congressional pay raises.

THE ELECTION OF 1992

Bush watched with alarm as the economic crisis deepened. In a poll taken in January 1992, eight in ten Americans rated the economy as "fairly bad" or "very bad." Most people—especially Democrats—blamed Bush. The president also faced harsh criticism from within his own party.

Beginning with Nixon's election in 1968, the Republican party had won the White House in five of six elections by building a coalition of ideologically diverse constituencies.

Republican Constituencies

———

Economic conservatives who had always voted Republican were joined by cultural conservatives, particularly fundamentalist and evangelical Christians who advocated "family values" and opposed abortion and homosexuality. The "Radical Right," people of extremely conservative views, also voted Republican. Reagan Democrats—blue-collar workers and one-time Democrats—had supported Bush in 1988 as Reagan's heir. White voters in the South who disliked the Democratic party's liberalism on civil rights issues could be counted on to vote Republican, as could young Americans aged eighteen to thirty who had come of age politically during the "make-money" frenzy of the Reagan years. Finally, there were the residents of America's ever growing suburbs, which in 1990 accounted for almost half of the nation's population. The sheer size of the suburban vote, which tended to be antitax and antigovernment, made this group the most significant of all. Prosperity, anticommunism, and Ronald Reagan held these constituencies together in the 1980s; by 1992, all three factors had disappeared.

Among the Democratic hopefuls in 1992 were William Jefferson "Bill" Clinton, governor of Arkansas; Paul Tsongas, former senator from Massachusetts; and Jerry Brown, former governor of California. By July, when the Democrats convened to nominate their candidate, Clinton had become the clear victor in the primaries. Born in 1946—the first baby boomer nominated for president by a major party—Clinton had opposed the Vietnam War and successfully exploited the selective service system to avoid being drafted (as had Vice President Dan Quayle, also of the Vietnam generation).

Bill Clinton

———

Clinton sought to move the Democratic party to the right to make it more attractive to white suburbanites, Reagan Democrats, and members of the business community. He hoped, said an ally, "to modernize liberalism so it could sell again." To this end, Clinton applauded private business as the engine of economic progress and endorsed reform to move people off welfare and to put more police officers on the streets. But in the liberal tradition, he also advocated greater public investment in the nation's infrastructure of roads, bridges, and communications; greater access to job-training projects and college educations; less costly and more inclusive health care; and a shift of funds from defense to civilian programs. He also took a "pro-choice" stand, declaring it a woman's right to choose abortion. His running mate, Tennessee Senator Albert Gore, was a baby boomer, a moderate Democrat, and a Vietnam War veteran. He had also gained a reputation as a specialist on environmental issues.

In 1992, the American people witnessed the most active third-party campaign since 1968, when George Wallace had run for president. H. Ross

H. Ross Perot
——

Perot, a Texas multibillionaire who had amassed his fortune in the computer industry, spoke in plain language about economic issues. His one-liners caught on with many people who thought a Washington outsider and successful businessman could fix the deficit and spark economic growth.

Meanwhile the Republicans renominated George Bush and Dan Quayle. At the Republican convention in August, Bush assumed the identity

Republican Attacks on Clinton
——

of guardian of family values. Cultural conservatism dominated the convention, at which speaker after speaker championed the traditional two-parent family, denounced unconventional lifestyles, and disparaged homosexuals—all the while suggesting that the Clintons had strayed outside acceptable boundaries. Bush's acceptance speech offered little to voters who wanted solutions to the nation's economic crisis.

The Bush-Quayle campaign strategy featured negative campaigning, particularly attacks on Clinton's character. Clinton's Vietnam draft status and alleged extramarital affairs drew constant criticism. Republicans caricatured him as "Slick Willie." The issue, Bush insisted, was "trust."

Claiming that he had ended the Cold War and highlighting triumph in the Gulf War, Bush asked Americans if they could trust the inexperienced Clinton to handle international affairs. Clinton rebutted that Bush's taking credit for the ending of the Cold War was like "the rooster who took credit for the dawn." Clinton also chastised Bush for befriending dictators, especially the "appeasement" of Saddam Hussein before the war. Debate on foreign relations was shallow, with neither candidate helping the American people to reorient to the transformed world. But domestic policy, not foreign policy, dominated the campaign.

On November 3, with the highest voter turnout (55 percent) since 1976, the Clinton-Gore ticket scored well in the Northeast, the Pa-

Clinton's Victory
——

cific coast, and the industrial heartland of the Midwest, and made inroads into the South (see map). Clinton-Gore also

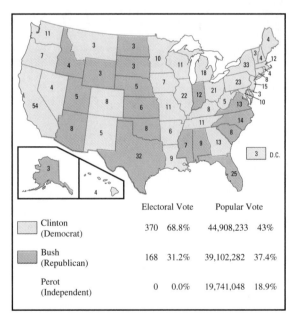

	Electoral Vote		Popular Vote	
Clinton (Democrat)	370	68.8%	44,908,233	43%
Bush (Republican)	168	31.2%	39,102,282	37.4%
Perot (Independent)	0	0.0%	19,741,048	18.9%

Presidential Election, 1992   *Although a minority of voters cast ballots for Bill Clinton, he won handily in the electoral college. Clinton's share of the popular vote was the lowest for anyone elected president since Woodrow Wilson won with a smaller percentage in 1912. Clinton took a majority of votes only in the District of Columbia and Arkansas, but Bush and Perot failed to win a majority of votes in any state. Exit polls revealed that the votes for Perot would have divided about evenly between Clinton and Bush had Perot not been in the race.*

The night the 1992 election tallies poured in, Hillary Clinton (left), Bill Clinton, Al Gore, and Tipper Gore celebrated the Democratic triumph in Little Rock, Arkansas. Dancing to rock 'n' roll, they declared a generational shift to more youthful leadership, reminding some observers of the transition from Eisenhower to Kennedy more than thirty years earlier. Sygma/Ira Wyman.

ran well in normally Republican strongholds: suburbs, high-tech areas, retirement communities, and the Sun Belt. Overall, the Democrats won 43 percent of the popular vote and 370 electoral votes, Bush and Quayle tallied 37 percent and 168 electoral votes, and Perot earned 19 percent but no electoral votes. Perot polled the largest popular-vote percentage for a third party since the Bull Moose party ran Theodore Roosevelt eighty years earlier.

Voters also changed their Congress. The Democrats remained in control of both houses, but four more women were sent to the Senate and nineteen more to the House. Voters also elected more African-American and Hispanic representatives. Many of the first-term members of Congress were—like Clinton—in their forties with advanced degrees, no military service, and considerable experience in politics at the state level.

One of Bush's last decisions smacked of the discredited past: just before leaving office, he pardoned former Secretary of Defense Caspar Weinberger and other Iran-contra figures who had been indicted on felony counts that charged them with lying to Congress and obstructing a congressional inquiry. Had nothing been learned from the Watergate scandal, asked the *Washington Post* columnist David Broder, especially "their duty to obey the law?" The veteran journalist added: "We have failed as a society to express our contempt and disgust for those who violate their oaths of office with such impunity."

Bush Pardon of Iran-Contra Figures

THE CLINTON PRESIDENCY

President Clinton could not reverse Bush's pardon, but he could try to mobilize the nation to pull itself out of its economic, social, and political doldrums. Clinton named to his cabinet a mix of seasoned politicos, young politicians, intellectuals, women, and minorities. He called for a national mission of shared sacrifice. He appointed Hillary Rodham Clinton to draft a plan for health-care reform. The new president immediately overturned Bush's "gag rule," which had prohibited abortion counseling in clinics that received federal funds. When Clinton announced that he planned to lift the ban on homosexuals in the military, the military brass joined Republicans in harshly criticizing the move. Seeing that the American people were evenly divided on the issue, and fearful of losing support for his economic proposals, Clinton delayed a decision for months; finally he accepted a compromise that prohibited discrimination against gays in the military but held them to a strict code of behavior. A Clinton trait soon emerged: when criticized, he often retreated to some middle ground, where few people seemed to stand with him. He alienated both liberals and conservatives.

The economic plan sent to Congress in February 1993 called for higher taxes for the middle class, a 10 percent surtax on individuals with taxable incomes greater than $250,000, **Clinton's Economic Proposals** an energy tax, and a higher corporate tax. Clinton promised to end business deductions for expense accounts, such as memberships in country clubs. He also proposed to cut government spending through a smaller defense budget and a downsized bureaucracy, and he offered an immediate stimulus to the economy through public projects.

Interest group lobbyists wasted no time in attacking the comprehensive plan. Republicans protested that Clinton was not cutting back enough on spending, and other critics hammered him for reneging on his campaign pledge to provide tax relief for middle-class Americans. Clinton fought back, and Congress, while killing the president's stimulus proposal, passed most of his requests.

Clinton's popularity dropped fast. People protested higher taxes and showed impatience with the slowness of his plan to revive the economy. Critics charged that Clinton was indecisive (backing down when pressed) and unwilling to take risks. Public-relations gaffes and late-hour White House abandonment of controversial appointees raised doubts about the president's management ability.

Throughout 1993 and 1994, a scandal dating to the mid-1980s dogged President Clinton. The scandal involved the failed Madison Guaranty Savings and Loan and the Whitewater **Whitewater** Development Company. Then-governor Bill Clinton and Hillary Rodham Clinton were partners in Whitewater with James McDougal, who also owned the Madison Guaranty Savings and Loan. Companies controlled by McDougal covered overdrawn Whitewater checks in excess of $100,000. Some Republicans speculated that McDougal did this so that the Clintons would not have to use their own money. In 1994, Senate Republicans sought a broad investigation of Whitewater, including the role of the Clintons. In a straight party-line vote, however, the Senate decided upon a narrow investigation, focusing on whether Clinton administration officials had either lied to Congress or interfered with the investigation of Whitewater.

Potentially more damaging to Clinton was the appointment by a three-judge panel of Kenneth Starr as the special prosecutor in the Whitewater case. Starr was a former appeals court judge and Bush administration official. He had the authority to open or reopen any aspect of the case.

In December 1994, Webb Hubbell entered into a plea bargain agreement with Starr. Hubbell was a longtime friend and political ally of the Clintons, the former managing partner of the law firm in which Hillary Clinton had been a partner, and until his resignation months prior to the plea bargain, an official in the justice department. Hubbell, in return for his cooperation in the Whitewater investigation, was allowed to plead guilty to one count of tax evasion and one count of mail fraud. At the time of the Hubbell deal, Starr was also looking into the financial dealings of Arkansas Governor Jim Guy Tucker and McDougal.

The president did move some of his agenda forward: he signed the "motor-voter" and family leave bills, persuaded Congress to pass a campaign finance reform bill, and reversed a Bush policy and announced that the United States would sign the international agreement protecting rare and endangered species. Clinton also signed into law measures dealing with the sale of firearms. The Brady bill (1993) required a short waiting period before the sale of handguns; a second law banned the sale of assault weapons. And in 1994, Clinton, with the votes of three Republican senators who broke with their party, secured the enactment of a $30.2 billion crime bill. The new law banned assault-style weapons and provided funds for building more prisons and increasing the size of urban police forces. When Byron R. White stepped down from the Supreme Court, Clinton appointed as justice Ruth Bader Ginsburg, an experienced women's rights advocate and federal appeals court judge. Clinton also appointed Stephen Breyer, a federal judge from Massachusetts, to the Supreme Court to replace Harry Blackmun. And with considerable opposition from his own party and organized labor, Clinton secured congressional approval of the North American Free Trade Agreement.

After eighteen months in office, it was becoming apparent that the president's health-care plan and welfare reform program would determine his success or failure on the domestic front. Virtually everyone— liberal and conservative, Democrat and Republican—agreed that the nation's health-care system was in a state of crisis and its welfare system in a state of failure. Different constituencies, however, had vastly different "solutions" to both problems.

The Health-Care Crisis

America's health-care crisis was basically twofold. First, 17 percent of the population lacked medical insurance. Added to these thirty-nine million Americans were millions more who were inadequately insured. Second, health-care costs were virtually out of control. Between 1980 and 1992, cost outlays for medical treatment in the United States tripled. Estimates were that by 1995 total health-care costs would reach $1 trillion—about 15 percent of the gross domestic product. The cost of health care, including expenditures for medical insurance, threatened the security of families, added to the national debt, and contributed to the lack of competitiveness of American companies in the global marketplace.

Clinton released his health-care plan in the autumn of 1993. The administration's proposal was complex, and many Americans had difficulty understanding exactly how the plan would work. It called for universal coverage, much of which would be attained by requiring employers to provide health insurance for their workers. Under this mandated system, employers would bear 80 percent of the cost of health insurance and employees the remaining 20 percent. Economically hard-hit employers—those having few workers—were to be eligible for government subsidies. Self-employed individuals would continue to pay the entire cost of their health insurance, but the payments would become fully tax deductible. The federal government would be responsible for unemployed workers.

When the plan was first unveiled, universal coverage appeared to have broad support. In addition to liberal groups, the American Medical Association, insurance lobbyists, major corporations, and the U.S. Chamber of Commerce recognized that medical costs had to be controlled. They agreed in principle that universal coverage was the means to do it. No agreement existed over how to pay for universal coverage or whether it should be implemented immediately or phased in.

Conservatives critics vehemently objected to the mandate system. There was also strong conservative criticism to both the plan's cost and its provisions for reproductive services. Simply put, conservatives wanted funding for abortions excluded from the list of covered services and perceived universal coverage as too expensive for both the government and the private sector.

In the end, the 103d Congress refused to enact health-care reform. Multiple factors, two of which are primary, contributed to Clinton's failed effort. First, his opponents were well financed. *Newsweek* estimated that they spent at least $300 million to lobby against the program. Second, the Clintons believed they could win with a liberal coalition based to a great extent on senior citizen groups and organized labor. This conviction led to the administration's refusal to compromise with moderates, making defeat inevitable. Still, the issue was not dead; it remained on the table for Congress to deal with in the future.

As Congress debated health care, President Clinton announced his plan for welfare reform. Initially created with the intent of helping people having difficult—but temporary—periods in their lives, the nation's welfare system instead seemed to trap them in a self-perpetuating cycle of poverty. The birth of children by unwed mothers, especially teenagers, was at the heart of the cycle. By the 1990s, unwed teenagers accounted for one-third of all births in the United States. Uneducated children without job skills were bringing infants into the world. The annual welfare cost of these teenage mothers and their children reached $34 billion. And the human tragedy was that those infants had virtually no chance of ever escaping poverty. The chances were that they would simply become the next generation of welfare mothers and juvenile criminals. Clinton proposed to break this cycle.

Welfare Reform

The plan announced by Clinton in June 1994 had a five-year price tag of $9.3 billion. In order to receive benefits, unwed teenage mothers would be required to live with their parents, identify the child's father, and remain in school. Those who were eighteen or older would be granted a two-year benefit period. During the two years, they were to receive job training and secure a job. At the end of the two years, all cash benefits would be stopped; food stamps would, however, continue. Like so many issues on the national agenda, welfare reform sparked heated debate that delayed action.

As Americans prepared to vote in November 1994, news analysts and pollsters projected Democratic losses. The scope of the Republican victory, however, was greater than most had anticipated. For the first time in forty years, the Republicans gained con-

The 1994 Elections

trol of the House of Representatives. In the process, Democrat Thomas S. Foley of Washington became the first sitting Speaker of the House since 1862 to lose an election. Overall, the Democrats lost more than fifty House seats. And while long-term Democrats such as Jack Brooks of Texas (twenty-one terms) and Dan Rostenkowski of Illinois (eighteen terms) went down in defeat, not a single incumbent Republican lost. Voters also gave Republicans a four-vote majority in the Senate. When Senator Richard Shelby, a Democrat from Alabama, changed parties two days after the election, the Republican majority increased. The Republican sweep was likewise felt at the state level. After the election, Republicans held a majority of the nation's governorships, including those of eight of the nine most populous states. Among these states, only Florida remained in Democratic hands.

Some used the words "Republican revolution" to describe the election's results. The election was not a revolution, but it certainly signaled a changing political agenda. The health-care and welfare proposals advanced by the administration faced strong opposition in the new Congress. And Clinton's political future seemed in danger. Voters had moved the nation in a conservative direction, and the president's reelection hopes would require him to move to the center of the political spectrum. Some worried about the political influence of the religious right, but buried in all the election statistics was a telling one that had little to do with moral crusades: 63 percent of the nation's white male voters had cast Republican ballots.

During the 1994 campaign, the Republican party made what it called a "Contract With America." Through that contract, which Republican leaders promised to act upon in the first one hundred days of the new Congress, ten major issues were addressed. Among the more controversial promises were a balanced budget amendment with a line-item veto, term limits for members of the House and the Senate, welfare reform, tax cuts, a repeal of 1993 tax increases on social security benefits, and the maintenance of a strong national defense system. Critics asked the obvious question: how could the budget be balanced, taxes be cut, and defense spending be maintained at a high level?

Although Clinton's first priority was domestic policy, he and his secretary of state, the veteran diplomat Warren Christopher, could not ignore the highly volatile multipolar world of the post–Cold War era. Iraq continued to cross Washington; in June 1993, Clinton ordered a Tomahawk cruise-missile attack against Baghdad in retaliation for an alleged Iraqi plot to assassinate former President Bush. Terrorism remained a constant danger; in early 1993, Islamic extremists bombed the World Trade Center in New York City. Russia needed vast amounts of foreign aid to stave off economic collapse and preserve steps toward democracy. At the Vancouver, Canada, summit meeting in April 1993 with Russian leader Boris Yeltsin, Clinton pledged American assistance.

America and a Multipolar World

Two problems—ethnic warfare and nuclear proliferation—seemed to dwarf other global issues. Ethnic hostilities were especially alarming, because they bespoke a future of instability in which the nation-state seemed less able to maintain order. Between January 1991 and June 1994, perhaps as many as a half million people were killed in ethnic rivalries. In what had once been Yugoslavia, there were at least 250,000 deaths from warfare among Serbs, Croats, and Bosnian Muslims. And in a matter of a few months in 1994, an estimated 200,000 men, women, and children were slaughtered in Rwanda's war between Hutu government soldiers and militiamen and Tutsis fighting for the Rwandan Patriotic Front. Tens of thousands more died in overcrowded refugee camps. The former Soviet Union, with literally scores of ethnic groups, also suffered bloodshed. The United States offered relief aid in many cases, but the needs remained too large.

In 1994, the nuclear proliferation issue focused on North Korea, where spent fuel rods from a nuclear reactor yielded enough plutonium to produce perhaps four or five nuclear weapons. After North Korea consistently refused to allow full inspection of its nuclear facilities by United Nations personnel, as required by the nonproliferation treaty of 1969, the Clinton administration pushed for international economic sanctions. Japan and the Peoples Republic of China, however, favored less stringent action than the United States. Meanwhile, some talked of war, and the South Korean government began conducting air raid drills for its people. The death of North Korea's long-time leader Kim Il Sung in mid-1994 further clouded the issue.

An October agreement between the Clinton administration and North Korea eased tensions. Under the agreement, the United States would help North Korea build light-water reactors from which it is more difficult to extract weapons-grade plutonium. In return North Korea would abandon its graphite-moderated reactors. Until the new reactors were on line, the United States would provide fuel oil for North Korea's power plants.

In parts of the world, tensions relaxed some. Elections were held in South Africa in 1994, and for the first time blacks and other people of color, as well as whites, were allowed to vote. Nelson Mandela—once an imprisoned freedom fighter and head of the African National Congress—was elected president of a new black-majority government. Even before he took office, Mandela, in a gesture of national reconciliation, reached out to his white and black opponents.

Also in 1994, a modest but significant change occurred in the Middle East. The Palestinian Liberation Organization (PLO), in accordance with an agreement signed earlier at the White House, became the authority in the Gaza Strip and the West Bank town of Jericho. The agreement provided for a less than fully independent Palestinian state. The PLO had only limited legislative powers, Israel maintained responsibility for external security, and four thousand Jewish settlers—with Israeli protection—were allowed to remain in Gaza. Still, the arrangement represented Israel's most significant concession in the occupied territories since the return of the Sinai to Egypt in 1979. In mid-1994, moreover, Jordan and Israel signed a peace accord. The peace process was, however, marred by violence. In Gaza, fundamentalist Muslims battled the PLO, and there, as elsewhere, acts of terrorism continued.

In Haiti a diplomatic team comprised of former president Jimmy Carter, retired General Colin Powell, and Senator Sam Nunn headed off a probable American invasion. At the last minute, as President Clinton was preparing to recall the diplomatic team and launch the invasion, Carter secured an agreement. The generals agreed to step down, paving the way for the October 1994 return of Jean-Bertrand Aristide. Approximately twenty thousand American troops occupied Haiti at the time of his return. They remained there until early 1995 when a United Nations force replaced them.

For the United States, the central questions in public debate on foreign policy were simple, but the answers were not: should or could the United States play the expensive role of global police officer while undertaking the expensive task of economic renewal at home? What mix of retrenchment and international activism, of unilateralism and multilateralism, lay ahead? Which foreign disturbances threatened vital U.S. interests and which did not?

Throughout American history, the closing decade of a century has been a time of turbulence and transformation. In the 1690s, as the colonists struggled to adjust to the Navigation Acts that governed their membership in the far-flung British mercantile empire, King William's War pitted the French and their Indian allies against British-Americans. Accusations of witchcraft in Massachusetts revealed political disorder and a society in stress. In the 1790s, a new republic with a new constitution confronted the Whiskey Rebellion, the Alien and Sedition Acts, the rise of partisan political parties, and entanglement in Europe's wars. The 1890s witnessed devastating depression, agrarian revolt, burgeoning cities, bloody labor strikes, the emergence of corporate giants, the onset of a major reform movement, and a new empire abroad that anti-imperialists considered a violation of U.S. principles.

As the twenty-first century beckoned, the 1990s too promised turmoil and adjustment for Americans. In charting their nation's future in a turbulent present, their many different memories of the past would guide them. In his 1993 inaugural address, President Clinton invoked Thomas Jefferson's prediction that "to preserve the very foundations of our nation we would need dramatic change from time to time." In the poem she read at the inauguration, Maya Angelou also spoke of the tenacious link between past and future:

> History, despite its wrenching pain,
> Cannot be unlived, but if faced
> With courage, need not be lived again.

SUGGESTIONS FOR FURTHER READING

The Bush Administration

Donald L. Bartlett and James B. Steele, *America: What Went Wrong?* (1992); Colin Campbell and Bert A. Rockman, eds., *The Bush Presidency* (1991); Michael Duffy and Don Goodgame, *Marching in Place: The Status Quo Presidency of George Bush* (1992); Otis L. Graham, *Losing Time: The Industrial Policy Debate* (1992).

Bush and the World

See works cited in Chapter 29; Graham Allison and Gregory F. Treverton, *Rethinking America's Security* (1992); Richard E. Benedick, *Ozone Diplomacy* (1991); Michael R. Beschloss and Strobe Talbott, *At the Highest Levels* (1993); James Chace, *The Consequences of Peace* (1992); David E. Fisher, *Fire and Ice: The Greenhouse Effect, Ozone Depletion, and Nuclear Winter* (1990); Edward M. Graham and Paul R. Krugman, *Foreign Direct Investment in the United States* (1989); Sheila K. Johnson, *The Japanese Through American Eyes* (1990); Paul Kennedy, *The Rise and Fall of the Great Powers* (1987); Jeffrey Lefebvre, *Arms for the Horn: U.S. Security Policy in Ethiopia and Somalia, 1953–1991* (1992); Joseph S. Nye Jr., *Bound to Lead* (1990); Kenneth A. Oye et al., eds., *Eagle in a New World* (1992); Robert W. Tucker and David C. Hendrickson, *The Imperial Temptation* (1992).

To follow recent topics, see *Great Decisions* (annual) and *Headline Series*, both published by the Foreign Policy Association; the *America and the World* series, published annually by *Foreign Affairs* magazine; and Worldwatch Institute's *State of the World*, published annually on environmental issues.

Latin America and North America

Kevin Buckley, *Panama* (1991); John Dinges, *Our Man in Panama* (1990); Guy Gugliotta and Jeff Leen, *Kings of Cocaine*

(1989); Gary Hufbauer and Jeffrey Schott, *North American Free Trade* (1992); Abraham F. Lowenthal, *Partners in Conflict*, rev. ed. (1990); Donald J. Mabry, ed., *The Latin American Narcotics Trade and U.S. National Security* (1989); Robert A. Pastor, *Whirlpool* (1992); Peter Dale Scott and Jonathan Marshall, *Cocaine Politics* (1991).

Persian Gulf War

Deborah Amos, *Lines in the Sand* (1992); Rick Atkinson, *Crusade* (1993); Lawrence Freedman and Efraim Karsh, *The Gulf Conflict* (1993); Stephen Graubard, *Mr. Bush's War* (1992); Roger Hilsman, *George Bush vs. Saddam Hussein* (1992); Alex Hybel, *Power over Rationality* (1993); John MacArthur, *Second Front: Censorship and Propaganda in the Gulf War* (1992); John Mueller, *Policy and Opinion in the Gulf War* (1994); Joseph S. Nye Jr. and Roger K. Smith, eds., *After the Storm* (1992); Michael Palmer, *Guardians of the Gulf* (1992); Jean Edward Smith, *George Bush's War* (1992); Philip M. Taylor, *War and the Media* (1992).

Politics and the Election of 1992

E. J. Dionne, *Why Americans Hate Politics* (1992); Alan Ehrenhalt, *The United States of Ambition* (1991); William Greider, *Who Will Tell the People?* (1992); Jerry Hagstrom, *Beyond Reagan* (1988); Kathleen Hall Jamieson, *Dirty Politics* (1992); Kevin Phillips, *The Politics of Rich and Poor* (1990); Ruy A. Teixeira, *The Disappearing American Voter* (1992).

Historical Reference Books by Subject: Encyclopedias, Dictionaries, Atlases, Chronologies, and Statistics

American History: General

John D. Buenker and Edward R. Kantowicz, eds., *Historical Dictionary of the Progressive Era, 1890–1920* (1988); Gorton Carruth, ed., *The Encyclopedia of American Facts and Figures* (1993); John Drexel, ed., *The Facts on File Encyclopedia of the 20th Century* (1991); Robert H. Ferrell and John S. Bowman, eds., *The Twentieth Century: An Almanac* (1984); George H. Gallup, *The Gallup Poll: Public Opinion, 1935–1971* (1972), *1972–1977* (1978), and annual reports (1979–); Bernard Grun, *The Timetables of History* (1991); Stanley Hochman and Eleanor Hochman, *A Dictionary of Contemporary American History* (1993); *International Encyclopedia of the Social Sciences* (1968–); R. Alton Lee, ed., *Encyclopedia USA* (1983–); Michael Martin and Leonard Gelber, *Dictionary of American History* (1981); Richard B. Morris, *Encyclopedia of American History* (1982); James S. Olson, *Historical Dictionary of the 1920s* (1988); Thomas Parker and Douglas Nelson, *Day by Day: The Sixties* (1983); Harry Ritter, *Dictionary of Concepts in History* (1986); Arthur M. Schlesinger, Jr., ed., *The Almanac of American History* (1983); *Scribner Desk Dictionary of American History* (1984); U.S. Bureau of the Census, *Historical Statistics of the United States* (1975); Philip P. Wiener, ed., *Dictionary of the History of Ideas* (1973).

American History: General Atlases

Geoffrey Barraclough, ed., *The Times Concise Atlas of World History* (1982); Robert H. Ferrell and Richard Natkiel, *Atlas of American History* (1987); Edward W. Fox, *Atlas of American History* (1964); Kenneth T. Jackson and James T. Adams, *Atlas of American History* (1978); Catherine M. Mattson and Mark T. Mattson, *Contemporary Atlas of the United States* (1990); National Geographic Society, *Historical Atlas of the United States* (1988); Charles O. Paullin,

Atlas of the Historical Geography of the United States (1932); U.S. Department of the Interior, *National Atlas of the United States* (1970). Other atlases are listed under specific categories.

American History: General Biographies

Lucian Boia, ed., *Great Historians of the Modern Age* (1991); *Dictionary of American Biography* (1928–); John A. Garraty, ed., *Encyclopedia of American Biography* (1974); *National Cyclopedia of American Biography* (1898–). Other biographical works appear under specific categories.

African Americans

Molefi Asante and Mark T. Mattson, *Historical and Cultural Atlas of African-Americans* (1991); Ingham, John N., *African-American Business Leaders* (1993); Bruce Kellner, *The Harlem Renaissance* (1984); Rayford W. Logan and Michael R. Winston, eds., *The Dictionary of American Negro Biography* (1983); W. A. Low and Virgil A. Clift, eds., *Encyclopedia of Black America* (1981); Charles D. Lowery and John F. Marszalek, eds., *Encyclopedia of African-American Civil Rights* (1992); Randall M. Miller and John D. Smith, eds., *Dictionary of Afro-American Slavery* (1988); Larry G. Murphy et al., eds., *Encyclopedia of African American Religions* (1993); Harry A. Ploski and James Williams, eds., *The Negro Almanac* (1989); Dorothy C. Salem, ed., *African American Women* (1993); Edgar A. Toppin, *A Biographical History of Blacks in America* (1971).

American Revolution and Colonies

Richard Blanco and Paul Sanborne, eds., *The American Revolution* (1993); Mark M. Boatner III, *Encyclopedia of the American Revolution* (1974); Lester J. Cappon, ed., *Atlas of Early American History: The Revolutionary Era, 1760–1790*

(1976); Jacob E. Cooke, ed., *Encyclopedia of the American Colonies* (1993); John M. Faragher, ed., *The Encyclopedia of Colonial and Revolutionary America* (1990); Jack P. Greene and J. R. Pole, eds., *The Blackwell Encyclopedia of the American Revolution* (1991); Douglas W. Marshall and Howard H. Peckham, *Campaigns of the American Revolution* (1976); Gregory Palmer, ed., *Biographical Sketches of Loyalists of the American Revolution* (1984); John W. Raimo, ed., *Biographical Directory of American Colonial and Revolutionary Governors, 1607–1789* (1980); *Rand-McNally Atlas of the American Revolution* (1974).

Architecture

William D. Hunt, Jr., ed., *Encyclopedia of American Architecture* (1980).

Business and the Economy

Christine Ammer and Dean S. Ammer, *Dictionary of Business and Economics* (1983); Douglas Auld and Graham Bannock, *The American Dictionary of Economics* (1983); Michael J. Freeman, *Atlas of World Economy* (1991); Douglas Greenwald, *Encyclopedia of Economics* (1982); John N. Ingham, *Biographical Dictionary of American Business Leaders* (1983); John N. Ingham and Lynne B. Feldman, *Contemporary American Business Leaders* (1990); William H. Mulligan, Jr., ed., *A Historical Dictionary of American Industrial Language* (1988); Glenn G. Munn, *Encyclopedia of Banking and Finance* (1973); Glenn Porter, *Encyclopedia of American Economic History* (1980); Richard Robinson, *United States Business History, 1602–1988* (1990). See also "African Americans" and "Transportation."

Cities and Towns

Charles Abrams, *The Language of Cities: A Glossary of Terms* (1971); John L. Androit, ed., *Township Atlas of the United States* (1979); Melvin G. Holli and Peter d'A. Jones, eds., *Biographical Dictionary of American Mayors, 1820–1980: Big City Mayors* (1981); Ory M. Nergal, ed., *The Encyclopedia of American Cities* (1980); David D. Van Tassel and John J. Grabowski, eds., *The Encyclopedia of Cleveland History* (1987). See also "Politics and Government."

The Civil War and Reconstruction

Mark M. Boatner III, *The Civil War Dictionary* (1988); Richard N. Current, ed., *Encyclopedia of the Confederacy* (1993); Patricia L. Faust, *Historical Times Encyclopedia of the Civil War* (1986); Kenneth C. Martis, *The Historical Atlas of the Congresses of the Confederate States of America: 1861–1865* (1994); James M. McPherson, ed., *The Atlas of the Civil War* (1994); Mark E. Neely, Jr., *The Abraham Lincoln Encyclopedia* (1982); Craig L. Symonds, *A Battlefield Atlas of the Civil War* (1983); Hans L. Trefousse, *Historical Dictionary of Reconstruction* (1991); U.S. War Department, *The Official Atlas of the Civil War* (1958); Jon L. Wakelyn, ed., *Biographical Dictionary of the Confederacy* (1977); Ezra J. Warner and W. Buck Yearns, *Biographical Register of the Confederate Congress* (1975). See also "The South" and "Politics and Government."

Constitution, Supreme Court, and Judiciary

Congressional Quarterly, *Guide to the Supreme Court* (1979); Leon Friedman and Fred I. Israel, eds., *The Justices of the United States Supreme Court, 1789–1978* (1980); Kermit L. Hall, ed., *The Oxford Companion to the Supreme Court of the United States* (1992); Richard F. Hixson, *Mass Media and the Constitution* (1989); Robert J. Janosik, ed., *Encyclopedia of the American Judicial System* (1987); John W. Johnson, ed., *Historical U.S. Court Cases, 1690–1990* (1992); Arthur S. Leonard, ed., *Sexuality and the Law* (1993); Leonard W. Levy et al., eds., *Encyclopedia of the American Constitution* (1986); Fred R. Shapiro, *The Oxford Dictionary of American Legal Quotations* (1993); Melvin I. Urofsky, ed., *The Supreme Court Justices* (1994). See also "Politics and Government."

Crime, Violence, and Police

William G. Bailey, *Encyclopedia of Police Science* (1994); Sanford H. Kadish, ed., *Encyclopedia of Crime and Justice* (1983); Michael Newton and Judy Ann Newton, *The FBI Most Wanted: An Encyclopedia* (1989); Michael Newton and Judy Ann Newton, *Racial and Religious Violence in America* (1991); Michael Newton and Judy Newton, *The Ku Klux Klan* (1990); Carl Sifakis, *Encyclopedia of Assassinations* (1990); Carl Sifakis, *The Encyclopedia of American Crime* (1982).

Culture and Folklore

Hennig Cohen and Tristam Potter Coffin, eds., *The Folklore of American Holidays* (1987); Richard M. Dorson, ed., *Handbook of American Folklore* (1983); Robert L. Gale, *A Cultural Encyclopedia of the 1850s in America* (1993); Robert L. Gale, *The Gay Nineties in America* (1992); M. Thomas Inge, ed., *Handbook of American Popular Culture* (1979–1981); Wolfgang Mieder et al., eds., *A Dictionary of American Proverbs* (1992); J. F. Rooney, Jr., et al., eds., *This Remarkable Continent: An Atlas of United States and Canadian Society and Cultures* (1982); Jane Stern and Michael Stern, *Encyclopedia of Pop Culture* (1992); Marjorie Tallman, *Dictionary of American Folklore* (1959); Justin Wintle, ed., *Makers of Nineteenth Century Culture, 1800–1914* (1982). See also "Entertainment," "Mass Media and Journalism," "Music," and "Sports."

Education and Libraries

Lee C. Deighton, ed., *The Encyclopedia of Education* (1971); Joseph C. Kiger, ed., *Research Institutions and Learned Societies* (1982); John F. Ohles, ed., *Biographical Dictionary of American Educators* (1978); Wayne A. Wiegard and Donald E. Davis, Jr., eds., *Encyclopedia of Library History* (1994).

Entertainment

Tim Brooks and Earle Marsh, *The Complete Directory to Prime Time Network TV Shows, 1946–Present* (1979); Barbara N. Cohen-Stratyner, *Biographical Dictionary of Dance* (1982); John Dunning, *Tune in Yesterday* (radio) (1967); Stanley Green, *Encyclopedia of the Musical Film* (1981); Larry Langman and Edgar Borg, *Encyclopedia of American War Films* (1989); Larry Langman and David Ebner, *Encyclopedia of American Spy Films* (1990); *Notable Names in the American Theater* (1976); *New York Times Encyclopedia of Television* (1977); Andrew Sarris, *The American Cinema: Directors and Directions, 1929–1968* (1968); Anthony Slide, *The American Film Industry* (1986); Evelyn M. Truitt, *Who Was Who on Screen* (1977); Don B. Wilmeth and Tice L. Miller, eds., *The Cambridge Guide to American Theatre* (1993). See also "Culture and Folklore," "Mass Media and Journalism," "Music," and "Sports."

The Environment and Conservation

Forest History Society, *Encyclopedia of American Forest and Conservation History* (1983); Robert J. Mason and Mark T. Mattson, *Atlas of United States Environmental Issues* (1990); World Resources Institute, *Environmental Almanac* (1992).

Exploration: From Columbus to Space

Silvio A. Bedini, ed., *The Christopher Columbus Encyclopedia* (1992); Michael Cassutt, *Who's Who in Space* (1987); W. P. Cumming et al., *The Discovery of North America* (1972); William Goetzmann and Glyndwr Williams, *The Atlas of North American Exploration* (1992); Clive Holland, *Arctic Exploration and Development* (1993); Adrian Johnson, *America Explored* (1974); Kenneth Nebenzahl, *Atlas of Columbus and the Great Discoveries* (1990). See also "Science and Technology."

Foreign Relations

Thomas S. Arms, *Encyclopedia of the Cold War* (1994); Gerard Chaliand and Jean-Pierre Rageau, *Strategic Atlas* (1990); Alexander DeConde, ed., *Encyclopedia of American Foreign Policy* (1978); Margaret B. Denning and J. K. Sweeney, *Handbook of American Diplomacy* (1992); Graham Evans and Jeffrey Newnham, eds., *The Dictionary of World Politics* (1990); John E. Findling, *Dictionary of American Diplomatic History* (1989); Stephen A. Flanders and Carl N. Flanders, *Dictionary of American Foreign Affairs* (1991); *Foreign Affairs Chronology, 1978–1989* (1990); Michael Kidron and Daniel Smith, *The New State of War and Peace: An International Atlas* (1991); Warren F. Kuehl, ed., *Biographical Dictionary of Internationalists* (1983); George T. Kurian, *Encyclopedia of the Third World* (1981); Edward Lawson, *Encyclopedia of Human Rights* (1991); Jack C. Plano and Roy Olton, eds., *The International Relations Dictionary* (1988); Bruce W. Watson et al., eds., *United States Intelligence: An Encyclopedia* (1990). See also "Peace Movements and Pacifism," "Politics and Government," "Wars and the Military," and specific wars.

Immigration and Ethnic Groups

James P. Allen and Eugene J. Turner, *We the People: An Atlas of America's Ethnic Diversity* (1988); Stephanie Bernardo, *The Ethnic Almanac* (1981); Francesco Cordasco, ed., *Dictionary of American Immigration History* (1990); Nicolás Kanellos, ed., *The Hispanic-American Almanac* (1993); Hyung-Chan Kim, ed., *Dictionary of Asian American History* (1986); Judy B. Litoff and Judith McDonnell, eds., *European Immigrant Women in the United States* (1994); Matt S. Meier, *Mexican American Biographies* (1988); Matt S. Meier and Feliciano Rivera, *Dictionary of Mexican American History* (1981); Sally M. Miller, ed., *The Ethnic Press in the United States* (1987); Stephan Thernstrom, ed., *Harvard Encyclopedia of American Ethnic Groups* (1980). See also "Jewish-Americans."

Jewish-Americans

American Jewish Yearbook (1899–); Jack Fischel and Sanford Pinsker, eds., *Jewish-American History and Culture* (1992); Geoffrey Wigoder, *Dictionary of Jewish Biography* (1991). See also "Immigration and Ethnic Groups."

Labor

Ronald L. Filippelli, *Labor Conflict in the United States* (1990); Gary M. Fink, ed., *Biographical Dictionary of American Labor* (1984); Gary M. Fink, ed., *Labor Unions* (1977); Philip S. Foner, *First Facts of American Labor* (1984).

Literature

James T. Callow and Robert J. Reilly, *Guide to American Literature* (1976–1977); *Dictionary of Literary Biography* (1978–); Eugene Ehrlich and Gorton Carruth, *The Oxford Illustrated Literary Guide to the United States* (1982); Jon Tuska and Vicki Piekarski, *Encyclopedia of Frontier and*

Western Fiction (1983). See also "Culture and Folklore," "The South," and "Women."

Mass Media and Journalism

Robert V. Hudson, *Mass Media* (1987); Joseph P. McKerns, ed., *Biographical Dictionary of American Journalism* (1989); William H. Taft, ed., *Encyclopedia of Twentieth-Century Journalists* (1986). See also "Constitution, Supreme Court, and Judiciary," "Entertainment," and "Immigration and Ethnic Groups."

Medicine and Nursing

Rima D. Apple, ed., *Women, Health, and Medicine in America* (1990); Vern L. Bullough et al., eds., *American Nursing: A Biographical Dictionary* (1988); Martin Kaufman et al., eds., *Dictionary of American Nursing Biography* (1988); Martin Kaufman et al., eds., *Dictionary of American Medical Biography* (1984); George L. Maddox, ed., *The Encyclopedia of Aging* (1987).

Music

John Chilton, *Who's Who of Jazz* (1972); Donald Clarke, ed., *The Penguin Encyclopedia of Popular Music* (1989); Edward Jablonski, *The Encyclopedia of American Music* (1981); Roger Lax and Frederick Smith, *The Great Song Thesaurus* (1984); Philip D. Morehead, *The New International Dictionary of Music* (1993). See also "Culture and Folklore" and "Entertainment."

Native Americans and Indian Affairs

Gretchen M. Bataille, ed., *Native American Women* (1992); Michael Coe et al., *Atlas of Ancient America* (1986); Mary B. Davis, ed., *Native America in the Twentieth Century* (1994); Frederick J. Dockstader, *Great North American Indians* (1977); *Handbook of North American Indians* (1978–); Sam D. Gill and Irene F. Sullivan, *Dictionary of Native American Mythology* (1992); J. Norman Heard et al., *Handbook of the American Frontier: Four Centuries of Indian-White Relationships* (1987–); Barry Klein, ed., *Reference Encyclopedia of the American Indian* (1993); Francis P. Prucha, *Atlas of American Indian Affairs* (1990); Paul Stuart, *Nation Within a Nation: Historical Statistics of American Indians* (1987); Helen H. Tanner, ed., *Atlas of Great Lakes Indian History* (1987); Carl Waldman, *Encyclopedia of Native American Tribes* (1988); Carl Waldman, *Atlas of the North American Indian* (1985).

The New Deal and Franklin D. Roosevelt

Otis L. Graham, Jr., and Meghan R. Wander, eds., *Franklin D. Roosevelt: His Life and Times* (1985); James S.

Olson, ed., *Historical Dictionary of the New Deal* (1985). See also "Politics and Government."

Peace Movements and Pacifism

Harold Josephson et al., eds., *Biographical Dictionary of Modern Peace Leaders* (1985); Ervin Laszlo and Jong Y. Yoo, eds., *World Encyclopedia of Peace* (1986); Robert S. Meyer, *Peace Organizations Past and Present* (1988); Nancy L. Roberts, *American Peace Writers, Editors, and Periodicals* (1991). See also "Wars and the Military" and specific wars.

Politics and Government: General

Erik W. Austin, *Political Facts of the United States Since 1789* (1986); Robert Benewick and Philip Green, eds., *The Routledge Dictionary of Twentieth-Century Political Thinkers* (1992); Mari Jo Buhle et al., eds., *Encyclopedia of the American Left* (1990); *The Columbia Dictionary of Political Biography* (1991); David DeLeon, ed., *Leaders of the 1960s: A Biographical Sourcebook of American Activism* (1994); Jack P. Greene, ed., *Encyclopedia of American Political History* (1984); Leon Hurwitz, *Historical Dictionary of Censorship in the United States* (1985); Bernard K. Johnpoll and Harvey Klehr, eds., *Biographical Dictionary of the American Left* (1986); Earl R. Kruschke, *Encyclopedia of Third Parties in the United States* (1991); Edwin V. Mitchell, *An Encyclopedia of American Politics* (1968); Philip Rees, *Biographical Dictionary of the Extreme Right Since 1890* (1991); Charles R. Ritter et al., *American Legislative Leaders, 1850–1910* (1989); William Safire, *Safire's Political Dictionary* (1978); Edward L. Schapsmeier and Frederick H. Schapsmeier, eds., *Political Parties and Civic Action Groups* (1981); Arthur M. Schlesinger, Jr., and Fred I. Israel, eds., *History of American Presidential Elections, 1789–1968* (1971); Robert Scruton, *A Dictionary of Political Thought* (1982); Jay M. Shafritz, *The HarperCollins Dictionary of American Government and Politics* (1992); Hans Sperber and Travis Trittschuh, *American Political Terms* (1962). See also "Cities and Towns," "Constitution, Supreme Court, and Judiciary," "States," and the following sections.

Politics and Government: Congress

Donald C. Brown et al., eds. *The Encyclopedia of the United States Congress* (1994); Congressional Quarterly, *Congress and the Nation, 1945–1984* (1965–1985); Kenneth C. Martis, *Historical Atlas of Political Parties in the United States Congress, 1789–1989* (1989); Kenneth C. Martis, *Historical Atlas of United States Congressional Districts, 1789–1983* (1982); Joel H. Silbey, ed., *Encyclopedia of the American Legislative System* (1994); U.S. Congress, *Biographical Directory of the United States Congress, 1774–1989* (1989).

Politics and Government: Election Statistics

Erik W. Austin and Jerome C. Clubb, *Political Facts of the United States Since 1789* (1986); Congressional Quarterly, *Guide to U.S. Elections* (1975); L. Sandy Maisel, ed., *Political Parties and Elections in the United States* (1991); Richard M. Scammon et al., eds., *America Votes* (1956–); Harold W. Stanley and Richard G. Niemi, *Vital Statistics on American Politics* (1990); G. Scott Thomas, *The Pursuit of the White House: A Handbook of Presidential Election Statistics and History* (1987).

Politics and Government: Presidency and Executive Branch

Henry F. Graff, *The Presidents* (1984); Richard S. Kirkendall, ed., *The Harry S Truman Encyclopedia* (1989); Leonard W. Levy and Louis Fisher, eds., *Encyclopedia of the American Presidency* (1993); Merrill D. Peterson, ed., *Thomas Jefferson: A Reference Biography* (1986); Robert A. Rutland, ed., *James Madison and the American Nation* (1994); Robert Sobel, ed., *Biographical Directory of the United States Executive Branch, 1774–1977* (1977). See other categories for various presidents.

Religion and Cults

Henry Bowden, *Dictionary of American Religious Biography* (1993); S. Kent Brown et al., *Historical Atlas of Mormonism* (1994); John T. Ellis and Robert Trisco, *A Guide to American Catholic History* (1982); Edwin S. Gaustad, *Historical Atlas of Religion in America* (1976); Samuel S. Hill, Jr., ed., *Encyclopedia of Religion in the South* (1984); Charles H. Lippy and Peter W. Williams, eds., *Encyclopedia of the American Religious Experience* (1988); J. Gordon Melton, *The Encyclopedia of American Religions* (1987); J. Gordon Melton, *Biographical Dictionary of American Cult and Sect Leaders* (1986); J. Gordon Melton, *The Encyclopedic Handbook of Cults in America* (1992); Mark A. Noll and Nathan O. Hatch, eds., *Eerdmans Handbook to Christianity in America* (1983); Arthur C. Piepkorn, *Profiles in Belief: The Religious Bodies of the United States and Canada* (1977–1979); Paul J. Weber and W. Landis Jones, *U.S. Religious Interest Groups* (1994). See also "African Americans."

Science and Technology

James W. Cortada, *Historical Dictionary of Data Processing* (1987); Clark A. Elliott, *Biographical Index to American Science: The Seventeenth Century to 1920* (1990); Charles C. Gillispie, ed., *Dictionary of Scientific Biography* (1970–); National Academy of Sciences, *Biographical Memoirs* (1877–); Roy Porter, ed., *The Biographical Dictionary of Scientists* (1994). See also "Exploration."

Social History and Reform

Mary K. Cayton et al., eds., *Encyclopedia of American Social History* (1993); Wayne R. Dynes, ed., *Encyclopedia of Homosexuality* (1990); Louis Filler, *Dictionary of American Social Change* (1982); Louis Filler, *A Dictionary of American Social Reform* (1963); Robert S. Fogarty, *Dictionary of American Communal and Utopian History* (1980); Joseph M. Hawes and Elizabeth I. Nybakken, eds., *American Families* (1991); Harold M. Keele and Joseph C. Kiger, eds., *Foundations* (1984); Mark E. Lender, *Dictionary of American Temperance Biography* (1984); Patricia M. Melvin, ed., *American Community Organizations* (1986); Alvin J. Schmidt, *Fraternal Organizations* (1980); Peter N. Stearns, ed., *Encyclopedia of Social History* (1993); Walter I. Trattner, *Biographical Dictionary of Social Welfare in America* (1986). See also "Crime, Violence, and Police."

The South

Robert Bain et al., eds., *Southern Writers: A Biographical Dictionary* (1979); Kenneth Coleman and Charles S. Gurr, eds., *Dictionary of Georgia Biography* (1983); William S. Powell, ed., *Dictionary of North Carolina Biography* (1979–); David C. Roller and Robert W. Twyman, eds., *The Encyclopedia of Southern History* (1979); Walter P. Webb et al., eds., *The Handbook of Texas* (1952, 1976); Charles R. Wilson and William Ferris, eds., *Encyclopedia of Southern Culture* (1986). See also "The Civil War," "Politics and Government," and "States."

Sports

Peter C. Bjarkman, ed., *Encyclopedia of Major League Baseball Team Histories* (1991); Ralph Hickok, *The Encyclopedia of North American Sports History* (1991); Zander Hollander, *The NBA's Official Encyclopedia of Pro Basketball* (1981); Frank G. Menke and Suzanne Treat, *The Encyclopedia of Sports* (1977); *The NFL's Official Encyclopedic History of Professional Football* (1977); David L. Porter, *Biographical Dictionary of American Sports: Baseball* (1987), *Basketball and Other Indoor Sports* (1989), *Football* (1987), and *Outdoor Sports* (1988); Paul Soderberg et al., *The Big Book of Halls of Fame in the United States and Canada* (1977); David Wallechinsky, *The Complete Book of the Olympics* (1984). See also "Culture and Folklore."

States

Roy R. Glashan, comp., *American Governors and Gubernatorial Elections, 1775–1978* (1979); John Hoffmann, ed., *A Guide to the History of Illinois* (1991); Joseph E. Kallenback and Jessamine S. Kallenback, *American State Governors, 1776–1976* (1977); Joseph N. Kane et al., eds., *Facts About the States* (1989); John E. Kleber et al., eds., *The*

Kentucky Encyclopedia (1992); Thomas A. McMullin and David Walker, *Biographical Directory of American Territorial Governors* (1984); Marie Mullaney, *Biographical Directory of the Governors of the United States, 1983–1987* (1988); Marie Mullaney, *Biographical Directory of the Governors of the United States 1988–1994* (1994); John W. Raimo, ed., *Biographical Directory of the Governors of the United States, 1978–1983* (1985); James W. Scott and Ronald L. De Lorme, *Historical Atlas of Washington* (1988); Benjamin F. Shearer and Barbara S. Shearer, *State Names, Seals, Flags, and Symbols* (1994); Robert Sobel and John W. Raimo, eds., *Biographical Directory of the Governors of the United States, 1789–1978* (1978); Richard W. Wilkie and Jack Tager, eds., *Historical Atlas of Massachusetts* (1991). See also "Politics and Government," "The South," and "The West and Frontier."

Transportation

Keith L. Bryant, ed., *Railroads in the Age of Regulation, 1900–1980* (1988); Robert L. Frey, ed., *Railroads in the Nineteenth Century* (1988). See also "Business and the Economy."

The Vietnam War

John S. Bowman, ed., *The Vietnam War: An Almanac* (1986); James S. Olson, ed., *Dictionary of the Vietnam War* (1988); Harry G. Summers, Jr., *Vietnam War Almanac* (1985). Also see "Peace Movements and Pacifism" and the next section.

Wars and the Military

William M. Arkin et al., *Encyclopedia of the U.S. Military* (1990); Charles D. Bright, ed., *Historical Dictionary of the U.S. Air Force* (1992); Andre Corvisier, ed., *A Dictionary of Military History* (1994); R. Ernest Dupuy and Trevor N. Dupuy, *The Harper Encyclopedia of Military History* (1993); Martin Gilbert, *Atlas of World War I* (1994); Holger H. Herwig and Neil M. Heyman, *Biographical Dictionary of World War I* (1982); John E. Jessup and Louise B. Ketz, eds., *Encyclopedia of the American Military* (1994); Michael Kidron and Dan Smith, *The State of War Atlas* (1983); Kenneth Macksey and William Woodhouse, *The Penguin Encyclopedia of Modern Warfare* (1992); James I. Matray, ed., *Historical Dictionary of the Korean War* (1991); Trevor Royle, *A Dictionary of Military Quotations* (1990); Roger J. Spiller and Joseph G. Dawson III, eds., *Dictionary of American Military Biography* (1984); Peter G. Tsouras et al., *The United States Army* (1991); U.S. Military Academy, *The West Point Atlas of American Wars, 1689–1953* (1959); Bruce W. Watson et al., eds., *United States Intelligence* (1990); *Webster's American Military Biographies* (1978); Bruce W. Watson and Susan M. Watson, *The United States Air Force* (1992); Bruce W. Watson and Susan M. Watson, *The United States Navy* (1991). See also "American Revolution," "The Civil War and Reconstruction," "The Vietnam War," and "World War II."

The West and Frontier

William A. Beck and Ynez D. Haase, *Historical Atlas of the American West* (1989); Doris O. Dawdy, *Artists of the American West* (1974–1984); J. Norman Heard, *Handbook of the American Frontier* (1987); Howard R. Lamar, ed., *The Reader's Encyclopedia of the American West* (1977); Doyce B. Nunis, Jr., and Gloria R. Lothrop, eds., *A Guide to the History of California* (1989); Dan L. Thrapp, *The Encyclopedia of Frontier Biography* (1988). See also "Literature" and "Native Americans and Indian Affairs."

Women

Anne Gibson and Timothy Fast, *The Women's Atlas of the United States* (1986); Maggie Humm, *The Dictionary of Feminist Theory* (1990); Edward T. James et al., *Notable American Women, 1607–1950* (1971); Lina Mainiero, ed., *American Women Writers* (1979–1982); Kirstin Olsen, *Chronology of Women's History* (1994); Barbara G. Shortridge, *Atlas of American Women* (1987); Barbara Sicherman and Carol H. Green, eds., *Notable American Women, The Modern Period* (1980); Helen Tierney, ed., *Women's Studies Encyclopedia* (1991); Angela H. Zophy and Frances M. Kavenik, eds., *Handbook of American Women's History* (1990). See also "African Americans," "Immigration and Ethnic Groups," "Medicine and Nursing," and "Native Americans and Indian Affairs."

World War II

Marcel Baudot et al., eds., *The Historical Encyclopedia of World War II* (1980); David G. Chandler and James Lawton Collins, Jr., eds., *The D-Day Encyclopedia* (1993); Simon Goodenough, *War Maps: Great Land Battles of World War II* (1988); Robert Goralski, *World War II Almanac, 1931–1945* (1981); John Keegan, ed., *The Times Atlas of the Second World War* (1989); Thomas Parrish, ed., *The Simon and Schuster Encyclopedia of World War II* (1978); Norman Polmer and Thomas B. Allen, *World War II: America at War* (1991); Louis L. Snyder, *Louis L. Snyder's Historical Guide to World War II* (1982); U.S. Military Academy, *Campaign Atlas to the Second World War: Europe and the Mediterranean* (1980); Peter Young, ed., *The World Almanac Book of World War II* (1981). See also "Wars and the Military."

DECLARATION OF INDEPENDENCE IN CONGRESS, JULY 4, 1776

When, in the course of human events, it becomes necessary for one people to dissolve the political bonds which have connected them with another, and to assume, among the powers of the earth, the separate and equal station to which the laws of nature and of nature's God entitle them, a decent respect to the opinions of mankind requires that they should declare the causes which impel them to the separation.

We hold these truths to be self-evident: That all men are created equal; that they are endowed by their Creator with certain unalienable rights; that among these are life, liberty, and the pursuit of happiness; that, to secure these rights, governments are instituted among men, deriving their just powers from the consent of the governed; that whenever any form of government becomes destructive of these ends, it is the right of the people to alter or to abolish it, and to institute new government, laying its foundation on such principles, and organizing its powers in such form, as to them shall seem most likely to effect their safety and happiness. Prudence, indeed, will dictate that governments long established should not be changed for light and transient causes; and accordingly all experience hath shown that mankind are more disposed to suffer, while evils are sufferable, than to right themselves by abolishing the forms to which they are accustomed. But when a long train of abuses and usurpations, pursuing invariably the same object, evinces a design to reduce them under absolute despotism, it is their right, it is their duty, to throw off such government, and to provide new guards for their future security. Such has been the patient sufferance of these colonies; and such is now the necessity which constrains them to alter their former systems of government. The history of the present King of Great Britain is a history of repeated injuries and usurpations, all having in direct object the establishment of an absolute tyranny over these states. To prove this, let facts be submitted to a candid world.

He has refused his assent to laws, the most wholesome and necessary for the public good.

He has forbidden his governors to pass laws of immediate and pressing importance, unless suspended in their operation till his assent should be obtained; and, when so suspended, he has utterly neglected to attend to them.

He has refused to pass other laws for the accommodation of large districts of people, unless those people would relinquish the right of representation in the legislature, a right inestimable to them, and formidable to tyrants only.

He has called together legislative bodies at places unusual, uncomfortable, and distant from the depository of their public records, for the sole purpose of fatiguing them into compliance with his measures.

He has dissolved representative houses repeatedly, for opposing, with manly firmness, his invasions on the rights of the people.

He has refused for a long time, after such dissolutions, to cause others to be elected; whereby the legislative powers, incapable of annihilation, have returned to the people at large for their exercise; the state remaining, in the mean time, exposed to all the dangers of invasions from without and convulsions within.

He has endeavored to prevent the population of these states; for that purpose obstructing the laws for naturalization of foreigners; refusing to pass others to encourage their migration hither, and raising the conditions of new appropriations of lands.

He has obstructed the administration of justice, by refusing his assent to laws for establishing judiciary powers.

He has made judges dependent on his will alone, for the tenure of their offices, and the amount and payment of their salaries.

He has erected a multitude of new offices, and sent hither swarms of officers to harass our people and eat out their substance.

He has kept among us, in times of peace, standing armies, without the consent of our legislatures.

He has affected to render the military independent of, and superior to, the civil power.

He has combined with others to subject us to a jurisdiction foreign to our constitution, and unacknowledged by our laws, giving his assent to their acts of pretended legislation:

For quartering large bodies of armed troops among us;

For protecting them, by a mock trial, from punishment for any murders which they should commit on the inhabitants of these states;

For cutting off our trade with all parts of the world;

For imposing taxes on us without our consent;

For depriving us, in many cases, of the benefits of trial by jury;

For transporting us beyond seas, to be tried for pretended offenses;

For abolishing the free system of English laws in a neighboring province, establishing therein an arbitrary government, and enlarging its boundaries, so as to render it at once an example and fit instrument for introducing the same absolute rule into these colonies;

For taking away our charters, abolishing our most valuable laws, and altering fundamentally the forms of our governments;

For suspending our own legislatures, and declaring themselves invested with power to legislate for us in all cases whatsoever.

He has abdicated government here, by declaring us out of his protection and waging war against us.

He has plundered our seas, ravaged our coasts, burned our towns, and destroyed the lives of our people.

He is at this time transporting large armies of foreign mercenaries to complete the works of death, desolation, and tyranny already begun with circumstances of cruelty and perfidy scarcely paralleled in the most barbarous ages, and totally unworthy the head of a civilized nation.

He has constrained our fellow-citizens, taken captive on the high seas, to bear arms against their country, to become the executioners of their friends and brethren, or to fall themselves by their hands.

He has excited domestic insurrection among us, and has endeavored to bring on the inhabitants of our frontiers the merciless Indian savages, whose known rule of warfare is an undistinguished destruction of all ages, sexes, and conditions.

In every stage of these oppressions we have petitioned for redress in the most humble terms; our repeated petitions have been answered only by repeated injury. A prince, whose character is thus marked by every act which may define a tyrant, is unfit to be the ruler of a free people.

Nor have we been wanting in our attentions to our British brethren. We have warned them, from time to time, of attempts by their legislature to extend an unwarrantable jurisdiction over us. We have reminded them of the circumstances of our emigration and settlement here. We have appealed to their native justice and magnanimity; and we have conjured them, by the ties of our common kindred, to disavow these usurpations, which would inevitably interrupt our connections and correspondence. They, too, have been deaf to the voice of justice and of consanguinity. We must, therefore, acquiesce in the necessity which denounces our separation, and hold them, as we hold the rest of mankind, enemies in war, in peace friends.

We, therefore, the representatives of the United States of America, in General Congress assembled, appealing to the Supreme Judge of the world for the rectitude of our intentions, do, in the name and by the authority of the good people of these colonies, solemnly publish and declare, that these United Colonies are, and of right ought to be, FREE AND INDEPENDENT STATES; that they are absolved from all allegiance to the British crown, and that all political connection between them and the state of Great Britain is, and ought to be, totally dissolved; and that, as free and independent states, they have full power to levy war, conclude peace, contract alliances, establish commerce, and do all other acts and things which independent states may of right do. And for the support of this declaration, with a firm reliance on the protection of Divine Providence, we mutually pledge to each other our lives, our fortunes, and our sacred honor.

JOHN HANCOCK
and fifty-five others

———

CONSTITUTION OF THE UNITED STATES OF AMERICA AND AMENDMENTS*

Preamble

We the people of the United States, in order to form a more perfect union, establish justice, insure domestic tranquillity, provide for the common defense, promote the general welfare, and secure the blessings of liberty to ourselves and our posterity, do ordain and establish this Constitution for the United States of America.

Article I

Section 1 All legislative powers herein granted shall be vested in a Congress of the United States, which shall consist of a Senate and a House of Representatives.

Section 2 The House of Representatives shall be composed of members chosen every second year by the people of the several States, and the electors in each State shall have the qualifications requisite for electors of the most numerous branch of the State Legislature.

No person shall be a Representative who shall not have attained to the age of twenty-five years, and been seven years a citizen of the United States, and who shall not, when elected, be an inhabitant of that State in which he shall be chosen.

Representatives and direct taxes shall be apportioned among the several States which may be included within this Union, according to their respective numbers, *which shall be determined by adding to the whole number of*

---

*Passages no longer in effect are printed in italic type.

free persons, including those bound to service for a term of years and excluding Indians not taxed, three-fifths of all other persons. The actual enumeration shall be made within three years after the first meeting of the Congress of the United States, and within every subsequent term of ten years, in such manner as they shall by law direct. The number of Representatives shall not exceed one for every thirty thousand, but each State shall have at least one Representative; *and until such enumeration shall be made, the State of New Hampshire shall be entitled to choose three, Massachusetts eight, Rhode Island and Providence Plantations one, Connecticut five, New York six, New Jersey four, Pennsylvania eight, Delaware one, Maryland six, Virginia ten, North Carolina five, South Carolina five, and Georgia three.*

When vacancies happen in the representation from any State, the Executive authority thereof shall issue writs of election to fill such vacancies.

The House of Representatives shall choose their Speaker and other officers; and shall have the sole power of impeachment.

Section 3   The Senate of the United States shall be composed of two Senators from each State, *chosen by the legislature thereof,* for six years; and each Senator shall have one vote.

Immediately after they shall be assembled in consequence of the first election, they shall be divided as equally as may be into three classes. The seats of the Senators of the first class shall be vacated at the expiration of the second year, of the second class at the expiration of the fourth year, and of the third class at the expiration of the sixth year, so that one-third may be chosen every second year; *and if vacancies happen by resignation or otherwise, during the recess of the legislature of any State, the Executive thereof may make temporary appointments until the next meeting of the legislature, which shall then fill such vacancies.*

No person shall be a Senator who shall not have attained to the age of thirty years, and been nine years a citizen of the United States, and who shall not, when elected, be an inhabitant of that State for which he shall be chosen.

The Vice-President of the United States shall be President of the Senate, but shall have no vote, unless they be equally divided.

The Senate shall choose their other officers, and also a President *pro tempore,* in the absence of the Vice-President, or when he shall exercise the office of President of the United States.

The Senate shall have the sole power to try all impeachments. When sitting for that purpose, they shall be on oath or affirmation. When the President of the United States is tried, the Chief Justice shall preside: and no person shall be convicted without the concurrence of two-thirds of the members present.

Judgment in cases of impeachment shall not extend further than to removal from the office, and disqualification to hold and enjoy any office of honor, trust or profit under the United States: but the party convicted shall nevertheless be liable and subject to indictment, trial, judgment and punishment, according to law.

Section 4   The times, places and manner of holding elections for Senators and Representatives shall be prescribed in each State by the legislature thereof; but the Congress may at any time by law make or alter such regulations, except as to the places of choosing Senators.

The Congress shall assemble at least once in every year, and such meeting *shall be on the first Monday in December, unless they shall by law appoint a different day.*

Section 5   Each house shall be the judge of the elections, returns and qualifications of its own members, and a majority of each shall constitute a quorum to do business; but a smaller number may adjourn from day to day, and may be authorized to compel the attendance of absent members, in such manner, and under such penalties, as each house may provide.

Each house may determine the rules of its proceedings, punish its members for disorderly behavior, and with the concurrence of two-thirds, expel a member.

Each house shall keep a journal of its proceedings, and from time to time publish the same, excepting such parts as may in their judgment require secrecy; and the yeas and nays of the members of either house on any question shall, at the desire of one-fifth of those present, be entered on the journal.

Neither house, during the session of Congress, shall, without the consent of the other, adjourn for more than three days, nor to any other place than that in which the two houses shall be sitting.

Section 6   The Senators and Representatives shall receive a compensation for their services, to be ascertained by law and paid out of the treasury of the United States. They shall in all cases except treason, felony and breach of the peace, be privileged from arrest during their attendance at the session of their respective houses, and in going to and returning from the same; and for any speech or debate in either house, they shall not be questioned in any other place.

No Senator or Representative shall, during the time for which he was elected, be appointed to any civil office under the authority of the United States, which shall have been created, or the emoluments whereof shall have been increased, during such time; and no person holding any office under the United States shall be a member of either house during his continuance in office.

Section 7   All bills for raising revenue shall originate in the House of Representatives; but the Senate may propose or concur with amendments as on other bills.

Every bill which shall have passed the House of Representatives and the Senate, shall, before it become a law, be presented to the President of the United States; if he approve he shall sign it, but if not he shall return it with objections to that house in which it originated, who shall enter the objections at large on their journal, and proceed to reconsider it. If after such reconsideration two-thirds of that house shall agree to pass the bill, it shall be sent, together with the objections, to the other house, by which it shall likewise be reconsidered, and, if approved by two-thirds of that house, it shall become a law. But in all such cases the votes of both houses shall be determined by yeas and nays, and the names of the persons voting for and against the bill shall be entered on the journal of each house respectively. If any bill shall not be returned by the President within ten days (Sundays excepted) after it shall have been presented to him, the same shall be a law, in like manner as if he had signed it, unless the Congress by their adjournment prevent its return, in which case it shall not be a law.

Every order, resolution, or vote to which the concurrence of the Senate and House of Representatives may be necessary (except on a question of adjournment) shall be presented to the President of the United States; and before the same shall take effect, shall be approved by him, or being disapproved by him, shall be repassed by two-thirds of the Senate and House of Representatives, according to the rules and limitations prescribed in the case of a bill.

Section 8   The Congress shall have power

To lay and collect taxes, duties, imposts, and excises, to pay the debts and provide for the common defense and general welfare of the United States; but all duties, imposts and excises shall be uniform throughout the United States;

To borrow money on the credit of the United States;

To regulate commerce with foreign nations, and among the several States, and with the Indian tribes;

To establish an uniform rule of naturalization, and uniform laws on the subject of bankruptcies throughout the United States;

To coin money, regulate the value thereof, and of foreign coin, and fix the standard of weights and measures;

To provide for the punishment of counterfeiting the securities and current coin of the United States;

To establish post offices and post roads;

To promote the progress of science and useful arts by curing for limited times to authors and inventors the ex-clusive right to their respective writings and discoveries;

To constitute tribunals inferior to the Supreme Court;

To define and punish piracies and felonies committed on the high seas and offenses against the law of nations;

To declare war, grant letters of marque and reprisal, and make rules concerning captures on land and water;

To raise and support armies, but no appropriation of money to that use shall be for a longer term than two years;

To provide and maintain a navy;

To make rules for the government and regulation of the land and naval forces;

To provide for calling forth the militia to execute the laws of the Union, suppress insurrections, and repel invasions;

To provide for organizing, arming, and disciplining the militia, and for governing such part of them as may be employed in the service of the United States, reserving to the States respectively the appointment of the officers, and the authority of training the militia according to the discipline prescribed by Congress;

To exercise exclusive legislation in all cases whatsoever, over such district (not exceeding ten miles square) as may, by cession of particular States, and the acceptance of Congress, become the seat of government of the United States, and to exercise like authority over all places purchased by the consent of the legislature of the State, in which the same shall be, for erection of forts, magazines, arsenals, dockyards, and other needful buildings; — and

To make all laws which shall be necessary and proper for carrying into execution the foregoing powers, and all other powers vested by this Constitution in the government of the United States, or in any department or officer thereof.

Section 9   *The migration or importation of such persons as any of the States now existing shall think proper to admit shall not be prohibited by the Congress prior to the year 1808; but a tax or duty may be imposed on such importation, not exceeding $10 for each person.*

The privilege of the writ of habeas corpus shall not be suspended, unless when in cases of rebellion or invasion the public safety may require it.

No bill of attainder or ex post facto law shall be passed.

No capitation, or other direct, tax shall be laid, unless in proportion to the census or enumeration herein before directed to be taken.

No tax or duty shall be laid on articles exported from any State.

No preference shall be given by any regulation of commerce or revenue to the ports of one State over those of another; nor shall vessels bound to, or from, one State, be obliged to enter, clear, or pay duties in another.

No money shall be drawn from the treasury, but in consequence of appropriations made by law; and a regular statement and account of the receipts and expenditures of all public money shall be published from time to time.

No title of nobility shall be granted by the United States: and no person holding any office of profit or trust under them, shall, without the consent of the Congress, accept of any present, emolument, office, or title, of any kind whatever, from any king, prince, or foreign state.

Section 10 No State shall enter into any treaty, alliance, or confederation; grant letters of marque and reprisal; coin money; emit bills of credit; make anything but gold and silver coin a tender in payment of debts; pass any bill of attainder, ex post facto law, or law impairing the obligation of contracts, or grant any title of nobility.

No State shall, without the consent of Congress, lay any imposts or duties on imports or exports, except what may be absolutely necessary for executing its inspection laws: and the net produce of all duties and imposts, laid by any State on imports or exports, shall be for the use of the treasury of the United States; and all such laws shall be subject to the revision and control of the Congress.

No State shall, without the consent of Congress, lay any duty of tonnage, keep troops or ships of war in time of peace, enter into any agreement or compact with another State, or with a foreign power, or engage in war, unless actually invaded, or in such imminent danger as will not admit of delay.

Article II

Section 1 The executive power shall be vested in a President of the United States of America. He shall hold his office during the term of four years, and, together with the Vice-President, chosen for the same term, be elected as follows:

Each State shall appoint, in such manner as the legislature thereof may direct, a number of electors, equal to the whole number of Senators and Representatives to which the State may be entitled in the Congress; but no Senator or Representative, or person holding an office of trust or profit under the United States, shall be appointed an elector.

The electors shall meet in their respective States, and vote by ballot for two persons, of whom one at least shall not be an inhabitant of the same State with themselves. And they shall make a list of all the persons voted for, and of the number of votes for each; which list they shall sign and certify, and transmit sealed to the seat of government of the United States, directed to the President of the Senate. The President of the Senate shall, in the presence of the Senate and House of Representatives, open all the certificates, and the votes shall then be counted. The person having the greatest number of votes shall be the President, if such number be a majority of the whole number of electors appointed; and if there be more than one who have such majority, and have an equal number of votes, then the House of Representatives shall immediately choose by ballot one of them for President; and if no person have a majority, then from the five highest on the list said house shall in like manner choose the President. But in choosing the President the votes shall be taken by States, the representation from each State having one vote; a quorum for this purpose shall consist of a member or members from two-thirds of the States, and a majority of all the States shall be necessary to a choice. In every case, after the choice of the President, the person having the greatest number of votes of the electors shall be the Vice-President. But if there should remain two or more who have equal votes, the Senate shall choose from them by ballot the Vice-President.

The Congress may determine the time of choosing the electors and the day on which they shall give their votes; which day shall be the same throughout the United States.

No person except a natural-born citizen, *or a citizen of the United States at the time of the adoption of this Constitution*, shall be eligible to the office of President; neither shall any person be eligible to that office who shall not have attained to the age of thirty-five years, and been fourteen years a resident within the United States.

In cases of the removal of the President from office or of his death, resignation, or inability to discharge the powers and duties of the said office, the same shall devolve on the Vice-President, and the Congress may by law provide for the case of removal, death, resignation, or inability, both of the President and Vice-President, declaring what officer shall then act as President, and such officer shall act accordingly, until the disability be removed, or a President shall be elected.

The President shall, at stated times, receive for his services a compensation, which shall neither be increased nor diminished during the period for which he shall have been elected, and he shall not receive within that period any other emolument from the United States, or any of them.

Before he enter on the execution of his office, he shall take the following oath or affirmation:—"I do solemnly swear (or affirm) that I will faithfully execute the office of the President of the United States, and will to the best of my ability preserve, protect and defend the Constitution of the United States."

Section 2 The President shall be commander in chief of the army and navy of the United States, and of the militia of the several States, when called into the actual service of the United States; he may require the opinion, in writing, of the principal officer in each of the executive departments, upon any subject relating to the duties of their respective offices, and he shall have power to grant reprieves and pardons for offenses against the United States, except in cases of impeachment.

He shall have power, by and with the advice and consent of the Senate, to make treaties, provided two-thirds of the Senators present concur; and he shall nominate, and by and with the advice and consent of the Senate, shall appoint ambassadors, other public ministers and consuls, judges of the Supreme Court, and all other officers of the United States, whose appointments are not herein otherwise provided for, and which shall be established by law: but Congress may by law vest the appointment of such inferior officers, as they think proper, in the President alone, in the courts of law, or in the heads of departments.

The President shall have power to fill up all vacancies that may happen during the recess of the Senate, by granting commissions which shall expire at the end of their next session.

Section 3   He shall from time to time give to the Congress information of the state of the Union, and recommend to their consideration such measures as he shall judge necessary and expedient; he may, on extraordinary occasions, convene both houses, or either of them, and in case of disagreement between them, with respect to the time of adjournment, he may adjourn them to such time as he shall think proper; he shall receive ambassadors and other public ministers; he shall take care that the laws be faithfully executed, and shall commission all the officers of the United States.

Section 4   The President, Vice-President and all civil officers of the United States shall be removed from office on impeachment for, and on conviction of, treason, bribery, or other high crimes and misdemeanors.

Article III

Section 1   The judicial power of the United States shall be vested in one Supreme Court, and in such inferior courts as the Congress may from time to time ordain and establish. The judges, both of the Supreme and inferior courts, shall hold their offices during good behavior, and shall, at stated times, receive for their services a compensation which shall not be diminished during their continuance in office.

Section 2   The judicial power shall extend to all cases, in law and equity, arising under this Constitution, the laws of the United States, and treaties made, or which shall be made, under their authority;—to all cases affecting ambassadors, other public ministers and consuls;—to all cases of admiralty and maritime jurisdiction;—to controversies to which the United States shall be a party;—to controversies between two or more States;—*between a State and citizens of another State;*—between citizens of different States;—between citizens of the same State claiming lands under grants of different States, and between a State, or the citizens thereof, and foreign states, citizens or subjects.

In all cases affecting ambassadors, other public ministers and consuls, and those in which a State shall be party, the Supreme Court shall have original jurisdiction. In all the other cases before mentioned, the Supreme Court shall have appellate jurisdiction, both as to law and fact, with such exceptions, and under such regulations, as the Congress shall make.

The trial of all crimes, except in cases of impeachment, shall be by jury; and such trial shall be held in the State where said crimes shall have been committed; but when not committed within any State, the trial shall be at such place or places as the Congress may by law have directed.

Section 3   Treason against the United States shall consist only in levying war against them, or in adhering to their enemies, giving them aid and comfort. No person shall be convicted of treason unless on the testimony of two witnesses to the same overt act, or on confession in open court.

The Congress shall have power to declare the punishment of treason, but no attainder of treason shall work corruption of blood, or forfeiture except during the life of the person attainted.

Article IV

Section 1   Full faith and credit shall be given in each State to the public acts, records, and judicial proceedings of every other State. And the Congress may by general laws prescribe the manner in which such acts, records, and proceedings shall be proved, and the effect thereof.

Section 2   The citizens of each State shall be entitled to all privileges and immunities of citizens in the several States.

A person charged in any State with treason, felony, or other crime, who shall flee from justice, and be found in another State, shall on demand of the executive authority of the State from which he fled, be delivered up, to be removed to the State having jurisdiction of the crime.

No person held to service or labor in one State, under the laws thereof, escaping into another, shall, in consequence of any law or regulation therein, be discharged from such service or labor, but shall be delivered up on claim of the party to whom such service or labor may be due.

Section 3 New States may be admitted by the Congress into this Union; but no new State shall be formed or erected within the jurisdiction of any other State; nor any State be formed by the junction of two or more States, or parts of States, without the consent of the legislatures of the States concerned as well as of the Congress.

The Congress shall have power to dispose of and make all needful rules and regulations respecting the territory or other property belonging to the United States; and nothing in this Constitution shall be so construed as to prejudice any claims of the United States, or of any particular State.

Section 4 The United States shall guarantee to every State in this Union a republican form of government, and shall protect each of them against invasion; and on application of the legislature, or of the executive (when the legislature cannot be convened), against domestic violence.

Article V

The Congress, whenever two-thirds of both houses shall deem it necessary, shall propose amendments to this Constitution, or, on the application of the legislatures of two-thirds of the several States, shall call a convention for proposing amendments, which, in either case, shall be valid to all intents and purposes, as part of this Constitution, when ratified by the legislatures of three-fourths of the several States, or by conventions in three-fourths thereof, as the one or the other mode of ratification may be proposed by the Congress; provided *that no amendments which may be made prior to the year one thousand eight hundred and eight shall in any manner affect the first and fourth clauses in the ninth section of the first article;* and that no State, without its consent, shall be deprived of its equal suffrage in the Senate.

Article VI

All debts contracted and engagements entered into, before the adoption of this Constitution, shall be as valid against the United States under this Constitution, as under the Confederation.

This Constitution, and the laws of the United States which shall be made in pursuance thereof; and all treaties made, or which shall be made, under the authority of the United States, shall be the supreme law of the land; and the judges in every State shall be bound thereby, anything in the Constitution or laws of any State to the contrary notwithstanding.

The Senators and Representatives before mentioned, and the members of the several State legislatures, and all executive and judicial officers, both of the United States and of the several States, shall be bound by oath or affirmation to support this Constitution; but no religious test shall ever be required as a qualification to any office or public trust under the United States.

Article VII

The ratification of the conventions of nine States shall be sufficient for the establishment of this Constitution between the States so ratifying the same.

Done in Convention by the unanimous consent of the States present, the seventeenth day of September in the year of our Lord one thousand seven hundred and eighty-seven and of the Independence of the United States of America the twelfth. In witness whereof we have hereunto subscribed our names.

GEORGE WASHINGTON
and thirty-seven others

Amendments to the Constitution*

Amendment I

Congress shall make no law respecting an establishment of religion, or prohibiting the free exercise thereof; or abridging the freedom of speech, or of the press; or the right of the people peaceably to assemble, and to petition the government for a redress of grievances.

Amendment II

A well-regulated militia being necessary to the security of a free State, the right of the people to keep and bear arms shall not be infringed.

Amendment III

No soldier shall, in time of peace, be quartered in any house without the consent of the owner, nor in time of war, but in a manner to be prescribed by law.

Amendment IV

The right of the people to be secure in their persons, houses, papers, and effects, against unreasonable searches and seizures, shall not be violated, and no warrants shall issue but upon probable cause, supported by oath or affirmation, and particularly describing the place to be searched, and the persons or things to be seized.

---

*The first ten Amendments (the Bill of Rights) were adopted in 1791.

Amendment V

No person shall be held to answer for a capital, or otherwise infamous crime, unless on a presentment or indictment of a grand jury, except in cases arising in the land or naval forces, or in the militia, when in actual service in time of war or public danger; nor shall any person be subject for the same offense to be twice put in jeopardy of life or limb; nor shall be compelled in any criminal case to be a witness against himself, nor be deprived of life, liberty, or property, without due process of law; nor shall private property be taken for public use without just compensation.

Amendment VI

In all criminal prosecutions, the accused shall enjoy the right to a speedy and public trial, by an impartial jury of the State and district wherein the crime shall have been committed, which district shall have been previously ascertained by law, and to be informed of the nature and cause of the accusation; to be confronted with the witnesses against him; to have compulsory process for obtaining witnesses in his favor, and to have the assistance of counsel for his defense.

Amendment VII

In suits at common law, where the value in controversy shall exceed twenty dollars, the right of trial by jury shall be preserved, and no fact tried by a jury shall be otherwise reexamined in any court of the United States, than according to the rules of the common law.

Amendment VIII

Excessive bail shall not be required, nor excessive fines imposed, nor cruel and unusual punishments inflicted.

Amendment IX

The enumeration in the Constitution, of certain rights, shall not be construed to deny or disparage others retained by the people.

Amendment X

The powers not delegated to the United States by the Constitution, nor prohibited by it to the States, are reserved to the States respectively, or to the people.

Amendment XI

[Adopted 1798]

The judicial power of the United States shall not be construed to extend to any suit in law or equity, commenced or prosecuted against one of the United States by citizens of another State, or by citizens or subjects of any foreign state.

Amendment XII

[Adopted 1804]

The electors shall meet in their respective States, and vote by ballot for President and Vice-President, one of whom, at least, shall not be an inhabitant of the same State with themselves; they shall name in their ballots the person voted for as President, and in distinct ballots the person voted for as Vice-President, and they shall make distinct lists of all persons voted for as President, and of all persons voted for as Vice-President, and of the number of votes for each, which lists they shall sign and certify, and transmit sealed to the seat of government of the United States, directed to the President of the Senate;— the President of the Senate shall, in the presence of the Senate and House of Representatives, open all the certificates and the votes shall then be counted;—the person having the greatest number of votes for President shall be the President, if such number be a majority of the whole number of electors appointed; and if no person have such majority, then from the persons having the highest numbers not exceeding three on the list of those voted for as President, the House of Representatives shall choose immediately, by ballot, the President. But in choosing the President, the votes shall be taken by States, the representation from each State having one vote; a quorum for this purpose shall consist of a member or members from two-thirds of the States, and a majority of all the States shall be necessary to a choice. And if the House of Representatives shall not choose a President whenever the right of choice shall devolve upon them, before *the fourth day of March* next following, then the Vice-President shall act as President, as in the case of the death or other constitutional disability of the President.

The person having the greatest number of votes as Vice-President shall be the Vice-President, if such number be a majority of the whole number of electors appointed; and if no person have a majority, then from the two highest numbers on the list the Senate shall choose the Vice-President; a quorum for the purpose shall consist of two-thirds of the whole number of Senators, and a majority of the whole number shall be necessary to a choice. But no person constitutionally ineligible to the office of President shall be eligible to that of Vice-President of the United States.

Amendment XIII

[Adopted 1865]

Section 1 Neither slavery nor involuntary servitude, except as a punishment for crime whereof the party shall have been duly convicted, shall exist within the United States, or any place subject to their jurisdiction.

Section 2 Congress shall have power to enforce this article by appropriate legislation.

Amendment XIV

[Adopted 1868]

Section 1 All persons born or naturalized in the United States, and subject to the jurisdiction thereof, are citizens of the United States and of the State wherein they reside. No State shall make or enforce any law which shall abridge the privileges or immunities of citizens of the United States; nor shall any State deprive any person of life, liberty, or property, without due process of law; nor deny to any person within its jurisdiction the equal protection of the laws.

Section 2 Representatives shall be apportioned among the several States according to their respective numbers, counting the whole number of persons in each State, excluding Indians not taxed. But when the right to vote at any election for the choice of Electors for President and Vice-President of the United States, Representatives in Congress, the executive and judicial officers of a State, or the members of the legislature thereof, is denied to any of the male inhabitants of such State, being twenty-one years of age and citizens of the United States, or in any way abridged, except for participation in rebellion, or other crime, the basis of representation therein shall be reduced in the proportion which the number of such male citizens shall bear to the whole number of male citizens twenty-one years of age in such State.

Section 3 No person shall be a Senator or Representative in Congress, or Elector of President and Vice-President, or hold any office, civil or military, under the United States, or under any State, who, having previously taken an oath, as a member of Congress, or as an officer of the United States, or as a member of any State legislature, or as an executive or judicial officer of any State, to support the Constitution of the United States, shall have engaged in insurrection or rebellion against the same, or given aid or comfort to the enemies thereof. Congress may, by a vote of two-thirds of each house, remove such disability.

Section 4 The validity of the public debt of the United States, authorized by law, including debts incurred for payment of pensions and bounties for services in suppressing insurrection or rebellion, shall not be questioned. But neither the United States nor any State shall assume or pay any debt or obligation incurred in aid of insurrection or rebellion against the United States, or any claim for the loss of emancipation of any slave; but all such debts, obligations, and claims shall be held illegal and void.

Section 5 The Congress shall have power to enforce, by appropriate legislation, the provisions of this article.

Amendment XV

[Adopted 1870]

Section 1 The right of citizens of the United States to vote shall not be denied or abridged by the United States or by any State on account of race, color, or previous condition of servitude.

Section 2 The Congress shall have power to enforce this article by appropriate legislation.

Amendment XVI

[Adopted 1913]

The Congress shall have power to lay and collect taxes on incomes, from whatever source derived, without apportionment among the several States, and without regard to any census or enumeration.

Amendment XVII

[Adopted 1913]

Section 1 The Senate of the United States shall be composed of two Senators from each State, elected by the people thereof, for six years; and each Senator shall have one vote. The electors in each State shall have the qualifications requisite for electors of [voters for] the most numerous branch of the State legislatures.

Section 2 When vacancies happen in the representation of any State in the Senate, the executive authority of such State shall issue writs of election to fill such vacancies: Provided, that the Legislature of any State may empower the executive thereof to make temporary appointments until the people fill the vacancies by election as the Legislature may direct.

Section 3 This amendment shall not be so construed as to affect the election or term of any Senator chosen before it becomes valid as part of the Constitution.

Amendment XVIII

[Adopted 1919; Repealed 1933]

Section 1 After one year from the ratification of this article the manufacture, sale, or transportation of intoxicating liquors within, the importation thereof into, or the exportation thereof from the United States and all territory subject to the jurisdiction thereof, for beverage purposes, is hereby prohibited.

Section 2   The Congress and the several States shall have concurrent power to enforce this article by appropriate legislation.

Section 3   This article shall be inoperative unless it shall have been ratified as an amendment to the Constitution by the legislatures of the several States, as provided by the Constitution, within seven years from the date of the submission thereof to the States by the Congress.

Amendment XIX

[Adopted 1920]

Section 1   The right of citizens of the United States to vote shall not be denied or abridged by the United States or by any State on account of sex.

Section 2   The Congress shall have power to enforce this article by appropriate legislation.

Amendment XX

[Adopted 1933]

Section 1   The terms of the President and Vice-President shall end at noon on the 20th day of January, and the terms of Senators and Representatives at noon on the 3rd day of January, of the years in which such terms would have ended if this article had not been ratified; and the terms of their successors shall then begin.

Section 2   The Congress shall assemble at least once in every year, and such meeting shall begin at noon on the 3d day of January, unless they shall by law appoint a different day.

Section 3   If, at the time fixed for the beginning of the term of the President, the President-elect shall have died, the Vice-President-elect shall become President. If a President shall not have been chosen before the time fixed for the beginning of his term, or if the President-elect shall have failed to qualify, then the Vice-President-elect shall act as President until a President shall have qualified; and the Congress may by law provide for the case wherein neither a President-elect nor a Vice-President-elect shall have qualified, declaring who shall then act as President, or the manner in which one who is to act shall be selected, and such persons shall act accordingly until a President or Vice-President shall have qualified.

Section 4   The Congress may by law provide for the case of the death of any of the persons from whom the House of Representatives may choose a President whenever the right of choice shall have devolved upon them, and for the case of the death of any of the persons from whom the Senate may choose a Vice-President whenever the right of choice shall have devolved upon them.

Section 5   Sections 1 and 2 shall take effect on the 15th day of October following the ratification of this article.

Section 6   This article shall be inoperative unless it shall have been ratified as an amendment to the Constitution by the Legislatures of three-fourths of the several States within seven years from the date of its submission.

Amendment XXI

[Adopted 1933]

Section 1   The eighteenth article of amendment to the Constitution of the United States is hereby repealed.

Section 2   The transportation or importation into any State, Territory, or Possession of the United States for delivery or use therein of intoxicating liquors, in violation of the laws thereof, is hereby prohibited.

Section 3   This article shall be inoperative unless it shall have been ratified as an amendment to the Constitution by conventions in the several States, as provided in the Constitution, within seven years from the date of submission thereof to the States by the Congress.

Amendment XXII

[Adopted 1951]

Section 1   No person shall be elected to the office of President more than twice, and no person who has held the office of President, or acted as President, for more than two years of a term to which some other person was elected President shall be elected to the office of President more than once. But this article shall not apply to any person holding the office of President when this article was proposed by the Congress, and shall not prevent any person who may be holding the office of President, or acting as President, during the term within which this article becomes operative from holding the office of President or acting as President during the remainder of such term.

Section 2   This article shall be inoperative unless it shall have been ratified as an amendment to the Constitution by the legislatures of three-fourths of the several States within seven years from the date of its submission to the States by the Congress.

Amendment XXIII

[Adopted 1961]

Section 1 The District constituting the seat of Government of the United States shall appoint in such manner as the Congress may direct:

A number of electors of President and Vice-President equal to the whole number of Senators and Representatives in Congress to which the District would be entitled if it were a State, but in no event more than the least populous State; they shall be in addition to those appointed by the States, but they shall be considered for the purposes of the election of President and Vice-President, to be electors appointed by a State; and they shall meet in the District and perform such duties as provided by the twelfth article of amendment.

Section 2 The Congress shall have the power to enforce this article by appropriate legislation.

Amendment XXIV

[Adopted 1964]

Section 1 The right of citizens of the United States to vote in any primary or other election for President or Vice-President, for electors for President or Vice-President, or for Senator or Representative in Congress, shall not be denied or abridged by the United States or any State by reason of failure to pay any poll tax or other tax.

Section 2 The Congress shall have the power to enforce this article by appropriate legislation.

Amendment XXV

[Adopted 1967]

Section 1 In case of the removal of the President from office or of his death or resignation, the Vice-President shall become President.

Section 2 Whenever there is a vacancy in the office of the Vice-President, the President shall nominate a Vice-President who shall take office upon confirmation by a majority vote of both Houses of Congress.

Section 3 Whenever the President transmits to the President pro tempore of the Senate and the Speaker of the House of Representatives his written declaration that he is unable to discharge the powers and duties of his office, and until he transmits to them a written declaration to the contrary, such powers and duties shall be discharged by the Vice-President as Acting President.

Section 4 Whenever the Vice-President and a majority of either the principal officers of the executive departments or of such other body as Congress may by law provide, transmit to the President pro tempore of the Senate and the Speaker of the House of Representatives their written declaration that the President is unable to discharge the powers and duties of his office, the Vice-President shall immediately assume the powers and duties of the office as Acting President.

Thereafter, when the President transmits to the President pro tempore of the Senate and the Speaker of the House of Representatives his written declaration that no inability exists, he shall resume the powers and duties of his office unless the Vice-President and a majority of either the principal officers of the executive department[s] or of such other body as Congress may by law provide, transmit within four days to the President pro tempore of the Senate and the Speaker of the House of Representatives their written declaration that the President is unable to discharge the powers and duties of his office. Thereupon Congress shall decide the issue, assembling within forty-eight hours for that purpose if not in session. If the Congress, within twenty-one days after receipt of the latter written declaration, or, if Congress is not in session, within twenty-one days after Congress is required to assemble, determines by two-thirds vote of both Houses that the President is unable to discharge the powers and duties of his office, the Vice-President shall continue to discharge the same as Acting President; otherwise, the President shall resume the powers and duties of his office.

Amendment XXVI

[Adopted 1971]

Section 1 The right of citizens of the United States, who are eighteen years of age or older, to vote shall not be denied or abridged by the United States or by any State on account of age.

Section 2 The Congress shall have power to enforce this article by appropriate legislation.

Amendment XXVII

[Adopted 1992]

No law, varying the compensation for the services of the Senators and Representatives, shall take effect, until an election of Representatives shall have intervened.

The American People and Nation: A Statistical Profile

Population of the United States

Year	Number of States	Population	Percent Increase	Population Per Square Mile	Percent Urban/ Rural	Percent Male/ Female	Percent White/ Non-white	Persons Per House-hold	Median Age
1790	13	3,929,214		4.5	5.1/94.9	NA/NA	80.7/19.3	5.79	NA
1800	16	5,308,483	35.1	6.1	6.1/93.9	NA/NA	81.1/18.9	NA	NA
1810	17	7,239,881	36.4	4.3	7.3/92.7	NA/NA	81.0/19.0	NA	NA
1820	23	9,638,453	33.1	5.5	7.2/92.8	50.8/49.2	81.6/18.4	NA	16.7
1830	24	12,866,020	33.5	7.4	8.8/91.2	50.8/49.2	81.9/18.1	NA	17.2
1840	26	17,069,453	32.7	9.8	10.8/89.2	50.9/49.1	83.2/16.8	NA	17.8
1850	31	23,191,876	35.9	7.9	15.3/84.7	51.0/49.0	84.3/15.7	5.55	18.9
1860	33	31,443,321	35.6	10.6	19.8/80.2	51.2/48.8	85.6/14.4	5.28	19.4
1870	37	39,818,449	26.6	13.4	25.7/74.3	50.6/49.4	86.2/13.8	5.09	20.2
1880	38	50,155,783	26.0	16.9	28.2/71.8	50.9/49.1	86.5/13.5	5.04	20.9
1890	44	62,947,714	25.5	21.2	35.1/64.9	51.2/48.8	87.5/12.5	4.93	22.0
1900	45	75,994,575	20.7	25.6	39.6/60.4	51.1/48.9	87.9/12.1	4.76	22.9
1910	46	91,972,266	21.0	31.0	45.6/54.4	51.5/48.5	88.9/11.1	4.54	24.1
1920	48	105,710,620	14.9	35.6	51.2/48.8	51.0/49.0	89.7/10.3	4.34	25.3
1930	48	122,775,046	16.1	41.2	56.1/43.9	50.6/49.4	89.8/10.2	4.11	26.4
1940	48	131,669,275	7.2	44.2	56.5/43.5	50.2/49.8	89.8/10.2	3.67	29.0
1950	48	150,697,361	14.5	50.7	64.0/36.0	49.7/50.3	89.5/10.5	3.37	30.2
1960	50	179,323,175	18.5	50.6	69.9/30.1	49.3/50.7	88.6/11.4	3.33	29.5
1970	50	203,302,031	13.4	57.4	73.5/26.5	48.7/51.3	87.6/12.4	3.14	28.0
1980	50	226,545,805	11.4	64.0	73.7/26.3	48.6/51.4	86.0/14.0	2.75	30.0
1990	50	248,709,873	9.8	70.3	75.2/24.8	48.7/51.3	80.3/19.7	2.63	32.8
1992	50	255,458,000	2.7	72.2	NA	48.8/51.2	83.3/16.5	2.62	33.4

NA = Not available.

Vital Statistics

Year	Birth Rate[a]	Death Rate[a]	Life Expectancy in Years					Marriage Rate	Divorce Rate
			Total Population	White Females	Nonwhite Females	White Males	Nonwhite Males		
1790	NA	NA	NA	NA	NA	NA	NA	NA	NA
1800	55.0	NA	NA	NA	NA	NA	NA	NA	NA
1810	54.3	NA	NA	NA	NA	NA	NA	NA	NA
1820	55.2	NA	NA	NA	NA	NA	NA	NA	NA
1830	51.4	NA	NA	NA	NA	NA	NA	NA	NA
1840	51.8	NA	NA	NA	NA	NA	NA	NA	NA
1850	43.3	NA	NA	NA	NA	NA	NA	NA	NA
1860	44.3	NA	NA	NA	NA	NA	NA	NA	NA
1870	38.3	NA	NA	NA	NA	NA	NA	NA	NA
1880	39.8	NA	NA	NA	NA	NA	NA	NA	NA
1890	31.5	NA	NA	NA	NA	NA	NA	NA	NA
1900	32.3	17.2	47.3	48.7	33.5	46.6	32.5	NA	NA
1910	30.1	14.7	50.0	52.0	37.5	48.6	33.8	NA	NA
1920	27.7	13.0	54.1	55.6	45.2	54.4	45.5	12.0	1.6
1930	21.3	11.3	59.7	63.5	49.2	59.7	47.3	9.2	1.6
1940	19.4	10.8	62.9	66.6	54.9	62.1	51.5	12.1	2.0
1950	24.1	9.6	68.2	72.2	62.9	66.5	59.1	11.1	2.6
1960	23.7	9.5	69.7	74.1	66.3	67.4	61.1	8.5	2.2
1970	18.4	9.5	70.9	75.6	69.4	68.0	61.3	10.6	3.5
1980	15.9	8.8	73.7	78.1	73.6	70.7	65.3	10.6	5.2
1990	16.7	8.6	75.4	79.4	75.2	72.7	67.0	9.8	4.7
1991	16.3	8.6	75.5	79.6	75.5	72.8	67.3	9.3[b]	4.8[b]

Data per one thousand for Birth, Death, Marriage, and Divorce rates.

NA = Not available.

[a]Data for 1800, 1810, 1830, 1850, 1870, and 1890 for whites only.

[b]Data for 1992.

Immigrants to the United States

Immigration Totals by Decade			
Years	**Number**	**Years**	**Number**
1820–1830	151,824	1911–1920	5,735,811
1831–1840	599,125	1921–1930	4,107,209
1841–1850	1,713,251	1931–1940	528,431
1851–1860	2,598,214	1941–1950	1,035,039
1861–1870	2,314,824	1951–1960	2,515,479
1871–1880	2,812,191	1961–1970	3,321,677
1881–1890	5,246,613	1971–1980	4,493,000
1891–1900	3,687,546	1981–1990	7,338,000
1901–1910	8,795,386	Total	56,993,620

Sources: U.S. Bureau of the Census, Historical Statistics of the United States, Colonial Times to 1970 *(1975); U.S. Bureau of the Census,* Statistical Abstract of the United States, 1993 *(1993).*

Major Sources of Immigrants by Country or Region (in thousands)

Period	Germany	Asia[a]	Italy	Britain (UK)	Ireland	Austria-Hungary	Canada	Mexico	Russia (USSR)[b]	Caribbean	Denmark, Norway, Sweden[c]
1820–1830	8	—	—	27	54	—	2	5	—	4	—
1831–1840	152	—	2	76	207	—	14	7	—	12	2
1841–1850	435	—	2	267	781	—	42	3	—	14	14
1851–1860	952	42	9	424	914	—	59	3	—	11	25
1861–1870	787	65	12	607	436	8	154	2	3	9	126
1871–1880	718	124	56	548	437	73	384	5	39	14	243
1881–1890	1,453	70	307	807	655	354	393	2[d]	213	29	656
1891–1900	505	75	652	272	388	593	3	1[e]	505	—	372
1901–1910	341	324	2,046	526	339	2,145	179	50	1,597	108	505
1911–1920	144	247	1,110	341	146	896	742	219	922	123	203
1921–1930	412	112	455	330	221	64	925	459	89	75	198
1931–1940	114	16	68	29	13	11	109	22	7	16	11
1941–1950	227	37	58	132	28	28	172	61	4	50	27
1951–1960	478	153	185	192	57	104	378	300	6	123	57
1961–1970	200	445	207	231	42	31	287	443	16	520	45
1971–1980	66	1,634	130	124	14	16	115	637	43	760	15
1981–1990	70	2,817	33	142	33	14	119	1,653	84	893	19
Total	7,062	6,161	5,332	5,075	4,765	4,337	4,077	3,872	3,528	2,761	2,518

Notes: Numbers are rounded. Dash indicates less than one thousand.

[a]Includes Middle East.

[b]Includes Finland, Latvia, Estonia, and Lithuania.

[c]Includes Iceland.

[d]Figure for 1881–1885 only.

[e]Figure for 1894–1900 only.

Sources: U.S. Bureau of the Census, Historical Statistics of the United States: Colonial Times to 1970 (1975); U.S. Bureau of the Census, Statistical Abstract of the United States, 1993 (1993); U.S. Immigration and Naturalization Service..

The American Economy

Year	Gross National Product (GNP) (in $ billions)	Steel Production (in tons)	Automobiles Registered	New Housing Starts	Foreign Trade (in millions of dollars)	
					Exports	Imports
1790	NA	NA	NA	NA	20	23
1800	NA	NA	NA	NA	71	91
1810	NA	NA	NA	NA	67	85
1820	NA	NA	NA	NA	70	74
1830	NA	NA	NA	NA	74	71
1840	NA	NA	NA	NA	132	107
1850	NA	NA	NA	NA	152	178
1860	NA	13,000	NA	NA	400	362
1870	7.4[a]	77,000	NA	NA	451	462
1880	11.2[b]	1,397,000	NA	NA	853	761
1890	13.1	4,779,000	NA	328,000	910	823
1900	18.7	11,227,000	8,000	189,000	1,499	930
1910	35.3	28,330,000	458,300	387,000 (1918 = 118,000)	1,919	1,646
1920	91.5	46,183,000	8,131,500	247,000 (1925 = 937,000)	8,664	5,784
1930	90.7	44,591,000	23,034,700	330,000 (1933 = 93,000)	4,013	3,500
1940	100.0	66,983,000	27,465,800	603,000 (1944 = 142,000)	4,030	7,433
1950	286.5	96,836,000	40,339,000	1,952,000	10,816	9,125
1960	506.5	99,282,000	61,682,300	1,365,000	19,600	15,046
1970	1,016.0	131,514,000	89,279,800	1,469,000	42,700	40,189
1980	2,742.0	111,835,000	121,600,000	1,313,000	220,783	244,871
1990	5,567.8	98,906,000	143,026,000	1,193,000	393,600	495,300
1992	6,045.8	92,900,000	144,213,000	1,200,000	448,200	532,700

[a]Figure is average for 1869–1878.

[b]Figure is average for 1879–1888.

NA = Not available.

Federal Spending and Debt

Year	Defense[a]	Veterans Benefits and Services[a]	Social Security[a]	Income Security[a]	Health and Medicare[a]	Education and Manpower[a]	Interest on Public Debt[a]	Federal Debt (dollars)
1790	14.9	4.1[b]	NA	NA	NA	NA	55.0	75,463,000[c]
1800	55.7	.6	NA	NA	NA	NA	31.3	82,976,000
1810	48.4 (1814 = 79.7)	1.0	NA	NA	NA	NA	34.9	53,173,000
1820	38.4	17.6	NA	NA	NA	NA	28.1	91,016,000
1830	52.9	9.0	NA	NA	NA	NA	12.6	48,565,000
1840	54.3 (1847 = 80.7)	10.7	NA	NA	NA	NA	.7	3,573,000
1850	43.8	4.7	NA	NA	NA	NA	1.0	63,453,000
1860	44.2 (1865 = 88.9)	1.7	NA	NA	NA	NA	5.0	64,844,000
1870	25.7	9.2	NA	NA	NA	NA	41.7	2,436,453,000
1880	19.3	21.2	NA	NA	NA	NA	35.8	2,090,909,000
1890	20.9 (1899 = 48.6)	33.6	NA	NA	NA	NA	11.4	1,222,397,000
1900	36.6	27.0	NA	NA	NA	NA	7.7	1,263,417,000
1910	45.1 (1919 = 59.5)	23.2	NA	NA	NA	NA	3.1	1,146,940,000
1920	37.1	3.4	NA	NA	NA	NA	16.0	24,299,321,000
1930	25.3	6.6	NA	NA	NA	NA	19.9	16,185,310,000
1940	17.5 (1945 = 89.5)	6.0	.03	15.9	.5	20.8	9.5	42,967,531,000
1950	32.2 (1953 = 59.4)	20.8	1.8	9.6	.6	.6	11.3	257,357,352,000
1960	52.2	5.9	12.6	8.0	.9	1.0	7.5	286,330,761,000
1970	41.8	4.4	15.5	8.0	6.2	4.4	7.3	370,918,707,000
1980	22.7	3.6	20.1	14.6	9.4	5.4	8.9	907,700,000,000
1990	23.9	2.3	19.8	11.7	12.4	3.1	14.7	3,233,300,000,000
1993	20.7	2.5	21.6	14.7	16.3	3.6	14.1	4,351,223,000,000

[a]Figures represent percentage of total federal spending for each category.

[b]1789–1791 figure.

[c]1791 figure.

NA = Not available.

Territorial Expansion
of the United States

Territory	Date Acquired	Square Miles	How Acquired
Original states and territories	1783	888,685	Treaty with Great Britain
Louisiana Purchase	1803	827,192	Purchase from France
Florida	1819	72,003	Treaty with Spain
Texas	1845	390,143	Annexation of independent nation
Oregon	1846	285,580	Treaty with Great Britain
Mexican Cession	1848	529,017	Conquest from Mexico
Gadsden Purchase	1853	29,640	Purchase from Mexico
Alaska	1867	589,757	Purchase from Russia
Hawaii	1898	6,450	Annexation of independent nation
The Philippines	1899	115,600	Conquest from Spain (granted independence in 1946)
Puerto Rico	1899	3,435	Conquest from Spain
Guam	1899	212	Conquest from Spain
American Samoa	1900	76	Treaty with Germany and Great Britain
Panama Canal Zone	1904	553	Treaty with Panama (returned to Panama by treaty in 1978)
Corn Islands	1914	4	Treaty with Nicaragua (returned to Nicaragua by treaty in 1971)
Virgin Islands	1917	133	Purchase from Denmark
Pacific Islands Trust (Micronesia)	1947	8,489	Trusteeship under United Nations (some granted independence)
All others (Midway, Wake, and other islands)		42	

Admission of States
into the Union

State	Date of Admission	State	Date of Admission
1. Delaware	December 7, 1787	26. Michigan	January 26, 1837
2. Pennsylvania	December 12, 1787	27. Florida	March 3, 1845
3. New Jersey	December 18, 1787	28. Texas	December 29, 1845
4. Georgia	January 2, 1788	29. Iowa	December 28, 1846
5. Connecticut	January 9, 1788	30. Wisconsin	May 29, 1848
6. Massachusetts	February 6, 1788	31. California	September 9, 1850
7. Maryland	April 28, 1788	32. Minnesota	May 11, 1858
8. South Carolina	May 23, 1788	33. Oregon	February 14, 1859
9. New Hampshire	June 21, 1788	34. Kansas	January 29, 1861
10. Virginia	June 25, 1788	35. West Virginia	June 20, 1863
11. New York	July 26, 1788	36. Nevada	October 31, 1864
12. North Carolina	November 21, 1789	37. Nebraska	March 1, 1867
13. Rhode Island	May 29, 1790	38. Colorado	August 1, 1876
14. Vermont	March 4, 1791	39. North Dakota	November 2, 1889
15. Kentucky	June 1, 1792	40. South Dakota	November 2, 1889
16. Tennessee	June 1, 1796	41. Montana	November 8, 1889
17. Ohio	March 1, 1803	42. Washington	November 11, 1889
18. Louisiana	April 30, 1812	43. Idaho	July 3, 1890
19. Indiana	December 11, 1816	44. Wyoming	July 10, 1890
20. Mississippi	December 10, 1817	45. Utah	January 4, 1896
21. Illinois	December 3, 1818	46. Oklahoma	November 16, 1907
22. Alabama	December 14, 1819	47. New Mexico	January 6, 1912
23. Maine	March 15, 1820	48. Arizona	February 14, 1912
24. Missouri	August 10, 1821	49. Alaska	January 3, 1959
25. Arkansas	June 15, 1836	50. Hawaii	August 21, 1959

Presidential Elections

Year	Number of States	Candidates	Parties	Popular Vote	% of Popular Vote	Electoral Vote	% Voter Participation[b]
1789	11	**George Washington**	No party			69	
		John Adams	designations			34	
		Other candidates				35	
1792	15	**George Washington**	No party			132	
		John Adams	designations			77	
		George Clinton				50	
		Other candidates				5	
1796	16	**John Adams**	Federalist			71	
		Thomas Jefferson	Democratic-Republican			68	
		Thomas Pinckney	Federalist			59	
		Aaron Burr	Democratic-Republican			30	
		Other candidates				48	
1800	16	**Thomas Jefferson**	Democratic-Republican			73	
		Aaron Burr	Democratic-Republican			73	
		John Adams	Federalist			65	
		Charles C. Pinckney	Federalist			64	
		John Jay	Federalist			1	
1804	17	**Thomas Jefferson**	Democratic-Republican			162	
		Charles C. Pinckney	Federalist			14	
1808	17	**James Madison**	Democratic-Republican			122	
		Charles C. Pinckney	Federalist			47	
		George Clinton	Democratic-Republican			6	
1812	18	**James Madison**	Democratic-Republican			128	
		DeWitt Clinton	Federalist			89	
1816	19	**James Monroe**	Democratic-Republican			183	
		Rufus King	Federalist			34	
1820	24	**James Monroe**	Democratic-Republican			231	
		John Quincy Adams	Independent Republican			1	

Presidential Elections, Continued

Year	Number of States	Candidates	Parties	Popular Vote	% of Popular Vote	Electoral Vote	% Voter Participation[b]
1824	24	**John Quincy Adams**	Democratic-Republican	108,740	30.5	84	26.9
		Andrew Jackson	Democratic-Republican	153,544	43.1	99	
		Henry Clay	Democratic-Republican	47,136	13.2	37	
		William H. Crawford	Democratic-Republican	46,618	13.1	41	
1828	24	**Andrew Jackson**	Democratic	647,286	56.0	178	57.6
		John Quincy Adams	National Republican	508,064	44.0	83	
1832	24	**Andrew Jackson**	Democratic	688,242	54.5	219	55.4
		Henry Clay	National Republican	473,462	37.5	49	
		William Wirt	Anti-Masonic	101,051	8.0	7	
		John Floyd	Democratic			11	
1836	26	**Martin Van Buren**	Democratic	765,483	50.9	170	57.8
		William H. Harrison	Whig			73	
		Hugh L. White	Whig	739,795	49.1	26	
		Daniel Webster	Whig			14	
		W. P. Mangum	Whig			11	
1840	26	**William H. Harrison**	Whig	1,274,624	53.1	234	80.2
		Martin Van Buren	Democratic	1,127,781	46.9	60	
1844	26	**James K. Polk**	Democratic	1,338,464	49.6	170	78.9
		Henry Clay	Whig	1,300,097	48.1	105	
		James G. Birney	Liberty	62,300	2.3		
1848	30	**Zachary Taylor**	Whig	1,360,967	47.4	163	72.7
		Lewis Cass	Democratic	1,222,342	42.2	127	
		Martin Van Buren	Free Soil	291,263	10.1		
1852	31	**Franklin Pierce**	Democratic	1,601,117	50.9	254	69.6
		Winfield Scott	Whig	1,385,453	44.1	42	
		John P. Hale	Free Soil	155,825	5.0		
1856	31	**James Buchanan**	Democratic	1,832,955	45.3	174	78.9
		John C. Frémont	Republican	1,339,932	33.1	114	
		Millard Fillmore	American	871,731	21.6	8	
1860	33	**Abraham Lincoln**	Republican	1,865,593	39.8	180	81.2
		Stephen A. Douglas	Democratic	1,382,713	29.5	12	
		John C. Breckinridge	Democratic	848,356	18.1	72	
		John Bell	Constitutional Union	592,906	12.6	39	
1864	36	**Abraham Lincoln**	Republican	2,206,938	55.0	212	73.8
		George B. McClellan	Democratic	1,803,787	45.0	21	

Presidential Elections, Continued

Year	Number of States	Candidates	Parties	Popular Vote	% of Popular Vote	Electoral Vote	% Voter Participation[b]
1868	37	**Ulysses S. Grant**	Republican	3,013,421	52.7	214	78.1
		Horatio Seymour	Democratic	2,706,829	47.3	80	
1872	37	**Ulysses S. Grant**	Republican	3,596,745	55.6	286	71.3
		Horace Greeley	Democratic	2,843,446	43.9	[a]	
1876	38	**Rutherford B. Hayes**	Republican	4,036,572	48.0	185	81.8
		Samuel J. Tilden	Democratic	4,284,020	51.0	184	
1880	38	**James A. Garfield**	Republican	4,453,295	48.5	214	79.4
		Winfield S. Hancock	Democratic	4,414,082	48.1	155	
		James B. Weaver	Greenback-Labor	308,578	3.4		
1884	38	**Grover Cleveland**	Democratic	4,879,507	48.5	219	77.5
		James G. Blaine	Republican	4,850,293	48.2	182	
		Benjamin F. Butler	Greenback-Labor	175,370	1.8		
		John P. St. John	Prohibition	150,369	1.5		
1888	38	**Benjamin Harrison**	Republican	5,477,129	47.9	233	79.3
		Grover Cleveland	Democratic	5,537,857	48.6	168	
		Clinton B. Fisk	Prohibition	249,506	2.2		
		Anson J. Streeter	Union Labor	146,935	1.3		
1892	44	**Grover Cleveland**	Democratic	5,555,426	46.1	277	74.7
		Benjamin Harrison	Republican	5,182,690	43.0	145	
		James B. Weaver	People's	1,029,846	8.5	22	
		John Bidwell	Prohibition	264,133	2.2		
1896	45	**William McKinley**	Republican	7,102,246	51.1	271	79.3
		William J. Bryan	Democratic	6,492,559	47.7	176	
1900	45	**William McKinley**	Republican	7,218,491	51.7	292	73.2
		William J. Bryan	Democratic; Populist	6,356,734	45.5	155	
		John C. Wooley	Prohibition	208,914	1.5		
1904	45	**Theodore Roosevelt**	Republican	7,628,461	57.4	336	65.2
		Alton B. Parker	Democratic	5,084,223	37.6	140	
		Eugene V. Debs	Socialist	402,283	3.0		
		Silas C. Swallow	Prohibition	258,536	1.9		
1908	46	**William H. Taft**	Republican	7,675,320	51.6	321	65.4
		William J. Bryan	Democratic	6,412,294	43.1	162	
		Eugene V. Debs	Socialist	420,793	2.8		
		Eugene W. Chafin	Prohibition	253,840	1.7		
1912	48	**Woodrow Wilson**	Democratic	6,296,547	41.9	435	58.8
		Theodore Roosevelt	Progressive	4,118,571	27.4	88	
		William H. Taft	Republican	3,486,720	23.2	8	
		Eugene V. Debs	Socialist	900,672	6.0		
		Eugene W. Chafin	Prohibition	206,275	1.4		

Presidential Elections, Continued

Year	Number of States	Candidates	Parties	Popular Vote	% of Popular Vote	Electoral Vote	% Voter Participation[b]
1916	48	**Woodrow Wilson**	Democratic	9,127,695	49.4	277	61.6
		Charles E. Hughes	Republican	8,533,507	46.2	254	
		A. L. Benson	Socialist	585,113	3.2		
		J. Frank Hanly	Prohibition	220,506	1.2		
1920	48	**Warren G. Harding**	Republican	16,143,407	60.4	404	49.2
		James M. Cox	Democratic	9,130,328	34.2	127	
		Eugene V. Debs	Socialist	919,799	3.4		
		P. P. Christensen	Farmer-Labor	265,411	1.0		
1924	48	**Calvin Coolidge**	Republican	15,718,211	54.0	382	48.9
		John W. Davis	Democratic	8,385,283	28.8	136	
		Robert M. La Follette	Progressive	4,831,289	16.6	13	
1928	48	**Herbert C. Hoover**	Republican	21,391,993	58.2	444	56.9
		Alfred E. Smith	Democratic	15,016,169	40.9	87	
1932	48	**Franklin D. Roosevelt**	Democratic	22,809,638	57.4	472	56.9
		Herbert C. Hoover	Republican	15,758,901	39.7	59	
		Norman Thomas	Socialist	881,951	2.2		
1936	48	**Franklin D. Roosevelt**	Democratic	27,752,869	60.8	523	61.0
		Alfred M. Landon	Republican	16,674,665	36.5	8	
		William Lemke	Union	882,479	1.9		
1940	48	**Franklin D. Roosevelt**	Democratic	27,307,819	54.8	449	62.5
		Wendell L. Willkie	Republican	22,321,018	44.8	82	
1944	48	**Franklin D. Roosevelt**	Democratic	25,606,585	53.5	432	55.9
		Thomas E. Dewey	Republican	22,014,745	46.0	99	
1948	48	**Harry S Truman**	Democratic	24,179,345	46.6	303	53.0
		Thomas E. Dewey	Republican	21,991,291	45.1	189	
		J. Strom Thurmond	States' Rights	1,176,125	2.4	39	
		Henry A. Wallace	Progressive	1,157,326	2.4		
1952	48	**Dwight D. Eisenhower**	Republican	33,936,234	55.1	442	63.3
		Adlai E. Stevenson	Democratic	27,314,992	44.4	89	
1956	48	**Dwight D. Eisenhower**	Republican	35,590,472	57.6	457	60.6
		Adlai E. Stevenson	Democratic	26,022,752	42.1	73	
1960	50	**John F. Kennedy**	Democratic	34,226,731	49.7	303	62.8
		Richard M. Nixon	Republican	34,108,157	49.5	219	
1964	50	**Lyndon B. Johnson**	Democratic	43,129,566	61.1	486	61.7
		Barry M. Goldwater	Republican	27,178,188	38.5	52	
1968	50	**Richard M. Nixon**	Republican	31,785,480	43.4	301	60.6
		Hubert H. Humphrey	Democratic	31,275,166	42.7	191	
		George C. Wallace	American Independent	9,906,473	13.5	46	

Presidential Elections, Continued

Year	Number of States	Candidates	Parties	Popular Vote	% of Popular Vote	Electoral Vote	% Voter Participation[b]
1972	50	**Richard M. Nixon**	Republican	47,169,911	60.7	520	55.2
		George S. McGovern	Democratic	29,170,383	37.5	17	
		John G. Schmitz	American	1,099,482	1.4		
1976	50	**Jimmy Carter**	Democratic	40,830,763	50.1	297	53.5
		Gerald R. Ford	Republican	39,147,793	48.0	240	
1980	50	**Ronald Reagan**	Republican	43,899,248	50.8	489	52.6
		Jimmy Carter	Democratic	35,481,432	41.0	49	
		John B. Anderson	Independent	5,719,437	6.6	0	
		Ed Clark	Libertarian	920,859	1.1	0	
1984	50	**Ronald Reagan**	Republican	54,455,075	58.8	525	53.1
		Walter Mondale	Democratic	37,577,185	40.6	13	
1988	50	**George Bush**	Republican	48,901,046	53.4	426	50.2
		Michael Dukakis	Democratic	41,809,030	45.6	111[c]	
1992	50	**Bill Clinton**	Democratic	44,908,233	43.0	370	55.0
		George Bush	Republican	39,102,282	37.4	168	
		Ross Perot	Independent	19,741,048	18.9		

Candidates receiving less than 1 percent of the popular vote have been omitted. Thus the percentage of popular vote given for any election year may not total 100 percent.

Before the passage of the Twelfth Amendment in 1804, the Electoral College voted for two presidential candidates; the runner-up became vice president.

Before 1824, most presidential electors were chosen by state legislatures, not by popular vote.

[a]Greeley died shortly after the election; the electors supporting him then divided their votes among minor candidates.

[b]Percent of voting-age population casting ballots.

[c]One elector from West Virginia cast her Electoral College presidential ballot for Lloyd Bentsen, the Democratic party's vice-presidential candidate.

Presidents and Vice Presidents

1. President	**George Washington**	1789–1797		22. President	**Grover Cleveland**	1885–1889
Vice President	John Adams	1789–1797		Vice President	Thomas A. Hendricks	1885–1889
2. President	**John Adams**	1797–1801		23. President	**Benjamin Harrison**	1889–1893
Vice President	Thomas Jefferson	1797–1801		Vice President	Levi P. Morton	1889–1893
3. President	**Thomas Jefferson**	1801–1809		24. President	**Grover Cleveland**	1893–1897
Vice President	Aaron Burr	1801–1805		Vice President	Adlai E. Stevenson	1893–1897
Vice President	George Clinton	1805–1809		25. President	**William McKinley**	1897–1901
4. President	**James Madison**	1809–1817		Vice President	Garret A. Hobart	1897–1901
Vice President	George Clinton	1809–1813		Vice President	Theodore Roosevelt	1901
Vice President	Elbridge Gerry	1813–1817		26. President	**Theodore Roosevelt**	1901–1909
5. President	**James Monroe**	1817–1825		Vice President	Charles Fairbanks	1905–1909
Vice President	Daniel Tompkins	1817–1825		27. President	**William H. Taft**	1909–1913
6. President	**John Quincy Adams**	1825–1829		Vice President	James S. Sherman	1909–1913
Vice President	John C. Calhoun	1825–1829		28. President	**Woodrow Wilson**	1913–1921
7. President	**Andrew Jackson**	1829–1837		Vice President	Thomas R. Marshall	1913–1921
Vice President	John C. Calhoun	1829–1833		29. President	**Warren G. Harding**	1921–1923
Vice President	Martin Van Buren	1833–1837		Vice President	Calvin Coolidge	1921–1923
8. President	**Martin Van Buren**	1837–1841		30. President	**Calvin Coolidge**	1923–1929
Vice President	Richard M. Johnson	1837–1841		Vice President	Charles G. Dawes	1925–1929
9. President	**William H. Harrison**	1841		31. President	**Herbert C. Hoover**	1929–1933
Vice President	John Tyler	1841		Vice President	Charles Curtis	1929–1933
10. President	**John Tyler**	1841–1845		32. President	**Franklin D. Roosevelt**	1933–1945
Vice President	none			Vice President	John N. Garner	1933–1941
11. President	**James K. Polk**	1845–1849		Vice President	Henry A. Wallace	1941–1945
Vice President	George M. Dallas	1845–1849		Vice President	Harry S Truman	1945
12. President	**Zachary Taylor**	1849–1850		33. President	**Harry S Truman**	1945–1953
Vice President	Millard Fillmore	1849–1850		Vice President	Alben W. Barkley	1949–1953
13. President	**Millard Fillmore**	1850–1853		34. President	**Dwight D. Eisenhower**	1953–1961
Vice President	none			Vice President	Richard M. Nixon	1953–1961
14. President	**Franklin Pierce**	1853–1857		35. President	**John F. Kennedy**	1961–1963
Vice President	William R. King	1853–1857		Vice President	Lyndon B. Johnson	1961–1963
15. President	**James Buchanan**	1857–1861		36. President	**Lyndon B. Johnson**	1963–1969
Vice President	John C. Breckinridge	1857–1861		Vice President	Hubert H. Humphrey	1965–1969
16. President	**Abraham Lincoln**	1861–1865		37. President	**Richard M. Nixon**	1969–1974
Vice President	Hannibal Hamlin	1861–1865		Vice President	Spiro T. Agnew	1969–1973
Vice President	Andrew Johnson	1865		Vice President	Gerald R. Ford	1973–1974
17. President	**Andrew Johnson**	1865–1869		38. President	**Gerald R. Ford**	1974–1977
Vice President	none			Vice President	Nelson A. Rockefeller	1974–1977
18. President	**Ulysses S. Grant**	1869–1877		39. President	**Jimmy Carter**	1977–1981
Vice President	Schuyler Colfax	1869–1873		Vice President	Walter F. Mondale	1977–1981
Vice President	Henry Wilson	1873–1877		40. President	**Ronald Reagan**	1981–1989
19. President	**Rutherford B. Hayes**	1877–1881		Vice President	George Bush	1981–1989
Vice President	William A. Wheeler	1877–1881		41. President	**George Bush**	1989–1993
20. President	**James A. Garfield**	1881		Vice President	Dan Quayle	1989–1993
Vice President	Chester A. Arthur	1881		42. President	**Bill Clinton**	1993–
21. President	**Chester A. Arthur**	1881–1885		Vice President	Albert Gore	1993–
Vice President	none					

Justices of the Supreme Court

	Term of Service	Years of Service	Life Span		Term of Service	Years of Service	Life Span
John Jay	1789–1795	5	1745–1829	William Strong	1870–1880	10	1808–1895
John Rutledge	1789–1791	1	1739–1800	Joseph P. Bradley	1870–1892	22	1813–1892
William Cushing	1789–1810	20	1732–1810	Ward Hunt	1873–1882	9	1810–1886
James Wilson	1789–1798	8	1742–1798	*Morrison R. Waite*	1874–1888	14	1816–1888
John Blair	1789–1796	6	1732–1800	John M. Harlan	1877–1911	34	1833–1911
Robert H. Harrison	1789–1790	—	1745–1790	William B. Woods	1880–1887	7	1824–1887
James Iredell	1790–1799	9	1751–1799	Stanley Matthews	1881–1889	7	1824–1889
Thomas Johnson	1791–1793	1	1732–1819	Horace Gray	1882–1902	20	1828–1902
William Paterson	1793–1806	13	1745–1806	Samuel Blatchford	1882–1893	11	1820–1893
*John Rutledge**	1795	—	1739–1800	Lucius Q. C. Lamar	1888–1893	5	1825–1893
Samuel Chase	1796–1811	15	1741–1811	*Melville W. Fuller*	1888–1910	21	1833–1910
Oliver Ellsworth	1796–1800	4	1745–1807	David J. Brewer	1890–1910	20	1837–1910
Bushrod Washington	1798–1829	31	1762–1829	Henry B. Brown	1890–1906	16	1836–1913
Alfred Moore	1799–1804	4	1755–1810	George Shiras, Jr.	1892–1903	10	1832–1924
John Marshall	1801–1835	34	1755–1835	Howell E. Jackson	1893–1895	2	1832–1895
William Johnson	1804–1834	30	1771–1834	Edward D. White	1894–1910	16	1845–1921
H. Brockholst Livingston	1806–1823	16	1757–1823	Rufus W. Peckham	1895–1909	14	1838–1909
Thomas Todd	1807–1826	18	1765–1826	Joseph McKenna	1898–1925	26	1843–1926
Joseph Story	1811–1845	33	1779–1845	Oliver W. Holmes	1902–1932	30	1841–1935
Gabriel Duval	1811–1835	24	1752–1844	William R. Day	1903–1922	19	1849–1923
Smith Thompson	1823–1843	20	1768–1843	William H. Moody	1906–1910	3	1853–1917
Robert Trimble	1826–1828	2	1777–1828	Horace H. Lurton	1910–1914	4	1844–1914
John McLean	1829–1861	32	1785–1861	Charles E. Hughes	1910–1916	5	1862–1948
Henry Baldwin	1830–1844	14	1780–1844	Willis Van Devanter	1911–1937	26	1859–1941
James M. Wayne	1835–1867	32	1790–1867	Joseph R. Lamar	1911–1916	5	1857–1916
Roger B. Taney	1836–1864	28	1777–1864	*Edward D. White*	1910–1921	11	1845–1921
Philip P. Barbour	1836–1841	4	1783–1841	Mahlon Pitney	1912–1922	10	1858–1924
John Catron	1837–1865	28	1786–1865	James C. McReynolds	1914–1941	26	1862–1946
John McKinley	1837–1852	15	1780–1852	Louis D. Brandeis	1916–1939	22	1856–1941
Peter V. Daniel	1841–1860	19	1784–1860	John H. Clarke	1916–1922	6	1857–1945
Samuel Nelson	1845–1872	27	1792–1873	*William H. Taft*	1921–1930	8	1857–1930
Levi Woodbury	1845–1851	5	1789–1851	George Sutherland	1922–1938	15	1862–1942
Robert C. Grier	1846–1870	23	1794–1870	Pierce Butler	1922–1939	16	1866–1939
Benjamin R. Curtis	1851–1857	6	1809–1874	Edward T. Sanford	1923–1930	7	1865–1930
John A. Campbell	1853–1861	8	1811–1889	Harlan F. Stone	1925–1941	16	1872–1946
Nathan Clifford	1858–1881	23	1803–1881	*Charles E. Hughes*	1930–1941	11	1862–1948
Noah H. Swayne	1862–1881	18	1804–1884	Owen J. Roberts	1930–1945	15	1875–1955
Samuel F. Miller	1862–1890	28	1816–1890	Benjamin N. Cardozo	1932–1938	6	1870–1938
David Davis	1862–1877	14	1815–1886	Hugo L. Black	1937–1971	34	1886–1971
Stephen J. Field	1863–1897	34	1816–1899	Stanley F. Reed	1938–1957	19	1884–1980
Salmon P. Chase	1864–1873	8	1808–1873	Felix Frankfurter	1939–1962	23	1882–1965

Justices of the Supreme Court, Continued

	Term of Service	Years of Service	Life Span		Term of Service	Years of Service	Life Span
William O. Douglas	1939–1975	36	1898–1980	Arthur J. Goldberg	1962–1965	3	1908–1990
Frank Murphy	1940–1949	9	1890–1949	Abe Fortas	1965–1969	4	1910–1982
Harlan F. Stone	1941–1946	5	1872–1946	Thurgood Marshall	1967–1991	24	1908–1993
James F. Byrnes	1941–1942	1	1879–1972	*Warren C. Burger*	1969–1986	17	1907–
Robert H. Jackson	1941–1954	13	1892–1954	Harry A. Blackmun	1970–1994	24	1908–
Wiley B. Rutledge	1943–1949	6	1894–1949	Lewis F. Powell, Jr.	1972–1987	15	1907–
Harold H. Burton	1945–1958	13	1888–1964	*William H. Rehnquist*	1971–	—	1924–
Fred M. Vinson	1946–1953	7	1890–1953	John P. Stevens III	1975–	—	1920–
Tom C. Clark	1949–1967	18	1899–1977	Sandra Day O'Connor	1981–	—	1930–
Sherman Minton	1949–1956	7	1890–1965	Antonin Scalia	1986–	—	1936–
Earl Warren	1953–1969	16	1891–1974	Anthony M. Kennedy	1988–	—	1936–
John Marshall Harlan	1955–1971	16	1899–1971	David H. Souter	1990–	—	1939–
William J. Brennan, Jr.	1956–1990	34	1906–	Clarence Thomas	1991–	—	1948–
Charles E. Whittaker	1957–1962	5	1901–1973	Ruth Bader Ginsburg	1993–	—	1933–
Potter Stewart	1958–1981	23	1915–1985	Stephen G. Breyer	1994–	—	1938–
Byron R. White	1962–1993	31	1917–				

*Appointed and served one term, but not confirmed by the Senate.

Note: Chief justices are in italics.

Index